FOUNDATIONS OF CAREER COUNSELING: A CASE-BASED APPROACH

Suzanne M. Dugger
University of Mississippi

PEARSON

Boston   Columbus   Indianapolis   New York   San Francisco   Amsterdam   Cape Town
Dubai   London   Madrid   Milan   Munich   Paris   Montréal   Toronto   Delhi   Mexico City
São Paulo   Sydney   Hong Kong   Seoul   Singapore   Taipei   Tokyo

Vice President and Editorial Director: Jeffery W. Johnston
Vice President and Publisher: Kevin M. Davis
Editorial Assistant: Marisia Styles
Executive Field Marketing Manager: Krista Clark
Senior Product Marketing Manager: Christopher Barry
Project Manager: Lauren Carlson
Procurement Specialist: Deidra Skahill
Senior Art Director: Diane Ernsberger
Cover Designer: Studio Montage
Cover Art: Shutterstock
Full-Service Project Management: Rashmi Tickyani, iEnergizer Aptara®, Ltd.
Printer/Binder: RR Donnelly/Willard
Cover Printer: Phoenix Color/Hagerstown
Text Font: Minion Pro

Credits and acknowledgments for material borrowed from other sources and reproduced, with permission, in this textbook appear on the appropriate page within the text.

Every effort has been made to provide accurate and current Internet information in this book. However, the Internet and information posted on it are constantly changing, so it is inevitable that some of the Internet addresses listed in this textbook will change.

Copyright © 2016 by Pearson Education, Inc. or its affiliates. All Rights Reserved. Manufactured in the United States of America. This publication is protected by Copyright, and permission should be obtained from the publisher prior to any prohibited reproduction, storage in a retrieval system, or transmission in any form or by any means, electronic, mechanical, photocopying, recording, or likewise. For information regarding permissions, request forms, and the appropriate contacts within the Pearson Education Global Rights & Permissions department, please visit www.pearsoned.com/permissions.

PEARSON and ALWAYS LEARNING are exclusive trademarks in the U.S. and/or other countries owned by Pearson Education, Inc. or its affiliates.

Library of Congress Cataloging-in-Publication Data
Dugger, Suzanne M. Hobson.
 Foundations of career counseling : A case-based approach / Suzanne M. Dugger, Eastern Michigan University. — First Edition.
   pages cm
 ISBN 978-0-13-707986-5 — ISBN 0-13-707986-9
 1. Vocational guidance—Psychological aspects. 2. Career development—Psychological aspects. I. Title.
HF5381.D8244 2015
378.1'9425—dc23

2015008145

10 9 8 7 6 5 4 3 2 1

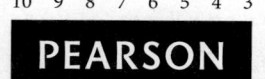

ISBN 10: 0-13-707986-9
ISBN 13: 978-0-13-707986-5

PREFACE

This text is designed for professors and counselor–educators interested in finding ways to excite graduate students about the theory and practice of career counseling. Written in an accessible and down-to-earth style, this text uses a case-based approach to engage students in the study of what can sometimes be rather dry content.

Beginning in Chapter 1, students connect with seven fictional clients. These realistic and engaging clients are diverse with regard to culture, settings, career concerns, and the personal and/or family issues that complicate their situations. To support student mastery of the content and skills involved in career counseling, Dugger follows these seven clients throughout the first thirteen chapters of the book. Rather than simply describing career development theories, the author demonstrates how they may be used to understand and assist the seven clients. Cultural, ethical, and legal issues are not only presented but are also explored in the context of these seven clients. Chapters about the career counseling process; intake interviews; and the use of tests, card sorts, and technology and information resources are especially rich because they contain transcripts, examples, and sample assessment results from simulated sessions with these fictional clients. So rich are these applications that many students become emotionally connected with the clients and remember their favorite "client" even years after taking the course.

Contributing to the engaging nature of this text are the author's down-to-earth writing style, her ability to explain complex concepts in everyday language, and her focus on the how-to's of implementing career development activities and providing career counseling. Dugger's counseling experience in K–12 schools, university counseling centers, and private practice supports her realistic portrayal of career challenges facing a wide variety of clients. This text allows future counselors to develop a deep knowledge base of both theory and techniques pertaining to career development interventions with elementary, secondary, and postsecondary students as well as with adults, including specific populations such as persons with disabilities, military veterans, ex-offenders, homemakers and caretakers, and even themselves. Indeed, this is the only major career counseling text on the market that includes a full chapter dedicated to the career development of students seeking graduate degrees in counseling.

For instructors, supplemental materials include an instructor's manual featuring interactive exercises for use in the classroom, author-developed PowerPoint slides for each chapter, a course syllabus and assignment descriptions that build on the seven clients featured in the book, quizzes and study guides for each chapter, and a test bank to support the development of midterm and final exams.

ACKNOWLEDGMENTS

No project of this magnitude is completed by a single individual. With deep appreciation, I wish to acknowledge the considerable support and meaningful contributions others have made toward the completion of this text:

- John Chandler Dugger III, my husband and best friend—Thank you for your loving support, inspiration, and practical suggestions.
- Jaclynn C. Tracy, department head, leadership and counseling, Eastern Michigan University—Thank you for your enthusiastic interest and investment in my scholarship.
- Office of the Provost at my former employer—Eastern Michigan University—Thank you for the support offered through a sabbatical leave and a faculty research fellowship. Both were essential to my completion of this project.
- Christine Woods, Eric Sweet, Kathleen Hucks, and Adrienne Seeley—Thank you for your work as my graduate assistants over the course of this project.
- All other family members, friends, and coworkers who demonstrated interest in this project and provided support along the way.

I would also like to thank the following individuals at Pearson for their involvement in and contributions to this project:

- Meredith Fossel, executive editor at Pearson—Thank you for convincing me to embark on this project, for your wise guidance and counsel, and for your enthusiasm.
- Kevin Davis, vice president and publisher at Pearson—Thank you for the guidance and invaluable feedback during the revision process.

I would also like to thank Rashmi Tickyani and Linda Clark of Aptara for their attention to detail and their involvement in the production process and Karen Slaght for her excellent proofreading.

Finally, I would like to acknowledge the following reviewers, whose feedback and suggestions were invaluable during the development and revisions of this first edition:

- Regine Talleyrand Abrams, George Mason University
- Mary L. Anderson, Western Michigan University
- Janet Froeschle Hicks, Texas Tech University
- Steven R. Jochim, University of Massachusetts–Boston
- Aaron Oberman, The Citadel
- Mark S. Parrish, University of West Georgia
- V. Scott Solberg, Boston University

BRIEF CONTENTS

SECTION I   **Introduction**
       Chapter 1   The History of Work, Globalization, and Contemporary Client Issues   1

SECTION II   **Theories of Career Development and Career Counseling**
       Chapter 2   Trait Factor Theories   17
       Chapter 3   Developmental Theories   34
       Chapter 4   Learning Theories   56
       Chapter 5   Narrative Theories   88

SECTION III   **Other Foundational Knowledge**
       Chapter 6   Cultural Dimensions of Career Development and Career Counseling   104
       Chapter 7   An Employment Law Primer for Career Counselors   138
       Chapter 8   Becoming an Ethical Career Counselor   158

SECTION IV   **The Practice of Career Counseling**
       Chapter 9   The Career Counseling Process   174
       Chapter 10   Intake Assessments   201
       Chapter 11   Standardized Tests   228
       Chapter 12   Card Sorts   268
       Chapter 13   Technology and Information Resources   294

SECTION V   **Setting-Specific Practices**
       Chapter 14   Career Development in K–12 Educational Settings   331
       Chapter 15   Career Development in Career and Technical Education Settings   353
       Chapter 16   Career Services in College Settings   370
       Chapter 17   Job Loss, Unemployment, and the Job Search Process   389
       Chapter 18   Adult Career Transitions and Specific Populations   410

SECTION VI   **Career Planning for Professional Counselors**
       Chapter 19   Charting Your Own Career Path as a Professional Counselor   441

CONTENTS

Section I Introduction

Chapter 1 The History of Work, Globalization, and Contemporary Client Issues   1

A Vocabulary Lesson   1
  Application Activity   2
The Profession of Career Counseling   2
A Brief History Lesson   3
  The Industrial Revolution   3
  Frank Parsons: The Father of Counseling   4
  The Digital Revolution   4
  Globalization   5
Changes in the World of Work   6
  Job Opportunities   6
  Postsecondary Training Needs   7
  Job Security and Career Stability   8
The Need for Career Counseling   9
Our Cast of Clients   9
Client 1: Wayne Jensen   10
  Welcome to Wayne's World   10
Client 2: Lily Huang Li Mei   11
  Helping Li Mei Blossom   11
Client 3: Lakeesha Maddox   11
  Doors and Windows   11
Client 4: Vincent Santiago Arroyo   12
  Caskets, Closets, and Careers   12
Client 5: Doris Bronner   12
  Embitterment Versus Empowerment   12
Client 6: Gillian Parker   13
  Golden Handcuffs   13
Client 7: Juan Martinez   13
  Bloques de Construcción para un Futuro Nuevo ("Building Blocks for a New Future")   13
Conceptualizing Contemporary Client Issues   14
  External and Internal Motivators for Career Counseling   14
  Interweaving Personal and Career Issues in Counseling   14
  The Role of Theory   15
Overview of the Text   15

Section II Theories of Career Development and Career Counseling

Chapter 2 Trait Factor Theories   17
Historical Roots   18
Holland's Person-Environment Fit Theory   20
Dawis and Lofquist's Theory of Work Adjustment   25
Comparison of Trait Factor Theories   30
Application to Our Cast of Clients   30
  Application of Holland's Theory   30
  Application of Dawis and Lofquist's Theory of Work Adjustment   32
Putting It All Together   33

Chapter 3 Developmental Theories   34
Roe's Theory of Personality Development and Career Choice   34
Bordin's Psychodynamic Model of Career Choice and Satisfaction   36
Ginzberg's Theory of Occupational Choice   37
  Initial Version of Ginzberg's Theory   37
  Revised Version of Ginzberg's Theory   38
Super's Life-Span, Life-Space Approach   39
  Super's Propositions   39
  Segment 1: Life Span   41
  Segment 2: Life Space   43
  Segment 3: Self-Concept   45
  Assessment of Life-Span and Life-Space Constructs   46
  Career Development Assessment and Counseling Model   46
Gottfredson's Theory of Circumscription, Compromise, and Self-Creation   48
  Process of Circumscription   48
  Process of Compromise   51
  Self-Creation: The Influence of Genetics   51
Application to Our Cast of Clients   52
  Application of Super's Life-Span, Life-Space Approach   52
  Application of Gottfredson's Theory of Circumscription, Compromise, and Self-Creation   54

Chapter 4 Learning Theories   56
Bandura's Foundational Learning Theories   56
  Social Learning Theory   57
  Social Cognitive Theory   57
Learning Theories of Career Development and Career Counseling   57
  Krumboltz's Learning Theories   57
  Social Cognitive Career Theory   65
  Cognitive Information-Processing Approach   75
Application to Our Cast of Clients   82
  Application of Krumboltz's Learning Theories   82
  Application of Social Cognitive Career Theory   85
  Application of the Cognitive Information-Processing Approach   86

Chapter 5 **Narrative Theories** 88
    Introduction 88
    Cochran's Narrative Approach to Career Counseling 89
        Elaborating a Career Problem 89
        Composing a Life History 89
        Founding a Future Narrative 90
        Constructing Reality 91
        Changing a Life Structure 91
        Enacting a Role 91
        Crystallization 91
    Savickas's Theory of Career Construction and Career Counseling 91
        Career Construction Theory 92
        Implications of CCT for Career Interventions 93
        Counseling for Career Construction Within a Life-Design Paradigm 94
    Application to Our Cast of Clients 100
        Brief Application of Narrative Theory 100
        Comprehensive Application to the Case of Gillian, by Thomas Eckert 101

Section III **Other Foundational Knowledge**

Chapter 6 **Cultural Dimensions of Career Development and Career Counseling** 104
    An Introduction to Culture 104
        Culture and *Diversity* Defined 104
        Career Development Theories: Cultural Considerations 105
        Culturally Encapsulated Assumptions 106
    Putting It All Together 107
    Differences Across Cultural Groups 107
        Differences in Worldview: Individualism Versus Collectivism 107
        Sociopolitical Inequities 107
        Socioeconomic Disparities 108
    Diversity Within Cultural Groups 110
        Identification with Multiple Cultures 110
        Immigration History 111
        Acculturation 111
        Identity Development 112
    Understanding Your Client as a Cultural Being 112
        The Cultural Formulation Approach 113
        Culture and Career Genograms 114
    Putting It All Together 120
    Understanding the Potential Impact of Culture 120
        Potential Impact of Culture on Career Development 120
        Potential Impact of Culture on Career Decision Making 121
        Potential Impact of Culture on Career Success 122

Responding Effectively to Cultural Dimensions in the Career Counseling Process   124
    Tip 1: Be Aware of Yourself and the World Around You   124
    Tip 2: Be Humble   124
    Tip 3: Get a Grip on Reality   124
    Tip 4: Think Critically   125
    Tip 5: Pay Attention to Nuances   125
    Tip 6: Actively Seek to Understand Your Client   125
    Tip 7: Take a Two-Pronged Approach   125
    Tip 8: Keep Learning   126
Application to Our Cast of Clients   126
    Wayne Jensen: Welcome to Wayne's World   126
    Lily Huang Li Mei: Helping Li Mei Blossom   127
    Lakeesha Maddox: Doors and Windows   129
    Vincent Santiago Arroyo: Caskets, Closets, and Careers   131
    Doris Bronner: Embitterment Versus Empowerment   133
    Gillian Parker: Golden Handcuffs   134
    Juan Martinez: Bloques de Construcción para un Futuro Nuevo (Building Blocks for a New Future)   135

Chapter 7 An Employment Law Primer for Career Counselors   138

Why Frank Parsons Cared About Employment Law   138
The Evolution of Employment Doctrine in the United States   140
Summary of Relevant Employment Laws   141
    Laws Pertaining to Hiring and Firing   141
    Laws Pertaining to Work Conditions   146
    Laws Pertaining to Unemployment and Inability to Work   148
    Laws Pertaining to Life After Retirement   152
Resources for More Information   153
Application to Our Cast of Clients   154
    Wayne Jensen: Welcome to Wayne's World   154
    Lily Huang Li Mei: Helping Li Mei Blossom   154
    Lakeesha Maddox: Doors and Windows   154
    Vincent Santiago Arroyo: Caskets, Closets and Careers   155
    Doris Bronner: Embitterment Versus Empowerment   155
    Gillian Parker: Golden Handcuffs   156
    Juan Martinez: Bloques de Construcción para un Futuro Nuevo (Building Blocks for a New Future)   156

Chapter 8 Becoming an Ethical Career Counselor   158

Step 1: Become Competent   158
Step 2: Obtain the Appropriate Credentials   159
    Licensure   159
    Certification   161
Step 3: Use General Ethical Principles as a Guide   163

Step 4: Read and Adhere to Ethical Codes 165
    Section A: The Professional Relationship 165
    Section B: Confidentiality, Privileged Communication, and Privacy 166
    Section C: Professional Responsibility 166
    Section D: Relationships with Other Professionals 166
    Section E: Evaluation, Assessment, and Interpretation 166
    Section F: Use of the Internet in the Provision of Career Services 167
    Section G: Supervision, Training, and Teaching 167
    Section H: Research and Publication 167
    Section I: Resolving Ethical Issues 167
Step 5: Use a Solid, Ethical Decision-Making Model 168
Step 6: Stay Up-to-Date 168
Application to Our Cast of Clients: Scenarios Warranting Ethical Consideration 169
    Wayne Jensen: Welcome to Wayne's World 169
    Lily Huang Li Mei: Helping Li Mei Blossom 169
    Lakeesha Maddox: Doors and Windows 169
    Vincent Santiago Arroyo: Caskets, Closets and Careers 169
    Doris Bronner: Embitterment Versus Empowerment 170
    Gillian Parker: Golden Handcuffs 170
    Juan Martinez: Bloques de Construcción para un Futuro Nuevo (Building Blocks for a New Future) 170
Application to Our Cast of Clients: Ethical Principles and Standards Pertinent to Client Scenarios 170
    Wayne Jensen: Welcome to Wayne's World 170
    Lily Huang Li Mei: Helping Li Mei Blossom 171
    Lakeesha Maddox: Doors and Windows 171
    Vincent Santiago Arroyo: Caskets, Closets and Careers 172
    Doris Bronner: Embitterment Versus Empowerment 172
    Gillian Parker: Golden Handcuffs 173
    Juan Martinez: Bloques de Construcción para un Futuro Nuevo (Building Blocks for a New Future) 173

Section IV The Practice of Career Counseling

Chapter 9 The Career Counseling Process 174
Stages of the Career Counseling Process 174
    Beginning Stage: Introduction 174
    Middle Stage: Identification and Implementation of Helping Strategies 177
    Ending Stage: Conclusion 181
Application to Our Cast of Clients 182
    Welcoming and Orienting Clients to Counseling: Lily Huang Li Mei 182
    Identifying Client Concerns and Goals: Lakeesha Maddox 185
    Gathering Background Information 185

Identifying Helping Strategies: Juan Martinez   187
Implementing Helping Strategies: Vincent Santiago Arroyo   190
Implementing Helping Strategies: Doris Bronner   194
Solidifying Client Progress: Gillian Parker   197
Preparing for the Future: Wayne Jensen   198

Chapter 10   Intake Assessments   201

Approaches to Intake Assessments   202
Content of Intake Assessments   203
   Basic Personal Information   203
   Concerns and Goals   204
   Education and Training   204
   Employment History   208
   Family Background   208
   Current Living Situation   208
   Challenges and Obstacles   213
   Personal Strengths and Sources of Support   213
   Cultural Formulation   214
   Current Health Status and Medical Information   215
Putting It All Together   217
Application to Our Cast of Clients   217
   Basic Personal Information: Wayne Jensen   218
   Concerns and Goals: Vincent Santiago Arroyo   218
   Education and Training: Gillian Parker   219
   Employment History: Doris Bronner   220
   Family Background: Lily Huang Li Mei   220
   Current Living Situation: Wayne Jensen   222
   Challenges and Obstacles: Lakeesha Maddox   222
   Personal Strengths and Sources of Support: Lakeesha Maddox   223
   Current Health Status and Medical Information: Juan Martinez   225
Putting It All Together   227

Chapter 11   Standardized Tests   228

Types of Standardized Tests Used in Career Counseling   228
Standardized Tests Related to Career Selection   229
   Standardized Tests Related to Interests   229
   Standardized Tests Related to Personality   235
   Standardized Tests Related to Work Values   239
   Standardized Tests Related to Abilities   241
Standardized Tests Related to Career Decision Making   249
   Career Beliefs Inventory   249
   Career Decision Scale   250
   Career Decision Self-Efficacy Scale   250
   Career Development Inventory   250

Career Factors Inventory 250
Career Maturity Inventory: The Adaptability Form 251
Career Thoughts Inventory 251
My Vocational Situation 251
Standardized Tests Related to Career Adjustment 252
ACT WorkKeys 253
Adult Career Concerns Inventory 253
Barrier to Employment Success Inventory, Fourth Edition 253
Becker Work Adjustment Profile: 2 253
BRIGANCE Transition Skills Inventory 254
Career Attitudes and Strategies Inventory 254
Career Futures Inventory–Revised 254
Job Observation and Behavior Scale 254
Job Stress Survey 254
Job Survival and Success Scale, Second Edition 255
Maslach Burnout Inventory, Third Edition 255
Minnesota Satisfaction Questionnaire 255
Minnesota Satisfactoriness Scales 255
Occupational Stress Inventory–Revised 256
Transition Behavior Scale, Third Edition 256
Transition Planning Inventory, Updated Version 256
Transition-to-Work Inventory, Third Edition 256
Workplace Skills Survey 256
Putting It All Together 257
Additional Resources 257
Application to Our Cast of Clients 258
Wayne Jensen: Welcome to Wayne's World 258
Lily Huang Li Mei: Helping Li Mei Blossom 259
Lakeesha Maddox: Doors and Windows 259
Vincent Santiago Arroyo: Caskets, Closets and Careers 262
Doris Bronner: Embitterment Versus Empowerment 263
Gillian Parker: Golden Handcuffs 264
Juan Martinez: Bloques de Construcción para un Futuro Nuevo (Building Blocks for a New Future) 265
Putting It All Together 267

Chapter 12 Card Sorts 268
Early Pioneers 268
Leona E. Tyler 268
Robert H. Dolliver 269
Subsequent Modifications 270

Using Theory 271
    Trait Factor Theory: Person-Environment Fit 271
    Trait Factor Theory: Theory of Work Adjustment 271
    Learning Theories 271
    Theory of Circumscription and Compromise 272
    Constructivist Theories 272
How-to Guide 272
    Step 1: Identify Your Purpose 272
    Step 2: Obtain or Create Cards 273
    Step 3: Identify the Categories or Continuum 273
    Step 4: Create Header Cards and a Corresponding Worksheet 273
    Step 5: Introduce the Card Sort and Explain the Process to Your Client 274
    Step 6: Observe While the Client Completes the Card Arrangement 274
    Step 7: Engage in Iterative Activities 274
    Step 8: Record the Results 275
    Step 9: Process the Activity 275
    Step 10: Engage in Closure Discussion 275
Demonstration with Our Cast of Clients 275
    Wayne Jensen: Wayne's Career-Related Values 275
    Lily Huang Li Mei: Occupational Interests 279
    Doris Bronner's Employability Skills 279
A Final Word 288
Purchasing Information 289

Chapter 13 Technology and Information Resources 294
Role of Counselors 295
Types of Information About the World of Work 295
Occupational Classification Systems 296
    Standard Occupational Classification System 296
    Other Occupational Classification Systems 298
Occupational and Labor Market Information 299
    National Career Development Association Content Guidelines 299
    Federal Government Resources 299
    State Government Resources 313
    Commercial Resources 315
    Other Sources of Occupational and Labor Market Information 319
Education and Training Information 321
    Importance of Postsecondary Education 321
    Selecting and Applying to an Educational Program and Paying for It 322
    Building Confidence by Building Skills 323
Skill-Building Information 323
    Employability Skills 323
    Job Searching Skills 324

Application to Our Cast of Clients   326
    Lily Huang Li Mei: Career Exploration and Selection of Academic Majors   326
    Wayne Jensen: Labor Market Information   327
    Juan Martinez: Occupational, Labor Market, and Short-Term Training Information   327
    Lakeesha Maddox: Career Options, Life Balance, and Networking   328
    Doris Bronner: Skill-Building Workshops   330

Section V Setting-Specific Practices

Chapter 14 Career Development in K–12 Educational Settings   331

American School Counselor Association National Model   331
Student Competencies in Career Development   332
Importance of Integrated Career Development Programs   333
Career Development Programs in Elementary Schools   333
    Developmental Considerations   333
    School Counseling Core Curriculum: Career Development Lessons for Elementary School Classrooms   334
    Schoolwide Events or Programs: Other Career Development Activities for Elementary Schools   335
    Educational Planning Activities for Elementary Schools   335
Career Development in Middle Schools   337
    Developmental Considerations   337
    School Counseling Core Curriculum: Career Development Lessons for Middle School Classrooms   337
    Schoolwide Events or Programs: Other Career Development Activities for Middle Schools   338
    Educational Planning Activities for Middle Schools   339
Career Development in High Schools   340
    Developmental Considerations   340
    School Counseling Core Curriculum: Career Development Lessons for High School Classrooms   340
    Schoolwide Events or Programs: Other Career Development Activities for High Schools   341
    Educational Planning Activities for High Schools: Postsecondary Planning   342
Putting It All Together   350

Chapter 15 Career Development in Career and Technical Education Settings   353

A False Dichotomy: Academic Rigor and CTE   354
History of Vocational Education in the United States   355
    Smith-Hughes Act of 1917   355
    Additional Early Legislation   355
    National Defense Education Act   356
    Expanding the Focus of Vocational Education   356
    Carl D. Perkins Vocational Education Act of 1984   356

Carl D. Perkins Vocational and Applied Technology Education Act of 1990 356
School-to-Work Opportunities Act 357
Carl D. Perkins Career and Technical Education Improvement Act of 2006 357
Vocational Education as a Tracking System 357
The New Career and Technical Education System in the United States 360
Career Clusters 360
Best Practice CTE Programs 360
Looking Ahead: The Future of CTE 362
The Career Counselor's Role in CTE 364
Advocating for CTE 364
Explaining Curricular Requirements 364
Facilitating Consideration of CTE Options 364
Assisting with the Postsecondary Search and Selection Process 365
Assisting CTE Students with Career Development Needs 367
Putting It All Together 367

Chapter 16 Career Services in College Settings 370

Developmental Considerations 371
Students Who Transition Directly from High School to College 371
Returning Students 373
Competencies and Standards 374
National Career Development Guidelines 374
CAS Program Standards for Career Services 374
Program Components 375
Career Counseling 375
Information and Resources on Careers and Additional Education 382
Opportunities for Career Exploration Through Experiential Learning 385
Job Search Services 385
Employer Relationship and Recruitment Services 386
Consultation Services to Faculty and Administrators 387
Collaboration 387
Putting It All Together 387

Chapter 17 Job Loss, Unemployment, and the Job Search Process 389

Job Loss and Unemployment 389
Unemployment: Definitions and Statistics 390
Psychological Reactions to Job Loss 391
Helping Strategies for the Unemployed 393
Addressing Psychological Reactions to Job Loss and Unemployment 393
Group Counseling Programs for the Unemployed 394
The Job Search Process 394
Technology and Information Resources to Support Job Searches 395
Putting It All Together 408

Chapter 18 Adult Career Transitions and Specific Populations 410

- Adult Career Transitions 410
  - Transition Factors 410
  - Types of Career Transitions 413
- Specific Populations and Their Career Service Needs in Community Settings 413
- People with Disabilities 414
  - Employment Statistics 414
  - Employment Challenges 415
  - Helping Strategies 415
- Military Veterans 417
  - Employment Statistics 417
  - Transition-Related Challenges 419
  - Helping Strategies 419
- Ex-Offenders 423
  - Incarceration and Employment Statistics 423
  - Employment Challenges 425
  - Helping Strategies 428
- Homemakers and Caretakers 432
  - Definitions and Statistics 432
  - Employment Challenges 435
  - Helping Strategies 436
- Providers of Career-Related Services in Community Settings 438
- Career Service Sites in the Community Setting 439
- Putting It All Together 440

Section VI Career Planning for Professional Counselors

Chapter 19 Charting Your Own Career Path as a Professional Counselor 441

- Step 1: Prepare Yourself 442
  - Gather Information 442
  - Adopt an Attitude of Self-Responsibility 443
  - Take Action to Prepare Yourself 444
  - Obtain Licensure and Other Credentials 446
- Step 2: Engage in a Job Search Process 449
  - Define the Parameters of Your Job Search 450
  - Identify Key Elements and Unique Strengths to Highlight in Your Application 451
  - Develop and Compile Application Materials 453
  - Launch Your Job Search 458

Step 3: Adjust to Your New Career 461
 Conduct and View Yourself as a Professional Counselor 461
 Acclimate to Your New Workplace 462
 Keep Learning 462
Step 4: Engage in Long-Term Career Planning 463

Appendices 467

Appendix A Historical Highlights of Vocational Guidance, Career Development, and Career Counseling in the United States 468
Appendix B National Career Development Association Counselor Competencies 470
Appendix C National Career Development Association Code of Ethics 472
Appendix D American School Counselor Association Student Standards in the Career Development Domain 497
Appendix E National Career Development Guidelines Framework 499
Appendix F Secretary's Commission on Achieving Necessary Skills (SCANS)–Employability Skills 508
Appendix G Sample Form for an Educational Development Plan 510

References 511
Author Index 539
Subject Index 544

CHAPTER

1

The History of Work, Globalization, and Contemporary Client Issues

Greetings, and welcome to the wonderful world of career counseling! My name is not Julie McCoy and I am not the cruise director on the once popular television show, *The Love Boat*. However, my role is somewhat similar. As the author of this text, I will accompany you on your first voyage into the world of career counseling and serve as a very informative tour guide. Continuing with the cruise ship metaphor, I hope to welcome you aboard, introduce you to all of the major sites (i.e., topics) along the way, help you learn quite a bit about each of them, be sensitive to times when you might get lost or seasick (i.e., bored or intimidated), and help you have such a good time (learning about career counseling) that you will want to return for similar cruises (additional courses in career counseling) in the future. And, to stretch this metaphor, perhaps you'll fall in love on this cruise and decide to specialize in career counseling.

As you can surely tell by now, this is not your ordinary text. I don't know about you, but I have, once or twice in my life, found it difficult to stay awake and maintain interest while reading a text. Although I could certainly write a much more serious and impressive-sounding text filled with lots of big words, I'm not sure you would want to read it. Realizing that you will learn much more from a text you actually read than from one that gathers dust on your shelf, I have chosen a more colloquial writing style with the hope of maintaining your interest. Obviously, I cannot predict how much you have on your plate with regard to competing responsibilities, how much sleep you get, and so forth. Those factors alone can make it difficult to keep up with and maintain interest in schoolwork. By the end of this text, however, I hope that you will agree that I have done my job by presenting some admittedly difficult concepts in a user-friendly, accessible writing style.

Don't make the mistake of thinking that a user-friendly writing style means the content is dumbed down. To the contrary, the content of this text exceeds that of most introductory texts on career counseling, both in terms of volume and in terms of conceptual complexity. As such, this text is appropriate for use in both master's and doctoral courses. There is a lot of information to learn, and you may struggle at times to digest all that you read. Thus, I encourage you to pace yourself as you read, take notes, and employ sound study skills as you make your way through this text and the course for which it is assigned. (Nobody ever said graduate school would be easy!)

A VOCABULARY LESSON

As we embark on this journey together, a quick vocabulary lesson may be useful. Within the world of career counseling, many different terms related to the world of work are used. At times, words like *job*, *work*, and *career* may seem interchangeable. However, each has a slightly different meaning. In reviewing the terms and definitions in Table 1.1, notice the differences.

TABLE 1.1 Vocabulary

Term	Definition
avocation	Unpaid activities during leisure time; avocations may include hobbies or other activities for which others get paid (e.g., woodworking) but for which one is unpaid and engages in during leisure time.
career	Numerous definitions of *career* exist, but most agree that this is a broad category referring to the series or sequence of one's vocational activities over the course of a lifetime. Two important elements of this definition are that *career* is a broad category and that a career spans a lifetime. There is generally agreement that *career* is integral to one's sense of self and that, ideally, one's career provides a form of self-expression and satisfaction. Different opinions exist whether this term is specific to vocational activities or whether it also includes avocational activities.
job	The specific set of tasks performed by an individual worker. The term *job* usually refers to paid positions, but payment isn't required.
lifestyle	The overall balance of vocational and avocational activities at any given point in time. The term *lifestyle* definitely includes vocational and avocational activities. It also focuses on the relative balance of competing roles (work, family, social, leisure), which can vary over time.
occupation	A term that represents a broader grouping of jobs that require similar skills and involve similar tasks. National labor market statistics usually address this broader category of occupations as opposed to very specific jobs. The term *occupation* is specific to paid work.
vocation	Paid employment in a job or occupation.
work	The expenditure of energy and effort. *Work* occurs during paid employment (e.g., at one's job) as well as during unpaid activities (e.g., housework, yard work). When used in the context of the *world of work*, it refers to paid employment.

Application Activity

To help cement the terms in Table 1.1 and the nuanced definitions in your mind, think about how each term applies to you. For example, identify some work you have recently done. It might be unpaid, undirected work involving your autonomous decision to complete a dreaded task such as finally cleaning your refrigerator. It might be unpaid but directed work such as reading this chapter when it was assigned by your instructor. Or it might include work your employer asked you to do as part of your paid position. As you complete this application activity, think about the various jobs you have had over the course of your life. Have they required similar skills and involved similar tasks, meaning that these various jobs might all be subsumed within a given occupational category? Also, what are the differences between what you are seeking as a career and what you have done vocationally up to this point? Finally, how do your career aspirations fit with your ideal lifestyle? What kind of balance between your vocational and avocational activities would you eventually like to have?

My hope is that, as you responded to the questions in the application activity, you started thinking about the importance of paid work in your own life. Although each of us likely wishes that we had already won a lottery jackpot so that paid employment would be unnecessary, the reality for the vast majority of us is that we need a vocation in order to meet our living expenses. Of course, many jobs provide an opportunity to earn a living. And the standard of living afforded by one's employment varies greatly depending on the pay and benefits, or perks, associated with any given job. How easily we subsist, comfortably we live, successful we feel, and satisfied we are depends a great deal on the nature of our work. The profession of career counseling is dedicated to assisting people with these types of issues. For example, career counselors help increase the likelihood that people will choose work that serves as a source not only of subsistence but also of satisfaction and success. Sadly, I've known people who did more research choosing a cell phone than choosing a college major and who put more time into planning a wedding than actively managing their future career development. Career counselors seek to change that.

THE PROFESSION OF CAREER COUNSELING

As you can surely surmise without the aid of a text, the profession of career counseling focuses on helping people with career-related issues. What you may not know, however, is what these issues might be and how to help people with them. This text is dedicated to addressing

TABLE 1.2 Career-Related Issues Addressed by Career Counselors
1. Early career development
2. Employment
3. Career success and satisfaction
4. Life balance

these topics in great detail. In this chapter, I offer a sneak peak. Table 1.2 shows four major categories of career-related issues addressed by career counselors. Career counselors (1) work to support the early career development needs of young people, (2) help people find employment, (3) assist people in finding success and satisfaction in the world of work, and (4) assist people in addressing life-balance issues.

A variety of terms are used to describe the work of career counselors. For example, services focused on supporting the early career development needs of young people are often referred to as *vocational guidance* or *career development* activities. Services focused on helping people find jobs are usually called *employment counseling*. Services focused on helping people find success and satisfaction in the world of work or helping people address life-balance issues are referred to as *career counseling*. The overall profession of career counseling subsumes more focused activities such as vocational guidance and employment counseling.

Today, in the aftermath of the Great Recession in the 21st century, you likely need little convincing about the importance of this work. You are probably quite aware of the unemployment statistics that have besieged our nation as a result of this recession and are all too familiar with the impact on every generation of workers. High school students worry about whether a college degree is necessary to earn a living. Young adults struggle to earn enough to get their own place and leave their parents' home. College students worry about finding a full-time job, especially one with benefits, after graduating with their degrees. Experienced workers worry about being laid off, downsized, outsourced, or otherwise unemployed. People approaching retirement age have concerns about whether social security benefits will be eliminated, whether their retirement savings will be sufficient, and whether they can safely exit the workforce to enter the next phase of their life and make room in the workforce for the upcoming generation. In fact, now is a good time to consider specializing in career counseling. The profession of career counseling emerged in similar economic times in the early 1900s. To help you put the history of this profession in perspective, I offer the following history lesson.

A BRIEF HISTORY LESSON

Career counselors benefit from an awareness of how the world of work has changed over time. Therefore, this history lesson is designed to help you recognize the societal changes that have affected our nation's economy and world of work and that ultimately created the need for the profession of career counseling. I will also draw parallels between those early societal changes and more recent changes and examine the similarly profound impact each had on the world of work. As you read through this history lesson, note the role of technology.

The Industrial Revolution

To start us off, think back to the U.S. History class(es) you likely took in high school. You may or may not remember learning about the Industrial Revolution (1820–1870), but the changes during this period had a remarkable influence on the nature of work in the United States. Prior to the Industrial Revolution, one could say that people inherited rather than chose their career (Baruch, 2006). In those times, people generally earned an income by working for themselves or a family business, and those who worked for someone else generally worked for a farmer because the United States had a largely agrarian economy (an economy that relies on farming) prior to the Industrial Revolution. There weren't many opportunities for career decision making. As Coutinho, Dam, and Blustein (2008) explained, "[B]efore the industrial revolution, work and family were closely tied; often people's work lives were determined by their parents' work, and work was done in the home or fairly close to it" (p. 9). Social class was a major determining factor, and only wealthy or otherwise privileged individuals were in a position to make a career decision geared toward personal fulfillment rather than simply doing what their parents had done (Hees, Rottinghaus, Briddick, & Conrath, 2012, p. 334).

This situation changed as a result of numerous technological advances, such as the expansion of the railroad transportation system; the development of mass production techniques such as the assembly line; and the development of human ability to produce, store, and use electricity. These technological advances changed the very nature of work, making it more efficient for companies to build large plants in cities where workers could engage in the mass production of items. Railroads allowed for the efficient transportation of supplies as well as manufactured products, and electricity allowed for the extension of the workday.

Those were interesting times in the world of work. Many people moved from the rural areas where their families lived to cities where they could easily find work in the manufacturing industry or in larger companies based in an urban area (Coutinho et al., 2008; Hees et al., 2012). In addition, a huge influx of immigrants sought work and a better life in the United States (Herr, 2013). The overall impact of the Industrial Revolution is that it offered "more individuals greater opportunity to pursue personally satisfying careers that provided a sense of security and dignity by matching their values and interests" (Hees et al., 2012, p. 334).

These changes resulted in an increased need for career development and career counseling, primarily because workers were no longer locked into the occupations of their families and instead now had many potential career paths from which to select. Now, career counselors were needed to assist people with determining the types of work they might find most fulfilling. In this sense, vocational guidance services were particularly useful. Additionally, the need for career development and career counseling really hit a peak when the economic recession of 1873 hit. This recession directly contributed to the development of the career counseling profession in two ways. First, people found themselves out of work and in dire need of assistance in finding a job (i.e., employment counseling). Second, as luck would have it, Frank Parsons, the eventual founder of the counseling profession, was directly influenced by this recession.

Frank Parsons: The Father of Counseling

To make a long story short, a man named Frank Parsons lost a high-paying job as an engineer for the railroad when the recession hit. Ironically, corruption in the railroad industry is often blamed for this particular recession (Zytowski, 2001). In any case, poor Frank couldn't find another high-paying job and finally ended up in a very low-paying, working-class job (Pope & Sveinsdottir, 2005). His experiences and observations at that time heightened his awareness of profound socioeconomic disparities in society and sensitized him to the career development needs of the general population (O'Brien, 2001).

These experiences eventually prompted Parsons to focus intently on career development issues. More specifically, Parsons took a two-pronged approach to improving the well-being of the nation's citizens. One prong involved contextually focused social justice activities in which Parsons advocated for better working conditions and more equitable pay for workers (Baker, 2009; O'Brien, 2001). The other prong involved person-focused activities in which Parsons promoted the incorporation of career development and career preparation into educational settings and in which he advocated for systematic methods of assisting individuals with the choice of a vocation (Davis, 1969). He articulated his thoughts in a book entitled, *Choosing a Vocation* (Parsons, 1909), and you will learn more about Parsons's theory in Chapter 2.

Parsons's book literally served as the foundation for the career counseling profession as well as for the wider counseling profession. To this day, Frank Parsons is regarded as the father of vocational guidance, the father of career counseling, and the father of counseling. With his establishment of guidelines to support the vocational guidance of young people and to systematize career counseling for adults, Parsons made a lasting contribution that served as the very foundation of our profession. You see, before Parsons, there was no profession of counseling. Rather than focusing on aiding people with mental illness (which was, at that time, the exclusive purview of psychology), Parsons focused on assisting people with normal, developmental needs. Their adjustment in adulthood, after all, depended in no small part on their ability to find gainful employment that they would find meaningful and satisfying. Indeed, Parsons recognized what are now referred to as spillover effects (Fabian, 2009, p. 426). Specifically, he recognized that one's work satisfaction frequently spills over and affects one's overall life satisfaction and, conversely, that one's life satisfaction affects one's disposition, performance, and well-being at work.

In the years following publication of *Choosing a Vocation* (Parsons, 1909), the profession of career counseling flourished. The world, after all, had changed dramatically. Technological advances had literally transformed the world of work and the nature of society in the United States. Indeed, our country shifted from an agrarian-based economy to a manufacturing-based economy. Accompanying this shift, the population of the United States became more mobile. Instead of living in one rural area for a lifetime, it now became customary for people to move to cities to find work.

If this is sounding terribly familiar, that tells me you're paying attention and noticing the similarities between those old school times and today's world. Think about it. The Industrial Revolution was sparked by technological advances that dramatically changed the nature of work and expanded the mobility of workers. This should sound familiar: Our world has recently experienced a digital revolution that has had just as dramatic an effect on the nature of work as the Industrial Revolution. Another parallel is that technological advances served as the catalyst for both the Industrial Revolution and the digital revolution, dramatically changing the nature of work and expanding the mobility of workers.

The Digital Revolution

The digital revolution, which involved the transformation of information from physical to electronic, digital format, first began around 1980 and accelerated considerably in the late 1990s with the advent of the Internet. This transformation has affected the recording and transmission of a wide array of information. Although you are likely aware of the impact such changes have had on your daily life, you may be less aware of how this digital revolution changed the world of work. As I see it, the digital revolution has had three primary effects on the world of work: It (1) increased individual productivity and effectiveness, (2) altered the nature and expanded the boundaries of the workplace, and (3) contributed directly to the rapid acceleration of globalization by making it technologically feasible.

With regard to individual productivity and effectiveness, you cannot fully understand the impact of digital technology unless you have typed a paper (using a real, old-school typewriter), gotten to the last line or so of the page, made a grievous typing error, and had to remove the page and retype it in its entirety on new paper. Word processing on a personal computer or tablet is immeasurably more efficient, even without the benefit of a spell checker. The keys push more easily, corrections can be made prior to printing, content can be cut and pasted, and so forth. Digital technology has also improved individual productivity in jobs not involving the writing process. Consider, for example, the time it would take to check a superstore's inventory manually. With the benefit of handheld scanners, an employee can now simply walk the aisles and use the scanner to record each item on the shelves. This information is then magically (okay, digitally) transmitted to a central computer that can track the inventory and determine ordering needs. The result is a quicker, more accurate census of a store's inventory. As just one more example, even farmers have become more productive and effective as a result of digital technology. Newer tractors, for example, utilize digital technology to map fields and to allow the tractors to use global positioning satellite (GPS) systems to drive themselves in a pattern that spreads seed, applies fertilizer, or harvests crops most efficiently. This saves time and fuel and maximizes use of the land, all of which increase the farmer's productivity and effectiveness.

A second way in which the digital revolution has had a major impact on the world of work is that it has altered the nature and expanded the boundaries of the workplace. Rather than requiring that employees complete all of their work at the employment site, the digital revolution now allows for substantial work to be completed off site. A magazine photo editor, for example, may receive and respond to mockups on her smartphone while traveling in a cab. An office worker may access and work with a company database from home while on flex time. Paradoxically, rather than shortening a workday, this development has had the opposite effect. Because the physical boundaries of many workplaces have been expanded, many workers now put in their eight hours at their place of employment *and* work after hours, on weekends, and even on vacation (yikes).

In addition to expanding the boundaries of a local workplace, the technological advances associated with the digital revolution have also had the effect of allowing for collaboration across great distances. Using workflow software and digital transmission of data, companies can now outsource an amazing number of tasks to other countries. In an outstanding book that traces technological and sociopolitical factors contributing to economic globalization, Pulitzer Prize–winning author Thomas Friedman (2005) provided numerous examples of such outsourcing. You are likely aware of the fact that many of the telephone calls you make to place catalog orders or to seek customer service are actually transferred to call centers in India. What you may not be aware of, though, is how widespread outsourcing has become. Did you know, for example, that accounting firms in the United States outsourced approximately 100,000 U.S. tax returns as far back as 2004? You may have thought you were having the firm down the street do your tax return, but the truth is that the digital revolution allows that firm to scan your documents, have someone in another country prepare the tax return (at a far lower hourly rate), and provide them to you with no mention of having outsourced the work. (Shocking, right?) Similarly, Friedman explained that, "in many small and some medium-size hospitals in the U.S., radiologists are outsourcing reading of CAT scans to doctors in India and Australia" (p. 16). Thus, a third major way in which the digital revolution has affected the world of work is that it directly contributed to the rapid acceleration of globalization by making it technologically feasible. So just what is globalization? Let's take a look.

Globalization

At the most basic level, globalization simply refers to interactions across national borders; these interactions have the effect of making the world a smaller place. A more formal definition was offered by Arnett, who defined globalization as "a process by which cultures influence one another and become more alike through trade, immigration, and the exchange of information and ideas" (Arnett, 2002, p. 774). Economists generally define globalization more narrowly as "the integration of economies through the exchange of goods, capital, people (labor), and knowledge" (Paredes et al., 2008, p. 156).

Of course, globalization has been happening since time began or at least since people began claiming national borders. Even so, experts generally trace the beginning of globalization back to 1492, the year Columbus set sail in search of a more efficient trade route to India (Friedman, 2005). In this first wave of globalization, the sponsorship of national governments was generally needed. In the case of Columbus, for example, he was able to make his voyage only with the financial sponsorship of Spain. The second era of globalization roughly coincided with the beginning of the Industrial Revolution and continued until 2000. In this era, corporations and companies tended to sponsor globalization efforts (Friedman, 2005). These efforts were generally motivated by a search for new markets (in which to sell goods or services) and for new labor (people to work at a lower cost to the employer). For example, it might surprise you to know that General Motors (GM) actually sells more cars outside the United States than within it. Although we hear and read a lot of media grumblings about the sales of foreign cars in the United States, we don't often hear that GM was China's largest foreign automobile manufacturer in 2008 or that it is currently the third largest in Korea. All told, GM has facilities for the manufacturing, assembly, distribution, and so on, of automobiles and trucks in 62 other countries, and a whopping 72.3% of the sales revenue in 2011 came from sales outside the United States (General Motors, 2012). Who knew, right?

A basic concept related to globalization, therefore, is that the economic well-being of the United States is affected by our country's balance of importing and exporting goods and services; by the international banking system; by the cost of labor both here and abroad; and by our ability to harness, develop, and share knowledge through the use of technology. Indeed, everyone seems to agree that the explosion of technological innovation associated with the digital revolution has fueled the most recent wave of globalization.

In this era, spanning from 2000 until the present day, globalization has not required national or corporate sponsorship (Friedman, 2005). Thanks in large part to the amazing technological capacity available through personal computers, the Internet, and cell phones, individuals and small groups now have the ability to go global on their own. Of course, the efficiency with which national governments and multinational companies can go global has also increased exponentially as a result of these same technological advances.

CHANGES IN THE WORLD OF WORK

It should be clear from my brief history lesson that the world of work in the United States has experienced dramatic changes over time. In the following sections, I will address three major changes in the world of work: (1) job opportunities, (2) postsecondary training needs, and (3) job security and career stability. My hope is that the history lesson helped you understand technological and sociological contributions to these changes. In addition, I hope you will recognize that, with each historical shift, the changes have been neither all good nor all bad. Instead, some changes have been more positive than others, and the impact of each change has benefited some workers and challenged others.

As a side note, it is really important for counselors-in-training to become increasingly tolerant of ambiguity and to think critically rather than dichotomously. Rarely is any person, event, or situation all good or all bad. Instead, life is complicated and people are complex. As you read about the changes in the world of work, I therefore challenge you to think about how each change might be positive or represent progress (at least for some people) as well as to recognize how each change could challenge or cause hardship (at least for some people). To do this, you will need to move far beyond the simplistic rhetoric so frequently produced by some members of the media. Do I have you interested? Let's see how you do in identifying the complexities related to each type of change in the world of work.

Job Opportunities

The United States, especially as a developing nation, enjoyed a long-standing reputation as the land of opportunity; however, it now faces steep competition from other countries. Citizens in developing nations such as China and India represent an inexpensive labor pool and compete against workers in the United States, especially for unskilled jobs (Gibson & Mitchell, 2006; Harmon, 1996). Developing nations are also investing tremendous amounts in higher education and are producing the majority of the world's engineers (The White House, 2011). Jobs in the manufacturing sector of our economy were once plentiful and relatively high paying, but this is not true today because of technological advances and globalization. In contrast, opportunities within knowledge-based professions such as information technology, health sciences, and engineering have increased. Whereas career opportunities for women and minorities were once limited by stereotypes, biases, and outright discrimination, there are now more opportunities for women and minorities. (Even so, more progress is needed.)

So how did you do? I am guessing that the negative elements of these changes were easy to recognize, but what positive elements did you identify? For example, I assume you recognize the negative challenges associated with increased competition, including the loss of relatively high-paying manufacturing jobs in the United States as a result of the outsourcing of these manufacturing jobs to very poorly paid workers in developing countries. I hope you also recognize potentially positive elements as well. For example, the transfer of low-skill jobs to developing countries is not new. In fact (news flash!), the transfer of low-skill jobs reflects progress (not decline) on the part of the United States (Friedman, 2005). This progress allows for the level of work completed in the United States to be at a higher, more complex level than the work we outsource. Friedman (2005) used the following example to illustrate this by quoting one of his colleagues in India. This colleague, whose name is Jaithirth (Jerry) Rao, was focusing on the practice of outsourcing the preparation of U.S. tax returns to India and offered the following explanation:

> The accountant who wants to stay in business in America will be the one who focuses on designing creative complex strategies, like tax avoidance or tax sheltering, managing customer relationships. . . . He or she will say to his [sic] clients, "I am getting the grunt work done efficiently far away. Now let's talk about how we manage your estate and what you are going to do about your kids. Do you want to leave some money in your trusts?" It means having the quality-time discussions with clients rather than running around like chickens with their heads cut off from February to April, and often filing for extensions into August, because they have not had the quality time with clients. (Friedman, 2005, pp. 13–14)

Outsourcing work allows accountants in the United States to avoid the distinctly unpleasant grunt work of tax season. Such work takes little skill and a lot of time. The negative side, of course, is that there are likely people in the United States who would jump at the opportunity to do that grunt work. However, the wages they expect are far higher than what will be paid in India. The costs and benefits of this situation can be analyzed from many perspectives. From the perspective of highly trained accountants, the benefits outweigh the costs because they (a) avoid doing the grunt work and (b) make a profit from the difference between what they charge the client and what they pay the worker in India. From the perspective of people in the United States who would want that job, the costs outweigh the benefits because that job is not available to them. There is no doubt that lower skill workers with limited education fare the worst in this scenario and thus experience the highest unemployment rates (Hees et al., 2012). From yet another angle, the social justice perspective calls into question the ethics involved in this situation. News reports abound regarding the terrible working conditions and poor wages paid by U.S. employers to workers in developing nations (Harrison & Scorse, 2006; Workers Rights Consortium, 2013). As we will discuss later in this text, U.S. employers are not bound—unfortunately—to abide by U.S. employment laws (regarding minimum wage, child labor, worker safety, etc.) in their offshore holdings.

With these few examples, I hope you are better able to understand the complexity involved in these changes within the world of work. Let's look at another category of change, one that is directly related to what we just discussed regarding the impact of globalization on lower-skill workers with limited education. Again, think about how each change might be positive or represent progress (at least for some people) and about how each change could challenge or cause hardship (at least for some people).

Postsecondary Training Needs

Whereas workers with limited education (high school or less) could once earn a livable wage and support a family, this is much less likely in today's world of work. Postsecondary education or training is increasingly necessary for career success and financial stability (Carnevale, 2008; Symonds, Schwartz, & Ferguson, 2011). However, whereas any college degree was once a virtual assurance of career success, this is no longer the case (Gibson & Mitchell, 2006). Instead, the competition for jobs has increased, and employers pay greater attention to the college's reputation, one's academic major, one's career-related experiences, and one's actual skills. In addition, advanced degrees are increasingly required.

Perhaps more than ever before, people need to have a high level of skills in order to succeed in the world of work. Many times, these skills are developed in the course of formal education. Obviously, though, people can and do develop strong, marketable skills and succeed in the world of work without formal postsecondary education. Bill Gates, the founder of Microsoft, and Mark Zuckerberg, the founder of Facebook, come to mind. Both dropped out of college but have done reasonably well for themselves (wink). LeBron James has succeeded in the National Basketball Association (NBA) with only a high school diploma. Some may mistakenly conclude that this means postsecondary education isn't important for career success; however, I argue the opposite. For most of us regular folks, formal education represents our best access to knowledge and skill development. I would contend that, although they were each able to develop extremely high levels of skill outside the confines of a college classroom, Mark Zuckerberg, Bill Gates, and LeBron James cannot be described as regular folks. The bottom line is that, one way or another, a higher skill level is now more essential to career success than in previous generations. This should make intuitive sense given that many of the lower skill jobs are outsourced to developing nations.

The importance of lifelong learning cannot be overemphasized. The new world of work not only requires a higher level of skill and education at the point of entry but also requires continual learning and skill acquisition. Although this has always been true in some sense, workers in previous generations could usually obtain any additional skills or training through their employer. This is now much less common. Employers who once provided or paid for such training are now increasingly likely to expect employees to take individual responsibility for their continuing education. Rather than depending only on mentoring and professional development offered by their employer, savvy workers today take personal responsibility for their continued education and skill development.

Job Security and Career Stability

Another way in which globalization has changed the world of work relates to the level of job security and career stability one can reasonably expect. These changes affect everyone along the career development spectrum, including young people preparing to enter the world of work, seasoned workers who have established career trajectories, and workers preparing (or at least hoping) to exit the world of work via retirement.

Young people approaching or entering adulthood could once reasonably expect to achieve as much or more career success and financial stability than their parents, but this is no longer the case. Instead, the current cohort of young adults faces a postrecession world in which career success is more elusive and in which they may very well fare more poorly than their parents (Gibson & Mitchell, 2006). Whereas the career decision-making process was once geared toward a single decision point at which a person selected a lifelong career path, change is now the norm. Because people will hold multiple jobs and work in different careers over the course of their lifetimes, learning how to make good career decisions is more important than ever.

In the case of seasoned employees, globalization has affected the stability of already established careers, the psychological relationship between employees and employers, and their bargaining power. Whereas employees were once in a strong position to bargain collectively and negotiate for wages or salaries, they are now in a much weaker position. This has been, in large part, a direct result of globalization because employers may now choose to utilize foreign labor sources in developing nations rather than pay U.S. wages and/or union-negotiated wages to U.S. workers.

Right-to-work legislation has passed in many states and is likely to reduce employee bargaining power.

Another way in which globalization has affected the stability of already established careers involves the commitment and loyalty of employers to their employees. Whereas employers once rewarded workers for their hard work and loyalty with job security and career progression within the organization, they are now more likely to eliminate positions despite a worker's success and tenure with the organization (Coutinho et al., 2008; Hees et al., 2012). Commitment to organizational performance and profit now overshadows loyalty to long-term employees. Employer efforts to cut costs and increase profits have resulted in downsizing; outsourcing; and an increased reliance on part-time, contingent, and temporary workers who do not qualify for perks such as health benefits (Coutinho et al., 2008; Herr, 2013). Even high-performing workers who demonstrate hard work, loyalty, and honesty can find themselves the victims of downsizing, offshoring, restructuring, and so forth (Hees et al., 2012).

As a result of these changes, the psychological contract involving employer–employee loyalty has been broken (Coutinho et al., 2008, p. 9). Employers no longer assume responsibility for the long-term well-being of their employees (Harmon, 1996, p. 38). Long-time workers can no longer count on holding their jobs until retirement (Jacobs & Blustein, 2008). Rather than seeking career advancement opportunities primarily within their current organization, ambitious employees today must consider advancement opportunities that require leaving their current employers and may also require moving to another geographic area. In short, workers in today's market are increasingly "mobile and rootless" (Gibson & Mitchell, 2006, p. 9) and need to demonstrate higher degrees of self-directedness in managing their career trajectories.

This requires a paradigm shift. In the old paradigm, it was reasonable to envision a single career decision point and an entire career within a single organization or industry. In the new paradigm, movement into new organizations for career advancement is the norm, and it is necessary for workers to demonstrate increased levels of self-directedness as it pertains to their career trajectories. Two concepts associated with such a paradigm shift are the "boundaryless career" (Arthur & Rousseau, 1996, p. 5) and the "protean career" (Hall, 1976, p. 201). A *boundaryless career* is not constrained by the boundaries of an individual organization or employer. Instead, a boundaryless career "revolves around opportunities across organizational boundaries" and has also "been interpreted by others as interfirm mobility" (Briscoe & Hall, 2006, p. 6). Whereas the concept of a boundaryless career focuses on the location of advancement opportunities (e.g., in other organizations), the concept of the protean career focuses on the internal mind-set of an employee. The *protean career* emphasizes the importance that "the individual rather than the organization takes on the responsibility for one's own career and for transforming one's own career path" (Baruch, 2006, p. 129).

The world of work has also changed with regard to retirement. Whereas workers could once reasonably expect to retire comfortably by the age of 65 (and some much earlier), this is no longer the case (Gibson & Mitchell, 2006). Instead, many workers find themselves unable to afford retirement at age 65. Factors contributing to this include the loss of net worth as a result of the economic recession's impact. The security of pensions is now in question, and many worry about whether social security retirement benefits will continue to offer a sufficient financial safety net.

As we conclude our discussion of the changes that have transpired within the world of work, I hope it is self-evident that, even though there are some positive elements to these changes, they have also resulted in tremendous stress and anxiety for workers (Baruch, 2006). I contend that the need for career counselors is greater than ever before to help alleviate this stress and anxiety.

> "Because we are in no better position than our clients to control the economy in which we function, we need to find ways to help individuals deal with change. We must all find ways to increase our comfort with the fact that the world of work is changing more rapidly than ever before and to increase our sense of control over our own lives and destinies within an increasingly complex social and economic environment."
>
> ~ Harmon, 1996, p. 39 ~

THE NEED FOR CAREER COUNSELING

The radical changes that have occurred in the world of work and the pressing need for assistance with career planning, job searching, and career management translate into a strong need for career counselors. Herr (2013) echoed this sentiment:

> Most workers in the future will need to reinvent their careers to keep up with a fast changing workplace. They will need to cope with the complexities of the job market and find positions suited to their talents and interests. Workers will be more dependent than ever on career counselors. (p. 277)

This text is therefore dedicated to assisting you in acquiring the knowledge and developing the skills you will need to fill such a role.

In the hopes of engaging you more deeply, I have incorporated seven case studies into this text. In the final section of this chapter, I will introduce you to seven hypothetical clients. Their cases represent a wide variety of presenting concerns and a range of contemporary career-related issues. My hope is that they will help you understand the breadth of this exciting field. Then, as we progress through each chapter, we will revisit these cases in order to apply chapter concepts.

OUR CAST OF CLIENTS

As a graduate student working toward a counseling degree, you will soon face the challenge of applying what you learn in didactic classes and from text to real clients. Although it's been many years, I still vividly remember my first practicum experience and my early work with "real" clients. I remember my response when clients said something totally unexpected—being quite sure no book or class had ever addressed that particular scenario and struggling to conjure up a reasonable response.

I also remember experiencing a sudden, deep realization that real-life clients were so much more complex than those portrayed in the nifty little case studies I had read. Looking back at those case studies, it occurred to me that this was, in part, because most of the case studies were but a couple paragraphs in length. Indeed, the case scenarios in many texts tend to be very brief, and the texts' discussions tend to give no more than a page or two of attention to any given client.

As simplistic as the cases may have been, I recall often feeling bewildered when reading them. I wondered how in the world the counselor knew what to do with the client in the case study and why I couldn't figure out what to do with my real clients. Surely, the simplicity of the case studies and the unidimensional client descriptions made counseling seem so easy when reading the books. However, there was something else that was missing. Specifically, many texts seem to lack an in-depth application of the theories and techniques described within them. I wanted to know *how* to use the theories I read about, *how* to conceptualize a client, and *how* to use any given technique.

To be sure, no text, class, or graduate program can prepare you for every possible scenario you will encounter with your future clients, and it is difficult to capture the complexity of clients on paper. As any seasoned counselor will tell you, there is never a surefire formula to tell you how to succeed with a client. Nonetheless, this text represents my attempt to remedy these issues. To help you better understand how to grapple with client complexity and actually apply theories, conceptualize clients, and utilize techniques, I will use the same seven clients throughout the entire text. In this chapter, you will be introduced to these seven clients. Although the descriptions you'll read in this chapter will seem much like the case scenarios you may have read in other books, this is just the beginning of our work with these clients. Here in Chapter 1, you'll simply get a sneak peek at them.

In Chapters 2 to 5, we'll revisit these seven clients and explore ways to use theories to understand their career development history and counseling needs. In Chapter 6, we'll discuss cultural dimensions of these clients and the implications of culture for our work with them. In Chapters 7 and 8, you'll learn about various employment laws and ethical standards relevant to each client. Later, in Chapters 9 to 13, we'll examine the counseling process along with specific helping strategies used in career counseling, and I will demonstrate how a counselor might actually use various assessments and interventions with our cast of clients.

My hope is that this approach will approximate the complexity of working with clients while simultaneously demonstrating the practical aspects of how to apply theory, how to conceptualize clients, and how to use techniques to help them. As the book progresses, you'll become increasingly familiar with our clients, their histories, and their needs. Just as you learn more about a real-life client in each session with him or her, you'll gain more insight into these textbook clients each week of your class. And just as it is important in real life to remember what your client has shared with you in previous sessions, you will want to remember what you've learned about our cast of clients in each chapter of this text.

Now, I'd like to introduce our cast of clients.

THE FINE PRINT

The clients in this text are fictitious. Any resemblance to real people, living or dead, is entirely coincidental.

CLIENT 1: WAYNE JENSEN

Welcome to Wayne's World

Unlike the slackers in the Hollywood movie *Wayne's World,* Wayne Jensen is hard-working both on and off the job. A 40-year-old Caucasian male, Wayne has been working on a factory line for the Ford Motor Company since graduating from high school. Although he is not particularly challenged by his job, Wayne takes pride in doing his job well and in being a good provider for his family. Indeed, his status as a member of the United Auto Workers (UAW) union has allowed him to earn a surprisingly high salary for someone with no more than a high school diploma. Including overtime pay, Wayne makes just under $100,000 a year.

He owns his own home in a relatively new subdivision and is able to pay child support consistently to his ex-wife. In fact, he has enough disposable income to own a new, chromed-out Harley Davidson motorcycle with customized accessories and to have given his daughter a brand-new Mustang convertible last year for her 16th birthday. Wayne has, in a way, viewed himself as a perfect example of the American dream. He has worked hard all his life, showing up to work on time every day, doing a hard day's work, and never complaining. His hard work has paid off with a very comfortable lifestyle—until now.

Now, things are different. Detroit's Big Three automakers just barely escaped extinction. In recent years, their financial problems are detailed nearly every night on the evening news. Plants are closing, workers are laid off, and contractual retirement benefits are even being threatened. Two of the big three have actually gone through bankruptcy proceedings, and it took a federal government bailout to save them. Despite having 22 years of seniority and being a union employee, Wayne sees the writing on the wall and decides to seek career counseling. He says he needs a plan B.

THINK AHEAD. Given this introduction to Wayne, think ahead to your first counseling session with him. What feelings might he have had when making the appointment to see you and when arriving for his first appointment? What issues do you believe might be important to discuss? What types of easy advice do you think he may have already received from his friends, family members, and coworkers? How might the similarities and differences between you and Wayne influence the development of rapport? How might you establish a connection with Wayne so that he has a positive first impression of you and of counseling?

A note about easy advice may be warranted. All too often, novice counselors are so invested in being helpful to their clients that they are tempted to offer easy advice. A sure sign is your impulse to offer possible solutions after only a very brief introduction to a client's concerns. Remember that this easy advice generally tends to be the same advice your clients could get (and probably have already received) from many other, nonprofessional sources. Parents, siblings, friends, coworkers, bartenders, and even the person sitting beside them on the airplane could all offer that easy advice. Clients come to professional counselors for something else: something more fitting, more thoughtful, and generally more complex.

CLIENT 2: LILY HUANG LI MEI
Helping Li Mei Blossom

For several weeks, Li Mei hadn't been sleeping well. Concerned about sleep problems, her frequent headaches, and general lack of energy, this Taiwanese-American sophomore at Chapman University finally decided to make an appointment at the student health services center. To Li Mei's surprise, even after ordering a number of lab tests, the physician could find nothing physically wrong with her. She was even more surprised when the physician referred her to the campus office for personal counseling. The idea of seeing a counselor was not particularly comfortable, but Li Mei complied.

She just hoped her parents wouldn't find out because she felt that this would be yet another way she would disappoint them. For most of her life, 19-year-old Li Mei felt like a disappointment. Overshadowed by the many successes of her older siblings, Li Mei knew she couldn't possibly measure up. Although Chapman University is a highly respected college, Li Mei was keenly aware that she was admitted only after being placed on the wait list. In contrast, her 21-year-old sister was recruited by and awarded a full scholarship to Stanford University, where she was earning all As in the engineering curriculum and also competing on the Stanford women's swimming and diving team as an accomplished diver. Her 25-year-old brother was now in his third year of medical school at Johns Hopkins and aspires to become a neurosurgeon.

Although she had been a fine student in high school, with a 3.2 grade point average (GPA) at a highly rated, private high school near her home in Flushing, New York, and was involved in a number of extracurricular activities, Li Mei wasn't a National Merit exam finalist like her brother and sister and didn't have the grades for schools like Stanford and Johns Hopkins. She also didn't have the same drive. After all, why bother? As the youngest and least accomplished child in the Huang family, Li Mei often felt invisible. For months now, Li Mei had felt increasingly discouraged. Lately, it was all she could do to make it to her classes, and it was next to impossible to see the point. After all, she didn't even know what she wanted to do. How was she supposed to declare a major?

THINK AHEAD. Imagine that you work in the counseling center at the college and are preparing for your first appointment with Li Mei. What thoughts do you have as you read her name and see that she was referred by a physician at the college's health clinic? What questions come to mind? What feelings might she have when arriving for her first appointment? How might the similarities and differences between you and Li Mei influence the development of rapport? How might they influence your ideas about how to help her?

CLIENT 3: LAKEESHA MADDOX
Doors and Windows

It was about 8:00 p.m. when Lakeesha heard the knock on the door. She was feeling more than a bit annoyed because she had finally managed to get both of her children to bed and didn't want them awakened. Contributing to her irritability was the fact that her husband hadn't yet arrived home from work. Terrence normally came home around 6:15 and Lakeesha looked forward to their shared time with the children each evening. Although cherishing the opportunity to stay home with their two little ones, this 27-year-old African American housewife and mother also admittedly craved her husband's adult companionship and found relief when they were both home to care for the children.

That was six months ago. The officer at the door regretfully informed Lakeesha that her husband had died in a multicar collision on the expressway while on his way home from work. That knock, and the message that followed, left Lakeesha stunned, disoriented, and numb. How she would have managed to care for the children without the help of the ladies from church, she didn't know. It took weeks for the message to sink in and it was weeks more before she could talk about it.

Now, though, she had to talk about it. She needed to think about her children and find a way to provide for them. She knew that the life insurance money would only last so long. For that reason, she decided to return to her alma mater, Spelman College, for some career counseling.

When asked what she hoped to get out of counseling, several tears trickled down her cheeks as Lakeesha softly explained that she was looking for a window. Deeply religious, Lakeesha was clinging to the hope offered by a quotation she had often heard: "When the Lord closes a door, somewhere He opens a window."

THINK AHEAD. Given this introduction to Lakeesha, think ahead to your first counseling session with her. What will it be like for you to have Lakeesha as a client? How might the similarities and differences between you and Lakeesha influence the development of rapport with her? How might the career counseling process with Lakeesha be like the career counseling process with other students and alumni who seek career services at Spelman College? How might it be different? How might you prioritize her needs?

CLIENT 4: VINCENT SANTIAGO ARROYO
Caskets, Closets, and Careers

Some might say that Vincent Santiago Arroyo's career path began with a casket. When he was only three years old, Vincent's father died a hero's death. As a firefighter in New York City, Vincent's father perished on September 11, 2001, while attempting a valiant rescue of workers trapped inside the second tower of the World Trade Center. Although Vincent has but distant memories of his father, he has grown up in awe of him. Many a family gathering has included a moment of silence to honor his father's heroism and, to this day, Vincent's mother still lights a candle for her late husband each Sunday before Mass.

Now 17 years old and a junior in high school, Vincent works every day after school at the *bodega* (corner grocery) in order to help his mother with the bills and rarely feels that he has time to do homework. As a result, Vincent maintains mostly Cs and Ds, but his school counselor told him he was still on track to graduate next year and to pursue his dream of joining the military after high school.

Perhaps this dream represents a desire to honor his father's sacrifice. Perhaps it stems from wanting to also experience the admiration shown to Vincent's fallen hero. Perhaps it reflects a desire to defend his country from the terrorism that claimed his father's life. Whatever the reason, Vincent has long dreamed of joining the Marines.

Now, though, there is a problem. For several years, Vincent has been fighting an increasing awareness that something's not right about himself. Although he hates to admit it, he's figured out that he's gay. At his most recent meeting with his school counselor, he shares this disappointing news with her and asks her opinion about whether he should continue pursuing his dream of joining the Marines. Vincent knows about the military's past "don't ask, don't tell" policy and, despite its recent repeal, has concerns about the military's long-standing opposition to gay soldiers. Vincent said this wouldn't be a problem for him right now because he is still "in the closet" and really doesn't want anyone to know. He wonders, though, how long he can keep the secret.

THINK AHEAD. Given this introduction to Vincent, think ahead to the variety of issues that may be involved in career counseling. What career issues does Vincent present? What personal issues may also need to be addressed? As is often the case, this client presents with a career issue that is closely intertwined with personal issues. Indeed, Vincent's first career goal was inspired by a personal tragedy, and another personal issue now threatens his pursuit of this goal. Also think ahead and identify cultural issues and their relevance to your work with Vincent. How might the racial, ethnic, religious, and sexual orientation dimensions of Vincent's cultural identity affect his career development and your counseling process with him? How might the similarities and differences between you and Vincent influence the development of rapport? Given the relatively recent repeal of the "don't ask, don't tell" policy in the U.S. military, how relevant are Vincent's concerns about being gay and seeking a military career?

CLIENT 5: DORIS BRONNER
Embitterment Versus Empowerment

Embitterment was written all over Doris Bronner's face the first time you met with her. You could hear it in her tone of voice, see it in her body language, and hear it in her words. In response to your opening inquiry about her reason for seeking career counseling, Doris barked, "It's not fair!" with an angry tone that seemed almost accusatory. This 53-year-old Caucasian female soon revealed that she was referred for employment counseling after discovering that she would not be eligible to receive unemployment insurance benefits because Nebraska law requires that recipients be unemployed through no fault of their own.

Several months ago, Doris was fired from her job as a secretary at the insurance agency for which she had worked the past 14 years. Since then, she has been fired from two other temporary jobs. The truth, although she certainly wouldn't volunteer this, is that Doris was not a model employee. At the insurance agency, for example, Doris often arrived late for work, offering no explanation to her supervisor, and she rarely completed an assignment on time. In fact, when confronted by her supervisor regarding slow turnaround times on assignments, Doris would argue that she was terribly busy and would then purposely slow down. The quality of her work was mediocre at best and her attitude was poor.

From Doris's perspective, though, it isn't fair that her new boss at the insurance agency expected so much and that another secretary and an insurance agent both voiced complaints about her. It isn't fair that she was let go so quickly at her two temp jobs without being given an opportunity to prove herself. It isn't fair that her husband is angry that she got fired, especially after all he has put her through. It isn't fair that she knows her husband cheats on her, and it isn't fair that she feels trapped in this unhappy marriage for financial reasons. It isn't fair that, at 53 years of age, she now finds herself unemployed without a good reference to get a new job, and it isn't fair that she doesn't qualify for unemployment insurance benefits. It just isn't fair, and Doris is angry and bitter.

THINK AHEAD. Given this introduction to Doris, think about your immediate, internal reaction to her demeanor when asked about her reason for seeking career counseling. What might you feel when confronted with her anger and bitterness? How might you best respond? What career issues does Doris present? What personal issues may also need addressing? How might you balance the need to establish and maintain rapport with your need to confront some difficult issues such as attitude and performance problems?

CLIENT 6: GILLIAN PARKER
Golden Handcuffs

At 36 years of age, it seems that Gillian Parker has everything going for her. It's actually been that way for quite some time. When graduating from high school in the Tacoma, Washington, area, Gillian was voted most likely to succeed and most popular, and these titles seem to have been appropriately bestowed upon her. Well liked, academically successful, and active in extracurricular activities, Gillian was the total package. Nobody was surprised when she was accepted to Cornell University, the highly prestigious Ivy League college.

Nor were they surprised when she was just as successful in college. Immediately after completing her undergraduate degree, Gillian sat for the exam and became credentialed as a certified public accountant (CPA) at 22 years of age. She then completed Cornell's highly esteemed MBA program before accepting a position with Ernst and Young, one of the nation's big four accounting firms. Once again, Gillian rose to the challenge. She was well liked by the firm's managing partners and received a number of choice assignments as an auditor. Although they involved relocating, these assignments seemed well worth it because they helped Gillian climb the corporate ladder quickly. After 12 years of grueling but rewarding effort, Gillian was made partner and was delighted to return to her home state of Washington. The Ernst and Young firm's Washington office was located in Seattle, only an hour from her parents in Tacoma.

Making upward of $250,000 a year, Gillian was doing quite well. She enjoyed the respect of her colleagues, the appreciation of her clients, and the satisfaction of a job well done. Personally, life was also going well. Very happily married now for three years, Gillian and her husband lived in the Green Lake neighborhood, where they shared a luxurious home with a large enough yard for their sheltie, Lance, to enjoy.

In a challenging economy in which the unemployment rate exceeds 10%, Gillian feels incredibly fortunate.

Lately, though, Gillian has also been feeling twinges of dissatisfaction. Aware that her next assignment will likely involve relocating to Europe for a three-year stint, Gillian questions whether the rewards of her career are worth the effort and sacrifice. She and her husband have talked about the possibility of starting a family, and Gillian is beginning to grow weary from the long days of work and the likely need to relocate every three to five years.

THINK AHEAD. Think ahead to what Gillian needs and what you have to offer. Given that few career counselors earn anywhere near Gillian's income, what issues may arise within you as you welcome her as a client and seek to help her? How might the similarities and differences between you and Gillian influence the development of rapport? What types of responses do you think Gillian may have already received from her friends and family members when revealing her growing dissatisfaction with her career? How might Gillian's husband and family react to the possibility that she might choose to change careers, even if this means a reduction in income and benefits? How might you help Gillian capitalize on her strengths as she explores her career options with you?

CLIENT 7: JUAN MARTINEZ
Bloques de Construcción para un Futuro Nuevo ("Building Blocks for a New Future")

When you first met Juan Martinez, you were immediately struck by the unlikely combination of his physical appearance and way in which he gingerly eased himself into the seat across from you. Had you not watched him wince and exclaim, "¡Oh, mi dolor de espalda!" ("Oh, my aching back!") as he carefully lowered himself into the chair, you would have found Juan's physique rather imposing, even intimidating. With his tattooed biceps bulging from his T-shirt, Juan looked every bit the part of a weathered construction worker. In fact, hard construction labor had been Juan's vocation since he left high school at the age of 16.

Born and raised in Fort Worth, Texas, Juan was the oldest of seven children. As undocumented and unskilled laborers who had emigrated from Mexico, his parents struggled to put food on the table. They were secretly relieved when Juan decided to leave school to accept work with a local construction company in order to contribute to the family income. Never one to complain and unquestionably loyal to his family, Juan worked tirelessly and he happily shared his income with his parents until he married at the age of 23. By then, several of his siblings had left home and his parents were better able to manage family expenses.

As the parents of two, Juan and his wife Carlita have had a much easier time than either of their parents. Juan's construction job, though physically brutal, has paid well and has grown to nearly $16 per hour. Including Carlita's income as a part-time housekeeper for a local hotel, the Martinez family has enjoyed a combined household income of nearly $40,000, which in Juan's words, is "*mucho dinero.*"

However, *eso ere antes, y esto es ahora* ("that was then, and this is now"). As a result of the past 16 years of heavy lifting on the job, Juan's 34-year-old back would tolerate it no more. With a herniated disc in his lower back, Juan was no longer able to perform the required tasks of his job and had no choice but to stop. Despite receiving some payments from worker's compensation, Juan and Carlita could no longer afford the mortgage on their modest home. Juan therefore decided to avail himself of the vocational rehabilitation benefits available through Texas worker's compensation system.

THINK AHEAD. Imagine that you work in a state-operated office that specializes in vocational rehabilitation counseling. Think ahead to what it might be like for Juan to need your services. Consider his working-class background, identification as a "man's man," preference for speaking in Spanish, and lack of familiarity with the counseling process. How might the similarities and differences between you and Juan influence the development of rapport? How might you use metaphor to help Juan understand career counseling? What questions do you have regarding the work-related nature of his injury? How might you help Juan identify new career options for which his back injury won't serve as a barrier?

CONCEPTUALIZING CONTEMPORARY CLIENT ISSUES

Now that you have been introduced to the seven clients who will be featured in this text, you have a better idea of the types of reasons clients may seek career counseling. As you have seen from these clients, people seek career counseling for a wide variety of reasons. Internal and external factors both contribute to client decisions to seek counseling, and the most effective counselors address both career and personal issues in the career counseling process.

External and Internal Motivators for Career Counseling

Clients sometimes seek career counseling due to external factors. These factors generally involve something that occurs in the client's life that results in the client's need for assistance with regard to careers. Wayne, for example, is responding to external factors related to economic globalization and its impact on the auto industry. He anticipates a high likelihood of being laid off from his job. Lakeesha's need to enter the world of work and her decision to seek career counseling is motivated by external factors: the sudden, unexpected death of her husband and her need to provide for her children. Doris is another client who is responding primarily to external factors when initially seeking career counseling. She was fired from a job and is not eligible for unemployment benefits.

Clients may also seek career counseling in response to internal factors. These factors may involve normal developmental challenges or may signify internal psychological or physical changes in the client that result in a need for career assistance. As a sophomore in college, Li Mei is likely experiencing some normal developmental challenges with respect to choosing a college major and career path. Vincent is also experiencing some normal developmental challenges as a junior in high school who is attempting to identify his postsecondary plans and his career path. Although older and already on a successful career path, Gillian also faces normal developmental challenges as she struggles with decisions related to family planning and prioritizing family and career. In contrast, Juan has experienced a physical injury that prevents him from continuing in his chosen career and he therefore needs a new career direction.

When conceptualizing clients, it can be useful to think about both the external and internal factors that may have motivated their decision to seek career counseling. It can also be useful to identify and consider the various career and personal issues that may exist for your clients. Indeed, although it is common for counselors to distinguish between personal counseling and career counseling, such a demarcation with real-life clients is generally not very useful.

Interweaving Personal and Career Issues in Counseling

Rather than presenting with only personal problems or with only career problems, many clients present with both. Given the importance of career identity in U.S. society, this should come as no surprise. Here in the United States, we often identify so closely with our chosen occupation or current job that our job title can become the central way in which we identify ourselves to others. What we do for a living often affects our lifestyle, our self-esteem, and other aspects of our sense of personal well-being. In turn, our personal well-being (including mental health and self-esteem) often affects our work performance and career satisfaction.

It is important to recognize and address the various career and personal issues that exist for your clients, whether they initially came to you for personal counseling or for career counseling. Note that the seven clients featured in this text all need career counseling but also have a variety of personal issues.

Wayne, for example, is facing the likelihood of being laid off from a job due to no fault of his own. Think about what this would be like for a client. Feelings might include anger, frustration, and fear. Self-esteem may be affected, and symptoms of depression or anxiety may become manifest. Rather than focusing exclusively on helping Wayne find a plan B with the idea that this is only career counseling, a competent career counselor will also assess continually for the need to address other, more personal issues.

In Li Mei's case, the need to attend to such issues is easier to recognize. She is experiencing considerable somatic symptoms, but a physician has already ruled out physiological causes and has referred her for personal counseling. This suggests that her somatic symptoms are likely indicative of some depression or anxiety. Li Mei also seems to be struggling with self-esteem issues associated with the relative success of her older siblings. Given Li Mei's age, stage in life, and need to declare a major, a wise counselor would assist Li Mei not only with her needs for personal counseling but also with her needs for assistance with career development.

It is apparent that Lakeesha also has a need to address issues commonly discussed in personal counseling settings. She is clearly grieving her husband's tragic death and likely has deep feelings related to this loss as well as to her sudden need to enter the world of paid employment. It would be foolhardy for a counselor to attempt to provide only career counseling to Lakeesha.

The same could be said of a counselor who works with Vincent. It is unclear whether Vincent has any need for personal counseling related to his father's death, but Vincent certainly has some need for personal counseling related to his sexual orientation. In addition to needing guidance with immediate postsecondary plans and a decision about whether to enlist in the Marines, Vincent also has a need for a counselor who understands gay identity development and who can skillfully assist him in integrating his racial, ethnic, religious, and sexual orientation identities.

Doris is unlikely to reveal, at least initially, her history of poor work performance, so a counselor might assume that the unhappiness Doris presents in the first session stems primarily from being fired. Upon learning more about Doris and her work history, the counselor may then consider the possibility that Doris's poor work performance and eventual job loss was caused by her unhappiness and general dissatisfaction with her marriage and life in general. In Doris's situation, it will be difficult to ascertain the direction of causation. Either way, though, it is clear that she has a need for both career counseling and personal counseling.

Gillian also has a need to address both career and personal issues in the career counseling process. Unlike most clients who seek career counseling, Gillian currently has a high-paying job at which she excels and from which she seems to derive a great deal of satisfaction. There is no looming layoff and, because she is now a partner (part owner), Gillian could realistically count on having her job for the rest of her career. However, Gillian is wrestling with the issues related to her competing goals of being successful in her job and expanding the time she has available to have children and engage in family life. She needs a counselor with knowledge of both personal counseling and career counseling.

Juan may struggle with being unable to do the heavy lifting required in the construction industry and equate this with being unable to do "man's work." He views the ability to provide for his family as of paramount importance and will likely feel pressure to find another way to provide equally well. Juan may also experience some emotional reactions to his physical injury. A competent career counselor will continually assess for the need to address psychological issues rather than focusing exclusively on helping Juan identify a new career path.

The Role of Theory

Considering these two perspectives (internal versus external motivating factors and career versus personal issues) is a good first step as you begin to conceptualize clients who seek career counseling. An important next step is to conceptualize clients using theory. Personal issues may be conceptualized according to psychological theories, and career issues can be conceptualized according to career development theories. In Chapters 2 to 5, we'll turn our attention to career development theories.

OVERVIEW OF THE TEXT

At the beginning of this chapter, I likened myself to a cruise director. Continuing with that metaphor, you have now completed your orientation session (Chapter 1) and the ship is now ready to set sail. In preparation for our voyage, I offer a brief overview of what you can expect for the remainder of the cruise.

As stated above, the next four chapters will address a variety of career development theories. Chapter 2 will focus on a category of career development theories comprising the trait factor approach. Next, Chapter 3 will introduce you to developmental theories of career development. Learning theories of career development and career counseling will be the topic of Chapter 4, and Chapter 5 will end this textbook's coverage of theories with an introduction to narrative approaches to career counseling. At the end of each chapter, we'll then revisit our seven clients and use various theories to better understand their career development history and their counseling needs.

In Chapters 6 to 8, we will continue exploring foundational concepts related to the practice of career counseling. Specifically, Chapter 6 will address cultural dimensions of career counseling. Chapter 7 will introduce you to elements of employment law particularly relevant to the practice of career counseling, and Chapter 8 will offer guidelines for becoming an ethical career counselor. Again, each chapter will conclude with a discussion of our seven clients so as to assist you in understanding how to actually apply the course concepts.

Chapters 9 to 13 will be dedicated to putting these foundational concepts to work in the actual practice of career counseling. Chapter 9 will begin with an overview of the career counseling process. Next, Chapter 10 will teach you how to conduct intake assessments within the context career counseling. The profession of career counseling is well known for its use of standardized tests, and this will be the focus of Chapter 11. Chapter 12 is dedicated to exploring the use of vocational card sorts with clients. Finally, Chapter 13 will teach you about how to use a wide variety of technology and information resources in career counseling.

Once again, each chapter will conclude with a discussion of our seven clients so as to assist you in understanding how to actually apply the course concepts.

Chapters 14 to 18 will then focus on specific settings in which career counseling is practiced. In Chapter 14, you will learn about career development in K–12 educational settings. Chapter 15 is dedicated to Career and Technical Education, which may occur in K–12 as well as community college settings. Next, Chapter 16 explores career services in college settings. Chapters 17 and 18 focus upon career counseling in community settings. Specifically, Chapter 17 explores the number one topic addressed in community settings: job loss, unemployment, and the job search process. Chapter 18 is dedicated to other types of adult career transitions and specific populations in need of career services in community settings. These populations include people with disabilities, military veterans transitioning to civilian employment, ex-offenders transitioning from prison settings, as well as homemakers and caretakers transitioning into paid employment.

Chapter 19 is dedicated to you and your own career development needs. In that chapter, I will offer specific steps for charting your own career path as a professional counselor. These steps will include preparation, job searching, and adjusting to your new career.

Should you have any questions along the way, please do not hesitate to ask the ship's captain (your professor). Should he or she be unable to offer the assistance you are seeking, please feel free to email your favorite cruise director.

CHAPTER 2

Trait Factor Theories

> **STUDY TIP**
>
> In preparing this chapter, I have synthesized a tremendous amount of material, which means that there will be a lot of concepts, a lot of vocabulary, and a lot of references. However, I have attempted to simplify and organize these theories by supplementing my narrative description of them with figures and tables. My hope is that these illustrations and tables will render the theories more understandable. I have also offered ideas of how two of the most prominent theories might be applied to each person in the seven cases. That is my part of the partnership. Your professor's part involves offering deeper explanations, facilitating discussion and experiential activities, and illustrating more specific applications of these theories. And your part, as the student, is to read the material and study it. Given that we will be addressing a number of theories that feature specific concepts, there is really no way to avoid the use of what may sometimes seem like lofty, technical vocabulary. To master the vocabulary and associated concepts, you may find it useful to take notes and/or make flashcards. Upholding your part of the partnership will serve you well in terms of your course grade, your performance on the National Counselor Examination (which has traditionally focused heavily on theory), and your eventual practice of career counseling.

The field of counseling includes several theories. Some theories, known as personality theories, are ways to explain the development of one's personality and to understand how various life events and experiences may affect personality development. Other theories, known as counseling theories or models of helping, represent ways to explain the helping process and to illustrate how a counselor may be most effective in assisting clients. There are also a number of lifespan development theories that focus on explaining various aspects of human development, including cognitive development, moral development, and psychosocial development.

Although all these types of theories will be useful to you as a career counselor, Chapters 2 to 5 in this text focus on another type of theory; these chapters focus specifically on theories that seek to explain career development and career decision making. Consider the following list of questions:

- How do people make occupational and career choices?
- Why is any given person better suited to some occupations and careers than to others?
- What factors contribute to a person's level of success and satisfaction in a given occupation or career?
- How can counselors help people make career choices that are most likely to result in their success and satisfaction?

Career development theories seek to answer these very questions.

The first, and the foundational, category of career development theory to be introduced involves a number of trait factor theories. These theories, which are the topic of this chapter, focus specifically on matching people with jobs by assessing each person's traits and identifying complementary work environments. In the context of these theories, *traits* refer to relatively stable characteristics of an individual and may include abilities, interests, personality, values, and so on (Lent, 2005). *Factors* refer to relatively stable features of a career or work environment that are generally related to job success.

I will begin by providing a brief historical overview of societal changes that contributed to the need for career development theories and of early pioneers who laid the foundation for the development of trait factor theories. I will then turn to the trait factor theory of John Holland, which is the theory that has arguably had the greatest influence on career counseling (Rayman & Atanasoff, 1999). Finally, I will present information about the theory of work adjustment (TWA; Dawis & Lofquist, 1984) and the generalized version of TWA, which is known as the theory of person-environment congruence (PEC; Dawis, 2002).

Historical Roots

THE INDUSTRIAL REVOLUTION. The origins of, and indeed the need for, career development theories can be traced back to the Industrial Revolution in the United States (Osipow & Fitzgerald, 1996). Prior to the Industrial Revolution, people didn't necessarily make vocational choices. Instead, when they were old enough to work, they generally followed the path taken by their same-sex parent. For example, this might have involved continuing to work on the family farm, becoming active in operating a father-and-son business, or working as a homemaker just like one's mother did.

However, the Industrial Revolution (which occurred during the years 1820 to 1870) resulted in tremendous changes in the world of work. As factories were built to accommodate the mass production approach, many people left their hometowns and moved to cities in pursuit of new career opportunities. Simultaneously, the United States experienced a large influx of immigrants, many of whom also sought work in these same cities. In the context of these revolutionary changes, the need for vocational guidance (as it was then called) became increasingly apparent. People now had vocational choices and needed assistance with selecting an occupation suited to them. With the pioneering efforts of Jesse B. Davis in schools and Frank Parsons in community settings, experimentation with approaches to providing such assistance began in earnest (Baker, 2009).

FRANK PARSONS. After establishing the nation's first vocational guidance programs, known as the Breadwinner's Institute and later the Boston Vocational Bureau, Frank Parsons began to record his thoughts about the process of helping people find suitable work. Parsons organized these beliefs into a now classic book, *Choosing a Vocation,* which was published in 1909 just months after his death. To this day, the major concepts presented in his book remain the foundation of nearly all career interventions. As a result, the counseling profession recognizes Frank Parsons as the father of vocational guidance. Because vocational guidance (now called career counseling) preceded the development of all other forms of counseling, including school counseling, college counseling, and clinical mental health counseling, Frank Parsons is also considered the father of counseling. Sadly, Parsons did not live long enough to realize the legacy he would leave when he planted the seeds that would grow into the counseling profession.

What were these concepts that played such an integral role in the establishment of our profession? To begin with, Frank Parsons articulated a number of beliefs about why he viewed vocational guidance as so important. His five key principles are listed in Table 2.1. As you read them, you'll surely recognize from Parsons's wording that the workplace was predominately limited to men in 1909. Although that has now changed and Parsons's exclusive attention to men is outdated, the basic elements of his five principles continue to have contemporary relevance. As you read them, see if you agree.

The first and third principles both articulate Parsons's belief that proactively choosing a vocation is preferable to taking any job one can get. Although financial circumstances back then and still today sometimes result in

TABLE 2.1 Frank Parsons's Fundamental Beliefs About Vocational Guidance

1. It is better to choose a vocation than merely to hunt for a job.
2. No one should choose a vocation without careful self-analysis, thorough, honest, and under guidance.
3. The youth should have a large survey of the field of vocations and not simply drop into the convenient or accidental position.
4. Expert advice, or the advice of men who have made a careful study of men and vocations and the conditions of success, must be better and safer for a young man than the absence of it.
5. Putting it down on paper seems a simple matter, but it is one of supreme importance in study.

Source: Excerpted from: Parsons (1909, p. viii) Parsons, F. (1909). *Choosing a vocation.* Boston, MA: Houghton Mifflin Company.

a pragmatic need to take any job one can get, the idea that it is preferable to have a choice has been maintained over time. The second and fourth principles point to Parsons's belief that choosing a vocation with expert guidance is preferable to choosing a vocation without such guidance. These concepts provide the rationale for the establishment of our profession. Indeed, this entire text is designed to equip you to provide such guidance. Parsons's fifth principle communicated his belief that using a written format for portions of the guidance and counseling process is essential.

In addition to articulating his beliefs about the need for vocational guidance, Parsons (1909, p. 5) also specified three steps for assisting a person in choosing a vocation. These steps, which are summarized in Table 2.2, represent Parsons's best known and most lasting contribution.

Although many career development theories have since been developed, the matching concept underlying the three steps outlined in the table continues to serve as the foundation for many career counseling theories and has been recognized as the most durable concept in career counseling (Zunker, 2006, p. 25). Although this concept may seem like common sense to you, it was not so easily apparent in 1909. The opportunity to choose a career rather than follow in a parent's footsteps was relatively new, and Parsons was helping people understand how to take advantage of their opportunity to make vocational choices. He was helping them identify the important factors to consider, both with regard to self-understanding and to developing an awareness of the world of work.

DIFFERENTIAL PSYCHOLOGY AND THE STANDARDIZED TESTING MOVEMENT. When conceptualizing the process of choosing a vocation, Parsons relied primarily on a person's self-report and used interviews and informal checklists as his primary means of assessment. It was not until the concepts and techniques of differential psychology were applied to Parsons's process of vocational guidance that the first group of trait factor theories emerged (Osipow & Fitzgerald, 1996; Williamson, 1972). The origins of differential psychology are often attributed to Alfred Binet, whose work resulted in the 1916 publication of the Stanford Binet Intelligence Scales and earned him recognition as the father of standardized testing (DuBois, 1970, as cited in Campbell & Borgen, p. 87).

The testing movement gained momentum during World War I due to the U.S. army's development of the Army Alpha and the Army Beta tests of cognitive ability (verbal and performance-based, respectively). In developing these tests, the army modified Binet's approach in order to create group-administered tests of cognitive ability for the purpose of guiding its placement of military personnel.

After World War I, the University of Minnesota took the lead in further developing approaches for vocational assessment. The Minnesota Mechanical Abilities Project began in the 1920s and focused on assisting immigrants with finding work. During the Great Depression, in 1931, the Minnesota Stabilization Research Institute was established. It focused on interest and ability assessments to assist unemployed people with finding work and/or retraining programs (Osipow & Fitzgerald, 1996).

With the application of standardized testing techniques to the measurement of individual differences, differential psychology soon broadened its scope beyond the study of intelligence to the measurement of a wide variety of individual differences. Perhaps most applicable to career counseling and the early development of trait factor theory, differential psychology included attention to differences in intelligence, abilities, interests, and personality. Because of

---

TABLE 2.2 Summary of Frank Parsons's Three Steps to Choosing a Vocation

Step 1: Understand Yourself
- Aptitudes and abilities
- Interests
- Resources
- Limitations
- Other qualities

Step 2: Understand the World of Work
- Requirements and conditions of success
- Advantages and disadvantages
- Compensation
- Opportunities
- Prospects in different lines of work

Step 3: Use "True Reasoning" to Find a Good Match Between You and the World of Work

Source: Adapted from Parsons, F., *Choosing a vocation* (1909, p. 5). Boston, MA: Houghton Mifflin Company.

their emphasis on assessment and matching, trait factor theories have also been called actuarial approaches to counseling. And because the early foundational work on trait factor theory was conducted in Minnesota, trait factor theories are sometimes referred to as the Minnesota point of view (Sharf, 2010). One key Minnesotan involved in the efforts to develop sound vocational assessment approaches was E. G. Williamson.

E. G. WILLIAMSON'S TRAIT FACTOR APPROACH TO VOCATIONAL GUIDANCE. Williamson worked at the University of Minnesota and focused on developing techniques to assist college students with the selection of a major and a career. His books, *How to Counsel Students* (Williamson, 1939) and *Vocational Counseling* (Williamson, 1965), represent two more classic contributions to the field of career counseling in general and to the development of the trait factor approach to career counseling in particular. In his book *How to Counsel Students*, Williamson articulated six steps of the counseling process. As you can see in Table 2.3, Williamson took a decidedly direct, expert, and medical model approach to vocational assessment.

Whereas Parsons (1909) pointed to the importance of a good fit between a person and a job and Williamson (1939) articulated types of vocational problems and the steps for assisting clients with solving these problems, neither approach was developed enough to be considered a full-fledged theory. The first so-called real trait factor theory was offered by John Holland (1997), and we will explore it further in this chapter.

Holland's Person-Environment Fit Theory

Although Holland was also trained in the Minnesota tradition, which emphasized assessment and empirical rather than theoretical models (Spokane & Cruza-Guet, 2005), he perceived a need for a theoretical model of career development with practical applications. He sought to meet this need through the development of a theory, which he first published in 1959 (Holland, 1959) and has continually updated since then. By all accounts, Holland's theory represents a major contribution to our understanding of career development, and Rayman and Atanasoff (1999) contend, "[A]rguably, no theory of career development has had a greater influence on the practice of career counseling and education than Holland's" (p. 114). In fact, Holland's theory has become so foundational to the practice of career counseling that most refer to his theory simply as Holland's theory, but some also refer to it as a person-environment fit theory. Holland (1997) called it a theory of vocational personalities and work environments. Whatever it's called, Holland's theory represents a foundational contribution to our understanding both of career development and of the career counseling process.

TABLE 2.3 Williamson's Six-Step Process of Trait Factor Counseling

1. Analysis
   - Use interviews and tests to collect a variety of data about the student.
2. Synthesis
   - Synthesize the information from these assessments to identify strengths, weaknesses, and challenges for the student.
3. Diagnosis
   - Identify the student's problem. Four types of career problems articulated by Williamson are:
     - No vocational choice
     - Uncertain vocational choice
     - Unwise vocational choice
     - Conflict between abilities and vocational interests
4. Prognosis
   - Inform the student of a variety of options and provide a prediction of success for each option.
5. Counseling
   - Assist the student in using resources to achieve and adjust well to the option chosen.
6. Follow-Up
   - Follow up with the student to determine his or her level of success and satisfaction with vocational choice. Offer additional assistance as needed.

Source: Based on Brown (1990, pp. 20–23). Trait and factor theory. In D. Brown, L. Brooks, & Associates, *Career choice and development: Applying contemporary theories to practice* (2nd ed., pp. 13–36). San Francisco, CA: Jossey-Bass.

TABLE 2.4 Key Elements of Holland's Theory

1. People develop a relatively stable personality type as a result of complex interactions between themselves and the environment.
2. There are six primary categories by which an individual's personality may be understood.
3. These same six categories may be used to describe work environments.
4. Standardized assessment instruments and procedures may be used to determine an individual's personality type and the type of work environment.
5. The better the match (congruence) between a person's personality and the person's work environment, the more satisfied, successful, and stable that person will be.
6. Secondary concepts may be used to increase our ability to predict how satisfied, successful, and stable a person will be within a specific type of work environment.

In classic trait factor fashion, Holland emphasized the importance of the match between a person's personality type and that person's work environment (hence the person-environment fit theory). However, Holland went far beyond the work of early pioneers such as Parsons and Williamson by developing a model for personality development, developing a typology of personality and work environments, identifying specific assessment instruments and procedures with which to evaluate people and occupations, and conducting a tremendous amount of research to validate his theory. Table 2.4 identifies several key elements of Holland's theory.

PERSONALITY DEVELOPMENT ACCORDING TO HOLLAND. Although the six personality types and work environment types represent the most central concept of Holland's theory, it is also important to understand Holland's explanation of how personality develops. Holland suggested that personality development results from ongoing interactions between a person and that person's environment. With respect to the environment, Holland placed emphasis on a person's home, school, relations, and friends and also acknowledged the important contribution of a person's culture and community (Holland, 1997, p. 19). He explained that, as a person grows and develops from infancy, there is a two-way interaction between that person and his or her environment in which the person affects the environment and the environment influences the person.

Personal characteristics specifically named by Holland begin with heredity and cultural dimensions such as "age, gender, ethnicity . . . social class, physical assets or liabilities . . . [and] intelligence" (Holland, 1997, p. 13). As an infant develops, Holland contends, the interaction between these personal characteristics and the environment results in the infant's initial preference for some activities over others. As the infant and then young child engages in these activities, the interactions continue to occur and result in the sequential development of interests, competencies, and dispositions. Holland explained that the result of these interactive experiences is the development of personality. Holland defined personality as including one's "self-concepts, perception of self and world, values, sensitivity to environmental influences, and personality traits" (Holland, 1997, p. 19). Holland's illustration of this process of personality development is shown Figure 2.1.

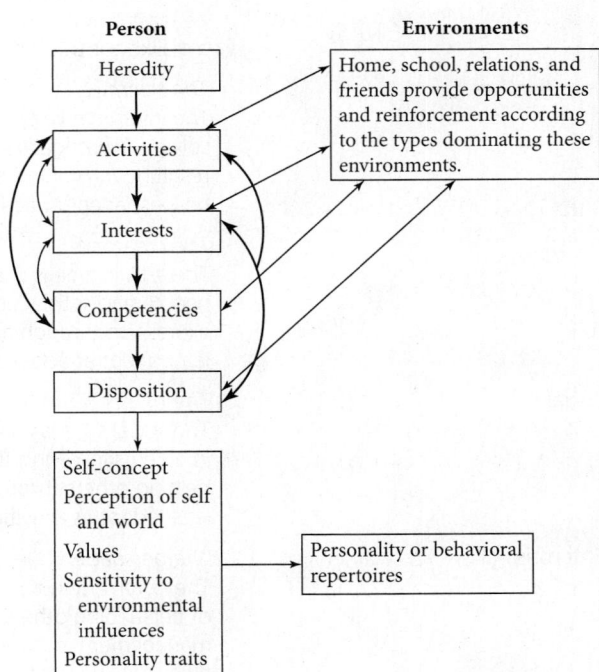

FIGURE 2.1 Holland's Model of Personality Type Development
Source: Reproduced by special permission of the Publisher, Psychological Assessment Resources, Inc., from *Making Vocational Choices,* Third Edition, Copyright 1973, 1985, 1992, 1997 by Psychological Assessment Resources, Inc. All rights reserved.

HOLLAND'S SIX PERSONALITY TYPES. Holland believed that the resultant personality could be categorized in accordance with six vocational personality types. Although Holland acknowledged that each person has a unique personality, he proposed that six personality types could be used to categorize most people effectively. The six types (often referred to as RIASEC) that were posited by Holland are shown in Table 2.5 alongside their respective one-letter abbreviation and brief description. Note that the italicized titles (e.g., *the doer*) included in each description were not put forth by Holland but instead represent my own, unauthorized way of describing each type.

Application Activity. As a worker, which of these six vocational personality types seems to resonate with your own personality? Can you look back at jobs you've had in the past, guess which environmental type best describes each job, and use these concepts to understand better the level of satisfaction you experienced in each job? As a future career counselor, think about the seven clients you "met" in Chapter 1. Even with the short introduction to them, can you formulate guesses about which vocational personality types each might have?

Assessment of Personality Types. Although Holland (1997) clarified that a person's vocational personality type could be assessed using qualitative methods involving careful attention to the person's expression of preferences regarding vocational aspirations, academic interests, and so forth, the primary means by which career counselors

TABLE 2.5 Holland's Six Personality Types

Type	Abbreviation	Description
Realistic	R	*The doer* The realistic type is characterized by a preference for practical, concrete, hands-on activities in accordance with a specific sequence or routine. Realistic people find satisfaction in careers requiring them to do something, usually involving physical activity focused on building, installing, repairing, or growing something. Realistic types may be least adept at activities characteristic of social occupations and often communicate a dislike for traditional academic settings and abstract or intellectual conversations.
Investigative	I	*The scientist* The investigative type is characterized by a preference for rational thinking and problem solving. Investigative people find satisfaction in careers and academically related pursuits resulting in problem solving and/or the creation of knowledge. Investigative types may be least adept at activities characteristic of enterprising occupations.
Artistic	A	*The creator* The artistic type is characterized by creativity and an enjoyment of self-expression. Artistic people find satisfaction in careers offering unprescribed situations that allow for self-expression through activities such as writing, art, music, and acting. Artistic types may be least adept at activities characteristic of conventional occupations.
Social	S	*The helper* The social type is characterized by interpersonal interests. Social people find satisfaction in careers involving the establishment of interpersonal relationships for the purpose of helping others through activities such as teaching or counseling. Social types may be least adept at activities characteristic of realistic occupations.
Enterprising	E	*The persuader* The enterprising type is characterized by the use of interpersonal skills for the purpose of persuading others. Enterprising people find satisfaction in careers involving leadership, management, and sales and place value on influence and financial gain. Enterprising types may be least adept at activities characteristic of investigative occupations.
Conventional	C	*The systematizer* The conventional type is characterized by a preference for the use of systematic procedures and organization. Conventional people find satisfaction in careers requiring systematic approaches to the management and/or analysis of data, information, or processes. Conventional types may be least comfortable with the unprescribed work style and activities characteristic of artistic occupations.

tend to assess vocational personality type are quantitative largely because Holland and others have developed a number of surprisingly simple and remarkably practical assessment instruments for this purpose. Examples of specific instruments that are commonly used to assess a person's vocational personality type in accordance with Holland's theory include the Vocational Preference Inventory, the Self-Directed Search, and the Strong Interest Inventory. These instruments will be among those discussed in Chapter 11.

Human Complexity and Holland Codes. When identifying these six personality types, Holland was not suggesting that only six types of people exist in the world. Rather, Holland clarified that people could best be understood in accordance with their similarity to each of the six types using a rank-ordering process in which the type most similar to a person would be listed first and the type least similar to a person would be listed sixth. For you mathematically inclined counselors-to-be, a factorial calculation of 6! results in 720 different permutations, meaning that Holland's typology allows for the classification of people into 720 six-letter categories. Pragmatically, however, Holland's actual practice has been to classify people (and occupations) using a two- or three-letter code. This code represents the top two or three types most similar to a person, arranged in rank order. For example, if a person is most similar to the social type, then the artistic type, and then the enterprising type (in that order), that person's two-letter type would be SA and that person's three-letter type would be SAE. These two- or three-letter codes have become known as Holland codes.

HOLLAND'S SIX MODEL ENVIRONMENTS. Holland (1997) believed that work environments could also be categorized using the RIASEC schema because people of a given personality type are drawn to and tend to dominate the corresponding environment type. In other words, realistic personality types are drawn to and tend to dominate realistic environments, and so forth. The climate, expectations, and work demands in a given environment stem from a cyclical, interactive process between the work environment and the personality types of the people most typical in that work environment. Given this conceptualization, it should not be surprising that the descriptions of each model work environment shown in Table 2.6 bear close resemblance to the descriptions of each personality type shown earlier in Table 2.5. As you review the following descriptions, note that Holland reserved the word *type* for people and used the term *model environments* when discussing the six work environments.

Assessment of Work Environments. This idea of defining an environment by considering the most dominant personality types employed in it led to Holland's development of the environmental assessment technique (EAT; Astin & Holland, 1961). A second, more formal approach to determining the Holland code of work environments involves use of the Position Classification Inventory (PCI). This instrument was developed by Gottfredson and Holland (1991) and differs in focus from the EAT. Whereas the EAT categorizes occupations via the assessment of employees in each occupation, the PCI is "an eighty-four-item assessment of the job requirements, skills, perspectives, values, personal characteristics, talents, and key behaviors performed in a particular job" (Spokane, Luchetta, & Richwine, 2002, p. 387).

Although a counselor or researcher could employ these techniques to determine the type of various work environments, much of this work has been done for you. Relying primarily on the EAT process but also using the PCI approach, Gottfredson and Holland (1996) identified a two- or three-letter Holland code for every occupation listed in the *Dictionary of Occupational Titles* (DOT, U.S. Department of Labor, 1991). They published this information in a widely used resource called the *Dictionary of Holland Occupational Codes* (DHOC; Gottfredson & Holland, 1996). In addition to identifying the Holland code for each occupation, this resource also offers an estimate of what Holland called the occupational level (Holland, 1997, p. 49) and others have called cognitive complexity (Gottfredson & Holland, 1996; Reardon, Vernick, & Reed, 2004). The Occupational Information Network (O*NET) website (onetonline.org), a more contemporary resource operated in partnership with the U.S. Department of Labor, also provides this same type of information for occupations. Holland codes may be found within the Interests section of O*NET Descriptors, and information about the occupational level or cognitive complexity may be found within the Job Zone section of O*NET.

CONGRUENCE AND THE MATCHING OF PERSONALITY TYPES AND MODEL ENVIRONMENTS. The matching process is central, of course, to the trait factor approach to career counseling and is a key concept in Holland's theory. In fact, the basic goal of Holland's theory and other trait factor theories is to assist people in finding a line of work that is well matched to themselves. Holland contended that people would be most satisfied and successful when employed in a model environment closely matched to their personality types. He called this concept congruence. Whether helping clients identify compatible careers to pursue or helping them understand sources of satisfaction or frustration in their current

TABLE 2.6 Holland's Six Model Environments

Type	Abbreviation	Description
Realistic	R	Dominated by people of the realistic personality type, the realistic environment is characterized by work demands and opportunities that involve practical, concrete, hands-on activities in accordance with a specific sequence or routine. Careers associated with the realistic work environment usually involve physical activity focused on building, installing, repairing, or growing something.
Investigative	I	Dominated by people of the investigative personality type, the investigative environment is characterized by work that requires rational thinking and problem solving and results in new knowledge or solutions to problems. Careers associated with the investigative work environment usually involve the scientific or scholarly exploration and analysis associated with the hard sciences or social sciences.
Artistic	A	Dominated by people of the artistic personality type, the artistic environment is characterized by an unstructured work environment and work that requires creativity and self-expression. Careers associated with the artistic work environment usually involve activities such as writing, art, music, and acting.
Social	S	Dominated by people of the social personality type, the social environment is characterized by work that requires the establishment of interpersonal relationships for the purpose of helping others. Careers associated with the social work environment usually involve activities focused on enhancing the welfare of others, such as teaching or counseling.
Enterprising	E	Dominated by people of the enterprising personality type, the enterprising environment is characterized by work that requires the use of interpersonal skills for the purpose of persuading others in order to achieve personal or organizational gain. Careers associated with the enterprising work environment usually involve ambitious activities such as business, politics, or administration.
Conventional	C	Dominated by people of the conventional personality type, the conventional environment is characterized by work that requires the use of well-organized, systematic procedures. Careers associated with the conventional work environment usually involve the methodical management and/or analysis of data, information, or processes such as in accounting, logistics, or clerical work.

careers, Holland suggested first exploring the degree of congruence between the client's personality type and potential and/or current work environments.

SECONDARY CONCEPTS WITHIN HOLLAND'S THEORY: CAVEATS TO CONSIDER. Embedded in Holland's theory is an assumption that personality is a relatively stable characteristic. Although Holland (1997) acknowledges that some people do change types over time, he believes that most people do not. The stability of a person's personality type is important in trait factor theories because it has implications for the effectiveness with which vocational predictions can be made (Hansen, 2005). Some people, however, have types that are more predictable than others. In an attempt to account for this variation, Holland (1997) articulated several secondary concepts. He explained that "the purpose of these secondary concepts is to moderate or qualify predictions or explanations that are derived from the main concepts" of his theory (Holland, 1997, p. 4). In other words, Holland offers these constructs as a way to understand his theory's effectiveness in predicting any given person's vocational aspirations, choices, success, satisfaction, and stability. The secondary concepts are described in the following subsections.

Consistency and Calculus. In conceptualizing each of these personality types and the model environments, Holland believed some types are more similar than others. Figure 2.2 shows a hexagonal diagram that Holland developed to illustrate the degree of similarity between each type. On the diagram, the shorter the distance between two types, the more similar Holland considered them. Conversely, the greater the distance between two types, the more different Holland considered them. As an example, the realistic (R) type would be considered most similar to the conventional (C) and the investigate (I) types; it would be most different from the social (S) type. Note in

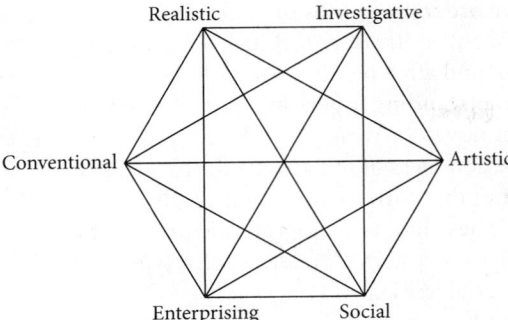

FIGURE 2.2 Holland's Hexagon
Source: Reproduced by special permission of the Publisher, Psychological Assessment Resources, Inc., from *Making Vocational Choices,* Third Edition, Copyright 1973, 1985, 1992, 1997 by Psychological Assessment Resources, Inc. All rights reserved.

the figure that the lines between RC and RI are of equal length and shorter than any other lines connected to R, and the line between RS is longer than any other lines connected to R.

Holland proceeded to articulate the implications of his premise that some types are more similar than others by using concepts he called consistency and calculus. Within Holland's theory, "*consistency* is the degree of relatedness" between the types (Holland, 1997, p. 4). In regard to a three-letter Holland code, examples of highly consistent types would include RIA and CES. You'll note that these letters are adjacent to one another on the hexagon in Figure 2.2. In contrast, SIC and EIR are examples of less consistent three-letter types. Holland maintained that vocational predictions lend themselves better to people with highly consistent types than to people with less consistent types.

A second concept related to the degree of similarity between types is calculus. This concept is directly related to the hexagonal shape in Figure 2.2 and specifies that the greater the distance between any two types, the less similar and less theoretically related are those two types. Holland (1994) provided actual calculations and correlation coefficients for each relationship, but a discussion of these is beyond the scope of this text. For our purposes, Holland believed that the degree of relatedness—both between personality types and between environment models—could be determined mathematically. He also applied the concept of calculus to exploring the degree of similarity between personality types and environment models. Calculus represents a mathematically based geometric model for representing the similarity or difference between each of the personality types and/or environmental models.

Differentiation. When using a standardized assessment instrument such as the Self-Directed Search (SDS; Holland, Fritzche, & Powell, 1994) or the Vocational Preference Inventory (VPI; Holland, 1985) to determine an individual's personality type, the individual receives a numerical score on each of the six types. Holland believed that knowing the difference between the person's highest numerical score and lowest numerical score is also useful in the career counseling process, and he referred to this concept as differentiation. The greater the difference between the highest and lowest scores, the greater the degree of differentiation. Holland proposed that higher levels of differentiation resulted in a greater ease of predicting a person's vocational aspirations, choices, success, satisfaction, and stability.

Identity. The concepts of consistency and differentiation each offer insight into how well defined a person is with regard to the six personality types. Holland contended that people with well-defined personalities are not only more predictable with regard to their vocational aspirations and choices but also with respect to how satisfied, successful, and stable they will be in their chosen vocations. He developed the concept of identity as another way to capture this concept, which is defined as "the possession of a clear and stable picture of one's goals, interests, and talents" (Holland, 1997, p. 5). To quantify this construct, Holland developed another standardized test called My Vocational Situation (MVS; Holland, Daiger, & Power, 1980); a person's score on this instrument is considered the person's identity score. People with higher identity scores have clearer and more stable goals, interests, and talents. Therefore, Holland's theory is more effective in making predictions about the vocational aspirations, choices, success, satisfaction, and stability of people with higher identity scores.

Think Ahead. Given this introduction to Holland's theory, think ahead to how you might use this theory with each person in our cast of clients. Without yet having the benefit of assessment results, what guesses can you make about the personality types of each client? Which clients might benefit most from an assessment of their personality type and an exploration of congruent work environments?

Dawis and Lofquist's Theory of Work Adjustment

A second major trait factor theory of career development is the theory of work adjustment (TWA; Dawis & Lofquist, 1984). Whereas Williamson's (1939) efforts focused on the vocational guidance needs of college students, immigrants, and the unemployed, and Holland's theory emerged from his work with high-achieving high school and college students, Dawis and Lofquist's theory stemmed from their work with vocational rehabilitation clients as part of the University of Minnesota's Work Adjustment Project (Dawis, 2005). Vocational rehabilitation focuses on the vocational guidance and employment preparation needs of people with disabilities, whether the disabilities are lifelong or, as in the case of our client Juan Martinez, acquired later in life.

Like Holland's theory, TWA is a trait factor theory that focuses on the goodness of fit between a person and the work environment. However, TWA differs from Holland's theory in two important ways. First, whereas Holland focused on vocational interests as indicators of vocational personality types, the TWA conceptual model does not include interests or personality. Instead, TWA focuses on a person's needs and values and on his or her skills and abilities. Second, whereas Holland focused on what people are looking for in careers, the TWA focuses on both what people are looking for in careers and what employers are looking for in their workers. As such, TWA offers an important expansion of the trait factor category of career development theories.

TRAITS AND FACTORS FEATURED IN TWA. Three primary traits are addressed in TWA. Each of these traits represents a set of relatively stable, though certainly not unchangeable, characteristics of a person. First, TWA is interested in a person's needs and values with regard to work. These may range from the very basic, biological needs for survival to more existential values such as altruism. Needs and values are useful in understanding why a person works, what types of work-related rewards are especially important to her or him, and what types of reinforcement needs a person has. The person's level of satisfaction can be understood in terms of the goodness of fit between the person's needs and values and the types of rewards and reinforcements offered by a particular work environment. Second, TWA is interested in a person's skills and abilities. In TWA, skills refer to "repeatable behavior sequences in response to prescribed tasks" (Dawis, 2005, p. 12), and abilities are viewed as higher order categories of skills. Dawis (2002) identifies several ability areas: perceptual, cognitive, motor/psychomotor, and affective abilities. Skills and abilities are useful in understanding a person's potential satisfactoriness as an employee in various work environments, depending on the goodness of fit between the person's skills and abilities and the work environment's skill requirements.

These first two traits are the primary focus of TWA, but the theory also addresses a third type of trait involving style variables. Dawis (2005) explains that the style variables all have some relationship to elements of time. For example, referring to a person as P, Dawis identifies and defines the four style variables: "*celerity* is how quickly P typically responds, *pace* is how much energy P typically expends per unit time, *rhythm* refers to the typical pattern of pace over time, and *endurance* is how long P can typically maintain response" (p. 14). Style variables are useful in further understanding the fit between a person and a given work environment by comparing the person's time-related styles to the demands of the environment. Table 2.7 summarizes these three traits and the corresponding work environment factors according to TWA.

TWA refers to the goodness of fit between these traits and factors as the level of correspondence (Dawis, 2002). In presenting TWA theory, Dawis (2005) offers two separate but related models: (1) the predictive model and (2) the process model. The predictive model uses the level of correspondence to predict a person's satisfaction with a given job or career as well as that person's likelihood of being satisfactory to the employer in that work environment. The process model uses some additional concepts to understand what happens when there is dissatisfaction on the part of either the employee or the employer.

TWA also acknowledges the relevance and importance of several other factors, although it does not focus on them. Acknowledging the complexity of humans, Dawis observes that "it is not surprising to find other variables besides TWA variables that can predict satisfaction, satisfactoriness, and tenure" (Dawis, 2005, p. 14). Dawis (2005) identifies these as vocational interests, personality, family culture, and the labor market.

TABLE 2.7 Person's Traits and Environmental Factors of TWA

Person's Traits	Environmental Factors	Variables Affected by Level of Correspondence
Needs and values	Reinforcers	Person's level of satisfaction with job
Skills and abilities	Skill and ability requirements	Person's level of satisfactoriness to employer
Style factors	Style	Person's level of satisfaction and satisfactoriness

Source: Based on Dawis (2005). The Minnesota theory of work adjustment. In S.D. Brown, & R.W. Lent (Eds.). *Career development and counseling: Putting theory and research to work* (pp. 3–23). Hoboken, NJ: John Wiley & Sons, Inc.

TABLE 2.8 TWA Assessments

Instruments for Assessing a Person's TWA Traits

Needs/values	Minnesota Importance Questionnaire
Skills/abilities	General Aptitude Test Battery*

Instruments for Assessing the TWA Factors in an Environment

Reinforcers	Minnesota Job Description Questionnaire
Skill/ability requirements	Occupational Aptitude Pattern

Instruments for Assessing Outcomes

Satisfaction	Minnesota Satisfaction Questionnaire
Satisfactoriness	Minnesota Satisfactoriness Scales

Source: Based on Dawis (2005), The Minnesota theory of work adjustment. In S.D. Brown, & R.W. Lent (Eds.). *Career development and counseling: Putting theory and research to work* (pp. 3–23). Hoboken, NJ: John Wiley & Sons, Inc.
*No longer in print.

Assessment of TWA Traits and Factors. Consistent with other trait factor theories, TWA also makes extensive use of assessment instruments. For each of the traits and factors identified in Table 2.7, Dawis (2005) identifies an assessment instrument that can be used to quantify them (see Table 2.8). Dawis (2005) cautions, however, that "one misconception in the field is that research on TWA can be done only with these instruments" (p. 15). I would also like to reassure you on the following point: You can use TWA with career counseling clients without using these instruments.

THE TWA PREDICTIVE MODEL. The TWA predictive model is designed to help career counselors and clients understand the dynamics related to a person's satisfaction in a given job and the degree to which a person is deemed satisfactory on the job. As you've likely surmised, TWA predicts that the level of correspondence between a person's traits and the work environment is directly related to the level of satisfaction a person experiences in a given job and to the degree to which a person is deemed satisfactory on the job. The TWA model is complex, however, because it addresses several variables. It recognizes that a lack of correspondence across any of the three dimensions can result in a person's dissatisfaction or that person's unsatisfactoriness.

In the event that there is a high level of correspondence across the three person-environment dimensions, TWA predicts that the person would experience satisfaction and that the work environment would find the person a satisfactory employee. This would result in maintenance behaviors on the part of the person and the environment and would likely lead to a long tenure, meaning that the person would stay in that work environment for a long period of time. In contrast, if there is a lack of correspondence across any or all of the three person-environment dimensions, TWA predicts that the person would experience dissatisfaction and that the work environment would find the person an unsatisfactory employee. This would result in adjustment behaviors on the part of whoever is dissatisfied (either the person and/or the work environment). Success with the adjustment behavior on the part of the person and/or the work environment would result in greater satisfaction and/or satisfactoriness and support a person in remaining on the job (a longer tenure). In contrast, insufficient adjustment on the part of the person and/or the environment would result in continued dissatisfaction and/or unsatisfactoriness and may result in the person quitting or being fired. Figure 2.3 illustrates the TWA predictive model.

THE TWA PROCESS MODEL. The TWA process model begins where the predictive model leaves off. It specifically addresses the process of work adjustment and seeks to answer the question, "What happens when a worker is dissatisfied or unsatisfactory?" This question is especially pertinent given that most people who seek career counseling are likely experiencing low levels of correspondence in at least one dimension and are likely feeling dissatisfied or having difficulty performing at a level satisfactory to their employers.

High levels of dissatisfaction or unsatisfactoriness can result in a worker quitting or being fired, but this obviously doesn't happen every time. Employees sometimes remain in dissatisfying jobs, and employers sometimes retain unsatisfactory employees. And sometimes circumstances change and the employee or employer becomes more satisfied. In these cases, adjustment behaviors on the part of the employee and/or employer generally occur in order to achieve more satisfaction via higher levels of correspondence. The way in which these adjustment behaviors occur is the focus of the TWA process model.

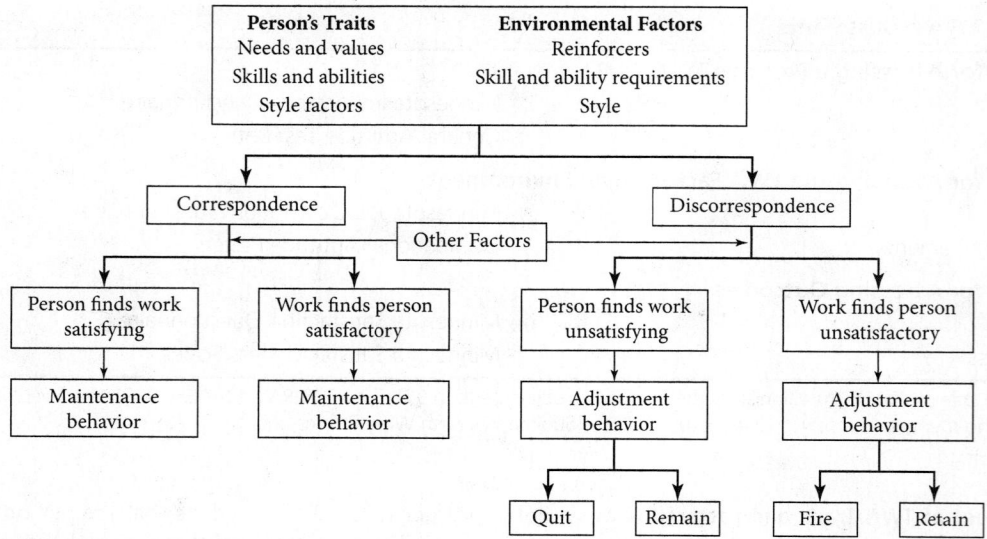

FIGURE 2.3 TWA Predictive Model
Source: Based on Dawis, R.V. (2005). The Minnesota theory of work adjustment. In S.D. Brown, & R.W. Lent (Eds.). *Career development and counseling: Putting theory and research to work* (pp. 3–23). Hoboken, NJ: John Wiley & Sons, Inc. [Figure 1.2, p. 8].

Keeping their focus on the career counseling client (the person), Dawis and Lofquist (1984) developed their process model to emphasize the person's response to dissatisfaction or unsatisfactoriness. Specifically, they identify four types of adjustment styles. The first is called flexibility and is defined as "the degree of discorrespondence tolerated before becoming dissatisfied enough to engage in adjustment behavior" (Dawis, 2005, p. 9). People with higher levels of flexibility not only master a full range of yoga poses, they can also tolerate low levels of correspondence with regard to their needs/values and their personal styles longer than others.

At some point, though, even the most flexible people may reach a level of dissatisfaction at which they decide to engage in adjustment behaviors in an attempt to increase the level of correspondence and satisfaction. In this case, people have three options: (1) Change their employer or their job, (2) change themselves, or (3) leave the situation. The remaining adjustment styles are related to these three options.

Attempts to adjust by changing one's employer or job involves the adjustment style known as activeness. Activeness refers to a person attempting to change the nature of the work environment. This can occur by changing either the types of reinforcers available in the work environment (in order to experience more satisfaction when the job meets their personal needs or values better) or the skill requirements of the job (in order to be viewed by the employer as more satisfactory). Attempts to adjust by changing oneself involve the adjustment style known as reactiveness. Reactiveness refers to a person attempting to change oneself in order to increase levels of correspondence. This adjustment style tends to involve attempts to improve one's skill levels or to modify one's personal behaviors. Improving one's skill levels can result in better meeting the employer's skill requirements and thus one's satisfactoriness. Improving one's skill levels can also result in more satisfaction by getting one's needs better met by the work environment. It is important to note that Dawis and Lofquist (1984) recognized that people do indeed respond both actively and reactively in any given situation. As such, it is not a matter of which adjustment style reflects an individual but rather the level to which that individual demonstrates each of these adjustment styles.

Let's explore an example of active and reactive adjustment behaviors. An important need for a person may be related to money. A person may be in a job in which the pay is not sufficiently meeting his or her needs. In exhibiting an active adjustment style, the person could simply request a raise. In exhibiting a reactive adjustment style, the person could respond to his or her dissatisfaction with the pay by enrolling in a training program in order to gain the knowledge and skills necessary for a promotion within the same company.

People differ with regard to how long they will attempt such adjustment strategies before they decide to

TABLE 2.9 TWA Adjustment Styles in Response to Dissatisfaction or a Lack of Correspondence

Colloquial Expression	TWA Adjustment Style	Description
"Put up with it."	Flexibility	How long a person can tolerate a lack of correspondence before engaging in adjustment behavior.
"Change them."	Activeness	Adjustment behavior involving attempts to change the nature of the work environment.
"Change yourself."	Reactiveness	Adjustment behavior involving attempts to change oneself.
"Keep trying."	Perseverance	How long a person engages in adjustment behaviors before leaving the situation.

Source: Based on Dawis (2005), The Minnesota theory of work adjustment. In S.D. Brown, & R.W. Lent (Eds.). *Career development and counseling: Putting theory and research to work* (pp. 3–23). Hoboken, NJ: John Wiley & Sons, Inc.

leave the situation. TWA identifies this as its fourth adjustment style and calls it perseverance. People with higher levels of perseverance spend more time trying to adjust than do people with lower levels of perseverance before deciding to leave the situation (usually by quitting). Although not specifically addressed by Dawis (2005), one's ability to leave the situation by quitting is also influenced by other factors, especially those pertaining to socioeconomic status and the labor market.

See Table 2.9 for the basic concepts and dynamics represented in the TWA process model expressed in colloquial language. The cyclical and interactive nature of the concepts within the TWA process model is illustrated in Figure 2.4.

EXPANSION OF TWA AND A NEW NAME: PERSON-ENVIRONMENT CORRESPONDENCE THEORY. In recent years, TWA (Dawis & Lofquist, 1984) has been expanded. Rather than focusing on the level of correspondence between people and environments only in work environments, the expansion recognizes the value of applying these same concepts regarding person-environment fit to other

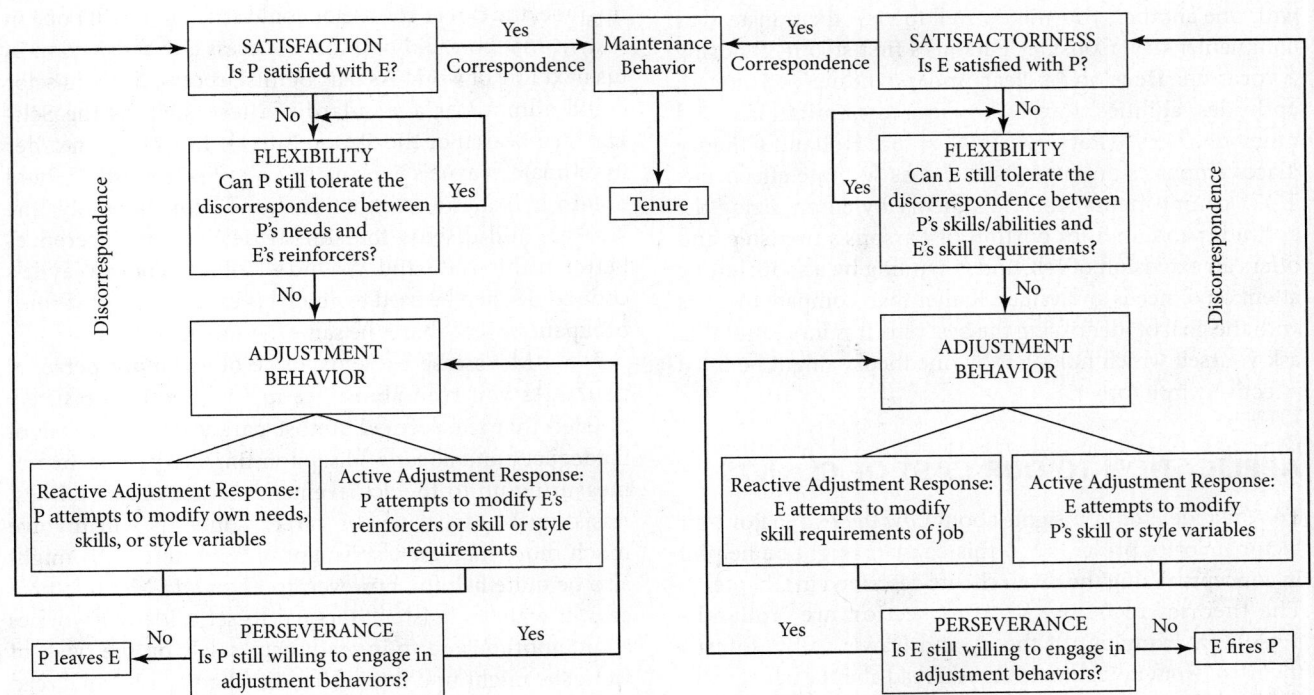

FIGURE 2.4 TWA Process Model

Source: Based on Dawis, R.V. (2005). The Minnesota theory of work adjustment. In S.D. Brown, & R.W. Lent (Eds.). *Career development and counseling: Putting theory and research to work* (pp. 3–23). Hoboken, NJ: John Wiley & Sons, Inc. [Figure 1.3, p. 10].

environments. This expanded theory is called person-environment correspondence (PEC) theory (Lofquist & Dawis, 1991) and is described by Dawis (2002) as the "generalized version of the theory of work adjustment" (p. 427). In addition to being useful in understanding work environments, PEC theory can be applied to many other environments, including social environments.

Think Ahead. Given this introduction to TWA (Dawis & Lofquist, 1984), think ahead to how you might use this theory with each person in our cast of clients. Which clients present with complaints of dissatisfaction? Which clients might struggle with being deemed unsatisfactory by their employers? Answers to these questions should help you identify which clients might benefit most from the application of TWA approaches to career counseling.

Comparison of Trait Factor Theories

As a counselor in training, you may now find yourself wondering about the implications of the differences between Holland's theory and Dawis and Lofquist's theory of work adjustment, and you may find yourself trying to determine which theory is better. Although it is tempting to compare theories in this way, I would encourage you instead to find the value in each theory. In this chapter, for example, rather than viewing the trait factor theories as being in competition with one another, you will do well to view them instead as complementary. Consider Parsons's first step in choosing a vocation: Develop "a clear understanding of yourself, aptitudes, abilities, interests, resources, limitations, and other qualities" (Parsons, 1909, p. 5). Holland's theory places emphasis on interests and does so quite effectively. TWA complements Holland's theory by emphasizing the aptitudes and abilities portion of Parsons's first step and offers an extension of self-understanding by also including attention to needs and values. Rather than compare theories with the goal of identifying the best one, it is more useful to ask yourself which holes left by one theory might be filled effectively by another.

APPLICATION TO OUR CAST OF CLIENTS

To conclude, I offer insights about how the two major trait factor theories presented in this chapter might be helpful in conceptualizing the seven clients described in Chapter 1. The theories to be used in this section are Holland's person-environment fit theory and Dawis and Lofquist's theory of work adjustment. As you read about each of these theories in this chapter, you were asked to think ahead about the relevance and potential application of each of these theories to our clients. Let's see now how our thoughts compare.

Application of Holland's Theory

When you think of Holland's theory, you should immediately think of trait factor matching approaches and recall that this theory focuses on matching an individual's traits with factors related to success and satisfaction in the workplace. You should also remember that the major premise of Holland's theory is that both people and work environments can be conceptualized in accordance with their similarity to six different styles, organized in a hexagonal shape and referred to with the acronym RIASEC. How might this theory apply to our cast of seven clients?

Let's begin with Wayne. You'll recall that Wayne has worked on an automotive assembly line since graduating from high school. Rather than doing any serious career exploration or engaging in self-assessment in order to determine what types of careers might best fit him, Wayne followed in his father's footsteps and took a job at Ford. His decision to enter career counseling was prompted by the economic downturn in Michigan and his anticipation of needing a plan B, but a career counselor could talk with Wayne about the ways in which he found his job on the assembly line rewarding and/or frustrating and introduce the concept of using career counseling not to find just any job but instead to find a job that would be even more satisfying. Reframing the plan B as an opportunity for an upgrade, the career counselor could strive to instill hope in Wayne that he could find more success and satisfaction in his next line of work. As part of this process, the counselor could administer a standardized test, such as the Self-Directed Search or the Strong Interest Inventory, in order to estimate Wayne's personality type. The counselor could obtain a Holland occupational code for assembly-line workers and discuss the similarities and/or differences between this code and Wayne's Holland code. Wayne's code could then be used to guide his exploration of various occupations that share the same or similar codes.

Li Mei's case presents some other, more personal issues. As you read about her in Chapter 1, you surely noticed that she seemed almost paralyzed by a sense of inadequacy and a fear of disappointing her parents by not measuring up to the achievements of her older siblings. Assisting Li Mei with her career concerns will involve much more than an assessment of her interests. It might also be quite helpful, however, to engage Li Mei in a process in which she is encouraged to set aside her worries about aptitude and to instead focus solely on the types of work she might find interesting. In Chapter 12, you'll read about how a counselor could do just that. In that chapter, the counselor will facilitate Li Mei's completion of a vocational card sort in which each occupation or work activity reflected on the cards is associated with a Holland model work environment. In this way, Li Mei can begin to consider what she might enjoy doing without regard to whether she believes she would be good at it.

Lakeesha was working as a stay-at-home mom at the time of her husband's death, but remember that she had graduated with a bachelor's degree in psychology from Spelman College. She had chosen this major after attending a career assessment session with some of her sorority sisters. She still had her results from the Self-Directed Search and shared them with her new counselor at the alumni career services office. She indicated that the results (SE) still seemed to be a good reflection of her vocational personality type. Rather than the career counseling efforts focusing on a determination of occupational interests, the new counselor could integrate these results and focus on other issues.

Vincent's school counselor, of course, recognized that Vincent's primary concern involved addressing his budding awareness of being gay and exploring how this might affect his long-standing hopes of a career in the U.S. Marine Corps. Using a matching approach early with Vincent would not be appropriate. At some point in the counseling process, however, Vincent may decide that he'd like to identify and explore some other, nonmilitary vocational options. At that point, it would be quite appropriate to help Vincent determine his Holland code and to teach him how to identify and explore occupations with this code. Because Vincent is still in high school, commonly used resources such as the *Dictionary of Holland Occupational Codes* or the online O*NET system will likely be less appealing to him. It would be wise for his school counselor to use materials already available to students. For example, his school might have a site license for Bridges, which is a program that includes an informal interest assessment based on Holland's theory and offers career suggestions that match well with the student's interest codes and is widely used in K–12 settings. (You will learn more about this program in Chapters 13 and 14.)

In reading about Doris in Chapter 1, you surely recognized that she has a history of poor performance and attitude problems at work and likely wondered about the potential impact of her marital issues on her work performance. A career counselor might be tempted to focus solely on personal and attitudinal issues, but I believe that this would be a mistake. Although these issues clearly need to be addressed, a career counselor should also consider the possibility that another factor may be contributing to these problems. Perhaps there is a poor match between Doris's vocational personality type and the clerical/secretarial positions she has held. It would be useful to conduct an assessment of Doris's vocational interests and personality by using an instrument such as the Self-Directed Search (SDS) or the Strong Interest Inventory (SII). As you will learn in Chapter 11, such an assessment will reveal that Doris's interests (SAR) do not match well with her past job responsibilities in the role of a secretary (CE).

With Gillian, however, such an assessment would not likely be useful. She has already found a position in which she has been successful and satisfied. There is no need to find a better match between her vocational interests and personality and her occupation. In talking with Gillian, the career counselor discovers that this was no coincidence. Gillian reveals that she visited the Cornell Career Services office her first semester on campus. Over the course of several visits with a career counselor there, Gillian identified accounting as an area of strong interest. Like any good accountant worth her salt, Gillian had organized all of the assessment data from her career counseling experience into a spreadsheet, which included her SII results and indicated that her Holland code was CEI. Application of Holland's theory to Gillian's case simply involves recognizing that one explanation for her high degree of success and satisfaction as an accountant is the perfect match between Gillian's code (CEI) and the Holland occupational code for accountants (CE).

In Juan's case, career counseling is necessitated by a medical condition that rendered Juan unable to continuing performing his job as a laborer. Whereas some clients seek career counseling because of difficulties identifying occupations of interest or because of dissatisfaction with choices already made, this is not true in Juan's case. His desire to find a new line of work is unrelated to satisfaction or dissatisfaction. In fact, based on the information shared in Chapter 1, we have no idea whether Juan liked his job as a laborer and this would be important to determine. It would also be useful to determine Juan's Holland code in order to compare it to the occupational code for construction laborers and thus gain insight into one factor that likely contributes to Juan's level of satisfaction or dissatisfaction. In talking with Juan about these issues, the counselor learned that Juan had actually enjoyed his construction job but admitted that the physical nature of the job was taking its toll on him as he aged, even before the back injury. The administration of the SDS suggested that Juan's Holland code was RC and, when looking up the occupational code for construction laborers, Juan's counselor discovered that this occupation shared the exact same code. Thus, it should not come as a surprise that Juan enjoyed the position. This insight helped the counselor recognize that the goal with Juan was not to find a career that would fit his vocational interests and personality better; rather, it was to find a career that would be better suited to his physical limitations.

Application of Dawis and Lofquist's Theory of Work Adjustment

When you think of TWA, you should think immediately of trait factor matching approaches. In contrast with Holland's theory (which focuses on vocational interests and personality), TWA focuses on a worker's needs for reinforcement and the work environment's skill requirements. Therefore, assessments should focus on client needs and values and on skills and abilities. Also in contrast with Holland's theory, TWA not only addresses the quality of the match in order to predict worker satisfaction, success and stability; its process model also addresses the adjustments that may be made when the worker and/or employer are dissatisfied. Let's turn to an application of these constructs to our cast of clients.

In Wayne's case, the career counselor interested in applying TWA would continue with the approach of reframing the plan B as an opportunity for an upgrade. The counselor would primarily utilize the TWA predictive model and seek to assess Wayne's needs/values and his abilities. The counselor might choose to administer the Minnesota Importance Questionnaire in order to better understand what rewards and reinforcements Wayne would like to experience as a result of his work. A card sort can also be used to assess these values. In Chapter 12, the counselor working with Wayne will administer a card sort based specifically on the TWA work values. In this chapter, you'll learn how to use this card sort, and you'll find that the rewards Wayne is most attracted to are achievement, relationships, support, recognition, working conditions, and independence.

A similar approach could be used with Li Mei to assess her work needs and values. This would be useful in understanding what types of work Li Mei would experience as rewarding. Perhaps more pertinent in Li Mei's case, however, is TWA's emphasis on abilities. Li Mei has expressed her subjective feelings of inadequacy. In doing so, however, she tends to compare herself with her two older siblings, both of whom are highly accomplished. Although Li Mei has clearly taken a number of scholastic aptitude tests (such as the PSAT and the SAT) and has failed to qualify for the National Merit Scholarships like her siblings, she has never taken a vocationally oriented aptitude test. It might be useful with Li Mei to administer a vocational aptitude test such as the Differential Aptitude Test (DAT) or the General Aptitude Test Battery (GATB) in order to get a more objective estimate of her aptitudes. A goal of primary importance to Li Mei is to identify occupations in which she will be most likely to experience a high degree of success, and these standardized tests may be useful in this regard.

With Lakeesha, TWA could be useful in helping her identify the types of work she might find most rewarding. Although financial considerations and her need to provide for her children are clearly a priority, it would be ideal to help Lakeesha identify other aspects of a job that would also contribute to her sense of well-being. Administration of the Minnesota Importance Questionnaire or use of the O*NET Work Importance Locator card sort would be useful ways to assess this.

With Vincent, the TWA predictive model's emphasis on worker needs and values certainly has relevance and could help Vincent identify rewards he values most. As an adolescent with little life experience, however, he may not know these values yet. This is especially true given that he is in the midst of a major transition with regard to identity development. The TWA predictive model's emphasis on employer requirements and a worker's satisfactoriness may be more germane for Vincent, especially given his coming to terms with a gay identity and his worry about the military's attitude toward gay soldiers (in spite of the repeal of "don't ask, don't tell"). Vincent is wise to consider whether he would be satisfactory to his employer in the event that he entered the Marines and later chose to come out as a gay man. TWA's process model also has relevance because it indicates that, if Vincent were to disclose his gay identity, his employer may well be dissatisfied with Vincent. One possible outcome, of course, would involve Vincent being fired or discharged from the military.

Doris's case also involves discorrespondence between her skills and performance and the employer's expectations. From what we learned in Chapter 1, it is clear that Doris's employers have been dissatisfied with her attitude and performance, with the result that Doris has been fired from at least one job. It is unclear, however, whether Doris lacked the skills necessary to perform her job responsibilities, whether her failure to perform them were purely based on motivation and attitude, or whether her failure to perform them reflected TWA style variables. For example, the style variable of celerity, which refers to how quickly an employee typically responds, seems to have been a problem with Doris. If Doris were willing, it might be quite helpful to have her former employer complete the Minnesota Satisfactoriness Scales in order to gather feedback about the sources of dissatisfaction leading to Doris's termination. Assessments such as the DAT or GATB that are focused on vocational skills and assessments and on more general employability skills would be helpful in understanding Doris's unsatisfactoriness as an employee of the insurance agency.

In Gillian's case, there seems to be good reason to believe that she has been a very satisfactory employee and that there is little need to assess her skill sets or aptitudes.

Thus, the TWA concept of satisfaction becomes more relevant with Gillian. This is suggested by the fact that Gillian has been questioning whether the rewards of her career are worth the effort and sacrifice. To understand these complex issues, a TWA assessment such as the Minnesota Satisfaction Questionnaire would be useful to gain an understanding of the aspects of her current job that she finds satisfying or dissatisfying. Maybe Gillian does not particularly value pay as much as she might value other rewards. In this case, an assessment would offer some explanation of why Gillian might consider leaving a position that yields such a high income.

As we conclude our application of TWA, you may recall that TWA was actually developed in the context of vocational rehabilitation counseling; thus, it has most historical relevance to Juan's case. It also has practical relevance. In addition to identifying occupations that Juan may find satisfying, TWA also places emphasis on ensuring that Juan will be satisfactory to his employer with regard to his skills, abilities, and style variables. Thus, assessments of his work values and abilities are in order. It would appear that Juan was a satisfactory worker until his back problems became so pronounced that he was unable to continue in his position as a construction laborer. Like many clients with acquired disabilities who seek rehabilitation counseling, Juan lost the ability to use skills he previously had (such as heavy lifting and use of a hammer drill) and this had a direct impact on his satisfactoriness as a worker and ultimately on his tenure. One important focus of TWA will be determining his current skill set, identifying work he can do at this point in time, and on assessing aptitudes that might be developed with additional training to lead to an even more satisfying job for Juan.

PUTTING IT ALL TOGETHER

In this chapter, you learned a lot about trait factor theories of career development. At this point, you should be able to identify which theorist is associated with which theory, articulate the basic concepts associated with each theory, and recognize and explain various figures and illustrations related to the theories. My hope is that the application to our cast of seven clients allowed you to connect the relevance of these theories to the actual practice of career counseling. Keep in mind, of course, that the applications I suggested are not all inclusive. There are many more ways to apply each theory than could fit in a single chapter. Additionally, there are other career development theories with which you need to be familiar. In the next chapter, we will turn our attention to developmental theories of career development.

CHAPTER 3

Developmental Theories

> In Chapter 2, you learned about trait factor theories, which focus on the here-and-now matching of a person's traits with factors associated with various careers. In this chapter, you will learn about developmental theories. These theories focus on (a) understanding how early experiences affect the development of a person's career proclivities and choices, and (b) how people develop within their careers over time. Trait factor theories emphasize a static snapshot of relatively stable traits; developmental theories emphasize the process of change over time.

Over the years, there have been a number of theories put forth that focus, in one way or another, on the role of early childhood experiences and/or life-span development in a person's career choices and level of satisfaction within various careers. In this chapter, you will learn about five of these theories. As we begin, I'd like to acknowledge that these theories are only loosely related, much less so than the trait factor theories addressed in Chapter 2. Instead of being categorized as developmental theories, they could also be conceptualized as needs-based, relational, or personality-focused theories. I've chosen to group them together and to label them as developmental theories, however, because each of them addresses the impact of early childhood development and/or the evolving career choices that are made over the course of life-span development.

ROE'S THEORY OF PERSONALITY DEVELOPMENT AND CAREER CHOICE

Based largely on her training and experience as a clinical psychologist, Anna Roe (Roe, 1957; Roe & Lunneborg, 1984) developed a theory that one's occupational choices were largely determined by early childhood experiences and the nature of parenting received. More specifically, Roe explored the impact of three types of parenting styles, as shown in Table 3.1.

Roe believed that the type and subtype of parenting style resulted in the child's *major orientation* either toward persons or not toward persons, and she proposed that this affected the child's eventual occupational interests. More specifically, Roe believed that the nature of the parent–child relationship affected an individual's psychological needs, and she conceptualized these needs in accordance with Maslow's hierarchy of needs. Roe proposed that a person's most salient psychological needs then determined the direction of occupational interest,

TABLE 3.1 Types of Parenting Styles According to Roe

Types	Subtypes
Emotional concentration on child	Overprotective concentration
	Overdemanding concentration
Avoidance of child	Emotionally rejecting avoidance
	Neglectful avoidance
Acceptance of child	Casual acceptance
	Loving acceptance

Source: Based on Roe & Lunneborg (1984, p. 42) Roe, A., & Lunneborg, P.W. (1984). Personality development and career choice. In D. Brown, L. Brooks, & Associates (Eds.), *Career choice and development: Applying contemporary theories to practice* (pp. 31–60). San Francisco: Jossey-Bass.

and the intensity of those needs determined the level a person would likely achieve. In keeping with this hypothesis, Roe (Roe, 1957; Roe & Lunneborg, 1984) developed an occupational classification system involving eight occupational groups (showing direction of occupational interest) and six occupational levels (showing level of achievement. Her occupational classification system is presented in Table 3.2.

Next, Roe developed a rather complex diagram to illustrate her theory's prediction about how the various types and subtypes of parent–child relationships would affect the child's eventual vocational choice in adulthood. Specifically, she categorized careers in accordance with the early childhood experiences that might serve as "early determinants of vocational choice" (Roe, 1957, p. 216). As you can see in Figure 3.1, occupational groups are arranged at the outer edge of the figure. The major orientation, subtype of parent–child relationship, and type of parent–child relationship are specified in the inner layers of the diagram. Although this diagram includes attention to the parenting style and to the occupational group most likely to be chosen, it does not include a prediction of the occupational level to be achieved. The level achieved would be determined by the intensity of a person's needs as a result of early childhood experiences with parents.

By her own admission, however, Roe had "no experience in career counseling" (Roe & Lunneborg, 1984, p. 32). Perhaps because of this, her theory has failed to be upheld by empirical research (Sharf, 2010), and Roe's theory has not had a major impact on the actual practice of career counseling (Brown, 2002). However, it is useful for you to know about this needs-based, developmental theory and to recognize that it may make some intuitive sense, even if research has failed to uphold the idea that the nature and quality of parent–child relationships are directly related to a child's eventual career choice. Roe's work, however, inspired a number of other career development theories related to the impact of early childhood, the role of needs, and the relevance of personality development. Several of these theories made attempts to apply psychoanalytic and psychodynamic theories of personality development in order to understand vocational choice and satisfaction, the most "ambitious" of which was put forth by Bordin, Nachmann, and Segal (1963; as cited in Osipow & Fitzgerald, 1996, p. 23).

TABLE 3.2 Roe's Occupational Classification System

Occupational Group	Occupational Levels
Group I: People	Level 1: Professional and managerial 1
Group II: Business contact	Level 2: Professional and managerial 2
Group III: Organization	Level 3: Semiprofessional and small business
Group IV: Technology	Level 4: Skilled
Group V: Natural phenomena	Level 5: Semiskilled
Group VI: Science	Level 6: Unskilled
Group VII: General cultural	
Group VIII: Arts and entertainment	

Source: Based on Roe & Lunneborg (1984, pp. 34–37) Roe, A., & Lunneborg, P.W. (1984). Personality development and career choice. In D. Brown, L. Brooks, & Associates (Eds.), *Career choice and development: Applying contemporary theories to practice* (pp. 31–60). San Francisco: Jossey-Bass.

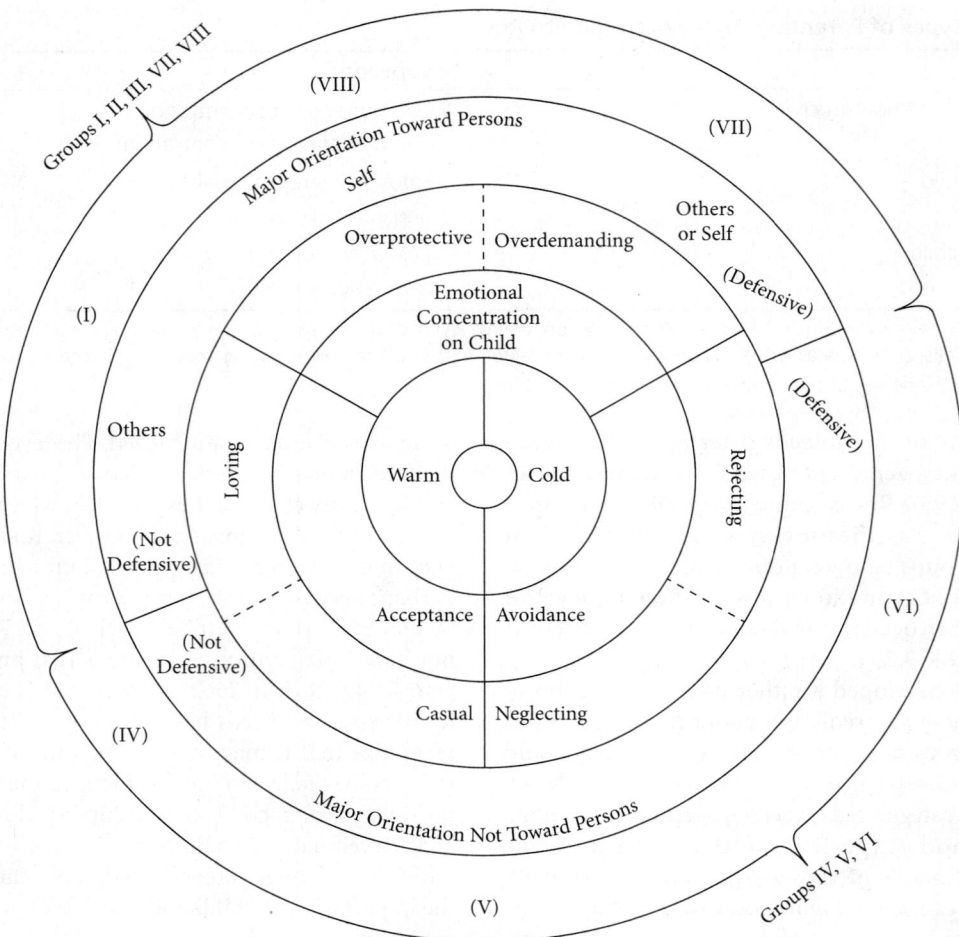

FIGURE 3.1 Roe's Model: Early Determinants of Career Choice
Source: Roe, Anne, From Early determinants of vocational choice. *Journal of Counseling Psychology,* Vol 4(3), Fal 1957, 212–217. Page 216. American Psychological Association. Reprinted with permission.

BORDIN'S PSYCHODYNAMIC MODEL OF CAREER CHOICE AND SATISFACTION

Edward Bordin had a strong interest in understanding why some individuals have difficulty in making career choices, and he was interested initially only in blending the matching concept prevalent in the trait factor theories with the ideas about self-concept made popular by Carl Rogers. Bordin was later influenced to a tremendous degree, however, by the psychoanalytic tradition when he accepted a position at the University of Michigan. His theory offers a unique blending of these three approaches, with an emphasis on psychodynamic issues. At the heart of Bordin's theory is his "framework for mapping occupations from the point of view that their intrinsic work requirements give the individual a way of being that is consonant with the dynamics and structure of his or her personality" (1984, p. 96). In other words, Bordin believed that a person's developmental experiences resulted in a personality that could be described in psychodynamic terms and that could also be understood as self-concept. He further believed that individuals seek expression of their unconscious personality structure and their conscious self-concept via their occupational choice. Bordin suggested that one reason individuals may exhibit difficulty in making career decisions could be that they are also experiencing difficulties with regard to their self-concept and/or personality development.

A major psychodynamic element of Bordin's theory is his contention that people may not be conscious of what they find intrinsically satisfying but may instead be motivated by unconscious desires and needs. He stated that "the theory proposes that the participation of personality in work and career is rooted in the role of play in human life" (1984, p. 96). Bordin explained that one's preference regarding *play* activities is based on what one finds "intrinsically satisfying" and suggested that people seek such satisfaction in all aspects of their life, including work.

Bordin's theory also addresses the conflicting goals of the id and ego, both of which are recognized as part of personality structure within the psychoanalytic and psychodynamic traditions. Although some people are fortunate enough to find work that truly feels like play, most people find that work requires *effort,* and they experience conflict between their desire to play or rest with the external pressures and practical needs to work. The "unquenchable urge" (Bordin, 1984, p. 97) toward spontaneity, play, and rest represents the id portion of the personality, whereas the "external pressures" (Bordin, 1984, p. 99) and the reality-based need to work represent the ego portion of the personality. Consistent with psychodynamic theory, Bordin believed that the superego (one's conscience) develops as a result of the internalization of reality-based expectations. Bordin referred to the "internalization of external pressures" as *compulsion*, and this concept is consistent with the superego within psychodynamic theory.

Bordin's theory is considerably more complex than can be fully addressed in this text, but the most basic premise of it can be summarized by the third proposition of his theory. This proposition states that "a person's life can be seen as a string of career decisions reflecting the individual groping for an ideal fit between self and work" (1984, p. 101). Although this proposition certainly sounds similar to those of the trait factor tradition, Bordin's emphasis on early experiences and personality structures such as the id, ego, and superego render it developmental and psychodynamic in nature.

As in the case of Roe's theory, empirical evidence supporting his theory is scant. Bordin (1984) was quick to acknowledge, however, that he never intended his theory to explain career choice fully. Rather, he clarified that his goal was simply to elucidate the "participation of personality in career development" (p. 96) and as a supplement to other theories addressing the many other factors influencing career choice.

Ultimately, the implications of Bordin's theory for the practice of career counseling are twofold. First, if a person has major problems in personality structure (i.e., a personality disorder), that person is likely also to experience vocational difficulties. In that case, traditional career counseling is unlikely to resolve adequately either the person's career issues or the person's other issues. More extensive psychotherapy focused on personality reconstruction would be recommended in lieu of the career counseling approaches described in this text. Second, if a person does not have major problems in personality structure and instead is presenting primarily with career concerns, the treatment modality most consistent with Bordin's theory (psychoanalysis) would not be the treatment of choice (Osipow & Fitzgerald, 1996). The major contributions of Bordin's theory are to increase our awareness of the involvement of personality structure in all areas of a person's life, including work, and to identify situations in which traditional career counseling approaches are unlikely to be effective.

GINZBERG'S THEORY OF OCCUPATIONAL CHOICE

Eli Ginzberg, a professor of economics at Columbia University, and his colleagues found little "merit in the psychoanalytic formulation, which holds that one's occupational choice is determined by unconscious needs" and also criticized the environmentalists' exclusive focus on the labor market (Ginzberg, 1988, p. 360). Perceiving and, in an unpopular move, publicly asserting lack of an adequate theoretical base to guide vocational counselors, Ginzberg and his colleagues set out to develop a general theory of occupational choice. Beginning in the 1930s (during the Great Depression when unemployment was at its peak) and continuing it for the better part of two decades, Ginzberg worked with an interdisciplinary research team to study "the role of work in modern society, from both the viewpoint of the individual and of the group" (Ginzberg, 1952; as reprinted in Ginzberg, 1988, p. 359). In 1951, they published their theory (Ginzberg, Ginsburg, Axelrad, & Herma, 1951). Twenty years later, based on research findings that were published in the intermediate two decades, Ginzberg offered a restatement of the theory that involved major revisions of several key concepts of the initial version of their theory. For historical accuracy, both versions will be described briefly in this section.

Initial Version of Ginzberg's Theory

The initial version of the theory by Ginzberg et al. (1951) was developmental in nature and focused on the occupational decision-making process that occurred approximately between the ages of 11 and 21. They identified three periods, with several stages within the periods, to explain how individuals make occupational choices. These stages are summarized in Table 3.3.

FANTASY CHOICES. The *fantasy* period represented the first period, occurring up until age 11, during which

TABLE 3.3 Ginzberg's Process of Occupational Choice

Age Range	Period	Stages
Younger than 11 years	Fantasy choices	None
11–17 years	Tentative choices	Interests
		Capacities
		Values
		Transition
17–21 years	Realistic choices	Exploration
		Crystallization
		Specification

Source: Based on Ginzberg (1984, p. 42).

Ginzberg stated that a child "believes he [sic] can be whatever he wants to become" (1952; as reprinted in Ginzberg, 1988, p. 360). Ginzberg and his colleagues put almost no emphasis on this period but instead focused on the latter two periods.

TENTATIVE CHOICES. The second period, between the ages of 11 and 17, was thought to consist of *tentative* choices and included four stages. In the first stage of the tentative period, the child's *interests* were viewed as the primary source of tentative choices. In the second stage of the tentative period, the child's *capacities,* or abilities, were viewed as the primary source of tentative choices. In the third stage, the child's *values* were viewed as the primary source of tentative choices. Notice how these three stages (interests, capacities, and values) resemble the ideas put forth in the major trait factor theories. Ginzberg identified subjectivity as the theme of the tentative period and explained that, between the ages of 11 and 17, children and adolescents tend to identify vocational aspirations based on their subjective sense of self because they are not yet able to consider external, objective factors such as the labor market. However, in the fourth and final stage of the tentative period—the *transition* stage—the adolescent's attention begins to focus on the reality of postsecondary education or employment.

REALISTIC CHOICES. Ginzberg suggested that, at approximately age 17, adolescents enter into the third and final period of occupational choice. The focus of this period is on making *realistic* choices through a process that necessarily involves *compromise* between one's interests, capacities, and values and the reality involving the pros and cons about various careers. The first stage of the realistic period is the *exploration* stage, during which an adolescent "seeks for the last time to acquaint himself [sic] with his alternatives" (1952; as reprinted in Ginzberg, 1988, p. 361). An exploration of the reality of various career options takes place at this time and results in the adolescent making a final occupational choice. This is known as the *crystallization* stage. Once the occupational choice has been made, a person enters into the third and final stage of the realistic period: *specification*. Ginzberg (1984) suggested that this final stage involved a fine-tuning process during which a person becomes more specific about the sectors, settings, and specializations of her or his occupational choice that are most appealing to her or him.

In addition to specifying this progression toward occupational choice, the initial Ginzberg theory featured three other basic elements: "Occupational choice is a process; the process is largely irreversible; and compromise is an essential aspect of every choice" (1952; as reprinted in Ginzberg, 1988, p. 360). The periods and stages described above and portrayed in Table 3.3 represent the process of occupational choice. With the exception of the age ranges, this conceptualization has remained a useful contribution to the way we think about the developmental process of career decision making. The other two elements, however, have not withstood the test of time (or research) and were targeted in the revision of the theory.

Revised Version of Ginzberg's Theory

Holland made numerous changes to his theory based on research findings, and Ginzberg did the same. In the 1972 revision of his theory, Ginzberg offered reformulations of each of the three basic elements of the theory: the process, its irreversibility, and the inevitable compromise. With regard to the process, Ginzberg removed any references to specific ages and stated that "we no longer consider the process of occupational decision-making as limited to a decade; we now believe that the process is open-ended, that it can coexist with the individual's working life" (1972, p. 169). His initial theory was based on studies of upper-class, well-educated young men who generally had the luxury of choosing one specific occupation early in life and remaining in it as they continued to climb the corporate ladder over the course of their careers, but now Ginzberg (1972) cited research on other groups, including workers in lower income brackets, racial minorities, and women, as contributing to his new perspective regarding the process.

This same research served as partial motivation for the second major revision of Ginzberg's theory. He eliminated the concept of irreversibility from his theory and explained:

> While we still feel that the multiple educational and occupational decisions that a young person makes between his [sic] childhood and his 21st or 25th year have a cumulative effect on his occupational prospects, we now feel that it is wrong to see these decisions as having an irreversible impact on his career. (Ginzberg, 1972, p. 171)

In eliminating this concept, Ginzberg acknowledged that decisions can be and are reversed. In cases when a person has made a number of choices that might seemingly eliminate college attendance as an option, these same people mature or become inspired later in life to pursue a college education and professional position. In cases when a person has made a seemingly firm vocational choice, family circumstances or changes in the labor market prompt consideration of other career options.

The final major revision offered by Ginzberg (1972) consisted of a reframing of the concept of compromise. Ginzberg originally described compromise as a "static concept" (p. 171) that was based on the assumption of a single occupational choice at the point of crystallization, but he revised this to allow for a more dynamic process. To capture this nuance, he chose the word *optimization* and noted that this allowed both for "changing desires and . . . changing circumstances" (p. 171). Thus, Ginzberg's theory transitioned from an initial view of occupational choice as a time-limited, irreversible process occurring between the ages of 11 and 21 that culminated in a single occupational choice necessarily involving compromise to a revised view of occupational choice as "a lifelong process of decision-making in which the individual seeks to find the optimal fit between his career preparation and goals and the realities of the world of work" (1972, p. 172).

SUPER'S LIFE-SPAN, LIFE-SPACE APPROACH

Ginzberg was an economist, and his theory stemmed from a multidisciplinary approach, but Super's entire career was dedicated to vocational guidance. First working for the YMCA Employment Department (1932–1935) and then as director of the Cleveland Guidance Service (1935–1936), Super realized his passion for providing vocational guidance to unemployed people (Savickas, 1994). This prompted him to seek a doctorate in educational psychology and guidance through the Teachers College at Columbia University before accepting a faculty position at Clark University. While in this position, in 1939, Super published his first articles related to career development. This marked the beginning of what was to become a prolific career for Super. Indeed, Super's segmental theory is identified as "the leading developmental approach" (Niles & Harris-Bowlsbey, 2009, p. 41). In just over a decade, his contributions were noteworthy enough that Super was elected president of the American Psychological Association.

Clearly not appreciative of the way in which Ginzberg "shocked and even unintentionally annoyed many members of the National Vocational Guidance Association by stating, at the annual convention, that vocational counselors attempt to counsel concerning vocational choice without any theory as to how vocational choices are made" (Super, 1953, p. 185), Super used the beginning of his 1952 presidential address to the American Psychological Association to offer a number of criticisms of the theory put forth by Ginzberg. In this same speech, however, Super (1953) also reluctantly agreed with Ginzberg that the field lacked an adequate theoretical base and sought to help fill this void by offering propositions in a theory of his own.

Super's Propositions

Although Super updated these propositions a number of times (1957, 1981, 1984, 1988), a meta-analysis of the various versions revealed that "Super's theoretical propositions have not changed substantially in 40 years" (Salamone, 1996, p. 180). The most recent set of Super's theoretical propositions is presented in Table 3.4. Although it is long and somewhat repetitious, you will want to take time to read each proposition carefully. As you do so, consider how strongly you agree or disagree with each.

For the remainder of his career, Super dedicated himself to elaborating on these propositions. As he did so, he published various articles and book chapters in which he offered new models and graphic illustrations specific to a number of these propositions. Despite devoting himself to this endeavor for several decades and being recognized as one of the premier

TABLE 3.4 Super's Theoretical Propositions

1. People differ in their abilities and personalities, needs, values, interests, traits, and self-concepts.
2. People are qualified, by virtue of these characteristics, each for a number of occupations.
3. Each occupation requires a characteristic pattern of abilities and personality traits, with tolerances wide enough to allow some variety of occupations for each individual as well as some variety of the individuals in each occupation.
4. Vocational preferences and competencies, the situations in which people live and work, and hence their self-concepts change with time and experience, although self-concepts as products of social learning are increasingly stable from late adolescence until late maturity, providing some continuity in choice and adjustment.
5. This process of change may be summed up in a series of life stages (a "maxicycle") characterized as a sequence of Growth, Exploration, Establishment, Maintenance, and Disengagement, and these stages may in turn be subdivided into periods characterized by developmental tasks. A small (mini) cycle takes place during career transitions from one stage to the next or each time an individual's career is destabilized by illness or injury, employer's reduction in force, social changes in human resource needs, or other socioeconomic or personal events. Such unstable or multiple-trial careers involve the recycling of new growth, reexploration, and reestablishment.
6. The nature of the career pattern—that is, the occupational level attained and the sequence, frequency, and duration of trial and stable jobs—is determined by the individual's parental socioeconomic level, mental ability, education, skills, personality characteristics (needs, values, interests, and self-concepts), and career maturity and by the opportunities to which he or she is exposed.
7. Success in coping with the demands of the environment and of the organism in that context at any given life-career stage depends on the readiness of the individual to cope with these demands (that is, on his or her career maturity).
8. Career maturity is a psychosocial construct that denotes an individual's degree of vocational development along the continuum of life stages and substages from Growth through Disengagement. From a social or societal perspective, career maturity can be operationally defined by comparing the developmental tasks being encountered to those expected based on the individual's chronological age. From a psychological perspective, career maturity can be operationally defined by comparing an individual's resources, both cognitive and affective, for coping with a current task to the resources needed to master that task.
9. Development through the life stages can be guided, partly by facilitating the maturing of abilities, interests, and coping resources and partly by aiding in reality testing and in the development of self-concepts.
10. The process of career development is essentially that of developing and implementing occupational self-concepts. It is a synthesizing and compromising process in which the self-concept is a product of the interaction of inherited aptitudes, physical makeup, opportunity to observe and play various roles, and evaluations of the extent to which the results of role-playing meet the approval of supervisors and peers.
11. The process of synthesis or compromise between individual and social factors, between self-concepts and reality, is one of role-playing and of learning from feedback, whether the role is played in fantasy, in the counseling interview, or in such real-life activities as classes, clubs, part-time work, and entry jobs.
12. Work satisfactions and life satisfactions depend on the extent to which an individual finds adequate outlets for abilities, needs, values, interests, personality traits, and self-concepts. Satisfactions depend on establishment in a type of work, a work situation, and a way of life in which one can play the kind of role that growth and exploratory experiences have led one to consider congenial and appropriate.
13. The degree of satisfaction people attain from work is proportional to the degree to which they have been able to implement self-concepts.
14. Work and occupation provide a focus for personality organization for most men and women, although for some individuals this focus is peripheral, incidental, or even nonexistent. Then, other foci, such as leisure activities and homemaking, may be central. Social traditions, such as sex-role stereotyping and modeling, racial and ethnic biases, and the opportunity structure, as well as individual differences, are important determinants of preferences for such roles as worker, student, leisurite, homemaker, and citizen.

Source: Super, D.E., Savickas, M.L., & Super, C.M. (1996). The life-span, life-space approach to careers. In D. Brown, L. Brooks, & Associates (Eds.), *Career choice and development: Applying contemporary theories to practice* (3rd ed., pp. 121–178). San Francisco: Jossey-Bass. (p. 123–126).

career theorists, Super never offered a fully integrated theory of career development. Instead, he described his contributions as a "segmental theory" consisting of "a loosely unified set of theories dealing with specific aspects of career development taken from developmental, differential, social, and phenomenological psychology and held together by self-concept or personal-construct theory" (Super, 1984, p. 194).

Segment 1: Life Span

In a segment designed to elaborate on proposition 5, Super's life-span model provides an explanation of the developmental stages through which people traverse from childhood into adulthood. The model has relevance to the way in which people develop a sense of themselves and the types of work that they find most appealing. Super believed that the life cycle consisted of five stages: (1) growth, (2) exploration, (3) establishment, (4) maintenance, and (5) disengagement. The developmental tasks and substages associated with each of these stages are summarized in Table 3.5 and are described below.

GROWTH STAGE. Super's conceptualization of career development begins with the growth stage, which spans the ages of 4 to 13. During this period, children face several developmental tasks essential to career development. To develop a sense of occupational interests, they must begin to shift from a primary focus on the present and develop interest in what the future might hold for them. They must also develop a belief that they have some control over, choice regarding, and responsibility for what they will do in the future. More specific to the world of work, it is important that they develop a desire to be successful and an interest in achieving, first at school and later at work. Finally, they must develop skills, habits, and attitudes necessary for success at school and work.

In addition to these developmental tasks, which are more competency-based, Super also articulated substages that relate more closely to the eventual selection of a career direction. In this regard, Super believed that children age 4 to 13 progress through the substages of curiosity, fantasy, interests, and capacities during the growth stage. Driven initially by their natural curiosity, children not only ask the endless list of questions characteristic of this life stage, they also entertain fantasies of adulthood that often include various occupational roles. They pretend to be doctors, firefighters, truck drivers, teachers, business owners, and

TABLE 3.5 Super's Life-Span Model

	Growth	Exploration	Establishment	Maintenance	Decline/Disengagement
Ages (in maxicycle)	4–13	14–24	25–44	45–65	66–75
Developmental Tasks	• Developing future orientation • Developing sense of personal responsibility for one's future • Developing achievement orientation with respect to school and work • Developing employability skills and attitudes	• Crystallizing • Specifying • Implementing	• Stabilizing • Consolidating • Deciding whether to stay in career of choice or to pursue another career • Advancing	• Holding on • Keeping up • Innovating	• Deceleration • Retirement planning • Retirement living
Substages	• Curiosity • Fantasies • Interests • Capacities	• Tentative • Transition • Trial (Recycling)	• Stabilizing • Consolidating • Frustration or Advancement	• Holding • Stagnating or Updating • Decelerating or Innovating	• Specialization or Disengagement • Retirement
Related Constructs	• Self-Concept	• Career Maturity	• Career Adaptability • Recycling		

Source: Based on Super, Savickas, & Super (1996, pp. 131–135).

so on. Complementing this *fantasy* play, children begin learning more about the world of work as a result of their interactions at school and in the community. These experiences lead to a child's exploration of various occupational possibilities, with children learning more about the world of work by seeking information and/or interacting with "key figures" (Super, 1990, p. 233). These experiences result in a child's development of interests and their pursuit of these interests, which lead in turn to a child's ability to develop capacities in line with these interests or to a child's inability to develop some capacities and their rejection of the corresponding interests. As a result of their progression through the substages of curiosity, fantasy, interests, and capacities, children emerge from the growth stage and progress to the exploration stage.

EXPLORATION STAGE. The exploration stage of Super's life-span model was theorized to span from ages 14 to 24, a period in which young adults are faced with three primary developmental tasks: crystallizing, specifying, and implementing their career choices as they progress through the substages called tentative, transition, and trial. Super postulated that, by age 14, adolescents have developed relatively stable self-concepts based on what they have learned about themselves, others, and the world around them during the growth stage. Entering the exploration stage, adolescents are now able to focus more on learning about occupations of interest. Specifically, they are able to begin crystallizing their career interests by publicly identifying tentative occupational choices; continuing to gather information about the various occupations of tentative interest to them; and making educational, avocational, and vocational choices consistent with these interests. Whereas crystallizing involves the identification of careers of most interest, specification involves the decision-making process. The crystallizing of tentative choices leads to transition and trial experiences that serve either to increase or to decrease interest in the respective occupations and ultimately to a career decision point at which young adults specify an intended career direction. Super referred to an adolescent's "readiness to make educational and vocational choices" as career maturity (Super, Savickas, & Super, 1996, p. 132). Once they make a career choice, young adults transition to the next stage of career development and begin the process of implementing their career decision by obtaining the necessary education or training and obtaining a job in their chosen field. In the next stage, they begin to establish themselves in their careers of choice.

ESTABLISHMENT STAGE. As the name suggests, the establishment stage of career development involves the process of becoming established within one's career of choice. After obtaining a job, the process of stabilizing begins. This substage includes getting oriented to the policies and culture of the workplace, learning about the specific tasks required in the position, and performing them well enough to survive the probationary period and keep the job. Once stabilized, an employee enters the consolidation substage. In this substage, the employee's focus shifts from maintaining stable employment and being good enough to making a name for oneself. Establishing oneself as an employee with a good attitude, reliable work habits, and good performance is the concern in the consolidation substage. If successful in this substage, the employee may (or may not) seek advancement to a related position involving more responsibility, prestige, and, ahem, more pay.

If unsuccessful in the consolidation substage, the employee is likely to experience frustration and have difficulty in achieving advancement and may consider whether to remain in this career or pursue a different one. Super identified this reconsideration as a common midlife experience, leading either to a person's progression in the maintenance stage of career development (in the event that the choice is to remain with the initial career choice) or to a recycling process in which a person returns to the exploration stage in order to begin the process of choosing a different career to pursue. In the latter case, the person's age will not be consistent with the age ranges specified in Table 3.5 because the person has temporarily moved out of the maxicycle into a minicycle. As an adult recycles through the earlier stages of exploration and establishment, the concept of career maturity is replaced by the concept of career adaptability, which is more appropriate to adult career development. The term refers to a person's "readiness to cope with the predictable tasks of preparing for and participating in the work role and with the unpredictable adjustments prompted by changes in work and working conditions" (Savickas, 1997, p. 254). Once established in a career (whether one's first career choice or a later career choice achieved through the recycling process), the adult worker will then enter the maintenance stage of career development.

MAINTENANCE STAGE. Super conceptualized the maintenance stage as spanning from age 45 to 65 and involving the developmental tasks of "*holding on, keeping up,* and *innovating*" (Super, Savickas, & Super, 1996, p. 134), but he also acknowledged other possibilities during this stage of career development. As already described, a person might not transition from the establishment stage to the maintenance stage because of a decision not to hold on but rather to move on to a different career, and thus the person would recycle through the exploration and establishment stages. Assuming that a person does decide to hold on to the career already achieved, the employee enters the maintenance stage and faces the challenge of keeping one's job. The next substage in Super's model involves the employee's stagnation or updating of skills. In this substage, the employee either maintains the skill set already possessed (stagnates) or engages in a purposeful attempt to stay up to date by enhancing his or her knowledge base and skill set.

This decision (to stagnate or to update) generally determines the direction of the next substage: innovation or deceleration. With innovation, the employee may combine new knowledge and skills with the broader perspectives gained through years of experience to develop new processes or approaches to the work. This may actually result in a person's development of a specialization or area of expertise during late career stages and extend his or her time in the maintenance stage. In contrast, employees who do not engage in innovation instead enter the substage of deceleration, which marks one's entry into the final stage of career development, initially called decline (Super, 1984) and now called disengagement (Super, Savickas, & Super, 1996).

DECLINE/DISENGAGEMENT STAGE. Super conceptualized three developmental tasks associated with the disengagement stage of career development. First, as already mentioned, the substage of deceleration marks a transition during which employees manifest a declining capacity for work and a transition toward retirement. This substage often involves the relinquishing of responsibilities to less senior employees who are invested in establishing and advancing themselves. Next, the employee experiences greater focus on retirement planning. Close attention to the economy and stock market, consultation with financial advisers, consideration of moving after retirement, and development of leisure activities that can be maintained following retirement mark this substage. Super's life-span model ends when a person enters retirement living.

MAXICYCLES AND MINICYCLES. Super referred to these five stages across the span of a person's life, from birth to death, as a maxicycle (a term that has sometimes drawn giggles from even the most mature graduate students). Super also identified a number of substages, developmental tasks, and transitions that occur within the maxicyle stages. Super recognized that our life paths and career paths are not always best conceptualized as a singular progression along one path. Whether motivated by internal or external factors, people sometimes make major changes in their lives and career paths and may even change direction altogether. When this occurs, Super suggested that people recycle through the same five stages. He described this process as a minicycle. To illustrate this concept, Super created a ladder diagram (see Figure 3.2) that included the ages, transition points, stages, and substages involved in a maxicycle. He clarified that a minicycle would occur during each transition.

Segment 2: Life Space

Although we often introduce ourselves by including our job title and although our work certainly plays a large role in how we define ourselves, Super also recognized that career is (or should be) only one part of our lives. In an effort to articulate how career fits within one's life and how the degree of investment in career waxes and wanes over the course of a person's life, Super (1981) introduced his life-space model. He identified four theaters in which people function and nine roles they may play in any one or more of these theaters (see Table 3.6).

Super (1980) acknowledged that his lists of theaters and roles are not all-encompassing or all-inclusive. The list of theaters, for example, does not acknowledge that some people may be involved in other theaters such as a community of worship, a retirement community, or a social club, and some people may not enter the theater of work. In addition, there may be an overlap between or among the theaters. Much of this text was written in my home while I was on sabbatical, which reflects an overlap for my work and home theaters.

Super (1980) also recognized that his list of roles is not all-encompassing because some people may play other roles (e.g., some may also be an aunt or sibling). His list of roles is not all-inclusive because some people may not play all nine roles (e.g., some may not become parents or may not live long enough to retire and become a pensioner).

As you can imagine, Super's (1980) articulation of these theaters and roles represented a major contribution to the field of career counseling in that it helped place career in the wider context of a person's life. This segment is the life-space portion of the life-span, life-space approach. The life-span part of the model stemmed from Super's recognition that the relative importance of each of the nine roles changes over the course of a person's life. For example, the role of a child tends to be of major importance early in life (ages 0 to 18) and then takes a backseat to other roles for quite awhile. Later in life, this role may reemerge as a major one when one's parents reach an age at which they require considerable time and attention. Super invented the term *leisurite* because "no standard term [was] available to describe the position and role of one engaged in the pursuit of leisure-time activities" (1980, p. 283), but it is a role that may be central in the life of a child and then reemerge in importance when a person is retired.

Super believed that the relative importance of each role, what he called role salience, varied not only over the course of a person's lifetime but also in accordance with the individual. In other words, people may have different preferences, priorities, and/or life circumstances. The centrality of work can vary across people (with some people choosing to work 60 hours a week and others choosing to work far less), and the centrality of any other role can also vary as a function of personal preference or life situation.

44 Chapter 3

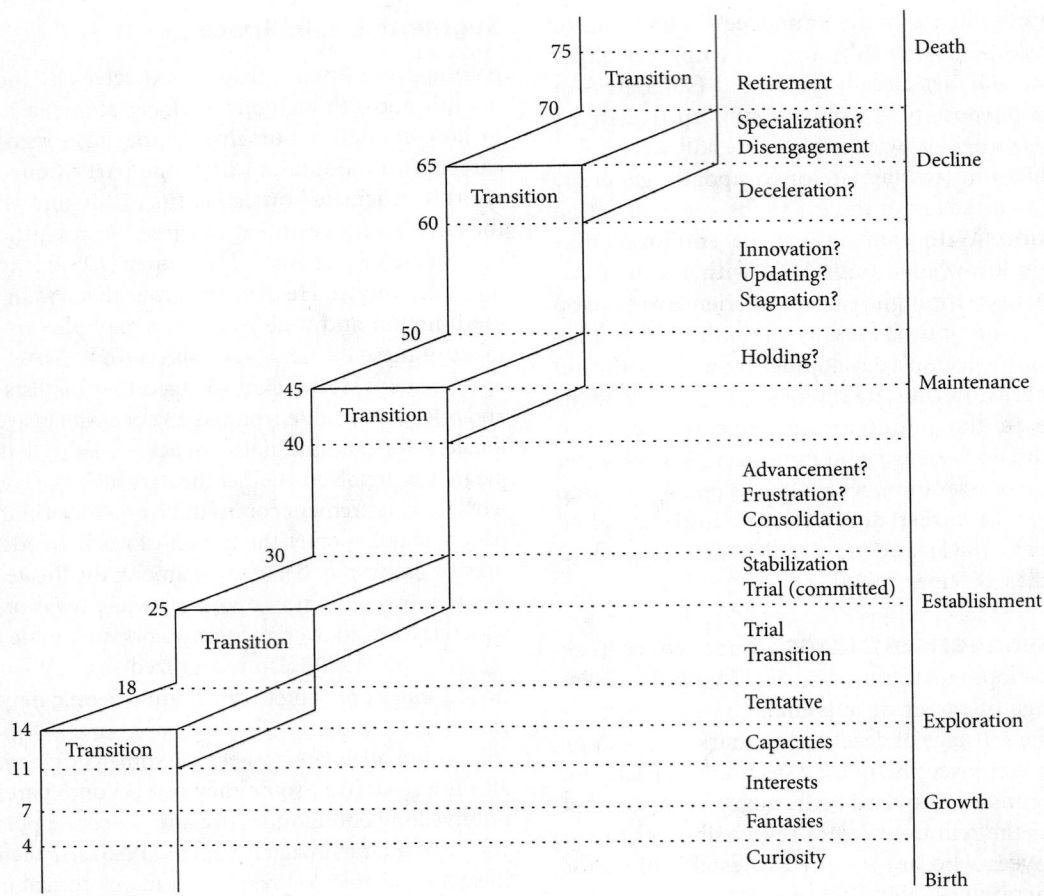

FIGURE 3.2 Super's Ladder-of-Life Stages
Source: Super, D.E. (1984). Career and life development. In D. Brown, L. Brooks, & Associates (Eds.), *Career choice and development: Applying contemporary theories to practice* (pp. 192–234). San Francisco: Jossey-Bass. Figure 2, p. 202.

TABLE 3.6 Theaters and Roles in Super's Life-Span, Life-Space Approach

Theaters	Roles
1. Home	1. Child
2. Community	2. Student
3. School	3. Leisurite
4. Workplace	4. Citizen
	5. Worker (paid or unpaid)
	6. Spouse
	7. Homemaker
	8. Parent
	9. Pensioner

Source: Based on Super (1980, pp. 283–284) Super, D.E. (1980). A life-span, life-space approach to career development. *Journal of Vocational Behavior*, 16, 282–298. Elsevier BV.

Developmental Theories

LIFE-CAREER RAINBOW. To illustrate the relative centrality of the nine roles (life space) over the course of a person's lifetime (life span), Super introduced the life-career rainbow. The outer edge of the rainbow identifies the life-span development stages and the second layer of the rainbow identifies the corresponding ages identified in the life-span model. The inside layers represent the one to nine roles that comprise a given person's life space, arranged in what Super considered the most likely chronological order. He suggested varying the width and/or varying the depth of color of each layer in order to reflect the centrality of role importance over time for a specific individual.

Figure 3.3 offers a retrospective depiction of a life-career rainbow for one person, with the layer width and shading used to show the relative centrality of that person's roles over the course of his or her life. This person's life space involved six roles over the course of his or her life span. Notice how the width of each band expands and contracts over the course of the person's lifetime. In Figure 3.3, for example, the role of student was especially pronounced during what appears to be the high school years. Notice that it disappears entirely between the ages of 25 and 30 and that this role becomes prominent at three more points later in the person's life. Notice also that the role of worker disappears between the ages of 45 and 47 and that the student role is fully expanded during this same time (perhaps this person has returned to graduate school to become a professional counselor).

Segment 3: Self-Concept

Rather than saying, "I provide counseling," most of us are much more likely to say, "I am a counselor." In the first statement, an occupation is something we do; in the second statement, an occupation is something we are, a defining part of our identity. The idea that we define ourselves in relation to the kind of work we do is widely recognized today, but this wasn't always the case. In fact, Super helped articulate the connection between self-concept and career, and he conceptualized several constructs worthy of attention. In the broadest sense, Super conceptualized a self-concept system consisting of occupational self-concept as well as other role-specific self-concepts associated with the roles in his life-space model. The occupational self-concept was central to Super's career development theory and was defined as "the constellation of self-attributes which the individual considers vocationally relevant," whether or not these attributes "have been translated into a vocational preference" (Super, 1963, p. 19).

IMPLEMENTATION OF SELF-CONCEPT AS THE GOAL OF CAREER CHOICE. A major premise of Super's theory that distinguishes it from other developmental theories involves the central role of self-concept in career choice. Super believed that the choice of a career should be viewed as a way in which a person attempts to express his or her

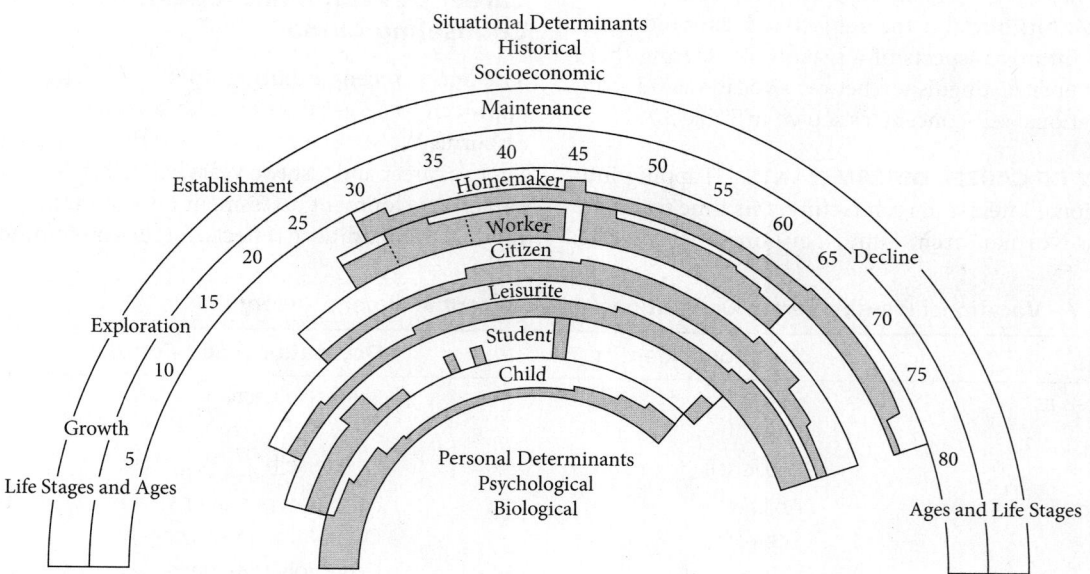

FIGURE 3.3 Super's Life-Career Rainbow
Source: Super, D.E. (1984). Career and life development. In D. Brown, L. Brooks, & Associates (Eds.), *Career choice and development: Applying contemporary theories to practice* (pp. 192–234). San Francisco: Jossey-Bass. Figure 1, p. 201.

self-concept. According to Super, Savickas, and Super (1996), "life-span, life-space theory conceptualizes occupational choice as implementing a self-concept, work as a manifestation of selfhood, and career development as a continuing process of improving the match between the self and situations" (p. 139). In addition to asserting the importance of self-concept in the process of selecting a career path, Super (1950) also pointed to its importance in the process of adjusting to that selection. When a career choice is consistent with a person's self-concept, Super (1950) suggested, there are higher levels of vocational adjustment and satisfaction. In contrast, vocational maladjustment results when a career choice is inconsistent with a person's self-concept.

OBJECTIVE VERSUS SUBJECTIVE WAYS OF KNOWING ONESELF. Reflective of his interest in supplementing differential psychology with phenomenological perspectives in order to better understand the matching process, Super also devoted attention to the difference between objective and subjective ways of knowing oneself, and he suggested the need to supplement objective assessments with subjective assessments. Whereas trait factor theorists placed emphasis on the objective assessment of aptitudes and interests and the provision of information about the world of work, Super advocated going beyond this rational, assessment-based approach. He suggested that the phenomenological construct of self-concept is assessed less easily in an objective manner and that effective career counseling needs to address not only facts and logic (as reflected in the trait factor tradition) but also the subjectively assessed emotional and intuitive aspects of a person. In offering these thoughts, Super distinguished between vocational identity and occupational self-concept, as shown in Table 3.7.

ARCHWAY OF CAREER DETERMINANTS. Tapping into his avocational interest in architecture, this time using the shape of a Norman arch, Super developed yet another illustration related to his life-span, life-space approach to career development (Super, 1990). In the *Archway of Career Determinants*, Super highlights the central role of self-concept by positioning it at the top and center of the archway. He also uses this model to show both individual and contextual factors that influence the development of career choice in addition to self-concept. This archway, which is shown in Figure 3.4, features psychological determinants on the left column and societal determinants on the right column. The base acknowledges the foundational impact of biographical life experiences as well as geographical contextual factors. Reflecting once again his interest in complementing rather than competing with other theories, Super identifies the "cement" holding the stones of this archway as learning theory (Super, 1990, p. 204).

Assessment of Life-Span and Life-Space Constructs

Consistent with other major theories of career development, Super's life-span, life-space approach also makes extensive use of assessment instruments. These instruments tend to focus on the primary stage of interest to Super: the exploration stage. Table 3.8 identifies the instruments most closely associated with Super's approach, and these instruments will be discussed in more detail in Chapter 11.

Career Development Assessment and Counseling Model

The most recent addition to the life-span, life-space approach to career development was published by Super, Osborne, Walsh, Brown, and Niles (1992) toward the end of Super's career and just two years before his death. Called the career-development assessment and counseling (C-DAC) model, this addition reflects Super's recommendations

TABLE 3.7 Vocational Identify Versus Occupational Self-Concept in Super's Theory

	Vocational Identity	**Occupational Self-Concept**
Experienced as	Self-as-object	Self-as-subject
	"me"	"I"
	Public self	Private self
Consisting of	Abilities	Self-concept systems
	Interests	Occupational self-concept
	Values	Other role self-concepts
Measured by	Objective assessments	Subjective assessments
Associated with	Trait factor theory	Life-span, life-space approach

Source: Based on Super, Savickas, & Super (1996, pp. 137–141) Super, D.E., Savickas, M.L., & Super, C.M. (1996). The life-span, life-space approach to careers. In D. Brown, L. Brooks, & Associates (Eds.), *Career choice and development: Applying contemporary theories to practice* (3rd ed., pp. 121–178). San Francisco: Jossey-Bass.

Developmental Theories **47**

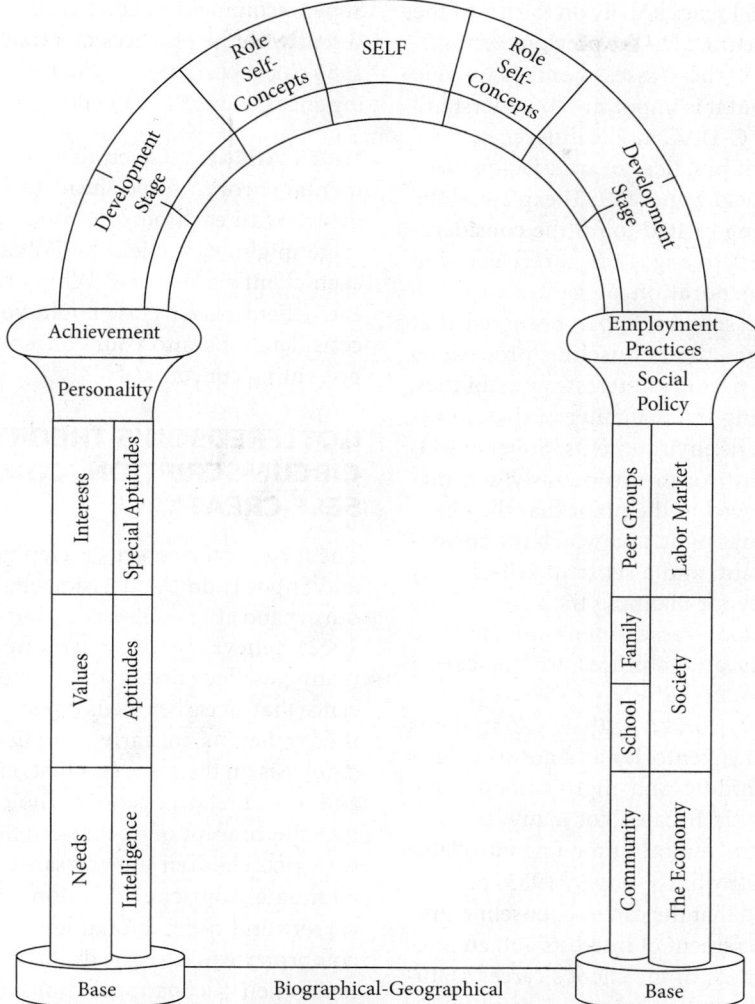

FIGURE 3.4 Super's Archway of Career Determinants
Source: Super, D.E. (1990). A life-span, life-space approach to career development. In D. Brown, L. Brooks, & Associates (Eds.), *Career choice and development: Applying contemporary theories to practice* (2nd ed., pp. 197–261). San Francisco: Jossey-Bass. Figure 7.1, p. 200.

TABLE 3.8 Assessments Specific to the Life-Span, Life-Space Approach

Construct	Instrument
Worker role salience	Salience Inventory (SI)
Career maturity	Career Development Inventory (CDI)
Career adaptability	Adult Career Concerns Inventory (ACCI)
Values	Values Scale (VS)
Career decision making	Career Decision Scale (CDS)

regarding how to integrate the three segments of his theory, assess the related constructs, and use this information to facilitate the career development and career counseling processes with clients. Super et al. (1992) identified assessment as the modality necessary to transform the theory reflected in Super's various segmental models for practical use. Thus, the C-DAC model relies heavily on the use of the various assessment tools identified in the previous section.

A thorough review of these assessments is outside the scope of this chapter, but it is important to understand that assessment in Super's C-DAC model differed considerably from the assessment practices of trait factor theorists. In a much earlier article, Super (1983) explained the primary differences as being related to (a) the consideration of a person's readiness to engage in career decision making and (b) the incorporation of values into the matching portion of assessments. Super observed that trait factor theorists begin the counseling process by immediately measuring a person's interests and abilities, with the next step involving the matching of these traits with factors in various work environments. Super (1983) suggested that such an approach erroneously assumes that individuals have matured to the point that they have stable traits, a future orientation within which the consideration of careers is relevant, and a sense of self-efficacy and personal responsibility for planning their future, and that they are ready to apply assessment information regarding their interests and abilities to the career decision-making process.

As anyone who has worked with K–12 students knows, the career interest inventories and aptitude tests administered in many middle and high schools yield results that are not very useful because, for many students, "occupational futures are too remote or too uncontrollable for planning to seem worthwhile" (Super, 1983, p. 557). Therefore, Super suggested that the career counseling process begin not with an assessment of interests and abilities but rather with an assessment of the client's career maturity (in the case of adolescents) or career adaptability (in the case of adults). The C-DAC model recommends the administration of the Career Development Inventory (CDI; Super, Thompson, Lindeman, Jordaan, & Myers, 1979, 1981) to assess career maturity or the Adult Career Concerns Inventory (ACCI; Super, Thompson, & Lindeman, 1988) to assess career adaptability. These instruments assess the client's readiness to engage in career decision making. The C-DAC model also calls for the assessment of role salience using the Salience Inventory (SI; Nevill & Super, 1986) to ascertain the importance of the worker role to the client.

If this combination of early assessments suggests that the client is not yet ready to engage in career decision making, the C-DAC model calls for attention to developing the client's awareness and facilitating the exploration necessary to achieve readiness. Only at the point of readiness does the C-DAC model suggest utilizing interest and ability assessments. From that point onward in the counseling process, Super recommended adherence to a matching process consistent with the practices of a trait factor counselor (Super, 1983; Super et al., 1992), with the notable addition of including an assessment of values (Super et al., 1992).

THINK AHEAD. Given this introduction to Super's segmental theory, think ahead to how you might use this theory with each person in our cast of clients. In which stage might each client be? What roles might constitute each client's life-space? Which roles would you imagine each client plays? How might you integrate self-concept considerations into your conceptualization of the clients' presenting concerns?

GOTTFREDSON'S THEORY OF CIRCUMSCRIPTION, COMPROMISE, AND SELF-CREATION

The focus of the career development theories by Ginzberg and Super is on the decision-making process that occurs during and after adolescence, but Gottfredson (1981, 1996, 2002) believes people have often already eliminated so many possible careers and occupational levels by adolescence that an earlier focus is necessary. Thus, Gottfredson's theory begins in early childhood and places primary emphasis on the processes that occur between the ages of 3 and one's first occupational choice in early adulthood. She uses the concept of circumscription to explain the process by which children unnecessarily (but often permanently) eliminate from consideration a wide variety of possible careers and occupational levels. She uses the concept of compromise to describe the process by which young adults make their occupational choice from among the alternatives that, as a result of the circumscription process, they still view as appropriate options.

Process of Circumscription

Gottfredson was very interested in the how developmental experiences and socialization result in children eliminating certain fields of work and certain occupational levels from consideration. Gottfredson referred to this process of eliminating options as circumscription and defined it as "the process by which youngsters . . . progressively eliminate unacceptable [vocational] alternatives in order to carve out . . . a zone of acceptable [occupational] alternatives from the full menu that a culture offers" (2002, pp. 92–93). As a result of this process, many otherwise attractive occupations have already been eliminated from consideration simply due to perceptions of sextype, prestige, and difficulty levels by the time an adolescent begins the self-assessment and career exploration processes leading to career decisions. In a carefully constructed theory based in part on knowledge of cognitive development in childhood and adolescence, Gottfredson articulated four stages of the circumscription process. In each of the first three stages, a person rejects (or eliminates from consideration) a certain range of occupations as unacceptable. This elimination process results in the circumscription (or narrowing) of the options remaining.

STAGE 1: ORIENTATION TO SIZE AND POWER. Between the ages of three and five, children's cognitive development results in an increasing awareness of patterns. Gottfredson noted that this shift results in a recognition of size and power differences among people, with adults tending to be bigger and more powerful than children. Children at this age also begin to perceive a pattern that adults have jobs and children go to school. This cognitive developmental period also involves a shift from magical thinking to more awareness of reality. As a result of these shifts, children begin thinking about potential adult roles differently. Once this cognitive shift is made, children no longer respond to the question, "What do you want to be when you grow up?" with fantasy roles such as a transformer action figure, a fairy princess, a horse, or a Muppet but rather with titles of adult occupations. This is the first circumscription of possible roles and involves the rejection of make-believe or otherwise impossible roles.

STAGE 2: ORIENTATION TO SEX ROLES. Between the ages of six and eight, children move from the preoperational to the concrete operational level of cognition. Categorization is a major feature of this stage of cognitive development, and children at this stage tend to force things into one category or another. As a result, their thinking tends to be dichotomous in nature, with everything being categorized as all good or all bad. With respect to sex roles, children at this stage of development tend to see activities, clothes, and even colors as "only for girls" or "only for boys." Gottfredson believes that children apply this same gender-based dichotomous thinking to careers and identify some careers as only for boys and others as only for girls. She explains that these children, "being particularly rigid and moralistic, . . . often treat adherence to sex roles as a moral imperative. Vocational aspirations at this stage reflect a concern with doing what is appropriate for one's sex. Both sexes believe their own sex is superior" (2002, p. 96). This is the second circumscription of possible roles and involves the rejection of occupations the child views as inappropriate for his or her sex. Gottfredson indicates that this circumscription results in the establishment of a tolerable-sextype boundary.

STAGE 3: ORIENTATION TO SOCIAL VALUATION. According to Gottfredson, children become increasingly cognizant of prestige and social valuation between the ages of 9 and 13. She suggestd that, by age 13, most adolescents "rank occupations in prestige the same way adults do, and they understand the tight links among income, education, and occupation" (2002, p. 97), and she referred to this as a "common cognitive map of occupations" (1981, p. 551). In addition to becoming cognizant of the prestige levels associated with various occupations, children also develop a perception of their family's socioeconomic and prestige levels and have "learned which occupations their own families and communities would reject as unacceptably low in social standing" (p. 97). Taking these two factors (the prestige level of various occupations and their family's socioeconomic expectations) into consideration, children then set what Gottfredson termed a tolerable-level boundary that specifies the point at which an occupation is associated with too low a prestige level to be considered. This represents the floor in terms of occupational level. Taking into account the education level associated with various occupations, children also set what Gottfredson termed a tolerable-effort boundary that specifies the point at which an occupation requires too much effort to attain. This represents the ceiling in terms of occupational level. This stage results in the third circumscription of possible roles and involves the rejection of occupations the child views as being too low on a social level or requiring too much effort.

STAGE 4: ORIENTATION TO THE INTERNAL, UNIQUE SELF. Gottfredson believed that, by the time a person is of an age and cognitive developmental level (what Super would call career maturity) to consider vocational options in the context of his or her unique personality, interests, values, and personality, he or she has already eliminated a number of vocational options. The zone of acceptable alternatives that comprises occupations still under consideration during stage 4 is bordered by the sextype, social prestige level, and effort boundaries that are established as a result of the circumscriptions that occur in the first three stages. During this fourth stage, Gottfredson theorized, adolescents are becoming increasingly aware of themselves as unique individuals, particularly with regard to internal traits such as personality, interests, and values.

Because they may lack self-knowledge, however, they benefit from activities that result in increased self-understanding. In the realm of career development, activities designed to aid understanding their career-relevant aspects such as interests, personality, abilities, and values are especially useful when there is also assistance in connecting them with specific occupations and/or postsecondary educational pursuits. The circumscription that occurs during this fourth stage involves the elimination of occupations that don't match well with a person's interests, ability patterns, personality, or work-related values.

The overall process of circumscription is illustrated in Figure 3.5. The horizontal axis is associated with stage 2 of Gottfredson's theory and consists of a continuum representing the sextype of occupations, ranging from very masculine to very feminine. Rising up from this continuum is a tolerable sextype boundary for a "hypothetical middle-class boy of average intelligence" (Gottfredson, 1981, p. 557). The vertical axis is associated with stage 3 of Gottfredson's theory and consists of a continuum representing the prestige level of occupations, ranging from low to high. Stemming from this continuum are two boundaries. The tolerable-effort boundary represents the ceiling, and the tolerable-level boundary represents the floor of the zone of acceptable alternatives. Notice that these boundaries do not necessarily have to be straight. For example, the tolerable-sextype boundary has a slight curve, reflecting the idea that a higher prestige level occupation could be a bit more feminine than a lower prestige level job and still be acceptable.

IRREVERSIBILITY OF CIRCUMSCRIPTION. A key idea in Gottfredson's theory is that these circumscriptions are more or less permanent. Although we are likely relieved that children permanently reject early on the idea of becoming a fairy princess or superhero when they grow up, Gottfredson views it as unfortunate that the circumscriptions occurring in stages 2 and 3 will not be revisited in the absence of a specific prompt to do so. In other words, she considers the tolerable sextype boundary, the tolerable-level boundary, and the tolerable-effort boundary to be relatively permanent. In Gottfredson's words, "once rejected according to an earlier criterion (i.e., sextype, prestige level, effort required), these rejected options will not be reconsidered except in unusual circumstances" (1981, p. 556). As a result, only occupations falling within *the zone of acceptable alternatives* are generally considered during the period when many have historically assumed that most career development decisions are made. During stage 4, then, only a narrow range of occupations remain open for consideration. Within this range, Gottfredson believes, people identify more idealistic aspirations and more realistic aspirations, with the more realistic aspirations involving occupations of lower prestige and difficulty than the more idealistic aspirations. At this point people shift their focus away from defining their own vocational aspirations and toward the realities associated with achieving them. In Gottfredson's theory, this transition marks a shift from the process of circumscription to the process of compromise.

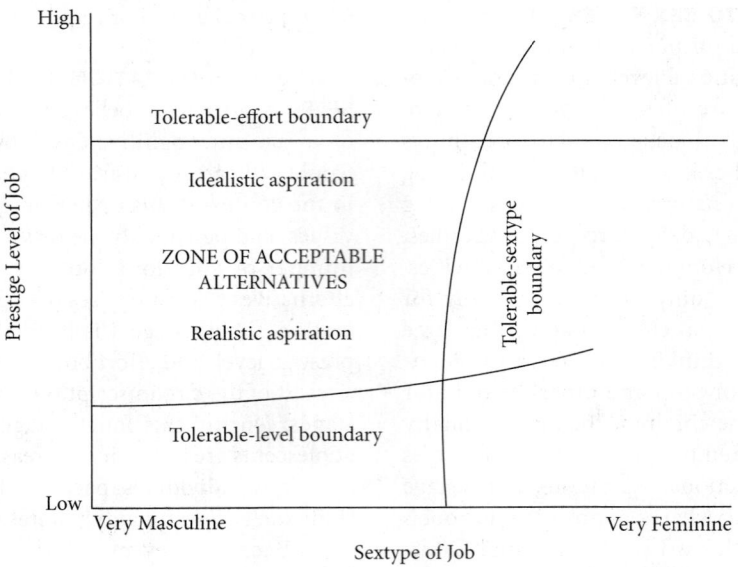

FIGURE 3.5 Circumscription of Aspirations According to Perceptions of Job–Self Compatibility

Source: Use of Figure 4, page 557, from Circumscription and compromise: A developmental theory of occupational aspirations. Gottfredson, Linda S. *Journal of Counseling Psychology,* Vol 28(6), Nov 1981, 545–579. American Psychological Association (APA). Reprinted with permission.

Process of Compromise

Gottfredson explained, "[W]hereas circumscription is the process by which individuals reject alternatives they deem unacceptable, compromise is the process by which they abandon their most-preferred alternatives" (2002, p. 100). She believed that compromise occurs most frequently in response to situational or external barriers or challenges that interfere with a person's ability to achieve his or her most idealistic aspirations. At the core of compromise are a person's perceptions of the attainability of any given occupation. In addition to being related to level of difficulty and effort required, attainability is affected by the existence of barriers. Common barriers might include a lack of money to pay for the college education necessary to enter a given profession, a family situation requiring immediate entry into paid employment instead of college, and actual or perceived discrimination making entry into a vocation of choice unduly difficult. Gottfredson (2002) describes two types of compromise—anticipatory and experiential—and explains that the distinction is based on whether a person actually experiences external constraints that interfere with her or his ability to achieve her or his most idealistic aspirations or whether the person simply anticipates the constraints.

As part of her theory, Gottfredson (2002) articulated several principles of compromise. She cautions, however, that these principles are most relevant to people when they are "just launching their adult lives" (p. 107) and feel a great deal of investment in the acceptability of their public selves. Once people feel more secure about themselves and their lives, they may be willing to make vocational choices based on their private selves, regardless of whether their aspirations are considered acceptable with regard to sextype, prestige level, and so on. When preparing to enter an occupational field early in life, people tend to be highly cognizant of the boundaries of acceptability established during the circumscription process and of the external constraints of reality. As a result, Gottfredson says, young people make compromises according to several principles.

The first principle is that people establish "conditional priorities" that govern what they are most likely to sacrifice when making a compromise regarding occupational goals (2002, p. 104). The second principle is that people will often compromise and settle for an occupation they view as good enough in lieu of engaging in a difficult process of information gathering and decision making in order to find the best possible choice for themselves (p. 106). The third principle is that a person will avoid making any choice at all if none of the available choices seem good enough. Gottfredson explains that "avoidance may take many forms, including searching for more alternatives, persevering with an untenable choice, reconsidering the tolerable-effort boundary, or simply delaying decisions or commitments (remaining 'undecided') for as long as possible" (p. 106). Gottfredson's fourth principle of compromise is that, if necessary, people may make psychological accommodations by changing their view of themselves. She believes that people are most likely to reconsider fields of work they had circumscribed as uninteresting, less likely to reconsider fields of work they had circumscribed as being at too low a social level or too high in difficulty, and least likely to reconsider fields they had circumscribed as being of an unacceptable sextype.

THINK AHEAD. Given this introduction to Gottfredson's theory, think ahead to how you might use this theory with each person in our cast of clients. In doing so, consider the sex-role, prestige, and effort boundaries each client may have established by adolescence. Think about how each client may have circumscribed potentially good careers for themselves and about how you might help these clients expand their zones of acceptable alternatives. Also consider how perceived barriers may have affected each client's choice of occupational pursuits.

Self-Creation: The Influence of Genetics

In the most recent extension of her theory, Gottfredson (2002) has added considerable attention to the influence of genetics. Whereas the rest of her theory focused on the role of socialization as the major influence on a person's vocational choices, Gottfredson has now shifted her focus dramatically to include attention to recent behavioral genetic research and the implications for this research on our understanding of how vocational aspirations develop (2002, p. 110). Citing research and reviews by Bouchard (1998); Plomin, DeFries, McClearn, and McGuffin (2001); Wachs (1992); Betsworth et al. (1994); and Betsworth and Fouad (1997), Gottfredson (2002) has concluded that socialization theory has effectively been disproved and that there is a need to acknowledge the important role of genetics in influencing life outcomes. Indeed, one could say that Gottfredson has reversed herself and drawn the conclusion that innate learning abilities rather than socialization are primarily responsible for gaps in academic and career achievement.

Whereas the foundational aspects of her theory emphasized the importance of sex-role stereotypes and socioeconomic status on the career aspirations of young people, Gottfredson has shifted her focus to intelligence levels and how they differ across racial groups (Gottfredson, 2005, 2011). If you are raising your eyebrows and feeling discomfort as you read this, you are not alone. Gottfredson's latest focus has indeed been highly controversial. In fact, her new focus has been so controversial that Gottfredson (2010) claims that even her own university has attempted to silence her.

Why the controversy? In her more recent publications, Gottfredson now focuses almost exclusively on racial group differences in intelligence. Calling the idea of equal potential a "collective fraud" and an "egalitarian fiction" (Gottfredson, 2000, p. 19), Gottfredson explains that this is the "frequent but false assertion that intelligence is clustered equally across all human populations, that is, that there are, on average, no racial-ethnic disparities in developed mental competence" (p. 19). She indicates that "studies in the United States and other developed nations converge on mean IQs of roughly 85, 100, and 106 for Blacks, Whites, and East Asians, respectively" (Gottfredson, 2005, p. 526). In addition to noting these between-group differences, Gottfredson (2011) suggests that her own theory of circumscription and compromise, along with other "social privilege" theories, are mistaken in their claims that social inequality is "manufactured or magnified by differences in advantages that siblings share (e.g., parental income)" (p. 557). She further explains that "social inequality is inevitable when a society's members vary in a genetically conditioned trait such as g [general intelligence], which is highly useful and therefore confers a competitive advantage and garners social rewards" (p. 570).

Gottfredson's more recent publications therefore reflect her belief that genetic characteristics may (a) be useful in understanding how within-group differences in vocational aspirations occur despite two people being raised in very similar environments and (b) reduce our estimate of the relative influence of our learning experiences. She hypothesizes that the genetic makeup of a person not only affects what she or he brings into the world (intelligence levels, aptitudes, personality traits, etc.) but also affects the kinds of environments and learning experiences a person seeks. More specifically, she suggests that "individuals [seek and create] environments that bring out and reinforce their genetic proclivities" (Gottfredson, 2002, p. 115). The concept of self-creation therefore refers to the complex manner in which she believes genetics influence a person to create a life consistent with one's genetic makeup. This concept has resulted in Gottfredson's addition of self-creation to the title of her theory. Until 2002, it was known as the theory of circumscription and compromise, but Gottfredson now calls it as the theory of circumscription, compromise, and self-creation.

Although this most recent extension of her theory about the influence of genetics has not been widely embraced by the counseling profession, Gottfredson challenges our field to continue expanding its understanding of career development by also focusing on biological and genetic factors. This is in stark contrast to the learning theories of career development, which will be described in the next chapter. Only time will tell whether other theorists will incorporate behavioral genetic research into their theories of career development.

APPLICATION TO OUR CAST OF CLIENTS

As in Chapter 2, this chapter concludes with an application of theories to our cast of clients. It is my hope that this final section will help you in understanding how seemingly abstract theories can have direct relevance to the practice of counseling. When you read about each of these theories earlier in this chapter, you were asked to think ahead about the relevance and potential application of each of these four theories to our clients. Let's see now how our thoughts compare.

Application of Super's Life-Span, Life-Space Approach

When you think of Super's theory, you should immediately recall that it is a segmental theory addressing stages of career development over the life span, the various roles and theaters in which people invest their time and energy, and the ways in which people attempt to implement their self-concepts within their chosen careers. You should also remember that Super made extensive use of graphic illustrations, including the ladder, the life career rainbow, and the archway of career determinants. Super's expansive approach could be applied to our cast of clients in numerous ways.

For example, a career counselor might conceptualize Wayne as being in the maintenance stage in his career as an assembly-line worker at the Ford factory. Because of external factors (the economy), however, Wayne is recycling back to an exploration stage with an interest in developing another career option. A career counselor using Super's approach might also note that Wayne apparently did very little career exploration in his youth and instead followed in his father's footsteps. Thus, the counselor may be curious about Wayne's level of readiness to make career decisions, whether this readiness is called career maturity (referring to Wayne's readiness in his youth) or adaptability (referring to Wayne's readiness at this point in his life). The career counselor may choose to administer an instrument such as the Adult Career Concerns Inventory to assess this.

Administration of the CDI may be quite useful when working with Li Mei. Li Mei attended a prestigious high school in which college attendance was the postsecondary norm and academic pursuits were the focus. Rather than delivering a guidance curriculum including in-depth career exploration and development, her well-intentioned but misguided school counselors focused almost exclusively on preparing students to excel on college entrance exams, on the college application process, and on the pursuit of scholarships. Although Li Mei succeeded by getting into college, she arrived at Chapman University with no sense whatsoever of what to major in or of what career she wanted to pursue. Li Mei's scores on the CDI will likely reflect this lack of career maturity and guide the counselor toward emphasis on the exploration stage of career development in Super's life-span approach.

A counselor using Super's approach with Lakeesha would most likely begin by focusing on life-space issues. At the time of her husband's death, Lakeesha worked as a stay-at-home mother, raising their two children, running the household, and managing the family budget. The three most prominent roles in her life-career rainbow were spouse, homemaker, and parent. These would be followed, at a distance, by child, leisurite, and citizen, and the roles of student, worker, and pensioner would not be included. Now, faced with the need to become the sole breadwinner for the family and to be a single parent to her children, Lakeesha faces a dramatic change in her life space. The career counselor would clearly acknowledge and support Lakeesha in her grieving process, but it would also be useful to frame this loss within the context of the life-career rainbow. Perhaps the counselor could have Lakeesha draw two rainbows, with one reflecting the way she and her husband had envisioned her roles over time and with the other reflecting how she might restructure her life and change the patterns of role salience now. Super's life-span model pertains to Lakeesha because she will need to recycle through exploration, get a job, and begin the process of establishment.

Vincent's coming-out process served as the impetus for his reconsideration of his long-standing career plans of become a Marine, and Super's self-concept theory may be particularly useful with him. It might be helpful to use the archway model to begin exploring the various factors that contributed to Vincent's desire to enter the military, with attention to both columns of the arch: the left column representing aspects of him as an individual and the right column representing contextual factors. This exploration could include a discussion of family dynamics and the impact of 9-11 on Vincent's career aspirations. Super believed that a career represents a way in which people attempt to implement their self-concept, so the archway model could then be used to explore how Vincent's growing awareness of himself as a gay man might affect and be affected by a career in the military. Also, of course, the counselor would want to facilitate Vincent's recycling back through the exploration stage of career development to assist him in either reaffirming his desire to enter the military or identifying another career option of greater appeal to him.

Although Doris's situation is complicated by personal issues in her life, a career counselor could use Super's life-span approach to explore her stage of career development prior to being fired. Doris is 53 years of age and had been at the insurance agency for 14 years, so it is likely that she had gone from the establishment stage to the maintenance stage. Within this stage, you'll recall that the developmental tasks include holding on, keeping up, and innovating. Doris seems to have had difficulty with these challenges. Instead of keeping up by updating her skills, she seems to have stagnated, and instead of innovating, she appears to have decelerated. The career counselor working from Super's approach may be interested in exploring whether Doris is experiencing the common midlife crisis in which people often question whether they want to remain in their chosen occupation or pursue a new direction. In the event that Doris expresses no interest in finding a new career direction, the focus of counseling would be on the importance of the developmental tasks involved not only in the maintenance stage but also in the establishment phase. Both will be of utmost importance to Doris as she strives to be successful in her next job.

Gillian's case would be ideal for working within Super's life-space approach. Gillian has been highly successful in navigating through the life stages of exploration, establishment, and maintenance. She has enjoyed a great deal of professional success, holds a position as partner with a major accounting firm, and shows no signs of decline. In that sense, one might expect Gillian to be satisfied with her career. The problem, of course, is not with her career but rather with her life space. Gillian's life-career rainbow has been dominated by the role of worker, and she is reaching a point in her life at which she wants to invest more time into her role as a spouse and becoming a parent. Knowing that there are only 24 hours in a day, and knowing that parenting can be hard when frequent relocations are the norm in your career, Gillian has some choices to make. Approaching them from a life-space perspective would likely be effective and well received.

Super's approach would recognize in Juan's case that Juan had previously been in the maintenance stage in his work as a construction laborer. When faced with a health condition necessitating a new career direction, Juan was forced to recycle and enter a minicyle in which he revisits the exploration stage, identifies a new career direction, gets a job, and begins the establishment stage. As with Wayne, the Adult Career Concerns Inventory may be useful to assess Juan's readiness to engage in this process.

Application of Gottfredson's Theory of Circumscription, Compromise, and Self-Creation

When you think of Gottfredson's theory, you should immediately recognize that it is a developmental theory with emphasis on the ways in which young people eliminate career options early in their lives based on sex roles, prestige, and difficulty levels and on the ways in which compromises are made later in life in response to real or perceived barriers. More recently, Gottfredson has acknowledged the role of genetics and heritable traits in the complex interactions between people and their environments. Her theory can be applied in numerous ways and may offer insights regarding our cast of clients.

A career counselor may find it useful to identify what Wayne considers as the zone of acceptable alternatives. As a teen, he likely would have identified some jobs as too feminine for him, others as too difficult, and some as too low in prestige (or at least income). As a mature adult, however, Gottfredson's theory recognizes that people may be more willing to pursue a career (a public self) that is more congruent with their private selves. This would be useful to explore with Wayne because he may now be willing to expand the zone of acceptable alternatives to include some careers he would not have viewed as acceptable earlier in his life. As Wayne identifies careers of potential interest, a counselor working from Gottfredson's theory may be interested in having him articulate the types of factors contributing to the compromises he makes. How much training, for example, is he willing to complete in order to pursue a new career?

With Li Mei, a career counselor might use the metaphor of being caught between a rock and a hard place to describe her career dilemma. Working within Gottfredson's theory, the counselor may sense that the tolerable-level boundary for Li Mei is quite high because her family considers only high-prestige careers as being acceptable. In addition, Li Mei lacks self-confidence when she compares her abilities to those of her siblings, so she may have set a relatively low tolerable-effort boundary. The result is that these two boundaries are very close together, and Li Mei feels trapped between the two, believing herself to be unable to achieve the types of careers that would be acceptable to her family. Expanding this zone of acceptable alternatives will be essential to broadening the career exploration process with Li Mei.

In working with Lakeesha, a career counselor is most likely to begin by focusing on her immediate concern to enter the workforce relatively quickly and thus ensure her ability to support her family. Lakeesha may be willing to make some compromises by initially accepting a position with less prestige than she'd prefer. She'll then want to continue job hunting in areas of interest to her and in which her bachelor's degree in psychology will be an asset. In the event that Lakeesha in interested in positions requiring additional education, she will need to make a decision about whether to pursue additional education and weigh the choices between her more idealistic and more realistic aspirations.

As a counselor working with Vincent, I would be curious to explore the types of jobs he previously viewed as appropriate with regard to sextype, and I would wonder whether the tolerable sextype boundary has changed now that he identifies as gay. Vincent's heart has been set on becoming a Marine, which would be considered a stereotypically masculine career path. Now, however, he is less certain about this path. Is this solely due to his perceptions that antigay sentiments are still pervasive within the military? Is another factor prompting his reconsideration related to perceptions of sextype and his stereotypes of careers appropriate for gay men? Such a discussion might yield useful insights into Vincent's career beliefs and an opportunity to explore the ways in which his zone of acceptable alternatives has been affected by his coming-out process.

As already mentioned, it would be a mistake to approach Doris's performance problems as being indicative only of motivational and personal problems. A career counselor working with Gottfredson's theory could explore more deeply the issues related to the lack of a match between Doris's interests (Social-Artistic-Realistic [SAR]) and her work responsibilities as a secretary (Conventional-Enterprising [CE]). Note the use of Holland's codes in these designations. In doing so, a career counselor would recognize that conventional jobs (such as Doris's job as a secretary) are considered the most feminine (see Figure 3.5). At age 53, Doris was likely subject to more limiting messages about what occupations were appropriate for females, so one might speculate that Doris initially sought a job as a secretary because "that's what women do." Indeed, this might offer some insight into the complex sociopolitical factors contributing not only to Doris's career choice but also to her bitterness.

Gillian hasn't experienced difficulty with making an occupational choice or with experiencing career success; thus, the circumscription and compromise portions of Gottfredson's theory may be less germane in her case. A career counselor could still apply the theory, however, by exploring ways in which Gillian is reconsidering her tolerable-effort boundary. Until now, Gillian has not perceived the effort involved in obtaining her position or of excelling in it to be overly taxing. Now, however, as she anticipates parenthood, she is reconsidering whether the time and the frequent relocations required in her position will continue to be acceptable.

Juan is faced with the task of finding another occupation that he will enjoy and find rewarding, and in which he will be successful. He knows he can no longer continue with a career as physically rigorous as the work involved in his job as a construction laborer; however, he doesn't know what else he might like to do. As a client without a high school diploma, Juan will undoubtedly find himself limited with respect to educational requirements. It will be helpful for the career counselor to talk with Juan about entry requirements for various jobs. In doing so, it may be useful to discuss the tolerable-effort boundary and to explore his willingness and ability to get additional education. Such a conversation will have a direct impact on whether Juan pursues his idealistic aspirations or compromises to pursue his more realistic aspirations.

CHAPTER 4

Learning Theories

> The theories presented in Chapters 2 and 3 focused on the importance of relatively stable personal traits and the impact of our early developmental experiences on our career choices and level of career satisfaction, respectively. The learning theories presented in this chapter will focus, however, on how our past and present learning experiences influence our beliefs about ourselves, our level of self-efficacy, and the impact of these cognitive processes on our career choices and level of career satisfaction.

Henry Ford, the great American industrialist who founded the Ford Motor Company, is often credited with saying, "Whether you think you can or you think you can't, you're right." Although we can find ample evidence to discredit this claim among many of the apparently overconfident and undertalented potential contestants vying for a spot on the popular television show *American Idol*, the basic essence of Ford's sentiment bears consideration. Consider your own reactions to Ford's statement. What are the implications of this idea in understanding your own academic and career development and success?

Certainly, our level of self-confidence and a particular kind of self-confidence known as self-efficacy have an impact on our willingness to consider various educational and career paths, on the goals we set for ourselves, and even on the level of success we experience when striving to reach those goals. Each of the learning theories presented in this chapter devotes significant attention to the messages we internalize about ourselves and the world of work. A basic idea prominent in each of these theories is that the messages we internalize in response to learning experiences have an effect on the choices we make regarding our career direction and the level of success we attain when performing work-related tasks. Although the theories may use different vocabulary to describe it, an important element of these theories involves the impact of our learning experiences on our level of self-efficacy. Therefore, before we turn to the learning theories of career development and career counseling, a review of the literature on self-efficacy is in order. This literature is most closely associated with the work of Albert Bandura.

BANDURA'S FOUNDATIONAL LEARNING THEORIES

The famous psychologist Albert Bandura developed two learning theories that are foundational not only to psychology but also to education and career counseling. The first, social learning theory (SLT), addresses the idea that people learn not only as a result of their actual, direct experiences but also as a result of their observations of other people's experiences. The second, social cognitive theory (SCT), introduced the concept of self-efficacy.

Social Learning Theory

Although it is now common knowledge, the ideas that people learn by observing others and that these lessons have an impact on motivation were not always prominent in mainstream psychology. Albert Bandura first coined the term *social learning*. Although a thorough discussion of his social learning theory (Bandura, 1961, 1977b, 1978) is beyond the scope of this text, a key concept involved observational learning, also called vicarious learning. Through a series of experiments, Bandura was able to demonstrate empirically that people can learn not only through direct experiences involving their own behaviors and associated consequences (in keeping with the principles of classical and operant conditioning) but also by observing models, their behaviors, and the consequences of those behaviors.

Social learning theory has been used in multiple disciplines, including education and psychology, to understand the way in which people learn through observation of others. It has also directly affected the field of career counseling. Concepts related to social learning theory are also incorporated into the other career development theories presented in this chapter. Bandura developed another theory, however, that had an even greater impact on these career development theories.

Social Cognitive Theory

After making his mark with SLT, Bandura next turned his attention to the development of his social cognitive theory (Bandura, 1977a, 1986). Whereas SLT emphasizes the impact of observation and modeling on a person's learned behaviors, the focus of SCT is on how an individual's internal processing of information affects his or her behavior. Two major aspects of Bandura's SCT are most germane to the learning theories of career counseling: (1) the triadic, reciprocal nature of causation and (2) self-efficacy.

Triadic reciprocality is a complicated way of saying that people, their behaviors, and their environment interact in a complex, bidirectional model, with each influencing the other (Bandura, 1977b, 1986). Bandura used the triangular diagram shown in Figure 4.1 to illustrate this concept, with P representing a person, B representing that person's behavior, and E representing that person's environment.

Second, SCT expanded SLT by examining the way in which "children and adults operate cognitively on their social experiences and . . . how these cognitive operations then come to influence their behavior and development" (Grusec, 1992, p. 781). The specific cognitive operation Bandura focused on was self-efficacy, and he was interested in how self-efficacy pertains to human

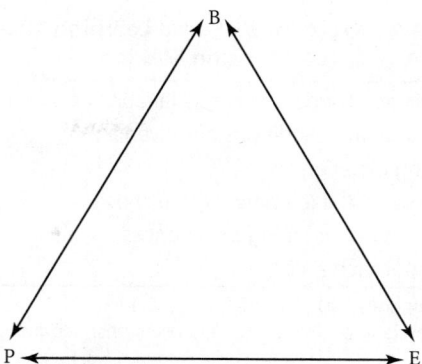

FIGURE 4.1 Triadic Reciprocality
Source: Bandura, Albert, *Social foundations of thought and action: A social cognitive theory,* 1st Ed. © 1986, p. 24. Reprinted and electronically reproduced by permission of Pearson Education, Inc. Upper Saddle River, New Jersey.

agency. To put it simply, Bandura believed that the way people think about themselves and the level of confidence they have in their ability to perform any given task has an impact on the degree to which they believe they can affect their current and future circumstances. He defined perceived self-efficacy as "a judgment of one's capability to accomplish a certain level of performance" (Bandura, 1986, p. 361). As you will see, Bandura's concepts of triadic reciprocality and self-efficacy play a prominent role in the career development theories presented in this chapter.

LEARNING THEORIES OF CAREER DEVELOPMENT AND CAREER COUNSELING

Krumboltz's Learning Theories

Although most career development theorists have continued to refine their theories over time based on new data and insights, they generally have kept the same title and focus for their theory. This is not the case with Krumboltz's learning theories. Instead, as his theory has evolved, Krumboltz has altered the name of his theory to reflect its focus more closely. In this section, you will learn about three particularly prominent iterations of Krumboltz's theory.

SOCIAL LEARNING THEORY OF CAREER DECISION MAKING. Krumboltz developed perhaps the earliest career development theory to focus on the impact of both direct and observational learning experiences on one's beliefs about oneself. He first published *A Social Learning Theory of Career Selection* (Krumboltz, Mitchell, & Jones, 1976) and soon thereafter renamed it as *A Social Learning Theory of Career*

TABLE 4.1 Krumboltz's Social Learning Theory of Career Selection: Four Factors That Influence the Nature of Career Decision Making

1. Genetic endowment and special abilities
2. Environmental conditions and events
3. Learning experiences
    a. Instrumental learning experiences
    b. Associative learning experiences
4. Task approach skills

Source: Krumboltz, J.D., Mitchell, A.M., & Jones, G.B. (1976). A social learning theory of career selection. *The Counseling Psychologist*, 6, 71–81. Copyright © 1976 by Sage Publications. Reprinted by Permission of SAGE Publications.

Decision Making (SLTCDM; Krumboltz, 1979). Krumboltz explained that this theory was "designed as a first step toward understanding more precisely what specific kinds of learning experiences contribute to the development of occupational preferences" (Krumboltz et al., 1976, p. 17). In this theory, Krumboltz and his colleagues identified "four [primary] factors that influence the nature of career decision making" (p. 71). These factors are presented in Table 4.1.

Although acknowledging the importance of innate personal characteristics (such as race, sex, and various forms of intelligence or special abilities) and environmental circumstances (ranging from job market trends to labor laws, to natural disasters, to the school and community in which one is raised), this theory focused primarily on the impact of learning experiences. This, of course, is consistent with the title of the theory. Within the category of learning experiences, Krumboltz explored in detail both the direct types of learning experiences addressed by Skinner's (1938) behaviorism and the indirect types of learning experiences described in Bandura's social learning theory. Krumboltz termed these instrumental and "associative learning experiences," respectively.

Instrumental Learning Experiences. Krumboltz explained that instrumental learning experiences (ILEs) occur when an "individual acts on the environment in such a way to produce certain consequences" (Krumboltz et al., 1976, p. 72). Similar to Skinner, Krumboltz believed it was important to understand the antecedents of a person's behavior, the actual behavior, and the consequences of the behavior. Unlike Skinner, Krumboltz was interested in both overt (observable) and covert (internal) behaviors. To capture the essence of instrumental learning experiences, Krumboltz used an H-shaped diagram. In Figure 4.2, you will see Krumboltz's general model (excerpted from Krumboltz et al., 1976) as well as a specific example related to our client Wayne. This second diagram is used to provide an example of one direct, instrumental learning experience that may have influenced Wayne's choice of careers or, at the very least, his decision not to go to college.

Associative Learning Experiences. Krumboltz coined the term *associative learning experiences* (ALEs) and explained that they include Bandura's concept of "observational learning in which the individual learns by observing real or fictitious models" as well as Skinner's concept of "the pairing of stimuli through the classical conditioning paradigm" (Krumboltz et al., 1976, p. 72). To represent associative learning experiences, Krumboltz used an O-shaped diagram. Three such diagrams are presented in Figure 4.3. The diagram on the left illustrates the general model, the diagram in the middle illustrates an associative learning experience involving the pairing of two stimuli, and the diagram on the right illustrates an associative learning experience involving observation of a model. Specifically, the middle diagram illustrates an associative learning experience that may have influenced Gillian's choice of careers, and the diagram on the right illustrates an associative learning experience that may have influenced Vincent's choice of careers.

Self-Observation Generalizations. Another important element of the SLTCDM involves the impact of learning experiences on what Krumboltz and colleagues called self-observation generalizations (SOGs). They defined a SOG as "an overt or a covert self-statement evaluating one's own actual or vicarious performance in relation to learned standards" (1976, p. 74). As you have likely surmised, the concept of self-observation generalizations is very similar to Bandura's concept of self-efficacy. Both involve internalized beliefs about one's capacity to perform at a given level. To represent self-observation generalizations, Krumboltz used a triangle. Figure 4.4 shows Krumboltz's general model as well as a specific example related to our client Li Mei.

Krumboltz's Model of Instrumental Learning Experiences

Antecedents	Behaviors	Consequences	Antecedents	Behaviors	Consequences
Genetic endowment Special abilities and skills		Verbal feedback from self and/or others Direct observable results of actions	Wayne, age 16, is a white male living in a working middle-class family. He is reasonably intelligent and is a good at working with his hands.		The student he sits next to encourages him to try harder because "algebra is required for college." Wayne also receives an at-risk notice from counselor.
Task or problem	Covert and overt actions	Convert reactions to consequences (cognitive and emotional responses)	Wayne enrolls in a high school algebra class. He finds the subject matter boring and difficult.	Wayne's effort in the class wanes, and he earns a D+ for the first card marking.	Wayne feels discouraged and concludes that he is not college material. He meets with the counselor and drops the class.
Planned and unplanned environmental (e.g., social, cultural, or economic) conditions or events		Impact on significant others	Wayne's family happens to live in the metro Detroit area. In class, he happens to sit next to a straight A, college-bound student.		Wayne's father was understanding and reassured him that people can make a very good living without going to college.

General Model*   **Example for Wayne**

FIGURE 4.2 Krumboltz's Model of Instrumental Learning Experiences

Source: Krumboltz, J.D., Mitchell, A.M., & Jones, G.B. (1976). A social learning theory of career selection. *The Counseling Psychologist,* 6, 71–81. Copyright © 1976 by Sage Publications. Reprinted by Permission of SAGE Publications.

Task Approach Skills. The final major concept addressed by Krumboltz's SLTCDM involves task approach skills. Krumboltz defined these skills as "cognitive and performance abilities and emotional predispositions for coping with the environment, interpreting it in relation to self-observation generalizations, and making covert or overt predictions about future events" (Krumboltz et al., 1976, p. 74). Examples of task approach skills include "work habits, mental sets, perceptual and thought processes, performance standards

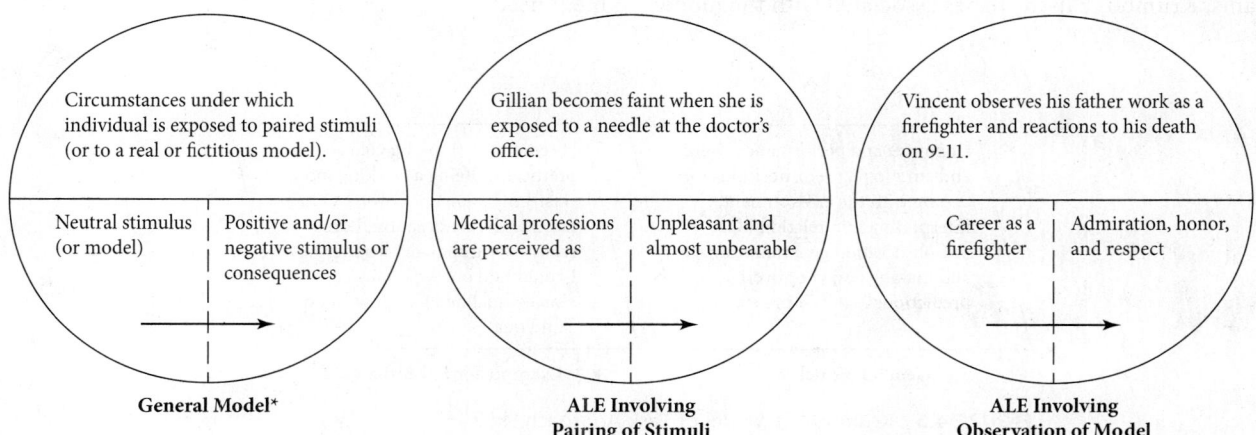

FIGURE 4.3 Krumboltz's Model of Associative Learning Experiences

Source: Krumboltz, J.D., Mitchell, A.M., & Jones, G.B. (1976). A social learning theory of career selection. *The Counseling Psychologist,* 6, 71–81. Copyright © 1976 by Sage Publications. Reprinted by Permission of SAGE Publications.

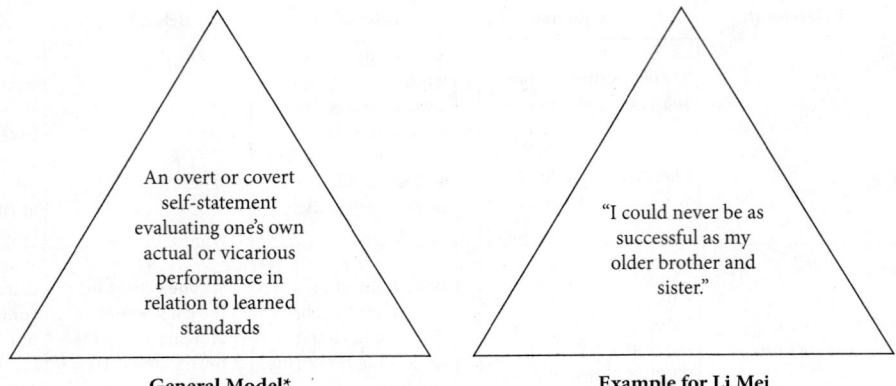

FIGURE 4.4 Krumboltz's Model of Self-Observation Generalizations
* *Source:* Krumboltz, J.D., Mitchell, A.M., & Jones, G.B. (1976). A social learning theory of career selection. *The Counseling Psychologist,* 6, 71–81. Copyright © 1976 by Sage Publications. Reprinted by Permission of SAGE Publications.

and values, problem orientating, and emotional responses" (p. 74). To represent task approach skills, Krumboltz used a parallelogram. Figure 4.5 shows Krumboltz's general model as well as a specific example related to our client Lakeesha.

Putting It All Together. Krumboltz used these four concepts (instrumental learning, associative learning, self-observation generalizations, and task approach skills) to explain the process of career selection (Krumboltz et al., 1976) or, as he called it in the next iteration of his theory (Krumboltz, 1979), the process of career decision making. Specifically, he created diagrams to illustrate the various types of circumstances and learning experiences that may affect a person's career choices. In these diagrams, Krumboltz used shapes associated with the model for each of these concepts. Figure 4.6 provides one such illustration. This diagram is intended to illustrate the factors and learning experiences that contributed to Juan's career choices.

LEARNING THEORY OF CAREER COUNSELING. The next major iteration of Krumboltz's learning theory occurred with his publication of the learning theory of career counseling (LTCC; Mitchell & Krumboltz, 1996). Rather than considering LTCC as a replacement of his earlier social learning theories, Krumboltz described this theory as an extension of these earlier theories. It retains all of the major elements of the earlier social learning theories and adds information about how career counselors can intervene to assist clients with their career development needs.

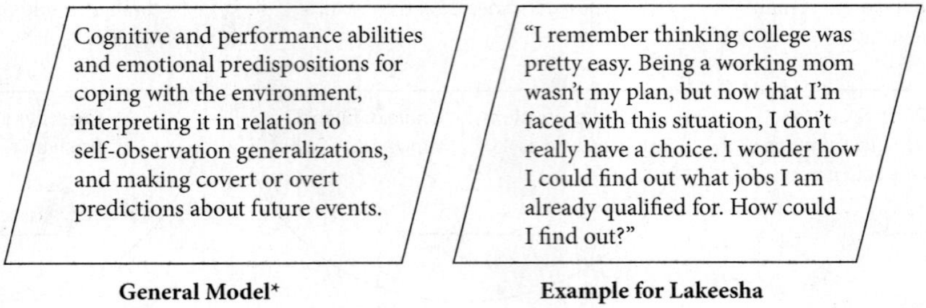

FIGURE 4.5 Krumboltz's Model of Task Approach Skills
* *Source:* Krumboltz, J.D., Mitchell, A.M., & Jones, G.B. (1976). A social learning theory of career selection. *The Counseling Psychologist,* 6, 71–81. Copyright © 1976 by Sage Publications. Reprinted by Permission of SAGE Publications.

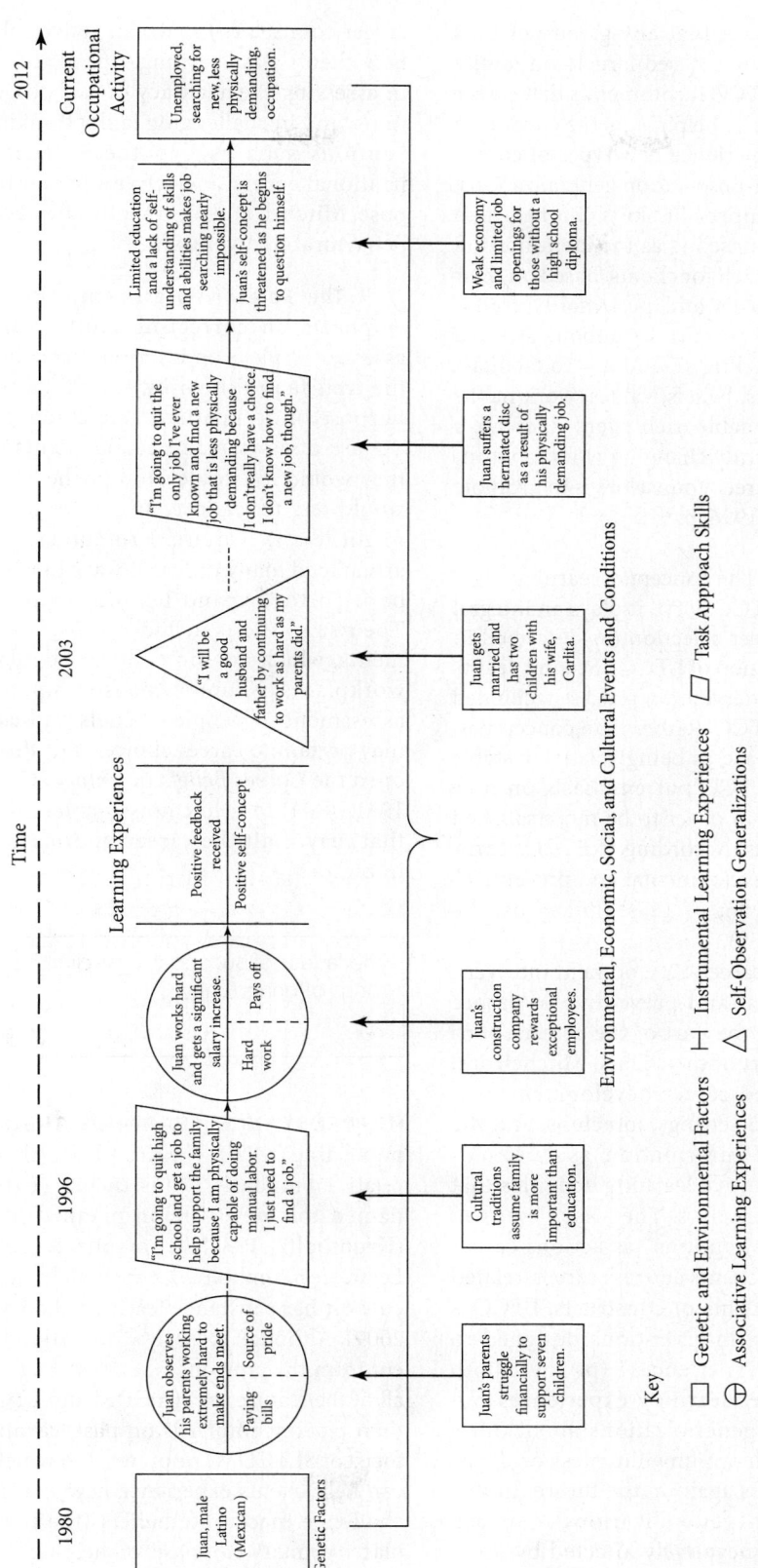

FIGURE 4.6 Illustration of Krumboltz's Social Learning Theory in Action

Source: Krumboltz, J.D., Mitchell, A.M., & Jones, G.B. (1976). A social learning theory of career selection. *The Counseling Psychologist*, 6, 71–81. Copyright © 1976 by Sage Publications. Reprinted by Permission of SAGE Publications.

In recognition of the fact that any given person's learning experiences are limited, based largely on family and environmental factors, LTCC recommends that career counselors take an active role in helping clients encounter new learning experiences, experience new types of consequences, develop accurate self-observation generalizations, and strengthen their task approach skills. Rather than viewing the goal of career counseling as the identification of "a suitable occupational match for clients, based on their existing interests, values, skills and personality traits" (Mitchell & Krumboltz, 1996, p. 252), Krumboltz asserted that the goal of career counseling should be "to facilitate the learning of skills, interests, beliefs, values, work habits and personal qualities that enable each client to create a satisfying life within a constantly changing work environment [and that] the task of career counselors is to promote client learning" (Krumboltz, 1996, p. 61).

The Roles of Learning. The concept of learning plays two important roles in the LTCC. First, it plays an integral role in explaining initial career selection (as described in the social learning theory portion of LTCC). Second, learning is also a key goal in the intervention process facilitated by career counselors using LTCC. Rather than conceptualizing clients and the workplace as being relatively stable entities, counselors using LTCC put emphasis on how clients can learn and change in order to be more satisfied with their work environments. According to LTCC, learning interventions may be "developmental and preventive" (Mitchell & Krumboltz, 1996, p. 257) or they can be "tailored and remedial" (p. 259).

Almost by definition, career development interventions that are developmental and preventive in nature involve psychoeducation on the part of the career counselor and learning on the part of the clients. Mitchell and Krumboltz (1996) identified career development programs provided within K–12 settings, job clubs, and the provision of occupational information as examples of developmental and preventive learning activities that can be offered by career counselors. They also described "tailored and remedial interventions" as actions career counselors may take to help clients address career-related problems. In keeping with its major constructs, LTCC is most interested in tailoring interventions designed to challenge "faulty learning experiences" (p. 259). Both instrumental and associative learning experiences can result, of course, in faulty generalizations about one's capabilities and may result in an unwillingness or disinclination to try such activities again in the future. In this way, both self-observation generalizations and task approach skills can also be negatively affected by these faulty learning experiences. Therefore, LTCC encourages career counselors to take an active role in understanding how clients' past learning experiences have affected them, in assessing the accuracy of self-observation generalizations, and in challenging faulty thinking. Cognitive interventions such as hypothesis testing, disputation of irrational beliefs, and reframing may be used for this purpose. Mitchell and Krumboltz also recommend the use of behavioral interventions.

The Role of Assessment. Because LTCC places emphasis on correcting faulty learning experiences, assessment plays an important role in the theory. Unlike the trait factor theories, which use assessments for the purpose of occupational matching, LTCC recommends the use of assessments to aid clients in identifying skills they would like to develop further, areas of interest they would like to explore, and other personality styles they might like to acquire. Krumboltz and Vidilakas (2000) articulated many different ways in which assessments can be used to "expand learning opportunities" (p. 315). Their suggestions included the use of 360-degree assessments, which are increasingly popular in contemporary workplaces. Krumboltz also emphasized the need for assessment of people's beliefs and assumptions as they may pertain to career choices. For this purpose, he developed the *Career Beliefs Inventory* (CBI; Krumboltz, 1988, 1991, 1994) to help counselors identify inaccurate beliefs that may limit the career options a client is interested in exploring.

> The ladder of success is best climbed by stepping on the rungs of opportunity.
>
> ~ Ayn Rand ~

HAPPENSTANCE LEARNING THEORY. Shortly after publishing his LTCC, Krumboltz changed the name and relative emphasis of his theory (Krumboltz, 1998). He named this new version planned happenstance theory (Krumboltz, 1998; Krumboltz & Levin, 2004; Mitchell, Levin, & Krumboltz, 1999), which theory evolved into his current happenstance learning theory (HLT; Krumboltz, 2009). Although these new titles sound dramatically different from the previous two titles, the theory actually retains all of the features of SLTCDM and LTCC. However, rather than placing emphasis on past learning experiences (the focus of SLTCDM) or on ways in which a career counselor can help clients experience new learning experiences and challenge inaccurate beliefs (the focus of LTCC), HLT places primary emphasis on helping clients make the most out of chance events.

Central Concepts in Happenstance Learning Theory.

Chance events. A major theme of HLT is that chance (or happenstance) has a major influence on a person's career development more often than not. As you consider this proposition, think about your own career development and how chance may have influenced your direction. How did your family's circumstances and the environment in which you were raised (clearly elements of your experience that were not of your own choosing) affect your career interests and aspirations? What types of unpredictable events occurred early in your life, and how might they have influenced your career development? What types of unexpected opportunities and/or barriers have arisen later in your life and influenced your career direction? If you are like most people, a number of unplanned events and happenstance situations likely affected the types of learning experiences and the types of opportunities you had. Indeed, a central concept of HLT is that "chance events inevitably play a major role in everyone's career" (Mitchell et al., 1999, p. 115). Instead of using the counseling process to minimize the impact of such chance events on client career development, HLT calls for career counselors to help clients increase the likelihood of potentially beneficial chance events and to capitalize on these opportunities.

Learning. Although HLT calls for career counselors to place primary emphasis on helping clients make the most out of chance events, the role of learning also remains central to the theory. Specifically, HLT (Krumboltz, 2009) addresses the importance of learning from two perspectives. First, HLT posits that people behave the way they do because of instrumental and associative learning experiences that occur in the context of their environment (including familial, peer, educational, and societal environments) and their genetic makeup (p. 137). Second, HLT identifies learning as the overall goal of career counseling as well as the goal of career assessments. In fact, Krumboltz states that "counselors are educators" (2009, p. 141) and implores them to take an active role in teaching their clients how to interact in their worlds so that they encounter new situations and learning experiences that may result in new career opportunities.

Action. Happenstance learning theory also emphasizes the importance of action within the career counseling process. Krumboltz (2009) observed, "Naming a future occupation is amazingly simple and can be faked.... The hard part is taking the actions necessary for achieving the goal—not just stating it" (p. 142). HLT therefore calls on career counselors to define their success not by a client's identification of a career goal but instead by a client's achievement of a satisfying and successful career and on clients to engage in action outside counseling sessions each and every week. These actions may include active exploration of career possibilities, behaviors to increase the likelihood of potentially beneficial chance events, and/or engaging in the behaviors necessary to accomplish a goal.

Indecision/open-mindedness as an asset. Krumboltz criticized the trait factor approaches for pathologizing indecision and suggested that it is more productive to embrace indecision than to view it only as a problem to be solved. In fact, because indecision is often a loaded word with negative connotations, this theory recommends using the word *open-minded* rather than *undecided* or *indecisive* (Mitchell et al., 1999). Because of this theory's emphasis on the value of recognizing and capitalizing on chance events, indecision becomes an asset to clients rather than a problem to be solved. Clients who have identified a single career goal and are focused exclusively on achieving that goal may be less likely to recognize and capitalize on chance events by taking risks and changing directions. Clients who have not yet made a firm decision may be more open-minded to a range of possibilities, more flexible with regard to their direction, more optimistic about the potential options, and more willing to take the risks needed to capitalize on unplanned opportunities.

Open-mindedness is also important from a longer-term perspective. Selecting a single career path for one's life may be unrealistic and undesirable. Such a goal may be unrealistic because circumstances change. The world of work and the nature of individuals may change. A company could go out of business. Entire industries (such as those devoted to production of the manual typewriters or floppy disk drives) may become obsolete. An acquired injury could render an individual unable to continue working within a chosen career. In addition, selecting and remaining in a single career for one's entire work life may be undesirable. One's interests or work-related values may change. For instance, a person may seek a career featuring physical risk and adventure early in life but later start a family and desire a career offering more safety and security. Open-mindedness can serve as an asset not only in the short-term process of looking for work but also in the long-term process of managing one's career development. Mitchell and colleagues (1999) therefore recommend that counselors reassure clients that they "do not need to plan [their] whole life right now" but can instead "take it one step at a time and evaluate [their] options as [they] proceed" (p. 124).

Using Happenstance Learning Theory in Career Counseling. Career counselors wishing to use planned happenstance theory approach the counseling process in ways that may surprise clients. Clients often seek career counseling with the expectation that the counselor will help them identify the best career path for them and assist them in making progress toward a specific career goal. When clients express this expectation, Mitchell et al. (1999) recommend responding as follows:

> If I had a way to identify the perfect occupation for you, believe me, I'd do it right now. Instead let's start a learning process that will expand your options and teach you how to take advantage of events you never could have anticipated. (p. 121)

In addition to helping clients understand that the goal of a career counselor isn't to help them select *the* single best career option for them, HLT suggests that career counselors engage in the following steps (see Table 4.2).

The first step, the orientation of clients to the counseling process, is typical of most career counseling approaches in that all clients need to understand what to expect of the counselor and the counseling relationship. Career counselors practicing HLT should include in this orientation an introduction to the importance of unplanned events not only in the client's past experiences but also in the counseling process. The second step also closely resembles other approaches to career counseling and simply involves understanding the client's concerns and framing them as a starting place. In doing so, HLT counselors pay special attention to understanding the types of activities that energize the client.

The third and fourth steps most clearly distinguish HLT from other approaches to career counseling. In the third step, the counselor encourages clients to reflect on ways in which chance experiences may have been beneficial to their career satisfaction, success, or opportunities. In addition to placing value on these chance experiences, the third step also involves helping clients gain insight from those experiences possibly to guide their future actions. The fourth step continues to focus on chance events, this time with a future orientation. In this step, the counselor teaches clients "to reframe unplanned events into career opportunities" (Krumboltz, 2009, p. 147). During this step, clients learn to become more aware of chance situations, identify ways to increase the likelihood of experiencing situations in which an unplanned opportunity may arise, and be prepared to capitalize on those opportunities. Specific skills useful in this step include "curiosity, persistence, flexibility, optimism and risk taking" (Mitchell et al., 1999, p. 118).

Finally, the fifth step of HLT involves identifying and addressing any faulty beliefs that may be interfering with the client's progress in counseling. For example, some clients may suffer from unnecessarily low self-efficacy, which may affect their ability and/or willingness to pursue potentially satisfying career options.

THINK AHEAD. Given this introduction to the Krumboltz's learning theories, think ahead to how you might use them with each person in our cast of clients. Consider, for example, what types of instrumental and associative learning experiences may have influenced each client's initial career choice and also how these learning experiences may have affected each client's self-observation generalizations and task approach skills. Think about what types of developmental interventions may have helped each client develop positive, accurate self-observation generalizations and sound task approach skills. Imagine what types of remedial interventions might help each client to unlearn faulty beliefs and strengthen task approach skills. Consider how the role of unpredictable, chance events has played a part in each client's career development. Answers to these questions should help you identify which clients might benefit most from the application of these approaches to career counseling.

> One important key to success is self-confidence.
> An important key to self-confidence is preparation.
>
> ~ Arthur Ashe ~

TABLE 4.2 Steps for Employing Planned Happenstance Learning Theory in Career Counseling

1. Orient client expectations.
2. Identify the client's concerns as a starting place.
3. Use client's successful past experiences with unplanned events as a basis for current actions.
4. Sensitize clients to recognize potential opportunities.
5. Overcome blocks to action.

Source: Krumboltz, J.D., (2009). The happenstance learning theory. *Journal of Career Assessment, 17,* 135–154. Copyright © 2009 by Sage Publications. Reprinted by Permission of SAGE Publications.

Social Cognitive Career Theory

First published in 1994 by Lent, Brown, and Hackett (1994), social cognitive career theory (SCCT) is another learning theory in career development. SCCT is founded on principles put forth by Bandura's social cognitive theory and grew out of early research on self-efficacy as it pertains to the career development of females (Hackett & Betz, 1981). Since then, a tremendous amount of research has guided the development of the theory and its application to both career development and career counseling interventions (Lent, 2005; Lent & Brown, 1996a, 1996b, 2002; Lent, Brown, & Hackett, 1996, 2000, 2002).

SCCT focuses on the triadic reciprocal relationship among people, their behaviors, and their environment in order to understand a person's career interests, choices, and performance. In doing so, SCCT pays particular attention to person variables (self-efficacy, outcome expectations, and performance goals) as well as to contextual factors both early in life (distal) and present-day (proximal). Although thorough coverage of this theory is beyond the scope of this chapter, this section will address four primary elements: person variables, contextual factors, triadic reciprocity, and SCCT's models.

PERSON VARIABLES IN SCCT. An important feature of SCCT is its attention to the ways in which characteristics of a person can and do influence his or her career development. SCCT approaches this from two perspectives. First, like most other career development theories, SCCT recognizes the impact of personal characteristics such as one's biological sex and race, one's sociological identification with regard to gender and ethnicity, and other factors such as disability status. Lent, Brown, and Hackett (1994) explained that, although these characteristics may have some direct impact on career development, they have a greater interest in how these characteristics might interact with the environment, thereby resulting in different types of learning experiences and opportunities. Second, SCCT calls attention to three specific cognitive processes occurring within people and affecting their career development: (1) self-efficacy, (2) outcome expectations, and (3) personal goals. These three cognitive processes represent the cornerstone of SCCT.

Self-Efficacy. Earlier in this chapter, you learned that Bandura defined perceived self-efficacy as "a judgment of one's capability to accomplish a certain level of performance" (Bandura, 1986, p. 361). In the context of SCCT, self-efficacy is defined similarly. However, Lent (2005) cautioned against conceptualizing self-efficacy as a stable, globalized trait. Instead, he explained, SCCT takes the perspective that self-efficacy may change over time and may differ across situations. Consider your own self-efficacy. It likely differs depending on the task you are asked to perform. Most of us feel quite confident about our own abilities to perform at a high level in some areas and much less confident with respect to other areas. For example, you may see yourself as quite adept at tasks such as reading or writing and much less adept at utilizing computer aided design (CAD) programs. Broadening this analogy from specific tasks to careers, your self-efficacy as a prospective counselor is likely higher than as a prospective design engineer.

In addition to varying across situations, self-efficacy may also change over time as a result of learning experiences. Indeed, self-efficacy is thought to develop from both direct and vicarious learning experiences and to change over time as a result of new learning experiences. Often, these new learning experiences involve a person's attempt to perform a given task. When the performance is better than anticipated, self-efficacy may increase. When it is worse than predicted, self-efficacy may decrease. As an example, you may find that your level of self-efficacy varies tremendously during your practicum experience. When a session seems to go well, you may experience a spike in your self-efficacy and may even feel like "super counselor." Conversely, when a session goes poorly, you may question your abilities and may even wonder if you made a mistake in pursuing a career as a counselor. Such fluctuations in self-efficacy are normal, especially for beginning counselors.

SCCT also recognizes that the relationship between self-efficacy and performance is complex and fully bidirectional. Other factors, such as the way a person interprets these situations, also have an impact. For example, how you feel about yourself as a prospective counselor also depends on the cognitive filters you use to interpret your performance in any given session. If you attribute successes to luck, your self-efficacy is less likely to spike than if you attribute your successes to your own skill and knowledge. Similarly, your self-efficacy is less likely to plummet if you attribute failures to external, random causes than if you attribute them to stable, internal deficits.

Outcome Expectations. Another cognitive person-variable that holds great importance in both SCT and SCCT involves a person's outcome expectations. Lent, Brown, and Hackett (2002) explained as follows:

> Outcome expectations are personal beliefs about the consequences or outcomes of performing particular behaviors. Whereas self-efficacy beliefs are concerned with one's capabilities (Can I do this?), outcome expectations involve the imagined consequences of

performing given behaviors. (If I do this, what will happen?) Outcome expectations include several types of beliefs about response outcomes, such as beliefs about extrinsic reinforcement (receiving tangible rewards for successful performance), self-directed consequences (such as pride in oneself for mastering a challenging task), and outcomes derived from the process of performing a given activity (for instance, absorption in the task itself). (p. 262)

In short, self-efficacy regarding one's ability to perform a given behavior or reach a given goal is but one factor influencing a person's decision about whether to engage in the behavior. Another factor involves that person's predictions about the likely outcomes of the behavior. Two students, for example, may each have a high level of confidence in their ability to earn an A in their math class. If self-efficacy were the only influencing factor, we would predict that both students would then engage in the behaviors necessary to earn the A. Outcome expectations, however, also play an influential role. If one student predicts positive outcomes (eligibility for a college scholarship, a sense of pride, and enjoyment of the challenge) but the other student predicts negative outcomes (being ridiculed by friends as a geek, feeling socially isolated, or having to miss social events to study), we would predict that the student with the positive outcome expectations would be more likely than the student with negative outcome expectations to engage in the behaviors necessary to earn the A. SCCT posits that the same principle applies to career development.

Personal Goals. A third personal determinant addressed by SCCT involves a person's goals. Lent et al. (2002) explained:

> Goals may be defined as the determination to engage in a particular activity or to effect a particular future outcome (Bandura, 1986). By setting personal goals, people help to organize, guide, and sustain their own behavior, even through overly long intervals, without external reinforcement. Thus goals constitute a critical mechanism through which people exercise personal agency or self-empowerment. (p. 263)

When thinking about your own career development, consider the importance of your goals. In addition to having confidence in your ability to complete a master's degree and believing that such an accomplishment would yield positive outcomes, you also needed to establish the goal of completing the degree. Without that goal, you would be left with only a feeling that "I could get that degree if I wanted to" rather than with an actual degree. It took a decision, though, to prompt you to initiate the process of enrolling in a degree program. That decision can be conceptualized as goal setting.

To summarize, a primary feature of SCCT involves its belief that people can and do exert considerable influence over their career development. SCCT refers to this as human agency (Bandura, 1989) and identifies three variables as especially important in the exercise of human agency: self-efficacy, outcome expectations, and personal goals. In addition to identifying ways in which these person variables may have a direct impact on career-related behaviors, SCCT also recognizes that these variables may affect one another as well. This is illustrated in Figure 4.7 and represents a new application of Bandura's concept of triadic reciprocality.

CONTEXTUAL FACTORS IN SCCT. In addition to understanding how personal variables influence career behavior, SCCT is concerned with how environmental variables influence career behavior. SCCT refers to these environmental variables as contextual factors, and two types of contextual factors are addressed by this theory. First, SCCT is interested in how the context of learning experiences earlier in one's life may affect the development of the personal determinants (self-efficacy, outcome expectations, and personal goals). SCCT refers to these as distal contextual factors. Second, SCCT recognizes that career-related behaviors are also influenced by current environmental factors, close to the point at which decisions are made. SCCT refers to these as proximal contextual factors (Lent et al., 2000).

Distal Contextual Factors. Distal contextual factors are, by definition, more distant from the career decision points. Lent et al. also referred to them as background contextual affordances and explained that these factors "affect the learning experiences through which career-relevant self-efficacy and outcome expectations develop" (Lent et al., 2000, p. 37). In other words, the social and cultural context in which people are raised makes a difference in the types of career-related exposure they experience, the types of role models to which they have access, the quality and emphasis of education they receive, and the types of behaviors that are rewarded or discouraged.

Drawing from the work by Astin (1984) and Vondracek, Lerner, and Schulenberg (1986), SCCT also acknowledges that both objective and subjective distal contextual factors should be considered. "Examples of objective factors include the quality of the educational experiences to which one has been exposed and the financial support available to one for pursuing particular training options" (Lent et al., 2000, p. 37). The way one

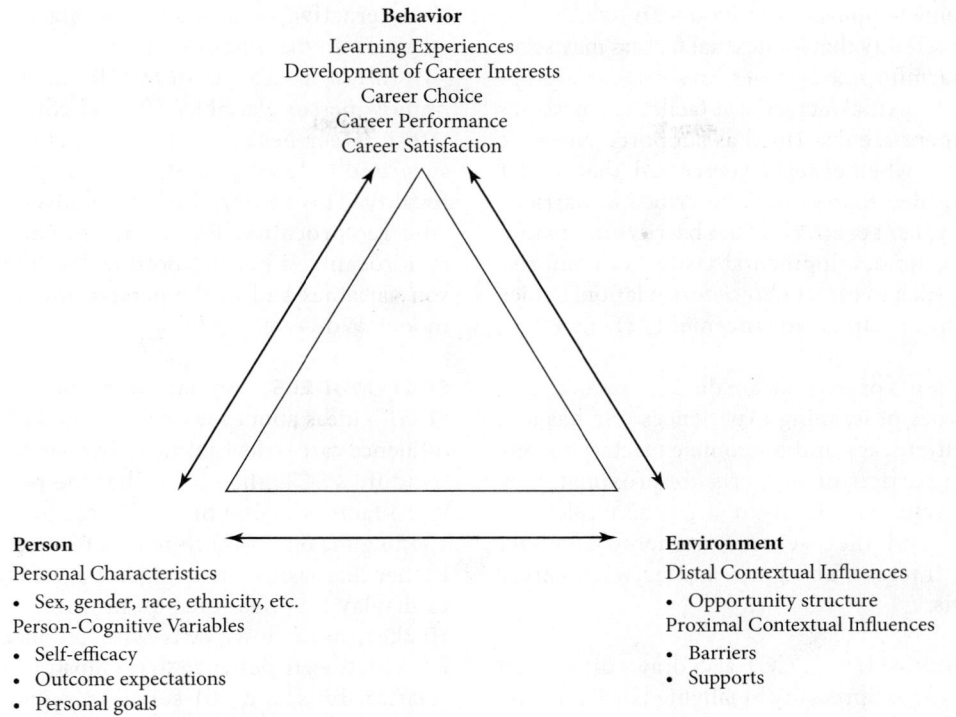

FIGURE 4.7 Triadic Reciprocality in Social Cognitive Career Theory

subjectively perceives contextual factors also matters. How individuals perceive and interpret various environmental variables has an impact on their development of self-efficacy and outcome expectations and ultimately on their career choices. This is yet another way SCCT emphasizes the role of human agency in career development. Rather than viewing people simply as products of their objective, distal environments, SCCT recognizes the active role people can take by how they "make sense of, and respond to, what their environment provides" (Lent et al., 2000, p. 37).

Proximal Contextual Factors. SCCT also acknowledges the very real impact that one's immediate environment—what SCCT refers to as proximal contextual factors—can have on one's career choices. SCCT states that proximal contextual factors serve a moderating role in which they either support or hinder one's ability to translate career interests into career goals or to transform career goals into career actions. As explained by Lent et al.:

> It is posited that people are less likely to translate their career interests into goals, and their goals into actions, when they perceive their efforts to be impeded by adverse environmental factors (e.g., insurmountable barriers or inadequate support systems). Conversely, the perception of beneficial environmental factors (e.g., ample support, few barriers) is predicted to facilitate the process of translating one's interests into goals and goals into actions. (Lent, Brown, & Hackett, 2000, p. 38)†

Even with the most ideal distal contextual influences, a person may feel thwarted by current circumstances with regard to his or her ability to realize career aspirations.

For example, a person may develop an interest in becoming a teacher but decide against it because of current environmental conditions. In this case, the distal contextual factors may have supported the requisite self-efficacy, outcome expectations, and personal goals necessary for the person to articulate an interest in becoming a teacher. Articulating the interest would represent one career-related behavior. The next career-related behavior might be to choose education as a college major. In this case, though, the person might encounter proximal contextual factors that are perceived as barriers. Such barriers might include a lack of money to attend college, lack of family support for this career aspiration, or a flooded job market for teachers.

---

†*Source:* Lent et al 2000, p. 38. Lent, R.W., Brown, S.D., & Hackett, G. (2000). Contextual supports and barriers to career choice: A social cognitive analysis. *Journal of Counseling Psychology, 47,* 36–49. American Psychological Association. Reprinted with permission.

Barriers and Supports. As you can see, SCCT addresses the possibility that contextual factors may serve a helpful or a harmful role in a person's career development. Positive contextual factors that facilitate a person's career development are described as supports. Negative contextual factors, whether real or perceived, that hinder a person's career development are described as barriers. More specifically, Lent et al. "consider barriers in relation to the more specific developmental tasks that comprise career progress, such as career choice formulation, choice implementation, or career advancement" (Lent et al., 2000, p. 39).

When supports or barriers are distal in nature, they influence the types of learning experiences one has and the resultant self-efficacy and outcome expectations one develops. When barriers or supports are proximal, they influence one's actual or perceived ability to implement career choices, and they serve a moderating effect between career interests and goals and between career goals and actions.

TRIADIC RECIPROCALITY. SCCT also draws directly on the model of triadic reciprocality highlighted by Bandura's social cognitive theory. The model in Figure 4.1 illustrated an interactive relationship among a person (P), that person's environment (E), and that person's behavior (B). In our discussion of SCCT thus far, we've focused on how person variables (P) and contextual (E) factors affect career behaviors (B). You shouldn't be terribly surprised to learn that SCCT also applies triadic reciprocality. This theory, though, involves two layers of triadic reciprocality. Figure 4.8 illustrates how triadic reciprocality is present both in the interactions of person variables and in the person-environment-behavior model. Wowzers!

SCCT MODELS. So far, this chapter has addressed SCCT's ideas about how person and contextual variables influence career development. In keeping with its roots in Bandura's SCT, the idea is that the relationship among these factors is one of triadic reciprocality, with each affecting the other (which reflects ties with Bandura's SCT). Rather than using a triangular diagram (as in Figure 4.8) to display this relationship, however, Lent, Brown and Hackett used flowcharts with feedback loops. These flowcharts were designed to (a) illustrate triadic reciprocal relationships and (b) serve as segmental models to explain the development of career interests, the making

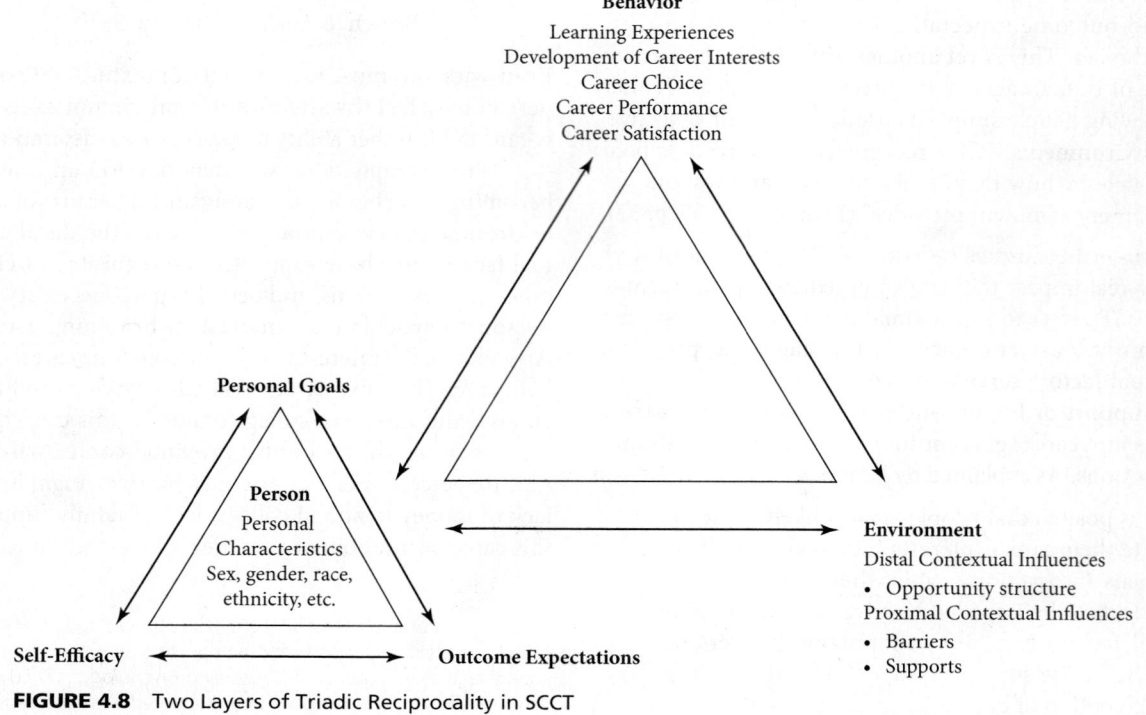

FIGURE 4.8 Two Layers of Triadic Reciprocality in SCCT

of career choices, and the quality of career performance. Lent explained:

> In SCCT, (1) the development of academic and career interests, (2) the formation of educational and vocational choices, and (3) the nature and results of performance in academic and career spheres are conceived as occurring within three conceptually distinct yet interlocking process models (Lent et al., 1994). In each model, . . . the basic theoretical elements—self-efficacy, outcome expectations, and goals—are seen as operating in concert with other important aspects of persons (e.g., gender, race/ethnicity), their contexts, and learning experiences to help shape the contours of academic and career development. (Lent, 2005, pp. 105–106)

Interest Model. Understanding how academic and career interests develop is of great interest to SCCT. In keeping with a learning theory perspective, SCCT explores ways in which learning experiences unfold and affect a person's interests. However, rather than suggesting that interests are a direct result of associative and instrumental learning experiences (*à la* Krumboltz's SLTCDM), SCCT is particularly interested in how the person variables of self-efficacy and outcome expectations mediate the relationship between learning experiences and the development of interests. This relationship is illustrated in the SCCT interest model shown in Figure 4.9.

The basic idea underlying this interest model is that people are constantly engaged in this feedback loop.

They enter every situation with a given level of self-efficacy and outcome expectations specific to the current situation and shaped by prior learning experiences. When levels of self-efficacy are high and outcome expectations are positive, a person is more likely to experience interest in that activity, decide to engage in it, and experience performance outcomes as a result of engaging in it. These outcomes then circle back and modify one's self-efficacy and outcome expectations regarding that particular activity. If the performance outcomes are positive, self-efficacy and outcome expectations are reinforced and increase interest and subsequent involvement in that type of activity. On the other hand, if the performance outcomes are negative, self-efficacy and outcome expectations are modified and decrease interest and subsequent involvement in that type of activity. Although SCCT acknowledges that ability and values also play a part in this process, the theory focuses on how these factors "funnel through self-efficacy and outcome expectations" (Lent, 2005, p. 107). Indeed, the primary focus of SCCT's interest model is on how those person variables mediate learning experiences and affect interest development.

Choice Model. Clearly, there is more to understanding one's career development than identifying interests. At the point of initial career selection, people may have many interests but choose to pursue only one of them in a formal academic or career setting. In today's world of work, it is common for individuals to have multiple careers over the course of their lifetime. This results, of course, in multiple choice points. These new choices are sometimes motivated internally, perhaps in conjunction with changing interests, needs, values, and/or abilities. Alternatively, these new

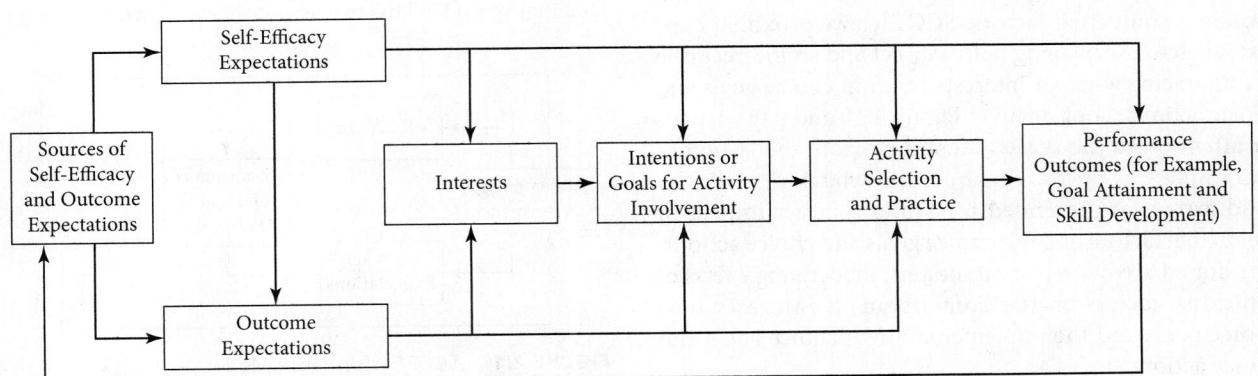

FIGURE 4.9 SCCT Interest Model

Source: From Lent, R.W. (2005). A social cognitive view of career development and counseling. In S.D. Brown, & R.W. Lent (Eds.), *Career development and counseling: Putting theory and research to work* (pp. 101–127) (p. 106) Copyright © 1993 is owned by Lent, Brown and Hackett.

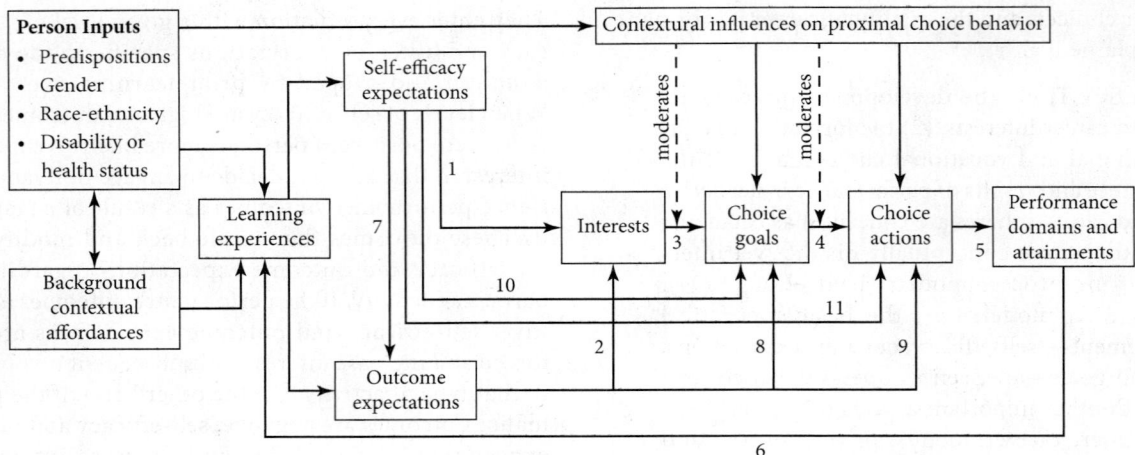

FIGURE 4.10 SCCT Choice Model

Source: From Lent, R.W. (2005). A social cognitive view of career development and counseling. In S.D. Brown, & R.W. Lent (Eds.), *Career development and counseling: Putting theory and research to work* (pp. 101–127) (p. 108) Copyright © 1993 is owned by Lent, Brown and Hackett.

choices may be externally motivated by the presentation of new opportunities, the encountering of barriers such as discriminatory promotion practices, or the experience of a layoff.

In explaining the career choice process, both at the point of initial career selection and at later points of career decisions, SCCT offers a second segmental model: the choice model. As shown in Figure 4.10, the choice model posits that interests feed into choice goals and that choice goals next feed into choice actions, which result in some level of performance attainment. The performance outcomes then trigger a feedback loop, which influences one's self-efficacy and outcome expectations, which in turn affect one's level of interest. An additional and very important element of the SCCT choice model involves how this ongoing feedback loop is affected by distal and proximal contextual factors. SCCT views proximal contextual factors as playing both a direct and an indirect role in influencing whether interests result in choice goals and choice actions. Look again at Figure 4.10 and pay particular attention to the arrows stemming from the "Contextual influences on proximal choice behavior" box. The solid arrows are intended to signify a direct impact of contextual factors on both choice goals and choice actions. The dotted arrows represent indirect, moderating effects of contextual factors on the conversion of interests into choice goals and the implementation of choice goals into choice actions.

Even though a person may develop specific career goals consistent with his or her interests, that person may be subject to contextual factors that directly influence the viability of this career choice. Lent explains, "In certain cultures, for example, individuals may defer their career decisions to significant others in the family, even where the others' preferred career path is not all that interesting to the individual" (2005, p. 110). Another example of a direct influence might be a lack of financial resources necessary to obtain training to enter a specific career. Contextual factors may also indirectly affect a person's career choices by helping or hindering the establishment of goals based on interests or taking action in accordance with goals. SCCT's choice model suggests that this process is helped by "strong environmental supports and weak barriers in relationship to [a person's] preferred career paths" and hindered by a lack of support and strong barriers (Lent, 2005, p. 110).

Performance Model. The third and final segmental model put forth by SCCT is called the performance model (see Figure 4.11). This model is concerned with the quality

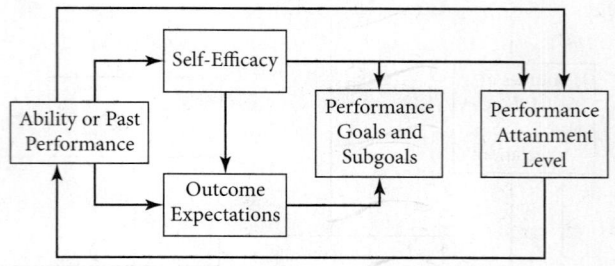

FIGURE 4.11 SCCT Performance Model

Source: From Lent, R.W. (2005). A social cognitive view of career development and counseling. In S.D. Brown, & R.W. Lent (Eds.), *Career development and counseling: Putting theory and research to work* (pp. 101–127) (p. 111) Copyright © 1993 is owned by Lent, Brown and Hackett.

of a person's performance as well as with the degree of persistence a person demonstrates in performing a given career activity. It also employs a feedback loop.

In this performance model, the elements of career development addressed by the interest model and the choice model are not displayed. Instead, this model focuses attention on the way in which ability and past performance affects people's level of self-efficacy and outcome expectations, how these personal determinants then influence the performance goals people set for themselves, and how their actual level of performance then serves to modify their self-efficacy and outcome expectations.

For example, let's apply the performance model to your situation. As a graduate student, you entered this course with your own unique set of abilities and knowledge of how you've performed as a student in other courses. Your sense of your own abilities and your experiences in other classes likely affected your level of self-efficacy and your outcome expectations. In other words, you entered this class with some level of confidence and anticipated the outcomes of taking this particular course. You may have felt completely confident and anticipated doing well or rather concerned about passing. According to SCCT, your self-efficacy and outcome expectations would affect the performance goals you set for yourself. Do you set a goal of earning an A or do you set a goal of passing the class with no lower than a C—? The goals you set influence to some extent the level of performance attainment, but other factors are also involved. Is this an especially difficult course? Is the grading based on a curve? Did you over- or underestimate your ability to succeed and the likely outcomes of your effort? At the end of the semester, you will have a grade: a metric of your performance attainment level. This grade will then cycle back through the feedback loop and become data regarding your past performance, influence your self-efficacy, outcome expectations, and so on, in future courses.

Thus, the SCCT performance model addresses the ways in which your abilities and past performances affect your self-efficacy as well as the way in which your level of self-efficacy then affects the level of performance goals you set for yourself. All these factors influence your ultimate level of performance in a given activity. An additional element of this model involves the degree of persistence or stability a person demonstrates. The basic idea is that people will demonstrate more persistence in activities in which they are satisfied with their performance outcomes. Once again applying the model to yourself, poor grades in a number of courses will likely decrease your persistence in your academic program. You may withdraw from the program, based on decreased levels of self-efficacy and outcome expectations, or you could be dismissed from the program. Although SCCT recognizes that poor performance isn't the only reason a person may not persist in a given activity (e.g., a better opportunity may arise), it suggests that persistence is one indicator of sufficient quality of performance.

APPLICATION OF SCCT IN THE CAREER COUNSELING PROCESS. As you can see, SCCT represents a comprehensive theory that may prove quite useful in understanding a person's career development path. SCCT provides recommendations for how career counselors might use theory-based interventions to help (and not just understand) clients with their career development needs. In this section, you will learn how career counselors can use SCCT to develop interventions in the career counseling process, and to support effective career development in youth.

SCCT addresses a number of ways in which counselors can assist clients with career difficulties (Brown & Lent, 1996; Lent & Brown, 2002). SCCT's recommendations for counseling interventions are based on three tenets, each of which flows logically from the theory itself. First, it recognizes that self-efficacy isn't always reflective of a person's true abilities and that outcome expectations are not always consistent with reality. As a result, "some (perhaps many) clients enter counseling having already eliminated potentially rewarding occupational possibilities because of faulty self-efficacy beliefs or outcome expectations" (Brown & Lent, 1996, p. 355). The second tenet that guides SCCT career counseling interventions addresses the ways in which faulty self-efficacy beliefs and/or inaccurate outcome expectations may be modified. Because SCCT believes that these constructs develop largely as a result of learning experiences involving past "performance accomplishments" (p. 355), modifying them will require new (more successful) performance accomplishments and/or reinterpretation of past performance accomplishments. The third principle underlying SCCT career counseling interventions is that the progression of career-related interests into career choices (goals or actions) is affected by a person's perceptions of proximal contextual barriers. Although a person may be interested in a given career, he or she may choose not to pursue it because of perceived barriers.

Interventions to Support Reconsideration of Low-Interest Occupations. The first approach recommended by SCCT is to focus on areas of client disinterest to determine whether the disinterest indicates a premature foreclosure based on inaccurate self-efficacy beliefs or outcome expectations. It is not sufficient, according to SCCT, to explore with clients only those career options in which they express interest. Instead, SCCT counselors are also curious about areas in which a client does not express interest. To identify the most likely areas of premature foreclosure based on faulty self-efficacy beliefs or inaccurate outcome expectations, SCCT recommends that career counselors conduct an analysis of discrepancies among a client's interests, aptitudes, and values (Brown & Lent, 1996). The goal is to identify areas in which clients might have an interest *if* they believed they could be successful in that career or that the career would yield outcomes of value to them.

A career counselor might identify such discrepancies in several ways. For example, the counselor might compare a client's results on standardized tests of career interests, aptitudes, and needs/values. For careers in which the client reports little or no interest, the results might suggest that the client has the necessary aptitude to succeed and that the career would meet the client's outcome needs, so the counselor would talk with the client about the reasons for disinterest. At times, of course, such a discussion will result in the counselor discovering that the client has the requisite self-efficacy and accurate outcome expectations but simply considers that particular career path uninteresting. If this conversation reveals that, despite the aptitude to be successful (as objectively measured), the client has low self-efficacy beliefs, the counselor would then seek to challenge those faulty self-efficacy beliefs. If this discussion suggests that the client's disinterest is based on inaccurate outcome expectations, the counselor would then seek to provide more accurate information to correct those outcome expectations.

Another way a counselor could identify such discrepancies would be with the use of a modified card-sort technique. You will learn more about the use of card sorts in Chapter 12. For now, though, it is sufficient to know that a common example of a card sort invites clients to sort a stack of cards (each containing the name of an occupation) into columns according to interest levels. In the classic use of card sorts, the counselor and client then focus on occupations represented by cards in the highest level of interest columns. In the modified approach suggested by Brown and Lent (1996), they would instead focus on the occupations in the column representing the least amount of interest. Specifically, a counselor would then ask the client to:

> sort these occupations into more specific categories reflecting self-efficacy beliefs (i.e., "might choose if I thought I had the skills"), outcome expectations (i.e., "might choose if I thought it offered me things I value"), definite lack of interest (i.e., wouldn't choose under any circumstance"), or other. Occupations sorted into the self-efficacy and outcome expectation subcategories are then explored for accuracy of skill and outcome perceptions; further testing or information-gathering may be used for these purposes. (Brown & Lent, 1996, p. 360)

Brown and Lent suggest that, although standardized tests would be one obvious way to determine accuracy of self-efficacy beliefs, other informal approaches could also be used. For example, they described an activity in which clients complete a self-rating of skills and also ask three friends or coworkers to rate them (the client) on those same skills. In this way, discrepancies between self-perceptions and others' perceptions of skills could be identified.

Interventions for Modifying Inaccurate Self-Efficacy Beliefs. Once faulty self-efficacy beliefs are identified, the second type of counseling intervention recommended by SCCT involves attempts to correct them. One way to correct them, of course, would be simply to confront the client's inaccurately low self-efficacy beliefs with objective data indicating high levels of capability. Doing so might also involve comparing a client's scores on a standardized test with normative data to get an objective sense of the quality of the client's performance. Lent and Brown (2002) explained, though, that "SCCT [and SCT] both point to perceived performance accomplishments as generally being the most potent source of information for altering self-efficacy beliefs" (p. 91). Thus, SCCT suggests that counselors encourage clients to seek new opportunities to test one's abilities, with the hope that clients will succeed in these opportunities, thereby having reason to adjust their self-efficacy beliefs. Lent and Brown also note that, in cases in which clients interpret objectively successful experiences as failures due to cognitive distortions, it may be necessary to focus attention on those distortions.

Interventions for Addressing Perceived Barriers. The third type of counseling interventions prescribed by SCCT (Brown & Lent, 1996; Lent & Brown, 2002) is focused on addressing perceived proximal contextual barriers. In such situations, clients may perceive barriers that affect their ability or willingness to move from interests to choice goals and from choice goals to choice actions. Interventions in this category of interventions may involve determining whether the perception of barriers reflects reality or developing strategies for managing or overcoming barriers. Either way, these interventions begin with a discussion of the client's career interests and any barriers they perceive for each occupational interest. One way to facilitate discussions about perceived barriers is to "adapt Janis and Mann's (1977) decisional balance sheet procedure to help . . . clients identify possible consequences, for themselves and their significant others, related to their preferred option(s)" and "then [to] focus on those anticipated negative consequences that might serve as choice implementation barriers" (Lent & Brown, 2002, p. 90). A simple conversation with your client could also be used to identify perceived barriers.

When barriers are identified, reality testing might first be employed. For example, if a client is interested in a career requiring a college education but perceives a lack of financial resources as a barrier to attending college, it may be useful to explore actual costs associated with a variety of colleges and to estimate his or her eligibility for financial aid. Similarly, if a client is interested in a career area but identifies a tight job market as a barrier, reality testing would involve accessing occupational information resources to determine the rate of growth and/or the average number of job openings each year or to conduct informational interviews with employers for that career. Occupational data is available in national as well as state-specific forms, and you will learn about using such resources in Chapter 13. In many instances, of course, the reality of barriers is harder to assess. In such cases, Lent and Brown (2002) suggest that counselors assist clients with estimating the probability of encountering the barrier and whether the barrier will be insurmountable.

SCCT also emphasizes the importance of helping clients realize that, although obstacles may actually be present and encountered, they may also be overcome. Career counselors can help clients anticipate possible barriers and develop action plans to overcome them. This type of intervention basically involves focused, anticipatory problem solving. As an example, a client might express an interest in becoming a chef but perceive a barrier related to transportation. The client might live in a small town with few restaurants, and she or he may realistically anticipate the need to commute in order to find work in the culinary industry. One barrier in this case could be a concern about having an old car and worrying that it might break down. Reality testing would first be used to determine whether the client would likely need to commute in order to find work as a chef. The client could also have his or her car inspected to determine the likelihood of an impending problem. Problem solving might then include determining whether a car pool or public transportation would be possible in the event that the car breaks down and the establishment of a plan to set aside money from each paycheck for an auto repair or replacement fund.

DEVELOPMENTAL APPLICATIONS OF SCCT. In addition to suggesting ways in which counselors can assist clients with career difficulties, SCCT addresses ways to support the career development of youth (Brown & Lent, 1996; Lent & Brown, 2002). The theory focuses on developmental applications appropriate for use with children and early adolescents, and on other applications more appropriate for use with people in their late adolescence and early adulthood.

Childhood and Early Adolescence. SCCT recommends developmental applications for use with children and early adolescents (i.e., elementary and middle school students) by drawing directly on its interest model. Recall that, according to this model, career-related interests develop as a result of learning experiences and a child's resultant self-efficacy and outcome expectations. Also recall that SCCT believes that young people may foreclose consideration of a wide variety of careers based on faulty self-efficacy beliefs or inaccurate outcome expectations. In keeping with these tenets, "SCCT suggests that psychoeducational interventions designed to promote optimum career development (or to prevent future choice or adjustment problems) need to focus not only on students' emergent interests, values, and talents but on the cognitive bases of these characteristics" (Lent et al., 2002, p. 287).

SCCT suggests that the career development of youth can be enhanced by addressing these very concepts. As Lent explained, "The four sources of efficacy information can be used as an organizing structure for psychoeducational interventions" (2005, p. 117), with primary emphasis placed on the role of personal performance accomplishments in influencing self-efficacy beliefs. For example, students can be assisted in developing a wide variety of skills in order to enhance their personal performance accomplishments. Direct instruction, practice, and gradually increasing levels of difficulty can assist young people in developing both competence and confidence. Other strategies may involve modeling skill acquisition and career exploration and providing encouragement (i.e., social support and persuasion) for youth to "attempt new tasks, to persist despite initial setbacks, and to interpret their performances favorably" (p. 117). Attention to the potential impact of physiological states of arousal on self-efficacy might involve helping students manage anxiety that could lower their performance. An example might be a classroom guidance lesson or counseling intervention geared toward addressing test anxiety in elementary school students, written by yours truly under my maiden name: Hobson (1996).

A second developmental application for use with youth involves providing them with accurate information on which to base outcome expectations. Classroom guidance lessons (to be discussed in Chapter 14) should provide students with exposure to a great deal of information about potential careers. Lent notes that such exposure is "key to fostering acquisition of realistic outcome expectations (i.e., beliefs about the working conditions and reinforcers available in diverse occupations)" (Lent, 2005, p. 118). Accurate information about a broad range of careers is essential.

Indeed, whether focusing on self-efficacy or on outcome expectations, a key concept involves accuracy. In order for children to avoid the development of faulty self-efficacy beliefs, they need to receive accurate feedback about their performance and developing abilities (Lent et al., 2002, p. 287). After all, a high level of self-efficacy combined with a low level of skill is not useful. Likewise, a low level of self-efficacy despite high levels of ability and performance is also problematic. SCCT argues that it important for students to develop an accurate sense of their relative strengths and weaknesses. When efficacy levels exceed performance, students may need to receive direct feedback regarding deficits in their abilities or performance. Two potential solutions to this discrepancy exist. First, self-efficacy beliefs can be adjusted downward to match abilities or performance more closely. Second, focused effort on skill development could improve performance results and thus warrant the existing level of self-efficacy. In cases in which performance and abilities exceed self-efficacy beliefs, attention should be paid to helping students acknowledge their own successes and thereby develop more accurate attributions.

Late Adolescence and Early Adulthood. SCCT recommends developmental applications for use with people in their late adolescence or early adulthood (i.e., high school students and young adults) by echoing the recommendations just offered and by drawing directly on its choice model. Assuming that students emerge from early adolescence with accurate self-efficacy beliefs and outcome expectations on which to base their career interests, the focus of developmental applications of SCCT with students in their late adolescence and early adulthood is on the career choice-making and implementation processes.

Psychoeducational interventions designed to help students recognize the varied career options that might be well suited to their interests, abilities, and values are especially important. Such interventions will surely include considerable career exploration and will also likely include the teaching of a career decision-making model. SCCT refers to the identification of tentative career goals as the transformation of interests into choice goals.

The next step involves the transformation of choice goals into choice actions or implementation. Goal setting becomes especially important at this point. Lent (2005) explains that long-term goals such as career aspirations are more likely to be achieved if the student is also assisted in establishing the short-term goals necessary to achieve her or his career aspirations. For example, if a student aspires to become an attorney, short-term goals would include graduating from high school, taking and succeeding in college preparation courses, applying and being admitted to college, and so forth. In addition to breaking long-term goals into short-term goals, Lent recommends that students be encouraged to make their short-term goals "clear, specific, proximal" and public (p. 121). Lent et al. (2002) recommend that all students need assistance in this regard, whether they are planning to transition directly from school to work and those aspiring toward postsecondary education.

Because proximal contextual barriers have both direct and indirect effects on choice behavior, another type of developmental application recommended by SCCT focuses on the potential barriers and supports a student might experience. Psychoeducational interventions focused on barriers and supports are viewed as essential. In the preceding section about counseling interventions, you learned about a number of strategies for anticipating potential barriers, developing strategies for managing or overcoming barriers, and for identifying sources of support.

For example, many high school students express an intention to attend college and want a career requiring a college education, but many of these same students may lack accurate information about what it takes to gain admission to college and succeed there (ACT, 2010). Assistance with setting the short-term goals necessary to become ready for college will be useful in this case, but it may not be sufficient. Students may also face a number of barriers or lack sufficient support related to the college admissions process. Programs such as KnowHow2Go (knowhow2go.acenet.edu) are designed to assist students in understanding the steps necessary to make college a reality. The first step described in this program encourages the student to "be a pain" and proceeds to address the very issue of overcoming barriers and enlisting support. The fourth step in this program helps students "put [their] hands on some cash," thereby directly addressing financial barriers (knowhow2go.acenet.edu/#aa). Such strategies are quite consistent with SCCT recommendations for developmental applications.

THINK AHEAD. Given this introduction to SCCT, think ahead to how you might use this theory with each person in our cast of clients. For each client, think specifically about how learning experiences may have affected his or her self-efficacy. Think about how distal and proximal contextual factors may have affected each client. Next, consider how self-efficacy and contextual factors may have influenced the client's career interests, choices, and performance. Given these insights, how might you use SCCT strategies to assist each client?

> Making good decisions is a crucial skill at every level.
> ~ Peter Drucker ~

Cognitive Information-Processing Approach

The final learning theory of career development to be presented in this chapter comes from Peterson, Sampson, Lenz, and Reardon, 2002; Peterson, Sampson, and Reardon, 1991; Peterson, Sampson, Reardon, and Lenz, 1996; and Sampson, Reardon, Peterson, and Lenz, 2004. The cognitive information-processing approach(CIP) differs from the learning theories presented earlier in this chapter because of its very specific focus. CIP was developed by career counselors at Florida State University. Faced with the daunting task of helping college students through a critically important decision-making process, these counselors developed an approach specifically focused on helping clients learn to make decisions about current career problems or choices and on teaching these same clients career decision-making skills for use with future career problems or choice points (Peterson et al., 1996; Sampson et al., 2004). In presenting the rationale for this theory, the authors observe that helping clients with the decision-making step of Parsons's (1909) three-step model for vocational choice has received considerably less attention than helping clients understand themselves and understand the world of work. Thus, they begin with a model for understanding a person's decision status.

CIP DECISION STATUS TAXONOMY. CIP offers a taxonomy designed to categorize people according to their decision status: (1) decided, (2) undecided, and (3) indecisive (Peterson et al., 1996; Sampson et al., 2004). Within these categories, CIP identifies some subcategories, while acknowledging that the career counseling needs of clients in each category and/or subcategory differ. Figure 4.12 illustrates the categories and subcategories of the CIP decision status taxonomy.

The decided category consists of people who have committed, either publicly or privately, to a specific career choice and includes three subcategories: decided–confirmation, decided–implementation, and decided–conflict avoidance.

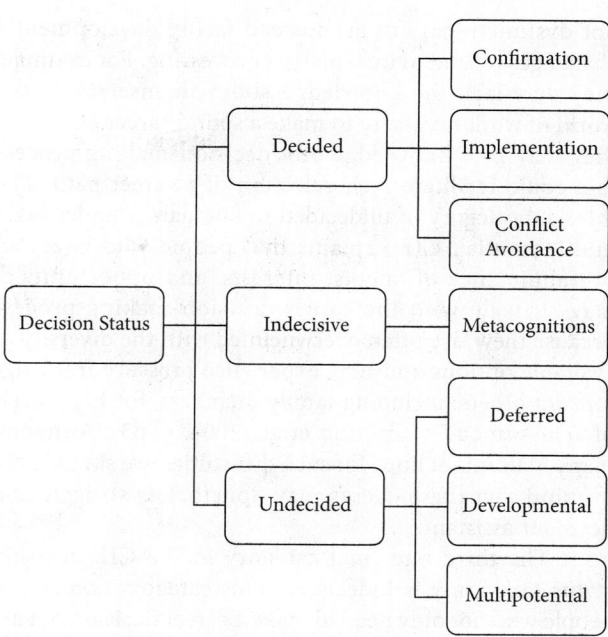

FIGURE 4.12 CIP Decision Status Taxonomy

Although, at first glance, you may wonder why a decided individual would ever seek career counseling. CIP suggests that such individuals may be seeking confirmation that the choice they have made is well suited to them or they may be seeking assistance with the implementation of their choice. Some people may make a public commitment to a choice because of external pressure but may not actually be confident in their choice. CIP describes such individuals as decided–conflict avoidant and suggests that they need the type of career assistance typically offered to clients in the undecided or indecisive categories.

The undecided category consists of people who "have not made a commitment to a specific occupational choice due to gaps in the knowledge for choosing" (Sampson et al., 2004, p. 82). This category includes three subcategories: deferred choice, developmental, and multipotential. The subcategory of undecided–deferred choice refers to situations in which the person has no urgent need to make a choice and thus has the luxury of delaying the decision. This is often the case with students in high school or just beginning their college education. As you can imagine, such individuals do not generally seek career counseling. However, career counselors may encounter them while conducting classroom guidance lessons (in a K–12 school setting) or doing outreach (in a college setting). In contrast, the undecided–developmental subcategory represents people who have reached a point at which they feel a need to make a career choice but feel unable to do so. CIP explains that these people are typically not dysfunctional but are instead facing developmental challenges related to information processing. For example, they may lack the knowledge about themselves or the world of work necessary to make a sound career choice, or they may lack knowledge of a decision-making process that could facilitate their selection of a career path. The third subcategory of undecided individuals is undecided–multipotential. CIP explains that people who have "an overabundance of talents, interests, and opportunities" may struggle with the career decision-making process because they "are often overwhelmed with the diversity of available options and may experience pressure from significant others, including family members, for high levels of achievement" (Sampson et al., 2004, p. 83). Although many of us might hope for such difficulties, we should bear in mind that these clients may nonetheless struggle and need our assistance.

The third and final category in the CIP decision status taxonomy is indecisive. This category consists of people who not only need to make a career decision but are also struggling with "a maladaptive approach to problem solving in general that is accompanied by a dysfunctional level of anxiety" (Sampson et al., 2004, p. 83). Specifically, they may struggle with "excessive negative self-talk, attention deficits, or confused thought processes" (p. 83). Peterson et al. (1991) noted that indecisive individuals may also be struggling with psychological conditions that affect their ability to engage in a career decision-making process.

As you read through these various types of decision status, you may have recognized yourself. You may have also noticed references to concepts associated with cognitive psychology. CIP is specifically designed to address "the actual thought and memory processes involved in solving career problems and making career decisions" (Peterson et al., 1996, p. 427) by drawing from the fields of cognitive psychology and cognitive science. In fact, the next section focuses on a hallmark feature of CIP that is based directly on research in these fields.

THE PYRAMID OF INFORMATION-PROCESSING DOMAINS. Central to CIP is its attention to the way in which individuals take in and process information. Indeed, CIP theorists believe that information processing lies at the heart of sound career decision making. CIP organizes the two primary career decision-making operations of (1) information gathering and (2) information processing into a hierarchical structure. This structure resembles a pyramid and has three segments (see Figure 4.13). CIP offers two versions of this pyramid: one for use by counselors and one for use by clients.

At the base of the pyramid are the knowledge domains of self-knowledge and occupational knowledge. The middle layer of the pyramid is the decision-making skills domain, which involves the acquisition of generic information-processing skills and the use of these skills to make a career decision. The top of the pyramid reflects the

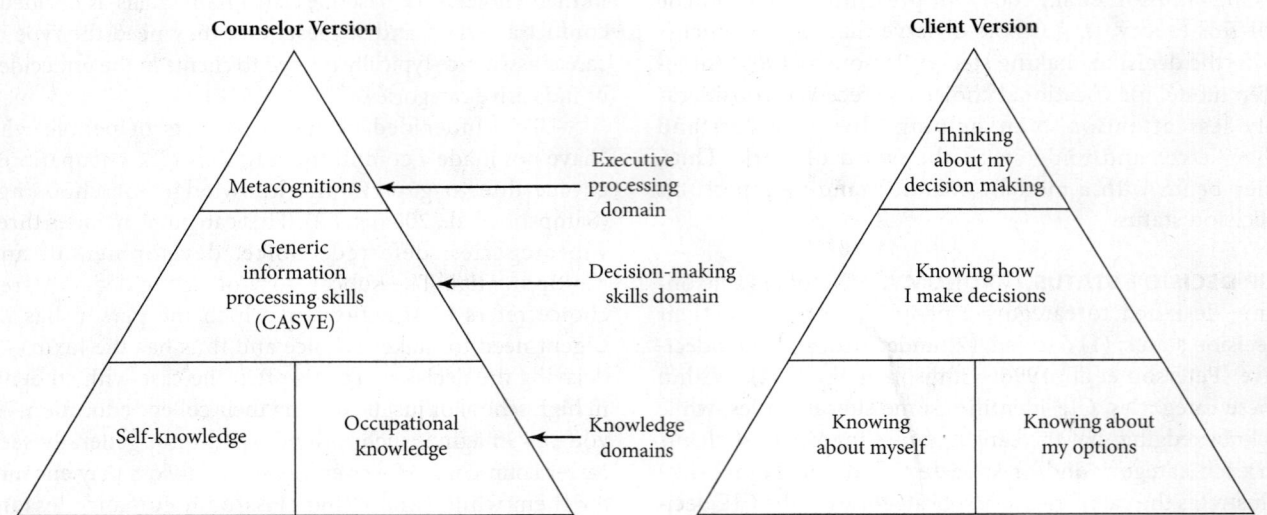

FIGURE 4.13 CIP Pyramid of Information-Processing Domains
Sources: Counselor Version: Peterson, G.W., Sampson, J.P., Jr., & Reardon, R.C. (1991). *Career development and services: A cognitive approach.* Pacific Grove, CA: Brooks/Cole. (p. 28). - Client Version: Sampson, J.P. Jr., Peterson, G.W., Lenz, J.G., & Reardon, R.C. (1992). A cognitive approach to career services: Translating concepts into practice. *The Career Development Quarterly,* 41, 67–74. (p. 70) Copyright: NCDA.

executive-processing domain and recognizes the importance of metacognitions. Notice how the first layer of this pyramid represents the first two steps offered by Parsons (understand yourself and understand the world of work). In contrast to other career counseling approaches that emphasize these steps, CIP emphasizes Parsons's third step of decision making as shown in the top two layers of the pyramid.

Knowledge Domains: Self-Knowledge and Occupational Knowledge. Consistent with other theories of career development, CIP also recognizes the importance of helping clients acquire and apply self-knowledge when engaging in the career decision-making process. Self-knowledge in the context of CIP includes interests, skills, and values (Sampson et al., 2004). CIP also recognizes the importance of helping clients expand their awareness of the occupational options available to them. Unique to CIP, though, is its conceptualization of how self-knowledge and occupational knowledge are stored and modified over time.

With regard to self-knowledge, CIP believes this form of knowledge is acquired based on episodes or experiences and one's interpretation of those experiences. Over time, new episodes or events may reinforce one's prior interpretation or may challenge them, thereby resulting in a reinterpretation of oneself—what CIP refers to as reconstruction (Peterson et al., 2002, p. 321). This concept is consistent with the cognitive processes of assimilation, accommodation, and equilibration that were initially conceptualized by Piaget (1985). Our past experiences and interpretations may influence the way in which we interpret new experiences. In both cases, CIP recognizes that the conclusions we reach about ourselves are partly based on actual experiences and partly based on subjective, unverifiable interpretations.

In contrast, CIP views occupational knowledge as largely objective and verifiable. Rather than being based on a series of experiences in which one develops beliefs about oneself, occupational knowledge is based on the acquisition and organization of facts and ideas about various occupations. In organizing this information, people may connect subordinate ideas with a broader concept by engaging in what Peterson et al. (2002) called schema specialization, or they may develop an understanding of how various broad concepts may be subsumed within an even broader category via a process Peterson et al. labeled schema generalization (p. 323). As you can see, the way in which CIP conceptualizes self-knowledge and occupational knowledge is quite different from the theories discussed so far. Instead of focusing on how or where to help clients gather information about themselves and the world of work, CIP is interested in how such information is processed, organized, stored, and modified over time. Indeed, this is consistent with the theory's name: the cognitive information-processing approach. Emphasis on information processing continues into the next levels of the pyramid as well.

Decision-Making Domain: Generic Information-Processing Skills. As Parsons noted, it is not enough simply to understand oneself and the world of work. In addition, it is important to know what to do with this information. Perhaps more than any other theory, CIP places a great deal of emphasis on helping clients develop decision-making skills. These skills are described as generic because they represent basic problem-solving and decision-making skills that can be applied to a wide variety of problems (Peterson et al., 2002), but CIP focuses specifically on how to apply them to career-related problems. The decision-making model offered by CIP includes five specific processes: communication, analysis, synthesis, valuing, and execution. These five processes are referred to by the acronym CASVE, which is "pronounced *kasha'vy*" (Peterson et al., 2002, p. 323).

CASVE and the CIP career decision-making model. The career decision-making model of CIP resembles a square flowchart (see Figure 4.14). Each segment in the counselor version correlates directly with the CASVE acronym: communication, analysis, synthesis, valuing, and execution. Note also that CIP offers a second version of this model in which the concepts in CASVE are translated into client-friendly and career-specific terms.

The first step of the CIP decision-making process is communication (C). In the counselor version of the diagram depicted in Figure 4.14, internal or external cues indicate that a problem exists. Internal cues may include dissatisfaction with one's current job, which may be associated with feelings of depression, increased absenteeism, or even somatic symptoms. In contrast, external cues may include job loss, the need for more income to meet expenses, pressure from a family member, or even a university timeline for selection of an academic major. The diagram also identifies a gap as part of this first stage. This concept reflects CIP's definition of a career problem as "a gap between an existing state of indecision and a more desired state" (Peterson et al., 2002, p. 315). When a person processes the internal and/or external cues and becomes aware of a gap between current reality and what he or she wants, that person realizes that a career decision needs to be made. This is reflected in the client version of the decision-making model with "knowing I need to make a choice." In this stage, clients are challenged to become keenly aware of thoughts and feelings related to their

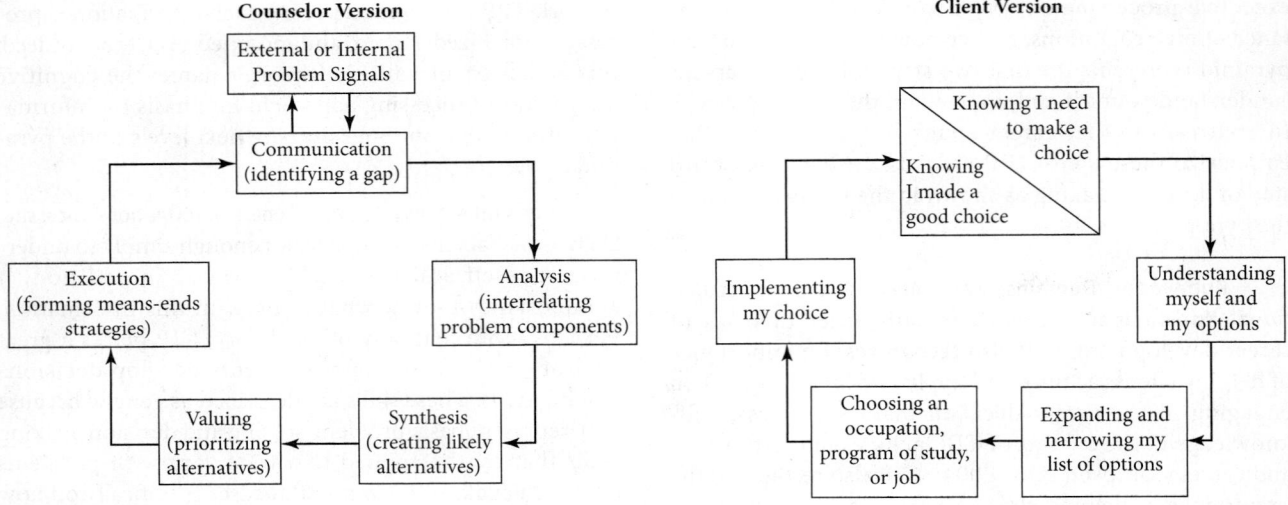

FIGURE 4.14 CIP Decision-Making Model: CASVE

Sources: Counselor Version: Peterson, G.W., Sampson, J.P., Jr., & Reardon, R.C. (1991). *Career development and services: A cognitive approach*. Pacific Grove, CA: Brooks/Cole. (p. 33). - Client Version: Sampson, J.P. Jr., Peterson, G.W., Lenz, J.G., & Reardon, R.C. (1992). A cognitive approach to career services: Translating concepts into practice. *The Career Development Quarterly,* 41, 67–74. (p. 70).

current career and to conceptualize goals for the career counseling process.

The second stage of the CIP decision-making model involves analysis (A). This is a reflective and information-gathering stage. In the counselor version, this involves an exploration of the causes of the problem, an attempt to analyze various factors related to the problem, and an examination of how those factors may relate to one another. This stage is reflected in the client version of the decision-making model with "understanding myself and my options." In this stage, clients are challenged to understand how their individual characteristics, contextual circumstances, and the nature of any given career interact to influence their career and life satisfaction. This stage may involve a great deal of assessment and occupational exploration.

The third stage of the CIP decision-making model involves synthesis (S). In the synthesis stage, clients use the knowledge and understanding gained in the second stage to engage first in divergent thinking in an attempt to brainstorm many possible solutions and then in convergent thinking to distill these possible solutions down to a manageable list of realistic options from which to choose. CIP refers to these processes as elaboration and crystallization. In the counselor version of the CASVE model, this stage involves brainstorming possible solutions to any type of problem. In the client-friendly version, this stage is described as "expanding and narrowing my list of options." In this stage, clients are challenged to consider a wide range of possible options before narrowing them down to a list of realistic options from which to choose.

The process of choosing from an array of options is the focus of the next stage: valuing (V). In the counselor version of the CASVE model, this stage involves a person identifying priorities and using them to evaluate options. It may also involve a person gaining some direct experience with various options (through informational interviews, job shadowing, etc.) in order to engage in some reality testing to ensure accurate understanding of each option before engaging in the valuing process. Note that, in CIP, this valuing process is not necessarily rational in nature. Unlike Parsons's approach of using true reasoning (Parsons, 1909, p. 5), the authors of CIP note that this valuing process may be cognitive or affective and rational or intuitive in nature (Sampson, 2008; Sampson et al., 2004). In CIP, the best choice for any given client depends on that client's priorities and values, so in this stage, CIP emphasizes that "each viable course of action is evaluated and prioritized according to one's value system" (Peterson et al., 2002, p. 326). More specifically, CIP encourages a client to consider "[w]hich alternative is the best course of action for me, and in some cases, my significant others, my cultural group, community, or society?" (p. 326). In the client-friendly version, this stage is described as "choosing an occupation, program of study, or job."

The fifth and final step of the CIP decision-making model is execution (E). This stage involves implementation of the decision that has been made. In the counselor version of the model, this involves forming means-ends strategies. The decision that has been made often represents a goal. As we all know, however, choosing a goal and reaching it are two different things. It is essential not only to choose a goal but also to develop a plan to achieve it. The steps in such a plan represent the means by which a person hopes to achieve the desired end. This is reflected in the client version of the model with "implementing my choice." In this stage, clients are challenged to develop a plan consisting of "intermediate steps, milestones, and subgoals to reach a career goal such as to complete a degree, obtain a first job, or pass a proficiency test" (Peterson et al., 2002, p. 326).

After implementing the plan, clients return full circle to the beginning of the model. If the selected option solves the problem effectively (by helping the client achieve a desired state and eliminating the previously existing gap), the client model suggests that clients will enjoy "knowing that I made a good decision." If the decision made does *not* adequately address the client's problem (with a gap remaining between the client's new current state and the client's desired state), the client continues through another cycle of the CASVE model.

Table 4.3 is offered as a tool to help you synthesize the two versions of the CIP decision-making models. We have now discussed the knowledge domains at the bottom of the CIP pyramid of information-processing domains and the CASVE decision-making domain in the middle of the pyramid. We turn now to the top of the pyramid.

Executive-Processing Domain: Metacognitions. In addition to addressing cognitive information-processing skills related to decision making, CIP also focuses on the role of higher-order metacognitions that consist of "regulatory and integrative processes" (Peterson et al., 2002, p. 327). Metacognitions basically refer to ways in which people think about and affect the nature of their own thinking. CIP is specifically interested in three primary types of metacognitions. The first type addressed by CIP is self-talk. Not unlike SCCT's focus on self-efficacy, CIP recognizes that the ways in which clients think about themselves affect their motivation and ability to engage in a sound career decision-making process. For example, clients who tell themselves that they can learn to apply decision-making and/or problem-solving skills to their career situations will have a far different experience in CIP career counseling than those who tell themselves that they are incapable of making a good decision for themselves.

A second metacognition addressed by CIP is self-awareness. Peterson et al. (2002) explain that self-awareness is important because it allows clients to "recognize such executive processes as the existence of debilitating negative self-talk, the need for more self or occupational knowledge, one's place in the problem-solving process, or the concurrent affective states that accelerate, retard, or confound the process" (pp. 327–328).

The third metacognition addressed by CIP involves monitoring and control. By using this form of

TABLE 4.3 The CIP Decision-Making Model

CASVE	Counselor Version	Client Version	Questions to Be Answered
C: Communication	Identifying a gap	Knowing I need to make a choice	• What am I thinking and feeling about my career choice at this moment? • What do I hope to attain as a result of career counseling?
A: Analysis	Interrelating problem components	Understanding myself and my options	• What are the reasons for the gap between my present state of indecision and a more desired state of decidedness?
S: Synthesis	Creating likely alternatives	Expanding and narrowing my list of options	• What are the possible courses of action I could take to reduce or eliminate the gap?
V: Valuing	Prioritizing alternatives	Choosing an occupation, program of study, or job	• Which alternative is the best course of action for me, and in some cases, my significant others, my cultural group, community, or society?
E: Execution	Forming means-ends strategies	Implementing my choice	• How can I transform my first choice into an action plan and set the plan into motion?

Source: Peterson, G.W., Sampson, Jr., J.P., Lenz, J.G., & Reardon, R.C. (2002). A cognitive information processing approach to career problem solving and decision making. In D. Brown, L. Brooks, and Associates, *Career choice and development* (4th ed.) (pp. 312–369). San Francisco: Jossey-Bass.

metacognition, clients are able to keep track of where they are in the career decision-making process and gauge when they have enough information or skill to move to the next step in the process. Research by Bullock-Yowell, Peterson, Reardon, Leierer, and Reed (2011) suggests that attention to negative career thoughts in the executive-processing domain is especially important when a client is also experiencing high levels of career and life stress.

CIP SEVEN-STEP DELIVERY SEQUENCE. CIP also offers concrete recommendations for the provision of career counseling services. It does so by identifying seven specific steps. As you read about these steps, notice that the decision-making taxonomy, the pyramid of information-processing domains, and especially the CASVE decision-making model play a major role in guiding the provision of career counseling services from the CIP approach. You will also become familiar with another concept specific to CIP: the individual learning plan. The seven steps of the CIP delivery sequence are listed in Table 4.4 and are described in the following subsections.

Initial Interview. The first step, the initial interview, involves a brief discussion of why the client is seeking services. This conversation may occur between a counselor and client but could also be conducted by an appropriately trained paraprofessional working in a career center. Sampson (2008) suggests initiating the conversation with a simple question such as "What brings you here today?" (p. 9). Peterson et al. (2002) recommend that a full range of attending and rapport-building skills be used during the brief assessment and also suggest that the client-friendly CASVE model be shown to the client. This allows the career professional to orient the client to the CIP approach and to gather information about client needs related to career problem solving and decision making.

TABLE 4.4 CIP's Seven-Step Delivery Sequence

1. Initial interview
2. Preliminary assessment
3. Definition of problem and analysis of causes
4. Formulation of goals
5. Development of an individual learning plan
6. Completion of the individual learning plan
7. Summative review and generalization

Source: From Sampson, J.P. Jr. (2008). *Designing and implementing career programs: A handbook for effective practice.* Broken Arrow, OK: National Career Development Association. (pp. 13–14) Copyright © 2008 by National Career Development Association. Reprinted by permission.

Preliminary Assessment. Before beginning to engage clients in the career problem-solving and decision-making process, however, career counselors practicing within the CIP model should understand client readiness. Sampson, Peterson, Reardon, and Lenz (2000) suggest that a preliminary assessment regarding client readiness can be useful in "selecting a *level* (self-help, brief staff-assisted, or individual case managed) and type (e.g., workshop, group counseling, individual counseling) of career intervention that is congruent with client readiness" (p. 149). In addition to assessing readiness, the preliminary assessment may involve the gathering of information typically collected during career counseling intake sessions (which are discussed in Chapter 10 of this text).

Assessment of client readiness. CIP conceptualizes client readiness in two ways. First, CIP counselors consider a person's decision status using the taxonomy discussed earlier. Next, CIP counselors want to conduct a preliminary assessment of a client's capability with regard to career decision making and of the complexity of the client's situation. Depending on the results of this assessment, a client may be offered self-service options, or he or she may be guided toward brief staff-assisted services or toward individual case-managed services. CIP captures these concepts in a two-dimensional model of readiness for career decision making (see Figure 4.15).

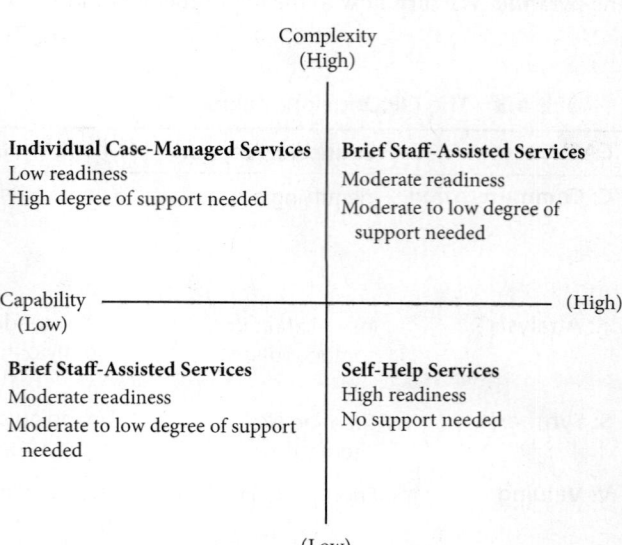

FIGURE 4.15 CIP's Two-Dimensional Model of Readiness to Make Career Decisions
Source: Sampson, J.P. Jr., Peterson, G.W., Reardon, R.C., & Lenz, J.G. (2000). Using readiness assessment to improve career services: A cognitive information-processing approach. *The Career Development Quarterly, 49,* 146–174. (p. 161).

According to CIP, one's readiness to engage in effective career decision making depends in part on one's individual characteristics (capability) as well as on external, contextual factors (complexity). One's capability depends on both cognitive and affective factors, which include possessing adequate levels of motivation to engage in the processes of learning about oneself and the world of work, a willingness to learn and utilize a formal decision-making model, the ability to "think clearly about one's career problem, its causes, and alternative course of action," self-efficacy related to one's abilities to problem-solve and to implement solutions, "an acceptance of personal responsibility for making a career decision," and an ability to engage in metacognitions about the potential impact of positive and negative thinking or self-talk and to monitor one's progress through the decision-making process (Sampson et al., 2004, p. 68).

In addition to recognizing that internal, individual characteristics affect one's readiness to engage in career decision making, CIP also recognizes that a variety of external, contextual factors can make the career decision-making process more or less complex (Sampson, 2008; Sampson et al., 2004). These external influences on complexity are organized into four categories: family, social, economic, and organizational. Family factors, for example, include a person's level of responsibility, the roles being juggled, and the level of support (or pressure) from family members. Social factors include social supports; cultural capital; and experiences of privilege, discrimination, or oppression. Economic factors include personal financial circumstances as well as societal economic conditions. Organizational factors are relevant only to people who are already employed. They include the stability, supportiveness, and opportunity structures within one's current place of employment.

Simply talking with clients is one way to assess the complexity dimension of their readiness. Sampson et al. (2004) suggest using the *Career Thoughts Inventory* (CTI; Sampson, Peterson, Lenz, Reardon, & Saunders, 1996a). This assessment instrument is frequently used to assess career readiness because it measures "three types of negative thoughts . . . decision making confusion (DMC), commitment anxiety (CA), and external conflict (EC)" (Paivandy, Bullock, Reardon, & Kelly, 2008, p. 475). The DMC and CA constructs represent aspects of the capability dimension of career readiness; the EC scale represents aspects of the complexity dimension of career readiness.

As shown in Figure 4.15, clients who have high capability for career decision making and low levels of complexity affecting the decision-making process have a high level of readiness and likely do not need individual career counseling. Instead, they may be guided toward self-help services involving use of materials and resources housed within a career center. In contrast, clients who have low capability for career decision making and high levels of complexity affecting the decision-making process have a low level of readiness and may benefit most from individualized attention and career counseling. CIP refers to this as individual case-managed services (Sampson et al., 2004, p. 81). Clients with a moderate level of readiness may benefit sufficiently from brief staff-assisted services (p. 81). In short, by assessing client readiness, CIP practitioners may quickly determine the entry point for any given client to begin using services in a career center.

Definition of Causes and Analysis of Problems. The third step of the delivery sequence involves activities to help define the client's career problem and to analyze causes of the problem. Although the word *problem* typically has a negative connotation, this is not the case in CIP theory. Instead, a career problem simply refers to "a gap between an existing state of indecision and a more desired state" (Peterson et al., 2002, p. 315). For example, this gap could be related to employment ("I don't have a job now but need to find one"), to career direction ("I have no idea what I want to be when I grow up, but I need to figure it out"), or to choice of college majors ("I need to declare a major by the end of the semester, but I'm not sure whether I want to major in political science or psychology"). In addition to identifying the problem/gap, this step also involves a discussion of various factors that may be causing the problem or inhibiting the solution.

Formulation of Goals. The fourth step of the delivery sequence involves the establishment of goals. In this stage, the counselor and client work together to determine what the client wants to achieve as a result of the career counseling services. The goals are generally written using CIP concepts. For example, a client may want to increase self-knowledge or occupational knowledge, to develop or improve decision-making skills, or to decrease the impact of negative thoughts on the process of choosing a career path.

Development of an Individual Learning Plan. The fifth step of the delivery sequence involves the development of an individual learning plan (ILP). In this document, the client specifies goals (from the fourth step) and identifies specific activities designed to meet those goals. ILPs may include some activities focused on using career center resources to achieve short-term goals related to the current problem as well as longer-term goals such as completing a degree in order to become qualified for entrance into a specific career. When developing the ILP, the counselor and client should collaborate. Counselors possess the expertise to offer suggestions about resources, services, and activities that may be helpful to the client, and clients need to take ownership of the plan and make a commitment to completing each activity. The activities in the ILP can be conceptualized according to the pyramid of information-processing domains. For example, if a client needs to enhance self-knowledge, activities might include taking an interest inventory or completing a values card sort. Activities to expand occupational knowledge may involve computer- or Internet-based programs such as Occupational Information Network (O*NET; onetonline.org). In the context of CIP, at least one activity tends to focus on the development of decision-making skills, and the CASVE model tends to be used for this purpose. Finally, activities designed to address dysfunctional or negative career thoughts within the executive-processing domain may include use of the CIP workbook, which is designed to help clients employ cognitive-restructuring strategies. The workbook, *Improving Your Career Thoughts: A Workbook for the Career Thoughts Inventory* (Sampson et al., 1996b), is intended as a supplement to the CTI. Figure 4.16 provides an example of a completed ILP.

Completion of the Individual Learning Plan. Once the ILP is developed, the client completes the sixth step: executing the ILP. Although some of the activities listed on the ILP may be completed with a counselor present, other activities may be completed by the client as independent homework. This allows the client to take ownership of the process and to develop the skills necessary to engage in a similar process in the future. As you'll recall, CIP not only helps clients solve current problems but also equips them with the skills necessary to solve similar problems in the future. Even with these outside activities, however, the counselor should remain available to meet with clients in order to monitor their progress through the ILP. During this process, counselors should also help clients connect their ILP with the pyramid and the CASVE decision-making model (Sampson et al., 2004). By doing so, counselors assist clients with developing metacognitive skills to understand where they are in the career problem-solving process.

Summative Review and Generalization. After completing their ILP, clients reach the seventh and final step of the delivery sequence: summative review and generalization. In this step, the counselor and client discuss the results of the ILP and the process thus far, and they determine whether the process has resolved the client's career problem. If so, the focus shifts to an exit discussion of how the client can generalize the knowledge gained in this process. Generalization includes ways to continue through the execution phase of the CSAVE model as well as ways in which clients may use the skills to address future problems, whether they are career or personal in nature. If the process thus far has not solved the client's career problem, however, it becomes necessary to recycle through the process. This entails returning to step 3 to ensure adequate understanding of, as well as agreement about, the client's problem, a reformulation of goals, and the design and implementation of a new ILP.

APPLICATION TO OUR CAST OF CLIENTS

In this chapter, you were asked to think ahead about the relevance and potential application of each theory to our clients. You'll now have an opportunity to see how your thoughts compare with mine because this chapter concludes with an application of theories to our cast of clients. In this section, I'll offer insights about how the theories presented by Krumboltz and SCCT, as offered by Lent, Brown, and Hackett, might be helpful in conceptualizing our Cast of Clients. My hope is that these sample applications will help you develop a greater sense of mastery over these theories.

Application of Krumboltz's Learning Theories

When you think about Krumboltz, you should immediately think of his early application of social learning theory to career decision making and to the career counseling process. You should recall his initial focus on associative and instrumental learning experiences, self-observation generalizations, and task approach skills. You should also realize that happenstance learning theory (HLT) represents Krumboltz's most recent extension of his learning theories and that it emphasizes the role of chance events on career development and ways in which clients may be helped to seek out and capitalize on such chance events. Krumboltz describes HLT as an extension and not a replacement of his previous theories, so this section refers to all of his theories with the acronym HLT. As you will see, though, the early concepts of social learning theory will be included in our application. With that caveat, let's explore how Krumboltz's learning theories might apply to our cast of clients.

Let's begin with Wayne. If you look back at Figure 4.2, you'll see a diagram illustrating instrumental learning experiences that Wayne experienced in high school. These experiences led him to develop a self-observation generalization that he was not college material. In fact, Wayne did not go to college but instead transitioned directly from high school into the world of work. Specifically, he has worked on an automotive assembly line since graduating from high school and is now seeking assistance in anticipation of a layoff. From an HLT perspective, one can perceive the role of happenstance in Wayne's career development as including the facts that he just happened to grow up in a suburb of Detroit, once known as the automobile capital of the world, and that he just happened to have a father who worked for Ford. One could say that Wayne took advantage of this happenstance

Goal(s): 1. Understand personal barriers to decision making

2. Clarify self-knowledge and occupational knowledge

3. Improve decision-making skills

Activity	Purpose/Outcome	Estimated Time Commitment	Goal	Priority
Individual counseling	Clarify issues and help with resource use	1 hour each session	1, 2, 3	1
CTI Workbook sections 1, 2, & 3	Challenge and reframe negative thinking	1½ hour	1	2
CTI Workbook section 4	Enhance decision-making skills	½ hour	3	3
Monitor thoughts related to a real decision	Learn about the decision-making process	1 hour	3	4
Occupational card sort	Clarify self-knowledge and generate options	1 hour	2	5
SDS: CV	(Same as above)	1 hour	2	6
Summary of self-knowledge	Clarify self-knowledge	½ hour	2	7
Career key	Identify information resources	15 minutes	2	8
Choices	Obtain occupational information	1 hour	2	9
Information interviews with land surveyor and computer programmer	Obtain more specific occupational information	2 hours	2	10

This plan can be modified by either party based on new information learned in the activities of the action plan.

The purpose of this plan is to work toward a mutually agreed upon career goal. Activities may be added or subtracted as needed.

Student: *JoeWilliams*   Date: 10/16/02   Career Adviser: *Marilyn Abbey*   Date: 1/16/02

FIGURE 4.16 Sample Individual Learning Plan

Source: From Sampson, J.P. Jr., Reardon, R.C., Peterson, G.W., & Lenz, J.G. (2004). *Career counseling & services: A cognitive information processing approach*. Belmont, CA: Brooks/Cole. Copyright © 2004 by James P. Sampson. Reprinted by permission.

by accepting gainful employment with the automaker right out of high school. On a less positive note, Wayne is now anticipating another chance event: a layoff related to an unprecedented recession for the state of Michigan and the auto industry. Rather than await the layoff with passivity, Wayne is taking a proactive approach by seeking career counseling, thereby exhibiting promising task approach skills. An HLT counselor would likely help Wayne to reframe the pending layoff as a potential career opportunity, encourage him to remain open-minded about future possibilities, and suggest that he utilize his task approach skills to explore other areas of interest to him. The HLT counselor may also find it useful to challenge Wayne's self-observation generalization of not being college material.

Moving on to Li Mei's case, you will recall that one prominent stressor for Li Mei is her need to choose a college major. Rather than trying to help Li Mei choose a major as soon as possible, however, the HLT counselor will likely attempt to depathologize Li Mei's indecision and reframe it as open-mindedness. For Li Mei, one barrier to choosing a major is the prominence of negative self-generalization observations. As shown in Figure 4.4, Li Mei has concluded that she could never be as successful as her siblings. It is clear that the belief is self-limiting because Li Mei seems almost paralyzed at the prospect of choosing a major and pursuing a career as long as she believes that she will never be as successful as her older brother and sister. An HLT counselor will likely find it necessary to confront Li Mei's faulty learning experiences. To help identify Li Mei's inaccurate beliefs, the counselor may choose to administer the *Career Beliefs Inventory*.

Whereas negative self-observation generalizations figure prominently in Wayne and Li Mei's cases, this is not true for Lakeesha. As illustrated in Figure 4.5, Lakeesha found college rather easy and does not seem to struggle with self-doubt regarding her capabilities; thus, the learning theory of HLT is less pertinent to her case. Of great relevance to Lakeesha's career development, though, is the role of happenstance. She and her husband had planned for her to work as a stay-at-home mom until their children graduated from high school, but her husband's unexpected death has resulted in her need for paid employment. Although HLT counselors are generally quick to point out the potentially positive elements of chance events, doing so with Lakeesha at the onset of counseling would be insensitive and ineffective. Instead, an HLT counselor may gently observe that Lakeesha's conceptualization of "looking for a window when a door has shut" is consistent with HLT's valuing of open-mindedness and interest in identifying potential opportunities, even in the wake of a tragic event.

Although Vincent also experienced negative chance events (the tragedy of the 9-11 terrorist attack on his city and the resultant death of his father), these events seem to have resulted in positive learning experiences for Vincent. As one example, Figure 4.3 illustrates an associative learning experience based on his observation of models. Specifically, in observing the admiration and respect bestowed on his father, Vincent came to associate the career of firefighting with honor, respect, and admiration. These are clearly rewards that Vincent would like to experience as part of his career, and the question that has arisen is whether he can achieve this as a gay man in the Marines. An HLT counselor might encourage Vincent to explore whether he can identify any Marines (or firefighters, for that matter) who he perceives as being more like him (i.e., gay) and also reaping the rewards of honor and respect he so desires.

Both the happenstance and the learning components of HLT are relevant to Doris's case. In terms of learning experiences, Doris has had numerous instrumental learning experiences at work, and she has received a considerable amount of negative feedback about her performance. In addition to contributing to negative self-observation generalizations, these have also contributed to very poor task approach skills. Rather than attempt to strengthen her work habits, Doris has allowed them to wither. Instead of holding herself to high performance standards and values, she seems to have resigned herself to substandard performance. A counselor working from a learning theory perspective may explain Doris's negative self-observation generalizations as reflecting her inability to fathom reaching an acceptable performance level. In Krumboltz's language, Doris likely needs "tailored and remedial" interventions to counter this self-defeating learning cycle. For example, Doris may benefit tremendously from behavioral interventions (such as values clarification exercises) designed to develop her task approach skills. Complementing this remedial approach might be more hopeful interventions that tap into the happenstance perspective. The HLT counselor may, for example, engage Doris in a discussion about activities about which she is curious and interested. Next, the counselor may help Doris think about possible career opportunities related to these activities and encourage her to join clubs as an attempt to become more open to happenstance. Discussions could include ways in which Doris could prepare herself to engage in networking conversations in order to test the waters for chance career opportunities.

Gillian seems to represent an objective picture of success and certainly is not in need of developing more positive self-observation generalizations or task approach skills as they pertain to her chosen career. That does not mean, however, that HLT is irrelevant to her case. From a learning theory perspective, many instrumental and associative learning experiences influenced Gillian's choice of careers. For example, Gillian had an associative learning experience in which she paired the sight of needles with negative somatic symptoms (as shown in Figure 4.3), Although she had the academic ability to become a physician, Gillian came to view such a career path as unattractive and unbearable. From a happenstance perspective, Gillian is in an ideal situation. She is not desperate for immediate employment and has the luxury of time to explore other opportunities. An HLT counselor would likely discuss the idea of planning for happenstance or, in other words, positioning herself in situations in which it is more likely for chance opportunities to arise. If one possible option of interest would be working as an accountant at a much smaller firm, Gillian may choose to begin attending luncheons and conferences in which networking is possible.

Finally, let's talk about Juan. Although some may not see it this way, Juan has always thought of himself as a success. As a 16-year-old, he had begun working to help his parents pay the bills. As a construction worker, he received much praise for his reliability and good work. The result was a series of instrumental learning experiences through which Juan learned that he is a good worker and a good provider (as shown in Figure 4.6), He translated this into positive self-observation generalizations related to him as an employee as well as a husband. Circumstances have changed, however; unable to engage in physically strenuous work because of his back injury, Juan is experiencing a tremendous sense of loss, and his self-observation generalizations are now at risk. An HLT counselor may encourage Juan to reframe this loss as an opportunity and attempt to tap into Juan's very strong task approach skills.

Application of Social Cognitive Career Theory

When you think of social cognitive career theory (SCCT), you think immediately about triadic reciprocality and the interactions among a person, the environment, and a person's behaviors, and, within the person, the interactions among that person's level of self-efficacy, personal goals, and outcome expectations. You should also recall that counseling interventions tend to reflect attention to inaccurate self-efficacy beliefs and/or perceived contextual barriers. As we apply SCCT to our cast of clients, you will notice some overlap between SCCT's focus on self-efficacy beliefs with HLT's attention to self-observation generalizations.

Let's say that Wayne has expressed an interest in pursuing a career in the skilled trades, possibly as an electrician or as a heating, ventilation, and air conditioning (HVAC) technician. Both require licensure in Michigan, and you indicate that the local community college happens to offer associate degree programs for each field. Wayne immediately responds that he could never succeed in a college class. An SCCT counselor would wonder whether Wayne's self-assessment is accurate and might suggest that Wayne go to the community college to take the placement test to find out. Because of SCCT's stance that the best way to alter self-efficacy beliefs is to gain new experiences on which to base them, the counselor might then suggest that Wayne try a single course to find out if he can handle it.

You have probably already predicted that an SCCT counselor would target Li Mei's poor self-efficacy beliefs. The fact is that her comparison sample—her older brother and sister—is not representative of average college students. Although Li Mei might indeed be unable to match their academic prowess, her standardized test scores (650 in math, 580 in critical reading, and 610 in writing on the SAT) suggest that she is above average when compared to other students applying for college. Because Li Mei is having difficulty even making it to class, however, it is unlikely that her performance accomplishments in her first semester at Chapman will improve her self-efficacy beliefs unless she also adjusts her outcome goals. Thus, some intensive counseling focused on Li Mei's feelings about her role within her family is warranted.

Counseling with Lakeesha is less likely to address self-efficacy and more likely to address contextual barriers. Although Lakeesha has an appropriately high level of confidence in her abilities, she has major concerns about child-care issues: She cannot imagine how she could work full-time and take care of her two children. An SCCT counselor would conceptualize this as a proximal contextual barrier and assist Lakeesha in identifying strategies for overcoming this barrier through focused, anticipatory problem solving. Brainstorming options might identify several strategies. Lakeesha may decide to join an online group of working mothers and start a conversation thread about how they manage child-care issues with preschool children. She might also talk with some of her fellow church members to explore their interest in providing child care for her. Yet another option would be to explore employment opportunities working from home. It is important, of course, that the counselor refrain from offering simple advice to Lakeesha and focus instead on facilitating *her* engagement in a problem-solving process.

As with Lakeesha, perceived contextual barriers are prominent for Vincent. In reviewing the SCCT choice model in Figure 4.10, you will see that Vincent had reached the point of transforming his interests into a choice goal of joining the Marines. However, he is now questioning whether to take the next step of transforming his choice goals into choice action, and Vincent's hesitance is directly related to his perception of a proximal contextual barrier. The barrier he perceives is a homophobic culture within the Marine Corps. Although the repeal of the "don't ask, don't tell" policy lessened the barrier to some degree, Vincent questions whether he could serve safely and successfully if he decides to come out. An SCCT counselor would likely encourage Vincent to do some reality testing, perhaps by contacting gay members of the military to learn about their experiences. If the barrier does indeed seem quite real, an SCCT counselor will assist Vincent in problem solving, perhaps by developing strategies for dealing with homophobia and exploring nonmilitary career options in which he may be safer.

Doris's case refocuses us on the impact of low levels of self-efficacy. In her case, however, it may very well be that Doris lacked the skills necessary to perform her job responsibilities as a secretary. As the office became increasingly technology-oriented, Doris may have experienced difficulties keeping up. If this is the case, an SCCT counselor would want to assist Doris in identifying strategies for skill building. After all, the goal is to have an accurate and high level of self-efficacy, not to have high self-efficacy without strong skills. In addition to focusing on skill building, an SCCT counselor may also become aware of Doris's fears related to proximal contextual barriers. Specifically, Doris may worry that, at 53 years of age, she is too old to be hired again and too old to learn a new job. Again, when addressing perceived barriers, an SCCT counselor would encourage reality testing and facilitate problem solving.

In Gillian's case, strengthening skills or self-efficacy isn't necessary. Gillian is struggling, however, with what she perceives as a contextual barrier. As she becomes increasingly interested in starting a family, Gillian has developed a preference for having a stable residence, which conflicts with the demands of her work (i.e., frequent relocation). Thus, Gillian is now trying to decide whether to continue implementing her choice action (working as a partner at Ernst and Young) or to recycle through the choice model to consider other options. From an SCCT perspective, there would be no need for Gillian to engage in reality testing because the need for frequent relocation has already been firmly established. Thus, some problem solving and possible recycling through the choice process would be in order.

To conclude our application of SCCT, we now turn to Juan's case, where SCCT's attention to both distal and proximal contextual barriers is warranted. Distally, Juan was raised in a family with few resources. Born and raised in Fort Worth, Texas, Juan was the oldest of seven children. As unskilled laborers who had immigrated from Mexico, his parents struggled to put food on the table. Juan decided to leave school at the age of 16 so that he could begin contributing to the family income. Juan's case illustrates how the social and cultural context in which he was raised affected the types of career-related exposure Juan experienced, the types of role models he encountered, the education he received, and the outcome expectations he developed. As a result, Juan's outcome expectations have always focused on earning a livable wage rather than on experiencing personal fulfillment from his job. Now, because of his back injury, Juan is uncertain whether he can continue earning a livable wage. This back injury represents a person input, and the physical requirements of the construction industry constitute a proximal contextual barrier. Juan's limited English proficiency also represents a person input, and he may face some contextual barriers when seeking jobs requiring English proficiency. An SCCT counselor would use such constructs in conceptualizing Juan's case and would encourage reality testing and problem solving to address the proximal barriers.

Application of the Cognitive Information-Processing Approach

You should immediately recall that the cognitive information-processing (CIP) approach is a theory focused on decision making and problem solving. CIP categorizes clients according to their decision-making status and readiness and uses this information to identify the level of services appropriate to clients' needs. You should also associate CIP with a seven-step delivery sequence that is based on information-processing domains and uses the CASVE decision-making process and individual learning plans (ILPs) as two primary interventions. Now, let's explore how CIP might be used with each of our clients. As a caveat, the following discussion will not be exhaustive. Although each element of CIP is applicable to each of our clients, only a couple of elements will be applied in each client discussion.

To begin, CIP would categorize Wayne as undecided–deferred on its decision status taxonomy. Although he wants to explore other career options, he is engaging in this process anticipating layoff. Without the urgency posed by unemployment, Wayne has some time to engage in career counseling before making a decision. Wayne would also benefit from an introduction to the client version of Figure 4.14 in order to understand the components of career decision making. As a high school student, Wayne didn't engage in a thorough decision-making process because an opportunity to work for Ford Motor Company arose. Now, as he attempts to choose a new direction, Wayne will benefit from learning about himself, learning about the world of work, and employing the CASVE decision-making process.

A CIP counselor would categorize Li Mei as indecisive on the decision-making taxonomy. Her scores on the *Career Thoughts Inventory* would likely reveal considerable commitment anxiety and place her in the low capability range of client readiness. Indeed, Li Mei's case demonstrates the first assumption of CIP: that emotions as well as thoughts are important to address because emotions affect a client's readiness to engage in a decision-making process. Rather than focusing on the decision-making process, a CIP counselor would be wise to develop an ILP with Li Mei that placed initial, primary emphasis on addressing Li Mei's negative thinking. Use of the *My Career Thoughts* workbook would be quite appropriate with Li Mei.

Lakeesha would be categorized as undecided–developmental because she is now facing a decision about entering the job market as a result of her husband's death. She has relatively high capability because she is motivated to engage in the career counseling process, willing to do what it takes to make a decision and implement it, and has strong metacognitive skills. In contrast, Lakeesha's life situation is fairly complex because she will be faced with issues such as juggling responsibilities as a single parent with paid employment. Lakeesha will likely benefit a great deal from an ILP that emphasizes the CASVE decision-making model. It is likely that the analysis phase of the CASVE model, and specifically occupational exploration, will be prominent in Lakeesha's counseling process. After exploring her options, Lakeesha would then proceed through the synthesis, valuing, and execution phases of the CASVE mode.

Vincent might be best categorized as decided–confirmation on the CIP decision status taxonomy. He has already made a decision to pursue a career in the Marines but now wants to confirm whether this remains a good choice for him given his growing identification as a gay man. Coming out to himself represents an internal cue that prompted his awareness of a gap and the existence of a career problem. With Vincent, an ILP emphasizing deeper exploration of the Marines as a career option for him as a gay man and broader exploration of other, perhaps more gay-friendly, occupations would be useful. The ILP will also likely emphasize the valuing phase of the CASVE model, with the counselor assisting Vincent in exploring how his values may influence his decision making.

In Doris's case, the external cues of being fired from her job and finding herself ineligible for unemployment insurance benefits resulted in a gap that prompted her awareness of a career problem. Doris is likely to score high on all three scales of the *Career Thoughts Inventory*. Specifically, her anger and bitterness are likely to interfere with her decision-making ability (DMC scale); she is likely to have a sense of futility and feel a great deal of anxiety related to being fired and having to look for a new job without a good reference (CA); and the lack of support from her husband, the stressors in her home environment, and her belief that she is too old to begin a new career will result in high scores with regard to external conflict (EC). Because her bitterness is so prominent in her initial presentation, it may be helpful to develop an ILP that emphasizes negative thinking patterns and perhaps utilize the *My Career Thoughts* workbook.

Juan seems to convey a positive attitude accompanied by pragmatism and openness to any career option that will allow him to support his family. He would be categorized as undecided–developmental on the CIP decision status taxonomy because he is uncertain how to solve his career problem but has an immediate need to do so. Although he has a good attitude and a strong willingness to participate in the career counseling process, Juan's readiness to make a decision may be compromised by the high level of complexity in his situation: He lacks a high school diploma, has limited English proficiency, and has physical limitations. Juan's ILP will likely focus on the CIP decision-making model, and it would be helpful to translate the client version of Figure 4.14 into Spanish.

Gillian's case illustrates the third assumption of CIP: that career development and decision making is a lifelong process. Although Gillian went through the decision-making process as an undergraduate at Cornell and has enjoyed a great deal of success and satisfaction in her career, an internal cue has signaled the existence of a developing career problem. Specifically, Gillian is increasingly interested in starting a family and less willing to relocate, so her level of satisfaction at Ernst and Young is waning. Gillian's ILP would likely emphasize the CASVE model with specific emphasis on the analysis phase. After exploring other career options, Gillian can apply her already honed decision-making skills.

CHAPTER 5

Narrative Theories

> Life has no meaning *a priori*. . . . It is up to you to give it a meaning, and value is nothing but the meaning that you choose.
>
> ~ Jean-Paul Sartre ~

INTRODUCTION

The meanings we make of our work and the narratives we compose about our lives have significant relevance to our career success and satisfaction. Let me tell you a story to illustrate this point. Many versions of this story exist, and the original source is unknown, but it generally goes like this:

> Once upon a time, three bricklayers were working when a child approached. Curious, the child approached each of the bricklayers individually and asked what they were doing. The first replied, "I'm laying bricks." The second said, "I'm earning a living." And the third said, "I'm building a cathedral."

As you reflect on this story, what are your reactions? Notice the implications of each story for the bricklayers' career success and satisfaction. Also notice that all three responses hold truth, as would many other responses. One could argue convincingly, in fact, that the objective truth is largely irrelevant because our individual realities are determined by our subjective perceptions and interpretations of our life experiences.

Such ideas are reflective of the postmodern paradigm. Hansen (2004) explained, "The general assertion of postmodernism is that meanings are created, not discovered, by observers (Leary, 1994). . . . Postmodernism . . . maintains that observers can never transcend their perceptual sets. Thus, knowledge always represents some combination of the observer and the observed; truths are created, not discovered" (p. 131). Therefore, the focus of postmodern theories is on how each individual's identity is constructed in a relational context. When applied in career counseling settings, postmodern counselors can work with clients to reconstruct and/or deconstruct their past and coconstruct their future (Savickas, 2012). This chapter will focus on one type of postmodern approach: narrative theories of career development and career counseling. Specifically, it will introduce you to Cochran's narrative approach to career counseling and to Savickas's career construction theory. Reading the following works by these authors may be helpful:

Cochran, L. (1997). *Career counseling: A narrative approach.* Thousand Oaks, CA: Sage Publications. (Cochran's narrative approach to career counseling)

Savickas, M. L. (2011a). *Career counseling.* Washington, DC: American Psychological Association. (Savickas's career construction theory and counseling for career construction)

COCHRAN'S NARRATIVE APPROACH TO CAREER COUNSELING

Cochran's (1997) narrative approach to career counseling positions clients as both narrator and protagonists in their life stories. It is designed to assist clients with constructing their future career paths by examining their life stories, exploring the subjective meanings and purposes that have been dominant thus far, and authoring the next chapters of their lives. This approach reflects the belief that meanings are best explored through stories and verbal dialogue. Rather than positioning the counselor as expert, Cochran's approach is designed to empower clients to tap into their own "practical wisdom" (1997, p. 24). He explains that this "practical wisdom is intimately related to one's life story through changing circumstances of life" (p. 24) and observes that some life stories are better than others. Some people, for example, suffer career problems because their stories are unrealistic or unattainable or because they feature themes of failure, disappointment, and/or defeat. Cochran suggests that "the task of career counseling is to help persons tell richer, more continuous, coherent, plausible, and productive stories" (p. 24). In contrast to themes of failure, disappointment, or defeat, a major theme of a productive story is a theme of self-efficacy or what Cochran calls a "sense of agency, a person's sensed capacity to bring about desirable outcomes or carry out a task" (p. 29).

Cochran (1997) provides a detailed rationale for and description of his narrative approach in his book, *Career Counseling: A Narrative Approach*. This chapter's brief coverage of his theory will focus on the "repertoire of episodes" (p. 42) from which a counselor may select for the purpose of meeting various needs. Specifically, Cochran describes seven episodes (see Table 5.1), that may be selected to meet three basic client needs. He cautions against using them in a step-by-step, prescribed manner and explains that "different clients require different episodes and/or a different coordination and ordering of episodes" (p. 42). Keep this understanding in mind, even though this chapter describes the episodes in order.

Elaborating a Career Problem

An important element in any career counseling is to work with clients to establish a shared understanding of the career problem that prompts the client to seek counseling. Cochran (1997) calls this elaborating a career problem. His definition of a career problem shares much in common with the definition offered by the cognitive information-processing (CIP) approach. Cochran suggests that a career problem involves a gap between what is desired and what is anticipated:

> A career problem occurs when a current course of action signals a qualitative difference between possible career futures. A person seeks career counseling when current courses of action indicate that a course of life has gone, is going, or is threatened with going off course, indicating a gap between what is and what ought to be. (Cochran, 1994, p. 207)

To understand a client's career problem from a narrative perspective, it is essential to listen carefully for themes in the client's life story. What, specifically, seems to be the gap? Is the gap already realized (e.g., wanting a job but not having one), or is it anticipated in the future (e.g., wanting a fulfilling job but not anticipating it given the current path one is traveling)? Cochran (1997) suggests that elaboration of the career problem be approached flexibly depending on client needs and recommends a variety of techniques that may be used to elaborate the career problem. Certainly, dialogue (storytelling and sharing of anecdotes) between the client and counselor is an important vehicle in narrative therapy. Cochran also recognizes the utility of a variety of other techniques, including traditional standardized tests and a constructivist approach to using vocational card sorts, which will be described in Chapter 12.

Composing a Life History

A life history may be conceptualized from an objective and/or subjective framework. From an objective perspective, a person's life history may resemble a chronology of events that a counselor may analyze to identify patterns and recognize occupationally relevant traits that can be used to match clients with occupations, much as is done by trait-factor theorists. From a subjective perspective, a person's life history includes more than a list of events; the subjective history also includes the meanings associated with those events and the stories behind them. Rather

TABLE 5.1 Episodes Within Cochran's Narrative Approach

1. Elaborating a career problem.
2. Composing a life history.
3. Founding a future narrative.
4. Constructing reality.
5. Changing a life structure.
6. Enacting a role.
7. Crystallizing a decision.

approaching the life history as an objective, fact-based, information-gathering process, narrative career counselors are more interested in the way clients subjectively present and experience their life histories.

Two key elements of composing a life history from a narrative approach are the importance of meaning and the rewriting of the life history in order to create a "unifying plot" (p. 60). With regard to meaning, narrative career counselors care a great deal about the meanings that clients make in response to past experiences as well as future possibilities. The unifying plot emerges from the patterns of meaning, and Cochran recommends that the client and counselor collaborate in understanding the implications of the life history as first presented by the client and then rewriting, so to speak, the life history to hold more promising and supportive implications. In other words, Cochran suggests that counselors help clients to reframe their life histories to reflect themes of self-efficacy, ability, hope and promise.

To begin the process of eliciting a client's life history, Cochran again relies primarily on dialogue with the client. He also describes six informal assessment techniques that may also be useful: (1) life line, (2) life chapters, (3) success experiences, (4) family constellation, (5) role models, and (6) early recollections (1997, pp. 74–79).

Founding a Future Narrative

When composing (and recomposing) the life history, the counselor and client work as coauthors to create a story about the client's past that holds personal meaning, has a unifying theme, and highlights sources of strength and promise for the future. When founding a future narrative, the counselor and client once again work together as coauthors, but this time, they focus on extending the unifying plot into the future chapters of a client's life.

Extending the plot into the future involves deciding from among various future scenarios, none of which will be perfect or satisfy all of a client's needs, interests, values, and so forth. As a result, the challenge facing the counselor and client is to make choices about which possible career path to chart for the future so that they:

> weave together, in a whole composition, the [client's] most fundamental motives, outstanding strengths, and salient interests and values. The central desires aroused in the past are to be fulfilled in the future. The core strengths cultivated in the past are to be put to purposeful use in the future. And the interests and values forged in past experiences are to be refined and extended in the future. (Cochran, 1997, p. 84)

Cochran suggests the use of two primary approaches, in tandem, for the purpose of constructing the future narrative: eliciting client visions for the future and portraying a future narrative.

ELICITING CLIENT VISIONS FOR THE FUTURE. Cochran suggested that the first step in founding a future narrative is to use a variety of techniques to elicit from clients their visions for the future. For example, Cochran described using the lifeline technique to gather a client's life history (past until present) and also recommended using this same technique for the client to map a future that would be optimally satisfying. He made a similar recommendation for extending the life chapters and success experiences exercises into the future. Cochran also described ways to utilize guided fantasy techniques as well as guidance material to assist clients in envisioning rewarding future career paths involving fulfilling meanings and plots.

PORTRAYING A FUTURE NARRATIVE. Once a counselor has elicited a client's vision for the future, the next step in founding a future narrative is for the counselor to create a future narrative to present to the client. Cochran (1997) refers to this as "portraying a future narrative" (p. 91). Creating the portrayal involves the counselor's development of a written report that incorporates key themes and meanings already communicated by the client, presentation of the written report to the client for the client's reaction, and subsequent collaboration with the client to weave together a script for the client's future that the client can own and find optimal.

Cochran suggests that the written report (which then serves as fodder for discussion) include five sections. The first and most important section should be a mission statement that captures the key themes in the client's life and the client's optimal occupational mission. The remaining four sections consist of a list of the client's strengths, a description of the client's work needs, acknowledgment of any client vulnerabilities, and a list of possible solutions to the client's career problems. This written report should draw, as much as possible, on the client's own words and stories and should never come as a complete surprise to the client; however, the client will likely have reactions to the report. These reactions then guide the collaboration between the counselor and client with the goal of creating a viable script for the client's future and writing, so to speak, the next chapter(s) of the client's life story.

Because the future narrative founded in this episode is not considered a firm, definitive choice but rather a preliminary vision for the client's future, the next three steps of Cochran's (1997) narrative approach to career counseling involve ways to help clients take the actions necessary to confirm their desire to pursue the future narrative they founded. The action episodes include constructing reality, changing a life structure, and enacting a role. Cochran explains that this action phase of career counseling often involves a client engaging in each of these action episodes simultaneously.

Constructing Reality

The action episode of constructing reality involves the client's active exploration of the desired future narrative. CIP calls for reality testing, and Cochran's narrative approach calls for clients to engage in activities that allow clients to experience the realities of the career that interest them directly. He suggests that clients evaluate the viability of the career path for them, have experiences that allow them to determine whether they can really imagine themselves employed in that field, and integrate the realities of a career path into their ideal narrative for their future.

Rather than relying on distant, passive methods to explore the career envisioned, the episode of constructing reality involves "active immersion in, or engagement with, an occupation" (Cochran, 1997, p. 106). For example, clients may go into the work setting to job-shadow, conduct informational interviews, or volunteer. The benefits of this active involvement not only include gathering information but also developing a sense of self-efficacy related to the career and having a basis in reality to determine whether one truly identifies with and can imagine working and feeling fulfilled in a given career.

Changing a Life Structure

Choosing or changing career paths often necessitates changing of life structures. These life structures may be external or internal. Changing external life structures generally involves changing situational circumstances. External life structures, for example, may relate to daily schedules, child-care arrangements, commuting requirements, or division of labor within the home. In contrast, changing internal life structures generally involves changing oneself. This may involve changing one's behavior, changing which skills to develop further, or challenging one's self-defeating beliefs.

Enacting a Role

Cochran (1997) explains that "enacting a role is concerned with actualizing ideals in the present through searching for and engaging in activities that are meaningful and enjoyable" (p. 113). One's desires and needs result in interests that, in turn, help lay the groundwork for the future narrative to which one aspires; thus, Cochran suggests that clients begin making intentional choices about how they spend their time. If their true interests lie in the future narrative they have founded, they will find themselves drawn to related activities. Engaging in those activities allows the person to experience them enough to test and use these experiences to guide them toward other enjoyable activities. This cyclical process may, Cochran suggests, result in abandonment, adoption, or fine-tuning of the future narrative to which one aspires.

Crystallization

As a result of the action episodes, clients find themselves ready to commit to the future narrative they constructed or back at the beginning, where they need to redefine their career problem, develop a new future narrative, and so on. This process, you'll surely recognize, closely resembles the cyclical nature of the communication, analysis, synthesis, valuing, and execution (CASVE) decision-making model associated with CIP (Peterson, Sampson, Reardon, & Lenz, 1996). When the action episodes confirm the client's hope that the path envisioned in the future narrative will indeed close the gap, crystallization is achieved. Cochran (1997) explains that, once a client reaches crystallization, "all one requires . . . is enough of an orientation to begin enacting a career plot, embarking on the next steps to shape a course of life in work" (p. 125). This orientation, Cochran suggests, represents the end of the career counseling process.

> You must have control of the authorship of your own destiny. The pen that writes your life story must be held in your own hand.
>
> ~ Irene C. Kassorla ~ [†]

SAVICKAS'S THEORY OF CAREER CONSTRUCTION AND CAREER COUNSELING

Savickas's (2011a) approach to career counseling represents a social constructionist, postmodern theory. Paralleling his belief that people actively construct their lives and author their narrative about themselves and their careers, Savickas's theory has evolved over time, resulting in the refinement of earlier versions (Savickas, 2002, 2005).

[†]From *Wisdom for the Soul: Five Millennia of Prescriptions for Spiritual Healing*, (Gnosophia Publishers, 2007), by permission of the publisher.

This chapter will present the most current version of his theory as described in his book about career counseling (Savickas, 2011a) and other recent publications (Savickas, 2011b, 2011c, 2012; Savickas et al., 2009). The discussion will begin by describing career construction theory (CCT) and its views about self and self-development. Next, are implications of CCT for career interventions, and then Savickas's model for career counseling within the paradigm of life design.

Career Construction Theory

According to Savickas (2013), "the theory of career construction explains the interpretive and interpersonal processes through which individuals construct themselves, impose direction on their vocational behavior, and make meaning of their careers" (p. 147). Note in this quotation that a postmodern conceptualization of self and identity serves as the foundation for CCT (Savickas, 2011a, 2011b, 2011c). Therefore, we'll begin with a discussion of how CCT views the self in the context of career development.

SELF-DEVELOPMENT FROM A SOCIAL CONSTRUCTIONIST PERSPECTIVE. Consistent with the social constructionist perspective, Savickas argues that the self is not a stable entity within a person waiting to be discovered or actualized. Instead, CCT suggests that the self is actively constructed by a person based on a person's relational experiences, that person's self-reflection and meaning making, and the contextually influenced stories that person develops about her- or himself. As a narrative approach, CCT also emphasizes the importance of language in self-making. Savickas explains:

> In a sense, we live inside language. Words provide a resource for living that enables thinking and meaning making. Words do not come to adhere to an essential, pre-existing self. Rather, language provides the words for the reflexive projects of making a self, shaping an identity, and constructing a career. (2013, p. 148)

Depending on a person's ability to be self-reflective, use language to author his or her life stories, and be active in constructing the future, various dimensions of self may be dominant. Specifically, Savickas (2011b) identifies three views of self: self as actor, self as agent, and self as author. He suggests that these views initially correspond with age and offer differing conceptualizations of self that have implications for career counselors.

SELF AS ACTOR. According to Savickas (2011b), the self as actor emerges in infancy and early childhood. Lacking the ability for metacognition, young children can best be described as actors who, without a great deal of forethought, engage in behaviors (actions) that are shaped in large part by their family environment and the roles available to them. As they are assimilated into the family, children gravitate toward a pattern of behaviors that tend to elicit descriptions by family members, and children in turn tend to internalize a belief that these characteristics are true about themselves. In this way, young children may come to resemble various personality types, and the associated traits may be construed as objective qualities. What others may view as the child's objective personality traits simply reflect socially constructed categories used to describe the child's behavior. As social constructions, these categories are created within a particular family, cultural, and community context. These labels do not describe who a child *is*; they simply described how the child has *acted*.

In the context of career, CCT posits that a person's early sense of career self is based on the internalization of traits others have attributed to him or her as well as on more active attempts to model the self after parents (guides) and role models. Savickas (2013) refers to these as core processes of self-construction and labels them as introjection of guides (parents) and incorporation of models (role models). Especially important to Savickas's approach to career counseling is his belief that, "as children, we select role models who portray tentative solutions to our main problems and dominant preoccupations" (2013, p. 152). Children tend to choose role models with whom they identify, and they tend to model their own behaviors after the role model. Part of this process may involve repetitive role playing of the model's work-related activities and behavior. Though others may interpret the role-played behaviors as reflective of a child's vocational personality, a social constructionist perspective views them simply as behaviors chosen and interpreted in a social environment. Savickas (2013) refers to this as a child's reputation and indicates that reputation rather than personality type is described by models such as Holland's (1997) typology.

SELF AS AGENT. The self as agent emerges as children mature and become increasingly able to engage in metacognition and self-direction. When children are ready to enter school and continue developing into adolescence, they become better able to make choices and set goals. As they set goals, invest effort, and experience success and failure, their sense of agency develops. Subjective feelings of motivation, self-efficacy, and self-control become driving forces influencing a person's choices.

In the context of career, the self as agent becomes important as a child uses a sense of agency to set goals, choose courses, and exercise control over her or his educational and occupational plots. Each new experience involving the exercise of agency affects the development of one's career narrative and the story one develops about one's life in educational and occupational contexts. Savickas (2013) indicates that one's sense of agency is activated by a need to adapt to three types of challenges that may arise. First, and most pertinent to adolescence, vocational development tasks (such as the expectation of developing a postsecondary plan and entering the workforce as a young adult) require the adaptation and the exercise of agency. Second, once a person is in the workforce, occupational transitions also require adaptation and the exercise of agency. Third, a special type of occupational transition—a work trauma—also requires adaptation and the exercise of agency. Savickas (2013) notes that work traumas tend to be undesirable and unanticipated occupational transitions. Whether facing a vocational development task, an occupational transition, or a work trauma, a person's successful adaptation depends on his or her "readiness, resources, responses, and results" (p. 8).

SELF AS AUTHOR. Savickas (2011b) suggests that the self as author emerges in late adolescence because "society expects late adolescents and young adults to begin to integrate their action and agency into a unified life story and a unique identity" (p. 180). People are no longer being defined by their objective actions or subjective sense of agency; the self as author is regarded as an ongoing project about which people weave together their past experiences into life stories and construct new chapters of their lives. One element of the life story, of course, involves the narratives we construct regarding our lives at work.

The stories we develop about ourselves and our educational and/or occupational plot have great relevance, of course, to our career development. Savickas (2011a) refers to these stories as our narrative identity (p. 20) and as identity narratives in more recent work (Savickas, 2013, p. 163). In either case, the narrative "tells a life history that revises identity over time without losing its essential meaning. It tells a life story about self, a narrative of becoming oneself in response to the continuous changes that occur during the life course" (Savickas, 2011a, p. 21). Consistent with the postmodern belief that reality is constructed, each version of the narrative can be considered true. Rather than showing interest in discovering a person's objective self and true identity, CCT is interested in the meanings one makes and the stories one authors.

Implications of CCT for Career Interventions

The goal of CCT is to assist clients in assuming an active role in authoring their career stories. Thus, CCT interventions focus on the self as author. However, Savickas also describes career interventions that focus on the self as actor and the self as agent. Indeed, in developing and offering his theory, Savickas does not "throw the baby out with the bath water." Rather than offering a wholesale rejection of modernist approaches such as those offered by Holland and Super, Savickas acknowledges their value. Explaining that he is "not a radical postmodernist" (personal communication, July 11, 2012), Savickas points to pragmatic reasons for valuing various approaches. Specifically, he places value on various approaches depending on the needs of the client and on the historical era and its corresponding world of work. In offering his theory, therefore, Savickas (2011a) reconceptualizes career interventions and suggests that three types of services (vocational guidance, career education, and career counseling) are offered by career counselors (see Figure 5.1).

VOCATIONAL GUIDANCE. Savickas refers to the first type of service as vocational guidance. He explains that this type of service is based on an "objective perspective of individual differences [that] views clients as actors who may be characterized by scores on traits" (Savickas, 2011a, p. 8). He indicates that this type of service is most closely associated with trait factor approaches and was ideal in the era of industrialization, when there was a need to match individuals with occupations based on their interests and abilities. Savickas also suggests that this approach continues to be useful with adolescents, young adults, and other clients needing assistance in

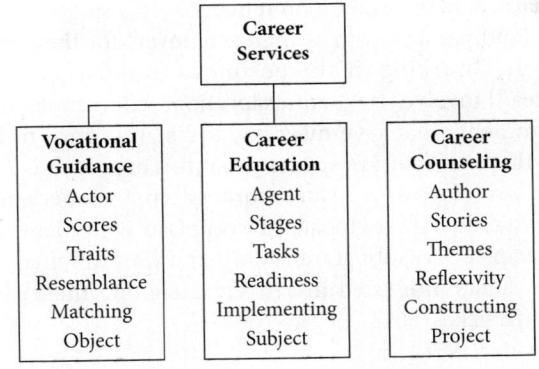

FIGURE 5.1 Career Services as Conceptualized by Career Construction Theory
Source: Savickas, M.L. (2011a). *Career counseling.* Washington, DC: American Psychological Association. (Figure 1.1 on p. 7). Savickas, M.L. (2011a). *Career counseling.* Washington, DC: American Psychological Association. Reprinted with permission.

identifying a good occupational match for their interests, values, skills, and needs.

CAREER EDUCATION. Savickas refers to the second type of career services as career education. He explains that this type of service is based on a "subjective perspective of individual development" and "views clients as agents who may be characterized by their degree of readiness to engage in developmental tasks appropriate to their life stages and who may be helped to implement new attitudes, beliefs, and competencies that further their careers" (2011a, p. 8). He indicates that this type of intervention is closely associated with developmental and learning theories and was ideal in the era of corporate America, when "workers could count on bureaucratic organizations to provide a grand narrative about how their lives would unfold" (Savickas, 2012, p. 13). Savickas indicates that career education services continue to be well suited to helping people understand and further their career development within a single organization and/or a single career path.

CAREER COUNSELING. Savickas refers to the third type of career services as career counseling, by which he refers specifically to counseling for career construction (2011a) and life designing (2012). He explains that this type of service is based on a "project perspective of individual design" in which clients are viewed "as authors who may be characterized by autobiographical stories and who may be helped to reflect on life themes with which to construct their careers" (2011a, p. 8). He indicates that this type of service calls for a social constructionist, narrative approach to career counseling and argues that this approach is ideal for the global economy of the 21st century. Whereas individuals could once count on remaining in a single occupation (and perhaps with a single employer) for their entire careers, "working in the postmodern global economy [instead] involves frequent dislocations from employment assignments that give meaning and significance to life" (2011a, p. 9). Savickas suggests that this approach is especially useful with "insecure workers" (p. 9) experiencing the instability of the globalized workplace, with clients who are facing occupational transitions and work traumas, and with clients interested in actively designing their career lives (Savickas, 2012).

Counseling for Career Construction Within a Life-Design Paradigm

Savickas notes that, although we all have an occupational plot consisting of the education we have achieved and the jobs we have held, we generally invest little attention in the nature of our career story—our identity narrative—until we approach transition points or changes that may alter the direction of our occupational plot. As already described, these points may occur when clients anticipate the need to complete a vocational development task or when they face an occupational transition or work trauma. At these points, clients have the opportunity to revisit their career stories, construct the next chapter in the story, and revise past chapters. Although clients' past occupational plots (the objective chronology of their respective educational and work histories) remain the same, the meanings they make and the stories they construct may change over time.

Counseling for career construction, which Savickas (2012) frames within a paradigm of life designing, represents a way for counselors to assist clients. The general process of life designing involves four major activities. First, this counseling approach begins with the construction of an identity narrative of the client's story up to the present day and deconstruction as needed. Second, the counselor engages in reconstruction efforts to weave together a synthesized version of the client's story to date. Third, the counselor and client work together to coconstruct a new story, including the next chapter. This is quite similar to what Cochran (1997) refers to as founding a future narrative. Fourth, the client engages in action necessary to bring the new chapter to life. The following sections will describe the practical application of this process using Savickas's (2011a) counseling for the career construction approach, framed within the paradigm of life designing (Savickas, 2012). Figure 5.2 provides a summary of the stages of Savickas's counseling for career construction. Each stage will be discussed in the following subsections.

CONSTRUCTION. Construction refers to the process of taking stock of one's current situation and constructing a story to make sense of it. Dislocation from one's previous story (generally prompted by a vocational development task, occupational transition, or work trauma) precipitates the need to construct a new story. Savickas suggests that people may construct a new story on their own or they may seek career counseling at this point. When people seek career counseling, Savickas begins the counseling process with construction activities. Specifically, he begins by asking, "How can I be useful to you as you construct your career?" (2011a, p. 49). During the initial session, he also asks clients to describe the precipitating circumstance and their goals.

Career Story Interview. Next, CCT counselors conduct a career story interview. The career story interview consists of five topics the counselor addresses in order to gather information from the client in the form of micronarratives, or short stories. Over decades of practicing career counseling, Savickas has experimented with a variety of questions; he has

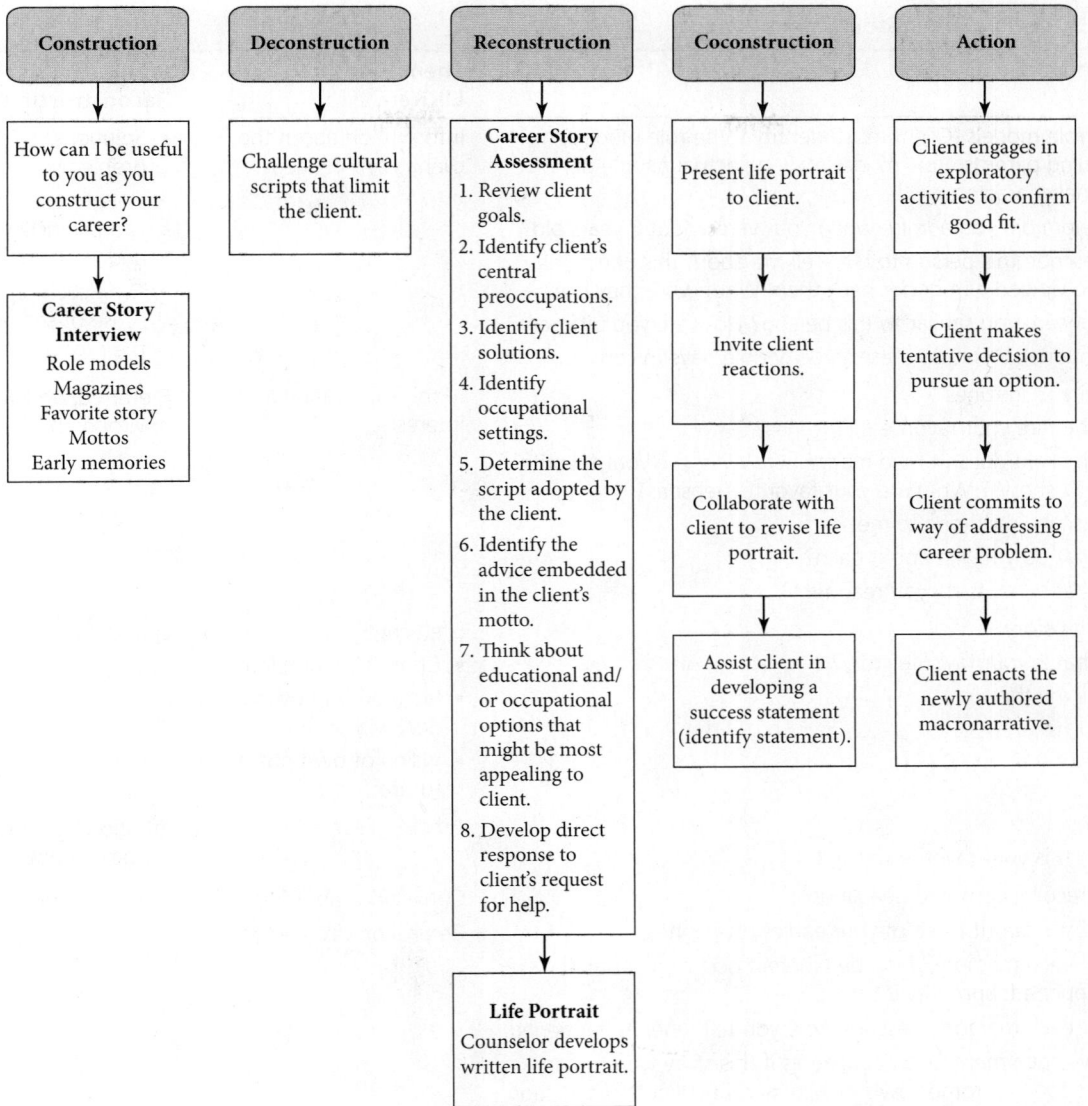

FIGURE 5.2 Counseling for Career Construction

concluded that questions related to the following five topics are most effective in eliciting the thematic material from clients necessary to understand their narrative identity (he recommends addressing these topics in sequence; see Table 5.2):

1. Role models
2. Magazines
3. Favorite story
4. Mottos
5. Early recollections

The topic of role models involves asking clients to identify and describe three of their role models in their early childhood, with a specific focus on what qualities of each role model were admired by the client. Although Savickas (2011a) suggests asking about role models the client had at the age of 6, eliciting information about early role models is more important than the client's specific age. You'll recall that CCT places importance on the introjection of guides (parents) and the incorporation of models in a person's early construction of self. The questions related to role models are designed to elicit information about the client's self-concept.

The second topic relates to a client's favorite magazines or, if the client rarely reads magazines, favorite television shows or websites. Savickas (2011a) explains that preferences related to media outlets are reflective of how

TABLE 5.2 The Career Story Interview

Topic and Questions	Thematic Material Elicited	Implications for Reconstruction

1. Early role models (Client must identify three role models, not including parents. Role models may be actual people or fictional characters):
   a. Whom did you admire when you were about 6 years old?
   b. Describe this person to me. Tell me about this person as you viewed him or her back then. What were they like?
   c. How are you similar to this person? How are you different?
   d. Optional: What do these three people have in common?
	Information about the client's self-concept	• Solutions to current problems.
		• How to use one's own characteristics to address life challenges.
		• The development of a sense of self around the preoccupation.

2. Favorite magazines
   a. What are your favorite magazines?
      • If client doesn't read magazines: What are your favorite TV shows? What are your favorite websites?
   b. Describe each one to me.
   c. What do you like about each?
   d. What sections do you read first?
	Manifest vocational interests	Preferred work environments.

3. Favorite story
   a. What is your favorite story?
   b. Tell me the story.
	Life Script
	• Central life problem
	• Ideas about how to deal with it
	• Vision of own possible future
		Life script.
		Core essence.

4. Mottos a. What is your favorite saying?	Advice to self	Intuition about direction for next chapter.

5. Early recollections and headlines
   a. Tell me about three of your earliest memories.
   b. For each memory, describe where it occurred, what happened, and how it turned out.
   c. For each memory, describe how you felt when it happened.
   d. Give each memory a headline as if this story were going to appear in tomorrow's newspaper (headline must include a verb).
	Convictions about life
	Central preoccupation
		Central preoccupation.
		Central essence of self.

people spend their time. People generally choose to do things they enjoy, so their selection of any given magazine will likely reflect their interests. Using Holland's (1997) RIASEC model, for example, one might conceptualize some magazines being more social in nature (e.g., celebrity magazines) and others being more enterprising in nature (e.g., business or finance magazines). Questions related to favorite magazines are designed to elicit information about the client's vocational interests.

The third topic addresses the client's favorite story. After the client identifies the story, the counselor should ask the client to tell the story. This is intended to help the counselor understand the salient aspects of the story from the client's perspective. Questions related to the favorite story are believed to elicit information about the client's central life problem, ideas about how to solve it, and visions of her or his possible future.

The fourth topic involves asking clients to share their favorite sayings or mottos. Savickas (2011a) suggests that this motto represents the client's best advice to him- or herself. This advice can be used to guide development of the client's next chapter in life.

The fifth and final topic in the career story interview focuses on the client's early recollections. Clients are asked to share three of their earliest memories and to tell the story about what was happening in each, how they felt, and so forth. After telling the stories, clients are asked to give each story a headline. Savickas (2011a) suggests that these early recollections reveal a client's central preoccupation and his or her convictions about life.

DECONSTRUCTION. Because identity is formed through the process of the self interacting within a social context, most stories that a client shares are influenced to some degree by their respective cultures. Indeed, cultural truths often inform one's worldview. Most of the time, culture simply influences and reflects how clients see themselves, and in turn, they reveal themselves through the career story interview. At times, however, counselors may realize that some of the cultural scripts adopted by clients do not serve them well. Savickas suggests that problematic cultural scripts may limit "the range of possible selves and styles of living that individuals may adopt . . . by forcing individuals to adhere to cultural assumptions, behavioral norms, gender stereotypes, and social inequalities" (2011a, p. 110).

Counselors will want to help clients explore the veracity of their scripts. Savickas (2011a, 2013) refers to this process as deconstruction, a process in which a counselor assists clients in questioning some potentially limiting, culturally based scripts embedded within the stories they have constructed. Counselors may discuss with clients what a story "overlooks, omits, forgets, or inadequately addresses" in order to help clients "expose assumptions and question the certainties of their favorite stories" (Savickas, 2011a, p. 111).

RECONSTRUCTION. During the career story interview, the counselor focuses on asking questions, probing for deeper understanding, and deconstructing distortions if they become apparent. Although each topic is designed to elicit specific thematic material, this material isn't interpreted during the career story interview process. Instead, the counselor uses time between the first and second sessions to assess the information gathered before attempting to reconstruct and, if necessary, further deconstruct the client's narrative identity. Thus, the next step of counseling for career construction involves the counselor privately assessing and synthesizing the information gathered during the career story interview.

Career Story Assessment. The assessment process described by Savickas (2011a) is designed to assist the counselor in taking the small stories (micronarratives) shared by the client during the career story interview, assessing them for thematic meaning, and synthesizing them into a macronarrative that addresses the career concerns presented by the client in the initial session. Savickas recommends a specific assessment routine. First, counselors should review the client's goals. Revisiting client responses to the initial question about how they hope the counselor can be useful to them serves this purpose. This time, the counselor can use the information gleaned from the career story interview to understand the themes embedded in the client's responses.

Second, counselors should identify the client's central preoccupations or concerns as revealed by the client's early recollections, with specific interest in the verb associated with the first recollection shared. Savickas believes that these early recollections point to memories and lessons so deeply embedded within a client's consciousness that they define the "central force in a client's life" (2011a, p. 74) and capture a person's basic essence. The early recollections offer clues about how people may "implant their spirit into the mundane activities of daily living" (p. 75), such as work.

Third, the counselor should identify client solutions by reviewing the adjectives clients use to describe their role models and the lessons they learned from them. For example, if a client describes each of her role models with adjectives such as *determined, tenacious,* and *persistent,* these word choices can shed light on the client's orientation to problem solving. Solutions to her current career problem will likely be solved by tapping into those same characteristics within herself. Savickas explains that, "as architects of their own character, individuals select role models who provide blueprints for how to solve problems that they themselves now face" (2011a, p. 83).

The fourth step in the assessment process is to identify occupational settings of likely interest to the client. Savickas maintains that these settings are revealed by the client's favorite magazines, television shows, or websites and how the client describes each one. During the analysis phase, counselors should pay particular attention to how these favorites pertain to "the places in which they want to work, the people with whom they wish to interact, the problems they prefer to address, and the procedures they would like to use" (2011a, p. 100). Although Savickas acknowledges that this assessment can also be conducted using standardized interest inventories, he maintains that a discussion of favorite magazines is more effective because the magazines reveal a client's manifest interests, whereas an interest inventory measures reported interests. Given that what we say (report) can differ markedly from what we do (manifest), knowing where a client actually focuses leisure time (e.g., reading a magazine) may be more accurate than responses to a standardized test.

The fifth step in the assessment process is to determine the script adopted by the client, which is achieved through analysis of the client's favorite story "to learn which cultural tales clients reproduce and which truths reverberate in their lives" (Savickas, 2011a, p. 104). Clients may use these stories to guide them in life, both in terms of the meanings they construct and the choices they make. Revealing psychodynamic elements underlying his approach to counseling, Savickas likens the setting revealed in one's favorite magazine to an "objective holding environment" and the script evident in one's favorite story to a "subjective holding environment" (Savickas, 2011a, p. 105).

The sixth step in the assessment process is to identify the advice embedded within the client's favorite saying or motto. This step is similar to Cochran's concept of practical wisdom. Savickas explains that "each client possesses an inner wisdom with which to guide himself or herself. The deep meaning of a personal truth encapsulated in a motto becomes evident against the backdrop of the client's current situation" (2011a, p. 112). Although clients may feel stuck or confused with regard to the career problem that prompted them to seek assistance, Savickas maintains that they likely already possess the inner wisdom needed to guide them to resolution.

At the point of seeking assistance, however, clients are generally uncertain about how to proceed in the authoring of their career story. The purpose of the career story interview is to guide clients through a series of questions that elicit micronarratives reflective of their core self-concepts, their central preoccupations, work settings of interest to them, scripts that have guided them, and advice they have for themselves. Ferreting out these meanings from the micronarratives, however, may require the skill of a narrative counselor. After completing the assessment routine, the counselor's next task is to synthesize the micronarratives into a tentative macronarrative that can be presented to the client. Savickas calls this macronarrative a "life portrait" (2011a, p. 117).

In preparation for developing the life portrait, the seventh step in the assessment process consists of the counselor thinking about educational and occupational options that may be most appealing to the client. One approach is to categorize the client's favorite magazines in accordance with Holland's (1997) RIASEC model. With the Holland code suggested by the client's favorite magazines, a counselor can brainstorm and/or use vocational guidance resources to identify a variety of occupations and areas of study that may be well suited to the client's manifest interests.

The eighth and final step in the assessment process (also part of the preparation for developing the life portrait) is to develop a direct response to the client's request for help. This step requires revisiting the client's goals and how the client indicated that the counselor could be useful. Savickas observed that the question underlying the client's goals are typically "about clarifying some issue that makes [him or her] hesitant about moving forward" (2011a, p. 116).

With these eight steps complete, the counselor is now ready to develop a life portrait.

Development of a Life Portrait. The development of a life portrait involves the counselor creating a macronarrative of the client's life story based on the micronarratives shared by the client during the career story interview. During this process, the counselor taps into the client's central problem or preoccupation revealed via early recollections, the client's self-concept and ways of using him- or herself as a resource for addressing life problems as revealed in the discussion of role models, the client's manifest interests ascertained by the discussion of favorite magazines, the client's life scripts as discerned from the favorite story, and the client's best advice to him- or herself as reflected by the client's favorite motto. Savickas explains that "the idea is to let the client's life speak, and specifically speak to the issue at hand" (2011a, p. 69). In creating the macronarrative, the counselor should strive to stay close to the stories shared by the client while weaving them together. The life portrait should also have a positive bent "that enhances a sense of vitality, reveals meaning, and portrays a life that matters" (p. 68).

Savickas recommends a particular set of steps for developing the life portrait. He suggests that the first topic of the story should tie into the client's preoccupation as indicated by early recollections. After communicating the preoccupation, the life portrait should then describe "how the client has built a self to manage that preoccupation" (2011a, p. 123) using information about the client's role models. The story should then shift to identification of the clients' various preferred educational or vocational settings. Next, the life portrait should integrate the client's script and core essence, drawn from the client's favorite story. Finally, the life portrait should draw on the client's motto to apply his or her best advice to the career issue that precipitated counseling.

In composing the life portrait, a counselor may find that more than one macronarrative could be developed to capture accurately meanings communicated during the career story interview. In this case, Savickas suggests that counselors select the story that is most likely to be of practical use to the client. Counselors should remember that the story they develop as a client's life portrait is not intended to capture any objective truth or to prescribe any advice and that the counseling process does not end with the composition of the life portrait. Instead, it proceeds to a process in which the counselor and client work together to revise the macronarrative to the point at which the client can "own" it. Savickas refers to this collaborative process as coconstruction.

COCONSTRUCTION. The counselor generally completes the reconstructive process of assessing the client's macronarratives and transforming them into a life portrait between the first and second session. The second session begins with the counselor checking with the client to see whether he or she has gained any clarity or would like to add something since the first meeting. Next, the counselor presents the life portrait in the form of an oral story, using as many words, phrases, and themes from the career story interview as possible. Savickas recommends that counselors do this clearly, concisely, and tentatively.

Although a counselor hopes that the life portrait will resonate with the client, Savickas indicates that it is insufficient for clients to adopt the life portrait as presented by the counselor. Instead, it is important for the counselor and client to collaborate in the revision of this macronarrative, which allows the client to claim authorship of the macronarrative. During the process of revision, the macronarrative needs to be altered to add new meaning and hope. Specifically, "the coconstruction of the life portrait seeks to incorporate the current dislocation in a way that increases the possibility of transformation and development" (Savickas, 2011a, p. 129). In other words, the macronarrative is revised to challenge old meanings, to reframe sense of self in the best possible light, and to see possibilities for being true to oneself while navigating the circumstances that prompted the client to seek assistance. During this process, clients generally realize their own answers to the questions they posed at the beginning of the first session.

Once the life portrait is presented and revised, the next step in the coconstruction process is to transform the client's new insights into intentions for action. This transformation begins when addressing the client's "central narrative—that is, the career theme and occupational plot" (Savickas, 2011a, p. 131). Savickas recommends using a technique to help amplify intention. This technique is basically a sentence completion exercise in which a client identifies the actions needed to achieve happiness and success. Savickas refers to this as an identity statement. An example of an identity statement is "I will be happy and successful when I help people find and pursue more meaningful directions in their lives." An identity statement clarifies the occupational or educational direction desired by the client. This leads naturally to the client expressing an intention to take action. The hope is that the client will begin engaging in this action between the second and third counseling sessions.

ACTION. Because "action, not verbal expressions of decidedness, prompts further self-construction and life design" (Savickas, 2011a, p. 135), the conclusion of counseling for career construction necessarily involves clients acting on the insights gained during the coconstruction process. Cochran (1997) defined action as including reality testing, modifying life structures, and/or enacting roles.

Savickas discusses the importance of engaging in exploratory activities that may help a client confirm a goodness of fit with a desired occupational path or gain more clarity about which specific path may be most desirable.

Assuming that the client engages in at least some exploration between the second and third sessions, the third session is ideal for discussing the insights gained as a result. This session should also prompt the client to make a tentative decision and to commit to a way of addressing the career problem originally posed to the counselor. In a case involving a vocational development task, the decision may involve pursuit of education; the commitment may be to apply for admission to a specific program. In a case related to occupational transitions, the decision may be to remain in the same occupation but to seek a job with a new employer; the commitment may be to prepare job-hunting materials (e.g., résumés, cover letters) and engage in a vigorous job search.

Taking these kinds of actions is not easy for some clients. Savickas (2011a) acknowledges that some clients may struggle with enacting their newly authored macronarrative. This hesitation may be due to internal issues such as the client's attitudes, beliefs, and competencies or to external issues such as contextual barriers. In such cases, conclusion of the counseling process would be premature after the third session, and Savickas recommends additional sessions to address these issues. When the client exhibits the ability to engage in the actions necessary to achieve the vision laid out in the macronarrative, the process of counseling for career construction moves toward conclusion.

When preparing to conclude the counseling process, the counselor should revisit the client's initial reason for seeking assistance. One suggestion is to remind the client about how she or he responded in the first session when asked, "How can I be useful to you in constructing your career?" and then to ask the client whether the counseling has been useful. If the client indicates that counseling has been useful and appears able to take the actions necessary to achieve the vision laid out in the macronarrative, the process of counseling for career construction with this client is ready to end.

THINK AHEAD. Given this introduction to these two theories of career counseling, think ahead to how you might use the narrative approach with our cast of clients. How might each client feel derailed by his or her life story to date? How might you assist each client in reframing his or her life story to create a new narrative that is tied together with themes meaningful to the client? What type of future narrative do you imagine each client might construct? Answers to these questions should help you identify ways in which clients might benefit from narrative approaches to career counseling.

APPLICATION TO OUR CAST OF CLIENTS

Unlike Chapters 2 to 4, in which each major theory was applied in similar depth to each client, this chapter provides a brief description about how narrative theories, from both Cochran and Savickas, may be applied to six of our clients (Gillian is the exception). The chapter concludes with a more intensive application of Savickas's career construction theory to the case of Gillian. My hope is that this combination of brief sample applications and one in-depth application will help you develop a greater sense of mastery over how to use narrative theories in career counseling.

Brief Application of Narrative Theory

Starting with Wayne, you will recall that Wayne has a strong work ethic. This work ethic will be reflected, in all likelihood, in at least some of his micronarratives. For example, during the career story interview, Wayne identifies his favorite saying as a quotation attributed to Vince Lombardi: "If you're early, you're on time. If you're on time, you're late. If you're late, don't bother showing up." A narrative career counselor would observe that this saying has guided Wayne throughout his career at Ford Motor Company. He has been employed at Ford for 22 years, consistently arriving on time, putting in a hard day's work, and generally working overtime. A narrative career counselor might also speculate that the advice reflected in this quotation has guided Wayne to pursue career counseling in advance of any layoff notification. Indeed, exploring career options early will allow Wayne to anticipate a career transition.

Li Mei's case offers rich narrative material for exploration in career counseling. The career theme prevalent in her micronarratives is one of inadequacy and failure to live up to family standards. Whether Li Mei's parents are actually disappointed in her is irrelevant. From a postmodern perspective, Li Mei's subjective reality—her belief that she is a disappointment to her parents—is of much more concern. Li Mei's response to the career story interview question about her favorite story is rather revealing. She identified *The Ugly Duckling* by Hans Christian Andersen. When telling the story to the counselor, Li Mei described a baby duckling that didn't fit in with its siblings. The mother and father duck were very disappointed to see such an ugly duckling in their brood, and the poor little duckling felt inferior to its siblings. Li Mei's face lit up as she shared the exciting conclusion to the story. She explained that the ugly little duckling grew up into the most beautiful swan and spent the rest of its life enjoying the admiration of others. In reading Li Mei's retelling of the story, you may think to yourself that she didn't tell the story quite the way you remembered it, but this doesn't matter. Arriving at an objective truth is not the goal of the postmodern approach. Instead, we are interested in Li Mei's subjective understanding of the story. You can likely imagine how this story may pertain to Li Mei's life script and her core essence.

At the onset of counseling, in response to the counselor's question about what she hoped to get out of it, Lakeesha volunteered her favorite saying: "When the Lord closes a door, somewhere He opens a window." This motto, of course, represents Lakeesha's best advice to herself. The next chapter of her life will likely involve occupational exploration and identification of potential employment options. In response to the question about role models, Lakeesha identified Oprah Winfrey. When asked to describe her, Lakeesha explained that Oprah had endured some very difficult times, but she was tough and she persevered to create a life admired by millions of people. When asked about whether she was similar to Oprah, Lakeesha indicated that they had both been through tough times: Oprah had endured childhood sexual abuse, and Lakeesha was still reeling from the tragic death of her husband. Lakeesha also noted that they are both African American women, are interested in what motivates human behavior, and are committed to the welfare of children. This description might offer insight into how Lakeesha could use her own characteristics to address life challenges. Indeed, toughness and perseverance are likely to be essential. Cochran's episode of changing a life structure would also be quite useful with Lakeesha.

With Vincent, a narrative career counselor may use a technique recommended by Cochran to explore Vincent's personal ideas of career heavens and career hells. Vincent may respond that career heaven involves any career in which he can help others and that any career of social irrelevance (a career that doesn't involve directly helping others) represents his idea of career hell. In elaborating the idea of helping, Vincent may home in on protecting and/or rescuing others as his most heavenly type of career. This concept may be extended in helping Vincent found a future narrative and may lead to a search for a wide array of careers that could embody Vincent's conception of career heaven.

In response to the question about mottos, Doris indicated that her favorite saying is "In the end, it's not going to be how many breaths you took, but how many moments took your breath away." Given the abrasive way in which Doris interacted with the counselor at the onset of counseling, this response may be somewhat surprising. From another perspective, it may reflect Doris's preoccupation with her age. This saying also represents Doris's best advice to herself. When the counselor probed a bit and asked Doris how many moments in the past year had taken her breath away, Doris looked crestfallen. Realizing that she could not remember a moment like that in the past year, Doris became aware of how truly unsatisfying her entire life had become. Doris felt miserable at home with her alcoholic, inattentive, and unfaithful husband, and she felt nearly as miserable at work. She realized that, in founding her future narrative, she wanted to find a job that might include moments that would take her breath away. Hints about her manifest interests were apparent in her favorite magazines: *Quilt* and *Nature*. Perhaps a job in a sewing store, nature center, or zoo could offer Doris experiences that could take her breath away.

Because the nuance of words and working is so important in narrative career counseling, it would be very helpful to talk with Juan using Spanish. When a career counselor fluent in Spanish asks Juan about his favorite magazines, he reveals that he doesn't like to read much. As a follow-up, the counselor may then inquire about Juan's favorite television show and learn that Juan's very favorite show is *Extreme Makeover: Home Edition*. In fact, there is even a Spanish version of this show, *Cambio Radical*, on one of the cable stations. He also reports enjoying *This Old House*. Even though he doesn't understand all of the English, Juan enjoys watching the home restorations. From a narrative perspective, this information is important. Although Juan finds himself unable to engage in the heavy physical labor in the construction industry, his vocational interests were well matched to that type of job. In forming a future narrative, Juan will likely be attracted to similar occupations but will need to pursue something he is physically able to do. With the assistance of a back brace, for example, he may be able to work in a position not requiring heavy lifting, perhaps at a store such as Lowes or Home Depot. His years of experience could be quite valuable when assisting customers and offering advice. Although his English proficiency is limited, he is generally able to follow directions given in English and could assist the many Spanish-speaking customers who live in the area.

It is my hope that these brief examples offer you a glimpse of the ways in which you could use narrative theory to provide career counseling to Wayne, Li Mei, Lakeesha, Vincent, Doris, and Juan. The richness of this approach, of course, is found within the content of client stories. The stories for six of our clients were necessarily limited in scope because of the limited space in this chapter. This chapter will conclude with a more comprehensive application of Savickas's career construction theory as it applies to Gillian.

Comprehensive Application to the Case of Gillian, by Thomas Eckert[†]

According to Savickas, the career story interview begins much as any initial counseling session would. The counselor simply asks the client "to articulate and elaborate" what he or she is seeking from the counseling experience (Savickas, 2011a, p. 59). In this way, a client is given the opportunity to relay important information regarding his or her occupational dilemma. The opening question also gives the career construction counselor a chance to assess the client's presentational style and emotional tone. During this beginning phase, it is especially important to validate and affirm the client, in support of establishing a working alliance. Once a level of rapport is established, the counselor begins a more formal sequence of questions. These questions serve as a relatively quick narrative assessment, yielding information relating to a client's self-concept, preferred work environments, narrative scripts, self-motivation skills, and personal theme (Savickas, 2011a).

The first formal question of the career story interview pertains to whom the client admired during childhood or young adulthood, other than his or her parents. Those admired might come from the client's own life, or they might be fictional characters, famous people, historical figures, or what have you. By asking the client to describe his or her role models, we implicitly learn about the client's self-concept. In other words, the client unwittingly uses role models to describe his or her own ideals. As Savickas (2011a) notes, "[I]t is not *whom* the client admires but *what* the client admires" (p. 67). A counselor can further clarify self-concept by asking how the client is similar to each role model, and in what ways they differ.

Gillian, for example, identified "Sacagawea" as an early role model. When asked to elaborate upon her choice, Gillian said that Sacagawea, the Shoshone Indian guide who accompanied the Lewis and Clark expedition in the Northwest United States, was "full of strength and determination. She was an agent for peace." When asked to name another admired person, Gillian said that she had always followed Hillary Clinton's story. "Hillary is a woman of strength who is always reaching new heights," said Gillian. "And yet she's always been grounded and, family-oriented, and she understands the value of community."

The second question of the interview is less about self-concept and more about preferred settings. A client's answers to this question indirectly reveal which kinds of

---

[†] The following application example was written by Thomas Eckert, one of my former graduate students, and is reprinted with his permission. Thank you, Tom.

settings, including occupational settings, are personally suitable for pursuing purpose and fulfilling values (Savickas, 2011a). Traditional approaches to career counseling assess preferred environments through interest inventories, or simply by asking the client about ideal work environments. Career construction counselors, on the other hand, assess preferred environments by asking a client about his or her favorite magazines and/or websites (Savickas, 2011a). Favorite magazines and websites convey relevant spheres of interest and reflect environments in which the client feels most comfortable.

Gillian named three favorite magazines. The first was *Wired Magazine,* which she said helps her "to stay on the cutting edge as far as technological developments are concerned." The second magazine she named was *Success Magazine,* which she said helps her to "stay motivated," and to "think more independently" with regard to her future. The third magazine she chose was *Ms.* magazine, which she picked because "it represents women's strengths, and it talks about how women today balance all kinds of activities and challenges."

The next question in the interview elicits a client's favorite story, be it from a book, movie, TV show, or what have you (Savickas, 2011a). Here the counselor asks the client to briefly relay a favorite story in his or her own words. In this way, the client highlights subjectively important aspects of the story and thus unwittingly hints at his or her own narrative theme. The counselor clarifies the client's theme by listening for the central problem of the story. The protagonist's approach to the story's central problem will tend to reflect the client's approach to his or her life and career. In other words, a person is attracted to a certain kind of story because in some way it speaks to his or her central preoccupation. It is this preoccupation which fuels purpose, thus influencing an individual's occupational plot and career theme.

In response to the "favorite story" question, Gillian singled out the television series *Lost.* When asked about the story, she responded: "I really liked the character of the doctor. He was thrown into this totally unexpected situation, and he took it upon himself to get everyone working together to survive. He knew he had to be a leader. But to do so, he had to figure himself out. He had to go inside his mind and work out his issues, . . . like those he had with his father, who had recently died. He had to let go of his hang-ups and become more balanced. The more he worked on himself, the more he led."

Gillian also offered a second story. She fondly recalled crawling into bed as a little girl, turning out the lights, and waiting for her mother to come tuck her in. "Sometimes she would come in with a lit candle and talk to me. That was our time; . . . it was like our little secret." When prompted to tell the story, Gillian responded in this way: "I happen to have some Indian blood in me; my mom is part Suquamish Indian. I remember one night she came in and put a blanket over me—an Indian throw—and started to tell me all about our Suquamish ancestry. She told me about their customs, their values, their views about nature and spirituality. It all seemed so magical to me; they seemed so strong, and yet so balanced, so peaceful. It made me feel proud. She taught me that the females were leaders because they brought balance and harmony to the tribe. And she read Indian poetry to me. My favorite was called "Go Forward, Be Brave." I still have the book after all these years."

The next question in the career story interview focuses on self-given advice. This information is attained by asking a client to share any personal mottos or wise sayings that he or she frequently uses (Savickas, 2011a). The question is meant to get inside the client's internal dialogue and clarify a method of self-motivation. When asked to identify a personal motto, Gillian responded with "Go Forward, Be Brave," the title of the Indian fable received from her mother.

The final and most personal question of the interview asks about early memories (Savickas, 2011a). This part is saved for last, because it naturally deepens the dialogue. When a counselor asks about a client's early recollections, the aim is to access the deepest layers of narrative information. The client is asked to provide detail, including setting, action, results, and emotional content. Because these early recollections sit at the base of the life story, the details often tell us something about a client's root preoccupation. Like personal parables, they uniquely illuminate the macronarrative theme. They speak to the career theme as well, inasmuch as one's career is driven by a central preoccupation. Writes Savickas (2011a), "[p]ractitioners seek to learn clients' convictions about life by considering nuclear scenes in which clients encapsulate their life stories. These scenes, in the form of early recollections, present to the practitioner a client's perspective on life" (p. 63).

When prompted, Gillian provided the following early recollection: "I'm an only child, so I always discovered things on my own. I remember the first time I wandered off alone. I was probably three years old. We were at our lakeside cottage in the summertime, on the beach. My parents were talking to some folks from a neighboring cottage, so I wandered off without anybody noticing. I came around a patch of high grass and foliage, and entered into a little cove. I was greeted by a giant swan, just a few feet away, looking me right in the face. There were about a half-dozen little baby chicks clustering all around her. I was terrified, because she was way bigger than I was. She puffed up and made a frightening noise, and then ambled off toward the lake. All the chicks filed themselves into a straight line behind her and followed her out. I ran back to my parents to tell them what I'd seen."

When asked to convey her feelings in relation to the memory, Gillian said, "I'm not sure why that experience sticks out. I guess it was my first taste of independence. And then, of course, the swan made quite an impression. She was so big, strong, beautiful. She had everything under control, with all her little babies following behind her. I was just so excited. I guess I've always been a nature lover."

The "early recollections" question brings the formal career story interview to a close. Aside from facilitating valuable narrative information, the interview gradually transitions the client into a narrative mode of thinking and feeling. A client's shared "early recollection" is a first foray into narrative exploration. The counselor is now in a position to reinforce storytelling behavior, and to elicit further micronarrative material. As such, the remainder of the first session is dedicated to eliciting new and relevant stories from the client.

The second session, which should take place approximately a week after the first, requires some preparation on the part of the counselor. Between sessions, the counselor is charged with analyzing and curating the client's stories. This process entails weaving smaller stories into a larger story, and identifying a theme. The theme, and underlying rationale, is presented to the client at the beginning of the second session. But rather than impose the theme upon the client, the counselor initiates dialogue. The purpose of this dialogue is to "coconstruct" an "authorized" theme (Savickas, 2011a). Here the client and counselor work together to refine and expand the career theme. Savickas (2011a) notes that "the actual intervention involves rebalancing the occupational plot and career theme" (p. 45). *Rebalancing* means recalibrating the theme so as to create narrative coherency among past, present, and the possible horizon of the future.

As earlier noted, Gillian's theme revolves around strength, independence, and leadership. These insights represent a starting point for dialogue, initiated at the beginning of the second session. As such, the second session is mostly dedicated to narrative processing. As Gillian explores her narrative material, she increasingly realizes that she wants to bring balance into her career theme. She wants to dilate the meaning of her story. As noted before, she wants to raise a family, connect with her community, and have more control over how she spends her time.

Gillian now recognizes that her responses during the career story interview directly apply to her current occupational transition. She sees that her "early recollection" was a parable describing her evolving independence. She knows that her ancient discovery, the great swan, represents "strength, beauty, natural balance, family . . . all the things I'm after today." She realizes that her magazine choices reflect a desire for total self-sufficiency, while her early role models exude values which she still longs to manifest. And though the realization causes her much anxiety, she also recognizes that her current role at Ernst & Young, while partially fulfilling, will never quite get her where she wants to go.

So, like the doctor in *Lost*, Gillian is bravely facing her unexpected transition, and digging deeper than she has before. In the midst of her narrative introspections, Gillian comes out with this: "I've always thought of myself as an independent person. But, in truth, I've always had someone telling me what to do. First it was my father, and then it was the firm. Deep down, I want to be free of it all. I want to be in business for myself. I've just been too scared to do it. But maybe it's time. Maybe it's time to do it my own way . . . my work, my life, my family . . . all of it. Maybe that's what this is all about." As Gillian continues to clarify her thoughts, she gains confidence in her new direction. She realizes that she possesses all the skills, and has all the connections, which are necessary to transition successfully into private practice as an accountant and business consultant. "It would take some work," she says, "but I'd be *home*. My schedule would be mine. My *life* would be mine." Gillian goes on to describe how her potential consulting practice might bring her closer to the community. "It would be so fulfilling to help local businesses grow and thrive!"

By the end of the second session, Gillian's gut-sense tells her that she is on the right track. The idea of setting forth on her own fills her with new meaning and energy. The counselor, recognizing that narrative coherency has been achieved, moves the session into its final phase. The latter portion of the second session is dedicated to identifying action steps. Gillian agrees to outline her plan, initiate various research activities, and contact a variety of potentially helpful people. A third and final session is scheduled for three weeks, simply to review progress. After the counselor draws the session to a close, Gillian rises and gradually moves toward the door. "Yes, I feel good about this, thank you," she says, before pausing, as if falling back into her head. As she leaves, a familiar phrase escapes from her lips: "Go forward, be brave."

CHAPTER 6

Cultural Dimensions of Career Development and Career Counseling

Not so long ago, the counseling and psychology professions paid little to no attention to the implications of culture in the counseling process. That the same was true within the field of career counseling is evidenced by Brown's (2002) observation that "career development theorists have all but ignored the career development of ethnic and cultural minorities" (p. 48). There was an assumption, though largely unstated, that the theories and techniques of career counseling were universal and equally applicable to all people regardless of their cultural background (Young, Marshall, & Valach, 2007). Now, of course, such a claim seems naïve.

Replacing this culture-blind, etic approach in counseling has been an increasing emphasis on an emic awareness of the ways in which culture affects our experiences in and assumptions about the world, our standards of normality, our priorities, our ways of being and behaving, and our help-seeking behaviors. Rather than neglecting the importance of culture, counselor training programs now emphasize the importance of developing the multicultural competencies counselors will need to be effective with clients across a broad spectrum of diversity. It is likely that your training program requires a specific course dedicated to this subject matter and also that every course in your training program addresses cultural issues to some extent. Indeed, such an approach is specified by the American Counseling Association's (ACA) *Code of Ethics* requirement that "counselor educators infuse material related to multiculturalism/diversity into all courses and workshops for the development of professional counselors" (American Counseling Association, 2005, F.6.b.). This chapter will focus on cultural dimensions related to career development and career counseling.

AN INTRODUCTION TO CULTURE

Culture and *Diversity* Defined

Culture may be defined as "membership in a socially constructed way of living, which incorporates collective values, beliefs, norms, boundaries, and lifestyles that are cocreated with others who share similar worldviews comprising biological, psychosocial, historical, psychological, and other factors" (American Counseling Association, 2005, p. 20). Cultural identity involves not only a person's race and ethnicity but also national origin, immigration and citizenship status; age and generational cohort; biological sex, socialized gender and gender identity; sexual orientation; physical and psychological disabilities; social class and socioeconomic issues; and religious/spiritual beliefs (Corey, Corey, & Callahan., 2011). Each of these cultural dimensions may affect a person's career development and decision making as well as experience of the workplace and level of career success. Each has implications for the counselor–client interactions over the course of the career counseling process.

The issue of whether a client is a member of dominant or nondominant cultures is particularly important because the norms and worldviews of dominant cultures are generally also dominant within our beliefs about work, our career development theories, and our career counseling approaches. Table 6.1 lists a variety of dominant and nondominant cultural groups in the United States with which your clients may identify.

THINK AHEAD. Given this introduction, think ahead about how these various elements of culture could affect a person's career development. How, for example, might one's cultural affiliations affect a person's views about work and career? How might they affect a person's career aspirations and decision making? How might these cultural dimensions affect a person's experience of the workplace and level of career success? Which cultural dimension(s) might be most salient for each person in our cast of clients?

Career Development Theories: Cultural Considerations

In Chapters 2 through 5, I introduced a variety of theories. These theories serve as the foundation of our understanding of career development and the career counseling process. Although some of the theories (e.g., social cognitive career theory; Lent, Brown, & Hackett, 1994) explicitly address cultural factors, other theories give little explicit attention to cultural factors and instead take a rather etic approach to explaining career development and to guiding the career counseling process (Brown, 2002). Perhaps most important, many of the career development theories are based on culturally encapsulated assumptions that are reflective of dominant culture (Arthur & Collins, 2011; Wrenn, 1962).

TABLE 6.1 Dominant and Nondominant Cultural Groups in the United States

	Dominant Cultural Group	Nondominant Cultural Group
Race/ethnicity	European American	African American
		Asian American
		Latino and Latina American
		Native American
Immigration and citizenship status	Established	Recent
	Voluntary	Involuntary
		Refugee
		Disenfranchised native
	Documented	Undocumented, illegal, no visa
		Undocumented, expired visa
Social class	Middle class	Lower class
	Upper class	
Gender/gender identity	Male	Female
		Transgender
		Nonbinary
Sexual orientation	Heterosexual	Gay/lesbian
		Bisexual
Disability status	No disability	Visible disability
		Nonvisible disability
Religion	Christian	Jewish
		Muslim
		Buddhist
		Hindu
		Other
		Atheist
		None

Culturally Encapsulated Assumptions

Gysbers, Heppner, and Johnston (1998, as cited in Flores & Heppner, 2002) noted that "the field of career counseling has been built largely on a framework of western European tenets that have dramatically influenced career theory, research and practices" (Flores & Heppner, 2002, p. 182). They proceeded to identify five specific tenets as examples of culturally encapsulated assumptions. "These tenets include (a) individualism and autonomy; (b) affluence; (c) the structure of opportunity being open to all; (d) the centrality of work in people's lives; and (e) the linearity, progressiveness, and rationality of the career development process" (Flores & Heppner, 2002, p. 182). Today, the tenet involving a linear, progressive, and rational career development process is no longer the norm for most people, so I present a slightly different set of culturally encapsulated assumptions in the paragraphs below. It is my contention that the following five culturally encapsulated assumptions frequently underlie career development theories and threaten those theories' applicability to diverse clientele. Although these assumptions may hold true for many clients from dominant cultures and for some clients from nondominant cultures, they are far from universally applicable. Indeed, a foundational premise within the discipline of multicultural counseling involves the importance of recognizing other truths. Let's take a look.

INDIVIDUALISM VERSUS COLLECTIVISM. The first assumption involves an a priori valuing of individualism and autonomy. This assumption is evident when counselors universally encourage clients to make their own, independent career decisions and when they tie the idea of career maturity to a client's ability and willingness to make career decision autonomously (Leong, 2010; Sue & Sue, 2008). However, collectivism rather than individualism is the norm for several racial and ethnic groups (Hartung, Fouad, Leong, & Hardin, 2010; Mau, 2004).

CENTRALITY VERSUS NONCENTRALITY OF WORK. The second assumption, reflective of dominant U.S. culture and embedded within many career development theories, is that work is central to an individual's identity and should be a primary focus in one's life. This "relative importance of work and career in an individual's life" is referred to as work salience (Diemer et al., 2010, p. 620). As just one example of this assumption in action, consider how frequently people in the United States introduce themselves by identifying their name and occupation. It can be a mistake, however, to assume that career is central to a client's life and identity or that work is a means by which to implement one's self-concept. Blustein and his colleagues argue convincingly that the field of career counseling is geared primarily to middle-class clients for whom this is true (Blustein, Coutinho, Murphy, Backus, & Catraio, 2011). In "highlighting the reality that not every job seeker has the opportunity to implement his or her self at work" (p. 213), these authors suggest that it is essential for career counselors to recognize that work may have a much different meaning for working-class clients than it does for middle-class clients.

AFFLUENCE VERSUS SPIRITUALITY AND SUBSISTENCE. The third culturally encapsulated assumption is that affluence is a common goal and a measure of one's success and that status and power are best "measured by economic possessions" (Katz, 1985, p. 618). However, affluence is far from a universal indicator of success. Instead, Sue and Sue note that "many racial/ethnic minority groups in this country are strongly spiritual. African Americans, Asian Americans, Latino/Hispanic Americans, and Native Americans all place strong emphasis on the interplay and interdependence of spiritual life and healthy functioning" (2008, p. 226).

EQUITABLE VERSUS INEQUITABLE OPPORTUNITY STRUCTURE. The fourth assumption is that there is an equitable opportunity structure in the United States in which all citizens have an equal opportunity to succeed in education and the world of work. Rather than acknowledging structural oppression, discriminatory practices, and other inequities, this assumption is that all people have equal access to the so-called American dream. Directly challenging this assumption, Sue and Sue note that "racial/ethnic minorities and other marginalized groups (women, gays/lesbians, and the disabled) in our society live under an umbrella of individual, institutional, and cultural forces that often demean them, disadvantage them, and deny them equal access and opportunity" (2008, p. 84).

PERSONAL AGENCY VERSUS SOCIOPOLITICAL DETERMINANTS. The fifth assumption follows from the fourth and proposes that, given the allegedly equitable opportunity structure, one's success is determined by one's individual talents and work ethic. Key to this assumption is a valuing of the Protestant work ethic (Katz, 1985) and a belief that hard work will lead to success. This assumption attributes success or failure to the individual's exercise of personal agency and dismisses the potential impact of sociopolitical determinants. In contrast, people from nondominant cultures who experience an inequitable opportunity structure often experience a very different reality in which factors such as discrimination and other contextual barriers make career success much more difficult to achieve, even with the determined, persistent exercise of personal agency.

PUTTING IT ALL TOGETHER

Career counselors should be vigilant in considering ways in which these five culturally encapsulated assumptions may influence their beliefs about work, career decision making, and career success. Career counselors should actively question the societal messages they have internalized about opportunity structure and personal agency. With these ideas in mind, let's turn to a closer examination of several differences across cultural groups that have pronounced implications for our understanding of career development and our approach to career counseling.

DIFFERENCES ACROSS CULTURAL GROUPS

Career counselors should be aware of how clients of various cultures may differ from one another and understand the implications of such differences on one's career development and on the career counseling process. These include differences in worldview, sociopolitical inequities, and socioeconomic disparities.

Differences in Worldview: Individualism Versus Collectivism

A primary way in which cultural groups may differ involves worldview. Particularly relevant to the career counseling process is the relational dimension of worldviews that may differ with regard to the value placed on individuality, independence, and autonomy (Hartung et al., 2010, Sue & Sue, 2008). The dominant, European American culture in the United States tends to place a high value on these qualities and embraces a philosophy of individualism (Mau, 2004). Within this worldview, individuals are viewed as the "smallest unit of survival" (Leong, 2010, p. 384). Many in the United States believe that career decisions should be made autonomously, with a primary focus on the individual's needs and desires, and that career success is best evaluated by how much satisfaction the individual derives from work and by what the individual achieves or accomplishes at work. As noted in our earlier discussion of culturally encapsulated assumptions, the valuing of individualism is deeply embedded within many of our profession's theories of career development and often guides our work with clients (Young et al., 2007).

In many cultures, however, the individual is not the primary psychosocial unit (Sue & Sue, 2008). For much of the world, the family or the community is recognized as the primary "psychosocial unit of operation" (Sue & Sue, 2008, p. 141), and value is placed on "the subordination of personal goals for the sake of attaining the goals of the group/community" (Leong, 2010, p. 384). This worldview is generally referred to as collectivism. In the context of career counseling, a collectivist worldview holds that career decisions should be made collectively, with a primary focus on the family's and perhaps the community's needs, and that career success is best evaluated by how much it benefits the family and wider community.

Counselors should therefore consider each client's worldview and relative valuing of individualism and collectivism as it pertains to career issues. Otherwise, clients from collectivist cultures "may find that the career counseling process overlooks some of their primary considerations and, in fact, feel pressured to discard considerations of their family or community" (Arthur & Popadiuk, 2010, p. 436).

Sociopolitical Inequities

Another important element of becoming culturally competent involves developing a deep awareness of sociopolitical inequities that exist between dominant and nondominant cultures. Simply put, this requires understanding that members of dominant, privileged groups live in a world in which their cultural group does not regularly experience structural oppression or discrimination evidenced by access to fewer resources, fewer opportunities, and perceptions of themselves as "lesser than." In this context, members of dominant groups live in an opportunity-based world in which they have access to an opportunity structure that includes abundant resources. These resources are apparent in educational settings, in the availability of role models and mentors similar to oneself, social capital, and an unlimited range of occupational opportunities. In contrast, sociopolitical realities including structural oppression and discrimination are all too familiar to many members of nondominant, minority groups. Although this may be debated by some naïve or incendiary radio talk show hosts, the existence of sociopolitical inequities is now broadly recognized within the profession of career counseling.

Reflecting this, Leong (2010) observed that "the fact that members of minority groups experience limited opportunities is rarely debated, and there is a large body of work on how such barriers affect vocational development" (p. 382). For example, Diemer et al. (2010) explained that sociopolitical inequities include "macrolevel inequities, such as structural racism and the asymmetrical distribution of resources, that limit access to microlevel resources, such as educational and occupational opportunities, supports, and social capital" (p. 619). In this context, members of nondominant groups live in a barrier-based world in which they lack equal access to an opportunity structure featuring abundant resources. The lack of resources is apparent in substandard educational settings, the paucity of role models and mentors similar to oneself, and the lack of social capital. This lack of resources serves as one type of barrier, and discriminatory practices represent another.

Such sociopolitical inequities also have an impact on the development of occupational self-concept, the perception of barriers to career success, the levels of occupational self-efficacy and volition, and the level of work salience embraced as part of the career development process (Blustein et al., 2011; Diemer & Hsieh, 2008; Diemer et al., 2010). These researchers also argue that these factors both result from and contribute to a continuing cycle of economic impoverishment. This cycle has the effect of limiting socioeconomic mobility (Blustein et al., 2011; Diemer & Hsieh, 2008; Diemer et al., 2010). One clear impact of the interaction between sociopolitical inequities and vocational development is on the economic well-being of individuals across cultures. These economic disparities both contribute to and result from career development difficulties, and it is clear that nondominant cultural groups suffer economically in greater proportions than do dominant cultural groups.

Socioeconomic Disparities

A third way in which cultural groups often differ involves economic well-being. Although there are rich and poor individuals within every cultural group, socioeconomic disparities between cultural groups are evident. Indicators of economic well-being can be measured in a number of ways, including annual income, wealth, and poverty rates. As you will see in this section, such indicators confirm the existence of significant disparities across cultures in the United States. Let's take a look.

INCOME. National data collected by the U.S. Census Bureau and the Pew Research Center provide ample evidence that members of nonminority groups, especially people of color and persons with disabilities, fare much worse when it comes to earning a living. Figure 6.1 shows how median annual incomes differ by race/ethnicity, sex, and disability status. The 2012 median household income differs significantly across race (Fry, 2013). There is also a significant gap in the earnings of full-time, year-round workers by sex, with females earning on average only 77% of what males earn (DeNavas-Walt, Proctor, &

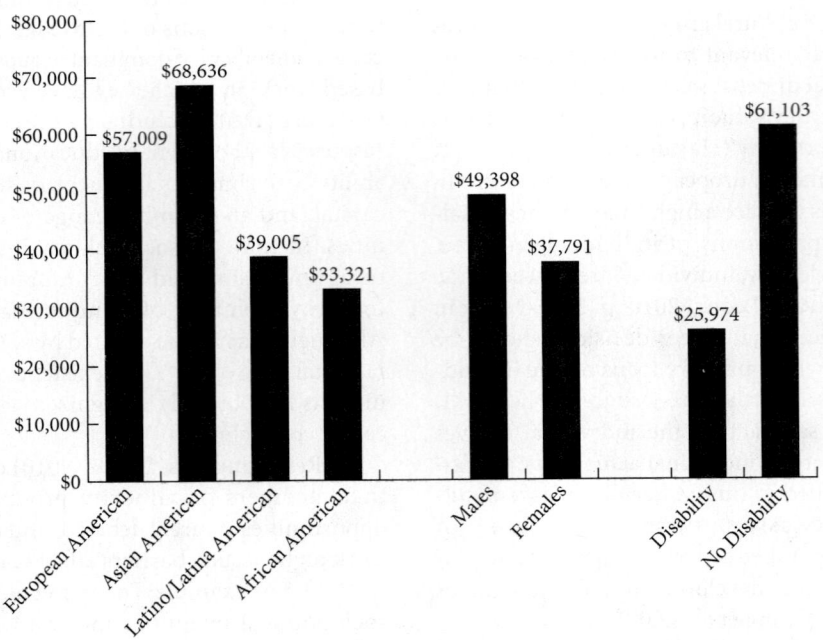

FIGURE 6.1 Income Inequities Across Cultural Groups: Median 2012 Annual Household Income
Source: DeNavas-Walt, Proctor, and Smith, 2013.

Smith, 2013). Finally, people without disabilities earn substantially more than people with disabilities (DeNavas-Walt et al., 2013).

WEALTH. Economic disparities are evident not only in annual income levels but also in accrued wealth, which is defined as assets minus debts (Kochhar, Fry, & Taylor, 2011, p. 1). Figure 6.2 shows that the gaps in wealth are even more astounding than the gaps in annual income. When including home equity, the total median wealth of European American households is a whopping 17.5 times the total median wealth of an African American household (U.S. Census Bureau, 2011). When excluding home equity, the total median wealth of European American households is 15.7 times the total median wealth of an African American household. These differences in wealth may serve to perpetuate long-term inequality due to the ability of wealthier families to "pass on monetary resources and social capital at a higher rate" than poorer families (King & Madsen, 2007, p. 396).

POVERTY RATES. Significant gaps also exist in the poverty rates across cultural groups. As shown in Figure 6.3, more than 25% of all African Americans and Latino Americans live in poverty compared to less than 10% of European Americans. These statistics reveal that African Americans and Latino Americans are nearly three times more likely to live in poverty than European Americans. Also astounding are the statistics showing that people with disabilities have more than double the poverty rate as people without disabilities. A notable gap in poverty rates exist between the sexes, with females more likely to live in poverty than males.

As you can see from these data regarding income, wealth, and poverty rates, significant economic disparities across cultures exist. Such indicators of economic well-being, often discussed in the context of socioeconomic status (SES) or social class, have clear implications for career development. For example, Rojewski and Kim (2003) found that educational aspirations are highly correlated with SES, with teens in the highest SES quartile being four times more likely than other teens to aspire to college and to obtain postsecondary education. These authors explained that the "considerable role of SES on determining postsecondary transition status, and hence occupational and educational aspirations, should be thoughtfully considered. SES can influence career decision-making and attainment by opening and closing opportunities, as well as shaping occupational self-concept and decision-making" (p. 106).

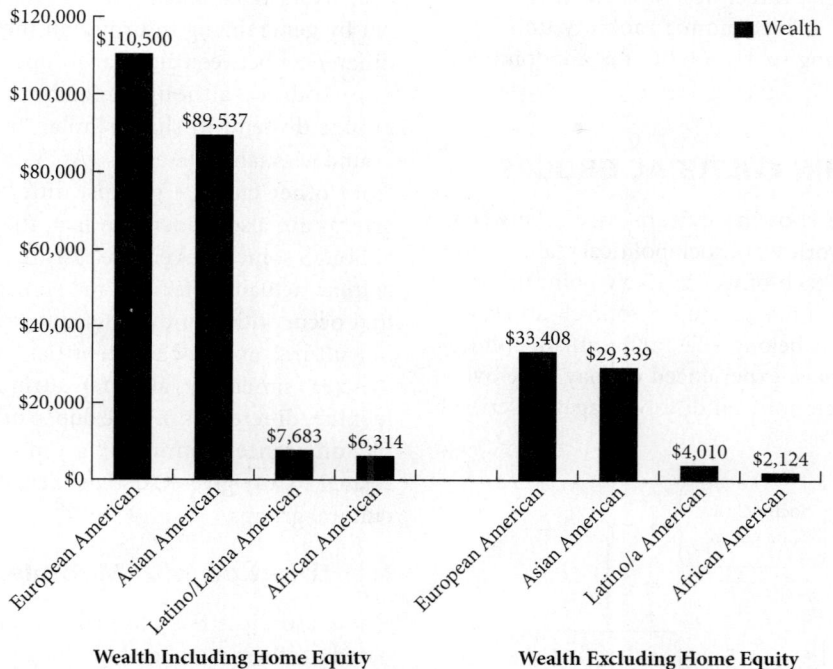

FIGURE 6.2 Wealth Inequities Across Cultural Groups: Assets Minus Debts
Source: U.S. Census Wealth_Tables_2011 - http://www.census.gov/people/wealth/

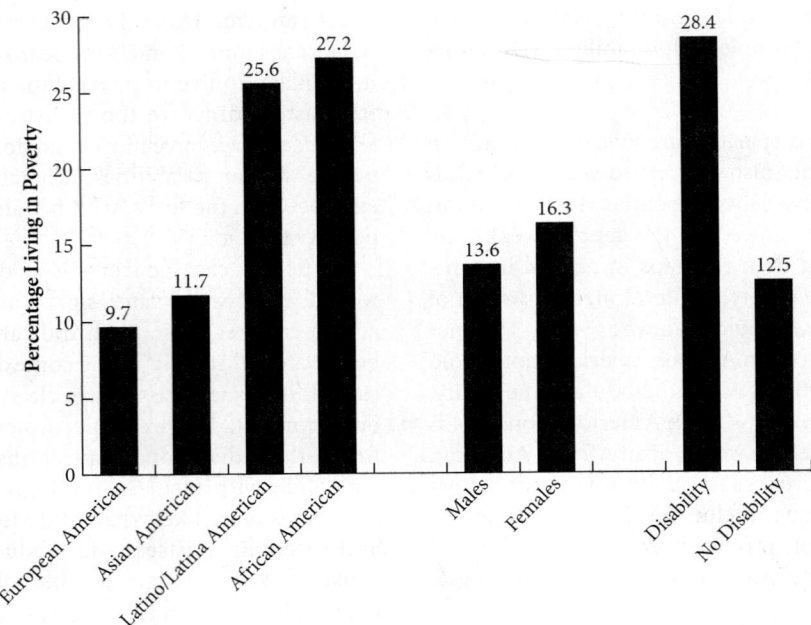

FIGURE 6.3 Poverty Rates Across Cultural Groups
Source: DeNavas-Walt, Proctor, and Smith, 2013.

Figure 6.4 shows triadic interactions occurring among these three factors, with each affecting the other (Blustein et al., 2011; Diemer & Hsieh, 2008; Diemer et al., 2010). To the extent that career development represents a path toward upward socioeconomic mobility, this cycle has the effect of limiting such mobility for nondominant cultural groups.

DIVERSITY WITHIN CULTURAL GROUPS

Despite the evidence showing culture-based, between-group differences in worldview, sociopolitical realities, and economic well-being, each of us can likely point to many exceptions. In fact, you may consider yourself an exception. Although you may belong to a nondominant cultural group, you may not have experienced or may have overcome the types of sociopolitical disadvantages described above and may be faring quite well, thank you, with regard to economic well-being and career success. Clearly, exceptions exist to almost every rule, and it is essential that counselors avoid making assumptions about any given client by generalizing information they have learned about differences between cultural groups.

Indeed, although members of various cultural groups do tend to share similar "values, beliefs, norms, boundaries, and lifestyles" (ACA, 2005, p. 20) that differ from other cultural groups, differences *within* cultural groups are also evident. In fact, the concept of diversity, although sometimes erroneously used as another word for *culture*, actually refers to "the similarities and differences that occur within and across cultures and the intersection of cultural and social identities" (ACA, 2005, p. 20). Whereas similarities are often attributed to shared cultural identity, differences may be due to other factors. For example, differences within any given cultural group may be related to any given person's identification with multiple cultural groups.

Identification with Multiple Cultures

One reason it is risky to make assumptions about clients based on their membership in a specific cultural group is that people often identify with more than one dimension of culture (Leong, 2010). For instance, culture "can be associated with a racial or ethnic group as well as with gender,

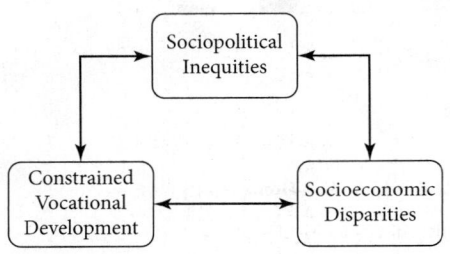

FIGURE 6.4 Potential Barriers to Socioeconomic Mobility

religion, economic status, nationality, physical capacity or disability, and affectional or sexual orientation" (Corey et al., 2011, p. 115). With these dimensions of culture in mind, any given person may hold membership in a culture specific to race/ethnicity, gender, SES, and so forth. A European American, middle-class male may be quite different from a European American male firmly embedded within the lower social class whose family history reveals generations of poverty. One of these European Americans might feel (and be) part of the dominant culture of the United States, but the other may quite accurately feel (and be) disadvantaged.

Immigration History

Differences within and between cultural groups may also be understood in the context of the recency with which one's family entered the United States and the circumstances surrounding the immigration (Leong, 2010). Yakushko, Backhaus, Watson, Ngaruiya, and Gonzales (2008) elaborated on the variety of circumstances that may prompt immigration. Specifically, they observed that migration from another country may be voluntary or forced and "there are three broad categories of relocation that are officially recognized in the United States: (a) legal immigration, (b) refugee relocation; and (c) undocumented or illegal immigration" (p. 367). Yakushko and colleagues contend that the career development concerns of clients whose families have relocated to the United States will differ depending on the recency and circumstances of the immigration, especially when their proficiency in English is limited. For example, a first-generation born Mexican American whose parents entered the United States without documentation may differ significantly from a person whose parents emigrated from Spain in the early 1800s, although both people may identify as Latino. Similarly, an African American whose ancestors were brought forcibly to the United States as slaves may differ significantly from an African American whose family voluntarily immigrated to the United States from Uganda two generations ago, especially with regard to cultural mistrust (Bullock-Yowell, Andrews, & Buzzetta, 2011).

Acculturation

Another source of difference within and between cultural groups involves acculturation. Acculturation involves the degree to which any given person identifies with the nondominant culture within which he or she was raised and the degree to which that person identifies with the dominant, mainstream culture (Berry, 1997; Miller & Kerlow-Myers, 2009). Although the concept of acculturation has primary relevance to situations in which individuals are raised in one culture before coming into contact with another culture (e.g., a person raised in a Latino culture in Guatemala moves to an almost exclusively white neighborhood in Iowa), it also has relevance to situations in which individuals are raised in nondominant cultures existing within a larger dominant culture. In both cases, individuals face decisions about the extent to which they continue engaging with and adhering to the norms of their nondominant culture of origin and the extent to which they engage with and adhere to the norms of the dominant culture. These decisions have a direct impact on the degree of change that results from the opportunity to engage with another culture. Thus, *acculturation* is defined as "the alterations that result from continuous direct contact between two or more different cultural groups and/or individual members thereof" (Fox, Merz, Solorzano, & Roesch, 2013, p. 270).

Rather than assuming that all clients from a particular nondominant culture share a common belief system and worldview, career counselors are wise to consider the strategies each individual client chooses with regard to acculturation. Figure 6.5 shows four primary strategies that people tend to use when faced with such decisions.

Clients who maintain a high level of engagement with their nondominant culture of origin and who reject opportunities to engage in and affiliate with the dominant culture are more likely to hold the traditional values and beliefs of their culture of origin. In contrast, other clients may reject the norms and traditional values of their nondominant culture of origin and fully embrace the values and beliefs of the dominant culture. One client may embrace a collectivist worldview and approach to career decision making, and another client from the same culture

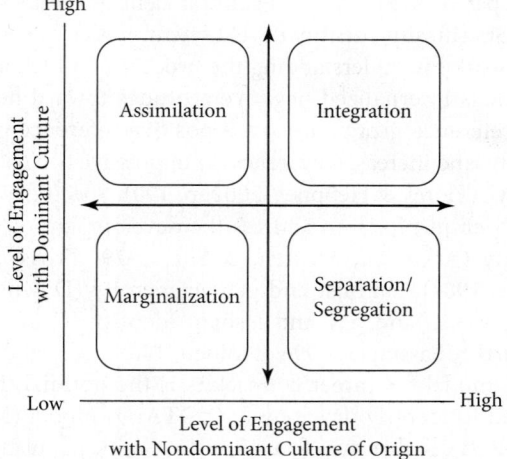

FIGURE 6.5 Strategies of Acculturation
Source: Based on Berry, J.W. (1997). Immigration, acculturation, and adaptation. *Applied Psychology: An International Review,* 46, 5-68. Berry, J.W. (1997).

may have adopted an individualistic worldview and approach to career decision making. Although these clients may share a culture of origin, they may differ significantly with regard to acculturation strategies.

As already noted, these acculturation strategies may have an impact on career decision making. Research findings also suggest some relationship between acculturation strategies and self-efficacy beliefs, educational aspirations and expectations, career aspirations, the value placed on work that allows for the implementation of self-concept, and job performance ratings (Flores, Navarro, & DeWitz, 2008; Miller & Kerlow-Myers, 2009). For example, describing youth who have thus far utilized a separation strategy of acculturation, Constantine, Kindaichi, and Miville (2005) indicated that "Black and Latino youth who have strong feelings of ethnic loyalty may anticipate and experience profound social costs in the pursuit of higher education" and they may also "experience a sense of disloyalty to their peer group and community in pursuing college" (p. 264). To the extent that members of nondominant cultures perceive college attendance as requiring a high level of engagement—and possible assimilation or integration—with the dominant culture, preferred acculturation strategies may have a profound impact on the perception of viable and desirable educational and career aspirations.

Identity Development

Differences within cultural groups may also be understood in the context of identity development. A course you take that is dedicated to multicultural counseling will surely teach, in great depth, about identity development models. These models provide a means by which to conceptualize how a person's experience of cultural identity develops over time. Specifically, identity development models "provide a framework for understanding the process by which a person sheds internalized negative attitudes toward her/his own reference group, accepts a positive reference group identity, and increases awareness of oppressive behaviors in society" (Flores & Heppner, 2002, p. 190). Specific models have been put forth to address the development of racial identity (Atkinson, Morten, & Sue, 1979; Cross, 1971; Helms, 1984), feminist and gender identity (Downing & Rush, 1985), and gay and lesbian identity (Cass, 1979; McCarn & Fassinger, 1996; Troiden, 1989). A particularly useful model for career counselors is the optimal theory applied to identify development (OTAID) model (Myers et al., 1991). Rather than focusing on a specific population or type of identity development, the OTAID model is inclusive and is designed to address the identity development of a wide range of cultural identities subject to oppression by dominant cultural groups. Advantages of this model include its relevance to the full range of nondominant groups identified earlier in Table 6.1 and its recognition that our various identities (e.g., race, sex, disability status, social class) are "interrelated and interdependent" (Myers et al., 1991, p. 59).

Research findings suggest that identity development is important to the development of self-efficacy beliefs for members of nondominant racial and ethnic groups as well as for females (Gushue & Whitson, 2006). Tovar-Murray, Jenifer, Andrusyk, D'Angelo, and King (2012) reported research findings that "demonstrated that African American college students who have a strong racial and ethnic identity reported higher levels of vocational identity, career hopes, and career decidedness" (p. 260). Research findings also highlight the importance of identity development to one's ability to manage and overcome potential career barriers such as sexism, racism, and discrimination (Byars-Winston, 2010; Gushue & Whitson, 2006). Byars-Winston explained that higher levels of identity development "helps African Americans adapt to their environment" by serving the functions of "bonding, buffering, and bridging" (Byars-Winston, 2010, p. 446). High levels of identity development, for example, allow for bridging because individuals with strong identity development are more secure in their own identity and more comfortable interacting effectively with members of the dominant society.

UNDERSTANDING YOUR CLIENT AS A CULTURAL BEING

Although a more thorough discussion of differences within and between cultural groups is beyond the scope of this text, you should understand several basic concepts essential to understanding your client as a cultural being. First, rather than treat every client in a culture-blind fashion and focusing simply on individual differences, it is important to understand the role of culture in each client's life. Specifically, you will want to understand the various cultural groups with which each client identifies; the relative importance of each cultural identity on each client's overall sense of self; the cultural worldview, values, and norms that may guide each client; and the sociopolitical and socioeconomic realities that may inform each client's experience of the world. Second, you will want to recognize that the worldview, values, and norms of any given culture are not universally adopted by all members of that culture in the same way and that all members of a given culture do not experience the same sociopolitical and socioeconomic realities. Factors that influence any given person's adoption of and adherence to cultural norms include individual differences, immigration history and circumstances, level of acculturation, and stage of identity development.

Commenting on the importance of career counselors gaining an in-depth, nuanced understanding of each client that incorporates attention to cultural dimensions, Heppner and Fu (2010) stated, "[I]t is critical for counselors to not only understand that all vocational behavior is an act in context but more so to understand how to truly integrate the role of culture" into their understanding of the "choices and life journeys of their clients" (p. 488). Thus, you will benefit from using a systematic approach to exploring your clients' cultural identities and their implications for career development. The cultural formulation approach (CFA) provides such an approach.

The Cultural Formulation Approach

The CFA, initially introduced by the American Psychiatric Association (2000) as part of the *Diagnostic and Statistical Manual of Mental Disorders* (*DSM-IV-TR*), has since been adapted for the profession of career counseling (Leong, 2010). In addition to being offered as a general model for career assessment (Leong, 2010), the CFA has also been applied to specific racial and ethnic groups. For example, it has been applied to career counseling with African Americans (Byars-Winston, 2010), Native Americans/ American Indians (Juntunen & Cline, 2010), Asian Americans (Leong, Hardin, & Gupta, 2010), Latina and Latino clients (Flores, Ramos, & Kanagui, 2010), and international students (Arthur & Popadiuk, 2010).

A CULTURAL FORMULATION APPROACH TO CAREER ASSESSMENT. Leong's (2010) cultural formulation approach to career assessment called for career counselors to incorporate five elements into their assessment of clients (see Table 6.2). Specifically, Leong (2010) and his colleagues (Arthur & Popadiuk, 2010; Byars-Winston, 2010; Flores et al., 2010; Juntunen & Cline, 2010; Leong, Hardin, & Gupta, 2010) encouraged counselors to consider five cultural dimensions when developing a case conceptualization of their career counseling clients. They advised counselors to begin by considering each client's cultural identity. First and foremost, this involves understanding which cultural dimensions are most salient to a client's sense of self and assessing the degree to which a client identifies with the dominant culture (Leong, Hardin, & Gupta, 2010). Next, they recommended that counselors seek an understanding of how each client's career problems might be conceptualized within his or her culture. Particularly important to this portion of the CFA is determining whether clients adhere to an individualistic or collectivist approach to "self-construal" and to career decision making (Leong, 2010, p. 380). Also, career counselors should not assume a shared understanding of career, work, and jobs but should instead invite clients to articulate their ideas about such concepts as well as about the career development process in general (Flores et al., 2010, p. 414).

Explaining the third step of the CFA, Leong and his colleagues drew attention to the importance of assessing how contextual and psychosocial factors specific to each client's culture might contribute to the client's sense of self as well as her or his career problems. Using terms from social cognitive career theory (SCCT), such factors include both distal and proximal contextual factors (Lent et al., 1994). With regard to distal factors affecting a client's sense of self, Leong explained that a "restriction in the range of possible selves occurs both directly (e.g., by explicitly being told that women should not be ambitious or that Asian Americans should not go into theater)" as well as "indirectly (e.g., by the lack of available role models for a particular path" (Leong, 2010, p. 382). Proximal contextual factors may include a lack of financial resources for additional education, a perception of discriminatory hiring practices within a field of interest, or affiliation with a culture in which members are discouraged from seeking career or academic success.

The fourth element of the CFA involves a consideration of the implications of cultural dynamics on the development of an effective counseling relationship. It should come as no surprise that the level of cross-cultural trust is an important element related to the effectiveness of any counseling relationship. Simply knowing about cultural differences between a career counselor and client, however, does not allow one to predict the level of cross-cultural trust that will exist or develop. Addressing racial and/or ethnic differences between clients and counselors, Byars-Winston summarized the complexities affecting trust level:

> African Americans who are highly bonded to their in-group and have low interest or experience in bridging with out-groups may find it difficult working with non-Black therapists. Conversely, those who are highly bonded to an out-group (non-Black) or have high bridging (bicultural) skill may be comfortable working with non-Black therapists. (2010, p. 453)

TABLE 6.2 The Original Cultural Formulation Approach to Career Assessment

1. Cultural identity
2. Cultural conception of career problems
3. Cultural context and psychosocial environment
4. Cultural dynamics in the counseling relationship
5. Overall cultural assessment

Source: Based on Leong, F.T.L. (2010). A cultural formulation approach to career assessment and career counseling: Guest editor's introduction. *Journal of Career Development*, 37, 375–390.

In essence, this example points to the importance of understanding each client's stage of identity development and preferred acculturation strategy.

Being relevant and having a clue about sociopolitical realities and cultural values can also be important to the establishment of one's credibility as a career counselor. For example, Daire, LaMothe, and Fuller (2007) suggested that white counselors working with black college students be certain to address, in the first session, socioeconomic gaps and point to career counseling as a means by which to pursue jobs of higher income and status. They suggested that addressing these important topics in the first session may "generate client 'buy in' for career counseling services" and increase the likelihood of African Americans returning for a second session (p. 279). Orienting clients to the career counseling process, understanding their expectations, and respecting worldview differences (especially with regard to individualism versus collectivism) are also important to the development of an effective, cross-cultural career counseling relationship (Flores et al., 2010).

Leong and his colleagues suggested that these elements be supplemented with an overall cultural assessment. Together, these elements (shown in Table 6.2) constituted the substance of Leong's 2010 cultural formulation approach to career assessment for use in developing case conceptualization.

THE CULTURAL FORMULATION INTERVIEW IN CAREER COUNSELING. What was lacking in Leong's (2010) approach, as well as the original Cultural Formulation Approach featured in the DSM-IV (APA, 2000) upon which Leong's approach was based, was a specific strategy for discussing cultural issues with clients. This omission was remedied with the publication of the DSM-5 (American Psychiatric Association, 2013). The DSM-5 includes a Cultural Formulation Interview that is useful in understanding cultural dimensions of people's psychological problems. Instead of only addressing content areas involved in a cultural formulation, the DSM-5 includes a Cultural Formulation Interview. Specifically, this interview is organized into four sections: (1) cultural definition of the problem; (2) cultural perceptions of cause, context and support; (3) cultural factors affecting self-coping and past help seeking; and (4) cultural factors affecting current help seeking. For each section, the interview protocol provides the counselor with background information, specific verbatim questions to ask, and guidelines for probes. Whereas this interview is specifically intended for use by counselors in assessing cultural issues associated with mental disorders and related treatment, it can be adapted for use in the career counseling process. Toward this end, in Table 6.3, I offer the following examples of questions which may be used in a career counseling context.

Culture and Career Genograms

Another way in which career counselors can understand their clients as cultural beings is to engage them in creating and discussing a culture and career genogram. A genogram is a visual diagram of an individual's family history, generally spanning at least three generations. Similar to a family tree, genograms include biographical data such as important dates for each individual (birth, death) as well as for relationships (marriages, divorces, separations, etc.). When used in the context of family therapy, genograms include additional symbols to identify the nature of relationships between people (i.e., distant, close, enmeshed) as well as the presence of physical disabilities and/or mental disorders.

Although originating within the field of family therapy (Bowen, 1978), genograms have since been modified for a wide variety of purposes within the counseling profession (Magnuson & Shaw, 2003). For example, genograms have been used in counseling to (1) understand cultural norms within a family system and cultural influences on an individual (Hardy & Laszloffy, 1995; Kelly, 1990 and (2) conceptualize career-related patterns within a family system in order to facilitate career development and decision making (Chope, 2005; Malott & Magnuson, 2004; Moon, Coleman, McCollum, Nelson, & Jenson-Scott, 1993; Okiishi, 1987). Combining these two approaches (understanding cultural norms and conceptualizing career-related patterns), genograms have also been recommended for effective multicultural career counseling (Kakiuchi & Weeks, 2009; Penick, 2000; Sueyoshi, Rivera, & Ponterotto, 2001).

Because the creation and discussion of a culture and career genogram is an interactive exercise involving a visual display, both clients and counselors tend to find the activity nonthreatening, enjoyable, and enlightening (Magnuson & Shaw, 2003; Moon et al., 1993). To introduce the activity, counselors briefly explain the nature and purpose of a genogram. Counselors can also describe it as a special kind of family tree that will be used to understand cultural and familial messages about career development.

COLLECTION OF INFORMATION. Next, it is useful to gather information from the client about his or her family members (Chope, 2005). In doing so, you may want to complete a chart, such as the one shown in Table 6.4,

TABLE 6.3 A Cultural Formulation Interview for Career Counseling

Career Concerns

The initial step in developing a cultural formulation of your clients' career concerns is to inquire about their definition of the problem. Such questions prompt clients to describe their concerns in their own words:

- Using your own words, how would you describe your career concerns?
- If you were to explain your career concerns to your family or friends, what would you say? Also, what would you say is causing or contributing to your career difficulties?
- Conversely, how might your family or friends describe your career situation? Also, what would they say is causing or contributing to your career difficulties?

Contextual Supports and Barriers

Generally speaking, people with career concerns don't exist in a vacuum. Therefore, the next step is to inquire about your clients' perception of any stressors and supports related to their career problem, including those that may be related to their cultural identity (American Psychiatric Association, 2013).

- In dealing with your career concerns, to whom have you been able to turn for support? What other sources of support do you have in your life?
- Besides your career concerns, what other stressors do you have in your life?
- What contextual challenges or barriers will you need to overcome in order to resolve your career concerns or achieve your career goals?
- Let's talk about cultural identity. By that, I am referring to race, ethnicity, the primary language you speak, gender, religion, sexual orientation and disability status. How would you describe your cultural identity? Which of these are most important in the way you define yourself?
- Are there any ways in which you believe your cultural identity affects your career situation, either positively or negatively?

Approaches to Coping

Finally, it is essential to explore cultural dimensions that may affect your clients' coping strategies. Coping strategies may involve autonomous efforts to cope as well as a more collectivist approach of seeking help from others.

- Up until this point, what have you done on your own to address your career concern?
- Up until this point, what other sources of help have you sought in an attempt to deal with your career concern?
- Have your friends or family suggested any other coping strategies or sources of help?
- What prompted you to seek career counseling? How is career counseling viewed by your friends and family or within your culture?
- Do you have any concerns that cultural differences may interfere with my ability to help you?

---

during a session or assign it to the client as an outside activity. In either case, additional rows should be added as necessary. My personal preference is to assign the chart as an outside activity because it allows clients to consult with family members and thus gather information they may not know. For example, when doing a cultural and career genogram in my class, one student commented about how little she knew about her relatives' occupations. As we talked, it became apparent that many of her relatives did not consider their occupation to be central to their identity. Although she knew many of them liked their jobs, she sensed that this was due to the social aspects and positive relationships they enjoyed with their coworkers.

As a practical tip, be sure to explain the chart thoroughly to clients if you ask them to complete it outside of session. Although the Gender and Age columns are self-explanatory, you will want to explain that the Culture column refers to whatever aspect of culture is most salient to each individual. For one family member, being African American may be most salient. For another, being Baptist may be most salient. And for yet another, being female

TABLE 6.4 Family Information for Use in Developing Culture and Career Genograms

	Name	Gender	Age	Culture	Education	Occupation
Siblings						
Parents and/or stepparents						
Cousins						
Aunts and uncles						
Grandparents						

may be most salient. The Education column is designed to elicit information about the highest level of education completed and, if appropriate, the area of study (e.g., college major, occupational certification). The Occupation column should be completed with information about what each family member does or did for a living. It is important to communicate that parenting and homemaking may also be recorded in this column for family members who do not or did not work outside the home. This column may be left blank for those family members (e.g., children, adolescents, and college students) who have not yet entered the workforce.

CREATION OF THE BASIC GENOGRAM. The next step in developing a culture and career genogram involves the sketching or computer generation of a diagram that captures the information gathered in the previous step. Traditionally, genograms feature a common set of symbols. Although use of these symbols isn't entirely necessary and I have certainly developed genograms with elementary school students by drawing stick figures, the symbols are helpful because they serve as a type of shorthand when communicating with other mental health professionals. Figure 6.6 identifies some of the most commonly used genogram symbols.

Two additional customs are worth noting. First, in representing heterosexual couples, it is customary to place the male on the left and the female on the right. Second, in representing sibling groups, it is customary to place children on a continuum from oldest on the left to youngest on the right.

Generally speaking, it is most effective to draw or generate the genogram during a session, with the counselor doing the sketching in consultation with the client. If developing a three-generation genogram, you will want to plan on five lines or rows, with the top row consisting of the client's grandparents, the second line representing aunts and uncles, the third row identifying cousins, the fourth row representing the client's parents, and the bottom row consisting of the client and his or her siblings (Penick, 2000).

Cultural Dimensions of Career Development and Career Counseling   **117**

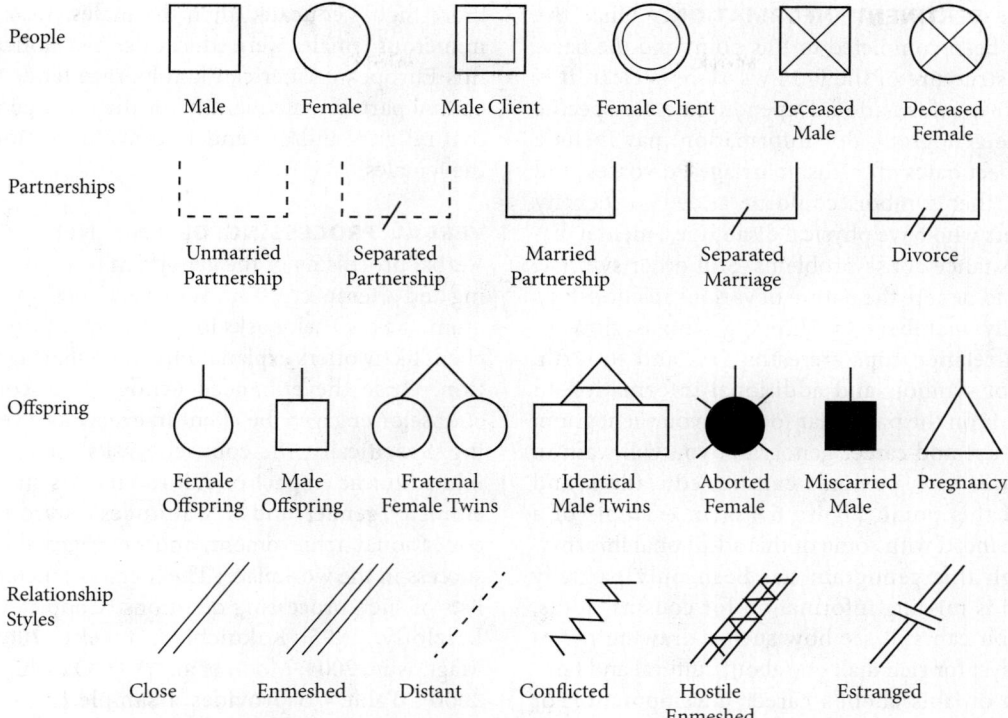

FIGURE 6.6 Common Genogram Symbols

An example of a five-line genogram is featured in Figure 6.7. In this genogram, you can tell that the client is a 48-year-old female who is the oldest of her sibling group. She has two brothers who are identical twins and a half-sister. On the next line up, you can see that her parents were divorced; her father subsequently had a significant, unmarried relationship resulting in the birth of the client's half-sister; and the client's mother is deceased. On the third line, you can see that the client has two cousins, both born to a paternal uncle. On the second line, you can see that each of her parents had a single sibling. On the first row, you can see that the client's only living grandparent is her paternal grandmother.

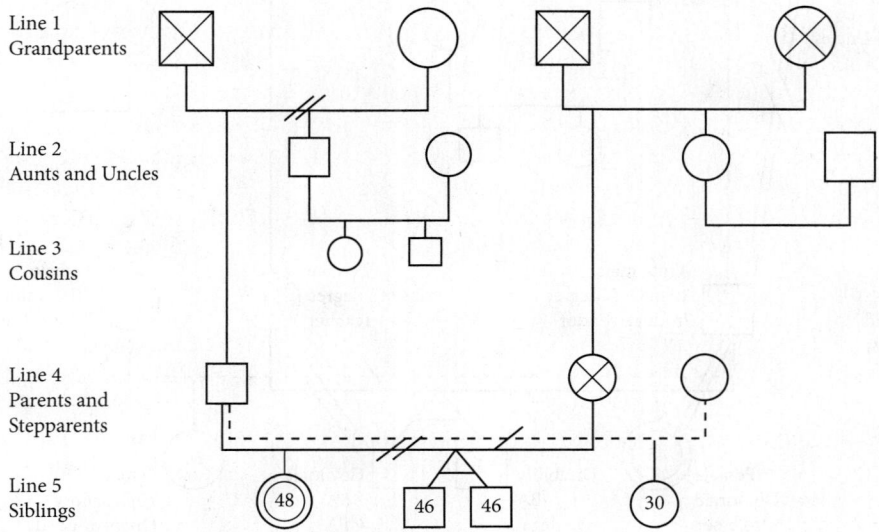

FIGURE 6.7 Basic Five-Line Genogram

ADDITION OF PERTINENT INFORMATION. Once the genogram has been completed to this point and the basic demographic structure of the family system is clear, it is time to add other information. Depending on the specific purpose of the genogram, this information may include symbols to reflect dates of births, marriages, divorces, and separations. Other symbols could be added to identify family members who have physical disabilities, mental disorders, or substance abuse problems. Still other symbols may be added to denote the nature of various relationships between family members by showing who is close to whom, which relationships are estranged, and so forth. Your choice of symbols and additional information to include depends on the particular focus of your genogram.

In a culture and career genogram, you will want to add notes about each person's culture, education, and occupation at this point. Figure 6.8 is an example of a genogram enhanced with some of this additional information. Although this genogram has been only partially enhanced and is missing information for cousins, aunts, and uncles, you can still see how such a drawing might serve as a catalyst for rich dialogue about cultural and family influences on this client's career development. For example, notice the pattern in which the females tend to be more highly educated than the males. Also observe that numerous females were educators. Also notice that, within this European American family, race tends to be a more central part of male identify for the older generations and that religion and/or gender seems to be more salient for the females.

VERBAL PROCESSING OF ENHANCED GENOGRAM. Verbal processing of the genogram is important both during and after its creation. While enhancing the basic genogram, the counselor asks for pertinent information and the client likely offers explanations while sharing this information. Once the enhanced genogram is completed, the counselor engages the client in even more verbal processing. Specifically, the counselor asks the client questions related to the impact of cultural factors such as race and ethnicity, gender, and SES; attitudes toward education and educational achievement; and messages about work and success in the workplace. The literature includes abundant lists of such processing questions (Chope, 2005; Hardy & Laszloffy, 1995; Kakuichi & Weeks, 2009; Malott & Magnuson, 2004; Moon et al., 1993; Okiishi, 1987; Penick, 2000). Table 6.5 provides a sample of such questions, organized by topic.

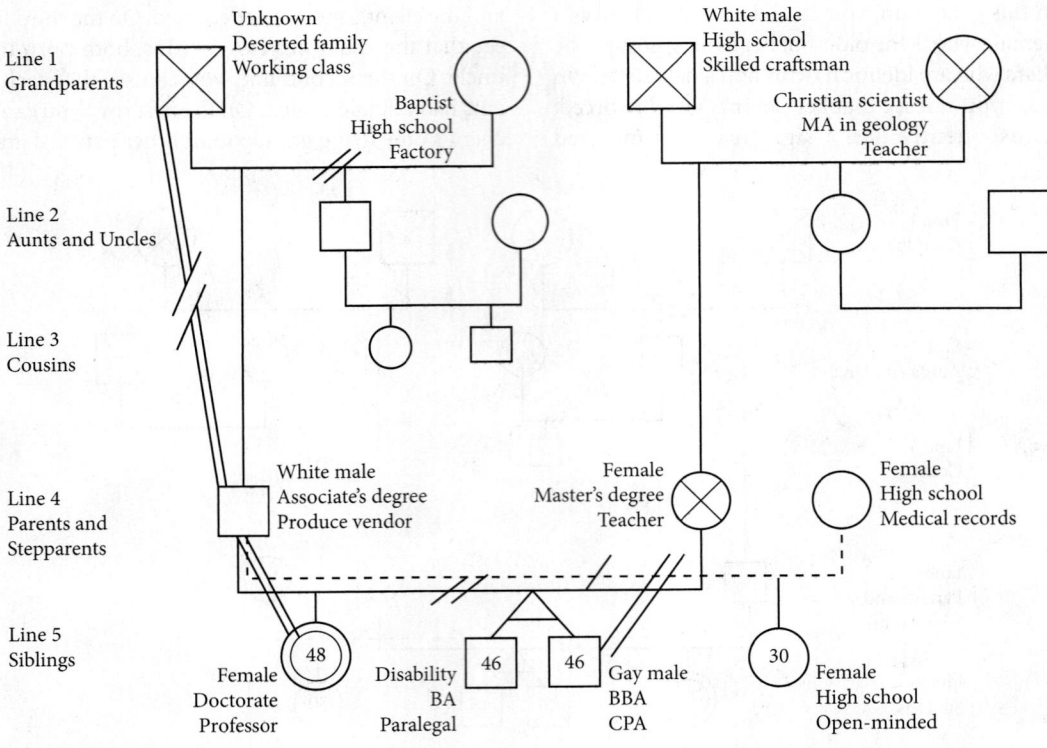

FIGURE 6.8 Enhanced Five-Line Genogram

TABLE 6.5 Sample Processing Questions for Culture and Career Genograms

Culture

- What are the major cultural groups represented in your family?
- How are success and failure defined in these cultures?
- What cultural expectations and views on education are you aware of?
- What cultural expectations and views on work or career are you aware of?
- Are there certain types of work or careers that are most valued within your culture?
- What types of opportunities do you perceive for people within your culture?
- What types of barriers do you perceive for people within your culture?
- How has oppression affected the cultural groups with which you identify?
- What prejudices or stereotypes do these cultural groups have about themselves?
- What prejudices or stereotypes do others have about these cultural groups?
- What issues divide members within your cultural groups?

Family

- Who would you identify as the leaders in your family?
- Whose opinions seem to matter most?
- How are success and failure defined in your family?
- Are educational and career expectations the same for each family member? If not, how do they differ?
- How have expectations differed in your family depending on gender, disability, or other cultural factors?
- How are these expectations communicated?
- How are career decisions made within your family?
- Are there any family rules or expectations that might limit your career options?
- How has your family viewed education? How is this communicated?
- Are there certain types of work or careers that are most valued within your family?
- What would your family identify as your strengths and weaknesses?
- What would family members say about you?

Role Models

- Who in your family is viewed as being most successful?
- Which family members do you view as role models? What do you admire most about them?
- Whom within your cultural groups do you view as role models? What do you admire most about them?
- In what ways do you see yourself as similar to these role models?
- In what ways do you see yourself as different from these role models?
- What types of support are available from these role models?

Sources: Chope, 2005; Hardy & Laszloffy, 1995; Kakuichi & Weeks, 2009; Malott & Magnuson, 2004; Moon et al., 1993; Okiishi, 1987; Penick, 2000.

Waldron and Loomis (2000) offered another strategy for exploring these issues. Describing their approach to processing genograms, these authors recommend that counselors invite clients:

> to imagine what each of [their family members] would tell [them] about "what to be." Then ask [them] to reflect on their family members' attitudes about work-related issues and, on a separate sheet of paper, to complete the following sentences for each of three to five people on their family trees:
>
> Work is . . .
>
> Money is . . .
>
> Success is . . .
>
> To be a good person . . .
>
> My advice to [you] about work is . . . (p. 69)

These questions and prompts are intended only to provide ideas for processing any given client's cultural and career genogram. As you begin to integrate genograms into career counseling, do not feel obliged to ask every question on this list, to limit yourself to these questions, or to follow exactly the prompts offered by Waldron and Loomis (2000). Instead, strive for enough familiarity with such questions and prompts to trust yourself to customize your verbal processing to your individual client's situation and needs.

PUTTING IT ALL TOGETHER

Both the CFA, which is based on the *DSM-IV* and adapted by Leong (2010) for use in career assessment, and the more recent cultural formulation interview in career counseling, which is based on the *DSM-5* and modified by me for use in career counseling, provide strategies for understanding your clients as cultural beings. Cultural and career genograms offer yet another strategy. After orienting your client to the purpose and nature of genograms and gathering background information, develop the genogram in close consultation with your client. Verbal processing of the genogram is essential to gaining a deeper understanding of your client and to helping your client gain insight about the cultural and familial factors that may influence career aspirations, career decision-making processes, and definitions of career success. Indeed, although having a textbook understanding of cultural concepts involving within- and between-group differences and developing an understanding of your client as a cultural being may be interesting in its own right, the reason these topics are important for career counselors is that cultural dimensions can have a very real impact on a person's career development, approaches to career decision making, work experiences, and experience of the career counseling process. We'll investigate these topics more closely in the next section.

UNDERSTANDING THE POTENTIAL IMPACT OF CULTURE

In the context of career counseling, culture may have an impact on three areas: (1) career development, (2) career decision making, and (3) one's experience of the workplace and career success.

Potential Impact of Culture on Career Development

When conceptualizing a client's career development, including early and persisting career aspirations as well as eventual career choices, counselors should recognize the potential impact of cultural dimensions. As shown in Figure 6.9, career development may be affected by cultural norms, societal messages, sociopolitical realities, and socioeconomic factors.

With regard to cultural norms, it is particularly important to consider how clients may have been socialized differently depending on their cultural identities. This socialization often results in the adoption of cultural norms that may influence one's beliefs about what constitutes success in life and about whether work and career are central to one's identity, success, and happiness.

In addition to being subject to within-group cultural norms, individuals are also affected by stereotypes and broader societal messages about what others like them can and should do occupationally. Depending on their identification with dominant or nondominant cultural groups, individuals will also experience differing availability of role models who resemble them and be exposed to different stereotypes about their cultural group(s). This may result in the circumscription process described by Gottfredson (1981) and likely affects career aspirations.

Differences in sociopolitical realities may also have a profound impact on a person's career development. As discussed earlier in this chapter, membership in dominant or nondominant cultural groups likely involves different experiences of the world with regard to opportunity structure. These different experiences involve varying levels of privilege and exposure to discrimination, which have implications for one's perceptions of contextual barriers and supports (Lent et al., 1994). Such factors may play a supporting or limiting role in the establishment of vocational expectations for oneself.

As discussed earlier, socioeconomic factors are likely to have a direct effect on the quality of educational resources and experiences one has early in life. The fact is that poor children tend to live in impoverished communities and attend underfunded schools (Blustein et al., 2002). Educational experiences play an important role in an individual's development of academic and career-related skills and in the development of self-efficacy beliefs and vocational expectations. Through their correlation with inferior educational experiences, socioeconomic factors play an important role in a person's career development (Baum & Flores, 2011).

The takeaway message is that culture can have both a direct and indirect impact on an individual's career development, including the relative valuing of educational achievement and career pursuits as well as one's career aspirations, objective skills and self-efficacy beliefs, and vocational expectations. Through such mechanisms, the very foundation of one's career development process is

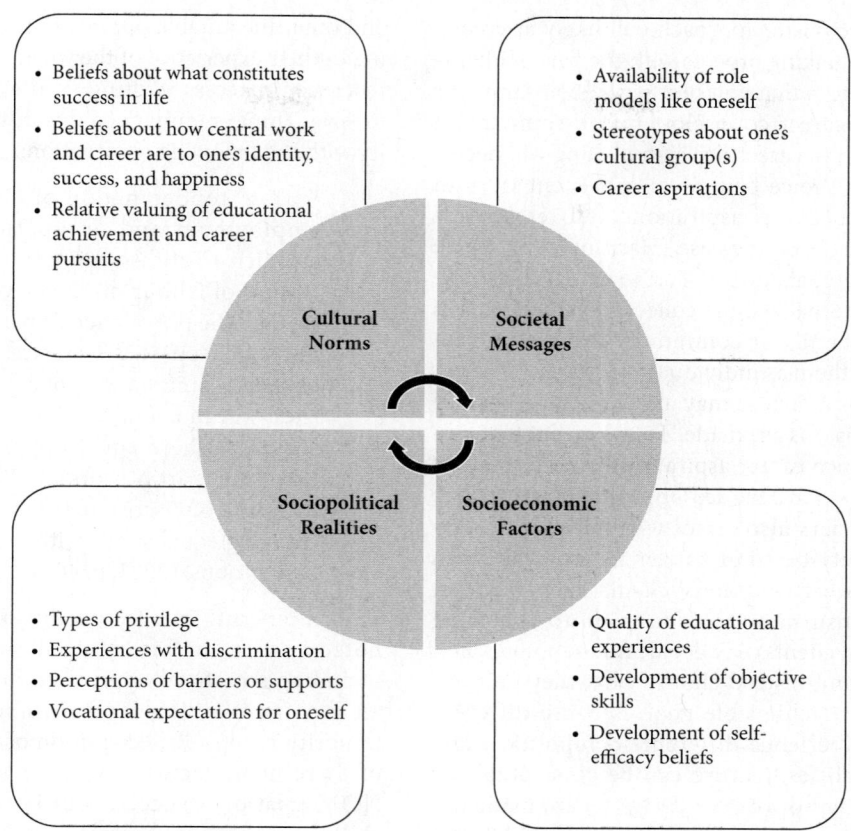

FIGURE 6.9 The Potential Impact of Culture on Career Development

established within a cultural context. Ultimately, the educational and career paths of interest and available to an individual are influenced by these factors.

Potential Impact of Culture on Career Decision Making

Cultural factors may also have an impact on the career decision-making process. Specifically, cultural factors may influence whether, how, and what career decisions are made. Let's begin by examining how cultural factors may affect whether career decisions are made. This involves the concept of volition or personal agency. Indeed, the very idea of career decision making presupposes volition, or feeling like one has opportunities to make choices and exercise personal agency. Although this premise serves as a major foundation of the profession of career counseling, à la Parsons' *Choosing a Vocation* (1909), Blustein and his colleagues argue that the idea of proactively making career choices in an attempt to implement one's self-concept "does not apply to all workers, particularly those forced to take any job available to them in order to earn a living" (Bluestein at al., 2011, p. 217). In fact, they suggest that the concept of volition is applicable only to a minority of workers around the world: workers who enjoy the privilege associated with being a member of a dominant culture within a developed nation (Blustein, 2001; Blustein et al., 2011). Therefore, career counselors should consider the possible impact of socioeconomic and sociopolitical factors on each client's ability to exercise volition and engage in a career decision-making, as opposed to a job-hunting, process.

When one can exercise volition and make career decisions, his or her culture's preference for individualism or collectivism may affect how career decisions are made (Mau, 2004). To summarize our already extensive discussion of these worldviews, clients who subscribe to an individualistic approach will likely approach the career decision-making process with the goal of identifying a career direction that will be personally satisfying. Their own individual interests, work values, skills, and personality traits will be among the most important factors in selecting career paths of interest. In contrast, clients who subscribe to a collectivistic approach will likely approach the career decision-making process with the goal of identifying a career direction that will best serve their family or community. Some career counselors may assume that a collectivist approach to career decision making will necessarily result in the choice being less consistent with an individual client's personal aspirations, but researchers have not found this to be the case (Hartung et al., 2010; Leong, 2010; Leong et al., 2010). To the extent that these individuals have internalized the collective values, what is beneficial to their family or community will feel subjectively rewarding to them as individuals.

Finally, cultural factors may also have an influence on what career decisions are made. To the extent that cultural factors influence career aspirations, they also affect what career decisions are made. Opportunity structures and perceived barriers also affect whether career decisions are opportunity-based or barrier-based. Even when aspiring to lofty career ambitions, clients may face what they perceive as insurmountable barriers to achieving them. In such cases, clients may decide not to pursue their ideal career goals and instead choose what they perceive as a more realistic, achievable goal. Because different cultural groups experience different sociopolitical and socioeconomic realities, culture can be conceptualized not only as affecting how career decisions are made but also as determining what career decisions are made. This is reflected in concepts such as the tolerable effort boundary (Gottfredson, 1981) and proximal contextual barriers (Lent et al., 1994).

Potential Impact of Culture on Career Success

A third major way in which cultural dimensions can affect our clients is with regard to their experience of the world of work and ultimately their career success. Although a pure meritocracy in which success at work is determined only by a worker's skills and effort may represent an ideal (Tomei, 2003), the reality is that achieving career success is much more complicated than simply having the skills and working hard. As you have learned, career success is also related to factors such as the goodness of fit between a worker's skills and the skill requirements of the occupation (Dawis & Lofquist, 1984), other life roles that compete for a worker's time and attention (Super, 1980), and even happenstance events that may result serendipitously in a worker being in the right place at the right time (Krumboltz, 2009).

EVIDENCE OF DISCRIMINATION AND INEQUITY. Sadly, that is not the all of it. In addition, cultural dimensions involving workers' experiences of oppression, discrimination, and other inequitable opportunity structures also contribute to their experience of the world of work and ultimately to career success. Writing in the *International Labour Review*, Tomei summarized this disturbing, universal reality with the following observation:

> Formal condemnation of discrimination in employment and occupation is universal and firm. Yet discrimination is an enduring feature of labour markets everywhere in the world. The prevalence of particular forms of discrimination—based on race, sex or religions—or their manifestations may vary across countries, within countries, over time. But even in societies where equal opportunity practices have been part of working life for some time, members of discriminated groups are far from enjoying equal status with members of dominant groups. (2003, p. 401)

This is certainly true for people in the United States. As noted earlier in this chapter, sociopolitical realities, including structural oppression and discrimination, are all too familiar to many members of nondominant, minority groups. In recognition of the differential impact of these many factors on career success, Brown noted, "[O]ccupational success will be related to job-related skills acquired in formal and informal educational settings, job-related attitudes, SES, participation in the work role, and the extent to which discrimination is experienced" (2002, p. 52).

At this point, I would not be surprised if you have what I refer to as a "yes, but" reaction such as, "Yes, I know there has been a long history of oppression, but discrimination? That's illegal." You are right that there has been a long history of oppression. You are right that many forms of workplace discrimination in the United States are illegal. In fact, you will be learning about several laws against workplace discrimination when you read Chapter 7, which focuses on what career counselors need to know about employment law. However (and I know you saw this one coming), your "yes, but" reaction is ultimately wrong because it makes an assumption that laws against workplace discrimination are followed consistently. Let's take a look.

Although you may not know the details right now, you probably know that it is illegal in the United States to discriminate in the workplace. As a preview of what you will learn in Chapter 7, one of the most important laws prohibiting discrimination in the workplace is the Civil Rights Act of 1964. Specifically, Title VII of this law, "prohibits the refusal or failure to hire any individual, or the discrimination against any individual with respect to compensation, terms, conditions, or privileges of employment because of that individual's race, color, religion, sex, or national origin" (Cihon & Castagnera, 2011, p. 114). You are right: Employment discrimination on the basis of factors such as race, religion, and sex is indeed illegal.

A full 40 years following the passage of this landmark legislation, Bertrand and Mullainathan (2004) published experimental research demonstrating the persistence of discrimination in the hiring process. In this fascinating but disturbing article, the authors report on an empirical research study in which they sent out 5,000 résumés in response to 1,300 job postings for a wide variety of jobs. They sent out two levels of résumés: qualified and highly qualified. These résumés were identical except for two variables: the applicant's name and address. With regard to the name, the researchers randomly assigned "very White sounding names (such as Emily Walsh or Greg Baker) to half the résumés and very African American names (such as Lakisha Washington or Jamal Jones to the other half" (p. 992). They also randomly assigned the address so that some of these hypothetical applicants lived in "wealthier (or more educated or Whiter) neighborhoods" (p. 992).

The results of this study provided astounding evidence for discrimination in the hiring process. Applicants with the "white-sounding" names were 50% more likely to receive calls for interviews. Living in "better" neighborhoods helped white applicants much more than African American applicants with regard to callbacks. Although the higher quality résumés for both groups were more likely to result in calls for interviews, the "gap between Whites and African Americans [actually widened] with résumé quality" (Bertrand & Mullainathan, 2004, p. 992). These results provide compelling evidence for what many people of color already know as a result of firsthand or vicarious experience: Even though it has been illegal for more than 50 years, discrimination in the hiring process still exists. Obviously, getting hired has great implications for career success.

"But what about compensation and advancement," you ask. Good question. Earlier in this chapter, I presented recent data demonstrating significant gaps in income across race, gender, and disability status (Figure 6.1); wealth (Figure 6.2); and poverty rates (Figure 6.3). These data make it clear that career success, at least as measured by these financial indicators, is experienced differentially by various cultural groups. An important question, however, is about the source of these gaps. You may wonder whether these gaps are due to career choices people make with regard to postsecondary education, types of employment sought, or hours worked. In other words, are these gaps due to factors that just happen to correlate with cultural demographics or are they due to discrimination?

The American Association for University Women (2013) addressed this question with regard to gender pay gaps:

> After accounting for college major, occupation, economic sector, hours worked, months unemployed since graduation, GPA [grade point average], type of undergraduate institution, institution selectivity, age, geographical region, and marital status, *Graduating to a Pay Gap* found that a 7 percent difference in the earnings of male and female college graduates one year after graduation was still unexplained. Similarly, *Behind the Pay Gap* found a 12 percent unexplained difference in earnings among full-time workers 10 years after college graduation. (p. 8)

Even after being hired, therefore, it appears that nondominant groups lose ground with respect to the pay gap.

In addition, women, people of color, and people with disabilities face challenges with regard to other forms of advancement. Based on the seminal work *Men and Women of the Corporation,* in which the concept of the glass ceiling was first articulated (Kanter, 1977), the U.S. Department of Labor created a Federal Glass Ceiling Commission. This commission described the glass ceiling as "the unseen, yet unbreachable barrier that keeps minorities and women from rising to the upper rungs of the corporate ladder, regardless of their qualifications or achievements" (Federal Glass Ceiling Commission, 1995a, p. 4) and labeled this as "discrimination" (p. 5). Examining the composition of company leadership positions within the Fortune 500 companies, the commission found that 95% or more of the senior managers in Fortune 500 companies were white males and also noted that, "where there *are* women and minorities in high places, their compensation is lower. For example, African American men with professional degrees earn 79% of the amount earned by white males who hold the same degrees and are in the same job categories" (Federal Glass Ceiling Commission, 1995b, p. iv).

These reports are dated, but similar findings have been published more recently. Calvert Investments, Inc. (2013) studied the companies comprising Standard & Poor's 100 (S&P 100) and found that, despite the fact that many of these companies had implemented diversity policies and reported actively recruiting minorities, a huge racial and gender gap still existed at the highest management levels. In 56% of these companies, not a single female or person of color was among the highest paid executives. Similarly, a recent study on the composition of Fortune 500 company corporate boards of directors found that 83.4% of the seats are held by males and 86.7% of the seats are held by Caucasians (Alliance for Board Diversity, 2012). It appears that the so-called glass ceiling (Kanter, 1977) has yet to be cracked and much more progress is needed to achieve the vision reflected in the 1964 civil rights legislation.

RESPONDING EFFECTIVELY TO CULTURAL DIMENSIONS IN THE CAREER COUNSELING PROCESS

As we conclude the content portion of this chapter, I offer some closing thoughts about responding effectively to cultural dimensions in the career counseling process. I've framed these closing thoughts as tips, which are listed in Table 6.6 and explained in the following subsections.

Tip 1: Be Aware of Yourself and the World Around You

My first tip is to strive toward increasing awareness of yourself and the world around you. To be prepared to respond to clients in a culturally effective manner, it is essential that you have an awareness of yourself as a cultural being, which includes awareness of how you identify across multiple dimensions of cultural identity (race/ethnicity, immigration and citizenship status, social class, gender, gender identity, sexual orientation, disability status, religion), as well as an awareness of which of these dimensions are most salient to you. It is also important for you to recognize the dimensions in which you are a member of a dominant cultural group and the dimensions in which you are a member of a nondominant cultural group (see Table 6.1). Self-awareness also requires that you have an understanding of your socialization experiences within each of these cultural dimensions and that you recognize how these experiences have resulted in certain worldviews and biases.

This tip includes the importance of becoming aware of the world around you: developing an awareness of how various cultural groups may differ with regard to worldviews, beliefs about work, and definitions of success. My hope is that this chapter has equipped you well in this regard, but I also highly recommend a quick read entitled, *Gaining Cultural Competence in Career Counseling* (Evans, 2008). Evans's work contains a full three chapters devoted in increasing awareness.

Tip 2: Be Humble

Almost by definition, the process of socialization into a culture—whether from birth, as in the case of racial and/or ethnic culture, or later in life, as is the case when coming out as gay or lesbian—results in a shared view of normality. This shared view of normality "incorporates collective values, beliefs, norms, boundaries, and lifestyles that are cocreated with others who share similar worldviews comprising biological, psychosocial, historical, psychological, and other factors" (ACA, 2005, p. 20). In short, people who share your cultural identity and socialization experiences may very well share similar beliefs about what is normal. Although this is a natural outcome of the socialization process, it is essential that, as a counselor, you recognize that your definition of normal is not *the* definition of normal. It is *a* definition and, more specifically, your culture's definition. Rather than doom yourself to cross-cultural ineffectiveness, this tip cautions you to be humble and to recognize that you and your culture don't have a monopoly on the rules of life. By being humble, you become not only aware but also appreciative of others' perspectives. These other perspectives may involve collectivist approaches to life in general and, more specifically, to issues such as arranged marriages and approaches to career decision making. They may also involve beliefs about whether work should be central to one's identity, and what constitutes the good life and success.

Tip 3: Get a Grip on Reality

My third tip encourages to you "get a grip on reality." By this, I am referring to the importance of increasing awareness to extend beyond abstraction and to include some of the unpleasant, even gritty, realities that are correlated with cultural group memberships. For many members of dominant groups, this requires recognizing and owning the injustice of one's privilege as a European American born in the United States, as a male, as a temporarily able-bodied

---

TABLE 6.6 Tips for Responding Effectively to Cultural Dimensions in the Career Counseling Process

1. Be aware of yourself and the world around you.
2. Be humble.
3. Get a grip on reality.
4. Think critically.
5. Pay attention to nuances.
6. Actively seek to understand your client.
7. Take a two-pronged approach.
8. Keep learning.

person, as a Christian, as a heterosexual, or as a member of the middle or upper class. For others, it requires recognizing ways in which you may be more subject to and affected by oppression than you would like to think. For members of nondominant groups, it may involve sociopolitical development to increase one's "recognition of the connection between external sociopolitical events/issues and one's life" (Diemer & Hsieh, 2008, p. 259). For all of us, it requires breaking through any self-protective walls of denial and incorporating a deep awareness of the sociopolitical and socioeconomic realities that can so negatively affect the career development and success of nondominant groups.

Tip 4: Think Critically

My fourth tip emphasizes the importance of thinking critically. You have probably noticed that this chapter did not include any sections dedicated to summarizing what you need to know about various cultural subgroups (e.g., African Americans, gays and lesbians, people with disabilities). Although this approach has some merit, I consider it foolhardy to even attempt to distill such knowledge into just a few paragraphs about each group. Therefore, rather than tempt you with the false hope of broad generalizations, I chose to focus on addressing the underlying concepts (worldviews, sociopolitical realities, socioeconomic factors) that often, but not always, distinguish one cultural group from another. In doing so, I hope to have inspired you to think critically about how any given client's cultural group memberships are intertwined with these between-group differences. I also hope you will think critically about how various counseling theories may reflect culturally encapsulated assumptions and therefore need to be adjusted for appropriate use with a diverse clientele. As one example, your critical thinking should influence your use of career development theories and decision-making models so that you are appropriately inclusive of family and/or community concerns when working with clients who embrace a collectivist worldview. As another example, you should adhere to sound assessment strategies when selecting and using standardized tests by thinking critically about whether the norming sample is representative of your client's cultural groups (Evans, 2008).

Tip 5: Pay Attention to Nuances

My fifth tip represents an extension of the fourth. In addition to thinking critically about issues such as the applicability of different theories to clients from various cultures, you will also want to pay attention to nuances to avoid overgeneralizing. For example, although the professional literature may identify "the salience of collectivist influences for virtually all Asian cultures" (Leong et al., 2010, p. 466), this does not mean that collectivist beliefs will hold true for every Asian American client. Instead, it is important to recognize that variation exists within every cultural group. It is important to avoid reliance on stereotypes and generalizations and instead to pay attention to nuances. In this chapter, I introduced several sources of variation that may provide clues to such nuances. Specific sources of variation include identification with more than one dimension of culture (race and ethnicity, gender, sexual orientation, etc.); immigration history and citizenship status; acculturation strategies; stages of identity development; and, of course, a person's idiosyncratic personality characteristics and personal life experiences.

Tip 6: Actively Seek to Understand Your Client

To discover the nuances described above, it is essential that you actively seek to understand your client, not only as an individual but also as a cultural being. Rather than treat every client in a culture-blind fashion by focusing simply on individual differences, it is important to understand the role of culture in each client's life. Specifically, strive to understand the various cultural groups with which each client identifies; the relative importance of each cultural identity on each client's overall sense of self; the cultural worldview, values, and norms that may guide each client; and the sociopolitical and socioeconomic realities that may inform each client's experience of the world. This doesn't happen by osmosis. Instead, it requires you as a counselor to actively seek this understanding. In doing so, you may use a cultural formulation approach to conceptualize clients, ask questions associated with the cultural formulation interview to elicit information directly from clients, or engage clients in developing culture and career genograms. You might also choose other strategies such as the career-in-culture interview (Ponterotto, Rivera, & Sueyoshi, 2000), the ecological approach offered by King and Madsen (2007), the cultural accommodation model of counseling (Leong, 2011), career counseling with underserved populations (Pope, 2011), and the model for culture-infused career counseling (Arthur & Collins, 2011).

Tip 7: Take a Two-Pronged Approach

My seventh tip is to take a two-pronged approach when selecting helping strategies for use with clients. Possible helping strategies will be introduced in Chapter 9, in the context of understanding the career counseling process. For now, suffice it to say that one prong will involve client-centered interventions that seek to empower clients to exercise personal agency. Such interventions may focus on helping clients learn about themselves, build skills, improve self-efficacy beliefs, develop more accurate outcome expectations, explore areas of curiosity, reconstruct life narratives, employ decision-making strategies, and so forth. These client-centered interventions stem from the various theories presented in Chapters 2 through 5. Such strategies are important for use in the career counseling process. However, in seeking to enhance your effectiveness, especially with clients from nondominant groups, you will also benefit from including a second prong in your counseling approach. This second prong involves society-focused interventions designed to address sociopolitical and socioeconomic inequities. Rather than "locate" career problems only within a client, culturally effective career counselors recognize that many career problems involve external, societal factors as well. The second prong of helping strategies should address these external, societal factors. Such interventions may include recognizing and acknowledging both distal and proximal contextual barriers (Lent et al., 1994), helping clients increase their "awareness of and motivation to change social and economic inequality" (Diemer & Hsieh, 2008, p. 258), increasing social capital and tapping into resources (Diemer et al., 2010), and recognizing and addressing discrimination in the workplace (Evans, 2008). Each of these strategies focuses on addressing external, environmental factors to help a client.

Tip 8: Keep Learning

Finally, I would encourage you to keep learning. No one is ever fully knowledgeable and equipped to be entirely effective—cross-culturally or otherwise. This is true regardless of your cultural identity and background. It is naïve to think that, simply because you are part of a nondominant cultural group, you possess the knowledge and skills to be effective with people from other cultures. Lest you find yourself at risk of falling into this trap, this tip encourages you to keep learning about the similarities and differences that exist between you and others within your own cultural groups as well as between you and others in other cultural groups.

For members of dominant groups, I recognize that there can be a sense of shame related to deficits in cross-cultural understanding. This might stem from discomfort about undeserved privilege, thinking you should already know things you don't know, or prejudice and biases you wish you didn't have. For those of you in dominant cultural groups, this tip encourages you to keep learning—and learning without unnecessary shame.

Remember, our biases and prejudices generally result from years of socialization, and it takes both time and effort to reeducate ourselves.

For all of us, cross-cultural understanding is an ongoing process, but only if we allow and/or push ourselves to keep learning. To provide effective career services to a wide range of clients, career counselors and counselors-in-training must commit to updating their understanding of how various cultural dimensions may affect the career development process and work experiences of those clients, and they must do so throughout their careers. An important part of the learning process involves application. Before you proceed to the next section, take a few minutes to jot down your ideas about how you might use the concepts presented in this chapter to understand and/or more effectively counsel each member in our cast of clients.

APPLICATION TO OUR CAST OF CLIENTS

To conclude this chapter, let's look at a variety of cultural dimensions as they might pertain to the career development or career counseling needs of each of our seven clients. My hope is that this section will help you understand how to apply some of the abstract concepts discussed in this chapter. For each client, I will begin by presenting demographic information regarding the various dimensions that contribute to his or her cultural identity. Next, I will speculate about which dimensions might be most salient for each client. I will also offer my thoughts about cultural implications for each client's career development and/or career counseling needs. Remember that these are hypothetical clients that I have fabricated for the purpose of illustration in this text. There is no right answer to questions about which cultural dimensions might be most salient or how they affect a client. The ideas that you brainstormed may be just as valid as the ones I present here.

Wayne Jensen: Welcome to Wayne's World

Wayne is a 40-year-old, Caucasian male of European American ancestry (see Table 6.7). His family has been rooted in the United States for seven generations, since his ancestors voluntarily emigrated from Germany. Wayne was raised as a Lutheran and still identifies as Christian, but he also describes himself as nonpracticing and admits that he hasn't been to church in over a decade. Wayne is employed in a working-class occupation, but his income from the Ford Motor Company is high enough that he qualifies as living within the middle-class socioeconomic bracket. As a Christian-affiliated, white male who identifies

TABLE 6.7 Dimensions of Wayne Jensen's Cultural Identity

Cultural Dimension	Wayne's Identification
Age	40 years
Gender/gender identity	Male
Race/ethnicity	Caucasian, European American with German ancestry
Immigration and citizenship status	U.S. Citizen, seventh-generation immigrants from Europe
Geographic region	Michigan, Midwest
Socioeconomic status/social class	Middle SES, working class
Sexual orientation	Heterosexual
Disability status	No disability
Religion	Nonpracticing Lutheran

as heterosexual and has no disability, Wayne is often viewed as being among the most privileged of our nation. Indeed, Wayne is part of the dominant cultural group across every cultural dimension identified in Table 6.1.

What, though, is the most salient dimension of Wayne's cultural identity? The truth is that Wayne doesn't really feel like he has a cultural identity. When asked directly, Wayne couldn't articulate any clear sense of cultural identity and only offered, "I dunno. I mean, I'm a mutt. I'm white, obviously, but I don't really think about it." This feeling of disconnection from cultural identity isn't unique to Wayne but is instead quite common, especially for Caucasians (Helms, 1992). Noting that this is the result of losing "one's links to a specific ethnic past, probably by means of acculturation or assimilation," Helms explained that the ability to lack conscious awareness of one's race and ethnic background is reflective of White privilege (p. 11).

Wayne does not feel privileged, however. From his perspective, he has worked hard for every dollar he has earned and for everything he has acquired. This approach to work (unbeknownst to Wayne) is reflective of his cultural upbringing. Specifically, Wayne exhibits adherence to the Protestant work ethic, which some believe serves as the foundation for capitalism (Weber, 1930) and can be credited for the success of the United States. In Wayne's mind, his approach to work is "normal" and just part of who he is and how things should be. In actuality, though, his definition of normal has been passed down through generations of family members. It reflects the Protestant work ethic that dates all the way back to Martin Luther, the founder of Wayne's religion. Who knew? Certainly not Wayne!

I would speculate that the generational transmission of the Protestant work ethic is likely the cultural dimension that has had the greatest influence on Wayne's career development. Rather than focusing on the prestige of an occupation, Wayne's family placed value on hard work in and of itself. Wayne's family has lived in southeastern Michigan for several generations, and this geographic location just happened to be the automotive manufacturing center of the world. The regional culture, if you will, placed a high value on working within the automotive industry, and any job within this industry was well rewarded for many years with a high union salary.

In terms of cultural implications for the career counseling relationship, it is important to think about the cultural identities of both the client (Wayne) and the counselor. Maybe both share dominant worldviews and experiences. If so, the establishment of the counseling relationship may be rather effortless. On the other hand, the career counselor may identify with primarily non-dominant cultures. In this case, the counselor may struggle to experience appropriate levels of empathy for Wayne due to reactions to his privileged, dominant cultural identity.

What about you? How easy or hard would it be for you to establish a trusting, supportive relationship with Wayne in which you empathize with his fears and possible anger about the pending layoffs? What strategies might you use to provide culturally effective counseling with Wayne?

Lily Huang Li Mei: Helping Li Mei Blossom

Li Mei is a 19-year-old, Asian American female of Taiwanese descent (see Table 6.8). Li Mei's parents were each raised in Taiwan but moved to the United States shortly after marrying so that her father could complete his graduate

TABLE 6.8 Dimensions of Li Mei Huang's Cultural Identity

Cultural Dimension	Li Mei's Identification
Age	19 years
Gender/gender identity	Female
Race/ethnicity	Asian, Taiwanese
Immigration and citizenship status	U.S. citizen, parents emigrated from Taiwan
Geographic region	Raised in Flushing, New York; attending college in California
Socioeconomic status/social class	Upper class
Sexual orientation	Heterosexual
Disability status	No disability
Religion	Nonpracticing Buddhist

studies at Stony Brook University in New York. After Li Mei's father earned his Ph.D. in engineering, he was offered a high-paying job in Flushing, New York, and the company sponsored his application for a work visa. When the work visa was granted, her parents decided to remain in the United States and, by the time Li Mei entered kindergarten, they had each become naturalized citizens of the United States. Li Mei's father was very well employed, and her family enjoyed the perks of an upper-class lifestyle. Li Mei and her siblings had the best of everything, including enrollment at the best private school in the area. With regard to other cultural dimensions, Li Mei identified as heterosexual (though she had never had a serious boyfriend) and had no disabilities. Although her family identified as Buddhist, they were not active practitioners of Buddhism.

The two most salient dimensions of Li Mei's cultural identity were her race and ethnicity and her family's social class. Interestingly, Li Mei's name reflects both of these dimensions. Within Taiwanese culture, it is common and even customary for parents to give their children two first names: a Chinese name and an English name. This is especially common for families aspiring to upward socioeconomic mobility because Chinese names are viewed as potential barriers to hiring and career success. In contrast, English names are associated with professional achievement and ambition. This custom also reflects recognition that many English-speaking Americans find it difficult to pronounce Asian names; thus, English names represent a form of social capital because they result in greater ease of interaction with dominant-culture Americans. Therefore, many children in Taiwan are raised with both an English name and a Chinese first name. When attending English cram school, these children use their English name almost exclusively.

Mr. and Mrs. Huang embraced this custom when their children were born, and each was given both an English name and a Chinese first name. Throughout their childhoods, the Huang children were addressed exclusively by their English names. As such, Li Mei has been called Lily her entire life. To her, this name represented her parents' desire for her and her siblings to achieve great career success. When she arrived at Chapman University, however, Li Mei shifted to her Chinese first name and seldom used her English name, Lily. A culturally attuned career counselor would recognize that it is highly unusual for a Taiwanese American with both an English name and a Chinese name to make such a shift. After learning that Li Mei grew up being called Lily and only recently switched to her Chinese name, a counselor would want to gently probe in the hope of better understanding the reasons for the change.

In terms of cultural dimensions most likely to influence Li Mei's career development, her family's high socioeconomic status and the high value that they place on academic success resulted in minimal barriers to learning early in her life. There were distal contextual barriers to negatively affect her academic preparation or her development of an orientation toward the importance of work. To the contrary, Li Mei's upbringing was privileged and resulted in many opportunities to excel. This included attendance at the finest private schools in the region, and Li Mei and her siblings excelled academically. Indeed, despite Li Mei's self-deprecation and low levels of academic and career self-efficacy, she gained admission to college, and to a relatively prestigious private college at that. Even so, Li Mei bore the burden of living in her siblings' shadow, did not view herself as living up to the "model minority" stereotype bestowed on Asian Americans (Leong et al., 2010, p. 473), and constantly feared bringing shame on her family (Kim, 2011). With regard to career decision making, the culturally astute counselor will want to be aware that even model minorities are subject to stereotypes that may serve as stressors during the career decision-making process.

For example, you will want to consider the possibility that Li Mei may have "internalized the model minority stereotype to such an extent that [she] perceives [her] lack of interest or aptitude in math as a personal failure" (Leong et al., 2010, p. 473). You will also want to tap into the knowledge that Asian American cultures tend, on the whole, toward a collectivist worldview. The implications of this for the career decision-making process are twofold. First, if Li Mei and her family do indeed hold a collectivist world view, it will be important to Li Mei that her choice of career be consistent with familial values and that she bring honor to her family rather than be a source of embarrassment or shame (Chang & O'Hara, 2013; Leong et al., 2010). Second, it would be culturally insensitive and inappropriate for you to view a collectivist decision-making style as dependent or less mature. You will want to recognize the importance of involving family members in the decision-making process rather than encouraging Li Mei to focus on her own individual preferences and make her choice of academic major and career path autonomously (Mau, 2004).

Finally, let's examine some cultural implications for the career counseling relationship. First, it is important to recognize that Li Mei's choice to seek help at the university's health center first is not uncommon for Asian Americans. Summarizing the literature on this phenomenon, Ruzek, Nguyen, and Herzog (2011) noted that "visiting the health center may be less shaming than visiting the counseling center because students believe they are seeking help for somatic symptoms, which are often perceived as more acceptable than mental health problems in Asian cultures" (p. 192). Second, you will want to demonstrate cultural understanding and respect by not focusing the session too much on Li Mei's struggles and the pressures she feels from her family because this could prompt her to "reveal deeply personal information . . . which may lead to loss of face or shame" (Kim, Li, & Liang, 2002, p. 343). Instead of inviting significant disclosure of possibly shaming information or attempting to help Li Mei gain insight into the reasons for her low levels of self-efficacy and her career decision-making difficulties, you may choose to focus your sessions more on problem solving and solution finding (Kim, 2011). It may also be useful to talk with Li Mei about your awareness that disclosure in counseling may be especially difficult for Asian Americans because of the potential loss of face. Although you may be wholly uncomfortable with the idea of being the leader of counseling sessions or being viewed as an expert, keep in mind that Asian cultures emphasize hierarchical relationships and that it may be important for you to assume a more directive role with Li Mei than you would with European American clients (Chang & O'Hara, 2013).

Lakeesha Maddox: Doors and Windows

Lakeesha is a 27-year-old, African American female (see Table 6.9). Although she is a U.S. citizen, Lakeesha is deeply aware of her African roots and the fact that her ancestors were forcibly brought to this continent as slaves. This awareness stems from both oral history within her family and seminars at Spelman College. In fact, Lakeesha's decision to apply to and attend this historically black college or university (HBCU) reflected her awareness of sociopolitical inequities and a desire to receive her college education at an institution dedicated to greater social

TABLE 6.9   Dimensions of Lakeesha Maddox's Cultural Identity

Cultural Dimension	Lakeesha's Identification
Age	27 years
Gender/gender identity	Female
Race/ethnicity	African American
Immigration and citizenship status	U.S. citizen, ancestors brought from Africa as slaves
Geographic region	Suburb of Atlanta, Georgia
Socioeconomic status/social class	Middle class
Sexual orientation	Heterosexual
Disability status	No disability but had gestational diabetes
Religion	Practicing Baptist

equality. Initially founded as the "Atlanta Baptist Female Seminary," Spelman College has "the distinction of being America's oldest historically Black college for women" (spelman.edu/about-us, para 1). While attending Spelman, Lakeesha experienced a great deal of identity development, with regard to both race and spirituality, and these dimensions became the two most salient of her cultural identity. With regard to other cultural dimensions, Lakeesha identifies as heterosexual and was firm in her Baptist beliefs. Lakeesha does not consider herself disabled. Although she developed gestational diabetes during her most recent pregnancy, Lakeesha indicates that the symptoms subsided following the birth of her youngest daughter and that she now carefully monitors her diet to minimize the elevated risk of later developing Type 2 diabetes. Lakeesha was raised in a middle-class family and, until now, has enjoyed a middle-class family income in her married life.

In thinking about these cultural dimensions, I would speculate that gender and race may have had the most influence on Lakeesha's career development. As an African American female, Lakeesha is well aware of how important it was to her parents for her to avoid becoming another statistic by getting pregnant out of wedlock. Indeed, her parents seemed to harp on this topic, even posting newspaper clippings to the refrigerator. Although this might seem like overkill (and certainly annoyed Lakeesha), her parents' fears were well founded. For example, national statistics indicate that 71% of black children in 2013 were born to unwed mothers (U.S. Department of Health and Human Services, 2015) and that 67% of black or African American children in 2013 lived in single-parent families (Annie E. Casey Foundation, 2014). With these statistics looming large in her parents' consciousness, Lakeesha constantly heard messages such as "finish school," "no sex before marriage," and "find a good man and settle down." In fact, Lakeesha was pretty sure that the only reason her parents agreed to pay for college was because they believed that this is where she would be most likely to "find a good man." They wanted her to find a beau who was going places, someone who would have a good education, get a good job, and be a good provider.

Who knew they might actually be right? Despite her skepticism, Lakeesha couldn't have been happier than she was in her life with Terrence. To her, Terrence was the perfect man, the perfect husband, a perfect father, and a wonderful provider. In Lakeesha's mind, everything had turned out perfectly. Lakeesha had internalized an image of a perfect family in which the wife stayed at home with the children and the husband worked outside the home to support the family. Truth be known, Lakeesha isn't sure she ever had a "real" career aspiration. Although she went to college, Lakeesha and her family viewed this as a means by which to become attractive to and marry "a good man." She had achieved her dream, but the accident changed everything and Lakeesha now needed to find a way to support her family.

Cultural dimensions likely to affect Lakeesha's immediate career decision making at this point most likely center on the need to balance her parental responsibilities with her need for income. In developing an effective counseling relationship with Lakeesha, you will want to ensure a respectful attitude toward the primacy of Lakeesha's parenting responsibilities. Far too often, career counselors can communicate a devaluation of full-time parenting as a career choice, perhaps by not even recognizing it as such. As Schultheiss noted, however, "many women have and will continue to define motherhood as a career" (Schultheiss, 2009, p. 26). To avoid making an ignorant comment such as "Oh, so you've never worked before," remind yourself that every mother is a working mother and that full-time parenting is an important career path; unfortunately for Lakeesha, it is simply no longer a financially viable one. She has become what Locke and Gibbon termed a "displaced new traditionalist" (Locke & Gibbon, 2008, p. 132). They defined such individuals as "women of the present era whose primary jobs were working in the home as wives and mothers, but whose marriages end as a result of divorce, separation, or widowhood" (p. 132).

In working with Lakeesha, it would be important to address issues of grief and loss not only over the death of her husband but also over the "shift in personal identity that will undoubtedly occur as she transitions from her role working within the home to working outside the home" (Locke & Gibbon, 2008, p. 134). Lakeesha has spoken of her collectivist worldview, so it will be important to recognize additional sources of support. These will likely include her faith, the women at her church, and her family. You will also want to be attuned to any concerns Lakeesha may have about discrimination based on race, sex, marital status, or family structure. Although I have not focused on these particular cultural dimensions in my discussion of Lakeesha, keep in mind that they could actually be just as or even more salient to her or to any client's situation. Remember that these are hypothetical clients that I have fabricated for the purpose of illustration in this text; my exploration of the cultural dimensions affecting them is necessarily limited by space. Also, remember that the ideas you brainstormed may be just as valid as the ones I present here for Lakeesha and for any of our seven clients.

Vincent Santiago Arroyo: Caskets, Closets, and Careers

Just as with every other client, Vincent's cultural identity involves numerous dimensions. As shown in Table 6.10, Vincent is a 17-year-old, Puerto Rican male living in the South Bronx. He is a practicing Catholic, and he and his mother light a candle before mass every week in memory of his father. With no known disabilities, Vincent is a strapping young man who appears ready for the physical challenge of boot camp should he decide to enlist in the Marines. Although every one of these characteristics is worthy of thorough exploration, I will focus this particular section on two other dimensions of Vincent's cultural identity: his socioeconomic status and his sexual orientation.

Because money has been really tight for his family since his father's death, Vincent got a part-time job at the local bodega in order to help with the bills. Each day after school, Vincent would rush to the bodega, where he would bag groceries, stock shelves, and sweep floors. While other kids his age were participating in extracurricular activities, Vincent was at work. It was with great pride that he presented his paycheck to his mother each week, and Vincent never seemed to begrudge the situation. He also rarely felt inclined to do homework, but neither he nor his mother was overly concerned with his grades. Vincent passed all his classes and was well liked by his teachers, most of whom knew about his father. He had well-founded confidence that he would graduate from high school, which was enough for him.

Note the very real impact of socioeconomic status (SES) on Vincent's career development. Rather than doing homework and focusing on academic achievement, Vincent was focused on making a financial contribution to his family. Although this was admirable and probably necessary, it also had a decidedly negative effect on Vincent's academic preparation. To the extent that academic skills serve as the foundation for career preparation, SES played a limiting role in Vincent's career development. Even if Vincent enlists in the military as he had planned, his academic development will likely play a limiting role in his career options in the Marines because all enlistees must take the Armed Services Vocational Aptitude Battery (ASVAB), and scores from this test are used to determine the Military Occupational Specialties (MOS) for which an enlistee is eligible (military.com). Each job in the Marines has a minimum qualifying test score. As a result, the lower one's test scores, the more limited one's career options within the Marines. Even so, the U.S. military "is an invaluable vehicle for economic mobility for many working-class families" (Pérez, 2010, p. 169), and "many young Latinas/os have regarded their participation in the military as a one [sic] pathway to first-class citizenship" (p. 170).

Now, of course, Vincent is not so sure about his long-time dream of joining the Marines. He took a huge risk in revealing to you, his career counselor, the reason for his uncertainty. The fact that he took such a chance with you suggests that you and your office may communicate an atmosphere of safety for all students. This is especially important to students and clients whose minority status is not visible (one simply cannot identify another's sexual orientation simply by looking at him or her). And one cannot predict a person's reaction to a disclosure of being gay simply by looking at him or her. However, environmental clues can be quite instrumental in communicating one's commitment to supporting students regardless of sexual

TABLE 6.10 Dimensions of Vincent Santiago Arroyo's Cultural Identity

Cultural Dimension	Vincent's Identification
Age	17 years
Gender/gender identity	Male
Race/ethnicity	Puerto Rican
Immigration and citizenship status	U.S. citizen, grandparents voluntarily emigrated from Puerto Rico to New York City
Geographic region	South Bronx barrio in New York City
Socioeconomic status/social class	Lower SES/working class
Sexual orientation	Gay, in process of coming out to self but not to others
Disability status	No disability
Religion	Practicing Catholic

orientation. Such clues may include a rainbow flag or a safe-space sticker on a door or bulletin board (Datti, 2009; Goodrich & Luke, 2009). One such sticker is featured in Figure 6.10 and is available through the Gay, Lesbian and Straight Education Network's (GLSEN) Safe Space Campaign (safespace.glsen.org).

Books and other print resources represent other environmental clues that may communicate to a student like Vincent that it is safe to come out to you. For example, you might include college resources such as the *LGBT-Friendly Campus Climate Index,* published by Campus Pride (campuspride.org), or *Your Queer Career* (Folds, 2013), in addition to *The Latino Student's Guide to College Success* (Valverde, 2012), on your bookshelf. Such environmental artifacts create a counseling atmosphere in which a student may feel comfortable coming out to a school counselor. This level of comfort is essential to developing an authentic counseling relationship.

You also need to be aware of how sexual orientation may affect Vincent's career development and decision making. Given that "the age of first awareness typically ranges from 8 to 11 years, and that the age of identifying as LGB typically ranges from 15 to 17 years" (DePaul, Walsh, & Dam, 2009, p. 301), early influences on Vincent's career development were likely limited to associative learning experiences and exposure to stereotypes, such as assumptions that all male nurses or hairstylists are gay (Datti, 2009). Another barrier to career development may be the scarcity of role models. Adams, Cahill, and Ackerlind (2005) observed that "LG youth may have fewer role models because many LG adults are not visible, instead choosing to remain closeted to protect their jobs" (p. 200). Whereas a textbook or teacher would think nothing of identifying a major historical figure as African American, that same textbook or teacher is likely to remain silent with regard to a major historical figure's sexual orientation (Hardy & Harley, 2009).

In addition to being aware of how sexual orientation may affect Vincent's career development, you need to be prepared with knowledge and resources to support his career decision making. As Goodrich and Luke (2009) noted,

> . . . when students do publicly identify as LGBTQ, school counselors need to integrate LGBTW experience into the academic, career, and personal planning. While understanding that identity should not "pigeonhole" a person, this can be done by assisting students in locating environments that support and affirm LGBTQ experience (teachers, courses, higher education settings, careers) and by facilitating conversations about self-advocacy. (p. 119)

In Vincent's case, this will require discussions and research about the experiences of gay soldiers in the military as well as the exploration of other careers in which he might find more safety and/or acceptance. For example, Vincent might be interested to know that the New York City Fire Department (FDNY) has recently increased its efforts to recruit gay firefighters (Kyle, 2010), and the department has a gay advocacy group called FireFLAG/EMS (fireflag.org). Having such discussions with Vincent are especially important given the likelihood that he will

FIGURE 6.10 Safe-Space Sticker
Source: safespace.glsen.org.

proceed through stages of gay identity development (Cass, 1979; Troiden, 1989) and reach a point where he is no longer satisfied being closeted and instead wants to be what I call "out loud and out proud." Thus, it is essential to talk with Vincent about the realities of discrimination, the risks and benefits of being out, ways to locate role models, and so forth. Although discussions of religion may or may not be appropriate within a school setting, it might be helpful to talk with Vincent about the fact that one need not choose between being gay or being Catholic. One organization dedicated to supporting LGBT individuals in reconciling their sexual orientation with their Catholicism is Dignity USA (dignityusa.org).

Doris Bronner: Embitterment Versus Empowerment

Doris is a 53-year-old Caucasian, heterosexual woman of Jewish descent (see Table 6.11). Entering the United States through Ellis Island, her great-grandparents emigrated from Germany in the late 1800s, just prior to the turn of the twentieth century. This was well before the Holocaust, and to Doris's knowledge, she had no relatives who perished at the hands of the Nazis. Her parents and grandparents nonetheless felt the emotional impact of this persecution. Whereas many other families living in the United States responded by strengthening their ties with the Jewish community, Doris's family responded with stronger efforts toward integration into mainstream U.S. culture. As a result, Doris did not receive a formal Jewish education and there was no bat mitzvah to commemorate her twelfth birthday. Although Doris had an awareness of being of Jewish descent, her identification as a Jew ended there.

Far more salient to Doris's cultural identity were her gender and her age/generational cohort. When Doris was growing up, many more societal messages communicated gender-based occupational constraints. She was still in high school when the Civil Rights Act of 1964 was passed to prohibit employment discrimination based on an "individual's race, color, religion, sex, or national origin" (Cihon & Castagnera, 2011, p. 114). Although this law directly addressed discrimination in the workplace, many inequities persisted within the educational realm. In fact, it wasn't until 1972, with the passage of Title IX of the Educational Amendments Act, that sex discrimination in educational institutions and programs was prohibited by federal law. Title IX required K–12 schools, colleges, and universities to ensure sex equity in both expenditures and opportunities in every imaginable way, ranging from academics to sports and other extracurricular clubs, such as scouts, to campus housing. By 1972, however, Doris had completed her high school education as well as a short certificate program in clerical work.

Doris's gender and generational cohort had a marked impact on her career development. Indeed, Doris was subject to more limiting messages about what occupations were appropriate for females. One might speculate that the circumscription process (Gottfredson, 1981) contributed directly to Doris's choice to seek a job as a secretary because "that's what women do." From another theoretical perspective, these gender-based occupational constraints represented distal contextual factors affecting Doris's vocational interests and career choices (Lent, Brown, & Hackett, 1994).

Now, though, times have changed, and females are better (though not adequately) represented across the spectrum of possible careers. It is much more common to

TABLE 6.11 Dimensions of Doris Bronner's Cultural Identity

Cultural Dimension	Doris's Identification
Age	53 years
Gender/gender identity	Female
Race/ethnicity	Caucasian/Jewish
Immigration and citizenship status	U.S. citizen, fourth-generation immigrants from Germany
Geographic region	Originally from Westwood, California (suburb of Los Angeles), but moved to Omaha, Nebraska, 20 years ago when husband was transferred
Socioeconomic status/social class	Lower middle class
Sexual orientation	Heterosexual
Disability status	No disability
Religion	Nonobservant

see female doctors, business owners, and scientists. Thus, time offers a benefit to Doris in the context of a wider array of acceptable career options. In another way, though, the progression of time has hurt Doris's employment prospects. As she ages, Doris has become keenly aware that she tends to be one of the oldest employees wherever she works. Now, especially with blemishes on her employment record, Doris fears that she is too old to be hired again. In addition to worrying about potential age discrimination, Doris has also internalized some ageist beliefs and finds herself thinking that she is too old to learn a new job.

With regard to the impact of Doris's cultural identity on the development of a counseling relationship, you would be wise to consider how the similarities and differences between the two of you may affect the counseling process. For example, if there is a substantial difference in your ages, how might this affect your credibility with Doris as well as your ability to understand her experiences (both past and present) of the world? As a little advice, it's generally not useful to express understanding of a client who is older than you by observing that he or she is about the same age as your parents or (egads!) your grandparents. Such a comment runs the risk of being demeaning to clients and/or of calling your credibility into question. Instead, it is more helpful to invite clients to share their experiences with you and to inquire about societal changes they have observed over the years. With Doris, for example, you might ask what career paths she considered while she was in high school. If they were all stereotypically feminine careers, you might comment on this and ask whether she just happened to have these interests or whether she felt some jobs were off limits to females at the time. You could then follow up by asking whether she feels that she has a greater range of options open to her now and, if so, whether she has any interest in those jobs that had previously been off limits.

Gillian Parker: Golden Handcuffs

Gillian is a 39-year-old, heterosexual female who has no disabilities (see Table 6.12). Gillian does not subscribe to any religious beliefs but instead considers herself agnostic. When Gillian's uncle became interested in genealogy a few years ago, he traced their family's history. This project led Gillian to discover that she is 11 generations removed from her ancestors, who emigrated from England to what were then the British colonies and later became the United States. Over the next 10 generations, there were several instances of intermarriage between her English ancestors and Native Americans. This resulted in Gillian being seven eighths English and one eighth Suquamish. However, despite being one eighth Suquamish Native American and fondly recalling some of the Native American stories her mother read to her as a child, Gillian tends to think of herself simply as white.

Gillian's primary identification with dominant, white culture may be attributed to generations of intermarriage and an assimilation process in which "the cultural differences between groups are incompletely passed on across the generations and eventually become so diluted that they ultimately disappear" (Huyser, Sakamoto, & Takei, 2010, p. 545). The truth is that, aside from those bedtime stories, Gillian grew up with fairly minimal exposure to Suquamish culture. It is important that Gillian grew up without feeling the emotional impact of the European colonization of North America and the subsequent displacement and disenfranchising of various Native American tribes. Perhaps most indicative was her family's

TABLE 6.12 Dimensions of Gillian Parker's Cultural Identity

Cultural Dimension	Gillian's Identification
Age	39 years
Gender/gender identity	Female
Race/ethnicity	Seven eighths English and one eighth Suquamish Native American
Immigration and citizenship status	U.S. citizen, eleventh-generation immigrants from England
Geographic region	Green Lake, Washington (suburb of Seattle)
Socioeconomic status/social class	Upper class
Sexual orientation	Heterosexual
Disability status	No disability
Religion	Agnostic

participation in annually celebrating a traditional American Thanksgiving. These occasions were replete with romanticized images of harmonious relations between the Native Americans and the Pilgrims as they joined together to share the bounty of the autumn harvest, a far cry from the reality of imperialistic genocide that actually marked these times (Zinn, 2010).

Indeed, Gillian has lived a life of privilege in part because she and her family members are perceived as Caucasian and in part because of her family's high SES. Whereas "unemployment is a crisis for many American Indian communities," with unemployment rates "ranging from 15% to 80%" (Juntunen & Cline, 2010, p. 398), nobody in Gillian's immediate family has been unemployed. Instead, her family members have consistently earned college degrees and tend to hold high-level, professional positions. For example, Gillian's father was a business executive for Boeing, and Gillian, of course, is an Ivy League graduate in a top position with Ernst and Young.

At this point in Gillian's life, the most salient cultural dimension related to her career development, career success, and career decision making is likely her gender. Until now, Gillian has felt unencumbered by gender issues that so frequently constrain the academic and career development of females. She excelled academically in every subject, including math, which is typically viewed as an area for males to succeed; she reached the pinnacle of academia by earning not one but two degrees in Ivy League institutions; and she achieved the highest level of professional success as an auditor when she was named partner in a Big Four accounting firm. These accomplishments can be attributed to both individual and contextual factors. Contextually, Gillian was raised in a family of privilege and enjoyed every opportunity for success. Gillian made her own choices all along the way, demonstrating persistence in her studies and tenacity in her work. She worked as many or more hours than her male counterparts.

Until now, Gillian's career development more closely resembled that of "men who often have a singular vocational focus when constructing their vocation self" than women who "develop aspirations for both career and family" (Heppner & Fu, 2011, p. 182). Now, though, with her biological clock ticking ever more loudly, Gillian finds herself contemplating a major change in her life: having children. This major change would introduce Gillian to the challenges faced by many working women who struggle to balance their work life with their family life. As she debates whether to add yet another role to her life space (Super, 1980), Gillian comes face to face with gender issues related to the world of work.

With regard to the development of a counseling relationship with Gillian, you will want to be attuned to the implications of cultural similarities and differences between the two of you. In Chapter 1, for example, I suggested that, because few career counselors earn anywhere near Gillian's income, it would be helpful for you to contemplate the issues that may arise as you welcome Gillian as a client and seek to help her. You may struggle with respect to self-confidence given that she is seeking career counseling but has obviously been quite successful in her career. (Remember, there is honor in all work: Juan's, yours, and Gillian's!) Additionally, you may also find yourself wrestling with stereotypes and misconceptions about upper-class people and may struggle to offer an appropriate level of empathy. Or perhaps you have strong feelings about ethnic pride and need to bracket your disapproval of Gillian's assimilation and identification with dominant, European American culture. You may have opinions about the importance of motherhood for a "complete" life or beliefs that women should not work while their children are young. If any or all these cases are true for you, you are responsible for being aware of your own biases and beliefs and for setting them aside in order to focus exclusively on assisting Gillian with making choices that are right for her.

Juan Martinez: Bloques de Construcción para un Futuro Nuevo (Building Blocks for a New Future)

Juan is a 34-year-old, Mexican American male living in Fort Worth, Texas (see Table 6.13). His parents were born and raised in Mexico, and met and married while living in Nuevo Laredo. Shortly after learning they were pregnant with Juan, they decided to emigrate from Mexico to the United States in the hope of providing a better life for their children. Having no sponsor in the United States and unlikely to get visas, they chose to cross the Rio Grande and enter the United States illegally, without documentation. Once safely across, Juan's parents were understandably terrified of being discovered and deported. They made their way to Fort Worth, Texas (far away from the Mexican border) and were able to find work there. Without a green card or work visa, Juan's parents were quite limited with regard to employment options and could take jobs only in which they were paid under the table. Although their family income was in the lower SES brackets, their standard of living in Fort Worth, Texas, far exceeded what they would have experienced had they remained in Nuevo Laredo, Mexico. These unskilled laborers were thankful to be in the United States and took solace in the knowledge that their children would be U.S. citizens.

TABLE 6.13 Dimensions of Juan Martinez's Cultural Identity

Cultural Dimension	Juan's Identification
Age	34 years
Gender/gender identity	Male
Race/ethnicity	Hispanic/Latino
Immigration and citizenship status	U.S. citizen, second-generation immigrants from Mexico
Geographic region	Fort Worth, Texas
Socioeconomic status/social class	Lower middle class
Sexual orientation	Heterosexual
Disability status	Herniated L4L5 disc
Religion	Nonobservant Catholic

As their family expanded, Juan's parents struggled to put food on the table, and their financial stressors increased as each of their seven children was born. As the oldest child in the family, Juan was well aware of the family's financial difficulties. Consistent with the Latino values of *familismo* and filial piety (Flores et al., 2010), Juan therefore decided to leave school at age 16 to find a job and contribute to the family income. He had worked, until his back injury, in the construction industry ever since.

With regard to other dimensions of his cultural identity, Juan would be categorized as heterosexual and, assuming dual incomes in his household, lower middle class. Although raised Catholic, Juan is best described as nonobservant. At his wife's insistence, Juan generally accompanies his family to midnight mass on Christmas Eve, but other than that, he can't remember the last time he attended mass, went to confession, said the rosary, or even prayed. Although Juan now has two herniated discs, he does not consider himself disabled. Most salient to his cultural identity are Juan's ethnicity as a Mexican American, his parents' undocumented status, and his family of origin's low SES. Each had a clear impact on Juan's career development and decision making.

For example, Juan's exposure to role models in the world of work was decidedly quite limited. His parents were unskilled laborers who worked seven days a week. They had little time nor money to expose Juan to the wider world around them. There were no trips to libraries or museums, no tickets for sporting events, no vacations to exciting places, and no money for extracurricular activities associated with school. Their entire social circle was comprised of other unskilled workers, and only Spanish was spoken at home. Although they hoped for Juan to do well in and behave at school, his parents could not help him with his homework because they spoke very little English and could not read it. Still worried about being discovered as undocumented, they largely avoided contact with the school and their children's teachers. Because their focus was necessarily on meeting daily subsistence needs and paying bills, Juan's parents couldn't even imagine sending their children to college. Even if Juan were interested in finishing high school and going to college, he would undoubtedly face barriers and complexities specific to being the child of undocumented immigrants (Baum & Flores, 2011).

Given that "educational attainment constitutes the bedrock of career development and choice" by opening up career options (Arbona, 1996, p. 48), Juan faced quite limited career options because he did not complete high school. Juan's reality was such that it wasn't practical for him to dream of careers. Instead, Juan needed to focus on practical, achievable jobs with which he could earn income with which to enjoy a reasonable standard of living. This, of course, is quite consistent with Blustein's writings about the psychology of work (Blustein et al., 2011).

Since making his initial choice to leave school and take a position in the construction industry, Juan has continued to experience the impact of cultural factors on his career success. Specifically, Juan's subsequent career success has been constrained by his limited proficiency in English and his lack of a high school education. Although Juan is a U.S. citizen, he may very well encounter discrimination when applying for jobs. Such discrimination is illegal, but potential employers may be less willing to interview and/or hire Juan. Their bias may be in response to his ethnicity (which is clearly evident even in Juan's name) or reflective of more recent anti-immigration sentiment in the United States and especially in border states such as Texas. Because he is unable to continue working in his previous position, cultural dimensions may also affect his psychological adjustment. "If he ascribes to traditional Latino gender roles, Juan may perceive his role of providing for his family financially as a direct reflection of his male identity" (Flores et al., 2010, p. 414).

To conclude our discussion of Juan, let's examine some cultural implications for a career counseling relationship with him. My hope is that you quickly realize the importance of considering the impact of Juan's English proficiency (and your Spanish proficiency) on your ability to counsel him effectively. Obviously, the ability to communicate and understand one another is essential to your ability to provide effective counseling services to Juan. Communication should be an important consideration in whether to continue meeting with Juan beyond your initial session, arrange for an interpreter, or refer Juan to a counselor who is fluent in Spanish. You will also want to recognize and safeguard against any biases you may hold with regard to Mexican immigrants, especially those who are undocumented or who are born to parents who are undocumented. The political climate in the United States, and especially in border states such as Texas, has shifted to one of often strong opposition to Mexican immigrants. Regardless of your personal beliefs or concerns about immigration, your job as a counselor is to help Juan as best you can.

I hope that you would convey what I believe to be an ultimate guiding principle: that there is honor in all work. It is far too easy to look down on—consciously or unconsciously—the ways that others make their living. As a construction laborer, Juan is vulnerable to such judgments but deserving of much better, and Juan has as much right as anyone to hold his head high and be proud of his efforts to support his family.

CHAPTER 7

An Employment Law Primer for Career Counselors

As a career counselor, you will likely have clients who are hoping to be hired, who are affected by issues in the workplace, or who have recently been fired. Depending on your work setting, you may also have clients who are facing unemployment and/or clients who have disabilities that affect the types of tasks they can perform on the job. When working with such clients, it is useful to know the laws related to their situations. This chapter will highlight a number of employment laws that may pertain to your clients' experiences. As you read this chapter, keep in mind that there is no expectation that you become an expert in employment law or that you commit all of these laws to memory. However, a basic understanding of these employment laws will serve you very well as a career counselor because such an understanding will allow you to recognize times when it is prudent to suggest to your client that he or she seek legal advice.

THE FINE PRINT

I am not an attorney and I don't even play one on TV. Reading this chapter will not qualify you to offer legal counsel.

WHY FRANK PARSONS CARED ABOUT EMPLOYMENT LAW

Before embarking on a discussion of specific employment laws, this chapter begins with a brief history featuring Frank Parsons's interest in employment law. Although nearly all counselors recognize Frank Parsons as the father of counseling and father of vocational guidance, many are unaware of Parsons's own career path. You may not have realized that, on leaving high school and enrolling in college at the ripe old age of 15, Parson had no intention of laying the foundation for career counseling but instead pursued a career as a civil engineer. After graduating at the age of 18 from Cornell University with a degree in civil engineering, Parsons accepted a prestigious position as an engineer with a railroad company, which was the highest paid occupation in the country at that time. Much to his dismay, he lost that job when the railroad company went bankrupt because of a major economic recession in 1873.

The economy was so depressed at the time that the only job Parsons could find was as a manual laborer for an iron rolling mill, and his job there consisted of "lifting and shearing iron and loading it on wagons—10 hours a day, 6 days a week, for $39 per month, with a 2-mile walk to work each day" (Pope & Sveinsdottir, 2005, p. 108). Although his time as a manual laborer lasted but a year, the experience made a lasting impression on him. Do the math, and you'll realize that Parsons made only $468 that year! In comparison to the $1,500 to $2,000 annual earnings he'd likely have made as a railroad engineer (Zytowski, 2001), Parsons now had firsthand experiences in the working worlds of the haves and have nots.

The contrasts among his initial entry into the high-paying job of a railroad engineer, the harsh realities of manual labor jobs such as the one he held at the iron mill, and the middle-class teaching position into which he next transitioned heightened Parsons's awareness of profound inequities, and he soon became a social activist (Zytowski, 2001). Parsons's next career shift involved the study and practice of law. In fact, he practiced as an attorney for nearly 20 years (Davis, 1969). Later, as a faculty member (first at Boston University and later at Kansas Agricultural College), Parsons taught courses in political economics as well as insurance law. Parsons often spoke out about political issues pertaining to employment and the economy. He took up the cause of working- and middle-class citizens in *Our Country's Needs* (Parsons, 1894, as cited in Pope and Sveinsdottir, 2005, p. 108). As detailed by Zytowski (2001),

> Parsons wrote that one eighth of the population owned seven eighths of the wealth. The highest paid occupation was the railroad engineer, $1,500 to $2,000 per year, whereas nine tenths of factory employees earned less than $1,000 per year, and women less than $350. Children as young as 10 worked as many as 14 hours a day in mines and textile mills. (p. 59)

In opposition to these disparate conditions, Parsons became "an advocate for youth, women, the poor, and the disadvantaged" (O'Brien, 2001, p. 66) who championed "a minimum wage and organized a national campaign to institute an 8-hour workday" (Mann, 1950; as cited in O'Brien, 2001). However, Parsons was fired from his faculty position because of his so-called subversive views supporting controversial issues such as "women's suffrage and government regulation of industry" (Baker, 2009, p. 200).

Clearly the epitome of someone who benefitted from "planned happenstance" (Mitchell, Levin, & Krumboltz, 1999), Parsons then changed careers yet again and began to focus on the career development needs of the middle- and working-class citizens about whom he cared so much. Specifically, he turned his attention toward public education and focused on the career development needs of youth (Davis, 1969). It was only at this point in his life that he developed his theories about vocational guidance and planning, and articulated what has become the foundation of trait factor theory. Sadly, Parsons likely did not recognize the legacy he would leave when he planted the seeds that would grow into the counseling profession. His book *Choosing a Vocation* (Parsons, 1909), which is most often recognized as the foundational publication precipitating the development of the counseling profession, was published after his death, with portions of it still in draft form (Baker, 2009).

Parsons perceived many inequities in the world of work and was passionate about remedying them. He argued for the importance of fair pay and better conditions (Baker, 2009; O'Brien, 2001) and called attention to the misuse of children for cheap labor (Zytowski, 2001). Had he not been fired from his faculty position, it is my belief that Parsons could have become an early leader in the development of employment law. Although he spent the remainder of his career focused on helping others through vocational guidance and planning activities, Parsons's passion for what would become employment law was clear.

Although the study of employment law is generally required when training for work in legal, human resources, and administrative positions, it is surprisingly uncommon when training to become a career counselor. This is especially surprising given the stance of the National Employment Counseling Association that

> . . . one of the traits that separate employment counselors from other types of counselors is their understanding of employment law and their commitment to protect the rights of the public. Indeed, as has been argued, if employment counselors are going to call themselves professional, they have an obligation to ensure that their clients receive up-to-date information about employment-related issues. (n.d.; cited in Von Borgen, Von Borgen, & Ballaré, 2008, p. 115)

Especially given Parsons's passion for such issues and the relevance of employment law to our clients' well-being, it is important for career counselors to have some basic understanding of it. This chapter will therefore help you become aware of employment laws and understand how they might be relevant to your work as a career counselor.

ACKNOWLEDGMENT

I would like to acknowledge the assistance and contributions of Patrick J. Cihon, associate professor of law and public policy at Syracuse University. As a coauthor of a widely used text on employment law (with J. O. Castagnera), Professor Cihon graciously shared his expertise with me as I prepared the remainder of this chapter, providing input and feedback throughout the writing process. You'll see his text (Cihon & Castagnera, 2011) widely cited throughout the remainder of this chapter, which reflects the extent of his assistance.

THE EVOLUTION OF EMPLOYMENT DOCTRINE IN THE UNITED STATES

As discussed earlier in this text, the technological advances during the Industrial Revolution (1820–1870) had a remarkable influence on the nature of work in the United States. Workers now had many potential career paths open to them, which resulted in the need for career development and career counseling. There was also a significant change in the way workers were paid. During the agrarian, pre-industrial economy,

> workers were subject to the "entire contract doctrine," which maintained that workers who quit their jobs or were dismissed before the end of the term of their employment contract forfeited any wages for the time worked. For example, if a worker hired for a year left [or was fired] after ten months, he [sic] would often find himself without pay for the period worked. (Stone, 2007, pp. 85–86)

Imagine that! Workers were hired for a fixed period of time, and to collect pay, those workers had to work the entire contract or otherwise not get paid. They had to remain healthy enough to continue working through the entire contract, they had to avoid any mistakes for which they might be fired, and they had to stay in the good graces of their employer. Clearly, there was considerable room for abuse of this policy, for example, the employer who fired an employee after most (but not all) of the contract period had been completed. Although obviously harsh and risky to those workers who entered into such jobs, the concept of accepting a job for a fixed period of time did make some sense during the agrarian economy. The fixed period most often revolved around the growing season.

After the Industrial Revolution, though, the entire contract approach didn't make as much sense. When workers moved to cities and got jobs in factories, they were generally hired for employment on an ongoing basis because factories didn't have seasons in the same way as farms. Rather than being hired for a fixed term of employment, workers were hired on an indefinite basis. As Stone (2007) explained, this resulted in a new common law approach to employment contracts:

> Beginning in the 1880s, a few state courts adopted the view that both parties to an employment contract of indefinite duration could terminate it at any time for any reason. This was termed the "at-will doctrine," and it quickly spread from state to state and became the overwhelmingly dominant common law. At its inception, the at-will doctrine was beneficial for unskilled workers because it mitigated the harshness of the nineteenth-century entire contract regime. It provided that a worker hired for an indefinite term had the right to be paid for the time worked, up to the moment he [sic] quit or was fired. (p. 86)

To this day, the at-will employment doctrine is dominant in the United States (Cihon & Castagnera, 2011; Stone, 2007). In the absence of a collective bargaining agreement or other written contract, the assumption (consistently upheld by courts) is that both the employer and employee are free to end the contract at any time. The employee is free to quit at any time and be paid for the time already worked, and the employer is free to fire the employee "at any time for any reason—or for no reason at all" (Cihon & Castagnera, 2011, p. 19) unless doing so violates a law. However, this caveat wasn't always in place.

Instead, the early implementation of the at-will employment doctrine allowed firing for literally any reason, and there were many abuses of this system, with the advantage consistently in favor of the employer. Although the development of at-will employment had the positive impact of protecting workers from losing pay for work they had already done, employers could still abuse the system and (legally) mistreat workers. For example, a worker might accept a job working for 50 cents per hour and do outstanding work, only to be informed by the employer that the new pay would be 10 cents per hour. If the worker complained or even asked for an explanation, the employer could fire him or her. Workers who raised concerns about safety issues or other working conditions also risked dismissal.

Because it was very risky for an individual worker to broach concerns with employers, employees began to join together in an attempt to bargain collectively with employers regarding issues like wages and working conditions. The at-will employment doctrine was so deeply embedded at the time that such collective activities were deemed criminal conspiracies and ruled illegal by the courts (Cihon & Castagnera, 2011). It wasn't until the formation of unions for the purpose of collective bargaining was legalized (with the passage of the National Labor Relations Act in 1935) that workers began to enjoy better protection under the law.

Since that time, a number of worker protections have been established in law, either by the promulgation of legislation or by common law via a judge's ruling. In many respects, each of these laws has had the effect of narrowing, or limiting, the at-will employment doctrine (Cihon & Castagnera, 2011). These protections, also known as employment laws, are the subject of the remainder of this chapter.

> This chapter provides a basic introduction to a variety of federal employment laws that may be pertinent to your clients in career counseling. Keep in mind that the following summary covers only federal laws. In some cases, a state law may offer your clients more protection than the federal law, so it is important that you also become aware of employment laws in the state in which you work.

SUMMARY OF RELEVANT EMPLOYMENT LAWS

In delineating these employment laws, I have organized this chapter according to likely concerns of clients who seek career counseling. First, clients may have concerns about issues that might affect their ability to get hired or about issues that may result in them being fired. Some of these practices may be illegal but nonetheless affect your client. Next, clients may raise concerns about the working conditions in their place of employment, and legal guidelines may pertain to such conditions. Other clients may have issues related to the inability to find work (unemployment) or the inability to perform work (disability). Some clients may benefit from knowing about laws pertaining to life after retirement. This organizational framework is illustrated in Table 7.1.

Laws Pertaining to Hiring and Firing

A number of important federal laws pertain to the hiring of employees in the United States. One such law addresses the citizenship requirements for legal employment. Another involves the use of and reliance on criminal background checks. Several laws prohibit various forms of discrimination in the hiring process as well as in the firing (discharging) of employees.

IMMIGRATION LAW. Immigration laws focus on who may legally enter into and reside in, study in, and work in the United States. The primary law was passed in 1952, but the "most recent major overhaul of U.S. immigration law" is the Immigration and Reform Control Act (IRCA) of 1986 (Cihon & Castagnera, 2011, p. 92). In career counseling,

TABLE 7.1 Counselor-Friendly Organization of Employment Laws in This Chapter

- Laws pertaining to hiring and firing
- Laws pertaining to work conditions
- Laws pertaining to unemployment or inability to work
- Laws pertaining to life after retirement

of course, many clients are interested in gaining employment. The first step toward this is being legally eligible for employment in this country. The IRCA requires that all employers with three or more employees "verify the work eligibility status of all applicants for employment" (American Bar Association, 2006, p. 272) by examining government-issued documents and completing an I-9 Form to record this verification process. Such documents may include a driver's license, social security card, birth certificate, passport, or other documents demonstrating eligibility for work. Applicants who were not born in the United States may provide other evidence of employment eligibility. Such documents may include evidence of naturalization or status as a resident alien (Cihon & Castagnera, 2011, p. 93).

A more recent law, the Immigration Act of 1990, has "expanded the protection of the IRCA to cover seasonal agricultural workers" and protect applicants from discriminatory practices in the document examination process by prohibiting employers "from requesting more or different employment-eligibility documents than are required under the IRCA and from refusing to honor documents that reasonably appear to be genuine" (Cihon & Castagnera, 2011, p. 214).

EMPLOYEE BACKGROUND CHECKS. Assuming your client is able to document eligibility for employment in the United States, the next step of the hiring process may include some sort of background check. Employers often check an applicant's references. Some employers may also conduct criminal background checks or financial credit checks. They may also request information about a prospective employee's medical history. As you talk with clients about the job-seeking process, they may have questions about or benefit from basic information about what is and is not legal in background checks.

With regard to reference checks, employers can and often do contact an applicant's references before extending offers of employment. However, because former employers likely know that it is illegal to provide "false or misleading references about former employees," many "will only verify that an employee worked for them for a particular period, and will not provide an assessment of that employee's performance" (American Bar Association, 2006, p. 53). Afraid of being sued by their former employees, these employers choose to err on the side of safety rather than to risk being accused of defamation.

According to Cihon and Castagnera (2011), criminal background checks are legal in a number of states and are even required for certain types of positions. For example, they identify eight states in which a criminal background check is required for employment in the areas of child care or day care. Other occupations in which criminal background checks may be required include law enforcement, state lottery commissions, nuclear power plants, and jobs within public schools. Obviously, in cases where state law requires criminal background checks, it is certainly legal (and actually required) for employers to avoid hiring people who do not pass the background check. This is particularly common for professions in which occupational licensing laws prohibit employment of ex-offenders—those who have criminal convictions and have completed their sentence (Thompson & Cummings, 2010).

It is important to note, however, that criminal records can consist not only of convictions but also of arrests that did not result in a conviction. The legality of basing hiring and firing decisions on criminal background checks depends in part on whether a decision is based on prior arrests or solely on actual convictions. Cihon and Castagnera (2011) explained that basing decisions on prior arrests that did not result in convictions may be legally untenable. Specifically, they stated that "refusing to hire applicants because of their arrest records (as opposed to convictions) may constitute . . . discrimination" and be prohibited by the Civil Rights Act of 1964 (Cihon & Castagnera, 2011, p. 318). The basis for this point is that some racial groups (or other protected classes of citizens) may be falsely arrested more often than others. Even so, some employers choose not to hire applicants without criminal convictions but with a history of arrests. Thompson and Cummings (2010) suggest that this is due in part to fears about "negligent hiring, in which employers in many states are held liable for any criminal actions committed by their employees" (p. 210).

Another type of background check can involve checking an applicant's credit rating and/or credit history. The American Bar Association (2006) explains that the legality of conducting financial credit checks and requiring good credit is questionable. Specifically, it indicates that, because "disproportionately more nonwhites than whites live below the poverty line," credit checks may be deemed discriminatory (p. 53). It also indicates that such checks may be found in violation of the Fair Credit Reporting Act.

Another type of background check that is sometimes attempted by employers involves collection of information about a prospective or current employee's medical history. However, the use of such "protected health information" for "personnel decisions" is prohibited by the Health Insurance Portability and Accountability Act (HIPAA; Cihon & Castagnera, 2011, p. 67). The Genetic Information Nondiscrimination Act of 2008 specifies that employers cannot require or even request employees or prospective employees to provide genetic information. In considering this law, it is important for you (and your career counseling clients) to understand that such information is not limited to DNA samples or actual genetic tests. Instead, one's "family medical history is included in the definition of genetic information because it is often used to determine whether someone has an increased risk of getting a disease, disorder, or condition in the future" (U.S. Equal Employment Opportunity Commission, 2014, para. 4).

Except for very specific occupational classifications, employees or potential employees cannot legally be required to provide such information. Even if the employee voluntarily provides such information, the employer is prohibited from using the information for employment decisions. Specifically, the U.S. Equal Employment Opportunity Commission (2014) states that the law:

> prohibits the use of genetic information in making employment decisions, restricts employers and other entities covered by Title II (employment agencies, labor organizations and joint labor-management training and apprenticeship programs—referred to as "covered entities") from requesting, requiring or purchasing genetic information, and strictly limits the disclosure of genetic information (U.S. Equal Employment Opportunity Commission, 2014, para. 2)

It is important to note that, although it is illegal for employers to discriminate on these health-related bases, it *is* legal for employers to make employment decisions on the basis of drug use and/or drug testing. With the exception of the Drug-Free Workplace Act (which requires certain federal government contractors and grant recipients to establish policies and programs to promote drug-free workplaces), federal law is relatively silent on the issue of drug testing. In contrast, many states have passed legislation allowing employers to require drug testing and to make employment decisions based on the results of drug testing. In an effort to protect employees, however, these laws also tend to be very specific about how employers implement such policies. Generally speaking, the laws require employers to make the drug-testing policy available to employees in writing and to allow for retesting before firing an employee who tests positive. Some states also require employers to provide opportunities for employees to participate in drug rehabilitation programs before firing them (Cihon & Castagnera, 2011).

NONDISCRIMINATION LAWS. With regard to laws that have curtailed the reach of the at-will employment doctrine, the landmark legislation is clearly the Civil Rights Act of 1964. Passage of this law marked a historical shift toward protecting workers from personnel decisions based on a variety of demographic characteristics. Title VII of the Civil Rights Act of 1964 "prohibits the refusal or failure to hire any individual, or the discrimination against any individual with respect to compensation, terms, conditions, or privileges of employment because of that individual's race, color, religion, sex, or national origin" (Cihon & Castagnera, 2011, p. 114).

Cases involving alleged discrimination are considered in two primary ways. One, called disparate treatment, involves the employer's direct (and presumably intentional) discrimination against an employee or applicant based on his or her race, color, religion, sex, or national origin (Cihon & Castagnera, 2011, p. 116). The other, called disparate impact, does not generally involve intentional discrimination. Instead, it results from a seemingly neutral policy that has a disparate impact on people of various races, colors, religions, sexes, or national origins (Cihon & Castagnera, 2011, p. 117). This concept was referred to earlier during the discussion of financial credit checks, with the caution that a seemingly neutral policy of requiring that employees have good credit may have a disparate impact because "disproportionately more non-whites than whites live below the poverty line"; in this case, credit checks may be deemed discriminatory (American Bar Association, 2006, p. 53).

This nondiscrimination law has some exceptions, however. First, this federal legislation does not apply to employers with fewer than 15 employees. Many states have antidiscrimination laws paralleling Title VII that *do* apply to employers with fewer than 15 employees. Thus, you should become familiar with your state's antidiscrimination laws. The other exception important to note is that the Title VII law allows "an employer to hire employees of a specific gender, religion, or national origin [but never race or color] when the business necessity—the safe and efficient performance of the particular job—requires it" (Cihon & Castagnera, 2011, p. 117). In such cases, however, the employer must be able to document that one of these factors is a bona fide occupational qualification (BFOQ), which is generally quite difficult to do (Cihon & Castagnera, 2011, p. 117).

In addition to discrimination based on race, color, gender, religion, or national origin (all of which are addressed by the Civil Rights Act of 1964), it is also illegal to discriminate on the basis of age. The Age Discrimination in Employment Act (ADEA) of 1967 "prohibits discrimination against individuals forty years of age and older" (American Bar Association, 2006, pp. 15–16). Discrimination might involve "the refusal or failure to hire, the discharge, or any discrimination in compensation, terms, conditions or privileges of employment because of an individual's age (Cihon & Castagnera, 2011, p. 246).

Examples of discrimination include forced retirement at a given age or assignment decisions that are based on an employee's age rather than current skill set.

Another prohibited form of discrimination in employment involves disability. In terms of federal laws, the Americans with Disabilities Act (ADA), first passed in 1990 and most recently amended in 2008, is the best-known legislation in this arena. Title I of this law "prohibits employment discrimination against qualified individuals with a disability, and requires employers to make reasonable accommodations to such individuals" (American Bar Association, 2006, p. 16). You should note two key points here. First is the issue of being qualified. To qualify, the employee (or potential employee) "has the burden of demonstrating his or her ability to meet all . . . requirements legitimately necessary" for the job (Cihon & Castagnera, 2011, p. 269). If a person with a disability cannot perform all requirements of a given job, it is not considered discrimination if an employer does not hire him or her. The second key point is also essential to consider: The person can be deemed qualified if, given "reasonable accommodations," she or he can perform all of the "essential functions of the job" (Cihon & Castagnera, 2011, p. 269). Accommodations are considered reasonable, however, only if they do not cause undue burden for the employer (American Bar Association, 2006, p. 115).

An additional piece of legislation that prohibits discrimination on the basis of disability is the Rehabilitation Act of 1973. Whereas the ADA legislation "applies to both private and public sector employers with fifteen or more employees but does not apply to most federal government positions" (Cihon & Castagnera, 2011, p. 267), the Rehabilitation Act focuses on protection of federal employees and those people working for employers who receive federal funding.

Because career counselors may encounter clients who also struggle with alcohol or other drug dependence, it is worth noting that both the ADA and the Rehabilitation Act contain specific exceptions regarding drug dependence. According to Cihon and Castagnera (2011),

> Section 104 of the ADA specifically excludes from the definition of "qualified individual with a disability" any persons who are currently engaged in the illegal use of drugs and allows employers to prohibit the use of alcohol and illegal drugs in the workplace. The Rehabilitation Act also excludes from its protection individuals who are alcoholics or drug abusers whose current use of alcohol or drugs prevents them from performing the duties of the job or whose employment constitutes a direct threat to the property or safety of others. (p. 285)

These laws do, however, prohibit discrimination against individuals who have had alcohol or drug dependence problems in the past but who are successfully abstaining from use. Neither the fact that someone has had substance abuse problems nor the fact that someone has participated in a substance abuse rehabilitation program can be used as a basis for employment decisions. As long as one is no longer using and as long as these previous issues no longer prevent adequate performance of one's job, the individual is protected from discrimination on this basis.

If you've been keeping track of the various classes of individuals who enjoy legal protection from employment discrimination, you may have noticed one notable omission. To date, there is no federal employment law specifically prohibiting discrimination on the basis of sexual orientation (American Bar Association, 2006). There have been many court cases regarding discrimination on the basis of sexual orientation, but in the absence of specific law, federal "courts have generally allowed public employers to refuse to hire homosexuals when the employer can show that the ban on homosexuals has some legitimate relationship to valid employment-related concerns" (Cihon & Castagnera, 2011, p. 189). However, many states and localities do have laws prohibiting discrimination on the basis of sexual preference or sexual orientation. If this issue is a concern for your client, it is essential that you check state and local statutes.

Perhaps the highest profile example of such discrimination, and one that could not be remedied by state or local statutes, existed within the U.S. military system until its repeal on July 22, 2011. The U.S. military had a longstanding unwillingness to enlist or commission gays, lesbians, and bisexuals and, under the Clinton administration, adopted the "don't ask, don't tell" policy. This policy called for the immediate, dishonorable discharge of military personnel who engaged in homosexual conduct or who even verbally admitted to identifying as gay, lesbian, or bisexual. Career (and school) counselors had to be aware that, in addition to the psychological and occupational impact, such a discharge could be financially devastating for an individual. Crompton (1993) cautioned that students who enroll in the military through the Reserve Officers' Training Corp (ROTC) program and are then "disenrolled because they are homosexual must repay military scholarship monies" (p. 10). In other words, if ROTC monies paid for 3 years of a student's college costs and it was then revealed that the student is gay, that student would be dishonorably discharged and required to repay the government for all monies expended on his or her behalf.

One could argue that such a policy resulted in the individual being put in a worse position compared to his or her starting point.

Laws do change, however, and the "don't ask, don't tell" policy was finally overturned. In September 2010, the Log Cabin Republicans ("the nation's original and largest organization representing gay conservatives and allies who support fairness, freedom, and equality for all Americans" [logcabin.org/about-us/, para. 1]) sued the United States claiming that the "don't ask, don't tell" policy is unconstitutional (*Log Cabin Republicans v. United States of America*, U.S. Dist. Ct. for Cent. Dist. Cal., 9/9/2010). The federal district court judge in this case found in favor of the plaintiffs and rendered a decision that the policy was unconstitutional. However, the case was appealed, and the policy was finally repealed on July 22, 2011, when President Obama finally signed it into law. The repeal of this policy serves as an excellent example of how important it is to remain current.

WRONGFUL DISCHARGE EXCEPTIONS TO AT-WILL EMPLOYMENT. As you have learned in this chapter, the at-will employment doctrine is the predominant form of employment in the United States. With very few exceptions, this doctrine means that the employer can fire an employee "for a good reason, a bad reason, or no reason at all" (Tomlinson & Bockanic, 2009, p. 77). However, few employees understand this; "80–90% of employees believe that the law of the United States is just cause" and think that they can be fired only for a good reason (Kim, 1997, as cited in Dannin, 2007, p. 8). In fact, however, only the states of Montana and Arizona require just cause for the termination of employees (Dannon, 2007). For all other states, just cause is not necessary for an employer to fire an at-will employee. It is important for career counselors to have a sound understanding of at-will employment and the exceptions to it. In general, however, an employer can legally fire a client "for a good reason, a bad reason, or no reason at all" unless one of the following exceptions exists: statuary exceptions, contract exceptions, and common law exceptions.

Statuary Exceptions. Statuary exceptions exist when specific laws have been passed to narrow the reach of the employment-at-will doctrine. Table 7.2 summarizes such statuary exceptions and is based primarily on information shared by Tomlinson and Bockanic (2009) and Cihon and Castagnera (2011).

Contract Exceptions. Two specific types of contracts narrow the reach of the at-will employment doctrine. These two exceptions are explained thoroughly by

TABLE 7.2 Statuary Exceptions to Employment-at-Will

National Labor Relations Act
- This law protects employees from being fired for participating in legal, collective bargaining or union activities.

Civil Rights Act of 1964, Title VII
- This statute protects employees from being fired for discriminatory reasons based on their race, color, religion, sex, and/or national origin.

Age Discrimination in Employment Act
- This law protects employees from being fired for discriminatory reasons based on their age if they are over age 40 (Cihon & Castagnera, 2011).

Occupational Safety and Health Act
- This statute protects employees from being fired for filing a complaint alleging unsafe working conditions.

Americans with Disabilities Act and Rehabilitation Act of 1973
- This law protects employees from being fired because of disabilities if the employee could perform the job with reasonable accommodations.

Family Medical Leave Act
- This statute protects employees from being fired or demoted after taking medical leave to which they are legally entitled. Such leave may be taken to attend to one's own medical needs or to attend to the medical needs of family members.

Pregnancy Discrimination Act
- This law protects employees from being fired because of "pregnancy, childbirth and other medically related conditions" (Tomlinson & Bockanic, 2009, p. 78).

Tomlinson and Bockanic (2009). Table 7.3 summarizes this information.

Common Law Exceptions. Some court cases have been brought in which individuals have sued their former employers successfully after being fired. In these suits, the former employees claimed that they should either be reinstated or compensated for wrongful discharge. In the absence of a particular type of contract or the absence of a specific statuary exception, these plaintiffs had to convince the court that, in spite of the dominance of the at-will doctrine, their firing was so appalling that it called for a finding against the employer. Such findings result in the establishment of common law (Cihon & Castagnera, 2011). These common law precedents have generally been established in state-level courts, however, so there may be some variation from state to state with regard to recognition of the common law shared below. Nonetheless, it is helpful to have some familiarity with the most widespread common law precedents. Table 7.4 presents four types of common law exceptions to the at-will employment doctrine and is based on information presented by Tomlinson and Bockanic (2009).

ADVANCE NOTICE OF MASS LAYOFFS. In some cases when workers lose their jobs, it is not their fault nor is it due to mistreatment by employers. Instead, workers may lose their jobs because their employer can no longer afford to employ them. Businesses fail and plants close. Although sad, it's reality. In these cases, though, some advance notice can be quite useful. Imagine how you'd feel if you arrived at work one day, just like you'd done every day for the past 10 years, only to find a sign on the door stating, "Plant closed." You and your coworkers would be literally left out on the street.

TABLE 7.3 Contract Exceptions to Employment-at-Will

Collective bargaining agreement (union contract)
- Most collective bargaining agreements include specific terms related to conditions of employment and conditions for advancement and termination. Such contracts protect employees from being fired for no reason and for bad reasons.

Express contract between employer and employee
- Some employment contracts meet very specific conditions necessary for an express contract. When "delineating the term of employment and/or conditions permitting discharge of the employee," such contracts supersede the at-will employment doctrine (Tomlinson & Bockanic, 2009, p. 78).

TABLE 7.4 Common Law Exceptions to Employment-at-Will
Implied covenant of good faith and fair dealing
• Some employees have successfully sued employers after being fired in spite of a good faith agreement.
Implied contracts
• Some employees have successfully sued employers after being fired when an implied contract existed (usually articulated in employee handbooks or other employer-developed documents that indicate that employees will be terminated only for just cause).
Tort claims
• Some employees have successfully sued employers after being fired for what they consider bad reasons, such as when employer behavior, either during or after employment, could be characterized as including "defamation, wrongful infliction of emotional distress, fraud, invasion of privacy, [or] assault and battery" (Tomlinson & Bockanic, 2009, p. 79).
Public policy claims
• Protects employees from being fired for "exercising [a] legal right or fulfilling [a] legal duty" (Cihon & Castagnera, 2011, p. 20). Examples include "refusal to commit perjury, . . . serving on a jury, blowing the whistle on employer misdeeds, or refusing to engage in criminal activity at the request of the employer" (Tomlinson & Bockanic, 2009, p. 80).

The federal Worker Adjustment and Retraining Act (WARN) was passed in 1988 to avoid these unfortunate situations. This law requires that any employer with at least 100 employees must warn employees in writing at least 60 days in advance of any upcoming mass layoffs, defined as involving "fifty or more employees [losing] their jobs during any thirty-day period," unless the employer's circumstances are so dire that they are considered a "failing firm" (Cihon & Castagnera, 2011, pp. 473–474). Although WARN does not give employees any input into the decisions regarding layoffs or the closing of plants or businesses, it still packs a punch. If an employer covered by WARN fails to give the 60-day notice, "the employer is required to pay each affected employee up to sixty days' pay and benefits" and can be subject to additional fines (Cihon & Castagnera, 2011, p. 474).

PUTTING IT ALL TOGETHER. This section has explored several categories of legislation relevant to the hiring and firing processes, and Table 7.5 provides a summary of these laws. Although your head may be swimming with the many laws described in this section, keep in mind that you do not need to become an expert in employment law or commit all these laws to memory. However, clients in career counseling often present with struggles to become hired or to having been fired. Although these concerns may sometimes be best attributed to a client's need for change (i.e., the development of strong employability skills), sometimes your client has received unfair and/or illegal treatment that has resulted either in not being hired or in being fired. A basic understanding of these employment laws will serve you very well as a career counselor as it will allow you to recognize times at which it is prudent to suggest to your client that he or she seek legal advice.

Laws Pertaining to Work Conditions

Several important federal laws pertain to the hiring and firing of employees in the United States, and several regulate

TABLE 7.5 Laws Pertaining to Hiring and Firing of Employees
Immigration law
• Immigration Reform and Control Act (IRCA) of 1986
• Immigration Act of 1990
Employee background checks
• Reference checks
• Criminal history
• Credit history
• Health history
Nondiscrimination laws
• Title VII of the Civil Rights Act of 1964
• Age Discrimination in Employment Act
• Americans with Disability Act
• Rehabilitation Act of 1973, as amended
Wrongful Discharge Exceptions to At-Will Employment
• States requiring just cause (Montana and Arizona)
• Statuary exceptions
• Contract exceptions
• Common law exceptions
Advance notice of mass layoffs
• Worker Adjustment and Retraining Act of 1988

work conditions. Generally speaking, these laws may be categorized into laws protecting workers from discrimination and/or harassment and laws protecting workers from unsafe or inhumane working conditions. Each set of laws is designed to ensure that the workplace is safe, humane, and nondiscriminatory.

LAWS PROTECTING WORKERS FROM DISCRIMINATION AND/OR HARASSMENT. As described in the previous section of this chapter, several employment laws prohibit discrimination. In addition to applying to the hiring and firing of employees, these same laws pertain to workplace conditions. Such working conditions may include the assignment of tasks, work schedule, level of compensation, opportunities for advancement, degree of supervision, and even dress code. In the interest of brevity, this section will not revisit the laws discussed earlier in the chapter by specifically enumerating their relevance to working conditions. Suffice it to say—just as it is illegal to hire, not hire, or fire someone on the basis of race, color, religion, sex, national origin, age, and/or disability status, it is also illegal to discriminate on these bases with regard to other working conditions such as pay, promotion requirements, and work schedules.

Several other laws are also designed to protect workers from discrimination. The Equal Pay Act is one such law. Passed in 1963, this law prohibits sex discrimination with regard to pay. The Equal Pay Act requires "equal pay for equal work." To be considered equal work, the work does not have to be identical; instead, the emphasis is on work that is equivalent. Specifically, the work must require the same "skills, effort and responsibilities . . . performed under similar working conditions" (Cihon & Castagnera, 2011, p. 155).

The Lilly Ledbetter Fair Pay Act is also worth noting. This law was enacted by Congress in 2009 to extend the period of time an individual has to file a complaint about discriminatory pay with the U.S. Equal Employment Opportunity Commission (EEOC). This period of time is defined rather narrowly by Title VII of the Civil Rights Act and by the Equal Pay Act, but the Lilly Ledbetter Fair Pay Act defines it more broadly. In all three laws, the individual has 180 days within which to file a complaint with the EEOC. However, Title VII and the Equal Pay Act start the clock, so to speak, at the point of performance evaluation. In contrast, the Lilly Ledbetter Fair Pay Act starts the clock "from the latest of three dates: when the discriminatory pay policy is adopted, when the employee becomes subject to the discriminatory pay policy, or when the employee is affected by the policy" (Cihon & Castagnera, 2011, p. 219).

The problem of sexual harassment also pertains to working conditions and discrimination based on sex. The EEOC has determined that sexual harassment violates the prohibition against discrimination on the basis of an individual's sex and is therefore considered a violation of Title VII of the Civil Rights Act of 1964. State laws prohibiting sex discrimination also prohibit sexual harassment. According to Cihon and Castagnera (2011),

> Sexual harassment is defined as unwelcome sexual advances, requests for sexual favors, or other verbal or physical conduct of a sexual nature, where the employee is required to accept such conduct as a condition of employment, the employee's response to such conduct is used as a basis for employment decisions such as promotion, bonuses, or retention, or such conduct unreasonably interferes with the employee's work performance or creates a hostile working environment. (p. 173)

A quid pro quo system in which the implicit or explicit message from the employer to the employee is, "I'll give you this if you give me that" would be an example of sexual harassment. In such systems, the targeted employee may benefit or suffer financially in some way (hours, pay, promotion, etc.) based on his or her acceptance of the sexual conduct. In contrast, the hostile working environment involves situations in which there is no financial reward or punishment for acceptance of sexual conduct but the employee is "subjected to unwelcome comments, propositions, jokes, or conduct that have the effect of interfering with the employee's work performance" (Cihon & Castagnera, 2011, p. 155). Whether directed at a female or male employee and whether directed toward someone of the same or opposite sex, unwelcome comments or behaviors of a sexual nature are inappropriate and constitute cause for legal action. Should a client come to you for career counseling and express dissatisfaction with his or her work due to sexual harassment, it is important that you also provide her or him with contact information for the EEOC to explore options for filing a complaint.

LAWS PROTECTING WORKERS FROM INHUMANE OR UNSAFE WORKING CONDITIONS. Recall that Frank Parsons expressed grave concerns about inadequate pay for manual labor positions, extremely long hours, unsafe working conditions, and the employment of children as cost-saving measures. Indeed, these working conditions were appalling and indicative of how much of an advantage the employment-at-will doctrine gave employers at the time. Since that time, a number of laws have been passed to protect workers from such mistreatment by employers in the United States.

The Fair Labor Standards Act (FLSA), passed in 1938, represents the preeminent legislation to ensure that workers in the United States are treated humanely. It does so by regulating the minimum wage, ensuring overtime pay for hourly workers, and regulating the employment of children. This law calls for a minimum wage (adjusted by the Department of Labor) for hourly workers, identifies the length of a full-time workweek as 40 hours, and insists that hourly workers be paid time and a half for working more than 40 hours in a week. Exceptions to this law exist, however: The minimum wage and overtime requirements generally don't apply to employees who are salaried (usually executives, administrators, or professionals) or to those who work on commission (Cihon & Castagnera, 2011).

The FLSA also addresses two major issues related to the employment of children. First, the law addresses the type of work children can do by prohibiting the employment of minors in jobs deemed "hazardous" (Cihon & Castagnera, 2011, p. 701). Second, FLSA limits the number of hours children under the age of 18 can work, with specific regulations for those between 16 and 18, those between 14 and 16, and those younger than 14. If you will be providing career development or career counseling to minors, perhaps in a school setting, it is essential that you familiarize yourself with these regulations.

One other piece of landmark legislation related to working conditions is the Occupational Safety and Health Act (OSHA). The elements of the law itself are fairly basic but incredibly important. First, OSHA drew attention to the importance of workplace safety and workplace dangers by calling for the systematic study of conditions contributing to workplace fatalities and illnesses, and the development of safety guidelines to avoid them. Second, OSHA called for the promulgation of standards to inform workers of workplace hazards and to specify safety precautions designed to protect workers. Third, OSHA protects workers from retaliation by employers for participating in OSHA activities, requesting OSHA information, refusing to engage in a work activity due to a safety concern, or making complaints to OSHA about work conditions (Cihon & Castagnera, 2011). OSHA reports that, as a result of such efforts, "workplace fatalities have been cut by more than 60 percent and occupational injury and illness rates have declined 40 percent" (Occupational Safety and Health Act, 2006, p. 4).

As we conclude this section about laws pertaining to working conditions, it is worthwhile to note that the laws shared here regulate the working conditions only in the United States. Although one might assume that the laws regarding discrimination, compensation, child labor, and workplace safety regulate the working conditions by all U.S. employers, this is not correct. U.S. employers are required to follow these laws only in their U.S. locations. Cihon and Castagnera (2011) observed that "globalization has put new pressure on American free enterprise, which all too often has succumbed to the lure of faraway places where sweatshops can be established to replace high-wage, frequently unionized factories in the United States" (p. 681). Career counselors with an interest in social justice and human rights issues may choose to engage in advocacy efforts to promote future legislation regarding the inhumane treatment of workers by any U.S. employer regardless of the location of the worksite (Sloan, 2005).

PUTTING IT ALL TOGETHER. Clients in career counseling often present with concerns related to dissatisfaction with their current job. When exploring such dissatisfaction, it is not enough to consider only the goodness of fit between the job and your client's interests, values, skills, and personality. As a responsible career counselor, you also want to bear in mind that the dissatisfaction may not be due to a poor fit between your client and the occupation itself but rather due to poor, and perhaps illegal, working conditions in his or her specific workplace. The blame for these poor working conditions may sometimes be best attributed to a "my boss is a jerk" situation. At other times, the situation might actually involve illegal practices by the employer. Table 7.6 will give you a basic understanding of the laws discussed in this section.

Laws Pertaining to Unemployment and Inability to Work

Some clients who seek career guidance or counseling do so because of an inability either to find work or to engage in the type of work they've done in the past. In the United States, several laws provide safety nets for such individuals (Cihon & Castagnera, 2011, p. 657). For individuals who are unable to find work, these safety nets include the ability to continue health insurance benefits and the ability to collect unemployment insurance benefits. For workers who are unable to engage in the type of work they've done in the past because of injuries or illnesses, these safety nets include worker's compensation and vocational

TABLE 7.6 Laws Pertaining to Working Conditions

Laws protecting workers from discrimination and harassment
- Title VII of the Civil Rights Act of 1964
- Age Discrimination in Employment Act
- Americans with Disability Act
- Rehabilitation Act of 1973, as amended
- Equal Pay Act of 1963
- Lilly Ledbetter Fair Pay Act of 2009

Laws protecting workers from inhumane or unsafe working conditions
- Fair Labor Standards Act of 1938
- Occupational Safety and Health Act

rehabilitation benefits. For workers who are unable to engage in any type of work because of injuries or illnesses, these safety nets include disability insurance benefits.

EXTENSION OF ELIGIBILITY FOR HEALTH CARE BENEFITS.
When losing a job, one loses more than the income associated with the job. As a future professional counselor, you surely recognize the psychosocial issues associated with job loss. A person's sense of identity, confidence, even esteem from others can all be at risk in times of unemployment. On a more pragmatic level, though, another important loss can be that of health insurance. For individuals and/or families who are in need of health care, such a loss can be devastating.

The Consolidated Omnibus Budget Reconciliation Act (COBRA) of 1985 was passed into law by Congress. This law affects people who either lose their job altogether (regardless of fault) and to people who lose their employer-based group health care due to a reduction in hours (generally to less than half-time; American Bar Association, 2006). In these cases, the law requires that the employer allow the individual the option to continue receiving health care benefits through the employer's group health plan. Individuals have up to 60 days to decide whether to take COBRA benefits. Under typical conditions, they can get these benefits for up to 18 months. In circumstances involving the death of or divorce from an employee, benefits may be continued for up to 36 months. To extend health care benefits through COBRA, however, the individual generally has to pay the entire premium associated with the group health plan. In most cases, the premium associated with the group health plan is considerably less than what the person would need to pay for an individual/family plan on his or her own.

UNEMPLOYMENT INSURANCE. You may be surprised to know that there is no federal law governing unemployment insurance benefits. Instead, using both state and federal monies, unemployment insurance programs are run by states, so you should learn more about your state's unemployment insurance program. Generally speaking, these state-based programs share many commonalities.

First, these benefits are available only to those individuals who are unemployed due to no fault of their own (American Bar Association, 2006; Cihon & Castagnera, 2011). Such situations include becoming unemployed "due to plant closure [or] natural disaster" (American Bar Association, 2006, p. 186). Depending on the state, an individual who voluntarily leaves a position with "good cause," such as relocating because of a spouse's job transfer, may also qualify (American Bar Association, 2006). In most states, however, employees who become unemployed as a result of being fired, quitting, or failing a drug test will likely have a difficult time collecting unemployment insurance benefits because they are often considered at fault in these situations (Cihon & Castagnera, 2011).

Second, unemployment insurance benefits tend to be based on the requirement that the recipient is available for work and actively seeking to become reemployed (American Bar Association, 2006). In reality, there is considerable variation in the seriousness with which recipients attempt to find work. At a minimum, most states require that the recipient become involved with a state-run employment agency to find work. Anecdotal evidence suggests that the intensity of the job search tends to increase only when unemployment benefits are about to expire or already have expired. Indeed, if you become a career counselor at a state employment agency, you will likely have many clients who seek your services only to document that they are actively seeking work. Such clients will demonstrate minimal investment in the career counseling and job-seeking process until expiration of benefits creates a sense of urgency for them. Although it may be tempting to develop a cynical attitude and question whether these clients really want to work, such an attitude will likely be demoralizing to you and unhelpful to your clients. Instead, you may want to utilize a motivational interviewing strategy. McCarthy and Cluss (2002) described uses of motivational interviewing in employment settings, and this approach could easily be modified for use with unemployed clients who demonstrate resistance and/or ambivalence about engaging in a vigorous job search.

Third, the length of time an individual can collect unemployment benefits usually has a limit. In most cases, state laws call for funding unemployment benefits for only 26 weeks. Remember, however, that the unemployment insurance system, although run by the respective state, is funded by state and federal monies. In difficult economic times, it is not uncommon for the federal government (Congress) to approve additional federal monies to be allocated specifically for the extension of unemployment benefits. For example, you may recall hearing about the U.S. Congress extending unemployment benefits for up to 96 weeks to ease the hardships during the recent recession the United States experienced. In such cases, these federal monies are then funneled through the states to the recipients of these benefits. The premise is that, when jobs are scarce, it is very difficult for the unemployed to find new jobs even if they are desperately trying to do so.

Another commonality across state unemployment benefit programs is that unemployment insurance benefits are based on the requirement that the recipient is indeed able to engage in work. Although this may seem obvious, you may sometimes work with clients who wish to apply for unemployment benefits but who may not be able to work. Most often, this situation occurs when a worker becomes unable to work due to an injury or illness. In these cases, the next set of safety nets—workers' compensation and/or social security disability—would be more appropriate for those individuals to seek.

WORKER'S COMPENSATION. Despite the progress that has been made with regard to workplace injuries and illnesses (Occupational Safety and Health Act, 2006), employees can and do suffer injuries while performing their work and/or develop illnesses as a result of their work. In fact, OSHA reports that, each year, "nearly 4.3 million people suffer non-fatal workplace injuries and illnesses" at an annual cost of "more than $156 billion" (Occupational Safety and Health Act, 2006, p. 5). Some of these injuries and illnesses result in a person's temporary or permanent inability to continue performing the job, whereas others do not. In either case, the employee should file an injury/illness report with his or her employer for the purposes of OSHA record keeping regarding such occurrences.

In addition, if the injury and illness does indeed result in a person's temporary or permanent inability to continue performing the job, he or she may also qualify for worker's compensation benefits. Although worker's compensation programs vary from state to state, they all generally provide two types of benefits for workers injured on the job: (1) replacement of lost income and (2) medical expenses related to the injury or illness (American Bar Association, 2006). Note also that it is generally not necessary for the employee to document that the injury or illness was the fault of the employer (i.e., negligence) in order to qualify for benefits. As long as the injury or illness occurred at work and as long as the employer participates in the worker's compensation insurance program (generally mandated for all employers but varies by state), the employee is usually covered. When providing career counseling services to clients who have been injured on the job, it is useful to inquire about whether they have filed an OSHA report and whether they have considered applying for worker's compensation benefits. In addition, they may qualify for vocational rehabilitation benefits.

VOCATIONAL REHABILITATION. As part of the Rehabilitation Act of 1973, the Rehabilitation Services Administration (RSA) was established by Congress. Its purpose is to administer a wide variety of programs intended to assist individuals with disabilities in a number of capacities, including "vocational rehabilitation, supported employment and independent living" (Rehabilitation Services Administration, 2010, para. 2). This federal agency also "oversees grant programs that help individuals with physical or mental disabilities to obtain employment and live more independently through the provision of such supports as counseling, medical and psychological services, job training and other individualized services" (Rehabilitation Services Administration, 2010, para. 4). Although many smaller grants are made to independent, nonprofit agencies, the majority of these funds are used to operate state vocational rehabilitation agencies in all 50 states. These state agencies provide vocational rehabilitation services (often staffed by career and/or vocational rehabilitation counselors) geared toward people whose ability to engage in gainful employment is limited by a disability.

Some people have acquired a disability; others have had lifelong disabilities. As you know, some workers who are injured on the job sustain serious and permanent injuries that prevent them from being able to continue in their former line of work. In addition to qualifying for worker's compensation benefits to supplant the income they would have been earning and to cover medical costs associated with the injury, these individuals will generally also qualify for free vocational rehabilitation counseling services through the state. Another group of individuals who will generally qualify are those who sustain an injury or develop a serious illness in a setting other than work. These individuals, of course, would not qualify for worker's compensation but will likely qualify for vocational rehabilitation services through a state agency. In each of these cases involving injuries or illnesses that are acquired either on or off the job, the focus of vocational rehabilitation counseling is to assist the client in identifying existing and potential skills with which they could resume gainful employment.

The third type of client generally eligible for vocational rehabilitation benefits is one with a lifelong or longstanding disability preceding his or her entrance into the workforce. In this case, vocational rehabilitation services are often offered in conjunction with special education services. As students approach the transition from the K–12 educational system, the emphasis on vocational rehabilitation services increases in an attempt to prepare them for entry into the workforce. These services are generally coordinated through the U.S. Department of Education's Office for Special Education and Rehabilitative Services.

SOCIAL SECURITY BENEFITS. In some cases, individuals sustain injuries or develop illnesses so severe that vocational rehabilitation services are insufficient to assist them in regaining their capacity to engage in gainful employment for an extended and indefinite period of time. In these cases, employees may be eligible for assistance from Social Security Disability Insurance (SSDI) and/or the Supplemental Security Insurance (SSI) programs. Although both programs require that recipients be disabled in accordance with very strict definitions (specified in Table 7.7),

TABLE 7.7 Qualification Requirements for SSDI and SSI

SSDI	SSI
Citizenship status	Citizenship status
• The person must be a U.S. citizen or be lawfully admitted for permanent citizenship in the United States with a valid immigration status.	• The person must be a U.S. citizen or be lawfully admitted for permanent citizenship in the United States with a valid immigration status.
Insured status	Insured status
• If age 32 or older, the person must have worked 5 of the last 10 years and paid Social Security contributions for at least 5 years. • If age 18 to 31, the person must have paid Social Security contributions, but the length of time is based on a graduated scale requiring the person to have worked and contributed for half of the time since turning 18. • Differs for blind persons.	• None. Insured status is not required for SSI.
Financial need	Financial need
• None. Financial need is not required for SSDI.	• The person must have demonstrated financial need. Factors such as household income, parental status, and marital status are considered.
Disabled status	Disabled status
• The person must meet requirements specified below, either steps 1 to 3 or steps 1, 2, 4, and 5, which are evaluated sequentially by the SSA.	• The person must meet requirements specified below, either steps 1 to 3 or steps 1, 2, 4, and 5, which are evaluated sequentially by the SSA.

Steps for determining disabled status:
1. Unable to engage in substantial gainful activity (defined in 2010 as earning $1,000/month or more, which is subject to change annually, unless a person is statutorily blind) since the alleged onset of the disability.
2. Existence of impairment or combination of impairments that would reasonably limit a person's ability to perform work activities.
3. Existence of impairment criteria as specified by the SSA Listing of Impairments (Appendix 1, Code of Federal Regulations). The criteria for these impairments are recognized by the SSA as being so severe from a medical standpoint, regardless of vocational factors, that the person qualifies as disabled without needing to meet the requirements listed below in steps 4 and 5. *Note:* If the individual meets requirements 1 and 2 but not 3, he or she must also meet requirements 4 and 5 as listed below in order to qualify as disabled for SSDI purposes.
4. Inability to perform any job he or she has held in the 15 years before disability as the job is generally performed in the national economy or as the individual had performed it.
5. Inability to perform a significant number of jobs in the national economy on a regular and sustained basis. Determination of this qualification depends on the person's age, education, skill level of past work, and what the SSA calls the person's residual functional capacity.

they differ in their legislative backing and in their focus. The SSDI program was established by Title II of the Social Security Act and it is best considered a worker's insurance program for people with disabilities that prevent their gainful employment. In contrast, the SSI program was established by Title XVI of the Social Security Act and is best described as a needs-based program for people with disabilities that prevent their gainful employment.

In thinking about client eligibility for such programs, the phrase "disabilities that prevent their gainful employment" is worth clarifying. Whereas the worker's compensation program pertains even to short-term injuries (such as a broken leg) that temporarily impede an employee's ability to do his or her job, the SSDI and SSI programs are intended only for longer-term disabilities. Specifically, "a disabling medical condition" for these programs "is one that is expected to last at least twelve months [or result in death] and prevent someone from gainfully working anywhere in the country" (American Bar Association, 2006, p. 88). The concept that someone must be unable to engage in any gainful employment is also important to note. As clarified by Cihon and Castagnera (2011, p. 669), "if the injured or ailing worker can do some sort of work, though not necessarily the same work as before the disability," he or she is unlikely to qualify for SSDI or SSI benefits. As you can see, obtaining these benefits is difficult because an employee must meet several qualifications. Table 7.7 summarizes the major qualification requirements for each program.

In the event that you become employed as a counselor in a setting such as a state vocational rehabilitation center or a center for independent living, you may encounter clients who have disabilities and for whom vocational rehabilitation services may not be sufficient to support them in being able to engage in gainful employment. In such cases, should your client not already be receiving SSDI and/or SSI benefits, you would be doing them a disservice by not providing them information about these programs. In both cases, you should refer them to the nearest Social Security Administration (SSA) office. Because SSA has no vested interest in advocating for your client and because of the enormous amount of paperwork and bureaucracy involved in qualifying for such benefits, you should also advise your client to seek the assistance of a social worker or attorney (with specific knowledge of the SSA application process) who can guide them through the process and advocate for her or his needs.

PUTTING IT ALL TOGETHER. This section has described an assortment of laws (summarized in Table 7.8) designed to provide a safety net for employees. An awareness and familiarity with these laws may be especially useful to you when counseling clients who have been laid off, who are unable to find work, or whose ability to perform work is affected by a disability. Should you become employed at a state employment agency or a vocational rehabilitation agency, familiarity with the laws described in this section is essential.

Laws Pertaining to Life After Retirement

Although an individual sometimes leaves employment prematurely due to more or less permanent disabilities, the more common reason to end employment involves an intentional decision to retire. On retirement, of course, bills and expenses continue to arise and must be paid, even though one is no longer drawing a paycheck or a salary from a job. Retirees must therefore rely on other sources of income, which may include social security retirement benefits, an employer-based pension plan, and one's own savings and/or investments.

SOCIAL SECURITY. Initially called the Old Age and Survivor's Insurance program, the social security program was established in 1935 (Cihon & Castagnera, 2011). Prior to its passage, there was no federal safety net for employees. When one retired, one had only one's savings and (rarely) a pension from an employer. As you can imagine, the idea of a long retirement once conjured up images of prolonged poverty in the absence of an extended family to rely on for support. With the establishment of the social security program, however, people who worked for at least 10 years and made contributions to the program were guaranteed some retirement income. Contributions are generally shared equally by the employer and the employee at the rate of 15.3% of the employee's income. The amount of retirement income, of course, is based on how long one works, how much one earns, how much one contributes to the program, and the age at which one retires.

Broadly speaking, the vast majority of workers in the United States become eligible for this retirement benefit. It should be noted, however, that not every employee is eligible for social security retirement benefits. One's employer must participate in the program and, although nearly all employers are required by law to do so, "exceptions exist for some government employees and railroad employees" (American Bar Association, 2006, p. 178). For example, Walsh (2010) reported that the states of Maine and Illinois do not participate in the social security program but instead have established pension plans for their state employees. As a result, state employees (including many university professors) in Illinois and Maine are unable to collect social security on retirement unless they have become fully insured (via work and contributions) in another state.

EMPLOYEE RETIREMENT INCOME SECURITY ACT. Another source of retirement income for some employees is an employer-based pension plan. There are two types of pension plans. One type is a defined-benefit pension. With this plan, the employee is guaranteed a monthly income of a certain amount, usually determined by a formula that takes into account the person's salary level and years of service. This income is guaranteed to the person from the date of retirement until the person's death. The benefits cannot be transferred to beneficiaries and instead end completely when the retiree dies. The other type of pension is called a defined-contribution plan. In this type of plan, the

---

TABLE 7.8 Laws Pertaining to Unemployment and Inability to Work

Unemployment
- Consolidated Omnibus Budget Reconciliation Act (COBRA) of 1985
- Unemployment insurance benefit programs

Inability to work
- Worker's compensation programs
- Vocational rehabilitation programs (Rehabilitation Act of 1973)
- Social Security Disability Insurance (SSDI)
- Supplemental Security Insurance (SSI)

employer and/or employee makes pretax contributions to a retirement plan, often to a 401(k) or 403(b) annuity account. In this case, on retirement, the employee is not guaranteed any specific amount of income. Instead, "the benefit due to an employee upon retirement depends on the amount of money in the account and the payout method selected" (American Bar Association, 2006, p. 103). When the retiree dies, whatever funds remain in the annuity account can be transferred to beneficiaries.

With both types of plan, the pension income is generally an addition to social security retirement income. Whereas almost all employers are required to participate in the social security system, there is no federal law requiring that employers offer pensions, and most do not. When they do offer a pension, however, there are strict regulations they must follow. These regulations are put forth by the Employee Retirement Income Security Act (ERISA) legislation. This law regulates private pension plans to ensure that the retirement benefits promised to employees are actually provided to them on retirement. Even if an employer later decides to discontinue a pension plan, the retirement funds promised to existing and vested employees must be secured through the Pension Benefit Guarantee Corporation (American Bar Association, 2006). Ironically, ERISA does not pertain to federal or state pensions and, as is evident in daily news articles, some of these plans are at risk as a result of the economic recession and the concomitant decline in the performance of investment funds (Walsh, 2010).

RESOURCES FOR MORE INFORMATION

This chapter has presented information about a wide variety of employment laws. Although you may be overwhelmed right now, there may a time when you want or need more information about the laws described in this chapter. As its title suggests, this chapter is only an introduction to these laws. Much more extensive information is available. In addition to print sources, a considerable amount of information is also accessible online. Table 7.9

TABLE 7.9 Online Resources About U.S. Employment Laws

Government Agencies	
Disability Resources	disability.gov
National Labor Relations Board – Unions	nlrb.gov
Occupational Safety and Health Administration	osha.gov
Social Security Administration (SSA) • Social Security Disability • Supplemental Security Income • Social Security Retirement	ssa.gov
SSA Code of Federal Regulations	ssa.gov/OP_Home/cfr20/cfrdoc.htm
Unemployment (to find state agencies)	servicelocator.org/OWSLinks.asp
U.S. Department of Labor	dol.gov
U.S. Equal Employment Opportunity	eeoc.gov
U.S. Office of Special Counsel—Immigration	justice.gov/crt/osc
Vet Success—Vocational Rehabilitation and Employment Program	vba.va.gov/bln/vre/
Vocational rehabilitation (to find state agencies)	wdcrobcolp01.ed.gov/Programs/EROD/org_list.cfm?category_cd=SVR
Worker's compensation (to find state agencies)	dol.gov/owcp/dfec/regs/compliance/wc.htm
Other Organizations	
American Bar Association—Public Resources	abanet.org/public.html?gnav=global_publicresources_lead
Employment Law Information Network	elinfonet.com
Find Law Employee Rights Center	employment.findlaw.com/
Workplace Fairness	workplacefairness.org

identifies a number of government agencies that provide oversight, handle complaints, and provide additional information about the laws discussed in this chapter. Links to websites for several other organizations that provide information about these laws are also listed.

APPLICATION TO OUR CAST OF CLIENTS

Now that you have some understanding of various laws that pertain to employment, let's explore how you might use this information with our clients. Although all of the laws presented in this chapter could be relevant hypothetically to each and every one of our clients, some will be more relevant than others. In this section, I'll share my ideas about which laws may be most relevant to each client. As you continue reading, consider whether you would talk with your clients about these laws or whether you'd simply keep them in mind as you meet.

Wayne Jensen: Welcome to Wayne's World

In my mind, two employment laws have the most relevance to Wayne. First, the National Labor Relations Act is clearly relevant to Wayne. As an assembly-line worker in an automobile factory and as a member of the United Auto Workers, Wayne has earned nearly $100,000 per year when including overtime pay. His level of income—nearly $100,000 per year when including overtime pay—is surely due in large part to the success of his collective bargaining unit, and collective bargaining wasn't legally protected until passage of the National Labor Relations Act in 1935.

Of course, the reason Wayne has sought career counseling is that he anticipates being laid off as a result of the economic woes besieging the Big Three automakers in Detroit. You should recognize immediately the relevance of the Worker Adjustment and Retraining Notification Act to Wayne's situation. As a result, you know that his employer will be required to give him a minimum of 60 days notice prior to a mass layoff.

Lily Huang Li Mei: Helping Li Mei Blossom

Because Li Mei is not currently working, employment law is less pertinent to her circumstances, and it is highly unlikely that a career counselor would find a need to address employment laws with her. Eventually, though, Li Mei, as a female and as a person of color, might find relevance in Title VII of the Civil Rights Act as it pertains to nondiscrimination. Similarly, the Equal Pay Act and the Lilly Ledbetter Fair Pay Act could become relevant should she believe she is being paid less as a female for the same work that comparable male employees perform.

Lakeesha Maddox: Doors and Windows

Recall that Lakeesha's husband was the breadwinner for the family until he died in an automobile accident. In this situation, though, Lakeesha should be informed of her legal right to continue the health care benefits that had been part of her husband's benefit package. COBRA gives her 60 days to make a decision about health care insurance. In instances involving divorce from or death of an employee, benefits are available up to 36 months. Although it is likely that Lakeesha will need to pay the health insurance premiums, she may choose to do this in order to ensure affordable health care for her and her two children. The 36 months of additional coverage should give Lakeesha enough time to obtain a job with health care benefits.

You should advise Lakeesha to contact an SSA office to inquire about survivor's benefits because, "[w]hen you die, certain members of your family may be eligible for survivor's benefits. These include widows, widowers (and divorced widows and widowers), children and dependent parents" (Social Security Administration, 2013, p. 4). Whether Lakeesha's husband worked long enough and/or paid enough into the system is unclear, but Lakeesha should certainly inquire about her family's eligibility for these benefits. If her family does qualify, the exact amount of the benefits would be calculated by the SSA. This agency "uses the deceased worker's basic benefit amount and calculates what percentage survivors are entitled to. The percentage depends on the survivors' ages and relationship to the worker" (Social Security Administration, 2013, p. 8). Widows with children under the age of 16 may be entitled to "75 percent of the worker's benefit amount," and each child may also receive "75 percent of the worker's benefit amount" (Social Security Administration, 2013, p. 9). However, there is a maximum family benefit. Although the maximum varies, it "is generally between 150 and 180 percent of the deceased's benefit amount" (Social Security Administration, 2013, p. 9).

Lakeesha also worries about finding a job. Specifically, she wonders whether anyone will want to hire her knowing that she has been a stay-at-home mom and that she now has sole responsibility for the care of her two daughters. She worries that prospective employers will choose other candidates who either don't have children or who have partners to help with the child care. You should recognize that such a practice is discriminatory, in accordance with Title VII of the Civil Rights Act of 1964. Because there are considerably more female stay-at-home parents and more single mothers than single fathers who serve as the head of household, making hiring decisions based on whether someone has been a stay-at-home parent or is a single parent would have a disparate impact on females. Such a practice would likely be found discriminatory on the basis of sex.

Vincent Santiago Arroyo: Caskets, Closets and Careers

You may think that immigration laws, as they pertain to eligibility for employment in the United States, are most pertinent to Vincent's case. Remember, however that Vincent is Puerto Rican. Because Puerto Rico is a territory of the United States, Puerto Ricans are also U.S. citizens. As such, the immigration laws will not pertain to Vincent any more than they pertain to all other U.S. citizens. Despite his U.S. citizenship, though, Vincent could experience discrimination on the basis of race, color, religion, sex, or national origin. If he were to express a concern about such discrimination, the Civil Rights Act of 1964 would be germane.

As far as we know, though, Vincent hasn't had a concern about discrimination related to race, color, religion, sex, or national origin. Rather, he worries about discrimination on the basis of sexual orientation. It is important for you to recognize that no federal law prohibiting employment discrimination on the basis of sexual orientation currently exists; however, such a law exists in the state of New York. Enacted in 2003, the Sexual Orientation Non-Discrimination Act (SONDA) "prohibits discrimination on the basis of actual or perceived sexual orientation in employment, housing, public accommodations, education, credit, and the exercise of civil rights" (State of New York Civil Rights Bureau, 2014, para. 1). It will be useful for a career counselor to share information with Vincent that New York and, as of 2012, 20 other states and the District of Columbia currently have nondiscrimination laws prohibiting employment discrimination based on sexual orientation (Human Rights Campaign, 2014). The remaining 29 states, however, offer no such protection.

Vincent is considering a career in the military, so he may take some comfort in the repeal of the congressional policy referred to as "don't ask, don't tell." Under this policy, Vincent (or any other soldier) would be at significant risk of discharge from the military in the event that he discloses his sexual orientation, he is observed engaging in same-sex romantic behavior, or he is "outed" by someone else. Even with the repeal, Vincent's concern may be well-founded because antigay sentiments may persist within the military. It is unclear whether future legislation will add sexual orientation to civil rights laws prohibiting discrimination.

One additional law with relevance to Vincent's case is the Fair Labor Standards Act, specifically its provisions regarding child labor. Recall that Vincent works at the corner grocery to supplement his family's income. Such work would be considered nonhazardous, and the FLSA regulations require that children be at least 14 years of age in order to be employed in nonhazardous work. Because Vincent is 17, it is legal for him to be engaged in such work. You may also wonder about the hours he can work. Federal law does not "limit the number of hours or times of day that workers 16 years of age and older may legally work, though many states do" (U.S. Department of Labor Wage and Hour Division, 2010, p. 2). This would prompt you, of course, to determine what state regulations might be relevant. The website of the New York State Department of Labor provides easy access to information about these regulations. There, you will learn that Vincent needs an employment certificate (also called working papers) and written permission from his mother in order to work in the bodega after 10:00 p.m. You will also learn that minors who are under 16 and are even more limited in the number of hours they can work. During the school year, they can work no more than four hours on weekdays and no more than eight hours on weekends, with Friday being considered part of the weekend. In addition, they cannot work more than six days per week and no more than 28 hours per week (New York State Department of Labor, 2014).

It is often necessary to know not only about federal employment laws but also whether there are any pertinent state laws. In Vincent's case, both federal and state laws are applicable with regard to both nondiscrimination and child labor laws.

Doris Bronner: Embitterment Versus Empowerment

In Doris's case, the two most relevant types of laws are exclusively state-based. Fired for poor performance and poor attitude, Doris was clearly angry when she arrived for her appointment with you after being told that she would not be eligible for unemployment insurance benefits. Almost immediately, she demanded to know whether this was true and to ask whether she should sue her former employer for wrongful discharge (a term she had heard while watching the television show *Judge Judy*). Especially in an emotional session like this, you'll be thankful you learned about employment law before fielding these questions from an irate client like Doris.

Although your ultimate response will be that Doris should consult an attorney who specializes in employment law, it is nonetheless useful for you to have an educated guess about the answers to her questions. First, your familiarity with the common law precedent known as the at-will employment doctrine will allow you to speculate that, in the absence of a contract specifying terms for discharge of an employee, employers do not need just cause to terminate an employee as long as the employer isn't violating any other laws in the process. This awareness might prevent you from making overly reassuring statements to Doris. Instead, you might ask whether she had a contract and, if so, what conditions for termination were specified in the contract. You might also ask her if she believes any laws were broken.

Because of your awareness that unemployment insurance benefits generally require that a person be unemployed due to no fault of his or her own, you should avoid reassuring Doris that she will certainly be able to collect unemployment. Instead, you should direct her to the state unemployment agency and you'll know to refer to Table 7.9 for that information. (This is, of course, good reason not to sell your books back at the end of a semester!)

You may wonder why you need to know this type of information if you're ultimately going to suggest that Doris also seek legal counsel. After all, the attorney can tell her this, right? True. However, imagine Doris's abrasive reaction in the event that your only response to her inquiries were that you weren't sure, you didn't know, and maybe she should consult an attorney. Already angry and likely at risk of projecting her own feelings of inferiority onto you, Doris may well berate you. She may question your credibility and speculate that you have nothing to offer her. Of course, she may do so anyway. If she does, though, you won't secretly agree with Doris that you don't know anything or that you don't have anything to offer. Rather, you'll be confident that you are indeed appropriately familiar with employment law. You can follow up by explaining what you do know and by offering a disclaimer that, because you aren't a lawyer, she'd be wise to verify this information with an attorney.

Gillian Parker: Golden Handcuffs

Gillian's case is ambiguous with respect to employment law. As you've learned in this chapter, employment laws have generally been promulgated in an attempt to protect employees from mistreatment by employers. But does Gillian have legal status as an employee? As a partner with her firm, she is actually considered a part owner of the company. Rather than being salaried, Gillian's income depends on how well the firm does in any given year. She pays income tax in Washington, where she resides, *and* in every state in which her firm does business. From a legal perspective, Gillian may not be protected by employment laws. In fact, there have been several court cases (*Clackamas Gastroenterology Association v. Wells*, 538 U.S. 440 (2003); *EEOC v. Kelley Drye & Warren, LLP*, No. 10 Civ. 0655 [S.D.N.Y. 2010]; *EEOC v. Sidley Austin Brown & Wood*, 315 F.3d 696 [7th Cir. 2002]; *Nationwide Mutual Ins. Co. v. Darden*, 503 U.S. 318, 323-25 [1992]) in which the question of whether partners are employees formed the core of the case. The courts have varied in their decisions about this question, with the degree of control or influence a partner has within a company being a primary factor influencing their decisions.

With Gillian, therefore, it is important that you bear in mind that the applicability of various employment laws may be debatable from a legal perspective because of her status as a partner with the firm. Even so, it is useful to consider which employment law may have the most relevance to Gillian's situation. She has clearly been very successful and seems to have no concerns about discrimination, injuries, or disabilities.

However, Gillian is now questioning her desire to remain with her accounting firm because she and her husband are thinking about starting a family. In this context, the Family and Medical Leave Act may be pertinent. This law "requires employers to grant eligible employees up to twelve weeks of unpaid leave within a twelve-month period, with the right to be reinstated to their jobs" (American Bar Association, 2006, p. 100). The purpose of the leave must be to attend to an employee's own medical needs; provide care for a family member, including a newborn baby; or adjust to a family member's deployment. However, "the employer may designate 'key employees' who may be denied leave under the act" (Cihon & Castagnera, 2011, p. 167). Even if Gillian were considered an employee, her firm could legally deny leave if it has designated her as a key employee.

The ERISA legislation may also pertain to Gillian's situation. Given her income of approximately $250,000, it is likely that Gillian and her husband have invested considerable money in pension funds in order to build a nest egg for retirement. Recall that ERISA is legislation designed to protect the solvency of such pension funds and thus ensure that the money Gillian has saved for retirement will indeed be available to her when she retires.

Juan Martinez: Bloques de Construcción para un Futuro Nuevo (Building Blocks for a New Future)

I hope that you recognize the relevance of worker's compensation laws to Juan. Because his back injuries seem to be a direct result of the heavy lifting and manual labor he engaged in as a construction worker, Juan likely qualifies for worker's compensation benefits. Also recall that states, rather than the federal government, administer this program.

It may come as a surprise to you that, in Texas, private employers do not have to participate in the worker's compensation program (Texas Department of Insurance Division of Workers' Compensation, 2014). In fact, only the state of Texas offers employers the choice of whether to participate in its state-based worker's compensation program. According to the Texas Association of Business (2014), more than 40% of employers are nonsubscribers. At your suggestion, Juan contacted his company's benefits office and learned that his employer did participate. Thus, Juan will want to contact the Texas worker's compensation office. Just as you would conduct such research for your real clients, you may want to take this opportunity to visit the Internet to gain more specific information for Juan. Specifically, find the address of the worker's compensation office nearest Fort Worth and see if you can find instructions in Spanish for filing a complaint.

Although you may have identified Social Security Disability Insurance as relevant to Juan's case, and it certainly wouldn't hurt for him to apply, the chances of him qualifying for these benefits are quite slim. Remember that the Social Security Administration has very specific criteria required for its disabled categorization and for SSDI benefits. Because Juan's injuries are not severe enough to render him unable to do *any* type of job, he is unlikely to qualify. Instead, the expectation would be that Juan find work in another occupation for which his injury would not serve as a barrier. Thus, Juan would also likely qualify for vocational rehabilitation resources. Such resources would be designed to assist him in reentering the workforce.

It may also be useful to acknowledge potential concerns Juan may have with immigration law. Although Juan was born in Texas and is a U.S. citizen, he may nonetheless encounter situations in which his citizenship is questioned. The racial tensions around legal and illegal immigration have been especially pronounced in the Southwest: Recent legislation in Arizona allows law enforcement officers to require individuals to produce proof of citizenship or proof of legal immigration on request. Juan may be offended when asked for proof of his citizenship and may ask you whether prospective employers can require him to produce it. Although it will be useful to reassure Juan that *all* new employees must produce such documents for the I-9 forms, it will be essential for you to use your counseling skills to respond empathically as well as to acknowledge and discuss the tensions contributing to Juan's reaction.

CHAPTER 8

Becoming an Ethical Career Counselor

No one enters the counseling profession with the intention of practicing unethically. The decision to become a counselor generally stems from a noble desire to help others. Even with this admirable motivation, though, ethical practice is anything but simple or easy; it requires a considerable knowledge base, commitment to constant self-examination, and a useful strategy for addressing complex situations in which ethical principles may conflict. Because of the complexity and importance of ethics in counseling, most Council for Accreditation of Counseling and Related Educational Programs (CACREP)–accredited programs in counseling require a specific course on ethics and also infuse attention to ethical issues into a variety of other courses (CACREP, 2009). In the interest of infusing ethics education into career counseling, this chapter will present the following six steps toward the ethical practice of career counseling:

1. Become competent.
2. Obtain the appropriate credentials.
3. Use general ethical principles as a guide.
4. Read and adhere to ethical codes.
5. Use a solid, ethical decision-making model.
6. Stay up-to-date.

STEP 1: BECOME COMPETENT

Issues related to competence are central to the ethical practice of counseling in general and career counseling in particular. Ethical counselors develop the knowledge and skills necessary to practice their profession competently and avoid areas of practice in which they lack sufficient competence. This textbook is designed to assist you in developing competence as a career counselor, with the assumption that you will also have opportunities to practice career counseling under supervision in practicum and/or an internship before graduating. In addition to understanding the general practice of career counseling, you will also need to understand the practice of career counseling in your chosen setting(s). After all, career counseling and/or career development activities are conducted in a wide variety of settings, including elementary, middle, and high schools; colleges; community agencies and private practices; state and government agencies; and corporations.

An important observation I would offer with respect to competence is that your counseling professors cannot make you competent. Rather, they can provide the knowledge, facilitate experiences, and offer feedback designed to help you become competent. Ultimately, the development of competence is up to you. At all times, you are responsible for completing the reading, doing the homework, and engaging in the experiences as part of your coursework. Under some circumstances, it may also mean reading additional resources, going to conferences, consulting with others, or even retaking a course.

For example, I chose to retake a course in diagnosis during my graduate studies. The first time I took the class, I had an outstanding experience and learned a great deal about cultural and feminist issues related to diagnosis. However, the *Diagnostic and Statistical Manual of Mental Disorders* (*DSM*; American Psychiatric Association, 2000) was neither required nor used in that first course. Although I earned an A in the class and met the curricular requirement for my degree, I chose to take it again with a faculty member who focused on use of the *DSM* in diagnosis. Fortunately, this second faculty member did not require that I enroll (or pay) a second time, and I learned a tremendous amount about how to use the *DSM* in the diagnostic process. Although you wonder why I would subject myself to retaking the class when I didn't have to, I hope you also recognize that this was an ethical choice. Knowing that I would eventually be responsible for diagnosing clients, it was my ethical responsibility to develop competence in this area of study, so I chose to retake the class and to attend conferences focused on this topic.

As you proceed through this course and your counseling program, it will be useful to track your own development of competencies. By knowing the competencies you are expected to develop and keeping track of them, you will be able to take ownership of your educational experience and ensure that you will be prepared to meet the variety of challenges presented by a career as a professional counselor. With respect to career counseling competencies, I recommend that you utilize the list of counselor competencies set forth by the National Career Development Association (NCDA; National Career Development Association, 2009), which are included in Appendix B. As you review this list, you will discover that NCDA takes a decidedly comprehensive view of the competencies necessary to be an effective career counselor. Indeed, the basic message is that a career counselor is competent in many areas and modalities of counseling, including the following:

- Career development theory
- Individual and group counseling skills
- Individual and group assessment
- Information, resources, and technology
- Program promotion, management, and implementation
- Coaching, consultation, and performance improvement
- Supervision
- Ethical and legal issues
- Research and evaluation

For each of these designated areas, NCDA identifies numerous specific competencies related to career counseling.

Clearly, a single course in career counseling cannot prepare you in all of these areas. Instead, you'll find many other courses in your counseling program pertinent to the development of these competencies. Create a competency checklist for yourself and review it at the end of every semester. Competence, after all, is at the heart of ethical practice.

STEP 2: OBTAIN THE APPROPRIATE CREDENTIALS

In addition to becoming competent, it is also necessary for you to acquire the credentials that are legally required to practice professional counseling, including career counseling. Two types of credentials are especially relevant to the practice of career counseling: (1) licensure and (2) certification. As you will learn in the following subsections, licenses are legally required, whereas certifications are voluntary.

Licensure

A license is a type of credential that (a) requires a minimum level of training and education, (b) offers title protection, and (c) has a legally defined scope of practice. With regard to the minimum level of training and education, most states require a master's degree in counseling with a minimum of either 48 or 60 credit hours of coursework in specific content areas. As you proceed through your graduate studies, it would be wise for you to read your state's licensure law along with the administrative rules that further define and explain the law.

Title protection refers to the law limiting the use of the professional title to individuals who have the license. Unfortunately for our profession, we share the title of counselor with many others: credit counselors, travel counselors, counselors-at-law, camp counselors, and even canine counselors; thus, the title of counselor is not protected. Rather, each state licensure law specifies the title(s) that are protected. For example, the title of licensed professional counselor is frequently protected under licensure laws, which means that only those individuals who have their state's professional counseling license can refer to themselves as licensed professional counselors. Check your state counseling law to determine what titles are legally protected. You may be specifically interested in determining whether your state legally protects the title career counselor. If it does not, this basically means that anyone can market themselves as career counselors even if their only qualification is that they once had a career.

The third element involved in licensure involves a protected scope of practice. A scope of practice refers to the various types of activities performed by a group of professionals. It is illegal to practice medicine without a license, and it is illegal in all 50 states to practice professional counseling without a license. Even if you have received a master's or doctoral degree in counseling and even if you do not call yourself a professional counselor (or whatever title is protected in your state), you cannot practice counseling (as it is defined by your state law) until you have a state-issued license.

Note, however, that career counseling is included as part of the protected scope of practice in only 27 states and the District of Columbia (American Counseling Association, 2010). These jurisdictions are identified in Table 8.1. Because laws do change, you should review periodicially the licensure law and administrative rules in your state for the definition of counseling and the activities that constitute the practice of counseling.

Also note that only those career professionals who possess a license can practice career counseling in these jurisdictions. However, there are several other types of recognized career professionals. Although they are not trained as professional counselors, they are trained and engaged in career development and career guidance functions. Such career professionals, however, are restricted in their activities. In addition to the legal requirements that they not practice in a protected scope of practice without a license, ethics also mandate that they must practice only within their boundaries of competence. This is highlighted in the NCDA *Code of Ethics* (National Career Development Association, 2007):

A.1.b. Differentiation Between Types of Services Provided

"Career planning" services are differentiated from "career counseling" services. Career planning services include an active provision of information designed to help a client with a specific need, such as review of a résumé; assistance in networking strategies; identification of occupations based on values, interests, skills, prior work experience, and/or other characteristics; support in the job-seeking process; and assessment by means of paper-based and/or online inventories of interest, abilities, personality, work-related values, and/or other characteristics. In addition to providing these informational services, "career counseling" provides the opportunity for a deeper level of involvement with the client, based on the establishment of a professional counseling relationship and the potential for assisting clients with career and personal development concerns beyond those included in career planning. All career professionals, whether engaging in "career planning" or "career counseling," provide only the services that are within the scope of their professional competence and qualifications. (p. 4)

C.2.c. Qualified for Employment

Career professionals accept employment only for positions for which they are qualified by education, training, supervised experience, state and national professional credentials, and appropriate professional experience. Career professionals hire for professional positions only individuals who are qualified and competent for those positions. (p. 15)[†]

To conclude this section, before you begin practicing as a career counselor, you should obtain your professional counseling license after acquiring your graduate degree and meeting any other state licensure requirements. This license allows you to practice professional counseling in your state legally. In addition to obtaining licensure to allow you to provide professional (personal and/or career) counseling, you may also wish to acquire certification.

[†]*Source:* From National Career Development Association Code of Ethics (2007):(p. 4)(p. 15) Copyright © 2008 by National Career Development Association. Reprinted by permission.

TABLE 8.1 States with Protected Scopes of Practice That Include Career Counseling

Alabama	Indiana	New Hampshire	South Carolina
Arizona	Kansas	New Mexico	Tennessee
Arkansas	Louisiana	North Carolina	Texas
Colorado	Maryland	North Dakota	Vermont
District of Columbia	Michigan	Ohio	Virginia
Florida	Missouri	Oregon	West Virginia
Idaho	Montana	Pennsylvania	Wyoming

Certification

As you have learned, counseling licenses are issued by a state and are legally required for the practice of counseling in that state. Licensing is how states regulate the profession, and it is an attempt to protect the public. Licensure, however, tends to set *minimum* standards that must be met in order to begin practicing a profession. In contrast, certification requirements tend to exceed the minimum standards and represent recognition by the profession. Table 8.2 offers a comparison of these two types of credentials.

It is often considered more prestigious to possess certification because it generally signifies that you have gone above and beyond the minimum standards set by licensure laws. Table 8.3 identifies several types of certification you may wish to obtain as a career counselor. Although the credentials issued by NCDA are actually referred to as special membership designations, they are, for all practical purposes, types of certification.

CERTIFICATION OFFERED BY THE NATIONAL BOARD FOR CERTIFIED COUNSELORS. The National Board for Certified Counselors (NBCC) describes itself as the "largest national counselor certification program in the world" (National Board for Certified Counselors, 2011, para. 2). At the current time, NBCC offers four types of certifications: (1) National Certified Counselor (NCC), (2) Certified Clinical Mental Health Counselor (CCMHC), (3) National Certified School Counselor (NCSC), and (4) Master Addictions Counselor (MAC). As a future career counselor, you may be especially interested in the NCC certification. A variety of options are available for obtaining this certification, ranging from options for graduate students in the process of completing their degrees, to options for graduates of CACREP-accredited programs and options for graduates of programs that are not CACREP-accredited. In addition to requiring specific coursework, the NCC credential requires passage of the National Counselor Examination (NCE), and it is necessary to document ongoing continuing education in order to maintain this credential.

TABLE 8.2 Comparison of Licensure and Certification

Licensure	Certification
• Required by law.	• Voluntary.
• Issued by states.	• Issued by professional associations.
• Goal is to protect public by regulating entrance into the profession.	• Goal is to recognize a professional's special training and expertise.
• Sets minimum requirements.	• Sets more stringent requirements.

TABLE 8.3 Certifications Currently Available to Career Counselors

Certification	Issuing Body
• National Certified Counselor (NCC)	• National Board for Certified Counselors (NBCC)
• Master Career Counselor (MCC)	• National Career Development Association (NCDA)
• Master Career Development Professional (MCDP)	• National Career Development Association (NCDA)
• Global Career Development Facilitator (GCDF)	• Center for Credentialing and Education (CCE)

For more information about the eligibility requirements for each certification, visit the NBCC website at nbcc.org.

The NBCC also used to credential National Certified Career Counselors (NCCC). However, it discontinued this certification option in 2000. "In response to NBCC's decision, NCDA established two special membership categories in 2001 to credential career counselors" (Brown, 2007, p. 422). These credentials will be described in the next subsection.

SPECIAL DESIGNATIONS FROM THE NATIONAL CAREER DEVELOPMENT ASSOCIATION. The National Career Development Association (NCDA) offers several special designation membership types. As indicated earlier, the Master Career Counselor (MCC) and the Master Career Development Professional (MCDP) special designations are, for all practical purposes, types of certification. They are voluntary; issued by a professional association; designed to recognize the training and expertise of the professional; and, as you can see in Table 8.4, they have standards that generally exceed licensure requirements.

NCDA also offers one other special designation membership type. Designation as a fellow represents not so much a certification as an honor bestowed by the association. The National Career Development Association (2014) explains:

> The term "Fellow" is a person of professional distinction within an academic institution or society. A Fellow is conferred to recognize outstanding and substantial contributions in science, teaching and training, practice, service, policy development, and political action. It is considered an honor to be awarded this distinction. (para. 9)[†]

[†]*Source:* From National Career Development Association (2014) (para 9). Copyright © 2008 by National Career Development Association. Reprinted by permission.

TABLE 8.4 NCDA Special Membership Designations (Certifications)

Master Career Counselor

NCDA members who hold a master's degree in counseling or related field may apply for the MCC category. NCDA members may apply for MCC throughout the year. Minimum requirements include:

- Two-year membership in NCDA (either professional or regular membership). This may be paid in advance to expedite the application process.
- Master's degree or higher in counseling or closely related field from a college or university that was accredited when the degree was awarded by one of the regional accrediting bodies recognized by the Council on Post-secondary Accreditation.
- Three years of post-master's experience in career counseling.
- Possess and maintain the NCC, state LPCC, RPCC, or licensed psychologist credential.
- Successfully completed at least three credits of coursework in each of the six NCDA Competency areas (career development theory, individual and group counseling skills, individual and group assessment, information/resources, diverse populations, ethical and legal issues).
- Successfully completed supervised career counseling practicum or two years of supervised career counseling work experience under a certified supervisor or licensed counseling professional.
- Document that at least half of the current full-time work activities are directly career counseling related.

Master Career Development Professional (MCDP)

NCDA members who are involved in the career development service field may apply for the MCDP category. NCDA members may apply for MCDP throughout the year. Minimum requirements include:

- Two-year membership in NCDA (either professional or regular membership). This may be paid in advance to expedite the application process.
- Master's degree or higher in counseling or closely related field.
- Three years of post-master's career development experience in training, teaching, program development, or materials development.
- Document that at least half of the current full-time work activities are directly career development related.

Source: From *Membership Categories-Special Designations*. Copyright © 2008 by National Career Development Association. Reprinted by permission. Retrieved from: http://associationdatabase.com/aws/NCDA/pt/sp/membership_categories_special.

Table 8.4 presents information only about the two NCDA special designations that constitute the equivalent of certification. As you can see, both the MCC and the MCDP requirements include a master's degree or higher in counseling or a closely related field. Individuals who hold either credential are likely to also qualify for licensure and to be competent in the practice of career counseling. The choice of obtaining one or the other, or both, certifications depends less on one's professional preparation and is more reflective of one's professional experience and responsibilities.

CERTIFICATION OFFERED BY THE CENTER FOR CREDENTIALING AND EDUCATION. In contrast to the NCC, the MCC, and the MCDP certifications (all of which are intended exclusively for professional counselors), the Center for Credentialing and Education (CCE) offers a certification initially designed for career paraprofessionals who are *not* trained as professional counselors (Brown, 2007). Specifically, CCE offers certification for Global Career Development Facilitators (GCDF). In developing the requirements for the GCDF credential, the CCE worked with NCDA and the National Occupational Information Coordinating Committee. This joint effort resulted in a credential initially called Career Development Facilitator (CDF), which evolved into the GCDF when this credential became available in 13 other countries in addition to the United States (Center for Credentialing and Education, 2010a).

As you can see in Table 8.5, not even a bachelor's degree is required for the GCDF. Instead, the requirements for the GCDF noninstructor credential include completion of a 120-hour training seminar and a specified number of hours of career development experience, which varies depending on the educational level of the applicant. In addition, there is another training seminar required for those individuals who wish to become GCDF instructors.

TABLE 8.5 CCE Global Career Development Facilitator (GCDF) Requirements

GCDF Non-Instructor

- Completion of an approved 120-hour training GCDF seminar
- Experience in career development activities (varies by educational level):

Education Level	Hours of Experience Required
Graduate degree	1,400
Bachelor's degree	2,800
Associate's degree	4,200
High school diploma/GED	5,600

GCDF Instructor

- Completion of an approved 120-hour training GCDF seminar
- Completion of an approved GCDF instructor training course
- Experience in career development activities (varies by educational level):

Education Level	Hours of Experience Required
Graduate degree	1,400
Bachelor's degree	2,800
Associate's degree	4,200
High school diploma/GED	5,600

Source: Based on http://cce-global.org/Downloads/Apps/GCDFapp-us.pdf

Because this credential is available to persons with no college degree, you may question its value to you as a future professional counselor. If your chosen specialty is career counseling, however, you may find it worthwhile to acquire the GCDF training as well as the certification. Another credential certainly couldn't hurt, of course, but the real value is in the additional training. Remembering that competence is at the very heart of ethical practice and recognizing that the career counseling class in your graduate program likely involves far fewer than 120 hours of instruction, you may choose to enroll in the GCDF training seminar in order to learn even more about career development activities. As an example of what is covered in the 120-hour training seminar, the Center for Credentialing and Education (2010b) identifies the following 12 competency areas that must be addressed within an approved GCDF curriculum:

- Helping skills
- Labor market information and resources
- Assessment
- Diverse populations
- Ethical and legal issues
- Career development models
- Employability skills
- Training clients and peers
- Program management and implementation
- Promotion and public relations
- Technology
- Supervision

STEP 3: USE GENERAL ETHICAL PRINCIPLES AS A GUIDE

Once you are appropriately trained and credentialed, you are ready to begin your career as a professional counselor. As you will undoubtedly find, the situations and circumstances you encounter will feel more complex than those you discussed in graduate school. In your efforts to practice ethically, you want to rely on general ethical principles as well as specific codes of ethics to guide your actions.

Five major principles are generally recognized as the foundation of the numerous ethical codes that have been promulgated by various professional associations within counseling. These were originally articulated in a seminal article by Kitchener (1984) and have since been expanded upon by other scholars (Remley & Herlihy, 2010). The five principles addressed by Kitchener are identified in Table 8.6.

The principle of autonomy emphasizes the importance that career counselors respect a client's "freedom of action" and "freedom of choice" (Kitchener, 1984, p. 46).

TABLE 8.6 Ethical Principles in Counseling as Articulated by Kitchener (1984)

1. Autonomy
2. Nonmaleficence
3. Beneficence
4. Justice
5. Fidelity

This principle becomes particularly important with respect to career decision making and is highlighted as an NCDA bedrock policy regarding career development: "Freedom of occupational and career choice is one of the most important birthrights of every U.S. citizen. This freedom must be protected and enhanced throughout life" (National Career Development Association, 2011, p. 1). As a career counselor, it is essential for you to recognize and respect clients' rights to make their own decisions and to avoid attempting to subvert their autonomy by imposing your values. For example, a career counselor may personally believe that mothers should stay home with their children in lieu of paid employment, at least until their children are in school, but it would be inappropriate and unethical to use the counseling relationship to steer a client in this direction. Instead, an ethical career counselor respects the client's autonomy and helps her make a decision in keeping with her own individual, familial, and cultural value systems. As another example, a career counselor may personally believe that all students should go to college in order to achieve the best career results, but it would be inappropriate and unethical to communicate this as the single best choice for a client. An ethical career counselor respects the client's autonomy and helps the student make a decision based on relevant statistical information and in keeping with his or her life circumstances as well as his or her own individual, familial, and cultural value systems.

The principle of nonmaleficence (pronounced non'ma-lef'ĭ-sens and not non-mal-feez-ense) is best captured by the expression, "Above all, do no harm" (Kitchener, 1984, p. 47). This principle is widely recognized as the foundation for the Hippocratic oath in the field of medicine and also serves as a foundation to the ethical practice of counseling. Career counselors should observe this principle whenever choosing a course of action. Any action that is likely to cause harm to a client should be avoided. Aside from the obvious harm that could be caused by a career counselor telling a client that he or she is a loser who will never amount to anything, many other actions also have the potential for client harm. For example, a career counselor who administers outdated standardized tests and compares a client's scores to outdated norms could cause harm to a client. A career counselor who engages in a sexual relationship with a client could cause harm to that client. Breaking confidentiality can also cause harm to clients, as can a failure to evaluate a depressed client for suicidal ideation based on the erroneous assumption that such an evaluation is unnecessary because the client came "only" for career counseling.

In contrast to nonmaleficence, the principle of beneficence calls on career counselors not only to avoid doing harm but also to help the client. Indeed, career counseling is a helping profession, and a career counselor's actions and decisions should be evaluated by the degree to which they are helpful. To maximize the degree to which you can help your clients, you should focus on the mastery of our profession's knowledge base and the development of skills and dispositions necessary for exceptional practice as a counselor. Indeed, Kitchener (1984) observed that "the concept of beneficence underlines the critical importance of competence in providing such services" (p. 49).

Next, the principle of justice refers to the importance that career counselors refrain from discriminatory actions and instead demonstrate "commitment to fairness in professional relationships" and "equitable treatment of all clients" (Remley & Herlihy, 2010, p. 10). Consistent with this ethical principle, the NCDA *Code of Ethics* states,

> Career professionals do not condone or engage in discrimination against any individual based on age, culture, mental/physical disability, ethnicity, race, religion/spirituality, creed, gender, gender identity, sexual orientation, marital/partnership status, language preference, socioeconomic status, any other characteristics not specifically relevant to job performance, or any basis prohibited by law. (National Career Development Association, 2007, Standard C.5., p. 15)[†]

The concept of equitable treatment refers not to the idea that career counselors should provide equal services to all clients regardless of these characteristics. Instead, it refers to the idea that career counselors should provide equally good services to all clients regardless of these characteristics.

The final ethical principle articulated by Kitchener (1984) was fidelity. This principle "involves the notions of loyalty, faithfulness, and honoring commitments" (Forester-Miller & Davis, 1996, para. 7). For example, career counselors should engage in a thorough informed consent process so that clients know in advance what to expect of them and of the counseling process. To be experienced as trustworthy, career counselors need to stay true to their word and to behave in accordance with the promises

---

[†]*Source:* From National Career Development Association Code of Ethics (2007), Standard C.5., (p. 15). Copyright © 2008 by National Career Development Association. Reprinted by permission.

made during this discussion. An additional example of how counselors can demonstrate fidelity is related to following through on agreements. If you tell a client you will have materials ready for the next session, be sure to have them ready. In short, you should do your homework, keep your promises, and keep your appointments.

STEP 4: READ AND ADHERE TO ETHICAL CODES

As you may know, the promulgation of ethical standards is considered necessary in order for an occupation to be considered a profession (Leahy, Rak, & Zanskas, 2009). Whereas most professions have a single code of ethics, counseling has numerous codes. Some might consider the counseling profession an overachiever in this respect, but most seem to view the existence of multiple codes as problematic (Brown, 2007; Herlihy & Remley, 1995; Niles & Harris-Bowlsbey, 2009). Herlihy and Remley (1995) observed, for example, that "the existence of multiple codes of ethics creates a confusing situation for professionals and consumers and is counterproductive to the efforts of counseling to establish itself as a true profession" (p. 130). Perhaps most poignantly, Brown (2007) lamented that

> [t]he ethical situation in the counseling profession is in a morass. Every association seems to feel duty bound to publish its own code of ethics. The result is that there are at least a dozen statements that deal with some aspect of ethical practice. (p. 421)

As a professional counselor, you will likely be subject to numerous codes of ethics, with the expectation that you adhere to *all* of them. For example, you will be subject first and foremost to the American Counseling Association's *Code of Ethics* (ACA, 2005). As a career counselor, you will also be subject to the NCDA *Code of Ethics* (National Career Development Association, 2007). Depending on your work setting and job responsibilities, you may also be subject to the ethical standards put forth by another organization or another division of ACA. These other sets of ethical standards include those from the American School Counselor Association (2010), the American Mental Health Counselors Association (2010), and the National Board for Certified Counselors (2005).

Be certain to identify the various codes of ethics to which you will be subject. Although this recommendation should be self-evident, you need to read each set of ethical standards. In fact, it's a good idea to reread them on a regular basis. The good news is that these various codes of ethics have much in common, building on the five ethical principles described earlier in this chapter. For the most part, the ACA *Code of Ethics* serves as the foundation, and the other codes of ethics are meant as specialty-specific supplements to the ACA Code. For example, "The NCDA Ethics Committee endeavored to follow the structure of ACA's Code so that the two codes would be compatible with each other, while developing, adding, and enhancing profession-specific guidelines for NCDA's membership" (National Career Development Association, 2007, p. 1).

Because this text is about career counseling, the remainder of this section will focus on the NCDA *Code of Ethics* (National Career Development Association, 2007). The full text of the NCDA *Code of Ethics* is included in Appendix C. For our purposes in this chapter, a brief description of the nine sections of the NCDA *Code of Ethics* is intended to orient you to the general content with the expectation that you will also read the entire code as a supplement to this chapter. Indeed, NCDA (2007) calls on you to do so in its *Code of Ethics*:

> **I.1.a. Knowledge**
>
> Career professionals understand the *NCDA Code of Ethics* and other applicable ethics codes from professional organizations or from certification and licensure bodies of which they are members and/or which regulate practice in a state or territory. Career professionals ensure that they are knowledgeable of and follow all applicable federal, state, local, and/or institutional statutes, laws, regulations, and procedures. Lack of knowledge or misunderstanding of an ethical responsibility is not a defense against a charge of unethical conduct. (p. 45)[†]

Section A: The Professional Relationship

The major thrust of this section of the NCDA *Code of Ethics* is the primacy with which career professionals are expected to treat client welfare. The ethical principles of autonomy, nonmaleficence, and beneficence are evident throughout this section. Specific attention is given to practicing only within the boundaries of one's competence, engaging in an informed consent process with career clients so that they understand the risks and benefits of working with you, practicing in a manner that is culturally and developmentally appropriate to your clients, avoiding other types of relationships with clients that could potentially harm them, addressing fees and payment for services in an ethical and culturally sensitive manner, and ending the counseling relationship appropriately.

[†]*Source:* From National Career Development Association (2007) Code of Ethics:I.1.a. Knowledge (p. 45). Copyright 2007 by National Career Development Association. Reprinted by permission.

Section B: Confidentiality, Privileged Communication, and Privacy

This section, as its name clearly indicates, addresses guidelines for respecting your clients' right to privacy (what they share with you) and their rights regarding what you might share with others (confidentiality being the ethical guideline and privileged communication referring to the legal guideline). A number of important scenarios are addressed in this section, including appropriate settings for the discussion of confidential information with supervisors or subordinates, the provision of information to insurers or other third-party payers, group work, record keeping, and the electronic transmission of confidential information. Emphasis is placed on the importance of a thorough discussion of the exceptions to confidentiality during the informed consent process.

Section C: Professional Responsibility

This section focuses on aspects of professionalism as they pertain to the work of career counselors. It begins by articulating the expectation that all career professionals are expected to read and understand the various codes of ethics pertaining to their work and also communicates the expectation that we become active members of professional associations and engage in ongoing continuing education. This section also pays significant attention to issues of professional competence, including not only the concept of practicing within one's boundaries of competence but also the expectation that career professionals accurately reflect these areas of competence when marketing their services or communicating their qualifications. Another major theme within this section involves our professional responsibility to avoid discriminative practices. The *Code* specifies the following:

> **C.5. Nondiscrimination**
>
> Career professionals do not condone or engage in discrimination against any individual based on age, culture, mental/physical disability, ethnicity, race, religion/spirituality, creed, gender, gender identity, sexual orientation, marital/partnership status, language preference, socioeconomic status, any other characteristics not specifically relevant to job performance, or any basis prohibited by law. (NCDA, 2007, p. 18)[†]

Although some counselors may erroneously believe that they can avoid working with some clients by claiming that doing so would be outside their boundary of competence, the NCDA expressly refutes this by communicating an expectation that career professionals become competent with regard to diversity issues.

[†]*Source:* From National Career Development Association (2007) 2007, C.5. Nondiscrimination (p. 18). Copyright 2007 by National Career Development Association. Reprinted by permission.

> **C.2.a. Boundaries of Competence**
>
> Career professionals practice only within the boundaries of their competence, based on their education, training, supervised experience, state and national professional credentials, and appropriate professional experience. Career professionals gain knowledge, personal awareness, sensitivity, and skills pertinent to working with a diverse client population. (NCDA, 2007, p. 15)[†]

This statement means that it is unethical for career counselors to refuse clients or to refer clients based on the clients' "age, culture, mental/physical disability, ethnicity, race, religion/spirituality, creed, gender, gender identity, sexual orientation, marital/partnership status, language preference, socioeconomic status, any other characteristics not specifically relevant to job performance"[‡] (NCDA, 2007, p. 18). Such practice constitutes unethical discrimination rather than an ethical decision to practice only within the boundaries of one's competence. If you lack competence in working with one (or more) of these specific types of clients, it is your ethical responsibility to become competent.

Section D: Relationships with Other Professionals

This section is divided into two separate subsections. It begins with a subsection focused on ethical relationships with your colleagues, your employers, and any employees you may have. Although the basic message is to "play nice with others," this section articulates concisely the importance of demonstrating professional respect, hiring competent employees, and resolving conflicts (even with employer policies) in a professional manner.

The second subsection addresses the practice of consultation. Sometimes, career professionals may be hired as consultants in order to assist a consultee (a colleague or an organization) in functioning more effectively with clients. The standards expressed in this section focus on issues of competence, the importance of understanding the consultee's circumstances and goals, and the need for informed consent.

Section E: Evaluation, Assessment, and Interpretation

This section presents ethical guidelines for the appropriate and culturally sensitive use of both quantitative and qualitative assessment tools, including clinical interviews,

---

[†]*Source:* From National Career Development Association 2007, C.2.a. Boundaries of Competence (p. 15) Copyright © 2007 by National Career Development Association. Reprinted by permission.

[‡]*Source:* From National Career Development Association (2007) p. 18 Copyright © 2007 by National Career Development Association. Reprinted by permission.

observations, and standardized tests. Emphasis is placed on the importance of being competent in the use of any assessment approaches you use; using only those assessment approaches that are appropriate to a given client's presenting concerns and cultural background; attending to psychometric issues such as reliability, validity, and norming samples when selecting standardized tests; engaging in sound administration, scoring, and interpretation practices; and procuring the client's informed consent prior to the assessment. This section also includes standards related to diagnosis and forensic evaluations.

Section F: Use of the Internet in the Provision of Career Services

This section focuses on the use of online technology and the Internet as a means of providing career services to clients, "the most common of which are email, newsgroups, bulletin boards, instant messaging, chat rooms, blogs (web logs), web cams (video cameras) and websites offering a wide variety of services" (NCDA, 2007, p. 27). Although such technologies can be used ethically in the career counseling process, NCDA maintains that "the Internet should typically be only one component of the career services process and then its use must be evaluated based on the client's personal and cultural context" (p. 27)[†]. Issues addressed in this section that might pique your curiosity include the importance of identifying a method to verify your client's identity each time you communicate online, the issue of whether you can assist a client online if the client resides in a state in which you are not licensed, and the risks to confidentiality inherent in electronic communication. As online technology continues to be integrated into the practice of professional counseling, new issues will surely be identified and will likely influence future revisions of our ethical standards.

Section G: Supervision, Training, and Teaching

Regardless of whether you are a graduate student being supervised during practicum and internship, a newly minted counselor in need of postgraduate supervision, or a seasoned counselor responsible for supervising others, this section of the *Code of Ethics* is pertinent to you. Indeed, whether you are in the role of a supervisor or a supervisee, it is important that you understand our profession's expectations of supervisors. This section articulates these expectations.

As you may know, supervisors have responsibilities to several constituencies. First and foremost, they are responsible for client welfare, and the primary responsibility for client welfare is emphasized within this section.

[†]*Source:* From National Career Development Association, (2007) p. 27. Copyright © 2007 by National Career Development Association. Reprinted by permission.

Supervisors are also responsible to their supervisees and seek to assist them with their professional development, and supervisors are responsible to the profession and possibly to an institution. In this latter role, they serve as gatekeepers in an attempt to ensure that only ethical and competent counselors enter and remain in the counseling profession. When client welfare is at risk because of a supervisee's behavior, the supervisor's primary obligation is to the client, not the supervisee. If a supervisee (either in graduate school or postgraduate) demonstrates insufficient competence and unwillingness or inability to remediate, the supervisor's responsibility is to the profession and to future clients who could be harmed by the supervisee's incompetence. Given these sometimes conflicting responsibilities, the ethical standards call for supervisors to provide supervisees with informed consent, including attention to the potential conflicts among these various roles and responsibilities.

Also, the practice of supervision involves a different set of knowledge and skills than does counseling and generally requires additional training. Recognizing this, NCDA calls on supervisors to become trained and competent in this area before serving as a supervisor. This section also includes ethical standards related to the relationships between supervisors and supervisees.

Section H: Research and Publication

Career counselors may also engage in research, sometimes as a way in which to evaluate the effectiveness of their services and sometimes as a way to contribute to the knowledge base of the profession. This section addresses ethical standards related to the conduct of such research. Not surprisingly, the welfare of clients and/or research participants is the primary focus of this section. In an effort to ensure the welfare of any clients or others who may participate in the research, this section articulates a number of expectations for researchers, including the use of sound research practices, ways in which to protect the rights of research participants, and the ethical reporting of results. To minimize the risk to research participants, NCDA strongly encourages researchers to submit research proposals to a review board (such as a human subjects institutional review board) prior to embarking on the research even if such a review is not required by one's employer.

Section I: Resolving Ethical Issues

This section calls on us to hold other career professionals and our employers to the standards articulated in the NCDA *Code of Ethics* (National Career Development Association, 2007) and offers guidelines for intervention when we perceive a possible violation by an individual or organization. A key concept is the importance of first directly expressing our concerns to the individual or organization and attempting to resolve the concerns informally. When this approach does not resolve your concerns, the standards call for you to persist with additional actions. "Such action might include referral to state or national committees on professional ethics, voluntary national certification bodies, state licensing boards, law enforcement or other appropriate institutional authorities" (NCDA, 2007, p. 46). In instances in which the ethical standards seem to conflict with a law, NCDA clearly indicates that career professionals should abide by the law. This section also encourages career professionals to seek consultation in instances in which they are uncertain about the most ethical course of action.

STEP 5: USE A SOLID, ETHICAL DECISION-MAKING MODEL

Although we make numerous ethical decisions every day in which the ethical action is easily identifiable, an ethical dilemma will sometimes arise. In such situations, the most ethical action is difficult to discern, often because there appears to be conflict among various ethical standards or principles that are pertinent to the circumstances. Kitchener (1984) defined an ethical dilemma more clearly as one in which there is no clear best action and perhaps "no course of action seems satisfactory" (p. 43). She also offered that "the dilemma exists because there are good, but contradictory ethical reasons to take conflicting and incompatible courses of action" (p. 43).

When faced with ethical dilemmas in which, by definition, you are uncertain about the best course of action, it is essential that you have a systematic strategy for resolving this uncertainty. A variety of such strategies are designed for the purpose of managing ethical dilemmas, and these strategies are referred to as ethical decision-making models. In addition to the ethical justification model presented by Kitchener (1984), numerous other models have been published in the counseling and psychology literature (Cottone, 2001; Forester-Miller & Davis, 1996; Frame & Williams, 2005; Garcia, Cartwright, Winston, & Borzuchowska, 2003; Hill, Glaser, & Harden, 1995; Tarvydas, 1998; Welfel, 2002).

For the most part, these models are more similar than they are different. With the exception of Cottone's (2001) model based on social constructivism, the foundation of each consists of a problem-solving model in which you begin by recognizing that there is a problem, proceed to gather information to develop a better understanding of the problem, identify possible solutions, engage in a cost-benefit analysis of each possible solution to determine the best option, implement the solution chosen, and evaluate the results. At any point in this process, consultation with a supervisor or colleague may be necessary. Each model puts emphasis, however, on different factors related to this problem-solving model. If you are unsure about which models appeal to you and would like to learn more, an excellent review of numerous models is offered by Cottone and Claus (2000). Ultimately, you want to select a model to guide your ethical decision making and become very familiar with its use.

Regardless of which ethical decision-making model you use to identify the best ethical choice, your next step is to implement it. Tarvydas (1998) cautioned that it is important to "anticipate and work out personal and contextual barriers to effective execution of the plan of action" and thus maximize the likelihood of your eventual satisfaction with the outcome (p. 89).

It is essential that you evaluate the results of your decision with regard to your own satisfaction with it as well as with regard to client welfare. If the results are unsatisfactory, you will need to reengage in the decision-making process and identify another, more suitable alternative.

STEP 6: STAY UP-TO-DATE

By following steps 1 to 5, you should be well prepared to begin your counseling career and to practice in a highly ethical manner. As stated at the beginning of the chapter, however, ethical practice requires a commitment to constant self-examination, and it takes work to maintain a high level of competence. After graduating, your level of competence will initially increase as you gain experience and continue to benefit from supervision. Over time, your knowledge base will become outdated and your skills may become rusty without continuing education and ongoing supervision. For this reason, our profession's ethical standards call for counselors to engage in continuing education on a regular basis. As one example, the NCDA *Code of Ethics* (National Career Development Association, 2007) states:

> **C.2.f. Continuing Education**
> Career professionals recognize the need for continuing education to acquire and maintain a reasonable level of awareness of current scientific and professional information in their fields of activity. They take steps to maintain competence in the skills they use, are open to new procedures, and keep current with the populations with whom they work. (p. 16)

APPLICATION TO OUR CAST OF CLIENTS: SCENARIOS WARRANTING ETHICAL CONSIDERATION

This section will focus on ethical principles and ethical standards rather than ethical dilemmas. Clearly, every ethical principle and ethical standard will not apply to your work with all clients, including the seven clients featured in this text. Nonetheless, it may be useful to consider each of our client scenarios and explore the application of at least one ethical principle or standard as it applies to that client's scenario. In the first portion of this section, a scenario deserving of ethical consideration will be presented for each of our seven clients. After reading each scenario, stop and reflect, take a few moments to review the five ethical principles articulated by Kitchener (1984), and identify the principle that seems most informative in guiding your response to each client's scenario. Consider which standards from the NCDA *Code of Ethics* (National Career Development Association, 2007) seem most applicable to each scenario. In completing this exercise, you will benefit the most if you jot down your thoughts. At the end of this chapter, each scenario will be revisited and discussed briefly.

Wayne Jensen: Welcome to Wayne's World

Imagine that you responded to Wayne's disclosure about having a chromed-out Harley Davidson with an expression of appreciation. On hearing your undeniable esteem for "hogs," Wayne spontaneously offers to take you for a ride some time. Although this may strike you as an especially appealing opportunity, I hope you also experience some internal discomfort at the thought. Whether this discomfort stems from a "rational-evaluative process" or a "feeling-intuitive process" (Hill et al., 1995), it should be interpreted as a signal that there may be ethical issues to consider. Review the five ethical principles articulated by Kitchener (1984) and identify the principle that seems most informative in guiding your response to Wayne's offer. Consider which ethical standards from NCDA seem most applicable.

Lily Huang Li Mei: Helping Li Mei Blossom

Recall from your first meeting with Li Mei that she was referred for counseling by a physician at the campus-based student health center. Although the idea of seeing a counselor was not particularly comfortable, Li Mei complied with the doctor's recommendation and made an appointment with you. In her first session, however, she expressed a hope that her parents wouldn't find out she was attending counseling and explained that this would be yet another disappointment for them. As you can imagine, Li Mei's expression of concern would offer an outstanding segue into a discussion of confidentiality in this initial session. In preparation for this discussion, determine which NCDA ethical standards are most pertinent. Identify which of the five ethical principles articulated by Kitchener (1984) are most relevant to your responsibility to maintain confidentiality.

Lakeesha Maddox: Doors and Windows

You keenly remember that sinking feeling in your stomach as Lakeesha tearfully shared details of her husband's tragic death during your first meeting with her. Just two months ago, you had that same sinking feeling as you sat at your spouse's side and listened as the physician disclosed that the biopsy revealed an incurable malignancy. Now facing the prospect of your spouse's death, you find it incredibly difficult to remain emotionally present with Lakeesha. As a college counselor who has tended to work with traditional, college-age students who have yet to establish their own families, this is the first time since your spouse's diagnosis that you've encountered a client situation that so clearly parallels your own. Which of Kitchener's principles seem most applicable to the counseling situation in which you now find yourself? Which NCDA ethical standards will likely offer you the most guidance?

Vincent Santiago Arroyo: Caskets, Closets and Careers

As a school counselor, you've always been fond of Vincent. Although he hasn't been the best student, he's attended school regularly, avoided disciplinary problems, and tries hard. As a fellow member of the same Catholic Church, you regularly see Vincent and his mother on Sundays. Also, your awareness of his father's death on 9-11 has deepened your compassion for Vincent, and you've secretly felt a great deal of admiration for his intention to join the Marines. Now, however, you find yourself struggling to feel the same connection with Vincent. How could Vincent be gay? As a devout Catholic, you want nothing more than to tell Vincent to go to confession and to seek forgiveness for his sins. As a counselor, though, you also know that you have a professional responsibility to do otherwise. You wisely seek a professional consultation with a colleague you trust to be objective. Working together, you begin by identifying the two general ethical principles (Kitchener, 1984) most relevant to this situation and then proceed to seek guidance from the NCDA ethical standards.

Doris Bronner: Embitterment Versus Empowerment

Lately, especially when faced with clients like Doris, you find yourself daydreaming about leaving your job. In the background, you imagine Johnny Paycheck singing his now classic rendition of "Take This Job and Shove It" (Paycheck, 1977, Side 1, Track 1). When you decided to pursue a job as a career counselor, this aspiration was born of a desire to help others. Lately, though, clients like Doris make you wonder why you ever thought you could make a difference. You're fed up, burnt out, and ready to tell Doris what you really think. Before you do, though, you find yourself in your supervisor's office being reprimanded after your supervisor overheard you in the staff lounge making inappropriate comments about Doris.

As a counselor-in-training eager to enter the profession and to help clients, you may find it hard to imagine ever behaving so inappropriately. Or maybe this scenario reminds you of similarly inappropriate behavior you've witnessed in others. Such scenarios do occur and should be recognized as what they are: inappropriate and unethical. Review the NCDA ethical standards and Kitchener's ethical principles. What stands out for you as most relevant in this situation?

Gillian Parker: Golden Handcuffs

As a career counselor in private practice, you are greatly enjoying your work with Gillian. The more you learn about her, the more you wish you could be friends. Indeed, despite the differences in your salaries, the two of you have a great deal in common. You are about the same age, seem to enjoy similar recreational activities, and your sessions are marked by an ease of communication. And you feel like you personally understand Gillian's struggle. Like Gillian, you faced the decision of whether to attempt to balance a career with having children. Thinking that your self-disclosure might be useful to Gillian, you tell Gillian about how you and your husband struggled with the decision but ultimately chose to start a family. Your daughter was born 4 years ago. You have been able to schedule your counseling sessions primarily in the afternoons and evenings, and your husband tends to be home from work by 5:30. However, you now find yourself wondering how you'll ever find time to see your daughter once she starts school. By the time school lets out, you'll be headed to work and won't return until her bedtime. You wonder whether you made the right decision, and you share this with Gillian as well.

Review the five ethical principles articulated by Kitchener (1984) and identify the principle that seems most relevant to your work with Gillian. Consider which ethical standards from NCDA also seem most applicable.

Juan Martinez: Bloques de Construcción para un Futuro Nuevo (Building Blocks for a New Future)

As a counselor working in Texas, the state vocational rehabilitation agency for which you work serves a large Latino population. Most of these clients have assimilated and speak English proficiently. Upon meeting with Juan, though, you instantly recognize that his English proficiency is limited and are concerned about this. You speak only a little Spanish, so out of a desire to be as helpful as possible to Juan, you explore other options. Once again, review the five ethical principles articulated by Kitchener (1984) and the NCDA *Code of Ethics* (National Career Development Association, 2007). Identify the principles and ethical standards that would seem most relevant to your work with Juan.

APPLICATION TO OUR CAST OF CLIENTS: ETHICAL PRINCIPLES AND STANDARDS PERTINENT TO CLIENT SCENARIOS

You have now considered each of our client scenarios and examined the relevance of various ethical principles and standards to each. Table 8.7 provides an overview of principles and standards that I hope you considered. When reading this section, compare your ideas about the ethical issues most pertinent to each client with the suggestions I offer.

In this section of the chapter, I offer a brief discussion of how these principles and standards apply to the corresponding client scenario; however, the absence of a principle or standard in Table 8.7 or the discussion that follows does not suggest the inapplicability of those principles or standards. Instead, you may have identified other viable and important principles and standards that I chose not to highlight in this portion of the text.

Wayne Jensen: Welcome to Wayne's World

Before responding to Wayne's offer to take you for a ride on his Harley Davidson, you should consider standard A.5.c. This standard addresses nonprofessional interactions or relationships with clients and states that "nonprofessional relationships with clients, former clients, their romantic partners, or their family members should be avoided by career professionals, except when the interaction is potentially beneficial to the client" (NCDA, 2007, p. 7). Just as sexual or romantic relationships can result in harm to a client, so can other nonprofessional interactions or relationships. In the interest of nonmaleficence,

TABLE 8.7 Application to Our Cast of Clients: Ethical Principles and Standards Pertinent to Client Scenarios

Client	Ethical Principles	NCDA Ethical Standards
Wayne	Nonmaleficence	A.5.c. Nonprofessional interactions or relationships
Li Mei	Fidelity	B.1.c. Respect for Confidentiality
		B.1.d. Explanation of Limitations
Lakeesha	Beneficence	C.2.g. Impairment
	Autonomy	C.2.e. Consultation on Ethical Obligations
Vincent	Autonomy	Introduction
	Justice	A.1.a. Primary Responsibility
		A.4.b. Personal Values
		C.2.a. Boundaries of Competence
Doris	Nonmaleficence	C.2.g. Impairment
		G.1.a. Client Welfare
		G.4.c. Standards for Supervisees
Gillian	Autonomy	C.2.e. Consultation on Ethical Obligations
	Beneficence	
	Nonmaleficence	
Juan	Justice	A.2.c. Developmental and Cultural Sensitivity

a counselor is generally wise to avoid nonprofessional interactions with clients. The professional relationship with clients is necessarily focused exclusively on the needs of the client, whereas nonprofessional relationships and interactions tend to be more mutual. Once the needs and desires of the counselor enter into a client–counselor relationship, the potential risk of harm to a client increases.

Lily Huang Li Mei: Helping Li Mei Blossom

Li Mei has clearly expressed concerns about confidentiality, especially as it pertains to information that may be shared with her parents. As a counselor, it is essential that you engage in a thorough discussion of confidentiality, including limits, as part of the informed consent process. Standard B.1.c. cautions that "career professionals do not share confidential information without client consent or without sound legal or ethical justification;" Standard B1.d. requires that, "at initiation and throughout the professional relationship, career professionals inform clients of the limitations of confidentiality and seek to identify foreseeable situations in which confidentiality must be breached" (NCDA, 2007, p. 10). Once you have discussed these issues thoroughly with Li Mei, the principle of fidelity requires that you keep your word by maintaining your commitment to confidentiality.

Lakeesha Maddox: Doors and Windows

Because you are currently experiencing considerable emotional distress related to your spouse's diagnosis of terminal cancer, you may be unable to separate your issues from Lakeesha's effectively and therefore may be unable to counsel her effectively. In this regard, your ability to adhere to the principles of autonomy and beneficence may be impaired. Standard C.2.g. addresses counselor impairment and states that "[c]areer professionals are alert to the signs of impairment from their own physical, mental, or emotional problems and refrain from offering or providing professional services when such impairment is likely to harm a client or others" (NCDA, 2007, p. 16). In this case, you may or may not be impaired to the point that you need to refrain from providing career counseling to any clients, but providing services to Lakeesha might be too much of a stretch for you at this point. In such a case, you would be wise to seek consultation with a supervisor or colleague and request assistance in assessing your level of impairment and determining the best course of action with Lakeesha. Standard C.2.e. addresses such consultations and states that "career professionals take reasonable steps to consult with other career professionals or related practitioners when they have questions regarding their ethical obligations or professional activities" (NCDA, 2007, p. 16).

Vincent Santiago Arroyo: Caskets, Closets and Careers

As a professional counselor, you must be able to recognize your own personal values and have be aware of how these values may subtly or overtly influence your conceptualization and treatment of clients. It is your professional responsibility to avoid imposing your personal values on clients. The principle of autonomy requires that you respect and honor your clients' rights to make decisions and take actions consistent with their own belief systems, not yours. The principle of justice calls on you to provide equally good, equally supportive, and equally respectful services to all clients regardless of a client's demographic characteristics or membership in traditionally underrepresented groups. Consistent with the principle of justice, the NCDA *Code of Ethics* includes the following nondiscrimination statement:

> NCDA opposes discrimination against any individual based on age, culture, mental/physical disability, ethnicity, race, religion/spirituality, creed, gender, actual or perceived gender identity or expression, actual or perceived sexual orientation, marital/partnership status, language preference, socioeconomic status, [and] any other characteristics not specifically relevant to job performance. (National Career Development Association, 2007, p. 1)

In Vincent's case, he has been in the process of coming out to himself and takes a risk disclosing such information to you, his school counselor. Regardless of your personal or religious beliefs, it is incumbent on you to avoid discriminating against Vincent (e.g., by refusing to work with him) and imposing personal values (e.g., by attempting to discourage him from being gay). Instead, it is your responsibility to demonstrate competence when working with Vincent around this diversity issue. NCDA addresses these responsibilities most succinctly in its introduction to Section A: The Professional Relationship:

> Career professionals encourage client growth and development in ways that foster the interest and welfare of clients and promote formation of healthy relationships. Career professionals actively attempt to understand the diverse cultural backgrounds of the individuals they serve. Career professionals also explore their own cultural identities and how one's cultural identity affects one's values and beliefs about the working relationship. (NCDA, 2007, p. 4)

Standard A.1.a. also reminds us that "the primary responsibility of career professionals is to respect the dignity and to promote the welfare of the individuals to whom they provide service" (NCDA, 2007, p. 4), and Standard A.4.b. cautions us against imposing our own values. Another relevant standard is C.2.a., which states that "career professionals gain knowledge, personal awareness, sensitivity, and skills pertinent to working with a diverse client population" (NCDA, 2007, p. 15).

You should have a working awareness of the stages of gay identity development (Cass, 1979). You should be prepared to help Vincent weigh his career options given his concerns about the military's previous "don't ask, don't tell" policy and the current climate for gay soldiers. Should Vincent want to explore sexual orientation issues, you should be prepared to assist him in doing so (Goodrich & Luke, 2009). This exploration may also include discussion of Vincent's multiple minority identities involving race, faith, and sexual orientation (Ziomek-Daigle, Black, & Kocet, 2007). It might be helpful to talk with Vincent about the fact that one need not choose between being gay and being Catholic. One organization dedicated to supporting lesbian, gay, bisexual, and transgender (LGBT) individuals in reconciling their sexual orientation with their Catholicism is Dignity USA (dignityusa.org).

Doris Bronner: Embitterment Versus Empowerment

The scenario with Doris highlights the potential for even well-intentioned counselors to experience burnout and to develop a related cynical and/or disrespectful attitude toward clients. In addition to the obvious potential for client harm and the relevance of the nonmaleficence principle, "the consequences of burnout, including therapeutic ineffectiveness, premature occupational attrition, depression, and substance abuse, are potentially serious for counselors, both personally and professionally" (Lambie, 2006, p. 32). In this scenario, your supervisor acted in Doris's best interest by intervening and confronting you.

Standard G.4.c. calls on supervisors to "make their supervisees aware of professional and ethical standards and legal responsibilities. Supervisors of post-degree career professionals encourage these individuals to adhere to professional standards of practice" (NCDA 2007, p. 33). Standard G.1.a. emphasizes that "[a] primary obligation of supervisors is to monitor the services provided by other career professionals or students for whom they have responsibility. Supervisors also monitor client welfare and supervisee performance and professional development" (NCDA, 2007, p. 32). With regard to the likely impairment stemming from your burnout, Standard C.2.g. states that "career professionals assist colleagues or supervisors in recognizing their own professional impairment. They provide consultation and assistance, when warranted, with colleagues or supervisors showing signs of impairment and intervene as appropriate to prevent imminent harm" (NCDA, 2007, p. 16).

Gillian Parker: Golden Handcuffs

Any time you find yourself wishing you were friends with a client, it's time for an ethical consultation because you are at risk of crossing a professional boundary in which you might act in accordance with your own needs rather than focusing exclusively on the needs of your client. Doing so can result in failure to help a client as much as you could (beneficence); harm to a client in the event that your needs conflict with the clients' needs (nonmaleficence); and overidentification with the client, which could prevent you from honoring the client's autonomy. Although your conscious intention in self-disclosing may have been to help Gillian feel understood, it is likely that an unconscious or subconscious motivation involved your desire for a more reciprocal relationship with your client. In this case, it is essential that you seek a consultation with a supervisor or colleague in order to explore your feelings and to safeguard your ethical practice. NCDA Standard C.2.e. states that "[c]areer professionals take reasonable steps to consult with other career professionals or related practitioners when they have questions regarding their ethical obligations or professional activities" (p. 16).

Juan Martinez: Bloques de Construcción para un Futuro Nuevo (Building Blocks for a New Future)

In the scenario involving Juan's limited English proficiency, the ethical principle of justice calls for counselors to provide equally good services to clients regardless of characteristics such as national origin and language preference. NCDA offers more specific guidance with regard to this issue. Standard A.2.c. addresses developmental and cultural sensitivity and states the following:

> Career professionals use clear and understandable language when discussing issues related to informed consent. When clients have difficulty understanding the language used by career professionals, they provide necessary services (e.g., arranging for a qualified interpreter or translator) to ensure comprehension by clients. The cost for such services, however, may be passed on to clients in accordance with federal, state, local, and/or institutional statute, law, regulation, or procedure. Thus clients should be given the opportunity to seek another career professional or to employ an interpreter or translator of their own choosing. (National Career Development Association, 2007, p. 5)

Unfortunately, the state vocational rehabilitation agency for which you work does not employ a translator; thus, it would be appropriate for you to discuss with Juan his other options. These options could include referring him to another counselor in the agency who speaks Spanish proficiently, having Juan bring someone (such as a family member or friend) who could translate for you in future sessions, or having Juan hire a translator to accompany him to sessions with you.

CHAPTER 9

The Career Counseling Process

In Chapter 1, you became acquainted with our cast of seven clients. Each of them (Wayne Jensen, Lily Huang Li Mei, Lakeesha Maddox, Vincent Santiago Arroyo, Doris Bronner, Gillian Parker, and Juan Martinez) was introduced as being in need of career counseling services. Now, with the benefit of what you learned in the first eight chapters of this text, you are ready to approach the study of the actual career counseling process. Imagine that any one of these clients is assigned to you, perhaps in your practicum experience. Think about what the career counseling process might look like. How will you begin the process? How will you facilitate your client's progress toward his or her goals? How might various theories influence your choice of helping strategies? What will you actually do as the counselor?

This chapter is designed to help you answer such questions. Exactly how you approach the career counseling process depends on the client, the career problem, other presenting concerns, contextual circumstances, and the type of theory or theories you choose to use with that particular client. The look and feel of the career counseling process can vary tremendously from client to client. Some commonalities tend to occur, however, in all career counseling relationships. Regardless of the theory used or the career problems addressed, career counseling experiences tend to involve a common set of stages and tasks.

STAGES OF THE CAREER COUNSELING PROCESS

The career counseling process, like any other counseling process, can be conceptualized according to stages. Hackney and Cormier (2013), for example, articulate a widely used stage model of the counseling process consisting of five stages: (1) relationship and rapport building, (2) assessment, (3) goal setting, (4) intervention, and (5) termination. Others have promoted stage models that are more focused on the practice of career counseling. Isaacson (1985), for example, addressed six elements of career counseling: (1) getting started, (2) dealing with change, (3) sizing up self, (4) learning about the world of work, (5) expanding or narrowing choices, and (6) making plans. Because it is my contention that a distinction between personal and career counseling is difficult if not impossible to draw, the stage model offered by this text is meant to be applicable to all counseling processes rather than only the career counseling process. This model consists of three stages that address eight counseling tasks, as shown in Table 9.1.

Beginning Stage: Introduction

All counseling relationships, whether focused predominantly on personal or career issues, begin with an introduction. During this stage, the counselor and client become acquainted with one another and determine whether to proceed with the counseling relationship. For you as the counselor, this entails orienting the client to your way of approaching the counseling process and gathering enough information about the client's situation, needs, and goals to determine whether you can be of adequate professional assistance to him or her. For the client, the introductory stage involves

TABLE 9.1 Stages and Tasks of the Counseling Process

Stages	Tasks
Beginning stage: introduction	Welcoming and orienting clients to counseling
	Identifying client concerns and goals
	Gathering background information
Middle stage: identification and implementation of helping strategies	Identifying helping strategies
	Implementing helping strategies
Ending stage: conclusion	Solidifying client progress
	Preparing for the future
	Evaluating the career counseling experience

sharing information about his or her situation, and needs and goals for the counseling process to determine whether to proceed in counseling with you. This section will describe three specific tasks for which the counselor is responsible during the introduction stage: (1) welcoming and orienting clients to counseling, (2) identifying client concerns and goals, and (3) gathering background information.

WELCOMING AND ORIENTING CLIENTS TO COUNSELING. As the saying goes, first things first. Before lunging full force into trying to help your client, it is important to take time to welcome and orient him or her to the counseling process.

Extending a Warm Welcome. As counselors, our ability to be of assistance to clients depends largely on our success in establishing a trusting relationship, one in which they are willing to reveal themselves and their concerns. Clients should feel warmly welcomed and cared about from their first contact with us—whether by phone or in person—and these feelings should persist throughout the counseling process. What does it take to achieve this?

First, be on time. As you learned in Chapter 8, the ethical principle of fidelity includes being consistently reliable. If you tell a client that you will be available to meet at 2:00, be ready to meet at 2:00. Second, give serious consideration to the way in which you greet the client in the reception area. Fortunately or unfortunately, there is no single correct way in which to do this. Instead, your greeting should be individualized and based on your best guess about what will be experienced by your client as approachable and respectful. With some clients, you will choose to use their first name. With other clients, you will choose to address them more formally by using their surname. There may also be times, especially when others are in the waiting room and you suspect confidentiality may be of concern to a client, that you approach a client and introduce yourself rather than calling his or her name. Third, however you greet clients, it is essential that your verbal and nonverbal communications are congruent. You may say, "I'm glad you're here," but your client won't believe it if the tone of your voice, your eye contact, and/or your body language suggest otherwise. One recommendation I offer is to ensure that there is a smile in your voice and on your face as you welcome a client. Finally, throughout every session with a client, you should convey a relaxed, attentive, fully present demeanor. To do otherwise, perhaps by seeming distracted or rushed, offers less than a welcoming environment.

Orienting Clients to Counseling. Just as with any other form of counseling, career counselors should begin every first session by letting clients know what to expect from the first session and by addressing informed consent issues. At a minimum, you should explain to the client how much time you will have together and what you will do during your first session. Here is an example:

> We have approximately 45 minutes to meet today and, as we get started, I'd like to tell you a little bit about what to expect from today's meeting. First, there are a few things about counseling that I would like to explain. After I explain them and answer any questions you might have, I'd like to have you tell me what has prompted you to seek assistance and how you hope I might be helpful. We will probably spend most of our meeting today talking about this, and I may ask some follow-up questions. Toward the end of the session, I'll tell you whether I think I can be of assistance and we can also talk about whether I feel like a good fit for you. If so, we can schedule a second appointment and begin working on the concerns that have prompted you to seek counseling.

Just this little bit of structuring can go a long way toward helping your clients feel more comfortable. Although the structuring statement may seem like common sense, remember that you are trained as a counselor and already know what to expect from a first counseling session. This isn't the case with most clients.

After providing some structure to the first session, counselors have a few things about counseling to explain. In our professional jargon, this explanation refers to the process of gaining a client's informed consent. It is important to note that addressing informed consent issues is just as crucial in career counseling as it is in personal counseling. As discussed throughout this text, career and personal issues often intersect, and career counseling often involves discussion of highly personal issues as well. Obtaining a client's informed consent at the onset of career counseling is an ethical imperative. Essential issues that must be addressed include the confidential nature of counseling relationships, limits to confidentiality, and client rights and responsibilities (including fee structure) during the counseling process. Counselors may also address issues such as their qualifications, any supervision they are received, their approach to counseling, any session limits and/or the typical number of counseling sessions they have with clients, alternatives to counseling, and so forth. Quite often, the informed consent discussion is guided by an agency's or school's standard disclosure statement.

In sharing this information, you should use easily understandable language as opposed to professional jargon. The goal is to present information in a way that allows your clients to make informed decisions about whether to proceed in counseling and about what they are willing to share with you. To make informed decisions, clients must fully understand what you are saying. This is best accomplished with the use of common, everyday language rather than with professional jargon that sounds impressive but may not be fully understood. For instance, rather than telling a client that you need to review informed consent information, you could rephrase by indicating that there are a few details about counseling you would like to explain before getting started. Although it is difficult to avoid using the word *confidentiality*, you can follow it immediately with an explanation of what it means. Here is an example:

> An important element of counseling is confidentiality. This means that I cannot tell others you are coming here or what we talk about in our sessions without your written permission. This will be true in all but a few, very unusual circumstances.

You would then, of course, proceed to use everyday language to explain the limits of confidentiality.

After sharing this information, answering any questions, and obtaining your client's informed consent to participate in counseling with you, the next step is to invite your client to share information with you.

IDENTIFYING CLIENT CONCERNS AND GOALS. A major focus of the initial session should be the concerns that have prompted your client to seek the assistance of a career counselor. Exactly how you initiate this conversation depends in part on your personal style, any theory-based preferences regarding how you conduct career counseling, and your reading of the client. For example, as you learned in Chapter 5, Savickas recommends starting with a particular question reflective of his constructivist, narrative approach to career counseling. Specifically, he begins by asking, "How can I be useful to you as you construct your career?" (2011a, p. 49). Many career counselors, however, do not begin with a theory-based approach in mind but instead use theories that seem especially well suited to each client's individual needs. In such a case, the conversation about a client's presenting concerns may be initiated more generically. Transitioning from the informed consent discussion, this prompt may sound like the following:

> Now that you understand a little more about the counseling process, I'd like to shift gears and hear about the concerns you were hoping to discuss in counseling. Could you tell me what has prompted you to seek assistance and how you hope I might be helpful?

At that point, of course, your job as counselor is to listen and respond so that you can broaden and deepen your understanding of the concerns shared by your client. You will likely rely on basic communication skills that serve as foundational counseling techniques. Sometimes referred to as microskills (Ivey, Ivey & Zalaquett with Quirk, 2012), they include basic attending skills, paraphrases, reflections of feelings, and appropriate use of questions. When using these skills, counselors should strive consistently to demonstrate empathy, unconditional positive regard, and genuineness—all of which were identified by Rogers (1957) as therapeutic conditions of growth.

Through your provision of these conditions and your use of these skills, you create an environment in which clients feel safe and encouraged to share thoughts and feelings about their career and personal issues. Rather than seeking to offer help too quickly, counselors are wise to first understand their clients' concerns. In the event that you have the impulse to offer possible solutions after only a very brief introduction to a client's concerns, remember that this easy advice generally tends to be the same advice your client could get (and probably already has received) from many other, nonprofessional sources. Parents, spouses, siblings, friends, coworkers, and even bartenders could all offer that easy advice. Clients come to professional counselors for something else: something more fitting, more thoughtful, and generally more complex. As such, refrain from giving in to this temptation. Listen intently and probe for deeper understanding.

GATHERING BACKGROUND INFORMATION. In addition to facilitating your client's disclosure of concerns and goals, the first and sometimes the second session tend to involve gathering background information. This portion of the counseling process is sometimes referred to as an intake assessment, and it is often more counselor-directed because it is focused on eliciting specific types of information from your client. Chapter 10 will provide an in-depth discussion of the intake assessment process. At this point, it is sufficient to understand that the intake information consists of background information related to your client's history and current status. Topics include education, employment, family, physical and mental health, and social supports.

You should conclude the initial session by communicating to your client whether you believe you can be of assistance and, if so, outlining a general strategy for the remainder of the counseling process. At that point, your client is in a position to decide whether to schedule another session and invest in the counseling process with you.

Assuming that the process does continue, the next task facing you as the counselor is to complete the intake assessment. This may involve having the client complete some paperwork between the first and second sessions and in continuing the intake assessment in the second session. Next, you will proceed to the second stage of the counseling process.

Middle Stage: Identification and Implementation of Helping Strategies

Although other stage models identify assessment and intervention as distinct stages separated by a goal-setting process (Hackney & Cormier, 2013), it has been my experience that these processes tend to overlap considerably during the counseling process. For example, client goals are discusseda in the very first session. In subsequent sessions, of course, these goals may be revisited and refined. Similarly, the introductory discussion of client concerns and the gathering of intake information represent a broad, preliminary assessment. In the second stage of the counseling process, often referred to as the working phase, more focused assessments may be useful. However, these assessments are quite difficult to separate from interventions. In many cases, the assessment itself becomes an intervention by virtue of the clarity or insight a client gains as a result of the assessment process. Interventions don't occur in counseling only after a thorough assessment has been conducted and clear goals have been articulated. Even the very act of listening intently to your clients and displaying interest and concern for their well-being, in other words, the establishment of a working alliance, is in fact an intervention. For this reason, I have chosen to combine these processes within a single stage: a middle stage focused on the identification and implementation of helping strategies.

IDENTIFYING HELPING STRATEGIES. After one to two sessions, counselors should have a fairly clear understanding of the client's presenting concerns, goals for the counseling process, and enough background information to begin identifying strategies that may be helpful to the client. These strategies should relate directly to the client's career problems and goals for the counseling, and the strategies may include additional assessments, career development techniques, and career counseling interventions. Table 9.2 lists several helping strategies appropriate to various career problems and counseling goals. This table is far from all-inclusive, but it does highlight some of the most common counseling goals and problems addressed in career counseling.

With regard to counseling goals, most clients seeking career counseling want assistance in choosing a career path, finding a job or a better job, or increasing their satisfaction or success in their career. When reviewing Table 9.2, notice that there can be some overlap, with some clients having more than one counseling goal. The table also illustrates how a variety of career problems may be associated with the same career goals. For example, although many clients seek career counseling for assistance in finding a job, they may present with vastly different career problems. Some are doing so because they are reaching a developmental transition point at which they are expected to seek employment. A developmental transition point is often associated with completion of an educational program, whether it be high school, college, or graduate school. Other clients seeking assistance in finding a job may do so after (or in anticipation) of job loss. Wayne and Doris fall within this category. Still others, like Lakeesha and Juan, are preparing to reenter the workforce following an absence from it.

After determining the client's goals and career problems, you are in a good position to identify helping strategies that may be most appropriate for your client's individual circumstances. Table 9.2 illustrates that helping strategies may include assessments as well as interventions. Although the following subsections will address assessments and interventions separately, keep in mind that these helping strategies tend to overlap considerably.

Assessments as Helping Strategies. When assessments are used as helping strategies, they are selected for particular clients for specific reasons. Such assessments may involve additional discussion (interviewing), standardized testing, or the use of informal assessments such as card sorts, questionnaires, and/or checklists. Regardless of the format of the assessments, they tend to have a specific focus when used as helping strategies. The selection of

TABLE 9.2 Identification of Helping Strategies

Sample Counseling Goals	Sample Career Problems	Sample Helping Strategies
• Choose a career path	• Developmental need to choose (e.g., a postsecondary option, college major, etc.) • Indecisiveness • Voluntary career transition • Involuntary career transition (e.g., job loss, obsolescence of job)	Assessments of self (interests, personality, work-related values, abilities, self-efficacy, maturity, etc.) • Interviews • Standardized tests • Card sorts • Informal assessments Techniques and interventions • Psychoeducation about career decision-making process • Occupational exploration (electronic and print resources, informational interviews, job shadowing experiences, etc.) • Planning for happenstance • Counseling interventions to address personal or contextual issues serving as a barrier to career choice
• Find a job	• Developmental need to enter job market (e.g., following graduation) • Layoff, job loss, unemployment • Reentry into workforce (e.g., after raising children, recovering from accident, completing incarceration, or returning from military service)	Assessments • Employability skills • Job qualifications Techniques and interventions • Psychoeducation about job search process • Assistance with résumé and cover letter writing • Mock interviews • Planning for happenstance • Counseling interventions to address personal, interpersonal, or contextual issues serving as a barrier to acquiring a job
• Find a better job • Become more satisfied at work	• Insufficient income • Lack of health care • Underemployment • Unsatisfactory working conditions • Interpersonal difficulties • Lack of fulfillment	Assessments • Work-related values and needs • Job satisfaction • Occupational stress Techniques and interventions • Guided imagery • Psychoeducation related to career trajectories • Narrative career construction • Planning for happenstance • Psychoeducation about conflict resolution, negotiation skills, assertiveness skills • Job search assistance • Use of counseling skills to address personal or contextual issues contributing to job dissatisfaction

Sample Counseling Goals	Sample Career Problems	Sample Helping Strategies
• Become more successful at work	• Poor performance evaluations • Job loss • Interpersonal difficulties	Assessments • Employability skills • Job qualifications Techniques and interventions • Guided imagery • Psychoeducation related to career trajectories • Narrative career construction • Planning for happenstance • Psychoeducation about conflict resolution, negotiation skills, assertiveness skills • Job search assistance • Counseling interventions to address personal or contextual issues interfering with optimal performance at work

these assessments is specific to the client's career problems and counseling goals and is also guided by the counselor's use of theories.

From a trait factor approach, the use of assessments as helping strategies would figure prominently in the counseling process. Holland's theory (1997) emphasizes the importance of interest/personality assessments. The theory of work adjustment (Dawis, 2005) emphasizes the use of values and ability assessments. Super's developmental theory (Super, Savickas, & Super, 1996) emphasizes an assessment of career maturity and readiness to make career decisions and may also call for objective assessments of vocational identity, subjective assessments of occupational self-concept, and a values assessment. Although not heavy on assessment, Gottfredson's theory (2002) would likely involve an interest assessment and at least an interview-based assessment to explore issues related to circumscription and compromise.

Both the learning theory of career counseling and happenstance learning theory (Krumboltz, 1996, 2009) recommend the use of assessments to aid clients in identifying skills they would like to develop further, areas of interest they would like to explore, and other personality styles they might like to acquire. Krumboltz (1988) emphasized the need to assess people's beliefs and assumptions as they pertain to career choices. Social cognitive career theory (SCCT; Lent, Brown, & Hackett, 2002) is especially focused on the match (or mismatch) between one's actual abilities and one's self-efficacy. Assessments that serve as helping strategies include the assessment of abilities and self-efficacy. This theory also emphasizes at least a conversational assessment of proximal barriers perceived by a client. From a cognitive information processing (CIP) approach, self-knowledge is important within the communication, analysis, synthesis, valuing, and execution (CASVE) model (Peterson, Sampson, Lenz, & Reardon, 2002) of career decision making. Assessments that might enhance a client's self-knowledge (i.e., interests, values, abilities) are regarded as helping strategies. CIP emphasizes the importance of assessing a client's readiness to make career decisions using instruments such as the Career Thoughts Inventory (Sampson, Reardon, Peterson, & Lenz, 2004).

Within Cochran's (1997) narrative approach to career counseling, assessments are used as helping strategies, especially with regard to eliciting a client's life history and a client's vision for the future. As you learned in Chapter 5, Cochran describes six informal assessment techniques that may also be useful: (1) life line, (2) life chapters, (3) success experiences, (4) family constellation, (5) role models, and (6) early recollections (1997, pp. 74–79).

The career story interview is the primary assessment used when counseling in accordance with career construction theory (Savickas, 2011a).

Techniques and Interventions as Helping Strategies. Table 9.2 also offers techniques and interventions that may be appropriate for clients presenting with various career problems and counseling goals. Career development techniques commonly used in career counseling include psychoeducation regarding a wide array of career-related topics, direct observation and feedback (e.g., mock interviews), the facilitation of occupational exploration, and education about decision-making models. Career counseling interventions may include the development and analysis of career timelines; guided imagery; the use of card sorts; the development and analysis of career-based genograms; bibliotherapy; modeling and role playing; the use of brainstorming and problem-solving techniques; the use of decision-making models; and the use of general counseling interventions such as cognitive reframing, the challenging of irrational thoughts, or even a discussion of introjected models.

In addition to assessments, theory may influence a counselor's choice of techniques and interventions. Using Holland's theory, for example, a counselor might provide psychoeducation regarding different types of people and model work environments and teach clients how to use Holland's RIASEC (realistic, investigative, artistic, social, enterprising, conventional) typology to guide their occupational exploration. Accordingly, counselors may teach clients how to use resources such as the Occupational Information Network (O*NET; onetonline.org) to search for jobs corresponding with their RIASEC type. A counselor relying on the theory of work adjustment (TWA) might provide psychoeducation about how the degree of correspondence between a person's needs and that person's work environment may explain a person's satisfaction and satisfactoriness in that work environment. TWA counselors may also teach clients how to use O*NET and to search for occupations most likely to meet their needs as measured by the Work Importance Locator. Depending on a client's concerns and goals, a counselor using Super's developmental theory (Super, Savickas, & Super, 1996) may facilitate conversations about the relative importance of various theaters and roles from the client's perspective and offer psychoeducation about life stages, maxicycles, and minicycles. As you learned in Chapter 3, the career-development assessment and counseling (C-DAC) model calls for attention to developing the client's awareness and facilitating the exploration necessary to achieve readiness prior to administering interest, ability, and value assessments that might be helpful in the career decision-making process (Super, Osborne, Walsh, Brown, & Niles, 1992). Gottfredson's theory (2002) would likely involve the use of techniques designed to broaden the zone of acceptable alternatives, question past circumscription, and address perceived barriers that seemingly necessitate compromise. Both psychoeducation and cognitive reframing techniques may serve these purposes.

Interventions consistent with the learning theory of career counseling (Krumboltz, 1996) include an examination of past learning experiences and seeking of new experiences with which to challenge potentially false self-efficacy beliefs. Counselors working from the happenstance learning theory perspective use cognitive reframing to help a client appreciate the benefit of remaining open-minded rather than berating themselves for being undecided. They may also use guided imagery to assist the client in envisioning opportunities of interest. Other strategies include the use of encouragement and perhaps role playing to support clients in readying themselves to recognize and capitalize on unplanned chance events. Interventions based on SCCT (Lent, Brown, & Hackett, 2002) likely address skill development and/or correction of inaccurate self-efficacy. Problem-solving techniques are also useful in addressing proximal barriers anticipated or experienced by a client. Psychoeducation represents an important intervention within the CIP approach (Peterson, Sampson, Lenz, & Reardon, 2002). As you learned in Chapter 4, this theory uses a number of diagrams to support psychoeducation related to career decision making and problem solving. CIP also uses the individual learning plan (ILP) as an intervention that is personalized for each client's particular needs. Within his narrative approach to career counseling, Cochran (1997) recommends the use of techniques such as the life line, life chapters, and success experience exercises. When these exercises are focused on the past to the present, they are considered assessments; when they are focused on the future, they are considered interventions. Interventions consistent with career construction theory (Savickas, 2011a) include the development and presentation of a life portrait and the coconstruction of future chapters in a person's life story.

To summarize, the helping strategies you choose should be based on a client's career problem and counseling goals; in addition, your choice will likely be influenced by the theory or theories you choose to use with any given client. Your choice of theories may also be influenced by the career problems and counseling goals expressed by your client.

Once you have identified helping strategies appropriate to your client's needs, it is time to implement them.

IMPLEMENTING HELPING STRATEGIES. Generally speaking, the time lapse between your identification and implementation of helping strategies is quite minimal. In fact, you may do both within a single session. It is worthwhile, however, to conceptualize these as two different tasks. For the most part, the process of identifying the helping strategies to use will be yours exclusively; however, it may be the topic of conversation in a supervision session. In contrast, the implementation process will reflect what you actually do to help your client.

In later chapters, you will learn more about how to implement a variety of helping strategies. Chapter 11 will focus on a wide variety of standardized tests that are often used as helping strategies in career counseling. In Chapter 12, you will learn about the use of card sorts. These may serve both as assessments and interventions. In Chapter 13, you will learn about how technology and career information resources may be used to assist your career counseling clients. For now, within the context of understanding the career counseling process, you need only understand that the implementation of helping strategies represents the core of career counseling and requires the most time. By using various helping strategies, you assist your clients in resolving or managing their career problems and in reaching their goals. Although both of these steps may occasionally be accomplished in a single session, the implementation of helping strategies more typically requires multiple sessions. As the sessions continue and your client approaches resolution of his or her concerns, the career counseling process moves into the final, concluding stage.

Ending Stage: Conclusion

Three primary tasks must be accomplished during the final stage of career counseling: You want to (1) help your clients solidify their progress, (2) assist clients in preparing for their future, and (3) evaluate the effectiveness of the career counseling process for that particular client. These tasks are often completed simultaneously in what others (Hackney & Cormier, 2013) call the termination process.

SOLIDIFYING CLIENT PROGRESS. One way to help clients solidify their progress is to invite them to compare how they were when they began career counseling and how they are now, as they are preparing to stop coming for sessions. A then-versus-now comparison includes the status of the problem(s) that prompted them to seek counseling and the goals they established for counseling. In addition to discussing objective facts, such as needing a job then and now having a job, this conversation should also address emotions; cognitions; self-confidence; self-awareness; and understanding of factors related to career selection, satisfaction, and success.

Simply identifying the changes that occurred is insufficient, however, for solidifying client progress. You must also engage the client in a discussion of *how* those changes were accomplished, including what occurred during the counseling sessions, such as your use of helping strategies. But the discussion should also be focused on what the client did and why it mattered. For example, after identifying a change as going from career indecision to selection of a career path, the discussion of how this change was accomplished shouldn't focus as much on the assessments and interventions you administered as on the impact of these helping strategies on your client. A discussion of how the change was accomplished should be on the client learning more about herself and her interests, abilities, and values and about their importance to career satisfaction and success, not on your use of various assessments and psychoeducation.

PREPARING FOR THE FUTURE. A second task in the concluding stage of career counseling is to assist clients in preparing for the future. Clients rarely if ever accomplish all of their work-related goals in the span of a single career counseling relationship. There is a difference between accomplishing their goals for career counseling and accomplishing all of their career goals. Thus, the concluding stage of career counseling should also assist clients in looking forward, identifying future goals, and in strategizing steps toward accomplishing those goals.

With clients who enter career counseling with the goal of selecting a career path, for example, the successful ending of the career counseling process likely occurs after a client has chosen a career path to pursue. This may involve the selection of a college major or the choice of a specific occupation of interest to the client. In either case, the client's work is not done, even though his or her goals for career counseling have been accomplished. After solidifying the client's progress through a then-versus-now comparison and a discussion of what the client did to achieve that progress, the counselor should also assist the client in preparing for the future. After a client has accomplished the counseling goal of selecting a career path, a future goal may be to become qualified for a desirable job within that career pathway. For some clients, this job may be an entry-level job for which they are already qualified. For others, this job may require additional education or preparation. For clients needing additional education, such steps may be applying and gaining admission to a training or degree program in that field; completing all coursework with high grades; and receiving strong reference letters from professors, trainers, and/or supervisors. Other steps may be to obtain a first job in their chosen career path, to be successful enough in that first job to qualify for a higher-level job, and so forth.

Because selection of a career path does not guarantee satisfaction or success in it, I would recommend including a step such as monitoring one's level of satisfaction in the chosen career when helping clients prepare for the future. Clients should be reminded that, in the event that they find themselves dissatisfied with their chosen career, they now know the steps they took to make that choice and can engage in a similar decision-making process in the future. They may do so on their own or by returning for additional career counseling.

EVALUATING THE CAREER COUNSELING EXPERIENCE. The final task to be accomplished as career counseling concludes is an evaluation of the career counseling experience for that particular client. This evaluation is important because it allows counselors to collect cumulative data useful in demonstrating accountability and effectiveness (e.g., to administrators, management companies, insurance companies, or grant providers) and to learn from our clients in order to improve future services. In evaluation parlance, these are referred to as summative and formative purposes, respectively.

To gather this data, use an *evaluation form* that you (and hopefully the other counselors in your agency, center, or department) administer consistently. Ideally, you can also include time in your final session for a discussion about whether career counseling was or was not as helpful as hoped. To do so, of course, you must know in advance that a given session will be your client's last one with you. A third strategy for evaluating the effectiveness of counseling involves self-reflection. Self-reflection should focus on what occurred over the course of the counseling process and specifically on what you did as a counselor to facilitate the process.

APPLICATION TO OUR CAST OF CLIENTS

This section will offer examples of how the counseling process may progress with our cast of clients, and it will do so in segments that parallel the stages and tasks of career counseling. I will begin with the initial stage and provide examples of how each of the three tasks associated with this stage may be addressed, with each example using a different member of our cast of clients (see Table 9.3).

I will begin with Li Mei and demonstrate the task of welcoming and orienting her to the counseling process. The following example will illustrate the task of identifying the concerns and goals that prompted Lakeesha to seek career counseling. Because gathering of background information will be the sole focus of Chapter 10, a client application of this step will be deferred. Moving next to the middle stage of the counseling process, an example of identifying assessments to be used as helping strategies with Juan will be provided. This will be followed by a demonstration of the implementation of a psychoeducational technique as a helping strategy with Vincent and a demonstration of a counseling intervention as a helping strategy with Doris. For the concluding stage of counseling, an example of solidifying Gillian's progress will be offered, and an example of preparing for the future will be demonstrated with Wayne.

Welcoming and Orienting Clients to Counseling: Lily Huang Li Mei

As already discussed, it is important to demonstrate the same warmth in welcoming a client for career counseling as for any other kind of counseling. In fact, in the case of Li Mei, you will be unaware that she needs career counseling until you begin meeting with her. As a student at Chapman University, Li Mei was referred to student psychological counseling services after meeting with a physician about sleep problems, frequent headaches, and general lack of

TABLE 9.3 The Counseling Process Applied to Our Cast of Clients

Stages	Tasks	Client Application
Beginning stage: introduction	Welcoming and orienting clients to counseling	Lily Huang Li Mei
	Identifying client concerns and goals	Lakeesha Maddox
	Gathering background information	This topic is deferred to Chapter 10.
Middle stage: identification and implementation of helping strategies	Identifying helping strategies • Assessments	Juan Martinez
	Implementing helping strategies • Psychoeducational techniques	Vincent Santiago Arroyo
	Implementing helping strategies • Counseling interventions	Doris Bronner
Ending stage: conclusion	Solidifying client progress	Gillian Parker
	Preparing for the future	Wayne Jensen

energy. As a counselor in this office, you are assigned to work with Li Mei.

Over lunch at your desk on the day of your first appointment with Li Mei, you review the chart (file) that was placed in your mailbox by a member of the support staff. Like many other charts for new clients, it was basically empty. The telephone intake form includes only her full name, student identification number, campus address and phone number, and an indication that she was referred by Dr. Lopez in Chapman's student health services. In mentally preparing for the appointment, you find yourself remembering the developmental challenges facing college freshmen and wondering how Li Mei is coping with each of the challenges. You also think about how best to greet Li Mei and remember that Asian American clients may be more comfortable seeking medical assistance than psychological assistance (Robinson-Wood, 2009). At that point, your phone rings and the receptionist reports that Li Mei has arrived for her 1:00 appointment. The start of your session appears in Table 9.4.

As you finish orienting Li Mei to the counseling process, you are ready to progress to the second task of the initial stage of counseling: the identification of client concerns and goals. With this introduction to Li Mei, you can envision how the conversation can shift very naturally to the concerns and reasons she is seeking counseling. As you will soon discover, Li Mei's concerns not only include personal concerns such as depressive symptoms, an existential crisis, and troubling family dynamics but also career concerns such as choosing an academic major, selecting a career path, and developing sufficient self-efficacy to succeed in her academic and career pursuits. As you come to realize the extent of Li Mei's concerns, you will undoubtedly find yourself grateful that your academic preparation program required a course in career counseling.

TABLE 9.4 Welcoming and Orienting Li Mei to Counseling

Entering the Reception Area

Counselor:	Ms. Huang?
Li Mei:	(Quietly, looking down) Yes.
Counselor:	(Extending a hand for a handshake and deciding on a formal introduction) Hello! I'm Dr. Yolanda Jamison. (Gesturing to client to follow the counselor back to the office) Please come in.
Li Mei:	Thank you.
Counselor:	(As tempting as it is to ask "How are you?" as both walk down the hallway to the office, Dr. Jamison wisely refrains from doing so. She realizes that this would either put the client in a position of beginning the counseling session in the hallway or responding with a socially polite but probably inaccurate "I'm fine.") My office is the third door on the left.

Arriving at the Door of Your Office

	Please make yourself comfortable. You can sit anywhere you like.
Li Mei:	Thank you. (Quickly surveying the office, Li Mei sees that her choices include a small loveseat, an upright wooden chair, or an upholstered easy chair. She chooses the upright wooden chair and positions herself on its very edge, sitting with excellent posture but looking down at the floor).
Counselor:	(Noticing her obvious discomfort) May I offer you a bottle of water?
Li Mei:	(Smiling meekly) No, thank you.

A Formal Introduction

Counselor:	All right, then. I'd like to start by giving you my business card and introducing myself. As I mentioned earlier, my name is Yolanda Jamison and I work here at Chapman University as a professional counselor. You can call me Yolanda or you can call me Dr. Jamison, whatever you prefer. And what about you? How would you like me to address you?
Li Mei:	My full name is Lily Huang Li Mei, but most of my friends here call me Li Mei.

(Continued)

TABLE 9.4 Welcoming and Orienting Li Mei to Counseling (*Continued*)

Structuring of the First Session

Counselor:	Well, Li Mei, I am so glad you've come in today and I'm looking forward to working with you. We have approximately 45 minutes to talk today, and I'd like to begin by telling you a little bit about what to expect from this session. First, there are a few things about counseling that I would like to explain. After I explain them and answer any questions you might have, I'd like to have you tell me what has prompted you to make an appointment for counseling and how you hope I might be helpful. We will probably spend most of our meeting today talking about this, and I may ask some follow-up questions. Toward the end of the session, I'll tell you whether I think I can be of assistance and we can also talk about whether I feel like a good fit for you. If so, we can schedule a second appointment and begin working on the concerns that have prompted you to seek counseling. How does that sound?
Li Mei:	That sounds okay. I've never been to counseling, so I don't really know what happens.
Counselor:	You're not alone. In fact, even some people who think they know about counseling have misconceptions about it. That's why I like to start with an explanation of what counseling is all about. (Li Mei looks a bit relieved and makes solid eye contact with you for the first time.) I guess the place to start is to tell you that counseling is a professional relationship in which I, as a trained professional counselor, work with you to address any concerns you may have. As I'm sure you know, when people have concerns in their lives, there are all sorts of people they may talk with. They may talk with family members, they may talk with friends, or they may seek professional assistance. All of these approaches can be useful. One advantage of seeking professional assistance is that mental health professionals have specialized training. My training as a professional counselor has equipped me with the knowledge and skills to help people with a wide variety of concerns. So, as we talk today, I'll be listening closely to the nature of your concerns to make sure I feel qualified to help you address them and reach your goals. If I believe a referral for more specialized services is needed, I will let you know. Otherwise, I will use my training to help you to the best of my ability. Another advantage of seeking professional assistance is that you and I don't already know each other. Although it can seem strange to talk to a stranger, there are actually some benefits to it. For example, I don't have any past history with you and I don't already have an opinion about choices you should make or the things you should do. Sometimes, friends and family members have very strong opinions about what they think you should do, and sometimes people worry that their friends and family members might get upset with them about certain things. As a professional counselor, instead of trying to get you to do what I think you should do, I'll listen very carefully to you with the goal of supporting you in whatever choices you make. In making your decisions, it is up to you whether to do so independently or to seek input from your family and friends. My role, though, will be neutral and I won't be offering you advice. And a third major benefit of seeking professional assistance is that counseling involves a confidential relationship. What that means is that I cannot share with anyone outside our counseling center the fact that you've made an appointment here or whatever we talk about. I can't tell your professors. I can't tell your parents. I can't tell your roommates. I can't tell your girlfriend or boyfriend. (Notice here the intentional language designed not to assume heterosexuality.) Unless you give me written permission to share information, I cannot tell anyone outside this counseling center what we talk about. And this is true in all but a few, very rare situations. Even though they are rare, though, I do like my clients to know right from the start what those situations are. That way, Li Mei, you will never have to wonder what I would tell versus what I would keep confidential. The situations in which I would need to break confidentiality and share information about our sessions together are primarily related to safety issues and legal situations. In terms of safety issues, I want you to know that, if I ever believe you are so suicidal that you are unsafe to yourself, I would need to involve others in order to ensure your safety. Similarly, if I ever believe you intend to seriously harm another person, I would need to involve others in order to ensure their safety. For example, if I believe you are abusing children or elderly people, I would need to inform the proper authorities. Do you have any questions about that?
Li Mei:	No, not really. That makes sense. Unless you have a concern about me being unsafe to myself or to someone else, you won't tell anyone else. Is that right?

Counselor:	That's right, with one other exception. If for any reason a judge in a court of law were to order me to disclose information, I would have to do so.
Li Mei:	That's okay. I can't see that happening.
Counselor:	I'm glad to hear that. Is there anything I've said so far that you wonder about?
Li Mei:	Well, could you explain a little more about not being able to tell my parents?
Counselor:	Sure. How old are you?
Li Mei:	I just turned 19.
Counselor:	As a 19-year-old, you are legally considered an adult. One benefit of that legal status is that our professional relationship and whatever you share with me is considered privileged information. What that means legally is that you and you alone get to decide whether I disclose information about our work together. And that holds true no matter what, except when a judge orders me to release information or when I have a safety concern. It means that, even if your parents pay your tuition, even if they were to call me on the phone and say, "Yolanda, we heard that Li Mei has come to see you. Is that true?," I can't tell them. I can't even tell them that I know who you are. Does that answer your question?
Li Mei:	(Looking visibly relieved) Yes.
Counselor:	That seems pretty important to you.
Li Mei:	Yes. I really don't want my parents to find out that I came here today.
Counselor:	Maybe that's a good place for us to shift gears. Now that I've told you a little about what to expect from counseling, why don't I stop talking and invite you to talk? You can tell me about your parents, about why you decided to come for a counseling appointment, or about anything else. You can start anywhere you like.
	(Transition to task of identifying client concerns and goals.)

Identifying Client Concerns and Goals: Lakeesha Maddox

In the this example, imagine that you are a counselor working in the career center at Spelman College. In this setting, of course, you fully expect clients to present with career concerns. As Lakeesha's case illustrates, however, such clients may also need to address personal concerns. Personal and career concerns intersect dramatically in many clients' lives.

In the beginning minutes of welcoming and orienting Lakeesha to counseling, you noticed that she seemed disengaged. Although Lakeesha nodded politely and seemed to understand everything you said, your discussion of professional counseling relationships, confidentiality, and so forth, seemed to be of little interest to her. Lakeesha just wasn't worried about the limits of confidentiality and felt like she had a pretty good handle on what counseling entails. But it was all she could do to refrain from bursting into tears the minute she sat down in your office. What appeared to reflect disinterest was actually more indicative of distraction. Lakeesha was so distracted by her emotional pain and her concerns that it was hard to feign interest in the logistics of the counseling process. As a professional counselor, you recognize the importance of orienting her to counseling. Noting her disengagement, though, you also make a mental note that it might be important later in the counseling process to revisit topics such as the limits of confidentiality. It appears that Lakeesha is now ready to talk. Let's listen to what transpires when the counseling session transitions to a focus on identifying client concerns (see Table 9.5).

During this brief exchange, you gathered a great deal of information from Lakeesha. You learned about the tragic death of her husband (the triggering event), about her need to find work (her career problem), and her hopes of finding work that will support her family financially without preventing her from providing her daughters with a good childhood (her goals). You have also suggested another goal: Lakeesha should seek support for herself as she struggles through the grief process. Understanding a client's triggering event, career problem, and goals for the counseling process is obviously essential.

Gathering Background Information

It would be premature, however, to jump from this basic understanding to a selection and implementation of helping strategies. First, you need to develop a deeper understanding of the client in context, which requires the gathering of background information, generally achieved through an intake assessment. Intake assessments, which are the focus of our next chapter, generally address a wide variety of topics. These topics might include a client's educational background, employment history, family background, physical and mental health issues, legal issues, and social supports. Because Chapter 10 focuses extensively on gathering this background information, a demonstration is not offered here. Know, however, that gathering the background information is essential prior to your selection and implementation of helping strategies. The background information ensures that your selection of helping strategies will be relevant and appropriate to your client's unique needs and circumstances. The following example seeks to illustrate the process of identifying helping strategies with Juan.

TABLE 9.5 Identifying Lakeesha's Concerns

Transition to Task of Identifying Client Concerns and Goals

Counselor:	Maybe that's a good place for us to shift gears. Now that I've told you a little about what to expect from counseling, why don't I stop and let you talk? I'd like to hear about the reasons you decided to seek career services, about any troubles you've been having, about what you hope to get out of counseling, or anything else you'd like to talk about. You can start anywhere you like.
Lakeesha:	(With several tears trickling down her cheeks) I . . . . Oh, I'm sorry. I told myself I wasn't going to cry and I can't even get a word out before I . . . I'm so sorry.
Counselor:	Lakeesha, there's absolutely no need to apologize. Whatever you're feeling, whatever you're going through, this is a safe place to express it.
	(Lakeesha closes her eyes and begins crying.)
Counselor:	(Softly) Go ahead. Let it out. (Remains silent as Lakeesha cries. It feels like an eternity but is actually about 45 seconds.)
Lakeesha:	(Regaining her composure) Okay, I think I'm okay. I'm so sorry to start this way. Obviously, I'm a mess.
Counselor:	What's obvious to me is that you're in a lot of pain. What's going on?

Identification of Trigger and Goals

Lakeesha:	(Long sigh) Well, I lost my husband about six months ago, and I came here because I really need to find a way to support my family.
Counselor:	(Choosing to address the content that seems most related to her tears) You lost your husband?
Lakeesha:	Yes, um. He was killed in a car accident. I still can't believe it.
Counselor:	So this was a really unexpected tragedy. I am so sorry for your loss.
Lakeesha:	Thank you. And yes, totally unexpected. This isn't at all what I had planned for my life. We were so happy. We met when I was here at Spelman and he was at Morehouse. That was . . . gosh, I guess it was almost eight years ago, and we married right out of college. Our five-year anniversary and reunion is coming up.
Counselor:	Five years of being married and now everything has changed.
Lakeesha:	Yes. We decided to start a family right away, so Terrence worked and I was a stay-at-home mom. We were like the *Leave It to Beaver* family.
Counselor:	So you have children?
Lakeesha:	Yes. Two girls. Nia and Nala. They're my babies. Nia is four and Nala is two.
Counselor:	I can't help but notice the tears welling up in your eyes as you talk about them.

Identification of Concerns

Lakeesha:	I, we, just wanted so much for them. We wanted them to have the perfect childhood. That's why we decided that I'd stay home with them while he worked. Now everything has changed. It's bad enough that they've lost their father, and now they won't have me at home either. I'm fully responsible for them now, and I just have to face the fact that I have to get a job.
Counselor:	So in addition to all of the sadness and loss related to Terrence's death, you're worried about how your need to work will affect your little girls.
Lakeesha:	Yes, exactly. And I'm worried about finding a job. I've never held a full-time job. I don't even know where to start.

Restatement of Goals

Counselor: Coming here is a great place to start. I'm so sorry you've found yourself in this situation, Lakeesha, but I'm happy to say that I think I can help you. Obviously, there's nothing I can do to bring Terrence back and I can only imagine how much you must hurt, but I do think I can help you find a way to support your family and still feel like you're being a good mother and taking good care of Nia and Nala.

Lakeesha: That would help a lot.

Identification of Another Goal

Counselor: I'd also like us to talk about ways you can take care of yourself through all this. It's not just your girls who have experienced a loss. You have, too. You've lost your husband. How are you dealing with all of this?

(Transition to intake assessment.)

Identifying Helping Strategies: Juan Martinez

As a professional counselor employed by the Texas Department of Assistive and Rehabilitative Services (DRS), you are quite experienced in providing career counseling services to people with "the presence of a physical or mental disability that results in a substantial impediment to employment" (dars.state.tx.us/drs/, para. 6, 7/16/2014). Juan Martinez certainly fits in this category, and you welcome the opportunity to work with him. Unlike some people who struggle with chronic back pain, Juan's goal isn't to collect Social Security Disability Insurance (SSDI). Instead, he very much wants to find a job so he can continue supporting his family. Juan has always taken great pride in being able to contribute financially to the well-being of his family. This was true when he quit school at the age of 16 to help his parents pay bills, and it's been true ever since. During the initial stage of counseling with Juan, you establish a strong working alliance with him, learn about the back pain that finally resulted in his inability to keep working as a laborer for a construction company, and clarify his goal of finding another way to make a living wage.

As a side note, it is important to understand the difference between the minimum wage and a living wage. The minimum wage, set by the federal government (and in some cases set higher by individual state governments), is the minimum hourly wage an employer can pay. In contrast, the living wage reflects the "minimum estimate of the cost of living for low wage families" (http://livingwage.mit.edu, para. 12, 7/16/2014). As you can imagine, this varies depending on where a family resides and the number of people living in a household. Living wage calculators are often used to estimate the living wage. Using the living wage calculator available through the Massachusetts Institute of Technology (http://livingwage.mit.edu), we will calculate the living wage for Juan and his family.

In Tarrant County, where Juan and his family reside, the living wage for a sole provider in a family of two adults and two children is $19.20 per hour or $39,936 per year (http://livingwage.mit.edu/counties/48439). Juan isn't a sole provider, however, because his wife Carlita works as a part-time housekeeper at a local hotel making the minimum wage of $7.25 an hour for 20 hours a week. Taking this into account, you do some quick calculations and determine that Juan would need to make $15.58 per hour in a full-time job for his family's combined income to be at the level of a living wage. This is commensurate, of course, with the nearly $16.00 per hour that Juan was making as a construction worker. It's higher, of course, than the minimum wage of $7.25 per hour. The challenge, therefore, is identifying employment options that would provide a living wage for Juan's family and also fall within his physical abilities. Many such jobs require intense physical labor, for which Juan is no longer suited, or higher level skills.

In identifying helping strategies that are likely to support Juan in achieving his goals, you recognize the need for a thorough assessment of Juan's abilities and skills. This assessment is important in order to define more clearly the types of jobs in which Juan could succeed and to set the parameters for occupational exploration. Fortunately, your office is well equipped to conduct such vocational assessments. The assessments will evaluate Juan's physical, cognitive, and language abilities as well as his readiness to pursue employment. You also believe an interest inventory would be useful in setting parameters that not only fall within Juan's abilities but also his interest areas.

Once the parameters are well defined, guided occupational exploration would be another appropriate helping strategy. The focus of the initial exploration should be on identifying occupations that are consistent with Juan's abilities and interests and that have the potential of paying a living wage. Psychoeducation about and assistance with a career decision-making process could also be helpful.

Once you have identified these strategies, it may be useful to present them to Juan on paper (see Figure 9.1). You may even choose to ask clients to sign such a form, often called a treatment plan, to indicate their agreement with the helping strategies you have proposed. Such a practice can be useful in keeping your sessions on track and in supporting client ownership of the process. Whether you use a form or not, the next step in the process would be to implement these helping strategies. Once you have done so, Juan should have a fairly clear idea of the job or jobs he would like to pursue. With this summary, let's listen to a discussion about the identified helping strategies for Juan (see Table 9.6).

TABLE 9.6 Identification of Helping Strategies for Juan

Transition Comments

Counselor:	During our first session, you explained to me about what happened to your back and why you've been out of work. You were also kind enough to answer a lot of questions.
Juan:	Yes, a lot of questions.
Counselor:	Thank you for answering them. You really helped me understand what kind of help you are looking for. Since that meeting, I did some homework and have some ideas about what I can do to help you.
Juan:	Okay.

Introduction of Counseling Plan

Counselor:	I wrote down my ideas on this paper [see Figure 9.1], and I'd like to start today by explaining them to you.
Juan:	Okay.
Counselor:	These are ideas about how I think I can help you achieve your goal of finding a job that pays well and that you can do without hurting your back anymore.
Juan:	Good.

Counseling Plan

Client: Juan Martinez _____   Client Number: _____

Counselor: _____   Date: _____

Goal: To find a job paying at least $15.00 per hour that I can perform successfully and without too much pain

Steps to Achieving Goal
1. Determine my requirements of job
    a. Determine my physical abilities and limitations.
    b. Determine other abilities and limitations.
    c. Determine areas of interest.

2. Explore occupations that meet my requirements

3. Decide on an employment goal
4. Identify plan for achieving goal
5. Complete the steps identified in the individualized plan for employment (IPE)

Helping Strategies
1. Use of assessments
    a. Vocational Evaluation
    b. Wonderlic Personnel Test
    c. Test of English Proficiency
    d. Valpar Career Ability Test
    e. Self-Directed Search

2. Guided use of Occupational Information Network (O*NET) occupational information network or Career Cruising to explore many options

3. Use of decision-making process
4. Develop an IPE
5. Provide the services specified in the IPE

Client Signature _____   Date _____

Counselor Signature _____   Date _____

FIGURE 9.1 Identification of Helping Strategies for Juan Martinez

Thorough Description of Each Element of the Plan

Counselor: See, up here (Points at Goal at the top of the figure), I put your goal here.

Juan: Hm, hm.

Counselor: And over here (Points at Steps to Achieving Goal), I made a list of the steps I think it will take to reach your goal.

Juan: Okay.

Counselor: First (Points at *determine my requirements of job*), it seems to me that we need to figure out what types of abilities you have and what types of limitations or barriers you have. For example, we already know your back is hurt pretty badly and you probably won't be able to use a job that requires you to operate a jack hammer.

Juan: That's for sure!

Counselor: So that's what this box says. (Still pointing at Determine my requirements of job)

Juan: That makes sense.

Counselor: It also says that we want to figure out not only what types of jobs you *can* do but also what types of jobs you would *enjoy* or find interesting. For example, you mentioned last week that you really like working outdoors. That's important to know.

Juan: Yes.

Counselor: And over here (Points at Use of assessments), I have notes about what I need to do to help you complete this step. There are several assessments that I know about that can help figure out your abilities and interests. My job in this step would be to use those assessments so that we can figure out what types of abilities you have, what types of limitations or barriers you have, and what types of jobs might be most interesting to you. Does that make sense?

Juan: Yes.

Counselor: After we figure that out, the next step (Points at Explore occupations that meet my requirements) would be for me to help you learn more about the jobs that seem to fit well with your abilities and interests. I have a specific tool (Points at Guided use of Occupational Information Network [O*NET]) that is really helpful in learning about different kinds of jobs. My job would be to help you use this tool to learn more about jobs you might want to consider.

Juan: Okay.

Counselor: And once you learn about possible jobs, the next step is for you to make a decision about the types of jobs you want to try for (Points at Decide on an employment goal). And my job would be to help you make some choices. (Points at Use of decision-making process) How does that sound?

Juan: Good, but what about getting the job?

Counselor: I'm glad you asked. That is actually the next step. (Points at Identify plan for achieving goal) We need to make a plan for how you could get the job. It might be an easy plan, like all you have to do is apply for a job and hopefully get it. Or it might be a harder plan, like you might need to go through a training program to get qualified for a job you've never done before. It really depends on the job you decide you want. (Points again at Decide on an employment goal)

Juan: Yea, I guess that makes sense.

Counselor: Here at the DRS, we use a special form for this plan. That form is called an individualized plan for employment. (Points) That form shows all the steps you will take to get the job. (Points at Complete the steps identified in the individualized plan for employment [IPE]) The form also shows you all the services our agency will provide to help you get that job (Points at Provide the services specified in the IPE).

Juan: Okay.

Check for Agreement and Understanding

Counselor: So how does this plan sound to you?

Juan: It sounds good. First we need to figure out what type of work I can do, right?

(*Continued*)

TABLE 9.6	Identification of Helping Strategies for Juan (*Continued*)
Counselor:	Yes. And also what type of work you might enjoy.
Juan:	And then I'll choose what type of job I want?
Counselor:	Yes, but before you choose, we will do some research. We will work together to learn about the different jobs you have to choose from. It might be that our list of possible jobs will include jobs you don't know about. So before you choose, we need to learn about them.
Juan:	Oh, yes. I forgot that part.
Counselor:	No problem. That's why I wrote it down, and I'll give you a copy of it to take with you, too.
Juan:	Thank you. And after I choose what type of job I want, you'll help me get the job. Is that right?
Counselor:	Yes. There will probably be things you need to do to get the job and there will probably be ways our agency can help you. We'll list all of those on the IPE form.
Juan:	Okay.
Counselor:	Ready to get started?
Juan:	Yes. Ready, Freddy.
Obtaining Formal Agreement	
Counselor:	(Laughs) Okay. I'll have you sign here and then we can get started.
Juan:	Okay.

Notice that the presentation of proposed helping strategies is relatively brief. Even so, it is an important step. By adding structure to your future sessions, this type of plan helps you and your client stay on track and monitor the client's progression toward the counseling goals. It also allows for greater clarity and accountability. It also tends to result in greater client ownership of and participation in the counseling process.

After identifying strategies you believe will help your clients achieve their goals and presenting the strategies to your clients in the form of a counseling plan, your next step is to actually implement the helping strategies. In the following two examples, you will see how a psychoeducational technique may be implemented as a helping strategy with Vincent, and a counseling intervention may be implemented as a helping strategy with Doris.

Implementing Helping Strategies: Vincent Santiago Arroyo

As a school counselor working with Vincent, you have been influenced by the career development assessment and counseling (C-DAC) model (Super, Osborne, Walsh, Brown, & Niles, 1992). In keeping with this theory, you were reluctant, when identifying helping strategies, to give Vincent an interest inventory to determine other occupations that might appeal to him. Doing so may be premature, and Vincent may not yet be ready to make career decisions. Therefore, while gathering background information, you choose to administer the school form of the Career Development Inventory (CDI; Thompson, Lindeman, Super, Jordaan, & Myers, 1988).

Vincent's scores reveal that he knows a great deal about the Marines. Until now, joining the Marines had been what the CDI refers to as his preferred occupation (PO). With this aspiration now under reconsideration, though, you want to understand Vincent's readiness to make a vocational choice. Specifically, you wonder what he knows about other occupations and about the career decision-making process in general. Vincent's CDI composite scores reveal a fairly high degree of readiness related to career decision attitudes (CDA) but a fairly low degree of readiness related to career decision knowledge (CDK). The scores on the decision making (DM) and knowledge of the world of work (WW) were both low.

Given these findings, you select helping strategies designed to help Vincent develop more understanding of career decision making and more knowledge about the world of work. You therefore decide to provide Vincent with some psychoeducation about career decision making and choose to use materials developed as part of the cognitive information-processing (CIP) approach (Sampson, Peterson, Lenz, & Reardon, 1992). Let's peek into the session in which you implement this helping strategy and teach Vincent about the communication, analysis, synthesis, valuing, and execution (CASVE) decision-making model (see Table 9.7). You learned about the CASVE model in Chapter 4.

TABLE 9.7 Implementing a Psychoeducational Technique as a Helping Strategy with Vincent

Acknowledgment of Career Problem

Counselor: You know, Vincent, it seems like, until now, you've always known what you wanted to be when you grew up.

Vincent: Yeah, until now, I just *knew* I'd go into the Marines. Arrghh! This is so screwed up.

Counselor: And now, with everything else you have to think about, you're just not sure the joining the Marines is for you. Have you given this any more thought since we met last week?

Vincent: I'll say! It's practically all I think about. I just feel . . . I don't know. It's just so screwed up.

Counselor: This whole thing must be pretty scary and confusing for you. You thought you knew who you were and what you wanted for your career. Now you're realizing some things about yourself that you didn't predict and are just not sure what it would be like to be a gay man in the military.

Vincent: (In a hushed voice) You haven't told anyone, have you?

Review of Confidentiality

Counselor: No, of course not. Vincent, I meant what I said about confidentiality. Obviously, your teacher knows you are coming to see me and so does the office secretary. But nobody knows what we are talking about unless you choose to tell them. Unless there is a very unusual situation, like if I have a serious concern about your safety or someone else's safety, I won't be telling anyone without your permission. This is your information, and it's up to you to decide who to tell.

Vincent: Okay. Thanks. I just don't want anyone to know.

Counselor: I understand. It probably surprised you when I made that comment about not being sure what it would be like to be a gay man in the military.

Vincent: Hm, hm.

Counselor: The reason I said it is that, until now, you've learned a lot about what it would be like to be a straight man in the military and you liked what you heard. Now that you've realized you're gay, though, you're not so sure.

Vincent: Exactly.

Further Definition of Career Problem

Counselor: And you're not even sure about how to go about making a decision.

Vincent: You got that right!

Counselor: I know I've visited your classroom before to talk about career decision making, but I'm guessing that maybe it didn't seem as important to you then as it does now. After all, you had already decided for sure what you were going to do.

Vincent: Yeah, I mean, no offense, but I don't really remember what you talked about. My bad.

Structuring of Session

Counselor: That's okay. I get it. How about today I teach you a little bit about the career decision-making process? I certainly can't make this decision for you, but I can help you learn effective ways to make career decisions. How would that be?

Vincent: That'd be great. I'd really appreciate it.

Counselor: All right then. Let's get started. I have a picture to show you. It is related to career decision making, and I think it might help you.

Vincent: Okay.

Presentation of the CASVE Model

Counselor: So here it is. (Shows Vincent a version of the CASVE model [see Figure 9.2])

Vincent: Hey, I do sorta remember you showing that in one of my classes.

(Continued)

| TABLE 9.7 | Implementing a Psychoeducational Technique as a Helping Strategy with Vincent (*Continued*) |

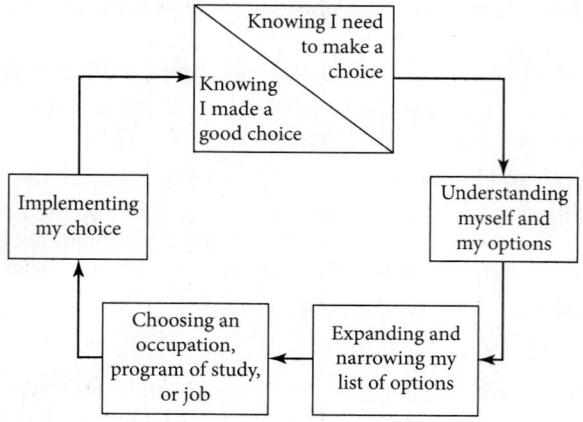

FIGURE 9.2 CIP Decision Making Model: CASVE
Source: Sampson, J. P. Jr., Peterson, G. W., Lenz, J. G., & Reardon, R. C. (1992). A cognitive approach to career services: Translating concepts into practice. *The Career Development Quarterly, 41,* 67–74. (Figure on p. 70.)

Counselor:	Great! So here's the deal. This picture basically provides a road map for the career decision-making process. You're here. (Points to Knowing I need to make a choice)
Vincent:	Yep. All along I thought I already made my choice, but now I guess things have changed.
Counselor:	Well, your understanding of yourself has certainly changed. After going through this whole process, you might decide to stick with your original plan and join the Marines, or you might make a different choice. By using this road map, though, you can be sure you are using a good process to make your decision.
Vincent:	Okay. What do I need to do?
Counselor:	Well, let's take a look. (Points to Understanding myself and my options). One thing that is important to making a good career decision is to understand yourself and your options. (Laughs) I guess you understand more than most about how a change in the way you understand yourself can affect what careers might be best for you.
Vincent:	Oh, yeah.
Counselor:	But this part (Pointing again to Understanding myself and my options) isn't just about understanding your sexuality. In the context of careers, it has a lot to do with understanding the types of things you enjoy doing, the types of rewards you want out of work, the types of things you're good at, and so forth. That's the part about understanding yourself. And the other part of this box is about understanding your options. Options refer to career possibilities, so this part means that it is also important that you learn about different career options before you make a decision. You may think you'd like to do a certain job but then, after learning more about it, you might decide you'd hate it.
Vincent:	Oh, yeah. Like that story you told us about how you wanted to be a professional football player when you were little but then realized that it hurt to run into other people or to get tackled into the ground. Then you decided you wouldn't like it.
Counselor:	(Laughs) That's funny that you remember that story. But yes, that's exactly right. Sometimes we know we have no clue about a job and we need to learn about it before we can decide whether we'd like it. But other times, we think we know about a job, but we're wrong. What we think we know about a job can just be wrong.

Vincent:	I get that. So before we decide for or against a job, we have to find out what it's really like.
Counselor:	Exactly. And, as we do so, we might end up crossing some jobs off our list and discovering other jobs we might be interested in. On this road map (Points), this is called expanding and narrowing our list of options.
Vincent:	I get it.
Counselor:	Another way to expand and narrow our options is to use criteria to judge each possible job. For example, you may have some "must haves" in a job. You might, for example, only want jobs in which you have to have a college degree and might not consider any jobs that don't require a college degree.
Vincent:	Well that won't be me!
Counselor:	Maybe not, but you may decide you have some other criteria. For example, you might decide you only want to consider careers in which it is safe to be openly gay.
Vincent:	Oh, I see what you mean. But, right now, I don't want nobody to know. Keepin' it on the down low, if you know what I mean. But I dunno. Maybe later I'll change my mind. I just dunno.
Counselor:	So that's another example of how you might use criteria to expand or narrow your options. And, just like every person is different, every person might have different criteria.
Vincent:	Got it.
Counselor:	So let's look at this next box. (Points at Choosing an occupation) Here's where the rubber meets the road. Here's where you make a decision. Using everything you've learned about yourself, everything you've learned about a whole bunch of possible careers, using criteria that are important to you, you make a decision about what you want to pursue.
Vincent:	But how do you decide?
Counselor:	Well, different people use different strategies to decide. I wouldn't recommend this, but some people flip a coin.
Vincent:	(Laughs) No, why would you do all this and then just flip a coin?
Counselor:	Exactly. The whole point here is that you are trying to make the best decision you can. And a coin certainly can't do that. But some people make a list of pros and cons of each job. Some people even give different points for each pro and con and use math to figure out what option gets the highest score. Other people make decisions more with their heart or their gut; they reflect on their choices until they figure out which one feels best for them. Other people talk with a parent, a teacher, or a close friend. Some people use all of these strategies.
Vincent:	And what if you make the wrong decision?
Counselor:	Then you learn from your experience and make a new decision. That's the great thing about career decisions. Your first career decision is just that: where you want to start. Some people like their first career so much that they stay in it forever. Other people change their careers later in their life, sometimes because they've changed, sometimes because they didn't like the career as much as they thought they would, and sometimes because it's too hard to find a job in the career they thought they wanted.
Vincent:	But if I choose the Marines, I can't exactly change my mind. That'd be an epic fail.
Counselor:	Well, you can change your mind all you want, but you can't get out of your obligation to the military. Once you're in, you have to stay in until the military discharges you.
Vincent:	That's a lot of pressure.
Counselor:	It's a really big commitment. And even though you're not exactly happy about realizing you're gay, at least you figured this out before you make a final decision about whether to join the Marines. This way, by knowing this part of yourself and using this road map (Points to the CASVE model), you can try your very best to make a decision that you'll be happy about.
Vincent:	Yeah, that makes sense. This will really help. (School bell rings) Oops. Gotta bounce. Mrs. Cranston hates it when we're late to her class.
Counselor:	Okay. Next time you come, we can start using this road map.
Vincent:	Sounds good.

Vincent's session illustrates the implementation of a psychoeducational intervention. At times during the career counseling process, you will undoubtedly do some teaching. Even when teaching, though, the relationship between you and a client is still a counseling relationship. Unlike a student–teacher relationship in which the teacher is in a position of grading a student's submissions and is driven by a curriculum, a counselor providing psychoeducation in the context of career counseling does not grade the client and is driven by the client's needs rather than by a curriculum. As personal issues arise, a counselor has the flexibility, knowledge, and skills to employ interventions that are more psychological in nature. The next client application illustrated this process.

Implementing Helping Strategies: Doris Bronner

Since the first day you met Doris, you knew your work with her wasn't going to be easy. As is sometimes the case with those who experience employment difficulties, Doris is her own worst enemy in many ways (Wall, 2008). For myriad reasons, Doris exudes bitterness, which has affected both her performance and her relationships at work. You realize that, at some point in the counseling process, her bitterness will need to be addressed. Today is the day. Borrowing a phrase from Singleton and Linton (2006), you decide to invite Doris to engage in some "courageous conversations."

When you read through the transcript with Doris, I hope that you noticed a balance between supportiveness

TABLE 9.8   Implementing a Counseling Intervention as a Helping Strategy with Doris

Acknowledgment of Career Problem

Counselor:	Doris, from everything you've shared with me, I get the picture that you harbor a great deal of resentment toward your former coworkers and boss and, I hesitate to say this, but I'm guessing they may have felt the same way toward you.
Doris:	I have to admit, you're probably right. I hated them, and they probably hated me.
Counselor:	And I'm guessing that, although you're pretty clear about your reasons for hating them, you might be a little confused about why they hated you.
Doris:	No, not really. I just think they had it out for me because of my age.
Counselor:	Are you sure that's all it was?
Doris:	What do you mean?
Counselor:	Well, in my experience, it's really quite hard to read people's minds. It's especially hard to know what they are thinking about us unless they tell us.
Doris:	Yeah, I know what you mean. But those witches wouldn't say things to my face. They'd rather talk about me behind my back.
Counselor:	Tell me about that. You had a sense that they were talking about you?
Doris:	Hm, hm. Sometimes when I'd go in the break room, it'd suddenly get quiet, and I always figured they had been saying something bad about me.
Counselor:	And you thought they were talking about your age?
Doris:	Well no, not really. They were probably just saying bad things about me.
Counselor:	Like what?
Doris:	I don't know, just bad things.
Counselor:	That's really unfortunate and, I'm sad to say, really common. I think it happens way too often in workplaces that people talk behind your back rather that coming to you when they have a complaint.
Doris:	I agree. It's really not fair.
Counselor:	It isn't fair. And it isn't effective. I mean, for me, I'd want to know if I were doing something that people disliked. Depending on what it was, I might continue doing it or I might make changes. But it's hard to make changes if I don't know what the other people are thinking.
Doris:	Exactly. They can be nice to your face and then back-stab you.

The Career Counseling Process **195**

Counselor:	Did you ever go to them and ask about it?
Doris:	No. I just got mad. If I'm really honest with you, I think my work suffered when I got mad. I just didn't even want to be there. I didn't want to help the agency. What's that called? Passive aggressive?
Counselor:	Yes, that's one description. But giving it a name doesn't really help solve the problem. I'm more interested in what you can do about it.
Doris:	What do you mean?

Goal Statement

Counselor:	Well, my goal is to help you, to help you be as effective as possible in whatever jobs you have in the future. Part of this, it seems to me, is finding a way to interact with your coworkers more effectively.
Doris:	(Sullenly) I guess . . . .
Counselor:	And I know this isn't easy for you to hear me say, but what you and I are doing, having an honest conversation about tough topics, is really important. I firmly believe that it's better to know what others think so that you then have the ability to make choices about how to respond.
Doris:	I guess that's right.

Introduction of Exercise

Counselor:	With that in mind, I'd like to propose some homework for you this week.
Doris:	(Tentatively) Okay. What is it?
Counselor:	This is up to you, of course, but I think it could be really helpful.
Doris:	Okay.
Counselor:	The homework is called "courageous conversations."
Doris:	Oh, you want me to talk to someone?
Counselor:	Yes. I'd like you to choose someone at the insurance agency where you used to work and invite that person to meet you after work.
Doris:	Now that's my kind of homework!
Counselor:	(Laughing) Don't get too excited. I haven't shared the hard part yet. I want you to ask someone at the insurance agency that you think would be the most honest with you, even if it's hard.
Doris:	Oh, that would probably be Chris or Wendy.
Counselor:	And I want you to have a courageous conversation with that person.
Doris:	What do you mean?
Counselor:	Well, I'd suggest that you take a list of questions with you. Take this list, for instance [see Figure 9.3]:
Doris:	(Tears well up in her eyes as she reads it) I . . . I can't do this.
Counselor:	Tell me about your tears.
Doris:	If they were honest, I . . . .
Counselor:	If they were honest, it might hurt?
Doris:	Yes. It would hurt.
Counselor:	You think you'd hear some things you wouldn't like?
Doris:	They just don't understand.
Counselor:	Don't understand what?

(Continued)

TABLE 9.8 Implementing a Counseling Intervention as a Helping Strategy with Doris (*Continued*)

Courageous Conversations with Coworkers

Conversation Starter

I know that people sometimes find it hard to communicate directly with their coworkers when there are difficulties, but I'm interested in learning more about how you have perceived me as a coworker and about the changes I could make to be more effective. I have some questions that I'd like to ask, and I promise to do my best to listen, even if some of what you say is hard to hear.

Courageous Questions
1. What words would people use to describe me as a coworker? I'd like you to identify two positive words and two negative words.
2. What is my greatest strength as a coworker?
3. What are two behaviors or traits that make me less effective as a coworker?
4. What are two things I could do to be more effective as a coworker?
5. Give me an example of when my reaction to something made me difficult to work with.
6. What are two things I could do to have better relationships with my coworkers?

FIGURE 9.3 Courageous Conversations with Coworkers
Source: Based on Wall, B. (2008). *Working relationships: Using emotional intelligence to enhance your effectiveness with others* (revised ed.). Mountain View, CA: Davies-Black Publishing. (Exercise 5, p. 33).

Doris:	(Getting choked up) I was doing the best I could.
Counselor:	I understand that. You were doing the best you could at the time. One of our goals is to help you gain the ability to do even better. And part of that involves understanding what people liked and disliked about you as a coworker.
Doris:	I understand that they think I sucked.

Restatement of Goal

Counselor:	I don't know what they thought. But even if they did think you sucked, I'm more interested in the reasons than a general conclusion. The reasons might point us in a useful direction, to something within your control, to something you could improve.
Doris:	I guess.
Counselor:	(Softly) Doris, this isn't about placing blame and it's not about finding reasons to judge you badly. It's about getting a clearer understanding of how you affect your coworkers so that we can focus our energy on things within your control.
Doris:	I understand, but I just can't do this. I just can't ask a coworker these questions.
Counselor:	You're not ready.
Doris:	No, not yet.

Balancing Challenge with Support

Counselor:	How would it be if you took these questions home with you this week and wrote out your own answers to them?
Doris:	That'd be better.
Counselor:	Do you think it could be helpful?
Doris:	I guess so.

and challenge. Striking such a balance is often a key to maintaining strong working alliances with clients. Erring on the side of too much support and too little challenge tends to result in unproductive, feel-good counseling. Clients keep coming but achieve little progress. In contrast, erring on the side of too little support and too much challenge tends to result in clients prematurely discontinuing counseling or in giving all the right answers in session without making corresponding changes in their actual lives. Though you may be tempted to hit some clients in the head with a two-by-four piece of wood (*I call it two-by-four therapy*), you really will be more effective by striving to balance challenge with support. The more challenging you are, the more support you also need to offer.

In the context of viewing this transcript as an example of the implementation of a helping strategy, it is important to understand that the courageous conversations exercise was not *the* intervention. Instead, the entire conversation with Doris was the intervention. The conversation as a whole represents an intervention in which the counselor gently confronted Doris with the idea that her past behaviors as a coworker may have been problematic and may need improvement. Whether or not Doris engages in a courageous conversation with one or more of her past coworkers, the questions posed in Figure 9.3 offer opportunities for Doris to gain insight and self-awareness. Of course, it would be ideal if Doris does ask a former coworker these courageous questions; however, it is important for you to recognize that not all counseling interventions go as smoothly as sometimes suggested in textbooks. Counselors face the challenge of remaining patient and persistent as they select and implement various helping strategies.

When counseling goes well, these helping strategies succeed in assisting clients with resolving their career concerns and reaching their counseling goals. When clients reach their goals, the counseling process transitions to the concluding stage. The first task in this stage is to assist clients in solidifying their progress.

Solidifying Client Progress: Gillian Parker

Unlike most of your clients, Gillian already has a job that most would envy. Indeed, Gillian's career has been marked by a level of success attained by few. When you first met Gillian, you wondered how you could possibly help her. After all, she had degrees and accomplishments that far exceeded yours. What she didn't have, though, was an objective listening ear, someone who would refrain from admonishing her to remain grateful for all she has or who would discourage her from even considering the possibility of leaving such an impressive position. You can allow Gillian to explore sources of career dissatisfaction, examine her options, and make some decisions. Now, as your sessions draw to a close, she reflects on her experiences in counseling (see the session in Table 9.9).

TABLE 9.9   Solidifying Gillian's Progress

Initiating Closure Conversation

Gillian:	If it's okay, I think this will be my last session with you.
Counselor:	That's completely up to you, Gillian. Do you feel like you've accomplished what you set out to by coming here?
Gillian:	Yes, I do, and I'd really like to thank you for your help.
Counselor:	You're very welcome. (Pause) Perhaps we can use our session today to recap our work together and to review your plans for the future. Before you leave today, I'd really appreciate it if you could complete a written evaluation of your experiences here.
Gillian:	I'd be happy to. It's been a really great experience.
Counselor:	Thanks. So talk to me about when you first made the appointment to see me, about what was going on for you and how you felt about career counseling.
Gillian:	Well, I honestly wasn't sure what to expect when I made our first appointment. I guess I made the appointment on a whim. I saw a flier at a local diner and noticed that it mentioned life planning. Before that, I had assumed career counseling was just résumé writing and job hunting and things like that. The reference to life planning, though, really resonated with me.
Counselor:	So at the point when you saw the flier, you had already been struggling internally with feelings of uncertainty about what you wanted for your future. And when you saw the reference to life planning on my flier, you realized that there are professional career counselors who help people with these things.

(Continued)

TABLE 9.9 Solidifying Gillian's Progress (*Continued*)

Gillian:	Exactly. And it may sound funny, but I was really impressed that your flier included a QR [quick response] code. It seemed like you might be state-of-the art, so I scanned it and the rest is history.
Counselor:	I'm really glad you came in.
Gillian:	Me, too. It's really helped me clarify what I want.
Counselor:	Yes, talk to me about that, about your lack of clarity when you first came here and about the insights you gained.
Gillian:	Hm. Well, if I were to pinpoint it, I'd say that I saw only two options when I first came here. The options were to remain as a partner with Ernst and Young and not start a family or to quit working so that I could start a family. And at that point, I didn't like either choice and I just felt so stuck.
Counselor:	And now?
Gillian:	Well, it's interesting. In some ways, I have more clarity and in other ways, I have more ambiguity. But now I'm comfortable with the ambiguity.
Counselor:	Explain that.
Gillian:	Before, I only saw two choices. Now, I see many more choices. For example, I've realized that I actually could start a family *and* remain as a partner. Before, I wasn't thinking that this was a very realistic option.
Counselor:	What changed?
Gillian:	One of the things that helped me the most was your suggestion that I talk with some of the female partners who have children and ask about how they manage it. Hearing about what has worked well and not so well for them was really helpful. Also, an added bonus of those conversations is that I feel so much less alone now. I feel like I have this cohort of female colleagues with whom it is safe to express myself. I hadn't realized how isolated I felt.
Counselor:	And even though each of you might make different decisions about whether to have children, whether to work as a parent, and how to juggle competing responsibilities, it's comforting to have a network of other professional women who get it, who understand the dilemma you're facing and can relate to your struggles.
Gillian:	Exactly.
Counselor:	So one thing that changed over the course of our work together involved developing this collegial support network and another thing that changed is that you became aware of more options to choose from. What else?
Gillian:	Well, another important change for me involves my perspective. When I started, I felt like I was facing a lose/lose decision. No matter what I chose, there would be a major loss. Now, although I do still see potential for major loss, I'm more optimistic. You might say that I've changed from having a lose/lose perspective to a win/win perspective.
Counselor:	And I know that must feel a lot better.
Gillian:	Absolutely.

Solidifying a client's progress simply requires you to facilitate the client's reflection on the changes that occurred over the course of the counseling relationship. This generally includes a then-versus-now comparison as well as a discussion about how the changes were accomplished. Later in this same session, Gillian might also talk about how helpful she found it to draw her own life space rainbow, examine the differential dominance of various roles over the course of her life, and consider various options for the distribution of life roles in her future. The conversations involved in solidifying a client's progress assist the client in developing an overarching conceptualization of what transpired in counseling and helps bring the counseling process to closure. An additional element of closure involves looking into the future.

Preparing for the Future: Wayne Jensen

The counseling process with Wayne involved approximately eight sessions, all of which were geared toward helping him develop a plan B in case his fears of being laid off from his long-standing job at Ford Motor Company are realized. The helping strategies you used with Wayne included psychoeducation regarding the career decision-making process; assessments of his interests, abilities, and values; and a considerable amount of occupational exploration. At the point at which counseling concludes, Wayne has identified a plan for becoming an electrician. In Table 9.10, he talks with the counselor about his future plans.

In the session shown in the table, Wayne and his counselor simply talked about his next steps. Other career counselors may encourage their clients to develop a written plan complete with anticipated completion dates for each step. Exactly how you address the task of helping your client prepare for the future depends on your personal style as well as your client's needs. At the very least, however, you want to discuss the steps your client will need to take after exiting counseling in order to achieve his or her goals.

TABLE 9.10 Planning for the Future with Wayne

Transition

Counselor:	So you've really come a long way since we first started meeting two months ago. Back then, you knew you wanted to have a plan B in case you get laid off, but you didn't really know your options.
Wayne:	And now I know my options and have settled on a pretty good plan B. You know, in learning about becoming an electrician, I've actually been getting excited about it. In some ways, it doesn't feel like a plan B. Who knows? If I finish the training program and get my license and I'm still working at Ford, maybe I can transfer off the line and get a higher level position there as an electrician. That'd be cool.
Counselor:	Yes, like a mixture of your plan A and your plan B.
Wayne:	I could have my cake and eat it, too.
Counselor:	Well, you know I certainly wish the best for you. I hope everything works out just the way you'd like.
Wayne:	Thanks. I appreciate it.
Counselor:	So talk to me about your next steps. We won't be meeting regularly anymore, so walk me through what comes next for you.
Wayne:	Sure. I did go over to the community college and put in an application. I also talked with someone there and got set up to take the first course in the certificate program for electricians.
Counselor:	Great. You've already registered for a course?
Wayne:	Yes, once the semester starts, it will meet on Tuesday nights, so that will be perfect with my work schedule.
Counselor:	So you've already taken care of that first step. Taking this course will give you an opportunity to gather even more information about exactly what's involved in becoming an electrician.
Wayne:	Right. I think I'm going to like it, but this will help me decide for sure.
Counselor:	And if you don't like it, you may want to reconsider some of the other options we have been talking about as possible new versions of a plan B.
Wayne:	Yes, and I could always come back to see you, right?
Counselor:	Of course. If this first plan B doesn't work out like you think it will, you now know the process you used to choose this one. You could use that same process to pick a new plan B or you could always come back to see me.
Wayne:	I think it's going to work out, though.
Counselor:	I sure hope so. So let's say that you get into this first course and you just love it. What's your next step?
Wayne:	Well, you had mentioned before that I could meet with an adviser at the community college. Is that right?
Counselor:	Absolutely. You could go to the academic advising center and meet with an adviser there, or you could figure out who runs the electrician training program and ask him or her to meet with you.
Wayne:	That might be better.
Counselor:	Maybe so. That person will probably be more familiar with exactly what courses you will need to become an electrician. Also, you may want to ask that person about apprenticeship and internship opportunities.

(Continued)

TABLE 9.10	Planning for the Future with Wayne (*Continued*)
Wayne:	Yeah, that person could really help me get my foot in the door somewhere.
Counselor:	Exactly.
Wayne:	So once I take all the courses, I can do the field experience requirement and then get my journeyman's license.
Counselor:	So to summarize, coming here for career counseling helped you decide that your plan B would be to go back to school to get trained as an electrician. To accomplish this, you've already taken the first step and applied to a program. You've even registered for the first course in the program.
Wayne:	May as well get this ball rollin'.
Counselor:	And so you have. And hopefully, you'll enjoy the courses and they'll confirm that becoming an electrician is a good option for you.
Wayne:	I think so.
Counselor:	And then you'll go get the field experience.
Wayne:	Yep, and then I'll get my journeyman's card.
Counselor:	Sounds like you have a plan.
Wayne:	Sounds like I do. Thanks so much for your help.
Counselor:	You're very welcome.

CHAPTER 10

Intake Assessments

Armed with the understanding of the overall career counseling process you gained from your diligent study of Chapter 9, you are now ready to embark on an exploration of the specifics. This chapter will introduce you to the process of gathering background information about your client. This process is part of the beginning stage of career counseling, and it is known as an intake assessment.

First, however, we will discuss what you need to understand about your clients in career counseling. In the following paragraphs, I've described five basic content areas: (1) current psychological state; (2) contextual information; (3) educational and occupational history; (4) factors related to career selection, success, and satisfaction; and (5) factors related to career decision making. These five content areas are described below and are summarized in Table 10.1.

Regardless of whether a client is seeking career counseling or wants to address more personal or social issues, you have a responsibility as a counselor to assess that client's current psychological state. You want to assess, for example, whether a client shows any signs of acute psychopathology, which would need to be addressed immediately. It is important to conduct a brief lethality assessment. Consider, for example, the possibility that Li Mei could be experiencing some suicidal ideation. Her sense of shame and her feelings of hopelessness might be so pronounced that she considers ending her life rather than continuing to live as a perpetual disappointment and embarrassment to her family. One major difference between career counselors and other career professionals (e.g., Global Career Development Facilitators [GCDF]) is that counselors have the training necessary to assess and address current psychological state.

Contextual information represents another important factor to assess. As you know, several career development and career counseling theories recognize the importance of contextual factors (Gottfredson, 2002; Lent, Brown, & Hackett, 1996; Savickas, 2012). Whether utilizing these particular theories or not, counselors do well to understand a client in context. Specifically, you want to seek an understanding of your clients in the context of their current family structure as well as their family of origin, their cultural identities, and the communities in which they reside.

Career counselors also want to understand their clients' educational and occupational history. This information likely has direct relevance to the client's presenting concerns and goals for counseling. Keep in mind that educational and occupational histories involve more than a chronology. In addition to wanting to know factual information such as the highest educational level achieved, grade point average, or college major, career counselors are also interested in the client's subjective history.

Career assessment generally focuses on factors related to career selection, success, and satisfaction. These factors include occupational interests and personality characteristics; work-related values and needs; strengths, aptitudes, and abilities; employability skills; and self-efficacy. As you have learned, different theories emphasize

TABLE 10.1 What You Need to Understand About Your Client

Category	Examples
Current psychological state	• Negative affect or emotions • Presence or absence of acute psychopathology • Lethality risk level
Contextual information	• Family context • Culture context • Community context
Educational and occupational history	• Highest level of education achieved • Indicators of academic success and aptitude • Employment history • Indicators of occupational success, satisfaction, and aptitude
Personal characteristics related to career selection, success, and satisfaction	• Occupational interests • Personality characteristics • Work-related values and needs • Strengths, aptitudes, and abilities • Employability skills • Self-efficacy • Career maturity • Physical and/or psychological conditions that may affect employment options • Other barriers that may affect employment
Factors related to career decision making	• Readiness • Beliefs • Maturity

different factors. Career assessment also addresses factors related to career decision making. Some address readiness to make career decisions (Sampson, Peterson, Reardon, and Lenz, 2000); others focus on people's beliefs and assumptions as they may pertain to career choices (Krumboltz, 1988). Also, it may be important to inquire about any physical and/or psychological conditions and any barriers that may affect employment options. Juan, for example, has a physical condition that limits his ability to succeed in occupations requiring heavy lifting. One barrier for Lakeesha could be her parental responsibilities because she has two young children.

Learning about your clients across these five dimensions takes time, and you may take comfort in knowing that the assessment process should span the entire course of the counseling relationship. The first step of this assessment process involves intake assessments at the beginning of the counseling relationship. Subsequent chapters will then address assessment strategies to be used over the course of the counseling relationship to better understand and/or address individual client needs.

APPROACHES TO INTAKE ASSESSMENTS

As counselors or counseling offices prepare to take in new clients, it is helpful to gather some information about them. In gathering this information, counselors use various approaches that differ in format, structure, and timing.

In terms of format variations, intake assessments may be conducted orally, in writing using a paper-based form, or in writing using a computer-based medium. Oral intake assessments involve a conversation—either by phone or in person—between the client and the counselor (or counseling office staff person). The counselor or counseling office staff person generally creates a written record of the conversation and the information gathered. In contrast, intake assessments may involve the clients themselves creating the written record either with a pencil-and-paper method or by keyboarding the information into a computer.

Structural variations for intake assessments can be defined as structured, semistructured, or open-ended. Open-ended intake assessments tend to rely on a conversation at the beginning of the counseling process in which the client is invited to share his or her concerns. The conversation is directed by the client, who is encouraged by the counselor using basic listening skills such as paraphrasing and reflection of feelings, and prompting if needed with open questions.

In contrast, structured intake assessments are guided by a predetermined set of topics and questions. The conversation is directed by the counselor who uses the preset structure to guide the client through a number of intake topics. In highly structured intake assessments, the topics are addressed in sequence.

Semistructured intake assessments blend the structured and open-ended approaches. The counselor assumes ultimate responsibility for guiding the intake process and for addressing predetermined topics, but she or he does so in a flexible manner in which the client often takes the lead. To the extent that the conversation naturally flows through relevant topics, the counselor allows the client to lead the discussion. The counselor then supplements this natural flow with more structured questions to ensure coverage of all intake topics.

Finally, intake assessments can take three primary temporal variations. Some counselors prefer to gather intake information from prospective clients prior to the first appointment. In such cases, counselors may send clients a questionnaire to complete and bring to their initial session, or they may ask clients to arrive early for their first session to allow them time to complete an intake questionnaire in the reception area prior to meeting with them. A second temporal variation involves counselors gathering intake information during the first session. This approach commonly consists of a semistructured interview in which the counselor asks questions and records the client's responses on an intake form or questionnaire. Rarely would a counselor sit with a client and watch him or her complete a written questionnaire. The third temporal variation (which you've probably guessed by process of elimination) involves having clients complete an intake questionnaire following their initial session with you.

CONTENT OF INTAKE ASSESSMENTS

Although intake assessments vary with regard to format, structure, and timing, they tend to address similar content. This section is designed to familiarize you with the content of an intake assessment in a career counseling context. Intake assessments are designed to collect a wide range of information from your client expeditiously, at the onset of the counseling relationship. Some of this information will be specific to the concerns that prompted your client to seek counseling. Other information may appear

TABLE 10.2 Content of Intake Assessments

- Basic personal information
- Concerns and goals
- Education and training
- Employment history
- Family background
- Current living situation
- Challenges and obstacles
- Strengths and sources of support
- Cultural formulation
- Current health status and medical information

more peripheral but may be useful in better understanding clients and ultimately addressing their concerns. Note that some intake assessments are more extensive than others. Depending on your needs in a specific setting, you may choose a more focused intake assessment. What follows is a discussion of the content that should be addressed in a comprehensive intake assessment. The basic sections typically included in an intake assessment are identified in Table 10.2.

Basic Personal Information

The vast majority of intake assessments begin with the collection of basic information. At a minimum, this information tends to include name; address; contact information; and an inquiry asking permission to leave messages, send emails, and/or send text messages. It is also common for intake assessments to request information about a person's demographic characteristics, and some will include questions about a client's fluency in English and eligibility for employment in the United States. Given increased concerns about identity theft, contemporary intake assessments rarely request a client's social security number. Figure 10.1 illustrates a sample section of an intake assessment form requesting basic personal information.

Note that, rather than offering a "laundry list" of demographic options, this form simply invites clients to specify their sex, relationship status, and race/ethnicity. Should you decide to identify the demographic options in a checklist fashion, you should take care to offer an inclusive, culturally sensitive range of options. For example, rather than listing only male and female as options, you also want to include transgender, intersex, and nonbinary options or, at the very least, include other as an option. Ensure that the relationship status item includes options relevant to same-sex couples. To do otherwise communicates a not-so-subtle but most likely unintended message

```
Name: _____  Date of Birth: _____
Street address: _____
City: _____  State: _____  Zip: _____
Phone number: _____  ☐ Home                       ☐ Cell
Permission to leave message?         ☐ Yes                        ☐ No
Permission to text appointment reminders?  ☐ Yes                  ☐ No
Email address: _____
Permission to send email?            ☐ Yes                        ☐ No

Optional Information:
Sex: _____
Relationship status: _____
Race/ethnicity: _____
Fluent in English?                   ☐ Yes                        ☐ No
Eligible for employment in United States?  ☐ Yes                  ☐ No
```

FIGURE 10.1 Basic Personal Information

to clients about what you and/or your organization consider as legitimate, normal options.

Concerns and Goals

Another common element of intake assessments involves the concern(s) the client wants to address in counseling and the level of difficulty the client is having with these concerns. Closely connected to client concerns is an identification of client goals, which focuses on what the client hopes to accomplish in counseling. Information about client concerns and goals may be elicited by using an open question or by using a checklist. Both approaches have advantages and disadvantages. The open question allows clients to use their own words without limiting their choices. For example, you might ask, "Why are you seeking career counseling?" or "What do you hope to accomplish through counseling?" Clients can respond to such questions however they like without feeling constrained by a set of predetermined options. In contrast, an advantage of the checklist is that the list of options may include concerns or goals clients have but may not have articulated. For example, a client may respond to an open question by identifying a need to choose an academic major. On a checklist, the client would check this option but may also check options such as "learn more about possible careers" or "address some personal concerns." Because each style of eliciting client concerns has compelling advantages, it is not unusual for counselors to use a combination approach, which is illustrated in Figure 10.2.

In this example, the checklist is sandwiched between two open questions. Notice that this example asks about the client's goals for counseling and also about the client's career goals.

Education and Training

Understanding a client's educational status, academic abilities, and training experiences is especially important when providing career counseling. This element of the intake assessment is generally more extensive when working with clients who present first with career concerns than when working with clients who seek counseling with an initial goal of addressing personal concerns. Figure 10.3 offers an example of a fairly extensive section pertaining to education and training.

Notice that the section about a client's high school experiences is especially detailed. This developmental phase is often associated with what Super (1990) described as the exploration stage during which students begin crystallizing their career interests by publicly identifying tentative occupational choices; continuing to gather information about the various occupations of tentative interest to them; and making educational, avocational, and vocational choices related to these interests. Consistent with the idea that careers should reflect, at least to some degree, a person's self-concept, the section about high school asks not only about academic success but also about favorite and least favorite subjects and about extracurricular activities in which the client participated. Note in Figure 10.3 that a wide variety of

What concerns or issues bring you to our office?
_____
_____
_____

How much of a struggle are these concerns for you?

Not a struggle or concern at all									Significant struggle or concern
1	2	3	4	5	6	7	8	9	10

Please check the specific area(s) in which you would like assistance:

- ☐ Choosing an academic major
- ☐ Confirming my choice of a major
- ☐ Learning more about possible careers
- ☐ Choosing a career path
- ☐ Accessing job market information
- ☐ Developing a résumé
- ☐ Improving my interviewing skills
- ☐ Other: _____
- ☐ Engaging in self-exploration
- ☐ Finding a job
- ☐ Finding a better job
- ☐ Becoming more satisfied at work
- ☐ Being more successful at work
- ☐ Overcoming challenges to career success
- ☐ Addressing some personal concerns

What would you like to accomplish in counseling?
_____
_____

What are your current career goals? (Even if you are uncertain, identify any thoughts you currently have about this area.)
_____
_____
_____

If you could do anything you wanted as a career, what would it be?
_____
_____
_____

FIGURE 10.2 Concerns and Goals

High School (Secondary) Education

What high school did you attend?   School name: _____
                                    Location: _____

Did you graduate from
high school?
☐ Yes
☐ No, but I have a GED diploma
☐ No. I left school after _____ grade.

FIGURE 10.3 Education and Training

(Continued)

How were your high school grades?

GPA: _____

Class rank: _____

☐ Mostly *A*s
☐ Mostly *B*s
☐ Mostly *C*s
☐ Mostly *D*s
☐ Mostly *E*s or *F*s

What types of courses did you take in high school? *(Check all that apply.)*

☐ Advanced placement
☐ College preparatory
☐ General education
☐ Career and technical education/vo-tech
☐ Special education

What was your favorite subject? _____

What was your least favorite subject? _____

In what types of extracurricular activities did you participate? *(Check all that apply.)*

☐ Academic
☐ Business
☐ Cultural
☐ Farming/4-H
☐ Journalism/yearbook
☐ Performing arts (band, choir, drama, etc.)
☐ Political
☐ Religious
☐ Sports
☐ Social
☐ Student government
☐ Other: _____
☐ Other: _____

On a scale of 1 to 10, how much did you enjoy high school?

Hated it									Loved it
1	2	3	4	5	6	7	8	9	10

Postsecondary Education

What types of postsecondary education have you had?

☐ Specialized training program: _____
☐ Some community college
☐ Community college degree (associate's degree)
☐ Some 4-year college
☐ 4-year college degree (bachelor's degree)
☐ Some graduate school
☐ Graduate school degree:
　　☐ Master's　　☐ Specialist　　☐ Doctorate

In what types of extracurricular activities did you participate during your postsecondary education? *(Check all that apply.)*

☐ Academic
☐ Business
☐ Cultural
☐ Farming/4-H
☐ Journalism/yearbook

☐ Performing arts (band, choir, drama, etc.)
☐ Political
☐ Religious
☐ Sports
☐ Social
☐ Student government
☐ Other: _____
☐ Other: _____

On a scale of 1 to 10, how much did you enjoy your postsecondary education?

Hated it									Loved it
1	2	3	4	5	6	7	8	9	10

Diplomas, Degrees, and Certifications

Use this space to list all of your diplomas, degrees, and certifications.

☐ GED diploma
☐ High school diploma
☐ Certificate or training program not requiring college:
    Area: _____
    Institution: _____
    Dates: _____
☐ College diploma
    ☐ Associate's degree
        Major: _____
        Institution: _____
        Dates: _____
    ☐ Bachelor's degree
        Major: _____
        Institution: _____
        Dates: _____
    ☐ Master's degree
        Major: _____
        Institution: _____
        Dates: _____
    ☐ Specialist degree
        Major: _____
        Institution: _____
        Dates: _____
☐ Doctoral degree
    Major: _____
    Institution: _____
    Dates: _____
☐ Advanced certificate or training program
    Area: _____
    Organization: _____
    Dates: _____
    _____

(Continued)

You as a Student

What ways of learning are effective for you?
(Check all that apply)

☐ Reading
☐ Taking notes
☐ Listening to a teacher explain
☐ Hands-on learning
☐ Trial and error
☐ Studying by myself
☐ Studying with a group
☐ Other: _____

On a scale of 1 to 10, how confident do you feel in your ability to learn?

Not confident at all   Very confident
1   2   3   4   5   6   7   8   9   10

On a scale of 1 to 10, how willing are you to consider seeking additional education or training?

Completely unwilling   Only if necessary   Very willing
1   2   3   4   5   6   7   8   9   10

FIGURE 10.3 Education and Training (*Continued*)

postsecondary educational experiences are recognized in this section. It concludes with asking about learning styles, the client's self-confidence as a learner, and the client's willingness to consider additional education or training.

Employment History

Career counseling intake assessments also emphasize a client's employment history, of course. Some counselors ask clients to provide a current résumé; others ask clients to complete forms asking about employment history. Still others simply engage clients in a discussion about their past employment experiences. Whatever your approach, you should take care to inquire not only about the chronology of a person's past employment but also about the quality of those experiences. For example, you will benefit from knowing how much your clients enjoyed each position, how successful they were in each, and why they left. You may also want to ask specifically whether the client has been fired or dismissed from any positions and, if so, the circumstances surrounding the discharge. Having a client explain (as I once did) that she has never held a job for longer than 90 days, meaning that she had never made it past the probationary period, can be particularly useful information. Figure 10.4 offers sample items that may be included in an intake assessment of a client's employment history.

Family Background

Most intake assessments also address the clients' family background. This section includes information about the client's childhood, parent(s), and siblings. It generally also includes inquiries about various issues or stressors that may have affected the family. Within a career counseling context, this portion of the intake assessment should also include attention to the educational achievement and employment history of parents and other significant adults in the client's life. It also provides an ideal opportunity to inquire about how decisions are made within the client's family to determine whether career decision making is viewed as an individual responsibility or a collective endeavor. Sample questions that may be included in the intake exploration of a client's family background are presented in Figure 10.5.

Current Living Situation

A discussion about the client's current living situation tends to flow easily from the previous exploration of family background. As you know, client ability to pay for housing is deeply affected by career well-being. For example, clients who have mortgages may experience great anxiety at the prospect of a layoff and may panic when they are suddenly unemployed. Having a mortgage may also limit a client's mobility or willingness to relocate for a specific job. Similarly, dissatisfaction with one's living situation may serve as an impetus to seek better-paying employment. In a striking example of how living situations can be affected by career status, one of my former clients sought counseling after being fired. Of primary concern to him was that his housing had been provided by his employer. Thus, getting fired also meant losing a place to live, and this particular client feared that he would once again need to live in his car. Figure 10.6 includes some items that may be included in an intake assessment of a client's living situation. In addition to inquiring about the people with whom the client resides, this section asks about the type of housing in which the client lives, the level of satisfaction the client feels with his or her living situation, and the client's willingness to relocate for a new job.

Are you legally eligible to work in the United States? ☐ Yes ☐ No
Have you ever been employed? ☐ Yes ☐ No
How many jobs have you held in the past 10 years? _____
Have you ever been terminated or fired from a job? ☐ Yes ☐ No
Have you ever been promoted? ☐ Yes ☐ No
Have you ever received a raise? ☐ Yes ☐ No
What has been your favorite job? _____
What has been your least favorite job? _____
What work-related accomplishment are you most proud of?
_____

Current Employment
Use this space to identify any job(s) you currently have.
Job title: _____
Employer: _____
Dates of employment: _____ to present
Job title: _____
Employer: _____
Dates of employment: _____ to present
Are you having any difficulties or stressors in your current job(s)? If so, what are they?
_____
_____
_____

Past Employment
Use this space to identify any other job(s) you have had in the past 5 years.
Job title: _____
Employer: _____
Dates of employment: _____ to _____
Reason you left: _____
Job title: _____
Employer: _____
Dates of employment: _____ to _____
Reason you left: _____
Job title: _____
Employer: _____
Dates of employment: _____ to _____
Reason you left: _____

FIGURE 10.4 Intake Assessment of Employment History

Grandparents

In the spaces below, provide information about your grandparents. Identify their first names, their relationship to you, their highest level of education completed, and the career or job they have held the longest. An example is provided.

First Name	Relationship	Education	Job/Career
Beverly	*Grandmother*	*Master's degree*	*Teacher*

Parents and/or Stepparents

In the spaces below, provide information about the parent(s) and/or stepparent(s) who raised you. Identify their first names, their relationship to you, their highest level of education completed, and the career or job they have held the longest.

First Name	Relationship	Education	Job/Career

Siblings

In the spaces below, provide information about your sibling(s). Identify their first name(s), their age(s), their highest level of education completed, and the career or job they have held the longest.

First Name	Age	Education	Job/Career

Significant Other

If you have a significant other, provide information about him or her. Identify his or her first name, the nature of your relationship, the highest level of education completed, and the career or job he or she has held the longest. Two examples are provided.

FIGURE 10.5 Intake Assessment of Family Background

First Name	Relationship	Education	Job/Career
James	Partner	Associate's degree	Pharmacist technician
Celeste	Wife	1 year of college	Full-time student

Family Messages

What messages about work and career did you receive from your family?

_____
_____
_____
_____

Family Role Models

When it comes to career matters, who in your family would you identify as your role models?

_____
_____

Why? _____
_____
_____

Family Decision-Making Style

When it comes to making your career-related decisions, what style of decision making is generally used in your family?

☐ Individual decision making: It is completely up to me

☐ Individual decision making with family input: I ultimately decide, but it is important to seek my family's input and advice before I decide.

☐ Family decision making with my input: My parents will make the decision with input from me.

☐ Family decision making without my input: My parents will make the decision for me.

☐ Family/community decision making: My parents will seek input from members of our community before making a decision.

Family Stressors

Many families are affected by stressful situations. Please identify the types of stress that have affected you and your family by checking all that apply.

Health-Related Stressors

☐ Chronic illness of a family member
☐ Physical disability of a family member
☐ Life-threatening illness of a family member
☐ Death of a family member
☐ Drinking problems or drug use by a family member
☐ Mental illness of a family member
☐ Emotional problems of a family member
☐ Other: _____

Relationship Stressors

☐ Frequent arguments in family
☐ Physical violence at home
☐ Separation of parents
☐ Divorce of parents
☐ Child abuse or neglect
☐ Conflict about cultural differences
☐ Other: _____
☐ Other: _____

(Continued)

Financial Stressors	Work-Related Stressors
☐ Arguments about money	☐ Arguments about work
☐ Difficulty paying bills	☐ Having a family member hate his or her job
☐ Loss of home due to foreclosure	☐ Having to move because of work
☐ Pressures to make more money	☐ Having a family member lose a job
☐ Other: _____	☐ Unemployment
☐ Other: _____	☐ Other: _____

FIGURE 10.5 Intake Assessment of Family Background (*Continued*)

With whom do you currently live? *Check all that apply.*	☐ By myself ☐ With my parent(s) ☐ With roommates ☐ With friends ☐ With a significant other ☐ With my school-age children ☐ With my adult children ☐ Other: _____
Where do you currently live?	☐ In a single family home that I/we own ☐ In a single family home that I/we rent ☐ In an apartment ☐ In a dormitory or residence hall ☐ In someone else's home ☐ I don't have a stable residence right now
How satisfied are you with your current living situation?	☐ Very satisfied ☐ Somewhat satisfied ☐ Somewhat dissatisfied ☐ Very dissatisfied
If you are looking for a job, would you be willing to move?	☐ Yes, and I would look forward to it. ☐ Yes, but I hope I don't need to. ☐ No, but I wish I could. ☐ No, I want to stay where I am.

FIGURE 10.6 Intake Assessment of Current Living Situation

Challenges and Obstacles

Because most clients perceive at least some issues that have the potential to affect their career planning and/or success negatively, intake assessments should also inquire about these issues. They may include a variety of personal challenges and environmental obstacles. Personal challenges may include academic issues, decision-making difficulties, emotional concerns, financial problems, health problems, legal troubles, and work history. Environmental obstacles may include discrimination, family issues, poor economy, or a tight job market. Figure 10.7 includes some items that may be included in an intake assessment of the challenges and obstacles perceived by clients.

Personal Strengths and Sources of Support

In addition to caring about the challenges and obstacles your clients may face, inquire about sources of strength

---

Please identify any challenges or obstacles that may affect your career planning or success.

- ☐ Academic issues
  - ☐ Lack of motivation
  - ☐ Learning problems
  - ☐ Low grades
  - ☐ Other: _____

- ☐ Decision-making difficulties
  - ☐ Indecisiveness
  - ☐ Pressure from others
  - ☐ Too few or no interests
  - ☐ Too many interests
  - ☐ Other: _____

- ☐ Discrimination

- ☐ Emotional concerns
  - ☐ Anxiety
  - ☐ Depression
  - ☐ Lack of confidence
  - ☐ Low self-esteem
  - ☐ Mental health
  - ☐ Other: _____

- ☐ Family issues
  - ☐ Aging parents
  - ☐ Child care
  - ☐ Family expectations
  - ☐ Other: _____

- ☐ Economic problems
  - ☐ Credit history
  - ☐ Debt
  - ☐ Personal finances
  - ☐ Poor economy
  - ☐ Tight job market
  - ☐ Other: _____

- ☐ Health issues
  - ☐ Physical challenges
  - ☐ Drinking and/or drug use
  - ☐ Other: _____

- ☐ Legal troubles
  - ☐ Criminal history
  - ☐ Driving record
  - ☐ Other: _____

- ☐ Work history
  - ☐ Gaps in my résumé /work history
  - ☐ Have been fired
  - ☐ Little or no work experience
  - ☐ Lack of good references
  - ☐ Other: _____

- ☐ Anything else you are concerned about: _____

What potential obstacles or challenges concern you the most?
_____
_____
_____

FIGURE 10.7 Intake Assessment of Challenges and Obstacles

and support. A section of an intake assessment requesting this information is illustrated in Figure 10.8. Responding to these types of questions may help clients recognize and articulate personal strengths such as determination, good health, and intelligence. It can also be useful in tapping into sources of support.

Cultural Formulation

As discussed in Chapter 6, it is also important to understand each client's cultural identity and to consider how cultural factors may also influence clients' career situations and career counseling needs. I recommend use of a modified version of the cultural formulation interview featured in the *Diagnostic and Statistical Manual of Mental Disorders* (*DSM-5*; American Psychiatric Association, 2013). Table 10.3 presents this modified cultural formulation interview protocol, and you may wish to revisit Chapter 6 for a more thorough discussion of it. For the purposes of this chapter, it is important to recognize that these questions should be included in your intake interviews either by asking them in

---

Personal Strengths

Everyone has strengths that will help them achieve their goals. Identify the strengths that you believe you possess.

☐ Determination
☐ Good health
☐ Intelligence
☐ Luck
☐ Motivation
☐ Persistence
☐ Other strengths:
_____
_____

☐ Academic success
☐ Financial resources
☐ Good references from past employers
☐ History of work-related success
☐ Strong support network
☐ Specific skills:
_____
_____

Sources of Support

When you go through tough times, who can you count on to be supportive?

☐ Family
  ☐ Husband/wife/partner
  ☐ Parents
  ☐ Siblings
  ☐ Children
  ☐ Other: _____

☐ Friends
  ☐ Boyfriend or girlfriend
  ☐ Best friend: _____
  ☐ Other friends: _____

☐ Religious supports
  ☐ God/Allah/Supreme Being
  ☐ Minister/priest/rabbi/clergy/other
  ☐ People at my place of worship

☐ Pet: _____

☐ Nobody

☐ Other: _____
_____

On a scale of 1 to 10, how well supported do you feel at this point in your life?

Not at all   Completely

   1   2   3   4   5   6   7   8   9   10

FIGURE 10.8 Intake Assessment of Personal Strengths and Sources of Support

TABLE 10.3   A Cultural Formulation Interview for Career Counseling

Career Concerns

The initial step in developing a cultural formulation of your clients' career concerns is to inquire about their definition of the problem. Such questions prompt clients to describe their concerns in their own words:

- Using your own words, how would you describe your career concerns?
- If you were to explain your career concerns to your family or friends, what would you say? Also, what would you say is causing or contributing to your career difficulties?
- Conversely, how might your family or friends describe your career situation? Also, what would they say is causing or contributing to your career difficulties?

Contextual Supports and Barriers

Generally speaking, people with career concerns don't exist in a vacuum. Therefore, the next step is to inquire about your clients' perception of any stressors and supports related to their career problem, including those that may be related to their cultural identity (American Psychiatric Association, 2013).

- In dealing with your career concerns, to whom have you been able to turn for support? What other sources of support do you have in your life?
- Besides your career concerns, what other stressors do you have in your life?
- What contextual challenges or barriers will you need to overcome in order to resolve your career concerns or achieve your career goals?
- Let's talk about cultural identity. By that, I am referring to race, ethnicity, the primary language you speak, gender, religion, sexual orientation and disability status. How would you describe your cultural identity? Which of these are most important in the way you define yourself?
- Are there any ways in which you believe your cultural identity affects your career situation, either positively or negatively?

Approaches to Coping

Finally, it is essential to explore cultural dimensions that may affect your clients' coping strategies. Coping strategies may involve autonomous efforts to cope as well as a more collectivist approach of seeking help from others.

- Up until this point, what have you done on your own to address your career concern?
- Up until this point, what other sources of help have you sought in an attempt to deal with your career concern?
- Have your friends or family suggested any other coping strategies or sources of help?
- What prompted you to seek career counseling? How is career counseling viewed by your friends and family or within your culture?
- Do you have any concerns that cultural differences may interfere with my ability to help you?

---

this specific sequence or by integrating them within the various sections of intake assessments addressed above.

Current Health Status and Medical Information

One additional topic generally included within the intake assessment process involves the client's current health status and medical information. In the context of career counseling, both physical and mental health conditions may affect a client's eligibility for certain types of work and/or her or his ability to perform various work-related tasks. Figure 10.9 offers one approach to inquiring about your clients' current health status and medical information.

On a scale of 1 to 10, how would you rate your current health?

Very Poor									Very healthy
1	2	3	4	5	6	7	8	9	10

Name of primary care physician: _____

Approximate date of last physical examination: _____

To your knowledge, do you have any *physical* conditions that may affect your ability to work or perform certain types of jobs? ☐ Yes ☐ No

Do you have any vision problems? ☐ Yes ☐ No

Do you have any hearing loss? ☐ Yes ☐ No

To your knowledge, do you have any *psychological* conditions that may affect your ability to work or perform certain types of jobs? ☐ Yes ☐ No

Have you ever attempted or considered suicide or had suicidal feelings? ☐ Yes ☐ No

Please check any areas in which you have been experiencing difficulties (*check all that apply*):

- ☐ ADHD
- ☐ Alcohol use
- ☐ Anger
- ☐ Anxiety
- ☐ Appetite
- ☐ Concentration
- ☐ Depression
- ☐ Drug use
- ☐ Energy
- ☐ Fatigue
- ☐ Headaches
- ☐ Hearing
- ☐ Irritability
- ☐ Mobility
- ☐ Pain
- ☐ Panic
- ☐ Sexual concerns
- ☐ Sleep
- ☐ Stomach
- ☐ Suicidal feelings
- ☐ Troubling thoughts
- ☐ Vision
- ☐ Weight
- ☐ Other: _____

Medications and Substance Use

Please list any prescription or over-the-counter medications you are currently taking.

Medication	Dosage	Reason

Which of the following do you currently use?

Type of drug   How much and how often?

☐ Alcohol _____

☐ Caffeine _____

☐ Nicotine _____

FIGURE 10.9 Intake Assessment of Current Health Status and Medical Information

Please identify any drugs you have used (even once) in the past 12 months (*check all that apply*):

- ☐ Amphetamines/speed
- ☐ Barbiturates
- ☐ Benzodiazepines
- ☐ Cocaine/crack
- ☐ Ecstasy/MDMA
- ☐ Hallucinogens
- ☐ Heroin
- ☐ Inhalants
- ☐ Marijuana/cannabis
- ☐ Methadone
- ☐ Methamphetamine
- ☐ Opiates
- ☐ Phencyclidine (PCP)
- ☐ Sedatives/downers
- ☐ Other: _____

On a scale of 1 to 10, how confident are you that you would pass a 10-panel urine screen (30-day) drug test if it were required as part of employment testing?

Not at all   Completely
1   2   3   4   5   6   7   8   9   10

On a scale of 1 to 10, how confident are you that you would pass a hair follicle (12-month) drug test if it were required as part of employment testing?

Not at all   Completely
1   2   3   4   5   6   7   8   9   10

PUTTING IT ALL TOGETHER

As with any counseling relationship, career counseling begins with an intake assessment. Although they may vary with regard to extensiveness, administration method, structure, and timing, intake assessments tend to address a set of common topics:

- Basic personal information
- Concerns and goals
- Education and training
- Employment history
- Family background
- Current living situation
- Challenges and obstacles
- Strengths and sources of support
- Cultural formulation
- Current health status and medical information

We'll examine these topical areas and in relation to our cast of clients next.

APPLICATION TO OUR CAST OF CLIENTS

This section will demonstrate the intake assessment process with our cast of clients by using segments that parallel the typical outline of topics. I will proceed through a typical intake assessment and address each content area, using a different member of our cast of clients as an illustration of each. In doing so, I will also vary the strategies used to collect this intake information. You can compare my approach to Table 10.4.

TABLE 10.4 Intake Assessment Process with Our Cast of Clients

Content Area	Client Application	Strategy Demonstrated
Basic personal information	Wayne Jensen	Intake form
Concerns and goals	Vincent Santiago Arroyo	Unstructured interview
Education and training	Gillian Parker	Semistructured interview
Employment history	Doris Bronner	Intake form
Family background	Lily Huang Li Mei	Semistructured interview
Current living situation	Wayne Jensen	Semistructured interview
Challenges and obstacles	Lakeesha Maddox	Intake form
Strengths and sources of support		
Current health status and medical information	Juan Martinez	Intake form

Basic Personal Information: Wayne Jensen

When Wayne called to make an appointment to meet with a career counselor, he was asked to arrive 15 minutes early to complete some paperwork. Just as requested, Wayne arrived promptly at 4:45 for a 5:00 appointment. The receptionist smiled, greeted him warmly, and thanked him for remembering to come early. He then provided Wayne with a pencil and a clipboard with an intake form attached, and instructed Wayne to fill out as much as he could. He assured Wayne that it was okay to leave items blank if he had questions or concerns about them. Once seated, Wayne quickly glanced through the pages before beginning to write. He noticed that the first page looked a lot like the forms one normally sees at doctor appointments and quickly completed it (see Figure 10.10).

A quick perusal of this form provides you with contact and demographic information. Notice that Wayne identified himself as a 40-year-old, divorced white male who lives in the small community of Woodhaven, in what is known as the downriver area of Detroit. Notice also that, although Wayne has a cell phone and is willing to receive text message appointment reminders, he appears to have no email address. You wonder about the implications of this for his computer literacy.

Concerns and Goals: Vincent Santiago Arroyo

Because Vincent is a student seeking assistance from his school counselor, it is unlikely that the counseling process would involve a formal intake assessment. It is also unlikely that the school counselor has not yet met Vincent (they have likely had occasional contact throughout his time in high school). For example, Vincent remembers his school counselor coming into various classes to talk about the Regents exams, study skills, bullying, and career planning. He and his mother also met with the school counselor early in his freshman year because his mother wanted to make sure the counselor understood the significance of 9-11 to Vincent. As a result of these various contacts, Vincent and his school counselor already know one another to some degree.

In fact, Vincent revealed a need for more extensive career and personal counseling during a routine career planning meeting with his school counselor. What could have been a simple review of career aspirations paired with a discussion of courses to take in his senior year turned into a counseling session. When the school counselor reviewed her notes from previous meetings and asked Vincent whether he was still planning to join the Marines immediately on graduation, he surprised her by expressing uncertainty. Sensing some deep emotion, the school counselor gently probed and waited patiently as Vincent talked about why he has been rethinking this career option. Vincent revealed that "something's not right" about him and that the Marines won't want him if they find out.

Ignoring the phone as it rang and putting aside any thoughts about the long list of students she needed to see, the school counselor realized that Vincent needed genuine counseling and began an open-ended exploration of Vincent's concerns and goals. Within this safe environment, Vincent

---

Basic Personal Information

Name: _Wayne Jensen_   Date of birth: _March 28, 1973_
Street address: _3048 Subdivision Drive_
City: _Woodhaven_   State: _MI_   Zip: _48183_
Phone number: _(734) 123-4567_   ☐ Home   ☑ Cell
Permission to leave message?   ☑ Yes   ☐ No
Permission to text appointment reminders? ☑ Yes   ☐ No
Email address: _None_
Permission to send email?   ☐ Yes   ☑ No

Optional:
Sex: _Male_
Relationship status: _Divorced_
Race/ethnicity: _White_
Fluent in English?   ☑ Yes   ☐ No
Eligible for employment in the United States? ☑ Yes   ☐ No

FIGURE 10.10 Wayne Jensen's Basic Personal Information

eventually verbalized that, as much as he hates the idea, he has realized he is gay. Although he knows that the military has repealed its "don't ask, don't tell" policy, Vincent worries that the Marines are still permeated by an antigay mentality. He can even understand it: After all, he doesn't like the idea that he's gay. He has come to realize, however, that it isn't a choice and it isn't going to change (Marcus, 2005).

After 45 minutes or so, Vincent has articulated two specific concerns. First, he has concerns about being gay. Second, he is now uncertain about what he wants to do when he graduates from high school. Together, Vincent and the school counselor formulated four goals: (1) to help Vincent come to terms with his realization that he's gay, (2) to gather information about what it might be like to be a gay Marine in the post–"don't ask, don't tell" era, (3) to explore other career options that might appeal to Vincent, and (4) to use a decision-making strategy to guide his career planning.

Education and Training: Gillian Parker

Clearly quite diligent, Gillian arrived for her first meeting with you having neatly and thoroughly completed all of the paperwork mailed her in advance by your office. You, in turn, used this paperwork to guide the initial session in a semistructured manner. You glance through the section about her education and training experiences, and the conversation shown in Table 10.5 took place.

Notice that this discussion of Gillian's education and training was conversational in nature and a far cry

TABLE 10.5 Discussion of Gillian's Education and Training Experiences

Transitioning to Education and Training

Counselor:	Let's shift gears and talk a little about your educational experiences.
Gillian:	(Laughs) Okay. As you can see from my materials, I'm officially a geek.
Counselor:	(Uncertain how to interpret Gillian's identification as a geek) Tell me about that. In your mind, is being a geek a source of pride or do you mean it more negatively?
Gillian:	Hm, both, I guess. I've always been an overachiever at school and, honestly, I actually liked school. That's why I described myself as a geek, and I'm okay with that. There were times in high school when I felt like the odd one out, but even then, I felt some pride in my achievements and accepted myself for who I am.
Counselor:	(Looking at Gillian's paperwork) Wow! I see here that you certainly were an overachiever. A 4.21 GPA is pretty impressive. I'm assuming some of your courses were weighted?
Gillian:	Yes. Getting As in my AP courses put me over the 4.0.
Counselor:	And you were the valedictorian?
Gillian:	Yes.
Counselor:	And it looks like you did a lot more than study. Tell me about your extracurricular activities.
Gillian:	Oh, gosh. Back then, it seems like I was involved in everything. I was an officer for the National Honor Society and vice president of our student council, participated on the debate and quiz bowl teams. I was involved in Junior Achievement, helped edit the yearbook, and played varsity tennis.
Counselor:	Good for you! That's incredible. I'm guessing you had many scholarship offers when it came time to go to college.
Gillian:	Yes, I had several offers for full scholarships. I was very lucky.
Counselor:	Come now, your accomplishments sound like they resulted from a lot of hard work and not just luck.
Gillian:	(Laughs somewhat nervously) Yes, that's true. I'd just hate to sound arrogant.
Counselor:	I get that. I'm guessing that some people react negatively to the degree of academic success you've experienced and make inaccurate assumptions about you.
Gillian:	Yes, especially because I went to an Ivy League school.
Counselor:	I noticed that. Tell me about how you chose Cornell.
Gillian:	Well, I was definitely interested in attending a prestigious school and I considered some other Ivy League colleges. After visiting Harvard and Yale, I just couldn't see myself there. I knew they were a bit more prestigious than Cornell, but their campuses felt too urban to me. I liked Princeton's campus and Cornell's campus much more. Upstate New York is so beautiful.

(Continued)

TABLE 10.5 Discussion of Gillian's Education and Training Experiences (*Continued*)

Counselor:	So part of your decision was based on the aesthetics of the environment.
Gillian:	Exactly. I knew I would get a top-notch education at any of those schools, so I also considered the college campus and the college town. Urban, downtown campuses just don't appeal to me as much.
Counselor:	So the overall feel and lifestyle mattered to you.
Gillian:	That's exactly right. You know, I've never really thought of it like that. Now that I do, though, it occurs to me that one reason I'm so happy living in Green Lake is the lifestyle it affords. I love having such easy access to nature.
Counselor:	That's an interesting insight about the priorities that influence your decisions.

from a formulaic question-and-answer interview. One advantage of having clients complete forms in advance of the initial session is that the paperwork provides you with many pertinent facts and allowed for more flexible conversation. Gillian's academic success and self-confidence as a learner was abundantly clear from her paperwork. She identified her grade point average (GPA), the chronology of her schooling, her extracurricular involvement, and so forth. This written portion of the intake assessment could be supplemented with a broader discussion of Gillian's educational experiences, self-perception, and decision making. Notice in this conversation that environmental aesthetics and the associated lifestyle contribute to Gillian's decision about which college to attend. As Gillian struggles with what to do regarding her current position and the anticipated move to Europe, this insight may prove beneficial.

Employment History: Doris Bronner

When Doris made the appointment to see you, she was asked to arrive 15 minutes early to complete the paperwork; however, she forgot to come early and actually arrived 10 minutes late. Thus, you chose to meet with her for the remaining 40 minutes of her time slot and to send her home with the paperwork to complete prior to her second session. The first session was decidedly unstructured because Doris seemed to have a lot to say in response to your opening inquiry about why she had sought career counseling. Doris began by saying, "It's not fair!," with an angry tone of voice that seemed almost accusatory. She proceeded to complain about how she was treated poorly at her former job, how it was all because the new boss was so unreasonable, how she didn't deserve to get fired, and the injustice of the Nebraska law preventing her from receiving unemployment insurance benefits because she was fired. In an attempt to find something positive about her life and to shift the intake assessment to her personal life, you summarized how poorly things have been going in her work life and expressed hope that things were more positive for her at home. It soon became clear that Doris was equally unhappy with her home life. She spoke about how she would leave her cheating, no-good husband if she could, how the only thing he is good for is money, and how unfair it is that he has the nerve to be angry with her for getting fired.

As the end of your first session approached, it became clear that this intake assessment would likely span at least two sessions because you realized that the two of you had covered very little of the content you normally address in this process. You concluded the session with an empathic communication about how difficult it must be to feel like everyone is against her and assured Doris that you were looking forward to being on her side and working with her to help her find a new job. You stated that the first step toward that goal involved having Doris complete some standard paperwork. You apologized that the packet was lengthy but commented that it should be easy for Doris given her years of experience handling large volumes of paperwork as a secretary. This strategy was successful because Doris did indeed bring the completed packet to her second appointment.

In reviewing the section about her employment history (see Figure 10.11), you noticed a pattern of Doris disliking her jobs and another pattern of her viewing external factors (bosses, coworkers, guests, patients, work environments) for her dissatisfaction. Though it is certainly feasible that Doris had been the victim of misfortune by having primarily awful jobs, it is also necessary to consider the possibility that Doris was the common denominator and played an active role in her dissatisfaction. Rather than drawing a conclusion this early in the counseling process, you wisely choose to hold both hypotheses as possibilities.

Family Background: Lily Huang Li Mei

Early in your first session with Li Mei, you could sense the weight of family expectations and her fear that she couldn't live up to them. You therefore decided to focus on family background in the intake assessment process. Explaining that it might be useful for you to understand the education levels and career paths of her family members, you asked Li Mei to tell you about each of her grandparents, parents,

Employment History

Are you legally eligible to work in the United States? ☑ Yes ☐ No
Have you ever been employed? ☑ Yes ☐ No
How many jobs have you held in the past 10 years? _____
Have you ever been terminated or fired from a job? ☑ Yes ☐ No
Have you ever been promoted? ☐ Yes ☑ No
Have you ever received a raise? ☑ Yes ☐ No
What has been your favorite job? __Ice cream parlor__
What has been your least favorite job? __Secretary at insurance agency__
What work-related accomplishment are you most proud of?
   __I've shown that I can put up with a lot.__

Current Employment
Use this space to identify any job(s) you currently have.
Job title: __Unemployed__
Employer: _____
Dates of employment: _____ to present
Job title: _____
Employer: _____
Dates of employment: _____ to present
Are you having any difficulties or stressors in your current job(s)? If so, what are they?
   __There was a lot of stress in my former job. My boss was a jerk. Now I am stressed out because I need to find another job. Also, I am not getting unemployment benefits like I should be.__

Past Employment
Use this space to identify any other job(s) you have had in the past 5 years.
Job Title: __Secretary__
Employer: __Joe Schmoe Insurance Agency__
Dates of Employment: __1999__ to __2013__
Reason you left: __Boss__

Job Title: __Receptionist__
Employer: __TLC Doctor's Office__
Dates of Employment: __1996__ to __1998__
Reason you left: __Didn't want to be near sick people__

Job Title: __Secretary__
Employer: __Housing-4-You Real Estate Office__
Dates of Employment: __1991__ to __1996__
Reason you left: __Hated it, too much paperwork__

Job Title: __Waitress__
Employer: __Alice's Restaurant__
Dates of Employment: __1986__ to __1991__
Reason you left: __Too hectic, rude guests, bad hours__

FIGURE 10.11 Doris Bronner's Employment History

and siblings. In response, Li Mei explained that her paternal grandfather, Wei, had attended the very prestigious National Taiwan University (NTU) and worked as an engineer; her paternal grandmother, Xiùlán, graduated from National Taiwan Normal University (NTNU) and worked as a teacher. Each valued education tremendously and pushed their children to excel academically, insisting that they take night classes to supplement their day school. Li Mei's father, Frank, was the only child in the family to score well enough on the national university entrance exams to gain admission to NTU, where he completed an undergraduate degree in engineering. Frank's role as a source of family pride became even more pronounced when he was accepted to graduate school in the United States.

On her mother's side of the family, Li Mei's grandfather, Gāng, and grandmother, Ling, had a secondary school education but nothing more. Her maternal grandparents worked together selling goods at the Shida Night Market in Taipei and were regularly assisted by their children. In fact, this is how Li Mei's parents met. Li Mei's mother, Xiá, was helping at the night market when her future father, Frank, happened by. A student at the nearby NTU, Frank frequented the night market because it offered inexpensive food and entertainment. Soon, Xiá and Frank became quite close and, with the permission of their parents, became engaged. They married soon after Frank graduated from NTU and lived in Taipei for only a short while before moving to the United States so that Frank could continue his schooling at Stony Brook University in New York.

Soon after, Xiá became pregnant, and she and Frank decided that she would not work so she could be home to raise their children. While Frank was still a student at Stony Brook, Li Mei's brother (Kevin/Qiáng) and sister (Joyce/Yi-chun) were born. After earning a doctorate in electrical engineering, Frank accepted a high-paying job in nearby Flushing, New York. Li Mei was born the next year. When all the children were school age, Xiá began working part-time for a local florist. Although she enjoyed the work, Xiá always felt a bit inadequate because she had not attended university like her very accomplished husband. Together, Xiá and Frank were determined that all their children would go to college.

Kevin, the oldest, did not disappoint. He completed his undergraduate degree at Columbia University and, at 25 years of age, was now in his third year of medical school at Johns Hopkins and hoped to become a neurosurgeon. Joyce (Li Mei's sister) was recruited by and awarded a full scholarship to Stanford University. She was earning all As in the engineering curriculum and also competing on the Stanford women's swimming and diving team as an accomplished diver.

Overshadowed by the many successes of her older siblings, Li Mei struggled with her academic self-concept and was embarrassed to have been wait-listed before finally being admitted to the decidedly less prestigious Chapman University. Feeling like an outsider, Li Mei began distancing herself from her family once she arrived on campus. Perhaps most symbolic of this distancing was her decision to shift from using Lily as her first name—as she had all her life—to using her Chinese given name of Li Mei.

Current Living Situation: Wayne Jensen

Rather than including a form about a client's current living situation in the intake paperwork, you elected to simply ask Wayne about it during your initial session. He reported that he owns a home in a new subdivision in the Downriver area of Detroit (a working-class neighborhood) and has a mortgage. He explained that he bought the house approximately three years ago, when he and his wife divorced. Although he lives there alone, he has a bedroom for his 16-year-old daughter, who spends every other weekend with him. He described himself as somewhat satisfied with his living situation but said that he would like to see his daughter more often. When asked if he would be willing to move for a new job, he quickly responded that he would not be willing to move out of the immediate area because this would make it more difficult to spend time with his daughter.

Challenges and Obstacles: Lakeesha Maddox

You intended for the first session with Lakeesha to be semistructured, but you chose not to pose many of the questions you normally ask because of her obvious need to emote. Rather than redirect her toward career-focused topics, you wisely chose to listen empathically to the story of her husband's fatal accident and to inquire more about him, their marriage and family, and her grief process. Lakeesha clearly had much more grieving to do, and you were relieved to hear that she had also joined a support group through her church. Toward the end of your session, Lakeesha identified her need to find gainful employment sufficient to support her family, but she admitted to feeling terrified. Offering reassurance, you expressed confidence that the two of you could work together to achieve her goals and asked her to complete a packet about herself prior to your next session. She agreed and returned with a full complement of forms. Included in this was a section that addressed the challenges and obstacles she was facing.

After completing the form shown in Figure 10.12, Lakeesha was surprised to feel a bit of relief. She had been so focused on the obstacles facing her that she felt rather

Please identify any challenges or obstacles that may affect your career planning or success.

Academic issues
- ☐ Lack of motivation
- ☐ Learning problems
- ☐ Low grades
- ☐ Other: _____

Decision-making difficulties
- ☐ Indecisiveness
- ☐ Pressure from others
- ☐ Too few or no interests
- ☐ Too many interests
- ☐ Other: _____
- ☐ Discrimination

Emotional concerns
- ☐ Anxiety
- ☐ Depression
- ☐ Lack of confidence
- ☐ Low self-esteem
- ☐ Mental health
- ☑ Other: _Grief_____

Family issues
- ☐ Aging parents
- ☑ Child care
- ☐ Family expectations
- ☐ Other: _____

Economic problems
- ☐ Credit history
- ☐ Debt
- ☐ Personal finances
- ☐ Poor economy
- ☐ Tight job market
- ☐ Other: _____

Health issues
- ☐ Physical challenges
- ☐ Drinking or drug use
- ☐ Other: _____

Legal troubles
- ☐ Criminal history
- ☐ Driving record
- ☐ Other: _____

Work history
- ☐ Gaps in my résumé/work history
- ☐ Have been fired
- ☑ Little or no work experience
- ☐ Lack of good references
- ☐ Other: _____
- ☐ Anything else you are concerned about:
  _____

What potential obstacles or challenges concern you the most?

Finding employment that will pay enough to support my family. Also I am worried about child care and having quality time with my girls

FIGURE 10.12 Lakeesha Maddox's Challenges and Obstacles

hopeless. What she hadn't realized was how many other challenges or obstacles she could—but didn't—face. She felt pleased to realize that, whereas other people might have academic problems, difficulties making decisions, bad credit, health issues, and legal troubles, she wasn't concerned with any of these areas. In fact, in your second session with her, she commented that this form helped her realize that she "could be a lot worse off."

Personal Strengths and Sources of Support: Lakeesha Maddox

Another source of hope for Lakeesha was the form addressing strengths and sources of support. Her completed form is shown in Figure 10.13 Lakeesha described herself as highly motivated, persistent, and determined to provide a good life for her daughters. She also reported being in

---

Personal Strengths

Everyone has strengths that will help them achieve their goals. Identify the strengths that you believe you possess.

- ☑ Determination
- ☑ Good health
- ☑ Intelligence
- ☐ Luck
- ☑ Motivation
- ☑ Persistence
- ☐ Other strengths: _____

- ☑ Academic success
- ☑ Financial resources *(life insurance)*
- ☐ Good references from past employers
- ☐ History of work-related success
- ☑ Strong support network
- ☐ Specific skills: _____

Sources of Support

When you go through tough times, who can you count on to be supportive?

- ☐ Family
  - ☐ Husband/wife/partner
  - ☑ Parents
  - ☐ Siblings
  - ☐ Children
  - ☑ Other: *cousin*
- ☐ Friends
  - ☐ Boyfriend or girlfriend
  - ☑ Best friend: *Chantelle*
- ☑ Other friends: *Desiree, Naomi*

- ☑ Religious supports
  - ☑ God/Allah/Supreme Being
  - ☑ Minister/priest/rabbi/clergy/other
  - ☑ People at my place of worship
- ☐ Pet: _____
- ☐ Nobody
- ☑ Other: *neighbor*

On a scale of 1 to 10, how well supported do you feel at this point in your life?

Not at all 1 2 3 4 5 6 7 ⑧ 9 10 Completely

FIGURE 10.13 Lakeesha Maddox's Personal Strengths and Sources of Support

relatively good health despite having diabetes, and she recognized that the money from her husband's life insurance is a luxury many others don't have. Lakeesha also reported that she had a reasonably strong GPA at Spelman and described herself as "smart enough." Lakeesha also has a strong support network.

In reviewing this form with Lakeesha, you commented about how many sources of support she has and invited her to talk about each one. She explained that Chantelle, Desiree, and Naomi were "sort of double counted" because they are also the ladies at the church who have been so wonderful to her since her husband died. Had it not been for them, she explained, she didn't know how she would have managed to care for her children. When you asked Lakeesha about the numeric rating, she clarified that she really couldn't ask for better people in her life, but she couldn't rate it as a 10 because her husband Terrence was by far her biggest source of support.

Current Health Status and Medical Information: Juan Martinez

Given Juan's choice to seek vocational rehabilitation services, the emphasis on health and medical issues will be strong. In fact, Juan will likely be asked to provide additional documentation of his ailments and will probably be asked to sign an information release form to allow the vocational rehabilitation office to contact his physician. At the onset, however, only basic medical information is collected as part of the intake assessment.

As Juan's counselor, you were pleased that he arrived with his paperwork completed (see Figure 10.14). You used the first session to discuss it with him. You began by asking Juan to explain his reasons for rating his overall health as a 5 out of 10. He explained that he is "really messed up" because of his back; other than that, he's pretty healthy. Following up on this explanation, you asked if the back injury is what he meant when he checked yes on the item about having a physical condition that may affect his ability to work. Affirming this, Juan described the heavy lifting and use of heavy tools that had been required on his job as a construction laborer. When he explained that his back pain is so severe that he can no longer work his old job in construction, this resonated with you as true. After all, you had watched him wince and exclaim, "¡Oh, mi dolor de espalda!" ("Oh, my aching back!") as he carefully lowered himself into the chair across from you. Although some clients seeking vocational rehabilitation services may feign the extent of their impairment, this was not your sense with Juan. Supporting your intuition was the

---

Current Health Status and Medical Information

On a scale of 1 to 10, how would you rate your current health?

Very poor   Very healthy

1   2   3   4   ⑤   6   7   8   9   10

Name of primary-care physician: _Dr. Montgomery_

Approximate date of last physical examination: _Last month_

To your knowledge, do you have any *physical* conditions that may affect your ability to work or perform certain types of jobs?   ☒ Yes   ☐ No

Do you have any vision problems?   ☐ Yes   ☒ No

Do you have any hearing loss?   ☐ Yes   ☒ No

To your knowledge, do you have any *psychological* conditions that may affect your ability to work or perform certain types of jobs?   ☐ Yes   ☒ No

Have you ever attempted or considered suicide or had suicidal feelings?   ☐ Yes   ☒ No

Please check any areas in which you have been experiencing difficulties *(check all that apply)*.

- ☐ ADHD
- ☐ Alcohol use
- ☐ Anger
- ☐ Anxiety
- ☐ Appetite
- ☐ Concentration
- ☐ Depression
- ☐ Drug use
- ☒ Energy
- ☒ Fatigue
- ☐ Headaches
- ☐ Hearing loss

FIGURE 10.14 Juan Martinez's Current Health Status and Medical Information

(Continued)

☐ Irritability	☒ Stomach
☐ Mobility	☐ Suicidal feelings
☒ Pain	☐ Troubling thoughts
☐ Panic	☐ Vision
☐ Sexual concerns	☐ Weight
☐ Sleep	☒ Other: _Back_

Medications and Substance Use

Please list any prescription or over-the-counter medications you are currently taking.

Medication	Dosage	Reason
Ibuprofen	800 mg	Back
Tums	Only sometimes	Stomach

Which of the following do you currently use?

Type of Drug How Much and How Often?

☒ Alcohol _4 to 5 beers on weekends_
☒ Caffeine _2 cups of coffee in morning_
☐ Nicotine _____

Please identify any drugs you have used (even once) in the past 12 months.
Check all that apply.

☐ Amphetamines/speed	☐ Hallucinogens	☐ Methamphetamine
☐ Barbiturates	☐ Heroin	☐ Opiates
☐ Benzodiazepines	☐ Inhalants	☐ Phencyclidine (PCP)
☐ Cocaine/crack	☐ Marijuana/cannabis	☐ Sedatives/downers
☐ Ecstasy/MDMA	☐ Methadone	☐ Other:

On a scale of 1 to 10, how confident are you that you would pass a 10-panel urine screen (30-day) drug test if required as part of employment testing?

Not at all   Completely

1   2   3   4   5   6   7   8   9   **(10)**

On a scale of 1 to 10, how confident are you that you would pass a hair follicle (12-month) drug test if required as part of employment testing?

Not at all   Completely

1   2   3   4   5   6   7   8   9   **(10)**

FIGURE 10.14 Juan Martinez's Current Health Status and Medical Information (*Continued*)

fact that he endorsed only a few areas of difficulty (low energy, fatigue, pain, stomach, and back) and reported taking only two medications (prescription ibuprofen for pain and over-the-counter antacids for occasional stomach pain).

Based on your experience that clients sometimes admit details about themselves aloud but not on paper, you also engaged Juan in a discussion of any legal or illegal drugs he may be using. He firmly denied any use of illegal drugs and expressed complete confidence that he would pass drug tests. Juan indicated that his former employer routinely tested for drugs and that he had never failed one. He explained that, especially because he quit school and went to work at such a young age, he never fell in with crowds that did drugs. Instead, he considers himself a family man and takes great pride in being a good provider and role model for his children. Juan did acknowledge, however, that he starts every day with two cups of coffee and that he drinks beer and watches sports nearly every weekend.

PUTTING IT ALL TOGETHER

As you reflect on this chapter, consider the ways in which you might vary your approach to intake assessments. Also consider what additional information about each of our clients you might find useful. After all, assessment does not end with the intake; it persists throughout the counseling process. As discussed in Chapter 9, you may choose to use assessments as helping strategies later in the counseling process. These helping strategies may involve the use of standardized tests (which will be discussed in Chapter 11) or the use of other, less formal approaches to assessment. Examples of less formal approaches are culture and career genograms (Chapter 6) and vocational card sorts (Chapter 12).

CHAPTER

11 Standardized Tests

Standardized tests are frequently used in the context of career counseling. In fact, at one time, standardized tests dominated the field so much that phrases such as "test and tell" (Cochran, Vinitsky, & Warren, 1974, p. 659) and "three interviews and a cloud of dust" (Crites, 1981, p. 49) were used to describe the practice of career counseling. The sad reality was that many career counselors met with a client, administered a battery of tests, and used the test results to point the client in a career direction that seemed well matched to his or her individual characteristics as revealed by the test. My hope is that you recognize that such an approach is way less than desirable.

Although tests can indeed be useful, they are only one tool and should not be relied on exclusively. Precisely for this reason, this text includes not only this chapter on standardized tests but also three other chapters addressing alternative ways in which counselors can gather information from and develop an understanding of clients. Chapter 6 introduced you to the use of cultural formulation interviews and to culture and career genograms. In Chapter 10, you learned about the use of intake interviews and forms. In Chapter 12, you will learn about the use of card sorts. This breadth of coverage reflects my belief that the best career counselors employ multiple assessment procedures. I hope to convince you, however, that *testing* isn't a bad word or an undesirable practice in career counseling. Counselors should strive to use a wide variety of assessment approaches to best serve their clients. In this chapter, you will learn about how standardized tests may be used.

Before we begin, a word of warning is in order. This chapter is long, and it contains what may be an overwhelming amount of information. After introducing you to the skills needed to use standardized tests, I will present information about more than 80 standardized tests. This portion of the chapter is intended to read like an annotated bibliography. Do not try to remember or even take notes on each of these tests. Instead, focus your attention on the range of tests that exist in each category. Notice their varying emphases and the different types of clients for which the tests are intended. You will see that each section includes a table summarizing this information, which I hope you will find helpful. Later, when you are actually practicing as a counselor and have occasion to use a standardized test, these tables and the annotated descriptions of each test should serve as a useful reference. For now, though, your focus should be on the big picture rather than on the details.

TYPES OF STANDARDIZED TESTS USED IN CAREER COUNSELING

In addition to understanding the basic skills involved in standardized testing, counselors should be aware of the various types of standardized tests that may be used when providing career counseling. As shown in Table 11.1, standardized tests used in career counseling are organized into three primary categories. First are the tests used to assist clients with career selection, including tests of occupational interests; personality characteristics; work-related values; and estimates of academic achievement, scholastic aptitude, and vocational aptitude. Second are tests that address factors related to the process of making career decisions, including assessments of career readiness, career maturity, and career beliefs. There are tests used to understand career adjustment, including those designed to assess career concerns, employability skills, career stress, and job satisfaction. The remainder of this chapter will be devoted to identifying and describing tests within each of these categories. In addition to identifying the categories of standardized tests used in career counseling, Table 11.1 indicates which tables later in the chapter address each category.

STANDARDIZED TESTS RELATED TO CAREER SELECTION

A common reason people seek career counseling is for assistance in selecting a career path. Indeed, this was the sole focus of Parsons's (1909) foundational book, *Choosing a Vocation*. To this day, career selection remains a primary focus of career counseling. Not surprisingly, an enormous number of standardized tests have been developed for this purpose. Some are classics that have been revised multiple times in order to remain current. Others are relative newcomers that have been published more recently and are still being vetted by the profession. These tests include those focused on interests; personality characteristics; work-related values; and estimates of academic achievement, scholastic aptitude, and vocational aptitude.

Standardized Tests Related to Interests

Interest inventories are likely the most common type of standardized test used in career counseling. These tests focus on the activities in which a person is interested by inquiring about that person's likes and dislikes, preferences, and current involvement in various activities. Questions about likes and dislikes generally list a variety of academic subjects, occupations, and activities. For each item, clients are asked to select from choices such as "like," "dislike," or "uncertain." Questions about preferences generally present clients with pairs of academic subjects, occupations, or activities and ask clients to identify which item in the pairing they prefer or like best. When tests ask clients to report on their likes, dislikes, and preferences, they are measuring expressed interests, which simply means that the client self-reports these interests (Whiston, 2009).

Expressed interests may differ from manifest interests, which are interests that are evident in a person's behavioral choices (Whiston, 2009). For example, a client may identify music as an interest but may rarely listen to or perform music. In this case, music is an expressed interest, but this interest would not be manifest in his or her choices. To assess manifest interests, some interest inventories also ask clients to identify activities in which they are currently involved. The choices generally consist of activities one could do in or outside a work setting to determine vocational and avocational interests. Manifest interests may also be assessed through observations and interviews.

To be sure, a vast number of standardized tests exist for the purpose of assessing an individual's interests in the context of career counseling. Rather than offer a comprehensive, overwhelming list of such tests, this section will provide you with a more manageable listing of interest inventories. Table 11.2 lists interest inventories and identifies the various populations with which each test may be used. Next, I will offer a brief description, in alphabetical order, of each of these tests. As you read through the information on these

TABLE 11.1 Types of Standardized Tests Used in Career Counseling, by Table in This Chapter

Standardized tests related to career selection	
• Standardized tests used to assess interests	Table 11.2
• Standardized tests used to assess personality	Table 11.3
• Standardized tests used to assess work-related values	Table 11.4
• Standardized tests used to assess ability	
◦ Standardized tests used to assess academic ability	Table 11.5
◦ Standardized tests used to assess vocational aptitude	Table 11.6
Standardized tests related to career decision making	Table 11.7
Standardized tests related to career adjustment	Table 11.8

TABLE 11.2 Standardized Tests Used to Assess Interests*

Interest Inventory	Populations			
	K–12 School Settings	College Settings	Community Settings	Special Needs
Ashland Interest Assessment	MS/HS		X	X
Campbell Interest and Skill Survey	HS	X	X	
Career Assessment Inventory	X	X	X	
Career Directions Inventory	HS	X	X	
Harrington-O'Shea Career Decision-Making System	MS/HS	X	X	
Interest, Determination, Exploration, and Assessment System	MS/HS		X	X
Jackson Vocational Interest Inventory	HS	X	X	
Kuder Career Interests Assessment	MS/HS	X	X	
Occupational Attitude Survey & Interest Schedule	MS/HS	X		X
O*NET Interest Profiler	HS	X	X	
Pictorial Inventory of Careers Pathfinder	MS/HS		X	X
Reading-Free Vocational Interest Inventory	MS/HS		X	X
Self-Directed Search	HS	X	X	X
Self-Directed Search Career Explorer	MS			
Strong Interest Inventory	HS	X	X	
Unisex Edition of the ACT Interest Inventory	MS/HS		X	
Wide Range Interest and Occupation Test	E/MS/HS	X	X	X
World of Work Inventory	MS/HS	X	X	X

*E = elementary school, MS = middle school, and HS = high school.

standardized tests, keep in mind that my intention is not for you to memorize them. My goal is simply to familiarize you with them enough to heighten your awareness of various options. If certain tests pique your curiosity, I hope you will take steps to learn more about them.

ASHLAND INTEREST ASSESSMENT. The Ashland Interest Assessment (AIA; Jackson & Marshall, 1997) is an interest inventory specifically designed for use with clients who have special needs that will likely serve as barriers to employment. These special needs may include "educational, physical, emotional, cognitive, or psychiatric conditions such as learning disabilities, developmental disabilities, brain injuries, or chronic psychiatric problems" (McCowan & McCowan, 2001, para. 1), all of which have the potential to limit a person's employment prospects. The AIA requires only a third-grade reading level, and its content focuses on career options likely within reach of people with significant employment barriers. For example, respondents may be asked to identify whether washing floors or showing watches to customers would be more interesting to them (McCowan & McCowan, 2001). Counselors working with special needs populations in school or community settings may find the AIA quite useful in assessing interest patterns associated with careers likely in reach. The AIA is published by and available for purchase from Sigma Assessment Systems, Inc.

CAMPBELL INTEREST AND SKILL SURVEY. As its title suggests, the Campbell Interest and Skill Survey (CISS; Campbell, 1992) is a standardized test that assesses both interests and skills related to career selection. The test is divided into two parts, one focused on interests and the other focused on skill confidence related to academic subjects and specific work activities. Part 1, the interest assessment, includes 200 items addressing vocational interests. Results of the interest assessment are reported on three scales: orientation scales, basic interest scales, and occupational scales. Seven orientation scales reflect broad areas of interest (influencing, organizing, helping, creating, analyzing, producing, and adventuring). The publisher states that these orientation scales use different words but can be likened to the RIASEC (realistic, investigative, artistic, social, enterprising, conventional) model developed by Holland (1997) and addressed in Chapter 2. The 29 basic interest scales identify more specific areas within each of the seven orientations. For example, the helping orientation scale includes the basic scales of adult development, counseling, child development, religious activities, and medical practice. The occupational scales section of CISS identifies the degree of similarity between the test taker's interest patterns and the interest patterns of happily employed workers in 58 different occupations. The test requires at least a sixth-grade reading level and is designed for use with people 15 years of age and up. Thus, the CISS can be used with high school students. In practice, though, it is used much more widely with adults in college and community settings. The CISS is published by and available for purchase from Pearson Assessments.

CAREER ASSESSMENT INVENTORY. The Career Assessment Inventory–The Enhanced Version (CAI; Johansson, 2003a) is an interest inventory that yields three types of results: six general theme scales that rate an individual's interests according to Holland's RIASEC typology, 25 basic interest area scales that rate an individual's more specific interests in categories distributed among the six RIASEC types, and 111 occupational scales that compare an individual's interest to people employed in specific occupations. It is worth noting that the original version of the CAI was designed for use with people not interested in seeking careers that would require a college education. This version still exists and has been updated as the Career Assessment Inventory–Vocational Version (Johansson, 2003b). In contrast, the enhanced version (Johansson, 2003a) was developed to include careers requiring a college education as well as those not requiring postsecondary education. Both versions require at least an eighth-grade reading level. They are published by and available for purchase from Pearson Assessments.

CAREER DIRECTIONS INVENTORY. The Career Directions Inventory (CDI; Jackson, 2003) is an interest inventory developed by the same Douglas Jackson who developed the Jackson Vocational Interest Survey (JVIS). As you will learn later in this section, the JVIS is most appropriate for use with adolescents and adults intending to pursue postsecondary education. In contrast, the CDI has a broader target audience including both individuals interested in college and individuals with or without a high school diploma who intend to seek immediate employment rather than postsecondary education (Goldman, 2007). It is one of the few interest inventories intended for use with people who aspire to blue-collar, technical, or skilled jobs (Maddux, 2007). The CDI requires at least a sixth-grade reading level and consists of 100 items. Each item presents three work-related activities. Test takers must identify which of the three activities they like best and which of the three they like least. Results are presented for 15 basic interest scales and seven general occupational themes. The occupational themes correspond roughly with Holland's RIASEC typology, with the addition of an occupational theme focused on serving. The job clusters section of CDI identifies the degree of similarity between the test taker's interest patterns and the interest patterns of happily employed workers in 27 job clusters. Unlike most interest inventories, the results also identify the degree of similarity between the test taker's interest patterns and the interest patterns of students enrolled in 100 different education or training programs (which the CDI refers to as educational specialty groups). The extended interpretive report also provides information to encourage additional career exploration within each of the respondent's top three job clusters. The CDI is published by and available for purchase from Sigma Assessment Systems, Inc.

HARRINGTON-O'SHEA CAREER DECISION-MAKING SYSTEM–REVISED. The Harrington O'Shea Career Decision Making System–Revised (CDM-R; O'Shea & Feller, 2000) is an interest inventory with two versions. The CDM-R Level 1 is intended for use in school settings with middle school students and with those who have limited reading skills. The CDM-R Level 2 is intended for use with students in high school or college and with adults in community settings. Both versions classify results according to six career interest areas that parallel the RIASEC typology developed by Holland (1997). Both versions also address 18 career clusters distributed across the six career interest areas. In addition, Level 2 of the CDM-R provides test takers with information about college majors and postsecondary education related to their strongest career interest areas and career clusters. A major selling feature of the CDM-R involves its attention to emerging jobs such as those in the science, technology, engineering, and math (STEM) areas. Unlike more dated interest inventories, the CDM-R seeks to predict job opportunities likely to exist in 2020. Also laudable are the efforts of the developers to ensure that the results are relevant to diverse populations in and outside the United States. The CISS is published by and available for purchase from Pearson Assessments.

INTEREST, DETERMINATION, EXPLORATION, AND ASSESSMENT SYSTEM. The Interest, Determination, Exploration, and Assessment System (IDEAS; Johansson, 1993) is an interest inventory most often used in school settings with middle and high school students. An adult version of IDEAS is also available and can be used to assist clients who are preparing to reenter the world of work. Both versions are designed to provide a broad overview of vocational interests in accordance with Holland's RIASEC typology. Ideally, the IDEAS interest inventory should be used as part of career development units; a companion workbook helps students understand their Holland code and assists them with career exploration. IDEAS represents an abbreviated version of the Career Assessment Inventory (CAI) discussed above (Miller, 1992). Whereas the CAI consists of 370 items, IDEAS contains only 128 items. This obviously allows for quicker administration, but there is a cost. The results for IDEAS only report student interests in 16 occupational areas distributed across the six RIASEC themes. When working with adults, you will need to make a decision about whether to use a short, quick interest inventory such as IDEAS or to use a test that yields more detailed, extensive results. The IDEAS is published by and available for purchase from Pearson Assessments.

JACKSON VOCATIONAL INTEREST SURVEY. The Jackson Vocational Interest Survey (JVIS; Jackson, 1999) is singularly focused as an interest inventory and enjoys considerable respect for its psychometric properties and test construction process (Sanford, 2003; Steinberg, 2003). Although the tagline on its website is "turn your interests into a career" (jvis.com), the JVIS does not seek to match response patterns on the JVIS to specific occupations. Instead, it focuses on the relationship between interests and occupational clusters. For example, rather than matching interests with specific occupations such as nursing, physician, radiological technician, and so on, the JVIS matches them with occupational clusters such as medical service, office work, life science, and business. Thus, the results are quite useful in encouraging future exploration within identified clusters of occupations and/or areas of additional education (i.e., college majors). The interpretive report not only identifies clusters but also lists specific activities students may take to learn more about areas of interest. This emphasis on additional career exploration activities represents a major advantage of the JVIS when used in a school setting. Although the JVIS may be used with adult populations, the fact that just over two thirds of its norming sample involved secondary school students (Steinberg, 2003) suggests the utility of this instrument in K–12 settings, too. Generally speaking, the JVIS is most appropriate for use with students who intend to pursue a college education. The JVIS is published by and available for purchase from Sigma Assessment Systems, Inc.

KUDER® CAREER INTERESTS ASSESSMENT. As part of the Kuder® Career Planning System (KCPS), the Kuder® Career Interests Assessment (KCIA; Kuder, Inc., 2012a) interest inventory is particularly useful in K–12 settings. Indeed, the KCPS includes programs geared toward students in elementary school (Kuder Galaxy), those in middle and high school (Kuder Navigator), as well as college students and adults (Kuder Journey). The KCIA (2012a) is the most recent version of Kuder's career interest assessment and has evolved from what was once called the Kuder General Interest Survey. Because students may lack sufficient awareness of various occupations to express occupational preferences meaningfully, the KCIA does not ask students to do so. Instead, it asks students to rate their level of interest in various activities. Specifically, they are asked to respond to groups of three activities by indicating which activity they would most like to do and which activity would be their second favorite. Respondents are instructed to imagine that they have the necessary skills and training to perform each activity so that their selections are based only on interest and not on skills confidence. The results are based on the match between student interests and the interests of people working within various occupations. A major advantage of the KCIA is the ease with which the results report can be understood. The interpretive report offers students an easy-to-read snapshot of how closely their interests match the six RIASEC areas in Holland's typology and the 16 national career clusters. A second major advantage of this interest inventory is that it is designed to be used in conjunction with the skills and values inventories that are also part of KCPS. Kuder refers to this tripartite assessment process as "career development on a three-legged stool" (Zytowski, 2006, p. 1). Indeed, students using the KCPS are able to take standardized tests addressing their interests, skills, and values. These assessments are published by and available for purchase from Kuder, Inc.

OCCUPATIONAL ATTITUDE SURVEY & INTEREST SCHEDULE. As its name suggests, the Occupational Attitude Survey & Interest Schedule (OASIS-3; Parker, 2002) is designed to assess both aptitudes and interests. The interest portion of the OASIS-3 is generally referred to as the Interest Schedule. It presents test takers with 240 items, half of which are job titles requiring a varying degree of education (such as livestock rancher or chemist) and half of which are job activities (such as design and write computer programs). Respondents must identify whether they like, dislike, or feel neutral toward each item. Results indicate the strength of each test taker's interest (in comparison to the norming sample) in 12 occupational areas: artistic, scientific, nature, protective, mechanical, industrial, business detail, selling, accommodating, humanitarian, leading-influencing, and physical performing. In his expert review of the OASIS-3, Michael (2005) offered particular praise for the solid test construction and impressive psychometric qualities of this test. Because the norming sample was limited to students in middle school, high school, and college, the OASIS-3 is best limited to use with these populations. Whitfield and Cato (2009) also note that the OASIS-3 is appropriate for use with special populations. The OASIS-3 is published by and available for purchase from Pro-Ed.

O*NET INTEREST PROFILER. The Occupational Information Network (O*NET) Interest Profiler was developed by the U.S. Department of Labor Employment and Training Administration (2001b). In Chapter 13, you will learn about O*NET, which is a website developed by the U.S. Department of Labor as an online replacement of *The Dictionary of Occupational Titles* (U.S. Department of Labor, 1991) and is described as the "nation's primary source of occupational information" (onetcenter.org/overview.html, para. 1). In addition to providing access to occupational information, the O*NET website also grants free access to three assessment instruments, one of which is the O*NET Interest Profiler. This interest inventory may be taken online or with a downloadable print version. It presents 180 items and asks test takers to respond with like, dislike, or unsure. The results categorize a person's interests in accordance with Holland's RIASEC typology. In addition to being available free of charge, another benefit of the O*NET Interest Profiler is that test takers can also use the O*NET website to enter results for use in searching for information related to their Holland code. Chapter 13 contains more information about how to use this site in conjunction with test results. Appropriate for use with individuals 14 years of age and older, the O*NET Interest Profiler and supporting documentation (such as a User's Guide and Score Report) may be downloaded from onetcenter.org/IP.html.

PICTORIAL INVENTORY OF CAREERS PATHFINDER. The Pictorial Inventory of Careers (PIC) Pathfinder (Talent Assessment, 2007) is rare among interest inventories in that it requires no reading whatsoever. Instead, it involves video presentations of "real life work scenes" (talentassessment.com/pages/PIC, para. 1). After viewing each segment, students rate whether they would like or dislike that type of work. Results are organized according to 17 career areas such as agricultural, electrical/electronics, and protective services. In addition to identifying areas of strong interest or disinterest, the PIC also identifies career areas about which students report having limited knowledge. This inventory has two versions, one for mainstream populations and the other for special needs populations. Indeed, the lack of reading requirements renders the PIC quite useful with special populations, where it is most commonly used. It is marketed for use in developing transition plans (which will be discussed in Chapter 17).

The PIC is published by and available for purchase from Talent Assessment, Inc.

READING-FREE VOCATIONAL INTEREST INVENTORY. The Reading-Free Vocational Interest Inventory (R-FVII:2; Becker, 2000) is another rare inventory that requires no reading. This test is paper-based and consists of 55 items. Each item shows pictures of three different work tasks and asks test takers to identify which of the three drawings they would prefer to do. Because the job tasks presented in the R-FVII:2 are limited to those at unskilled, semiskilled, and skilled levels, this interest inventory is most appropriate for use with individuals who have significant work limitations due to cognitive ability or functional impairment, which may include individuals in "junior high, senior high, vocational/technical schools, sheltered work centers, and other job training and work placement career centers" (proedinc.com/customer/productView.aspx?ID=3052, para. 4). Scores are reported for 11 interest areas distributed across five clusters. For example, the mechanical cluster includes the automotive and building trades interest areas. The R-FVII:2 was published by Elbern Publications and is available for purchase from both Pro-Ed and Pearson Assessments.

SELF-DIRECTED SEARCH. Whether or not the Self-Directed Search, Fourth Edition (SDS; Holland, Powell, & Fritzsche, 1997), is truly "the world's most widely used career interest test," as sometimes touted, it is clearly at or near the top of the list. It has been translated into at least 25 different languages and claims to have been used by "more than 30 million people worldwide" (self-directed-search.com, para. 1). Developed by Holland himself, this interest inventory is designed to yield a three-letter Holland code in accordance with Holland's own RIASEC typology. The SDS can be taken and scored by individuals without the involvement of a career counselor and outside the context of career counseling. The SDS comes in three forms (Brown, 2001). Form R is the "regular" version and is intended for use with students in high school or college and with adults who may have limited experience in the world of work. Form E is the "easy" version; it is written at the fourth-grade level and is appropriate for use with clients who have reading difficulties. Form CP is the "career planning" version and is intended for use with those who have significant work experience. This group may include professional-level employees and adults interested in a new career. All three forms of the SDS are published by and available for purchase from Psychological Assessment Resources (PAR), Inc. The SDS may also be taken online at self-directed-search.com.

SELF-DIRECTED SEARCH CAREER EXPLORER. In addition to the three forms of the SDS described above, a middle school version of the Self Directed Search (SDS) is also available. It is the SDS Career Explorer (SDS CE; Holland & Powell, 1994). This interest inventory is designed for students from 11 to 17 years of age and is written at a third-grade reading level. Like the SDS, the SDS CE is designed to yield a Holland code in accordance with Holland's own RIASEC typology. Rather than offering a three-letter Holland code like the SDS, however, the SDS CE offers only a two-letter Holland code. Supplemental materials such as the *Careers Booklet* and the *Exploring your Future* booklet make the SDS CE easy to use in a classroom setting for lessons related to career development. The SDS CE is published by and available for purchase from Psychological Assessment Resources (PAR), Inc.

STRONG INTEREST INVENTORY. The Strong Interest Inventory (SII; Donnay et al., 2005) is also among the most widely used interest inventories. Its use is especially common in college settings, and the publisher indicates that more than 70% of colleges offer the SII (cpp.com/products/strong/index.aspx). It currently comes in three versions. One is simply labeled Form R, which comes in a College Edition Form R and a High School Edition Form R. All are written at the ninth-grade reading level and are considered appropriate for use with people 14 years of age and older. The SII consists of 291 items distributed across six sections: occupations, subject areas, activities, leisure activities, people, and personal characteristics. For each item, respondents are asked to select from five options: strongly like, like, indifferent, dislike, and strongly dislike. Scores on the SII are presented in four sections. First, the General Occupational Themes section yields a Holland code based on the six RIASEC areas. Second, the Basic Interest Scales addresses a person's interest in 30 occupations distributed across the six RIASEC areas. These first two sections indicate the strength of the test taker's interest in comparison to the general population. The third section of SII results are reported on occupational scales. This section compares a test taker's interest patterns to people already employed and satisfied in a variety of occupations. This section involves samples of satisfied workers in 260 different occupations. The fourth section of results involves personal style scales and addresses the test taker's preferred work style, learning environment, leadership style, level of risk taking, and team orientation. Because of the complexity of scoring, it is necessary to purchase scoring software, mail response forms to the publisher for scoring, or take the SII online through CPP. The SII is published by and available for purchase from

Consulting Psychologists Press (CPP), Inc. It can also be taken online through skillsone.com, which is owned and operated by CPP, Inc.

UNISEX EDITION OF THE ACT INTEREST INVENTORY (UNIACT). Because it is attached to several of the achievement tests offered by ACT, the Unisex Edition of the ACT Interest Inventory (UNIACT) is an interest inventory commonly administered to students in middle and high school. Specifically, UNIACT is part of three ACT tests: the ACT Explore, which is generally taken in eighth or ninth grade; the ACT PLAN, which is typically taken in 10th grade; and the ACT, which is usually taken at the end of 11th grade but can also be taken at the beginning of 12th grade. As part of its College and Career Readiness System, ACT includes the UNIACT as part of each of these three academic achievement tests. The inclusion of the UNIACT with these achievement tests represents a primary advantage to school counselors because no additional costs are associated with it. Another advantage of the UNIACT is that it does not ask students to rate their interest in specific occupations. Because students may or may not be familiar with a wide range of occupational titles, the UNIACT instead relies on items that relate to work but are likely more familiar to students. For example, rather than asking students to rate their interest in phlebotomy, corresponding work-related activities might be drawing blood or, more broadly, helping sick people. The results of the UNIACT correspond with Holland's typology as well as with a visual display of occupational types developed by ACT. This visual display is called the ACT World-of-Work Map, and you will learn more about it in Chapter 13. The UNIACT is published by ACT, Inc. It is not available for purchase by itself. Instead, as described above, it is a companion to the ACT, PLAN, and EXPLORE.

WIDE RANGE INTEREST AND OCCUPATION TEST, SECOND EDITION. The Wide Range Interest and Occupation Test (WRIOT-2; Glutting & Wilkinson, 2003) is another interest inventory that requires little or no reading. Thus, it is a suitable instrument for use with children as young as nine years of age, people with disabilities, and people with limited reading proficiency. Even so, the publisher indicates that the test is appropriate for use with everyone, from unskilled laborers to highly skilled professionals. The test consists of 238 pictures, representing various work situations, which are shown to test takers either in a hard-copy test booklet or on a computer using the test's compact disk (CD). Respondents are asked to identify whether they like, dislike, or feel undecided about the work situation being depicted in each picture. Results from the WRIOT-2 are reported on three scales. First, the WRIOT-2 organizes results according to the six Holland Type Scales. Second, the occupational clusters portion of the WRIOT-2 reports interests in 17 career areas. Third, the interest clusters portion of the WRIOT-2 reports "needs, motives, and values influencing occupational choice" (Bugaj, 2005, para. 2). The WRIOT-2 is published by and available for purchase from Pearson Assessments.

WORLD OF WORK INVENTORY. The World of Work Inventory (WOWI; Ripley, Neidert, & Ortman, 2004) consists of three scales, one of which is an interest inventory. Specifically, the WOWI's Career Interest Activities (CIA) scale asks test takers to indicate whether they like, dislike, or feel neutral about 136 different activities. The CIA scale results show the test taker's level of interest in 17 occupations. The WOWI is published by and available for purchase from World of Work, Inc. It can also be taken online at wowi.com. An advantage of using the WOWI is that it addresses both interests and work-related temperament and aptitudes. As you will see in the upcoming sections, the use of standardized tests for assistance with career selection should not be limited to interest inventories; they should also address personality characteristics, work-related values, and skills and aptitudes.

Standardized Tests Related to Personality

Although they are used less frequently than interest inventories, standardized tests related to personality are also commonly used in career counseling. Whereas interest inventories generally ask respondents to rate their interest in various occupations and work-related activities, personality inventories ask test takers to identify how well various items describe them as individuals. The goal is to assess various factors that represent different personality traits.

Although some personality tests are designed to assess for psychopathology, such tests are generally not used in a career counseling context. Career counseling emphasizes the use of personality tests that measure normal variations in personality. On these tests, it is impossible for the results to identify diagnosable disorders or severe disturbances in personality. If you, as a counselor, are concerned that a client may suffer from a personality disorder or another diagnosable disorder, you would use other assessment strategies and standardized tests for assessment. In contrast, your goal in using the personality tests presented in this chapter should be to understand how your clients' personality traits or types may affect them in the context of work. Even with this in mind, an important caveat is worth mentioning. School counselors

TABLE 11.3 Standardized Tests Used to Assess Personality*

Personality Inventory	Populations			
	K–12 School Settings	College Settings	Community Settings	Special Needs
California Psychological Inventory, Third Edition	HS	X	X	
Clifton StrengthsFinder	HS	X	X	
Jackson Personality Inventory–Revised	HS	X	X	
Myers-Briggs Type Indicator	HS	X	X	
Murphy Meisgeier Type Indicator for Children	E/MS/HS			
NEO Personality Inventory–3	MS/HS	X	X	
Sixteen Personality Factor	HS	X	X	
World of Work Inventory	MS/HS	X	X	X

*E = elementary school, MS = middle school, and HS = high school.

considering the use of any kind of personality test—whether designed to measure normal personality or to assess for psychopathology—should be aware that state laws and/or school district policies may require written consent of the student's parents or guardians prior to administration of such tests.

Table 11.3 lists standardized tests that may be used to assess an individual's personality in the context of career counseling. In the following subsections, I will describe briefly each of these tests, in alphabetical order.

CALIFORNIA PSYCHOLOGICAL INVENTORY, THIRD EDITION. One personality test used in career counseling is the California Psychological Inventory (CPI; Gough & Bradley, 1996). Although the CPI was developed using some of the items from the Minnesota Multiphasic Personality Inventory (MMPI), these two instruments vary dramatically with regard to purpose. The MMPI is widely used to identify disturbances in personality and psychopathology. In contrast, the CPI is designed to assess normal dimensions of personality, and the results are intended to describe how others may perceive the test taker. The long form of the CPI has 434 items and is known as the CPI 434. The short form has 260 items and is known as the CPI 260. Both forms can be used in career counseling, with the short form designed specifically for use in employment settings (Whitfield, Feller, & Wood, 2009). According to Gough (1995), however, both versions of the CPI have direct relevance to career counseling. In particular, the four lifestyles identified by the CPI are associated with differing levels of satisfaction and success in various careers: "Alphas seek and do best in managerial and leadership roles, Betas function well in supportive/ancillary positions, and Gammas look for and are adept in creating change. Deltas work best alone, in fields such as art, literature, and (depending on their ability) mathematics" (Gough, 1995, p. 101). In marketing the CPI 434, the publisher focuses primarily on its usefulness in developing leaders and helping workers become more aware of their strengths and weaknesses. The CPI is written at an eighth-grade reading level and may be used with students in high school or college and with adults in the workplace. Atkinson (2003) noted that high school students represented a full 50% of the norming sample and college students represented another 16.7%. School counselors considering the CPI should be aware, however, that state laws and/or school district policies may require written consent of the student's parents or guardians before administering this or any other personality test. The CPI is published by and available for purchase from Consulting Psychologists Press, Inc.

CLIFTON STRENGTHSFINDER 2.0. Some personality tests may feel intimidating or even scary to some clients, even with the assurance that the tests measure only normal dimensions of personality; however, the name of the Clifton StrengthsFinder (CSF; Asplund, Lopez, Hodges, & Harter, 2009) focuses on the positive. In fact, the instrument reflects the strengths-based approach of the counseling profession at large as well as the field of positive psychology. The CSF was developed specifically for helping people understand and capitalize on their strengths and talents and for assisting employers in selecting and developing "the right people for the right jobs" (Lopez & Tree, 2009, p. 390). This test is offered only in an online format (strengthsfinder.com). Respondents are presented with 180 pairs of descriptors, and they must identify which descriptor from each pair best describes them. These items are designed to assess 34 potential talents, and the results report identifies a person's top five talents. Examples of these 34 talents include: belief, which refers to deeply held and unwavering core values that guide behavior and provide motivation; discipline, which refers to an appreciation of routine and structure, and an ability to create order in one's life; and the delightfully named woo, which refers to the enjoyment of and skill at "meeting new people and winning them over" (Asplund, Lopez, Hodges, & Harter, 2009, p. 28). According to Lopez and Tree (2009), "Clifton believed that these talents were naturally recurring patterns of thought, feeling, or behavior" and "strengths were viewed as developed talents" (p. 390). In career counseling, of course, it can be useful to identify a client's top five talents and then discuss ways in which these talents may be developed into actual strengths through the acquisition of knowledge and skills. The CSF is published by Gallup and available for purchase from the Gallup Strengths Center at strengthsfinder.com or gallupstrengthscenter.com.

JACKSON PERSONALITY INVENTORY–REVISED. The Jackson Personality Inventory–Revised (JVI-R; Jackson, 1994) is a standardized test designed specifically for use in career counseling and personnel selection. Like the other personality inventories presented in this chapter, the JPI-R does not measure psychopathology but instead addresses only dimensions of normal personality. Test takers respond to 300 true/false items addressing 15 different personality traits. The JVI-R results are organized into five dimensions, and the 15 personality traits are distributed across them. These categories are analytical, emotional, extroverted, opportunistic, and dependable. Its goal is to be useful in career counseling, and the developers of the JPI-R had three norming groups: students, blue-collar workers, and senior executives. Zachar (2009) suggests that one major use of JPI-R involves the consideration of whether a person's personality style is well matched to various careers under consideration. For example, a person who scores low on the analytical cluster may not be well suited to careers such as engineering or actuarial work, and a person who scores high on the extroversion scale may enjoy careers demanding high levels of sociability and social confidence. The JPI-R is published by and available for purchase from Sigma Assessment Systems, Inc.

MYERS-BRIGGS TYPE INDICATOR AND MURPHY MEISGEIER TYPE INDICATOR FOR CHILDREN. Despite a lack of critical acclaim for its psychometric properties (Fleenor, 2001; Mastrangelo, 2001), the Myers-Briggs Type Indicator (MBTI) is a widely used personality test with educational, interpersonal, and career applications. In fact, its manual indicates that the MBTI is the "most widely used personality inventory in history" (Briggs Myers, McCaulley, Quenk, & Hammer, 1998, p. 9). Its purpose is to assess dimensions of personality in accordance with the theory of Carl Jung (1923). Specifically, the 93 items on the MBTI Form M are designed to assess a person's preferences with regard to four dimensions of normal personality: source and focus of energy, perception and the taking in of information, judging and the making of decisions, and orientation to the outer world. These preferences are then organized into a single "type" that is identified by four letters, each of which refers to the person's preferences on each of the four dimensions of personality. The premise of the MBTI is that this four-letter type is more than the sum of its parts and that each type involves unique "type dynamics" based on the interaction of the various preferences. Supplemental materials for use with the MBTI are abundant. In career counseling, for example, the *Introduction to Type and Careers* (Hammer, 1993) is particularly useful. A one-page handout is dedicated to each of the 16 types and addresses type-specific strengths, challenges, and suggestions with regard to goal setting, information gathering, networking, and decision making. Although the MBTI may be administered to those 14 years of age and older, counselors working with children and adolescents may prefer to use the Murphy-Meisgeier Type Indicator for Children (MMTIC; Murphy & Meisgeier, 2008). The MMTIC also offers a career report designed especially for use with school-age youth. The MBTI is published by and available for purchase from Consulting Psychologists Press (CPP), Inc. The MMTIC is published by and available for purchase from the Center for Applications of Psychological Type (CAPT; capt.org).

NEO PERSONALITY INVENTORY–3. The NEO Personality Inventory–3 (NEO-PI-3; Costa & McCrae, 2010) is a standardized test designed to assess five domains of personality: neuroticism, extraversion, openness to experience, agreeableness, and conscientiousness. These domains have come to be recognized as the five major factors of personality and comprise the five-factor model (FFM) of personality (McCrae & Costa, 1991). Like the other personality inventories presented in this chapter, the NEO-PI-3 does not measure psychopathology but instead addresses only dimensions of normal personality. Designed for use with those 12 years of age and older, the NEO-PI-3 consists of 241 items.

McCrae and Costa (1991) suggest that the NEO-PI may be useful in career counseling in several ways. First, an individual's personality traits can be compared to the demands of occupations under consideration. Needless to say, a person who scores exceptionally low on conscientiousness may struggle to be successful in jobs demanding just that (e.g., air traffic control). Second, when an interest inventory yields flat results and few interests, the results of the NEO-PI-3 may be used to suggest careers well matched to an individual's personality profile and thereby worthy of exploration. Third, NEO-PI-3 scores may be useful in understanding personality dynamics that may be contributing to a desire to change careers. Reed, Bruch, and Haase (2004) also found correlations between NEO-PI scores and self-efficacy about career searches, information-seeking behaviors, and self-exploration.

A NEO Job Profiler is now available. Described as a tool for determining the "personality requirements of different occupations" (Costa, McCrae, & Kay, 1995, p. 123), the NEO Job Profiler is marketed as a way for employers to select job candidates well suited to a given position. The NEO-PI-3 is published by Sigma Assessment Systems, Inc. and is available from this publisher as well as from other vendors. It may also be taken online at sigmaassessments.com.

SIXTEEN PERSONALITY FACTOR. The Sixteen Personality Factor (16PF; Cattell, Cattell, & Cattell, 2002) Questionnaire is a personality test that, as its name suggests, measure 16 primary dimensions of normal personality. The 16PF yields scores on five global factors (extraversion, anxiety, tough-mindedness, independence, and self-control). Although the 16PF can be used in clinical settings, the top two uses specified by the publisher fall within the purview of career counseling: Its results can be used to guide clients in choosing careers and to guide employers in the selection of personnel. When using the 16PF, counselors can select from among several results reports that address issues related to careers. Pearson Assessments offers two such reports: the Basic Interpretive Report and the Human Resource Development Report. The Basic Interpretive Report contains a section about vocational activities. It provides a graphic display of how similar the client's personality structure is to each of the six Holland themes (RIASEC). The Human Resource Development Report is more specific to an individual's potential for management positions. It contains sections about leadership style, interpersonal interaction styles, decision-making style, initiative, and personal adjustment. The publisher of the 16PF, the Institute for Personality and Ability Testing, Inc. (IPAT; ipat.com), offers a number of other reports, including the Career Development Report, the Career Success Report, the Competency Report, the Leadership Coaching Report, the Management Potential Report, and the Teamwork Development Report. Due to space considerations, only the first two IPAT reports will be described here.

The Career Development Report is intended to help people better understand themselves as workers, with the goal that the insights gained from the 16PF will be useful in planning for the future. It contains sections dedicated to problem solving, coping with stressful conditions, communicating and interacting with others, preferences with regard to roles in the work setting, and general vocational and avocational interests. It concludes with a summary of considerations related to personal effectiveness and suggestions for further exploration. Newly available for the 16PF is the Career Success Report, which is designed for use with college students. This report contains sections addressing personality-based strengths and challenges, prospective occupations, and suggestions for additional career exploration. Whereas the Basic Interpretive Report uses Holland's RIASEC categories in its section addressing vocational activities, the Career Success Report uses the categories from the CISS (Campbell, 1992). The 16PF may be used with individuals as young as 16 years of age, but an adolescent version—the 16PF Adolescent Personality Questionnaire—is also available. The APQ Guidance Report associated with the adolescent version includes information relevant to career planning. Both the 16PF Questionnaire and the 16PF Adolescent Personality Questionnaire are published by the Institute for Personality and Ability Testing, Inc. (IPAT; ipat.com). They are available for purchase from IPAT as well as from other vendors, including Pearson Assessments.

WORLD OF WORK INVENTORY. The World of Work Inventory (WOWI; Ripley, Neidert, & Ortman, 2004) consists of three scales, one of which is a measure of temperament. This scale consists of 96 items, and it assesses an individual's versatility, adaptability to repetitive work, and adaptability to performing under specific instructions, and how dominant, gregarious, isolative, influencing, self-controlled, valuative, objective, and subjective an individual is. The WOWI refers to these factors as Job Satisfaction Indicators (JSIs), and Jenkins (2005) explained that they are "based on the Dictionary of Occupational Titles" and represent "12 temperament factors that relate to job satisfaction" (para. 4). As already mentioned, an advantage of using the WOWI is that it addresses both work-related temperament and interests and aptitudes. The WOWI is published by and available for purchase from World of Work, Inc. It can also be taken online at wowi.com.

Standardized Tests Related to Work Values

Another area of assessment that has great relevance to career selection involves work-related values. Work-related values refer to what we find most desirable about work. Few jobs offer everything a person could possibly want. Thus, career seekers and workers are all faced with trade-offs. Our work values reflect the benefits of work that we hold most important. For some, a primary value is income. This may reflect the pure necessity of paying bills in order to sustain oneself, or it may reflect a valuing of the lifestyle a high income can offer. For others, a primary value may involve contributing to the welfare of others. Still others may place primary value on flexibility to be free to raise their children or engage in recreational activities. With these examples in mind, think about the trade-offs involved in various occupations. Imagine, for instance, a very highly paid position that requires up to 70 hours of work each week. Those who place value on income or prestige may feel quite satisfied with such a job, and those who place value on flexibility may hate it despite the income.

Table 11.4 lists standardized tests that may be used to assess an individual's work-related values. This table will be followed by brief descriptions, in alphabetical order, of each of the tests.

CAREER ANCHORS SELF-ASSESSMENT. The Career Anchors Self-Assessment (Schein, 2006c) is a values inventory designed for use by people who already have significant work experience and, because of the norming samples, is most appropriate for those with higher-level jobs and education. Designed for use in MIT's graduate program in management, it has been widely used to assist students in MBA programs and higher-level professionals with mid-career planning. In this instrument, an anchor represents a primary work-related value: "the one thing a person would refuse to give up if forced to make a choice among alternative occupational pursuits" (Robertson, 1998, para. 1). With just 40 items, this instrument assesses an individual's prioritization of eight possible career anchors: technical/functional competence, general managerial competence, autonomy/independence, security/stability, entrepreneurial creativity, service/dedication to a cause, pure challenge, and lifestyle. After taking the assessment and submitting it for scoring, respondents receive an interpretive report that identifies a person's primary career anchor, lists the anchors in rank order for the respondent, and describes each anchor in easily accessible language. There is also a Career Anchors Participant Workbook designed for use with the self-assessment. The Career Anchors assessment materials are published by and available for purchase from Pfeiffer (pfeiffer.com), an imprint of John Wiley Sons, Inc.

KUDER WORK VALUES ASSESSMENT. The Kuder Work Values Assessment (KWVA; Kuder, Inc., 2012d) is also part of the Kuder® Career Planning System (KCPS). The KWVA was derived directly from the Super Work Values Inventory–Revised (SWVI-R), an instrument no longer in print but highly esteemed. In fact, the interpretive report produced by Kuder still retains *Super's Work Values Inventory–Revised* (kuder.com/downloads/SWV-Report.pdf) as a title. The KWVA is a 25-item values inventory that is designed to assess 12 different work values (such as variety, creativity, security, and challenge). The interpretive report lists your expressed values in rank order of

TABLE 11.4 Standardized Tests Used to Assess Work-Related Values*

Values Inventory	Populations			
	K–12 School Settings	College Settings	Community Settings	Special Needs
Career Anchors Self-Assessment		X	X	
Kuder Work Values Assessment (also known as Super's Work Values Inventory—Revised)	MS/HS	X	X	
Minnesota Importance Questionnaire	HS	X	X	
O*NET Work Importance Profiler	HS	X	X	
Values Preference Indicator	HS	X	X	X
Work Motivation Scale	HS	X	X	

*MS = middle school, and HS = high school.

importance. The report also includes a "person match" section that identifies the people (by occupation) for the norming sample whose values profile most closely matches yours. The report also identifies 10 occupations that are most likely to meet your value expectations. One caution in using this instrument is that it does not limit the number of values that can be rated as important or require that respondents prioritize them. Robinson and Betz (2008) found that some respondents, especially the younger ones, displayed a tendency to rate all values as important. Pointing out that the "achievement of some values—for example, Security or Lifestyle—may reduce the ease of achieving others, such as Income or Mental Challenge" (p. 469), they explained that, although a respondent may highly value all of the options, it is not realistic to think that any job could equally satisfy all of the values. Thus, a high, flat profile warrants additional discussion focused on prioritization of work values. This test is published by and available for purchase from Kuder, Inc.

MINNESOTA IMPORTANCE QUESTIONNAIRE. The Minnesota Importance Questionnaire (MIQ; Rounds, Henly, Dawis, Lofquist, & Weiss, 1981) is a values inventory that corresponds directly with the theory of work adjustment (TWA; Dawis & Lofquist, 1984). As you'll recall from Chapter 2, a major premise of this theory is that worker satisfaction is a function of the match (or mismatch) between a worker's vocational needs/values and the work-related reinforcers associated with his or her job. The MIQ is designed to assess a person's needs and values in accordance with TWA. Specifically, it assesses six overarching values (achievement, altruism, autonomy, comfort, safety, and status), with 20 needs distributed across them. A person's scores on the MIQ can be compared with the Occupational Reinforcement Patterns associated with various jobs. The MIQ is written at the fifth-grade level and can be used in high schools, colleges, and community settings. Although the instrument is quite dated, it continues to be available for purchase from Vocational Psychology Research at the University of Minnesota (psych.umn.edu/psylabs/vpr/). It also serves as the foundation for the more recently developed O*NET Work Importance Profiler, which will be described next.

O*NET WORK IMPORTANCE PROFILER. The O*NET Work Importance Profiler was developed by the U.S. Department of Labor Employment and Training Administration (2002). In addition to providing access to occupational information, the O*NET website also grants free access to three assessment instruments, one of which is the O*NET Work Importance Profiler (WIP). Just like the MIQ, the WIP is a values assessment designed to assess work-related values in accordance with the theory of work adjustment (TWA; Dawis & Lofquist, 1984). Using slightly different language but referring to the same constructs, the WIL measures the relative importance of six work-related values: achievement, independence, recognition, relationships, support, and working conditions. Also like the MIQ, the WIP assesses a variety of vocational needs distributed across these six value areas. The WIP is a computer-administered values inventory that presents respondents with sets of items and asks them to rank-order the items within each set. In addition to being available free of charge, another benefit of the O*NET WIP is that test takers can also use the O*NET website to enter results for use in searching for information related to their work values. Chapter 13 contains more information about how to use this site in conjunction with test results. Appropriate for use with individuals 14 years of age and older, the computer software necessary to administer and score the O*NET Work Importance Profiler and a user's guide may be downloaded at onetcenter.org/WIP.html. Note that this assessment also comes in a paper-and-pencil version called the Work Importance Locator (WIL; U.S. Department of Labor Employment and Training Administration, 2001c). The WIL is not a standardized test, however; it is a card sort. It is included here to emphasize its connection with the WIP and MIQ. The WIL was introduced in Chapter 2 and will also be discussed in depth in Chapter 12.

VALUES PREFERENCE INDICATOR. The Values Preference Indicator (VPI; Robinson & Keis, 2011) is a values inventory designed to assess the relative importance of 21 values. Examples of values targeted by the VPI include accomplishment, creativity, instruction, recognition, and spirituality. The "test" is actually a 12-page booklet that guides people through an exploration and assessment of their values and then addresses implications of the results. The VPI is published by and available for purchase from Consulting Research Group International, Inc.

WORK MOTIVATION SCALE. The Work Motivation Scale (WMS; Brady, 2008) is a values inventory designed for use with adolescent and adult clients. Previously called the Work Orientation and Values Survey (WOVS; Brady, 2002), the WMS has direct application to career selection, career planning, and job seeking. Specifically, the WMS assesses the relative importance of four work motives (survival and safety, affiliation, self-esteem, and fulfillment) and eight values (earnings and benefits, working conditions, coworker relations, supervisor relations, managing others, task orientation, mission orientation, and success orientation). The WMS consists of 32 items, each describing a motive or work value and requiring that the respondent rate its importance on a Likert scale. Interpretive materials then guide the client through understanding the implications of the results to her or his current job as well as to the process of career selection. The WMS is published by and available for purchase from JIST Publishing.

Standardized Tests Related to Abilities

Thus far, we've discussed three types of standardized tests often used to assist clients with career selection: interest inventories, personality tests, and assessments of work-related values. For the most part, these three types of tests address factors related to worker satisfaction with a chosen career. In contrast, the fourth and final type of standardized test often used to assist clients with career selection focuses not so much on worker satisfaction as on satisfactoriness. Specifically, an individual's success and satisfactoriness as an employee depends in large part on having the ability necessary to perform the tasks and responsibilities associated with the job. Two primary types of ability tests are used in career counseling: those assessing academic ability and those assessing vocational ability.

TESTS OF ACADEMIC ABILITY. As you probably know, some people say we live in the era of no child left untested. For the most part, this observation refers to the widespread use of academic achievement tests within the K–12 school system. Indeed, the plethora of academic achievement tests administered to K–12 students every year is overwhelming. Some are group-administered measures designed to assess student achievement. Others are diagnostic tests used for the purpose of identifying areas of giftedness or learning difficulties. Such tests are beyond the scope of this text. In this chapter, my coverage of academic ability tests is limited to those most likely to be used in a counseling context.

Tests of academic ability are used in the context of career counseling for two basic reasons. First, most jobs require some level of academic skill. They may require, for example, the ability to read, write, and perform basic math functions. Especially when working with clients who have not completed any postsecondary education, you may find it useful to establish their level of academic proficiency. Their proficiency levels will have an impact on the types of jobs they will be able to perform satisfactorily. Second, some careers require higher levels of education (e.g., college or graduate school) for entry. In such cases, tests of academic ability may be useful in gauging a client's likelihood of success in gaining admission to postsecondary programs and completing them satisfactorily.

Table 11.5 lists standardized tests that may be used to assess an individual's academic abilities. As you read the following descriptions of each test, pay particular attention to whether each test is geared more toward use with clients for the purpose of estimating current proficiency or geared more toward predicting potential for future academic success in pursuing higher levels of education. As you read, think about why this matters in a career context; for example, think about our clients from Chapter 1 and how their academic abilities may affect their respective career options.

ACT, Inc. Tests. Three standardized tests of academic ability are published by ACT, Inc. Each one serves as an objective measure of a student's knowledge and is part of the ACT College & Career Readiness system. First, the ACT Explore is given to students in eighth or ninth grade. It consists of four sections: English, math, reading, and science. The Explore Student Score Report provides information about how a student's scores on this test compare to other students in the United States, how a student's scores compare to scores demonstrating college readiness, how a student's planned coursework for high school compares to the recommended core coursework needed to become college ready, and student-reported needs for academic and career support. It also provides career interest results from the UNIACT interest inventory described earlier in this chapter.

The ACT Plan is generally taken by students in 10th grade whether they aspire to attend college or to seek employment after graduating from high school. Just like the Explore, the Plan objectively assesses academic achievement and aptitude in English, math, reading, and science. The Plan Student Score Report provides information about how a student's scores on this test compare to other students in the United States, how a student's scores compare to scores demonstrating college readiness, and how a student's planned coursework for high school compares to the recommended core coursework needed to become college ready. It also provides career interest results from the UNIACT interest inventory described earlier in this chapter.

The third major test published by ACT, Inc. is the actual ACT test and is probably the one with which you are most likely familiar. Although it is widely considered a college entrance examination, the ACT is also administered in several states (e.g., Colorado, Illinois, Kentucky, Michigan, Tennessee, and Wyoming) to *all* high school students in the respective states. The ACT test is normally taken in junior year, but some students opt to retake it in their senior year in an effort to improve their scores and increase their chance of admission to the college of their choice. Just like the Explore and the Plan, the ACT test objectively

TABLE 11.5 Standardized Tests Used to Assess Academic Ability*

Academic Achievement Tests	Populations			
	K–12 School Settings	College Settings	Community Settings	Special Needs
ACT, Inc. Tests • ACT Explore • ACT Plan • ACT Test	E/MS/HS			
Adult Basic Learning Examination			X	X
Basic Achievement Skills Inventory	E/MS/HS	X	X	
College Board Tests • PSAT/NMSQT • SAT • AP • CLEP	HS		X	
Graduate School Exams • GRE • MCAT • LSAT • GMAT		X	X	
Tests of Adult Basic Education (TABE) Forms 9 and 10 (HS)	X		X	X
Wonderlic Assessments • Wonderlic Contemporary Cognitive Abilities Test • Wonderlic Scholastic Level Exam • Wonderlic Basic Skills Test			X	X

*E = elementary school, MS = middle school, and HS = high school.

assesses academic achievement and aptitude in English, math, reading, and science. It also includes an optional writing test. The composite score as well as the scores for each subsection of the ACT Test are reported on a scale of 1 to 36. The Student Report provides information about how a student's scores on this test compare to other students in the United States, how a student's scores compare to scores of students currently enrolled at the colleges in which they have expressed interest, and how these scores compare to information stemming from the UNIACT interest inventory described earlier in this chapter. Counselors may find it helpful to have information available about the average ACT score of incoming freshmen for a variety of colleges. This information can be useful in helping students put their scores into perspective as they think about their likelihood of admission to various colleges.

All three of these tests—the ACT Plan, the ACT Explore, and the ACT Test—are part of ACT's College and Career Readiness Program. ACT, Inc. has recently launched a new test as part of this same program. It is called the ACT Aspire.

Whereas the ACT tests of academic ability are most commonly used to assess whether students are on track and/or ready for college work, the next two tests of academic ability are more likely to be used with clients not aspiring to postsecondary education. These tests determine whether students have the academic skills necessary to meet job-specific requirements in reading, writing, and arithmetic.

Adult Basic Learning Examination, Second Edition. The Adult Basic Learning Examination (ABLE; Karlsen & Gardner, 1986) is a test of academic achievement that is designed for use with adults who have completed at least one year but no more than 12 years of formal schooling. It consists of just 45 items and yields scores on six subtests: vocabulary, reading comprehension, spelling, language, number operations, and problem solving. The test has three levels. The Level 1 version demands the least reading ability (with many items read aloud to the test taker), and Level 3 requires the most reading ability. Results are presented in percentile ranks, stanines, and grade equivalents. The scores provide an estimate of a person's academic proficiency levels and are useful in determining the types of jobs he or she will be able to perform satisfactorily. The ABLE is regarded as one of "the two preeminent batteries available to assess adults' educational achievement" (Fitzpatrick, 1992, para. 14). It is published by and available for purchase from Pearson Assessments.

Basic Achievement Skills Inventory. The Basic Achievement Skills Inventory (BASI; Bardos, 2004) is a group-administered test of academic abilities that focuses on reading, written language, and math. The BASI has four levels, which allows it to be administered to children as early as third grade as well as to adults up to age 80. Whereas the comprehensive version has diagnostic uses (e.g., assessing for learning disabilities), counselors will likely prefer the survey version of the BASI, which is designed to provide a quick snapshot of an individual's academic achievement and ability. Separate interpretive reports are available for K–12 students, college students, and adults. When used with adult clients, BASI scores provide an estimate of a person's academic proficiency levels and are useful in determining the types of jobs they will be able to perform satisfactorily. The BASI is published by and available for purchase from Pearson Assessments.

College Board Tests. The College Board is another organization that, like ACT, Inc., publishes tests that are most commonly used to assess whether students are on track and/or ready for college work. In fact, the College Board (collegeboard.org) is an organization that has focused extensively on promoting student readiness for college. For instance, it does a great deal of work in training school counselors to promote a college-going culture. College readiness examinations, however, probably represent the College Board's best-known program. Two such tests are particularly well known and are described here.

First, the Preliminary SAT/National Merit Scholarship Qualifying Test (PSAT/NMSQT) is a standardized test of academic ability that is typically administered to high school students in their sophomore and junior years. When taken in 10th grade, the PSAT provides students with early performance feedback that may be useful in guiding their selection of coursework and preparation for later exams. Students who wish to compete for a National Merit Scholarship (nationalmerit.org) typically must also take the PSAT/NMSQT during their junior year to qualify. In the context of career counseling, the PSAT/NMSQT offers one source of data regarding a student's academic ability and an early prediction about the student's likelihood of earning admission to a college. The PSAT/NMSQT score report presents scale scores ranging from 20 to 80. The results are also accompanied by national percentile ranks. Students who take the PSAT/NMSQT are granted access to *My College QuickStart,* which helps students understand their PSAT scores and develop plans for preparing for the SAT, and also includes career development modules. For instance, it includes a personality test, a list of colleges that offer majors of interest to the student, and extensive information about various majors and careers.

Second, what was originally called the Scholastic Aptitude Test and later renamed the Scholastic Assessment Test is now simply known as the SAT. The SAT is a standardized test that is normally taken by high school students in their junior year, although some students opt to retake it in their senior year in an effort to improve their scores and increase their chance of admission to the college of their choice. As a college admissions test, the SAT is designed to assess a student's readiness for college. It consists of three sections: critical reading, mathematical reasoning, and writing. The SAT score report presents scale scores ranging from 200 to 800. These scores are also accompanied by national percentile ranks. Counselors may find it helpful to have information available about the average SAT scores of incoming freshmen for a variety of colleges. This information can be useful in helping students put their scores into perspective as they think about their likelihood of admission to various colleges.

Both the PSAT/NMSQT and SAT are published by The College Board. They are unavailable for direct purchase and are available only through approved testing sites.

In addition to these two exams, the College Board offers several other tests of academic ability and achievement. Although they are administered less frequently than the PSAT/NMSQT and the SAT, counselors aspiring to work with high school students and/or adults who wish to pursue a college degree will benefit from an awareness of these tests. First, numerous SAT Subject Tests are available. These tests assess knowledge in specific academic areas (U.S. history, world history, literature, mathematics, biology, chemistry, physics, and specific languages such as French, German, Italian, Latin, modern Hebrew, Spanish, Chinese, Japanese, Korean, and Spanish). These subject area tests can be useful in helping students choose from among various college majors and, when the scores are especially high, in strengthening a student's application to highly selective colleges. Second, the College Board also administers the Advanced Placement (AP; professionals.collegeboard.com/testing/ap) examinations. Depending on their scores on AP exams, students may earn college credit and/or advanced placement at many universities. Finally, the College Board also administers the College-Level Examination Program (CLEP; clep.collegeboard.org/). Whereas students typically must take an AP course in high school in order to take the corresponding AP exam, the CLEP exams are open to anyone (high school students and adults) who desire an opportunity to earn college credit via an examination.

Graduate School Exams. Counselors working with people interested in seeking a college degree will likely find the examinations offered by ACT, Inc. and/or the College Board quite useful and important. These tests will be less useful, however, when working with clients who already have college degrees. After all, the results of a test designed to predict a person's ability to succeed academically in college aren't very relevant after a person has already succeeded in earning a college degree. This does not mean, however, that tests of academic ability are no longer useful with such clients. Indeed, some of these clients may be interested in pursuing careers that require a degree at the graduate level. It is important that career counselors also have an awareness of examinations designed to assess a person's capacity to earn a graduate degree. Four tests are commonly used for this purpose.

First, what used to be called the Graduate Management Admissions Test is now simply referred to by its acronym: GMAT (Graduate Management Admissions Council, 2012). This test is intended specifically for students who are interested in pursuing a master's degree in business administration (MBA). It consists of four sections: quantitative, verbal, analytical writing, and a newly introduced section on integrated reasoning. The composite or total score on the GMAT ranges from 200 to 800. Scores on the verbal and quantitative subtests range from 0 to 60. Scores on the analytic writing subtest range from 0 to 6, and scores on the integrated reasoning subtest range from 1 to 8. The test is published by the Graduate Management Admissions Council and is unavailable for purchase. Test takers must register and take the GMAT at an authorized testing center.

Second, what used to be called the Graduate Record Examination is now known simply as the GRE. A major revision of this test was published in 2011, and the test's official name is the GRE Revised General Test (Educational Testing Service, 2011). This test is used by many graduate programs nationwide as a measure of a person's academic ability to perform graduate work. Because the GRE is a common admissions requirement for graduate programs in counseling, you may very well have taken this test. Although the GMAT has historically been the test of choice for individuals interested in business school, the GRE is now marketing itself for both general graduate degree programs *and* business schools. The test consists of three sections: verbal reasoning, quantitative reasoning, and analytical writing. Before the 2011 revision, GRE scores were based on a scale much like the SAT, with scores on the verbal and quantitative scales ranging from 200 to 800. The 2011 revision meant a major change in how scores are reported. Now, scores on the verbal and quantitative scales are reported on a scale ranging from 130 to 170, and scores on the writing section are reported on a scale from 0 to 6. In addition to the GRE Revised General Test are several GRE Subject Tests. Specifically, they are offered in biochemistry, and cell and molecular biology; biology; chemistry; computer science; literature in English; mathematics; physics; and psychology. Scores on these tests are on a scale ranging from 200 to 990. The GRE Revised General Test and the GRE Subject Tests are published by the Educational Testing Service (ETS) and are unavailable for purchase. Test takers must register to take these exams at an approved testing site.

Third, the Law School Admission Test (LSAT; Law School Admission Council, 2012) is a standardized test required by many law schools as part of their admissions process. This test is designed to assess a person's reading comprehension, ability to engage in analytic reasoning, ability to engage in logical reasoning, and ability to write. The LSAT score is reported on a scale of 120 to 180. Percentile ranks accompany the score. The LSAT is published by the Law School Admissions Council and is unavailable for purchase. Test takers must register to take these exams at an approved testing site.

Fourth, individuals wishing to attend medical school generally must take the Medical College Admission Test (MCAT). The new MCAT 2015 exam consists of four sections: (1) biological and biochemical foundations of living systems; (2) chemical and physical foundations of biological systems; (3) psychological, social, and biological foundations of behavior; and (4) critical analysis and reasoning skills. Scores for each of these sections are reported on a scale of 1 to 15. A total score is also reported. The MCAT is published by the Association of American Medical Colleges and is unavailable for purchase. Test takers must register to take these exams at an approved testing site.

Tests of Adult Basic Education. The Tests of Adult Basic Education (TABE; CTB/McGraw-Hill, 2004) involve objective assessments that are designed to measure skills needed for success in the workplace and life in general.

Specifically, these tests measure basic skills in reading, math, language, language mechanics, vocabulary, and math. Advanced tests in science, social studies, algebra/geometry, and writing are also available. Because the TABE has several levels (literacy, easy, medium, difficult, and advanced), it is necessary first to administer the TABE Locator Test to determine the most appropriate version of the TABE for a particular individual. Results of the TABE may be used to screen potential employees, assess worker skills, identify training needs, and assess language proficiency. Within educational settings, the TABE may be used to assess a person's readiness to take the General Equivalency Diploma (GED) exam. The TABE is published by and available for purchase from CTB/McGraw-Hill.

Wonderlic Tests. Wonderlic, Inc. (wonderlic.com) produces numerous tests of academic ability with relevance to the practice of career counseling. Perhaps most relevant are the Wonderlic Contemporary Cognitive Ability Test (WCCAT; Wonderlic, Inc., 2007a), the Wonderlic Scholastic Level Exam (WSLE; Wonderlic, Inc., 1999), and the Wonderlic Basic Skills Test (WBST; Wonderlic, Inc., 2011). WCCAT and WSLE, which differ only slightly, are considered tests of ability; the WBST is considered an achievement test. For all three tests, the test manual provides the median composite scores associated with various occupations, so this information could be quite useful in career counseling.

The WCCAT, formerly called the Wonderlic Personnel Test–Revised (WPT-R; Wonderlic, Inc., 2007a, 2007b), is marketed to employers for use in the selection of personnel. Its publisher describes it as "the most respected and widely used cognitive ability test in the world" (wonderlic.com/assessments/ability/cognitive-ability-tests/contemporary-cognitive-ability-test, para 1). In his expert review of the test, Geisinger (2001) acknowledges its "long history of use in employment settings, both personnel offices of companies and employment agencies" (para. 1). Even the National Football League (NFL) uses the classic version of this test, and it is required of nearly all players eligible for the draft. This test contains only 50 items, and examinees have only 12 minutes to take it. Although it takes very little time and no special skill to administer, the WCCAT offers a surprisingly robust estimate of general cognitive ability, complete with percentile ranks and an estimated full-scale intelligence quotient (IQ) equivalent. The WCCAT is available in both a paper and an online version.

The WSLE, previously referred to as the Scholastic Level Exam, is also a 50-item exam that allows examinees a maximum of 12 minutes. It, too, results in a surprisingly robust estimate of general cognitive ability, complete with percentile ranks and an estimated full-scale intelligence quotient (IQ) equivalent. Like the WCCAT, the WSLE is also available in both a paper and an online version. In fact, the WSLE and the WCCAT/WPT exams are "essentially the same test" (Geisinger, 2001, para. 1). The primary difference involves marketing. Whereas the WCCAT is marketed for employment settings, the WSLE is marketed for educational settings. Both forms offer an estimate of general cognitive ability and require a minimum amount of time for examination and no special skills to administer them.

In contrast with the WCCAT and the WSLE, both of which purport to measure general cognitive ability (that is, intelligence), the WBST is designed to measure basic verbal and math skills. This test, which requires 20 minutes for administration, is most appropriate for use with those who have not earned a high school diploma or GED or those who have been out of school long enough perhaps to have forgotten some basic academic skills (Power, 2009). The WBST offers a composite score, a verbal subtest score (based on items addressing word knowledge, sentence construction, and information retrieval), and a quantitative score (based on items addressing explicit, applied, and interpretive problem solving). Whereas scores on the WCCAT and WSLE are offered in percentile ranks and IQ estimates, scores on the WBST are presented as GED levels and grade-level equivalents. The test manual also provides the median composite scores associated with various occupations, so this information could be quite useful in career counseling.

TESTS OF VOCATIONAL APTITUDE. Another set of tests that purport to measure ability are tests of vocational aptitude. These tests generally include sections that address academic ability but also include sections addressing other skills needed in various work settings. Table 11.6 lists standardized tests that may be used to assess an individual's vocational aptitudes and/or career readiness.

Whereas all of the tests of academic ability described so far involve objective measurement of ability, this is not the case with tests of vocational aptitude. As you will see, some of these tests do involve objective measurement, but others simply ask clients to rate their ability in different areas. Objective ability tests present items requiring the application of skill, and each item has a right and a wrong answer. The score therefore represents, objectively, the test taker's performance on the test. In contrast, items on self-report measures have no right and wrong answers; the items present various tasks and ask clients to self-report their level of skill in performing those tasks. Such tests often refer to skills confidence rather than to skills or aptitudes. As you read about each

TABLE 11.6 Standardized Tests Used to Assess Vocational Aptitude*

Tests	Populations			
	K–12 School Settings	College Settings	Community Settings	Special Needs
Ability Explorer	MS/HS	X	X	
Armed Services Vocational Aptitude Battery	HS	X	X	
Campbell Interest and Skills Survey	HS	X	X	
Differential Aptitude Tests	MS/HS	X	X	
General Aptitude Test Battery	HS	X	X	
Kuder Skills Confidence Assessment	MS/HS	X	X	
Occupational Attitude Survey & Interest Schedule (OASIS)	MS/HS	X		X
O*NET Ability Profiler	HS	X	X	
Skills Confidence Inventory	HS	X	X	
Valpar Career Ability Test (a sample test is available at valparint.com/VCAT.HTM)	HS		X	
World of Work Inventory	MS/HS	X	X	X

*MS = middle school, and HS = high school.

of the following tests, note which of the tests represent objective measures and which are self-report measures on which respondents rate the quality of their knowledge or skills in different areas.

Ability Explorer, Third Edition. The Ability Explorer (AE; Harrington, Harrington, & Wall, 2012) is an assessment that relies on a person's self-report rather than offering an objective test of abilities. It can be used with middle school and high school students as well as adults. Although a plethora of objective tests of academic achievement and aptitude are administered to students every year, students are rarely asked to assess their own abilities. The AE does just that, and rather than focusing only on academic subject areas, the AE focuses on 12 work-related abilities that are identified by the U.S. Department of Labor. Specifically, it invites respondents to assess their artistic, clerical, interpersonal, language, leadership/persuasive, manual/technical, musical/dramatic, numerical/mathematical, organizational, scientific, social, and spatial abilities. Interpretive materials include *Careers Finder*, which assists clients in understanding the connection between their abilities and the demands of various occupations. The AE is published by and available for purchase from JIST Publishing, Inc.

Armed Services Vocational Aptitude Battery. The Armed Services Vocational Aptitude Battery (ASVAB; U.S. Military Entrance Processing Command, 1997) offers an objective assessment of academic and vocational aptitudes. Specifically, it measures aptitudes in four domains (verbal, math, science and technical, and spatial) and consists of 10 subtests (general science, arithmetic reasoning, word knowledge, paragraph comprehension, math knowledge, electronics information, auto information, shop information, mechanical comprehension, and assembling objects). The ASVAB is typically offered to high school students as well as young adults in college or community settings who are considering military career options. Results are presented in two forms. First, the overall ASVAB scores (using all subtests) are presented as T scores, with 50 as the mean and a standard deviation of 10. Second, the results from four specific subtests (arithmetic reasoning, math knowledge, paragraph comprehension, and word knowledge) are used as the Armed Forces Qualification Test (AFQT). This score identifies the AFQT category (ranging from I to V) which is based on the percentile rank of an examinee's score. AFQT scores are extremely important to individuals seeking to join the military because they are used to determine (a) a person's eligibility to join the military, (b) the types of training and benefits a person can receive in the military, and (c) the choices of military occupational specialties from which a person can choose. Although the ASVAB is obviously designed specifically for use within the military, it can also be quite useful in civilian settings such as high schools. In fact, ASVAB has invested tremendous resources in developing a career exploration program (asvabprogram.com/) for use in schools. This program includes free administration of the ASVAB, an interest assessment, and several career exploration tools. Within this context, ASVAB attends not only to military occupations but also to the full array of civilian occupations available within the 16 career clusters developed by the U.S. Department of Education.

Campbell Interest and Skills Survey. As its title suggests, the Campbell Interest and Skill Survey (CISS; Campbell, 1992) is a standardized test that assesses both interests and skills related to career selection. The test is divided into two parts, one focused on interests and the other focused on skill confidence related to academic subjects and specific work activities. Part 2, the skills assessment, includes 120 items addressing skills associated with various occupations. Respondents are asked to rate their level of skill for each item on a Likert-type scale. This, of course, represents a self-report of skill rather than an objective measure of ability. Nonetheless, it provides useful information. The interpretive report provides a visual display of how the test taker's level of interest and skills confidence compare with one another on each of the seven orientation scales and 29 basic scales described earlier in this section. The report also shows how one's interests and skills compare to the norming sample. Based on these comparisons, the CISS interpretive report offers a suggestion that the student/client pursue, develop, explore, or avoid various areas. In areas of high interest and high skill, a recommendation of "pursue" is offered. In areas of high interest but lower skill, a recommendation of "develop" is provided. In areas of high skill but less interest, clients are advised to "explore." In areas of low interest and low skill, a recommendation to "avoid" is made. The CISS is published by and available for purchase from Pearson Assessments.

Differential Aptitude Tests. The Differential Aptitude Tests, Fifth Edition (DAT; Bennett, Seashore, & Wesman, 1992) are designed as objective assessments of vocational aptitudes. Appropriate for use with middle school students, high school students, and adults, the DAT reports scores on eight subtests that comprise three domains. The general cognitive abilities domain is based on the verbal reasoning and numerical ability tests. The perceptual abilities domain is based on the abstract reasoning, mechanical reasoning, and space relations tests. The clerical and language skills domain is based on the spelling, language usage, and separate clerical speed and accuracy tests. The DAT may be administered as the complete battery of eight tests or as a partial battery consisting only of the verbal reasoning and numerical ability tests. In addition to raw scores, score reports include percentile ranks and stanines separated by sex. The DAT is published by and available for purchase from Pearson Assessments. It can also be purchased with a career interest inventory to support career development activities in K–12 school settings.

General Aptitude Test Battery. What used to be called the General Aptitude Test Battery (GATB; United States Employment Service, 1986) has since been revised and renamed as the O*NET Ability Profiler (U.S. Department of Labor Employment and Training Administration, 2001a). Because references to the GATB continue to permeate our professional literature, however, I have chosen to briefly describe it here. Its replacement, the O*NET Ability Profiler, will be described later in this section. The GATB, which was last published in 1986, was an objective measure consisting of 12 separate tests designed to assess ability in nine areas: general learning ability, verbal aptitude, numerical aptitude, spatial aptitude, form perception, clerical perception, motor coordination, finger dexterity, and manual dexterity. Given its replacement by the O*NET Ability Profiler, its use in the United States is now quite limited, but the GATB continues to be used in Canada. It remains available for purchase from Nelson Education, Ltd. (assess.nelson.com/group/gp-gatb.html).

Kuder Skills Confidence Assessment. Another part of the Kuder Career Planning System (KCPS), the Kuder Skills Confidence Assessment (KSCA; Kuder, Inc. 2012b) is a self-report instrument with which respondents rate their own skills. The KSCA is designed for use with students, and the Kuder® Skills Confidence Assessment–Adult (KSCA-A; Kuder, Inc., 2012c) is intended for use with adult clients. Each version of this test contains 56 items that describe work-related activities. Test takers are asked to identify their level of confidence in their ability to perform each task. The Likert-type scale gives four options, ranging from "I don't think I could ever learn how to do this task" to "I can already do this task" (Schenck, 2009, p. 168). The interpretive report organizes results in accordance with the 16 national career clusters. In addition to providing a graphic display of the clusters rank-ordered according to the respondent's skill confidence, the report also provides a percentile rank comparing the respondent's self-efficacy in each area to other people her or his age. The report concludes with an identification of 10 occupations that are well matched to the respondent's areas of skill confidence. In addition, Kuder, Inc. also offers a composite report. For each of the 16 career clusters, this composite report shows a graphic display of the respondent's level of interest and skill confidence, along with the percentile ranks for each. The KSCA and KSCA-A are both published by and available for purchase from Kuder, Inc.

Occupational Attitude Survey & Interest Schedule. As noted earlier in this chapter, the Occupational Attitude Survey & Interest Schedule (OASIS-3; Parker, 2002) is designed to assess both aptitudes and interests. The aptitude portion of the OASIS-3 is generally referred to as the Aptitude Survey. It is an objective measure of ability that uses 250 items to assess ability in six areas: general ability, verbal aptitude, numerical aptitude, spatial aptitude, perceptual aptitude, and manual dexterity. Bunch (2005) indicated that the OASIS-3 Aptitude Survey is based on the General Aptitude Test Battery (GATB) described earlier in this section. Because the norming sample was limited to students in middle school, high school, and college, the OASIS-3 is best limited to use with these populations. Whitfield and Cato (2009) also note that the OASIS-3 is appropriate for use with special populations. The OASIS-3 is published by and available for purchase from Pro-Ed.

O*NET Ability Profiler. In addition to providing access to occupational information, the O*NET website (onetcenter.org/overview.html, para 1) also grants free access to three assessment instruments, one of which is the O*NET Ability Profiler. As indicated earlier in this chapter, the O*NET Ability Profiler was developed from the GATB and has now replaced it. Written at the sixth-grade level and intended for use with people at least 16 years of age, the Ability Profiler is an objective measure of ability and contains 11 subtests. The entire test takes approximately 2½ hours to administer, but the subtests are separately timed and the test can therefore be administered over two days. The score report combines results from subtests and yields scores for nine ability areas: verbal ability, arithmetic reasoning, computation, spatial ability, form perception, clerical perception, motor coordination, manual dexterity, and finger dexterity. In addition to offering percentile ranks for these nine abilities, the score report also provides a list of occupations that may be well suited to the test taker's abilities. This, of course, encourages further exploration of occupations that may not have otherwise been considered. One drawback of the O*NET Ability Profiler is that the O*NET website does not allow users to enter Ability Profiler results in order to search for occupations. As you recall, the other two O*NET assessment instruments (the Interest Profiler and the Work Importance Profiler) do allow for entering results data. The O*NET Ability Profiler and supporting documentation (such as a user's guide, instrument materials, and answer sheets) may be downloaded from onetcenter.org/AP.html.

Skills Confidence Inventory. The Skills Confidence Inventory, Revised Edition (SCI; Betz, Borgen, & Harmon, 2005) is a vocational ability test based on self-report. This instrument is designed to assess self-confidence in one's ability to perform a variety of work-related tasks. These tasks are organized into the six RIASEC areas of Holland's typology. In fact, the Skills Confidence Inventory is available only in conjunction with the Strong Interest Inventory. This package, called the Strong Inventory and Skills Confidence Inventory (Betz, Borgen, & Harmon, 2005), results in an interpretive report that reports not only vocational interests for the Strong Interest Inventory (as described earlier in this chapter) but also skill confidence for each of the general occupational themes. In an easy-to-read graphic display, this report visually contrasts an individual's interest and skills confidence in the realistic, investigative, artistic, social, enterprising, and conventional areas. Based on the relationship between interest and skills confidence for each area, the report also identifies priorities for career exploration. High priorities are the RIASEC areas in which a person expresses high interest and high skills confidence. Low priorities are the areas in which a person expresses low interest and low skills confidence. When a person expresses strong skills confidence but less interest in a given RIASEC area, the report identifies that area as a possible option if interests develop and suggests careful consideration of that area. When a person expresses strong interest but less skills confidence in a given RIASEC area, the report identifies that area as a good option if confidence in skills can be increased. Because the SCI is based in part on self-efficacy theory, an increase in skills confidence may require an improvement in skills *or* an increase in confidence to more accurately reflect skills already possessed.

Valpar Career Ability Test. The Valpar Career Ability Test (VCAT; Valpar International, 2004) is designed to measure academic and vocational aptitudes. With regard to academic ability, the VCAT tests three areas of general educational development (GED): reasoning, math, and language. It also tests seven aptitudes: general learning ability, numerical ability, verbal ability, spatial perception, form perception, clerical skills, and color discrimination. Although it also includes a brief interest assessment, this is not the focus of the VCAT. The VCAT is published by and available for purchase from Valpar International.

One advantage of the VCAT is that it is administered online and can be offered on a per administration basis. For counselors needing only occasional use of this instrument, this is a cost-effective method.

Valpar International also offers a software-based aptitude test called the Aviator 3 (Valpar International, 2002). This instrument assesses the same areas as the VTAC (academics, aptitudes, and interests), but it requires the purchase of software for each computer on which the test may be administered. Both VTAC and Aviator 3 may be combined with the Aviator Dexterity Modules in order to assess motor coordination, manual dexterity, and finger dexterity also.

World of Work Inventory. The World of Work Inventory (WOWI; Ripley, Neidert, & Ortman, 2004) consists of three scales, one of which measures abilities. Specifically, the WOWI's Vocational Training Potentials (VTP) scale consists of 98 items that assess abilities in six areas: verbal, numerical, abstractions, spatial-form, mechanical-electrical, and clerical. As already mentioned, an advantage of using the WOWI is that it addresses abilities *and* interests and work-related temperament. The WOWI is published by and available for purchase from World of Work, Inc. It can also be taken online at wowi.com.

STANDARDIZED TESTS RELATED TO CAREER DECISION MAKING

Parsons (1909) identified the first step in choosing a vocation as developing an understanding of yourself. Tests designed to help clients understand themselves are those I have categorized as tests related to career selection, including tests related to interests, personality, work-related values, and abilities. These, of course, were the focus of the previous section of this chapter. We will now transition to Parsons's third step and examine tests focused specifically on factors that affect a person's career decision-making process. Some of these tests address beliefs, thoughts, and self-efficacy; others address career maturity; and still others address vocational identity. Regardless of the specific constructs assessed, all of instruments included in this section share a common focus on difficulties associated with making a career decision.

Table 11.7 lists standardized tests related to the career decision-making process. The table will be followed by brief descriptions, in alphabetical order, of each of the tests.

Career Beliefs Inventory

The Career Beliefs Inventory (CBI; Krumboltz, 2009) is a standardized test designed to facilitate the exploration of problematic beliefs that may interfere with a person's career decision making and/or career development. Initially developed by Krumboltz for use in conjunction with his learning theory of career counseling (LTCC; Mitchell & Krumboltz, 1996), the CBI is now used in a variety of career counseling contexts. It is appropriate for use with adults as well as students in middle school, high school, and college. The instrument addresses 25 beliefs distributed across five categories: my current situation, what seems necessary for my happiness, factors that influence my decisions, changes I am willing to make, and effort I am willing to initiate. The score report offers both a graphic

TABLE 11.7 Standardized Tests Related to Career Decision Making*

Tests	Populations			
	K–12 School Settings	College Settings	Community Settings	Special Needs
Career Beliefs Inventory	MS/HS	X	X	
Career Decision Scale	HS	X		X
Career Decision Self-Efficacy Scale	HS	X	X	
Career Development Inventory	MS/HS	X		
Career Factors Inventory	X	X	X	
Career Maturity Inventory	MS/HS			
Career Thoughts Inventory	HS	X	X	
My Vocational Situation	HS	X	X	

*MS = middle school, and HS = high school.

display of results and a narrative description of results and their implications. These results are best used as a springboard for discussion with clients about their beliefs and potential impact. The CBI is published by and available for purchase from Consulting Psychologists Press, Inc. It may also be purchased from and taken online through Mind Garden (mindgarden.com).

Career Decision Scale

The Career Decision Scale (CDS; Osipow, Carney, Winer, Yanico, & Koschier, 1987) is a standardized test designed to measure a person's level of career indecision and to identify factors contributing to indecision. It may be used in the context of career counseling to guide the counselor in addressing any perceived barriers to decision making. Because "indecision scores [should] decrease following career counseling interventions" (Herman, 1985, para. 5), the CDS may also be used to measure the effectiveness of various counseling strategies. The CDS consists of just 19 items. Two of these items measure a person's certainty with regard to career choice, and the remaining items focus on factors contributing to indecision. The CDS is normed on students in high school and college and is specifically intended only for use with individuals between 14 and 23 years of age. Osipow and Winer (1996) indicated that it may also be used with special populations. It is published by and available for purchase form Psychological Assessment Resources, Inc.

Career Decision Self-Efficacy Scale

The Career Decision Self-Efficacy Scale (CDSE; Betz & Taylor, 1994) is designed to measure, as its title so aptly indicates, people's degree of self-efficacy related to their ability to make a good career decision. Hackett and Betz (1981) conducted some landmark research on the role of self-efficacy in career development, and their work laid the foundation for the later development of social cognitive career theory (Lent, Brown, & Hackett, 1994). There are two versions of the CDSE: A 50-item CDMSE is the standard, and a 25-item short form of the CDSE is also available. Both versions address self-efficacy beliefs in five areas: self-appraisal, occupational information, goal selection, planning, and problem solving. Although the CDSE is normed exclusively on college students, the publisher indicates that it may be used with people 16 years of age and older. It is published by and is available for purchase from Mind Garden (mindgarden.com).

Career Development Inventory

Described as "the best current measure of career choice competencies" (Savickas & Porfeli, 2011, p. 357), the Career Development Inventory (CDI; Super, Thompson, Lindenman, Jordaan, & Myers, 1979, 1981) is a standardized test designed to assess an individual's readiness to make career decisions. It is based directly on Super's model of "readiness to make educational and vocational choices," which he termed career maturity (Super, Savickas, & Super, 1996, p. 132). As you will recall from Chapter 3, the Career-Development Assessment and Counseling (C-DAC) model (Super, Osborne, Walsh, Brown, & Niles, 1992) specifically calls for the use of the CDI to assess career maturity. There are two forms, one designed for students in middle or high school (Super, Thompson, Lindenman, Jordaan, & Myers, 1979) and the other designed for college students (Super, Thompson, Lindenman, Jordaan, & Myers, 1981). Each form is divided into two parts. Part 1 of the CDI addresses a person's "career orientation" and includes "four scales: career planning, career exploration, decision-making, and world of work" (Osborn & Zunker, 2006, p. 197). Part 2 of the CDI is focused on a person's knowledge of the occupation in which she or he is currently most interested. Because middle school students generally have not yet solidified a career decision enough to have researched the occupation extensively, Part 2 is only recommended for high school and college students. Scores represent a person's attitude in the areas of career planning and career exploration and a person's competencies in the areas of decision making, knowledge of the world of work (breadth), and knowledge about the occupation of greatest interest (depth). The CDI was published by Consulting Psychologists Press, Inc., but it is no longer available for purchase; however, it is available free of charge from Vocopher (vocopher.com).

Career Factors Inventory

The Career Factors Inventory (CFI; Chartrand, Robbins, & Morrill, 1997) is another standardized test designed to assess a person's readiness to make a career decision. This instrument provides results on four common sources of career indecision: a need for more self-knowledge, a need for more information about the world of work, anxiety about making a career choice, and generalized indecisiveness. Because it takes only 10 minutes to administer and can be self-scored, the CFI can be quite useful as a screening device with any client whose goal is to make a career decision. The publisher indicates that it can be used with "high school students, new and returning college students, employed individuals engaged in second-career planning, and unemployed individuals seeking work" (cpp.com/en/strongproducts.aspx?pc=82, para. 1). The CFI is published by and available for purchase from Consulting Psychologists Press, Inc.

Career Maturity Inventory: The Adaptability Form

The Career Maturity Inventory: The Adaptability Form (CMI Form C; Crites & Savickas, 2012) represents a recent, significant revision of the original Career Maturity Inventory. Savickas and Porfeli (2011) explained that the CMI was "initially administered in 1961" and was actually "the first paper-and-pencil measure of vocational development" (p. 355). The CMI was revised by Crites in 1978, and an adult version of the CMI was published by Crites and Savickas in 1996. Although each of these revisions remained closely tied to the original format and content of the CMI, the most recent version reflects a major change. With this newest version, Crites and Savickas (2012) incorporated the concept of adaptability from the career construction theory (Savickas, 2005), which you studied in Chapter 5. Specifically, the CMI Form C consists of 24 items that address three dimensions of adaptability: concern, curiosity, and confidence. Savickas and Porfeli (2011) reported that the CMI Form C yields five scores:

> The first score is a total score for career choice readiness based on the 18 items in the Concern, Curiosity, and Confidence Scales. It measures an individual's degree of adaptability in career decision making and readiness to make occupational choices. The next three scores are for the Concern, Curiosity, and Confidence Scales. The Concern Scale measures the extent to which an individual is oriented to and involved in the process of making career decisions. The Curiosity Scale measures the extent to which an individual is exploring the work world and seeking information about occupations and their requirements. The Confidence Scale measures the extent to which an individual has faith in her or his ability to make wise career decisions and realistic occupation choices. The fifth score is for the Consultation Scale, which measures the extent to which an individual seeks assistance in career decision making by requesting information or advice from others. (p. 360)

The CMI Form C copyright is held by Crites and Savickas (2012), and it is available free of charge from Vocopher (vocopher.com).

Career Thoughts Inventory

The Career Thoughts Inventory (CTI; Sampson, Peterson, Lenz, Reardon, & Saunders, 1996a) is an integral part of the application of *A Cognitive Information Processing Approach to Career Problem Solving and Decision Making* (CIP; Peterson, Sampson, Lenz, & Reardon, 2002; Sampson, Reardon, Peterson, & Lenz, 2004). As we discussed in Chapter 4, the CIP theory conceptualizes readiness for career decision making using a two-dimensional model involving both capability and complexity. The CTI addresses both dimensions. Specifically, "there are three types of negative thoughts measured by the CTI: decision making confusion (DMC), commitment anxiety (CA), and external conflict (EC)" (Paivandy, Bullock, Reardon, & Kelly, 2008, p. 475). High scores on the DMC subscale suggest an "inability to sustain the decision making process as a result of disabling emotions and/or a lack of understanding about the decision making process itself," and high scores on the CA subscale relate to "the inability to make a commitment to a specific career choice, accompanied by generalized anxiety about the outcome of the decision making process" (Sampson, Peterson, Lenz, Reardon, & Saunders, 1999, p. 4). The DMC and CA constructs represent aspects of the capability dimension of career readiness. Sampson, Peterson, et al. (1999) note that the CTI's external conflict (EC) subscale measures "the inability to balance the importance of one's own self-perceptions with the importance of input from significant others, resulting in a reluctance to assume responsibility for decision making" (p. 4). Thus, this subscale has relevance to contextual complexity.

The CTI score report offers results for each of these subscales along with a composite score. A companion workbook is also available and offers activities designed to help clients recognize and challenge negative career thoughts and thinking patterns. The CTI instrument is appropriate for use with high school students at least 17 years of age, college students, and adults. It is published by and available for purchase from Psychological Assessment Resources.

My Vocational Situation

My Vocational Situation (MVS; Holland, Daiger, & Power, 1980) is a standardized test designed to identify difficulties related to career decision making. It consists of three sections. The first assesses difficulties related to vocational identity, the second section screens for difficulties related to a lack of occupational information, and the third section screens for difficulties related to perceived barriers to achieving one's career goals. When used at the initial contact with a student or client, the MVS can provide valuable insight into his or her needs. Some clients may need assistance in crystallizing their vocational identity before making a career decision, whereas others may simply need access to resources offering occupational information. Still others may need support in overcoming perceived obstacles. Although the MVS has received some criticism for the sections addressing occupational information and barriers, largely due to the brevity of those sections (Lunneborg, 1985), the Vocational Identity Scale section has much stronger psychometric support (Holland, Johnston, & Asama, 1993). The MVS was published by Consulting Psychologists Press. Although it is now out of print and unavailable for purchase, it is available free of charge for noncommercial use through the University of Maryland at education.umd.edu/EDCP/schoolassess/Tools/MVS/MVS.pdf.

STANDARDIZED TESTS RELATED TO CAREER ADJUSTMENT

As you have surely surmised from the many tests already discussed in this chapter, the field of career counseling has invested tremendously in the development of standardized tests to assist people who need help with career selection or are experiencing difficulties with career decision making.

Many people seek career counseling for these reasons; however, others seek career counseling due to adjustment difficulties. For one reason or another, they anticipate or experience stress, dissatisfaction, or performance difficulties at work, and these difficulties prompt them to seek your help. Although they may assume they simply need a new career and may initially voice a request for assistance in choosing a new career, you as the counselor should first understand the nature of their difficulties. Maybe they will ultimately decide to pursue another career, but it may also turn out that they need assistance with career adjustment.

Thus, a third type of standardized test commonly used in career counseling addresses issues of career adjustment. Such tests may focus on work readiness and employability skills, career concerns specific to occupational stress or in the broader context of life, and job satisfaction. Table 11.8 lists standardized tests related to career adjustment. The following subsections provide brief descriptions of each test.

TABLE 11.8   Standardized Tests Related to Career Adjustment*

Tests	Populations			
	K–12 School Settings	College Settings	Community Settings	Special Needs
ACT WorkKeys	HS		X	X
Adult Career Concerns Inventory				
Barrier to Employment Success Inventory		X	X	X
Becker Work Adjustment Profile	X			X
BRIGANCE Transition Skills Inventory	MS/HS			X
Career Attitudes and Strategies Inventory		X	X	
Career Futures Inventory				
Job Observation and Behavior Scale			X	X
Job Stress Survey			X	
Job Survival and Success Scale	HS	X	X	
Maslach Burnout Inventory		X	X	
Minnesota Satisfaction Questionnaire			X	
Minnesota Satisfactoriness Scales			X	
Occupational Stress Inventory			X	
Transition Behavior Scale	MS/HS			X
Transition Planning Inventory	MS/HS			X
Transition-to-Work Inventory	HS	X	X	
Workplace Skills Survey	HS	X	X	

*MS = middle school, and HS = high school.

ACT WorkKeys

The ACT WorkKeys assessments (ACT, Inc., 2012) represent the skills analysis component of the ACT Work Readiness System. Whereas the other ACT assessments addressed in this chapter involve tests of academic ability, WorkKeys focuses specifically on the skills needed for success in the workplace. These skills include foundational skills, which "measure cognitive abilities, as well as personal skills that allow for a prediction of how an employee will perform on the job" (Osborn, 2009, p. 217). Specifically, eight foundational skills are assessed by WorkKeys: reading for information, applied mathematics, locating information, applied technology, business writing, listening for understanding, workplace observation, and teamwork. WorkKeys also assesses soft skills, which include fit, talent, and performance. Fit refers to whether the results suggest a good fit between the test taker's interests and values and the careers under consideration. The talent scale focuses on attitude and behaviors that suggest the openness to feedback necessary to build on basic skills and learn higher-level skills. The performance scale is designed to screen for high-risk and/or unsafe employee behaviors such as drug use, aggression, stealing, and absenteeism. The WorkKeys assessments may be used in counseling settings to measure an individual's foundational and soft skills. The results can be compared to the skill requirements for the various careers under consideration in order to estimate the individual's readiness for immediate entry into each career. A major benefit of the WorkKeys Assessment System is that it also includes a training component called KeyTrain (act.org/workkeys/keytrain/), which can be used when deficits are identified. Using this system, individuals can focus on the specific areas in which they need further development. Individuals can also obtain a National Career Readiness Certificate (NCRC; act.org/products/workforce-act-national-career-readiness-certificate/) based on their scores on the WorkKeys assessments in applied mathematics, reading for information, and locating information. The WorkKeys assessments are published by ACT, Inc. and are available in online and for site-based administration.

Adult Career Concerns Inventory

A common point at which many individuals experience career adjustment concerns involves career transitions, especially those that are unplanned or involuntarily. As you recall from Chapter 3, Super's theory introduced the concepts of career adaptability; maxicycles; and recycling through a minicycle of exploration, establishment, maintenance, and disengagement (Super, Savickas, & Super, 1996). These concepts have great relevance to career adjustment, and the Adult Career Concerns Inventory (ACCI; Super, Thompson, & Lindeman, 1988) was designed by Super and his colleagues to assess the stages of a maxicycle or minicycle of most concern to individuals experiencing career adjustment issues. The ACCI consists of 61 items distributed across Super's four stages: exploration, establishment, maintenance, and disengagement. Clients rate their level of concern about each item, and the results provide a numeric and visual representation of the difficulties being experienced in each stage. Scores are also offered for the substages within each stage of Super's theory. Specific types of career interventions are recommended for difficulties in each stage. For example, adults with strong concerns related to the exploration stage will benefit from counseling interventions focused on self- and occupational exploration. Clients experiencing the greatest concerns in the maintenance stage may improve their job satisfaction by engaging in continuing education to help them maintain their currency and skill in their profession. The ACCI was published by Consulting Psychologists Press. Although it is now out of print and unavailable for purchase, it is available free of charge for noncommercial use through Vocopher (vocopher.com).

Barrier to Employment Success Inventory, Fourth Edition

The Barriers to Employment Success Inventory, Fourth Edition (BESI; Liptak, 2011) is intended for use with clients experiencing difficulties obtaining and/or keeping jobs. It is designed to assess five categories of possible barriers: personal and financial barriers, emotional and physical barriers, career decision-making and planning barriers, job-seeking knowledge barriers, and training and education barriers. The BESI can be self-administered and self-scored by clients, but it is best used within a counseling context. It provides a straightforward means of identifying issues interfering with employment and facilitates a discussion of those issues. In addition to the inventory to identify barriers, the BESI includes sections designed to help clients identify strategies and develop plans to overcome barriers. The BESI is published by and available for purchase from JIST Publishing.

Becker Work Adjustment Profile: 2

The Becker Work Adjustment Profile: 2 (BWAP; Becker, 2005) is a standardized test designed specifically for special populations, including people who have severe cognitive impairment, learning disabilities, physical disabilities, mental disorders, and economic disadvantage. Rather than being completed by a student or client, the BWAP is completed by an adult who is familiar with the student or client's typical behaviors and who can thereby base ratings on past observations. These ratings result in a composite score reflecting a person's overall work adjustment and in scores on four scales: work habits and attitudes, interpersonal relations, cognitive skills, and work performance skills. These scores can be useful in assessing a person's readiness for employment and for determining areas in which a person may need further development and/or ongoing support in order to adjust successfully to an employment setting. The BWAP is published by Elbern Publications and is available for purchase from vendors such as Program Development Associates (disabilitytraining.com).

BRIGANCE Transition Skills Inventory

The BRIGANCE Transition Skills Inventory (TSI; Brigance, 2010) is an assessment instrument designed specifically for use with middle school and high school students who are receiving special education services. It is a recent revision that combines elements of the former BRIGANCE Diagnostic Life Skills Inventory (Brigance, 1994) and the BRIGANCE Diagnostic Employability Skills Inventory (Brigance, 1995). As you will learn in Chapter 14, federal law requires that schools assist such students with the development of transition plans. These plans are directly related to future career adjustment issues because they outline what students will do following their completion of high school. This may include transition to postsecondary education, work, or sheltered work settings. The TSI assesses students in four domains related to transition planning: academic skills, awareness of postsecondary opportunities, capacity for independent living, and ability to access community services and be a good citizen. The Brigance TSI is published by and available for purchase from Curriculum Associates (curriculumassociates.com).

Career Attitudes and Strategies Inventory

The Career Attitudes and Strategies Inventory (CASI; Holland & Gottfredson, 1994) is an inventory that addresses nine elements related to career adjustment. Specifically, it consists of 130 items designed to assess job satisfaction, work involvement, skill development, dominant style, career worries, interpersonal abuse, family commitment, risk-taking style, and geographical barriers. Gottfredson (1996) described the CASI as "a systematic way of asking, 'how has your career been going?'" (p. 370). Whereas asking this question in a session may result in a nonspecific response such as "pretty well" or "not so good," the CASI requires a response that addresses numerous factors related to career adjustment. Scores on the CASI may be useful in identifying issues worthy of attention in career counseling and may help predict the degree of stability a person may experience in his or her career. The CASI is published by and available for purchase from Psychological Assessment Resources, Inc.

Career Futures Inventory–Revised

A revision of the earlier CFI (Rottinghaus, Day, & Borgen, 2005), the Career Futures Inventory–Revised (CFI-R; Rottinghaus, Buelow, Matyja and Schneider, 2012) is an instrument designed to assess aspects of career adaptability. Rottinghaus, Buelow, Matyja, and Schneider (2012) explain that career adaptability refers to Super's concept of "how adults adjust to the challenges of a changing world of work" (p. 124). Building on Savickas's theory of career construction, the authors of the CFI-R acknowledge that the world of work may change—and therefore require adaptation—due to normal developmental transitions (e.g., college graduation), job changes (e.g., job loss or promotion), or personal crises (e.g., serious injury affecting ability to work). Scores are reported on five subscales: career agency, negative career outlook, occupational awareness, support, and work–life balance. A relatively new instrument, the CFI-R was not yet on the market at the time of this writing.

Job Observation and Behavior Scale

The Job Observation and Behavior Scale (JOBS; Rosenberg & Brady, 2000) is an instrument designed to assess the quality of work adjustment being demonstrated by employees who have recently transitioned from school into work. It is particularly well suited for use with special populations and can be used in supported and sheltered work environments as well as competitive employment settings. The JOBS is completed by an employer or supervisor rather than a student or client. On each of the 30 items, the evaluator rates the employee both on the quality of his or her performance and on the level of support being provided to the employee in that area. Also for each item, the evaluator indicates whether the employee is using any adaptive technology or devices to perform each task. The items comprise three subscales: work-related daily living activities (e.g., hygiene, punctuality), work-required behavior (e.g., tolerating stress, demonstrating initiative), and work-required job duties. The JOBS is published by and available for purchase from the Stoelting Company (stoelting.com).

Job Stress Survey

The Job Stress Survey (JSS; Spielberger & Vagg, 1999) approaches the assessment of career adjustment by assessing sources of occupational stress. The authors explain that not only are workers motivated to reduce their level of stress (and thereby experience better career adjustment) but also employers should be motivated to attend to unnecessary stressors in the workplace because occupational stress can cause absenteeism, errors, and ultimately less productivity and profit for the employer. The 30 items on the JSS address events or duties that are generally considered stressful. For each item, respondents are asked to rate (a) how much stress they experience in response to that event or duty and (b) how frequently they have experienced that event or duty in the preceding six months. The JSS results in an overall score for job stress and two sets of subscale scores: one for stress attributed to the nature of the job and the other for stress due to insufficient support from the employer/organization. The JSS is published by and available for purchase from Psychological Assessment Resources.

Job Survival and Success Scale, Second Edition

Drawing heavily on Goleman's (1995, 1998) theory of emotional intelligence, the Job Survival and Success Scale, Second Edition (JSSS; Liptak, 2009), is based on the premise that succeeding at work not only requires getting the job via the use of job search skills and performing the job well using job-specific skills but also the demonstration of emotional intelligence. The JSSS focuses on skills related to emotional intelligence. Its 60 items are evenly distributed across five scales addressing emotional intelligence skills: dependability, responsibility, human relations, ethical behavior, and getting ahead. The JSSS can be used proactively, with high school and college students in advance of a job search, to allow for interventions designed to develop areas of weaknesses in the use of emotional intelligence skills. It may also be used with people who are already employed but not experiencing the level of success they desire. The JSSS is published by and available for purchase from JIST Publishing.

Maslach Burnout Inventory, Third Edition

Another factor influencing career adjustment is burnout. The Maslach Burnout Inventory, Third Edition (MBI; Maslach, Jackson, Leiter, & Schaufeli, 1996), is designed to assess for burnout. The MBI comes in three forms: the MBI-Human Service Survey (MBI-HSS) for people employed in human services, the MBI-Educators Survey (MBI-ES) for people employed as educators, and the MBI-General Survey (MBI-GS) for people employed in any other occupation. Each form of the MBI measures factors related to burnout and yields scores on the following three scales: emotional exhaustion, depersonalization, and personal accomplishment. Because burnout is most common among people who have been employed for an extended period of time, the MBI is most appropriate for use in the community setting. It could also be useful, however, in the college setting with returning students seeking a career change. The MBI can no longer be purchased from its original publisher (Consulting Psychologists Press); instead, the MBI is now available for purchase from MindGarden (mindgarden.com).

Minnesota Satisfaction Questionnaire

Although the most recent revision of the Minnesota Satisfaction Questionnaire (MSQ; Weiss, Dawis, England, & Lofquist, 1977) is dated, it is still available for purchase because it continues to offer surprisingly relevant information about the sources of work satisfaction that may contribute to career adjustment. As you recall from Chapter 2, the theory of work adjustment (TWA; Dawis & Lofquist, 1984) emphasizes the importance of worker satisfaction and worker satisfactoriness. The MSQ is designed to measure the level of worker satisfaction and is based on the TWA premise that satisfaction depends on how well the rewards of a job meet the needs of the worker. Respondents are asked to rate how satisfied they are with 100 aspects of their job, and these ratings result in scores on 21 different scales: ability utilization, achievement, activity, advancement, authority, company policies and practices, compensation, coworkers, creativity, independence, moral values, recognition, responsibility, security, social service, social status, supervision—human relations, supervision—technical, variety, working conditions, and general satisfaction. The MSQ was published by and remains available for purchase from the University of Minnesota. Purchasing information is available at psych.umn.edu/psylabs/vpr/msqinf.htm.

Minnesota Satisfactoriness Scales

Like the MSQ just described, the most recent revision of the Minnesota Satisfactoriness Scales (MSS; Gibson, Weiss, Dawis, & Lofquist, 1970) is also dated. It is still available for purchase because it continues to offer surprisingly relevant information about elements contributing to or detracting from a worker's satisfactoriness. These elements may also affect the quality of one's career adjustment. As you recall from Chapter 2, the theory of work adjustment (TWA; Dawis & Lofquist, 1984) not only emphasizes the importance of worker satisfaction but also worker satisfactoriness. The MSQ is designed to measure the degree of worker satisfactoriness and is based on the TWA premise that satisfactoriness depends on how well a worker's abilities match the ability requirements of a job. The MSQ is completed by the employee, but the MSS is generally completed by the employee's supervisor or boss; however, it may also be completed by a coworker. In rare instances, when an employee uses the MSS to rate him- or herself, the validity of the results obviously depend on the accuracy of the employee's self-perceptions and self-report. In addition to yielding a general satisfactoriness score, the MSS also offers scores on four subscales: performance, conformance, dependability, and personal adjustment. The MSS was published by and remains available for purchase from the University of Minnesota. Purchasing information is available at psych.umn.edu/psylabs/vpr/mssinf.htm.

Occupational Stress Inventory–Revised

The Occupational Stress Inventory–Revised (OSI-R; Osipow, 1998) approaches the assessment of career adjustment by attending to factors related to occupational stress. The OSI-R consists of three questionnaires. First, the Occupational Role Questionnaire measures the level and identifies the sources of occupational stress experienced by the test taker. It yields scores on six scales, each representing a different source of occupational stress: role overload, role insufficiency, role ambiguity, role boundary, responsibility, and physical environment. The second questionnaire in the OSI-R is the Personal Strain Questionnaire, which yields scores on four scales, each representing a different type of impact resulting from occupational stress: vocational strain, psychological strain, interpersonal strain, and physical strain. The third questionnaire in the OSI-R is the Personal Resources Questionnaire, which yields scores on four scales, each representing a strategy for coping with occupational stress: recreation, self-care, social support, and rational/cognitive coping. The OSI-R is published by and available for purchase from Psychological Assessment Resources.

Transition Behavior Scale, Third Edition

The Transition Behavior Scale, Third Edition (TBS-3; McCarney & Arthaud, 2012), is an instrument that focuses on future career adjustment and attempts to predict a student's success in navigating the transition from high school to the world of work and in living independently. It is intended specifically for use with middle school and high school students who are receiving special education services as part of the transition planning process. The TBS-3 has two forms. The School Version involves having a school staff member rate the student or client's typical behaviors; the Student Version is a self-report measure on which students rate themselves. The TBS-3 provides scores on three subscales: work-related, interpersonal relations, and social/community expectations. A *TBS IEP and Intervention Manual* (McCarney, 1989) is also available to assist school personnel in addressing areas of weakness in order to prepare students for transitioning. The TBS-3 is published by and available for purchase from Hawthorne Educational Services.

Transition Planning Inventory, Updated Version

The Transition Planning Inventory, Updated Version (TPI-UV; Clark & Patton, 2006), is another instrument that focuses on future career adjustment and attempts to predict a student's success in navigating the transition from high school to the world of work and in living independently. At least three people should use the TPI-UV to rate a student, and specific forms should be used: a Student Form for self-rating, a Home Form for parents to rate the student, and a School Form for teachers and other school personnel to rate the student. The TPI-UV provides scores on three subscales: employment, further education, communication, interpersonal relationships, leisure activities, community participation, health, daily living, and self-determination. The TPI-UV is published by and available for purchase from Pro-Ed, Inc.

Transition-to-Work Inventory, Third Edition

The Transition-to-Work Inventory, Third Edition (TWI-3; Liptak, 2012), is an instrument designed for use with a wide variety of clients. It is certainly appropriate for transition planning with students, but it is also appropriate for use with adults who are in transition. Adults may be experiencing transitions while searching for a new job, seeking a change, or preparing to reenter the workforce after absences due to a wide variety of reasons (e.g., parenting, incarceration, military service, unemployment). In contrast with the other transition-focused tests described in this chapter, the focus of the TWI-3 is not on evaluating a person's readiness for work; the TWI-3 is more similar to an interest inventory. It results in scores related to the 16 career clusters and facilitates exploration of careers to maximize the chances of satisfactory career adjustment following the transition. The TWI-3 is published by and available for purchase from Jist Publishing.

Workplace Skills Survey

As its title indicates, the Workplace Skills Survey (WSS; Industrial Psychology International Ltd, 1998) is an assessment of skills needed to succeed in the workplace. It can be used in educational, counseling, or employment settings not only to assess current skills but also to guide instruction about expected skills. The WSS yields a composite score as well as scores on six scales: work ethics, communication, teamwork, problem solving, adapting to change, and technological literacy. The WSS was originally published by Industrial Psychology International Ltd but it can no longer be purchased from this publisher; the WSS is now available for purchase from MetriTech (metritech.com) and from the Stoelting Company (stoelting.com).

PUTTING IT ALL TOGETHER

At this point in the chapter, I encourage you to pat yourself on the back and congratulate yourself because we covered a lot of ground in this section. First, you learned about standardized tests related to career selection. This large category includes tests that assess interests, personality, work-related values, academic abilities, and vocational aptitudes. Next you learned about standardized tests related to career decision making. These tests usually assess thoughts, emotions, and circumstances that influence decision making. You also learned about standardized tests related to career adjustment. Some of these tests focused on work readiness and employability skills; others focused on sources of job satisfaction and/or occupational stress.

I hope that you did not memorize these lists. My goal was simply to familiarize you with them enough to heighten your awareness of various options. In this way, you'll have a global sense of your testing options. As you encounter clients with various needs, you'll then be aware of these resources and you can refer to this text again. The next section provides even more resources.

ADDITIONAL RESOURCES

This chapter has presented a great deal of information about a number of standardized tests. Although my guess is that you are overwhelmed right now, you may want or need more information about the tests described in this chapter, and some additional resources would be valuable.

Test publishers often provide a great deal of information about the tests they develop and sell. In addition to identifying the purpose of each instrument, publishers tend to include additional information that your colleagues may not be able to provide. For example, some publishers identify the age range and reading level for which the instrument is appropriate, the length of time it takes to administer the test, administration and scoring options, and training requirements for users. Some publishers also identify supplemental materials that may be useful for providing additional information to your clients. Many publishers also provide sample interpretive reports for various instruments. A list of several test publishers and their websites is provided in Table 11.9.

TABLE 11.9 Examples of Career Counseling Test Publishers

Publisher	Website
Consulting Psychologists Press, Inc.	cpp.com
Creative Organizational Design	creativeorgdesign.com
CTB/McGraw-Hill	ctb.com
Educational Testing Service	ets.org
JIST Publishing, Inc.	jist.com
Kuder, Inc.	kuder.com
National Career Assessment Services, Inc.	kuder.com
National Occupational Competency Testing Institute	nocti.org
Paradigm Publishing	paradigm.emcpublishingllc.com
Pearson Assessments	pearsonassessments.com
Pro-Ed, Inc.	proedinc.com
Psychological Assessment Resources, Inc.	parinc.com
Scholastic Testing Service	ststesting.com
Sigma Assessment Systems	sigmaassessmentsystems.com
Talent Assessment, Inc.	talentassessment.com
U.S. Department of Labor	onetcenter.org
Vocational Research Institute	vri.org
Western Psychological Services	wpspublish.com
Wonderlic, Inc.	wonderlic.com

One disadvantage of using test publisher catalogs or websites when selecting tests is that the publishers seem convinced that every test they offer is of outstanding quality. As you will surely learn in the assessment class you take as part of your master's degree program, this certainly isn't the case and you will want to rely on other, more objective information when choosing a test. Table 11.10 lists some general resources related to standardized testing (which will be explored in depth in your assessment course) as well as two books specific to assessment in career counseling that I highly recommend.

APPLICATION TO OUR CAST OF CLIENTS

To help solidify your understanding of how standardized tests may be helpful in career counseling, let's take a look at how they might be used with our cast of clients. For each of our seven clients, I offer a brief overview of the kinds of tests that may be useful, and then provide more detailed information about how the results of one specific test may benefit each client.

Wayne Jensen: Welcome to Wayne's World

When meeting with Wayne, you are struck by his proactive approach to career management. Rather than passively await a layoff or assume a victim mentality, Wayne is demonstrating foresight in his anticipation of the layoff and his desire to search for a plan B. As you recall, Wayne followed in his father's footsteps and accepted a job at the Ford Motor Company immediately after high school graduation. Thus, Wayne never really engaged in career development activities while in high school. Now, though, his options are wide open and he is really unsure what direction to pursue should the layoff come to fruition. In this case, you might wisely choose to do an array of assessments with Wayne. Standardized tests related to interests and abilities might be particularly helpful.

With this in mind, let's say that you have Wayne take both the Self-Directed Search (SDS) and the Ability Explorer (AE). An advantage of both is that they can be self-administered and self-scored, which means that you can send them home with Wayne to complete between sessions and reduce the length and cost of career counseling for him. Conscientious as he is, Wayne returns with both instruments completed and is eager to learn from you what the results mean. You first review his SDS results and see that Wayne's Holland code is RIS (see Table 11.11).

Next, you examine his Ability Explorer results and are instantly struck by how consistent Wayne's self-reported abilities are with the interests suggested by his SDS results. Specifically, his highest level of interest is in realistic activities, and these activities tend to require

TABLE 11.10 Resources for Additional Information about Standardized Tests Used in Career Counseling

General Resources

Educational Testing Services Database
- ets.org/test_link/find_tests/

Mental Measurements Yearbook
- Available at your university library and online at buros.org/mental-measurements-yearbook

Tests in Print
- Available at your university library and online at buros.org/tests-print

Tests: A Comprehensive Reference for Assessments in Psychology, Education and Business
- Maddox, T. E. (2008). *Tests: A comprehensive reference for assessments in psychology, education and business* (6th ed.). Austin, TX: PRO-ED.

Resources Specific to Career Counseling

Using Assessment Results for Career Development
- Osborn, D. S., & Zunker, V. G. (2006). *Using assessment results for career development* (7th ed.). Belmont, CA: Brooks/Cole, Cengage Learning.

A Counselor's Guide to Career Assessment Instruments
- Whitfield, E. A., Feller, R., & Wood, C. (2009). *A counselor's guide to career assessment instruments* (5th ed.). Broken Arrow, OK: National Career Development Association.

TABLE 11.11 Results from Wayne's SDS and Ability Explorer

Self-Directed Search (SDS)	Ability Explorer
Realistic (R)	Manual/technical
Investigative (I)	Numerical/mathematical
Social (S)	Interpersonal

manual or technical abilities, which are Wayne's highest reported skill area. His second highest level of interest is in investigative activities, which tend to require numerical or mathematical abilities and these are Wayne's second highest reported skill area. His third highest level of interest is in social activities, which tend to require interpersonal abilities and are Wayne's third highest reported skill area. Such consistency between interests and abilities doesn't always occur, of course. In Wayne's case, though, he is fortunate to feel that his abilities are well matched to his occupational interest areas.

It would make sense to focus occupational exploration on these areas. As Wayne reads over the list of occupations consistent with a manual/technical–numerical/mathematical ability pattern, he notes three of particular interest to him: electricians; heating, air conditioning, and refrigeration mechanics and installers; and plumbers, pipefitters, and steam fitters. In the next stage of the career counseling process, you will likely teach Wayne how to explore information about each of these occupational areas.

Lily Huang Li Mei: Helping Li Mei Blossom

In getting to know Li Mei, you quickly begin to realize that her low levels of self-efficacy seem to be affecting not only her self-esteem but also her academic performance and her struggles with choosing a major. Because self-efficacy involves beliefs about oneself, you decide that it might be useful to administer the Career Beliefs Inventory (CBI) to Li Mei. This standardized test is designed to facilitate the exploration of problematic beliefs that may interfere in a person's career decision making and/or career development. Li Mei agrees to take the CBI, and her results reveal several beliefs that may interfere with her career development and ability to make a decision. These results are shown in Table 11.12. The first column of the table indicates the CBI scale and the second column describes the corresponding belief that has the potential to cause difficulty for Li Mei.

In discussing these beliefs with Li Mei, you will want to emphasize how her current beliefs could be problematic and identity beliefs that may be more helpful in facilitating her career development and decision making. Ideas for more helpful beliefs are identified in column three of the table. For example, review the information in Table 11.12 about self–other comparisons. To be sure, Li Mei has superstar siblings, both of whom were National Merit Scholarship finalists. Comparing herself to her siblings isn't really fair. More accurately, such a comparison isn't representative of how Li Mei compares to the rest of her peers.

To give more substance to the idea of comparing herself to average, normal college students, you may want to incorporate some other standardized test results into your discussion. In this case, you may use data already available to you: Li Mei's SAT scores. Although the annual means and standard deviations vary slightly from year to year, a general rule of thumb for the SAT is that each scale (math, critical reading, and writing) is normed to have a mean of 500 and a standard deviation of 100. This is reflected in the National Average column of Table 11.13.

Looking at the next column, notice that Li Mei's scores are notably higher than these national averages. Her scores are also higher than the average incoming freshman's scores at Chapman University. By helping Li Mei realize that her scores are clearly above average in comparison to the national pool of students and to students at Chapman, you may boost her confidence. As down as she is on herself, though, Li Mei may challenge this observation with the reality that she was waitlisted before being admitted. In response, however, you may also present the fact that her high school GPA of 3.2 was lower than the average GPA (3.5) of admitted students to Chapman. In this context, you might talk with Li Mei about the possibility that her low self-confidence has been interfering with her ability to achieve (GPA) to the level of her ability (SAT score). This might help frame self-confidence, rather than ability, as the actual problem.

Lakeesha Maddox: Doors and Windows

You may recall from Chapter 1 that Lakeesha had taken the Self-Directed Search while she was a student at Spelman College. At that time, her results suggested a Holland Code of Social-Artistic (SA) and this seems to resonate with her today. You decide, however, to have her take the Campbell Interest and Skills Survey (CISS) both to reaffirm this occupational interest pattern and, perhaps more important, to ascertain areas in which she is

TABLE 11.12 Potentially Problematic Beliefs Revealed by Li Mei's Career Beliefs Inventory Results

CBI Scale	Potentially Problematic Belief	More Helpful Belief
Acceptance of uncertainty	Li Mei believes that she should have already chosen a major and career path by now.	It may be useful for Li Mei to reframe her indecision as open-mindedness and to allow herself time for career exploration before making a decision.
College education	Li Mei believes that a college degree is essential to finding a good job and a respectable career.	Although college may be the path Li Mei has chosen and the only one acceptable to her parents, good jobs and respectable careers don't always require a college degree.
Peer equality	Li Mei believes that outperforming others, including her peers and siblings, is key to deserving respect from herself and others.	Rather than using the accomplishments of others as a metric of her success, Li Mei might be better served by competing with herself.
Responsibility	Li Mei believes that experts such as you can tell her what major and career she should choose.	Although career counselors can certainly help guide clients through the career exploration and decision-making process, Li Mei is ultimately responsible for choosing her career path.
Approval of others	Li Mei believes that it is essential that others, such as her parents, approve of her choice of major and career.	Although Li Mei greatly values her parents' opinions and desires their approval, it is also important to choose a major and career that she will find satisfying.
Self–other comparisons	Li Mei finds herself frequently comparing herself to her siblings, which contributes to a negative self-perception.	Rather than comparing herself to her siblings, who happen to be "off the chart, Li Mei would be wise to compare herself to average, normal college students. Another helpful strategy would be to shift her comparisons away from others and instead focus on comparing herself in the present with herself in the past and striving toward self-improvement.

especially confident in her skills. You also ask Lakeesha to take the 16PF personality test to take personality factors into consideration.

Rather than adhering to Holland's RIASEC typology, the CISS uses Campbell's interest orientations schema. As shown in Table 11.14, these two systems are quite similar. Aside from differences in word choice (e.g., *artistic* versus *creating*), the primary substantive difference is that Campbell has divided Holland's realistic type into two orientations: producing and adventuring.

Both the CISS and 16PF yield results using Campbell's orientations. Whereas the 16PF yields these orientations based on broad activity interests, the CISS bases them on interests *and* skills confidence. Table 11.15 presents select portions of Lakeesha's results on each of these instruments.

Let's begin by comparing the interest results for the CISS and the 16PF. You find that Lakeesha's responses to the items on these two tests resulted in the same rank order of interest orientations, with helping and creating as the areas of highest interest. This is slightly different from Lakeesha's early SDS results showing her top interests as social (helping) and enterprising (influencing). Part of this difference may be explained, though, by the skills confidence portion of the CISS. Notice that Lakeesha's results

TABLE 11.13 Li Mei's SAT Scores in Context

SAT Section	National Average	Li Mei	Chapman University
Math	500	650	606
Critical reading	500	580	601
Writing	500	610	598

Standardized Tests

TABLE 11.14 Campbell's Orientations Compared to Holland's Typology

Holland's Typology		Campbell's Interest Orientations	
R	Realistic	P	Producing
		A	Adventuring
I	Investigative	N	aNalyzing
A	Artistic	C	Creating
S	Social	H	Helping
E	Enterprising	I	Influencing
C	Conventional	O	Organizing

suggested much fewer skills confidence than interest in creative activities. Based on the comparisons of skills confidence and interests, the CISS recommends that Lakeesha pursue careers in the helping and influencing orientations, that she consider developing skills in the creating orientation, and that she further explore careers in the organizing and analyzing orientations because she has high skill confidence but less reported interest.

After discussing the CISS orientation results with Lakeesha, you then decide to focus on the basic scales for the two orientations for which the CISS recommended pursuit.

In Table 11.15, you can see that basic scales for each of these orientations are listed. After examining Lakeesha's CISS individual profile report, you describe the type of careers associated with each basic scale, show Lakeesha how her interests and skills confidence compared for each basic scale, and invite Lakeesha to respond. She expresses excitement about the idea of working in a religious setting but expresses less enthusiasm about working with children all day only to return home to take care of Nia and Nala. Lakeesha also seems quite interested in careers within the business sector and expresses curiosity about whether her degree in psychology would allow her to work in advertising, marketing, or even customer service. Lakeesha wonders aloud about whether working at a hotel might be a good fit for her. You assure her that all of these possibilities are worthy of further exploration and indicate that such exploration will be the focus of upcoming sessions.

Before launching into exploration, though, you want to ensure that the two of you have time to digest the results yielded from these two assessments. You then transition to the 16PF Career Development Report. You explain to Lakeesha that this report not only identifies some careers that may be well matched to her personality patterns but also provides information about her problem-solving resources, her patterns for coping with stress, her styles of interacting with others, her preferences for work settings

TABLE 11.15 Selected Results from Lakeesha's CISS and 16PF Tests

Selected Results from Campbell Interest and Skills Survey

Orientations	Interests	Skills	Recommendation
Pursue	Helping (70)	Helping (65)	Pursue
Pursue	Creating (65)	Creating (40)	Develop
Pursue	Influencing (62)	Influencing (60)	Pursue
Develop	Organizing (45)	Organizing (55)	Explore
Explore	Adventuring (40)	Adventuring (30)	Avoid
Develop	Analyzing (38)	Analyzing (55)	Explore
Avoid	Producing (35)	Producing (30)	Avoid
Basic scales in helping (in alphabetical order)	Adult development		
	Child development		
	Counseling		
	Medical practice		
	Religious activities		
Basic scales in influencing (in alphabetical order)	Advertising/marketing		
	Leadership		
	Law/politics		
	Public speaking		
	Sales		

(Continued)

TABLE 11.15 Selected Results from Lakeesha's CISS and 16PF Tests (*Continued*)

Selected Results from 16PF		
Career Activity and Career Field Interest Scores	Helping	
	Creating	
	Influencing	
	Organizing	
	Venturing	
	Analyzing	
	Producing	
Career fields consistent with activity interests	Child development	Social service
	Counseling	Art
	Fashion	Performing arts
	Music/dramatics	
Occupations consistent with activity interests	Interior decorator	Broadcaster
	Speech pathologist	English teacher
	Social worker	Musician
	Child-care worker	Artist, fine
	Guidance counselor	Artist, commercial
	Special education teacher	Writer/editor
	Elementary school teacher	Reporter
	Foreign language teacher	Minister
	Librarian	High school counselor
	Art teacher	Community service director
	Occupational therapist	Religious leader
Occupations in which others share Lakeesha's personal lifestyle patterns	Advertising executive	Buyer
	Paralegal	Corporate trainer
	Media executive	Bank manager
	Public relations director	Hotel manager
	Fitness instructor	Marketing Director
	Human resources director	

and roles within organizations, and suggestions for becoming even more effective at work and in relationships. Because of the extensiveness of this report, you ask Lakeesha to take it home with her, read over it carefully, highlight any areas she would like to discuss in more depth, and bring it back to the next session.

Vincent Santiago Arroyo: Caskets, Closets and Careers

Because Vincent is, in many ways, approaching the career exploration process for the first time, you decide that it would be worthwhile to have him take the Kuder Career Interests Assessment and the Kuder Skills Confidence Assessment. Taking both assessments requires a total of just 16 minutes on average, and this was the case with Vincent as well. In reviewing the results, you decide to focus on the composite report, which shows, in rank order, the clusters and pathways in which Vincent's results suggest the most interest and skills confidence (see Figure 11.1).

To explain these results to Vincent, of course, you first have to understand them yourself. You therefore used the time between the session in which Vincent took these tests and the session in which you interpreted them to study the results. You refreshed your memory about the

Standardized Tests **263**

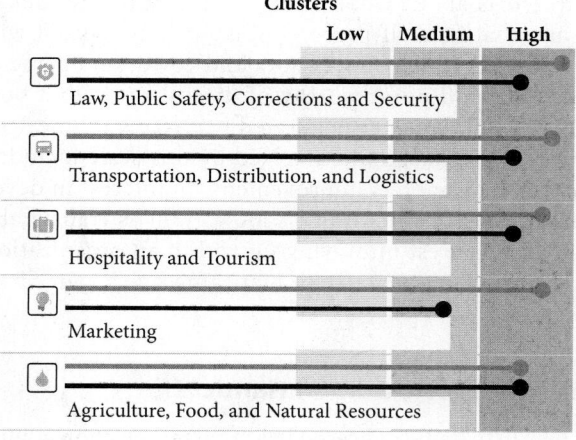

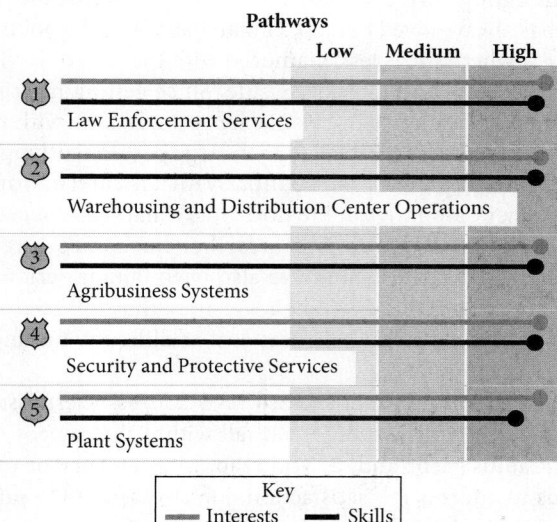

FIGURE 11.1 Vincent's Kuder Interest and Skills Confidence Composite Report

Source: From Kuder (2002). *Kuder Interest and Skills Confidence Composite Report.* Copyright © by 2002 by Kuder. Reprinted by permission.

difference between clusters and pathways so that you can explain to Vincent that there are 16 career clusters used nationally.

Of these 16, the results report shows the five in which Vincent's responses on the Kuder assessments suggest the greatest interest and skills confidence. The top line for each cluster indicates skills confidence and the bottom line reflects interest. You explain to Vincent at the next session that each of the clusters has a variety of pathways and that the display at the bottom of Figure 11.1 shows the five pathways for which Vincent's responses on the Kuder

assessments suggest the greatest interest and skills confidence. Notice that two of these pathways (law enforcement systems; security and protective services) fall within his highest ranked cluster (law, public safety, corrections, and security).

When Vincent sees these results, he smiles broadly. He is especially pleased to see that the results seem consistent with his long-standing interest in military service. Vincent is also excited to learn that there were a variety of civilian careers that would also match well with his interests and skills confidence. Although he laughs at the results related to agriculture and jokes about a city boy becoming a farmer, Vincent expresses a great deal of interest in learning more about careers related to public safety, corrections, security, and law enforcement. As you share the results with Vincent, you remind him that no test could possibly tell him what career he should choose or what path he should take. Instead, the tests are meant only to suggest a variety of occupations that seem well suited to his interests and skills, and that the next step is to do some additional career exploration to learn more about them before making a decision. The two of you agreed that Vincent would spend the next couple of weeks searching online to learn more about these occupations. You show Vincent how to use the Kuder Navigator website (kudernavigator.com) to explore occupations that were suggested by his assessment results, provide him with a handout identifying other useful career exploration websites, and give him a worksheet on which he can take notes about the occupations he explores.

Doris Bronner: Embitterment Versus Empowerment

In listening to Doris lament the many travesties she experienced while working at the insurance agency and the injustice of having been fired, you imagine that there are two sides of this story. From Doris's perspective, of course, she was misunderstood, mistreated, and unfairly fired. You wonder, though, whether Doris may be unaware of how others perceived her work and workplace behavior. Earlier in the counseling process, you expressed this curiosity to Doris, and she admitted that her supervisor and coworkers likely have a different perspective. At that point, you had asked Doris to engage in a "courageous conversation with one of her coworkers (see Chapter 9). However, Doris just wasn't able to bring herself to contact a coworker to complete this assignment.

Still believing that it might be useful for Doris to find out how she was perceived, you ask Doris whether she would be willing to sign a release to allow you to send a rating scale to her former boss at the insurance agency. You indicate that the rating scale is called the *Job Survival and Success Scale* (JSSS) and explain that you would like her to complete it and thus rate her own job survival and success skills. You suggest that it would be helpful for her former boss to complete it. This strategy would involve no direct contact between them; you could mail the rating scale along with the release and a letter requesting the supervisor's assistance, and he could mail the rating scale back to you. Doris expresses some reluctance and fear about what her former boss will say, but she ultimately agrees to your suggestion.

Just to make sure, though, you wait until your next session to have her sign the release form. You begin this session by recapping your reasons for wanting information about how Doris was perceived at the insurance agency, and you show Doris the JSSS along with letter of request you have prepared. After reviewing these materials, Doris agrees and signs the information release form. You then have Doris complete the JSSS and, after the session, you send the rating scale to her former supervisor.

To your delight, you receive a completed rating scale back from Doris's former boss within a week. Attached to the rating scale was a handwritten note expressing hope that the information will be helpful to Doris and wishing her the best. You get the sense that the supervisor cares about Doris's welfare and suspect that it may have been difficult for him to fire her. In preparation for your next session with Doris, you prepare a summary of how the two sets of ratings compare (see Table 11.16).

Based on these results, you note two specific topics you would like to discuss in your next session with Doris. First, Doris's self-ratings are consistently higher than the ratings offered by her former boss. Although Doris rated herself as at least average on four of the five scales, her former supervisor rated her as at least average on only one scale. Thus, it will be important to talk with Doris about what it might take in future jobs to ensure that her self-perception is more consistent with the ways in which supervisors and coworkers perceive her. A second point worthy of discussion is that both Doris and her former boss rated her as low on the "getting ahead" scale. Skills assessed by this scale include a focus on continuous improvement, an interest in developing skills specific to one's job as well as transferable skills, an interest in moving up within an organization, and a conscious practice of managing one's own career development.

Gillian Parker: Golden Handcuffs

Rather than being concerned with career selection, Gillian is struggling with issues of career satisfaction. Although she has always loved her job, Gillian has reached a point in her life where she is less enamored with the idea of having her career be the center of her life. Since getting married, Gillian has been able to balance her personal life with her work life, but this has been due in large part to working in the same city as her husband. With an international assignment looming on the horizon, Gillian has concerns about what this would mean for her husband's career. Gillian and her husband have also been talking seriously about having children. When she adds that to the equation, Gillian anticipates a great deal of difficulty finding a work–life balance.

Few, if any, standardized tests address these issues directly. Gillian's issues would fall within the category of work adjustment and, as you read, this category of tests tends to address job satisfaction, job stress, and the satisfactoriness of employees. Having made partner on the fast track and consistently received outstanding feedback on her performance, Gillian is clearly much more than satisfactory as a worker. Tests focused on occupational satisfaction wouldn't be appropriate because Gillian has always enjoyed her work as an auditor, and tests focused on occupational stress wouldn't likely yield any information

TABLE 11.16 Comparison of Doris's Self-Rating and Supervisor Rating on the Job Skills Survival Scale

	Doris's Self-Ratings		Supervisor's Ratings of Doris	
Scale	Score	Range	Score	Range
Dependability	42	High	31	Average
Responsibility	33	Average	17	Low
Human relations	31	Average	20	Low
Ethical behavior	41	Average	23	Low
Getting ahead	22	Low	18	Low

Gillian hasn't already articulated in her sessions with you. A test focused on work transitions wouldn't fit because Gillian has not made a decision to leave her job. She is, however, considering the possibility of making some changes in her work life. If pushed to select a test for you to administer to Gillian, I might choose to administer the Career Anchors Self-Assessment.

This assessment seeks to identify a person's career anchor, which Schein (2006a) defines as "that one element in a person's self-concept that he or she will not give up, even in the face of difficult choices" (p. 6). You therefore describe this test to Gillian, provide her with login information to take the test online, and ask her to download and read the results report and bring it to your next session. You make a note to bring a copy of the *Career Anchors Participant Workbook* (Schein, 2006a) for Gillian's next session.

Gillian takes the assessment and brings her results report with her to the next session. Table 11.17 summarizes Gillian's results. When you ask Gillian to describe her reactions to the instrument and results, she describes them as "fascinating." She is particularly struck by how close her scores are on the technical/functional competence (TF) and the lifestyle (LS) scales. Gillian explains that the test "hit the nail on the head" by identifying how important it is to her to be at the top of her game by exercising her technical and functional competence. She indicates that she has always taken great pride in being recognized for her expertise and competence. When asked for her reactions to her high score on the lifestyle scale, Gillian remarks that this would never have been that important to her before, meaning before she married her husband and before they started thinking about having children. Indeed, the *Career Anchors* assessment captures her conundrum perfectly.

You are glad to hear this, of course, and express as much. You explain to Gillian that the value of this instrument is not only in assessing current issues but also in guiding future decisions. Specifically, as Gillian weighs her options, she will want to consider the degree to which each option allows her to honor her TF anchor but also addresses her LS needs. As an example, because the TF anchor is generally associated with people who "derive [their] sense of identity from the exercise of [their] skills and are most happy when [their] work permits [them] to be challenged in these areas" (Schein, 2006b, p. 3), Gillian would likely find herself rather dissatisfied with an easy accounting job, even if it allowed her to avoid relocation and/or cut back on her work hours. The degree to which possible options allow Gillian to exercise her skills and to feel challenged should be a metric by which she assesses them.

Juan Martinez: Bloques de Construcción para un Futuro Nuevo (Building Blocks for a New Future)

Near the beginning of your work with Juan, the two of you developed a counseling plan (see Figure 9.1 in Chapter 9). As part of the plan, you agreed that it was important to determine his physical abilities and limitations, his other abilities and limitations, and his areas of interest. You identified a number of standardized tests he would take. One of these was the Valpar Computerized Ability Test (VCAT). You chose the VCAT for several reasons, including the availability of the test in both English and Spanish, and the audio option which allows test takers to hear the directions through the computer's speakers. This assessment of Juan's academic and general educational development aptitudes would be less likely to reflect his English language proficiency and more likely to reflect his actual abilities. Given that you will be testing Juan's English proficiency with another test, the VCAT's Spanish and audio options are particularly appealing to you. As an added bonus, the VCAT also includes a pictorial interest assessment.

After ensuring that Juan understood how to use the computer's mouse and space bar to answer questions on this computerized aptitude test, you administer the VCAT to him. After he completes the test, you use the remainder of the session to debrief and discuss his reactions to it, with the agreement that you will present the results report at your next session. During the debriefing discussion, one of the questions you ask Juan is whether any of the jobs that he saw in the interest assessment caught his eye.

TABLE 11.17 Gillian's Results on the Career Anchors Self-Assessment

Gillian's Anchor	TF: Technical/functional competence is:	
Gillian's Scores:	TF: Technical/functional competence	26
	LS: Lifestyle	25
	EC: Entrepreneurial creativity	17
	SE: Security/stability	14
	CH: Pure challenge	13
	AU: Autonomy/independence	11
	SV: Service/dedication to a cause	11
	GM: General managerial competence	9

TABLE 11.18 Juan's Results on the Valpar Computerized Ability Test

Interest Survey Results

Top three interest areas: Industrial Mechanical Protective

Ability Test Results

Academic subjects

Subtest	Grade Level (3, 5, 7, 9, 11, 13)
Reading = 7	
Spelling = 5	
Vocabulary = 7	
Mathematics = 8	
Editing	No Data

General educational development (GED) scores

Factor	Low (1, 2, 3, 4, 5, 6) High
Reasoning	
Mathematical	
Language	

Vocational aptitude scores

Aptitudes	Low (5, 4, 3, 2, 1) High
General learning ability	
Verbal	
Numerical	
Spatial perception	
Form perception	
Clerical perception	
Color discrimination	

Source: From Valpar International Corporation (2002). *Valpar Career Ability Test (VCAT) Individual Report.* Copyright © 2002 by Valpar International Corp. Reprinted by permission.

Although he can't remember all of them, Juan indicates that he got some good ideas from this part of the test. For example, he had not thought about it until now, but jobs involving the operation of motor vehicles appeal to him. Specifically, he notices jobs such as bus driver, crane operator, and truck driver. You jot these down as he talks and make a mental note to discuss them during next week's test interpretation.

In preparation for that session, you print out Juan's VCAT individual report and create a brief summary of the aptitude testing results. This summary is displayed in Table 11.18.

The results from the pictorial interest assessment are consistent with Juan's previous enjoyment of the construction industry and his newly piqued curiosity about jobs such as bus driver, crane operator, and truck driver. The results from the VCAT ability test indicate that his academic skills have slipped somewhat in the 16 years since he attended high school. Juan would likely need to take some adult education classes to refresh these skills prior to taking the GED. The results also suggest that it would be most appropriate to search occupations within Job Zone 1 to identify only those jobs not requiring higher education and perhaps not requiring a high school diploma or GED certificate. In terms of vocational aptitude, Juan's spatial perception is notable and suggests that he could be highly successful in occupations requiring spatial perception skills.

PUTTING IT ALL TOGETHER

This chapter introduced you the use of standardized tests in career counseling. Standardized tests are only one type of assessment you may use to understand and assist your clients, but they remain an important helping strategy in the career counseling process. As you begin to integrate testing into your counseling practice, you will find a wide array of standardized tests well suited to career counseling. My hope is that you will leave this chapter with a number of takeaways:

- The range of standardized tests related to career selection
- The range of standardized tests related to career decision making
- The range of standardized tests related to career adjustment
- How some of these tests were used with our hypothetical cast of clients and how they can be used with your future clients

At this point in the text, you've now learned about three important approaches to understanding and helping clients with career issues: the career and culture genogram, the intake assessment, and standardized tests. Whether clients wish to talk about career or personal issues, you will likely find a need to use each of these approaches frequently. Other assessment and intervention strategies are also important; in Chapter 12, you will learn how to use card sorts in counseling.

CHAPTER 12

Card Sorts

This chapter will introduce you to the use of card sorts in career counseling. As the name suggests, this technique involves having a client sort through a deck of cards and arrange the cards in various ways. Sorting the cards, explaining reasons for card placement, identifying themes, and discussing the process can serve as both assessment and intervention. Clients and counselors alike tend to enjoy card sorts and find them useful in the career counseling process.

Some card sorts in career counseling involve as few as seven cards (Athanasou & Hoskiug, 1998), but most include many cards, with some consisting of a hundred or more. Depending on the purpose of the card sort, each card generally features a specific occupational title, a skill or aptitude, or a career-related value. In addition to the name of the occupation, skill, or value, each card may include supplemental information, for instance, a description or example of the occupation, skill, or value, and perhaps a code. Some vocational card sorts include a code consistent with Holland's typology (RIASEC: realistic, investigative, artistic, social, enterprising, conventional) to help with the counselor's analysis of the card arrangement.

EARLY PIONEERS

Leona E. Tyler

The card-sort technique was first introduced in 1960 during a presidential address to the American Psychological Association's (APA's) Division of Counseling Psychology by psychologist Leona E. Tyler. Tyler did not develop the card sort as a career counseling technique but rather as a way to understand individuals by understanding their choices and the way they organized them. The card sort she described in her presidential address and subsequent publication (1961), however, was quickly recognized as an important contribution to the field of career counseling.

Tyler's occupational card sort involved three major elements: (1) the cards, (2) the categories, and (3) the process used for the card sort. Tyler's card sort consisted of 100 cards, each of which contained the name of a different occupation, and the categories she used were Would Not Choose, Would Choose, and No Opinion. The process she used began with the following instructions:

> I would like you to place over here in the *Would Not Choose* column all of the occupations you see as out of the question for a person like you and to place in the *Would Choose* column those you can see as possibilities for a person like you. If you can't make a decision, place the card under *No Opinion*. (Tyler, 1961, p. 195)[†]

[†]*Source:* Tyler, L.E. (1961). Research explorations in the realm of choice. *Journal of Counseling Psychology,* 8, 195–201. American Psychological Association. Reprinted with permission.

Interest inventories typically instruct clients to rely solely on their interests and how much an occupation appeals to them when responding; however, Tyler recognized instead that a client may have many reasons for placing an occupation in a column. These reasons might involve level of interest, perceived level of skill or aptitude, cultural factors, or even practical considerations. In fact, the next part of Tyler's process involved talking with clients about the reasons for card placements. Specifically, after clients completed their initial placement of all 100 cards into the three categories, Tyler would remove the cards in the No Opinion column and say to the client:

> Now I would like you to break up these big groups into smaller groups of occupations that for some reason go together in your mind. Place those you reject for one reason into one group, those you reject for another reason into a second group, and so on. On the positive side, place those you would choose for one reason in one group, those you would choose for another reason into a second group, and so on. There are no rules about the number of groups you should come out with or about the number of cards in each group. (Tyler, 1961, pp. 195–196)†

By asking clients to group the cards into these thematic groups and assign meaning to them, Tyler clearly took a constructivist approach. Career counselors who prefer a more narrative or constructivist approach may be especially interested in using the card-sort technique with clients.

After her clients completed this step and created groups for the Would Choose and Would Not Choose categories, Tyler asked them to explain what each group represents and then asked follow-up questions. Tyler also asked her clients to identify "which of the negative groups and which of the positive groups" they saw as most important for themselves (p. 196).

Because the card sort was never intended to be a standardized assessment, which would require certain levels of reliability and validity along with standardized content and a standardized form of administration (Goldman, 1983), this technique is especially amenable to modifications. Indeed, modifications have abounded ever since.

†*Source:* Tyler, L.E. (1961). Research explorations in the realm of choice. *Journal of Counseling Psychology, 8,* 195–201. American Psychological Association. Reprinted with permission.

Robert H. Dolliver

Soon after Tyler (1961) published her article about the occupational card sort, an aspiring doctoral student named Robert H. Dolliver chose to focus on card sorts in his dissertation research (Slaney & MacKinnon-Slaney, 2000). One could say that Dolliver's dissertation and the 1967 article that stemmed from it made Tyler famous for her development of the card-sort technique. Whereas Tyler referred to her method simply as "Choice Patterns—A New Technique" (1961, p. 195), Dolliver gave her technique a title that stuck. Throughout his article, he referred to "the Tyler technique" as the "Tyler Vocational Card Sort (TVCS)" (p. 916), and references to the TVCS have appeared in the literature ever since.

In his dissertation work, Dolliver made several modifications to and extensions of the card-sort technique initially introduced by Tyler. In addition to coining the phrase "vocational card sort" and describing it as "a structured interview technique" (Dolliver, 1967, p. 916), Dolliver made several other important contributions. To begin with, he changed the names of the categories (see Table 12.1). Although these category names are only slightly different, Dolliver's categories are preferable because they allow for more ambivalence or conflicting reasons in each of the first two categories. The initial instructions that Dolliver offered were also slightly different from Tyler's approach. He described the Might Choose category as being for "occupations you might actually choose, or that have some specific appeal to you, or that seem appropriate for a person like you" (Dolliver, 1967, p. 917). Conversely, the Would Not Choose column was for occupations the client would not choose, that do not have appeal, or that seem inappropriate for a person like him or her. The In Question grouping was for "those occupations about which you are indifferent, uncertain, or in question" (p. 917).

In the next iteration of the card-sort method, Dolliver paralleled Tyler by asking clients to group the first and third column cards into themes. He extended this stage, however, by including processing questions. For example, if a client identified a theme in the Would Not Choose column by saying that one of the grouping themes involved sales, the counselor would ask the client to elaborate on what it is about sales she or he dislikes.

Dolliver added two more steps to Tyler's method. Following completion of the thematic groupings, Dolliver asked clients to return to the Might Choose column and

TABLE 12.1 Card-Sort Categories

Tyler	Would choose	No opinion	Would not choose
Dolliver	Might choose	In question	Would not choose

rank-order the 10 occupations they most prefer. Next, he presented clients with a checklist called Requirements for an Ideal Job (Rosenberg, 1957; as cited in Dolliver, 1967), which he used to explore aspects of a job that would be motivating to them. Using the rank-ordering process once more, Dolliver asked clients to rank-order these work motives. He concluded the process by asking clients to review the sheet on which he recorded his notes about the card arrangements, the groupings, and the work motives, and then invited them to clarify or correct the notes as needed.

Dolliver's modifications and expansions of Tyler's original technique represent important contributions to the development of the card-sort technique (Slaney & MacKinnon-Slaney, 2000). I propose that Tyler and Dolliver might collectively be considered the "parents" of the vocational card-sort technique. Indeed, their work formed the foundation for future developments of this approach. Important developments were soon to come.

Subsequent Modifications

A notable weakness of Dolliver's approach involved the source of the occupations that were listed on his cards. In developing his card sort, Dolliver did not use Tyler's original 100 cards (whose source for the occupations was not identified). Instead, he used the 51 occupations that appeared on the *male* scale for the Strong Vocational Interest Blank (SVIB). Relying exclusively on the male scale of the SVIB left Dolliver open to criticisms related to the use of the card sort with women and the inherent sexism of the card sort he developed. Several addressed this problem. Dewey (1974), for example, developed the Non-Sexist Vocational Card Sort. In addition to using both male and female scales as sources for occupational titles, she modified the names of the occupations as necessary to render them gender-neutral. For example, she changed the word *salesman* to *salesperson* (Dewey, 1974, p. 312).

Slaney (1978) developed a slightly different method for his Vocational Card Sort (VCS). His unique contribution was the introduction of six cards containing the names of the six Holland types (RIASEC) and descriptions of each type, and cards representing each of the basic interest scales on the Strong Campbell Interest Inventory (SCII). Before having clients complete the card sort according to Dewey's methodology, Slaney asked clients "to rank the six cards according to 'how similar you believe each type is to the way you are'" (Slaney, 1978, p. 522) and to sort the basic interest scale cards into three categories representing the client's level of interest in each of the titles. Similarly, Williams (1978) greatly expanded the number of occupations listed on the cards (to 144) and published an article that drew attention to the flexibility of the card-sort technique.

Jones (1979) was interested in using the card-sort technique with junior and senior high school students and developed a card sort called the Occu-Sort (O-S; which is also referred to as the Occ-U-Sort [O-U-S]). The O-S was described as a "self-guided career exploration system," and it consisted of 60 cards (Jones & DeVault, 1979, p. 384). In addition to the name of the occupation, the front of each card included the occupation's Holland code and another code referring to the level of education required for that occupation. The back of each card included the most recent *Dictionary of Occupational Titles* description of the occupation.

In 1980, even Holland himself became involved in the card-sort business with his publication of the Vocational Exploration and Insight Kit (VEIK; Holland & Associates, 1980; Takai & Holland, 1979), which basically consisted of a vocational card sort combined with the Self-Directed Search (Takai & Holland, 1979). In addition to evenly distributing the occupational titles across the six RIASEC types, Holland gave considerable attention to the processing questions used to prompt client insight and encourage further vocational exploration. As one example, Holland's card sort included "a specific step developed to confront a person with the role that sex, race, religion, or social class may have played in sorting occupational titles" (Takai & Holland, 1979, p. 313).

Moore, Gysbers, and Carlson (1980) published the Missouri Occupational Preference Inventory (MOPI), a card sort intended for use with high school students. The MOPI consisted of 180 cards that are evenly distributed across three levels of educational requirements (high school, high school plus additional training, and college) and included occupations for all six Holland types, although they were not evenly divided among these types (Slaney & MacKinnon-Slaney, 2000). One major departure from the Tyler/Dolliver methodology is that Moore, Gysbers, and Carlson changed the categories for sorting the cards to Like, Undecided, and Dislike.

A very similar categorization was used by the final card sort to be addressed in this history section: the Missouri Occupational Card Sort (MOCS), which was created by Hansen and Johnston (1989). Like many of its predecessors, the MOCS was designed to be consistent with the Holland typology and consisted of 90 cards, which were evenly distributed across the RIASEC categories. The name of the occupation appeared on the front of the card, and occupational information appeared on the back. This card sort was geared specifically to the needs of college students to help them learn more about themselves and the world of work and to "expand or restrict the range and/or the appropriateness of occupations" they were considering (Bikos, Krieshok, & O'Brien, 1998, p. 139).

Notice that the change in categories reflected in the MOPI and the MOCS could have significant effects on the client's placement. When moving to this language, the card sort becomes much more exclusively about the assessment of the client's interests rather than being open to the client's broader reasons for choosing an occupation. For example, consider a client who likes the idea of becoming a singer and has fantasies of winning on the television show *American Idol*. On the MOCS or MOPI card sorts, she might place "professional singer" in the Like column. On the previous versions of the card sort, however, she might place this same card in the Would Not Choose column based on her near certainty that she lacks the skills; her career-related values of having a job that is stable, safe, and secure; her introverted personality; or practical considerations.

Later in this chapter, in the section called How-to Guide, you'll see that one of the steps involved in doing a card sort is to identify the categories into which your client sorts the cards. Notice here the importance of carefully selecting appropriate categories to serve your purpose in using a card sort. If your purpose is to focus only on a client's interests at that point in time, using the Like, Neutral/Undecided, and Dislike columns may be ideal. If your purpose is broader, you may want to consider using Might Choose, In Question, and Would Not Choose as your categories. You can also identify other categories that would better meet your client's needs.

USING THEORY

Even when using a technique such as a card sort, theory can guide your work. For example, Dolliver used Kelly's personal construct theory, a theory of personality (Kelly, 1955; as cited in Dolliver, 1967). This theory is recognized as the origin of contemporary constructivist theories of career development (Sharf, 2010). This section will explore how some of the career development theories discussed in Chapters 2 to 5 might influence your use of card sorts.

Trait Factor Theory: Person-Environment Fit

As discussed in the previous section, the vast majority of early card sorts were designed around Holland's typology, with occupations distributed across the six RIASEC types. Thus, it is nearly impossible to separate these early approaches to the card sort from Holland's theory. Contemporary uses of card sorts are often guided by trait factor theory and focus on occupational interests. In this approach, each card generally includes an occupational title and is classified as representing one of the Holland RIASEC types. The client then sorts these cards into columns, which might be specifically focused on level of interest and use headings such as Like, Neutral/Undecided, and Dislike (Moore, Gysbers, & Carlson, 1980, Hansen & Johnston, 1989). Given this theory's emphasis on matching people with their environments, the results of the card sort could be used to help clients better understand their personal Holland code and guide their exploration of occupations and careers that have similar Holland codes.

Trait Factor Theory: Theory of Work Adjustment

As discussed in Chapter 2, the theory of work adjustment (TWA; Dawis & Lofquist, 1984) is concerned with both the person's satisfaction with the job *and* the person's satisfactoriness. For maximum satisfactoriness, TWA points to the need for a good match between the person's abilities and the skill requirements of the job. To facilitate maximum satisfaction, TWA calls attention to the match between the person's work-related values (needs) and the reinforcers associated with the occupation (Sharf, 2010).

One card sort designed specifically around the satisfaction portion of TWA theory is the *O*NET™ Work Importance Locator* (U.S. Department of Labor, Employment and Training Administration, 2000a). This card sort is available free of charge through the Occupational Information Network (O*NET), an Internet-based resource developed and maintained by the U.S. Department of Labor (onetcenter.org/WIL). Using this card sort, clients can identify their work-related values and needs in accordance with TWA. Specifically, the card sort allows clients to calculate scores in the following six areas: (1) achievement, (2) independence, (3) recognition, (4) relationships, (5) support, and (6) working conditions. These areas represent the client's needs. In the next step, the counselor helps the client identify and explore occupations or careers that offer reinforcement in the areas most important to the client.

Learning Theories

To my knowledge, no card sorts designed around any of the social learning theories of career development have been published for commercial use. Remember, however, that one major benefit of card sorts involves how amenable they are to modification. To use a card-sort activity from a learning theory perspective, you can design your own header cards to accompany already existing cards that name specific skills or activities, or you can design an entire set of cards. If you are using already existing cards that name specific activities or occupations, header cards would help clients identify their beliefs about the rewards of those activities or occupations (outcome expectations) and/or their beliefs about their ability to succeed in them (self-efficacy). Counselor-created categories could include headings such as Rewarding, Uncertain, and Unrewarding or headings such as Have Skills to Succeed, Could Learn Skills to Succeed, and Couldn't Learn Skills to Succeed. Given the emphasis in these theories on the importance of a client's beliefs about the likely results of various behaviors and activities, the results of card sorts using headers such as those suggested here could be used to help clients articulate their beliefs. In facilitating the follow-up discussion, the counselor may or may not want to challenge these beliefs.

Theory of Circumscription and Compromise

As discussed in Chapter 3, Gottfredson (1981) made a key contribution to our understanding of career development by drawing our attention to the role that two diversity-related factors play in our willingness to consider various occupations or careers as acceptable options. Specifically, she addressed the early tendency of many people to circumscribe their career options based on perceived gender-role incongruence and their perceptions of the prestige associated with given occupations. Gottfredson also believed that, later in their career development, people also compromise and decide not to pursue certain careers that were still on the table, so to speak. Compromises may occur based on internal factors, such as a "mismatch between [a person's] interests and abilities" (Gottfredson, 1981, p. 571), the level of effort required to attain a goal, or external factors (e.g., when there is a mismatch between a person's preferred career direction and the job market). If guided by the theory of circumscription and compromise, a counselor might choose to use a card sort to explore circumscription by having clients sort the cards into categories such as Too Masculine, Just Right, and Too Feminine or categories such as Not Good Enough for Me, Just Right for Me, and Too Good for Me. Similarly, a counselor can use a card sort to explore compromise by having clients sort cards into categories related to the zone of acceptable alternatives. Such categories might include Too Hard to Attain, Just Right, and Too Easy or Job Market Wise, Not Sure, and Job Market Unwise. The follow-up discussion can also address the dynamics of circumscription and/or compromise.

Constructivist Theories

As explained in Chapter 5, constructivist career development theories include Cochran's (1997) narrative approach and Savickas's (2002) career construction theory. Both theories emphasize how individual clients make (construct) meaning of their experiences, the role of work in their lives, and the meaning of their career-related problems.

Although Sharf (2010) seems to credit Cochran (1997) with the first application of constructivist theory to the use of vocational card sorts, I contend that Tyler's (1961) card sort included constructivist elements. Tyler was interested primarily in understanding individual differences, and her approach to card sorts featured a distinctly constructivist element. Dolliver (1967) was even more specific about using the constructivist approach with card sorts, specifically integrating and articulating components of Kelly's personal construct theory (Kelly, 1955; as cited in Dolliver, 1967). Thus, it is appropriate to credit Tyler (1961) and Dolliver (1967) with the initial application of constructivist theory to vocational card sorts.

However, Cochran (1997) did elaborate on the application of constructivist theory in his narrative approach to career counseling. He explicitly demonstrated, with case examples, how a constructivist career counselor could assist clients in identifying themes and meanings associated with their categorization and grouping of cards and related to their career dilemmas. Cochran gave examples of how counselors might help clients recognize polarities associated with their groupings in the Accept column and the Reject column in order to identify constructs. For example, a counselor might help a client recognize a theme in the Accept column as "being able to take credit for good results" and a theme in the Reject column as a "fear of being held accountable for bad results" (Cochran, 1997, p. 45). In this way, clients can begin to realize the meanings they associate with various occupations and careers, and to think critically about them.

HOW-TO GUIDE

Although this section provides you with some basic instructions (a how-to guide) for using the card-sort technique with any client and any career development theory, a note of caution is important. I encourage you to view this section not as a sure-fire formula for success but rather as a general set of guidelines that you can apply in most circumstances. It is essential that counselors use critical thinking skills and demonstrate flexibility when using techniques or following guidelines for the application of techniques. Both are important to enhance your ability to meet the needs of any given client and to allow you to adapt counseling approaches so that they fit well with your own personal style. See Table 12.2 for a step-by-step guide to using card sorts in career counseling. I will explain each step in more detail in the following subsections.

Step 1: Identify Your Purpose

Because card sorts can be used for a variety of purposes, your first step in using them is to identify your purpose. You might want to (a) assess your client's expressed occupational

TABLE 12.2 Steps for Using a Card-Sort Technique
1. Identify your purpose.
2. Obtain or create cards.
3. Identify the categories or continuum.
4. Create header cards and a corresponding worksheet.
5. Introduce the card sort and explain the process to your client.
6. Observe while the client completes the card arrangement.
7. Engage in iterative activities.
8. Record the results.
9. Process the activity.
10. Engage in closure discussion.

interests, self-reported skills and aptitudes, or career-related values; (b) gain an understanding of the central constructs or meanings that are important to your client with regard to career; (c) help your client organize his or her thinking about various elements related to career selection; or (d) encourage your client to explore a wider range of possible careers.

Step 2: Obtain or Create Cards

Once you have determined your purpose for the card sort, obtain or create a deck of cards designed for that purpose. Most likely, you will seek or develop cards that focus on (a) occupational titles, (b) skills or activities involved in occupations, or (c) career-related values. A variety of card sorts are available commercially at surprisingly affordable cost, and a list of commercial vendors is included at the end of this chapter. Because card sorts are not standardized assessments, you may choose to create your own cards.

Step 3: Identify the Categories or Continuum

Next, identify the categories or continuum you will be using for the card sort. Your decision is likely to depend not only on your purpose but also on the theory guiding your work. For example, you might want to use a card sort to conduct an assessment of occupational interests in accordance with Holland's person-environment fit theory. In this case, the cards would identify jobs (e.g., nurse, firefighter, teacher, chemist) and/or occupational activities (e.g., typing, working outdoors, solving problems, using numbers), with each job or occupational activity corresponding with one of the six types posited by Holland (realistic, investigative, artistic, social, enterprising, and conventional). The client is then asked to read each card and place it in a column reflecting one of the categories you have preselected. So far in this chapter, we have used three categories, but more are certainly possible. Table 12.3 illustrates four possible column headers that you could use if your purpose is to explore a client's occupational interests.

Other possibilities are also available. For example, rather than using columns, some card sorts have clients sort the cards into two-dimensional categories. This approach can be used when exploring more than one dimension related to the cards. For example, a counselor may want to use a skills card sort to explore a client's interests in and perceived aptitude or skill level for given occupations. Or a counselor may wish to use a card sort in which each card specifies a job-related skill or activity. In this case, the counselor might want to explore a client's self-reported skill level and get a sense of how much she or he enjoys using that skill or engaging in that activity. Table 12.4 illustrates possible card arrangement categories for both scenarios. The counselor could also plan on using an iterative, two-step process, with the first step involving sorting the cards according to level of skill and the second step involving sorting some of the cards (generally those the client identifies as relative strengths) according to how much a client enjoys using the skills.

Step 4: Create Header Cards and a Corresponding Worksheet

Once you've conceptualized your card sort by determining your purpose and identifying the categories, columns, or continuum, you need to create the physical header cards to place on the table in front of your client. You also need to create a worksheet with the same category titles. This worksheet will be used later in the counseling process to record the results of the card sort.

TABLE 12.3 Possible Column Headings for a Card Sort				
Might Choose		In Question		Would Not Choose
Interesting		Uncertain		Not Interesting
Like		Neutral/Undecided		Dislike
Very Attractive	Attractive	Neutral/Unsure	Unattractive	Very Unattractive

TABLE 12.4 Two-Dimensional Card-Sort Categories

	High Interest	Low Interest
High Skill		
Low Skill		

Job Titles

	Like Using	Dislike Using
High Skill		
Low Skill		

Skills or Activities

Step 5: Introduce the Card Sort and Explain the Process to Your Client

Invite clients to read each card and place it in the category that best fits at the current time. It is important to encourage your clients to place each card in a way that most accurately reflects them as they are now rather than how they think they should be or the way others want them to be. The upcoming section called Demonstration with Our Cast of Clients includes transcribed portions of a counseling session in which the counselor introduces the card sort and explains the process.

Step 6: Observe While the Client Completes the Card Arrangement

Counselors differ in the way they interact with clients as they place cards. Some prefer to remain silent and allow the client to concentrate and work through all the cards before discussing the placements. Other counselors ask clients to think aloud about reasons for their placement of cards throughout the process. Others interact with clients during the process, voicing observations and asking questions while the client places the cards. What you decide to do during this step depends on you and your personal style as well as your perception of how each approach might affect or influence your client.

As your client places the cards, you may want to record the card placement on the worksheet you created in step 4. You can also delay recording the results until after your client completes additional activities.

Step 7: Engage in Iterative Activities

You may wish to have your client engage in additional activities at this point. These activities serve an iterative function by taking the activity to another level of analysis and card arrangement. For example, in the tradition of Tyler, Dolliver, and more contemporary constructivists, you may decide to ask your client to reorganize the cards into subgroups representing themes or reasons for placing them in their respective categories. Another iterative activity could involve having your client rank-order a category of cards in terms of relative importance. Here are some suggestions for introducing these iterative activities:

- *Thematic Arrangement (General):* I'm curious about any themes you can identify within the group of cards you placed in the Very Important category.
- *Thematic Arrangement (Specific):* "Now I would like you to break up these big groups into smaller groups of occupations that for some reason go together in your mind. Place those you reject for one reason into one group, those you reject for another reason into a second group, and so on. On the positive side, place those you would choose for one reason in one group, those you would choose for another reason into a second group, and so on. There are no rules about the number of groups you should come out with or about the number of cards in each group" (Tyler, 1961, pp. 195–196).
- *Rank-Ordering:* At this point, you've placed all of the career-related values cards into these categories reflecting relative importance. Next, I'd like to focus on the cards you included in the Most Important category. Obviously, all of the cards you put into this category are very important to you, but I would like you to rearrange the cards so that they are rank-ordered. Put the most important at the top and arrange them in decreasing importance.
- *Second Level of Sorting:* Next, I'd like you to review the cards in your Like Very Much category and separate them into gender-typical and gender-atypical categories.

Step 8: Record the Results

At this point, record the results of the card sort if you haven't done so already. Most counselors use the worksheet created in step 4. It can be helpful to make a duplicate copy of this worksheet so that your client can have one. You can place your copy in the client's file for future reference.

Step 9: Process the Activity

Whether or not you interact with your client during the card placement activity, it is essential that you process the activity with your client afterward. Open-ended ways to initiate this processing include the following:

- What was this activity like for you?
- I noticed that you seemed to struggle with where to place the ____ card. What was going on for you?
- Walk me through this process and your reasons for placing cards where you did.
- I'm curious about any insights you've gained so far in this activity.

Step 10: Engage in Closure Discussion

After processing the activity in the ways that best fit your purpose and theory, it is time for closure. You can talk about the information you've gained as a result of this activity or invite the client to offer any additional insights. Tell the client how you will use the results by connecting this activity with the client's goals and his or her next steps.

DEMONSTRATION WITH OUR CAST OF CLIENTS

Now that you have a solid understanding of the card-sort technique, let's explore how to use it with clients. This section of the chapter demonstrates the use of card sorts with clients and explores three different elements: career-related values, occupational interests, and employability skills. We will examine how card sorts might be used with only three of our clients, but I encourage you to think about how you can use them with the remaining four clients.

Wayne Jensen: Wayne's Career-Related Values

Table 12.5 shows how a counselor could introduce the card sort with Wayne Jensen. The counselor in this example uses Dawis and Lofquist's (1984) theory of work adjustment (TWA) and has chosen to use a card sort called the O*NET™ Work Importance Locator. This card sort is designed specifically around the TWA and is distributed by the U.S. Department of Labor, Employment and Training Administration (2000a) via the Occupational Information Network (O*NET).

One important element of this theory involves the relationship between employee values and their job satisfaction. The goal of this card sort is to help Wayne identify work-related values and rewards that might result in a more satisfying second career for him. After identifying his career-related values, the counselor can help Wayne identify and explore occupations consistent with his values.

TABLE 12.5 *Transcript of Session with Wayne: Value Card Sort*

Reviewing Last Session

Counselor:	As we were ending our session last week, we got to talking about how you never really explored other career opportunities when you were in high school. You always assumed you would follow in your father's footsteps and, when he was able to get you a job at Ford, you jumped at the opportunity and never looked back.
Wayne:	That's right. It just seemed like a natural progression. Both my father and my grandfather worked at Ford. I guess you could say it runs in the family. (Grins)
Counselor:	(Chuckles) Yes, it certainly does seem like there's been quite a family tradition and that, for the most part, it has allowed each of you to make a very comfortable living. I can understand why that would have been an attractive option for you.
Wayne:	Oh, a very comfortable living. I sure could've done a lot worse. But now, geez, I could be really screwed. Maybe I should have considered other career options way back then.
Counselor:	(Instilling hope) But here you are now, ready to explore those other options. You might be surprised to find another career that affords you a decent living and that you actually enjoy and find meaningful. I remember you saying earlier that the only thing you really enjoy about your current job is the paycheck, so maybe your plan B will be an upgrade.
Wayne:	That'd be great, but I really have no idea what it would be.
Counselor:	That's okay. Before we jump into identifying other career possibilities, it's useful to figure out what you'd really like to get out of your next career. Besides money, that is.

(Continued)

TABLE 12.5 Transcript of Session with Wayne: Value Card Sort (*Continued*)

Wayne: I get what you're saying. Of course, I want to find a way to keep bringing home a good paycheck, but I'd also like to have a job I'm proud of.

Counselor: Yes, that's close to what I mean. Everyone has different career-related values and looks for different types of rewards from their ideal jobs. I have an activity for us to do today that might help identify what you'd most like to get out of your next career.

Wayne: Okay. What do I need to do?

Introducing the Card-Sort Concept

Counselor: Well, I've brought a set of 20 cards to get us started. Each card identifies and describes a different quality or reward associated with various jobs. As you read each card, imagine your *ideal* job and think about how much you'd like to have a job like the one described on the cards. We'll examine each one.

Wayne: That sounds pretty easy.

Counselor: Yep. So I'll be quiet for a few minutes as you read the cards.

Wayne: Okay.

(The counselor remains quiet as Wayne sorts through and reads each card, noticing that he appears pensive as he carefully considers each one.)

Wayne: (Finishes reading) Wow. Those are some pretty interesting ideas. I haven't thought about jobs like that before.

Counselor: That's one of the neat things about career counseling. It gives you an opportunity to consider several important issues that can make a difference in the quality of your work life. So now that you've read through and thought about each card, I want you to arrange them on this paper. [See Figure 12.1.]

Counselor: (Continues) There are 20 cards and 20 squares, and you can have only four cards per column. You'll see that the column to the far left (Points) is for the four work values you consider most important in your ideal job and that the far right column (Points) is for the four work values you consider least important in your ideal job. Does that make sense?

Wayne: Sure does. I get it.

Counselor: Great. Then let's get started. Talk me through each card and your reasons for putting it in any given square. As you do, I'll watch and take a few notes.

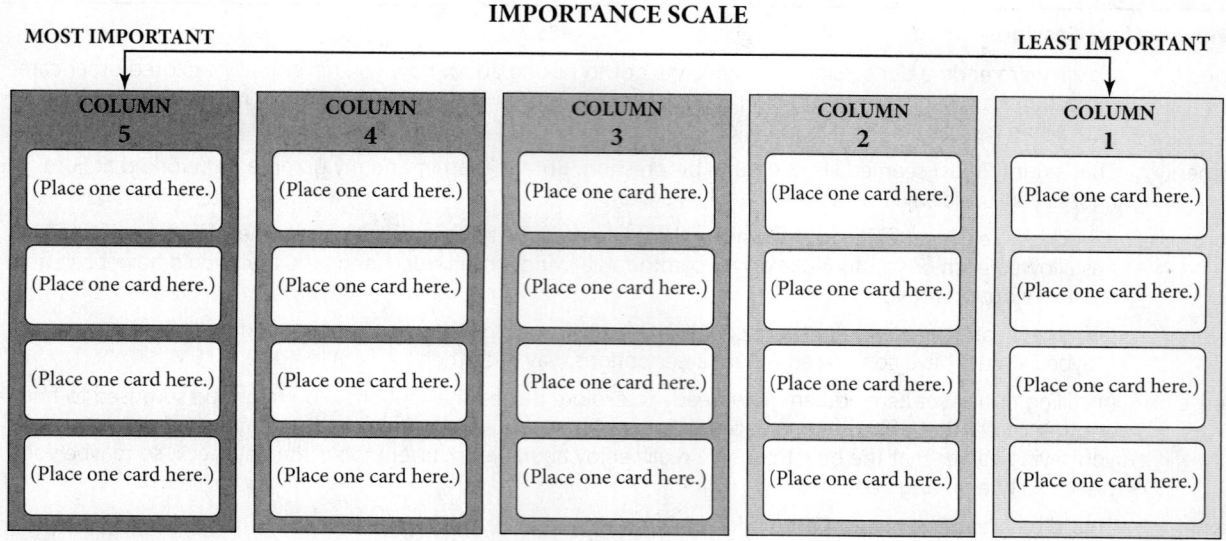

FIGURE 12.1 Blank Sheet for Work Value Card Sort
Source: U.S. Department of Labor, Employment and Training Administration.

Wayne: Okay.

(For the next 10 minutes or so, Wayne sorts through the deck of cards and places each into one of the five columns. As he does so, he comments occasionally about the reasons he is putting a card in a given category. For example, in response to the card indicating that "on my ideal job, it is important that I would never be pressured to do things against my sense of right and wrong," Wayne talked about how disturbed he was when he would see coworkers stealing company property or wasting company time. He reported that he'd like a job in which his coworkers knew right from wrong.)

Wayne: Alright. I think I'm done. (Pauses while he looks over his arrangement) Yes. I'm done. (Once he is done, the cards are arranged as shown in Figure 12.2.)

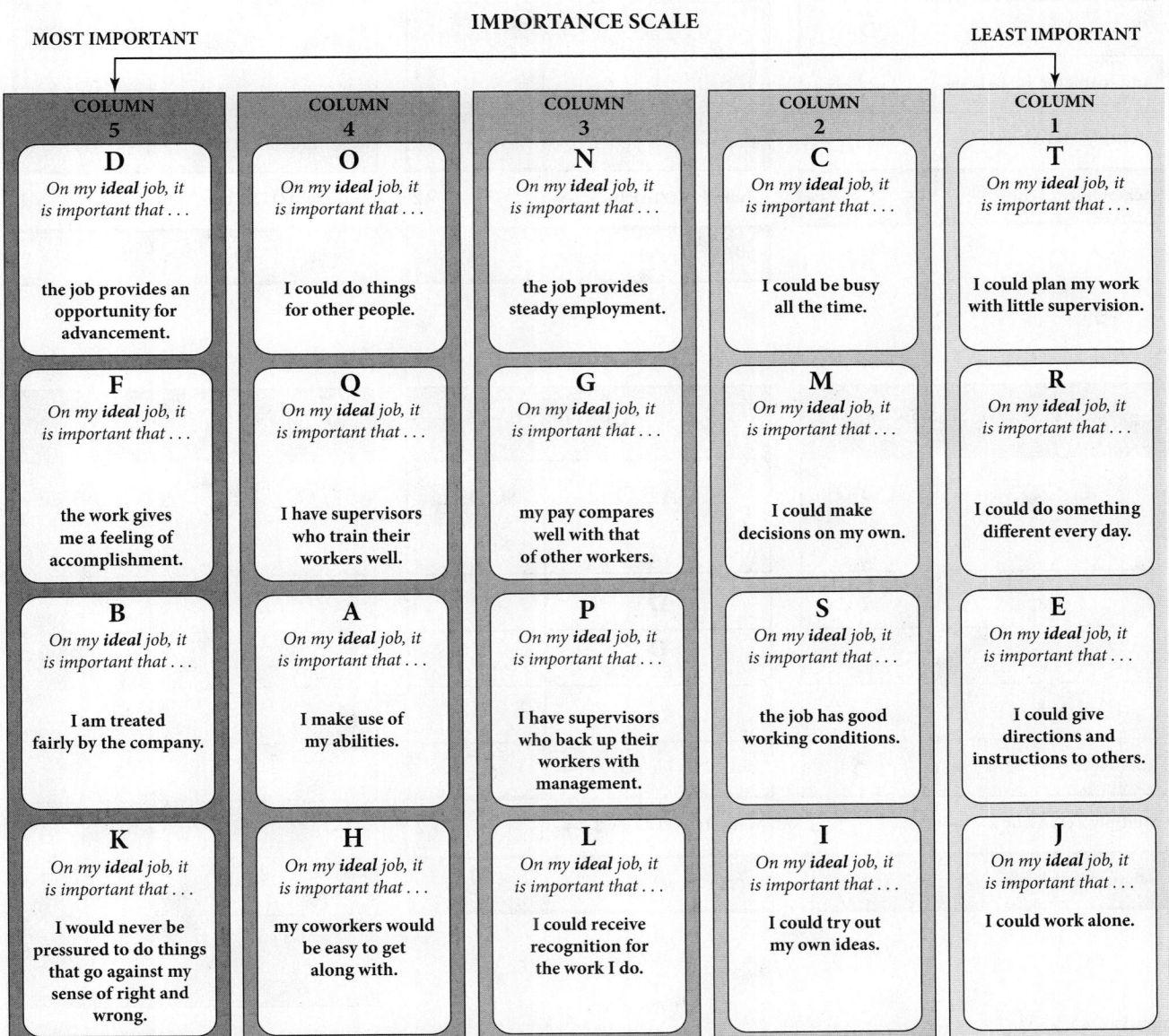

FIGURE 12.2 Completed Sheet for Work Value Card Sort
Source: U.S. Department of Labor, Employment and Training Administration.

(Continued)

TABLE 12.5 Transcript of Session with Wayne: Value Card Sort (*Continued*)

ACHIEVEMENT	
CARD	SCORE Column Number
A	4
F	+ 5
Add scores for TOTAL →	9
Multiply TOTAL by 3 →	×3
Achievement Score →	= 27

INDEPENDENCE	
CARD	SCORE Column Number
I	2
M	+ 2
T	+ 1
Add scores for TOTAL →	5
Multiply TOTAL by 2 →	×2
Independence Score →	= 10

RECOGNITION	
CARD	SCORE Column Number
D	5
E	+ 1
L	+ 3
Add scores for TOTAL →	9
Multiply TOTAL by 2 →	×2
Recognition Score →	= 18

RELATIONSHIPS	
CARD	SCORE Column Number
H	4
K	+ 5
O	+ 4
Add scores for TOTAL →	13
Multiply TOTAL by 2 →	×2
Relationships Score →	= 26

SUPPORT	
CARD	SCORE Column Number
B	5
P	+ 3
Q	+ 4
Add scores for TOTAL →	12
Multiply TOTAL by 2 →	×2
Support Score →	= 24

WORKING CONDITIONS	
CARD	SCORE Column Number
C	2
G	+ 3
J	+ 1
N	+ 3
R	+ 1
S	+ 2
Add scores for TOTAL Working Conditions Score →	= 12

FIGURE 12.3 Work Value Worksheet
Source: U.S. Department of Labor, Employment and Training Administration.

Processing

Counselor: Great. Thanks for doing this. What was it like for you?

Wayne: I liked it. It made me think a lot about what I really want from a job. As I look at these cards, I realize that my job on the line isn't very fulfilling to me. Don't get me wrong. The pay has been great and I shouldn't complain. But I can see now why you said my next career might be an upgrade.

Counselor: That's definitely what we're shooting for. Let's look at what your card arrangement suggests about your career-related values. (Places a piece of paper on the table) This scoring sheet (see Figure 12.3) is designed to use your card placement to calculate your scores with respect to six specific work values.

Wayne: Cool.

In the remainder of the session, the counselor scores the card sort and explains the results to Wayne. As shown in Figure 12.3, achievement was his strongest work value, followed by relationships, support, recognition, working conditions, and independence. To help Wayne explore the potential value of these results, the counselor asks Wayne to do homework before their next session. Wayne receives the Work Importance Locator Score Report from the counselor and is asked to read through it (U.S. Department of Labor, Employment and Training Administration, 2000a). The counselor explains that the report includes a listing of occupations associated with each of the six work values and asks Wayne to circle any occupations in which he might have interest, giving special attention to the occupations listed as meeting achievement, relationships, or support needs.

Lily Huang Li Mei: Occupational Interests

The preceding example of a client application included a demonstration of how a counselor might introduce the card sort to Wayne. The introduction to the use of a card sort, of course, depends on the purpose of the card sort and the types of categories used for the activity. In Table 12.6, the counselor explains to Li Mei how to do a card sort focused solely on occupational interests. The counselor will use the Occupational Interests cards from the Knowdell Card Sort (Knowdell, 2014) materials but will modify the categories for Li Mei sorting. Another modification is that the counselor chose not to utilize the Holland codes on these cards because of the unexplained discrepancy between the codes on the cards and the Holland interest codes on O*NET for the same occupations.

In this session, the counselor used an already established and commercially available card sort. She modified the activity, though, to meet the needs of her client. Whereas the card sort comes with header cards for five categories (Definitely Interested, Probably Interested, Indifferent, Probably Not Interested, and Definitely Not Interested), the counselor instead chose to have Li Mei sort the cards into only three categories (Interesting, Uncertain, and Not Interesting). Adaptations like this one are certainly appropriate and can result in the more effective use of the card sort with a given client. It is also acceptable for counselors to create their own deck of cards. Doing so may be especially useful when a client has unique issues not addressed by established and commercially available card sorts.

Doris Bronner's Employability Skills

The counselor has created a set of cards that are geared specifically toward employability skills, including the specific responsibilities Doris has had in her secretarial positions as well as more general employability skills. To create these cards, the counselor examined the items on Doris's last performance evaluation, reviewed a number of other performance evaluation forms she found on the Internet, and reviewed the skills identified by the Secretary's Commission on Achieving Necessary Skills (SCANS; Secretary's Commission on Achieving Necessary Skills, 1991). Borrowing items from these varied sources, the counselor created cards for the employability skills identified in Figure 12.6.

While interviewing Doris in Chapter 10, we learned that her troubles at work weren't limited to having been fired from her job as a secretary at the insurance agency for which she had worked the past 14 years. Doris reluctantly admitted that she began working with a temp agency after being fired but that she was let go from both of the secretarial assignments she had received. As a result, the temp agency had notified her that it would no longer place her. Clearly, Doris was not performing at a satisfactory level in these positions. What is less clear, though, is why Doris wasn't performing satisfactorily. In Table 12.7, the counselor engages Doris in a card sort designed to help both of them understand factors related to her performance

TABLE 12.6 Transcript of Session with Li Mei: Occupational Interest Card Sort

Reviewing Last Session

Counselor: I've been thinking about our last session and how discouraged you feel whenever you think about college majors and possible careers. It seems to me that a big part of the reason you get discouraged is that you automatically jump into comparing yourself to your brother or sister.

Li Mei: Yes, I suppose that's true. It seems to me that anything I could do, they could do better.

Counselor: Do you see how that type of thinking could interfere with your serious consideration of any majors or career directions?

Li Mei: I guess so.

Counselor: If it's okay with you, I'd like to put those types of thoughts on hold today. Instead of thinking about what you'd be good at or whether your siblings might be better than you, today I'd like to have you focus exclusively on what appeals to you, what you find interesting.

Li Mei: Okay, but I really don't know what careers appeal to me.

Counselor: Actually, that's really normal for college students. It's not unusual for people to feel stuck when they are asked to identify careers that they might like to explore. It's like their brain doesn't know where to start. To help you think about what appeals to you and what you might find interesting, I have an activity for us to do today. The neat thing about this activity is that it brings the ideas to you and you get to sort through them.

Li Mei: Okay. (Still seems skeptical but is willing to try it)

Introducing the Card-Sort Concept

Counselor: For this activity, I have a deck of cards. (Gestures) Each card identifies and describes a different occupation or career. As you read each card, I'd like you to pay attention to your reaction to the idea of doing that occupation or career. I don't want you to think about how good you'd be or whether your siblings would be better at it. I only want you to think about how appealing or interesting the occupation or career seems to you.

Li Mei: That might be hard, but I'll do my best.

Counselor: Great. I want you to read each card and place it into one of these categories: Interesting, Uncertain, or Not Interesting. (Places header cards on the table, as shown in Figure 12.4.) The Interesting column is for jobs or activities that have some appeal to you and that you might enjoy doing in a career. The Not Interesting column is for jobs or activities that you definitely dislike and would not enjoy doing in a career. And the Uncertain column is for when you can't decide or when you don't know enough about the job or activity to have a sense of whether you might find it interesting.

Li Mei: I understand. And you don't want me to consider how good I'd be at it when I place the cards, right?

Counselor: Exactly. That's really important today. Let's focus only on your level of interest, and we can address skills and aptitudes some other time. Are you ready to start?

Li Mei: Yes.

Interesting	Uncertain	Not Interesting

FIGURE 12.4 Blank Sheet for Work Value Card Sorting

Counselor: Great. Go ahead and place the cards. As you do, I'll be quiet and watch.
Li Mei: Okay.
(For the next 15 minutes or so, Li Mei sorts through the deck of cards and places each into one of the three categories. Once she is done, the cards are arranged as shown in Figure 12.5.)
Li Mei: (Smiling broadly) Alright, I'm done.

Processing

Counselor: Tell me about that smile.
Li Mei: (Giggles) I'm smiling because I totally had a light-bulb moment while doing this activity. All along, I've been feeling like I have no idea whatsoever what I want to do with my life. But when I looked through all of these cards, I realized that I'm not as clueless as I thought.
Counselor: Well, I never thought you were clueless, but tell me what you mean.
Li Mei: I mean, look at all the cards I put over here. (Points at the Not Interesting pile)
Counselor: Yes, there *is* a huge number of occupations over here. Are these occupations pretty much off the table in terms of your willingness to consider them as serious possibilities?
Li Mei: Definitely off the table.
Counselor: Let's take a few minutes to look at the types of occupations you put in this Not Interesting pile. What themes seem to describe these cards?
Li Mei: Well, there are a lot of jobs in that category that are at too low a level. I don't mean to be disrespectful, but I was raised to see only jobs that require at least a college degree as possibilities. Is that what you mean by a theme?
Counselor: Exactly. So some of these jobs are off the table because they don't require enough education, and maybe because they aren't associated with as much respect?
Li Mei: Yes, that's true. It's more than how much education is required. My parents would just die if I chose some of these careers. And it's not just them. I'd be embarrassed to have some of those jobs. I'm sorry. I don't mean to be rude.
Counselor: It's not rude. We're working together to find a career direction that fits for *you*, and if that's how you feel about some of these jobs, it's probably a good decision not to consider them. Are there any other themes that you see over here? (Points again at the Not Interesting column)
Li Mei: Yes. Some of the occupations are there because I'm just not interested in them, like the cards that say lawyer, politician, and stockbroker. I see them as too cut-throat and competitive. And some of them are too pure science for me, like physicist, chemist, and statistician.
Counselor: Great insights. Even in talking about the careers you're *not* interested in, we can reach some conclusions. You want a career that is associated with higher levels of education and prestige but that doesn't involve pure science or seems too cut-throat. Is that it?
Li Mei: (Smiles) Yes, exactly.

Interesting	Uncertain	Not Interesting
Accountant	College professor	99 other occupations
Architect	Foreign language teacher	
Dentist	Veterinarian	
Engineer		
Librarian		
Optometrist		
Pharmacist		
Physician		

FIGURE 12.5 Completed Sheet for Work Value Card Sorting

(Continued)

TABLE 12.6	Transcript of Session with Li Mei: Occupational Interest Card Sort (*Continued*)
Counselor:	There's that smile again.
Li Mei:	I just feel so good right now. It's like a weight has been lifted off my shoulders.
Counselor:	Doing this card sort has helped you realize that you really do have some clear ideas about what you want and don't want in a career.
Li Mei:	Yes. I guess I got so caught up in feeling inadequate that I couldn't even think about what I wanted. I'm so glad we did this.
Counselor:	I'm glad, too. But let's take this a step further. Are there any themes you see in the Interesting category?
Li Mei:	(Pauses and thinks for 15 seconds or so) I guess one theme I see is that a lot of the jobs in science are hands on. Also, there are several jobs in health care. Oh, and both accountants and librarians sort of organize information, I guess.
Counselor:	Very interesting observations. I think you're right on target. (Attempts to build confidence) The hands-on jobs you mentioned are called applied sciences as opposed to pure sciences. And yes, there are health care jobs and jobs that involve organizing information. What would you think about using this next week for these ideas to settle in for you, to see if any of these careers seem more or less appealing to you as you go through the week?
Li Mei:	I think that would be good.
Counselor:	And once you've had an opportunity to ponder them, maybe you will want to explore some or all of them more deeply. I can help with that by providing some resources containing good, reliable information about various occupations.

TS	**Technical Skills**
	• Employ tools of the job competently
	• Follow proper safety procedures
	• Use information and communications technology effectively
	• Possess strong technical skills and knowledge
WQ1	**Work Quality**
	• Complete work with accuracy and precision
	• Complete work with thoroughness and neatness
	• Demonstrate reliability—work is consistently done well and on time
	• Am responsive to requests for service
	• Follow up on and follow through with assignments
	• Demonstrate sound judgment and make good decisions
	• Correct errors
	• Recognize and learn from mistakes, taking appropriate action to reduce errors
WQ2	**Work Quantity**
	• Complete the amount of work expected
	• Complete assignments on schedule
	• Set priorities appropriately to meet important deadlines
	• Properly use materials and equipment to effectively and efficiently complete varying workload in a timely fashion

PB   **Professional Behaviors**
- Demonstrate regular attendance with rare absences
- Arrive at work early or on time, am at workstation when scheduled and remain at workstation for the duration of shift
- Work hard to reach goals, even if task is unpleasant
- Am viewed as having a positive attitude
- Follow instructions in professional manner
- Seek additional training and development

SM   **Self-Management Skills**
- Remain focused and productive, reliable and dependable without needing constant supervision
- Demonstrate initiative and act without needing direction
- Am able to plan and organize
- Am flexible and adaptable
- Can handle unexpected situations calmly and efficiently to minimize problems
- Manage stress and conflict to ensure minimal impact on quality or quantity of work

IS   **Interpersonal Skills**
- Demonstrate good interpersonal skills with coworkers
- Demonstrate good interpersonal skills with supervisors
- Demonstrate good interpersonal skills with clients
- Work well with others (positive and productive)
- Am viewed as accessible and approachable
- Understand and make the most of the relationships at work

CS   **Communication Skills**
- Communicate effectively in written format (memos, email, etc.)
- Communicate effectively in oral format (face-to-face, phone, etc.)
- Communicate accurately and honestly in an open, candid, and respectful manner
- Demonstrate tact and diplomacy in communications

TP   **Team Player**
- Am viewed as a team player
- Participate and make contributions in team activities
- Demonstrate commitment to team success
- Demonstrate enthusiasm and passion for the company/business
- Contribute positively to team/company morale and spirit
- Demonstrate a commitment to company by adhering to its stated values, policies, and procedures
- Take personal responsibility to resolve problems, even those not of my own making

FIGURE 12.6 Employability Card Sort

284 Chapter 12

TABLE 12.7 Transcript of Session with Doris: Employability Skills Card Sort

Reviewing Last Session

Counselor: Thanks, Doris, for bringing in your performance evaluation last week. I know you have a lot of anger about having been let go, and I imagine it might have been hard for you to share that evaluation with me.

Doris: Well, I wouldn't say it was hard. I just didn't see the point. Obviously, they wanted to fire me and they wrote up the evaluation to make it seem like I deserved to get fired.

Counselor: In your mind, they were out to get you and the evaluation wasn't accurate.

Doris: That's right. Ever since Brian became the new manager, I could tell he was out to get me. He just didn't like me.

Counselor: How do you make sense of what happened in the two temp jobs you had after Brian fired you from the insurance agency?

Doris: (Looking down and sounding deflated) I don't know. Maybe they were ageist. Maybe they talked to Brian. I don't know.

Introducing the Card Sort

Counselor: That's okay. I don't know, either, but I have an activity for us to do today that might help us figure it out. I have brought a deck of cards that we'll be using today. Each card specifies a different skill that tends to be associated with success at work and positive performance evaluations. Regardless of what the job is, these are skills and behaviors that employers tend to expect.

(Doris crosses her arms, knits her brows, and looks skeptical.)

Managing Resistance

Counselor: You've commented that you didn't respect the evaluation that Brian did and that you felt it was unfair. With this activity, you'll have an opportunity to evaluate yourself. Now, because it's just you and me and I'm on your side, there's no need to try to make yourself look extra good. I'm not your employer and I'm not in a position to interview you. (Chuckles) Come to think of it, I work for you. I'm *your* counselor.

Doris: (Laughs) Hey, that's right. You'd better watch out!

Counselor: That's true, you know. I have to walk a really fine line. On the one hand, in order to have you not fire me, you need to feel supported and understood, and not judged. On the other hand, for you to get your money's worth, you need to walk out of here different than you were when you walked in. In your case, things obviously haven't been going well at work. You've now been fired from three jobs in a row, and you came in for career counseling to change this. It's not that you want a different career; you just want the career you've chosen to go better for you. I want that, too.

Doris: (Looking up) I *do* want that. I just don't know what to do.

Explaining the Card Sort

Counselor: Well, let's see what we can discover today. With this activity, we'll be doing some detective work. As I said, each of these cards specifies a different skill that tends to be associated with success at work and positive performance evaluations. I want you to read each card and think about it. I want you to think about whether you have the skill or know how to do the behavior identified on the card. That's the first thing to think about. If you do have the skill, I want you to think about how consistently you demonstrated it in your job at the insurance agency. Remember, it's just you and me here, and I'm on your side. The more honest you can be with yourself and with me, the better our detective work will be. Our goal is simply to figure out what's been going wrong. We won't be judging you or criticizing you. Does that make sense?

Doris: Yes, but it sounds like you're trying to soften the blow. This is going to be hard, isn't it?

Counselor: Yes, I'm guessing that some parts of it might be hard. If it gets too hard or too upsetting, though, let me know and we can take a break.

Doris: All right.

Counselor: So, as you read each card and think about it, I want you to place it in one of the following columns. (Points to the blank sheet shown in Figure 12.7) In this way, we'll get a visual image of what skills you see yourself as having and how consistently you think you demonstrate them. Do you have any questions?

I have this skill and almost always demonstrate it at work.	I have this skill and sometimes demonstrate it at work.	I have this skill but rarely demonstrate it at work.	I have this skill but do not demonstrate it at work.	I don't have this skill.

FIGURE 12.7 Blank Sheet for Employability Skills Card Sort

Doris: No. I understand what you want me to do.

Counselor: All right, then. Here are the cards. While you work on this, I'm going to stay silent so that you can really look inside and think back about what skills you have been using and how consistently you've been using them. After you're done, we can talk about what the process was like for you and what it all means.

Doris: Okay. Here goes. (Works on the activity for approximately 20 minutes. At the end, her cards were arranged as shown in Figure 12.8.)

Processing the Activity

Counselor: Thanks, Doris, for doing this activity. As I watched, I could see that this wasn't easy for you. At one point, I even thought I saw you tear up just a bit.

Doris: I did. In fact, I almost lost it. All of a sudden, I realized that I probably deserved those bad evaluations. Look how few cards I put in the first column. (Points at the Almost Always Demonstrate column) That's not good, is it?

Counselor: No, not so good in terms of job performance. Employers tend to expect that most of these skills or behaviors are demonstrated pretty consistently by all of their employees. The good part, though, is how honestly you answered when placing these cards. Even with everything I said before you started, I'm guessing there could still be a temptation to put more cards over here. (Points at the Almost Always Demonstrate column)

Doris: Mm hmm! I *was* tempted. But then I figured, what the hell. Who am I kidding here? As you said, I can walk out of here in the same boat I started in or I can figure out what's been going wrong. Looking at this, I can see that *a lot* has been going wrong.

Counselor: It looks that way. The good news is that there are also only a few cards over here. (Points at the Don't Have This Skill column) We can talk about these cards a bit later and figure out how to help you develop these skills. As homework for our next session, though, I'd like to have you focus on the skills you *do* have but don't always use. This is where the detective work comes in. I'd like you to think about each of these skills and figure out the reasons you aren't using them consistently.

Doris: What do you mean?

Assignment of Homework

Counselor: (Shows worksheet) Well, there is usually a reason we don't use a given skill. What we'll do is list each skill in these middle three columns (Points at card sort), and I'll ask you to identify the reason or reasons you don't always demonstrate each skill at work. For example, whether or not you demonstrate the skill may depend on the task. You may like some parts of your job better than others and may simply avoid doing tasks you don't like. Or you may choose to demonstrate the skills with some people at work more than with other people at work. Another reason is that it might depend on your mood. When we're in a bad mood, it may be harder to use some of the skills we have. Or there may be more than one reason for any given skill. I'd like to get a sense of what's been going on for you so that we know what to work on. (Responding to Doris's nonverbal communication) What's that smile about?

(Continued)

TABLE 12.7 Transcript of Session with Doris: Employability Skills Card Sort (*Continued*)

I have this skill and almost always demonstrate it at work.	I have this skill and sometimes demonstrate it at work.	I have this skill but rarely demonstrate it at work.	I have this skill but do not demonstrate it at work.	I don't have this skill.
Follow proper safety procedures	Complete work with accuracy and precision	Demonstrate reliability—work is consistently done well and on time	Seek additional training and development	Remain focused and productive, reliable and dependable without needing constant supervision
Possess strong technical skills and knowledge	Follow up on and follow through with assignments	Am responsive to requests for service	Demonstrate initiative and act without needing direction	Manage stress and conflict to ensure minimal impact on quality or quantity of work
Work hard to reach goals, even if task is unpleasant	Complete work with thoroughness and neatness	Complete the amount of work expected	Use information and communications technology effectively	Properly use materials and equipment to effectively and efficiently complete varying workload in a timely fashion
Demonstrate a commitment to company by adhering to its stated values, policies, and procedures	Demonstrate sound judgment and make good decisions	Arrive at work early or on time, am at workstation when scheduled and remain at workstation for the duration of shift		
	Correct errors	Am viewed as having a positive attitude		
	Recognize and learn from mistakes, taking appropriate action to reduce errors	Am flexible and adaptable		
	Employ tools of the job competently	Can handle unexpected situation calmly and efficiently to minimize problems		
	Complete assignments on schedule	Am viewed as accessible and approachable		
	Set priorities appropriately to meet important deadlines	Am viewed as a team player		
	Demonstrate regular attendance with rare absences	Demonstrate enthusiasm and passion for the company/business		
	Follow instructions in professional manner	Contribute positively to team/company morale and spirit		
	Demonstrate good interpersonal skills with coworkers			

	Demonstrate good interpersonal skills with supervisors			
_____	_____	_____	_____	_____
	Demonstrate good interpersonal skills with clients			
_____	_____	_____	_____	_____
	Work well with others (positive and productive)			
_____	_____	_____	_____	_____
	Understand and make the most of relationships at work			
_____	_____	_____	_____	_____
	Communicate effectively in written format (memos, email, etc.)			
_____	_____	_____	_____	_____
	Communicate effectively in oral format (face-to-face, phone, etc.)			
_____	_____	_____	_____	_____
	Communicate accurately and honestly in an open, candid, and respectful manner			
_____	_____	_____	_____	_____
	Demonstrate tact and diplomacy in communications			
_____	_____	_____	_____	_____
	Participate and make contributions in team activities			
_____	_____	_____	_____	_____
	Demonstrate commitment to team success			
_____	_____	_____	_____	_____
	Take personal responsibility to resolve problems, even those not of my own making			
_____	_____	_____	_____	_____

FIGURE 12.8 Completed Sheet for Employability Skills Card Sort

Doris: It just never occurred to me that there might be a reason I don't do what I'm supposed to do. And you're right. Sometimes my husband puts me in a bad mood before I even get to work and that sets the stage for a really bad day. I love this. There's a reason. You're brilliant!

Identification of Next Steps

Counselor: I'm glad you feel that way, but don't get too excited. A reason isn't a free pass. Although it will be helpful to understand the reasons you haven't been demonstrating these skills consistently, we will then face the challenge of helping you learn to demonstrate them consistently, regardless of what the task is, who the people are, or what your mood is.

Doris: Ah, well. (Still smiling) Even so, this makes me feel a little better. Should I just put check marks on the worksheet or should I add notes?

Counselor: Actually, if you want to add notes of explanation for some of them, that'd be terrific. There's not a lot of space on the worksheet, but a couple of key words would be useful.

(Continued)

TABLE 12.7 Transcript of Session with Doris: Employability Skills Card Sort (*Continued*)

Skill	Depends on Task	Depends on Pension	Depends on Mood
_____	_____	_____	_____
_____	_____	_____	_____
_____	_____	_____	_____
_____	_____	_____	_____
_____	_____	_____	_____
_____	_____	_____	_____
_____	_____	_____	_____
_____	_____	_____	_____
_____	_____	_____	_____
_____	_____	_____	_____
_____	_____	_____	_____
_____	_____	_____	_____
_____	_____	_____	_____
_____	_____	_____	_____
_____	_____	_____	_____
_____	_____	_____	_____
_____	_____	_____	_____
_____	_____	_____	_____
_____	_____	_____	_____
_____	_____	_____	_____

FIGURE 12.9 Reasons for Inconsistent Skill Usage

problems. Notice that the counselor uses this activity not only as an assessment but also as an intervention to gently challenge Doris about the need for change.

Doris's work is far from over. By using this card-sort technique, however, the counselor was able to facilitate Doris's recognition that her past performance evaluations may have been accurate reflections of her performance. With the explanation of how each card represents a different skill that tends to be associated with success at work and positive performance evaluations, the counselor was able to educate Doris about employability skills without taking on the role of a teacher in the counseling process. This card sort served as an intervention involving gentle confrontation and education, and as an assessment tool by helping Doris articulate skill deficits as well as skills she was not demonstrating consistently at work.

A FINAL WORD

When reading these client applications, you may have noticed that the sources of the card sorts varied. The counselor with Wayne used the O*NET™ Work Importance Locator, a work values card sort distributed free online by the U.S. Department of Labor. With Li Mei, the counselor used the Knowdell Occupational Interests Card Sort, which is available for purchase from Career Research & Testing, Inc. The counselor working with Doris developed her own card sort geared specifically toward Doris's situation and needs. Each of these approaches is a viable option. To assist you in identifying available card sorts, the following section provides information about several, already established card sorts.

PURCHASING INFORMATION

This section provides basic information regarding several card sorts that are currently available. In reviewing them, note that some of the card sorts described earlier in this chapter, such as the vocational card sort that was part of Holland's Vocational Exploration and Insight Kit (VEIK; Takai & Holland, 1979), are no longer commercially available. Note also that this section includes card sorts that are developed and widely used by human resources professionals and consultants specializing in leadership development and/or organizational effectiveness. I believe their inclusion in this book is essential. The card sorts demonstrated in this chapter helped clients who are focused on career selection or transition (Li Mei and Wayne, respectively) or on meeting the basic requirements of work (Doris), but career counselors can also assist clients with development and advancement. These clients will not be focused on finding a good fit or maintaining employment but on excelling in their chosen fields. Some card sorts for these purposes have therefore been included. The card sorts in Tables 12.8 to 12.11 are categorized according to their topical focus.

THE FINE PRINT

This list of commercially available card sorts is for informational purposes only. Inclusion in this section is not intended as an endorsement of the product. Prices and availability may change from the date of this publication.

TABLE 12.8 Categories of Commercially Available Card Sorts

Career Selection or Transition
- Interests
- Skills
- Career-related values
- Other

Career Success and Development of Leadership Potential
- Competencies and learning styles
- Personality and personal styles

Post-Career and Retirement Card Sorts

TABLE 12.9 Career Selection or Transition Card Sorts

Interests

Knowdell Card Sorts: Occupational Interests $21.75
Publisher: Career Research & Testing, Inc.
Description: Developed by Richard L. Knowdell, this card sort focuses on post-career interests. The website describes it as "a low-cost technique for quickly identifying and ranking occupational interests. Clarifies the high-appeal jobs and fields; the degree of readiness, skills and knowledge needed; and the competency-building steps for entry or progress within an occupation. The kit includes 110 occupational cards and a manual. The manual includes guidelines for counselors and group facilitators, an overview of interests and their role in career decision making, detailed instructions for the individual user and optional activities for clarifying career-related interests" (careernetwork.org/career_assessment_instr.html#Occupational, para.13). The Planning Kit includes the manual, one deck of cards, and one worksheet. Additional decks of cards are available for discounted prices.
Note: There is an unexplained discrepancy between the codes on the cards and the Holland interest codes on O*NET for the same occupations.
Purchasing Information: careertrainer.com

Missouri Occupational Card Sort (MOCS) $30.00
Publisher: University of Missouri, Career Planning and Placement Center
Description: The MOCS was designed to be consistent with the Holland typology and consists of 90 cards, evenly distributed across the RIASEC categories, with the name of the occupation on the front of the card and occupational information on the back. This card sort is geared specifically to the needs of college students in order to help them learn more about themselves and the world of work. The cost includes one set of cards and a user's manual.
Purchasing Information: http://career.missouri.edu/career-assessments

(Continued)

TABLE 12.9 Career Selection or Transition Card Sorts (*Continued*)

Career Selection or Transition
Skills

Knowdell™ Card Sorts: Motivated Skills Card Sort $17.00

Publisher: Career Research & Testing, Inc.

Description: Developed by Richard L. Knowdell, this card sort focuses on transferrable skills used in various careers. The website describes it as "a quick and easy way to identify the areas that are central to personal and career satisfaction and success. Based on experience, feedback and instinct, clients use the cards to assess their proficiency and motivation in 51 transferable skills areas" (careernetwork.org/career_assessment_instr.html#Motivated, para. 9). The Planning Kit includes the manual, one deck of cards, and one worksheet. Additional decks of cards are available for discounted prices.

Purchasing Information: careertrainer.com

Skillscan™ Advance Pack $22.00

Publisher: Skillscan™

Description: This company sells two card sorts. Both are intended to for counselor-directed use. The Advance Pack is intended for use with college students and adults and "the cards consist of 60 transferable skills that fall into six major skill categories. Each skill card is denoted by an icon and color to designate the category it belongs to. Each deck includes nine category cards to use in identifying proficiency level, preference level, skill development and an optional 'No Longer Can Use' category card. This card is useful for clients who have sustained injuries that prevent them from using certain skills" (skillscan.com/catalog/23/advancepack). This pack might be especially useful in rehabilitation counseling. Additional materials, including profile forms, a facilitator manual, and a CD that includes reproducible handouts and PowerPoint presentations, are also available.

Purchasing Information: skillscan.com/

Skillscan™ Professional Pack $16.00

Publisher: Skillscan™

Description: This company sells two card sorts. Both are intended to for counselor-directed use. The Professional Pack is appropriate not only for adults but also for high school students. In this pack, "the cards consist of 64 transferable skills that fall into seven major skill categories. Each skill card is denoted by color to designate the category it belongs to. Each deck includes six category cards to use in identifying competence, preference level and optional skill development" (skillscan.com/counselors#professional-pack). Additional materials, including profile forms, a facilitator manual, and a CD that includes reproducible handouts, are also available.

Purchasing Information: skillscan.com/

University of Minnesota Skills Card Sort Free

Publisher: Unknown

Description: This card sort is available online through the University of Minnesota's College of Continuing Education. Unlike most card sorts, this version is completely virtual, with no physical cards to manipulate. Instead, cards are arranged on a computer monitor using a mouse. The website states that the purpose of this card sort is to help students "identify and prioritize [their] skills" (http://cce.umn.edu/Information-Center/Advising-and-Career-Services/Career-and-Lifework-Planning/index.html).

Access Information: cce.umn.edu/cardsort/skills/

Career Selection or Transition
Career-Related Values

Executive Leadership Values Assessment: Card Game Free

Publisher: CO2

Description: Developed by this Minneapolis-based executive coaching firm, this card sort is available online and results in an 8-page report that summarizes an individual's values and identifies his or her six core values. Unlike most card sorts, this version is completely virtual, with no physical cards to manipulate. Instead, cards are arranged on a computer monitor using a mouse.

Access Information: co2partners.com/cardgame

Knowdell™ Card Sorts: Career Values Card Sort Planning Kit $18.70

Publisher: Career Research & Testing, Inc.

Description: Developed by Richard L. Knowdell, this card sort focuses on career-related values. The website describes it as "a simple tool that allows your clients to prioritize their values in as little as five minutes. Fifty-four variables of work satisfaction—such as time freedom, precision work, power, technical competence and public contact—are listed and described. This is an effective tool for job seekers, those fine-tuning their present jobs and career changers at all ages and stages" (careernetwork.org/career_assessment_instr.html#Career, para. 5). The Planning Kit includes the manual, one deck of cards, and one worksheet. Additional decks of cards are available for discounted prices.

Purchasing Information: careertrainer.com

Personal Values Card Sort Free

Publisher: None (public domain)

Description: Developed by Miller, C'de Baca, Matthews, and Wilbourne (2001), this card sort is designed to assist clients in identifying their personal values. Although this card sort does not focus specifically on career-related values, it may nonetheless have relevance within career counseling. According to the materials, "this instrument is in the public domain and may be copied, adapted and used without permission."

Acquisition Information: motivationalinterviewing.org/content/personal-values-card-sort

University of Minnesota Values Card Sort Free

Publisher: Unknown

Description: This card sort is available online through the University of Minnesota's College of Continuing Education. Unlike most card sorts, this version is completely virtual, with no physical cards to manipulate. Instead, cards are arranged on a computer monitor using a mouse. The website states that the purpose of this card sort is to help students "reflect on what is important [to them] in a work setting" (http://cce.umn.edu/Information-Center/Advising-and-Career-Services/Career-and-Lifework-Planning/index.html).

Access Information: cce.umn.edu/cardsort/values/

O*NET™ Work Importance Locator Free

Publisher: U.S. Department of Labor (O*NET)

Description: This card sort assesses career-related values in accordance with the Theory of Work Adjustment (Dawis & Lofquist, 1984). The website describes it as "a self-assessment career exploration tool that allows customers to pinpoint what is important to them in a job. It helps people identify occupations that they may find satisfying based on the similarity between their work values (such as achievement, autonomy, and conditions of work) and the characteristics of the occupations. The O*NET Work Importance Locator measures six types of work values: achievement, independence, recognition, relationships, support, and working conditions" (onetcenter.org/WIL.html, para. 1–2). The O*NET website allows users to download the cards, a card sorting worksheet, a score report, and a user's guide.

Acquisition Information: onetcenter.org/WIL.html

Career Selection or Transition
Other

Intelligent Careers Card Sort® $75.00

Publisher: Intelligent Careers Card Sort®

Description: Like most constructivist approaches to career counseling, this card sort defies categorization. It is based on the philosophy that every individual is unique and purposely avoids categorization or typing of interests, values, personality or other career-related factors. Instead, the three sets of cards that comprise the ICCS® help individuals clarify their own values related to work and help them explore ways to transition into the world of work. One deck of cards (blue "knowing why" cards) focuses on values. One deck (yellow "knowing how" cards) "explore the steps the individual is taking to gain technical/professional skill and expertise" (Wnuk & Amundson, 2003, p. 276). The third deck of cards (green "knowing whom" cards) helps individuals explore ways in which their existing and future relationships with others could be useful in supporting their career entry or advancement. This card sort is administered solely online now with volume discounts offered to educational institutions and nonprofit agencies.

Acquisition Information: intelligentcareer.net/

TABLE 12.10 Career Success and Development of Leadership Potential Card Sorts

Competencies and Learning Styles
Personality and Personal Styles

Choices Architect® Sort Card Deck — $90.00

Publisher: Lominger Limited, Inc.

Description: This card sort is most often used by consultants focused on organizational effectiveness, with emphasis on hiring practices and personnel selection. It also has relevance to career counseling. According to its website, this card sort is "used by organizations to identify, validate and select those who are the most learning agile, who make sense of work and personal experiences and add those lessons to their lifelong learning portfolio" (http://store.lominger.com/store/lominger/en_US/pd/productID.127299200, para. 1). Certification (achieved through training with Lominger) may be required for purchase of this card sort.

Purchasing Information: http://store.lominger.com/

EQ & Leadership — £5.00 ($8.50)

Publisher: LearningMatters.com

Description: This English card sort is intended for "executives at all levels in the organization wishing to understand the part emotional intelligence plays in learning and displaying leadership characteristics" (http://learningmatters.com/idx/1048/, para. 3). Based on Daniel Goleman's work, this card sort focuses on "the leadership attributes of being Coercive, Authoritative, Affiliative, Democratic, Pacesetting and Coaching" (http://learningmatters.com/idx/1048/, para. 4).

Purchasing Information: http://learningmatters.com/idx/1048/.

Note: The cost on the website is listed in British pounds. Upon payment via the Internet, the card sort is available for immediate download.

Leadership Architect® Sort Card Deck — $90.00

Publisher: Lominger Limited, Inc.

Description: This card sort is most often used by consultants focused on organizational effectiveness, with emphasis on developing individuals as leaders. It also has relevance to career counseling. According to its website, this card sort is "made up of single cards devoted to each of 67 Leadership Architect® Competencies, 19 Career Stallers, and 7 Global Focus Areas. Each card includes the skilled, unskilled, and overused skill definitions" (http://store.lominger.com/store/lominger/en_US/pd/productID.152409700, para. 1). The competencies "provide a common language to help users identify the skills and behaviors needed to succeed" (http://store.lominger.com/store/lominger/en_US/pd/productID.152409700, para. 3). Certification (achieved through training with Lominger) may be required for purchase of this card sort.

Purchasing Information: http://store.lominger.com/

Strategic Effectiveness Architect™ Card Deck — $175.00

Publisher: Lominger Limited, Inc.

Description: This card sort is most often used by consultants focused on organizational effectiveness, with emphasis on developing individuals as leaders. It also has relevance to career counseling. According to its website, this card sort focuses on helping "organizations create a sustained increase in ROI [return-on-investment] by aligning people practices to firm strategy and customer value" (http://store.lominger.com/store/lominger/en_US/pd/productID.127297700, para. 1). Certification (achieved through training with Lominger) may be required for purchase of this card sort.

Purchasing Information: http://store.lominger.com/

Life Styles Inventory™ — $75.00

Publisher: Human Synergistics

Description: This Australian card sort is most often used by consultants focused on organizational effectiveness, with emphasis on developing individuals as leaders. It also has clear relevance to career counseling as well. The LSI 1 focuses on how an individual's thinking styles affect his or her behavior, whereas the LSI 2 focuses on the impact of an individual's behaviors on others. Both card sorts yield results that are plotted on the Human Synergistics Circumplex map, a visual presentation of scores on three scales: constructive styles, passive/defensive styles, and aggressive/defensive styles.

Product Information: humansynergistics.com/Products/IndividualDevelopment/LifeStylesInventory

Purchase Information: nefried.com/Products/Assessments/HSI.htm

Winning Colors® Communicards $9.95

Publisher: Winning Colors®

Description: This card sort is most often used within educational settings and can be used with both adults and children. It also has relevance to career counseling. According to the website, this card sort is designed for the purpose of "identifying behavioral strengths" (winningcolors.com/2.pdf, p. 1) of self and others and focuses upon communication and leadership behaviors. The cards address four categories of behavioral strengths: planning/thinking (green color, part of people), building/leading (brown color, bear and bull parts of people), relating/team building (blue color, dolphin part of people), and adventuring/taking action (red color, tiger part of people). The website cautions that this card sort should not be confused with type theory personality assessments (including True Colors) and explains that, "the Winning Colors® time-tested behavior recognition process is based on Behavior Modification, Client Centered Therapy, Neurolinguistics, Rotter's Locus of Control and common sense" (winningcolors.com/promo, para. 15).

Purchase Information: mymap4success.com/store

TABLE 12.11 Postcareer and Retirement Card Sorts

Knowdell™ Card Sorts: Leisure/Retirement Activities $17.00

Publisher: Career Research & Testing, Inc.

Description: Developed by Richard L. Knowdell, this card sort focuses on postcareer interests. The website describes it as "an easy to use and approachable tool to aid in the transition from formal employment to a meaningful retirement lifestyle. Forty-eight common pastimes, from cultural events to meditation, from entertaining to group leadership, are listed and described. Cards can be used to determine current frequency as well as preferred activity patterns. The manual provides explicit instructions for using the card sort, an overview of the concepts and issues of retiring, summary and worksheets for processing the exercises and eight supplementary activities for dealing with aging and retirement. A useful resource for organizational pre-retirement programs" (careernetwork.org/career_assessment_instr.html#Leisure, para. 1). The Planning Kit includes the manual, one deck of cards, and one worksheet. Additional decks of cards are available for discounted prices.

Purchase Information: careertrainer.com

Third Quarter of Life Card Sorts $35.00

Publisher: AdultMentor.com

Description: Developed by Richard L. Haid, this card sort focuses on postcareer issues. The website indicates that this card sort "was designed to help people become more aware of important issues they may face in the third quarter of life, and it helps them build on current strengths to design a future that will truly work for them. The Third Quarter of Life Card Sorts let users quickly identify the possibilities—as well as the barriers—which need to be considered to create a plan for moving ahead. They give users the tools that provide a sense of direction and healthy optimism by helping the surface current Concerns, identify Strengths, and discover Passions" (http://adultmentor.com/3qlcs.html, para. 1–2). The kit consists of three decks of cards (addressing concerns, strengths, and passions), a response sheet and directions, a key, and a user guide.

Purchase Information: http://adultmentor.com/3qlcs.html or dickhaid@adultmentor.com

CHAPTER 13
Technology and Information Resources

The use of technology and information resources is another integral part of the career counseling process. In addition to addressing the importance of self-understanding, all major theories of career development also recognize the importance of information about the world of work (Gore & Hitch, 2005). Harkening back to ol' Frank Parsons (1909), for example, you will recall that an understanding of self is but the first step in his classic matching model. After all, what good does it do to understand your skills, interests, and so forth, if you do not know about the variety of careers that might fit well with your personal characteristics? Parsons specified that the second step of his matching model requires an understanding of the world of work, and he identified career information as an essential prerequisite to choosing a vocation. Also acknowledging the importance of career information to the process of choosing a vocation, McCormac (1989) observed that "up-to-date and accurate career information has been viewed as a key component of career decision-making since the Parsonian matching model appeared in the early 1900s" (p. 129). In this chapter, I extend this premise and suggest that information about the world of work is not only important to career selection but also to career launching, job searching, and continued career development.

As a counselor, you must be prepared to help clients in understanding not only their personal characteristics but also the world of work, and how the interaction between their personal characteristics and work factors may affect their career success and satisfaction. But here's the rub. For you to help clients gain this awareness and understanding, you have to know where to find career information and become familiar with it. This chapter is designed to help you do just that.

To get started, see how you do in answering the following eight questions:

1. What is the difference between an occupation and a job?
2. Approximately how many occupations exist in the United States?
3. What are the top three resources containing occupational information for use in career counseling?
4. What is the difference between occupational information and labor market information?
5. Is the projected growth rate higher for accountants or actuaries?
6. Just what is an actuary, anyway?
7. What type of training is needed to become a lineman [sic]?
8. How might you determine the top five jobs that don't require a four-year college degree?

If you are like most graduate students enrolled in counseling programs, you may be stumped by at least a few of these questions, and that's okay. No sweat. As a future counselor, though, you will want to know exactly where you can find answers to these and the many other questions your clients may have. The good news is that, by the end of this chapter, you will be able to answer most of these questions and others like them in under a minute. All you will need is Internet access and the knowledge of where to go for credible information.

In this chapter, I will provide you with an overview of the various types of information about the world of work, how this information is used in counseling, and where it comes from. I will also address finding this information online and in print, and will introduce you to a selection of recommended resources for use in career counseling. That's my end of the bargain. Your end of the bargain is to participate in learning this material by completing quick activities during your reading of this chapter. Every so often, I will include an application activity to help anchor this information. By completing these activities when prompted, you will (a) ensure that you don't fall asleep while reading what can otherwise be dry material, (b) develop the skills in assessing and using technology and information resources in counseling, and (c) increase your retention of the material.

This chapter will begin with an overview of the role of counselors related to the use of technology and information resources. It will then focus attention on four types of information about the world of work: (1) various classification systems used to organize information about the world of work, (2) occupational and labor market information, (3) information about the education and training needed to enter and advance within various occupations, and (4) information about building employability skills and conducting job searches.

ROLE OF COUNSELORS

In the career counseling process, counselors have three major roles related to the use of technology and information resources. First, counselors are responsible for identifying credible sources of information. Doing so requires an awareness of the various types of information resources, both hard copy and electronic, and an understanding of the appropriate uses of those resources in the career counseling process. It requires keeping up to date about these resources to ensure that the information provided by them is current. It also requires the information literacy necessary to distinguish between solid, accurate, and reliable information and information that is not credible (Zalaquettt & Osborn, 2007). The need to evaluate credibility of sources is especially important with regard to electronic resources (Osborn, Dikel, Sampson, & Harris-Bowlsbey, 2011). Whereas print publication of materials is generally contingent on external, professional evaluation of the quality and credibility of those materials, anyone can post information to the Internet. Thus, critical thinking skills and information literacy are necessary and especially important for the evaluation of material found on the Internet.

A second important role for counselors is to help clients gain access to relevant information. In a physical career center, this may entail guiding a client toward a specific resource or resource section or identifying a particular chapter in a relevant book. This may also involve asking a client to visit a particular website between sessions. In helping clients gain access to any of these resources, counselors must assess client readiness and ability to use these resources independently. This holds true both for digital and physical information resources. Simply handing a book to a client or directing a client to a website containing information is not sufficient. Instead, counselors need to orient clients to the materials, show them how to use the materials, and facilitate their use of this information in the career counseling process. Many career counselors provide instructional handouts or worksheets to clients as they utilize a variety of information resources.

In addition to helping clients access these information resources, counselors play an important role in helping clients make effective use of information. Indeed, a third important role for counselors is to help clients process the information they obtain and to help them apply that information to their particular situation. Rather than assuming that clients will know what to do with the information they gather or understand how to use it to resolve their concerns or reach their goals, counselors should engage clients in a discussion of their findings. Especially in this age, the availability of information can be overwhelming. Gathering information is only one step of the process. Digesting and synthesizing this information so that it becomes useful is another.

TYPES OF INFORMATION ABOUT THE WORLD OF WORK

Every counselor should be familiar with four primary types of information about the world of work:

1. Occupational classification systems
2. Occupational and labor market information
3. Education and training information
4. Skill-building and job search information

Occupational classification refers to systems used to organize information about occupations. Counselors need a basic understanding of these systems to help clients expand their understanding of the world of work. Counselors also need access to descriptive information about the nature of a wide variety of occupations as well as data regarding pay and projected demand for workers in those occupations. This type of information is called occupational and labor market information. Because many jobs require specific types of education and training, career counselors also need an awareness of informational resources to help clients identify appropriate education and training programs. Career counselors also need access to resources designed to assist clients in developing employability and job-hunting skills.

OCCUPATIONAL CLASSIFICATION SYSTEMS

Earlier in this chapter, I asked the following questions related to occupational information: (1) What is the difference between an occupation and a job? (2) Approximately how many occupations exist in the United States? My assumption is that you and your classmates generated a variety of definitions for *occupation* and *job* and that your guesses about the number of occupations in the United States varied widely. Although I will suggest a correct response for each of these questions, the answer to these questions ultimately depends on the occupational classification system you use to guide your response. My suggestion is that you rely on the Standard Occupational Classification (SOC) system to answer these questions because this system is now mandated for all federal agencies (Emmel & Cosca, 2010). In keeping with this recommendation, this section of the chapter focuses primarily on the SOC. Several other classification systems will also be identified.

Standard Occupational Classification System

Just as you and your classmates may have generated a variety of definitions for *occupation* and *job* and offered many different estimates of the number of occupations in the United States, so too has our government. Until 2000, federal agencies in the United States used vastly different systems to classify occupations. Examples of such systems include the *Dictionary of Occupational Titles* (DOT), the Occupational Employment Statistics (OES) system, the Standard Occupational Classification (SOC) system, and the U.S. Census occupational classification system (Gore & Hitch, 2005; Herman & Abraham, 1999). These varied systems resulted in different definitions of *occupation*; the identification of widely varying numbers of occupations; and numerous difficulties related to systematic data collection, sharing, and analysis. Before 2000, the correct answers to the questions posed earlier could vary dramatically depending on which classification system one used. The DOT, for example, identified more than 12,000 occupations; the OES system collected data on only about 800 occupations (Herman & Abraham, 1999).

The U.S. government made a decision to adopt a single classification system for use by all federal agencies. The work of developing such a system was conducted by the Standard Occupational Classification Revision Committee and resulted in a revised SOC in 2000. Since then, all federal agencies have been required to use the SOC for data collection, linking, and information dissemination. State, regional, and local agencies are also encouraged to use it. The SOC was most recently revised in 2010 (Emmel & Cosca, 2010).

I encourage you to rely on the standard definition of *occupation* that is now used by the U.S. government and specified in the Standard Occupational Classification (SOC) system. As you read the following, see if your earlier guess matches these official definitions of *occupation* and *job*:

> An occupation is a category of jobs that are similar with respect to the work performed and the skills possessed by the incumbents. A job is the specific set of tasks performed by an individual worker. "Turnpike toll collector" is an example of a job that corresponds to the occupation 41-2011 Cashiers. (U.S. Bureau of Labor Statistics, 2010, p. 2)

In other words, an occupation is a broader group of jobs that require similar skills and involve similar tasks. Now that you know one occupation recognized by the SOC is cashier and one job within this occupation is turnpike toll collector, take a minute and brainstorm other jobs that may also be subsumed within the occupation of cashier. Once you have done so, you may wish to complete an initial application activity by visiting the online version of the SOC (bls.gov/soc/2010) to see what other illustrative examples of cashiers are offered. While you're there, you may also wish to check out the occupation of counselor.

The SOC's approach to defining occupations by the skills needed and tasks performed is especially useful to career counselors because it facilitates the process of helping clients identify other jobs for which they may already be qualified. Another benefit of grouping jobs into broader categories of occupations is that this results in a manageable number of occupations that are tracked by our government and detailed in official occupational information resources. Whereas the DOT (last published in 1991) identified in excess of 12,000 occupation titles and was not very useful in identifying other jobs for which a client may also be qualified, the SOC has identified a very manageable 840 occupations in its attempt to classify "all occupations in which work is performed for pay or profit" in the United States (U.S. Bureau of Labor Statistics, 2010, p. ii).

As shown in Figure 13.1, these 840 detailed occupations are then combined into increasingly broad groupings to allow for varying levels of disaggregation in the collection and dissemination of occupational information and data. At the broadest level, the 840 occupations are organized into 23 major groups, which are identified in Table 13.1.

840	Detailed occupations
461	Broad occupations
97	Minor groups
23	Major groups

FIGURE 13.1 Standard Occupational Classification System Groupings

As you read the list of major groups identified in Table 13.1, try to guess which major group includes career counselors. Also notice that a numeric code is applied to each major group in the SOC and that the last four digits of every major group are 0000. You have probably surmised that the first two digits of the SOC code are used to denote the major group and may wonder what the other digits represent. Figure 13.2 shows that the remaining four digits are used to denote increasingly detailed groupings of workers.

Note in the figure that career counselors fall within the major group of community and social service occupations and within the more specific occupation of educational, guidance, school, and vocational counselors. Different job titles are often used to refer to very similar jobs; thus, there are many more job titles than there are occupations (this partly explains why the now defunct DOT contained more than 12,000 titles and the SOC includes only 840 occupations). To address job title variation, the SOC website also includes a direct match title database. If you search this database for career counselor, you would find that the SOC identifies this as a direct match for educational, guidance, school, and vocational counselors.

TABLE 13.1 Standard Occupational Classification (SOC) Major Groups

SOC Code	Major Group Title
11-0000	Management occupations
13-0000	Business and financial operations occupations
15-0000	Computer and mathematical occupations
17-0000	Architecture and engineering occupations
19-0000	Life, physical, and social science occupations
21-0000	Community and social service occupations
23-0000	Legal occupations
25-0000	Education, training, and library occupations
27-0000	Arts, design, entertainment, sports, and media occupations
29-0000	Health care practitioners and technical occupations
31-0000	Health care support occupations
33-0000	Protective service occupations
35-0000	Food preparation and serving-related occupations
37-0000	Building and grounds cleaning and maintenance occupations
39-0000	Personal care and service occupations
41-0000	Sales and related occupations
43-0000	Office and administrative support occupations
45-0000	Farming, fishing, and forestry occupations
47-0000	Construction and extraction occupations
49-0000	Installation, maintenance, and repair occupations
51-0000	Production occupations
53-0000	Transportation and material moving occupations
55-0000	Military-specific occupations

Source: U.S. Bureau of Labor Statistics. (2010). 2010 SOC User Guide. Washington, DC: Author. (p. xiv)

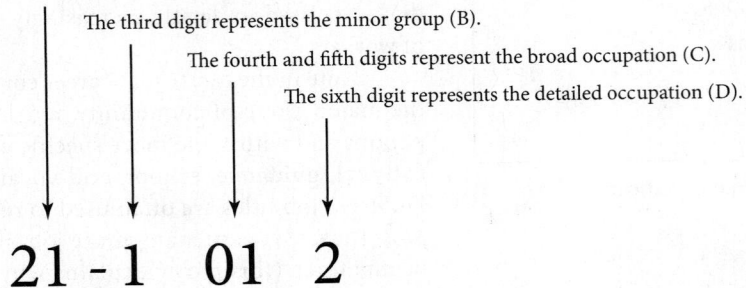

FIGURE 13.2 Standard Occupational Classification (SOC) Coding System
Source: U.S. Bureau of Labor Statistics

Other Occupational Classification Systems

The SOC is clearly the "gold standard" for occupational classification systems in the United States, but you should be aware of other systems. The SOC is most useful to career counselors in understanding the organization of and using government-based resources related to the world of work, but other systems tend to be most useful in providing psychoeducation to clients. Examples of the most prominent occupational classification systems are identified in Table 13.2.

HOLLAND'S OCCUPATIONAL CLASSIFICATION SYSTEM. As you learned in Chapter 2, Holland's (1997) person-environment fit theory is based in part on his development of an occupational classification system involving six primary types of model work environments denoted by RIASEC (realistic, investigative, artistic, social, enterprising, conventional) and illustrated with a hexagon. With Holland's classification system, occupations can be organized into any one of the six model work environments. In the interest of providing a more nuanced classification of occupations, Holland also identified a two- or three-letter Holland code for every occupation listed in the *Dictionary of Occupational Titles* (DOT: U.S. Department of Labor, Employment and Training Administration, 1991). He published this information in a widely used resource called the *Dictionary of Holland Occupational Codes* (DHOC; Gottfredson & Holland, 1996). In addition to identifying the Holland code for each occupation, this resource also offers an estimate of what Holland called the "occupational level" (Holland, 1997, p. 49) and others have called "cognitive complexity" (Gottfredson & Holland, 1996; Reardon, Vernick, & Reed, 2004). Holland's classification system organizes occupations based on the interests and personality styles of workers most likely to be satisfied and successful in them and on the level of difficulty associated with them.

This occupational classification system is especially useful to assist clients in using assessment results from instruments such as the Self-Directed Search or the Strong Interest Inventory to guide their consideration and exploration of various occupations. Later in this chapter, you'll learn how one of the most widely used resources for occupational and labor market information, the Occupational Information Network (O*NET) website (onetonline.org), also allows users to search for occupations using the

TABLE 13.2 Prominent Occupational Classification Systems

Classification System	Developer
Standard Occupational Classification (SOC) system	U.S. Department of Labor
Holland's occupational classification system	John Holland
National career clusters and pathways	States Career Clusters Initiative
World-of-work map	ACT, Inc.

classification system based on Holland's RIASEC typology and the *Dictionary of Holland Occupational Codes*.

WORLD-OF-WORK MAP. Expanding on Holland's typology, ACT developed an occupational classification system called the world-of-work map. This map may be viewed online at www.act.org/wwm/. This circular map is divided into 12 sections that resemble slices of a pie, and 26 occupational clusters are distributed among these sections. The dot associated with each occupational cluster is designed to denote that cluster's spatial placement and relative emphasis on data, things, ideas, and people, as well as association with each Holland model work environment. This occupational classification system is especially useful for middle and high school counselors because the world-of-work map is used to display results from the Unisex Edition of the ACT Interest Inventory (UNIACT; ACT, 2009). The UNIACT is an interest inventory automatically included with the three ACT achievement tests, which are part of ACT's College and Career Readiness System. The world-of-work map is useful in helping students understand the implications of their academic achievement and self-reported occupational interests and may be used to guide students' ongoing exploration of occupational options.

NATIONAL CAREER CLUSTERS AND PATHWAYS. Another prominent occupational classification system most often used in K–12 school settings was developed by the States Career Clusters Initiative, which is now known as the National Association of State Directors and Career Technical Education Consortium (NASDTE; n.d., 2013). As shown in Table 13.3, this organization has identified 16 career clusters and 79 career pathways that are subsumed within these clusters. Both the clusters and pathways in this classification system are organized according to the knowledge and skills needed. The distinction between them is that clusters align with industry needs, and pathways address needs within specific professions or occupations (Virginia Department of Education, 2012). The national career clusters and pathways system has been adopted by the U.S. Department of Education (Stone & Lewis, 2012).

Although developed within the narrower field of career technical education (CTE), the national career clusters are widely used with all students in middle schools and high schools. Specifically, they often become an integral component of the academic and career planning process and are featured in many career development materials geared toward K–12 students (Achieve Texas, 2007; Barge, 2012; Hobson & Phillips, 2004; Virginia Department of Education, 2012). You will learn more about the use of the national clusters as an occupational classification system in Chapters 14 and 15.

OCCUPATIONAL AND LABOR MARKET INFORMATION

In addition to understanding classification systems, career counselors must also be proficient in accessing and using occupational and labor market information. The term *occupational information* refers to information about what any given occupation entails; *labor market information* refers to the projected demand and compensation for workers in a given occupation. In tandem, occupational and labor market information is essential to supporting accurate awareness and understanding of one's vocational options. Without this information, career aspirations and decision making may be based on faulty assumptions and misperceptions. Indeed, the breadth, depth, and accuracy of the occupational and labor market information to which one is exposed or has access affects one's early career aspirations, initial career selection, and ongoing career development and decisions. It is extremely important to supporting career development and to providing career counseling.

National Career Development Association Content Guidelines

So what types of occupational and labor market information do people need? The National Career Development Association (National Career Development Association, n.d.) developed "Guidelines for the Preparation and Evaluation of Career and Occupational Literature" to address this very question. This document includes content guidelines that specify the types of occupational and labor market information NCDA recommends; these guidelines are summarized in Table 13.4.

Career counselors should seek informational resources that not only provide descriptive information but also address entry requirements, career progression and advancement opportunities, and labor market information such as typical earnings and employment outlook. Such resources are even more helpful when they support continued exploration by identifying other occupations for consideration and other sources of occupational information. Although this is a tall order, the good news is that several reputable resources provide this very information.

Federal Government Resources

The three primary resources with which every career counselor should be familiar are O*NET OnLine, the *Occupational Outlook Handbook*, and America's Career InfoNet.

OCCUPATIONAL INFORMATION NETWORK AND O*NET ONLINE. A product of the U.S. Department of Labor, the Occupational Information Network (O*NET) is an

TABLE 13.3 National Career Clusters

16 National Career Clusters and Pathways

Agriculture, Food, and Natural Resources
- Food products and processing systems
- Plan systems
- Animal systems
- Power, structural, and technical systems
- Natural resources systems
- Environmental service systems
- Agribusiness systems

Education and Training
- Administration and administrative support
- Professional support services
- Teaching/training

Hospitality and Tourism
- Restaurants and food/beverage services
- Travel and tourism
- Lodging
- Recreation, amusements, and attractions

Manufacturing
- Production
- Manufacturing production process development
- Maintenance, installation, and repair
- Quality assurance
- Logistics and inventory control
- Health, safety, and environmental assurance

Architecture and Construction
- Design/preconstruction
- Construction
- Maintenance/operations

Finance
- Securities and investments
- Business finance
- Accounting
- Insurance
- Banking services

Human Services
- Early childhood development and services
- Counseling and mental health services
- Family and community services
- Personal-care services
- Consumer services

Marketing
- Marketing management
- Professional sales
- Merchandising
- Marketing communications
- Marketing research

Arts, A/V Technology, and Communications
- Audio and video Technology and film
- Printing technology
- Visual arts
- Performing arts
- Journalism and broadcasting
- Telecommunications

Government and Public Administration
- Governance
- National security
- Foreign service
- Planning
- Revenue and taxation
- Regulation
- Public management and administration

Information Technology
- Network systems
- Information support and services
- Web and digital communications
- Health, safety, and environmental assurance
- Programming and software development

Science, Technology, Engineering, and Mathematics
- Engineering and technology
- Science and mathematics

Business Management and Administration
- General management
- Business information management
- Human resources management
- Operations management
- Administrative support

Health Science
- Therapeutic services
- Diagnostic services
- Health informatics
- Support services
- Biotechnology research and development

Law, Public Safety, Corrections, and Security
- Correction services
- Emergency and fire management services
- Law enforcement services
- Legal services
- Security and protective services

Transportation, Distribution, and Logistics
- Transportation operations
- Logistics planning and management services
- Warehousing and distribution center operations
- Facility and mobile equipment maintenance
- Transportation systems/infrastructure
- Planning, management, and regulation
- Health, safety, and environmental management
- Sales and service

TABLE 13.4 NCDA Content Guidelines for Occupational and Labor Market Information

Descriptive Information

Duties and nature of the work	• Purpose • Activities • Skills, knowledge, interests, and abilities • Specializations
Work setting and conditions	• Full range of possible settings • Physical, psychological, and social environment • Geographic regions • Time commitments and scheduling • Travel or relocation requirements

Entry Requirements and Career Progression

Preparation required	• Type and level of training or education • Experience requirements • Skills, knowledge, interests, and abilities • Typical and alternative forms of preparation
Special requirements or considerations	• Bona fide occupational qualifications • Credential requirements • Desirable qualities • Lifestyle considerations
Methods of entry	• Typical method of entry • Alternative routes
Usual advancement possibilities	• Opportunities for career progression • Requirements for advancement

Labor Market Information

Earnings and other benefits	• Wage and salary ranges • Geographic differences in wages or salary • Typical benefits
Employment outlook	• Projected growth rate • Projected number of new hires • Department of Labor projections

Recommendations for Further Exploration

Related occupations	• Occupations that involve similar skills, interests, and so on
Sources of additional information	• Organizations and associations • Publications • Audio and video material • Websites

Source: Based on National Career Development Association. (n.d.). *Guidelines for the preparation and evaluation of career and occupational information literature*. Broken Arrow, OK: Author. Retrieved on June 22, 2013 from http://ncda.org/aws/NCDA/pt/fli/4729/false

incredibly important resource for career counselors. The O*NET system includes several applications related to the career counseling process (only one of which is O*NET OnLine), such as:

- Career Exploration Tools: The O*NET assessment instruments are described in Chapter 11.
- O*NET-SOC Taxonomy and Code Connector: O*NET's connection to the Standard Occupational Classification system.
- My Next Move and Mi Próximo Paso: A career exploration program available in both English and Spanish and designed for use by students and job seekers.

- My Next Move for Veterans: An application to support veterans as they transition into the civilian workforce.
- Career Ladders and Lattices: Tools to assist people in understanding opportunities for advancement within a given career and opportunities for lateral moves into related occupations.
- Podcasts: Audio presentations available via the Internet that address a variety of career-related topics ranging from the use of O*NET in welfare-to-work programs to the use of O*NET in helping young people with disabilities transition from school into the world of work.
- O*NET OnLine: An application dedicated to the provision of occupational and labor market information.

The focus of this chapter is on occupational and labor market information, so I will focus on O*NET OnLine. However, as an application activity, you will benefit from visiting the O*NET Resource Center's website at onetcenter.org and familiarizing yourself with its wealth of resources.

Using O*NET OnLine to Access Occupational and Labor Market Information. O*NET OnLine is an application dedicated to the provision of occupational and labor market information. As you read this section about the various features of O*NET OnLine, you will also benefit from exploring them on the website (onetonline.org). Doing so will allow you to develop the skills necessary to use this resource to benefit yourself as well as future clients. Figure 13.3 illustrates the home page for O*NET OnLine.

FIGURE 13.3 O*NET Online Home Page
Source: ONET OnLine. National Center for ONET Development, n.d. Web. 23 Aug. 2014. http://www.onetonline.org/. ONET OnLine is sponsored by the - http://www.onetonline.org/ U.S. Department of Labor

As you explore this website, consider using it to answer some of the questions posed at the beginning of this chapter, such as:

1. Is the projected growth rate higher for accountants or actuaries?
2. Just what is an actuary?
3. What type of training is needed to become a lineman (an occupational title used for both men and women)?

To begin, enter *actuary* into the Occupation Quick Search window at the top right of the O*NET OnLine home page. When you do so, the next screen will identify a number of occupations most closely matched to *actuary*, and this listing will include *actuaries*. Notice a numeric code for each of the occupations listed. These are O*NET-SOC codes. The first six digits represent the SOC code, and the last two digits have been added by O*NET to classify occupations further. Next, click on "actuaries" to access occupational and labor market information about this occupation. An impressive amount of information will be displayed. Table 13.5 identifies the categories of occupational and labor market information provided by O*NET.

By skimming through the summary report of this information, you will soon understand the meaning of *actuary*. You may also wish to do the same for *accountants* in order to develop a more nuanced sense of the similarities and differences between these occupations. To determine which of these occupations has a higher projected growth rate, click on or scroll down to the wages and employment trends section of the summary report. At the time of this writing, the projected growth rate for actuaries was 20 to 28%, and the projected growth rate for accountants was 10 to 19%. Thus, the projected growth rate for actuaries is higher than for accountants. It is also important to notice the number of projected job openings. Notice that projections indicate there will be many more job openings for accountants than for actuaries. Specifically, the U.S. Bureau of Labor Statistics predicts that there will be 452,100 new job openings for accountants but only 18,900 new job openings for actuaries.

Note how little time it took to open this website and obtain this information for two different professions. All of a sudden, you feel amazingly well-equipped to access information about nearly any occupation. Although you likely knew what an accountant does and may or may not have known what an actuary does, you probably couldn't have offered nearly the degree of detail provided by O*NET OnLine.

In addition to descriptive information and labor market information, O*NET OnLine offers information about the training and experience needed to enter each occupation. It does this most thoroughly in its job zones section (see Table 13.6). O*NET OnLine uses job zones to address the level of preparation and training needed to enter any given occupation, including overall experience, job training, education, and a specific vocational preparation (SVP) code (National Center for O*NET Development, 2008). SVP codes were used in the DOT and ranged from 1 to 9. Occupations with an SVP code of 1 required only a brief demonstration; occupations with an SVP code of 9 required more than 10 years of education beyond a high school diploma or GED (National Center for O*NET Development, 1999).

For another application activity, see if you can answer my question about the training needed to become a lineman. Note that, despite the sexist title of this occupation, both men and women can and do work as linemen (Whitaker, 2013). To determine the training needed to enter this occupation, enter "lineman" into the occupation quick search. This time, you will see that no such job title matching "lineman" appears in the list of occupations. However, you will also see a relevance score of 100 for "electrical power-line installers and repairers." This indicates that the

TABLE 13.5 Occupational and Labor Market Information Provided by O*NET OnLine

Descriptive Information
- Tasks
- Tools and technology
- Knowledge
- Skills
- Abilities
- Work activities
- Work context
- Work styles
- Work values

Entry Requirements and Career Progression
- Job zone
- Education

Labor Market Information
- Wages and employment
- Job openings

Recommendations for Further Exploration
- Additional information

Source: ONET, OnLineNET Online, U.S. Department of Labor.

TABLE 13.6 O*NET OnLine Job Zone Descriptions

Job Zone One: Little or No Preparation Needed

Overall experience	No previous work-related skill, knowledge, or experience is needed for these occupations. For example, a person can become a cashier even if he or she has never worked before.
Job training	Employees in these occupations need anywhere from a few days to a few months of training. Usually, an experienced worker can show you how to do the job.
Job zone examples	These occupations involve following instructions and helping others. Examples include taxi drivers, amusement and recreation attendants, counter and rental clerks, cashiers, and waiters and waitresses.
SVP range	Below 4.0 (no more than 3 months of training)
Education	These occupations may require a high school diploma or GED certificate. Some may require a formal training course to obtain a license.

Job Zone Two: Some Preparation Needed

Overall experience	Some previous work-related skill, knowledge, or experience may be helpful in these occupations but usually is not needed. For example, a teller might benefit from experience working directly with the public, but an inexperienced person could still learn to be a teller with little difficulty.
Job training	Employees in these occupations need anywhere from a few months to one year of working with experienced employees.
Job zone examples	These occupations often involve using your knowledge and skills to help others. Examples include sheet metal workers, forest firefighters, customer service representatives, pharmacy technicians, salespersons (retail), and tellers.
SVP range	4.0 to < 6.0 (6 to 12 months of training)
Education	These occupations usually require a high school diploma and may require some vocational training or job-related coursework. In some cases, an associate's or bachelor's degree might be needed.

Job Zone Three: Medium Preparation Needed

Overall experience	Previous work-related skill, knowledge, or experience is required for these occupations. For example, an electrician must have completed three or four years of apprenticeship or several years of vocational training and often must have passed a licensing exam in order to perform the job.
Job training	Employees in these occupations usually need one or two years of training involving both on-the-job experience and informal training with experienced workers.
Job zone examples	These occupations usually involve using communication and organizational skills to coordinate, supervise, manage, or train others to accomplish goals. Examples include funeral directors, electricians, forest and conservation technicians, legal secretaries, interviewers, and insurance sales agents.
SVP range	6.0 to < 7.0 (1 to 2 years of training)
Education	Most occupations in this zone require training in vocational schools, related on-the-job experience, or an associate's degree. Some may require a bachelor's degree.

Job Zone Four: Considerable Preparation Needed

Overall experience	A minimum of two to four years of work-related skill, knowledge, or experience is needed for these occupations. For example, an accountant must complete four years of college and work for several years in accounting to be considered qualified.
Job training	Employees in these occupations usually need several years of work-related experience, on-the-job training, and/or vocational training.
Job zone examples	Many of these occupations involve coordinating, supervising, managing, or training others. Examples include accountants, human resources managers, computer programmers, teachers, chemists, and police detectives.
SVP range	7.0 to < 8.0 (2 to 4 years of training)
Education	Most of these occupations require a four-year bachelor's degree, but some do not.

Job Zone Five: Extensive Preparation Needed

Overall experience	Extensive skill, knowledge, and experience are needed for these occupations. Many require more than five years of experience. For example, surgeons must complete four years of college and an additional five to seven years of specialized medical training to be able to do their job.
Job training	Employees may need some on-the-job training, but most of these occupations assume that the person already has the required skills, knowledge, work-related experience, and/or training.
Job zone examples	These occupations often involve coordinating, training, supervising, or managing the activities of others to accomplish goals. Very advanced communication and organizational skills are required. Examples include librarians, lawyers, aerospace engineers, physicists, school psychologists, and surgeons.
SVP range	8.0 and above (4 to 10 years of training)
Education	A bachelor's degree is the minimum formal education required for these occupations. However, many also require graduate school. For example, they may require a master's degree, and some require a Ph.D., M.D., or J.D. (law degree).

Source: National Center for ONET OnLineNET Development. (2008). Procedures for ONET OnLineNET job zone assignment. Raleigh, NC: Author. U.S. Department of Labor

official SOC job title is a direct match for the title you entered. Therefore, click on "electrical power-line installers and repairers" to access occupational and labor market information about linemen. Information about the training needed to become a lineman will be most clearly identified in the job zone section. Here, you will discover that this occupations falls within job zone 3 and may require training through vocational schools, apprenticeships, associate's degrees, or on-the-job experience. By following links within the additional information section, you may access the website for the National Joint Apprenticeship and Training Committee for the Electrical Industry (NJATC, njatc.org) to learn about apprenticeship programs specifically designed to prepare people for this career. The Tennessee Valley Authority also offers a lineman apprentice program (tva.com/employment/ops_maint/lineman.htm).

At this point, I hope you feel confident in your ability to use O*NET OnLine to access occupational and labor market information about any occupation. You may use this online application to access and print out information for clients who may lack the skills or Internet access needed to use O*NET OnLine, and to teach more digitally literate clients how to use the system on their own.

Thus far, however, we have focused on searching for information using the name of a given occupation. In many cases, though, clients will not know which occupations they want to explore. Instead, they need assistance in identifying possible occupations that may be a good fit for them, and we explore this topic next.

Using O*NET OnLine to Identify Additional Occupations to Explore. One way to identify additional occupations for clients to consider is to use the O*NET OnLine Advanced Search application. This application, shown in the upper portion of Figure 13.4, allows users (counselors, clients, or anyone else) to search for occupations that match one's interests, work-related values, skills and abilities, and other characteristics. This is especially useful if you have assessment results for a client. For example, you may want to search for jobs that match a client's Holland code. To do so, you can go to the advanced search application and search by interest. After you select the first letter of the Holland code, additional windows appear, which allows you to select the second and third letters of the Holland code. Sometimes, you will want to use all three letters; sometimes this search will result in very few occupational matches, and you will find it more useful to use only two letters. Once the list of occupational matches to a Holland code appear, you can limit the results to a given job zone.

A second way to identify additional occupations for clients to consider is to use the O*NET OnLine Find Occupations application. This application, shown in the lower portion of Figure 13.4, allows users to search for occupations that fall within a variety of categories. For example, one can search for occupations falling within any one of the 16 national career clusters, within a specific industry, within a job family, and even within a specific science, technology, engineering, and math (STEM) discipline. This application also facilitates searches for occupations that fall within a given job zone, are recognized as having a bright outlook for rapid growth, and/or are considered part of the green economy.

OCCUPATIONAL OUTLOOK HANDBOOK. The *Occupational Outlook Handbook* (OOH; U.S. Bureau of Labor Statistics, 2013) is a second essential resource for occupational and labor market information. The U.S. Bureau of Labor Statistics describes the OOH as "the Nation's premier source for career information" (bls.gov/ooh/home.htm, para. 1).

306 Chapter 13

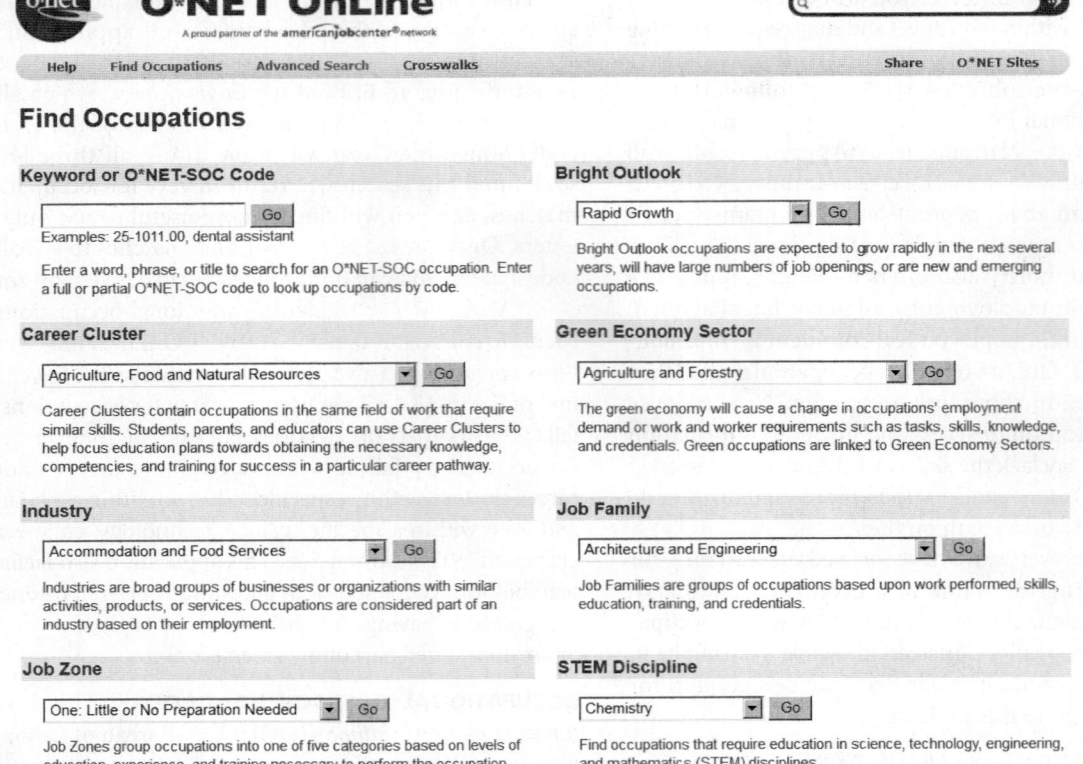

- Abilities
- Interests
- Knowledge
- Skills
- Work Activities
- Work Context

FIGURE 13.4 Search Options Using O*NET OnLine

Sources: http://www.onetonline.org/search/ and http://www.onetonline.org/find/ U.S. Department of Labor

The OOH is produced by the U.S. Bureau of Labor Statistics but, as a public domain resource, it is available for purchase from numerous publishers. Each publisher tends to offer its own supplemental chapters within its publication of the OOH, but the actual content of the OOH remains the same across all versions, regardless of publisher. The OOH is updated every other year, so each edition of the OOH identifies a two-year time span. For example, the edition available at the time of this writing is the 2013–2014 edition.

Although there is certainly overlap in the information available in the OOH and on O*NET OnLine, there are some differences. In contrast to O*NET, which features a wide variety of applications relevant to the career counseling process, the sole focus of the OOH is on providing occupational and labor market information. O*NET is available online only; the OOH is available both online and in print (book). The online and print formats of OOH are available in both English and Spanish.

OOH Occupational and Labor Market Information. Organized in accordance with the 23 major groupings of the SOC, the OOH presents occupational and labor market information about "hundreds of occupations that provide the overwhelming majority of jobs in the United States" (U.S. Bureau of Labor Statistics, 2013, p. 24). Specifically, 90% of the workers in the United States are employed in occupations included in the OOH. Because the OOH provides information for each of these occupations in a uniform format, the result is an easy-to-read resource. Table 13.7 identifies the sections included for each occupation listed in the OOH.

OOH Earnings and Job Outlook Information. A major feature of the OOH, as evidenced by its title, is attention to the outlook and earnings associated with each occupation. Whereas the wage and salary information is relatively easy to understand, the outlook information can be less so. In providing projections about the employment outlook for any given occupation for the decade, the OOH uses phrases to denote various degrees of growth or decline. Table 13.8

TABLE 13.7 Occupation and Labor Market Information Provided by the *Occupational Outlook Handbook*

Quick Facts
- Median pay
- Entry-level education
- Work experience in a related occupation
- On-the-job training
- Number of jobs
- Job outlook
- Employment change

Descriptive Information
- What workers in a particular occupation do
- Work environment

Entry Requirements and Career Progression
- Education
- Important qualities
- Training (optional)
- Licenses (optional)
- Certification (optional)
- Work experience (optional)
- Advancement (optional)

Labor Market Information
- Pay
- Job outlook

Recommendations for Further Exploration
- Contacts for more information
- Similar occupations

TABLE 13.8 Job Outlook Definitions in the *Occupational Outlook Handbook*

OOH Projected Changes	Definition
Grow much faster than average	Increase at least 29%
Grow faster than average	Increase 20 to 28%
Grow about as fast as average	Increase 10 to 19%
Grow more slowly than average	Increase 3 to 9%
Little or no change	Decrease 2% to increase 2%
Decline slowly or moderately	Decrease 3 to 9%
Decline rapidly	Decrease 10% or more

provides a key to the phrases used by the OOH to describe projected changes, with an indication of the percentage increase or decrease associated with each category.

In addition to providing this information, the OOH sections on job outlook may also identify factors contributing to the anticipated growth or decline of an occupation.

This section of the OOH also features a chart that provides a visual indication of how the projected growth for a given occupation compares to related occupations as well as all occupations. As you can imagine, such information can be quite useful to clients when attempting to select from among related occupational options. Figure 13.5 provides

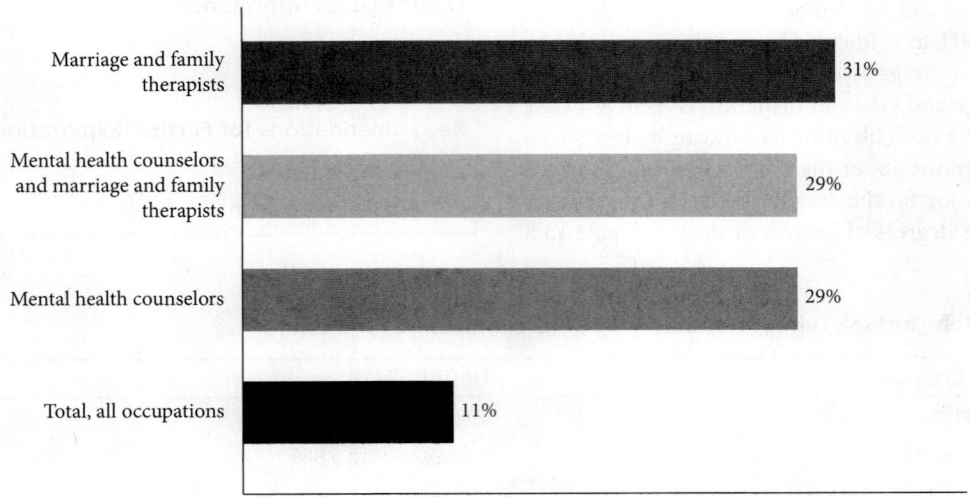

FIGURE 13.5 OOH Charts Regarding the Job Outlook for Counselors in 2015

Source: http://www.bls.gov/ooh/Community-and-Social-Service/School-and-career-counselors.htm#tab-6 and http://www.bls.gov/ooh/community-and-social-service/mental-health-counselors-and-marriage-and-family-therapists.htm#tab-6 U.S. Bureau of Labor Statistics.

an example of such charts and focuses on the job outlook for school, career, and mental health counselors.

Digging Deeper with Occupational Employment Statistics. You may want to narrow down or customize the data from OOH, maybe because you want statistics for a very specific occupation within an SOC occupation type, you want to identify where the job openings are expected to be, or you wish to determine which industries employ the most workers from a given occupation. These types of information are indeed available. Most of the OOH earnings and outlook data draw on the Occupational Employment Statistics (OES) generated by the U.S. Bureau of Labor Statistics. The good news is that (a) this data is available online (bls.gov/oes/current/oes_str.htm); (b) with the right know-how, you can create customized reports; and (c) you can get the right know-how from an easy-to-read article in which Cunningham (2013) offers step-by-step instructions for accessing industry profiles, accessing geographic profiles, and creating customized tables from this online data. Read that and you'll officially be a savvy person who knows how to dig deeper into OOH data using the OES.

Here is an example illustrating one possible way to use OES data in conjunction with the OOH. Let's say that a client came in for career counseling and asked you whether school counselors or college counselors earn more. This is a difficult question because of the way in which the SOC classifies these professions. Specifically, the SOC identifies both professions as falling within the same occupation: 21-1012, educational, guidance, school, and vocational counselors. In keeping with the mandate that all federal agencies use the SOC classification system, O*NET OnLine and the OOH both present earnings and outlook data for this occupational grouping. O*NET uses this exact title, and the OOH uses an abbreviated version: school and career counselors. Even a search specifically for college counselors results in the presentation of this combined category based on the idea that a college is a school. Although there are great reasons for the SOC's distillation of 840 careers, your client wants more specific information. You will be well equipped to provide this information because you will have read this text, read the article by Cunningham (2013), and even practiced online.

Although you may use the OOH to determine that the 2013 median annual wage for school and career counselors is $53,610, this does not answer your client's question about whether school or college counselors tend to earn more. To determine this, you will need to go directly to the source of this data: the OES website at bls.gov/oes/current/oes211012.htm. Figure 13.6 displays the type of information you will receive upon doing so. First, notice that the data provided is always somewhat out of date. In February, 2015, for example, this site provided data for May 2013. This should not be terribly surprising because it takes considerable time for the federal government to analyze and disseminate the data. Next, notice that OES presents two types of annual wage estimates: the median wage and the mean wage. OES reports a 2013 median wage of $53,600 and a 2013 mean wage of $56,160. These wage figures are for all educational, guidance, school, and vocational counselors, regardless of the setting or industry in which they are employed.

The industry profile for this occupation gives you the information you need to answer your client's question. This industry profile is displayed in the final segment of Figure 13.6, which shows the average mean wages for five different settings: K–12 schools, four-year colleges, community/junior colleges, vocational rehabilitation agencies, and other community agencies. Notice how easily you can now respond to your client's question. This data suggests that, for this occupation, the highest average salaries are in the K–12 school setting ($63,100), the next highest salaries are in junior/community colleges ($56,510), and the third highest salaries are in the four-year colleges and universities ($49,320). From this data, you can indicate that the national data suggest that (a) school counselors earn more on average than college counselors, and (b) college counselors at junior/community colleges tend to earn more than college counselors at four-year colleges and universities. Of course, this information is based on the data posted at the time of this writing. As another application exercise, go to the OES website to see what the current data is when you read this section of the chapter.

AMERICA'S CAREER INFONET. America's Career InfoNet is a web-based application that offers occupational and labor market information to support career exploration. (It is also developed and maintained by the U.S. Department of Labor.) America's Career InfoNet features tabs related to other elements of the career development process. For example, the section on salary and benefits includes information about compensation levels for various occupations *and* the costs of relocating, financial issues related to pursuing additional education or training, health care benefits, and unemployment insurance. Other sections provide resources related to seeking education and training, job searching, résumés, and interviewing. America's Career InfoNet also includes an application designed to help users access services from state-based employment agencies and locate other resources.

★ U.S. Bureau of Labor Statistics

Occupational Employment Statistics

Occupational Employment and Wages, May 2013

21-1012 Educational, Guidance, School, and Vocational Counselors

Counsel individuals and provide group educational and vocational guidance services.

National estimates for this occupation
Industry profile for this occupation
Geographic profile for this occupation

National estimates for this occupation: Top

Employment estimate and mean wage estimates for this occupation:

Employment (1)	Employment RSE (3)	Mean hourly wage	Mean annual wage (2)	Wage RSE (3)
241,870	0.9 %	$27.00	$56,160	0.8 %

Percentile wage estimates for this occupation:

Percentile	10%	25%	50% (Median)	75%	90%
Hourly Wage	$15.31	$19.68	$25.77	$33.42	$41.77
Annual Wage (2)	$31,850	$40,940	$53,600	$69,520	$86,870

Industry profile for this occupation: Top

Industries with the highest published employment and wages for this occupation are provided. For a list of all industries with employment in this occupation, see the Create Customized Tables function.

Industries with the highest levels of employment in this occupation:

Industry	Employment (1)	Percent of industry employment	Hourly mean wage	Annual mean wage (2)
Elementary and Secondary Schools	124,590	1.50	$30.34	$63,100
Colleges, Universities, and Professional Schools	49,260	1.68	$23.71	$49,320
Junior Colleges	19,740	2.59	$27.17	$56,510
Vocational Rehabilitation Services	11,930	3.69	$18.95	$39,420
Individual and Family Services	6,430	0.46	$18.90	$39,320

FIGURE 13.6 Selected Industry Profile Information from the Occupational Employment Statistics
Source: Occupational Employment Statistics – July 19, 2013 http://data.bls.gov/cgi-bin/print.pl/oes/current/oes211012.htm. U.S. Bureau of Labor Statistics.

Using America's Career InfoNet to Access Occupational and Labor Market Information. For occupational and labor market information, though, the career exploration portion of America's Career InfoNet is most relevant. Like O*NET OnLine, America's Career InfoNet allows a user to search for information by entering the name of a specific occupation and browse for occupations in various categories. Table 13.9 identifies the information provided by America's Career InfoNet for any given occupation.

A feature offered by America's Career InfoNet worth noting is the section containing career videos (these videos are not offered by O*NET OnLine or the OOH). These short videos may be especially attractive to clients who prefer to gain information via methods other than reading. Another unique feature of America's Career InfoNet is its requirement that users select a state when searching for occupational information. This allows America's Career InfoNet to offer labor market information on both the national and state level. Because this is such a useful feature, O*NET OnLine actually links to this site when users seek both state and national information regarding wages and employment trends.

State data is useful in helping clients understand how an occupation's typical earnings in their particular state compare to the national average salary. This information may also be useful to clients who are considering relocation. Consider, for example, a graduate student pursuing a degree and career in mental health counseling. If this student happened to live near the state border between Alabama and Georgia, or lived in a northern state but was considering a move to a warmer state, information about the relative compensation of mental health counselors in

TABLE 13.9 Occupational and Labor Market Information Provided by Career InfoNet

Descriptive Information

Occupation description

Career video

Knowledge, skills, and abilities

Tasks and activities

Tools and technology

Entry Requirements and Career Progression

Education and training

Typical education needed for entry

Typical work experience needed for entry

Typical on-the-job training needed for entry

Related instructional programs

Distribution of educational attainment

Colleges, training schools, and instructional programs for this occupation

Short-term training finder

Education resources

Financial aid adviser

Workforce Investment Act (WIA)–eligible training provider list

Labor Market Information

State and national wages

State and national trends

Recommendations for Further Exploration

Related occupation profiles

Web resources

Related content

Source: CareerOneStop, U. S. Department of Labor http://www.careerinfonet.org.

---

more than one state might be useful. Figure 13.7 provides this data from America's Career InfoNet. It should be noted, however, that America's Career InfoNet does not display the state comparisons in this manner; I created this figure after conducting two separate searches on America's Career InfoNet and grouping the online information in this single figure.

In addition to caring about compensation levels, of course, clients care about the employment outlook and job openings. For an application activity, visit the America's Career InfoNet site and determine the number of job openings for mental health counselors projected for Alabama and Georgia. Alternatively, of course, you may wish to seek this same information for the states you are considering for your future career.

Using America's Career InfoNet to Search for Jobs by Educational Level. A question frequently posed by clients is about the best jobs available for their education level. Implicit in this question is a communication that the client is uninterested in obtaining additional education and/or feels an urgent need for employment prior to obtaining any additional education. This type of inquiry is so common that one of my eight questions listed at the beginning of this chapter was, "How might you determine the top five jobs that don't require a four-year college degree?" Responses involving an explanation about the importance of finding a good fit for one's interests, skills, personality, and values are likely to seem evasive to clients; they often (a) want a concrete answer and (b) will test your credibility early in the counseling process. Fortunately, America's

State and National Wages

Location	Pay Period	2013				
		10%	25%	Median	75%	90%
United States	Hourly	$12.43	$15.47	$19.51	$25.15	$32.22
	Yearly	$25,900	$32,200	$40,600	$52,300	$67,000
Alabama	Hourly	$13.17	$15.81	$19.11	$25.12	$29.14
	Yearly	$27,400	$32,900	$39,700	$52,200	$60,600
Georgia	Hourly	$11.43	$15.53	$20.45	$24.86	$28.75
	Yearly	$23,800	$32,300	$42,500	$51,700	$59,800

FIGURE 13.7 America's Career InfoNet Comparison of State and National Wages for Mental Health Counselors

Source: CareerOneStop, U. S. Department of Labor. http://www.careerinfonet.org/occ_rep.asp?next=occ_rep&Level=&optstatus=111111111&jobfam=21&id=1&nodeid=2&soccode=211014&stfips=01&x=86&y=13#SectionOp2 and http://www.careerinfonet.org/occ_rep.asp?next=occ_rep&Level=&optstatus=111111111&jobfam=21&id=1&nodeid=2&soccode=211014&stfips=13&x=32&y=16#SectionOp2

Career InfoNet provides the tools you need to answer this question concretely and pass this credibility test.

First, you need to know the client's current level of education. You also need to know how the client defines *top jobs* or *best jobs*. Some clients may be referring to the highest paying jobs. Others, may be referring to the fastest growing occupations, or the occupations with the most projected openings or those employing the most workers. With these two pieces of information (your client's current level of education and the way he or she defines *best jobs*), you can answer the question in a matter of minutes by using America's Career InfoNet, where you can select "occupation information" to see a screen similar to Figure 13.8. Both on the side bar and in the body of this screen, America's Career InfoNet offers the opportunity to search for "top occupations" in a number of categories. By selecting any one of these categories, you will then be asked to specify an education level. America's Career InfoNet will then provide national data to answer your question and will also offer the option of obtaining state-specific information.

For an application activity, imagine that you are a school counselor in North Carolina. A student who is adamant about wanting to pursue no more than an associate's degree approaches you and asks specifically what occupations requiring only an associate's degree are the highest paying in North Carolina. To answer this question, go to careerinfonet.org, select "occupational information," click on the link for the highest paying occupations, select "two-year or associate's degree." When the national data appear, click on "select a state" and choose North Carolina. Figure 13.9 shows the 25 highest paying occupations in North Carolina requiring a two-year or associate's degree. Obviously, the data may have been updated between my writing and your reading of this text. Then be sure not to compare the median salary of counselors in North Carolina to this list.

OTHER FEDERAL RESOURCES.

CareerOneStop Videos. An additional federal resource for occupational information involves a large online selection of videos at careeronestop.org/Videos/default.aspx. These videos can be accessed as part of the CareerOneStop website, which is operated in conjunction with the American Job Center Network. These videos are available free of charge, and I encourage you to visit the website and watch some of them. Most are less than two minutes in length and are closed-captioned for viewers with hearing difficulties. Table 13.10 provides a brief description of the videos available from CareerOneStop.

MyFuture.com. Another federal resource for occupational and labor market information with which you should be familiar is a Web-based application called MyFuture.com (myfuture.com/careers/). This resource was developed and is maintained by the U.S. Department of Defense. It relies on data from the U.S. Department of Labor, the U.S. Department of Education, and the U.S. Department of Commerce. The basic information it

Occupation Information

The reports below may require selecting criteria including occupation, state, and education level.

Occupation Profile | Top Occupations by Wages & Trends | Compare Wages & Trends

- **Occupation Profile**
  Create a customized occupation profile. Available data include wages, employment trends, knowledge, skills, and abilities (KSAs), education and training, and web resources. National, state, and local information is available, as well as trend and wage comparisons across occupations and geographical areas.

- **Military to Civilian Occupation Translator**
  The Military to Civilian Occupation Translator helps service members match military skills and experience to civilian occupations.

- **Tools and Technology**
  Find a list of cutting-edge machines, equipment, tools, and software that workers may use in specific high-growth and in-demand occupations.

Top Occupations by Wages & Trends

- **Fastest-Growing Occupations**
  Find the fastest-growing occupations. Includes details about employment, wages, and education.

- **Occupations with the Most Openings**
  Create a list of occupations with the most openings by state or nationwide. Includes details about employment, number of estimated openings, wages, and education.

- **Occupations with the Largest Employment**
  Find national and state occupations with the largest employment. Includes details about employment, earnings, and education.

- **Occupations with Declining Employment**
  Create a list of occupations with the largest declines in employment by state or nationwide. Includes details about employment, earnings, and education.

- **Highest-Paying Occupations by Median Hourly Wage**
  Find the highest-paying occupations. Includes details about wages and education.

FIGURE 13.8 America's Career InfoNet Options for a Job Search by Education Level
Source: CareerOneStop, U. S. Department of Labor. http://www.careerinfonet.org/Occ_Intro.asp?id=1&nodeid=1

provides is quite similar to the information available from O*NET OnLine, the OOH, and America's Career InfoNet. It differs, however, in that it allows users to search all careers or only those careers found in the military, which, of course, represents the application's ties with the Department of Defense. Other search options include searching by industry (organized by the 16 national career clusters), by type of work (data, people or things), or by field of study.

State Government Resources

Many states also maintain their own career information delivery systems (CIDS). Historically, these were developed in collaboration with the National Occupational

Your Selections:

Find Related Content...

Education Level: **Two-year/associate's degree** Change Education Level

State: **North Carolina** Change State Change to National

These are the occupations with a typical entry-level education of an '**associate's degree**' with the highest median hourly wages in 2013. Select an occupation to learn more about it in the Occupation Profile.

Highest-Paying Occupations by Median Hourly Wages

Displaying Records 1 - 25 of 47   Next 25 >   Show All Records

		Median wages, 2013	
#	Occupation	Hourly	Annual
1	Air Traffic Controllers	$48.24	$100,300
2	Radiation Therapists	$35.50	$73,800
3	Nuclear Technicians	$35.26	$73,300
4	Funeral Service Managers	$34.82	$72,400
5	Dental Hygienists	$32.22	$67,000
6	Nuclear Medicine Technologists	$31.68	$65,900
7	Magnetic Resonance Imaging Technologists	$31.38	$65,300
8	Diagnostic Medical Sonographers	$30.49	$63,400
9	Cardiovascular Technologists and Technicians	$29.44	$61,200
10	Web Developers	$28.97	$60,300
11	Computer Network Support Specialists	$28.68	$59,700
12	Registered Nurses	$28.12	$58,500
13	Aerospace Engineering and Operations Technicians	$27.92	$58,100
14	Occupational Therapy Assistants	$27.41	$57,000
15	Engineering Technicians, Except Drafters, All Other	$27.09	$56,300
16	Physical Therapist Assistants	$26.59	$55,300
17	Electrical and Electronic Engineering Technicians	$26.29	$54,700
18	Radiologic Technologists	$25.33	$52,700
19	Respiratory Therapists	$25.28	$52,600
20	Mechanical Engineering Technicians	$23.58	$49,000
21	Architectural and Civil Drafters	$23.30	$48,500
22	Mechanical Drafters	$23.29	$48,400
23	Medical Equipment Repairers	$23.15	$48,200
24	Industrial Engineering Technicians	$23.09	$48,000
25	Avionics Technicians	$23.08	$48,000

Next 25 >

FIGURE 13.9 America's Career InfoNet Search for Highest Paying Jobs Requiring a Two-Year or an Associate's Degree in North Carolina

Source: CareerOneStop, U. S. Department of Labor. http://www.careerinfonet.org/oview5.asp?next=oview5&Level=edu4&optstatus=&jobfam=&id=1&nodeid=7&soccode=&ShowAll=&stfips=37.

TABLE 13.10 CareerOneStop Videos

Category	Description
Career and cluster videos	Videos about approximately 550 occupations organized according to the 16 national career clusters.
Career videos in Spanish	Videos about approximately 300 occupations organized according to the 16 national career clusters.
Skill and ability videos	Videos about 23 skills and abilities employers seek in their employees.
Industry videos	Videos about careers within six popular industries: automotive aftermarket, computer and data processing, health services, insurance, motor vehicle and equipment manufacturing, and retail sales.
Work option videos	Videos about nontraditional careers, including high-paying jobs that do not require college degrees and jobs that involve working outdoors.

Source: CareerOneStop, U. S. Department of Labor. http://www.careeronestop.org/Videos/default.aspx.

Information Coordinating Committee (NOICC). Before its federal funding was discontinued in 2000, the NOICC assisted each state in developing a state occupational information coordinating committee (SOICC; Lester, Woods, & Carlson, 2013). These committees developed CIDS to ensure that both state and national occupational information was available to citizens in their respective states. An alphabetical listing of the 36 state-based CIDs still in operation is available on the CareerInfoNet's Career Resource Library website at careerinfonet.org/crl/library.aspx?LVL2=45&LVL3=n&LVL1=23&CATID=400&PostVal=3.

Of these 36 CIDS, 21 were developed by a center called *intoCareers* (University of Oregon, 2013). This center at the University of Oregon specializes in the development and support of career information systems specifically for state agencies. Each of these systems is customized to include state data and to address state needs. You can learn more about *intoCareers* and its many state partners at intocareers.com.

Commercial Resources

Although the government-based resources described above provide occupational and labor market information sufficient to meet most counselors' and clients' needs, the following commercial resources may also be useful. Many of these resources are particularly useful in supporting the career exploration and decision making of young people in K–12 and college settings. Other commercially available resources focus on specific types of jobs that may appeal to a segment of your client population. The two largest commercial publishers of career-related material designed to provide occupational and labor market information are JIST Works, Inc. (jist.com) and Ferguson's, which is an imprint of Infobase (infobasepublishing.com). Several computer-assisted career guidance systems (CACGS) are also available commercially. This chapter introduces you to four of the most popular CACGSs on the market: Bridges/XAP, Career Cruising, the Kuder Career Planning System, and SIGI^3.

JIST WORKS RESOURCES.

Best Jobs **Series.** JIST Works, Inc. publishes 15 different books in its *Best Jobs* series. Although they contain little or no new information beyond what you can obtain from the federal government resources we described earlier, they offer some advantages. As you can see in Table 13.11, these books feature titles that may be particularly appealing to some of your clients. Some clients may struggle with the OOH because it is organized by the 23 SOC major groups. Some clients are less concerned about the industry or job cluster they will work in and are much more concerned about factors such as pay, stress, or education requirements. The books in the *Best Jobs* series are organized to address these factors.

The second advantage of this series is that, although you could certainly create these lists yourself using information from O*NET OnLine and the OOH, the editors of JIST Works have done it for you. Indeed, in order to create these groupings, they have done a lot of number crunching and disaggregated a lot of data from the federal resources.

A caution in using such resources, and any others for that matter, is that many clients become enamored with the median income cited in these books. This is especially true, of course, for books such as the *250 Best-Paying Jobs* (Shatkin & Farr, 2010). To their credit, though, the authors of these books caution readers against assuming that they, too, will make this amount of money should they pursue any given career listed in these books. They advise readers

TABLE 13.11 Best Jobs Series from JIST Works

Earnings and Outlook
250 Best-Paying Jobs
150 Best Jobs for a Secure Future
Best Jobs for the 21st Century

Education
200 Best Jobs for College Graduates
50 Best College Majors for a Secure Future
300 Best Jobs without a Four-Year Degree
200 Best Jobs through Apprenticeships

Employer
150 Best Federal Jobs
150 Best Jobs for the Military-to-Civilian Transition

Lifestyle/Values
150 Best Low-Stress Jobs
150 Best Jobs for a Better World
200 Best Jobs for Renewing America

Trait/Factor
200 Best Jobs for Introverts
150 Best Jobs for your Skills
50 Best Jobs for your Personality

Source: Based on JIST Publishing, 875 Montreal Way, St. Paul, MN 55102 http://jist.emcp.com/career-exploration.html?jist_product_series=169&limit=all

to "understand the limits of the data" (Shatkin, 2013, p. 3) provided by each book. Referring specifically to the annual earnings information, Shatkin explained:

> This sounds great, except that half of all people in that occupation earned less than that amount. For example, people who are new to the occupation or with only a few years of work experience often earn much less than the median amount. People who live in rural areas or who work for smaller employers typically earn less than those who do similar work in cities (where the cost of living is higher) or for bigger employers. People in certain areas of the country earn less than those in others. (p. 3)

This caution may go unread by clients as they dive right into the lists and the occupational information rather than reading the preface. Thus, it is useful for counselors to explain these caveats to clients whenever discussing median salaries.

Pocket Guide Series. The Pocket Guide series is another compilation offered by JIST Works, Inc. This series is specifically related to the level of education required for entry into a profession. Each pocket guide provides information on the 50 best careers for a given education level. The six guides address careers requiring (1) short-term, on-the-job training; (2) moderate-term, on-the-job training; (3) long-term, on-the-job training; (4) postsecondary vocational training; (5) two-year college degrees; and (4) four-year college degrees. The information about each job in these pocket guides includes a brief description of the job and working conditions; identification of the most closely associated Holland model work environment (first letter only); and labor market information such as annual earnings, growth rates, and projected job openings. These resources are sold in packages of 25, but free samples are also available from the publisher.

Young Person's Occupational Outlook Handbook. With its title, the *Young Person's Occupational Outlook Handbook* (U.S. Department of Labor, 2010) barely needs a description. Also published by JIST Works, this book is organized just like the OOH, with occupational descriptions organized into each of the SOC's 23 major groups. The occupational and labor market information for each career is contained on a single page in an easy-to-read style appropriate for students in grades 4 to 9. In addition to providing information from the OOH, each page also identifies subjects to study and suggests ways for students to discover more about the occupation. For example, this handbook suggests the following for students interested in learning more about the occupation of construction laborer: "Offer your services to your family or neighbors the next time they are planning a construction project. You might help build a porch or deck, pave a driveway, or haul materials to and from the worksite" (U.S. Department of Labor, 2010, p. 225). After all, what better way to understand what an occupation involves than to observe and help someone working in that occupation?

INFOBASE/FERGUSON RESOURCES. Infobase Publishing is another company that offers a wide range of books and materials to support career development and exploration. Most of these materials are published by Infobase under the imprint of Ferguson. A visit to the Infobase website (infobasepublishing.com) reveals a vast array of such materials, including 19 different sets or series of books focused on career exploration and numerous career-related reference materials. In this chapter, however, I will describe only three examples to illustrate the range of materials available.

Encyclopedia of Careers and Vocational Guidance. The *Encyclopedia of Careers and Vocational Guidance* (Ferguson, 2011) consists of more than 4,000 pages of occupational and labor market information distributed across five volumes. A popular resource for libraries and career centers alike (Easton, 2010), this resource is currently in its 15th edition and is most appropriate for high school students and recent high school graduates. The first volume provides career guidance information related to career preparation, job seeking, and employment information; a list of career resources for people with disabilities; a list of internships, apprenticeships and other training programs; and an overview of the remaining four volumes in the encyclopedia. Volumes 2 to 5 provide occupational and labor market information. Like most encyclopedias, these volumes are organized alphabetically. The information provided for each occupation includes:

- Descriptive Information
  - Quick facts
  - Overview
  - Job description
  - Work environment
  - History of the occupation
- Entry Requirements and Career Progression
  - Job requirements
  - Training and education
  - Employers
  - Starting out
  - Advancement
- Labor Market Information
  - Earnings
  - Outlook
- Recommendations for Further Exploration
  - Exploring
  - Additional information

***Careers in Focus* Series.** The *Careers in Focus* series is also published by Infobase/Ferguson and contains the same categories of information in *Encyclopedia of Careers and Vocational Guidance* (see the bullet list in the previous section). Instead of being organized into five large and possibly intimidating volumes of an encyclopedia set, though, the career articles in the *Careers in Focus* series are distributed in booklet form across 71 volumes. These booklets are most appropriate for high school students and recent graduates who are engaged in career exploration and decision making. Each booklet contains information about 16 to 25 occupations related to a specific set of interests or a specific industry. Examples include animal care, comic books and graphic novels, meteorology, and geriatric care.

***Discovering Careers* Series.** The *Discovering Careers* series is appropriate for elementary and middle school students in grades 4 to 9. This 18-volume series provides occupational and labor market information. Colorful and child-friendly, these descriptions facilitate early career exploration and expand awareness of career possibilities. Each volume is focused on a specific career area, and examples include animals, fashion, math, movies, and sports.

Streaming Video Collections. In addition to the many sets, series, and collections of print material, Infobase Publishing offers two streaming video collections designed to provide occupational and labor market information. The *Career & Technical Education* streaming video collection includes 1,000 full-length videos and 9,000 video clips. These videos are most appropriate for middle school and high school students. The *Master Career & Technical Education Streaming Video* collection is designed for use in college settings; the *Careers & Trades* collection is designed for use by public libraries.

CANDIDCAREER.COM. CandidCareer.com is another noteworthy resource for Web-based information about careers. This company offers site licenses primarily to colleges and universities. Its website features a large selection of videos about thousands of careers. Each career video addresses the following:

- Job description
- Loves and challenges
- How to prepare
- Interviewee's story
- Final advice
- Full-length interview
- Career advice

COMPUTER-ASSISTED CAREER GUIDANCE SYSTEMS. With the exception of videos, most of the career information resources offered by JIST Works and Infobase are formatted as books or booklets. Some of them are available as ebooks as well as in hard copy, but they are books nonetheless. Another popular approach to providing occupational and labor market information is through computer-assisted career guidance systems (CACGS). These systems tend to be geared toward young people (middle school, high school, and college students) who are in need of career exploration to support their continued career development, decision making, and planning. CACGS were first introduced as software programs that were then loaded onto school computers so that students could use those computers at school to explore careers. Now, these programs tend to be Web-based, with the school purchasing a site license and the ability to provide students with access codes. Students with Internet access can therefore access their school's CACGS at home or their favorite coffee shop. (Since when did students start drinking coffee?) Students without Internet access can use their school's CACGS while at school or in a public library. The costs associated with these programs tend to vary depending on the size of a school's student population. This chapter will introduce you to four of the most popular CACGSs on the market: Bridges/XAP, Career Cruising, the Kuder® Career Planning System, and *SIGI³*.

Bridges/XAP. Bridges (bridges.com) is a CACGS with a long history of supporting career exploration and development for K–12 students. In 2006, it partnered with XAP (xap.com) to offer similar products for use outside the K–12 setting. For the K–12 setting, Bridges/XAP offers several versions of its CACGS, each designed for a different age group. *Paws in Jobland* is designed for use in elementary schools and focuses on expanding students' career awareness. *Choices Explorer* is designed for use in middle schools and early in high school to support students' career exploration. *Choices Planner* is designed for use in high schools to assist students with career decision making and planning. *Transitions* is also designed for use in high schools and focuses on postsecondary planning. For the college setting, Bridges/XAP offers *Choices Planner for Career Transitions*. This program supports students in the transition from high school to college. For the community setting, Bridges/XAP offers another version of *Choices Planner for Career Transitions*. This CACGS is designed to support adults in exploring their career options, making career decisions, and searching for jobs.

Career Cruising. Career Cruising (careercruising.com) is another CACGS that began with a primary focus on the K–12 educational setting but has since expanded by adding products more closely aligned with the needs of college students and adults. For the K–12 setting, Career Cruising offers several versions of its CACGS, each designed for a different age group. For example, *ccSpark!* and *ccTheRealGame* are recommended for use in elementary schools. For middle school students, *ccSpringboard* and *ccTheRealGame* are most appropriate. These same products are appropriate for use with high school students. *ccPathfinder* is designed to assist high school students with course planning, and *ccAchieve* focuses on postsecondary planning and the college application process. For the postsecondary setting, Career Cruising recommends *ccSpringboard*, which is designed to support the career exploration and decision making of college students. For people already in the workforce, Career Cruising recommends use of *ccSpringboard* and also offers *ccInspire*. This CACGS supports adults in exploring their career options, making career decisions, and searching for jobs.

DISCOVER®. Previously offered by ACT, Inc. but now discontinued, the DISCOVER® program was a CACGS used to help middle and high school students engage in career exploration, decision making, and planning. DISCOVER was discontinued in September 2012, but it is mentioned here because it was a very popular and widely cited program that is still (erroneously) identified as active in other career counseling texts (Brown, 2012; Niles & Harris-Bowlsbey, 2013; Sharf, 2014; Zunker, 2012).

Kuder Career Planning System. The Kuder® Career Planning System (KCPS; kuder.com/product/kuder-career-planning-system/) is a CACGS with a long history of supporting career exploration and development for K–12 students. The KCPS has since added a program designed for postsecondary students and adults. For the K–12 setting, the KCPS offers several versions of its CACGS, each designed for a different age group. *Kuder® Galaxy* is designed for use in elementary schools and focuses on expanding students' career awareness. *Kuder® Navigator* is designed for use in middle schools and high schools to support students' career exploration, career decision making, and planning. *Kuder® Journey* is designed for students in postsecondary settings and adults in agency settings. A useful feature of *Kuder® Journey* is that it invites each user to select a profile from an impressive array of choices: "postsecondary student, first-time job seeker, career changer, veteran or active member of the military, adult with a disability, ex-offender, or retired person" (Kuder, 2013, para. 6). The program then modifies its features to meet the unique needs of each profile.

***SIGI³*.** Whereas the CACGSs discussed so far have historically been used in K–12 settings and have only recently expanded their offerings to include products designed for use in college and community settings, *SIGI³* has always been designed for use primarily in postsecondary settings such as community colleges, four-year colleges, and agencies. Thus, it doesn't offer myriad products, each geared toward a different age group; instead, there is a single *SIGI³* program.

Although this very popular CACGS is referred to simply by its acronym, it may help to know that *SIGI* stands for System of Integrated Guidance and Information (sigi3.org). Currently in its third edition, *SIGI* was developed by the Educational Testing Service (ETS) and has been in use since the 1980s. Now owned by Valpar International Corporation, *SIGI³* claims to offer "the most in-depth occupational information available" (sigi3.org/SIGI3-Features.html, para. 1) and also offers labor market information related to wages and employment projections.

An especially useful feature of $SIGI^3$ is that it allows for side-by-side comparison of occupations. Unlike the other CACGSs, $SIGI^3$ provides an option for individuals to purchase a license to use $SIGI^3$ for their own personal (individual) use. At the time of this writing, the cost for an individual license was $17.95 (sigi3.org/individual) for the first 90 days and $4.95 for a 60-day renewal. This may be an especially useful option for counselors who do not intend to specialize in career counseling (thereby justifying an organization-wide site license) but who may nonetheless see the occasional client seeking these career services. Providing an individual client with access to a CACGS such as $SIGI^3$ would be a useful supplement to your sessions because you could assign homework using the system to facilitate the client's exploration process.

OTHER USES OF CACGS. Thus far in this chapter, we have been exploring the value of CACGS in providing access to the occupational and labor market information needed to expand career awareness, facilitate career exploration, and support career decision making. By definition, though, CACGS do much more. In the career exploration and decision-making realm, CACGSs also tend to include brief assessments of the user and, in trait factor fashion, use the assessment results to yield a set of occupations for the user to explore and consider. Most of these CACGSs rely primarily on assessments of interests and self-reported skills. Although it also offers self-assessments of interests, personality, and skills, $SIGI^3$ emphasizes the use of career values in its identification of possible matches. Users can then access occupational and labor market information about any career on the list of suggestions offered by the CACGS. They can also enter the name of any occupation (regardless of whether it appears on the list of matches for them) or search by categories (e.g., "bright outlook" or "green occupations") or by clusters.

CACGS are also relevant to career planning. Most CACGS intended for use in middle or high school settings include a feature allowing students to create a four-year plan of the courses they need to take to pursue their career of interest after graduating from high school. In fact, many middle schools and high schools purchase site licenses for a CACGS specifically to take advantage of the educational development plan feature. Looking beyond high school graduation, most CACGS also include a feature to facilitate user exploration of postsecondary education and training opportunities related to the career(s) in which users are most interested. Many CACGS also include modules related to employability and job-seeking skills. Because they offer a single point of entry to such resources, CACGS may be likened to a one-stop shopping experience. Rather than needing to locate and access numerous, stand-alone websites and other resources, each focused on a specific type of information about the world of work, users can access a broad range of information through a single CACGS.

Other Sources of Occupational and Labor Market Information

Moving from high tech to high touch, it is important to acknowledge that books, websites, and CACGS are not the sole sources of occupational and labor market information. People and workplaces represent other important sources of information. Both you and your clients can learn a lot by talking with people about the work they do and from opportunities to observe them on the job. Such experiences can prompt an individual to seek additional information about an occupation from the books, websites, and CACGS discussed earlier in this chapter. Sometimes people may initially become interested in an occupation based on what they have read about it; in such cases, they may benefit tremendously from talking with people employed in that occupation and from observing such workers in action. Career counselors often recommend and/or facilitate several activities designed to help clients better understand a specific occupation as well as the world of work in general, and we turn to this topic next.

CLASSROOM PRESENTATIONS, CAREER DAYS, AND FIELD TRIPS. All students have some exposure to the world of work via the adults in their lives. At a minimum, these adults generally include parents, other family members, adults who live in the child's neighborhood, and adults who work at the school. This exposure is often limited, however, by socioeconomic status, class, gender roles, and prestige. To counteract these limiting factors, most elementary and middle schools attempt to broaden the exposure of all students to adults within the world of work through classroom presentations, career days, and field trips. Because these types of activities are featured most frequently in K–12 educational settings, more detailed descriptions and discussion of them will be reserved for Chapter 14. Many schools use such strategies as a way to broaden student exposure to a wide range of careers and to equip students with some beginning knowledge of occupational and labor market information related to careers. Keep in mind that these strategies are much more effective when they include a wide range of careers, advance preparation (with both the students and the workplace), and follow-up processing activities.

INFORMATIONAL INTERVIEWS. Informational interviews are yet another way to gather information about an occupation. These interviews are not job interviews and should not be viewed (by the interviewer or the interviewee) as attempts to get a job. The sole purpose of an informational interview should be to gather additional information about an occupation or career path. Whereas classroom visits and field trips tend to be most useful in expanding awareness of career possibilities and reinforcing the connection between school and work, informational interviews tend to be most useful in reality testing and in gathering data beyond what is available in print resources. Crosby (2002; Crosby & Dillon, 2010) identified several benefits of conducting informational interviews and explained that they can help you:

- learn more about the realities of working in a particular occupation;
- decide among different occupations or choose an occupational specialty;
- focus career goals;
- discover careers you never knew existed;
- uncover your professional strengths and weakness;
- find different ways to prepare for a particular career (Crosby, 2002, p. 32)
- gather ideas for volunteer, seasonal, part-time, and internship opportunities related to a specific field (Crosby & Dillon, 2010, p. 23)

When encouraging clients to conduct informational interviews, counselors should avoid assuming that clients understand their purpose, potential benefits, and preparation needed. Counselors must educate clients about the nature of informational interviews, help them identify potential interviewees, and advise them about appropriate ways to initiate contact to request an informational interview. Counselors should also encourage clients to prepare for the interviews by researching the occupation as well as the employer, and making a list of questions they would like to ask. Crosby recommended asking questions about the occupation, working conditions, and necessary education or training. Crosby also emphasized the importance of dressing and behaving professionally during the interview. In recognition that a sample size of one (interviewee) may result in an inaccurate perception of an occupation, Crosby recommended conducting interviews with multiple employees in an occupation under consideration. To help clients prepare for informational interviews, provide them with an article such as Crosby's original (Crosby, 2002) or updated (Crosby & Dillon, 2010) articles. Both are user-friendly and are written for job seekers rather than counselors.

JOB SHADOWING. Job shadowing involves watching people as they work. The client accompanies the employee and observes him or her performing the job. Although employees may obviously be on their best behavior during job shadowing, these experiences nonetheless allow clients to develop a deeper understanding of what it is like to work in a given occupation. Reading about an occupation or even seeing examples on television does not always serve this purpose. For example, job shadowing has allowed many a would-be veterinarian to experience some of the less attractive aspects of this occupation and to realize that, although he or she loves animals, working with sick and dying animals can be more emotionally difficult than anticipated. Many high schools and some middle schools offer job-shadowing programs, and Chapter 14 includes an in-depth discussion and step-by-step instructions for implementing job shadowing programs in an educational setting. These same instructions can easily be modified for use in community settings. Adult clients who are considering a specific occupation may benefit from the opportunity to observe employees as they perform duties associated with that occupation.

Simulations. Simulations, in which an individual is asked to perform the tasks and duties involved in an occupation while under observation, are another means by which one can gather occupational information. Even more than job shadowing, simulations allow an individual to experience what it is really like to perform an occupation. They also allow others to assess the individual's likelihood of success in performing the tasks required in an occupation and thus offer a testing ground in which individuals can determine how satisfied they may be in a given occupation and be evaluated by individuals in that same occupation. Simulations are used most frequently in vocational rehabilitation settings (McCormac, 1989). You will learn more about vocational rehabilitation counseling in Chapter 17.

Work Experience. A probably obvious source of occupational and labor market information is actual work experience. Whether accrued as a "real" job or during one's K–12 or college education, work experience allows an individual to experience what a job entails firsthand. This experience offers good insight into the nature of a given industry and the level of the position one holds. For instance, working as a cashier at McDonald's offers insight into the fast-food industry and working as a cashier but perhaps not much information about working as a restaurant manager in the same establishment.

EDUCATION AND TRAINING INFORMATION

Although occupational and labor market information plays the most prominent role in career counseling, other types of information can also be important in supporting clients' career development. For example, clients may benefit greatly from information about education and training. Such information may address the education and training necessary for entry into a career of interest; the various educational institutions through which one can obtain such training; and pragmatic information regarding the admissions process, success in higher education, and financial aid. These topics will be addressed in depth in Chapters 14 and 15, so only a brief description is provided here.

Importance of Postsecondary Education

Both student and adult clients may need information about the importance of education and training for career success in general as well as the required education and/or training necessary for entry into a specific career. Figure 13.10 shows a clear relationship among education attainment, unemployment rates, and earnings.

Despite anecdotal evidence to the contrary, the national data are clear and have been consistent for years: People with higher levels of postsecondary education enjoy higher average earnings and lower unemployment rates than people with lesser education. Although all of us have heard stories about college graduates who are disappointed in their subsequent earnings and about people who have earned a great deal despite their lack of postsecondary education, it is important to remember that such people are also included in these national surveys. I would encourage you to view the national data as more credible than anecdotal stories.

Even authors of books such as *300 Best Jobs Without a Four-Year Degree* (Shatkin, 2013) acknowledge these data. In a warning related to understanding the data presented in his book, Shatkin reminded readers that the earnings quoted for various occupations are medians, meaning that half of all people working in those occupations make less than the quoted amounts. He also specifically recommended that readers consider additional education. Specifically, he stated, "I encourage you to get as much education and training as you can. You used to be able to get your schooling and then close the schoolbooks forever, but this isn't a good attitude to have now" (p. 80). Given the reality of today's workplace as reflected in national statistics and in cautions from authors like Shatkin, counselors should emphasize the increasing importance of obtaining some form of postsecondary education to become competitive in today's labor market.

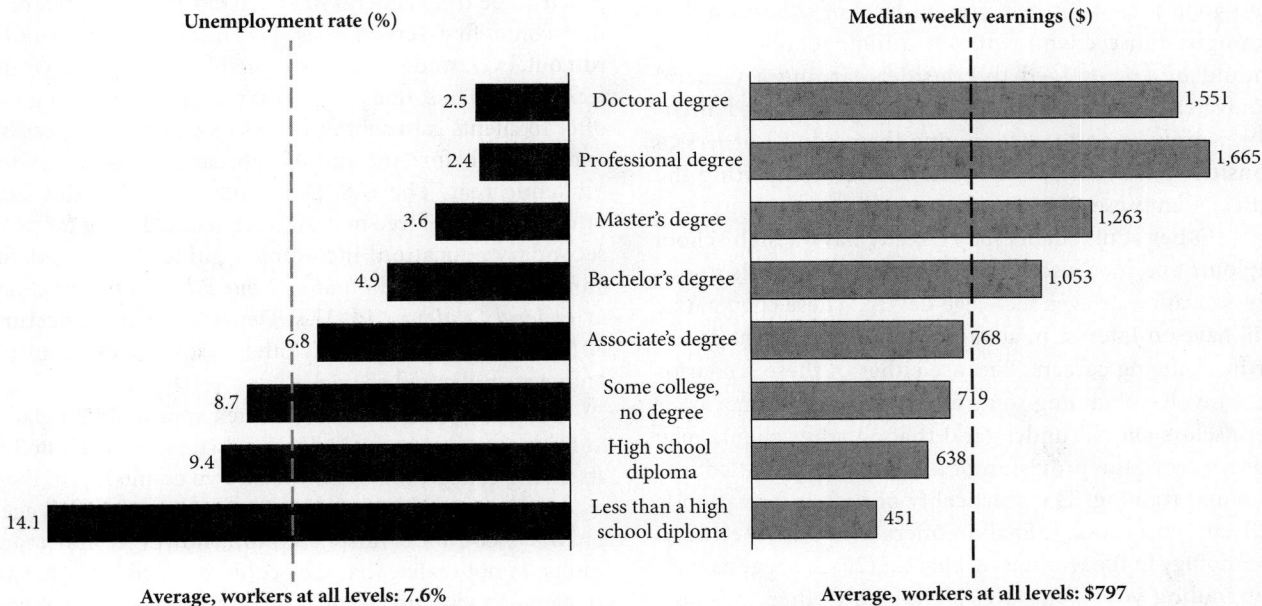

FIGURE 13.10 Relationship Among Educational Attainment, Unemployment Rates, and Earnings as of 2011
Source: Bureau of Labor Statistics, Current Population Survey U.S. Bureau of Labor Statistics. (2012). New school year, old story: Education pays. *Occupational Outlook Quarterly*, 56(3), 36.

When working with students in the K–12 setting, counselors will want to identify a full range of options for postsecondary education. This education may consist of two- or four-year college degree programs, occupational certificate programs, military training programs, registered apprenticeships, or some other form of training. When working with college students, counselors will likely focus more attention on providing information about the link between various academic majors and potential occupations, on assisting students with their selection of college majors, and providing information about graduate school options. Resources that may be useful in addressing academic majors include books such as *You Majored in What?* (Brooks, 2010) and a commercially available series of informational handouts on 80 academic majors entitled *What Can I Do with This Major?* This series is produced and sold by the University of Tennessee Career services (whatcanidowiththismajor.com) for a nominal fee.

Adult clients seeking career services may also need information about postsecondary education and training. When working with adults, career counselors will likely inquire about clients' past education history, including degrees, and help them assess transferrable skills. Career counselors may also find it useful to help adult clients understand the increasing importance of postsecondary and/or continuing education. This is especially true for clients for whom it has become increasingly difficult to find good jobs with their present level of education. For example, those clients without a high school diploma should be encouraged to consider earning a General Equivalency Diploma (GED) certificate. Increased attention is now given to encouraging these adult learners to consider postsecondary education after completing the GED (Alamprese, 2005).

Other adult clients may already have a high school diploma and may also have completed some postsecondary education or even a college degree. These clients may still have an interest in advancing in their current career or in changing careers. Because either of these scenarios may involve obtaining some additional education, career counselors should understand that all adult clients may benefit from the provision of information about education and training. The practicality of such information is reflected in a message Shatkin offers to adults. Specific to technology in the workplace, Shatkin (2013) suggests that, "upgrading your computer skills—and other technical skills—is particularly important in our rapidly changing workplace, and you avoid doing so at your peril" (p. 80). Oh, if Doris had only heeded such advice years ago!

Selecting and Applying to an Educational Program and Paying for It

In addition to helping student and adult clients understand the importance of postsecondary education and identifying options best suited to them, it is important for counselors to help clients learn about how to select and apply to an educational program and how to pay for additional education. Many counselors in high school settings conduct classroom presentations and encourage use of CACGS to address these needs. Initiatives such as KnowHow2Go (knowhow2go.org) have developed websites and other resources to help students translate their interest in postsecondary education into actions that realize this goal. Such resources are equally applicable to working with adult clients interested in pursuing additional education.

With regard to paying for postsecondary education, the College Board offers an online calculator (netpricecalculator.collegeboard.org) designed to help prospective college students, regardless of their age, estimate the total costs associated with attending a college of interest to them. I believe that all clients who have an interest in pursuing postsecondary education for credit should submit an application for federal financial aid. The application, called the Free Application for Federal Student Aid (FAFSA), is available at fafsa.gov. It is important to refer students specifically to this website because some other sites charge a fee to file the FAFSA, which, as its name indicates, is supposed to be free. Federal financial aid is distributed on a first-come, first-served basis. When the available monies run out, even students who are eligible will not receive any federal aid. Thus, one of the best pieces of advice you can offer to clients is to submit the FAFSA as soon as possible and always before the end of February for the following academic year. The U.S. Department of Education also offers a variety of free materials related to paying for postsecondary education, including a guide that is updated annually and entitled *Funding Your Education: The Guide to Federal Student Aid* (U.S. Department of Education, 2011). This guide and many other resources are available online at studentaid.ed.gov.

Although these resources often appear at first glance to be designed only for high school students interested in attending college, this is untrue on two counts. First, these materials are pertinent to prospective students of all ages. This is a common misperception, however, and many adults do not realize that they could be eligible for federal or state financial aid. Second, the use of federal student aid is not limited to paying for college. Federal student aid can be applied toward the cost of attending "an eligible college, technical school, vocational school, or graduate school"

(U.S. Department of Education, 2011, p. 1). In all cases, however, students must "be enrolled or accepted for enrollment as a regular student leading to a degree or certificate in an eligible program" (p. 7). This generally means that the student must be admitted (or seeking admission) to a program that leads to a specific credential or degree. In contrast, federal student aid cannot be used to pay for non-credit or enrichment classes or even for classes taken for credit but outside a degree program.

Although school counselors receive considerable training related to issues such as financial aid, other counselors who may provide career services to adults will also benefit from this type of knowledge. An important takeaway message is that these resources may be used with adult clients as well as with high school and/or college students. Counselors in community settings also need to be aware of programs designed specifically for adults wishing to pursue postsecondary education. Michigan, for example, actively promoted its Return to Learn initiative, which was run through its No Worker Left Behind program and funded with federal monies (Schultz, 2010). When these monies dried up, however, the program was discontinued. Career counselors must stay abreast of changes in financial aid options and programs.

Building Confidence by Building Skills

Clients often come to career counselors very concerned about their employment prospects. Such lack of confidence and trepidation about job searching is often well founded because, quite frankly, some clients lack the education, training, and/or skills needed to thrive in the labor market. Recall that, according social cognitive career theory (SCCT; Lent, Brown & Hackett, 1994), which was covered in Chapter 4, the most appropriate response to low levels of self-efficacy is not always to be a client's cheerleader or to search for and challenge irrational beliefs; the key is to determine whether the low levels of self-efficacy are warranted. If they are not, your job is to challenge irrational beliefs and provide new experiences that allow for the correction of low self-confidence. When low levels of self-efficacy are warranted, your job is to assist clients in identifying ways to improve their skills.

SKILL-BUILDING INFORMATION

Skill building is vital in helping clients build their confidence and ensuring that their confidence is well founded. Formal education and training can clearly result in better job prospects and a concomitant increase in self-confidence. Two other forms of skill building may also achieve these results. Education and training tend to focus on the acquisition of job-specific knowledge and skills, but the skills addressed in this section involve the general employability skills needed for any job as well as the skills needed to conduct an effective job search. Career counselors need to know (a) what these skills are and (b) where to find resources to help clients develop these skills.

Employability Skills

In everyday language, employability skills consist of a set of general, foundational skills that make an individual employable over a sustained period of time. In more technical terms, employability skills are "transferable core skill groups that represent essential functional and enabling knowledge, skills, and attitudes required by the 21st century workplace. They are necessary for career success at all levels of employment and for all levels of education" (Overtoom, 2000, p. 1).

A key idea involves the enduring importance of employability skills. These skills are necessary not only to render someone career- or work-ready at the entry stage of one's career, they are also essential to a person's continued employability, professional growth, and adaptability (North & Worth, 2004). It is one thing to be hired for a job; it is quite another to retain a job. Job retention and success are contingent on having the job-specific technical skills (or ability to learn them) necessary to perform the work tasks satisfactorily and on demonstrating more general skills expected of all employees regardless of their job title or work responsibilities. Employability skills do not decline in importance; they remain important throughout one's career regardless of one's position or level of education. Employability skills are essential not only for the success of each individual worker but also for the collective workforce and thus the nation's success "in building a globally competitive workforce" (Bates & Phelan, 2002, p. 121).

SECRETARY'S COMMISSION ON ACHIEVING NECESSARY SKILLS. These more generalized employability skills are so important to career- or work-readiness and to the overall quality of the nation's workforce that the U.S. Department of Labor appointed a commission in 1990 to identify the general work skills required by employers: the Secretary's Commission on Achieving Necessary Skills (SCANS). Its work resulted in the publication of five major reports (Secretary's Commission on Achieving Necessary Skills, 1991a, 1991b, 1991c, 1992, 1993). Although there have been other attempts to categorize employability skills (Bailey, 1990; Carnevale, Gainer, & Melzer, 1990; O'Neil, 1997), the reports generated by the

SCANS commission still represent the nation's authoritative statement of the employability skills needed by today's workers (ACT, 2000; Bates & Phelan, 2002; U.S. Department of Labor, 2013).

Drawing on analyses of job requirements and on interviews with a wide range of stakeholders (including managers, business owners, public employers, union representatives, and workers themselves), this commission identified the set of employability skills listed in Table 13.12 and described in much greater detail in Appendix F. These skills are organized into a set of foundational skills and a set of workplace competencies.

Importance of SCANS skills in career counseling. Career counselors may utilize the SCANS reports in two primary ways. First, counselors who work mostly with students in K–12 or college settings may use their knowledge of the SCANS skills to select psychoeducational activities designed to help young people develop a full range of employability skills prior to their entry into the world of work. The importance of integrating such psychoeducational lessons into school curricula cannot be overemphasized. A large-scale study culminating in the Workforce Readiness Report Card recently found that employers are dissatisfied with the quality of new workers entering the workforce (Casner-Lotto & Barrington, 2006). These authors explained that "[e]mployers expect young people to arrive in the workplace with a set of basic and applied skills, and the Workforce Readiness Report Card makes clear that the reality is not matching expectations" (p. 10). This is true not only of young people entering the workforce straight out of high school but also of college graduates.

Second, counselors who work primarily with adults may use their knowledge of the SCANS skills to assess the degree to which clients possess and consistently use various employability skills and the extent to which employability skills may be contributing to difficulties getting or keeping jobs. For example, career counselors may find it useful to discuss employability skills such as the SCANS skills with clients who have lost jobs or failed to earn promotions due to inadequate performance. It may also be useful to be aware of curricular materials designed to help people develop stronger employability skills. One organization that has done considerable work developing such a curriculum is SkillsUSA (skillsusa.org). This organization offers two different curricula: one intended for high school students and the other for postsecondary students and/or adults. The high school version, the Professional Development Program, is available both in workbook and online formats. The postsecondary/adult version, the Career Skills Education Program, is available only online.

Job Searching Skills

Thus far, this chapter has addressed the use of technology and information resources primarily in the context of career exploration, decision making, and preparation. After people make career decisions and take the steps necessary to prepare for them, most eventually reach a point where they need to invest in launching their chosen careers. It's true that some will have jobs fall into their lap as a result of their superior qualifications, useful connections, and social capital, or just plain happenstance. Those people, of course, are unlikely to need or seek your career counseling services in the first place. In contrast, many of our clients anticipate launching their careers with trepidation and worry that their hard work may not pay off with a good job in a career of their dreams.

Because assisting clients with job searching is such a critical component of career counseling, a thorough discussion of this topic will be reserved for Chapter 17, which is dedicated to assisting clients with the job search process and to supporting clients through job loss and out of unemployment. For the purposes of this chapter, I will provide only a brief overview of the types of technology and information resources available for use in equipping clients with job search skills. Career counseling centers both in education and community settings commonly feature a wide variety of technology and information resources designed to help clients develop materials for their job search. Some of these resources focus on the preparation of résumés, cover letters, and other written documents generally required when applying for jobs (Curtis & Simons, 2004). Other resources are designed to build skills in oral self-presentation. These resources focus on interviewing skills as well as the development and delivery of so-called elevator speeches (Howell, 2006; Sjodin, 2012). The development of networking skills is another common focus. Such resources may address the practice of informational interviewing, the use of social media networks such as LinkedIn, and strategies for tapping into the hidden job market (Lock, 2005; Mathison & Finney, 2010; Rockawin, 2012; Schepp & Schepp, 2010). Career counselors should be aware of resources for locating job openings for clients. These resources may be physically located on college campuses or in community-based employment offices, or they may be online. Again, Chapter 17 will provide much more detail about the job search process in general as well as the technology and information resources that career counselors and their clients may use to prepare for and implement a job search.

TABLE 13.12 SCANS Employability Skills

Foundational Skills

Basic skills	Reading
	Writing
	Arithmetic
	Mathematics
	Listening
	Speaking
Thinking skills	Creative thinking
	Decision making
	Problem solving
	Seeing things in the mind's eye
	Knowing how to learn
	Reasoning
Personal qualities	Responsibility
	Self-esteem
	Social
	Self-management
	Integrity/honesty

Workplace Competencies

Resources	Allocates time
	Allocates money
	Allocates material and facility resources
	Allocates human resources
Information	Acquires and evaluates information
	Organizes and maintains information
	Interprets and communicates information
	Uses computers to process information
Interpersonal	Participates as a member of a team
	Teaches others
	Serves clients/customers
	Exercises leadership
	Negotiates to arrive at a decision
	Works with cultural diversity
Systems	Understands systems
	Monitors and corrects performance
	Improves and designs systems
Technology	Selects technology
	Applies technology to task
	Maintains and troubleshoots technology

Source: Secretary's Commission on Achieving Necessary Skills. (1991). What work requires of schools: A SCANS report for America 2000. Washington, DC: U.S. Department of Labor. (ED332054)

APPLICATION TO OUR CAST OF CLIENTS

This chapter will conclude with my final application to five members of our cast of clients. Because the remaining chapters are setting-specific, they will not include client applications. However, my hope is that you and your instructors will discuss implications of each of the subsequent chapters for the clients we have been following since Chapter 1. To end this chapter, let's explore how you might use technology and information resources with Li Mei, Wayne, Juan, Lakeesha, and Doris. As you read these client applications, think about how similar types of technology and information resources might benefit Vincent and Gillian.

Lily Huang Li Mei: Career Exploration and Selection of Academic Majors

In Chapter 12, you read about the use of an occupational card sort with Li Mei in which she was asked to sort occupation titles into categories reflecting her level of interest. Although Li Mei began this exercise with the belief that she had "no idea" what careers might interest her, the card sort activity allowed her to realize that there were many occupations she considered completely "off the table" and that the occupations in which she might be interested shared some common themes. Specifically, Li Mei realized that she wants a career that is associated with higher levels of education and prestige, and is more hands on, or applied. Two particular occupations that emerged as promising were careers within the health care industry and careers focused on the organization and management of information (such as an accountant or librarian).

With these new insights, Li Mei feels less daunted by the task of selecting a career transition. However, she still lacks sufficient information about these career areas. As a counselor, you believe Li Mei would benefit from learning more about these occupation areas. You decide to introduce Li Mei to O*NET and show her how to use this system to learn more about various occupations of possible interest to her. You ask Li Mei to list at least three occupations she would like to explore. In response, Li Mei identified a desire to explore the following occupations: dentist, ophthalmologist, accountant, and librarian. Next, you show Li Mei how to access the O*NET OnLine. Using the "advanced search by interest option," you enter the first two letters of Li Mei's Holland code (CI) and then choose job zones 4 and 5. Both require at least a college degree and meet Li Mei's expectations for a certain level of prestige. You show the list to Li Mei and ask her to scan it and note any others that, on first glance, she may want to add to her own list. From the list of conventional/investigative occupations for job zone 5, Li Mei expresses some interest in archivist and pharmacist. From the list of conventional/investigative occupations for job zone 4, Li Mei expresses some interest in actuary and auditor. This results in a grand total of eight occupations for Li Mei to begin exploring.

To avoid overwhelming her, you decide to ask Li Mei to focus on learning more about only these eight occupations in the week between this session and the next. You show her how to enter the name of each occupation in O*NET OnLine's Quick Search and how to scroll through the information for each occupation. You suggest that Li Mei print out the results for each of these occupations and that she use highlighters to color code her reactions to what she reads. Li Mei responds by expressing an intention to use green, her favorite color, to highlight aspects of the description she finds appealing and yellow to highlight aspects of the description she finds unappealing. She seems eager to get started and you express curiosity about how she'll react to these various occupational possibilities.

As Li Mei leaves your office, you smile in recognition of how dramatically her demeanor has changed since her initial session with you. Li Mei seemed hopeless, depressed, and anxious in her first session, but she now appears hopeful and curious about possibilities. After all, Li Mei has identified a variety of career options that would meet her parents' expectations with regard to prestige, are different enough from her siblings' career pursuits to avoid any direct competition, and actually seem interesting to her.

As Li Mei continues to clarify her level of interest based on the O*NET OnLine information, plans for additional occupation exploration should include taking related courses at Chapman University in Orange, California. For example, if Li Mei continued to have dual interests in business-related occupations such as accounting and health care careers in pharmacy, you might assist her in exploring the recommended course sequence for both degree programs at Chapman. You might suggest that she take one course from each program track to see how she really likes the area of study. Within the accounting track, Li Mei might take MGSC 207: Introduction to Business Analytics. Within the pre-pharmacy track, Li Mei might take CHEM 140: General Chemistry I. You also want to encourage Li Mei to engage in other forms of occupational exploration. This might consist of informational interviews and job shadowing with professionals working within careers of interest to her. As Li Mei engages in reading more about career options, taking courses associated with them, and interacting with professionals working in those careers, she will be in a much better position to select a career direction and academic major with which she will be satisfied.

Wayne Jensen: Labor Market Information

Whereas Li Mei is a young adult just beginning to choose a career direction, Wayne has long been employed in a career he has enjoyed. Instead of needing to find a career direction of interest to him, Wayne's focus is much more pragmatic. Although his first choice would be to remain in his current position working for Ford, Wayne fears the possibility of a layoff and feels the need for a plan B. In selecting a plan B career option, Wayne is most concerned about maintaining his standard of living and his ability to support his family. Labor market information is of primary concern to him. Wayne needs to know which occupations will allow him to get "the biggest bang for his buck" by offering the best pay for the least investment of time, money, and energy in retraining.

In light of these priorities, you decide to focus on using America's Career InfoNet with Wayne. As you learned earlier in this chapter, this Web-based system includes features to search by labor market factors such as growth rate and wage ranges. You begin with an initial assessment of Wayne's digital literacy by asking him about his comfort and experience in using the Internet. Wayne tells you that he routinely accesses the Internet on his smartphone as well as at home, where he has a wireless router and high-speed Internet. In addition to playing games and reading news online, Wayne is a member of an online group of motorcyclists and has used mapping features to survey routes for upcoming motorcycle rallies.

With your laptop, you introduce Wayne to the website for America's Career InfoNet and specifically to its section dedicated to career exploration. You explain to Wayne that the link for "occupation information" in this section offers the types of information he will need to choose a new career. You then click on "top occupations by wages & trends" and explain that this link leads to important labor market information. Wayne immediately recognizes the likely value of this information because it includes listings of the highest paying jobs as well as information about whether various occupations are growing or declining. After all, Wayne does not want to select a new occupation facing layoffs or downsizing.

He begins by choosing the link for "highest paying occupations by median hourly wages." This link is especially useful because it allows the user to identify an education level and thus yield realistic results for him or her. Clearly, Wayne cannot prepare quickly for an occupation such as anesthesiologist (the highest paid occupation for those with a master's degree or higher) because he currently holds only a high school degree. In selecting "high school" as his education level, Wayne is able to obtain a list of the highest paying occupations into which he could transition with relatively little training. As he surveys the results, he notices several occupations of possible interest. You then show him how to access wage range information about each occupation and how to circle back through the site and access the occupation profile to learn more about the employment outlook and training requirements for each occupation of possible interest.

Confident in Wayne's ability to navigate the America's Career InfoNet site, you then provide him with a simple worksheet on which he can record information in the week to come. This worksheet includes separate columns for the name of each occupation, the wage ranges, employment outlook, and training needs. When he returns the following week, he brings with him his completed worksheet, which is summarized in Table 13.13.

This worksheet provides labor market information for six specific occupations. Based on this data, Wayne immediately eliminates elevator installer and repairer, power distributor and dispatcher, and power plant operator from consideration because of their employment outlook. He expresses the most interest in transportation, storage, and distribution manager for several reasons: It (1) offers the highest wage range, (2) is close to his residence, and (3) has a training program that is relatively short, and (4) the working conditions seem more suited to him than those for a lineman. Nonetheless, you encourage him to watch the videos about each job that are included on the America's Career InfoNet site and to conduct informational interviews with people employed in each occupation.

Juan Martinez: Occupational, Labor Market, and Short-Term Training Information

Although Juan is unable to continue working as a construction laborer, his years of consistently good performance have earned him a positive reputation within the local market of construction supervisors. They recognize Juan as a hard worker and reliable employee, and were disappointed when he was forced to resign due to his back injuries and inability to continue performing the job. Because this is the only job he has ever held since his entry into the workforce at age 16, Juan lacks knowledge about how to pursue new employment. He was wise, though, to seek assistance from the vocational rehabilitation office.

As part of the counseling process described in Chapter 9, Juan underwent a number of assessments, and the results confirmed what Juan already knew: Even though it was hard work, Juan loved his former job and would have happily continued in it had it not been for the unbearable pain. At this point, though, heavy lifting and hard labor are simply out of the question. The second helping strategy listed in his counseling plan involves the use of O*NET OnLine to explore occupational options. Because the testing clearly confirmed his satisfaction with the construction industry, you decide to enter "construction" in

TABLE 13.13 Wayne's Worksheet of Labor Market Information

Occupation	Wage Range		Employment Outlook		Short-Term Training
Transportation, storage, and distribution managers	$ 50,100 $ 79,400 $132,100	10% Median 90%	+4% 60	Growth rate Job openings	Henry Ford Community College in Dearborn, Michigan, has a program shorter than one year in logistics, materials, and supply chain management.
Elevator installers and repairers	$ 25,200 $ 38,200 $ 86,700	10% Median 90%	−7% 10	Growth rate Job openings	Henry Ford Community College has a program shorter than one year in industrial mechanics and maintenance technology.
Power distributors and dispatchers	$ 44,300 $ 67,000 $ 88,600	10% Median 90%	−1% 20	Growth rate Job openings	Couldn't find any programs in Michigan.
Power plant operators	$ 47,200 $ 65,100 $ 75,200	10% Median 90%	+1% 70	Growth rate Job openings	Couldn't find any programs in Michigan.
Electrical power-line installers and repairers (also known as linemen [sic])	$ 44,300 $ 65,100 $ 80,200	10% Median 90%	+5% 100	Growth rate Job openings	Lansing Community College in Lansing, Michigan, has a 1- to 2-year program in lineworker and in electrical and power transmission installation.
Electrician	$ 31,200 $ 56,600 $ 76,000	10% Median 90%	+6% 550	Growth rate Job openings	Kaplan Career Institute in Dearborn, Michigan, has a 1- to 2-year program. Jackson College in Jackson, Michigan, has a program shorter than one year and a 1- to 2-year program.

the "occupation quick search" on O*NET OnLine. These results are displayed in Figure 13.11.

You review this list with Juan and discuss the nature of each occupation. You express specific interest in whether Juan considers himself able, both with regard to physical labor and training, to do each occupation. Juan was familiar enough with some occupations to address this question. The two of you clicked on the name of some of the occupations to learn more about them. As a result of this conversation, Juan became particularly excited about the idea of becoming a construction equipment operator. He talked about how most construction sites utilize front-end loaders and cranes and indicated, with more excitement than he had felt in a long time, a belief that he could perform this job without undue amounts of pain.

The counseling process continued with deeper exploration of these occupations as possibilities, and Juan's interest in pursuing work as a crane operator grew. At your suggestion, Juan conducted some informational interviews with construction supervisors and crane operators to learn more about the requirements for this job. Juan's former supervisor was excited to hear of his interest and explained that all crane operators are legally required to be certified. He recommended a specific training program that provides training and preparation for the certification examination. Juan eagerly contacted the company offering this training and learned of several upcoming sessions. Because of the clear potential of such training to allow Juan to resume working, you were able to include this training on Juan's individualized plan for employment (IPE) and to secure federal vocational rehabilitation monies to pay for the training.

Lakeesha Maddox: Career Options, Life Balance, and Networking

When Lakeesha attended Spelman, psychology had seemed like the perfect major. She found the coursework fascinating, but now she wondered what she could possibly do with a bachelor's degree in psychology. As a career counselor at Spelman College, you want to address this concern directly and to reassure Lakeesha that her degree in psychology relates to a wide variety of professions. Spelman has purchased a site license to "What Can I Do with This Major? (http://whatcanidowiththismajor.com/major/psychology/)," and you share it with Lakeesha. It reveals a wide range of areas in which psychology majors may find employment, including human services, research, education, human resources, and business

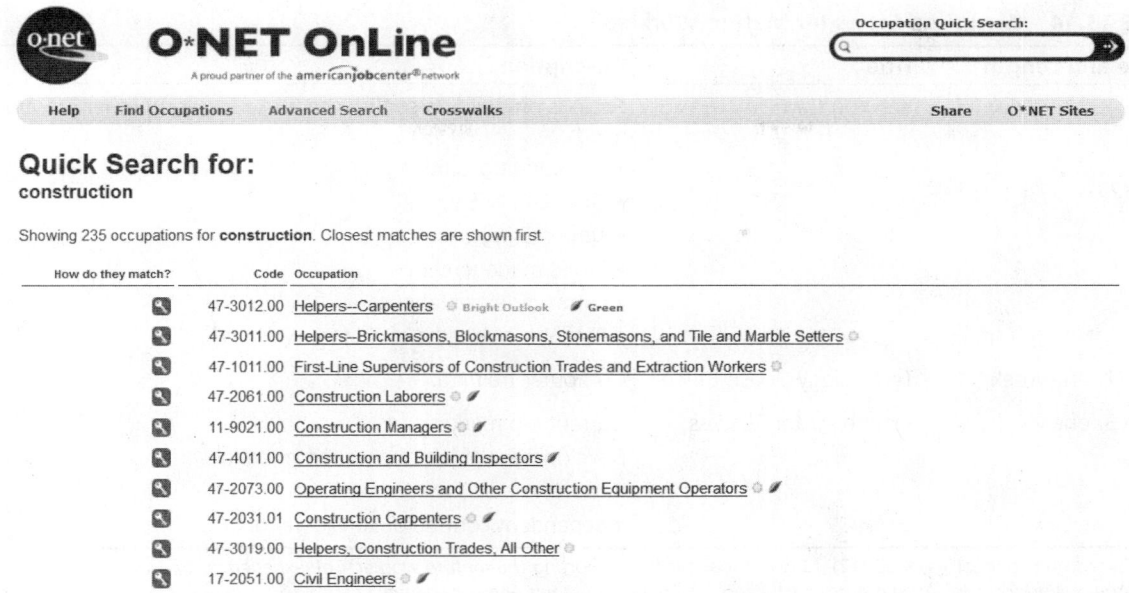

FIGURE 13.11 O*NET OnLine Results Related to Construction
Source: ONET OnLine U.S. Department of Labor http://www.onetonline.org/find/result?s=construction&a=1

and industry. You decide to print out the entire entry for psychology and ask Lakeesha to highlight all areas and employers that might be of potential interest to her.

Lakeesha wasn't interested in direct care occupations within human services. Instead, she gravitated more toward the idea of getting a job within advertising, marketing, or customer service, and she wondered whether working at a hotel might be a good fit for her. She wondered, though, how she could possibly balance a full-time job in any of these fields with her responsibilities to her daughters. In response, you suggest that she begin by reaching out to an area network of working mothers. You provide her with a website (workingmoms.meetup.com/cities/us/ga/atlanta/) that lists a variety of such groups in the Atlanta, Georgia, area. Lakeesha is stunned to see such a long list of support groups, many of which seem perfect for her, and agrees to contact at least three of them in the coming week. Her goal is to connect with other working mothers who can provide some emotional support for her through this major life transition as well as information about strategies for finding work.

When Lakeesha returns for her next session, she nearly bounces into your office. With a wide smile full of hope, Lakeesha announces that she thinks she may have found a window. Although two of the groups she contacted seemed anything but a good fit, the third group she contacted seemed just what she was looking for. After a long telephone call with the group's organizer, Lakeesha took a chance and attended an evening meeting. In addition to finding some kindred spirits in the group, Lakeesha received some great suggestions. One was to contact an organization called Mom Corps Atlanta (momcorps.com/atlanta). Another was to look into employment opportunities with the Turner Broadcasting System (TBS). Lakeesha learned that TBS has been recognized as one of the best companies for working mothers (Working Mother, 2011) and expressed relief to know that some companies recognize the challenge of life balance.

Lakeesha now has some broad ideas of the types of jobs she might want to pursue and some much-needed hope that it is possible to balance work and family responsibilities. Before she is ready to take the next step and begin searching for employment opportunities, though, Lakeesha needs to prepare several documents for the job search process. You provide Lakeesha with a worksheet designed to collect information for résumé writing. This worksheet includes a section dedicated to transferrable skills and a section dedicated to accomplishments and successes that her references can use. Because Lakeesha has not held a paying job since graduating from Spelman, these types of information may be particularly important.

Your plans for future use of technology and information resources with Lakeesha include assisting her with the creation of a Web-based résumé in order to combat likely assumptions about a former stay-at-home mom having outdated skills. You also plan to help Lakeesha understand the value of networking and informational interviews in identifying employment opportunities.

TABLE 13.14 Workshop Series for Mature Workers

Module and Length	Title	Description
Module 1: four days	Yes You Can	Focus is on building confidence and addressing other emotional needs: • Work-life transitions • Grief and loss • Time management • Stress management • Employer expectations • Potential strengths of mature workers
Module 2: one week	Technology Doesn't Byte	Computer training.
Module 3: one week	Setting up for Success	Current job market. Development of job application materials. Interviewing skills. Independent contractor considerations.

Source: Based on Klein-Collins, R. (2012). *New approaches for supporting the mature worker: The experiences of the U.S. Department of Labor's Aging Workforce Initiative grantees.* Chicago, IL: Council for Adult and Experiential Learning.

Doris Bronner: Skill-Building Workshops

Doris has a clear need to build some skills and change her attitude. Some of her difficulties may stem from her unhappy marriage and others from a lack of fit between the conventional jobs she has held and her social/artistic interests, but it occurs to you that it is also important to consider developmental issues. Because Doris has frequently commented about how difficult it is to be older than her boss, you wonder whether Doris is struggling with the aging process as it intersects with her career development (or lack thereof). Your awareness of this possibility has been heightened because you recently attended a breakout session on this very topic while at a conference last month. This session was presented by counselors at Goodwill Industries in Houston who described a week-long workshop series for mature workers (Klein-Collins, 2012). Table 13.14 describes the content of this workshop series, which seems suited to Doris's needs.

The first module of the workshop has the potential to help Doris reconcile some of the emotions likely contributing to her poor attitude and performance at work. The second module's focus on building computer skills offers an opportunity for Doris to upgrade her technology skills and this, according to Holland (2013), is absolutely essential for older workers. Doris clearly needs to find another job. The third module of this workshop addresses this need.

You decide to email one of the presenters from Goodwill Industries in Houston. In your note, you explain that you provide career counseling in Omaha, Nebraska, and inquire about their willingness to share their curriculum with you so that you might use it to provide similar workshops for aging workers in the Omaha area. Within a day, the presenter emails you the full curriculum.

After carefully reviewing it, you approach your supervisor to (a) share the materials and (b) ask to add an item to your next staff meeting agenda regarding interest in offering such a group. When you present to the staff meeting, some staff members oppose adding anything new to the agency's offerings; others are enthusiastic about the opportunity. Your supervisor selects three counselors to head this initiative and agrees to advertise the workshop.

I share this example to illustrate some realities of being a counselor. First, necessity truly is the mother of invention. Time and time again, you will encounter clients whose needs prompt your acquisition of new knowledge and your development of new approaches. Second, there isn't always a need to reinvent the wheel. In many cases, you can find materials to guide your addition of services, and you will generally find other counselors quite willing to share their materials as long as they are not in direct competition with you. Third, to be responsive to changing client needs, counselors need to become comfortable with the chain of command and the procedures for suggesting new approaches within any given agency or educational setting.

Each place you work will have its own politics, early adopters, and employees who need to be in an attitude adjustment workshop alongside Doris. To stay on the cutting edge, attend conferences. Doing so will allow you to connect with other energetic counselors who continue to embrace their responsibility for ongoing professional development and to get concrete ideas of programs and interventions that might benefit your current and future clients.

CHAPTER

14

Career Development in K–12 Educational Settings

As we begin this chapter and shift our focus to career development in educational settings, it may be useful to reflect on the purpose of education. Take a few minutes to brainstorm a list of reasons that a national government would fund public education and your thoughts about why a society would pass legislation mandating education for all youth. Also articulate your thoughts about why parents might invest their own money to provide a private education for their children and why young (or not so young) adults would pay money and take out loans to finance a college education.

What are the outcomes anticipated from such investments? Surely, our societal goal in mandating and financing elementary and secondary education isn't merely to prepare our young people to do well on standardized tests of academic aptitude or achievement. And our primary goal in investing our own time and money in nonmandatory education is not to obtain a piece of paper we can frame and hang on our wall. So why exactly do we—as individuals, as families, and as a society—invest in education?

My hope is that one reason that you brainstormed involved preparing ourselves and our young people to become productive citizens. An important goal of education is to equip our citizens with the knowledge and skills necessary to produce or perform something of value in order to support themselves and/or others. For many, if not most, people, supporting oneself requires entry into and success within the world of work. Thus, career preparation lies at the very heart of education.

Beyond focusing on academic subjects, though, how do schools strive to prepare students for entry into a career? Clearly, the answer to this question varies dramatically across school districts, state lines, and national borders. In some schools, the connection between academic courses and careers is more evident than in others. Efforts and activities focused specifically on career development vary tremendously. Because of this variation, what you read in this chapter may differ considerably from what you've observed within the schools where you or your family members have attended and/or worked. In this chapter, you'll learn about best practices as they pertain to career development in K–12 educational settings. My hope is that, should you accept employment as a counselor in an educational setting, you would aspire to facilitate the wide variety of career development activities for students as described in this chapter.

AMERICAN SCHOOL COUNSELOR ASSOCIATION NATIONAL MODEL

Contemporary school counselors plan their time and organize their activities in accordance with the American School Counselor Association (ASCA) National Model (American School Counselor Association, 2012). This model conceptualizes the services of a school counselor as including direct and indirect services. With regard to direct services, the ASCA National Model is designed to ensure that 100% of students receive the services of a school counselor through systematic school counseling core curriculum and individual student planning activities.

The school counseling core curriculum addresses the academic, career, and personal-social development needs of all students, and it is competency based. The primary emphasis of individual student planning activities is on helping students develop their own individual plans with regard to education (including postsecondary education) and career. Contemporary school counselors functioning within the framework of the ASCA National Model provide responsive services (such as individual and group counseling) to students who seek them. Indirect services consist of other appropriate school counselor activities related to the overall functioning of the counseling program and the school as a whole. These responsibilities, referred to as delivery systems, are addressed in detail in *The ASCA National Model: A Framework for School Counseling Programs* (American School Counselor Association, 2012) and are, for the most part, beyond the scope of this text. For now, however, it is important for you to recognize that school counselors today are expected to pay a great deal of attention to the career development needs of students and that these needs are addressed most frequently through a comprehensive school counseling core curriculum and through individual student planning activities.

STUDENT COMPETENCIES IN CAREER DEVELOPMENT

The career development activities within K–12 settings are guided by two organizations: the American School Counselor Association (ASCA) and the National Occupational Information Coordinating Committee (NOICC). Both organizations approach career development with the belief that specific competencies should be developed beginning in childhood and continuing into adulthood. In using these frameworks, school counselors are encouraged to specify the grade levels at which each competency will be targeted, the methods and materials used to help students achieve each competency, and the person(s) responsible for facilitating the career development activity or lesson. In other words, school counselors should not rely on hit-or-miss strategies and simply hope that students have opportunities to achieve the competencies recommended by ASCA and NOICC. Instead, they should work with the other counselors in their district to develop a systematic, K–12 approach in which various competencies are targeted at specific grade levels to ensure that all competencies are addressed with all students by the end of their time in the K–12 setting.

Table 14.1 identifies the ASCA student standards in the career development domain. For each competency, ASCA also identifies indicators, or ways in which students should be able to demonstrate mastery of each competency. For example, Competency C.1: Acquire Knowledge to Achieve Career Goals has seven indicators. Students should be able to indicate mastery of this competency by showing that they can:

1. Understand the relationship between educational achievement and career success
2. Explain how work can help to achieve personal success and satisfaction
3. Identify personal preferences and interests influencing career choice and success
4. Understand that the changing workplace requires lifelong learning and acquiring new skills
5. Describe the effect of work on lifestyle
6. Understand the importance of equity and access in career choice
7. Understand that work is an important and satisfying means of personal expression (American School Counselor Association, 2012)

TABLE 14.1 ASCA Student Standards in the Career Development Domain

Standard A:	Students will acquire the skills to investigate the world of work in relation to knowledge of self and to make informed career decisions.	
	Competency A1:	Develop Career Awareness
	Competency A2:	Develop Employment Readiness
Standard B:	Students will employ strategies to achieve future career goals with success and satisfaction.	
	Competency B1:	Acquire Career Information
	Competency B2:	Identify Career Goals
Standard C:	Students will understand the relationship [among] personal qualities, education, training, and the world of work.	
	Competency C1:	Acquire Knowledge to Achieve Career Goals
	Competency C2:	Apply Skills to Achieve Career Goals

Source: Copyright National Career Development Association (NCDA). Reprinted by permission from American School Counselor Association. www.schoolcounselor.org

The complete list of the ASCA Student Standards in the Career Development Domain is included in Appendix D.

In addition to the ASCA Student Standards in the Career Development domain, school counselors also refer to the National Career Development Guidelines (NCDG) Framework. These guidelines, which were developed by the National Occupational Information Coordinating Committee (1992), served as the basis for the ASCA standards (Lester, 1999).

The most recent revision of the National Career Development Guidelines (NCDG; Kobylarz, 2004) are arranged into three categories: the personal social domain, the educational achievement and lifelong learning domain, and the career planning domain (see Table 14.2). The three ASCA domains (academic development, career development, and personal-social development) parallel the NCDG domains. For each of the goals reflected in Table 14.2, the NCDG also identifies numerous indicators by which an individual should be able to demonstrate achievement of the goal. These indicators appear in Appendix E.

IMPORTANCE OF INTEGRATED CAREER DEVELOPMENT PROGRAMS

School counselors believe that *all* students deserve to benefit from an integrated career development program. Thus, career development programs should be geared toward helping 100% of students develop the career development competencies described above. The career development program is psychoeducational in nature and should be integrated as an essential part of the total school curriculum. Doing so requires coordination and collaboration among elementary, middle, and high school counselors as well as between counselors and other school personnel.

Generally speaking, integrated career development programs are delivered via three types of activities: (1) classroom guidance lessons within the school counseling core curriculum, (2) schoolwide events or programs, and (3) educational planning activities. This chapter provides information about career development programs at the elementary, middle, and high school levels. Each section begins by addressing basic developmental considerations before turning to an exploration of classroom guidance lessons, schoolwide programs or events, and educational planning activities.

CAREER DEVELOPMENT PROGRAMS IN ELEMENTARY SCHOOLS

Developmental Considerations

Yes. You read that right. Career development programs should indeed begin in elementary school. Clearly, it is unreasonable to think that elementary school students

TABLE 14.2 National Career Development Guidelines

Domain PS:	**Personal Social Development Domain**	
	Goal PS1:	Develop understanding of self to build and maintain a positive self-concept.
	Goal PS2:	Develop positive interpersonal skills including respect for diversity.
	Goal PS3:	Integrate growth and change into your career development.
	Goal PS4:	Balance personal, leisure, community, learner, family, and work roles.
Domain ED:	**Educational Achievement and Lifelong Learning Domain**	
	Goal ED1:	Attain educational achievement and performance levels needed to reach your personal and career goals.
	Goal ED2:	Participate in ongoing, lifelong learning experiences to enhance your ability to function effectively in a diverse and changing economy.
Domain CM:	**Career Management Domain**	
	Goal CM1:	Create and manage a career plan that meets your career goals.
	Goal CM2:	Use a process of decision making as one component of career development.
	Goal CM3:	Use accurate, current, and unbiased career information during career planning and management.
	Goal CM4:	Master academic, occupational, and general employability skills in order to obtain, create, maintain, and/or advance your employment.
	Goal CM5:	Integrate changing employment trends, societal needs, and economic conditions into your career plans.

Source: Copyright National Career Development Association (NCDA). Reprinted by American School Counselor Association. www.schoolscounselor.org

are ready to commit to any specific career direction. However, the elementary school years are the ideal time to begin developing the self-knowledge and understanding of the world of work that will assist in career planning later and even to begin developing employability skills (Magnuson & Starr, 2000). The career development needs of elementary school students primarily involve the need for increased awareness: awareness of themselves and their unique characteristics, awareness of the world of work and the wide variety of careers available, and awareness of behaviors associated with success both in school and work environments.

Especially at the elementary school level, it is essential that these topics must be addressed in developmentally appropriate ways in order to be effective. Whether providing personal counseling or career guidance, a counselor working in the elementary setting must be keenly aware and specially trained to engage children in developmentally appropriate ways. For example, activity-based lessons are recommended in lieu of lecture-style lessons, and the use of concrete, hands-on materials is more effective than relying on abstract words and concepts. Elementary school counselors may engage students in puppet plays, art projects, skits, and sharing circles while facilitating career development activities.

Career development theories also offer insight into developmentally important concepts. For example, at the elementary school level, career development competencies tend to build on children's natural curiosity, engage them in fantasy, and enhance their self-awareness of their interests (Super, 1984); develop their sense of self-efficacy (Lent, Brown, & Hackett, 1994); broaden their awareness of careers in the world; and seek to prevent circumscription based on sex role stereotypes (Gottfredson, 1981). Let's look at the kinds of activities that may be incorporated into an elementary school career development program.

School Counseling Core Curriculum: Career Development Lessons for Elementary School Classrooms

Some career development lessons focus on enhancing elementary school students' understanding and awareness of themselves. For example, one activity might consist of having students use magazines, scissors, and glue to create a collage of activities they enjoy. Processing questions could invite students to recognize how they each have different activities they enjoy and to connect these activities with school subjects and/or jobs, thereby enhancing student awareness not only of their interests but also of the connection among interests, school, and work. Discussion about the difference between vocational and avocational interests (in child-friendly language, of course) could also occur.

Other career development lessons and activities help students become more aware of the connection between school and work. As part of a unit in math, for example, students may be invited to play a detective game in which the winning team identifies the most careers that use math. In addition to naming the careers, the game rules may specify that the team must also tell how math is used in that job. Chefs, for example, may use fractions when following a recipe, professional golfers use addition when calculating their scores, and taxi drivers must be able to use math to count change for customers.

Still other career development lessons at the elementary school level focus on increasing student awareness of the variety of career possibilities. In addition to introducing students to career clusters, career guidance lessons at the elementary school should also increase student awareness of more specific careers in order to broaden their awareness of the wide variety of careers (Akos, Niles, Miller, & Erford, 2011). Elementary school students have limited awareness of careers, and these careers reflect primarily the careers to which they have had exposure: careers of family members, and careers they observe at school, in their everyday lives, and on television.

Not surprisingly, many children aspire to careers based on their admiration of people in their lives or based on media glamorization of various careers. For instance, when asked what they want to be when they grow up, many youngsters point toward careers as professional athletes, and this aspiration often seems to consternate and/or amuse the adults in their lives. Rather than harshly confronting children with the unfavorable odds of success in this pursuit (NCAA, 2013), career counselors would be wise to view this as an opportunity to broaden career awareness. One such lesson might involve students brainstorming a list of careers related to sports. This list would likely highlight a variety of professional sports, but it could also include careers such as umpire or referee, broadcaster or announcer, advertiser, concession vendor, groundskeeper, sports medicine professional, trainer, coach, photographer and so forth. Such a lesson could be incorporated into a physical education class, a writing unit (in which students learn to write a five-paragraph essay about a different sports-related career), or a computer unit in which students find online information about a sports-related career. Processing questions might also help students consider other, non-sport-related careers requiring similar aptitudes or characteristics (e.g., physical strength, endurance) and commensurate levels of physical activity (e.g., firefighters, construction workers).

Consistent with Gottfredson's (1981) findings regarding circumscription related to sex roles, it is essential that discussions include examples of both male and female workers in the occupations explored.

Schoolwide Events or Programs: Other Career Development Activities for Elementary Schools

In addition to classroom guidance lessons, school counselors should facilitate other career development activities in the school. These activities generally involve more than one classroom at a time. They may focus on a specific grade level, a specific group of students, or the entire student population.

Holding a schoolwide or grade-level career day or career fair is a popular career development activity in many elementary schools. As Beale and Williams (2000) noted, however, conducting such an event effectively requires a great deal of forethought and planning. It is not sufficient simply to invite random parents or adults in the community to converge on a specific day to share information about their careers. Counselors should be purposeful and selective when identifying guest speakers. Drawing from career development theory, for example, one approach would be to have guest speakers representative of each Holland work environment: realistic, investigative, artistic, social, enterprising, and conventional (RIASEC; Holland, 1997). Another approach would be to invite at least one guest speaker for each of the career clusters. Other factors to consider include the level of education necessary for entry into the profession, the inclusion of people considered gender nontraditional for a given profession, and the inclusion of role models who share characteristics with your student population. Such characteristics might be racial/ethnic backgrounds, disability status, or socioeconomic status during childhood. In their wonderfully practical article focused on career days, Beale and Williams (2000) provided many additional pointers for planning an elementary school career day and even included ideas for involving parents in the processing of career information. Should you decide to plan a career day, this article will surely be of use to you.

Whereas career days tend to be focused broadly, with the intent of increasing student awareness of a wide variety of careers across the spectrum, other career development activities may be more focused. Moore (2010), for example, offered ideas for a fifth-grade entrepreneur fair. Stating that "small companies account for 99.7 percent of employer-owned firms and create 60 to 80 percent of the new jobs in recent years in the United States"

Moore (2010) argued for the importance of schools increasing attention to entrepreneurship "as a viable career option" (p. 8). A simulation game called the Mini-Society is a "nationally recognized program . . . [that] allows students to learn basic economic concepts by creating their own micro-economy in the classroom" (Center for Economic & Financial Education, 2014, para. 1). A list of similar programs in each state is available from the Consortium for Entrepreneurship Education (2014).

Many schools have responded to the need for increased national achievement in the science, technology, engineering, and math (STEM) disciplines by offering a career day focused on STEM careers. Other schools infuse career development lessons about STEM careers into their academic curriculum. As shown in Table 14.3, several child-friendly websites focus on STEM careers. I hope you'll explore at least some of websites in the table. The NASA websites may be of particular interest because NCDA president Rich Feller has worked closely with NASA on these projects.

Another, more focused approach involves grade-level field trips to specific places of employment. Such an approach should be used systematically, with each grade level visiting a different workplace and students being exposed to a wide variety of positions in each workplace. As with all such activities, preparing students in advance and processing with them afterward is essential. If visiting a car dealership, for example, it would be useful for students to have an opportunity to talk with a wide variety of employees, ranging from the mechanics to the salespeople, to the cashiers, to the owner. If students are prepared with questions about how each person uses reading skills and math skills and about the training required in order to hold such a job, for example, the field trip will be much more effective. It is also useful to forewarn the employees that such questions will likely be asked during your visit so that they may prepare answers.

Educational Planning Activities for Elementary Schools

Another element of successful career developmental programs involves attention to educational planning. In this context, an important goal is to engage elementary school students in the consideration of postsecondary education. Contrary to what you might think, conversations about college and other postsecondary options are not premature in an elementary school setting. Rather, such activities are especially important for students whose family members have not attended college. The Plano Independent School District (2007) in Texas, for example, features a college week. Age-appropriate activities for such

TABLE 14.3 Child-Friendly Websites Focused on STEM Careers

Title	Website
Biology4Kids!	biology4kids.com/
Cool Science Careers	coolsciencecareers.rice.edu/
Design Squad Nation	pbskids.org/designsquad/
Engineer Girl	engineergirl.org/
Girl Scouts STEM	girlscouts.org/stem
iON Future	changetheequation.org/inspiring-youth-0
NASA	nasa.gov/audience/forstudents/k-4/index.html
	nasa.gov/audience/forkids/kidsclub/flash/index.html
Science Bob	sciencebob.com/index.php
The Fun Works	thefunworks.edc.org/SPT--homegraphic.ohp
Wonderville	wonderville.ca/

an event might include a large bulletin board near the cafeteria. The bulletin board might engage students in guessing which of their teachers attended which college, with teacher photos on one side and college logos and/or information on the other. Students could supply their answers on corresponding worksheets, and the answers would be revealed on the last day of the week using strings of yarn to connect teachers with the college(s) they attended. Another bulletin board might feature a map (of the United States or of the state in which the elementary school is located) and college-age photos of each teacher around the perimeter of the map. Yarn strings could then connect each photo with the geographic location of the college each teacher attended. Students can guess each teacher's identity and which college she or he attended. On the final day, teachers can wear some college apparel to reveal their alma maters.

Another activity may involve each classroom being assigned a specific college. The students could learn about the college, decorate the outside of the classroom door to reflect that college, write paragraphs or draw pictures about the college, and so on. Students could also learn about specific majors and learn about careers connected with those majors. A pen pal system could also be established, with elementary school students writing to students at that college. A pen pal system would most likely be established through a specific organization, for example, a service club, an honors college, a sorority or fraternity, or student government. While learning how to write a letter (an academic lesson), students would be simultaneously learning about postsecondary education and reaping career development benefits.

The fifth-graders at Detroit Service Learning Academy recently completed a service learning project known as the College-Bound Initiative. This project had a dual focus, with attention to both promoting college awareness in the fifth-graders and supporting high school seniors. The fifth-graders held a college-bound walk; they solicited donations and sponsorships, and they each received a T-shirt featuring the words *college bound* and bearing the logos of several nearby universities. Use of the donations was explained on the school's website:

> In today's economy it is hard for parents to send even their high achieving students to college, with all the tools and supplies needed to have a successful college experience. Our goal is to partner with Henry Ford High School and sponsor 20–30 seniors with College Bound Kits. These kits will include all supplies needed for a dorm room (bedding, toiletries, towels, face towels, microwaves, irons, etc. [sic] Our students will also host a College Bound Walk at Belle Isle where they will raise money for 2–3 scholarships for first semester books. (Detroit Service Learning Academy, 2011, para. 8)

Another popular activity in elementary schools involves the designation of a stuffed animal to accompany teachers or families on trips. While on the trip, the person in charge of the stuffed animal takes photos of the stuffed animal and writes explanatory sentences or paragraphs for them. On returning to school, the photos and descriptions are added to an album that sits beside the stuffed animal in a central location. Students and visitors can sit with the stuffed animal and look through the album to learn about its travels. To focus such an activity on college attendance or career development, the character may be aptly named, preferably with a gender-ambiguous name (e.g., Chris the College Student or Terry the Tireless Worker). Chris the College Student would visit colleges and be photographed at various college locations: perhaps studying at the library, taking notes during class, carrying a backpack across campus, watching a basketball game in the school gym, or having a slice of pizza in the student union. Chris's album would therefore feature photos of Chris at various colleges and engaged in typical college activities. Chris might even get a college T-shirt to wear. Terry the Tireless Worker may go to work with parents. While at work, the parent would photograph Terry "doing" work tasks typical for that position. Terry's album would therefore feature photos of Terry doing a wide variety of jobs, along with written descriptions of each and the tasks involved in that job.

As we conclude this section about career development activities in the elementary school, you should have a better sense of the types of age-appropriate activities that are engaging and effective in facilitating the career development of elementary students. In addition to ensuring age-appropriateness of the activities, counselors should maximize their value with follow-up activities rather than treating any of them as isolated events. Counselors should also pay particular attention to the need for preplanning a curriculum to ensure the systematic coverage of the full range of career development competencies over the course of a student's K–12 experience. Collaborative efforts allow the middle school counselors to build on what students have learned in their elementary school years.

CAREER DEVELOPMENT IN MIDDLE SCHOOLS

Developmental Considerations

Whereas the career development in elementary school revolves around the need for increased career awareness, the developmental needs of middle school students include a need for more specific career exploration (Magnuson & Starr, 2000) and self-understanding (Peterson, Long, & Billups, 1999). Thus, career development programs in middle schools generally include assessment activities designed to help students crystallize their sense of self (especially with respect to their academic interests and aptitudes). Once they have crystallized this self-knowledge, students benefit from an opportunity to engage in more in-depth exploration of specific careers. Such exploration is particularly helpful to the extent that it not only familiarizes students with careers of possible interest but also helps students understand the education and training needed to obtain such careers.

When students perceive a direct connection between education and future careers, they may experience school as more relevant to their lives, which, in turn, may result in them investing more energy in their scholastic efforts and selecting more rigorous coursework (Orthner et al., 2010). This is important because educational development plans are generally developed during the middle school years and have considerable impact on students' preparedness for college preparatory coursework during high school.

School Counseling Core Curriculum: Career Development Lessons for Middle School Classrooms

As is true at the elementary school level, a high-quality middle school counseling program should include a systematically designed and delivered school counseling core curriculum. Such a curriculum should address students' needs for academic development, career development, and personal/social development. Consistent with the developmental needs discussed above, it is common for middle school classroom guidance lessons to include a focus on enhancing student self-understanding as it pertains to career development.

Some units likely involve the administration and interpretation of various assessment instruments. For example, a unit might include the administration and interpretation of the Self-Directed Search Career Explorer, a standardized test designed for use in middle school or junior high settings that results in a two-letter Holland code (Osborn & Reardon, 2006). The results may then be used in future classroom guidance lessons to help students identify careers that share their Holland code and to guide their exploration of these careers.

When using standardized tests, however, school counselors should note several precautions. First, it is important to consult with the school administrator or legal counsel regarding whether written parental consent is necessary prior to the administration of such instruments. State laws vary, so a prudent school counselor will seek guidance in this regard. Second, ethical assessment practices require that counselors provide clients (students) with the results of assessments in a manner that is understandable and usable by the client (student). It is not sufficient simply to give students a score or even to provide them with a handout. Instead, it is necessary for school counselors to ensure that the information provided to students and/or their parents is in an understandable and usable format. School counselors should pay particular attention to the need to put test results into context for students and their families.

Far too often, I hear people share memories of taking some standardized test while in middle or high school and indicate that the results told them that they should enter a particular career. The person telling the story is usually communicating a belief that the career suggested by the test was surprising or even ridiculous and that the testing experience was worthless. Of course, career tests are not designed to tell clients what career they should pursue. Rather, they are designed to identify careers that may be a particularly good fit for clients, with the idea that clients then need to explore those careers to make a determination. Because of their cognitive developmental level, middle school students may be particularly susceptible to oversimplifications and dichotomous thinking. The savvy counselor should take extra precautions to help students understand very clearly that the test results are *not* intended to tell them what they should be when they grow up. Rather, they are intended to expand students' awareness of themselves and to identify types of careers that may or may not be a good fit for them. It is my experience that this cannot be overemphasized.

Another important element of a middle school career development program involves teaching students about employability skills. A variety of curricular resources are available for this purpose, and lessons in this category generally involve life skills and personal characteristics for success. One such lesson, for example, is offered by the Network for Teaching Entrepreneurship (NFTE; nfte.com) and addresses employability skills such as reliability, enthusiasm, accuracy, and initiative. Other such lessons are available from the State of Oklahoma's (2014) CareerTech website, including an entire set of lessons focused on employability skills.

Other classroom guidance lessons to facilitate the career development of middle school students involve helping students explore careers of potential interest. At this stage, it is particularly important to teach students how to access information about various careers and to assist them in processing the information they obtain. Chapter 13 presented various sources of information about the world of work. Many websites support career exploration by K–12 students. One, for example, is designed by the National Institutes of Health (2014) to help middle and high school students explore careers in the health and medical sciences. The U.S. Bureau of Labor Statistics (2014) offers a website on which students can identify school subjects they like and then identify careers related to those subjects.

As you can see, with the myriad Internet-based resources available, school counselors can easily obtain a wide selection of career exploration resources free of charge. Other costs, though, are associated with using such free resources. First, it takes time to seek out such resources, especially because website addresses frequently change. Second, it takes time and expertise to compile and sequence the resources and activities to meet the various career development standards targeted at each grade level. Time may also be needed to adapt the materials to the middle school level. Reproducing various worksheets for use in the classroom may be costly. Given the costs associated with this approach, many school districts choose to invest in a site license for commercially available career exploration systems that contain the curricula and materials necessary for use with elementary, middle, and high school students in all of the major career development areas.

Several computer-assisted career guidance systems (CACGS), such as Bridges/XAP, Career Cruising, and the Kuder Career Planning System, were discussed in Chapter 13. In the classroom environment, counselors or teachers can help students navigate these CACGS and use various print materials that are also available from the program developers. A particularly strong feature of most CACGS is a section that facilitates student exploration of specific careers. Students can generally select from an impressive array of occupations and access information that is developmentally appropriate and engaging. In addition to written information, many of these programs include short videos of people actually employed in the occupation, photos of people performing work tasks in the occupation, or interviews with employees. Each of these programs includes a feature focused on educational planning. Thus, the connection between career aspirations and the education and training necessary to achieve them is evident.

Schoolwide Events or Programs: Other Career Development Activities for Middle Schools

In addition to classroom guidance lessons, middle school counselors often facilitate other career development activities. One popular activity involves a simulation game in which students engage in real-life activities associated with adulthood. One such game, which was created by the Business and Professional Women's (BPW) Clubs of Indiana (Caniglia & Leapard, 2009), was previously known as the Reality Store. Although many counselors continue to use the name Reality Store, this simulation game is now officially called Life Unplugged as a result of a merger between BPW and the Michigan Women's Foundation. It used to be provided to districts free of charge under the sponsorship of state-based BPWs, but the new website (life-unplugged.org) indicates a nominal charge now for the materials.

Although competing versions of this type of game vary, they tend to share much in common (Jarvis, 2004). Each game is generally designed to build on previous career development lessons in which students learn about career pathways and identify careers of interest to them. The games tend to begin with a student selecting a career and then being invited to experience simulated life as it might be for someone with that career. Emphasis is placed on finances and lifestyle choices, so students learn about the salaries and benefits associated with various careers and the costs associated with adult life responsibilities and opportunities. On getting the virtual job, students go to different booths or stations to pay for their living expenses, including universal expenses (such as taxes, housing, utilities, food, and transportation) as well as other expenses associated with life choices (including savings, child care, student loans, insurance, and vacations) or unanticipated life circumstances (such as medical expenses, windfalls, or disasters). These games allow students to learn about the costs associated with adulthood through simulated experiences of receiving paychecks, paying bills, and making purchases. Reality games allow students to realize the importance of preparing oneself for a job that will afford them the lifestyle they desire and the impact of various choices on lifestyle.

Another career development approach used in middle schools involves service learning projects, which also afford an opportunity for students to engage in career exploration and develop employability skills (Kerka, 2000; Stott & Jackson, 2005). For example, the Colorado Department of Education (2010) offers a service learning toolkit for use in K–12 schools. This toolkit offers several service learning strategies that may facilitate career development. Middle school students may participate in a service learning project involving the preparation or delivery of meals for the elderly. In conjunction with this project, they may explore careers related to nutrition, dietetics, or gerontology. A counselor may facilitate students' reflection on this service learning project and ask them to consider how well this activity matched their interests, personality, values, and/or skills. Yet another approach would be to have students rate themselves on various employability skills required by such an activity. These skills may include punctuality, reliability, teamwork, and interpersonal skills. Regardless of the nature of the service learning project, counselors can capitalize on them by encouraging students to explore related careers, reflect on the match between the service learning activity and their own attributes, and assess the employability skills they need.

By providing students with classroom guidance lessons focused on their career development needs and offering other career development opportunities, such as the Life Unplugged game or service learning projects, middle school counselors can ensure that their students arrive at high school prepared to make the curricular and career choices that will soon face them. The key, of course, is not to relegate career development to a single course, a single unit, or a single lesson but instead to deliver a preplanned, sequential career development program that spans the entire time a student spends in middle school.

Educational Planning Activities for Middle Schools

It is important to recognize that educational planning and career development "are intrinsically bonded" (Trusty, Niles, & Carney, 2005, p. 136). Another key aspect of career development in the middle school involves assisting students with educational planning, which is most clearly articulated with educational development plans (EDPs), also known as four-year plans, six-year plans, or programs of study. The completion of these EDPs often begins with classroom presentations by the counselor that build directly on previous units and focus on career-related assessments and career pathways. Completion of an EDP may also include individual or small-group meetings with the counselor.

School counselors will surely learn about EDPs in their specialization coursework. Appendix G includes a sample EDP form (Hobson & Phillips, 2004). Note that this form begins with identification of career pathways and careers of interest to the student that are based on assessment results. The EDP also includes an area for specifying educational or training goals and the school's graduation requirements. The form contains space where a student can identify planned coursework for each semester of middle and/or high school. Modifications of such a form are likely from one district to the next. For example, in the sample, the school's graduation requirements are mandated by the statewide Michigan Merit Curriculum legislation. Other states participating in the American Diploma Project (achieve.org/adp-network) will likely have statewide graduation requirements. As such, the graduation requirement portion of the sample EDP included in Appendix G would need to be modified to reflect your state's or school district's graduation requirements. This sample form is based on six class periods per day arranged in accordance with semesters. Your school year, however, may be organized into trimesters, or your school days may be organized in a block schedule.

Another career development program focused on educational planning is called Gaining Early Awareness and Readiness for Undergraduate Programs (GEAR UP).

The GEAR UP program generally begins in middle school and continues into high school. GEAR UP is a federally funded (by the U.S. Department of Education) program "designed to increase the number of low-income students who are prepared to enter and succeed in postsecondary education" (U.S. Department of Education, 2014, para. 1). GEAR UP grants are available to states as well as to partnerships, which most often involve a collaborative effort between a university and a school district. Although GEAR UP specifically targets postsecondary education, an important element of many GEAR UP programs addresses the connection between career aspirations and postsecondary education. An implicit goal of GEAR UP programs is to target students who may otherwise not consider postsecondary education as a viable option due to circumscription. The programs use interventions not only to increase their academic preparedness but also to broaden their zone of acceptable alternatives when it comes to career aspirations (Gottfredson, 1981).

CAREER DEVELOPMENT IN HIGH SCHOOLS

Developmental Considerations

As you now know, career development programs seek to broaden career awareness at the elementary school level and to facilitate deeper exploration of careers and oneself at the middle school level. These elements of career development programs serve as the foundation for the educational and career planning that is needed at the high school level in preparation for the implementation of these plans at the postsecondary level (Arrington, 2000). Table 14.4 illustrates how the relative emphasis on each of these elements shifts from one educational level to the next.

Therefore, students enter high school ideally with a broad awareness of career options, a fairly solid sense of their career-related interests and skills, and significant knowledge about several potential careers of interest to them. Students are now prepared to begin the process of education and career planning. In fact, an initial planning step should actually occur in middle school with the drafting of an EDP involving selection of courses that a student will take during high school. Before discussing educational planning in greater depth, however, let us first look at other career development activities that should occur during high school.

School Counseling Core Curriculum: Career Development Lessons for High School Classrooms

Because school counselors may have the opportunity to deliver only a few lessons to each high school classroom, the lessons are often focused on short-term educational planning. For example, high school counselors may visit classrooms to help students understand the school's graduation requirements and the concept of course credit. They may also visit classrooms to assist in updating each student's EDP and provide information about the scheduling of classes for the upcoming semester or academic year.

Under more ideal circumstances, school counselors also conduct lessons focused on self-assessment of career-related values, interests, personality, and skills. These lessons build on similar lessons conducted during middle school; they allow students either to confirm or to modify past assessment results and help students plan for entry into specific careers matched to these personal variables. It is also useful for high school counselors to deliver guidance lessons focused on employability skills. Such lessons teach students about qualities and behaviors (such as good attendance, reliability, and persistence) typically rewarded in the workplace and help students recognize that demonstrating these same qualities and behaviors in high school affect the letters of recommendation they will receive and can predict postsecondary success. Other employability skills to be targeted at the high school level include guidance in résumé writing, completing job applications, and interviewing.

To help high school students develop their career plans, additional classroom guidance lessons regarding career options are often needed. As a result of such lessons, students should understand the career pathways of interest to them, know specific career options at each educational level within these pathways, and develop a plan for achieving various career options. Because not all students aspire to careers requiring a college degree, the high school counseling core curriculum should also familiarize all students with the breadth of postsecondary options available to them, including immediate entry into the workplace, career colleges or trade schools, a wide variety of options within the military, community colleges; four-year colleges or universities; and alternative 13th-year/gap-year options (Torpey, 2009).

It should be clear by now that significant content needs to be delivered to all high school students with

TABLE 14.4 Relative Emphasis of Career Development Programs at Each Educational Level

Elementary	Awareness
Middle school	Exploration
High school	Planning
Postsecondary	Implementation

respect to career development (Fitzpatrick & Costantini, 2011). As you've learned in this chapter, high school students need an opportunity to revisit, confirm, and/or modify their self-understanding of various career-related factors; develop a sound understanding and mastery of employability skills; and gain knowledge specific to each postsecondary educational and career option. Alas, school counselors continue to struggle to gain access to classrooms frequently enough to offer sufficient attention to these important topics. This lack of access is due in part to teacher reluctance to sacrifice curricular time for the purpose of guidance lessons. It can also be attributed to a vast array of nonguidance duties routinely assigned to school counselors and the "absurdly high student-counselor ratios in many public schools" (Johnson, Rochkind, Ott, & DuPont, 2010, p. 14). As noted by Johnson, et al. (2010),

> Much of their [counselors'] day is devoted to administrative tasks, discipline issues, untangling scheduling snafus . . . overseeing testing programs, along with lunch duty, attendance monitoring, and substitute teaching. Under the current system, public schools often seem to assume that counselors can juggle a whole roster of duties and still effectively assist hundreds of students in planning their future. (p. 76)

The problem of administrator assignment of nonguidance duties to school counselors probably won't be solved any time soon. Suffice it to say, though, that a high school counselor's effectiveness in supporting the career and educational planning needs of students is affected by teacher willingness to grant access to their students, the variety of competing responsibilities assigned to a counselor by the administration, the counselor's training and expertise in career counseling and postsecondary planning, and the counselor's choices with regard to the use of time. The following section will address ways, in addition to classroom guidance lessons, in which high school counselors may use their time to facilitate students' career development needs.

Schoolwide Events or Programs: Other Career Development Activities for High Schools

Far too few high school counselors report extensive use of classroom guidance presentations as a means of addressing the career development needs of students, but it is my opinion that far too many high school counselors rely on individual meetings with students. Although the concept of providing individual career counseling to each high school student is, on the surface, an attractive prospect, I contend that these meetings tend to be so brief and infrequent that they can only be likened to an assembly-line approach to education and career planning. Calling each student to the counselor's office during his or her junior year for an individual meeting (which often lasts no more than 20 minutes and rarely an hour) to discuss his or her career aspirations, high school EDP, and postsecondary options is highly inefficient and, I dare say, highly ineffective. It is no wonder, then, that "most students, even those who successfully complete college, give their high school guidance counselors fair or poor ratings" with respect to career guidance and postsecondary planning (Johnson et al., 2010, p. 5). As these same authors concluded, "having 'the meeting' clearly doesn't mean that the counselors fulfilled the students' needs and expectations" (p. 5). This is especially true if the students feel that the counselor doesn't know them and if the meeting is performed in a perfunctory manner.

How can high school counselors meet student needs in the areas of career and education planning more effectively? My preference would be to see every counselor conducting classroom guidance lessons related to career development on a regular basis so that each student experiences such a lesson and has direct contact with the counselor at least once a month. Other career development activities are worthy of strong consideration, and we discuss them next.

FRESHMAN CONFERENCES. First, I recommend that counselors hold meetings with every student and his or her parents early in the ninth-grade year instead of waiting until a student's junior year. To ensure that these meetings are personal rather than perfunctory, the counselor should use this time to become acquainted with the student and parents, provide information about the services offered by the counseling department, and explain the importance of beginning to think about postsecondary options as a freshman. To assist with gathering information and understanding the needs of each student, counselors should request that students and their families prepare for the meeting by completing a set of worksheets that address a wide variety of factors relevant to career and education planning. The worksheets may include a so-called brag sheet, in which a student identifies accomplishments and areas of interest, including hobbies; an interest inventory; a questionnaire about prior school experiences; and a questionnaire about career aspirations. By opening the door early, so to speak, freshmen have an opportunity to establish a relationship with the counselor immediately on arriving at high school, and parents can become aware of the counselor as an important resource for postsecondary planning. One outcome is that students will be more likely to seek out the counselor a number of times prior to the typical junior year meeting.

CAREER FAIRS. Another important practice for school counselors is to conduct highly visible career development programs. One of these programs may consist of a career fair (which we also discussed in relation to elementary and middle school students). Career fairs allow students yet another opportunity to expand their awareness and exploration of potential careers. Counselors may use career fairs to help students develop greater self-confidence in their ability to attain the skills necessary to be successful in various careers (Kolodinsky et al., 2006) and to help students crystallize their postsecondary plans.

JOB-SHADOWING PROGRAMS. Job-shadowing programs, though sometimes offered at the middle school level, are more common career development activities at the high school level (Lozada, 2001; Reese, 2005). These programs allow students to explore more deeply a specific occupation of interest by going into a workplace to observe employees performing their regular work duties and to talk with these employees about the work they do, education and training needed, and keys to success (Arrington, 2000).

Job-shadowing opportunities can be offered in short- and longer-term approaches. Short-term approaches often allow students an opportunity to shadow an employee on a single day, generally for three to six hours (Mariani, 1998). A common day used by schools for this purpose is Groundhog's Day. Started in 1999, the National Groundhog Job Shadow Day program was developed by "a coalition that included America's Promise–The Alliance for Youth, Junior Achievement, the Association for Career and Technical Education, the Society for Human Resource Management, the U.S. Department of Education, and the U.S. Department of Labor" (Hopkins, 2010, para. 7). Now affiliated most closely with Junior Achievement, this national program offers an array of useful materials to assist schools and job sites with the management of the job-shadowing program.

In contrast to one-day events, longer-term job-shadowing programs persist over an extended period of time during which students may complete lengthier shadowing experiences within a single work setting and/or participate in job-shadowing experiences in several work settings. Frawley (2009), for example, described a five-week job-shadowing experience conducted over the summer. It focused attention on positions held by skilled workers in a manufacturing company. Over the course of five weeks, students shadowed employees working in various positions and departments within a single company. This rotation allows students to observe and talk with employees who do a variety of skilled jobs.

Whether offered in a short- or longer-term format, job-shadowing programs are often organized by a counselor or a school-to-work coordinator who has developed a wide network of job sites where students may shadow. As with career fairs, the success of job-shadowing programs "is contingent on careful planning and effective follow up" (Lozada, 2001, p. 30). I highly recommend the article by Mariani (1998) for all counselors interested in developing a job-shadowing program because the article expands on each of the steps listed in Table 14.5.

Educational Planning Activities for High Schools: Postsecondary Planning

Regardless of their specific career goals, *all* students need assistance with education planning. This assistance should go beyond attention to the students' EDPs, graduation requirements, and high school coursework by including significant attention to planning for education beyond high school. This section highlights several elements of postsecondary educational planning that should occur in high schools.

TABLE 14.5 Steps for Offering a Job-Shadowing Program

1. Identify and develop partnerships with a wide variety of job sites where students are interested in job shadowing.
2. Disseminate information about the job-shadowing program to identify interested students.
3. Assess students in understanding their career interests.
4. Match students with job shadowing sites based upon their career interests.
5. Conduct an orientation session for students.
6. Have students contact the site and site employee whom they will shadow.
7. Shadow the employee for the allotted period of time.
8. Have students follow up with the site and site employee after the job-shadowing experience.
9. Collect and analyze evaluations from students and site employees.

Source: Based on Mariani, M.J. (1998). Job shadowing in junior and senior high school. *Occupational Outlook Quarterly, 42*(2), 42–45.

STAGES OF POSTSECONDARY PLANNING. Much of the literature on the process of postsecondary planning and selection is based on a three-stage model developed and refined by Hossler and colleagues (Hossler, 1984; Hossler & Gallagher, 1987; Hossler, Schmit, & Vesper, 1999). The Hossler model includes the three stages of predisposition, search, and choice, and I suggest adding a fourth stage to Hossler's model: a preparation stage positioned between the predisposition and search stage.

Predisposition Stage. The National Postsecondary Education Cooperative (2007) describes predisposition as "the self-reflective stage culminating in the decision to pursue postsecondary education" (p. 6) and explains that "individual and environmental background factors have the strongest influence at this stage, informing one's self-image, preferences, and inclinations" (p. 6). In reading this description, I hope you recognize the relevance of various career development theories to a student's inclination to pursue postsecondary education. Whether focusing on circumscription, self-efficacy, or other theory-based constructs, counselors should recognize the impact they may have on a student's postsecondary interests and aspirations. It is hoped that career development activities at the elementary and middle school levels facilitate students' dispositions toward seeking postsecondary education.

Preparation Stage. As already mentioned, this stage represents my addition to Hossler's model. Findings regarding the lack of college readiness in many students who aspire to earn bachelor's or graduate degrees (ACT, 2010) are alarming, and I believe that counselors must play an important role in encouraging students to take rigorous courses and in supporting attempts within their districts to establish more challenging academic standards. Indeed, having a predisposition toward college and being equipped with college search and selection strategies is insufficient. Students also need to take the appropriate coursework and master course content to prepare for success in whatever college they eventually attend. Within this context, it is especially important for counselors to aid high school students (those who are predisposed toward college attendance and those who may eventually choose other postsecondary options) to understand the importance and relevance of academic preparation. More specifically, effective career development programs in high schools should help students understand the connection between their performance in high school and their postsecondary plans. Students need to recognize the importance of their selection of coursework, high school grade point average (GPA), mastery of subject matter, and performance on standardized tests.

The importance of these issues for college-bound students may seem obvious, but this is not the case. Using the ACT college entrance examination as an example, let's look at the findings regarding college readiness. Between 2006 and 2010, the ACT was taken by approximately 1.57 million students, representing about 47% of the total high school student population in the United States. Although some states mandate that all students take the ACT as part of an exit requirement from high school, it is more likely that only those students who are predisposed toward college attendance choose to sit for this exam. Thus, 82% of the ACT test takers between 2006 and 2010 expressed the intention of earning at least a bachelor's degree in college. If any group of high school students were likely to understand the importance of academic preparation to their postsecondary plans, it should be this one; however, the ACT reported that only "seventy-one percent of all 2010 ACT tested high school graduates took at least a minimum core high school curriculum to prepare them for college" (ACT, 2010, p. 4). This suggests that 11% of ACT test takers who aspired to a four-year college did not understand the importance of taking the appropriate college-bound classes. Even more disappointing is ACT's finding that "only 24% of all 2010 graduates met all four ACT College Readiness Benchmarks, meaning that 76% were not adequately prepared academically for first-year college courses in English Composition, College Algebra, social sciences, and Biology" (ACT, 2010, p. 19). The data from ACT also reveal a sizable achievement gap with respect to race/ethnicity. Only 4% of African Americans, 11% of Hispanics, and 12 % of American Indian/Alaskan Native students achieved scores that met all four of the college readiness benchmarks in 2010 (ACT, 2010). Not surprisingly, in all racial/ethnic samples, students who took the core curriculum scored higher with regard to college readiness.

These data reveal the alarming number of students who plan to attain a bachelor's degree but are not meeting college readiness standards and are not taking the right courses. For this reason, school counselors should not assume that college-bound students have a firm understanding of the connection among the courses they take in high school, mastery of the content, performance on standardized tests, and readiness for college coursework. It is essential that counselors help college-bound students to recognize the connection between their performance in high school and their likelihood of postsecondary success. Students should be encouraged to take the most rigorous curriculum they can handle.

School counselors also need to help other, non-college-bound students understand the importance of these issues. Students aspiring to attend community colleges, career colleges, and trade schools and to join the military also need a solid foundation in core academic subjects in order to maximize their opportunities for success. For example, many assume that students who do poorly in high school can count on military options as a second chance to exhibit their full potential, but a study published by the Education Trust (Haycock, 2010) "shatters the comfortable myth that academically underprepared students will find in the military a second-chance pathway to success" (Haycock, 2010, p. 1). Recruits need to pass the Armed Forces Qualifying Test (AFQT), which is drawn from the academic sections of the Armed Services Vocational Aptitude Battery (ASVAB), in order to qualify for enlistment. In addition, they should know that the incentives, positions (military occupational specialties), and training opportunities available to them within the military may be severely curtailed by poor academic preparation and/or low AFQT scores (Theokas, 2010).

All students—even those who have noncollege postsecondary plans such as the military—therefore need to understand the relevance and importance of their high school academic success and to invest their energy into preparing academically for their post-secondary pursuits. As part of an effective career development program in high school, counselors should be proactive about helping students understand the relevance of their academic preparation for any postsecondary plans.

With this message as a backdrop, counselors should then assist students with the next stage of Hossler's model: the search stage. Counselors should familiarize students with the full breadth of postsecondary education options available to them.

Search Stage. The search stage involves just that: counselors helping students identify and explore various postsecondary options that fit with their career aspirations. The National Postsecondary Education Cooperative (2007) explains that the search stage is "characterized by the gathering of information about college in general and specific colleges, and culminates in a 'choice set' of preferred college options" (p. 6). To accomplish this, specific lessons should assist students in determining the type and extent of postsecondary education necessary to achieve their career goals.

With regard to the type of postsecondary education, school counselors should give ample attention not only to the traditional four-year college education but also to other types of postsecondary education and training. To be sure, obtaining some type of postsecondary education is increasingly necessary to ensure at least a middle-class lifestyle. In 1973, when 72% of jobs in the United States were filled by people with a high school diploma or less, only a high school diploma was needed "as a passport to the American Dream" (Symonds, Schwartz, & Ferguson, 2011, p. 2). At that time, 60% of people with a high school diploma were able to earn a middle-class living. In comparison, in 2007, only 41% of the jobs in the United States were filled by people with a high school diploma or less, and as discussed in Chapter 13, the value of postsecondary education is becoming increasingly significant with regard to earning potential.

It is projected that, by 2018, approximately two thirds of all jobs in the United States will require postsecondary education (Carnevale, 2008; Symonds, Schwartz, & Ferguson, 2011). In response to these projections, many states are raising high school graduation requirements, adopting more rigorous curricular standards, and embracing what has become known as a "college for all" mentality (Carnevale, 2008; Rosenbaum & Person, 2003; Symonds, Schwartz, & Ferguson, 2011). The message received by students, however, seems to be that the only acceptable option is to attend a four-year college and earn at least a bachelor's degree (Rosenbaum & Person, 2003; Symonds, Schwartz, & Ferguson, 2011).

A bachelor's degree from a four-year college doesn't have to be their only option. Symonds, Schwartz, and Ferguson (2011) published a widely disseminated Harvard study entitled *Pathways to Prosperity: Meeting the Challenge of Preparing Young Americans for the 21st Century*. Citing projections from the Georgetown University Center on Education and the Workforce, these authors explained that, between 2008 and 2018, nearly half of the projected job openings requiring postsecondary education

> will go to people with an associate's degree or occupational certificate. Many of these will be in "middle-skill" occupations such as electrician, and construction manager, dental hygienist, paralegal and police officer. While these jobs may not be as prestigious as those filled with B.A. holders, they pay a significant premium over many jobs open to those with just a high school degree. More surprisingly, they pay more than many of the jobs held by those with a bachelor's degree. In fact, 27 percent of people with post-secondary licenses or certificates—credentials short of an associate's degree—earn more than the average bachelor's degree recipient. (pp. 2–3)

Although projections state that two thirds of jobs by 2018 will require postsecondary education, this does not mean that all these jobs will require a bachelor's degree or higher. In fact, the Georgetown Center projections are that, of all jobs in the United States in 2018, approximately one third will require a bachelor's degree or higher, approximately one third will require some other form of postsecondary education or training, and approximately one third will require a high school diploma or less (Symonds, Schwartz, & Ferguson, 2011). These authors caution educators and counselors not to convey a simplistic college-for-all message but instead to embrace and communicate the potential value of other, more career-focused postsecondary education.

One postsecondary education option that should be shared with students involves attendance at a career college, vocational school, or trade school. Vocational and trade schools, for example, may provide the postsecondary education necessary for entrance into a career in the health care industry, business industry, personal-care industry, or transportation industry, to name just a few. With regard to career colleges, "there are close to 3,000 career college campuses operating in the United States offering a variety of academic programs designed to prepare students for high-impact careers in vital economic sectors, including healthcare, business, and information technology" (Imagine America Foundation, 2008, p. 7). Therefore, career and technical education should be presented to all students as a viable and respectable secondary and postsecondary option. (This option will be discussed in greater depth in Chapter 15.)

The military also offers a variety of postsecondary options that may be of interest to students, and presentations about postsecondary education should include them. In addition to general enlistment options within the Army, Navy, Air Force, and Marines, numerous options for postsecondary education within the military should be addressed. For example, students should be informed of the Reserve Officer Training Corps (ROTC), National Guard, military colleges such as the Citadel, and military academies such as the U.S. Military Academy at West Point. These latter options may also be addressed within the context of sharing information about four-year colleges and universities.

With regard to the educational options available through community colleges, students should be presented with information about associate degree programs and certification programs. Counselors should inform students of dual enrollment opportunities available through community colleges and share information relevant to attending community colleges with the intention of transferring to a four-year college (Bragg, 2006; O'Connor, 2006). In this context, students should learn about articulation agreements between community colleges and four-year universities in order to maximize the likelihood of their community college credits being accepted as transfer credits.

When sharing information with students about four-year colleges and universities as postsecondary options, counselors should help students understand the different types of colleges. At a minimum, counselors should familiarize students with the differences between public and independent/private colleges, in-state and out-of-state colleges (and tuition rates), national universities versus regional colleges, and proprietary versus nonproprietary colleges. Counselors should help students understand how to choose a college that will be a good fit for them (Antonoff & Friedeman, 2006) and ways in which they may search for and explore colleges of interest. Table 14.6 lists a variety of search engines designed specifically for college searches.

Another way to help students search for and explore colleges is to conduct college fairs or accompany students to a nearby college fair (National Association for College Admission Counseling, 2008). Holding a college fair involves inviting admissions officers and/or recruiters from a wide variety of colleges to attend. Some fairs are full-day events, beginning within a schoolwide assembly in which each college representative is provided an opportunity to share briefly with students some information about his or her college. The purpose of the presentation portion of the program is to ensure that all students have some information about each college represented at the fair before deciding which colleges to investigate in more depth. Following the presentations, college representatives remain at assigned tables on which they can display materials and at which they talk with interested students. At this point, students can circulate through the fair and approach

TABLE 14.6 College Search Engines

Big Future	bigfuture.collegeboard.org/college-search
College Navigator	nces.ed.gov/collegenavigator/
College Net	cnsearch.collegenet.com/cgi-bin/CN/index
College Quest	collegequest.com/
College Source	collegesource.org/
College View	collegeview.com/
Peterson's	petersons.com/ugchannel/code/searches/srchCrit1.asp

representatives for more information about their respective college. Another way of conducting a college fair is to schedule it in the late afternoon or evening, thereby making it more likely that parents can also attend. In this model, college representatives staff tables featuring information about their college and interact with students and/or parents, answering questions and promoting their institution. The College Board (2009) offers guidelines for counselors wishing to organize a college fair and suggests that counselors begin the planning process at least nine months in advance.

Because of the time involved in planning such an event, some high school counselors choose not to host a college fair at their school but instead prefer to encourage students and their families to attend a college fair hosted by the National Association for College Admission Counseling (NACAC; nacacnet.org). This association organizes and hosts college fairs across the country each year, and the fairs tend to feature a wider array of colleges than any single high school can attract to their own private fair. NACAC also sponsors performing and visual arts college fairs. Clearly, the decision of whether to hold a college fair at your school or to encourage students to attend an externally operated college fair depends in large part on proximity of the external college fairs.

Yet another approach to helping students explore their postsecondary options involves hosting recruiter visits at a high school. These recruiters may represent four-year colleges, community colleges, trade schools, or the military, and they generally initiate contact with schools and seek permission to visit on a specific day. Students are then informed of which recruiters will be present in their building, and they have the opportunity to sign up for group and/or individual sessions with the recruiter in order to learn more about that specific school or branch of the military. Counselors are wise to encourage students to visit the schools they are strongly considering for their postsecondary education.

Choice Stage. The National Postsecondary Education Cooperative (2007) explains that, "in the choice stage, students and their families interpret the collected information within the context of their personal and social circumstances, resulting in decisions about whether to apply to college, which colleges to apply to, and which college to attend" (p. 6). At this point, school counselors should help students with the choice stage by addressing strategies of how (and how not) to select a college or other postsecondary educational opportunity. Unfortunately, most students report dissatisfaction with the amount of assistance they receive from their school counselors regarding the selection process. Specifically, Johnson et al. (2010) found that only 30% of students rated their high school guidance counselors as good or excellent with respect to helping them decide which school was right for them, far less than the 67% of students who offered ratings of fair or poor. This seems to be a clear indicator that students feel the need for more assistance with the choice stage of Hossler's model of postsecondary planning and selection.

The College Board (2009) recommends two types of assistance at this stage. First, students need help in deciding where to apply. Second, they need assistance in understanding how to make a final selection once they know which schools have admitted them and have received information about the financial aid packages offered by each school. In helping students decide where to apply, counselors should equip students with tools for searching for information about various schools. Counselors should also help students narrow down the list of colleges to which they will apply. This decision will be based in part on the students' perception of goodness-of-fit and also in part on the perceived likelihood of admission. In this context, the College Board (2009) recommends that counselors encourage college-bound students to apply to:

- One or two safety colleges: colleges to which they will almost certainly be admitted.

- Some "probables": colleges where their GPA, test scores, and other features look very similar to those of recent entering classes.

- A reach (or two): colleges where they meet the criteria for admission but may not have the stellar qualifications of most first-year students. (p. 14)

Students also need assistance with estimating the likelihood of being admitted to any given institution of higher education. Counselors should teach students to seek information about each college's freshman class. Specifically, most colleges publish data regarding the academic credentials of their most recently admitted class of students. At a minimum, this data generally includes information about high school GPA and average test scores on the ACT and/or SAT. *Note:* The Big Future website (bigfuture.collegeboard.org) provides much more detailed information about standardized test scores for each university's freshman class than you can generally find elsewhere. To find this data, enter the college's name and select the section about applying to that college, and you will see a tab for SAT and ACT scores. Students can then compare their own GPA and test scores in order to make an educated guess about the likelihood of being admitted. This process helps students apply to safety schools, likely schools, and reach schools.

Counselors continue to have a vital role when students (and their tuition-paying parents, if applicable) make a final selection after receiving information about which colleges have admitted them and about the financial aid packages being offered. In the absence of such guidance, students may make the mistake of simply choosing the highest rated college (Crane, 2003); the closest college; or the college their boyfriend, girlfriend, or best friend plans to attend. Cautioning against relying on such selection criteria, Ziering (2010) offers (rather tongue-in-cheek) a more extensive list of criteria students should *not* use when choosing a college:

---

12 Ways Not to Choose Your College or University

Don't Choose a College or University Because:

1. Your boyfriend or girlfriend is going there.
2. Your friends are going there.
3. The tuition is low.
4. Because of its party-hearty reputation.
5. The college brochure or university guidebook showed all these fun students sitting under trees.
6. A computer college matching program said this was your best choice. (Although these can be very helpful in narrowing your choices, you need to make the final decision.)
7. You visited just that campus and didn't want to look elsewhere.
8. It's located in your city or state and you didn't consider other locations, even though you could have.
9. It's the one college you and your parents have heard of.
10. You know you'll be accepted there.
11. Because of its prestige.
12. It has the academic program you're looking for, so the campus atmosphere doesn't really matter.

http://ezinearticles.com/?12-Ways-Not-to-Choose-Your-College-Or-University&id=4793534

None of these criteria, of course, are likely to ensure the best possible fit for the student.

How, though, *should* students make a decision? What criteria should they use? Boshoven (2003; cited in Dugger & Boshoven, 2010) used the metaphor of buying a coat to help students and families understand the college selection process. First and foremost, Boshoven challenged "the notion that there is a perfect college that is somehow perfect for everyone and suggests that colleges, like coats, are not 'one size fits all'" (p. 288). This message tends to take some pressure off students and families by helping them realize that (a) no single college offers every student the best fit any more than one single coat offers the best fit for everyone, and (b) many colleges may offer a student a very good fit just as there are many coats that serve a person's needs quite well. Dugger and Boshoven suggested ways in which counselors can use the coat-buying metaphor to identify categories of criteria by which to judge the goodness of fit of any give college (see Table 14.7).

Other resources are available to help students and their families with selecting a school for their postsecondary education. For example, Antonoff and Friedemann (2006) have published a book entitled *College Match: A Blueprint for Choosing the Best School for You* as part of the popular Octameron series. Like Dugger and Boshoven (2010), Antonoff and Friedemann (2006) advise against basing postsecondary decisions on an assumption that "colleges are either good or bad" and instead suggest that students focus more on whether any given college is good or bad *for them* (p. 14). This book offers several different questionnaires and worksheets to help students rate themselves and understand their own college-related preferences. Counselors can share strategies offered in this and other similar books directly with students, or they can make these resources available to students directly. Counselors can also use worksheets from resources like the following when conducting classroom guidance lessons:

TRANSITION SERVICES FOR HIGH SCHOOL STUDENTS WITH DISABILITIES. Although all students need and deserve assistance with education and career planning for life beyond high school, such assistance is federally mandated for students with disabilities. The Individuals with Disabilities Education Act (IDEA) of 2004—the primary federal legislation related to special education—requires that schools assist all special education high school students age 16 and older with what is known as transition planning (Trolley, Haas, & Patti, 2009). Each student in special education must have an individualized

TABLE 14.7 Criteria for Buying a Coat and Selecting a College

Criterion	Buying a Coat	Selecting a College
Fit	The fit of a coat is somewhat subjective, with some people preferring them snug and others preferring them roomy enough to wear over a bulky sweater, but each person considers the quality of fit before purchasing a coat.	When selecting a college, fit may refer to the size of the student body, the size of the community in which the college exists, the number of curricular and extracurricular opportunities. The political atmosphere, religious affiliation, racial diversity, or existence of fraternities and/or sororities are other characteristics that might contribute to the fit of a college.
Feel	A coat can look perfect on the rack and technically fit but not "feel right." It may feel too stiff, too bulky, or too heavy. Buying a coat that fits but doesn't feel good to wear just isn't a good idea.	Although colleges can seem perfect for a student on paper (or the Internet), the true test comes when a student arrives on campus. When visiting a campus, students can often know immediately whether they like the feel of the school. To ensure that this "feel" barometer is accurate, students should visit campuses while classes are in session and visit several parts of the college (campus, an actual classroom, a residence hall, etc.).
Fashion/Flair	If fashion weren't a consideration, stores would offer only one or two coats in a myriad of sizes. Alas, fashion *is* a consideration, with consumers varying widely with respect to the styles they prefer.	Different colleges tend to be known for different strengths, and students have their own individual preferences. Some prefer a school known for its academic rigor; others are drawn toward a school known for athletic prowess. Schools with a reputation for strong programs in a student's area of career interest will likely enhance that student's interest.
Fiscal	Ever find the perfect coat only to look at the price tag, gasp, and then sigh with the knowledge that, no matter how perfect the coat, it's just not worth that much money to you? Have you decided to purchase a coat because its fit, feel, and fashion were "good enough," but the price was such a bargain that you deemed it the deal of the century?	Clearly, the cost of college *does* matter to all but the most affluent of students. In addition to considering the cost of tuition and room and board, students need to consider the availability of financial aid as well as employment opportunities and the cost of living in the surrounding community.

Source: Based on Dugger, S.M., & Boshoven, J.B. (2010). Secondary and post-secondary educational planning. In B. T. Erford (Ed.), *Professional school counseling: A handbook of theories, programs & practices* (2nd ed., pp. 274–294). Austin, TX: Pro-Ed, Inc.

education plan (IEP), and the IEP for high school students must address transition planning. Although earlier legislation (IDEA 1997) required the transition plan to be included in the IEP for all students 14 years of age and older, the current legislation (IDEA 2004) requires the transition plan to be included in the IEP for all students 16 years of age and older (Kosine, 2007; Sabbatino & Macrine, 2007).

Determining what types of postsecondary goals are appropriate and achievable for each individual student is important in creating a transition plan. The plan must identify "appropriate, measurable postsecondary goals based upon age-appropriate transition assessments that relate to training, education, employment, and where appropriate, independent living skills" (Kosine, 2007, p. 93). The transition plan should also specify which transition services are needed to help students reach these goals. Transition services may include additional schooling and/or vocational training:

Transition services are coordinated sets of activities that focus on improving student academic and functional achievement and facilitate movement from [high] school to postschool activities. Those activities may include postsecondary education, vocational training, integrated employment, continuing and adult education, adult services, independent living, or community participation. (Sabbatino & Macrine, 2007, pp. 33–34)

As a career counselor working within an educational setting, you will undoubtedly work with students who qualify for special education services. Therefore, you should understand the federal mandate for transition planning for these students and consider ways in which you can become actively involved in this process to help students achieve the goals established within their transition plans. Despite the legislative requirement for transition plans and transition services, students with disabilities often encounter tremendous difficulties obtaining and maintaining employment at a level that would qualify them as financially independent (Sabbatino & Macrine, 2007). Recall from Chapter 6 that adults with disabilities suffer from significantly higher unemployment and poverty rates.

To help students increase their likelihood of avoiding poverty, achieving independent living status, and meeting the postsecondary goals outlined in their transition plans, counselors should involve these students in all the activities described above. Classroom guidance lessons focused on self-understanding, employability skills, and career exploration are recommended. These students should also be involved in schoolwide programs such as service learning projects, job-shadowing programs, and internship experiences.

Estrada-Hernandez, Wadsworth, Nietupski, Warth, and Winslow (2008), for example, strongly recommended the use of internship programs to assist students with disabilities in solidifying career interests before making a commitment to any specific career direction and to help them develop employability skills. Sabbatino and Macrine (2007) recommended that these students experience "early training and paid-work experiences" (p. 35), and these authors provided details about a specific model entitled Start on Success. This model involved a partnership between universities and area high schools in which students with disabilities were placed in jobs at the university involving tasks such as unloading and organizing books, office work such as copying or filing, cafeteria work such as dishwashing and food preparation, and cleaning.

Nietupski et al. (2006) described another program designed to facilitate the transition of students with disabilities from school to employment. Targeting students with "middle range" disabilities, this program involved having them remain in high school for a fifth year. They called this year the "super senior" year (p. 17), and it focused exclusively on transition planning and transition services for students with disabilities. The Super Senior School-to-Work Transition Program involved a three-pronged approach accomplished during a student's fourth and fifth years in high school: (1) solid career planning activities that included self-assessments, exploration of work, and a matching process; (2) numerous, short-term experiences with the world of work accomplished through "job shadows [and] short-term job try-outs;" and (3) "extended paid internships/apprenticeships in the community" (Nietupski et al., 2006, p. 18). Although relatively small in scale (with 153 participants in the study), the outcomes of this approach to transition planning and preparation appear quite promising. Nietupski et al. (2006) reported that 82% of participants completed the program, and that 76% of these obtained paid employment, whereas only 39% of students who didn't complete the program were employed.

In addition to transition plans that focus on employment immediately after high school, counselors should understand issues related to college attendance by students with disabilities. Kosine (2007) noted that college attendance is becoming increasingly common for students with disabilities but lamented that matriculation rates far exceed graduation rates. She explained that "results of the National Longitudinal Transition Study . . . show that a higher percentage of students with learning disabilities drop out of school as compared with their nondisabled peers" (p. 94). It appears that many of these students drop out within the first year of postsecondary education, leading Kosine to conclude that "poor transition planning has been identified as a likely contributor to this problem" (p. 93).

An important strategy for increasing the college success and persistence rates of students with disabilities involves helping students understand the differences between the support services they received in the K–12 educational setting, in accordance with the IDEA (2004), and the support services they may obtain in the college setting in accordance with the Americans with Disabilities Act (ADA) and with Section 504 of the Vocational Rehabilitation Act (Kosine, 2007; McEachern & Kenny, 2007; Milsom & Hartley, 2005). Milsom and Hartley (2005) observed that,

[w]hile one could argue that students can successfully complete high school ignorant of the laws that help them, the same cannot be said for students in college. Because ADA and Section 504 mandate that postsecondary institutions provide support services only for individuals who request them, provided those individuals possess the appropriate documentation, students with learning disabilities must be aware of their rights and responsibilities. (p. 439)

Shaw, Madaus, and Banerjee (2009) offered further clarification that, at the postsecondary level, disability legislation places the burden of responsibility for obtaining evaluations, documenting disabilities, assessing the effectiveness of accommodations, and advocating for one's needs squarely on the shoulders of the students. Thus, counselors and special educators should take great care to help students prepare for postsecondary education by helping them understand these three types (IDEA, ADA, and Section 504) of disability legislation. In this context, students need to understand their rights and responsibilities. They may also need assistance in developing the self-advocacy skills for seeking support services on campus and/or accommodations from instructors. In a book geared specifically toward college-bound students with learning disabilities, Simpson and Spencer (2009) summarized the ways in which these rights, responsibilities, and advocacy roles differ between secondary and postsecondary educational settings.

In a highly practical article for counselors, McEachern and Kenny (2007) provide full outlines for two psychoeducational groups designed to assist high school students with disabilities with transition planning and preparation. One group is designed specifically for students who aspire to postsecondary education; the other group targets students wishing to transition directly into employment. The interventions suggested for both groups effectively address the various issues outlined in this section of the chapter.

As you can see from Table 14.8, many of these session topics would be pertinent not only to the special education population but also to the entire population of high school students. Primary differences include the need for self-determination and self-advocacy (including accessing support services) and the importance of understanding relevant legislation.

PUTTING IT ALL TOGETHER

To summarize this chapter, career development efforts in the K–12 setting share several common approaches. Table 14.9 provides a sample of activities identified in this chapter.

First, classroom guidance lessons should be delivered to all students as part of a coordinated school counseling core curriculum focused on the career development needs of students. At the elementary level, these lessons should

TABLE 14.8 Session Topics: Transition Groups for Students with Disabilities

Session	Transition to Further Education	Transition to Work
1	Awareness of self and others.	Awareness of self and others.
2	Self-determination and self-advocacy.	Self-determination and self-advocacy.
3	Making the right college choice.	Why work?
4	Understanding and navigating through admissions.	Finding the right job for me.
5	What I need to know about my legal rights.	How much do I need to make?
6	Accessing college support services.	The application process.
7	Choosing a college major.	The job interview.
8	Making new connections.	Making a plan and following it.
9	Ending yet getting started.	Ending yet getting started.

Source: Based on McEachern, A.G., & Kenny, M.C. (2007). Transition groups for high school students with disabilities. *The Journal for Specialists in Group Work,* 32, 165–77.

TABLE 14.9 Sample K–12 Career Development Activities Described in This Chapter

	Developmental Focus	School Guidance Curriculum	Schoolwide Events or Programs	Educational Planning Activities

Elementary	Awareness	• "What I like to do" collage
		• Detective game: How math is used in various careers?
		• Introduction of career pathways
		• Brainstorming of careers related to sports
			• Career day
			• STEM career day
			• Career fair
			• Field trips to places of employment
			• Traveling companions
			  • Workplace visits
				• College week
				  • Bulletin boards
				  • Classroom contests
				  • Pen pal system
				  • Service learning project for college-bound students
				• Traveling companions
				  • College visits

Middle School	Exploration	• Knowledge of self-assessments
		  • SDS CE
		  • DAT
		  • MMTIC
		• Employability skills
		  • Success traits
		  • Skills for success
		  • What do I need to be employable?
		• Careers in environmental sciences
		• Careers in medical and health sciences
		• BLS website
		• Career development and exploration programs
		• Computer-based programs
			• Reality store
			• Service learning projects
			• Delivery of food to elderly
				• EDPs
				• GEAR UP

High School	Planning	• Self-assessments
		  • Values
		  • Interests
		  • Personality
		  • Skills
		• Employability skills
		  • Behaviors
		  • Résumé writing
		  • Job applications
		  • Interviewing skills
		• Educational requirements of various career options
			• Freshman conferences
			• Career fairs
			• Job-shadowing programs
				• EDPs
				• Postsecondary planning
				  • Identifying postsecondary plans
				  • Preparing for postsecondary success
				  • College searches
				  • College selection
				• College fairs
				• Transition planning for students with disabilities

focus on expanding student awareness, the middle school lessons should focus on facilitating student exploration, and the high school lessons should assist students with planning. Second, schoolwide events or programs should be offered to provide additional support to the career development needs of students at each level, including career fairs, service learning projects, and job-shadowing programs. Third, educational planning activities should necessarily be tied to career development, for example, via college awareness activities at the elementary school level, the creation and revision of educational development plans (EDPs) at the middle and high school levels, the development of transition plans for students with disabilities, and significant attention to postsecondary planning at the high school level.

With regard to postsecondary planning, counselors should support student consideration of a wide variety of postsecondary education options. Rather than offering a dichotomous and biased choice of earning either a college degree or settling for a high school diploma, counselors should recognize and communicate the value of other postsecondary educational options including community college, military options, and vocational/trade school options. As explained in the chapter, these latter options fall within a category called career technical education (CTE). Chapter 15 focuses exclusively on CTE, a career development approach that is utilized at both the K–12 and the postsecondary educational levels.

CHAPTER 15

Career Development in Career and Technical Education Settings

You've already learned, in Chapter 14, about the increased need for postsecondary education. Specifically, you read projections that, by 2018, approximately two thirds of all jobs in the United States will require postsecondary education. We discussed how, in response to these projections, many states are raising high school graduation requirements, adopting more rigorous curricular standards, and embracing what has become known as a "college for all" mentality. I lamented that, too often, the message received by students is that the only acceptable option is to attend college and earn a bachelor's degree immediately after high school graduation. Such a message has profound implications for the future of career technical education (CTE). It seems to communicate to young people that their future financial well-being is contingent on obtaining at least a bachelor's degree and that college is the only reliable road to success. It also sends an implicit signal that CTE is unacceptable and paints it as a likely road to hardship.

As a future counselor, take a moment to reflect on these messages. First, were you already familiar with the college-for-all message currently being communicated to our young people? Second, do you personally and professionally believe that all students (excluding those with severe cognitive impairments) can succeed in college? Third, do you believe that college is the only reliable path to financial success? Your responses to these questions have a direct bearing on your opinion about whether counselors should promote CTE as a viable secondary and postsecondary option for young people.

One of the early leaders in the college-for-all movement was Robert Schwartz:

> Robert Schwartz has since 1996 been a lecturer on education at Harvard's Graduate School of Education, where he currently directs the Education and Management Program. From 1997 [to] 2002 he also served as founding President of Achieve, Inc., an independent, bipartisan, non-profit organization created by the nation's governors and corporate leaders to help states raise standards and improve performance in the schools. In its first five years Achieve conducted benchmarking studies of state standards, tests, and related education policies for 16 states; organized an interstate consortium to strengthen middle grades mathematics education; launched the American Diploma Project, an initiative with three other national organizations and five states to close the gap between high school exit requirements in reading, writing and mathematics and the real-world demands of colleges and high-skills workplaces; and hosted two National Education Summits. (The Aspen Institute, 2014, para. 1)[†]

The American Diploma Project lay at the heart of the college-for-all movement because it encouraged states across the nation to adopt more rigorous graduation requirements that constitute a college preparatory curriculum for all

---

[†]*Source:* From Robert B. Schwartz (2014) (The Aspen Institute, 2014, para 1). The Aspen Institute. Retrieved from http://www.aspeninstitute.org/people/robert-schwartz. Copyright © 2014 by The Aspen Institute. Reprinted by permission.

students. However, Schwartz has since changed his professional opinion. In a report that has shaken many educators and politicians who are invested in promoting the college-for-all agenda, Schwartz is now arguing against the wisdom of sending such a message. Schwartz, the very person who helped create the American Diploma Project and the college-for-all mentality, now cautions educators and counselors against conveying a simplistic college-for-all message.

In 2011, Symonds, Schwartz, and Ferguson (2011) published a widely disseminated Harvard study entitled *Pathways to Prosperity: Meeting the Challenge of Preparing Young Americans for the 21st Century*. When releasing this report, Schwartz issued the following statement:

> We are the only developed nation that depends so exclusively on its higher education system as the sole institutional vehicle to help young people transition from secondary school to careers and from adolescence to adulthood.... Unless we are willing to provide more flexibility and choice in the last two years of high school, and more opportunities for students to pursue program options that link work and learning, we will continue to lose far too many young people along the path to graduation. (Newseditor, 2011, para. 4)

As noted in Chapter 14, Symonds, Schwartz, and Ferguson (2011) clarified the data indicating that two thirds of all jobs in the United States will require postsecondary education by 2018. Specifically, they pointed out that this does *not* mean that two thirds of the jobs will require a bachelor's degree or higher. Instead, they noted that nearly half of the projected job openings requiring postsecondary education "will go to people with an associate's degree or occupational certificate" (p. 2). They also emphasized that many of the jobs at this level will "pay a significant premium over many jobs open to those with just a high school degree" (p. 3), and some may even pay more than the jobs held by those with a bachelor's degree. Schwartz and his colleagues recommend that educators and counselors embrace and communicate the potential value of other, more career-focused postsecondary education. In this vein, counselors should recognize and promote the potential value and viability of CTE.

Unger (2006) agrees. Although acknowledging that college graduates do indeed earn more on average than those who don't complete a college degree, Unger warns against concluding that this means that all students should aspire to college. Explaining that it is much easier to be admitted to most colleges than to graduate, Unger stated that "more than 40 percent of students who enroll in American colleges and universities quit without graduating . . . and end up in a career no-man's land. They have no college degree . . . and they haven't learned any skills to earn a living" (pp. 3–4). For this reason, Unger suggests that students consider all of their postsecondary options, including college as well as alternative forms of education such as CTE.

A FALSE DICHOTOMY: ACADEMIC RIGOR AND CTE

It is essential to understand that pursuing education and career preparation through CTE at the secondary or postsecondary levels does not necessarily involve less academic rigor than college preparatory curricula. Less rigorous academic options within CTE exist and will likely be attractive to students who struggle with academics; however, CTE also includes some very rigorous academic programs. In these cases, it isn't the degree of rigor that distinguishes CTE from traditional, college preparatory courses. Rather, the distinguishing factors involve (a) the clear connection of the academic material to careers and (b) the applied methodology used to teach the content. It is inaccurate to conceptualize college preparatory curricula as academically rigorous and CTE as not so. This would be an oversimplified, outdated, and false dichotomy.

If you are one of those people who believed, up until now, that CTE simply referred to a career training program track designed for the less academically able high school students, you are not alone. In fact, up until 2006, you may have been correct. In recent years, however, the field of CTE has changed dramatically. The National Association of State Directors of Career and Technical Education Consortium (NASDCTEc) and Association for Career and Technical Education (ACTE) explain:

> In 2006, the language "vocational and technical" was updated to "career and technical" education. This transition was more than just a name change. It represented a fundamental shift in philosophy from CTE being for those who were not going to college to a system that prepares students for both employment and postsecondary education. (National Association of State Directors of Career and Technical Education Consortium and Association for Career and Technical Education, 2009, p. 1)

Although many people still erroneously equate vocational education, or what is known today as CTE, with a program track intended for non–academically oriented and non-college-bound high school students, it is now a much broader approach to career development and preparation within educational settings (Dare, 2006). In its contemporary form, CTE now spans middle school, high school, and postsecondary settings. For that reason, information about CTE programs is presented in this text as a stand-alone chapter.

The remainder of this chapter addresses the evolution of CTE, from its origins as a vocational training track for high school students and adults (vocational education) to its contemporary format as a much more academically rigorous track system spanning middle school, high school, and postsecondary settings. This chapter also provides information about new developments that may portend a singular approach focusing on the provision of career and college preparation for all students. By reading this chapter, you will develop an appreciation of the potential value of CTE, an awareness of the changes that have occurred within CTE, and an understanding of the many ways in which counselors can use CTE to assist students with career development. We'll turn now to a history lesson designed to provide you with contextual information about the origins of vocational education, its central role in the American education system ranging from middle school to community college, and the impact of federal legislation on the establishment and development of vocational education programs.

HISTORY OF VOCATIONAL EDUCATION IN THE UNITED STATES

Vocational education, which can be defined as the transmission of knowledge and skills necessary for the performance of work, has been occurring in one form or another since the beginning of time. At its most basic level, vocational learning may involve a parent teaching the family business to a child or protégé (Scott & Sarkees-Wircenski, 1996). On a more formal basis, even prior to the establishment of a national system of vocational education in the United States, there were schools designed to teach the knowledge and skills necessary for the performance of work. For example, manual labor trade schools established in the late 1800s provided vocational training related to mechanical fields. So-called normal schools were established in 1839 to provide vocational training for teachers. And during this same time period, it became common for high schools to offer vocational training to female students in what became known as home economics and later as consumer and family studies.

Such vocational education efforts varied, however, from state to state, college to college, and high school to high school. It wasn't until federal legislation regarding vocational education was passed that the United States had a national system for vocational education. This began in 1914, when a federal law pertaining to agricultural education and home economics was passed by Congress. Known as the Smith-Lever Act of 1914, this law set the stage for the development of a national system of vocational education by addressing the issue of how such efforts might be funded. Specifically, this law created a partnership between state and national government in which both shared equally in the financing of agricultural education and home economics. With a cost-sharing system now in place, the stage was set for what most scholars consider the legislative establishment of a national system of vocational education in the United States.

Smith-Hughes Act of 1917

Most scholars trace the origins of a national system of vocational education in the United States back to 1917, when the federal government passed the Smith-Hughes Act. This law expanded the cost sharing established by the Smith-Lever Act to include national, state, and local governments and called for a partnership among them. The Smith-Hughes Act also established a Federal Board of Vocational Education; required schools to make vocational education and occupation-specific training available to students 14 years of age and older; and delineated specific responsibilities for local, state, and federal agencies as they pertained to the development and financing of vocational education.

Why was such a system important? Believe it or not, vocational education is viewed as essential to our national well-being, Scott and Sarkees-Wircenski (1996) explained:

> From the Smith-Hughes Act of 1917 to the current legislation, Congress has reaffirmed its belief that federal support for vocational education is an investment in the future of the nation's workforce. A high-skilled [sic] workforce is viewed as essential to maintaining the nation's standard of living, defense preparedness, economic strength, and leadership position in the free world. (p. 119)

At the heart of this legislation, therefore, was the need to prepare enough skilled workers to meet the needs of employers within the business and industry sectors. The Smith-Hughes Act of 1917 sought to meet employer needs through the vocational education of high school students.

Additional Early Legislation

Several other laws related to vocational education were passed in the next two decades. In general, these laws expanded vocational education beyond a focus on high school students. Over time, the focus of vocational education included military veterans returning from war (Smith-Sears Act of 1918 and Servicemen's Readjustment Act of 1944) and disabled persons (Smith-Bankhead Act of 1920 and Smith-Fess Act of 1920). Additional laws (George-Reed Act of 1929 and George-Ellzey Act of 1934) reaffirmed the purpose of vocational education as including the preparation of workers within fields such as home economics, agricultural education, and industrial education. Other laws expanded the purpose of vocational education to include the distributive occupations (George-Deen Act of 1936), which is now better described as marketing, management, and entrepreneurial occupations; health care (Health Amendments Act of 1956 and Health Professions Educational Assistance Act of 1963), and even fisheries (George-Barden Act of 1956).

National Defense Education Act

In 1958, another landmark piece of vocational education legislation was passed. Known as the National Defense Education Act (NDEA), this law was promulgated in direct response to Russia's success in launching *Sputnik,* the world's first satellite in orbit. This event caused great concern to the United States. Success in the so-called space race was considered to be of dire importance to national security, and the U.S. government therefore perceived a need to attract and train people to work within the aerospace industry. NDEA provided a great deal of funding to promote the training of individuals in science, math, technology, and foreign languages. This legislation also established funding for the training and hiring of school counselors, who were viewed as essential in identifying talented students and guiding them toward college majors that would prepare them for work in these fields. More specific to vocational education, though, Title VIII of the NDEA established funding for the development of areawide vocational schools. The purpose of these schools was to provide vocational education to high school and postsecondary students and older adults in order to prepare them as skilled assistants to the engineers and scientists needed to win the space race (Scott & Sarkees-Wircenski, 1996).

Expanding the Focus of Vocational Education

Until this point, the federal government invested in vocational education in an attempt to meet the nation's needs for skilled workers in various professions. Over time, though, the purpose of vocational education expanded to include assisting military personnel with reentry into the workforce, preparing persons with disabilities for gainful employment, and strengthening national defense by preparing workers for the aerospace industry.

Another type of expansion occurred during the 1960s. During this time, vocational education legislation also sought to reduce social unrest by meeting the needs of the unemployed and underemployed. Vocational education was viewed as equipping them with skills needed to be more gainfully employed. Examples of such legislation include the 1962 Manpower legislation (most recently funded as the Jobs Training Partnership Act [JTPA] of 1982) as well as the Vocational Education Act of 1963.

The Vocational Education Act of 1963 was of particular import because it provided a great deal of funding to support the expansion of vocational education in order to prepare more people with the skills they needed to enter and succeed in the workplace. Targeted populations included high school students unlikely to proceed to college, unemployed high school graduates and dropouts, current employees who needed additional training to succeed and/or advance in the workplace, and people with special education disabilities. This law required the establishment of advisory councils and work study programs, provided funding for the construction of vocational schools and the training of teachers as well as guidance counselors, and gave much more autonomy to states in using the funding in conjunction with funding for other vocational training programs. The Vocational Education Act of 1963 redefined vocational education and identified it as an educational track intended primarily to prepare non-college-bound students "for gainful employment as semi-skilled or skilled workers or technicians in recognized occupations" (Scott & Sarkees-Wircenski, 1996, p. 130).

Carl D. Perkins Vocational Education Act of 1984

Another significant piece of legislation was passed in 1984: the Carl D. Perkins Vocational Education Act. As described by Scott and Sarkees-Wircenski (1996), this legislation reaffirmed the federal government's belief that "effective vocational education programs are essential to the nation's future as a free and democratic society" (p. 145) and was designed to serve both economic and social goals. First, this legislation served an economic goal "to improve the skills of the labor force and prepare adults for job opportunities—a long standing goal traceable to the Smith-Hughes Act" (p. 145). Second, it attempted to achieve a social goal of ensuring "equal opportunity for adults in vocational education" (p. 145), with special attention to individuals with disabilities.

Carl D. Perkins Vocational and Applied Technology Education Act of 1990

When this legislation was reauthorized in 1990, a third goal was evident. New attention was paid to the need for a more technologically advanced workforce. The renamed Carl D. Perkins Vocational and Applied Technology

Education Act of 1990 established technical preparation (tech prep) programs, "which are cooperative arrangements that combine two years of technology-oriented preparatory education in high school with two years of advanced technology studies at a community college or technical institute" (Scott & Sarkees-Wircenski, 1996, p. 150). Spanning the K–12 and postsecondary educational settings, the tech prep programs established by vocational education legislation are an excellent example showing why CTE is deserving of its own chapter.

School-to-Work Opportunities Act

Using vocational education to meet the societal needs for specific types of workers was once again affirmed in 1994 with the passage of the School-to-Work Opportunities Act (STWOA). Designed to prepare students to meet the skill demands of the workplace, STWOA provided funding to support partnerships between schools and places of employment. To qualify for these funds, schools needed to establish partnerships with employers, provide both school-based and work-based learning opportunities for students, and engage students in "connecting activities" to help them understand the connection between school and work (Scott & Sarkees-Wircenski, 1996, p. 157). Examples of work-based learning opportunities include cooperative education, mentoring programs, and job-shadowing experiences (Stone & Aliaga, 2005).

Carl D. Perkins Career and Technical Education Improvement Act of 2006

In 2006, the most recently revised version of the Carl D. Perkins Career and Technical Education Improvement Act was passed with the goal of ensuring that schools "develop more fully the academic and career and technical skills of secondary education students and postsecondary education students who elect to enroll in career and technical education programs" (Perkins Act, 2006; as cited in Meeder, 2008, p. 4). Notice that this legislation specifically identified secondary and postsecondary levels of CTE. A key change from the previous Perkins Act is that the 2006 legislation emphasized tying together core academic coursework and CTE coursework by requiring that CTE students have "career and technical programs of study" (p. 4). Meeder (2008) explained that, prior to this legislation, high school students could "choose CTE courses without considering the academic courses necessary to pursue the career field at the postsecondary level, and select academic courses without making a connection to any area of career interest" (p. 4). By requiring a program of study, this legislation seeks to "ensure students are taking the right mix and sequence of CTE and academic courses" (p. 4). This requirement ensures that high school students who participate in CTE will be prepared to transition directly into postsecondary education at either a community college or four-year college and earn "a credential, certificate or degree" (p. 5). The 2006 Carl D. Perkins Career and Technical Education Improvement Act also added requirements for increased use of assessments, more accountability at the state and local levels, and modified requirements for tech prep, and added significant emphasis on ensuring that students leave CTE programs highly skilled for success in today's competitive workplace. In other words, a goal of this legislation is to promote the academic and career preparation necessary to ensure that our students graduate "college and career ready" (Meeder, 2008, p. 3).

As we conclude this history lesson, you may feel overwhelmed by the laundry list of laws that comprise the history of vocational education. Table 15.1 summarizes the laws described above. Also, be assured that this brief history has touched on only a select few laws; many other laws affecting vocational education were passed between the Smith Hughes Act of 1917 and the present day.

VOCATIONAL EDUCATION AS A TRACKING SYSTEM

From the passage of the Smith-Hughes Act in 1917 until the passage of the Carl D. Perkins Career and Technical Education Improvement Act in 2006, the United States had a system of vocational education. Until 2006, vocational education could reasonably be considered as a tracking system (Lewis & Cheng, 2006). As shown in Table 15.2, high school students generally had four options for their high school curriculum: a general track, vocational education/CTE track, college-bound track, or dual track (Fletcher & Zirkle, 2009; Stone & Aliaga, 2005).

Not surprisingly, such a tracking system has raised several concerns. The most common theme of these concerns involves the impact of educational tracking systems on social mobility. Of particular concern is the possibility—indeed, likelihood—that an educational tracking system in which only some students are prepared for and encouraged to attend college serves to preserve the current social order and maintain the achievement gaps between racial and socioeconomic groups (Dare, 2006; DeSena & Ansalone, 2009; Lewis & Cheng, 2006). Although a tracking system in which students are identified early, whether by the school, the parents, or the students themselves, as college-bound or not makes some sense on the surface, it is based on a false premise that the determination would be made solely on ability and aptitude.

TABLE 15.1 Select Examples of Vocational Education Legislation in the United States

Smith-Hughes Act of 1917

> This law represented the official establishment of vocational education within public schools. It established a Federal Board of Vocational Education; required schools to make vocational education and occupation-specific training available to students 14 years of age and older; and delineated specific responsibilities for local, state, and federal agencies as they pertained to the development and financing of vocational education.

National Defense Education Act (NDEA) of 1958

> This law was promulgated in direct response to Russia's success in launching *Sputnik,* the world's first satellite, and represented a national commitment to winning the space race. The NDEA funding promoted education in science, math, technology, and foreign languages and focused on both college-bound and non-college-bound students. With regard to non-college-bound students, Title VIII of the NDEA established funding for the development of areawide vocational schools. The purpose of these schools was to provide vocational education to high school and postsecondary students and older adults in order to prepare them as skilled assistants to the engineers and scientists needed to win the space race.

Manpower Development and Training Act (MDTA) of 1962

> This legislation represented an expansion of the purpose of vocational education. In addition to striving to meet employer needs for skilled workers, vocational education legislation during this time also sought to reduce social unrest by meeting the needs of the unemployed and underemployed.

Vocational Education Act of 1963

> This act was of particular import because it provided a great deal of funding to support the expansion of vocational education in order to give more people the skills they needed to enter and succeed in the workplace. Targeted populations included high school students unlikely to proceed to college, unemployed high school graduates and dropouts, current employees who needed additional training to succeed and/or advance in the workplace, and people with special education disabilities. This law also offered a definition of vocational education that persisted until 2006. This definition specified that vocational education focuses on the preparation of individuals to work in semiskilled or skilled occupations.

Carl D. Perkins Vocational Education Act (1984)

> This legislation reaffirmed the federal government's belief in the importance of vocational education to the nation's welfare. It pointed toward the economic and social benefits of vocational education by addressing the needs of the general populace for skills with which to gain employment and the needs of individuals with disabilities for vocational training.

Carl D. Perkins Vocational and Applied Technology Education Act (1990)

> The name change in the 1990 version of the Perkins legislation reflects an expansion on the 1984 Perkins Act by addressing the importance of vocational education in meeting the needs of employers for a more technologically advanced workforce. The 1990 legislation provided for the establishment of tech prep programs, which include two years of tech prep education in high school combined with an additional two years of tech prep education at a community college.

School-to-Work Opportunities Act (STWOA) of 1994

> Designed to prepare students to meet the skill demands of the workplace, STWOA provided funding to support partnerships between schools and places of employment. To qualify for these funds, schools need to establish partnerships with employers and provide students with both school-based and work-based learning opportunities.

Carl D. Perkins Career and Technical Education Improvement Act of 2006

> This version of Perkins legislation placed emphasis on ensuring that all students graduate both college- and career-ready. This law required that all CTE students have programs of study that ensure the appropriate combination of academic and CTE coursework necessary to prepare them to transition successfully into postsecondary education. It also called for more outcome assessments and greater accountability on the part of states and local educational agencies. It also expanded tech prep requirements.

TABLE 15.2 Common Academic Tracks Within High Schools

Track	Description
College preparatory	An academic track designed to provide students with the coursework and credits necessary to meet college admissions requirements.
Career and technical education (CTE)	An academic track designed to prepare students within a particular CTE occupational pathway that includes at least three CTE credits.
Dual	An academic track designed to prepare students who are both college- and career-ready. In this track, the student takes courses in both the college preparatory and the CTE tracks.
General	An academic track focused on receipt of a high school diploma. In this track, students take the minimum number of courses and credits required to graduate.

Source: Based on Fletcher, Jr., E.C., Zirkle, C. (2009). The relationship of high school curriculum tracks to degree attainment and occupational earnings. *Career and Technical Education Research*, 34(2), 81–102.

In addition to ability and aptitude, socioeconomic factors seem to play an especially important role. Specifically, higher socioeconomic status (SES) is correlated with a greater likelihood of choosing a college-bound track in high school and with college attendance, and SES is considered "one of the most important background characteristics" (Hossler & Gallagher, 1987, p. 210) contributing to a student's likelihood of aspiring to and enrolling in college. Mirroring this finding 20 years later, Palmer and Gaunt (2007) found that "the typical CTE student . . . is more economically disadvantaged than non-CTE students" (p. 35). Intertwined with socioeconomic factors is the race and/or ethnicity of students. Because more students of color are raised in lower SES families, it is difficult to separate the two. It seems that a disproportionate number of non-college-bound, vocational education students have been poor and/or racial and ethnic minorities (Fletcher & Zirkle, 2009). For this reason, vocational education programs have sometimes been viewed with considerable suspicion by educators and youth advocates, who are keenly aware of these achievement gaps. Some opponents express concerns that the "ideological intent" of vocational educational programs is to "shunt low-income, Black youth" into a "low class of working poor who stay off the streets" (Hemmings, 2007, p. 12).

To be fair, researchers do not blame only the existence of a tracking system for the fact that a disproportionate number of poor students and students of color have enrolled in the vocational education track and not entered college after high school. Researchers have also pointed consistently toward the role of social and cultural capital (Farmer-Hinton & Adams, 2006; Hemmings, 2007; Pérez & McDonough, 2008). Crediting Pierre Bourdieu and others for their contributions to our understanding of these constructs as they pertain to education and career development, Hemmings (2007) indicated that "cultural capital includes valued academic and mainstream cultural knowledge and, just as importantly, the cultural dispositions that are most conducive for success in various school settings" (p. 10). This form of capital can also be "derived from the cultural connections people make with books, computers, and other education-related objects as well as universities, libraries, and other education-related institutions (Grenfell & James, 1998; Robbins, 2000; cited in Hemmings, 2007, p. 10).

In contrast, social capital involves relationships with other individuals as well as social networks that "enable people to promote their own or others' educational achievement and attainment" (Hemmings, 2007, p. 10). Through these relationships, students internalize an expectation of educational success and also learn to use resources to attain such success. Such resources may be educational in nature (textbooks, tutors, test prep courses), but they may also be "auxiliary (e.g., psychological counseling, substance abuse treatment, medical services, legal assistance)" (p. 10) in nature. The basic idea is that students have contact with individuals and social networks that teach them the importance of and means to achieving educational success.

Given these concerns about vocational education being used as a tracking system that maintains the status quo, educators and school counselors are called on to be keenly aware of the messages we send to students and the possibility that their social and cultural capital resources may put them at a disadvantage when it comes to aspiring to the more advanced academic tracks in high schools. Farmer-Hinton and Adams (2006) implore school counselors to recognize their potential impact in becoming part of a student's social capital and helping them recognize the importance of college: "[S]chool counselors are institutional change agents who can share norms and resources about college access" (p. 101). In addition, there has been a movement to reform CTE and thus lessen the long-term implications of a tracking system, which is the topic we turn to next.

THE NEW CAREER AND TECHNICAL EDUCATION SYSTEM IN THE UNITED STATES

Although the title "career and technical education" was not formally established legislatively until 2006 with the passage of the Carl D. Perkins Career and Technical Education Improvement Act, efforts to reform the old vocational education system into a more academically rigorous enterprise spanning both high school and college began in earnest in 1990. The reform efforts were motivated by a variety of factors, including concerns about the impact of tracking as described above, as well as an increasing awareness of the importance of postsecondary education. As a result, the reform of vocational education into the new CTE system in the United States has had two major thrusts: (1) an increase in the academic rigor of CTE courses and (2) an expansion of CTE to include postsecondary education (Stone & Aliaga, 2005, p. 127).

Career Clusters

In addition to changes related to increased academic rigor and inclusion of postsecondary education within the CTE umbrella, the new CTE has also involved the identification of a set of career clusters across the country. As discussed in Chapter 13, this effort was undertaken by the States Career Clusters Initiative (SCCI). Prior to this initiative, some states had as few as six career pathways that were used; others had far more. The lack of consistency across state lines affected the implementation of national CTE initiatives. As a result of SCCI, however, there are now 16 career clusters and 79 associated career pathways nationwide. The 16 career clusters were identified and described in Chapter 13, and you may wish to review Table 13.3 to refresh your memory.

Best Practice CTE Programs

In reviewing contemporary approaches to CTE, Dare (2006) identified and described four "best practice programs that combine CTE courses with rigorous academic curricula" (p. 74). These best practice programs include tech prep, High Schools That Work, Project Lead the Way, and College and Career Transitions Initiative.

TECH PREP. Recall that tech prep programs were established as part of the Carl D. Perkins Vocational and Applied Technology Education Act of 1990. These programs "are cooperative arrangements that combine two years of technology-oriented preparatory education in high school with two years of advanced technology studies at a community college or technical institute" (Scott & Sarkees-Wircenski, 1996, p. 150). They span the boundary between high school and postsecondary education and infuse more academic rigor into coursework to ensure adequate preparation for postsecondary studies. With regard to academic rigor, the Center for Occupational Research and Development (2009) also emphasized that tech prep programs utilize a different approach to teaching academic subject areas. "A Tech Prep curriculum requires the same standards of academic accomplishment as college prep, but it teaches content through courses based on contextual learning methods" (p. 19). In doing so, the tech prep curriculum should address academic standards, general employability skills, and occupation-specific skills. Table 15.3 summarizes requirements for tech prep programs.

HIGH SCHOOLS THAT WORK. Another approach to CTE that has emerged as a best practice program involves the High Schools That Work (HSTW) approach (Dare, 2006). This approach was developed by the Southern Regional Education Board (SREB) in 1987 (Young & Cline, 2009). Like tech prep programs, the HSTW approach emphasizes increased academic rigor and the importance of preparing students for both college and careers. A major element of the HSTW approach involves the elimination of the "general" track as an option for students. Instead, students have the option of completing "a solid academic core and either an academic, a career/technical or a blended concentration" (Southern Regional Education Board, 2002, p. 1), with the academic track involving math and science and/or humanities concentrations within it (see Table 15.4).

PROJECT LEAD THE WAY. Whereas tech prep and HSTW programs offer students the opportunity to take CTE coursework in accordance with a variety of career

TABLE 15.3 Tech Prep Program Requirements

1. An articulation agreement between secondary and postsecondary consortium participants.
2. A 2 + 2 , 3 + 2, or 4 + 2 design with a common core of proficiency in math, science, communication, and technology.
3. A specifically developed tech prep curriculum.
4. Joint in-service training of secondary and postsecondary teachers to implement the tech prep curriculum effectively.
5. Training of counselors to recruit students and to ensure program completion and appropriate employment.
6. Equal access of special populations to the full range of tech prep programs.
7. Preparatory services such as recruitment, career and personal counseling, and occupational assessment.

Source: Excerpted from U.S. Department of Education, 2014, para. 7.

TABLE 15.4 High Schools That Work (HSTW) Curricular Requirements

"To complete the recommended HSWT curriculum, each student takes:
- At least four English courses with the content and performance standards of college-preparatory English
- At least three mathematics courses, including two courses with the content and performance standards of college-preparatory Algebra I, geometry, Algebra II, and trigonometry
- At least three science courses, including two courses with the content and performance standards of college-preparatory biology, chemistry, and physics or applied physics
- At least three college-preparatory-level social studies courses
- At least four courses in a planned career/technical concentration or additional course work in either mathematics and science, the humanities, or a blended concentration. A *career/technical concentration* consists of at least four credits in a planned sequence of quality career/technical courses in a broad field of study with students meeting standards on an external assessment. A *mathematics and science concentration* includes four or more credits each in mathematics and science courses with at least one credit at the Advanced Placement level. A *humanities concentration* includes four credits each in college-preparatory/honors English and social studies with at least one course at the Advanced Placement level, and four more credits drawn from foreign languages, fine arts, journalism, debate, or additional advanced-level courses in literature, history, economics, psychology, or another humanities area. A *blended academic and career/technical concentration* includes four college-preparatory English courses, three mathematics courses at the level of Algebra I and higher, three college preparatory-level lab science courses, and four courses in a planned series of career/technical courses.
- At least two courses in related academic and career/technical fields, including at least one-half credit in a basic computer course covering word processing, database entry, presentation software, and use of the Internet and e-mail. The computer technology course should be taken early in high school so that the student will be able to use technical skills in other classes."

Source: From Southern Regional Education Board. (2002). *High schools that work: An evidence-based design for improving the nation's schools and raising student achievement.* Excerpted from: http://publications.sreb.org/2002/02V07_2002_HSTW_Brochure.pdf, p. 4. Copyright © 2002 by Southern Regional Education Board. Reprinted by permission.

---

pathways, the focus of Project Lead the Way (PLTW) is narrower. The program describes itself as "the premier pre-engineering program for today's high schools" (Hughes, 2006, p. 39) and has more recently broadened this focus to include both engineering and the biomedical sciences. The PLTW pre-engineering program includes a middle school program called Gateway to Technology as well as a high school program called Pathway to Engineering. The PLTW Biomedical Sciences program offers a sequence of four specialization courses within the biomedical arena. Table 15.5 lists the courses offered within the PLTW program, and they are a far cry from the shop classes you might associate with vocational education of the past.

To offer the PLTW program, school districts must become certified. Similar to the legislative specifications for tech prep programs, the training of teachers and counselors is required by PLTW. Specifically, certification by PLTW requires a commitment by the school district to send all PLTW teachers for intensive two-week trainings for each course they will teach. Also, school counselors in PLTW-certified schools must attend one day of training to ensure their understanding of the program, with special attention to advising, placement, and college credit options. Because completion of the PLTW program can entitle students to college credit, certification by PLTW also requires strict adherence to the PLTW course curriculum. The opportunity to earn college credit by participating in the PLTW program reflects the two major thrusts of contemporary CTE programs: an increase in the academic rigor of CTE courses and an expansion of CTE to include postsecondary education.

COLLEGE AND CAREER TRANSITIONS INITIATIVE. The connection between high school CTE programs and postsecondary education is the primary focus of the final CTE program to be discussed in this chapter. Identified by Dare (2006) as a best practice program, the College and Career Transitions Initiative program focuses on the responsibility of community colleges to "play a greater leadership role in partnering with high schools to facilitate the transition of students into postsecondary education and employment, and to improve students' academic performance at both the secondary and postsecondary levels" (Dare, 2006, p. 76). This grant-funded program differs significantly from the other three best practice programs because it doesn't focus on the curricular offerings of high school as much as on the establishment of partnerships between community colleges and local educational agencies. Coordinated by the League for Innovation in the Community

TABLE 15.5 Project Lead the Way Coursework	
Middle School: Gateway to Technology	Design and Modeling Automation and Robotics Energy and the Environment Flight and Space Science of Technology Magic of Electrons
High School: Pathway to Engineering	Foundation Courses • Introduction to Engineering Design • Principles of Engineering • Digital Electronics Specialization Courses (electives) • Aerospace Engineering • Biotechnical Engineering • Civil Engineering and Architecture • Computer Integrated Manufacturing Capstone Course • Engineering Design and Development
High School: Biomedical Sciences	Principles of the Biomedical Sciences Human Body Systems Medical Interventions Biomedical Innovation

College, the College and Career Transitions Initiative program identifies the following purpose:

> Through partnerships of postsecondary institutions with secondary schools and employers, the CCTI will further the development of academically rigorous programs of study organized around broad occupational areas that initially include
>
> - Health science
> - Information technology
> - Education and training
> - Science, technology, engineering, and mathematics
> - Law, public safety, and security (league.org/league/projects/ccti/purpose.html, para. 2)

At this time, there are three community college–high school partnerships for each of these five career areas. Additional information about them, including CCTI toolkits for each site, can be found at league.org/league/projects/ccti/projects/.

LOOKING AHEAD: THE FUTURE OF CTE

The changes from vocational education programs of the past compared to the CTE programs in existence today have been dramatic. Increased academic rigor and preparation for postsecondary education have been major thrusts of this reform. An emerging emphasis on providing CTE to *all* students may foreshadow changes yet to come. In contrast to the college-for-all movement, calls for all students to be college-ready *and* career-ready are becoming increasingly common. Oakes and Saunders (2008) identified this argument as the "multiple pathways movement" (now called the linked learning approach) and explained the need for it as follows:

> Arguing that graduates who go directly to work need solid academic skills and those who go to college will also have careers, Multiple Pathways advocates seek to move beyond what they see as a tired debate between academic and vocational education and the traditional practice of tracking students into different high school courses, depending on whether they are seen as bound for college or work. (p. 5)

In essence, this approach emphasizes the importance that all students take rigorous academic coursework in high school, that contextualized learning is more effective than traditional instructional strategies, and that *all* students need to be prepared for success in college *and* careers. Although contemporary CTE programs have certainly addressed concerns about academic rigor and the importance of students enrolled in CTE programs having the preparation necessary to attend college if they choose, the current system can be likened to a "separate but equal" type of approach for students. Today's students still have the option of taking a college preparatory track, CTE track, general track, or dual track while in high school. Only this latter track—the dual track—requires students to take classes in both the college preparatory and the CTE tracks. Arguing that the preparation offered by each of these tracks is necessary for all students, proponents of the multiple pathways approach propose that schools reorganize so that the *only* track available to students is a combined, dual-like track:

> Students and their families choose from a variety of options, all of which lead students to the same destination: preparation to succeed in college *and* careers, not one or the other. All students graduate with the choice of a full range of postsecondary options. This single destination of the various pathways defies and seeks to change a long-standing high school hierarchy that makes college better than work and makes preparation for work the default for those who aren't expected to succeed in college. (Oakes & Saunders, 2008, p. 7)

The multiple pathways approach differs, however, from the dual track approach. Although each of these approaches call for all students to take courses that prepare them for both college and careers, only the multiple pathways approach specifies that *all* courses should be taught in a contextualized learning format and that students should choose from a variety of contexts (pathways) in which to learn their academic and career skills. For example, students might choose an arts and media pathway, and all courses would link their subject matter to this pathway. Other students might choose a health sciences pathway, and all courses would link their subject matter to this pathway. Figure 15.1 provides an overview of this approach.

Because contextualized learning lies at the heart of this approach, many have shifted from the term *multiple pathways*

What is Linked Learning?

Linked Learning transforms students' high school experience by bringing together strong academics, demanding career and technical education, and real-world experience to help students gain an advantage in high school, postsecondary education, and careers. Students follow industry-themed pathways, choosing among fields such as engineering, arts and media, or biomedicine and health.

Participation in Linked Learning prepares students to graduate from high school and succeed in a full range of postsecondary options—including two- or four-year colleges, certification programs, apprenticeships, military service, or formal job training. There is no one right way to implement a pathway. But whatever the strategy, each pathway embraces four guiding principles and four core components.

Guiding Principles

1. Pathways prepare students for postsecondary education *and* career—both objectives, not just one or the other.
2. Pathways lead to a full range or postsecondary and career opportunities by eliminating tracking and keeping all options open after high school.
3. Pathways connect academics to real-world applications by integrating challenging academics with a demanding technical curriculum.
4. Pathways improve student achievement.

Core Components

1. A challenging **academic component** prepares students for success—without remediation—in postsecondary programs. Pathways complement traditional learning with project-based instruction that links to real-world applications.
2. A demanding **technical component** delivers concrete knowledge and skills through a cluster of three or more technical courses.
3. A **work-based learning component** offers opportunities to learn through real-world experiences that enhance classroom instruction.
4. **Support services** include counseling and transportation as well as additional instruction in reading, writing, and mathematics to help students succeed with a challenging program of study.

FIGURE 15.1 Linked Learning Approach

Source: ConnectEd: The California Center for College and Career. (2010a). A fact sheet on linked learning. Berkeley, CA: Author. Retrieved from http://www.connectedcalifornia.org/downloads/LL_Fact_Sheet_web.pdf. http://www.connectedcalifornia.org/

to *linked learning* when referring to it (Hoachlander, Stearns, & Studier, 2008, p. 28). The multiple pathways/linked learning approach has been embraced particularly by an increasing number of school districts in the state of California, and more specific information about it can be obtained from ConnectEd: The California Center for College and Career (2010b, 2010a). The website for this organization is connectedcalifornia.org.

It is unlikely that all schools will transition to a linked learning, multiple pathways approach, but many will. These schools will likely house a number of "academies" that are organized according to various career pathways, and all students will need to choose one academy in which to study. One academy may focus on business, management, and administration; another academy may focus on human services; and another may focus on biomedical and health sciences. Students would then take all their courses within the academy of their choice; each course would be taught using the context (industry theme) of the academy and delivered in a project-based approach. Regardless of the postsecondary aspirations, all students would experience rigorous, college-preparatory coursework as well as career-specific training. At the completion of high school, all students would be considered college- *and* career-ready, with options to enter immediately into the workforce as a skilled worker, enroll in a postsecondary vocational training program, or enter college (Richmond, 2010). With the exciting prospects this approach has to offer, many educators have their eye on California and are watching to see the development and outcomes of the linked learning approach.

THE CAREER COUNSELOR'S ROLE IN CTE

Career counselors may play a variety of roles within CTE. If they are working in a K–12 educational setting, counselors may have several roles, including advocating for the importance of continuing to offer CTE options; explaining curricular requirements; assisting students and their parents in considering whether to participate in CTE programs during the students' secondary school experiences; assisting high school students and their parents, as well as clients in community settings, as they consider CTE programs as postsecondary options; helping high school students and community-based clients search for and select a CTE program to meet their postsecondary needs; and assisting CTE students and clients with career development needs.

Advocating for CTE

An important role of career counselors is to serve as advocates for the importance of continuing to offer CTE options. As schools are forced to tighten their budgets during tough economic times, decisions need to be made with regard to cutting programs. Although CTE programs are frequently spared such consideration due to the existence of state and national funding to help subsidize them, even they can be at risk of discontinuation due to funding issues. This is becoming especially true as state budgets shrink and our federal deficit climbs. Some schools may question the need for or value of CTE programs given the current push for academic rigor as part of the college-for-all movement. My hope is that the information contained within this chapter has convinced you of the need for and value of these programs, and that you are now equipped with information needed to advocate effectively for their continuation.

Explaining Curricular Requirements

Counselors will also have responsibilities related to helping others understand the curricular requirements associated with various programs. For example, school counselors may need to help students, parents, teachers, and even administrators understand the curricular requirements and/or articulation agreements associated with programs such as tech prep and the College and Career Transitions Initiative. Such requirements and agreements will pertain to high school graduation requirements, dual enrollment opportunities, and smooth transitions to community colleges. Counselors will also likely play an important role in developing the CTE programs of study for each student, as legislated by the 2006 Perkins legislation.

Facilitating Consideration of CTE Options

Career counselors will also need to be aware of the nature and purpose of contemporary CTE programs to assist students and their parents in considering whether to participate in CTE programs during middle and/or high school. Middle school counselors, for example, may be approached by students wanting to participate in PLTW coursework whose parents then express reluctance to consent to it. These parents may (accurately) consider their children as college-bound and (inaccurately) believe that this CTE program is intended for the less academically inclined students. Likewise, high school counselors will generally play an important role in helping students select courses to take, which requires knowledge of the full range of curricular options available to students, including CTE options.

High school counselors will also be called on to help students consider CTE options with respect to postsecondary education. Community-based counselors may have clients who are interested in pursuing additional education through a CTE program. Career counselors in both the high school and community settings will want to be informed about the various training options that exist within the CTE umbrella and be prepared to facilitate an exploration of these options, along with all other options for postsecondary education.

Assisting with the Postsecondary Search and Selection Process

Once high school students or community-based clients have decided that they want to seek postsecondary education in the form of CTE, career counselors play an important role in helping them search for and select the best program. This search and selection process parallels the college search and selection process discussed in Chapter 14. In some ways, however, counselors may find it more challenging to assist clients with the search and selection process for CTE programs because all professional counselors have attended college themselves but have not necessarily had any personal experience with CTE programs.

Effectively guiding high school students and community clients through the search and selection process first requires an awareness of the various settings within which CTE training programs are offered. In his book, *But What If I Don't Want to Go to College?,* Unger (2006) shares information about sources of what he calls "alternative education" (p. 17) but would be better described within the counseling profession as vocational education or CTE. Unger identifies three types of CTE training within secondary settings, eight types of CTE training within postsecondary educational settings, and two types of CTE training in employment settings (see Table 15.6).

As a career counselor, you should be aware that these types of CTE exist and collect an array of resources (electronic and hard copy) related to such programs in your geographic area. Familiarize yourself with search engines that may be used to assist students and clients in locating information about CTE training programs. Table 15.7 lists a variety of online resources for use in assisting students in searching for these types of postsecondary institutions.

Helping students and clients become aware of different settings in which they can obtain CTE training and assisting them in locating specific programs in their geographic area represents the "search" part of the search and selection process. Just as important, however, is the career counselor's role in assisting students and clients with the "selection" part of this process, and this part is particularly important with respect to postsecondary CTE training programs because of some highly questionable programs. Indeed, CTE training programs vary enormously with regard to accreditation status, quality, and costs. Unger (2006) shares his opinions about the advantages and disadvantages of each type of CTE training option identified in Table 15.6. He implores prospective students to be cautious, especially with regard to proprietary schools, which are schools that are privately owned and operated for profit.

> "Runaway schools that open one day and close the next are only one danger of proprietary schools. Of far greater danger is the unethical operator, who preys on high school dropouts, immigrants (legal and illegal) and poor, semiliterate students, convincing them to enroll and obtain government-backed student loans to pay for tuition. If, as is likely, the student drops out before completing the coursework, the school keeps the money, and the student is in debt to the government for every penny of the loan. The advent of big corporations into the trade-school industry has transformed it into a $7.5-billion-a-year cash machine. There are seven major chains: Apollo Group (34 states and Puerto Rico), Career Education Corporation (24 states), Corinthian Colleges (24 states), Education Management Corporation (24 states), ITT Educational Services (30 states), and Strayer Education (eight states). Each of the corporations pretends to set high, universal education standards in each of its schools, which used the national brand name to its benefit in local advertising. But a member school in one of the biggest national chains reportedly lured students to enroll with promises that they could expect starting salaries of $50,000 to $150,000 in their first year after graduation—more than enough to pay off student loans to cover tuition. Not one graduate that year, according to the California investigators, earned even $50,000; the average income of graduates turned out to be $26,000, while the average student debt was $74,000. So beware of proprietary school advertisements. The promises they make may be lies!" (Unger, 2006, p. 27)

The Federal Trade Commission (FTC) also offers similar cautions and has developed a brochure for prospective

TABLE 15.6 Sources of CTE Training

Secondary Education Settings	Description
CTE offered within comprehensive high schools	High schools in which students have an option to enroll in a vocational education track or a CTE program. Unger's comments about advantages and disadvantages are relevant to these "old school" programs but not to the newer CTE programs offered within high schools.
Specialized vocational/technical (vo-tech) high schools	High schools in which *all* students are enrolled in a vocational program. Students take all of their coursework (academic core and vocational) at these high schools.
Cooperative education programs in high schools	High schools in which students have an option to take vocational courses in the morning and work in the afternoon in a setting that allows for immediate application of what they have learned in school.

Postsecondary Educational Settings	Description
Tech prep programs	Spanning both secondary and postsecondary settings, tech prep programs involve vocational coursework beginning in high school and continuing into community college. Unger presents these as 2 + 2 programs, in which students take two years of vocational education in high school and two more in community college, leading to an associate's degree. From reading this chapter, you know that tech prep programs can also be offered in 3 + 2 and 4 + 2 configurations.
Cooperative education programs in colleges	Colleges at which traditional academic coursework is complemented by employment in related to a student's major. In some cases, students work part-time in the field while enrolled in classes. In other cases, students rotate between coursework and employment on a semester-by-semester basis.
Community colleges	Public two-year colleges offering academic coursework as well as vocational training in numerous configurations, including cooperative education, tech prep programs, associate degree programs and certificate programs.
Private, nonprofit junior (two-year) colleges	Private colleges offering many of the same types of vocational training as community colleges along with academic courses.
Technical schools	Two-year schools that are highly specialized and often quite costly, and offer only vocational training. Academic courses are not offered.
Private, proprietary (for-profit) trade schools	Private schools that generally have a specific occupational focus and offer intensive vocational preparation for entry into that specific field. Unger cautions that some of these schools entice students to enroll through dishonest advertising.
Four-year colleges and universities	Along with their extensive offerings in academic areas, many colleges and universities include vocational training programs and cooperative education opportunities.
Distance (online) learning	Replacing the correspondence courses of the past, distance learning offers students the opportunity for training without requiring physical presence in the classroom. Distance education generally offers all coursework online.

Postsecondary Work Settings	Description
Employer/union apprenticeship programs	Union-sponsored on-the-job training that involves a lengthy (generally 2,000-hour) apprenticeship involving paid hands-on training combined with education.
Employer-sponsored on-the-job training programs	On-the-job training offered by employers, trainees are taught to do a specific job while performing it under the supervision of current employees. This option involves little or no classroom instruction.

Source: Based on Unger, H.G. (2006). *But what if I don't want to go to college? A guide to success through alternative education* (3rd ed.). New York: Ferguson (pp. 18–32).

TABLE 15.7 Searching for Career Colleges, Trade Schools or Technical Schools: Online Resources

Career College Association	career.org/
Imagine America Foundation	imagineamericafoundation.com
National Commission for Cooperative Education	co-op.edu/
Peterson's Career College Search Engine	petersons.com/cca
U.S. Department of Education—College Navigator	http://nces.ed.gov/collegenavigator/
U.S. Department of Labor—Apprenticeships	doleta.gov/oa/apprentices.cfm
U.S. Department of Labor—Job Corps	jobcorps.gov/home.aspx
Vocational Information Center—Trade, Career, and Technical Schools	khake.com/page4.html

students. It has established a page on its website designed to promote consumerism. The website explains:

> While many private vocational and correspondence schools are reputable and teach the skills necessary to get a good job, others may not be as trustworthy. Their main objective may be to increase profits by increasing enrollment. They do this by promising more than they can deliver.
>
> For example, they may mislead prospective students about the salary potential of certain jobs or the availability of jobs in certain fields. They also may overstate the extent of their job training programs, the qualifications of their teachers, the nature of their facilities and equipment, and their connections to certain businesses and industries. (Federal Trade Commission, 2011, para. 2 and 3)

When assisting students and clients with the selection of a CTE training program, career counselors need to be aware of the advantages and disadvantages of various types of training programs and familiar with the specific offerings of various schools in the region. Career counselors should encourage caution in selecting any school and should urge students and clients to be savvy consumers and assist them in determining whether specific programs are accredited. Table 15.8 identifies several reputable sources of information regarding accreditation of CTE training programs as well as guidelines for consumers.

Assisting CTE Students with Career Development Needs

Like all students, CTE students need assistance with career development. Career counselors assist CTE students in developing their career plans and identifying the education necessary to achieve their goals. This may involve helping students move beyond simple selection of one of the 16 career clusters to identification of one or more of the 79 career pathways of most interest to them. Making such decisions, as you've learned in this text, includes the development of self-knowledge as well as an understanding of the world of work. Career counselors may assist CTE students in gathering and understanding information related to projected market demands for workers in specific pathways, salary or wages associated with various occupations, and training and/or credentials needed for entry into a given occupation. Career counselors also assist CTE students with the development of various employability skills, ranging from job searching to acceptable behaviors and demeanor in work settings.

PUTTING IT ALL TOGETHER

Career development has been at the heart of career and technical education since its inception. Originally called vocational education, this approach to education initially focused on the career development needs of students who were viewed as unlikely to attend college due to a lack of interest, ability, or financial resources. Vocational education represented a track for non-college-bound students and typically involved less academic rigor than the college preparatory curriculum.

Vocational education has historically enjoyed considerable funding from federal, state, and local resources because this education track has been designed to meet several needs that were deemed in the nation's best interest. These have included: (a) the need of employers for a skilled workforce, (b) the need of citizens for the training necessary to render them marketable and employable,

TABLE 15.8 Accreditation and Consumer Protection Resources

Regional Institutional Accrediting Associations and Commissions for High Schools, Community Colleges, Junior Colleges, Technical Institutes and Four-Year Colleges and Universities

Middle States Commission on Higher Education	msache.org
New England Association of Schools and Colleges	neasc.org
North Central Association of Schools and Colleges	ncacihe.org
Northwest Accreditation Commission	northwestaccreditation.org
Southern Association of Schools and Colleges	sacscoc.org
Western Association of Schools and Colleges	wascweb.org

Associations with Accreditation Directories

Accrediting Commission of Career Schools and Colleges	accsc.org/
Accrediting Council for Independent Colleges and Schools	acics.org
American Association of Community Colleges	aacc.nche.edu
Distance Education and Training Council	http://detc.org

U.S. Government Consumer Protection Sites

U.S. Department of Education	ed.gov/students/prep/college/consumerinfo/index.html
	ope.ed.gov/accreditation/
Federal Trade Commission	ftc.gov/bcp/edu/pubs/consumer/products/pro13.shtm

(c) the need of people with acquired or lifelong disabilities for training to increase their ability to be financially self-sufficient, and (d) the need to provide focused training opportunities to encourage entry into specific vocational areas of contemporary priority—whether science and engineering related to the space race of the late 1950s, new technology-based careers emerging in the 1990s, or green industries related to projected fuel shortages in the 21st century.

Partly due to concerns about the social implications of vocational education with regard to educational justice and partly in recognition of the increasing importance of more academic rigor for all students, vocational education evolved into what is now called career and technical education (CTE). The Carl D. Perkins Vocational and Applied Technology Education Act of 1990 marked the beginning of this reform by encouraging a postsecondary linkage and increased academic rigor, and the formal transition from vocational education to CTE was established legislatively in 2006 with the passage of the Carl D. Perkins Career and Technical Education Improvement Act. Contemporary, best-practice CTE programs now involve considerable academic rigor and are linked to postsecondary education. This chapter highlighted four such programs: tech prep, High Schools That Work (HSTW), Project Lead the Way (PLTW), and the College and Career Transitions Initiative.

As we look into the future of CTE, an emerging emphasis seems to be on providing CTE to *all* students. Calls to ensure that all high school graduates are college- and career-ready are increasingly common, and the leading approach toward this end is the multiple pathways movement (Oakes & Saunders, 2008). This educational and career development strategy, widely employed in California, is also called the linked learning approach. When graduating from a linked learning high school, all students would be considered college- and career-ready, with options to enter immediately into the workforce as a skilled worker, enroll in a postsecondary vocational training program, or enter college.

This chapter shared information regarding the career counselor's role in CTE. You learned that career counselors should advocate for the importance of continuing to offer CTE options; be prepared to explain CTE curricular requirements; assist students and their parents in considering whether to participate in CTE programs during the students' secondary school experiences; help high school students and community-based clients consider, search for, and select CTE programs as postsecondary options; and assist CTE students with career development needs. Indeed, our jobs are not done when a student identifies a career goal and specifies a postsecondary educational route to get there. Students also need our services to develop employability skills and thus enhance their ability to obtain and succeed in jobs. These needs will be evident in both college-bound and the non-college-bound students, whether or not they participate in CTE programs. In the Chapter 16, we will explore career development efforts in the college setting.

CHAPTER

16   Career Services in College Settings

I once attended a workshop in which the speaker described college as a very expensive form of career development. I thought, "Yes, he's right!" Until that point, simply getting into college may have been the student's primary career development goal (Schutt, Jr., & Schwallie-Giddis, 2008). As a result, a majority of students arrive at college uncertain of their career direction and undecided about their major (Cueso, 2005).

In fact, estimates are that "20 [to] 50% of students entering college are undecided about a major and that 75% change their major one or more times during their academic careers" (Gordon, 1995; cited in Berg-Kolin, Krueger, Thomas-Clark, & Fink, 2001, p. 31). This indecision may be due to a lack of experience with career development activities in their K–12 education, which were described in Chapter 14; a lack of readiness on the part of students to make a decision; or what Krumboltz called open-mindedness (Mitchell, Levin, & Krumboltz, 1999). In their thorough exploration of factors contributing to indecision, Gati, Krausz, and Osipow (1996) offered the revised taxonomy displayed in Figure 16.1.

To be sure, there are varying degrees of indecision (Gordon & Steele, 2003), and many reasons students may be undecided about their academic major and/or career direction. Readers particularly interested in this topic should read the article by Gati, Krausz, and Osipow (1996) as well as Gordon's (2007) premier text on the topic of undecided college students. Whatever the reason, students who arrive at college without a sense of career direction may spend an inordinate amount of time and money sampling courses and academic majors in search of their calling (Thompson & Feldman, 2010, p. 13). Although a linear path between college majors and career destinations does not necessarily exist (Brooks, 2010), such students could clearly benefit from career development activities and/or career counseling. In fact, student affairs professionals recognize this as a primary need for college students.

> The central developmental task demanded by society of college students is the independent choice of a career informed by the academic course of study. However, this developmental task, involving (1) an accurate assessment of the self, (2) a sophisticated understanding of the world of work, and (3) the ability to make good decisions, is not a simple one. Most students spend more time watching television or preparing to buy their next CD than immersing themselves in the career development process and preparing for decisions that may affect them for a lifetime. (Hoff, Kroll, MacKinnon, & Rentz, 2004, p. 108)

In the past, career counselors on college campuses have struggled to meet these needs. Considerable discrepancy existed between the percentage of students who have career development needs and the percentage of students who have sought assistance from college career centers, despite high levels of awareness that career services are offered on campus (Fouad et al., 2006; Ludwikowski, Vogel, & Armstrong, 2009). This may be changing, however, given heightened student awareness of the current economic conditions and the tight

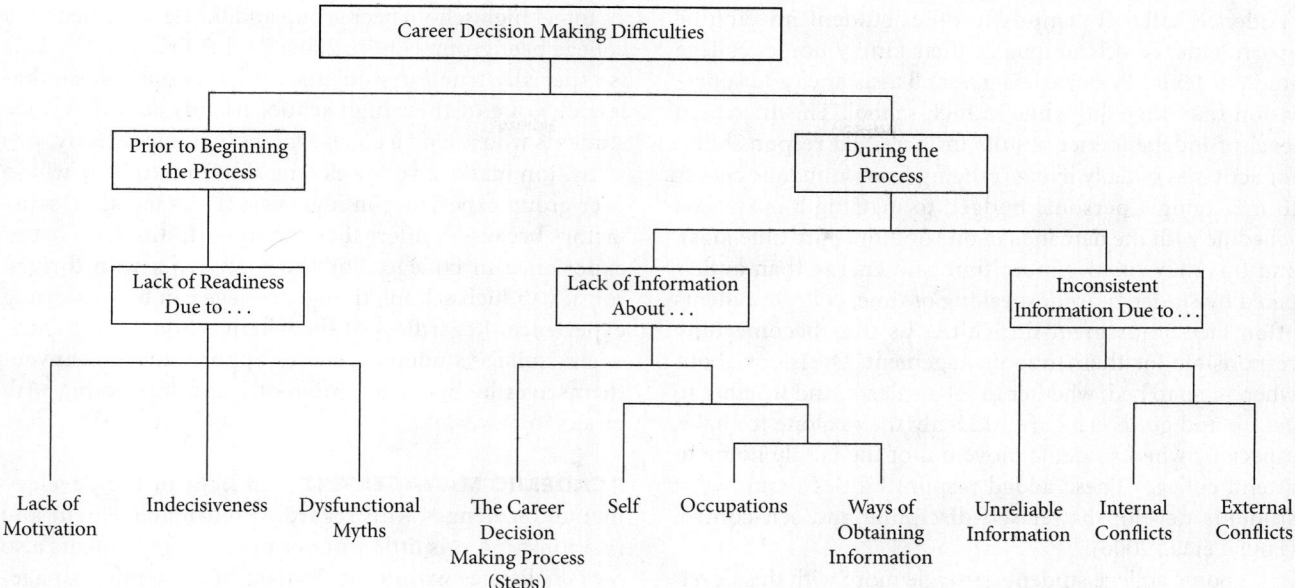

FIGURE 16.1 Revised Taxonomy of Career Decision-Making Difficulties
Source: From Gati, I., Krausz, M., & Osipow, S.H. (1996). A taxonomy of difficulties in career decision-making. *Journal of Counseling Psychology,* 43, 510–526. Published by the American Psychological Association. Reprinted with Permission.

job markets faced by new graduates (Kolowich, 2009; Lipka, 2008).

Indeed, career counselors on college campuses have a prime opportunity to extend their reach and help an even greater percentage of students. In doing so, college career counselors should focus not only on students new to campus (and likely undecided with regard to their academic major) but also on students who have already selected academic majors but who may be uncertain about career opportunities and job prospects associated with their major (Gordon, 2007). Graduate students and alumni may also need career services (Lehker & Furlong, 2006; Luzzo, 2000; Ryan, 1996).

In this chapter, you will learn about several factors influencing the provision of career services to students in college settings. These factors pertain to both the community college setting and the four-year college or university setting. This chapter will begin by addressing several development considerations that affect college students regardless of whether they are attending college immediately out of high school or have been out of the student role for an extended period of time. Next, we'll explore a set of student competencies and a set of program standards that have particular relevance to the provision of career services on college campuses. This chapter will provide you with information about the various program components that can and should be used to assist college students with their career development needs. Let's turn our attention first to developmental considerations.

DEVELOPMENTAL CONSIDERATIONS

Students Who Transition Directly from High School to College

Students who enter college immediately after high school face several developmental tasks. Most of these students have turned 18 and have graduated from high school, two signals of adulthood in our society. Many have long dreamed of reaching this developmental milestone and finally being recognized as adults, but the realities associated with the transition into adulthood and college attendance can be daunting. The transition into adulthood that occurs during the college years makes it particularly important for career counselors to recognize the importance of being aware of and addressing the personal as well as career concerns of college students. College students often experience challenges across several domains: self-management, relationship management, academic management, and career management.

SELF-MANAGEMENT. Many students experience considerably more responsibility and freedom in college compared to high school. Whether living on campus in a residence hall, off campus in other student housing or apartments, or off campus in their family home, college students tend to receive less parental assistance and supervision than they did while in high school. This increased level of independence results in increased responsibility for activities of daily living (ranging from mundane chores to managing a personal budget, to juggling a busy class schedule with the demands of one or more part-time jobs), and this may require more time and energy than anticipated by students. And, speaking of time, college students often face adjustment difficulties as they become fully responsible for their time management. Decisions about when to go to bed, whether to set an alarm, and whether to get up and go to class are suddenly theirs alone to make, especially when students move out of the family home to attend college. These added responsibilities require that students develop better self-discipline and self-control (Fouad et al., 2006).

Some college students struggle more with this developmental challenge than others. For some, these new freedoms are enthusiastically greeted by late nights out, missed morning classes, and disastrous academic results. For others, the increased responsibilities (often for financing their own college education) are overwhelming because they seem to require more than 24 hours in a day. On both ends of the spectrum, though, college students face self-management challenges.

RELATIONSHIP MANAGEMENT. Developmental challenges also exist with respect to relationship management. Students who enter college immediately after high school experience relational shifts within their families of origin and within their peer group. With regard to their families of origin, students may experience a wide variety of relational shifts. Some feel enormous pressure from their families to succeed in college and/or to pursue a specific academic major or career path. Students may struggle with reconciling their psychological needs for parental approval with their own individual preferences, and these conflicts may be complicated by cultural issues pertaining to individualism versus collectivism (DeVaney & Hughey, 2000). Other students may arrive at college and gain the safety and psychological distance necessary to address some problematic dynamics within their families of origin. Such issues may include parental substance abuse or childhood sexual abuse (Fischer et al., 2000; Wright, Crawford, & DelCastillo, 2009). As college students gain awareness of the impact of such experiences, they may have psychological and behavioral reactions that drain their time and energy.

With regard to relational shifts with peers, college students generally experience stress related to the loss of an intact high school peer group and the development of a college peer group (Entin, 2009; Paul & Brier, 2001). This is especially true for students who attend a college that few or none of their high school friends attend and for students who attend a college far from home. Clearly, this transition marks a very welcome shift for students whose peer group experience in high school was less than satisfactory because it offers them an opportunity for a better experience in college. For those students who thrived socially in high school, though, college can be a daunting experience. Regardless of their high school peer experiences, college students have an opportunity to reinvent themselves by behaving differently and interacting with others in new ways.

ACADEMIC MANAGEMENT. In light of the developmental challenges with regard to self-management and relationships, it is little wonder that college students also face challenges within the domain of academic management. Clearly, students' ability and inclination to focus on academics is affected by their increased freedom, increased responsibilities, distance from family of origin, and change in peer groups. College students are also challenged to adjust to a new academic structure and differing academic demands. Although some students arrive at college having already taken college classes through dual enrollment programs, most students experience significantly different academic structures in high school and in college.

In high school, most students are accustomed to attending school Monday through Friday from the morning until the afternoon, with late afternoons and evenings free for homework, recreation, extracurricular activities, and perhaps a part-time job. Traditionally, high school students shift from one class to another in accordance with a bell schedule, with classes being offered in a single building and scheduled one after the other until the end of the school day. In college, of course, classes are organized differently. Classes may meet for an hour three times a week, for three hours once a week, or even be offered online. Whereas high school teachers take attendance and this data is included on report cards, college instructors may or may not take attendance and this data is not included on grade reports or transcripts. College students may have large gaps of time between classes on any given day, and college classes are generally held in various buildings across campus.

College also differs from high school with respect to the use of syllabi and the nature of assignments. In high school, students likely rely on daily teacher communications about what they need to do, whereas college students are expected to use a syllabus to guide their completion of reading and assignments. Similarly, course grades in high school tend to be based on a greater number of small assignments and tests than in college.

Another significant difference related to academic management is that college students must select an academic major. Although some high schools (especially linked learning schools) require that students select a career pathway/cluster within which to take coursework (discussed in Chapter 15), this is not yet a common high school experience. High school students select coursework according to the nature of their postsecondary educational aspirations, with college-bound students tending to take the higher level courses. In college, of course, students must select an academic major, and they may feel and be unprepared to do so. High school students tend to share a common set of graduation requirements set forth by the school district, but college students must adjust to a structure in which the graduation requirements for their academic major differ significantly from the graduation requirements for their friends who have other academic majors. Collaboration with an academic adviser becomes imperative for college students to ensure that they progress toward graduation most efficiently, a challenge that involves awareness of graduation requirements for a particular major, course prerequisites, and course rotations.

CAREER MANAGEMENT. Career management represents a key developmental task for college students. As discussed earlier, developmental tasks in the career management domain include the choice of a career direction. Although the choice of an academic major and a career direction may be related, the extent of relationship varies widely across academic majors. For students choosing pre-professional majors such as occupational therapy, engineering, or elementary education, the link between academic major and career direction tends to be relatively well defined. For students choosing other majors, however, this may not be the case. Students majoring in English, psychology, or communication may have clear ideas about their intended career direction or may have very little idea of what they can or want to do with their degree.

One important developmental task for college students involves career selection. In addition, college students have several other career management needs. Students who have chosen a tentative major and identified an intended career direction may need assistance in confirming their choices or in realizing a need for a new choice. Other students need help in preparing for successful entry into the career of their choice. In addition to the academic knowledge and skills needed for career entry, students may also need assistance with regard to résumé and cover letter writing, job searching, portfolio development, and interviewing skills.

Returning Students

It is also important to acknowledge developmental considerations for college students who are not entering college directly from high school. According to Luzzo (2000), "between one third and one half of today's college students are returning adults—people over age 25 who have decided to return to school after spending several years outside the educational arena" (p. 191). Although the life circumstances and college experiences vary for these students, the considerations may be categorized in the same way: in accordance with self-management, relationship management, academic management, and career management.

With regard to self-management, returning students have accrued a variety of life experiences and have likely already mastered life-management tasks associated with adulthood. Rather than struggling to balance the temptations associated with increased freedom, the self-management challenges facing these students will more likely be associated with juggling numerous, compelling responsibilities, including work, child care, and other family responsibilities. Although serious about succeeding in college, these students may nonetheless struggle with self- and life management. In the event that these students have families of their own, relationship management issues may also stem from their need to take time away from their families in order to attend college and meet coursework expectations.

With regard to academic management, returning students often express concerns about feeling out of practice when writing papers and completing assignments. They may also communicate discomfort with the integration of new technologies into the academic environment. For example, many an older graduate student has shared with me his or her shock when discovering that course registration is now done exclusively over the Internet and shared surprisingly fond memories of the old-school arena registration process involving the collection of index cards for course sections. The increased use of online course management systems (such as BlackBoard or eCollege) and the administration of exams online can be daunting for returning students.

With regard to career management concerns, returning college students generally have a keen sense of the connection between their college attendance and their career aspirations. Whether or not they arrive with a specific career direction in mind, these students generally have a sense that they are seeking a college degree to improve their career outlook. Like other students, they may need assistance with choosing a career direction and also likely need assistance with résumé and cover letter writing, job searching, portfolio development, and/or interviewing skills.

COMPETENCIES AND STANDARDS

National Career Development Guidelines

Understanding the developmental considerations across the domains of self-management, relationship management, academic management, and career management is important for career counselors working on a college campus. Recognition of the developmental challenges in these various domains helps career counselors be sensitive to the difficulty involved in the transition to college, whether a student is transitioning directly from high school or is transitioning to college after an extended time away from school.

It is also important for career counselors to be aware of the career development competencies they should strive to help college students achieve. Developed and revised numerous times by National Occupational Coordinating Committee, the National Career Development Guidelines are presented in their entirety in Appendix E. Because these guidelines were already addressed in Chapter 14 (see Table 14.2), the emphasis in this chapter will be on a set of standards specific to college settings: the CAS Program Standards.

CAS Program Standards for Career Services

Career counselors on college campuses are guided by specific program standards developed by the Council for the Advancement of Standards (CAS). Hoff, Kroll, MacKinnon, and Rentz (2004) explained that CAS is "a consortium of 21 professional associations in higher education" (p. 113) that worked together to "standardize student affairs practice" (p. 114). These efforts resulted in the 1986 initial publication and several subsequent revisions of what are referred to as the CAS Standards. These standards are currently in their seventh revision, and any career counselor seeking employment or already employed in a college setting should read the chapter of the CAS Standards for Career Services (Council for the Advancement of Standards in Higher Education, 2012). Part 1 of these standards addresses the mission of career services units on college campuses. Table 16.1 shows some overlap between the mission of college career services as identified by the CAS Standards and the student competencies put forth in the National Career Development Guidelines, specifically as they pertain to ways in which career services units should seek to help students.

TABLE 16.1 Mission of College Career Services

Part I: Mission

The CAS Standards (2012) specify that the career services unit on each college campus should develop a mission statement. They further specify that:

"The stated mission should be to help students and designated clients to
- develop or clarify self-knowledge related to career choice and performance in the workplace
- develop understanding of the occupational information required to support career decision-making, including current and future trends and projections
- identify and select personally suitable academic programs and experiential opportunities that optimize future educational and employment options
- take responsibility for making informed career decisions and developing further education and employment plans
- understand how their professional interests and competencies relate to occupational and job requirements
- gain experience on or off campus for the purpose of exploring interests and developing their competencies
- develop effective job search and candidate presentation skills
- link with alumni, employers, professional organizations, and others who can provide opportunities to develop professional interests and competencies, integrate academic learning with work, and explore future career possibilities
- utilize technology throughout the career development and job search processes
- prepare to manage their careers after graduation" (p. 142).

Source: From *CAS Professional Standards for Higher Education* (8th ed.). Copyright © 2012 Council for the Advancement of Standards in Higher Education. Reprinted with permission. No part of the CAS Standards and Guidelines may be reproduced or copied in any form, by any means, without written permission of the Council for the Advancement of Standards.

PROGRAM COMPONENTS

Whereas school counselors look to the ASCA National Model (2003) and conceptualize their activities in accordance with the four delivery systems (responsive services, school guidance curriculum, individual student planning, and system support), career counselors working on college campuses conceptualize their activities in accordance with the program components specified by the CAS Standards. These program components are described in Part 2 of the Council for the Advancement of Standards in Higher Education (2012). Table 16.2 identifies the six components.

According to CAS, all these components *must* be offered by a college career services unit in order to ensure that the unit is able to "effectively accomplish its purpose" (2012, p. 145). The remainder of this chapter will be dedicated to describing the types of services that should be offered within each of these categories.

Career Counseling

Although this text has distinguished between career counseling and career development activities, the distinction between them is much less clear within the Council for the Advancement of Standards in Higher Education (2012). In fact, these standards seem to use the concept of career counseling as any activities that directly help students better understand themselves, learn about the world of work, and develop decision-making skills that result in the choice of an academic major and career direction. In addition to individual and group counseling, the CAS standards include a variety of psychoeducational career development activities within the umbrella of career counseling, and this section on career counseling will do the same. We will explore the provision of career development workshops, career development events, career development groups, career development courses, and individual career counseling within this section.

Note also that the Council for the Advancement of Standards in Higher Education (2012) emphasizes that it is essential that career counseling "be available at any stage of their career development" (p. 145). For example, incoming students may need career counseling to assist them with the selection of an academic major, students midway through their degree program may need career counseling to explore career opportunities related to their field of study, and students nearing graduation may need career counseling to prepare for the job search and transition into employment. The activities and opportunities described within this section on career counseling reflect attempts to meet the needs of students at varying points during their time in college.

CAREER DEVELOPMENT WORKSHOPS. It is common for college career centers to offer psychoeducational workshops on various topics related to career development. The workshops offered tend to span the entire spectrum of career development needs on campus but are generally offered as stand-alone sessions. Students may attend only one workshop or several. Such workshops might include the following, all of which have been offered recently by the college indicated in parentheses:

- Ace Your First Professional Interview (DePaul University)
- Assess Yourself Series: Skills, Values, Interests, Personality (Hofstra University)
- Career Decision Making (Middlesex County College)
- Choosing a Major or Career (Washington State University)
- Connecting Your Values to Career Satisfaction (DePaul University)
- Fastest Growing Career Fields (Riverside Community College District)
- Finding a Job During Tough Times (Lewis University)
- Map Out Your Career Path (George Brown College)
- Résumé Clinic (Cal Poly)
- Salary Negotiation (Drexel University LeBow College of Business)
- Social Media and the Online Job Search (Foothill College)
- The Changing Culture of the Workplace of America (Fullerton College)
- Working Overseas (Barton College)

Some of these workshops seek to enhance student self-understanding as it pertains to career selection, others focus on helping students become more aware of the world of work, some help students learn decision-making skills, and some seek to equip students with job-seeking skills.

Career development workshops are frequently offered within the centralized career services office on most college campuses. They can also be offered at various

TABLE 16.2 Program Components of College Career Services

1. Career counseling
2. Information and resources on careers and further education
3. Opportunities for career exploration through experiential learning
4. Job search services
5. Services to employers
6. Consultation and outcomes assessment

locations around campus, such as residence halls, dining halls, and student centers, or through collaboration between the career services office and other student affairs units on campus. The Foothill College Career Center (2014), for example, offers Career Workshops on Wheels and presents to groups in a wide variety of campus settings. Thus, the career center might be contacted by a student organization, a faculty member, an alumni organization, or even a community group with a request for a given workshop.

CAREER DEVELOPMENT EVENTS. The workshops already discussed tend to be relatively short in duration (generally one to three hours), are usually designed for relatively small groups, and tend to be offered frequently. In addition to such workshops, the career services unit on college campuses may organize and sponsor a variety of events related to career development. In contrast to the workshops, the events tend to be longer in duration (one to two days), are usually designed for large groups of participants, and tend to be offered only once or twice a year.

Many colleges, for example, hold an annual majors fair, which are geared primarily toward students who have not yet declared an academic major and those who are uncertain or undecided even if they have declared a major. These events are designed to provide a venue in which students may learn about a wide variety of academic majors and minors in a "convenient one-stop setting" (Berg-Kolin, Krueger, Thomas-Clark, & Fink, 2001, p. 31). In an exhibit hall setting, tables are arranged so that students can circulate through the fair and stop at tables or stations of interest. Most tables are sponsored by academic departments and are staffed by faculty and/or advisers who provide students with oral and written information regarding majors and minors available in their department. Some department tables are also staffed by student volunteers who have chosen a major within that department; these students provide an opportunity for undecided students to talk with other students who happen to have made a decision. Other stations at the majors fair generally include representatives of the academic advising office and the career services unit.

Another type of career development event is a mock interview day. Such an event has been offered with great success at St. Cloud State University (Ditlevson, 1995). Ditlevson explained that what distinguishes this annual, two-day event from the mock interview opportunities typically offered in college career centers is that it "provides each student with an opportunity to have a practice job interview with an experienced recruiter from an employer that covers that student's chosen career field" (p. 54). Student groups are surveyed by the career services office to identify the recruiters and employers to involve in this event. A student organization known as the Career Development Council (CDC) at St. Cloud State University provides student volunteers to give paraprofessional support in organizing and coordinating the event.

CAREER DEVELOPMENT GROUPS. Another way in which career counselors strive to meet the career development needs of students on campus involves the facilitation of groups, primarily in a psychoeducational format. Such groups are especially useful in addressing career development issues in greater depth than can be achieved through single-session workshops or events. When delivering workshops or events, career counselors may want to publicize the availability of related career development groups for students who would like to engage in career development activities to a greater extent. The range of possible topics for career development groups is wide. They may be focused on a specific NCDG competency (such as skills to prepare to seek, obtain, maintain, and change jobs), on a broader NCDG domain (such as the self-knowledge domain), or on a particular CAS standard (such as the transition to work or further education). Career development groups may also be geared toward a specific student population. For example, career development groups on college campuses have been geared toward a variety of student subpopulations, which may include students who are the first in their families to attend college (sometimes referred to as first time in any college [FTIACs]); international students; students who identify as lesbian, gay, bisexual, or transgender (LGBT); students with disabilities; student athletes; and graduate students (Hoff, Kroll, MacKinnon, & Rentz, 2004).

In designing such groups, career counselors should tie session topics to various competencies and/or standards and should develop content according to the professional literature. A group for college students might focus, for instance, on the self-knowledge domain; in this case, the career counselor would consult the NCDG framework to create sessions designed to help students achieve a specific competency within this domain. If choosing NCDG Competency 1, the goal of the group would be to help students develop and maintain a positive self-concept as it applies to career. Specific sessions might be dedicated to helping students assess and develop an accurate understanding of their interests, skills, work-related values, and personality characteristics, and guiding them to an understanding of how these qualities may relate to their success and satisfaction in various careers.

A career development group for LGBT students might focus on the job search process (NCDG Competency 7), with particular attention to LGBT issues. A session on résumé development might include a discussion of whether to include roles which might "out" the student during the job application process (Gelberg & Chojnacki, 1996). Although college students are generally encouraged to include leadership roles on their résumé, the president of the university's lesbian student association needs to make a decision about whether to include this on her résumé. Other sessions may focus on legal issues related to employment discrimination based on sexual orientation (Hetherington, 1991; Pope et al., 2004); ways to assess the workplace environment with regard to safety for and acceptance of LGBT employees (Gelberg & Chojnacki, 1996), including the existence of nondiscrimination statements, antiharassment policies, and domestic partner benefits (Kirby, 2002); specific tips for coming out most effectively in the workplace (Croteau & Hedstrom, 1993); and "panels of lesbians and gay men in the work force who can discuss their own career development strategies for dealing with job interviews, résumés, and work environments" (Pope, Prince, & Mitchell, 2000, p. 278).

Abundant resources regarding career issues specific to various special populations are easily accessible throughout the professional literature. You will find some of these resources by conducting a literature search through a library database system such as ERIC or PsychINFO. For example, if you are interested in addressing the career development needs of student athletes, such a search would quickly yield a number of useful articles (Keim & Strickland, 2004; Lally & Kerr, 2005; Lenz & Shy, 2003; Linnemey & Brown, 2010; Shurts & Shoffner, 2004). Rather than assuming that they understand the career development needs for specific populations, career counselors should be certain to seek resources while designing counseling groups. The same types of resources and ideas available within our research base should be used when developing workshops and career development courses. (Career development courses will be discussed in the next session.)

CAREER DEVELOPMENT COURSES. Many colleges also offer career development courses. These courses are often designed to assist students "in the deciding phase of selecting a major/career or wanting to confirm/change their major course of study" (Reese & Miller, 2010, p. 210). Others are focused on students approaching graduation, with the goal of preparing them for the transition to the world of work (McIlveen & Pensiero, 2008; Walls, 2002; Wood, 2004). Specialized courses may be offered within specific disciplines. For example, Folsom and Reardon (2003) reported that close to half of the business schools they surveyed offered "specialty career courses" designed to meet the specific career development and career planning needs of their students (p. 424).

Course Configurations. Career development courses may be offered in a traditional, hybrid, or online format and may be offered on a credit or no-credit basis. When offered for credit, such courses can frequently count toward a general education or similar requirement, thereby enhancing the attractiveness of such a course to students.

Courses to Assist Students with Career Decision Making.

Course titles. Many colleges offer a course designed to assist students with the career decision-making process. Intended primarily for students who are undecided about their academic major and/or career direction, these courses provide students an opportunity to participate in a full, integrated range of career development activities. Such courses may have a variety of titles. For example, Scott (2010) taught a mandatory freshman orientation course called Introduction to College Studies; Fouad, Cotter, and Kantamneni (2009) described a course entitled Foundations of Academic Success: Planning your Major and/or Career; Thompson and Feldman (2010) described a Let Your Life Speak course, which referred to the title of the text they used; Reese and Miller (2006) shared information about a course entitled Discovery: Career and Life Planning; and my university uses the title of Career Exploration and Decision Making. As you can see, such courses have many titles, and you might want to reflect on how you would title such a course if you were teaching it.

Foundational course content. More important than the title, of course, is the content of the class. Kern (1995) identified three primary content areas presented most commonly in such courses: "self-knowledge, which includes interests, abilities, and work values; occupational information, including ways to research occupations to gain knowledge of those occupations; and decision-making, which helps individuals learn how to make decisions appropriate for themselves" (p. 76). If these content areas sound familiar to you, they should. Once again, we see evidence of the endurance of Frank Parsons's (1909) basic premises for career counseling. Drawing from the work of Fouad, Cotter, and Kantamneni (2009), I suggest some additional content. I concur with these authors and believe that the foundational course content should include an introduction to the career planning process and a unit in which students "determine a tentative major/career choice and develop ongoing career planning goals" (p. 341).

Integration of career development theory. Others have suggested ways to use specific career development theories to guide course development. Reese and Miller (2006), for example, described the use of the cognitive information processing (CIP) model to build their course. (You learned about CIP in Chapter 4 of this text.) Their course addressed "four domains (self-knowledge, occupational knowledge, decision-making skills, and metacognitions) and a five-stage cycle that reflects information-processing skills as it applies to career decision-making" (Reese & Miller, 2006, p. 255). Such a course includes attention to all of the foundational content identified by Kern (1995) but would also address issues related to metacognitions and information-processing. Thus, Reese and Miller included assessments to measure students' sense of self-efficacy with regard to career decision making and to identify specific areas of difficulty in the decision-making process. They administered the Career Decision Self-Efficacy Scale–Short Form (CDMSES-SF; Betz, Klein, & Taylor, 1996) and the Career Decisions Difficulties Questionnaire (CDDQ; Gati, Krausz, & Osipow, 1996) to students in their class. These same instruments were used in the course described by Fouad, Cotter, and Kantamneni (2009). Osborn, Howard, and Leierer (2007) used CIP theory when developing their six-week course for freshmen. Their course focused more specifically on dysfunctional career thoughts (one source of career decision-making difficulty). They did so through the administration of the Career Thoughts Inventory (CTI; Sampson, Peterson, Lenz, Reardon, & Saunders, 1996a) and a corresponding book entitled *Improving Your Career Thoughts* (Sampson, Peterson, Lenz, Reardon, & Saunders, 1996b).

In contrast to these CIP approaches to the development of a career decision-making course, Grier-Reed and Skaar (2010) chose a postmodern approach. They used constructivist theory to guide their development of a career decision-making course. In keeping with the tenets of this theory, these authors sought to help students revisit their past experiences and the messages (scripts) about themselves and careers that they had internalized. Students were encouraged to consider reconstructing their past and present and to construct their future consciously. The course by Grier-Reed and Skaarwas (2010) was organized into three modules: exploring the past and present; (2) constructing the future; and (3) planning, action, and integration (p. 44).

Attention to spirituality and sense of calling. Another increasingly common way in which instructors have sought to build on the foundational content of a career decision-making course is by including existential and spiritual issues. Thompson and Feldman (2010) suggest that the traditional "step-by-step process of self-assessment, career exploration, and decision making" (p. 12) is often insufficient to assist students adequately with their career concerns. They explain that "many students . . . are exploring questions that extend beyond career exploration to issues of meaning and calling" (p. 12).

In addition to including the foundational content typically found in career decision-making courses, Thompson and Feldman included activities to promote self-reflection and insight, to help students consider the sources of meaning in their lives, and to discover their calling. They recommend use of the book *Let Your Life Speak: Listening for the Voice of Vocation* (Palmer, 2000).

Scott (2010) expressed similar concern about the importance of going beyond the more rational decision-making model typically found in career decision-making courses by addressing students' sense of calling. Although he began by teaching a more typically designed course and found it successful in increasing student retention at his university, Scott (2010) "sensed something was missing" (p. 102). Already familiar with and inspired by Palmer's (2000) book as well as *Career and Calling: Finding a Place for the Spirit in Work and Community* by Dalton (2001), Scott proceeded to author a similar book, *Vocatio: Discovering Your Personal Calling* (Scott, 2005) and to integrate these topics into his career decision-making course. In addition to including self-reflection activities in his course, Scott (2010) also encouraged students to identify "spiritual toxins" (p. 105). He did so by referencing Studs Terkel's (1974) classic book *Working* and asking students "to think of a job they had that felt like a 'Monday through Friday sort of dying,'" (Scott, 2010, p. 105), and facilitating exploration of the implications of such toxins on potential sources of career satisfaction and dissatisfaction.

Table 16.3 offers a sample outline overview of career development courses to assist students with career decision making.

TABLE 16.3 Sample Outline for Courses to Assist Students with Career Decision Making

- Introduction to Career Planning
- All About You!
  - Assessment of interests
  - Assessment of skills, aptitudes, and abilities
  - Assessment of personality type
  - Assessment of career-related values
- Focused Exploration
  - Identification of salient types of information
  - Using self-knowledge to focus your career exploration
  - Introduction to Occupational Information Network (O*NET) and other Internet resources
  - Informational interviews and job shadowing
- Finding Your Match(es)
  - Decision-making strategies
  - Development of academic and career plans
  - Next steps

Courses to Assist Students with the Transition from College to Work. Helping students select their academic major and identify their career aspirations is only one priority for college career counselors. Another is to prepare students to make a successful transition from college to employment (Gardner, Van der Veer, & Associates, 1998; Walls, 2002; Wood, 2004). As you will learn in the following paragraphs, this involves more than preparing students with job-seeking skills. Courses designed to assist students with the transition from college to work should address job search skills, employability skills, acclimation issues, and long-term career management.

Job search skills. Few college instructors enjoy as rapt attention from their students as when they address the topic of finding a job after graduating. Especially as graduation approaches, college students become increasingly concerned with the prospect of finding gainful employment (Wood, 2004), and the possibility of *not* finding a job is rather terrifying. In my experience, the unit focused on preparing students for the job search process therefore tends to be warmly welcomed and unusually well attended.

Several topics should be addressed in such a unit. First, students should learn *how to identify job openings*. In Chapter 17, you will learn about a wide variety of job-hunting resources and these should be shared with students. As discussed in that chapter, most job openings sought by college graduates are not posted in the newspapers. Although national search engines such as monster.com may post positions, they are unlikely to provide fruitful leads. Instead of recommending such resources, help students identify industry-specific venues in which job openings are posted, discuss the power of networking, and encourage them to participate in on-campus recruiting events.

Another important topic that should be addressed in a unit about job searching, of course, is the development of résumés. Students will understandably have many questions about this topic. For example, they will want to know what to include, how long it can be, and whether to print it on brightly colored paper. Other content you should address includes the various types of résumés (e.g., chronological versus functional), the idea of having more than one résumé for use when applying for different types of jobs, the importance of representing oneself accurately on all versions of résumés, and the need to proofread the résumé very carefully rather than relying on computer spell-check features. In the past, many instructors also taught students about scannable résumés, but even in 2002, this type of résumé was "becoming outdated because it is far easier to import an e-mailed résumé into a database than to scan a printed résumé" (Dixson, 2002). Instructors should now talk about the importance of converting résumés into portable document files (pdfs) to ensure that the formatting will not be lost in transmission.

Note that there are an overwhelming number of resources from which to gather tips for résumé construction, but not all of them will be useful to your students. Because standards vary significantly across professions, you should consult with faculty members in various academic departments on campus about this issue. You can also require students to schedule an appointment with a professor in their major to discuss résumé standards in the field. Students may also be encouraged to read a succinct article about writing effective résumés, such as the article by Kursmark (2002).

The completion of applications and the preparation of cover letters should also be addressed in a unit about the job search process. Tips about dressing appropriately when visiting a worksite to request an application, the value of taking an application home to complete, and the importance of legibility will likely benefit many students. Students will also have questions about how to respond to questions on the application. For example, a student had been fired from her past two jobs and wanted to know what to write in response to an item asking about the reason for leaving each job.

Davis (2002) identifies the cover letter as "probably the most important document a job seeker will ever write" (p. 21). At a minimum, a lesson about cover letters should familiarize students with the various types, emphasize that the letter be well written and organized, and discuss the general format of cover letters that will be sent in response to posted openings. If they are including a portfolio or other supporting documentation, students should be encouraged to mention this in their cover letter.

Once students have learned to identify job openings and how to prepare their résumés, applications, and cover letters, the unit about job seeking should turn to the topic of interviewing skills. Students should learn about the importance of presenting themselves (arriving on time, personal hygiene and grooming, style of dress, firmness of handshake, eye contact, etc.), ways to respond to common interview questions, and strategies for responding to challenging questions. It is helpful to encourage students to learn about the employer and job prior to the interview and to prepare specific examples to illustrate their strengths. Explain various interview formats. Students often anticipate that an interview involves a one-on-one conversation and may be surprised to encounter a group or panel interview or a behavior-based interview. It is also incredibly helpful to have students participate in mock interviews (Walls, 2002). Many career services offices on college campuses offer such an opportunity.

These interviews are generally recorded and include an opportunity for the student to view the recording and receive specific feedback from the career services staff person.

A final topic within a unit on job seeking involves the negotiation process after a job offer is received. Walls (2002) encouraged students to focus not only on the actual salary offered but on the "total compensation" included in the job offer (p. 121). Stating that "students are usually surprised that the benefits package can sometimes amount to nearly one-third of one's salary," Walls (2002) advises them to consider the value of benefits such as health insurance, retirement plans, and stock options (p. 121). He also encourages students to consider the relative value of a job offer (salary plus benefits) by considering the cost of living. Many a midwestern college graduate has been tickled to receive what sounds like an enormous salary offer only to discover that those dollars don't go nearly as far in a city like New York. Online tools for calculating cost of living can be found on the Internet (e.g., payscale.com/cost-of-living-calculator). Students will be surprised to hear that a salary of $30,000 in Ames, Iowa, is roughly equivalent to a salary of $69,782 in New York City when accounting for the cost of living.

Employability skills. Courses focused on assisting students with the transition from college to work should also address employability skills, including the variety of skills under the umbrella of employability skills. A useful resource to guide such a discussion is the list developed by the Secretary's Commission on Necessary Skills (SCANS; Secretary's Commission on Achieving Necessary Skills, 1991). Especially important to discuss with college students as they prepare to transition into the world of work are the personal skills (including the importance of demonstrating high levels of responsibility; hard work; persistence; self-control; and ethical, honest behavior), effective use of resources (especially their time as well as the employer's money, materials, and equipment), and interpersonal skills (including the importance of being a team player, demonstrating good customer service skills, using effective negotiation and conflict resolution skills, and working effectively with diverse others).

The most effective coverage of employability skills involves guest presentations by actual employers. Such presentations lend credibility to the message you want to communicate. As noted by McIlveen and Pensiero (2008), "delivery [of employability skills workshops] by industry professionals enabled students to have direct contact with the world-of-work and to hear what was expected in the contemporary graduate workplace" (p. 492).

Acclimation issues. Success and satisfaction in the workplace require more than subject area knowledge and skills and the demonstration of employability skills. Noting that "the transition from college to work is a significant and often difficult process for the traditional undergraduate student," Wendlandt and Rochlen (2008) identified several challenges often experienced in this transition (p. 151). First, they point to the differences between college culture and workplace culture and cited research findings that 79% of college "graduates felt they had little or no awareness of work culture prior to entry" (Sleap & Reed, 2006; cited in Wendlandt & Rochlen, 2008, p. 153). Therefore, courses geared toward helping students prepare for the transition into the world of work should include a unit designed to help students anticipate the culture of the workplace. Establishing appropriate coworker relationships, interacting effectively with people across a wide age range, adjusting to new expectations and forms of evaluation, and becoming accustomed to the workplace structure are all challenges students will face as they enter full-time, professional employment for the first time.

Graduates will likely experience a steep learning curve as they enter their first professional position, despite our best attempts to prepare our students with the knowledge and skills necessary to perform in our respective fields. In their discussion of this learning curve (what they labeled a "lack of experience and skills"), Wendlandt and Rochlen (2008) pointed primarily to the lack of employability skills such as communication skills and transferable skills (p. 154). Beyond that, however, it is likely that college graduates will also discover a need to learn considerable job-specific knowledge and skills to perform satisfactorily. For example, future counselors may have performed extremely well in their career development course, accepted a counseling position in a career services office in a college setting, and then needed to learn exactly how to use the assessment materials and/or software programs on that campus. Helping students anticipate the learning curve and normalizing it should be a goal of a career development course.

Another acclimation issue identified by Wendlandt and Rochlen (2008) involves inflated expectations. These authors indicate that graduates often experience significant differences between the realities of their new jobs and the way in which they envisioned them. Such discrepancies might relate to workplace culture, autonomy, excitement associated with the job, or the level of position they hoped to obtain. They summarized this challenge by stating that "research has indicated that graduating students are generally unfamiliar with the differences that exist between college and work and therefore anticipate little change. The inaccurate expectations they hold can be a cause of considerable disappointment, leading to job dissatisfaction" (p. 156).

Using catchier phrasing, Wood (2004) described this as "postparchment depression" (p. 71).

In addition to facing issues involving acclimation to their new job and employer, college graduates face issues related to the transition into full adulthood. For this reason, it is recommended that colleges participating in "the Senior Year Experience movement" address issues such as "effective life-planning and decision-making with respect to practical issues likely to be encountered in adult life after college (for example, financial planning, marriage and family planning)" (Cueso, 1997, as cited in Walls, 2002, pp. 117–118). At least one class session dedicated to such issues would therefore be quite appropriate. Walls (2002), for example dedicated one class session to personal financial planning, another to helping students understand "how their relationships with their classmates and significant others may change as a result of graduation and acceptance of a job that may well be far from most of their friends," (p. 121) and a third to the process of establishing and maintaining effective relationships in the workplace.

Long-term career management. Courses designed to assist students with the transition from college to work should also address long-term career management issues. Noting that "graduates must be able to proactively navigate the world of work and self-manage the career building process," Bridgstock (2009) points to the importance of preparing students with the knowledge and skills necessary for career management (p. 31). She summarizes long-term career management beautifully as

> an ongoing process of engaging in reflective, evaluative and decision-making processes using skills for self-management and career building, based on certain underlying traits and dispositional factors, to effectively acquire, exhibit and use generic and discipline-specific skills in the world of work. In the broadest sense, career management involves creating realistic and personally meaningful career goals, identifying and engaging in strategic work decisions and learning opportunities, recognizing work/life balance and appreciating the broader relationships between [sic] work, the economy and society. In the most proximal and immediate sense, it also includes the processes involved in obtaining and maintaining work. (pp. 35–36)

Within this summary are all of the major elements to be included in a career development unit. Students need to recognize that getting a job and being successful in it is an obvious first step. Beyond that, they also need to recognize and take advantage of opportunities, including the identification of a mentor, the request for a transfer to an office in which promotions might be more likely, and professional development opportunities. In addition, students need to learn how to develop long-term goals as they pertain both to their careers and their overall lives. Gillian, one of our cast of clients from Chapter 1, was very successful after graduating from college but eventually experienced a need to reevaluate her long-term goals and the balance between her work and family life. Students need to understand how to make career-related decisions in the future. The career decision-making models presented in this text will be useful to them.

Table 16.4 offers a sample outline for courses to assist students with the transition from college to work. Before we proceed to the next section, you may also want to take a moment now to check whether your university offers any career development courses and, if so, whether they seem to focus on assisting students with the career decision-making process or on preparing them for the transition from college to work.

INDIVIDUAL CAREER COUNSELING. The workshops, events, groups, and courses described above tend to be more psychoeducational in nature, but individual career counseling is not. College students may benefit from individual

TABLE 16.4 Sample Outline for Courses to Assist Students with the Transition from College to Work

- Overview of Transition Issues
- Getting the Job
  - Identifying job openings
  - Applications, cover letters, and résumés
  - Interviewing skills
  - Negotiation know-how
- Keeping Your Boss Happy: Employability Skills
  - SCANS skills
  - Guest presentations by actual employers
- Keeping Yourself Happy: Acclimation Issues
  - Understanding and adjusting to workplace culture
  - Managing the learning curve
  - Managing your expectations
  - Balancing your budget and your life
- Long-Term Career Management
  - Succeeding at work
  - Developing long-term goals
  - Recognizing opportunities
  - Making new decisions

counseling to assist them with their career development needs and decisions, regardless of whether they also partake of the career development opportunities described above. In an often-cited major meta-analysis, Whiston, Sexton, and Lasoff (1998) found individual counseling to be the most beneficial of all career counseling interventions. The provision of such counseling, of course, should be guided by the theories presented in this text and will likely employ many of the same career counseling techniques. For example, you've already seen how a career counselor worked with Li Mei, from Chapter 1, to assist her.

All of the interventions already described under the career counseling umbrella share a common quality. Though they may differ with respect to the degree of counseling versus psychoeducation involved, all involve face-to-face, person-to-person interaction. These interventions constitute an important component of any college's career services office. However, the services offered by such an office should extend beyond face-to-face career counseling and psychoeducation. The next section describes the second program component prescribed by the Council for the Advancement of Standards in Higher Education (2009). This component facilitates student interaction with hard-copy and online information and resources rather than with a career counseling staff member.

Information and Resources on Careers and Additional Education

College career services units should provide an opportunity for students to access information and resources relevant to careers as well as opportunities for additional education. To do so, the career services office should be involved in identifying, screening, collecting, and disseminating relevant information.

FORMATS OF INFORMATION AND RESOURCES.

Hard-Copy Materials. Although the digital age has decreased our reliance on hard-copy materials, the career services office still tends to house a significant number of tangible resources, including print materials such as published resources (magazines, journals, books); unpublished, compiled written materials (binders and files containing employer information, internship information, etc.); informational handouts about career-related topics; and assessment materials. Hard-copy materials also include video resources such as DVDs and CDs.

Online Digital Materials. Although most career services offices still maintain a sizable collection of hard-copy materials, they now tend to offer significant resources in an online digital format. Using the Internet as a repository for such resources, career services offices tend to develop and maintain impressive websites that not only identify the services offered by their office but also provide access to a huge range of information and resources. Adhering, of course, to copyright restrictions, career services offices may scan and upload some of their print materials. They may also provide several links to relevant resources. Advantages to the digital format include decreased costs and increased access. Indeed, barring server failures and other technological glitches, students have 24-hour access to the materials posted on the career services website. For those of you especially interested in the use of technology by college career services offices, Venable (2010) provides a thorough overview of the many technological resources that can be used to support student career development.

Computer-Assisted Career Guidance Systems. As discussed in Chapter 13, computer-assisted career guidance systems (CACGS) comprise a special category of digital materials. To supplement the discussion in Chapter 13, Table 16.5 offers some information about CACGS that are designed specifically for the college setting.

SELECTION CRITERIA. Especially with regard to the hard-copy and online digital materials, it is important that the career services office screen these sources of information to ensure that they are up to date, accurate, and credible. Hoff, Kroll, MacKinnon, and Rentz (2004) recommend several resources to guide decisions regarding which materials to select. First, the National Career Development Association (2000) has written *Guidelines for the Preparation and Evaluation of Career and Occupational Information Literature* as well as *Guidelines for the Preparation and Evaluation of Video Career Media* (National Career Development Association, 1992). Brown (2007) offers a thorough description of the history, features, advantages, and disadvantages of various CACGS. It is also important to ensure that the resources span a full range of topical areas. The Council for the Advancement of Standards in Higher Education (2012) specify that these resources should include materials relevant to several career-related categories.

CATEGORIES OF INFORMATION AND RESOURCES.

Self-Assessment and Career Planning. The first type of information and resources specified by CAS involves materials to "help students assess and relate their interests, competencies, needs and expectations, education, experience, personal background, and desired lifestyle to the employment market" (Council for the Advancement of Standards in Higher Education, 2012, p. 146). Career

TABLE 16.5 College-Specific Computer-Assisted Career Guidance Systems (CACGS)

CAPA Integrative Online System for College Major Exploration
- Based on the work of Nancy Betz in collaboration with Gail Hackett and, later, Fred Borgen.
- Intended specifically for use with undergraduate college students.
- Uses measures of interests and skills confidence to suggest academic majors for consideration by undecided college students.
- See the article by Betz and Borgen (2010) for more information.

FOCUS-2
- Originally developed by Donald Super and others and since acquired by Career Dimensions, Inc.
- Unlike other CACGS, FOCUS-2 is designed specifically for college settings.
- Offers a comprehensive career guidance and planning program, including units for self-assessment; exploration of career and educational opportunities; and assistance with decision making, career planning, and portfolio development.
- See focuscareer2.com/.

System of Integrated Guidance and Information (SIGI-3)
- Originally developed by Martin Katz at Educational Testing Service (ETS) and acquired by Valpar International Corporation.
- Offers a comprehensive career guidance and planning program, including modules for self-assessment; exploration of career and educational opportunities; and assistance with decision making, career planning, and transitioning from school to work.
- See sigi3.org.

counselors in college settings must first identify which self-assessment materials to offer. As discussed in Chapter 11, numerous standardized assessments are available across several dimensions related to self-knowledge. These include assessments of interests, career-related values, personality, aptitudes, and abilities.

The career services office also needs to decide which specific tests to purchase and the method(s) of appropriate administration. Purchasing decisions will likely be based on several factors. Psychometric factors, including the appropriateness of the norming sample, reliability, and validity, are very important. When selecting tests for self-guided use by students, factors related to the ease of use (including the clarity of instructions for taking and scoring the test as well as the usefulness of information to assist students in understanding and applying their test results) should also be considered. Practical issues such as the cost of assessment materials are also important (Whiston, 2009). Indeed, college career services units often need to weigh these factors against one another when making purchasing decisions. The most psychometrically sound instruments are likely to be the most expensive and are also likely require that a career counselor be involved in the administration and interpretation of the test. On the other end of the spectrum are numerous informal assessments that are available free of charge but are lacking in the psychometric research necessary to support their use. My recommendation is to avoid using these assessments and to bear in mind that, by providing access to them online or in hard-copy form, the career services office is implicitly communicating to students that the tests have met appropriate quality standards.

With regard to method(s) of appropriate administration, career counselors need to determine which tests can be used by students independently and which require counselor involvement. The use of some materials geared toward enhancing student self-knowledge requires face-to-face interactions between career counselors and students. This is particularly true for many of the standardized testing materials addressed in Chapter 11. Some self-assessment materials are appropriate, however, for self-administration. The Self-Directed Search (SDS; Holland, Powell, & Fritzche, 1997), for example, can be self-administered, self-scored, and self-interpreted. When providing students with access to assessment materials for self-guided use, however, career counselors are wise to (a) provide disclaimers to students and (b) communicate that additional assistance in understanding the implications of test results are available through the career services office. For example, it is useful to emphasize that no standardized test can tell students which major or career they should choose and also to communicate to students that the career services office is available to help them understand what their results do and do not mean and in developing a career plan.

The development of a sound career plan should also be based on information related to the world of work. This is the next category of information and resources specified by the CAS Standards.

Occupational and Job Market Information. Some college students select academic majors and career direction based solely on their own interests, career-related values, and other personal characteristics without regard to the realities of the job market and the likelihood of obtaining gainful employment on graduating. It has been my experience, however, that a majority of college students are concerned about finding a job in their chosen field after completing their degree. These students care not only about identifying a career in which they believe they will be satisfied and successful but also about choosing a career in which they will be able to find employment and support their desired lifestyle. Doing so, as Frank Parsons (1909) suggested, requires knowledge about oneself and about the world of work.

The Council for the Advancement of Standards in Higher Education (2012) indicates that college career services units should make information and resources about occupational and job market information available to students. As with the self-assessment materials described above, these resources may be hard copy or electronic. Hard-copy materials have historically included reference materials from the U.S. Department of Labor and the Bureau of Labor Statistics (such as the *Occupational Outlook Handbook*) along with written and video materials about various careers. As you learned in Chapter 13, however, it is now much more common for colleges to make such materials available online. Sites such as the Occupational Information Network (O*NET; onetonline.org) provide a wealth of information to assist college students in gathering information regarding careers as well as the job market. With the abundance of high-quality online materials providing occupational and job market information that are available free of charge, college career counselors do not have to balance the financial costs against the relative benefits of these materials in the same way they need to when selecting self-assessment materials.

Options for Further Study. To achieve their career aspirations, some college students need or want additional education. Community college students may identify a need to earn a bachelor's degree or beyond, undergraduates may decide to pursue a graduate or professional degree, and graduate students like you may have an interest in pursuing a doctorate. College career services offices should also make available information and resources regarding options for further study.

At community colleges, such information should include resources related to four-year colleges as well as to transfer options. Information regarding any articulation agreements is particularly important for these students. Articulation agreements are agreements that have been established between a community college and four-year colleges, and specify which courses at the community college will be accepted for credit by the four-year college and the equivalent course at the four-year college. Students benefit from knowing, for example, that English 110 at their community college will not transfer into the four-year university they hope to attend but that English 120 at their community college will transfer to the university as an equivalent of the university's English 100 course.

Resources should also be available for all students, regardless of their year in college, to assist them in searching for and selecting colleges for furthering their education. Such resources were discussed in depth in Chapter 14, in the section on school counselors' role in facilitating postsecondary planning, and these same strategies and resources are applicable in facilitating college student exploration of colleges and universities where students may obtain advanced degrees.

College students need to become aware of information related to admissions requirements for graduate and professional schools, just as high school students need to be aware of the coursework, grades, and test scores needed to gain admission to various colleges, College students need to understand what coursework and/or majors are most beneficial, what grades they need to achieve, and what entrance examinations they need to take. Therefore, in addition to providing resources to support the search process related to further education, college career services offices should also provide students with resources containing such information. Table 16.6 identifies the most common entrance examinations for graduate and professional schools in the United States.

TABLE 16.6 Graduate and Professional School Entrance Exams

Type of School	Acronym	Name of Test	Website
Graduate school	GRE	Graduate Record Exam	ets.org/gre/
	MAT	Miller Analogies Test	milleranalogies.com/
Business school	GMAT	General Management Admission Test	mba.com
Law school	LSAT	Law School Admission Test	lsac.org/JD/LSAT/about-the-LSAT.asp
Medical school	MCAT	Medical College Admission Test	aamc.org/students/applying/mcat/about/

Job Search Information. Although some college students seek to enter advanced degree programs immediately following their graduation, others want to transition directly into a job. The career services office on campus should have job search information and resources available to students. This information may include print materials as well as online resources such as those presented in Chapter 13. Specific topics that should be addressed include the process of searching for job openings, the application process (including the preparation of cover letters and résumés), and the interviewing process. Some colleges also provide information and resources related to the negotiation process once a job offer is received.

Employer Information. Closely connected to the provision of information about the job search process is the provision of information about prospective employers. Career services staff should collect and organize information about potential employers who may be interested in hiring graduates of the college. These potential employers include those that participate in on-campus recruiting events. By collaborating with the alumni affairs offices, career services staff can often gather data about other employers of the college's graduates.

Experiential Learning, Internship, and Job Listings. According to the Council for the Advancement of Standards in Higher Education (2012), "experiential education may include apprenticeships, cooperative education, internships, peer leadership experiences, service-learning, shadowing experiences, student teaching, undergraduate research, volunteer experiences, and work-study jobs and other campus employment" (p. 147). Such experiences can be invaluable in the career preparation process, and career services should provide students with access to information about them. This information may help students understand the value of such experiences, inform them of established programs on campus, or help them search for other such opportunities off campus. For example students interested in cooperative education may visit co-op.edu; those interested in apprenticeships may find useful information at http://www.dol.gov/apprenticeship/. In addition to providing information and resources about experiential learning opportunities, college Career Services should be involved in the establishment and coordination of such experiences. This responsibility is addressed in the next section of this chapter.

Opportunities for Career Exploration Through Experiential Learning

In addition to learning from their academic coursework, college students may benefit tremendously from experiential learning opportunities. The combination of academic and hands-on learning experiences may offer students a competitive edge when seeking employment (Unger, 2006). The Council for the Advancement of Standards in Higher Education (2012) specifies that the career services office on college campuses should be actively involved in making such opportunities available to students and identifies two forms of career services involvement: Career services may (1) administer experiential learning programs and (2) work with other units on campus as they administer experiential learning programs.

When administering experiential learning programs, career services should identify various opportunities for students to complete internships, participate in cooperative education programs, engage in service learning projects, complete apprenticeship programs, and so on. The majority of such opportunities will be off campus and all will provide students with an opportunity to learn by doing. Disney, for example, has a widely known and well-established internship program for college students, with specific internships geared toward a wide variety of college majors (wdwcollegeprogram.com). The Council for the Advancement of Standards in Higher Education (2012) cautions, though, that such experiences must also "provide students with opportunities to define both learning and career objectives and to reflect upon learning and other developmental aspects of their experience" (p. 147). Effective experiential opportunities not only provide students with the experience of doing something work related; they also provide students with an opportunity to reflect on the connection between their academic studies and their experiential projects and to apply insights to their future career plans.

Career services should collaborate with academic programs and other departments that may offer experiential learning programs. Student teaching programs, for example, are frequently administered by the college of education or the teacher education department within it. In this case, the career services office should offer its support of such a program via consultation or the sharing of resources.

Job Search Services

You've already learned that the information and resources component of career services should include information regarding the job search process. In addition, on-campus career services offices should be heavily involved in other functions related to job searching. The Council for the Advancement of Standards in Higher Education (2012) specifies that these "job search services may include offering site visits, campus recruiting, résumé referrals, information sessions, meetings with faculty members, access to alumni for networking, pre-recruiting activities, student access to employer information, posting job openings, and career and job fairs" (p. 148). Of course, such services will include assistance with résumé preparation and the development of interviewing skills. Both topics were addressed in the earlier section about career development courses, so they will not be revisited here. This section focuses on job fairs, on-campus recruiting, credential file services, and electronic portfolios.

JOB FAIRS. A common type of event coordinated by the career services office provides opportunities for students to meet with prospective employers in a job fair. Job fairs are frequently focused on a specific employment area. For example, a college may offer a job fair geared toward students seeking positions within education (teachers, counselors, administrators, speech and language pathologists, etc.), health or medical settings (nurses, physical therapists, occupational therapists, etc.), the business sector (accountants, human resources professionals, marketing specialists, etc.) or the informational technology arena (computer programmers, network specialists, systems analysts, etc.). Such job fairs are most successful when the career services office has developed strong working relationships with area employers and with administrators within the university's division of academic affairs, prospective employers have had good success when hiring graduates from the college, and students are prepared to make effective use of the job fair.

ON-CAMPUS RECRUITING. Hoff, Kroll, MacKinnon, and Rentz (2004) identify on-campus recruiting as "perhaps the most visible program provided by Career Services, particularly for students majoring in business, engineering, science, and education" (p. 125). Job fairs represent one type of on-campus recruiting, but it can also involve visits by one employer at a time. The focus of the visit may involve the employer meeting with faculty members to build relationships and a referral base. Another focus of an on-campus recruiting visit might involve the employer hosting an event at which interested students can learn more about career opportunities with that specific employer. The focus of the event could also involve actual interviews. In this case, an employer arranges with the career services office to be on campus on a particular day to interview applicants. Prior to the interview day, the career services office disseminates information and solicits applications and/or résumés from students. The employer then screens the applications and identifies specific students to interview. Hoff, Kroll, MacKinnon, and Rentz (2004) identify this option, involving an interviewing process, as "the most well-known" of the on-campus recruiting strategies (p. 127).

CREDENTIAL FILE SERVICES. Less common is the provision of credential file services, sometimes referred to as a dossier service. Generally speaking, career services serves as a repository for student credentials. These credentials might include the student's transcript, résumé, and even letters of reference. With these and a signed consent form in place, students or graduates in the process of applying for jobs or advanced degree programs can then contact the career services office to request that their credentials be sent on their behalf.

ELECTRONIC PORTFOLIOS. Although some colleges continue to offer credential file services, others have transitioned to an electronic portfolio system that contains similar types of documents. These electronic portfolios may be housed on campus-based servers associated with the college, but the career services office is otherwise uninvolved in the management of the portfolio. Rather than students or graduates contacting the office and requesting that certain documents be sent on their behalf, electronic portfolios are usually managed by the students or graduates themselves. Many universities choose to establish contracts with commercial companies such as Interfolio or ePortolio for this purpose; others have established contracts for course management systems that include an electronic portfolio feature for use by students and alumni. BlackBoard, eCollege, and Desire2Learn are examples of course management systems that include such a feature. Other universities, such as Florida State University and the University of California, San Diego, have developed their own electronic portfolio programs for use on campus (Ceperley & Schmidt, 2007; Lumsden, 2007).

Employer Relationship and Recruitment Services

In addition to providing services geared primarily to students and alumni, career services offices on college campuses should also provide services to employers. The Council for the Advancement of Standards in Higher Education (2012) specifies that

> [e]mployer relations and recruitment services may include: site visits; campus recruiting; résumé referrals; pre-recruiting information sessions with students; student access to timely employer information; posting and publishing of job and internship openings; on-site or virtual career/job fairs; experiential learning options which may include shadowing experiences, internships, externships, student teaching, cooperative education assignments; remote electronic interviewing options; employer participation in career planning, work-force readiness courses, career conferences, résumé preparation, practice interviews, and job search readiness workshops. (p. 149)

CAS cautions that career services offices should develop specific policies to guide their decisions about which employers to serve in these ways. Although CAS indicates that such policies should be "uniformly and consistently" applied to employers, CAS also recommends that staff members should also "understand the variety and diversity of needs and employment practices among businesses, corporations, government agencies, schools, and non-profit organizations" (p. 150).

Consultation Services to Faculty and Administrators

The final program component of career services specified by the Council for the Advancement of Standards in Higher Education (2012) involves the responsibilities of this unit for providing "faculty and administrative units with information, guidance, and support on career development, and employment issues and linkages with the broader community" (p. 151). Specifically, it encourages career services to be active in collecting and distributing the following types of career-related information to these constituencies:

- Employment trends and top employing organizations and on co-op and internship sponsors
- Employer feedback on the preparation of students for jobs, the curriculum, and the hiring process
- Appropriate ethical and legal guidelines for student referrals
- Guidance on effective strategies for engaging employers in programs offered by faculty and administrative units
- Career development issues and available resources
- Aggregate data on student learning, career-related and first-destination outcomes, and employer engagement for purposes such as accreditation, marketing, institutional development, and curriculum development
- Guidelines for serving as a reference and writing (Council for the Advancement of Standards in Higher Education, 2012, p. 151).

Collaboration

It is also essential that the career services office collaborate with other units on campus. For example, career services staff members may work closely with the admissions office and the transfer student office in the planning of orientation sessions and/or the preparation of welcome materials for new students, being certain to highlight the availability and location of career development and career counseling services. Each of these offices will also appreciate data from the career services office regarding the employment/placement rate of the college's graduates because such data can be useful in attracting and recruiting potential students.

Another important collaboration is between the career services staff members and the academic advising unit(s) on campus. These units should work together in the preparation of informational materials regarding career opportunities associated with various academic majors. Career counselors may also offer occasional training opportunities for academic advisers to help them recognize when referring a student for career counseling may be useful. Academic advisers will appreciate receiving disaggregated data regarding the employment/placement rate of students within various academic majors. Gathering such data, of course, requires collaboration among the career services office, alumni affairs office, registrar's office, and institutional research office. These units should work together to develop follow-up surveys regarding employment rates, salaries, and so on, of recent graduates as well as feedback from employers regarding the quality of preparation these graduates received in their academic programs. Because some graduates will inevitably encounter employment difficulties, the availability of career counseling for alumni is an important service to offer (Ryan, 1996).

PUTTING IT ALL TOGETHER

This chapter has explored the many career development needs presented by college students. You've learned that approximately 75% of college students are undecided about their academic major at some point during college, which is often accompanied by concomitant uncertainty about their career interests and aspirations. The majority of college students could benefit from career counseling and/or career development activities offered through the campus career services office. The National Career Development Guidelines and the CAS Program Standards are each useful in identifying the career development goals of such services.

Complicating their need for career services are developmental challenges faced by college students. These challenges occur not only in relation to career management but also to self-management, relationship management, and academic management. Career counselors working with college students should not only address career development issues but also listen for and perhaps inquire about other concerns that may be affecting the student's experience in college.

When focusing on career development issues with students, effective career counselors use a wide variety of approaches as outlined by the CAS Standards. Career counseling and career development activities should include workshops, events, groups, courses, and individual career counseling. In addition to these types of direct-service activities, the CAS Standards specify that a college's career services program should include several other components. Specifically, in addition to career counseling and career development activities, the program should include information and resources on careers and further education, opportunities for career exploration through experiential learning, job search services, services to employers, and consultation and outcomes assessment services.

Ultimately, the goal is to assist college students with support for their career development throughout the course of their academic studies. This support should begin with assistance in choosing an academic major and include preparation for and assistance with the job search process and the development of a long-term career management plan. These career development needs apply to undergraduate students, whether they have transitioned to college directly from high school or whether they are returning, nontraditional students, as well as to graduate students. You yourself may need some assistance with career development plans. With that in mind, the final chapter (Chapter 19) is dedicated to applying these same concepts to help you chart your own career path as a professional counselor.

CHAPTER

17

Job Loss, Unemployment, and the Job Search Process

The previous three chapters addressed the provision of career development interventions and career counseling services in educational settings, and it has been my experience that few graduate students in counseling programs require convincing about the need for such services. At some level, the need for career development interventions and career counseling in educational settings is self-evident. What can be less evident, though, is the need for career services in community settings. My observation has been that many graduate students who select a community counseling or clinical mental health track initially devalue the importance of taking a course on career counseling. They may do so quietly, behind the scenes, or they may openly question the value of the course for their future. Some of you, when enrolling in this course, never pictured yourselves as having a desire or need to provide career counseling. Instead, you may have envisioned a career in a community setting, perhaps as a clinical mental health counselor, helping clients with real issues, by which you probably meant diagnosable disorders and personal life problems.

I confess that my initial reaction to the idea of career counseling and to career issues, I dare say, was that they were boring, and I perceived the coursework as irrelevant to my future clinical work. My initial impressions, however, soon changed in the face of actual work experience. Even while working in private practice, I was amazed by how many clients needed at least some assistance with career issues. As just one example, my clients who suffered from moderate to severe depression certainly needed help combating suicidal urges, stabilizing their mood, recognizing signs of slippage, and addressing interpersonal and family issues contributing to and/or being affected by the depression. I had anticipated that. What I hadn't anticipated was that they would also need assistance with career issues. They needed assistance in processing the possible impact of depression on their performance at work, exploring the possible effect of work stressors on their depression, and making decisions about whether to disclose information about their struggles with depression to their employers. In the event that their depression became severe enough to interfere with their ability to work full-time, they needed documentation to warrant medical leave and/or job accommodations. And when they considered long-term career goals, they worried about the impact of a high-stress job on their ability to manage their symptoms. And this was in private practice, which is admittedly pretty far removed from the stark reality of providing career services in the community setting.

In community counseling, rest assured that career services are anything but boring or irrelevant for clients who have lost their jobs, face mounting debts and possible foreclosure, and worry about long-term unemployment. To these clients, career services are essential. With this in mind, this chapter is dedicated to career services in community settings that relate to job loss, unemployment, and the job search process.

JOB LOSS AND UNEMPLOYMENT

The most common goal for clients who seek career services in community settings is to find a job. In fact, it is so common that a specialized offshoot of career counseling, called employment counseling, exists to focus on these needs. Think for a minute about what types of clients might seek career services in community settings for assistance in transitioning back into the labor force. I'm guessing that the first clients who come to mind are those who have lost their jobs and need to regain employment. As people who are far cooler than me might say, *"True Dat."* Outsourcing; downsizing; offshoring; technological advancements resulting in job obsolescence; and our nation's recent, prolonged recession have resulted in many job losses and high unemployment rates. To be sure, nobody seems to be safe from job loss these days.

Because unemployment is such a pervasive problem and assisting such clients definitely falls within the scope of career counseling, Blustein, Kenna, Gill, and DeVoy (2008) called for increased attention to the preparation of career counselors in this area. They observed that our "traditional career theories . . . have focused on questions of career choice and implementation" and lamented that "the experience of those who are unemployed has been neglected" (p. 305) in the preparation of career counselors. I believe this criticism bears much merit because even a quick perusal of most textbooks reveals that they offer relatively little attention to this topic.

The fact is, though, that unemployment clearly represents the career challenge most likely presented by clients in community settings. To prepare for assisting clients with issues related to unemployment, counselors should understand how unemployment is officially defined and counted, the psychological impact of unemployment over time, and helping strategies that may be used to assist clients not only with the job search process but also with their emotional reactions and psychological needs.

Unemployment: Definitions and Statistics

Although the meaning of the word *unemployment* may seem obvious, the U.S. government uses some very specific definitions when collecting data and releasing statistics related to employment rates. Specifically, the U.S. Bureau of Labor Statistics (BLS) defines unemployment and limits this category to "people who are jobless, looking for jobs, and available for work" (U.S. Bureau of Labor Statistics, 2009, p. 4), clarifying that "looking for work" requires doing so within the past four weeks. Using this definition, the national unemployment rate in 2012 was 8.1%, which translates to estimates that "one out of every 12 Americans who are willing and able to work cannot find a job" (Business Roundtable, 2012, p. 1). This represents approximately 12 million people who are unemployed according to this narrow definition (U.S. Bureau of Labor Statistics, 2013b).

Should unemployment persist despite efforts to find work, even the most conscientious job seekers may become discouraged and stop looking for work (Amundson & Borgen, 1982; Business Roundtable, 2012). Once they have gone four weeks without looking for work, these individuals are no longer considered as unemployed. Yes, you read that correctly. Unemployed people who go one month or more without actively looking for a job are no longer considered unemployed, and they are no longer counted toward the national unemployment rate. People who haven't engaged in job searching for at least four weeks because of a belief that they won't find work are referred to as discouraged workers (U.S. Bureau of Labor Statistics, 2008). Discouraged workers are counted as marginally attached to the labor force. This category also includes people who want a job but who have not looked for work in the past four weeks for reasons such as enrollment in a training or education program or because of family responsibilities (U.S. Bureau of Labor Statistics, 2008). It is estimated that approximately 2.4 million people currently fall within the marginally attached category, with nearly 1 million specifically identified as discouraged (U.S. Bureau of Labor Statistics, 2013b).

Another category of long-term unemployed people are simply counted by the government as not in the labor force (U.S. Bureau of Labor Statistics, 2009). Kurtz (2013) described this group as "hopelessly unemployed" and explained that these individuals are not recognized by our government as unemployed, discouraged or marginally attached workers because they have "been jobless so long, they've fallen off the main government measures altogether" (para. 4). Kurtz is referring specifically to people who indicate that they would like a job but have not actively looked for work in the past year. An estimated 3.25 million Americans fall into this category, out of approximately 90 million adults who are counted within the broader category of "not in the labor force" (U.S. Bureau of Labor Statistics, 2013b). The "not in the labor force" category also includes approximately 40 million senior citizens and 47 million other adults who are not working and do not indicate that they want a job. Table 17.1 provides a summary of these definitions and statistics.

I hope to convey two takeaway messages. First, what the average person means by the word *unemployed* can differ dramatically from our federal government's definition. This is important mostly because unemployment insurance benefits are only available to those who meet the government's definition of *unemployed*. It is important for career counselors to recognize this government definition, but limiting the terms *unemployment* and *unemployed* to people who have been looking for work in the past four weeks is questionable for career

TABLE 17.1 Definitions and 2013 Statistics for Employment Classifications

Classification	Definition*	Number of People
Unemployed	"Persons aged 16 years and older who had no employment during the reference week, were available for work, except for temporary illness, and had made specific efforts to find employment sometime during the 4-week period ending with the reference week. Persons who were waiting to be recalled to a job from which they had been laid off need not have been looking for work to be classified as unemployed."	12,000,000
Discouraged	"Persons not in the labor force who want and are available for a job and who have looked for work sometime in the past 12 months (or since the end of their last job if they held one within the past 12 months) but who are not currently looking because they believe there are no jobs available or there are none for which they would qualify."	1,000,000
Marginally attached	"Persons not in the labor force who want and are available for work, and who have looked for a job sometime in the prior 12 months (or since the end of their last job if they held one within the past 12 months), but were not counted as unemployed because they had not searched for work in the 4 weeks preceding the survey. Discouraged workers are a subset of the marginally attached."	2,400,000
Not in the labor force	"Includes persons age 16 years and older in the civilian noninstitutional population who are neither employed nor unemployed in accordance with the definitions contained [herein]. Information is collected on their desire for and availability for work, job search activity in the prior year, and reasons for not currently searching."	90,000,000 total 3,250,000 who want a job but are not counted as unemployed, discouraged, or marginally attached

*Excerpted from: http://www.bls.gov/bls/glossary.htm. Bureau of Labor Statistics.

counseling purposes. Therefore, for the remainder of this chapter, I will use the terms *unemployment* and *unemployed* to refer to people who want a job but do not have one, regardless of the length of time since they last looked for work.

The second takeaway message involves the sheer number of people affected by joblessness. When combining all the categories of people who want but do not have jobs, regardless of how recently they have searched for work, we arrive at some staggering statistics. Approximately 18.65 million Americans, representing about 12% of the adult population, are unemployed. This translates to approximately one of every eight people who want jobs but do not have them. Clearly, unemployment represents a major career-related problem facing the community.

Psychological Reactions to Job Loss

People experiencing unemployment—however it is defined—are often in need not only of job search assistance from a paraprofessional but also of career counseling services provided by professional counselors (Donahue, 2009). Although some people may experience even involuntary "job loss as a blessing in disguise" (Zikic & Klehe, 2006, p. 391), many more experience involuntary job loss as a problem, loss, or even crisis (Guindon & Smith, 2002). Unemployment affects people not only financially but also psychologically, often resulting in grief reactions, identity crises, relational distress, and mental disorders such as depression or anxiety (Amundson & Borgen, 1982; Brewington, Nassar-McMillan, Flowers, & Furr, 2004; Donahue, 2009; Guindon & Smith, 2002;

Johnson & Jackson, 2011; Latack & Dozier, 1986; Murphey & Shillingford, 2012; Nicholson, 1984; Paul & Moser, 2009). It is simply insufficient for career counselors to attend only to the job search needs of unemployed clients (Donahue, 2009).

Thus, it is useful to understand the psychological reactions people may have to unemployment. Amundson and Borgen (1982) offered a particularly useful model for understanding the needs and experiences of their unemployed clients. This model, which resembles an "emotional roller coaster," is featured in Figure 17.1. The model begins at the point of job loss and suggests that the job loss generally triggers a grieving process (Amundson & Borgen, 1982, p. 563). The first segment of Figure 17.1 therefore depicts a theoretical illustration of the grief process following job loss. Keep in mind, though, that individual experiences of the grief process vary. For example, they may vary in duration as well as in emotional intensity. Grief reactions tend to be stronger for people who had been in the role of primary breadwinner (Papa & Maitoza, 2013) or for whom the worker role had been central to their identity (McKee-Ryan, Song, Wanberg, & Kinicki, 2005). When the job loss is anticipated rather than unexpected, individuals may experience anticipatory grief reactions prior to the job loss (Borgen & Amundson, 1987). Despite such individual variation, however, research has consistently found similarities between bereavement-related grief and the grief process following involuntary job loss (Anderson, Goodman, Schlossberg, 2012; Archer & Rhodes, 1995; Brewington et al., 2004; Donahue, 2009; Papa & Maitoza, 2013).

Applying Kübler-Ross's (1969) classic articulation of the stages of grief, Amundson and Borgen (1982) explained that the grieving process begins with a state of denial. This may be evidenced by numbness, feelings of shock, and reluctance to tell significant others about one's job loss. Anger represents the next stage in the grief cycle and may manifest in toward oneself, one's previous employer, the economy, or even government policies one blames for the job loss. In the bargaining stage, a person may attempt to be rehired by the former employer or engage in pleading prayers with a supreme being. When such bargaining fails to reverse one's fortune, a person moves into the depression stage and may exhibit depressive symptoms in mood, energy, thoughts, and behaviors. On reaching the acceptance stage of the grief cycle, a person embraces a more pragmatic approach and becomes ready to engage in a job search process.

The next segment of Amundson and Borgen's (1982) model focuses on psychological reactions to the job search process. During this process, clients may need informational support related to conducting self-assessments, exploring career possibilities, making decisions about career direction, searching for job openings, preparing application materials, and honing interviewing skills. They also likely need emotional support. As illustrated in the second segment of Figure 17.1, the emotions associated with the job search segment continue to resemble a roller

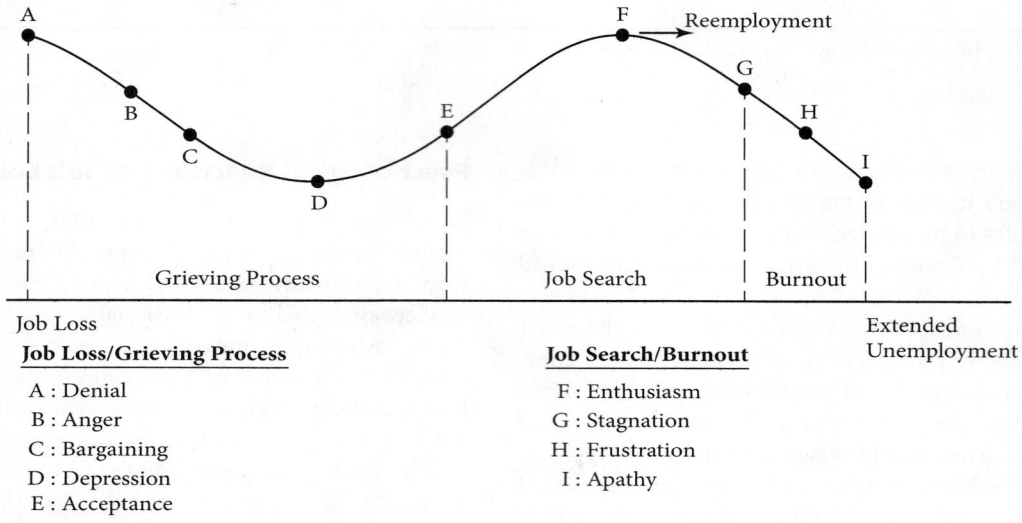

FIGURE 17.1 The Dynamics of Unemployment

Source: Amundson, N.E., & Borgen, W.A. (1982). The dynamics of unemployment: Job loss and job search. *Personnel and Guidance Journal,* 60, 562–564. (Figure 1, p. 563)

coaster. In emerging from the grief process, a person often feels enthusiastic and hopeful about the job search and is willing to put significant time and effort into looking for work. Ideally, this results in a person's reemployment and a happy ending to the story. Especially in tough economic times, however, even an enthusiastic job search may go unrewarded. Over time, this enthusiasm may wane in the face of unanswered job applications and rejection letters. The longer the job search remains unsuccessful, the more a person comes realize how difficult it may be to find desirable reemployment. If this occurs, a person may become increasingly discouraged and enter a stage in which job search efforts stagnate.

As with the grief process, individual experiences of the job search process may vary from the illustration in Figure 17.1. The job search process can vary in duration, with some people finding jobs right away and others reaching the point of stagnation. The pattern of the emotional roller coaster will also vary and will likely include a yo-yo effect related to the cycle of getting one's hopes up and having them dashed (Borgen & Amundson, 1987, p. 182). When this cycle of "rekindled hope . . . alternating with increased feelings of worthlessness" (p. 182) persists, a person may begin to experience burnout.

Burnout represents the third segment of Amundson and Borgen's (1982) model. Burnout is associated with long-term unemployment and is demonstrated emotionally and behaviorally. A person is likely to feel discouraged, frustrated, and eventually apathetic, at which point, that person is likely to invest much less time and energy looking for work and may even withdraw from the seemingly futile job search process altogether. A person may also engage in self-medicating behaviors such as drinking and drug use. It becomes increasingly difficult for a person who reaches the burnout stage to find reemployment. Feelings of worthlessness and futility combined with behavioral withdrawal from the job search process may result in a "self-fulfilling prophecy" (p. 563). Early in the burnout stage, a person is likely to meet the definition of a discouraged worker. If discouragement progresses to the point of apathy, a person may transition from being a discouraged worker to being among those not in the labor market and no longer looking for work.

HELPING STRATEGIES FOR THE UNEMPLOYED

As you've been reading about the emotional roller coaster associated with job loss and the job search process, I hope you've been thinking about what unemployed clients may need from a career counselor and how he or she can help them. In this section, I offer some general strategies to do just that. We then turn to a more specific discussion of how counselors can use technology and information resources to assist clients with the job search process.

Addressing Psychological Reactions to Job Loss and Unemployment

In terms of general strategies, it is important to begin by assessing all unemployed clients to determine where they are in the process delineated by Amundson and Borgen (1982). It is useful to gauge whether clients are in the grief process, have progressed to the job search stage, or are approaching the burnout phase. As you have surely surmised, unemployed clients often need far more than information and resources for conducting a job search.

If they come to you in the grief stage, for example, unemployed clients will benefit from attention to their emotional responses to job loss. You want to normalize their feelings, listen empathically, and allow time for them to experience the various stages of grief with you as a witness and for support. You also want to assess for more severe psychological reactions such as anxiety, depression, and even suicidal ideation. Failing to address grief reactions and instead pushing clients to begin a job search is likely to be ineffective and could inadvertently result in clients experiencing less success in achieving their goal of reemployment.

As clients emerge from the grief process and enter the job search stage, other forms of support will be needed. A comprehensive approach includes assistance with career development needs as well as support for the learning and use of job search skills (Donohue & Patton, 1998; Zikic & Klehe, 2006). Career development interventions should help clients:

- understand themselves as workers through the use of assessments,
- obtain and consider occupation and labor market information,
- explore career possibilities,
- make decisions about what types of jobs to seek, and
- develop an attitude of adaptability.

Interventions focused on job search skills should help clients:

- search for advertised job openings,
- develop and use networking skills to tap into the hidden job market,
- prepare application materials such as résumés and cover letters, and
- develop and hone their interviewing skills.

In addition to assisting clients with their career development needs and helping them build job search skills, counselors should also continue to provide empathic listening and emotional support. After all, it is important to help clients maintain their enthusiasm and hopefulness about their job search, modulate the yo-yo effect that can result from rejections, promote resilience, minimize discouragement, and avoid burnout.

When counseling clients who have reached the burnout stage, your goal is to revitalize their interest in searching for work. Doing so may require attention to their low self-efficacy beliefs and/or their negative outcome expectations (van Dam & Menting, 2012). Attending to perceived barriers, including discrimination and social justice issues, may also be important (Blustein, Medvide, & Wan, 2012). Fleig-Palmer et al. (2009) also recommended resiliency building activities especially for clients "who may be particularly vulnerable to additional challenges during the job search process" (p. 232).

In working with clients in any of these stages (grief, job search, or burnout), counselors should utilize both emotion-focused and problem-focused interventions (Eby & Buch, 1995; Haynie & Shepherd, 2010). In addition to doing this via individual counseling sessions, counselors may offer group counseling programs for the unemployed. One advantage is that the group members may offer each other social support.

Group Counseling Programs for the Unemployed

Group counseling for unemployed clients should also attend to clients' emotional reactions to unemployment rather than focusing exclusively on the dissemination of job search information. Research has borne out the importance of doing so. In a review of the most successful reemployment programs offered in group format, Saks (2005) reported that all the programs addressed psychological issues to some extent.

For example, Saks (2005) indicated that the Job Club program (Azrin & Besalel, 1980) has held up to empirical scrutiny over the years and that numerous research studies have found it to be among the most effective programs for helping people find jobs. In this program, clients "receive assistance in all areas of job search, including coping with discouragement, preparing résumés, obtaining and pursuing job leads, learning interviewing skills, scheduling time and record keeping, dress and grooming, and using the telephone for making inquiries and contacts" (Saks, 2005, p. 174). Although the Job Club program is primarily a behavioral, skill-building program, it also supports resilience by addressing ways to manage discouragement and to maintain motivation (Bhat, 2010).

Research has found that the JOBS Intervention Project (Caplan, Vinokur, Price, & van Ryn, 1989) is also quite effective in assisting unemployed people who are at high risk of developing depression not only with obtaining employment but also in achieving positive mental health outcomes (Vinokur, Price, & Schul, 1995). Although this group counseling program (Caplan et al., 1989) was "aimed specifically at enhancing job search skills, it also incorporated several components designed to enhance participants [sic] self-esteem and sense of control, job search self-efficacy, and inoculation against setbacks" (Vinokur et al., 1995, p. 40).

Murphey and Shillingford (2012) have also published information about an evidence-based approach to assisting unemployed clients. This particular program was designed for middle-age men and was organized around six "areas that research has shown to have a significant impact on unemployed men in particular" (Murphey and Shillingford, 2012, p. 85). Specifically, the group sessions are designed to help men with "expressing feelings; reducing depression, anger and anxiety; building social support; improving interpersonal communication; confronting unrealistic role expectations associated with the male gender; and providing an improved sense of control" (p. 85). When conducting these sessions, counselors offer emotional support, provide psychoeducation to build skills, and use a cognitive behavioral therapy approach to challenge irrational thoughts and problematic beliefs.

THE JOB SEARCH PROCESS

Thus far, this chapter has addressed the importance of understanding and attending to clients' psychological reactions to job loss and unemployment, and this may be achieved through the application of counseling skills in individual sessions as well as in counseling groups for the unemployed. It is my hope that you understand the importance of addressing the emotional needs of your unemployed clients and that you not simply serve as a disseminator of job search information. Even so, you will also need to be prepared to provide concrete assistance with the job search process. After all, a wonderfully compassionate counselor who can empathize with a client's reaction to job loss may be useless when it comes to helping that client find employment. Ideally, you should be prepared to do both: provide emotional support and provide psychoeducation and informational support for the job search process. It is essential that career counselors become aware of and skilled in using a wide variety of technology and information resources designed for this purpose.

Technology and Information Resources to Support Job Searches

This section focuses on the use of technology and information resources in the context of the job search process. Three types of clients will benefit from your knowledge of and skills in using these resources: (1) clients who have lost their jobs and are unemployed, (2) clients who have jobs but are looking for better jobs, and (3) clients who are nearing completion of their education and preparing to launch their careers.

All these clients may face the job search process with trepidation, and such worries are not necessarily irrational. The combination of an extended economic recession and the globalization of the workplace has resulted in significant challenges for job seekers. Within this milieu, career counselors are well positioned to play an important role in supporting clients through the job search process. To do so, it is essential that career counselors must be aware of and skilled in using a wide variety of technology and information resources designed for this purpose. The remainder of this chapter discusses several types of resources related to the job search process.

PREPARATION. Many of these informational resources pertain to the preparation of documents and other materials your clients will need to launch a successful job search. These documents should be tailored to your clients' specific employment goals. As a result, the first step of the job search process must be to clarify those goals.

Clarification of Goals. The first step of preparing for a job search is to clarify one's employment goals. Although many clients may initially indicate a willingness to take any job, chances are good that they have a specific type of position in mind. Also, the so-called spray and pray approach to job hunting simply doesn't work and results in an unnecessarily high rejection rate. Instead of taking this approach and sending résumés and applications for every posting found, clients will have a much more successful and tolerable experience with a targeted job search. To conduct such a search, though, clients must have a target at which to aim. Counselors should help clients identify the types of positions they want, the industries in which they would like to work, the employers for whom they would like to work, and the locations they are willing to consider. With these parameters in mind, clients are ready to develop a set of materials for use in the job search process and to tailor these materials to their targets.

Development of Job Search Materials. Before actually looking for job openings and submitting applications, clients should prepare a standard set of materials to be used in the application process. Typically, these materials include a résumé, cover letter, and list of references. It is also useful to prepare a document specifically designed for use in networking. Depending on the types of jobs a client is pursuing, other useful application materials may include a portfolio of work samples, a dossier of credentials, a set of recommendation letters, and a personal website featuring similar items. To support clients in preparing these materials, career counselors should stock their offices or career centers with psychoeducational handouts and books about these topics. If career counselors maintain a website, it is useful to include links to similar online materials.

Résumés. With the exception of clients who are seeking "unskilled, quick turnover" jobs, most employers require applicants to submit a résumé (U.S. Department of Labor, 2005b, p. 42). In preparation for a job search, therefore, most clients should develop a résumé. To help clients, career counselors should first assist them in identifying the content that will help them appear most qualified for the types of positions in which they are most interested.

Résumé content. Many counselors ask clients to complete a worksheet that asks for possible résumé content. Because all résumés should contain a common core of information consisting of the applicant's name, contact information, education, and employment history, these sections should all be included in a résumé worksheet. Résumé worksheets should also ask clients to provide information that is sometimes, but not always, included in résumés: for example, employment objective, military experience, honors or awards, licenses or other credentials, job-specific skills, and so on. With some clients, it will also be important to elicit information about their transferrable skills and employability skills. With ex-offenders who may question whether they have any skills, for instance, the U.S. Department of Labor (2005b) encourages development of a "background and experience list" and the consideration of the skills used even in hobbies (p. 36). For example, a hobby of playing sports may translate into the abilities to work as part of a team and to use basic arithmetic (as evidenced in scorekeeping); a hobby of repairing cars may translate into the ability to "diagnose mechanical problems" and to use tools (p. 36).

Next, counselors should help clients consider the skills and qualifications needed for the positions they want and examine the résumé worksheet to identify those skills and qualifications that the clients can accurately claim on a résumé. The goal of a résumé, of course, is to include and emphasize the content that will help clients demonstrate their qualifications for the types of positions in which they are most interested. Because the demands of different occupations and industries vary, it is acceptable for clients to develop two (or more) different résumés if they are interested in two very different types of positions. Each version must be truthful in its claims and must accurately reflect the client's education and experience, but the versions may vary with respect to the qualifications they emphasize.

Résumé format. After identifying the job goals and relevant content, career counselors can help clients think about the type of résumé that will likely serve them best. Three types of résumés are most commonly used: chronological, functional, and combination résumés (Curtis & Simons, 2004). The most common and generally most desirable type of résumé is chronological. Chronological résumés are generally divided into sections such as education, work experience, and so on, and the content within each section is organized in reverse chronological order. In other words, a person's most recent degree is listed first in the education section, and this is followed by the next most recent degree, and so on. The same holds true for experience, with a person's most recent job listed first, the next most recent job listed second, and so on. The sequencing of experiences is easily identifiable within chronological résumés, as are the specific positions an applicant has held, and the focus of chronological résumés is work experience. In contrast, a functional résumé is organized not to highlight a person's degrees or past jobs but rather to highlight transferrable skills. For any given skill the applicant wishes to highlight, the functional résumé provides details about pertinent education, work experience, and volunteer activities. Although these résumés also include sections on work experience and education, these sections are generally included at the end of the résumé. Generally speaking, a section with a title such as Skills and Accomplishments is the primary feature of functional résumés. Functional résumés tend to be most desirable for clients who have major gaps of time that would be unaccounted for on a résumé and that they wish to de-emphasize. However, because employers often react to functional résumés with an assumption that the candidate may have something to hide, career counselors should recommend them with caution. A combination résumé includes chronological and functional features. Curtis and Simons (2004) indicate that "the goal of the combination format is to showcase both a consistent employment record and a specific list of skills sets, incorporating a sound time frame to serve as the backbone of the résumé" (p. 27).

Résumé preparation. After selecting the most appropriate content and résumé format for a particular job search, clients are in a much better position to prepare the actual résumé. Clients have a choice between preparing the résumé themselves or paying someone else to do it. To support clients in preparing their own résumés, career counselors should have résumé-writing handouts and books available. For clients who may have great difficulty preparing their own résumé, using a résumé preparation service may be an attractive option. You may be surprised to know that there is a profession dedicated to résumé writing. The Professional Association of Resume Writers (parw.com) certifies individuals as Certified Professional Resume Writers (CPRWs).

High-Tech approaches to résumés. To assist clients in adding some flair to their résumés, career counselors may also wish to tap into newer technological approaches to résumé preparation. The standard résumé prepared on a PC is likely soon to seem as outdated as the résumé your grandparents prepared using a typewriter. As you review the high-tech trends in résumé development listed in Table 17.2, note those you have already incorporated into your own résumé. My guess is that at least a few of these high-tech trends will be new to you.

Many career centers purchase site licenses for online résumé writing programs and make these programs available for client use. Optimal Resume (optimalresume.com) and Visual CV (visualcv.com) are two examples. A note of caution: Clients must still take final responsibility for ensuring that the résumé is error-free, attractive, and easy to read even when using such snazzy programs. To assist them, many career counselors offer feedback on client résumés.

Another high-tech trend has developed in response to the increasing reliance employers place on applicant tracking systems (ATSs). An ATS is a computerized program that scans applicant résumés for key words. Only those résumés with a high enough match rate make it past the ATS and are read by human eyes. To increase the likelihood of résumés making it past the ATS, one strategy is to use white wording, which is the practice of adding a long list of possible key words (or even the complete job description included in the employer's posting) to a résumé in a very small, white font. When the résumé is printed out, these words do not appear (because they are in white font). They are recognized by the ATS, however, and result in more matches because of the chosen key words. A second strategy for getting past an ATS is to use an online program designed to maximize key words in a résumé. One such program is offered by Preptel and is called a Resumeter.

Career counselors should also be aware of some high-tech trends regarding contact information on résumés. Including a mailing address on a résumé is no

TABLE 17.2 High-Tech Trends in Résumé Development

Preparation
- Use of online programs such as OptimalResume.com and visualcv.com

Key Words and Applicant Tracking Systems
- Use of white wording
- Use of the Resumeter offered by Preptel.com to identify key words

Contact Information
- Elimination of mailing address (sole reliance on email address)
- Elimination of "old school" email addresses such as aol.com
- Elimination of fax numbers
- Elimination of multiple phone numbers (replaced with single, cell phone number)

Links to Supplemental Content
- Link to LinkedIn profile
- Link to Vizability.com business card
- Link to Web portfolio
- Quick response (QR) code
- Link to online elevator speech

longer required. Instead, it is now acceptable to include only an email address. Knowledge of this trend may benefit clients who are seeking positions in high-tech industries. Clients hoping to relocate may benefit from including only an email address because it may help them avoid being screened out due to geographic distance. Kursmark (2013) indicates that clients should also avoid using email addresses through older systems such as AOL and advises against including fax numbers because both could result in a perception that they are behind the times. A single telephone number is now preferred over the inclusion of multiple numbers for home, work, and cell phones.

An exciting high-tech trend in résumé development is the inclusion of links to supplemental content. In the past, potential employers have had access only to the written materials submitted by applicants. Now, however, technology has advanced to the point that resumes can contain links to additional content. Such links may provide employers with access to one's LinkedIn profile (to be discussed later in this chapter), a virtual business card highlighting specific Google links about oneself (vizability.com), a Web-based portfolio, or even a video-recording of a short introduction of the applicant. Another new trend is the inclusion of a scannable quick response (QR) code that also leads to supplemental content such as a LinkedIn Profile, web-based portfolio, video introduction of yourself, or video recommendation from a reference. Including such links on a résumé has two primary advantages. First, it provides potential employers with more information about you and your qualifications for the job you are seeking. Second, it demonstrates technological competence and an interest in staying on the cutting edge of new developments—two qualities generally desired by employers in any industry.

Example of a QR Code

Cover letters. Most clients applying for jobs should also develop a cover letter. The cover letter should accompany the résumé and, regardless of whether it will be printed out and mailed or sent electronically, it should be formatted as a formal business letter. I assume that you, as a prospective counselor, are well aware of how to write and format such letters. However, you should not assume that your clients know how to write these documents. Therefore, you should have materials available to support them in developing cover letters. Such materials generally identify each part of the letter (address, salutation, first paragraph, closing, etc.), share hints (e.g., addressing the letter to a specific person), and also provide sample letters.

Reference list. Helping clients create a reference list in preparation for a job search is also essential. Rather than listing the references on one's résumé, it is advisable to prepare a separate reference list. A header at the top of the page should be identical to the header used on the résumé, and the reference list should include each reference's name, job title, organization, work address, contact phone number, and email address. Generally speaking, a set of three professional references is sufficient. The selection of these individuals is critical and should be made in accordance with the following guidelines. First, each person on a client's reference list should be professional in nature. Friends and relatives are not acceptable as references, and it is far preferable to include current and/or former employers, supervisors, and instructors than it is to include clergy members, fitness instructors, and so forth. Second, each person listed as a reference should be willing and able to serve as a positive reference. To determine this, it is essential that clients make contact with each potential reference, communicate that they are launching a job search, and ask directly whether each person is willing to serve as a positive reference. Third, it is useful to provide each reference with materials to assist her or him in responding to any reference checks. At a minimum, these supporting materials should include a copy of one's current résumé. It may also be useful to include a brief summary of one's experiences working with the reference to remind her or him of the time frames during which you worked together, your accomplishments during that time, and so forth.

Once clients have completed their résumés, cover letter templates, and reference lists, they should convert these into portable document files (pdfs) to ensure that their formatting is retained when submitting materials electronically. With these materials in place, they will find it much easier to submit job applications.

Job applications. Some clients also benefit from psychoeducation regarding the proper completion of job applications. Many career counselors recommend that clients take the job applications with them, make a copy, and complete a first draft of the application on the copied version. Emphasis should be placed on legibility and neatness, correct spelling, carefully following directions, answering all items even if the only answer is "not applicable," and signing the application. Before completing applications online, a similar process should be used. In both cases, it is helpful to consult one's résumé to ensure consistency between the two documents.

Elevator speeches. First impressions count, and they often count a lot. When job searching, the opportunity to make a positive first impression may occur over the phone in a cold call, in an impromptu face-to-face encounter in an airport or elevator, or in the first few minutes of an interview. Rather than "winging it," clients will find that it pays to plan ahead to make a positive first impression. They should develop a short oral statement they can use to describe themselves and their goal quickly. Often referred to as an elevator speech or a 30-second commercial, this statement will be essential to your clients' ability to capture the listener's interest and prompt follow-up questions. Howell (2006) explained:

> An elevator speech is a short, pithy sentence or two that tells people, in a nutshell, what you do for a living. The catchy title "elevator speech" refers to the amount of time you have to generate interest with another person. For example, if you get on at the top floor of a forty-story building and ride down in an elevator nonstop to the lobby, it takes about twenty seconds. In that amount of time, you should be able to explain to another person—or a room full of people—what you or your business does. And if you do it well, what you say will engage your audience and prompt them to ask more questions. (p. ix)

Doing it well, of course, is the trick. Because this is easier said than done, it is helpful for career counselors to assist clients with the development of an elevator speech. It is essential that the speech deliver your client's "core message" (Pierson, 2006, p. 137) and that it be crafted effectively. With the idea that effectiveness is measured by the level of interest generated and the likelihood of the listener asking follow-up questions, Albertson (2008) offered examples of both good and bad openers. Instead of an accurate but uninteresting statement such as, "My name is Sharon. I sell life insurance and am a financial planner," (p. 2), Albertson recommends a much more intriguing statement such as, "I help middle-income families who struggle to save money reach the point where they can send their kids to college and also be prepared for a great retirement" (p. 3).

To help your clients develop effective elevator speeches, it will be useful for you to obtain and review written resources such as those offered by Albertson (2008), Howell (2006), and Sjodin (2012). It may also be helpful for you to search online for videos of elevator speeches. You will find many poor examples as well as some excellent ones. Some of the best examples were given at the elevator pitch competition sponsored by Wake Forest University (Mandel, 2013), where business school students from across the nation competed for a top prize of $30,000. You may want to try searching for elevator speeches given as part of this competition at (see 2012. elevatorcompetitionlive.com). It would be helpful for you to develop your own elevator speech. It will give you something to demonstrate for your clients as well as to use in your own upcoming job search.

Targeted opportunity profile. Although probably less familiar to you than résumés, cover letters, and reference lists, the targeted opportunity profile (TOP; Mathison & Finney, 2010, p. 136) is another document that may serve your clients particularly well during a job search. Some refer to TOPs as networking résumés, but Mathison and Finney describe them as un-résumés to highlight the very different purposes of these two documents. Whereas résumés are used to apply for jobs, TOPs are used to network with people who may have contacts at organizations, in industries, or with employers of interest or who may know of jobs in the hidden job market. Rather than being designed with the hope of getting an interview, the TOP is designed with the intention of equipping a networking contact with information about the type of position you are seeking, the skills you would bring to such a position, and a list of organizations at which you hope to get a job. The TOP is a professional document in which clients outline their job search game plan. When meeting with network contacts and conducting informational interviews, clients can provide the TOP to the individual with whom they are meeting and ask for recommendations of people to whom they might speak within their targeted industries and organizations.

Assisting Clients with Preparation of Job Search Materials. Clients vary in the level of assistance they need with regard to the preparation of application materials. Some may need the most basic education, including information about the various documents needed for a job search. Others may avail themselves of books and guides containing information about résumés, cover letters, and so forth. Still others may arrive at your office with polished documentation and need no assistance at all. To help the full range of clients, career counselors should acquire and become quite familiar with several resources related to job searching. Such resources are plentiful in bookstores and in exhibit halls at counseling association conferences. To remain current, counselors should consider attending conference sessions dedicated to topics such as résumé writing. Such sessions might introduce you to high-tech résumé techniques discussed earlier in this chapter, such as including a QR code at the top of a résumé (Kursmark, 2013), or establishing a professional social media presence.

Establishing a Professional Social Media Presence. Although there is no substitute for solid preparation and strong qualifications, job hunters who can harness the power of technology have a clear advantage over other similarly qualified applicants. In particular, the ability to use social media effectively is of paramount importance (Schepp & Schepp, 2010). As you will see in the following section, this requires much more than establishing a Facebook account or following celebrities on Twitter. Although some people equate social media with the recreational use of applications such as Facebook and Twitter, social media is a much broader entity. In the context of job hunting, it involves the management of one's digital footprint and the development of a personal brand using social media networks in order to develop a positive online reputation in one's field.

In the context of job searching, clients benefit most from social media outlets that allow for a high level of impression management. It is important to maximize the likelihood of social media searches resulting in positive impressions of your client because, regardless of whether your clients choose to use social media as part of their job search, it is becoming increasing common for employers to evaluate job applicants via social media (Strehlke, 2010). A digital footprint that makes a positive impression on potential employers increases the likelihood of job offers; a negative impression can result in "lost opportunities" (Strehlke, 2010, p. 38). Personal branding also allows for a focused impression on desired career direction and represents the ultimate in impression management.

Lorenz (2009) cited statistics indicating that "77 percent of recruiters run searches of candidates on the Web to screen applicants" and "35 percent say they've eliminated a candidate based on the information they uncovered" (para. 1). More recently, the television show *Top Recruiter TV* (2013) reported even stronger statistical evidence of the need for clients to consider the impact of their online profiles:

> According to a study commissioned by Microsoft, 79 percent of employers now conduct an online search of applicants. Fully 70 percent say they have turned down applicants by what they found online. However, only 7 percent of job applicants were concerned about their online reputations. (para. 1)

Because of statistics like these and the very real impact of digital footprints on job searches, Strehlke (2010) argued that it is important for contemporary career counselors to ask clients specifically about their online presence and their use of social media.

As a first step, therefore, it is important to encourage your clients to assess their current "digital footprint." To do so, clients should conduct Internet searches of their name using search engines such as Google and Bing and using social media outlets such as Facebook, Twitter, and LinkedIn. In conducting these searches, clients should ask themselves what type of impression the results might make on potential employers and whether these results would be more likely to "help or hinder" their job search (Strehlke, 2010, p. 43). Martin (2013) suggests several potential red flags that could result in lost employment opportunities, including search engine results that are unflattering, evidence that your client frequently complains and engages in negative conversations, content that an employer or the employer's customer base may find objectionable (including biased comments, inappropriate photos, and politically or religiously controversial statements), and even their association (e.g., liking something on Facebook) with a controversial cause or objectionable group.

Impression management lies at the heart of this inquiry. Once clients are aware of their current social media presence, they can determine whether it needs improvement, and they can identify strategies to present themselves more professionally. Aley (2013) offers tips, and her brief article may be quite a useful resource for your clients. Applications such as Reppler (reppler.com) and Brand Yourself (brandyourself.com) and professional companies such as Reputation.com are specifically designed to assist individuals with repairing undesirable online reputations. The goal is to have searches yield positive, professional results and either to eliminate or to push negative results so far down the list of search results that potential employers are unlikely to see them. This process is called search engine optimization (SEO), and the goal is to have only positive, professional results appear in the first three pages, for example, of a Google search (Richmond, Peters, & Woods, 2013).

The details of how to enhance one's professional social media presence are beyond the scope of this text. I encourage you to attend conference presentations and read books dedicated to this topic. Even so, it may be useful to know about some strategies for achieving this goal. Table 17.3 presents 10 strategies for enhancing one's online presence when preparing for a job search. As you review these strategies, consider ways in which you might use them in preparation for your own job search.

Although the list may be overwhelming, seriously consider implementing at least some of the strategies. At a minimum, establish your own LinkedIn profile. LinkedIn is the top way in which to enhance the likelihood of professional results from a Google search (Martinez-Moncada, 2012). This will assist you in establishing a professional presence of your own and prepare you to assist future clients in doing the same (Streufert & Richmond, 2013).

Preparation for Interviews. Clients may also benefit from psychoeducational materials and support related to the interview process. Most books, workbooks, and websites dedicated to the job search process give significant attention to the interview process. They tend to address a full range of topics, including proper attire, prompt arrival, interaction with the gatekeeper, management of anxiety, responding to difficult questions, responding to illegal questions, and so forth. Many of these materials also introduce readers to various types of interviews, including individual, group, and panel interviews; situational interviews; structured interviews; behavioral interviews; competency-based interviews; and stress interviews. Career counselors should therefore be certain that their bookshelves include such materials for use by clients wishing to prepare for the interview process. Examples of such resources include books by Martin (2012) and by DeLuca and DeLuca (2010), and websites such as best-job-interview.com and best-interview-strategies.com. All-encompassing job search websites such as The Riley Guide (rileyguide.com) and Quintessential Careers (quintcareers.com) also offer extensive information on job interviewing.

In addition to reading about the types of interviews and interview questions they may encounter, clients also benefit from practicing their interviewing skills. Levitt and Harwood (2010) reported that engaging in practice interviews results in as much as a 100% improvement in actual interview performance. To facilitate such practice, many career centers on college campuses offer mock interviews, which are generally conducted by staff members of the career center and are usually recorded. After the mock interview, the interviewer provides both positive and constructive feedback to the interviewee to promote more effective interviews in the future. In the absence of access to live mock interviewing, clients may also benefit from online practice interviews. Interview Stream (interviewstream.com) is a leading provider of online mock interviews. In addition to assisting clients in honing their interview skills, virtual mock interviews may also serve to reduce the anxiety many clients experience about job interviews (Rockawin, 2012).

TABLE 17.3 Top 10 Strategies for Enhancing Your Digital Footprint for Job Searching

Strategies	Social Media Platforms
1. Address content that may be viewed as negative, objectionable, or unprofessional.	
• Reevaluate and edit your profile information.	Facebook
• Remove all potentially objectionable photos, posts, likes, and associations with controversial groups.	Myspace
• Control access to your personal information and personal postings using privacy settings or codes.	
• Use privacy settings or codes to control your exposure via other peoples' postings and tags.	
• Remove your name from handles that you use for social purposes such as following celebrities and tweeting the details of your daily life.	Twitter
2. Add positive, professional content on social media sites traditionally used for more social purposes.	
• Join groups related to your profession.	Facebook
• Post updates regarding your professional activities.	Myspace
3. Establish and frequently use a Twitter account for professional purposes.	
• Include your name in your Twitter handle.	Twitter
• Include your resume keywords in your biographical information.	
• Follow professionals within your field.	
• Retweet professional tweets with which you want to be associated.	
• Post frequent, professional tweets of your own.	
• Include "follow me" and your Twitter handle on other social media accounts or postings.	
4. Establish and frequently use the professional networking site LinkedIn	
• Use of this site will have the largest impact on search engine optimization (SEO) and increase the likelihood of positive, professional results being yielded by Google searches.	LinkedIn
• Customize the URL for your public profile to include your name.	
• Include your résumé keywords in your profile.	
• Claim your skills and seek endorsements.	
• Ask supervisors and colleagues for recommendations.	
• Connect with professionals with whom you want to be associated.	
• Join groups in your profession and participate in discussions.	
5. Establish and frequently use other professional networking sites.	
• Use of these sites contributes to SEO and increases the likelihood of positive, professional results being yielded by Google searches.	Ryze
	Xing
• Zerply has especially strong impact on SEO.	Zerply
6. Use blogs to enhance your professional reputation.	
• Develop and frequently contribute to your own blog.	Blogger
• Serve as a guest author on others' blogs.	Tumblr
• Keep your postings professional and use them to highlight areas of expertise.	WordPress
• WordPress blogs have especially strong impact on SEO.	

(Continued)

TABLE 17.3 Top 10 Strategies for Enhancing Your Digital Footprint for Job Searching (*Continued*)

Strategies	Social Media Platforms
7. Use personal websites to enhance your professional reputation.	
• Establish a website with your name in the domain title.	Weebly
• Populate this website with content related to and featuring your areas of expertise.	Wix
• Include links to your other social media accounts (Twitter, LinkedIn, Facebook, blogs, etc.).	
8. Contribute to collaborative content sites.	
• Use your expertise to contribute postings to this question-and-answer style website.	Quora
• Submit blogged articles and other content to this site. If your submission is voted up and highly rated, this will enhance your online footprint.	Reddit
• Produce and post videos addressing areas of your professional expertise.	Vimeo
	YouTube
• Seek opportunities to contribute to entries about which you have expertise.	Wikipedia
9. Use social media sites dedicated to the management and enhancement of online reputation.	
• BrandYourself and Google+ have especially strong impact on SEO for Google searches.	About me
	BrandYourself
	Google+
	Klout
	Reppler.com
	Reputation.com
10. Use strategies to synthesize and manage your contacts across multiple social media applications.	Plaxo

Source: Based in part on Richmond, Peters & Woods (2013).

IMPLEMENTATION. Once your clients have clarified their employment goals, prepared a set of standard documents for use in the application process, optimized their online reputation, and honed their interviewing skills, they are ready to implement their job search. Tasks involved in the implementation of a job search include the identification of employment opportunities, the initiation of contact with employers, and management activities. Although this section addresses these tasks separately, they are not sequential in nature. Instead, clients are involved in all three tasks simultaneously throughout the job search process.

Identification of Employment Opportunities. An important part of implementing a job search is to invest considerable time in searching for employment opportunities. Clients should target two types of employment opportunities: (1) those posted as open positions and (2) those not posted as open positions. To be of optimal assistance to clients during their job search, career counselors should be well versed in both approaches to finding job leads.

Searching for posted positions. Posted positions include those advertised in the classified section of newspapers, listed by state-operated employment offices, identified as employment opportunities on employer websites, and listed online at job search websites. Obviously, career counselors should be equipped with handouts and information about various places their clients may find postings for open positions. As shown in Table 17.4, these job search sources are quite varied and range from state employment agencies to executive headhunter firms, from the want ads in a local newspaper to national, Web-based job banks.

TABLE 17.4 Job Search Sources for Posted Positions

Source	Examples
General Listings	
Newspaper classified section	Want ads
Government-operated employment offices	State employment security agencies
	One-stop centers
	Career One Stop
Electronic job banks and Web-based information about employers	CareerBuilder.com
	FlipDog.com
	GlassDoor.com
	Hotjobs.com
	Indeed.com
	LinkedUp.com
	Monster.com
	Quintcareers.com
	RileyGuide.com
	SimplyHired.com
Employment Agencies and Recruiting Firms	
Private employment and staffing agencies	Adecco Group
	Experis
	Kelly Services
	Manpower Group
Executive search and recruiting firms	Day & Associates
	Lonergan Partners
	Rice Cohen International
Employer- or Industry-Specific Sources	
Trade and professional associations and publications	American Society of Safety Engineers
	Chronicle of Higher Education
	Forbes
	UnionJobs.com
Corporate career centers	Cigna (careers.cigna.com)
	Procter and Gamble (pg.com/careers)
	Whirlpool (whirlpoolcareers.com)
Federal job agencies	USAJobs
	Federal Jobs Net
	Federal Career Central
Sources for Special Populations	
Employment agencies for people reflecting diversity	DiversityJobs.com
	Hire Diversity
	iHispano.com
	JewishJobs.com

(Continued)

TABLE 17.4 Job Search Sources for Posted Positions (*Continued*)

Source	Examples
Employment agencies for people reflecting diversity (continued)	LGBT CareerLink
	Urban League Jobs Network
	Workforce50.com
Employment agencies for people with disabilities	ABILITY Jobs
	Big Tent Jobs
	Hire Disability Solutions
Employment agencies for veterans	Hero 2 Hired (H2H)
	Military OneSource
	TurboTAP
Employment agencies for ex-offenders	ExOffenderReentry.com
	Federal Bonding Program
	National H.I.R.E. Network
Sources for Job Leads Outside the United States	
Job banks for international jobs	Antal International
	Giga Job
	OverseasJobs.com

Career counselors should also be prepared to assist clients in identifying employment opportunities that are not posted on sites such as those listed in Table 17.4. All of the jobs on those sites are advertised as open. This is a good place to start, and clients should certainly be encouraged to search for job leads using such resources. It is estimated, however, that 70% to 95% of all hiring is for positions that are *not* posted but accessed via the hidden job market (Lindgren, 1995; Lock, 2005; Mathison & Finney, 2010).

Networking to identify opportunities in the hidden job market. The hidden job market consists of employment opportunities that have not yet been posted or "advertised to the general public" (Lock, 2005, p. 14) as well as those that an employer might create to hire a specific individual who has the skills to meet his or her needs. Because the majority of job openings are filled before they are advertised, clients who focus their job search exclusively on responding to posted leads are limiting themselves unnecessarily. Career counselors should therefore help their job-seeking clients understand that the process of identifying employment opportunities includes not only searching for posted positions but also seeking opportunities within the hidden job market.

Finding such opportunities requires clients to network with people who already work in the industry where clients hope to find employment. Even better, clients should target specific employers for whom they would like to work and focus their efforts on identifying people to contact within those organizations. Networking is the name of the game when it comes to identifying employment opportunities in the hidden job market. This networking may be limited to telephone and face-to-face meetings or may be enhanced with communication via email and social media.

One way to network effectively for the purpose of finding job leads is to conduct informational interviews. The goal of such interviews is to identify people associated with a specific employer or within a given industry whom the client may contact as part of the job search. Let's say, for instance, that you have an interest in finding a job as a college counselor. More specifically, you want a job in a career center at a college in the Southwest. You live and go to school in Maine, however, and your network of first-degree contacts is limited to the northeast part of the country. Armed with a TOP summarizing your employment goals, qualifications, and the names of the employers you most want to work for, you may begin scheduling informational interviews with the counselors who work at your college. In scheduling these interviews, you make it clear that you are looking for advice for your job search rather than hoping to be hired by the career center at your college.

One of these interviews is with Jane Doe, a career counselor at your college with whom you conducted a career counseling group as part of your practicum experience. As shown in Figure 17.2, Jane Doe is considered a first-degree connection because you know her. When you meet with Jane, you present your TOP to her; explain your employment goal; briefly describe your training and qualifications; and identify the geographic region, industry, and employers for whom you would like to work. You then ask Jane whether she knows of any such job openings and also ask if she knows of anyone else you could contact to assist you in gaining the type of employment you are seeking. Jane responds by indicating that she doesn't know anyone who currently works at a university in the Southwest. However, she does know someone, Jim Smith, who used to work as a college counselor in Arizona. She gives you contact information for Jim Smith and explains that Jim moved from Arizona to Maine and works across town at another college.

As shown in Figure 17.2, Jim is considered a second-degree connection for you and he is a first-degree connection for Jane. You follow up and contact Jim, indicating that Jane Doe suggested that you meet with him. He schedules a meeting, and you are delighted when he tells you that he knows of a university in Arizona that is looking to hire career counselors. He provides you with the name of Bill Johnson, who is a third-degree connection to you. You are now in a position to contact Mr. Johnson directly and indicate that you were referred to him by a former colleague whom he respects. Your application is more likely to get a look, and the fact that you come recommended by someone Mr. Johnson knows increases your likelihood of getting an interview. Making such contacts represents the next step in implementing your job search plan.

Initiation of Contact. After identifying employment opportunities, clients need to initiate contact with the employers. The substance of this contact may involve inquiries about openings as well as submission of application materials, and the format of this contact may involve telephone calls, in-person visits, correspondence by mail or email, and online applications. To support clients as they initiate such contact, counselors may provide psychoeducation materials (e.g., scripts for phone calls). Counselors should also assist clients in understanding the importance of personalizing their documents each time they apply for a job. For example, although clients develop a cover letter during the preparation stage, it is important that they personalize the cover letter each time they apply for a job.

Management Activities. Career counselors should also provide clients with guidance regarding effective management of their job search process. Management of the job search process consists of (a) engaging in job search activities, (b) record keeping, and (c) addressing emotional needs related to the job search process.

Engaging in job search activities. A central task in managing the job search process is to engage continually and persistently in job search activities, including searching for job postings, networking to identify employment opportunities in the hidden job market, personalizing and submitting application materials, following up on applications already submitted, and attending interviews. Although the saying has become somewhat cliché, job searching is a full-time job (Balderrama, 2009).

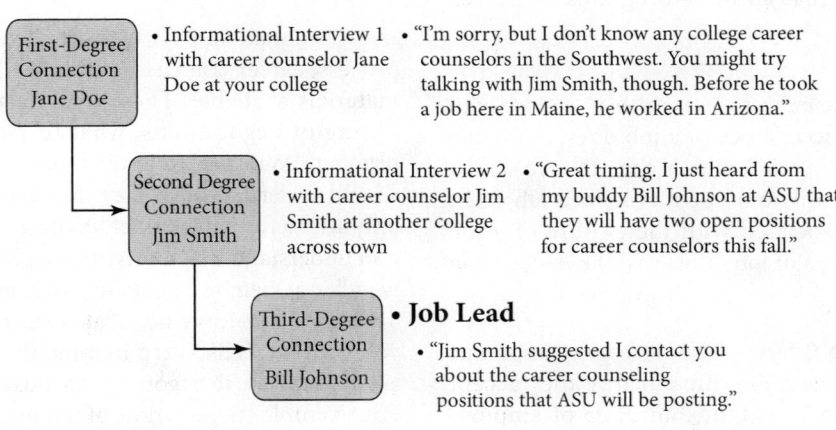

FIGURE 17.2 Networking

Counselors should help unemployed clients understand the importance of dedicating 40 hours per week toward their job search and encourage them to establish a weekly schedule for their job search activities. The schedule provides structure to job search activities and increases the likelihood that clients will allocate time to these activities.

Record keeping. Another important element in managing the job search process involves record keeping. Career counselors should teach their clients how to develop a record-keeping system in order to track all activities related to their job search. Tracking job search activities allows your clients to keep track of the jobs they have applied for, the application materials they have submitted, the networking they have done, the people they have contacted, and the interviews they have completed. A variety of free resources are available for this purpose. For example, Microsoft Word offers a free Excel template designed for job searching. The state of Minnesota (http://mn.gov/deed/job-seekers/) offers a variety of materials designed to manage the job search process (Minnesota Department of Employment and Economic Development, 2014). Web-based applications such as JibberJobber.com offer programs for the management of the job search process.

Addressing emotional needs. Because the job search process can be fraught with emotional ups and downs, it is also important to recognize that managing the job search process requires attention to emotional needs that arise. As trained professional counselors, career counselors are able to address their clients' emotional needs effectively during sessions. Clients may also benefit from participating in group counseling programs. Several reemployment programs are offered in a group format, and Saks (2005) reported that all these programs addressed psychological issues to some extent.

CLOSURE. The job search process comes to a close with a client's receipt and acceptance of a job offer. Although receipt of a job offer is often a client's goal, the job search process doesn't end until your client accepts a job offer. The primary tasks associated with the closure of a job search are the evaluation of job offers and the negotiation of terms.

Evaluation of Job Offers. Even if feeling desperate, all clients should evaluate job offers before they accept them. Once an employer extends an offer of employment, the client has an opportunity to ask for any additional information needed to make an informed decision about whether to accept the job offer. At a minimum, clients need to understand some specific information about the job offer. This minimal information includes the starting hourly wage or annual salary, the benefits package (e.g., health care, dental and vision coverage, life insurance, vacation time), the date and time the client would be expected to start work, the hours and location of the job, and the duties of the position being offered (Stebleton & Henle, 2011). Clients should also ask for the opportunity to review any agreements or contracts they need to sign as a condition of employment. Careful attention should be paid to contractual language as well as arbitration agreements, noncompetition agreements, and nondisclosure agreements (Lock, 2005). Before accepting any job offer, even verbally, clients should evaluate these documents and may even choose to have them reviewed by an attorney.

Other factors worth considering include the fit between the job and one's skills, interests, values, and career goals; advancement potential; the nature and culture of the employing organization; the employer's supervision and management philosophy; and pragmatic issues such as location and commuting time. To support clients in this process, career counselors may once again recommend technology and information resources. For example, Lock's (2005) book on job searching provides a questionnaire that clients may use to evaluate a single job offer as well as a decision matrix for use in choosing from among multiple job offers. If your client is considering a job requiring relocation, it will also be helpful to use a cost-of-living calculator to evaluate the salary being offered against the cost of living where the job is located.

Once your clients understand the details of a job offer, they may choose to accept the offer, reject the offer, or engage in a negotiation process.

Negotiation. To support clients in the negotiation process, career counselors should have psychoeducation materials available. These materials should address the timing of negotiations, what to negotiate, and how to negotiate. With regard to the timing of negotiations, clients should understand that they should begin discussing terms only after a formal job offer has been received. They should also understand that salary, although obviously important, is only one item to negotiate (Nielson, 2008). As shown in Table 17.5, one may negotiate over many other items. As you review this list, keep in mind that exactly which items are appropriate to negotiate depends on a variety of factors. For example, negotiation of some of the items, such as severance packages and company cars, will be appropriate only for some high-level positions.

TABLE 17.5 Negotiating a Job Offer

Negotiable Items	Examples
Financial compensation	• Starting salary or hourly wage • Conditions for future raises • Signing bonuses • Stock options • Severance packages • Retirement contributions
Health care benefits	• Health care coverage • Dental care coverage • Vision care coverage • Long-term health care coverage • Life insurance • Sick leave
Work schedule	• Start date • Vacation time • Flexible scheduling options • Telecommuting options • Reduced workload at beginning
Equipment	• Computer and related equipment • Software applications • Phone • Company car • Other work-related equipment
Continuing education	• Training • Memberships in professional associations • Conference expenses • Tuition reimbursement
Relocation	• Relocation expenses • Cost of living adjustment • Placement assistance for spouse/partner

Source: Based on Nielson, Troy, Career Trek: *The Journey Begins,* 1st Ed., © 2008, pp. 131–132. Reprinted and electronically reproduced by permission of Pearson Education, Inc. Upper Saddle River, New Jersey.

It is especially important to support clients while they negotiate starting salary or hourly wages because this process will have long-term ramifications for future raises (Stebleton & Henle, 2011). Coming full circle from the beginning of this chapter, occupational and labor market information are particularly useful at this point. Career counselors can assist clients in researching the wage ranges and median salaries for the position they are offered and the industry in which they will be working. Similar to the practice of determining *Kelley's Blue Book* value prior to finalizing the purchase of a car, this information allows clients to determine a realistic sense of their worth and provide data for use in the negotiation process. If an employing organization is unionized, clients should also be encouraged to contact a union representative to inquire about whether a job offer is acceptable. If an employing organization is a public institution, salary information for all employees is a matter of public record and clients should be encouraged to seek this information as part of the negotiation process. If a client wishes to negotiate a salary that will be higher than average, the client should be prepared with a list of reasons to justify the higher level of financial compensation.

Once a final offer of employment has been extended and accepted by a client, the client will be wise to write a formal letter of acceptance. In this letter, the client should thank the employer for the offer, clarify details that were negotiated, directly communicate acceptance of the offer, and convey enthusiasm about starting employment. A formal letter of acceptance marks the beginning of and sets the tone for an employee's future relationship with her or his new employer. Thus, clients should conduct themselves professionally throughout the negotiation and hiring process.

PUTTING IT ALL TOGETHER

Table 17.6 provides a review of the technology and information resources to use in the job search process. In preparation for the job search, clients should clarify their goals, develop a wide range of materials, consider ways to manage the impact of their digital footprint and to establish a more professional online presence, and hone their interviewing skills. A variety of technological and print resources are available for use in identifying employment opportunities, initiating contact with potential employers, and managing one's job search activities. Clients will benefit from psychoeducation materials regarding the evaluation and negotiation of job offers.

TABLE 17.6 Job Search Process

Stage	Tasks	Examples
Preparation	Clarification of goals	• Position • Industry • Employers • Location
	Development of materials	• Résumé • Cover letter • Reference list • Job applications • Elevator speech • Targeted opportunity profile
	Establishment of a professional social media presence	• Assessment of digital footprint • Impression management • Personal branding • Search engine optimization • Online networking
	Preparation for interviews	• Psychoeducation • Mock interviews
Implementation	Identification of employment opportunities	• Posted positions • Networking to identify opportunities in the hidden job market
	Initiation of contact	• Telephone calls • In-person visits • Correspondence by mail • Correspondence by email • Online applications
	Management activities	• Job Search Activities • Record Keeping • Emotional Needs

Stage	Tasks	Examples
Closure	Evaluation of job offers	• Accept • Reject • Negotiate
	Negotiation	• Financial compensation • Health care benefits • Work schedule • Equipment • Continuing education • Relocation

TABLE 17.6 Job Search Process (*Continued*)

CHAPTER 18

Adult Career Transitions and Specific Populations

The career counseling emphasis in educational settings is on career path selection, planning, preparation, and launching, but career counseling in community settings tends to have a much different focus. Instead of having an aspirational, future-oriented focus, career services in the community setting tend to be more pragmatic and focused on present-day needs. Chapter 17 focused on three types of pragmatic concern often addressed in community settings: job loss, unemployment, and job searching. This chapter builds on the material presented in Chapter 17 and explores other career challenges commonly addressed in community settings. As you will learn in this chapter, most career concerns addressed within community settings involve adult career transitions.

ADULT CAREER TRANSITIONS

As we discuss a variety of career challenges presented by specific populations in the community setting, it will be helpful for you to think about them in the context of transitions. Although transitions can be thought of in general terms as changes, a more specific definition may be useful. Drawing on Schlossberg's (1981) early writings about human adaptation to transitions, Anderson, Goodman, and Schlossberg (2012) defined a transition as "any event or nonevent that results in changed relationships, routines, assumptions, and roles" (p. 39). Many career changes, of course, fall within the scope of this definition because they involve a change in roles (e.g., from worker to nonworker or from worker at one job to worker at another job), a change in routines (e.g., whether your daily routine includes going to work or a change in the nature of your work responsibilities), a change in relationships (e.g., if and how you continue to interact with previous coworkers), and a change in assumptions (e.g., such as an assumption that you would hold a given job until retirement).

Transition Factors

Transitions may be experienced as positive or negative, and a variety of factors affect how easy or difficult any given transition is for an individual. These factors are described in the paragraphs below and also summarized in Table 18.1. Counselors should consider these factors in order to understand the potential impact of career transitions on their clients.

First, it is useful to understand the precursors to the transition. For example, it is useful to know how satisfied clients were with their previous job, career, or life role (Latack & Dozier, 1986). It is also useful to understand how central this previous role was to their sense of personal identity. As Haynie and Shepherd (2010) explained, "for an individual whose conception of self is strongly informed by his or her career, the termination of that career threatens self-identity and generates feelings of alienation, hopelessness, and despair" (p. 509). In addition to considering

TABLE 18.1 Factors in Adult Career Transitions

Precursors to the transition
- Degree of satisfaction with previous job, career, or life role
- Centrality of previous job, career, or life role to sense of personal identity
- Cultural and contextual background
- Current life context

Precipitants to the transition
- Trigger that prompted the transition
- Degree of choice (voluntary versus involuntary)
- Degree to which transition was foreseen (anticipated versus unanticipated)

Temporal issues
- Age (predictable versus unusual point in life span)
- Nature of onset (sudden versus gradual)
- Time constraints/sense of urgency
- Phase of transition process (moving out, moving through, moving in)

Impact of transition
- On roles, relationships, routines, and assumptions
- On psychological functioning and emotional well-being
- On self-image and self-efficacy
- On capacity for subsistence

Coping resources/capital
- Economic capital (financial resources)
- Human capital (education, experience, occupation-specific and transferrable skills)
- Social capital (relational supports, professional contacts, networking capacity)
- Psychological capital (self-efficacy, hopefulness, resilience)

---

precursors such as satisfaction and role centrality, it is also important to consider cultural/contextual background and current life context as precursors that affect the nature of a client's response to transitions (Fouad & Bynner, 2008). For example, how is a given career transition interpreted in the context of a client's culture? What else is going on in the client's life? Other life circumstances such as being in the process of a divorce or facing foreclosure can affect a client's experience of a transition.

Second, it is helpful to understand the precipitants to the transition. A priority, of course, is to understand what happened or could happen to prompt the transition. In addition to identifying this trigger, it is useful to think about whether the transition was voluntary or involuntary (Fouad & Bynner, 2008; Hopson & Adams, 1977) and whether the transition was anticipated or unanticipated (Schlossberg, 1981). As you examine Figure 18.1, think about the types of transitions that might fall within each quadrant and consider the implications of these factors on the challenges a client might experience in response to a career transition. Job loss, of course, would fall in the involuntary column. Notice, though, that it could be anticipated or unanticipated. Wayne, for example, one of the clients from Chapter 1, decided to seek career services in anticipation of a potential, involuntary job loss. In contrast,

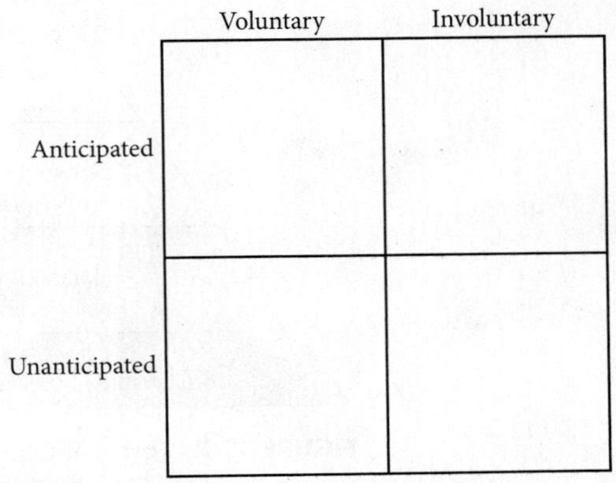

FIGURE 18.1 Precipitants for Career Transitions

Doris was fired unexpectedly; although her termination might have been foreseeable by some, Doris had not anticipated it. As you can imagine, the degree to which a career transition is chosen and the degree to which advance planning is possible can have tremendous effects on a client's experience of the transition and on his or her needs in the counseling process.

Third, it is important to consider temporal issues related to the transition. Temporal considerations include a client's age (Latack & Dozier, 1986), whether the transition occurs at a predictable time in the life span (Schlossberg, 1981), whether it came about suddenly or gradually, and whether the client has any time constraints or sense of urgency for completing the transition. It is also useful to consider where the client is in the transition process. Has the client come for services in anticipation (like Wayne) or consideration (like Gillian) of a change? Has the client only recently learned of an impending transition? Or has the client completed the transition (e.g., moved from one job to another) but is experiencing adjustment difficulties? In their integrative model of the transition process, Anderson et al. (2012) refer to these temporal phases as moving out, moving through, and moving in.

Fourth, it is also helpful to understand the impact of the transition on clients. Some of this depends, of course, on temporal issues and the precipitants for the transition (Figure 18.1). Schlossberg (2011) noted that even voluntary, anticipated career transitions can result in significant stress for clients. She argued, therefore, that "it is not the transition per se that is critical, but how much it alters one's roles, relationships, routines, and assumptions" (p. 159). In addition to considering the impact of a career transition on these factors, it is also important to understand the transition's impact on psychological functioning, emotional well-being, self-image, self-efficacy, and capacity for subsistence. Is the client suicidal, depressed, or anxious? How has the transition affected the client's self-perceptions? And, very important, is the client in need of referral to other community resources to address subsistence needs for food and shelter?

Fifth, it is important to consider the coping resources available to clients who are experiencing career transitions. These coping resources may be internal or external and can be conceptualized in accordance with the idea of capital. Luthans, Luthans, and Luthans (2004) developed a model to conceptualize various forms of capital. Although Luthans et al. initially developed their model for application in organizational settings, aspects of it have since been applied to career counseling (Fleig-Palmer, Luthans, & Mandernach, 2009). This model is shown in Figure 18.2 and features four types of capital.

Economic capital involves a client's current financial resources. Lakeesha, for example, has $100,000 from her husband's life insurance policy. In contrast, Juan has no savings whatsoever and has been living paycheck to paycheck. In the context of career transitions, human capital involves the personal assets a client can offer potential employers. This includes assets such as one's level and type of education, occupationally specific knowledge and skills, broader employability skills, and relevant occupational experience. Such assets are generally featured on a client's résumé. However, a successful job search doesn't depend

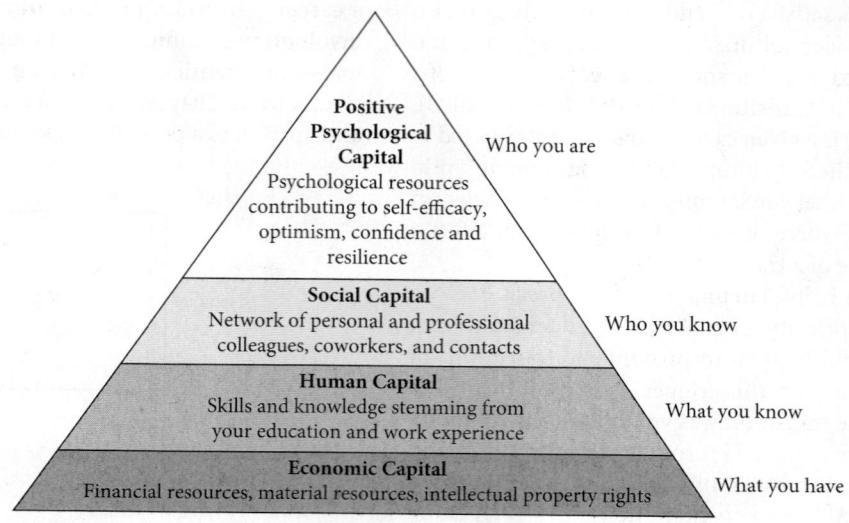

FIGURE 18.2 Forms of Capital
Source: Based on Luthans, F., Luthans, K. W., & Luthans, B. C. (2004). Positive psychological capital: Beyond human and social capital. *Business Horizons, 47,* 45–50.

only on what a client knows and can to offer an employer. As the saying goes, "it isn't only what you know but who you know." This reality is captured in the category of social capital. Supportive relationships serve as social capital, especially in times of need. Recall that Doris lacked these relationships and felt a lack of support even in her marriage, whereas Lakeesha received wonderful support from the women at her church. In addition to supportive relationships, social capital may include a network of professional contacts—people to whom one might reach out for assistance in finding work. A fair amount of research points to the importance of addressing social capital issues such as networking when assisting minority clients with their career development (Ao, 2007; Smith, 2005). It is helpful for career counselors to assist clients in recognizing and accessing the social capital they already have through networking activities and in further developing relationships to build additional social capital. The fourth and final category of capital articulated by Luthans et al. (2004) involves positive psychological capital. This consists of self-efficacy, hopefulness, and resilience, which they defined as "the capacity to 'bounce back' from adversity" (p. 47). Interventions to improve clients' levels of self-efficacy—about themselves in general, their work-related abilities, and themselves as job seekers—will be an important element of your work with clients. Encouraging clients to remain hopeful and persistent in their job searching is also necessary. Interventions to help clients build resilience will also be beneficial (Fleig-Palmer et al., 2009).

Types of Career Transitions

TRANSITIONS INVOLVING JOB LOSS AND UNEMPLOYMENT. An obvious example of career transitions frequently addressed in community settings is job loss. Because job loss and unemployment are, by far, the most common career issues addressed in community settings, especially in one-stop career centers (U.S. Department of Labor, 2013b), Chapter 17 was dedicated addressing these kinds of transition in great detail. It described the psychological reactions that often follow job loss as well as strategies for supporting clients through this transition and through the job search process. Although job loss is certainly a major reason for unemployment, clients may find themselves unemployed for other reasons and need assistance in finding work. Many of these clients face transition-related challenges involving complications in entering or reentering the workforce.

TRANSITIONS INVOLVING COMPLICATED ENTRY OR REENTRY. In an ideal world, there is a job for every person, a person for every job, and an opening for every job seeker. In our career development version of the American Dream, we teach our youth to be good students and to engage in the career exploration, planning, and preparation needed to enter the workforce and find a good job when they are ready. We assume that they will find jobs once they reach adulthood and complete whatever postsecondary education is needed to achieve their career goals. We assume that they will stay in the workforce until they retire or, in the event of job loss, they will reenter the workforce as soon as possible.

These assumptions, of course, are out of touch with reality. First, entry into the workforce isn't always so smooth. People who are ready to transition into the workforce for the first time may experience great difficulty doing so. Second, some people leave the workforce either voluntarily or involuntarily and later seek to rejoin it. Doing so, however, may not be easy. Career counseling may benefit clients who, for one reason or another, experience complications in entering or reentering the workforce. Moving from this abstract level of conceptualization, let's consider some concrete examples.

SPECIFIC POPULATIONS AND THEIR CAREER SERVICE NEEDS IN COMMUNITY SETTINGS

The majority of challenges addressed by career counselors in the community setting involve transitions related to unemployment and/or complicated entry or reentry, and a wide variety of specific populations tend to seek career services for assistance with these transitions. These subpopulations include people with disabilities, military veterans preparing to enter or reenter the civilian workforce, ex-offenders preparing to enter or reenter the workforce following incarceration, and homemakers or caretakers who are entering or reentering the workforce. Although people may seek career services in the community setting for many other reasons, this chapter focuses on these specific populations.

THE FINE PRINT

The information you are about to read about each of these specific populations is but a metaphoric drop in the bucket. Entire chapters and books have been dedicated to the career development concerns and appropriate career services for each of these groups. This section is intended only as an introduction and is offered with the hope that you will seek additional resources as you begin working with clients from each of these subpopulations.

PEOPLE WITH DISABILITIES

People with disabilities may experience unemployment due to transitional challenges in entering or reentering the workforce. For example, people with lifelong disabilities may face difficulties transitioning from educational settings into the workforce. Additionally, as in Juan's case, people who acquire a disability may find themselves unable to continue in their chosen occupation and may struggle with the transition process involved in moving out of their previous occupation, moving through the process of adjusting to their acquired disability and identifying a desirable and realistic new career path to pursue, and moving into a new occupation in that path (Anderson et al., 2012).

Factors related to these challenges were discussed in Chapter 6 in the context of culture and in Chapter 14 in the context of developing transition plans to prepare K–12 students with disabilities for postsecondary education and/or employment. Because many counselors in community settings will have clients whose disabilities affect them in the world of work and because numerous agencies and programs in the community setting are specifically designed to address the needs of people with disabilities, a discussion in this chapter is also warranted. To avoid replication, this chapter's coverage of people with disabilities focuses on employment statistics, employment challenges, and the career service needs of clients with disabilities.

Employment Statistics

As shown in Table 18.2, the Bureau of Labor Statistics (U.S. Bureau of Labor Statistics, 2012c) estimates that approximately 15 million persons with a disability between the ages of 16 and 64 are living in the United States within the civilian noninstitutional population. Of course, there are people with disabilities who are 65 or older, as well as people living in institutional settings because of chronic and/or severe disabilities. The BLS focuses exclusively on the noninstitutional population, however, because only those people living within the noninstitutional population are available for employment.

Of these 15 million people with a disability, only 4.8 million people indicate that they want a job and, if not employed, had looked for a job in the past year. This translates to a 32.2% participation rate in the labor force for persons with a disability. In comparison, there is a 76.9%

TABLE 18.2 Disability and Employment Statistics for People Age 16 to 64 Years

	Persons with a Disability	Persons with No Disability
Raw numbers		
Civilian noninstitutional population	15,047,000	184,842,000
Not in labor force	10,192,000	43,192,000
In labor force	4,854,000	141,650,000
Employed	4,067,000	129,155,000
Full-time	2,887,000	105,784,000
Part-time	1,180,000	23,371,000
Unemployed	787,000	12,495,000
Percentage rates		
Rate of participation in labor force[*]	32.2%	76.6%
Employment–population ratio[†]	27.0%	69.9%
Part-time employment rate[‡]	29.0%	18.0%
Unemployment rate[§]	16.2%	8.8%

Source: Based on U.S. Bureau of Labor Statistics. (2012). Persons with a disability: Labor force characteristics –2011. Retrieved May 11, 2013 from http://www.bls.gov/news.release/pdf/disabl.pdf
[*]Participation rate = number in labor force divided by civilian noninstitutional population.
[†]Employment–population rate = number employed divided by civilian noninstitutional population.
[‡]Part-time employment rate = number employed part-time divided by number employed.
[§]Unemployment rate = number unemployed divided by number in labor force.

participation rate in the labor force for persons with no disability. Of the 4.8 million people with a disability who indicate that they want a job, only 4.1 million have jobs: an unemployment rate of 16.2% for persons with a disability. In comparison, the unemployment rate for persons with no disability was 8.8%. Among those who are employed, 29.0% of persons with a disability are employed part-time (less than 35 hours per week), whereas only 18% of persons with no disability are employed part-time (U.S. Bureau of Labor Statistics, 2012d).

What does all this mean? In short, persons with a disability are 2.4 times less likely as persons with no disability to participate in the labor force and 2.6 times less likely to be employed. When they are employed, persons with a disability are nearly twice as likely to be employed part-time. The contrast between the unemployment rates of 16.2% and 8.8% for persons with and without a disability, respectively, make it patently clearly that people with disabilities face challenges related to gaining and maintaining employment.

Employment Challenges

Because disabilities involve some sort of functional impairment, it should be evident that one employment challenge faced by people with disabilities relates to the performance of activities required by some jobs. In Juan's case, for example, he now has a disability that prevents him from engaging in the heavy physical labor he once did in his construction job. The assessment of areas of ability, disability, and functional impairment is therefore a very important part of career counseling with clients who have disabilities (Flansburg, 2011; Parker & Bolton, 2005; Ryan, 2011; Witt, 1992). Although areas of ability, disability, and functional impairment are clearly very important for unemployed clients with disabilities, they are not the only employment challenges faced by people with disabilities. To be effective as career counselors, we must recognize and attend to more than just these clients' actual abilities and disabilities. The same is true, of course, when providing career counseling to any client. Specifically, we must also attend to our clients' emotional and psychological needs, cognitive factors such as self-efficacy, and contextual issues such as barriers and opportunity structure whenever engaging in career counseling. In each of these areas, clients with disabilities have some specific vulnerabilities that may affect them in a job search.

Helping Strategies

VOCATIONAL REHABILITATION COUNSELING. Although any professional counselor may have the opportunity to provide career services to people with disabilities, an entire specialization is dedicated to this area. This specialization is called rehabilitation counseling (Parker, Szymanski, & Patterson, 2005). Noting that "rehabilitation counselors are the only professional counselors educated and trained specifically to serve individuals with disabilities," the Commission on Rehabilitation Counselor Certification (2013) defines rehabilitation counseling as a "systematic process which focuses specifically on assisting persons with physical, mental, developmental, cognitive and emotional disabilities to achieve their personal, career, and independent goals in the most integrated setting possible through the application of the counseling process" (para. 1). Many community agencies employ rehabilitation counselors to assist clients with disabilities, and some agencies are dedicated to the provision of rehabilitation counseling. Some agencies specialize even more narrowly on the career concerns of clients with disabilities; they generally refer to themselves as providing vocational rehabilitation services.

Career counselors should know that such specialists and agencies exist and that one important strategy for assisting clients with disabilities is to encourage them to explore the services available through vocational rehabilitation agencies. Many of these agencies are government-funded and offer services to clients free of charge. To receive these services, however, clients must meet certain eligibility requirements. Generally speaking, these requirements are that a client must have a disability that serves as a significant barrier to employment, the client must need vocational rehabilitation counseling in order to obtain and maintain employment, and he or she must have the ability to benefit from the vocational rehabilitation services.

When providing career services to clients with disabilities, counselors (whether specialists in rehabilitation counseling or not) should practice according to the counseling process described in Chapter 9. This process should be supplemented with some specific assessments and interventions geared toward the needs of clients with disabilities. Both in the intake process and later, assessment is very important when providing career services to clients with disabilities. It is so important, in fact, that the term *vocational evaluation* is used to describe it (Flansburg, 2011).

VOCATIONAL EVALUATION. The goal of the vocational evaluation process is to identify "realistic career options and supports for persons with disabilities" (Flansburg, 2011, p. 114). This involves thorough evaluation of client abilities, strengths, disabilities, and areas of functional impairment. Depending on the nature of a client's disabilities, it may be necessary to use alternative assessment strategies instead of traditional standardized tests (Fabian & Liesener, 2005). Situational assessments, for example, involve observation of clients as they perform work-related tasks in simulated environments, vocational workshops, or actual job situations (Parker & Bolton, 2005).

The obvious purpose of this extensive assessment process is to determine the kinds of work a client with disabilities can do in order to identify realistic career options. An additional focus, however, may not be so obvious to you: The assessment process is also designed to identify accommodations that may be necessary in order for the client to perform various work tasks successfully.

IDENTIFICATION OF JOB ACCOMMODATIONS. As you learned in Chapter 7, the Americans with Disabilities Act not only prohibits discrimination in the hiring of persons with disabilities but also requires employers to make reasonable accommodations if these accommodations will allow a person to perform all the "essential functions of the job" (Cihon & Castagnera, 2011, p. 269). The identification of necessary accommodations is therefore an important element of providing career services to people with disabilities. Accommodations may include addressing accessibility issues in the workplace, allowing for modified work schedules, restructuring job requirements to eliminate nonessential tasks that a client is unable to perform, allowing or providing adaptive solutions (such as guide dogs or adaptive technology), allowing or providing support services (such as an interpreter), or allowing for telecommuting (Ryan, 2011; Witt, 1992).

Whereas rehabilitation counselors, especially those who work in vocational rehabilitation agencies, tend to have expertise in identifying such accommodations, you may not. A useful resource, however, is the Job Accommodation Network (JAN; askjan.org). This organization offers confidential consultation services to individuals, employers, and others (including counselors) free of charge. As it name suggests, JAN specializes in identifying accommodations for people with disabilities in the workplace. Rather than offering generic solutions, JAN is known for identifying customized solutions that meet the unique needs of the individual employee and employer. JAN also provides free, confidential consultation services to individuals, employers, and others who want assistance in understanding the requirements of the Americans with Disabilities Act (ADA) and other legislation pertaining to the employment of people with disabilities.

JOB SEARCH SUPPORT. In addition to using an expanded assessment process to determine the kinds of work a client with disabilities can do and helping clients identify accommodations they may need to negate the impact of functional impairments, career counselors should also help clients manage the job search process effectively (Gilbride & Hagner, 2005). Although the job search process is stressful and difficult for most people, people with disabilities face additional challenges when looking for work. Despite federal legislation prohibiting discrimination on the basis of disability (Americans with Disabilities Act, 1990, Americans with Disabilities Amendments Act, 2008), discriminatory hiring practices still exist, and people with disabilities are faced with an "uneven playing field" when applying for jobs (Ryan, 2011, p. 211), which may be due to factors such as misconceptions, stereotypes, and sociocultural attitudes toward disabilities (Livneh & Cook, 2005) or to concerns about the financial costs associated with ADA-mandated accommodations and litigation (DeLeire, 2000).

Therefore, job applicants with visible disabilities must contend with employer reactions to their disability during the interview process, and job applicants with nonvisible disabilities must wrestle with decisions about whether, when, and how to disclose their disabilities during the application process. Ryan (2011) recommends that people with disabilities that are not visible refrain from disclosing their disability until after receiving a job offer. In contrast, he advises clients whose disabilities are visible to address them early and directly in the interview. He explains that not doing so "may result in the interviewer going through the motions, trying to be careful not to break any laws, but focusing less on your answers" (p. 177). Bolles (1991) suggests a similar, proactive approach and encourages people with disabilities to recognize the fears a potential employer might have about hiring a person with a disability. He takes it a step further, though, by charging the applicant with the responsibility of disarming these fears. Although his book is dated, it addresses several, very realistic fears and offers terrific suggestions about what applicants could say to address them. One of these fears, as mentioned above, is that the employee will need very expensive accommodations. Ryan (2011) challenges this misconception and identifies a number of no- or low-cost accommodations. In fact, JAN has been collecting data about the costs and benefits of accommodations since 2004. Nearly 2,000 employers have participated in the study, and the findings indicate that "a high percentage (57%) of accommodations cost absolutely nothing to make, while the rest typically cost only $500" (Job Accommodation

TABLE 18.3 Job Search Sites Specific to People with Disabilities

Name	Website
ABILITY jobs	jobaccess.org
Careers & the disABLED Magazine	eop.com/mags-CD.php
Disability.gov	https://www.disability.gov/employment
Employer Assistance & Resource Network (EARN)	earnworks.com/
Federal Jobs Network	federaljobs.net/disabled.htm
Getting Hired	gettinghired.com
Lighthouse International	lighthouse.org/services-and-assistance/career-services
National Business and Disability Council	business-disability.com/job_seekers2.aspx
United Cerebral Palsy Employment and Training	ucpnet.org/employment-training.php
U.S. Office of Personnel Management	opm.gov/policy-data-oversight/disability-employment/
USA Jobs	https://help.usajobs.gov/index.php/Individuals_with_Disabilities

Source: Based in part on Holzer, H.J., Raphael, S., & Stoll, M.A. (2003, May).

Network, 2012, p. 3). Sharing such information during an interview may have a positive impact on an employer's hiring decision.

Another job search strategy involves the identification of employers who demonstrate an interest in recruiting and hiring people with disabilities. As an established professional counselor, of course, you will develop an awareness of local employers who fit this description. As shown in Table 18.3, several organizations have websites designed to assist people with disabilities in finding job openings with employers who demonstrate an interest in recruiting and hiring people with disabilities.

MILITARY VETERANS

Veterans represent another subpopulation who may experience unemployment due to transitional challenges in entering or reentering the workforce. The U.S. Department of Veteran Affairs (2013) defines a veteran as "a person who served in the active military, naval, or air service, and who was discharged or released under conditions other than dishonorable" (para. V1). They may have been drafted, enlisted voluntarily, entered through officer training programs, or been called up to active duty from the reserves. People who served only in the reserves and who were never called up to active duty are not defined as veterans and neither are people who served active duty but were dishonorably discharged.

If they meet the requirements listed, military service members become veterans when they leave active duty and transition back to civilian status. People who make this transition include those who are retiring from the military and seeking a second career, people who had planned to remain in the military until retirement age but are discharged because of injuries or disabilities sustained in the line of service, and relatively young people who elect or receive honorable discharge after only one term. Often, the top priority for these transitioning veterans is to secure employment (Clemens & Milsom, 2008). This priority is reflected in the military's preseparation counseling process. As part of this process, exiting military personnel are offered referrals to Transition Assistance Employment Workshops and to community agencies specializing in employment counseling (DD Form 2648, 2011). Counselors intending to provide career services in community settings should have some familiarity with the needs of veterans seeking to transition into the civilian workforce.

Employment Statistics

Approximately 1.4 million individuals are currently employed by the U.S. Military in active duty (U.S. Department of Defense, 2013). These active service members include the full range of personnel, from cadets and midshipmen to admirals and generals, and approximately 82% of these active service members are enlisted. By definition, these 1.4 million people serving in active duty fall outside the civilian labor force, and they are not included in the BLS statistics until they transition from the military into civilian life. At that point, they are counted as veterans within the civilian labor force. There are approximately

21.2 million veterans in the civilian noninstitutional population (U.S. Bureau of Labor Statistics, 2012a), and these veterans have served in various eras ranging from World War II to the current Gulf War Era II.

Since the 9-11 attacks on the World Trade Center and the Pentagon, which marked the beginning of the Gulf War Era II period, the United States has deployed more than 2 million soldiers to Iraq and Afghanistan (McBain, Kim, Cook, & Snead, 2012). As the withdrawal of troops and the reduction in force continues, many of these soldiers are choosing or receiving discharges from the military. For example, Ryan, Carlstrom, Hughey, and Harris (2011) reported that approximately 375,000 new veterans joined the civilian population in 2008 alone, and this pace of reentry is expected to continue.

These new veterans, of course, face the task of transitioning into the civilian labor force. Given that most of them joined the military between high school and their 21st birthday (Clemens & Milsom, 2008; Lighthall, 2012), these new veterans may never have worked in the civilian workforce. This could, understandably, make the transition more difficult. Even so, veterans tend to have a lower unemployment rate than civilians (National Center for Veterans Analysis and Statistics, 2010). This same pattern also holds true for veterans with disabilities. As shown in Figure 18.3, the 2012 unemployment rate for veterans with disabilities was actually lower than the rate for veterans without disabilities and lower than the rate for all civilians with or without disabilities. This stands in stark contrast with the civilian population in which the unemployment rate of people with disabilities is nearly double the rate for people without disabilities.

One could conclude from Figure 18.3 that veterans are faring well with regard to employment and question the need to tailor specific career interventions to this subpopulation. This figure clearly suggests that veterans are doing just fine or at least better than the rest of us when it comes to finding employment. However, these data reflect the employment status of all veterans, regardless of their age or when they served in the military. Thus, a closer look at the data is warranted. Figure 18.4 also compares the unemployment rates of civilians and veterans, but this time the data are disaggregated according to age and, for veterans, the service period in which they were on active duty. Given that future additions to the veteran population will likely come from the two Gulf War eras, this figure focuses specifically on them. For each age range, the first bar reflects the unemployment rate for nonveteran civilians, the second bar reflects the unemployment rate for all veterans, and the third and fourth bars reflect

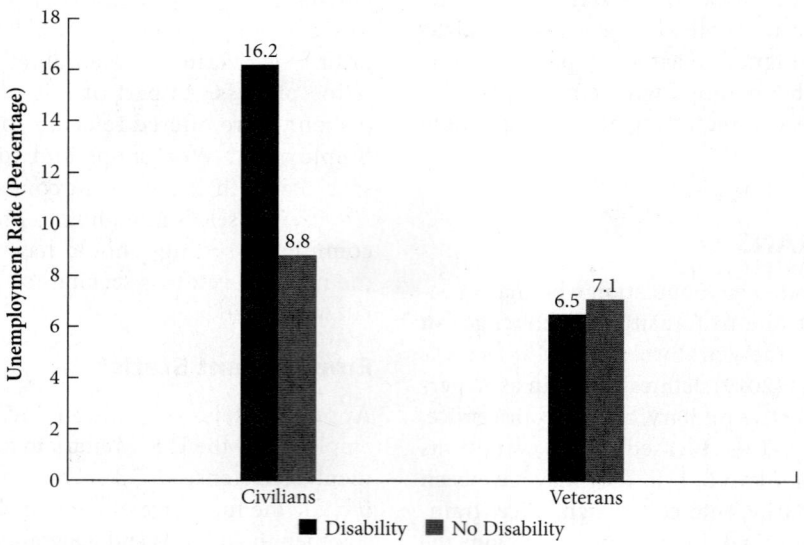

FIGURE 18.3 Unemployment Rates for 2012, by Disability Status and Veteran Status

Sources: Based on U.S. Bureau of Labor Statistics. (2012a). Employment Situation of Veterans – 2012. Retrieved May 22, 2013 from http://www.bls.gov/news.release/pdf/vet.pdf. U.S. Bureau of Labor Statistics. (2012c). Table 2. Employed full- and part-time workers by disability status and age, 2011 annual averages. Retrieved May 11, 2013 from http://www.bls.gov/news.release/disabl.t02.htm

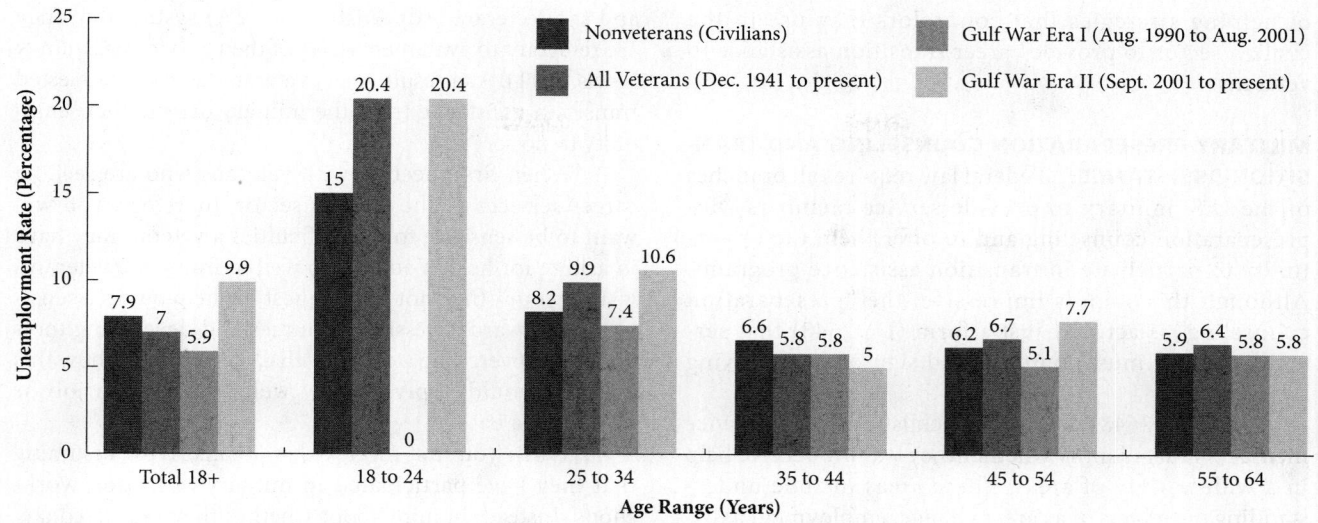

FIGURE 18.4 Comparison of Veteran and Civilian Unemployment Rates for 2012
Source: Based on U.S. Bureau of Labor Statistics. (2012a). Employment Situation of Veterans – 2012. Retrieved May 22, 2013 from http://www.bls.gov/news.release/pdf/vet.pdf

the unemployment rate for veterans from the two Gulf War eras.

As you can see, this comparison tells a much different story. Notice that, for individuals between the ages of 18 and 24, the unemployment rate for civilians is a troubling 15% and an even more alarming 20.4% for veterans from the Gulf War II era. Despite having served their country, these young veterans are encountering tremendous difficulties in obtaining and maintaining employment. To help you better understand factors that may contribute to these difficulties, the next section examines elements of the transition process they face.

Transition-Related Challenges

Surviving boot camp, acclimating to military life, and facing the possibility or reality of combat for the first time present incoming service members with transitional challenges, and so does the process of leaving the military (DiRamio, Ackerman, & Mitchell, 2008; Ryan et al., 2011). In many ways, veterans may experience a reverse version of culture shock (Carne, 2011) as they transition from military life back into civilian life.

With regard to their residence, for example, they experience a major transition in terms of the type of residence, geographic location, and the people with whom they live. Veterans also experience dramatic changes in how structured their daily routine is (from a high degree of structure to much less structure), in how decisions are made, and how much autonomy and independence they can exercise (from a clear chain of command and expected obedience to authority in the military to a civilian setting in which the questioning of authority and individual decision making is often embraced), in their sense of identity (Robertson, 2013), and even in how connected and understood they feel (from military camaraderie based in shared experiences and understanding of war to a sense that others [civilians] don't understand; DiRamio et al., 2008).

These transitions affect not only daily life but also a veteran's experience of the career exploration process and of the civilian workplace. In the career exploration process, for example, clients are often encouraged to focus on their individuality and uniqueness. This can challenge veterans accustomed to operating according to a military team mentality in which the expression of individuality is discouraged (Ryan et al., 2011). Similarly, veterans may experience challenges as they enter a civilian workplace in which employees may be expected to operate autonomously in a less structured context and in which expectations and guidelines are unclear (Freifeld, 2010). For veterans who choose to pursue a college education after leaving the military, the contrast may be even more pronounced (Carne, 2011). Therefore, counselors who provide career services to veterans must understand the many transitions they face.

Helping Strategies

This section provides an overview of the transition services offered by the military and identifies a wide variety of helping strategies that counselors may use in the civilian sector to provide career transition assistance to veterans.

MILITARY PRESEPARATION COUNSELING AND TRANSITION ASSISTANCE. Federal law requires all branches of the U.S. military to provide service members with preseparation counseling and to offer them the opportunity to participate in transition assistance programs. Although this sounds impressive, the "preseparation counseling" is actually just a form (DD2648) that service members must complete and sign prior to leaving the military.

The DD2648 form is a checklist on which service members must identify whether they want to receive help in a wide variety of areas. These areas include understanding the effects of a career change, employment assistance, relocation assistance, housing, education and training, physical and mental health well-being, health and life insurance, finances, reserve affiliation, veterans benefits, and disabled veterans benefits. Within the section on employment assistance, service members have the opportunity to attend a Department of Labor transition assistance program (TAP). This three-day workshop is held on military bases, and participants are taught about "job searches, career decision-making, current occupational and labor market conditions, and résumé and cover letter preparation and interviewing techniques," and they also receive "an evaluation of their employability relative to the job market" (U.S. Department of Labor [DOL], 2013c, para. 5). During this program, participants also receive a transcript of their military experience and training (DD Form 2586, 2010) and information about a number of websites and other programs designed to assist veterans in transitioning into the civilian labor force.

One might be impressed when reviewing this wide array of employment and transition assistance offered by the military; however, there is a surprisingly low rate of participation in these programs. Clemens and Milsom (2008) reported that only 33% of exiting Army personnel availed themselves of the opportunity to participate in transition workshops. Although the participation rate for other branches was higher (64% to 72%), it is clear that "many enlisted service members are not participating in transition assistance workshops" (p. 247).

One reason for this low participation rate may be reluctance on the part of a service member to admit a need or desire for help. Military personnel are trained to suppress their own needs and to maintain a tough, invincible exterior. Veterans may harbor enough distrust of the military and the Veterans Administration (VA) system that they are reluctant to avail themselves of their services (Caplin & Lewis, 2011). As a result, many veterans have not requested transition assistance from the military despite their eligibility to do so.

When first meeting with veterans who are seeking career services in the civilian sector, therefore, you will want to be sensitive to the difficulties a veteran may have in asking for help. You will do well to frame the veteran's visit to your office not as a request for help but as a sensible step toward accessing resources and developing tools needed to overcome a difficult challenge. (Notice how this wording could apply equally well to finding a job or defending a base.)

When you first meet with veterans, avoid assuming that they have participated in military transition workshops. Instead, inquire about whether they requested any employment assistance as part of the military's preseparation counseling process. Simply by knowing enough to ask such a question, you may gain some credibility. Next, of course, you need to provide solid career services to maintain this credibility. Although the services you provide need to be individualized and tailored to meet each veteran's unique needs, they tend to fall into five categories of helping strategies: career exploration activities, career counseling, vocational rehabilitation, job search support, and postsecondary education.

CAREER EXPLORATION ACTIVITIES FOR VETERANS. Because many entered the military immediately following high school graduation, veterans have often had fairly limited experiences with career development activities involving self- and occupational exploration (Clemens & Milsom, 2008). Therefore, they may have little understanding of the variety of existing career options; of the types of positions for which they may currently qualify; or about how factors such as their interests, personality, work-related values, and skills contribute to job satisfaction and success.

With regard to self-exploration, counselors should help veterans engage in self-exploration activities related to their interests, work-related values, personality, and skills. Assessment strategies, including interviews, standardized tests, and card sorts, may all be useful in this regard. Because job assignments in the military are primarily based on skills as assessed by the Armed Vocational Aptitude Battery (U.S. Military Entrance Processing Command, 1997), it is likely that veterans have a stronger grasp of how their skills relate to career selection and have more need for the assessment of their interests, values, and personality (Bullock, Braud, Andrews, &

TABLE 18.4 Military Skills Translators

Translator Resource	Website
Career One Stop	careeronestop.org/ReEmployment/veterans/i-want-to-match-my-military-skills-to.aspx
Department of Labor (DOL) Military to Civilian Occupation Translator	online.onetcenter.org/crosswalk/
Mil2FedJobs Federal Jobs Crosswalk	Mil2FedJobs.com
VA for VETS Military Skills Translator	https://mst.vaforvets.va.gov/mst/va/mos-translator
Vet Success List of Skills Translators	vetsuccess.gov/military_skills_translators

Phillips, 2009; Clemens & Milsom, 2008). However, veterans may also need assistance in understanding how the skills they used in the military may translate into skills that are useful in civilian jobs. Fortunately, several online tools may be used to assist with this translation. Table 18.4 provides a list of military skills translators that may be used for this purpose.

With regard to career exploration, veterans may benefit from the same types of occupational exploration opportunities as those provided in high school and college settings. Using sites such as Occupational Information Network (O*NET) can be particularly useful in helping veterans identify occupations that may be well suited to their interests, skills, and work-related values. For veterans who were satisfied with their job in the military and would like to continue in a similar line of work, some sites allow them to enter their job title or military occupational classification (MOC) and receive a listing of related civilian occupations. One such website is called Jobs2Vets Job Title Translator (jobs2vets.com/).

CAREER COUNSELING FOR VETERANS. Especially given that they face a number of simultaneous transitions as they exit the military, veterans may also benefit from counseling services to support them not only in their career transition but also with regard to other needs. They may feel overwhelmed by these transitions and communicate this to you, or they may conceal their emotional reactions. Either way, it is important to offer encouragement to veterans (DiRamio et al., 2008; Ryan et al., 2011). A strengths-focused way of offering such encouragement would be to indicate that veterans have already demonstrated the ability to make very difficult transitions by completing boot camp, adjusting to life in the military, and perhaps in surviving exposure to combat (DiRamio et al., 2008). It is also important, however, to acknowledge and address barriers to employment that may be affecting these clients. For example, veterans disproportionately experience barriers such as substance abuse, mental health issues, and homelessness (Bullock et al., 2009; Phillips, Braud, Andrews, & Bullock, 2007).

With these caveats in mind, you will likely proceed through the same stages of the counseling process as described in Chapter 9 and utilize a variety of career development theories (discussed in Chapters 2 to 5). For example, several authors have recommended use of the cognitive information processing (CIP) approach (Sampson, Lenz, Reardon, & Peterson, 1999) for use with veterans (Bullock et al., 2009; Clemens & Milsom, 2008; Phillips et al., 2007). Clemens and Milsom (2008) offered a particularly detailed example of how each step of the CIP process could be used with veterans, beginning with the initial interview and ending with closure of the counseling process. Another theoretical approach to career counseling that has been recommended for use with veterans is a narrative approach. Krieshok, Hastings, Ebberwein, Wetterstenand, and Owen (1999) advocated using narrative approaches to assist veterans in vocational rehabilitation settings.

VOCATIONAL REHABILITATION. Earlier in this chapter, you learned that vocational rehabilitation is a form of career counseling designed to assist people with lifelong or acquired disabilities. Many veterans, of course, will have acquired disabilities as a result of injury during service. Approximately 14% of all veterans have a service-related disability, and about 30% of Gulf War II veterans have a service-related disability (U.S. Bureau of Labor Statistics, 2012a). When working with veterans who have sustained service-related disabilities, counselors should also recommend vocational rehabilitation services. Vocational rehabilitation services designed specifically for veterans are offered under the auspices of the Department of Veterans Affairs by both the Veterans Health Administration and the Veterans Benefits Administration (Ostovary & Dapprich, 2011). These services have been quite successful:

The unemployment rate for veterans with a disability was actually lower in 2012 than the unemployment rate for veterans with no disability (U.S. Bureau of Labor Statistics, 2012a). The U.S. Department of Veterans Affairs (n.d.) reported that the 2011 average annual wages for veterans with disabilities, after completing vocational rehabilitation, was nearly five times higher than their salaries before participating in the VA vocational rehabilitation program.

JOB SEARCH SUPPORT. In providing job search support to veterans, career counselors will find that the strategies discussed earlier in this chapter and elsewhere in this book apply equally well to veterans. Like many other clients seeking career services in community settings, veterans may need help developing résumés and cover letters, identifying job leads, preparing for interviews, and so forth. Within these domains, however, veterans do have some unique needs.

For example, a typical job search skill we teach clients is how to create a résumé to demonstrate that they have the relevant education, skills, and work experience needed to perform a particular job to which they will apply. How, though, does a veteran who has never held a civilian job develop a résumé to accomplish this? A good place to start is with the veteran's DD214 (2000) because this document provides a list of "education and training received, positions held, [and] awards earned" (Clemens & Milsom, 2008, p. 253). Another document that contains similar information is the DD Form 2586 (2010). To assist veterans in creating a résumé for use in seeking civilian employment, it is useful to ask that they bring a copy of one or both forms. As they explain various military terms listed on these forms, you can assist them in identifying comparable civilian terms.

You may be of great value in helping veterans identify employability skills they will bring to any job. Military personnel, for instance, are required to arrive on time, properly dressed and ready to work. They respect authority, follow directions, work hard, and are unafraid of a challenge. They have been entrusted with a degree of responsibility seldom experienced by civilians and have literally been willing to sacrifice their lives for the greater good. Although they may be nervous about transitioning into the civilian labor force and may bring with them psychological and physical wounds, veterans are known to have a work ethic second to none. A discussion about this topic may be useful both in bolstering the veteran's self-confidence and in preparing them for interviews.

It may also be useful to recommend books to support veterans in their transition. For example, the *Military-to-Civilian Transition Guide* by Savino and Krannich (2011) focuses on career transitions. Career counselors should know about job search websites designed specifically for veterans. See Table 18.5 for such a list.

POSTSECONDARY EDUCATION FOR VETERANS. Given that only 10% of veterans had a bachelor's degree when they entered the military (Ryan et al., 2011), career counselors should explore whether veterans have an interest in postsecondary education or training. Many veterans are eligible for financial assistance through the Post 9/11 GI Bill, which "provides tuition and fees, monthly housing allowance, books and supplies, and living expense stipends to eligible veterans" (Ostovary & Dapprich, 2011, p. 66). These monies may be used to cover costs associated not only with four-year colleges but also with apprenticeships, trade schools, and even on-the-job training (Veterans Benefits Administration, 2012). In large part because of the Post 9/11 GI Bill, Gulf War era "veteran enrollments at U.S. colleges and universities reflect the highest numbers since the post–World War II era, when the first military educational benefit assistance programs were legislated in 1944" (Ostovary & Dapprich, 2011, p. 66).

In response, colleges and universities across the nation have been preparing to meet the needs of student veterans (DiRamio et al., 2008; Lighthall, 2012; McBain et al., 2012; Ostovary & Dapprich, 2011). Counselors play an important role in helping veterans select the type of postsecondary education best suited to them, choose a particular educational institution to attend, and succeed in their transition. To assist veterans in considering postsecondary education, use the same knowledge and skills discussed in Chapter 14. In helping veterans choose a particular educational institution to attend, it is useful to research various institutions to gauge how vet-friendly each institution is and to determine the nature and extent of veteran services offered at the school (Ostovary & Dapprich, 2011). It is useful to know, for example, whether a college has an office dedicated to the needs of student veterans, what types of veteran-specific programs and services are offered on campus, whether the college has a policy regarding tuition refunds in the event that a veteran is redeployed, and whether a college grants credit for military training and experience (McBain et al., 2012). With regard to helping veterans transition successfully into postsecondary education, DiRamio et al. (2008) recommend that veterans start taking courses slowly and work to remediate any rusty or deficient skills. Veterans transitioning into postsecondary education also benefit if they can connect with other student veterans, perhaps through student organizations

TABLE 18.5 Job Search Sites Addressing Veterans' Transition Needs

Name	Website
Career One Stop	careeronestop.org/ReEmployment/Veterans/
Corporate Gray	corporategray.com/
Feds Hire Vets	fedshirevets.gov/
Helmets to Hardhats	helmetstohardhats.org/
H2H Jobs	https://h2h.jobs/
Hire Veterans	hireveterans.com/
Hire Vets First	hirevetsfirst.dol.gov/
Jobs for Vets	jobsforvetsalpha.org
Jobs2Vets	jobs2vets.com/
Job Opportunities for Disabled American Veterans	JOFDAV.com
Monster Veteran Employment Center	military.com/veteran-jobs
My Next Move for Veterans	mynextmove.org/vets/
National Veteran's Business Development Corporation	veteranscorp.org
Recruit Military	RecruitMilitary.com
Troops to Teachers	proudtoserveagain.com
Turbo TAP	turbotap.org
Turbo TAP Employment Assistance	turboTAP.org/portal/transition/resources/Employment_Hub
USA Jobs (federal jobs for veterans)	https://www.usajobs.gov/Veterans
Vet Jobs	VetJobs.com
Vet Success Job Search	careeronestop.org/ReEmployment/Veterans/
Veterans Job Bank	https://www.nrd.gov/home/veterans_job_bank

(DiRamio et al., 2008; Lighthall, 2012). Although acknowledging that many veterans will be reluctant to disclose disabilities, Lighthall (2012) recommends that counselors encourage veterans to contact the appropriate office on campus to register their disabilities and to arrange for appropriate accommodations.

EX-OFFENDERS

Whereas today's veterans are generally welcomed back as heroes and offered gratitude for their service, ex-offenders often experience quite a different reception as they transition from incarceration back into society. Although they seek "a second chance and opportunity to demonstrate to their families and society that they can be good productive citizens" (Brown, C., 2011, p. 337), ex-offenders typically encounter significant challenges in making good on these aspirations. Because counselors in the community setting are highly likely to encounter at least some clients with criminal records and because of the profound interactions among employment, criminal convictions, and recidivism, it is essential that you have some understanding of the career counseling needs of this subpopulation.

Incarceration and Employment Statistics

As you read that last sentence, you may have been surprised by the statement that counselors in the community setting are highly likely to encounter at least some clients with criminal records. In a large-scale study of 673 clients seeking outpatient mental health services at 21 different agencies in California, Theriot and Segal (2005) found that 35.5% of those clients had criminal convictions and that more than half of these clients had felony convictions. This same study found that 32% of clients had spent time in jail and 6% had been in prison. These statistics suggest a much higher probability of counselors in community agencies seeing clients with criminal convictions and histories of incarceration than you might have suspected.

In addition to being heavily represented in clinical populations, ex-offenders are also common in the general population. Estimates are that 1% of the general population is currently incarcerated in the United States and that another 3% are on probation, parole, or otherwise "under some form of correctional control" (Schmitt & Warner, 2010, p. 2). If this seems high to you, consider that there was a 700% increase in incarceration rates in the 35 years spanning 1970 to 2005 (Shivy et al., 2007). Much of this increase is attributed not to an increase in the crime rate but instead to the enforcement of new government policies that were established as our nation decided to "get tough on crime" and to wage a "war on drugs" (Harrison & Schehr, 2004; Williams, 2013). In fact, drugs play an important role in these increased numbers, with 48% of offenders housed in federal prisons having convictions for drug-related crimes (Carson & Sabol, 2012), 75% of offenders and ex-offenders reporting substance abuse problems (Holzer, Raphael, & Stoll, 2003), and many offenders funding their expensive drug habits through illegal activities (Williams, 2013).

In addition to the consequences incurred by offenders, this high rate of incarceration presents high economic and social costs to our nation. The annual cost to our nation's economy is in the neighborhood of a whopping $57 to $65 billion (Schmitt & Warner, 2010). Socially, there is a disproportionate impact on racial minorities in the United States. It is estimated that 70% of all inmates are African Americans and Hispanic/Latino (Harrison & Schehr, 2004). In contrast to the 1% of the total population being currently incarcerated, 10% of all African American males are currently incarcerated, and a shocking 60% of African American males without high school diplomas will be incarcerated at some point in their lives (Brown, C., 2011).

Lest you erroneously conclude that these disparities are simply reflective of more crimes being committed by these racial minorities, consider the following:

> A common misconception is that African-Americans and Hispanics are committing more crimes and, thereby, deserve elevated rates of incarceration. However, as data from the U.S. Department of Health and Human Services reveals, 64% of crack users are White, while only 26% are Black. Nevertheless, by 1992 African Americans accounted for 91% of those who were sentenced under disparate drug laws (Dyer, 2000). (Harrison & Schehr, 2004, pp. 42–43)

This is especially important for you, as a future counselor, to understand. Whereas your training has or will surely emphasize the importance of embracing diversity and treating all clients with respect, I suspect some of you may mistakenly believe that this expectation doesn't hold firm when dealing with "criminals." On the contrary, the professional expectation is that you must indeed treat all clients with respect and that, when counseling clients who have criminal records, you take into account their individual histories and social justice disparities to serve as a foundation for empathy.

After all, it is highly likely that you will encounter clients with criminal records. Despite the mandatory sentencing requirements that have contributed to the dramatically increased incarceration rates, most offenders are eventually released. At this point, approximately 700,000 offenders are released from incarceration each year (Redcross et al., 2010). Do the math, and you'll realize that this translates to about 2,000 prisoners being released every day. Each of these individuals then faces the challenge of reentry. As part of their reentry process, they may very well seek counseling services to address various challenges and, regardless of their initial presenting concerns, will likely need assistance with career-related issues.

Study after study reveals that ex-offenders face enormous challenges when it comes to finding employment with which to support themselves without criminal activity (Harrison & Schehr, 2004; Holzer et al., 2003; Lichtenberger, 2012; Nally, Lockwood, & Ho, 2011; Piehl, 2009; Redcross et al., 2010; Shivy et al., 2007; Williams, 2013). Although there is widespread consensus that "stable employment is critical to a successful transition from prison to community" (Redcross et al., 2010, p. 2) and although ex-offenders understand the importance of finding gainful employment to avoid reincarceration (Nally et al., 2011), finding a job is difficult for an ex-offender. The unemployment rate for ex-offenders is approximately 70% (Nally et al., 2011), which means that 70% of ex-offenders who want a job and who are actively looking cannot find employment. To make things worse, when ex-offenders do get jobs, their wages tend to be extremely low (Holzer et al., 2003; Lichtenberger, 2012; Nally et al., 2011). What is extremely low? Nally et al. (2011) answered this question by explaining that "the most extraordinary finding in this study was that close to 50% of employed offenders had an annual income under $5,000" (2011, p. 52).

Table 18.6 summarizes these statistics. It is little wonder that many ex-offenders reengage in criminal behavior and face re-incarceration. "The most recent national statistics show that two-thirds of released prisoners are arrested and about half return to prison within

TABLE 18.6 Ex-Offender Statistics

Proportion of outpatient mental health clients that	
• have criminal convictions	35.5%
• have felony convictions	19%
• have spent time in jail	32%
• have spent time in prison	6%
Proportion of U.S. population that	
• is currently incarcerated	1%
• is on probation, parole, or other correctional control	3%
Proportion of U.S. incarcerated population that	
• is in prison for drug-related crimes	48%
• has substance abuse problems	75%
• does not have a high school diploma	68%
• has an eighth-grade education or less	14%
• is functionally illiterate	50%
• is African American or Hispanic/Latino	70%
Proportion of U.S. ex-offenders that	
• are unemployed	70%
• are employed but make less than $5,000 per year	50%
• will return to prison within three years	67%

three years" (Redcross et al., 2010, p. 2). However, the recidivism rate improves when ex-offenders are able to secure and remain employed in better-paying jobs (Brown, C., 2011). Counselors can play a very important role in helping ex-offenders reintegrate into their communities by providing career services. Before addressing strategies for doing so, though, it is also important to identify the various challenges ex-offenders experience with regard to seeking employment.

Employment Challenges

In identifying the factors that contribute to the difficulties ex-offenders face with regard to employment, I will borrow a conceptual model from Holzer and colleagues (2003). They organized the employment challenges faced by ex-offenders into two categories: (1) supply-side and (2) demand-side. Supply-side challenges consist of ex-offender characteristics; demand-side challenges include expectations or obstacles that exist within the hiring and workplace environment. Table 18.7 provides an overview of these challenges. We will discuss each one.

SUPPLY-SIDE CHALLENGES. Ex-offenders as a group are more likely than nonoffenders to suffer from several characteristics that negatively affect their employability, including poor educational backgrounds and academic skills, poor employability and job-specific skills, spotty employment histories, physical and mental health problems, substance disorders, lack of social capital, deficient interpersonal skills, and poor attitudes and choices. These characteristics often precede and contribute to the criminal activity that results in their incarceration and also negatively affects their employability. Additional supply-side challenges more specific to the postincarceration period include housing issues and transportation difficulties.

Education and Academic Skills. Ex-offenders' generally low level of education and academic skills seems to contribute a great deal to their difficulties in finding and maintaining employment both before and after incarceration (Brown, C., 2011; Harlow, 2003; Harrison & Schehr, 2004; Holzer et al., 2003; Nally et al., 2011; Piehl, 2009; Redcross et al., 2010). As you may have noticed in

TABLE 18.7 Employment Challenges Faced by Ex-Offenders

Supply-Side Challenges	Demand-Side Challenges
Insufficient education and academic skills	Legal restrictions
Insufficient job skills and spotty employment history	• Licensure restrictions
	• Hiring restrictions
Health, mental health, and substance disorders	
Lack of social capital	Employer reluctance to hire ex-offenders
Interpersonal skills, attitudes, and choices	Job requirements
Housing, subsistence, and transportation issues	

Table 18.6, 68% of incarcerated individuals do not hold a high school diploma, and 14% of incarcerated individuals dropped out of school before the ninth grade (Harlow, 2003). Approximately 50% of incarcerated individuals are "functionally illiterate" (Holzer et al., 2003, p. 5), which means that they cannot read and write well enough to complete basic tasks in contemporary society. Given our discussions in Chapters 14 and 15 about the importance of education to one's future employability and career options, the implications of these educational statistics should be clear: Ex-offenders who lack education and academic skills are at a major disadvantage in finding gainful employment both before and after their incarceration.

Job Skills and Employment History. With their lack of education and high rate of functional literacy, ex-offenders seeking jobs have limited skills to offer potential employers. In addition to lacking academic skills, ex-offenders also tend to lack marketable, job-specific skills as well as basic employability skills (Holzer et al., 2003; Nally et al., 2011; Redcross et al., 2010). This lack of academic, job-specific, and employability skills is associated with problematic employment histories even before incarceration (Holzer et al., 2003; Piehl, 2009). Ex-offenders report that, prior to incarceration, they are most often employed in unskilled or labor jobs in the "underground economy," in which they are paid "under the table," or they support themselves via illegal activities (Laux et al., 2011, p. 166). On the supply side of the employment equation, then, ex-offenders face employment difficulties because they lack the education, job skills, and stable work history generally sought by employers.

Health, Mental Health, and Substance Disorders. Ex-offenders may also struggle with mental health problems. It is estimated that 75% of ex-offenders have substance abuse problems and that 15% to 20% of ex-offenders struggle with other diagnosable mental disorders (Harrison & Schehr, 2004; Holzer et al., 2003; Shivy et al., 2007.) Substance abuse is particularly problematic because many offenders fund their expensive drug habits through illegal activities, placing them at double risk for re-arrest and reincarceration (Williams, 2013). Eighteen percent of female ex-offenders report a history of sexual victimization involving prostitution as minors, and 26% report having engaged in prostitution as adults (Laux et al., 2011). An estimated 18% of ex-offenders have hepatitis C, and 2% to 3% have AIDS or have tested positive for HIV (Holzer et al., 2003). Noting the unfortunate impact of such conditions on employability, Holzer and colleagues (2003) observed that "those with substance abuse and/or other health problems (both physical and emotional) are the least likely to be job-ready and will likely face few job offers or high discharge rates upon being hired" (p. 7).

Lack of Social Capital. Another employment challenge experienced by many ex-offenders involves their lack of social capital. Social capital is important with regard to role models and aspirations, and networking for job opportunities. Piehl (2009) found that inmates reported a paucity of positive role models in their youth. Their lack of exposure to adults who valued education, maintained employment, and modeled employability skills likely played a limiting role in ex-offender development and pursuit of career aspirations. Ex-offenders have often been raised in poor communities where few job opportunities existed, and they often return to these same communities following their release from prison. Their relational networks tend to be based in these locales, resulting in a dearth of social capital with which to network for the purpose of job hunting (Brown, C., 2011).

Interpersonal Skills, Attitudes, and Choices. Holzer et al. (2003) noted that ex-offenders may also hold attitudes and make choices that contribute to both pre- and postrelease employment difficulties. As an example, they observed that many ex-offenders may receive but decline job offers in lieu of making more money via illegal activities.

This preference for taking the easy way rather than the right way may also have been evident prior to one's incarceration. Factors such as a capacity for delayed gratification, an assumption of personal responsibility, and an internal locus of control may all contribute to poor choices that ultimately harm an ex-offender's employment prospects (Piehl, 2009). Also, ex-offenders may exhibit deficient interpersonal skills that affect their ability to interact appropriately in the workplace and to develop appropriate relationships with supervisors and coworkers (Nally et al., 2011).

Housing, Subsistence, and Transportation Issues. Following incarceration, many ex-offenders also experience housing and transportation barriers to employment. Regardless of one's ability to tolerate delays in gratification, the need for food and shelter following one's release from prison is urgent, and both cost money. Upon release, however, ex-offenders generally leave prison in debt to the courts (Shivy et al., 2007) and with very little money. The justice department does provide them with a release gratuity to aid them in their reintegration to society, but the amount is quite small. Specifically, the average release gratuity for those housed in state prisons is $69 (Harrison & Schehr, 2004) and may be as high as $500 for those being released from federal prison (Federal Bureau of Prisons, 2011). Either way, this is not a lot of money and understandably results in an urgent need for income, especially given that ex-offenders are ineligible to receive public assistance or food stamps (Harrison & Schehr, 2004; Hirsch et al., 2002, Brown, C., 2011). In the absence of getting a legal job right after release from prison, these factors may contribute to an ex-offender's choice to reengage in criminal activity.

You may be surprised to learn that federal law "requires the revocation or suspension of drivers' licenses for at least 6 months of any person convicted of a federal drug felony and thus prevents a large number of ex-offenders from seeking employment where driving is necessary" (Harris & Keller, 2005, p. 8). Thus, the lack of a driver's license and transportation difficulties may pose additional barriers to employment (Wazny, 2010). Seventy-three percent of ex-offenders participating in the Study of Violent Offenders Reentry Initiative reported a need for assistance with transportation (Visher & Lattimore, 2007). A lack of access to reliable transportation makes it difficult, of course, for an individual to get to work on time consistently.

Each of these supply-side challenges involves what an ex-offender has or does not have to offer to a potential employer. Each challenge affects an ex-offender's success in gaining and maintaining employment. In addition to these supply-side challenges, ex-offenders are also affected by a variety of demand-side challenges.

DEMAND-SIDE CHALLENGES. Ex-offenders experience challenges in finding employment as a result of expectations or obstacles that exist within the hiring and workplace environment. Holzer et al. (2003) referred to these as demand-side challenges, and this section addresses three specific challenges in this category: (1) legal restrictions against hiring ex-offenders, (2) employer reluctance to hire ex-offenders even in the absence of a legal prohibition against doing so, and (3) job requirements.

Legal Restrictions. Upon conviction with a felony, ex-offenders become automatically ineligible to work in a wide variety of licensed occupations because many licensure laws include legal restrictions against licensing ex-felons. Licensure boards generally revoke licenses when a licensee receives a felony conviction and refuse to issue new licenses to applicants who already have a felony conviction, often based on language requiring good moral character (Harris & Keller, 2005). This effectively prevents ex-offenders who have felony convictions from entering or reentering those licensed professions (Bushway & Sweeten, 2007; Harris & Keller, 2005; Harrison & Schehr, 2004; Holzer et al., 2003). Many states have laws prohibiting the hiring of ex-felons for a variety of unlicensed occupations.

What is the overall impact of these legal restrictions on the employability of ex-offenders? Bushway and Sweeten (2007) explained that, "through laws against hiring or licensing, ex-felons are barred from up to 800 different occupations across the United States" (p. 698), with the exact number varying from state to state. Criminal justice advocates are quick to criticize these bans as "blind to offense type" and question why "ex-felons are barred from being barbershop owners, commercial feed distributors, and emergency medical technicians in New York, as well as speech-language pathologists and cosmetologists in Florida" (Bushway & Sweeten, 2007, p. 698). It is therefore important, when assisting ex-offenders with career exploration, to determine whether various occupations under consideration have such licensing and/or hiring restrictions.

One additional legal restriction is worth noting. Federal legislation renders ex-offenders ineligible for federal financial aid (loans, grants, or work study) for a minimum of one year and possibly for life if they have drug convictions while attending college and were receiving financial aid (Federal Bureau of Prisons, 2011). This restriction may affect ex-offenders who wish to pursue a career requiring a college degree.

Employer Reluctance to Hire Ex-Offenders. Even in the absence of legal restrictions prohibiting the hiring of an ex-offender, many employers display reluctance to hire applicants who have a criminal history (Holzer et al., 2003; Redcross et al., 2010; Shivy et al., 2007). In fact, a full two thirds of employers have reported not only reluctance but complete unwillingness to "knowingly hire an ex-offender" (Shivy et al., 2007, p. 471). In addition to including an item on job applications inquiring whether an applicant has any criminal convictions, many employers also conduct criminal background checks as a routine procedure in their hiring process. These background checks reveal criminal convictions as well as arrest histories, and "thirty-eight states permit employers and licensing agencies to rely on arrests that do not lead to convictions in determining whether to hire or license" (Harris & Keller, 2005, p. 8).

One reason employers are so adamant against hiring people with criminal backgrounds is that they can be held liable for crimes committed by their employees. If they conduct a criminal background check and knowingly hire someone with a criminal background, employers may be considered negligent if that employee then commits a crime while in their employ. This is referred to as "negligent hiring" and "employers have lost 72% of negligent hiring cases with an average settlement of more than $1.6 million (Connerly et al., 2001)" (Holzer et al., 2003, pp. 8–9). Even employers who might otherwise be inclined to offer ex-offenders a second chance are understandably reluctant to hire them under these circumstances. This reluctance represents a second significant employment barrier for ex-offenders.

Job Requirements. A third demand-side challenge involves the requirements for any given job opening. Employers, of course, seek to hire the most qualified workforce they can. As indicated in our discussion of supply-side challenges, however, many ex-offenders have quite limited education, literacy rates, employability skills, and job-specific skills. When perusing lists of job openings, these ex-offenders therefore encounter many jobs for which they are ineligible. Sample job requirements that may represent an employment barrier for ex-offenders include requirements for a high school diploma, functional literacy, specific training, certifications or licensure, or a driver's license.

Although much as been written about the previous two demand-side barriers (legal restrictions and employer reluctance to hire ex-offenders), the importance of this barrier (job requirements) should not be minimized. As Piehl (2009) pointed out, many ex-offenders "had spotty or nonexistent employment records" prior to their first conviction (p. 2). She contended that the mismatch between the demand-side job requirements of the employer and the supply-side level of education and skills of the applicant is a better explanation for the extremely high unemployment rates of ex-offenders. Specifically, Piehl (2009) argued the following:

> Because inmates have poor outcomes both before and after prison, the employment restrictions noted earlier are probably not the primary driver of low employment rates, and thus removing or reducing legal impediments to employment is not likely to improve outcomes substantially. (p. 2)

Others concur with this argument and acknowledge that the employment difficulties experienced by many ex-offenders would exist even if they didn't have criminal backgrounds and that these employment difficulties are instead mostly attributable to the limited education and skills of ex-offenders (Harrison & Schehr, 2004; Holzer et al., 2003). Holzer et al. (2003) went further, though, and also emphasized the importance of employability skills. In doing so, they addressed both the impact of ex-offender attitudes and health conditions:

> Even where very little formal skill is required, basic "job readiness" is almost universally sought by employers. This personal quality involves the employer's expectation that the worker will show up every day and on time, will work hard and take some responsibility, will be generally trustworthy, etc. . . . Unfortunately, those with substance abuse and/or other health problems (both physical and emotional) are the least likely to be job-ready and will likely face few job offers or high discharge rates upon being hired. (p. 7)

Helping Strategies

Clearly, these challenges described in the preceding section are formidable. However, they are by no means insurmountable. Although you may feel overwhelmed at the prospect of providing career services to ex-offenders, a variety of helping strategies may be useful. And the good news is that you are already familiar with the vast majority of them. First, ex-offenders need assistance with career development needs. By helping ex-offenders envision their career options and make tentative career choices, you also give them some concrete aspirations to which they can aspire and increase the likelihood that they will be satisfied and successful in their future work. Second, ex-offenders need guidance related to career preparation. As already discussed, they tend to have deficits with regard to education, job skills, and employability skills. It is absolutely essential for counselors to help ex-offenders understand the importance of seeking education and developing skills in preparation for a job search. Third, on release, ex-offenders need assistance with career launching and job searching.

In the following paragraphs, I offer some caveats and pointers more specific to the needs of ex-offenders. This section then concludes with an identification of some specific programs and resources designed for use in supporting ex-offender reentry.

CAREER DEVELOPMENT. Helping strategies geared toward career development needs are too often neglected by those who work with ex-offenders (Brown, C., 2011; Thompson & Cummings, 2010; Vernick & Reardon, 2001). Often, however, ex-offenders have had very little exposure to career development interventions. This may reflect disengagement from their primary and secondary school experiences as well as their lack of exposure to career role models during their youth (Piehl, 2009). It can be quite helpful to engage ex-offenders in an exploration of themselves and the world of work and to expose them to career decision-making strategies.

In facilitating self-exploration, you may conduct assessments of their interests, skills, work-related values, and personality. Half of ex-offenders may be functionally illiterate, and you will want to take this into consideration when selecting assessment strategies. Attention to reading level is also important when helping ex-offenders explore the world of work. You may find, therefore, that assessment and career exploration materials traditionally used in K–12 settings may be more appropriate than higher level resources geared toward adults. For example, Career Cruising's assessments require minimal reading, and its exploration resources include videos for nearly every occupation included in its database.

With regard to occupational exploration with ex-offenders, it is important to help them understand the education and skill requirements for occupations of interest to them. It is important to determine whether there are any legal restrictions against them being licensed or hired for specific jobs in which they take an interest. As discussed earlier, ex-offenders may be ineligible to work in occupations that best fit their interest and skills due to legal restrictions (Brown, C., 2011). When introducing ex-offenders to career decision-making models, counselors should encourage them to include these pragmatic considerations in their decision making.

CAREER PREPARATION. One frequent outcome of career development interventions is a tentative career aspiration or plan. To achieve their goal, however, clients often need to engage in career preparation. Given what you have learned about the educational and skill levels of ex-offenders, it should be clear to you that this subpopulation tends to have significant needs in the area of career preparation. Without having the education and training needed to meet job requirements, ex-offenders are much more likely to have difficulty finding employment that offers "sustainable wages" and to go back to prison (Harrison & Schehr, 2004, p. 40). Indeed, the most effective protection against the high unemployment and recidivism rates cited earlier in this chapter are higher education and better job skills (Nally et al., 2011).

Therefore, the importance of helping offenders or ex-offenders understand the importance of completing more education and training programs cannot be overstated. Harrison and Schehr (2004) implore counselors to understand that "it is vitally important that ex-offenders have a marketable skill or trade to make them valuable to employers" (p. 57). Counselors should therefore take great care to assess ex-offenders' educational level both in terms of diplomas and degrees and in terms of academic skills. It is also important to encourage ex-offenders to complete additional education that will allow them to develop job-specific skills in demand in the current occupational marketplace.

It would be ideal if offenders complete this education while incarcerated so they have the education and skills needed to land a good job when they are released. The vast majority of prisons provide inmates with access to educational programs ranging from Graduate Equivalency Diploma (GED) completion programs to vocational training programs, to college courses (Harlow, 2003). If offenders do not avail themselves of these educational opportunities while in prison, however, counselors should strongly encourage them to do so following their release.

One other offender-specific caveat is in order. You learned earlier in this chapter that ex-felons with a drug conviction are ineligible for federal financial aid for a minimum of one year (Federal Bureau of Prisons, 2011). Many ex-offenders are aware of this barrier but believe that this is a lifetime ban for all felons and therefore do not consider any postsecondary education for which they would need financial aid. However, the legal ban on financial aid was modified in 2005 with the passage of the Second Chance Act, resulting in a narrowing of the ban

(Federal Bureau of Prisons, 2011). Since that time, the ban applies only to those whose conviction occurred while they were in college and were receiving federal financial aid. Ex-offenders who fall in this category and are thereby subject to this ban can actually regain eligibility after a minimum of one year and successful participation in substance abuse treatment (Bushway & Sweeten, 2007). Counselors should communicate this possibility to ex-offenders and encourage them to check into their potential eligibility rather than to assume that they cannot get financial aid (Hirsch et al., 2002).

An additional area of career preparation in which offenders and ex-offenders frequently need assistance involves employability skills. Psychoeducation interventions designed to help them understand and acquire employability skills are highly recommended. However, understanding and developing skills is different from actually using them. Because the consistent demonstration of such skills requires self-regulation skills involving delayed gratification, Piehl (2009) recommends the use of highly structured behavior modification interventions as part of a prerelease program to assist ex-offenders in developing these capacities.

CAREER LAUNCHING AND JOB SEARCHING. It is ideal if, prior to their release, ex-offenders engage in career development activities; identify suitable career aspirations; and acquire the necessary education, job-specific skills, and employability skills needed to launch a successful job search. In the real world, though, this doesn't always happen. It may be more common that ex-offenders arrive at your office seeking career services to get a job without having a sense of direction or the skills needed to do so. In such cases, career counseling can be viewed as a two-pronged process in which you simultaneously assist ex-offenders in getting a job and use helping strategies to assist them with their career development and career preparation needs. This section addresses some career-launching issues specific to the needs of ex-offenders.

First, you should ensure that these clients have the documents generally necessary for employment. Visher and Lattimore (2008) recommend that counselors ensure that ex-offenders have copies of their birth certificates and social security cards. If they do not have these, it will be important to help them obtain these documents. The Federal Bureau of Prisons (2011) provides contact information for each state's office for vital records and also recommends the following website: usbirthcertificate.net/google/. In addition to helping ex-offenders obtain such documents, it is useful to assist ex-offenders in creating a file containing these documents along with other basics such as a copy of their high school diploma or GED, any vocational training certificates they have earned, any college degrees they have earned, and transcripts from each of these educational programs (U.S. Department of Labor, 2005).

Second, psychoeducation about job searching, application completion, and résumé development are also important strategies for assisting ex-offenders in launching a career following their release from incarceration. With regard to job applications, for example, it is useful to discuss how best to respond to items asking if they have had any criminal convictions. Especially given employer reluctance to hire applicants with criminal histories, ex-offenders may be tempted to lie by not disclosing their convictions (Brown, C., 2011; Shivy et al., 2007). In a particularly helpful resource called the *Employment Information Handbook for Ex-Offenders*, the U.S. Department of Labor (2005) acknowledged that this is obviously up to them but recommended against lying on applications. This DOL handbook also recommended against too much honesty by advising ex-offenders "never [to] volunteer information that might be considered 'negative' by employers (i.e., criminal record, substance abuse history, job terminations)" when completing applications (U.S. Department of Labor, 2005). Instead, it suggests that ex-offenders respond to such questions with "will discuss." Similarly, job applications often ask applicants to indicate why they left their previous jobs. Instead of offering brutally honest responses such as "went to jail," the DOL handbook recommends that ex-offenders use more nebulous responses such as "relocated" or "contract ended" (U.S. Department of Labor, 2005). In developing its *Employment Information Handbook*, the Federal Bureau of Prisons (2011) Inmate Transition Program included these same DOL recommendations.

A third type of helping strategy related to career launching involves preparing for interviews. Because "the most dreaded part of the job search can be explaining a felony conviction to a potential employer" (U.S. Department of Labor, 2005; Federal Bureau of Prisons, 2011, p. 32), it is important to help ex-offenders prepare to do so. The *Employment Information Handbook for Ex-Offenders* (U.S. Department of Labor, 2005) provides several scripted examples of how ex-offenders could honestly and effectively respond to questions about their criminal history. "Addressing Felony Convictions in Job Interviews" identifies one possible response that also serves as an introduction to a fourth type of helping strategy.

> **Addressing Felony Convictions in Job Interviews**
>
> Interviewer: I see from your application that you have been convicted of a crime. Will you explain this to me? Tell me about it.
>
> Applicant: In my past, I was involved in drugs, but that is all behind me and I've taken control of my life. I have two years of experience in food service and want to stay in this industry and learn as much as possible. As a result of my past, when you hire me, your company is eligible for the Work Opportunity Tax Credit, which can save you up to $2,400. Are you familiar with this program?
>
> Source: U.S. Department of Labor. (2005). *Employment information handbook for ex-offenders*. Washington, DC: Author. Retrieved June 6, 2013, from exoffender.org/up/docs/Exohandbook.pdf (Appendix B).

The fourth type of strategy is to help ex-offenders learn about and tap into incentive programs that may be useful in securing employment, and two are available. First, a tax incentive program exists for employers who hire ex-offenders and other targeted groups (including veterans) who struggle finding employment. As mentioned, it is called the Work Opportunity Tax Credit, and information about it is available online at doleta.gov/business/incentives/opptax/. According to this website, employers can qualify for a tax credit of up to $2,400 for hiring an ex-felon.

The other type of incentive program uses bonding to encourage employers to hire ex-offenders. Employers who wish to hire an ex-offender can apply for a fidelity bond, which is "a business insurance policy that protects the employer against any loss of money or property due to employee dishonesty" (Federal Bureau of Prisons, 2011, p. 9). Ex-offenders can be bonded for up to $5,000 with no charge for the bonding, and the bond remains in effect for the first six months of an ex-offender's employment (Wazny, 2010). According to Wazny (2010), "approximately 40,000 applicants have obtained jobs due to being bonded and 99 percent have proven to be honest employees" (para. 2). The Federal Bonding Program is designed to incentivize the hiring of ex-offenders who serve time in state prisons, and the UNICOR Bond Program is designed to do the same for ex-offenders who serve time in federal prisons (Federal Bureau of Prisons, 2011). Information about the Federal Bonding Program and the UNICOR Bonding Program can be found online at bonds4jobs.com/ and unicor.gov, respectively.

Yet another strategy for career launching is a targeted job search. Nally et al. (2011) suggested that career counselors might want to encourage ex-offenders to focus their job search on the five occupational areas in which their research suggested that ex-offenders are most likely to obtain employment: manufacturing, wholesale and retail trades, construction, lodging and food services, and temporary help services. Nally and colleagues indicated that "temporary help agencies provided more jobs to post-release offenders than any other job sector" (p. 53) and speculated that this trend will continue. They did note, however, that temp jobs today require higher skill and education levels than in the past and therefore emphasized the importance of ex-offenders having these skills.

Another helping strategy to assist ex-offenders in securing employment involves referring them for vocational rehabilitation services. Recall that an estimated 75% of ex-offenders have substance abuse problems (Holzer et al., 2003), and substance disorders are among the qualifying conditions for vocational rehabilitation services. Note, however, that only those individuals who are in recovery qualify for these services. For those who do qualify, vocational rehabilitation services may include assessments, training, and support in finding and maintaining work.

The final strategy I offer for assisting ex-offenders in launching careers following their release from incarceration is to encourage their involvement in supervised reentry programs. According to the *Prisoner Reentry Toolkit*, "employers in need of qualified workers are more likely to hire ex-prisoners who are supervised by a reentry program than those who are not" (U.S. Department of Labor, 2013a, p. 1). Therefore, even if you are providing excellent career services to ex-offenders outside such programs, it may still be useful to encourage them to seek and participate in a structured reentry program (Wazny, 2010). This will take some research on your part, however, because available programs vary across states and communities. You will need to familiarize yourself with the programs available in your locale. Table 18.8 provides examples of reentry programs. This listing identifies just a few programs scattered across the country.

Krannich and Krannich (2005) identified other reentry programs and resources offered by government, associations, nonprofit/volunteer, and faith-based organizations (e.g.,

TABLE 18.8 Sample Reentry Programs for Ex-Offenders

Program	Location
AWEE Bridges to Jobs	Arizona
Boston Reentry Initiative (BRI)	Massachusetts
Center for Employment Opportunities (CEO)	New York
ComALERT	New York
Goodwill Easter Seals Prisoner ReEntry Initiative (PRI)	Minnesota
Michigan Prisoner Re-Entry Program	Michigan
Preventing Parolee Crime Program	California
Prisoner Reentry Transition Center	Oregon
Project RIO (ReIntegration of Offenders)	Texas
Project Return, Inc.	Tennessee
Re-entry One Stop Career Services (REOS)	Missouri
Safer Foundation	Illinois
Step-Up, Inc./Fitting Back In	Colorado
Virginia CARES	Virginia

U.S. Department of Labor, 2013a). They also recommended resources at the National Hire Network (hirenetwork.org), which are offered through its online clearinghouse.

Many of these programs are funded by grants targeting the rehabilitation of ex-offenders. Private foundations such as the Joyce Foundation offer such grants. Several federal agencies offer grants to nonprofit organizations interested in developing reentry programs for ex-offenders. The U.S. Department of Justice offers these grants through the Second Chance Act; the DOL, through the Reintegration of Ex-Offenders program (which is an outgrowth of its previous Ready4Work program); and the U.S. Department of Health and Human Services, through a variety of programs including its Offender Reentry Program (U.S. Government Accountability Office, 2012). In the event that you one day work in an agency and want to start a reentry program for ex-offenders, you may want to seek grant funding from agencies and foundations such as these.

HOMEMAKERS AND CARETAKERS

A subpopulation that often seeks career services in the community setting includes people who are transitioning into the paid workforce after an extended absence from it while doing unpaid work as homemakers or caretakers. Some of these individuals may have exited the paid workforce years earlier to devote themselves to other responsibilities; others may never have entered it. Some of these individuals may now be choosing to enter or reenter the paid workforce, and others may feel they have no choice.

Definitions and Statistics

If you are reading carefully, you have probably noticed that I have avoided any reference to gender. This is intentional. Although other resources on this topic focus exclusively on women who have focused exclusively on child care and/or homemaking, I have chosen a more inclusive approach. Rather than focusing here on reentry women, who, in this context, are defined as women who are voluntarily returning to the paid workforce after an extended absence of three or more years (Chae, 2002; Padula, 1994) or on displaced homemakers who are typically defined as women "whose sole responsibility has been working in the home and who [lose their] main source of income because of divorce, separation, or widowhood" (Locke & Gibbons, 2008, p. 32), I recognize that some stay-at-home parents and homemakers are male. Although stay-at-home fathers are far outnumbered by stay-at-home mothers, they do exist, and their numbers tripled from 1996 to 2008 (Dunn, Rochlen, & O'Brien, 2013; Helford, Stewart, Gruys, & Frank, 2012; U.S. Bureau of Labor Statistics, 2013). Specifically, females are stay-at-home mothers in 36.8% and males are stay-at-home fathers in 5.6% of all married, two-parent households with a child under the age of six (U.S. Bureau of Labor Statistics, 2013).

TABLE 18.9 Reasons for Career Transitions for Homemakers and Caretakers

Role	Caring for	Reasons for Career Transition

Homemaker and/or stay-at-home parent	• Children
	• Spouse/partner
	• Family home
		• Milestones for children
		  • Reaching school age
		  • Graduating from high school
		  • Moving out/empty nest
		• Subjective desire for career in the paid workforce
		• Financial need
		  • Loss of family income
		  • Insufficient family income
		  • Divorce
		  • Intimate partner violence
		  • Death of spouse/partner

Caretaker	• Seriously ill or disabled child • Seriously ill or disabled spouse or partner • Seriously ill, disabled, or aging parent or other relative (eldercare)	• Recovery of care recipient • Institutionalization of care recipient • Death of care recipient • Financial need

A second reason for my more inclusive approach to this topic is that stay-at-home parents/homemakers are not the only ones who choose to forego paid employment in order to dedicate themselves to caring for their family. People may withdraw from the paid workforce in order to serve as a caretaker for a seriously ill, disabled, or aging loved one. Table 18.9 presents several scenarios in which a person may serve in the role of homemaker and/or stay-at-home parent or caretaker and later seek to enter the paid workforce. In addition to identifying the care recipients for each role, this table also identifies a variety of reasons that could prompt homemakers or caretakers to reenter the paid workforce.

HOMEMAKERS AND/OR STAY-AT-HOME PARENTS. The stereotypic scenario involves an intact, two-parent family in which one parent is the sole breadwinner and the other does not engage in paid employment but instead assumes the role of homemaker, taking primary responsibility for child care and management of the household. Although 42% of first-time mothers return to work by the time their child is 3 months old and 64% return by the time their child is one year of age (Bianchi, 2011), others choose to remain out of the paid workforce to care for their children. As indicated earlier, females do represent the vast majority of homemakers, but approximately 17% of stay-at-home parents are now male (U.S. Bureau of Labor Statistics, 2013).

At some point, however, the stay-at-home parent and homemaker may want or need to transition into the paid workforce. This transition generally has a precipitant. For example, a couple may have planned for one person to be the stay-at-home parent until their youngest child enters kindergarten, until their youngest child graduates from high school, or until all of their children have moved out of the family home (thereby creating the so-called empty nest). In such cases, a developmental milestone represents the precipitant. In another scenario, a couple may have planned for one person to be the stay-at-home parent and homemaker indefinitely, but the stay-at-home parent reaches a point of wanting to work outside the home. This subjective desire for a career in the paid workforce can be a reaction to feeling isolated at home, yearning for the meaning/identity associated with paid employment, or the enjoyment associated with engaging in one's chosen line of work (Grant-Vallone & Ensher, 2011). Other such motivations for returning to work may be to feel a greater sense of equality within one's marriage, to serve as a role model for one's children, to satisfy one's own ambitions, or to benefit from the validation and intellectual stimulation associated with work (Cohen & Rabin, 2007). In all these scenarios, the transition into the paid workforce tends to be voluntary and welcomed. In such cases, the client seeking career services is referred to as a reentry parent (Chae, 2002; Padula, 1994).

With other precipitants, however, the transition into the paid workforce tends to be made out of financial necessity rather than desire. For example, the primary breadwinner may be laid off or may have an income insufficient to meet family expenses. Alternatively, a couple may divorce, which results in each of them needing income with which to support themselves and their separate households. In yet another scenario, entering the paid workforce may be the only way for a homemaker to leave a situation in which one is experiencing intimate partner violence (Chronister, Harley, Aranda, Barr, & Luginbuhl, 2011). And, as in Lakeesha's case, the primary breadwinner may die and the widow or widower may need to engage in paid employment to support the family. When a transition back to the workforce is precipitated by unwelcome factors involving financial need, the transitioning person is often referred to as a displaced homemaker (Watkins, 1988). Given that half of all marriages end in divorce and that 12% of all women become widowed at some point in their marriage (Locke & Gibbons, 2008), the displaced homemaker is a common precipitant for people to seek career services in community settings. Federal government legislation has required states to fund career services and special programs for displaced homemakers since the passage of the Vocational Technical Education Act of 1976 (Locke & Gibbons, 2008).

Caretakers. Some people choose to forego paid employment in order to dedicate themselves to serve in the role of caretaker for an ailing relative. Examples of possible care recipients include a child with a serious illness or disability, a spouse or partner whose disease or illness progresses to the point of needing enough care that he or she is unable to continue working outside the home, or an aging or ailing parent. According to the American Association of Retired Persons (AARP), 29% of the 2009 adult population reported caretaking responsibilities for an "adult or child with special needs" (Bianchi, 2011, p. 21). Table 18.10 provides data specifically about eldercare: who provides it and for whom.

Because of the difficulties associated with trying to balance both work and caretaking responsibilities (Kim,

TABLE 18.10 Percentage of U.S. Population That Provided Eldercare in 2011

By Sex		
	Males	15.4%
	Females	18.0%
By Age		
	15–24	12.8%
	25–34	10.1%
	35–44	13.2%
	45–54	23.3%
	55–64	22.4%
	65+	16.3%
By Care Recipient		
	Parent	42.4%
	Grandparent	19.1%
	Spouse/partner	4.3%
	Another relative	20.7%
	Nonrelative	25.4%

Source: Based on U.S. Bureau of Labor Statistics. (2011). American time use survey: Eldercare in 2011. Retrieved May 30, 2013 from http://data.bls.gov/cgi-bin/print.pl/tus/2011_eldercare_factsheet.htm

Ingersoll-Dayton, & Kwak, 2013), people may be motivated to leave paid employment and assume a full-time caretaking role. Financial considerations may also contribute to such decisions. When someone develops Alzheimer's disease, for example, it is not uncommon for them to reach a point in which it is unsafe for them to live alone. Although one option is placement in a nursing home, the costs may be prohibitive. With an average annual costs of $78,110 per year for a semiprivate room and $87,235 per year for a private room in a nursing home (Alzheimer's Association, 2013), leaving one's paid position in the workforce to care for one's parent may make the most financial sense.

Whereas people usually choose the homemaker role intentionally and may or may not plan to enter the paid workforce eventually, people who enter into the role of caretaker usually do so out of necessity and hope to return sooner rather than later. After an extended absence, both homemakers and caretakers likely need assistance in transitioning back into the paid workforce. In the next section, we explore some of the challenges related to this transition.

Employment Challenges

Homemakers and caretakers attempting to transition back into the paid workforce after an extended absence may face a variety of challenges. In this section, I address five clusters of employment challenges often experienced by homemakers and caretakers: (1) skills and education, (2) confidence, (3) networking and references, (4) others' perceptions, and (5) life balance. Although the nature of these challenges may vary based on an individual's socioeconomic status and financial situation (Bianchi, 2011), these five categories of employment challenges are very common.

SKILLS AND EDUCATION. One challenge for homemakers and caretakers involves their skills and education. These clients may have an insufficient level of education, they may lack up-to-date skills, or skills that were once sharp may have grown rusty (Helford et al., 2012; Locke & Gibbons, 2008; Watkins, 1988). With regard to education, homemakers and caretakers may face the same obstacles as entry-level workers. As you know, postsecondary education is increasingly necessary to obtain high-paying jobs. Especially in the case of displaced homemakers who may never have intended to seek paid employment, insufficient education is common. Locke and Gibbons (2008) indicated that nearly one in four displaced homemakers has not completed high school and that more than one in three displaced homemakers has no more than a high school education. Even those with college degrees, however, may find that the knowledge and skills they learned in college have since become obsolete. This is particularly common with regard to the use of technology in the workplace.

CONFIDENCE. Homemakers and caretakers preparing to reenter the labor force may also struggle with crises of confidence (Adams, 2012; Ericksen, Jurgens, Garrett, & Swedburg, 2008). Although their lack of confidence may be due in part to rusty or deficient skills, it can also be due to other factors. For example, a stay-at-home parent may have grown accustomed to introducing herself as "just a mom" and may struggle with owning a professional title. As children get older and less dependent, stay-at-home parents may struggle with feelings of worth even in the home setting (Cohen & Rabin, 2007). Others worry about competing with coworkers who are much younger and more recently educated. Even those who feel confident in their skills and abilities may be much less confident about convincing a potential employer to hire them.

NETWORKING AND REFERENCES. Generally speaking, a homemaker or caretaker has been networking with others engaged in similar activities. Stay-at-home parents, for example, may network with other parents to share play dates, child-rearing strategies, homework tips, carpooling, and so forth. People engaged in eldercare for extended periods are most likely networking with geriatric health professionals and family members to address various concerns. Thus, the networking process often used to identify job opportunities and informal referrals can pose a challenge. Identifying appropriate references who can speak about their current abilities may be difficult for those who have been absent from the workforce for extended periods. If the vast majority of one's time every day for the past decade has been spent at home caring for one's children, spouse, partner, or elder, it is difficult to maintain relationships with former colleagues and supervisors. The chasm between your respective realities and priorities seems to widen with each passing year. Even if you do maintain contact with former employers, their ability to speak in any meaningful way about your current skills is questionable at best. Thus, creating a reference list can pose quite the challenge for returning homemakers and caretakers.

OTHERS' PERCEPTIONS. Another challenge for homemakers and caretakers in returning to the workforce involves managing others' perceptions during the job search process and once hired. Employment gaps appear on résumés and may raise questions or concerns on the part of potential employers. Although this is an issue for both men and women, employment gaps related to child care can have an even more negative impact on men due to the dissonance with sex role stereotypes (Dunn et al., 2013; Helford et al., 2008). Potential employers may also react to employment gaps with concerns about whether one's skills are current, the degree to which a returning homemaker or caretaker will be committed to work, and the likelihood of work interruptions and absences as an employee attempts to balance work and care responsibilities (Cohen & Rabin, 2007; Kim et al., 2013).

Once hired, reentering homemakers and caretakers still need to manage others' perceptions. Water cooler references to the mommy track or the daddy track may reflect thinly veiled concerns about divided loyalties and one's commitment to work (Helford et al., 2008). As Cohen and Rabin (2007) noted, "Those taking a number of years off are rendered suspect in the eyes of others" and coworkers may wonder, "'Will she really put her nose to the grindstone after being at home?'" (p. 30). Even returning workers with graduate degrees may be surprised to detect coworker assumptions of their limited competence or seriousness about their career.

LIFE BALANCE. It can be difficult to refute others' concerns about divided loyalties when one is struggling to balance a new job with competing responsibilities at home. This is especially true for women returning to work. Research has consistently found that women continue to bear the burden of homemaker and child-care responsibilities even after returning to work (Ericksen et al., 2008). This phenomenon, in which women bear an inordinate proportion of household and child-care responsibilities even when working just as many hours outside the home as their husbands, is often referred to as the second shift (Hochschild, 2003). When one's return to work is precipitated by divorce or death, life balance challenges include adjusting to the many other changes that have occurred, which may include relocation, changes in one's social circle and support network, financial pressures, and grief reactions (Locke & Gibbons, 2008).

Helping Strategies

Now that you have a sense of the types of challenges that homemakers and caretakers may face as they attempt to transition back into paid employment, we conclude by exploring some helping strategies specific to each area of challenge. As in the previous section, this section addresses five categories of helping strategies: (1) skills and education, (2) confidence, (3) networking and reentry, (4) managing perceptions, and (5) finding a new life balance.

SKILLS AND EDUCATION. When working with homemakers and caretakers interested in returning to the paid workforce, it is important to help them conduct an inventory of their education and skills. You should help clients assess (a) the professional, work-related skills they had at the point they left their last job; (b) their current proficiency in using these skills; (c) skills they have developed since leaving their last job; and (d) the skills and levels of proficiency needed for the type of job they now hope to get. Special attention may be needed to assist these clients in recognizing that they have indeed learned new skills since leaving their job and in realizing the potential value of these skills in the marketplace. For example, transferable skills likely developed by stay-at-home parents include "multitasking, interpersonal skills, growing human capabilities, and habits of integrity" (Crittenden, as cited in Cohen & Rabin, 2007, p. 34).

As an outgrowth of this honest assessment of skills, counselors should help clients determine which skills may need updating and identify strategies for doing so (Adams, 2012; Cohen & Rabin, 2007). Given the fast pace of technological innovations in the workplace, for example, clients may benefit from enrolling in workshops or courses to improve their proficiency in the use of commonly used computer software. To remain up to date with the latest developments in their field, clients may also benefit from immersing themselves in recent literature related to their profession and attending conferences sponsored by professional associations for their industry (Chae, 2002). Other clients may decide they need additional formal education. Clients who are among the 22% of displaced homemakers who do not hold high school diplomas (Locke & Gibbons, 2008) may decide to enroll in a GED program. Clients who want to work in the informational technology (IT) field may decide to take an IT course at a local college to update their knowledge base. Others may choose to pursue a college or graduate degree as part of their transition back into the paid workforce. You or some of your classmates may be pursuing a graduate degree in counseling as part of this very transition.

CONFIDENCE. Although confidence is a broader concept than self-efficacy, the two share much in common, and I encourage you to draw on what you have already learned about improving self-efficacy as you seek strategies for helping clients build confidence. Recall from the coverage of social cognitive career theory (SCCT; Lent, Brown, & Hackett, 2002) in Chapter 4, improving self-efficacy and confidence involves a two-pronged approach. The first prong involves developing the skills necessary to warrant a high degree of confidence. The second prong involves developing accurate self-perceptions to give oneself credit for skills and positive qualities one already has. Updating skills and education (as discussed above) is therefore one important way to improve client confidence. Another way is to honor the time your client spent as a stay-at-home parent, homemaker, and/or caregiver as a career in and of itself rather than denigrating or marginalizing it (Schultheiss, 2009). This attitude should be evident in your conversations with clients and in your exploration of the transferrable skills they developed in these roles. You could also share Super's (1984) life-space rainbow and help clients recognize the value of all the roles, including homemaker and worker. Cognitive behavioral strategies to dispute irrational thoughts can be helpful in combating self-talk that threatens one's confidence.

NETWORKING AND REENTRY PROGRAMS. Because networking is such an important part of a contemporary job search, it is essential that career counselors encourage clients to do so rather than rely on "old school" methods of searching the newspaper classified section and mailing résumés in response to posted ads. Rather than simply encouraging returning homemakers and caretakers to begin networking, however, it is important to help them prepare to do so. Developing their skills and confidence renders clients better prepared to talk with others about their career aspirations and thereby serves as a foundation for future networking.

Developing a story to share with others is another important part of this preparation. The story should be true, of course, and should address one's former work life, one's absence from the paid labor force, what one gained from homemaking and/or caretaking experiences, why one wants to reenter the labor force, and what assets one has to offer. A narrative approach to career counseling can be useful in helping clients develop such a story (Locke & Gibbons, 2008). Cohen and Rabin (2007) recommend that clients begin by having conversations with a safe circle of friends to test and fine-tune their stories. They also recommend having more than one version of the story: a complete version, an elevator pitch version, and an even shorter version. Once ready to begin their networking, returning homemakers and caretakers should consider reconnecting with people from their past (e.g., friends from school, former coworkers, and former supervisors) and people with whom they have interacted more recently (perhaps through volunteer efforts).

In addition to networking, some returning homemakers and caretakers may explore the viability of reentry programs. These programs are generally geared toward highly educated female professionals and are often run by universities, corporations, and government agencies. The Harvard Business School (2013) offers a two-day reentry program for "women with high-powered degrees and professional expertise" (http://www.alumni.hbs.edu/careers/cyc.html para. 1); Goldman Sachs (2013) runs a 10-week "returnship program" designed to "develop talented individuals who, after an extended absence from the workforce, are seeking to re-start their career" (para. 3); and the National Association of Women Lawyers (2013) has an "on-ramp . . . initiative designed to help women lawyers who have left active practice re-enter the legal workplace" (para. 1). Cohen and Rabin (2011) provide a list of such programs across the nation as part of their business (iRelaunch; irelaunch.com/career reentry). iRelaunch holds an annual Return to Work conference (Cohen & Rabin, 2013) and, like the reentry programs described above, this conference targets highly trained, well-educated female professionals, with 95% of conference attendees being female and 75% of participants holding graduate degrees. For clients who do not fit these criteria, career counselors may want to offer group programs addressing topics relevant to reentry (Ericksen et al., 2008; McAllister & Ponterotto, 1992).

MANAGING PERCEPTIONS. Career counselors may also assist clients in developing strategies to manage the way they are perceived by potential employers, new bosses, and new coworkers. First, reentering homemakers and caretakers should be aware of how they may be perceived (addressed above). Second, they should understand that talk is cheap—that the only way to combat perceptions of them as having divided loyalties, less commitment to work, and outdated skills is to show people otherwise. Returning homemakers and caretakers should view their first year or so back in the paid workforce as an "investment period" (Cohen & Rabin, 2007, p. 146). During this time, they should go above and beyond to polish their skills and demonstrate to their coworkers and supervisors a level of commitment that they can trust. They should also avoid behaviors or comments that may lend credence to concerns about divided loyalties or inability to juggle work and family responsibilities. For example, they should avoid frequently identifying their children as a reason they cannot participate in an activity or project or as a reason they are absent or late for work (Cohen & Rabin, 2007).

TABLE 18.11 Providers of Career Services in Community Settings

Professional counselors	Generalists • Counselors whose clients seek assistance for a wide variety of issues, some of which will invariably involve career issues Specialists • Career counselors • Master career counselors • Master career development professionals • Vocational psychologists
Paraprofessionals	Global career development facilitators (GCDFs) • Credentialed by the Center for Credentialing and Education (CCE) Certified workforce development professionals (CWDPs) • Credentialed by the National Association of Workforce Development Professionals • nawdp.org/AM/Template.cfm?Section=Certification Offender workforce development specialists (OWDS) • Credentialed by the U.S. Department of Justice's National Institute of Corrections through a formal, collaborative relationship with the National Career Development Association • nicic.gov/Library/022173

FINDING A NEW LIFE BALANCE. These clients may indeed struggle with life balance issues as they make their transition back into the paid workforce. This is especially likely when stay-at-home parents seek employment while their children are still young enough to require child care. Obviously, one strategy to address this is to hire the best child-care providers one can afford. Another strategy involves preparing the family—children included—for their transition back to work. Children may learn to take on additional chores, spouses should increase their share of household responsibilities, and contingency plans should be established. As an example of a contingency plan, Cohen and Rabin (2007) recommend identifying a go-to person to whom children can turn when neither parent is available "for real or perceived crises, advice, homework help, or just someone close to hang out with for a while" (p. 147). Because children may experience the most adjustment issues at the onset of a parent's return to work, having a go-to person contingency plan is especially important during the investment period, when the parent needs to focus on demonstrating a high level of commitment to a new job. Lining up support is essential to a returning homemaker's success in making this transition (Ericksen et al., 2008).

When working with displaced homemakers for whom a divorce or death of a spouse of partner has prompted their need to enter the paid workforce, counselors should be prepared not only to address career management issues but also their possible need for emotional support. Their lives were thrown off balance by the divorce or death, and finding a new life balance includes adjusting to these changes. Returning homemakers or caretakers may need to revise their expectations of themselves and their standards for their homes. Household chores may be completed less frequently, spices may no longer be alphabetized, home-cooked meals may become less elaborate (or nonexistent), and the family can still survive.

PROVIDERS OF CAREER-RELATED SERVICES IN COMMUNITY SETTINGS

Each of the subpopulations discussed in this chapter experiences unique struggles that span the continuum of career and personal issues. They may all benefit not only from career development interventions but also from counseling with a professional who is qualified to address both career and personal issues at a deeper level. Not all providers of career services in community settings are qualified, however, to address both types of issues. Table 18.11 identifies a variety of providers who offer career-related services in community settings. Some of these providers are professional counselors who are qualified to address both career and personal issues at a deeper level; some are career paraprofessionals who are limited to the provision of career development interventions.

CAREER SERVICE SITES IN THE COMMUNITY SETTING

Now that we've established who most frequently seeks and who provides career counseling and other career services in community settings, you may be wondering exactly *where* these services are offered. Table 18.12 identifies several venues within community settings where career-related services are offered. These venues include government-operated agencies, community-based agencies, private practice, and corporate settings.

TABLE 18.12 Community Settings in Which Career Counselors May Be Employed

Government settings	State employment security agencies (SESAs)
	• Administer the federal-state unemployment insurance program
	• servicelocator.org/OWSLinks.asp
	One-stop career centers (also known as American job centers)
	• Serve as the state employment service offices with which all recipients of unemployment insurance benefits must generally register
	• Provide services to all citizens (whether unemployed or employed) who seek them
	• Tend to employ at least one staff member who specializes in assisting veterans, people with disabilities, and at-risk youth
	• servicelocator.org/onestopcenters.asp
	State vocational rehabilitation agencies
	• Specialize in the provision of vocational rehabilitation services
	• ed.gov/svr
Community-based agencies	Nonprofit organizations that are privately held but eligible for government funding
	Some examples of career services agencies with numerous offices across the country include:
	• JVS (jvs.org)
	• Goodwill Industries International, Inc. (goodwill.org)
	• Easter Seals Workforce Development Services (easterseals.com)
	• Centers for Independent Living (ncil.org)
	• Center for Employment Opportunities (ceoworks.org)
Private practice	For-profit entities that are ineligible for government grants
	• Sole proprietorships
	• Llimited liability companies (LLCs)
	• S corporations
Corporate settings	Corporate career development programs are a means by which a large corporate employer can retain and further develop talented staff members
	• Provide employees with systematic feedback on their performance
	• Make additional assessments available to identify their greatest strengths and passions
	• Help employees identify career advancement opportunities within the corporation
	• Maintain a list of job openings within the organization
	• Offer a training component by which employees can develop new skills and acquire new certifications
	• Facilitate mentoring programs

PUTTING IT ALL TOGETHER

It is my contention that all counselors in community settings should be prepared to address career issues presented by clients. Unlike other mental health professionals, counselors can take comfort and pride in the fact that their training programs include required coursework on career development and career counseling. If you are working as a generalist counselor in an agency or private practice, you will surely see clients who are concerned about their job or lack thereof.

I introduced you to several groups of people who frequently seek career services in the community setting. You learned about the career challenges sometimes experienced by people with disabilities, veterans and transitioning military service members, prisoners and ex-offenders, and homemakers and caretakers. For each of these populations, I provided employment statistics, an introduction to their unique challenges and needs, and an overview of helping strategies.

My hope is that the balance of breadth and depth in this section will prepare you to provide career services to a wide variety of people in community settings. You should understand, however, that this information is just a start. As you begin working with clients from these various subgroups, you should invest in learning even more about their specific challenges and about interventions that can help them.

The chapter identified the types of professional counselors and paraprofessionals who most frequently provide career services in community settings before concluding with an overview of the specific settings in which these services are provided. You should leave this chapter feeling convinced of the importance of professional counselors providing career services in government agencies, community-based agencies, private practice, and even corporate settings.

CHAPTER 19

Charting Your Own Career Path as a Professional Counselor

As a graduate student training to become a professional counselor, you likely approached this course with an interest not only in learning how to provide career counseling to others but also in applying insights to your own career development. After all, the very fact that you have chosen to enroll in a graduate degree program suggests that you are in the midst of a career development process of your own. You may have chosen to enter a master's degree program immediately after earning your undergraduate degree, in which case you are also anticipating your first professional position. Alternatively, you may have already considerable work experience and have chosen to enter a graduate degree program because you want to change careers and become a professional counselor. The motivations for entering your graduate program may be as varied as the students with whom you attend classes.

As we embark on this final chapter, the first question to consider is why *you* chose to apply for and enroll in a graduate degree program in counseling. Was your choice of academic programs the result of careful consideration? Had you participated in career development activities or career counseling in an effort to identify your desired career direction? Or was your choice based on happenstance? Perhaps you chose the program because a friend was planning to enroll, it sounded like fun, and you could carpool together. Perhaps you chose to apply to the program after taking what you thought would be a single class, but you found that you liked it so much you wanted to continue. Or perhaps, on some level, you chose the program to gain insight into and healing of relational wounds from your past. Reflecting on your initial motivation offers key insight that will help you understand why you are currently on this career path.

Beyond examining your initial motivation, however, you also want to reflect on whether you wish to remain on the path toward a career as a professional counselor. Whether you intentionally chose this path after careful consideration or stumbled upon it, the prospect of becoming a professional counselor may feel like a perfect fit for you, or you may now have some reservations about how successful and satisfied you will be as a counselor. As scary as that may sound, it sometimes happens that students enroll in a counseling program only to discover that the profession is not a good fit for them. Students may realize this as a result of their own dissonant feelings or beliefs. Something in the pit of their stomach or in the back of their head may be whispering that the profession of counseling is not for them. Some students may receive feedback from their professors and/or supervisors encouraging them to consider other career options. On rare occasions, students may actually be dismissed from counseling programs for academic or disciplinary reasons, thereby forcing them to explore other options.

So what about *you*? How good a fit does the counseling profession seem for you? Do you indeed want to continue on this career path? If you have any doubts whatsoever, take time now to seek some career counseling for yourself as a client. As a student, you likely have access to free career counseling services at your university. Use them. Share your concerns candidly with your counselor, and rest assured that these conversations will not be

TABLE 19.1 Steps for Charting Your Own Course as a Professional Counselor

1. Prepare yourself.
2. Engage in a job search process.
3. Adjust to your new career.
4. Engage in long-term career planning.

reported to the professors in your counseling program. Maybe career counseling will reaffirm your initial choice to pursue a career as a counselor, or maybe you will decide to go in another direction. Whatever the outcome, it is important that you allow yourself the opportunity to reconsider and confirm your career direction.

The remainder of this chapter is dedicated to those of you who decide to remain on the path toward a career as a professional counselor. Table 19.1 lists steps that will guide you as we explore what you can do now to enter the job market as prepared and marketable as possible, ways in which to manage the job search process, issues related to adjusting to your new career, and how to engage in long-term career management.

STEP 1: PREPARE YOURSELF

Rather than waiting until the semester before graduation to begin thinking about what it will take to become employed and successful as a professional counselor, it is wise to be proactive and to prepare well in advance. If you haven't already begun doing so, this section will provide you with ideas about what such preparation might entail.

Gather Information

To begin, gather information that will be useful in making choices about ways in which you still need preparation. Consistent with the classic contribution of Frank Parsons (1909), you should gather information about yourself as well as information about the job market for professional counselors.

INFORMATION ABOUT YOURSELF. Although you are far beyond needing the typical career assessments that cover interests and/or values, you can benefit from evaluating your relative strengths and weaknesses as a future counselor. This type of information can then inform decisions about how to prepare yourself to be as successful as possible in obtaining and performing in a position as a professional counselor.

The first source of such information is you. Take some time to reflect on what you perceive as your relative strengths and weaknesses. Begin by reviewing your academic transcript and noting the grades you have earned in various courses. I strongly encourage you to consult one or more listings of counselor competencies. As shown in Table 19.2, several professional associations concerned with the practice of professional counseling in various settings have promulgated competencies specific to those settings or specializations, and at least one of these listings should be relevant to your career aspirations. As a graduate student, you would be wise to review these competency listings early in your academic career in order to understand what will be expected of you on entry into the profession. When reviewing these competencies, identify your relative strengths and weaknesses, and use this information to guide your selection

TABLE 19.2 Counselor Competency Listings, by Organization

Issuing Organization	Title of Document
American School Counselor Association (ASCA)	School Counselor Competencies
Association for Assessment in Counseling (AACE)	Association for Assessment in Counseling (AACE) School Counselor Competencies
Association for Multicultural Counseling and Development (AMCD)	AMCD Multicultural Counseling Competencies
National Career Development Association	Career Counseling Competencies
National Career Development Association	Multicultural Career Counseling Competencies
National Association for College Admission Counseling (NACAC)	NACAC Statement on Counselor Competencies
National Employment Counseling Association (NECA)	National Employment Counseling Competencies
U.S. Department of Health and Human Services, Substance Abuse and Mental Health Services Administration (SAMHSA)	Addiction Counseling Competencies

of additional courses, additional readings, and supplemental experiences.

Another valuable source of such information is your academic adviser. As a graduate student intent on being as prepared and competent as possible after graduation from your counseling program, you should make an appointment to meet with your academic adviser in order to learn about his or her perceptions of your relative strengths and weaknesses. Of course, you should use such a meeting to discuss ways in which you might capitalize on your strengths and opportunities to become more knowledgeable or skilled in areas of weakness.

INFORMATION ABOUT THE WORLD OF WORK. While meeting with your academic adviser, you should also seek information about the realities of the work setting in which you hope to gain employment. To guide this part of your meeting, you may want to bring your résumé. By reviewing your current résumé, your adviser can help you identify additional academic, work, and volunteer experiences that may help you be more marketable after graduation. For example, your adviser may note that, although you are enrolled in a school counseling program, you only have experiences working or volunteering at the elementary school level. If you have any interest in becoming marketable for middle or high school counseling positions, your adviser might encourage you to seek some experiences at these levels prior to your graduation. If you aspire to become a career counselor in a nonprofit agency, your adviser might encourage you to take a course on grant writing because this skill is often a valuable selling point when seeking a position with a nonprofit.

In addition to seeking your adviser's opinions about how to be most marketable in the world of work, you may also want to conduct informational interviews with several area employers in the settings of interest to you. If you are interested in being a college counselor, you may want to interview the director of your university's career services unit as well as the director of your university's counseling and psychological services center. You may also want to meet with an administrator responsible for hiring counselors at nearby community colleges. Those interested in becoming school counselors may want to meet with principals and counselors who participate in the hiring process. If you are interested in career counseling in a government agency, you should identify various agencies employing career counselors and seek informational interviews there. In all such cases, adhere to the basics of informational interviewing as discussed earlier in this text and by Crosby (2010).

Another way to gather information about the world of work is via the same sources of occupational information about which you learned in Chapter 13. Sources such as the Occupational Information Network (O*NET; onetonline.org) will be useful in gathering information about the demands of the job as well as about labor and market information. If you are willing to relocate after earning your degree, for example, you may wish to compare the wages and employment information in several different states.

It is often beneficial to begin tracking job openings and reading job postings in your field long before you graduate. By doing so, you may be able to identify some commonly required or preferred qualifications that are not yet reflected in your repertoire or résumé. You can then use this knowledge of such qualifications in job postings to gain insight into ways in which you may better prepare yourself for the job search as well as for the realities of the job.

Adopt an Attitude of Self-Responsibility

Perhaps the most important step involved in preparing to enter professional counseling is to adopt an attitude of self-responsibility. Rather than viewing your professors, your adviser, and/or your program as being responsible for your preparation as a counselor, you will be wise to view yourself as primarily responsible. We can't simply flip open the top of our head and invite our professors to pour in the knowledge and skills we will need to master. In fact, I believe that students have a larger impact on their learning than their professors. What you do as a student and how you approach the learning process has a lasting impact on the quality of your education. Adopting an attitude of self-responsibility requires that you recognize, accept, and even embrace your ultimate responsibility for your preparation as a professional counselor. Chances are that there is no one more invested in your future than you.

The adoption of an attitude of self-responsibility should feel empowering. In essence, adopting such an attitude allows you to become an active participant in your preparation as a professional counselor rather than a passive recipient of education. Effective education involves a partnership between students and their teachers, but your role as a student is incredibly important. By recognizing the choices available to you and acting on them, you can exercise a great deal of control over your future as a counselor. At the least, these choices include which degree program you complete at what university, the approach you take to each of your courses, the types of relationships you establish with your adviser and professors, supplemental experiences you seek while completing your degree, and how you address any personal needs for counseling.

Take Action to Prepare Yourself

Common wisdom suggests, of course, that actions speak louder than words. Attitude will take you only so far toward becoming well prepared as a professional counselor. In addition to adopting an attitude of self-responsibility, you should ensure that your actions demonstrate this attitude. To assess the degree to which you have already been actively demonstrating responsibility for your preparation as a future counselor, consider the questions posed in Table 19.3.

As you responded to these questions, what reactions did you experience? Did your responses suggest that you have consistently made choices to become as well prepared as possible, or did they reveal some other opportunities to do so? Although you may have thought Table 19.3 might be better titled *Embrace Your Inner Counselor-Nerd*, I hope

TABLE 19.3 A Baker's Dozen: 13 Self-Assessment Questions to Gauge the Level of Responsibility You Demonstrate for Your Preparation as a Professional Counselor

Question	Yes	No
1. Before applying to a graduate program in counseling, did I compare the counseling programs offered by competing universities and select the program I thought would best prepare me?		
2. After admission, did I make an appointment to meet with an adviser to discuss my career goals, develop a program of study, and identify electives that might be best suited to my goals?		
3. Before registering for courses, do I seek "peer advising" to gather opinions about the advantages and disadvantages of taking any given course with a specific instructor and strive to take only those courses in which I am confident I will be well prepared, even if earning an A might be more difficult?		
4. Do I enroll in courses at a pace that allows me to develop mastery over the knowledge and skills being taught?		
5. At the beginning of the semester, do I introduce myself to each instructor and develop a healthy working relationship with him or her?		
6. While taking a course, do I complete assigned readings even if I will likely earn a good grade in the course without doing so?		
7. While taking a course, do I employ study strategies that are well suited to my individual learning style?		
8. When receiving constructive criticism from an instructor or supervisor, do I respond nondefensively and actively seek to understand how I can improve?		
9. In the unfortunate situation in which I take a course in which I learn less than I hoped, do I identify ways to compensate so that I learn the information and develop the skills I will need as a professional counselor?		
10. Do I seek other experiences to supplement my preparation as a counselor?		
11. Am I a member of the professional associations affiliated with my chosen profession (American Counseling Association, American College Counseling Association, American Mental Health Counselors Association, American School Counselor Association, National Career Development Association, etc.)?		
12. Have I attended any counseling-related conferences yet?		
13. Have I sought counseling to address unresolved issues that could potentially limit my effectiveness as a counselor?		

the questions helped you recognize the many ways in which you can actively influence the quality of your preparation. The following paragraphs elaborate on several themes reflected in Table 19.3, all of which relate to behaviors that have an impact on your preparation as a professional counselor.

ENGAGE IN SELF-CARE. First and foremost, it is essential that you engage in high-quality self-care to facilitate your preparation as a professional counselor. Throughout this text, you've read about the ways in which personal counseling and career counseling are fundamentally intertwined. A person's psychological well-being and personal life affects one's satisfaction and success at work, and a person's satisfaction and success at work affects one's psychological well-being and personal life. This maxim will be true not only for your future clients but also for you as a counselor.

You and your future clients will benefit from your choice to take care of yourself. At the most basic level, this requires that you engage in self-care activities on a regular basis to meet your needs for adequate sleep, nutrition, exercise, and so on. It also includes making choices to maintain or work toward a fulfilling interpersonal life with family, friends, and significant others. It may also entail your participation in counseling (as a client) to improve your psychological well-being. Counseling may benefit you in managing stress, reducing anxiety, overcoming depression, resolving relational wounds from your past, or making decisions about current relationships.

Becoming and staying healthy and satisfied with your own life is an essential step toward becoming an effective counselor. It is foundational in nature because the most important tool in the counseling process is *you*. Personal well-being is not enough, however, to ensure your effectiveness as a counselor. You will also need to be proactive and intentional regarding your formal preparation as a counselor.

BE INTENTIONAL IN YOUR SELECTION OF COURSES AND INSTRUCTORS. One important way in which you can influence your preparation is through your selection of courses and instructors. Although most of the courses you will take are likely required components of your graduate program of study, you will surely have some room for electives. Your selection of electives is important and should be guided by your career goals. For example, if you aspire to work in a community agency setting, you might fill your electives with courses about substance abuse, treatment planning, couple and family counseling, and so on. Someone who yearns to become an elementary school counselor might choose electives related to play therapy, classroom management, or parenting strategies. In other words, your choice of electives should be geared toward expanding your knowledge and skills in a way that will enhance your marketability and performance in your chosen counseling setting. In contrast, choosing electives on the basis of convenience or reputed easiness is unlikely to result in the quality of preparation you want and need when you enter the job market as a prospective new counselor.

Your selection of instructors is also essential. Though I wish I could say that all instructors are highly effective at teaching all courses, this is not reality. Some instructors are more effective at teaching some courses than they are at teaching other courses. Professor Plum may excel at teaching courses related to assessment and diagnosis but struggle when teaching courses on theory. Unless you happen to attend a graduate school in Lake Wobegon (where all the professors are strong, good-looking, *and* above average), you've surely discovered that some instructors are simply more effective than other instructors. Some professors are really effective with some types of students but not so effective with other types of students. The choices you make in this regard affect the quality of your preparation.

To assist you in selecting courses and instructors, my recommendation is that you consult with both your faculty adviser and your peers. Your faculty adviser should serve as an excellent resource in helping you identify electives that will be most beneficial to you, but he or she is unlikely to offer any advice with regard to selection of instructors. For such input, seek peer advising by talking with other students about their experiences with various instructors. Key to making effective use of such information, though, is to put the information into context. When talking with others, ask follow-up questions. What course did they have with the instructor? Did they like the instructor? Why or why not? Did they learn a lot? Listen for patterns related to the particular course being taught as well as the instructional style. Again, some professors are really effective with some types of students but not as effective with others. Similar to reading a movie critic's review of a new film, you need to take into account whether you have the same taste as the critic. With movies, shared appreciation of a particular genre might be a good indicator of shared taste. With instructors, shared appreciation of teaching style would suggest that you and your peer may have similar reactions to the same instructor.

PACE YOURSELF. Even when choosing all the "right" courses and instructors, though, the quality of your preparation will suffer if you do not pace yourself appropriately. To borrow a splendid metaphor offered by one of my colleagues, a counselor education program should not be approached like a hot dog eating contest. Enroll in courses at a pace at which you can take time to digest the information being presented and develop the skills being taught. By pacing yourself, you make a decision to allow yourself the time to become well prepared. An additional benefit of not racing through your program is that you'll feel less stressed and have more time for the other parts of your life.

EXCEL IN YOUR COURSEWORK. Becoming a well-prepared counselor does take time and energy. You will be much better prepared if you make a decision to invest whatever time and energy is necessary to master the knowledge and skills addressed in each of your courses. This involves the use of sound study skills and setting high expectations. Basics such as completing all assigned readings before class, taking notes on your reading, remaining fully engaged in each class meeting, starting assignments well in advance of due dates, and employing study strategies well suited to your learning style should be self-evident.

With regard to expectations, keep in mind that getting an *A* in a course does not necessarily mean you have mastered the knowledge and skills you need. All it means is that you have done enough in the course to earn an *A*. Instructor standards and university norms vary widely and greatly affect where the bar is set and what the expectations are for earning an *A*. As you've likely discovered, it is possible to learn more in a class in which you earn a *B* than in a class in which you earn an *A*. Thus, it is crucial that you recognize the difference. When learning a lot in a difficult class with high expectations, prioritize your learning over your grade point average (GPA). When you can earn an easy *A* with minimal effort, exercise responsibility for your learning and go above and beyond what is required for an *A*.

GO ABOVE AND BEYOND. Another way in which you can go above and beyond is to seek other experiences to supplement your preparation. The quality of your preparation can be improved by your choice to seek other learning opportunities. Consider the many ways in which you can help yourself become better prepared. You may choose to take additional coursework above and beyond what is required to earn your degree. You may choose to join one or more professional associations, receive and read the association journals, and attend conferences. You may choose to participate in a community-based program focused on cross-cultural relations, such as the Cultural Diversity and Historical Enrichment programs offered by the Eracism Foundation (eracismfoundation.org). You may decide to substitute-teach in order to gain more experience in school settings. You may choose to volunteer at a domestic violence shelter or to teach a career development course in a prison. As a prospective career counselor, you may choose to complete the training necessary for the optional global career development facilitator (GCDF) credential in addition to earning your master's degree and meeting licensure requirements.

The sky is the limit when it comes to identifying supplemental experiences to become better prepared for a career as a counselor. The types of experiences that will be most beneficial to you depend both on your own individual needs and on the demands of the specialized work setting in which you hope to work. To help guide your choice of supplemental experiences, therefore, rely on the insights you gained while gathering information about your own strengths and weaknesses as a prospective counselor and about the realities of the workplace and current expectations for counselors.

By following these guidelines, you will likely approach the job search process with a level of confidence based on being truly well prepared. Indeed, adhering to these recommendations will help protect you from experiencing postgraduation 20/20 hindsight about what you wish you had done to better prepare yourself. Rather than feeling such regrets, my hope is that you will embark on the next stage of career development—the job search—with eager anticipation. First, though, there is one more step to take to enter the field of counseling: You need to obtain licensure. Before turning our attention to the job search process, the next section of this chapter provides you with important information regarding licensure.

Obtain Licensure and Other Credentials

Because licensure is legally required to practice counseling, you need to become licensed before you begin working as a counselor. If you plan to launch a job search soon after graduating, you will need to apply immediately for your counseling license so that you can include licensure on your résumé and meet the legal requirements for employment as a counselor. Perhaps not so obvious, though, is the importance of obtaining licensure even if you plan to delay your job search and your entrance into a counseling position. For example, some graduates of our school counseling program plan to remain in their teaching positions for at least a year before seeking a counseling position, maybe because they are not yet ready to leave the classroom or because they are waiting until a counseling position becomes available in their current school district, or maybe some of our graduates qualify for licenses as school counselors and as professional counselors. They may plan to work as a school counselor and not see any immediate need for a professional counseling license. In such cases, it may be tempting simply to wait to apply for the counseling credentials. My advice: Don't wait.

RISKS OF DELAYING APPLICATION FOR LICENSURE. In waiting to obtain your credentials, you risk becoming ineligible for them because your eligibility for any given credential is based on whether you meet the requirements in place *at the time of your application*, not at the time of your graduation. In other words, if the requirements for a given credential change over time, you may find yourself ineligible for the credential at a later date. This means, of course, that you would also be ineligible for counseling positions requiring these credentials. Two examples are offered to illustrate this situation.

First, state-based requirements may change. The state laws governing the license as a professional counselor may change. Instead of requiring LPCs to complete a master's degree program of at least 48 credits, the new law may require at least 60 credits. Unless you are fortunate enough to fall within a grandfathering window, the fact that the state required a 48-hour master's degree when you graduated will not help you if you failed to apply for licensure when those regulations were in place. In this scenario, it is likely that you would need to take, at a minimum, an additional 12 credits of coursework to meet the new requirements for licensure. The state department of education's requirements for a school counseling credential may change. Instead of requiring a 600-clock-hour internship in a school setting, the new requirement may specify that the 600-clock-hour internship include experiences in elementary, middle, *and* high school settings. Again, the fact that the state did not specify that the school counseling internship include experiences at all three levels when you graduated will not help you if you failed to apply for licensure before the new regulations took effect. In this scenario, it is likely that you would need to complete a second internship providing for supervised experiences at the elementary, middle, and high school levels before qualifying for the school counseling credential needed for employment as a school counselor.

Second, university-based requirements may change. Generally speaking, the application process for a license requires that an applicant (a) meet specific training standards specified by state law; (b) pass an examination; and (c) receive a recommendation from an approved training program, which would be your university's counseling program. For universities to gain state approval of their training programs, they must submit their program requirements to the state. They must undergo periodic audits and must submit changes in requirements to the state. Thus, when providing a recommendation for an applicant to become licensed, the university is verifying that the applicant has met all requirements *currently* on record as constituting the approved training program. Even if the state laws governing licensure remain the same, the university's approved program requirements may change. This often occurs in response to new program accreditation requirements. For example, in response to new Council for Accreditation of Counseling & Related Educational Programs (CACREP) standards, a counseling program may add a requirement that all students take a course focused on crisis intervention and emergency preparedness. The new program requirements would then be submitted to the state and would constitute the new approved program. The fact that the university did not require such a course when you graduated will not make you eligible for that university's recommendation if you failed to apply for licensure before this requirement was added. In this scenario, you would need to take, at a minimum, a course focused on crisis intervention and emergency preparedness to meet the university's new requirements for a licensure recommendation.

Any delay in your application for counseling credentials puts you at risk of becoming ineligible for the credentials necessary to work as a counselor. For that reason, it is my recommendation that you apply for the credentials immediately after graduating. If you choose to delay this process, however, it is essential that you pay close attention to potential changes in state regulations and know that you will be held responsible for meeting new curricular requirements adopted by your university's training program.

LICENSURE APPLICATION PROCEDURES. I hope that you are now convinced of the merits of obtaining licensure immediately upon graduation whether or not you intend to seek a counseling position right away. To do so, contact your adviser to request information about how to obtain licensure in your state. Your adviser will likely refer you to the government agency websites related to the credentialing of counselors in your state. It is likely that separate agencies regulate the professional counselor licensure and school counselor licensure, and you may be eligible for more than one license. If this is the case, you need to obtain separate licensure application packets for each.

TABLE 19.4 American Counseling Association (ACA) Resources About State Licensure

Contact Information for State Boards/Agencies Issuing Licenses

These links provide contact information for the board or governmental agency that manages the licensure of counselors in each state. Application materials, laws, and administrative rules can be accessed from these sites.

Professional Counseling
counseling.org/knowledge-center/licensure-requirements

School Counseling
counseling.org/government-affairs/external-links/resources-for-school-counselors

Additional Resources

These resources provide more extensive information about each state's licensure requirements for professional counselors and school counselors. They are particularly useful to individuals interested in gaining licensure and becoming employed as counselors in another state. Notice the benefits of being an ACA member.

Licensure Requirements for Professional Counselors
Available online for ACA members only
Also available for purchase from ACA for nonmembers

A Guide to State Laws and Regulations on Professional School Counseling
Available online for ACA members only

Another source of such information is the American Counseling Association (ACA). ACA disseminates a variety of public policy resources via its website at counseling.org. Included in these resources are various documents pertaining to credentialing; some are accessible by the public and some are available only to ACA members. Table 19.4 identifies several of these documents. Such documents may be especially useful to individuals interested in gaining licensure and becoming employed as counselors in another state.

Although, as detailed in these resources, the licensure requirements vary from state to state, the application process will likely be similar for each license and each state. Most applications include a portion to be completed by the applicant and a portion to be completed by a faculty member, administrator, or certification officer at the university. In addition, you may be required to submit official transcripts, provide fingerprints and/or undergo a criminal background check, or even pass a drug test. Passage of a state or national examination is also a common licensure requirement.

LEGAL OBLIGATIONS ASSOCIATED WITH LICENSURE. As a new graduate, your focus is initially on the requirements for obtaining licensure. In addition to meeting the requirements and obtaining licensure, though, it is imperative that you learn about the legal obligations associated with possessing each of your licenses. It is important that you obtain and read the state's licensure law, the administrative rules for each type of license you seek, and the ongoing requirements for licensees.

Understanding the law and administrative rules is essential because you will be legally responsible for adhering to them the entire time you hold the license, and each state's laws and/or rules vary somewhat. For example, as of the time of this writing, LPCs in Michigan are not required to engage in continuing education, but they are required to provide all clients with a professional disclosure statement. In contrast, professional counselors and clinical professional counselors in Idaho must complete a minimum of 20 clock hours of continuing education each year, but they are not required to provide disclosure statements to clients. In Vermont, mental health counselors must provide disclosure statements to clients *and* they must complete at least 40 clock hours of continuing education every two years. Because of the variations and frequent changes in state laws and administrative rules, it is not sufficient to rely on guidelines described in textbooks; it is truly necessary that you invest the time and effort to familiarize yourself thoroughly with the regulations that govern your license.

If you obtain more than one license, it is also important to realize that you must adhere to the requirements for *all* of the licenses you hold; you cannot pick and choose which requirements to follow. This may seem self-evident, but counselors are sometimes surprised to discover vast differences in the licensure requirements and become confused about which to follow when. As an example, a counselor may obtain licensure as a professional counselor and as a school counselor. The laws regulating school counselors might require continuing education, whereas the laws regulating professional counselors may not. In this case, the school counselor licensure law has a higher standard, and the counselor with both these licenses must therefore meet the continuing education requirement. This is true even if this counselor is employed in a community setting. A well-intentioned (but uninformed) counselor in this situation might think that she or he needs to meet only the LPC licensure regulations while practicing in the community setting and "using" the professional counseling license. This assumption would be incorrect and illegal. Because this counselor "possesses" both licenses, she or he must adhere to the laws and administrative rules governing each of them. Possession, not use, is the key concept. Instead of focusing on which license you are "using" at any given time, you must instead focus on all licenses you "possess" at the time.

In addition to the legally required licenses that you learned in Chapter 8, you may qualify for several optional credentials (certifications). As a new graduate, it would be in your best interests to apply immediately for all credentials for which you qualify. Keep in mind, though, that you must also adhere to any requirements associated with those credentials. To keep track of the various credentialing requirements, you may find it useful to develop a tracking sheet, such as the one shown in Table 19.5. In the table, Jane Doe must meet several requirements whether or not she is employed as a school counselor, working in the community setting as a professional counselor, and/or engaged in facilitating the career development of clients in either setting. As long as she holds these three credentials, Jane must meet the requirements for all of them.

STEP 2: ENGAGE IN A JOB SEARCH PROCESS

In the not too distant future, you will be graduating from your counseling program, obtaining licensure, and embarking on a job search. Feeling (and being) well prepared and appropriately credentialed is an essential step toward a confident and successful job search. It is also helpful to understand the job search process

TABLE 19.5 Sample Worksheet to Track Credential Requirements

Counselor: Jane Doe
State: Michigan

Requirement	License 1: School Counselor	License 2: Limited License Professional Counselor	Certification 1: Master Career Development Professional	Requirements That Jane Doe Must Meet
Regulatory agency	Michigan Department of Education (MDE)	Michigan Bureau of Health Professions (MBHP)	National Career Development Association (NCDA)	(Not applicable)
Supervision	No	Yes, 100 clock hours of supervision by a licensed professional counselor (LPC) trained in the function of supervision	No	100 clock hours of supervision by an LPC trained in the function of supervision
Disclosure statement	No	Yes, to all clients	No	Yes, to all clients
Continuing education	Yes, 18 continuing education units, or 6 graduate credits every 5 years	No	Yes, 20 hours of continuing education every 5 years	Yes, of the amount and type necessary to meet the MDE *and* NCDA requirements
Other: association membership	No	No	NCDA membership	NCDA membership
Other: posting license	No	Yes, license must be posted in full view of clients	No	Yes, LPC license must be posted in full view of clients

within the profession of counseling. This section (which is designed to supplement the job search information already presented in Chapter 17) discusses defining the parameters of your job search, identifying key elements and unique strengths to highlight in your application, developing and compiling your application materials, launching your job search, and responding to offers of employment.

Define the Parameters of Your Job Search

Before beginning your job search, it is useful to make some decisions regarding the parameters of your job search. The idea is to identify factors related to the acceptability and attractiveness of various job openings. Although many new graduates of counseling programs have fairly wide parameters and may be willing to accept nearly any job, this varies tremendously, and some new graduates will have relatively narrow parameters. Regardless of how wide or narrow your parameters are, however, there is little reason to apply for a job that falls outside your range of acceptable parameters. It is helpful to approach the job search with specific parameters in mind and to apply only for positions that fall within the parameters you define.

Before turning to an exploration of specific parameters, note that the process of defining parameters will differ for everyone reading this text. Some will make decisions about job search parameters individually. Others will make these decisions in consultation (and perhaps negotiation) with significant others in his or her life. Some will view the parameters as firm and consistently apply only for positions that fall within his or her parameters. Some will view the parameters as flexible and may occasionally feel compelled to apply for positions even though they fall outside his or her parameters. Still others may begin by adhering strictly to the parameters for a set amount of time and, if not successful in obtaining a position within a certain period of time, will reexamine and likely expand the parameters in order to broaden the pool of acceptable positions. The following paragraphs discuss parameters related to the scope of a job search, the types of counseling positions applied to, the geographic location of jobs considered, and financial considerations.

PARAMETER 1: FACTORS RELATED TO THE BREADTH OF THE JOB SEARCH. First, determine the types of positions for which will you apply. Presumably, you are interested in obtaining a position as a counselor, but also consider whether you would be willing to apply for and accept a noncounseling position. This will likely be affected

---

My Own Job Search Experience with Safety, Target, and Reach Positions

After graduating from Harvard University with a bachelor's degree in psychology and a secondary teaching certificate, I moved to a college town in my home state of Michigan. My job search target involved teaching positions, and I was specifically interested in teaching psychology in a high school setting. Unfortunately, the job market for teachers—and especially for teachers in the social sciences—was quite saturated at the time. As a result, I found myself unable to land a job as a high school teacher. Fiercely independent and cognizant of my need for income, I expanded my job search and resorted to applying for safety jobs—jobs for which I was clearly overqualified. To my great dismay, the first paid position I held following my graduation was at Burger King. Fortunately, I had also expanded my job search to include reach positions. Within a month, I was offered—and gratefully accepted—a job as an elementary school counselor. Consistent with the theory of planned happenstance, it was this position that forever altered my career path. Had my career progressed as I had originally envisioned, I would probably still be teaching psychology in a high school setting. Instead, my willingness to apply for safety, target, and reach positions resulted in unplanned opportunities.

---

by how urgently you need to find a job and by the nature of the job market when you graduate.

In the event that you feel the need to apply for noncounseling positions, it may be helpful to frame your job search in much the same way as we framed the college application process in Chapter 14. Just as high school counselors may advise students to identify safety, target, and reach colleges, you may wish to conceptualize job openings in much the same way. Thus, you may apply for positions for which you are overqualified and would likely be underpaid because it is a relatively safe bet that you would be hired. Such a job would provide for your safety and survival needs and allow you to pay at least some of your bills. You will also apply for positions well matched to the academic preparation and experience of a new counselor. These positions are likely to be your primary targets within your job search. Finally, I hope you will apply for positions that may be a reach for someone of your academic preparation and experience.

Although the remainder of this chapter focuses on searching for jobs in your target and reach ranges, it is important to recognize that you may need to settle temporarily for a job in your safety category. If this is the case, of course, keep searching for jobs within your target and reach ranges. Let's proceed with our discussion of job search parameters.

PARAMETER 2: FACTORS RELATED TO THE TYPE OF COUNSELING POSITION. Assuming that your target range involves obtaining a position as a counselor, you should further define your job search parameters by being more specific. Are you interested in applying for positions as a career counselor? School counselor? College counselor? Clinical mental health counselor? Also, are you interested in full-time employment or part-time employment, or would either be acceptable to you?

Next, identify the settings for which are you prepared and interested in working. Again, be specific. If you are interested in a community setting, determine which types of counseling venues within the community setting would be of interest to you and would be well suited to your preparation. Venues within the community setting include private practices, private for-profit agencies, nonprofit community agencies, government-based agencies, health care and hospital settings, and so on. If you are interested in a school setting, determine which levels and types of educational institutions would be of interest to you and suited to your preparation. Levels include elementary, middle school or junior high, high school, community college, and four-year colleges. Types of educational institutions include public schools, charter schools, private schools, religiously affiliated schools, and proprietary schools.

Identify the types of clients with whom you are interested in working. Client types vary by age range, level of functioning, presenting concerns, level of motivation for counseling, and so on. Are you more interested in working with clients in one age range than another? Are you primarily interested in working with high-functioning clients or do you have a preference for working with more seriously disturbed clients? Are you hoping to specialize in working with clients with specific types of presenting concerns? Are you willing to work with involuntary clients who attend counseling as a requirement rather than of their own volition?

PARAMETER 3: FACTORS RELATED TO LOCATION. Another type of job search parameter is geography. Are you interested in positions located in rural, suburban, and/or urban areas? What is the maximum commute you are willing to consider? Are you willing to relocate? If so, are there specific geographic regions of greatest interest to you?

PARAMETER 4: FACTORS RELATED TO FINANCIAL CONSIDERATIONS. Another type of job search parameter involves financial considerations. What are your expectations with regard to income? Keep in mind that your income expectations may need to change depending on the cost of living in various geographic regions. Is it essential that the compensation package include benefits such as health insurance, dental coverage, and vision care? Are you interested only in salaried jobs, or are you willing to consider jobs in which your income is determined by the number of clients you see or the revenue you generate? Is it important to you to be classified for tax purposes as an employee, or are you interested in working as an independent contractor? Although these parameters will clearly become important during the negotiation process, it is also important to consider them as you launch your job search so you can be selective when applying for jobs. It will also increase the likelihood that job offers you receive will be acceptable with regard to compensation.

Now that you've defined the parameters of your job search, it may be tempting to launch right into it and begin searching and applying for positions. By establishing your job search parameters, you have determined what you are looking for in a job. Your decisions about whether to apply for any position will be based in large part on what the job has to offer you. Before applying for these jobs, however, it is also important that you are able to articulate to yourself and others what you can offer to the job.

Identify Key Elements and Unique Strengths to Highlight in Your Application

Job applications and their supporting documents (e.g., résumés, cover letters) serve two basic purposes. First, they provide the employer with the information necessary to determine whether you meet the minimum requirements for the job. Second, they provide prospective employers with additional information to determine whether they want to interview you for a position. In part, the employer's decision is based on a judgment about which candidates have the best education and experience and also on a perception of how good a fit you would be for the particular position as well as with the particular organization (department, school, agency, center, etc.). It is important that your application materials demonstrate your qualification for the position, but they should also serve as a snapshot of you as an individual and as a prospective employee. Therefore, as you prepare the supporting documents that you will need to include with your application materials, reflect on your own individual characteristics as a prospective counselor for the types of positions you will be seeking. The importance of doing so is articulated well by Hodges and Connelly (2010):

> Consider your cohort for a moment. Are you exactly like every other counselor with whom you attended classes? Of course not. Although you probably share some core interests, skills and values, you are an individual with interests, skills, and values that set you apart even from those who are in your career field. Those diverse interests and skills will help you to differentiate yourself from every other counselor who will join you in the job market. (p. 2)

The classmates with whom you are graduating will likely be competing with you for various job openings. Rather than framing this simply as a competition about which graduate is the best counselor, reframe it as an opportunity for each of you to find a job in which you happen to be the best fit. This fit depends on the nature of the job opening as well as on your individual characteristics. In addition to considering the interests, values, and skills that may distinguish you from other applicants, also reflect on how your various educational achievements and professional accomplishments will set you apart and make you more or less suited for any given job. Table 19.6 lists some elements that could be highlighted on a résumé, in a cover letter, or in other application materials. This list is based on graduate students with whom I have worked. It is by no means inclusive, but it should provide you with an idea of the breadth of distinguishing elements that a prospective counselor might choose to include on a résumé, in a cover letter, or in other application materials.

Any of these elements could have the effect of increasing or decreasing the likelihood of an applicant getting an interview, and including them comes with some inherent risk. Nonetheless, my belief in the concept of goodness of fit prompts me to focus on the potential benefits rather than the risks. To highlight the potential value

TABLE 19.6 Examples of Distinguishing Elements

Category	Counseling-Specific	Other
Interests	• Clients with disabilities • Group counseling • LGBT issues • Play therapy • Vocational card sorts	• Diving • Gardening • Mah-jongg • Poetry jamming • Poker
Values	• Advocacy • Parental involvement • Social justice • School guidance curricula	• Collaboration • Detail orientation • Risk taking • Travel
Skills	• Proficient in Zangle or PowerSchool • Proficient in using Strong Interest Inventory • Proficient in Career Cruising	• Grant writing • Fluent in French • Marketing • Public speaking • Website creation
Educational achievements	• 4.0 GPA • Academic award • Certified as trauma and loss specialist • Level I eye movement desensitization and reprocessing (EMDR) certification	• BA in gender studies • Doctorate in public health administration • Teacher certified for special education
Professional experience or accomplishments	• Elected as Chi Sigma Iota president • Interned at domestic violence shelter • Taught undergraduate career development course • Received group facilitation award as Wrapper of the Year	• Civil service employee • Environmental engineer • Teacher • Police officer • Residence hall director • Published novelist

of including such elements, it may be useful to share some real-life examples of how such elements might benefit a student or graduate in the job search process.

One student, for example, happened to have two daughters in high school. Both daughters participated on the high school swim and dive team and were nationally ranked divers. This student thus knew a tremendous amount about competitive high school sports and NCAA requirements for college eligibility. This interest and knowledge positioned her well for school counseling positions in which a department lacked a solid foundation in this aspect of student postsecondary advising. Another student happened to use a wheelchair to enhance his mobility. He also financed a good portion of his graduate degree with his (legal) poker winnings. Including this detail on his résumé would be one way to challenge a potential employer's conscious or unconscious preconceived notions about people with disabilities. Another student left a successful career as an engineer to become a school counselor. Her success and knowledge of the engineering field positioned her well to counsel students about career opportunities in the science, technology, engineering, and math (STEM) professions. Another student had significant experience working first as a residence hall adviser and later as a residence hall director. This experience was useful in obtaining a position as a college counselor. Still another student had a tremendous interest in play therapy. She had supplemented her master's degree by attending play therapy workshops offered through the The Center for Play Therapy at the University of North Texas (http://cpt.unt.edu), and she had also volunteered as a research assistant for a psychology professor studying attachment disorders. These experiences were of value in obtaining a position with an infant mental health agency. Another student entered our counseling program with a bachelor's degree in gender studies and found this academic background useful in securing employment with an agency focused on providing counseling services to women. Another student had exceptional skills in web design. Her résumé included a user-friendly URL leading to her own personal website and online portfolio. The agency to which she was applying for a counseling position was in desperate need of a respectable website, and her technology skills were a factor in their extension of a job offer.

Although your graduate degree and credentials as a counselor will certainly be necessary in your search for a counseling position, they will not likely serve to distinguish you from the many other applicants. Thus, it can be useful to identify key elements about yourself and your experiences that are important reflections of you and that you believe may help you secure an interview. With these ideas in mind, you are now ready to take on the task of actually crafting your résumé(s) and cover letter(s).

Develop and Compile Application Materials

When advising students preparing to enter the job market, I consistently advise them to develop and compile their application materials before initiating a job search. You can safely assume that nearly every potential employer will want you to submit your résumé and cover letter as part of the application process. If you launch your job search before preparing these documents, you are likely to discover jobs of interest and find yourself needing to throw together a résumé and cover letter quickly in order to meet an application deadline. Résumés and cover letters that are created on the spur of the moment are not likely to be as accurate, effective in highlighting your strengths, or professional in their presentation as those to which you give your full attention and the time necessary to create flawless documents.

The next step in your job search is to develop résumés and cover letters appropriate to the positions for which you anticipate applying. Of course, you will also want to compile other commonly requested materials, including a references list, recommendation letters, transcripts, and copies of your credentials.

RÉSUMÉS. Based on the parameters you established for your job search, you should have a clear idea about the types of positions for which you will apply. With this clarity, determine how many versions of your résumé and cover letter you are likely to need. If you plan, for example, to apply for jobs as a career counselor and as a school counselor, you would be well served by having two versions of your résumé. Each version must accurately reflect your training and experience, but the versions may vary with respect to emphasis. At the very least, if you include an objective on your résumé, one version's objective should reflect a desire to work as a career counselor and the other version should reflect a desire to work as a school counselor.

RÉSUMÉ CONTENT. Although a thorough discussion of résumé content is beyond the scope of this chapter, especially given the widespread availability of books on résumé construction, I offer a few comments. Specifically, counselor résumés generally include many of the content areas identified in Table 19.7. The five content areas in the first column of the table should be included in all counselor résumés, and a number of other content areas may also be incorporated into your résumé. Note that the titles of these content areas may vary. For example, instead of

TABLE 19.7 Résumé Content Areas for Counselors

Minimum Recommended	Optional Content Areas
Name	Counseling experience
Contact information	Committee memberships
Credentials	Core competencies
Education	Hobbies and interests
Employment history	Honors and awards
	Leadership experience
	Objective
	Professional development
	Professional memberships
	Publications
	Quotations
	References
	Summary of qualifications
	Teaching experience
	Volunteer work

Employment History, you may choose Professional Experience or simply Experience. Similarly, instead of Credentials, you may use Licensure and Certification. The sequence of these content areas and the relative emphasis you place on them will differ depending on whether you select a chronological, functional, combination, or other format for your résumé.

Contact Information. Remember that your contact information should create a positive impression with the employer both on review of your résumé and on attempting contact. Email addresses and phone numbers deserve special attention. Be sure to use an email address that is professional. Firstname.lastname@email.com will certainly create a more positive first impression than partygirl@email.com or worldsbestcounselor@conceited.com. I also advise against including the year in which you were born or graduated from high school in your email address because this provides potential employers with clues about your age.

With regard to phone numbers, ensure that a prospective employer who attempts to make contact with you will have a positive experience. Particularly important considerations include (a) the nature of your voicemail greeting and (b) the way in which calls are answered in person. Voicemail greetings should be in the job seeker's voice and should be professional. As you can imagine, greetings featuring music, your children's voices, or a rather sophomoric message are not likely to create a positive impression with an employer looking to hire a professional counselor. This same theme should guide the way in which you answer phone calls in person: Answer the phone in a professional manner. If somebody other than you may field the call, ask him or her to answer the phone professionally, take messages carefully, and deliver them to you immediately. Also, when engaged in a job search process, ensure that you check your email account and voicemail messages at least once daily.

Credentials. Few résumé guides on the market address the need for a section on credentials. Because counseling is a profession in which a license is required in order to work, however, I recommend that all counselors include this as a stand-alone section on their résumé. This will ensure that employers can easily ascertain your legal eligibility for the job opening.

For each credential, include the full name of the credential (e.g., Licensed Professional Counselor), any acronym or code (e.g., LPC), any specifiers (e.g., Grades K–12), the regulating body (e.g., Michigan Department of Education), your license number, and the year the license was first issued to you. In the event that you are job seeking before you actually have licensure, include this section with the same information except the license number and issuance date. In their place, identify the date (month and year) in which you anticipate receiving the license.

Education. As a job applicant with a graduate degree seeking professional positions, it is time to remove your high school education from your résumé. Employers will safely assume that you graduated from high school or earned a GED and that your academic aptitude is sufficient for college and graduate-level studies. You can save space on your résumé and avoid identifying your age by eliminating your high school education. The possible exception to this rule occurs when you are applying for a job in the town in which you attended high school; however, this information could also be shared in a cover letter.

Be sure to identify your graduate degree accurately. Ask your adviser exactly what degree you will receive on graduation. Many counseling programs, for example, offer several specializations or concentrations, such as community counseling, college counseling, school counseling, and rehabilitation counseling. If you attend such a program, it is important for you to clarify whether you will be receiving a graduate degree in one of those specializations (e.g., a master's degree in school counseling) or whether your degree will be in the overall category (e.g., a master's degree in counseling).

If your counseling program was accredited, you may want include this information in your section on education. For example, identifying your program as CACREP-accredited communicates that the quality of your training program has been externally validated. Many state licensure boards recognize this and therefore provide an expedited licensure process for applicants who have graduated from CACREP-accredited programs. If you happen to be applying for positions out of state, identifying your program as CACREP-accredited lets potential employers gauge the likelihood of you qualifying for licensure in their state.

Employment History. Regardless of whether you choose Employment History, Professional Experience, or something else as the title, this section of your résumé should be limited to professional work experiences. The fact that you had a paper route in middle school or worked at an ice cream joint in high school is not germane to your current job search. The only exception would be if you never had a professional job. For example, maybe you entered a graduate program immediately after completing your bachelor's degree. In such instances, you may want to include other work experience simply to demonstrate a history of successful employment. You may want to highlight any connections between the work you did and the position you are now seeking. An explanatory bullet list may be used for this purpose, for example:

- Used income to finance my graduate education
- Gained firsthand insight into careers in the manufacturing sector
- Utilized conflict resolution skills pertinent to my future career as a school counselor
- Developed additional multicultural competencies through interactions with diverse colleagues and clientele

These points render the inclusion of entry-level positions more relevant to your current job search than would identifying the various duties and responsibilities associated with each position.

Counseling Experience. Most students graduating from counselor education programs enter the job market with no professional, paid work experience as a counselor. Degree requirements for licensure ensure this as the norm; however, many graduate students worry about this lack of experience. Many new graduates seeking their first paid counseling position choose to include a section on their résumé entitled Counseling Experience. Another choice is Counseling and Related Experience. Table 19.8 shows that a variety of experiences may be included in such sections.

The table illustrates many ways that you may choose to include internship, practicum, or other predegree experiences on your résumé. Note that the entries vary with respect to sequence and relative emphasis. You may choose to emphasize the place at which you gained experience, your role or title at the time, or a combination of each. Such variations are illustrated in Table 19.8 simply to illustrate a range of style options. Whatever style you choose, of course, should be used consistently throughout your résumé.

RÉSUMÉ PROFESSIONALISM, PROOFREADING, AND APPEARANCE. As a job search tool, the quality of your résumé is of utmost importance. To create a positive first impression for potential employers, your résumé should be attractive, easy to read, and free of any errors. Of course, attractiveness is subjective. More important is that your résumé reflects your personality and preferences. Some applicants produce résumés that use a single, simple font and have a clean-cut, no-nonsense appearance. Other applicants create résumés that have a more complex appearance and flair. Such résumés might contain clip art, graphic designs, and italicized quotations in the margins. Résumés anywhere along this continuum may be attractive in appearance. I encourage you to develop your résumé in a manner you find both professional and attractive in appearance. Consider the statement your résumé's overall style may make about you.

Regardless of the stylistic features of your résumé, ensure that it is easy to read. Consider font size (not too small), white space (not too little), and easily identifiable sections. Unless you need a curriculum vitae (e.g., are launching a job search for an academic position within the professoriate), limit your résumé to no more than two or three pages. It is not necessary, however, to limit your résumé to a single page. Such guidelines—often included

TABLE 19.8 Sample Résumé Entries of Predegree Counseling Experiences

Internship Experiences

Urban Charter School Academy (K–8), City, State January to June 2012

School Counselor (Intern)—Provided individual and group counseling to middle school students. Assisted the counselor with scheduling, high school placement testing, and other counseling activities. Participated in educational development plans (EDPs). Worked closely with the school counselor, principal, teachers, and social worker. Met with parents and collaborated with school faculty on school projects such as career week and science fair. Coordinated peer mentor and study groups. Wrote student letters of recommendation. Coedited the school's newsletter. Successfully completed 627 (600 required) intern hours.

Counselor-in-Training Nearby University, City, State September to June 2012

Provided counseling services to college students with a wide range of presenting problems while meeting internship requirements for my master's degree program.

Nov. 2011– **School Counselor Intern at Suburban School** City, State
Apr. 2012 Worked with fifth- and sixth-grade counselor to implement state comprehensive guidance and counseling program. Developed and provided classroom guidance lessons, cofacilitated changing families group and homework help groups. Met individually with students for counseling and guidance.

Practicum Experiences

Your University Name of Your Practicum Site, City, State September to June 2012

Provided individual counseling sessions to a diverse client population. Administered assessments/tests, created client reports and case notes, and provided interventions and treatments. Participated in weekly group and individual supervision.

Counselor-in-Training September to June 2012

Name of Your Practicum Site, City, State

Provided individual counseling to diverse clients ranging in age from 18 to 51.

Other Experiences

Counselor-in-Training September to June 2010

Your University's Career Services Office

Served as cofacilitator of a series of career planning workshops.

Town Name LGBT Community Center September to June 2010

Counselor-in-Training

Served as a youth group facilitator for children with lesbian, gay, or bisexual parents.

---

in the commercially available résumé writing guides—are more appropriate for individuals seeking entry-level positions straight out of high school or college.

You may wonder why so many résumé writing guides emphasize the need for careful proofreading and question whether an error or two really makes a difference. Errors really do make a difference when it comes to résumés. In fact, even in the age of computerized spell checking software, "spelling errors are a primary reason why employers reject resumes" (Curtis & Simons, 2004, p. 179). Employers know that you've likely spent more time on your résumé than on most documents you will prepare while working for them. If you are unable to produce an error-free résumé, they understandably question your ability (or inclination) to produce consistent, high-quality work on behalf of their counseling agency, college, or school system.

Once you have perfected your résumé, ensure that its formatting will not be lost in the event that you submit application materials electronically. The most effective method is to convert your résumé into a portable document file (it will be saved with .pdf as an extension). By doing so, you can be sure that your résumé will appear the same regardless of the software type or version used by those who receive and/or print out your résumé. Convert all other application materials into pdf documents, including cover letters, lists of references, and recommendation letters.

Label your résumé (and all other documents) in a manner that renders your materials easy to identify. The transcript file name, for example, could read firstname.lastname.resume. You may not normally title documents in this fashion and may instead opt to label it as "resume" only, but keep in mind that this file will be saved onto someone else's computer rather than your own. Prospective employers will obviously receive many résumés and you want them to be able to locate yours easily.

OTHER APPLICATION MATERIALS.

Cover Letters. Before launching your job search, it is also useful to prepare at least one cover letter template. Ideally, you should develop a separate template for each type of counseling position for which you anticipate applying. Although you will certainly want to personalize your cover letters to include information specific to each job opening, these templates will render this task a simple matter of tweaking rather than a complex task of composing a new letter. In developing your templates, you will likely benefit from utilizing one of the many commercially available resources about résumés and cover letters.

List of References. Whether or not you include a statement such as "references furnished upon request" on your résumé, you should be prepared to provide a list of references. In anticipation of employer requests, it is wise to prepare the list in advance and to use the same format as your résumé. More difficult than creating this list, of course, is identifying the people who will serve as references for you.

As a prospective counselor, you should give careful consideration to your selection of references. Generally speaking, new graduates should include at least one person who has observed and supervised their clinical work (such as a practicum or internship supervisor); at least one professor who knows their academic performance and career goals; and a current or recent employer who knows their professionalism, ability to work on a team, and other factors related to successful employment. It is possible, however, that including your current or most recent employer as a reference could hurt rather than help you. This is most likely if the nature of your current or most recent work could be perceived as being questionable or inconsistent with your career aspirations. You need to use your best judgment about this. Unless you are applying for jobs in a parochial school or other organization with a religious affiliation, it is usually unwise to list a pastor, priest, rabbi, minister, and so on, as a reference. Also, you should avoid using any relatives or friends as references, even if they themselves are professional counselors.

Once you have identified the people you would like to include on your references list, you should always confirm, preferably in writing, each person's willingness to serve in this capacity. When asking permission to list people as references, you should also ask if they feel confident that they can serve as a strong, positive reference for you. To illustrate the importance of this, a professor recently reviewed an application for admission to a counseling program, and specifically on the written candidate rating form, one of the references for this applicant noted that, "although [this candidate] is kind, she lacks the innate capacity to form a therapeutic relationship with students." I imagine that this applicant would be shocked to know that one of her references basically communicated a belief that she is poorly suited to the counseling profession. Rather than assuming that your references will be strong and positive, you should confirm this.

When constructing your references list, include the person's name, title, workplace, address, phone number, and/or email address. As a practical matter, you should specifically ask each person on your list about the best phone number and/or email address to include. Professors, for example, may prefer that you include the direct number to their office rather than having employers call the department receptionist. If professors will be out of the office and difficult to reach by telephone for an extended period of time (e.g., summer vacation or sabbatical leave), they may suggest that you only include an email address.

Recommendation Letters. Many employers also request letters of recommendation. When approaching people with a request to serve as a reference, it is sensible to ask them for a letter of recommendation as well. Out of respect for the time it takes to write a high-quality letter of recommendation, you should ask at least a month in advance. At a minimum, you should provide the writer with a copy of your résumé and a brief description of the types of jobs you are seeking. It can also be helpful to provide writers with a summary of your work with them. For clinical supervisors, for example, it would be helpful to provide them with the beginning and ending dates of your supervised experience, a description of the clients with whom you worked (demographics, presenting concerns, diagnoses, etc.), a copy of the log sheet you used to track your hours, and a copy of any evaluations they did of your work. For professors, it is useful to provide a list of all courses you took with them, the semester in which you took each course, and the grade you earned. It might also be helpful to attach a copy of an assignment for which you received outstanding feedback from them. Although your former supervisors and professors could likely obtain this information on their own, doing so will require extra work on their part. You should do what you can to help your references with easy access to the information they need to write a solid, personalized letter of recommendation for you.

Transcripts and Credentials. You can anticipate needing to submit copies of your academic transcript(s) and copies of your counseling credentials (licenses and certifications). Take the time to scan and save these documents as pdf documents. It is also useful to have an official copy of each ready to give to employers on receipt of a job offer. In most cases, these official copies will be required for verification purposes by the human resources office.

With your application materials carefully developed, converted into pdf documents, and clearly titled, you are officially cleared for takeoff: You are finally ready to launch your job search. As you'll see in the following section, this process involves both organizational tasks and psychological challenges.

Launch Your Job Search.

Bolstered by solid preparation; in possession of appropriate credentials; and armed with carefully crafted résumés, cover letters, and other application materials, you are well prepared for the actual process of the job search. This process involves searching for job openings consistent with the parameters you have defined, tweaking and submitting your application materials, monitoring your email and voicemail for messages from prospective employers, knocking their socks off when you interview, and responding to offers of employment. Although this is admittedly easier to say than to accomplish, the steps you have already taken will undoubtedly serve you well during the job search. Remember, you have made choices throughout your graduate program to ensure that you are as well prepared as possible and have prepared an outstanding collection of application materials designed to highlight your individual strengths and assets as a prospective counselor. Now it is a matter of managing the job search process, both from an organizational and a psychological perspective.

ORGANIZATIONAL MANAGEMENT OF THE JOB SEARCH PROCESS. Perhaps the most valuable piece of advice I have heard regarding the organizational management of a job search is that job seekers should behave as if the job search is their job. Rather than approaching the job search as something to squeeze in when you have a little extra time, you will likely be more successful if you treat the job search as a high priority. Once you are ready to launch a job search, plan to invest a significant amount of time and energy in the job-seeking process. It may even be beneficial for you to establish a schedule for your daily activities. For example, you may allot two hours each morning to a careful Internet search for new job openings. You may allot another two hours each day for the completion and submission of applications. You may allocate another hour each day to follow up on applications you have already submitted. Other job search activities might include engaging in networking activities, sharpening your interview skills, and reading materials to develop your knowledge base.

Search for Job Openings.

Advertised job postings. When searching for job vacancies, you will want to identify sources of advertised job postings. In Chapters 17 and 18, we explored a variety of job search tools for clients, and these certainly apply to your job search as well. The website indeed.com, for example, tends to be a useful search engine for job openings, and this holds true for the counseling profession as well. Make use of other job search tools specific to your university, counseling specialization, and locale. Be sure to visit your university's career services office to gain access to its information regarding nearby job openings. Stay abreast of job openings posted by your professional counseling associations via online newsletters, their websites, and their print materials. I hope you researched local sources of job information after reading about these topics in Chapter 13. Now is the time to utilize these sources.

The hidden job market. Another strategy when job seeking involves attempts to tap into the hidden market—job openings for which there is no formal posting or advertisement (Hodges & Connelly, 2010). Such vacancies may not yet be advertised because of financial reasons (related to the cost of advertising), the opening emerged quite recently, or the employer prefers to recruit applicants rather than posting a solicitation for all comers. Some interns, for example, perform impressively enough that they receive job offers from their internship sites. In many of these cases, a job opening is usually not posted or advertised.

Because "estimates of how many people are employed through the hidden job market range upward of 65% of all new hires" (Bolles, 2004; cited in Hodges & Connelly, 2010, p. 9), you should not rely exclusively on advertised job postings during your job search. Instead, tap into the hidden job market. Networking is especially useful in this respect. Although this term sometimes conjures up images of a competitive business environment featuring the unsavory process of working a room, networking needn't be an unpleasant experience, even for counselors with a preference for introversion. In fact, given their human relationship skills, counselors are ideally equipped to use networking in the best sense of the word. In this context, networking involves tapping into already

> **Example of a Networking Email**
>
> Hello [person's name here]:
>
> I'm not sure whether you remember, but you were kind enough to meet with me last October to talk about the substance abuse recovery groups you run with adolescents. At the time, I was a student taking a class on substance abuse counseling at Rinkydink College, and my meeting with you helped me realize how much I would enjoy working with adolescents. Since then, I've taken two additional classes related to adolescent issues and treatment.
>
> I am writing to thank you for the inspiration and to let you know that I graduated in April with my master's degree in counseling. I have just received my limited license as a professional counselor and am in the process of job hunting. If you happen to hear of any open counseling positions—especially any involving work with adolescents—I'd be grateful if you would let me know and/or pass along my information. In case it would be helpful to you, I've also attached my résumé. Thanks again.

established relationships in order to communicate about your job search.

In addition to the people on your list of references, consider the various people with whom you have had contact over the course of your graduate program. How many of them are mental health professionals, administrators who hire them, or closely connected to them? Perhaps you conducted informational interviews with various counselors as part of a class assignment. Perhaps you met a high school principal while attending your daughter's softball game, or a number of counselors through your county's counseling association chapter. Perhaps you connected with some counselors while attending a conference. As part of your job search, consider tapping into this network: It could be as easy as sending a brief email.

Another way to network and thus access the hidden job market is to utilize social media platforms such as LinkedIn (linkedin.com). As discussed in Chapter 17, such networking strategies are becoming increasingly important for job searches.

Job searching and friendships: competition or collaboration? As you reach the end of your graduate program, you will likely find that you have made several close friends. You will be graduating at the same time and searching for jobs at the same time. Clearly, this has the potential to change the dynamics of your friendships because it introduces an element of competition to relationships that were previously experienced as primarily collaborative and supportive. As you begin your job search, you need to decide how to manage this new element in your relationships.

One professor routinely advises students not to tell any of their friends and classmates if they find out about a job opening. This advice makes some sense from the perspective that you may indeed be competing with those friends and classmates for the same positions. And you don't want to be become an enabler by saving your friends and classmates the trouble of searching for openings and rewarding their inaction by providing them with job leads.

On the other hand, following this advice can also heighten feelings of distrust and competition among your cohort. It can leave you feeling rather isolated and result in some decidedly awkward moments. Think about how you would feel exiting a job interview only to discover that your best friend is the next candidate waiting in the reception area.

In contrast, Rutter and Jones (2007) advocate for establishing "job clubs" for students preparing to graduate from counseling programs. A job club focuses on strengthening the job-seeking skills of participants and on creating a source of social support during the job search process. To gauge students' level of interest in job clubs, Rutter and Jones (2007) conducted a qualitative study using focus groups. Their "findings suggested that students had strong interest in a group that emphasized empowerment and collaboration, offered predictable social support, and provided training in specific job search skills" (p. 280). They also specifically assessed concerns about competition and found that "participants did not view as a major obstacle the possibility that club members may be competing for the same limited number of positions" (p. 285).

How *you* feel, though, may be different. For this reason, I encourage you to consider how you will manage the element of competition as you launch your job search. There is no single correct way to manage this element, but you should make the decision with some level of intentionality.

Apply for Positions. Whether or not you choose to let others know about openings you identify, the next step of the job search process is to apply for positions. This chapter has already addressed the two most pertinent issues related to applying for positions: the definition of parameters and the preparation of application materials. Now, it is simply a matter of personalizing and tweaking your cover letter and submitting whatever application materials are requested. When submitting your materials electronically, submit only pdf documents. When submitting your materials in print format, use only white or very light paper. It is common practice for employers to distribute copies of application materials, and darker shades of original paper result in decidedly unattractive copies. When delivering application materials in person, dress appropriately, as you would for an interview.

Interview and Follow-Up. The next step of the job search process involves invitations to interview. As with résumé writing, an abundance of literature on effective interviews exists. Hodges and Connelly (2010), for example, offer an outstanding chapter specific to the interview process in the profession of counseling.

This chapter touches briefly on only a few points. First, although it may sound cliché, remember that all interviews are two-way processes. Obviously, the employer is interviewing you and making judgments about your competence as well as your fit with the organization. Desperate as you may feel for employment, however, you also have the opportunity to use the interview as a way to evaluate how interested you are in accepting the job. Be prepared with three to four non-salary-related questions that may affect your level of interest in the job. Also, notice the interpersonal dynamics among those interviewing you and the overall atmosphere of the workplace.

Second, with this two-way evaluation in mind, the most effective way of using interviews to ensure a good fit between you and the job is to be yourself, and be your best self. This is different, of course, from being your whole self. Leave your bad habits and controversial opinions at home (unless they are deal breakers), but be genuine with what you do reveal and allow your personality to shine through. Avoid the temptation to role-play your perception of the ideal employee or to offer whatever responses you think the employer wants to hear.

Third, tap into the power of the follow-up contact. Regardless of how the interview seemed to go, the follow-up contact is an opportunity to enhance the likelihood that you will receive an offer of employment. In following up after an interview that seemed to go very well, you not only want to thank the employer for taking the time to meet with you but also communicate sincerely how good a fit it felt for you. After interviews that seemed to go dreadfully, you need to make a decision about whether you want the job. If you do *and* you are sure that the employer also had a negative impression of the interview, follow up and thank the employer for taking the time to meet with you, communicate an awareness that the interview went poorly, offer some explanation or additional information you forgot to share, and express a hope that he or she recognizes that the interview was not representative of the way you normally present yourself.

Psychological Management of the Job Search Process. The topic of dreadful interviews offers an opportunity to segue into a discussion about the psychological management of the job search process. The job search can be extraordinarily stressful. One source of stress is financial. The more you need a job financially, the more stressful the job search can be. Another source of stress is psychological. As discussed earlier in this text, our society puts a great deal of emphasis on employment, to the extent that people often define themselves by their jobs. You may be especially vulnerable to this when searching for a job right after you complete your graduate degree. You have invested a tremendous amount of time, energy, and money with the goal of becoming employed as a counselor. For some, the job search can also be stressful because it requires people to engage in uncomfortable behaviors such as self-promotion and talking with strangers. For others, it taps into still unresolved issues related to self-efficacy, adequacy, and self-esteem. Regardless of how prepared or well grounded you are, "the difficulties associated with finding employment can wear down even the most resilient jobseekers" (Vilorio, 2011, p. 3).

The good news, though, is that you are not just any resilient job seeker. You are a counselor, and you have the training and expertise to manage the stress associated with the job search. At a minimum, engage in basic self-care strategies such as caring for yourself physically with food, water, sleep, and exercise. A support system is also important. Share with at least one person (who is not financially affected by the success of your job search) your job search hopes, fears, worries, and triumphs. This may be a friend, family member, or mental health professional. Colleagues who can help you prepare for interviews and process them afterward can also be quite useful.

You have the knowledge and skills to identify and challenge your own understandable but irrational beliefs about the job search. For example, should you have a less than stellar interview, your irrational belief system might suggest, "I blew that interview. I'm such an idiot. I'm never going to get a job!" As a counselor, though, you know that such negative self-talk isn't likely to be of much use to you; instead, it's likely to cause you additional distress, lower your sense of self-efficacy, and reduce your effectiveness in future interviews. Although you may not avoid those types of negative thoughts altogether, you have the skills necessary to dispute them. In this scenario, you might replace your negative self-talk with, "I didn't blow that interview; it just didn't go as well as I'd hope." Or you may reframe it as "Yes, I blew the interview, but that doesn't mean that I'm an idiot or that I'll never get a job. Even amazing counselors like me occasionally blow an interview. I just need to calm down and be myself. The right job is out there for me." And it will be. At some point, you'll find yourself receiving an offer of employment.

RESPONDING TO OFFERS OF EMPLOYMENT. As excited as you will likely be when receiving a job offer, it is important that you approach this step of the job search process with as much care as you have exercised in each of the other steps along the way. Hodges and Connelly (2010) caution that, "if you accept immediately, you lose any leverage you have to review the entire compensation package and negotiate more favorable terms" (p. 79). By accepting on the spot, you are essentially accepting the offer without regard to the details. Salary and benefits are two obvious details you will want to learn about before making a commitment. You may also wish to consider factors such as start date, vacation time, office location, choice of supervisors, or even job title. For example, one graduate student encountered a situation in which the job offer came with a job title of talent connector. Uncomfortable with this, he negotiated for a title of career counselor before accepting the position.

Instead of accepting immediately on receiving the phone call, you might respond, "I'm delighted to hear that you'd like to hire me! I, too, felt a good fit with your [agency, school, etc.]. Could you share some details about the offer?" If the specifics shared at that point are acceptable to you, you can say, "I am excited to receive your offer and anticipate accepting it. I'd like to ensure that I've heard everything correctly, though, so if you could send me the offer in writing, I'll review it and let you know within a day or so." If there are some aspects of the offer that you would like to negotiate, you can begin by asking the employer if there is any room for negotiation. Hodges and Connelly (2010) advise that counselors "proceed gently and with some caution" (p. 81) when negotiating and understand that, "because counselors mostly work for nonprofit agencies or schools, the negotiable [salary] range is not like it is in the business world, particularly during times of economic turbulence when not-for-profits are particularly vulnerable to volatility in market fluctuations" (pp. 82–83). There is generally some room, however, to negotiate salary; a gentle way to explore this is to inquire about where the salary offer falls in the salary range for other counselors.

Once you are satisfied with the terms of an offer, you will want to accept it not only verbally but also in writing. You can then breathe a sigh of relief and celebrate a bit before you start your new job.

STEP 3: ADJUST TO YOUR NEW CAREER

After you accept the job offer and begin your new position, you will likely face some challenges with regard to adjustment. Both the transition from graduate school to professional employment and the process of acclimating to your place of employment will likely require some adjustment on your part.

Conduct and View Yourself as a Professional Counselor

With regard to the transition from graduate school to professional employment, you surely realize that working as a professional counselor is different than being a graduate student in a counseling program. You now have a different schedule, and you need dress appropriately for the setting and your position. You also need to conduct yourself as a professional. For the most part, these types of changes are easy to anticipate and to manage. Perhaps more difficult in the transition from graduate school to professional employment, however, involves your self-perception.

In practicum and internship, it is not uncommon for a counselor-in-training to encounter situations in which she or he determines that a client's needs necessitate a referral to a "real" counselor. The ability to make such referrals is important to ensure client welfare, but it also creates a cushion of comfort for the counselor-in-training. Once employed as a professional counselor, however, you *are* the "real" counselor to whom such clients are often referred. When you encounter a challenging client in your new position, referral remains an option, but it will be an option exercised far less frequently. You need to adjust to seeing yourself as a professional counselor and focus on *how* you can help the client rather than *if* you can help the client.

As you make this transition from counselor-in-training to "real" counselor, you may find your sense of self-efficacy fluctuating. Sometimes you will feel confident and competent, and sometimes you may feel completely inadequate and unprepared. Much of this fluctuation is normal. Some of it stems from normal developmental stages through which counselors progress. Now-classic research by Stoltenberg and Delworth (1987) revealed that counselors progress through developmental levels and that their level of motivation, self–other awareness, and sense of autonomy fluctuate in accordance with these levels.

Leach, Stoltenberg, Eichenfield, and McNeill (1997) found that counselor self-efficacy also fluctuates accordingly. Some of the fluctuation in self-efficacy is an artifact of the adjustment process. As you transition from graduate school to your first professional counseling position, you will undoubtedly come to the realization that graduate school does not prepare you for every situation you will encounter as a counselor. Although this stands to reason, it nonetheless can be a shocking realization once you are in the field. The shock may be such that you even find yourself questioning the value of your graduate education occasionally. Your graduate education has surely prepared you for many of the challenges you will face. Simply realize that you are not done learning.

Acclimate to Your New Workplace

The process of acclimating to your new place of employment also requires a period of adjustment on your part. The ease with which you acclimate depends in large part on how well you transition from the role of graduate student to professional counselor. Your ability to shift toward seeing yourself as a "real" counselor, to conduct yourself professionally, and to manage fluctuations in your sense of self-efficacy has an impact on your ability to acclimate to your new workplace. As a newly hired counselor, you neither want to come across as too confident nor too deferential. Moderation is the key.

After reading the prior section about fluctuating self-efficacy, you may be surprised to hear that coming across as too confident poses some danger, but this is indeed the case. When arriving at their new place of employment, many new graduates are full of enthusiasm and eager to use and share the knowledge they learned in graduate school. Having studied conscientiously throughout their graduate program, they sometimes feel (and perhaps are) better versed in the latest, greatest theories, techniques, and approaches to counseling than the counselors who have been in the field for many years. When their sense of self-efficacy is high, they may be eager to demonstrate their competence and to help their workplace become more current. Their colleagues and supervisors, however, may be considerably less excited to welcome a new coworker who seems to know it all or who continually makes suggestions about how to improve their new workplace. Although it may be true that you have some wonderful new ideas, also stay open to the importance of taking time to get to know your coworkers and learning about your new work setting before sharing your new ideas. Just as you would refrain from offering easy advice to clients in the first session and instead want to show respect and take the time to understand the complexities of their situation, you also want to take a similar approach at your new place of employment. After doing so, you might choose to make suggestions, or you might realize that the complexities of the situation are such that your initial ideas wouldn't be as helpful as you originally thought.

Just as you will want to avoid coming across as too confident, you also want to avoid seeming too deferential as you transition into the workplace. Although your new colleagues will understandably be irritated if you are constantly advising them to approach clients in newer, better ways, they are likely to have an equally negative reaction if you seem too uncertain about your knowledge and skills. This may be evident in constant questions about how to do things, frequent requests to refer clients, or even tearful meltdowns. You certainly need to ask questions, seek advice, and make occasional referrals, and a tearful meltdown is not unusual, especially early in a new counselor's tenure. You want to consider, however, the impression a high frequency of such behaviors can make. Again, moderation is the key.

Because many of your questions will relate to office management and procedural issues, an excellent way to avoid asking too many questions or making too many mistakes is to obtain the office manual as well as the policies and procedures handbook. Take them home and study them. Take the time to learn which form to use for what; how to operate the copy machine, even if it jams; and how to operate any specialized software in your workplace. Also take the time to learn who is responsible for what. Professors are no longer available to tell you what to read or to schedule exams that serve as a motivation to learn what may seem like trivial details. Part of the transition into your new position, however, requires that you identify what you need to know and that you take the time—generally off the clock—to learn it.

Keep Learning

You have surely noticed by now a pattern in the messages you've received from this text as well as from many of your professors. The importance of continued professional development cannot be overemphasized. In short, it is an absolute necessity that you keep learning in order to become more effective at meeting client needs and to stay abreast of new developments in your profession. As a supervisor during my doctoral internship once told me, graduation does not signify that we are "fully cooked" but rather we are only "half baked." As disappointing as this may be as you approach graduation, it is a non-negotiable fact. You do not have to continue enrolling in formal coursework, although this is certainly one good way to keep learning. There are many others as well. Join at least one professional association, consistently read its journals and magazines, and attend its conferences. Look for other conferences focused on topics of interest to you. Read books and journal articles about topics and challenges related to your clients. Participate in individual and/or group supervision to further develop your clinical insights and skills. By making a concerted, ongoing effort to keep learning, you will maximize the likelihood of your success with clients and your satisfaction with your career.

STEP 4: ENGAGE IN LONG-TERM CAREER PLANNING

A final step in charting your own career path as a professional counselor involves long-term planning. Whether you are taking this course early in your graduate program or are near graduation, it can be useful to think about your long-term career and life goals. Although your circumstances, priorities, or preferences may change over time, having a sense of longer-term goals can be helpful in guiding your choice of experiences along the way.

One technique often used to help undergraduate college students think about their long-term career plans may, if adapted, be of use to you as well. The exercise is called the five-year résumé and was developed by Laker and Laker (2007). As its name suggests, the activity involves asking undergraduates to develop a résumé to reflect where they would like to be in five years. Laker and Laker recommend going beyond the simple creation of such a résumé and suggest that the exercise span the entire course of a college semester. Specifically, they describe six parts of the exercise, which are listed in Table 19.9.

TABLE 19.9	**Steps in Laker and Laker's Five-Year Résumé Project**

1. Develop a current résumé.
2. Develop the résumé you would like to have in five years.
3. Based on the differences between your current and future résumé, identify long- and short-term goals you need to achieve and thus bridge this gap.
4. Develop a plan of action for achieving these long- and short-term goals.
5. Explore specifics related to the implementation of your action plan.
6. Summarize what you learned as a result of this exercise.

Source: Based on Laker, D., and Laker, R. (2007). The five-year resume: A career planning exercise. *Journal of Management Education, 31,* 128–141. Copyright © 2005 owned by Dennis R. Laker. Reprinted by permission.

The remainder of this section describes how you can adapt this activity to be more appropriate for your stage of life. You already have a current résumé, which is the first step recommended by Laker and Laker (2007). In contrast to the résumés constructed by undergraduate students, however, yours likely has much more substance. At the very least, it reflects completion of at least one college degree, and it may even reflect a great deal of experience in another career path.

The second step recommended by Laker and Laker (2007) encourages undergraduate students to create a résumé to reflect where they would like to be in five years, but I suggest modifying this step to involve the creation of a 10-year résumé. To begin, ask yourself where you would like to be professionally in 10 years. If you were to imagine seeking a new job in 10 years, what type of position would it be? Do you hope to become a school district's director of guidance? Do you hope to be a highly sought after career counselor in private practice? Do you hope to land a counseling job at a university in some wonderful destination location? Whatever your 10-year career goal, what would you like to be able to put on your résumé and thus enhance your chances of landing that dream job? In creating your 10-year résumé, be as specific as possible. To guide you in this process, Laker and Laker (2007) offered an extensive list of questions, which are displayed in Figure 19.1. Although the sections of your résumé may vary from those displayed in Figure 19.1, the questions should nonetheless be useful to you in considering the types of accomplishments you would like to be able to include on your résumé in 10 years.

The next step of the process is to identify the differences between your current résumé and your 10-year résumé. Laker and Laker (2007) recommended doing this to guide your identification of long- and short-term goals. For example, if your 10-year résumé shows that you worked as a counselor for three different organizations and that you took on increasing levels of responsibility at each, your long-term goal would involve the accrual of counseling experiences at three institutions within the next 10 years, and your first short-term goal would involve working at your present position for whatever period of time you specified on your 10-year résumé.

Laker and Laker (2007) suggested that you then create an action plan to help you achieve your long- and short-term goals. In other words, simply having the destination in mind and having goals is not sufficient. You must take action to achieve those goals. A quotation by Will Rogers captures the essence of this step: "Even if you're on the right track, you'll get run over if you just sit there" (Rogers, n.d.). When looking at your 10-year résumé, therefore, identify incremental concrete actions that you can take to help you reach your goals. For example, you may hope to become president of your state counseling association eight years from now. That is a terrific goal, but you will probably need to work toward it by serving in a progression of other leadership roles. Rather than doing nothing for six years and then nominating yourself for the presidency, you need an action plan. This plan may include becoming an active member of your local counseling chapter, seeking membership on one of the state

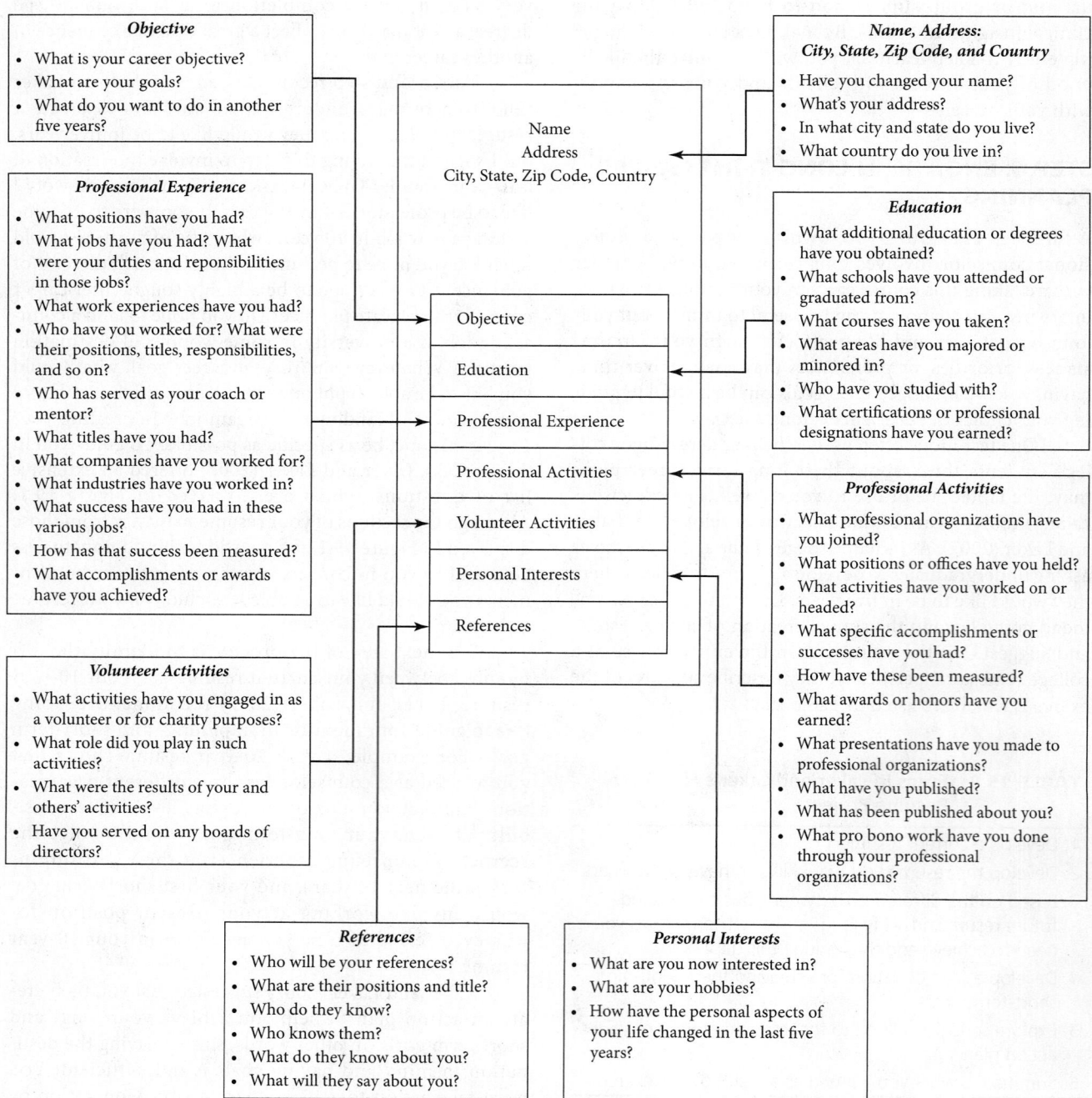

FIGURE 19.1 Questions to Guide the Creation of a Five- or Ten-Year Résumé

Source: Based on Laker, D., and Laker, R. (2007). The five-year resume: A career planning exercise. *Journal of Management Education*, 31, 128–141. (p. 140). Copyright © 2007 by Dennis R Laker. Reprinted by permission.

association committees, becoming a leader in one of the association's divisions, or even attending the governing board meetings as a guest simply to learn more about the operation of the association.

In developing your action plan, keep in mind that you won't necessarily know which steps could help you achieve your goals or how to accomplish the steps you do know about. Therefore, the next step recommended by Laker and Laker (2007) is to explore the specifics related to the implementation of your action plan. It may be quite helpful for you to consult with other counseling professionals—especially those in whose footsteps you might like to follow—to find out what steps they would recommend and how you can accomplish them. For example, you may aspire to a position that will require a doctorate. You may recognize this as a long-term goal but be uncertain about how to achieve it. This step therefore involves engaging in activities to help you identify the short-term goals and the specific steps you might take to achieve them. You may read a book about choosing doctoral programs, talk to people who have doctorates in counseling and/or related disciplines, or contact an adviser in a doctoral program to learn about admissions criteria for that program

The sixth and final step recommended by Laker and Laker (2007) is to summarize what you learned as a result of this exercise, and this recommendation is clearly geared toward the structure of an undergraduate course in which the five-year résumé project was an assignment. In adapting this exercise to better suit your needs, I recommend that you begin implementing your action plan and working toward your short-term goals. I also recommend that you revisit your 10-year résumé, your short- and long-term goals, and your action plan annually to ensure that they continue to reflect your aspirations and to be manageable given your life circumstances. If they do reflect your aspirations, the step of revisiting your plan can remind you of your goals and inspire you to take additional actions toward them. If they no longer match what you want, revisiting your plan will prompt you to revise it accordingly.

The End of Our Journey

As this chapter concludes, I'd like to congratulate you on finishing this text and the course for which it was assigned. Returning to the cruise ship metaphor with which we began, I hope you've learned a lot, enjoyed the cruise, and—even better—developed a passion for career counseling. As your future journeys take you to professional conferences, I hope our paths will cross and that we'll have the opportunity to meet in person.

Best wishes for a most fulfilling career as a professional counselor!

Suzanne M. Dugger, Ed.D.

Appendices

A. Historical Highlights of Vocational Guidance, Career Development, and Career Counseling in the United States
B. National Career Development Association Counselor Competencies
C. National Career Development Association Code of Ethics
D. American School Counselor Association Student Standards in the Career Development Domain
E. National Career Development Guidelines Framework
F. Secretary's Commission on Achieving Necessary Skills (SCANS)—Employability Skills
G. Sample Form for an Educational Development Plan

APPENDIX A

Historical Highlights of Vocational Guidance, Career Development, and Career Counseling in the United States

Year	Event
1883	Salmon Richards publishes *Vocophy*, which calls for vocophers to be placed in every town. He envisioned the role of the vocophers as providing vocational assistance to all.
1895	George Merrill experiments with vocational guidance at the California School of Mechanical Arts in San Francisco.
1898–1907	Jesse B. Davis instructs students about the world of work at Central High School in Detroit.
1907	Davis moves to a principalship in Grand Rapids, Michigan, where he encourages teachers to relate subject matter to vocations.
1905	Frank Parsons establishes Breadwinners' Institute, a continuing education center for immigrants and youth, in the Civic Service House in Boston, Massachusetts.
About 1908	Anna Y. Reed, working in Seattle, Washington, and Eli Weaver, in Brooklyn, New York, develop and organize vocational guidance programs in their respective schools.
1908	Philanthropist Mrs. Quincy Shaw organizes the Boston Guidance Bureau to provide assistance to young people based on the work of Frank Parsons, which stressed the importance of a systematic approach to selecting a vocation.
1909	Frank Parsons's book, *Choosing a Vocation*, is published posthumously. The book contains Parsons's tripartite theoretical model, which provided the basis for much of the vocational guidance in the first half of the 20th century.
1913	The National Vocational Guidance Association (NVGA) is established in Grand Rapids, Michigan.
1917	The first group intelligence test, the Army Alpha, is used as the basis for placement in World War I. This test leads to an explosion of test and inventory development in the 1920s and a more measured approach to test construction since. During the 1920s and 1930s, assessment devices became important tools to psychologists and counselors interested in helping people make career decisions.
1921	The *National Vocational Guidance Bulletin*, first published in 1915, begins publication on a regular basis. The journal becomes *Occupations: The Vocational Guidance Journal*.
1933–1935	New Deal programs, such as the Civilian Conservation Corps and Work Progress Administration, create employment and educational opportunities for youths and adults.
1939	The first edition of the *Dictionary of Occupational Titles* is published by the U.S. Department of Labor.
1939	E. G. Williamson publishes *How to Counsel Students*, one of the early primers regarding career counseling.
1951	NVGA merges with the American College Personnel Association, the Student

	Personnel Association for Teacher Education, and the National Association of Guidance Supervisors to form the American Personnel and Guidance Association. The NVGA journal, *Occupations*, becomes the *Personnel and Guidance Association* journal. The American School Counselor Association joins the group in 1952.
1951	Ginzberg, Ginzburg, Axelrad, and Herma publish the first theory of career development in their book *Occupational Choice: An Approach to a General Theory*.
1952	NVGA begins publishing the *Vocational Guidance Quarterly*, currently published as the *Career Development Quarterly*.
1953	Donald Super publishes "A Theory of Vocational Development" in the *American Psychologist*. His is the second developmental theory of career development but becomes the most influential.
1956	Ann Roe publishes *The Psychology of Occupations*, which contains her personality-based theory of career development.
1957	The National Defense Education Act provides money to train school counselors and support school counseling programs. The primary purpose of this legislation is to facilitate the recruitment of scientists, engineers, and mathematicians to aid in the U.S. response to the Soviet launch of the satellite *Sputnik*.
1959	John Holland publishes "A Theory of Vocational Guidance" in the *Journal of Counseling Psychology*, which lays the groundwork for his influential theory of vocational choice.
1963	The Vocational Education Act provides money for vocational guidance to vocational education students.
1982	The NVGA establishes competencies for career counselors.
1983	National Certified Career Counselor Certification is established by NVGA.
1984	NVGA changes its name to National Career Development Association (NCDA) and changes the name of its journal to *Career Development Quarterly*.
1984	The National Board for Certified Counselors assumes the management of the National Certified Career Counselor Certification program.
1987	NCDA holds its first national convention in Orlando, Florida, since becoming part of the American Personnel Association in 1951. Currently NCDA holds annual conferences.
1989	NCDA, in concert with the National Occupational Information Coordinating Committee (NOICC) and the Vocational Education Research Center at Ohio State University, commissions the Gallup Organization to poll Americans to ascertain their use of career development services and information; their perceptions of the availability and quality of these services; and their perceptions of various aspects of the workplace, including discrimination. NCDA and NOICC commission similar polls in 1992, 1994, and 2000.
1990	The Americans with Disabilities Act (ADA) is passed by Congress. The act ensures, among other things, equal access to job opportunities and training for people who have disabilities.
1994	School to Work Opportunities Act is passed by Congress. It provides impetus for public schools to develop challenging educational programs for all, relate academic subject matter to work, and help students identify their interests and make educational and career plans.
1994	U.S. Department of Labor launches an effort to develop an occupational classification scheme to replace the *Dictionary of Occupational Titles* (DOT). Technical reports detailing the development of the new system (Occupational Information Network [O*NET]) are published during the years 1995 to 1997, and the transition from the DOT to O*NET is completed by 2001.
2000	National Board for Certified Counselors opts to decommission the National Certified Career Counselor program. NCDA establishes a committee to explore the means of maintaining this program.
2001	NCDA establishes the Master Career Counselor membership category as a means of credentialing career counselors.

Source: This appendix is excerpted from pages 11–12 of Brown, D. (2012). *Career information, career counseling, and career development* (10th ed. Revised Printing). Upper Saddle River, NJ: Pearson Education, Inc.

APPENDIX B

National Career Development Association Counselor Competencies

National Career Development Association
Minimum Competencies for Multicultural Career Counseling and Development

(This document replaces the 1997 Career Counseling Competencies)
Approved by the NCDA Board–August 2009

INTRODUCTION

The purpose of the multicultural career counseling and development competencies is to ensure that all individuals practicing in, or training for practice in, the career counseling and development field are aware of the expectation that we, as professionals, will practice in ways that promote the career development and functioning of individuals of all backgrounds. Promotion and advocacy of career development for individuals is ensured regardless of age, culture, mental/physical ability, ethnicity, race, nationality, religion/spirituality, gender, gender identity, sexual orientation, marital/partnership status, military or civilian status, language preference, socioeconomic status, any other characteristics not specifically relevant to job performance, in accordance with NCDA and ACA [American Counseling Association] policy. Further, they will provide guidance to those in the career counseling and development field regarding appropriate practice with regard to clients of a different background than their own. Finally, implementation of these competencies for the field should provide the public with the assurance that they can expect career counseling and development professionals to function in a manner that facilitates their career development, regardless of the client's/student's background.

If you believe that you need assistance with performing at these minimum levels, or would like to further develop your skills in these areas, please visit the NCDA website www.ncda.org for contact information regarding sources for increasing your competence in dealing with individuals with different cultural backgrounds than yourself.

For those seeking a designation of competency, NCDA offers the Master Career Counselor and Master Career Development Professional Special Memberships. Visit www.ncda.org for more information.

THE MULTICULTURAL CAREER PROFESSIONAL

Career Development Theory

- Understands the strengths and limitations of career theory and utilizes theories that are appropriate for the population being served.

Individual and Group Counseling Skills

- Is aware of his/her own cultural beliefs and assumptions and incorporates that awareness into his/her decision-making about interactions with clients/students and other career professionals.
- Continues to develop his/her individual and group counseling skills in order to enhance his/her ability to respond appropriately to individuals from diverse populations.
- Is cognizant when working with groups of the group demographics and monitors these to ensure appropriate respect and confidentiality is maintained.

Individual/Group Assessment

- Understands the psychometric properties of the assessments he/she is using in order to effectively select and administer assessments, and interpret and use results with the appropriate limitations and cautions.

Information, Resources, and Technology

- Regularly evaluates the information, resources, and use of technology to determine that these tools are sensitive to the needs of diverse populations amending and/or individualizing for each client as required.
- Provides resources in multiple formats to ensure that clients/students are able to benefit from needed information.
- Provides targeted and sensitive support for clients/students in using the information, resources, and technology.

Program Promotion, Management, and Implementation

- Incorporates appropriate guidelines, research, and experience in developing, implementing, and managing programs and services for diverse populations.
- Utilizes the principles of program evaluation to design and obtain feedback from relevant stakeholders in the continuous improvement of programs and services, paying special attention to feedback regarding specific needs of the population being served.
- Applies his/her knowledge of multicultural issues in dealings with other professionals and trainees to ensure the creation of a culturally-sensitive environment for all clients.

Coaching, Consultation, and Performance Improvement

- Engages in coaching, consultation, and performance improvement activities with appropriate training and incorporates knowledge of multicultural attitudes, beliefs, skills and values.
- Seeks awareness and understanding about how to best match diverse clients/students with suitably culturally sensitive employers.

Supervision

- Gains knowledge of and engages in evidence-based supervision, pursues educational and training activities on a regular and ongoing basis inclusive of both counseling and supervision topics. Further, is aware of his/her limitations, cultural biases and personal values and seeks professional consultative assistance as necessary.
- Infuses multicultural/diversity contexts into his/her training and supervision practices, makes supervisees aware of the ethical standards and responsibilities of the profession, and trains supervisees to develop relevant multicultural knowledge and skills.

Ethical/Legal Issues

- Continuously updates his/her knowledge of multicultural and diversity issues and research and applies new knowledge as required.
- Employs his/her knowledge and experience of multicultural ethical and legal issues within a professional framework to enhance the functioning of his/her organization and the image of the profession.
- Uses supervision and professional consultations effectively when faced with an ethical or legal issue related to diversity, to ensure he/she provides high-quality services for every client/student.

Research/Evaluation

Designs and implements culturally appropriate research studies with regards to research design, instrument selection, and other pertinent population-specific issues.

NCDA Headquarters
305 N. Beech Circle
Broken Arrow, OK 74012
918/663-7060 Toll-free 866-FOR-NCDA
Fax: 918/663-7058
www.ncda.org

APPENDIX C

National Career Development Association Code of Ethics

Revised May 2007

The NCDA Ethics Committee gratefully acknowledges the American Counseling Association (ACA) and its Ethics Committee for permission to adapt their 2005 Code of Ethics. NCDA, one of the founding associations of ACA in 1952, is a current division of ACA. The NCDA Ethics Committee endeavored to follow the structure of ACA's Code so that the two codes would be compatible with each other, while developing, adding, and enhancing profession-specific guidelines for NCDA's membership. More information on ACA's Ethics Code can be found on their website (see the attached web references section).

The NCDA Ethics Committee gratefully acknowledges Cassandra Smisson for her assistance in reviewing the final draft of this code. As of June 2006, Ms. Smisson was pursuing a Ph.D. in Counseling Psych at Florida State University.

2005–2007 NCDA Ethics Committee Members

David M. Reile, Chair, Cheri Butler (Board Liaison); Greta Davis; Dennis Engels; Janice Guerriero; Janet Lenz; Julia Makela; Kristin M. Perrone-McGovern; James Sampson; Donald Schutt; Keley Smith-Keller

Nondiscrimination Statement
NCDA opposes discrimination against any individual based on age, culture, mental/physical disability, ethnicity, race, religion/spirituality, creed, gender, actual or perceived gender identity or expression, actual or perceived sexual orientation, marital/partnership status, language preference, socioeconomic status, any other characteristics not specifically relevant to job performance. (Statement adopted by the NCDA Board of Directors, May 2007)

2007 NCDA CODE OF ETHICS

Introduction & Purpose

While there are many ways to define and think about *ethics*, ethics and ethical behavior are basically about professionalism and transparency. The NCDA Ethics Code has been designed as a guide and resource for career practitioners. While it offers a set of principles that can be applied to wide range of settings and situations, it is not (nor can it be) comprehensive. If you are concerned about whether or not a particular practice is ethical, then you should not engage in that behavior without getting competent advice. More succinctly, when in doubt—don't; at least not without discussing the situation with others. Peer review isn't always going to give you perfect advice; but you can take comfort in knowing that you questioned your behavior before proceeding and allowed others to comment before taking action. There is safety and strength in the depth and breadth of opinions you seek before engaging in activity which may be untried or questionable. The Ethics Committee Members do not hold themselves up as definitive experts in all ethical matters. Further, we are not experts with regard to legal issues and cannot give legal advice. However, we encourage members of the National Career Development Association to contact us with questions. We are committed to working collaboratively to provide guidance where we can and to provide referrals as appropriate. You may reach us at ethics@ncda.org.

The National Career Development Association (NCDA) Code of Ethics serves five main purposes:

1. The *Code* enables NCDA to clarify to current and future members, and to those served by their members, the nature of ethical responsibilities held in common by its members.
2. The *Code* helps support the mission of NCDA.
3. The *Code* establishes principles that define ethical behaviors and practices of association members.
4. The *Code* serves as an ethical guide designed to assist members in constructing a professional course of action that best serves those utilizing career services and best promotes the values of the career profession.
5. The *Code* serves as a guide for those receiving career services so that they may understand what to expect from working with a career professional and to understand their rights and responsibilities as consumers of these services.

The *NCDA Code of Ethics* contains nine main sections that address the following areas:

Section A: The Professional Relationship

Section B: Confidentiality, Privileged Communication, and Privacy

Section C: Professional Responsibility

Section D: Relationships with Other Professionals

Section E: Evaluation, Assessment, and Interpretation

Section F: Use of the Internet in Career Services

Section G: Supervision, Training, and Teaching

Section H: Research and Publication

Section I: Resolving Ethical Issues

Each section of the *NCDA Code of Ethics* begins with an Introduction. The Introduction helps set the tone for that particular section and provides a starting point that invites reflection on the ethical guidelines contained in each part of the *NCDA Code of Ethics*. When career professionals are faced with ethical dilemmas that are difficult to resolve, they are expected to engage in a carefully considered ethical decision-making process. Reasonable differences of opinion can and do exist among career professionals with respect to ways in which values, ethical principles, and ethical standards would be applied when they conflict. While there is no specific ethical decision-making model that is most effective, career professionals are expected to be familiar with a credible model of decision-making that can bear public scrutiny and its application. (For one example of an ethical decision-making model from the Ethics Resource Center, see the attached web references section). Through a chosen ethical decision-making process and evaluation of the context of the situation, career professionals are empowered to make decisions that help expand the capacity of people to grow and develop.

NCDA has members in various career services positions (see Career Professionals), as well as in instructional (counselor educators, counseling psychology professors, etc.) and supervisory roles (Director, Associate Director, Career Supervisor, etc.). The term "career professional" will be used throughout this document both as a noun and as an adjective to refer to anyone holding NCDA membership and who is therefore expected to abide by these ethical guidelines.

Additionally, a brief glossary is given (see end of document) to provide readers with a concise description of some of the terms used in the *NCDA Code of Ethics*. NCDA Members who are affiliated with other professional associations (i.e., psychologists, school counselors, etc.) should also consult the ethics codes from those organizations and adhere to the highest standard of professional practice.

NCDA acknowledges and supports its members in their quest to achieve the highest academic and professional credentials appropriate to their work. Many NCDA members are trained credentialed counselors, psychologists, and/or educators with master's and/or doctoral-level degrees in counseling, psychology, or related disciplines. NCDA does not encourage or condone replacing these professionals with individuals who have lesser education, training, and/or credentials. However, NCDA acknowledges, respects, and welcomes individuals regardless of their training and educational backgrounds and recognizes the valuable contribution that all of its members make in the field of career development. Thus, NCDA opposes any statement, action, or activity, which implies a "second-class" status to any individuals within our association.

Section A: The Professional Relationship

INTRODUCTION Career professionals encourage client growth and development in ways that foster the interest and welfare of clients and promote formation of healthy relationships. Career professionals actively attempt to understand the diverse cultural backgrounds of the individuals they serve. Career professionals also explore their own cultural identities and how one's cultural identity affects one's values and beliefs about the working relationship. Career professionals are encouraged to contribute to society by devoting a portion of their professional activity to services for which there is little or no financial return (pro bono publico).

A.1. WELFARE OF THOSE SERVED BY CAREER PROFESSIONALS

A.1.a. Primary Responsibility The primary responsibility of career professionals is to respect the dignity and to promote the welfare of the individuals to whom they provide service.

A.1.b. Differentiation Between Types of Services Provided "Career planning" services are differentiated from "career counseling" services. Career planning services include an active provision of information designed to help a client with a specific need, such as review of a resumé; assistance in networking strategies; identification of occupations based on values, interests, skills, prior work experience, and/or other characteristics; support in the job-seeking process; and assessment by means of paper-based and/or online inventories of interest, abilities, personality, work-related values, and/or other characteristics. In addition to providing these informational services, "career counseling" provides the opportunity for a deeper level of involvement with the client, based on the establishment of a professional counseling relationship and the potential for assisting clients with career and personal development concerns beyond those included in career planning. All career professionals, whether engaging in "career planning" or "career counseling", provide only the services that are within the scope of their professional competence and qualifications. *(See C.2., C.4., E.2.a., F.7.)*

A.1.c. Records Career professionals maintain records necessary for rendering professional services as required by laws, regulations, or agency or institution procedures. Career professionals include sufficient and timely documentation in their records to facilitate delivery and continuity of services. Career professionals take reasonable steps to ensure that documentation in records accurately reflects client progress and the services provided. If errors are made in records, career professionals take steps to properly note the correction of such errors according to agency or institutional policies. Career professionals are encouraged to purge their files according to the time frame required by federal, state, local, and/or institutional statute, law, regulation, or procedure, particularly when there is no reasonable expectation that a client will benefit from maintaining the records any longer than required. Career professionals are expected to know and abide by all applicable federal, state, local, and/or institutional statutes, laws, regulations, and procedures regarding record keeping. *(See B.6., B.6.g., H.2.j.)*

A.1.d. Career Services Plans Career professionals and their clients work jointly in devising integrated career services plans (in writing or orally) that offer reasonable promise of success and are consistent with the abilities and circumstances of clients. Career professionals and clients regularly review career plans to assess their continued viability and effectiveness, respecting the freedom of choice of clients. *(See A.2.a., A.2.d.)*

A.1.e. Support Network Involvement Career professionals recognize that support networks hold various meanings in the lives of clients and consider enlisting the support, understanding, and involvement of others (e.g., family members, friends, and religious/spiritual/community leaders) as positive resources, when appropriate and with client consent.

A.2. INFORMED CONSENT IN THE PROFESSIONAL RELATIONSHIP *(See B.5., B.6.b., E.3., E.13.b., G.1.c., H.2.a.)*

A.2.a. Informed Consent Clients have the freedom to choose whether to enter into or remain in a professional relationship. To make informed choices, clients need adequate information about the working relationship and the career professional. Career professionals have an obligation to review in writing and orally the rights and responsibilities of both the career professional and the recipient of services prior to the beginning of the working relationship. Further, informed consent is an ongoing part of the professional relationship, and career professionals appropriately document discussions of informed consent throughout the working relationship.

A.2.b. Types of Information Needed Career professionals clearly explain to clients the nature of all services provided. They inform clients about issues such as, but not limited to, the following: the purposes, goals, techniques, procedures, limitations, potential risks, and benefits of services; the career professional's qualifications, credentials, and relevant experience; continuation of services upon the incapacitation or death of the career professional; and other pertinent information. Career professionals take steps to ensure that clients understand the implications of diagnosis (if applicable), the intended use of tests/assessments and reports, fees, and billing arrangements.

Clients have the right to confidentiality and to be provided with an explanation of its limitations (including how supervisors and/or treatment team professionals are involved); to obtain clear information about their records; to participate in the ongoing career services plans; and to refuse any services or modality change and to be advised of the consequences of such refusal.

A.2.c. Developmental and Cultural Sensitivity Career professionals communicate information in ways that are both developmentally and culturally appropriate. Career professionals use clear and understandable language when discussing issues related to informed consent. When clients have difficulty understanding the language used by career professionals, they provide necessary services (e.g., arranging for a qualified interpreter or translator) to ensure comprehension by clients. The cost for such services, however, may be passed onto clients in accordance with federal, state, local, and/or institutional statute, law, regulation, or procedure. Thus clients should be given the opportunity to seek another career professional or to employ an interpreter or translator of their own choosing. In collaboration with clients, career professionals consider cultural implications of informed consent procedures and, where possible, career professionals adjust their practices accordingly.

A.2.d. Inability to Give Consent When providing career services to minors or persons unable to give voluntary consent, career professionals seek the assent of clients to services, and include them in decision making as appropriate. Career professionals recognize the need to balance the ethical rights of clients to make choices, their capacity to give consent or assent to receive services, and parental or familial legal rights and responsibilities to protect these clients and make decisions on their behalf.

A.3. CLIENTS SERVED BY OTHERS

When career professionals learn that their clients are in a professional relationship with another mental health professional, they request a written release from clients to inform the other professionals and strive to establish positive and collaborative professional relationships, when necessary and appropriate.

A.4. AVOIDING HARM AND IMPOSING VALUES

A.4.a. Avoiding Harm Career professionals act to avoid harming their clients, students, trainees, and research participants and to minimize or to remedy unavoidable or unanticipated harm.

A.4.b. Personal Values Career professionals are aware of their own values, attitudes, beliefs, and behaviors and avoid imposing values that are inconsistent with clients' goals. Career professionals respect the diversity of clients, students, trainees, and research participants.

A.5. ROLES AND RELATIONSHIPS WITH CLIENTS *(See G.3., G.10., H.3.)*

A.5.a. Current Clients Sexual or romantic interactions or relationships with current clients, their romantic partners, or their family members are prohibited.

A.5.b. Former Clients Sexual or romantic interactions or relationships with former clients, their romantic partners, or their family members are prohibited for a period of 5 years following the last professional contact. Career professionals, before engaging in sexual or romantic interactions or relationships with clients, their romantic partners, or client family members after 5 years following the last professional contact, demonstrate forethought and document (in written form) whether the interactions or relationship can be viewed as exploitive in some way and/or whether there is still potential to harm the former client. In cases of potential exploitation and/or harm, the career professional does not enter into such an interaction or relationship.

A.5.c. Nonprofessional Interactions or Relationships (Other Than Sexual or Romantic Interactions or Relationships) Nonprofessional relationships with clients, former clients, their romantic partners, or their family members should be avoided by career professionals, except when the interaction is potentially beneficial to the client. *(See A.5.d.)*

A.5.d. Potentially Beneficial Interactions When a nonprofessional interaction with a client or former client may be potentially beneficial to the client or former client, the career professional must document in case records, prior to the interaction (or as soon as feasible), the rationale for such an interaction, the potential benefit, and anticipated consequences for the client or former client and other individuals significantly involved with the client or former client. Such interactions should be initiated with appropriate client consent. Where unintentional harm occurs to the client or former client, or to an individual significantly involved with the client or former client, due to the nonprofessional interaction, the career professional must show evidence of an attempt to remedy such harm. Examples of potentially beneficial interactions include, but are not limited to, attending a formal ceremony (e.g., a wedding/commitment ceremony or graduation); purchasing a service or product provided by a client or former client (excepting unrestricted bartering); hospital visits to an ill family member; and mutual membership in a professional association, organization, or community. *(See A.5.c.)*

A.5.e. Role Changes in the Professional Relationship When a career professional changes a role from the original or most recent contracted relationship, s/he obtains informed consent from the client and explains the right of the client to refuse services related to the change. Examples of role changes include, but are not limited to:

1. changing from providing individual career services to therapy, relationship or family counseling, or vice versa;
2. changing from a non-forensic evaluative role to a therapeutic role, or vice versa;
3. changing from a career professional to a researcher role (i.e., enlisting clients as research participants), or vice versa; and/or

4. changing from a career professional to a mediator role, or vice versa. Clients must be fully informed of any anticipated consequences (e.g., financial, legal, personal, or therapeutic) of role changes with a career professional.

A.6. ROLES AND RELATIONSHIPS AT INDIVIDUAL, GROUP, INSTITUTIONAL, AND SOCIETAL LEVELS

A.6.a. Advocacy When appropriate, career professionals advocate at individual, group, institutional, and societal levels to examine potential barriers and obstacles that inhibit access and/or the growth and development of clients.

A.6.b. Confidentiality and Advocacy Career professionals obtain consent prior to engaging in advocacy efforts on behalf of a client to improve the provision of services and to work toward removal of systemic barriers or obstacles that inhibit client access, growth, and development.

A.7. MULTIPLE CLIENTS When a career professional agrees to provide career services to two or more persons who have a relationship, the career professional clarifies at the outset which person or persons are clients and the nature of the relationships the career professional will have with each involved person. If it becomes apparent that the career professional may be called upon to perform potentially conflicting roles, the career professional will clarify, adjust, or withdraw appropriately from one or more roles. (See A.8.a., B.4.)

A.8. GROUP WORK *(See B.4.a.)*

A.8.a. Screening Career professionals screen prospective group participants. To the extent possible, career professionals select members whose needs and goals are compatible with goals of the group, who will not impede the group process, and whose well-being will not be jeopardized by the group experience.

A.8.b. Protecting Clients In a group setting, career professionals take reasonable precautions to protect clients from physical, emotional, or psychological trauma.

A.9. FEES AND BARTERING

A.9.a. Accepting Fees from Agency Clients Career professionals refuse a private fee or other remuneration for rendering services to persons who are entitled to such services through the career professional's employing agency or institution. The policies of a particular agency may make explicit provisions for agency clients to receive career services from members of its staff in private practice. In such instances, the clients must be informed of other options open to them should they seek private career services.

A.9.b. Establishing Fees In establishing fees for professional career services, career professionals consider the financial status of clients and the locality in which they practice. In the event that the established fee structure is inappropriate for a client, career professionals assist clients in attempting to find comparable services of acceptable cost.

A.9.c. Nonpayment of Fees If career professionals intend to use collection agencies or take legal measures to collect fees from clients who do not pay for services as agreed upon, they first inform clients of intended actions and offer clients the opportunity to make payment.

A.9.d. Bartering Career professionals may barter only if the relationship is not exploitive or harmful and does not place the career professional in an unfair advantage, if the client requests it, and if such arrangements are an accepted practice among professionals in the community. Career professionals consider the cultural implications of bartering and discuss relevant concerns with clients and document such agreements in a clear written contract. Career professionals must also be aware of local, state, and/or federal laws, including the tax implications of such an arrangement. Further, career professionals must make the recipients of their services aware of all applicable federal, state, local, and/or institutional statutes, laws, regulations, and procedures and should direct them to seek qualified counsel (i.e., attorney and/or accountant) in determining if such an arrangement is in their best interest.

A.9.e. Receiving Gifts Career professionals understand the challenges of accepting gifts from clients and recognize that in some cultures, small gifts are a token of respect and a way of showing gratitude. When determining whether or not to accept a gift from clients, career professionals take into account the nature of their relationship, the monetary value of the gift, a client's motivation for giving the gift, and the career professional's motivation for wanting or declining the gift.

A.10. TERMINATION AND REFERRAL

A.10.a. Abandonment Prohibited Career professionals do not abandon or neglect clients to whom they provide career services. Career professionals assist in making appropriate arrangements for the continuation of treatment, when necessary, during interruptions such as vacations, illness, and following termination.

A.10.b. Inability to Assist Clients If career professionals determine an inability to be of professional assistance to clients, they avoid entering into or continuing the relationship. Career professionals are knowledgeable about culturally and clinically appropriate referral resources and suggest these alternatives. If clients decline the suggested referrals, career professionals may discontinue the relationship.

A.10.c. Appropriate Termination Career professionals terminate a professional relationship when it becomes reasonably apparent that the client no longer needs assistance, is not likely to benefit from, or is being harmed by continued service provision. Career professionals may terminate the working relationship when in jeopardy of harm by the client, or another person with whom the client has a relationship, or when clients do not pay agreed upon fees. Career professionals provide pretermination career services and recommend other providers when feasible and necessary.

A.10.d. Appropriate Transfer of Services When career professionals transfer or refer clients to other practitioners, they ensure that appropriate clinical and administrative processes are completed and open communication is maintained with both clients and practitioners.

Section B: Confidentiality, Privileged Communication, and Privacy

INTRODUCTION Career professionals recognize that trust is a cornerstone of the professional relationship. Career professionals work to earn the trust of clients by creating an ongoing partnership, establishing and upholding appropriate boundaries, and maintaining confidentiality. Career professionals communicate the parameters of confidentiality in a culturally competent manner.

B.1. RESPECTING CLIENT RIGHTS

B.1.a. Multicultural/Diversity Considerations Career professionals maintain awareness and sensitivity regarding cultural meanings of confidentiality and privacy. Career professionals respect differing views toward disclosure of information. Career professionals hold ongoing discussions with clients as to how, when, and with whom information is to be shared.

B.1.b. Respect for Privacy Career professionals respect client rights to privacy. Career professionals solicit private information from clients only when it is beneficial to the working relationship.

B.1.c. Respect for Confidentiality Career professionals do not share confidential information without client consent or without sound legal or ethical justification.

B.1.d. Explanation of Limitations At initiation and throughout the professional relationship, career professionals inform clients of the limitations of confidentiality and seek to identify foreseeable situations in which confidentiality must be breached. *(See A.2.b.)*

B.2. EXCEPTIONS

B.2.a. Danger and Legal Requirements The general requirement that career professionals keep information confidential does not apply when disclosure is required to protect clients or identified others from serious and foreseeable harm or when legal requirements demand that confidential information must be revealed. Examples of when career professionals may divulge confidential information may include, but not be limited to, mandated reporting in cases of suspected or actual child or elder abuse, when a client has a communicable and life threatening disease or condition and may infect an identifiable third party, or when notifying a collection agency to recover unpaid fees from a client. Career professionals consult with other professionals, include attorneys, when in doubt as to the validity of an exception. *(See A.9.c., B.2.b., B.2.c & B.2.d.)*

B.2.b. Contagious, Life-Threatening Diseases When clients disclose that they have a disease commonly known to be both communicable and life threatening, career professionals may be justified in disclosing information to identifiable third parties, if they are known to be at demonstrable and high risk of contracting the disease. Prior to making a disclosure, career professionals confirm that there is such a diagnosis and assess the intent of clients to inform the third parties about their disease or to engage in any behaviors that may be harmful to an identifiable third party. *(See B.2.a.)*

B.2.c. Court-Ordered Disclosure When subpoenaed to release confidential or privileged information, career professionals endeavor to inform the client and to obtain written consent from the client or take steps to prohibit the disclosure, or have it limited as narrowly as possible, to minimize potential harm to the client. *(See B.2.d.)*

B.2.d. Minimal Disclosure To the extent possible, clients are informed before confidential information is disclosed and are involved in the disclosure decision-making process. When circumstances require the disclosure of confidential information, only essential information is revealed. *(See B.2.c.)*

B.3. INFORMATION SHARED WITH OTHERS

B.3.a. Subordinates Career professionals make every effort to ensure that privacy and confidentiality of clients are maintained by subordinates, including employees, supervisees, students, clerical assistants, and volunteers. *(See G.1.c.)*

B.3.b. Treatment Teams When client treatment involves a continued review or participation by a treatment team, the client will be informed of the team's existence and composition, information being shared, and the purposes of sharing such information.

B.3.c. Confidential Settings Career professionals discuss confidential information only in settings in which they can reasonably ensure client privacy.

B.3.d. Third-Party Payers Career professionals disclose information to third-party payers only when clients have authorized such disclosure and in accordance with federal, state, local, and/or institutional statute, law, regulation, or procedure.

B.3.e. Transmitting Confidential Information Career professionals take precautions to ensure the confidentiality of information transmitted through the use of computers, electronic mail, facsimile machines, telephones, voicemail, answering machines, and other electronic or computer technology.

B.3.f. Deceased Clients Career professionals protect the confidentiality of deceased clients, consistent with legal requirements and agency or institutional policies.

B.4. GROUPS AND FAMILIES

B.4.a. Group Work In group work, career professionals clearly explain the importance and parameters of confidentiality for the specific group being entered.

B.4.b. Providing Career Services to Multiple Family Members When providing career services to multiple family members (e.g., spouses/partners, parent and child, etc.), career professionals clearly define who is considered "the client" and discuss expectations and limitations of confidentiality. Career professionals seek agreement and document in writing such agreement among all involved parties having capacity to give consent concerning each individual's right to confidentiality and any obligation to preserve the confidentiality of information known.

B.5. CLIENTS LACKING CAPACITY TO GIVE INFORMED CONSENT

B.5.a. Responsibility to Clients When providing career services to minor clients or adult clients who lack the capacity to give voluntary, informed consent, career professionals protect the confidentiality of information received in the professional relationship as specified by federal and state laws, written policies, and applicable ethical standards.

B.5.b. Responsibility to Parents and Legal Guardians Career professionals inform parents and legal guardians about the role of career professionals and the confidential nature of the professional relationship. Career professionals are sensitive to the cultural diversity of families and respect the inherent rights and responsibilities of parents/guardians over the welfare of their children/charges according to law. Career professionals work to establish, as appropriate, collaborative relationships with parents/guardians to best serve the needs and welfare of their clients.

B.5.c. Release of Confidential Information When providing career services to minor clients or adult clients who lack the capacity to give voluntary consent to release confidential information, career professionals seek permission from an appropriate third party to disclose information. In such instances, career professionals inform clients consistent with their level of understanding and take culturally appropriate measures to safeguard client confidentiality.

B.6. RECORDS

B.6.a. Confidentiality of Records Career professionals ensure that records are kept in a secure location and that only authorized persons have access to records.

B.6.b. Permission to Record Career professionals obtain permission from clients prior to recording sessions through electronic or similar means (i.e., audio or video recording).

B.6.c. Permission to Observe Career professionals obtain permission from clients prior to allowing observation of sessions, review of session transcripts, or viewing recordings of sessions with supervisors, subordinates, faculty, peers, or others within a training environment.

B.6.d. Client Access Career professionals provide reasonable access to records and copies of records when requested by competent clients. Career professionals limit the access of clients to their records, or portions of their records, only when there is compelling evidence that such access would cause harm to the client and in accordance with federal, state, local, and/or institutional statute, law, regulation, or procedure. Career professionals document the request of clients and the rationale for withholding some or all of the record in the files of clients. In situations involving multiple clients, career professionals provide individual clients with only those parts of records that related directly to them and do not include confidential information related to any other client.

B.6.e. Assistance with Records When clients request access to their records, career professionals provide assistance and consultation in interpreting such records.

B.6.f. Disclosure or Transfer Unless exceptions to confidentiality exist, career professionals obtain written permission from clients to disclose or transfer records to legitimate third parties. Steps are taken to ensure that receivers of career services records are sensitive to their confidential nature. *(See A.3., E.4.)*

B.6.g. Storage and Disposal After Termination Career professionals store records following termination of services to ensure reasonable future access, maintain records in accordance with all applicable federal, state, local, and/or institutional statutes, laws, regulations, and procedures governing records, and dispose of client records and other sensitive materials in a manner that protects client confidentiality. When records are of an artistic nature, career professionals obtain client (or guardian) consent with regard to handling of such records or documents. Career professionals are encouraged to purge their files according to the time frame required by federal, state, local, and/or institutional statute, law, regulation, or procedure, particularly when there is no reasonable expectation that a client will benefit from maintaining the records any longer. Career professionals are expected to know and abide by all applicable federal, state, local, and/or institutional statutes, laws, regulations, and procedures regarding record keeping and disposal. *(See A.1.c.)*

B.6.h. Reasonable Precautions Career professionals take reasonable precautions to protect client confidentiality in the event of the career professional's termination of practice, incapacity, or death. *(See C.2.h.)*

B.7. RESEARCH AND TRAINING

B.7.a. Institutional Approval When institutional approval is required, career professionals provide accurate information about their research proposals and obtain approval prior to conducting their research. They conduct research in accordance with the approved research protocol.

B.7.b. Adherence to Guidelines Career professionals are responsible for understanding and adhering to state, federal, agency, or institutional policies or applicable guidelines regarding confidentiality in their research practices.

B.7.c. Confidentiality of Information Obtained in Research Violations of participant privacy and confidentiality are risks of participation in research involving human participants, however, investigators maintain all research records in a secure manner. They explain to participants the risks of violations of privacy and confidentiality and disclose to participants any limits of confidentiality that can reasonably be expected. Regardless of the degree to which confidentiality will be maintained, investigators must disclose to participants any limits of confidentiality that can reasonably be expected. *(See H.2.e.)*

B.7.d. Disclosure of Research Information Career professionals do not disclose confidential information that reasonably could lead to the identification of a research participant unless they have obtained prior consent of the person. Use of data derived from professional relationships for purposes of training, research, or publication is confined to content that is disguised to ensure the anonymity of the individuals involved. *(See H.2.a., H.2.d.)*

B.7.e. Agreement for Identification Identification of clients, students, or supervisees in a presentation or publication is permissible only when they have reviewed the material and agreed to its presentation or publication. *(See H.4.d.)*

B.8. CONSULTATION

B.8.a. Agreements When acting as consultants, career professionals seek agreements among all parties involved concerning each individual's rights to confidentiality, the obligation of each individual to preserve confidential information, and the limits of confidentiality of information shared by others.

B.8.b. Respect for Privacy Information obtained in a consulting relationship is discussed for professional purposes only with persons directly involved with the case. Written and oral reports present only data germane to the purposes of the consultation, and every effort is made to protect client identity and to avoid undue invasion of privacy.

B.8.c. Disclosure of Confidential Information When consulting with colleagues, career professionals do not disclose confidential information that reasonably could lead to the identification of a client or other person or organization with whom they have a confidential relationship unless they have obtained the prior consent of the person or organization or the disclosure cannot be avoided. They disclose information only to the extent necessary to achieve the purposes of the consultation. *(See D.2.d.)*

Section C: Professional Responsibility

INTRODUCTION Career professionals provide open, honest, and accurate communication in dealing with the public and other professionals. They practice in a nondiscriminatory manner within the boundaries of professional and personal competence and have a responsibility to abide by the *NCDA Code of Ethics*. Career professionals actively participate in local, state, and national associations that foster the development and improvement of the provision of career services.

Career professionals promote change at the individual, group, institutional, and societal levels that improves the quality of life for individuals and groups and removes potential barriers to the provision or access of appropriate services being offered. Career professionals have a responsibility to the public to engage in ethical practice. In addition, career professionals engage in self-care activities to maintain and promote their emotional, physical, mental, and spiritual well-being to best meet their professional responsibilities.

C.1. KNOWLEDGE OF STANDARDS Career professionals have a responsibility to read, understand, and follow the *NCDA Code of Ethics* and adhere to all applicable federal, state, local, and/or institutional statutes, laws, regulations, and procedures.

C.2. PROFESSIONAL COMPETENCE

C.2.a. Boundaries of Competence Career professionals practice only within the boundaries of their competence, based on their education, training, supervised experience, state and national professional credentials, and appropriate professional experience. Career professionals gain knowledge, personal awareness, sensitivity, and skills pertinent to working with a diverse client population. *(See E.2., G.2., G.11.c.)*

C.2.b. New Specialty Areas of Practice Career professionals practice in specialty areas new to them only after obtaining appropriate education, training, and supervised experience. While developing skills in new specialty areas, career professionals take steps to ensure the competence of their work and to protect others from possible harm. *(See G.6.e.)*

C.2.c. Qualified for Employment Career professionals accept employment only for positions for which they are qualified by education, training, supervised experience, state and national professional credentials, and appropriate professional experience. Career professionals hire for professional positions only individuals who are qualified and competent for those positions.

C.2.d. Monitor Effectiveness Career professionals continually monitor their effectiveness as professionals and take steps to improve when necessary. Career professionals in private practice take reasonable steps to seek peer supervision, as needed, to evaluate their efficacy as career professionals.

C.2.e. Consultation on Ethical Obligations Career professionals take reasonable steps to consult with other career professionals or related practitioners when they have questions regarding their ethical obligations or professional activities.

C.2.f. Continuing Education Career professionals recognize the need for continuing education to acquire and maintain a reasonable level of awareness of current scientific and professional information in their fields of activity. They take steps to maintain competence in the skills they use, are open to new procedures, and keep current with the populations with whom they work.

C.2.g. Impairment Career professionals are alert to the signs of impairment from their own physical, mental, or emotional problems and refrain from offering or providing professional services when such impairment is likely to harm a client or others. They seek assistance for problems that reach the level of professional impairment, and, if necessary, they limit, suspend, or terminate their professional responsibilities until such time as it is determined that they may safely resume their work. Career professionals assist colleagues or supervisors in recognizing their own professional impairment. They provide consultation and assistance, when warranted, with colleagues or supervisors showing signs of impairment and intervene as appropriate to prevent imminent harm to clients. *(See A.10.b., G.8.b.)*

C.2.h. Incapacitation or Termination of Practice When career professionals leave a practice, they follow a prepared plan for transfer of clients and files. Career professionals prepare and disseminate to an identified colleague or "records custodian" a plan for the transfer of clients and files in case of their incapacitation, death, or termination of practice. *(See A.1.c., A.10., B.6.g.)*

C.3. ADVERTISING AND SOLICITING CLIENTS

C.3.a. Accurate Advertising When advertising or otherwise representing their services to the public, career professionals identify their credentials in an accurate manner that is not false, misleading, deceptive, or fraudulent. *(See C.4.)*

C.3.b. Testimonials Career professionals who use testimonials do not solicit them from individuals who may be vulnerable to undue influence.

C.3.c. Statements by Others Career professionals make reasonable efforts to ensure that statements made by others about them or the services they provide are accurate.

C.3.d. Recruiting Through Employment Career professionals do not use their places of employment or institutional affiliations to recruit or gain clients, supervisees, or consultees for their private practices, unless they have permission. If permitted to solicit for their private practices, career professionals must make potential clients, supervisees, or consultees aware of the free or low-cost services already provided by them or others through their place of employment or institutional affiliation. *(See A.9.a.)*

C.3.e. Products and Training Advertisements Career professionals who develop products related to their profession or conduct workshops or training events ensure that the advertisements concerning these products or events are accurate and disclose adequate information for consumers to make informed choices.

C.3.f. Promoting to Those Served Career professionals do not use individual consultation, teaching, training, or supervisory relationships to promote their products or training events in a manner that is deceptive or would exert undue influence on individuals who may be vulnerable. However, educators may adopt textbooks and/or other materials they have authored or developed for instructional purposes.

C.4. PROFESSIONAL QUALIFICATIONS

C.4.a. Accurate Representation Career professionals claim or imply only professional qualifications actually completed and correct any known misrepresentations of their qualifications by others. Career professionals truthfully represent the qualifications of their professional colleagues. Career professionals clearly distinguish between paid and volunteer work experience and accurately describe their continuing education and specialized training. *(See A.1.b, C.2.a, E.9.c.)*

C.4.b. Credentials Career professionals claim only licenses or certifications that are current and in good standing.

C.4.c. Educational Degrees Career professionals clearly differentiate between earned and honorary degrees.

C.4.d. Implying Doctoral-Level Competence Career professionals clearly state their highest earned degree in counseling or a closely related field. Career professionals do not imply doctoral-level competence when possessing only a master's degree in counseling or a related field. Career professionals do not use the title "Dr." nor refer to themselves as "Dr." in a counseling or career services context when their doctorate is not in counseling or a related field.

C.4.e. Program Accreditation Status Career professionals clearly state the accreditation status of their degree programs at the time the degree was earned.

C.4.f. Professional Membership Career professionals clearly differentiate between current, active memberships and former memberships in associations.

C.5. NONDISCRIMINATION Career professionals do not condone or engage in discrimination against any individual based on age, culture, mental/physical disability, ethnicity, race, religion/spirituality, creed, gender, gender identity, sexual orientation, marital/partnership status, language preference, socioeconomic status, any other characteristics not specifically relevant to job performance, or any basis prohibited by law. Career professionals do not discriminate against clients, students, employees, supervisees, or research participants in a manner that has a negative impact on these persons.

C.6. PUBLIC RESPONSIBILITY

C.6.a. Sexual Harassment Career professionals do not engage in or condone sexual harassment. Sexual harassment is defined as sexual solicitation, physical advances, or verbal or nonverbal conduct that is sexual in nature, that occurs in connection with professional activities or roles, and that either

1. Is unwelcome, is offensive, or creates a hostile workplace or learning environment, and career professionals know or are told this; or
2. Is sufficiently severe or intense to be perceived as harassment to a reasonable person in the context in which the behavior occurred.

Sexual harassment can consist of a single intense or severe act or multiple persistent or pervasive acts.

C.6.b. Reports to Third Parties Career professionals are accurate, honest, and objective in reporting their professional activities and judgments to appropriate third parties, including courts, health insurance companies, those who are the recipients of evaluation reports, and others. *(See B.3., E.4.)*

C.6.c. Media Presentations When career professionals provide advice or comment by means of public lectures, demonstrations, radio or television programs, prerecorded tapes, technology-based applications, printed articles, mailed material, or other media, they take reasonable precautions to ensure that

1. The statements are based on appropriate professional literature and practice,
2. The statements are otherwise consistent with the *NCDA Code of Ethics,* and
3. The recipients of the information are informed that a professional relationship has not been established.

C.6.d. Exploitation of Others Career professionals do not exploit others in their professional relationships. *(See A.5.b., A.9.d.)*

C.6.e. Scientific Bases for Treatment Modalities Career professionals use techniques/procedures/modalities that are grounded in theory, are generally considered to be established professional practice in the fields of counseling and career development, and/or have an empirical or scientific foundation. Career professionals who do not must define the techniques/procedures as "unproven" or "developing" and explain the potential risks and ethical considerations of using such techniques/procedures and take steps to protect clients from possible harm. *(See A.4.a.)*

C.7. RESPONSIBILITY TO OTHER PROFESSIONALS

C.7.a. Personal Public Statements When making personal statements in a public context, career professionals clarify that they are speaking from their personal perspectives and that they are not speaking on behalf of all career professionals or the profession. *(See C.6.c.)*

Section D: Relationships with Other Professionals

INTRODUCTION Career professionals recognize that the quality of their interactions with colleagues can influence the quality of services provided to clients. They work to become knowledgeable about colleagues within and outside the profession. Career professionals develop positive working relationships and systems of communication with colleagues to enhance services to clients.

D.1. RELATIONSHIPS WITH COLLEAGUES, EMPLOYERS, AND EMPLOYEES

D.1.a. Different Approaches Career professionals are respectful of approaches to career services that differ from their own. Career professionals are respectful of traditions and practices of other professional groups with which they work.

D.1.b. Forming Relationships Career professionals work to develop and strengthen interdisciplinary relations with colleagues from other disciplines to best serve clients.

D.1.c. Interdisciplinary Teamwork Career professionals who are members of interdisciplinary teams delivering multifaceted services to clients keep the focus on how to best serve the clients. They participate in and contribute to decisions that affect the well-being of clients by drawing on the perspectives, values, and experiences of the profession and those of colleagues from other disciplines. *(See B.3.b.)*

D.1.d. Confidentiality When career professionals are required by law, institutional policy, or extraordinary circumstances to serve in more than one role in judicial or administrative proceedings, they clarify role expectations and the parameters of confidentiality with their colleagues. *(See A.5.e, B.1.c., B.1.d., B.2.c., B.2.d., B.3.b.)*

D.1.e. Establishing Professional and Ethical Obligations Career professionals who are members of interdisciplinary teams clarify professional and ethical obligations of the team as a whole and of its individual members. When a team decision raises ethical concerns, career professionals first attempt to resolve the concern within the team. If they cannot reach resolution among team members, career professionals pursue other avenues to address their concerns consistent with client well-being.

D.1.f. Personnel Selection and Assignment Career professionals select competent staff and assign responsibilities compatible with their knowledge, skills, and experiences.

D.1.g. Employer Policies The acceptance of employment in an agency or institution implies that career professionals are in agreement with its general policies and principles. Career professionals strive to reach agreement with employers as to acceptable standards of conduct that allow for changes in institutional policy conducive to the growth and development of clients.

D.1.h. Negative Conditions Career professionals alert their employers of inappropriate policies and practices. They attempt to effect changes in such policies or procedures through constructive action within the organization. When such policies are potentially disruptive or damaging to clients or may limit the effectiveness of services provided and change cannot be achieved, career professionals take appropriate further action. Such action may include referral to appropriate certification, accreditation, or state licensure organizations, or voluntary termination of employment.

D.1.i. Protection from Punitive Action Career professionals take care not to harass or dismiss an employee who has acted in a responsible and ethical manner to expose inappropriate employer policies or practices.

D.2. CONSULTATION

D.2.a. Consultant Competency Career professionals take reasonable steps to ensure that they have the appropriate resources and competencies when providing consultation services. Career professionals provide appropriate referral resources when requested or needed. *(See C.2.a.)*

D.2.b. Understanding Consultees When providing consultation, career professionals attempt to develop with their consultees a clear understanding of problem definition, goals for change, and predicted consequences of interventions selected.

D.2.c. Consultant Goals The consulting relationship is one in which consultee adaptability and growth toward self-direction are consistently encouraged and cultivated.

D.2.d. Informed Consent in Consultation When providing consultation, career professionals have an obligation to review, in writing and orally, the rights and responsibilities of career professionals and consultees. Career professionals use clear and understandable language to inform all parties involved about the purpose of the services to be provided, relevant costs, potential risks and benefits, and the limits of confidentiality. Working in conjunction with the consultee, career professionals attempt to develop a clear definition of the problem, goals for change, and predicted consequences of interventions that are culturally responsive and appropriate to the needs of consultees. *(See A.2.a., A.2.b.)*

Section E: Evaluation, Assessment, and Interpretation

INTRODUCTION Career professionals use assessment instruments as one component of the career services process, taking into account the client's personal and cultural context. Career professionals promote the well-being of individual clients or groups of clients by developing and using appropriate career, educational, and psychological assessment instruments.

E.1. GENERAL

E.1.a. Assessment The primary purpose of educational, psychological, and career assessments is to provide measurements that are valid and reliable in either comparative or absolute terms. These include, but are not limited to, measurements of ability, personality, interest, intelligence, achievement, skills, values, and performance. Career professionals recognize the need to interpret the statements in this section as applying to both quantitative and qualitative assessments.

E.1.b. Client Welfare Career professionals do not misuse assessment results and interpretations, and they take reasonable steps to prevent others from misusing the information these tools provide. They respect the client's right to know the results, the interpretations made, and the bases for career professionals' conclusions and recommendations.

E.2. COMPETENCE TO USE AND INTERPRET ASSESSMENT INSTRUMENTS

E.2.a. Limits of Competence Career professionals utilize only those testing and assessment services for which they have been trained and are competent in administering and interpreting. Career professionals using technology-assisted test interpretations are trained in the construct being measured and the specific instrument being used prior to using its technology-based application. Career professionals take reasonable measures to ensure the proper use of psychological and career assessment techniques by persons under their supervision. *(See G.1.)*

E.2.b. Appropriate Use Career professionals are responsible for the appropriate application, scoring, interpretation, and use of assessment instruments relevant to the needs of the client, whether they score and interpret such assessments themselves or use technology or other services.

E.2.c. Decisions Based on Results Career professionals responsible for decisions involving individuals or policies that are based on assessment results have a thorough understanding of educational, psychological, and career measurement, including validation criteria, assessment research, and guidelines for assessment development and use.

E.3. INFORMED CONSENT IN ASSESSMENT

E.3.a. Explanation to Clients Prior to assessment, career professionals explain the nature and purposes of assessment and the specific use of results by potential recipients. The explanation will be given in the language of the client (or other legally authorized person on behalf of the client), unless an explicit exception has been agreed upon in advance. Career professionals consider the client's personal or cultural context, the level of the client's understanding of the results, and the impact of the results on the client. *(See A.2.)*

E.3.b. Recipients of Results Career professionals consider the examinee's welfare, explicit understandings, and prior agreements in determining who receives the assessment results. Career professionals include accurate and appropriate interpretations with any release of individual or group assessment results. *(See B.2.c., B.5.)*

E.4. RELEASE OF DATA TO QUALIFIED PROFESSIONALS

Career professionals release assessment data in which the client is identified only with the consent of the client or the client's legal representative. Such data are released only to persons recognized by career professionals as qualified to interpret the data and in accordance with all applicable federal, state, local, and/or institutional statutes, laws, regulations, and procedures. *(See B.1., B.3., B.5.c., B.6.e.)*

E.5. DIAGNOSIS

E.5.a. Proper Diagnosis Career professionals take special care to provide proper diagnosis and do so only when making a diagnosis is appropriate and when properly trained. Assessment techniques (including personal interview) used to determine client care (e.g., locus of treatment, type of treatment/services, or recommended follow-up) are carefully selected and appropriately used.

E.5.b. Cultural Sensitivity Career professionals recognize that culture affects the manner in which clients' problems are defined. Clients' socioeconomic and cultural experiences are considered when making a diagnosis. *(See A.2.c.)*

E.5.c. Historical and Social Prejudices in the Diagnosis of Pathology Career professionals recognize historical and social prejudices in the misdiagnosis and pathologizing of certain individuals and groups and the role career professionals can play in avoiding the perpetuation of these prejudices through proper diagnosis and provision of services.

E.5.d. Refraining From Diagnosis Career professionals may refrain from making and/or reporting a diagnosis if they believe it would cause harm to the client or others.

E.6. INSTRUMENT SELECTION

E.6.a. Appropriateness of Instruments Career professionals carefully consider the validity, reliability, psychometric limitations, and appropriateness of instruments when selecting assessments.

E.6.b. Referral Information If a client is referred to a third party for assessment, the career professional provides specific referral questions and sufficient objective data about the client to ensure that appropriate assessment instruments are utilized. *(See B.3.)*

E.6.c. Culturally Diverse Populations Career professionals are cautious when selecting assessments for culturally diverse populations to avoid the use of instruments that lack appropriate psychometric properties for the client population. *(See A.2.c., E.5.b.)*

E.7. CONDITIONS OF ASSESSMENT ADMINISTRATION

E.7.a. Administration Conditions Career professionals administer assessments under the same conditions that were established in their standardization. When assessments are not administered under standard conditions, as may be necessary to accommodate clients with disabilities, or when unusual behavior or irregularities occur during the administration, those conditions are noted in interpretation, and the results may be designated as invalid or of questionable validity.

E.7.b. Technological Administration Career professionals ensure that administration programs function properly and provide clients with accurate results when technological or other electronic methods are used for assessment administration.

E.7.c. Unsupervised Assessments Unless the assessment instrument is designed, intended, and validated for self-administration and/or scoring, career professionals do not permit inadequately supervised use of any assessment.

E.7.d. Disclosure of Favorable Conditions Prior to administration of assessments, conditions that produce the most favorable assessment results are made known to the examinee.

E.8. MULTICULTURAL ISSUES/DIVERSITY IN ASSESSMENT

Career professionals use, with caution, assessment techniques that were normed on populations other than that of the client. Career professionals recognize the possible effects of age, color, culture, disability, ethnic group, gender, race, language preference, religion, spirituality, sexual orientation, and socioeconomic status on test administration and interpretation, and place test results in proper perspective with other relevant factors. *(See A.2.c., E.5.b.)*

E.9. SCORING AND INTERPRETATION OF ASSESSMENTS

E.9.a. Reporting In reporting assessment results, career professionals indicate reservations that exist regarding validity or reliability due to circumstances of the assessment or the inappropriateness of the norms for the person tested.

E.9.b. Research Instruments Career professionals exercise caution when interpreting the results of research instruments not having sufficient technical data to support respondent results. The specific purposes for the use of such instruments are stated explicitly to the examinee.

E.9.c. Assessment Services Career professionals who provide assessment scoring and interpretation services to support the assessment process confirm the validity of such interpretations. They accurately describe the purpose, norms, validity, reliability, and applications of the procedures and any special qualifications applicable to their use. The public offering of an automated test interpretation service is considered a professional-to-professional consultation. The formal responsibility of the career professional is to the individual/organization requesting the assessment, but the ultimate and overriding responsibility is to the client. *(See E.1.b., E.2.)*

E.10. ASSESSMENT SECURITY Career professionals maintain the integrity and security of tests and other assessment techniques consistent with legal and contractual obligations. Career professionals do not appropriate, reproduce, or modify published assessments or parts thereof without acknowledgment and permission from the publisher.

E.11. OBSOLETE ASSESSMENTS AND OUTDATED RESULTS Career professionals do not use data or results from assessments that are obsolete or outdated for the current purpose. Career professionals make every effort to prevent the misuse of obsolete measures and assessment data by others.

E.12. ASSESSMENT CONSTRUCTION Career professionals use established scientific procedures, relevant standards, and current professional knowledge for assessment design in the development, publication, and utilization of educational and psychological assessment techniques.

E.13. FORENSIC EVALUATION: EVALUATION FOR LEGAL PROCEEDINGS

E.13.a. Primary Obligations When providing forensic evaluations, the primary obligation of career professionals is to produce objective findings that can be substantiated based on information and techniques appropriate to the evaluation, which may include examination of the individual and/or review of records. Career professionals are entitled to form professional opinions based on their professional knowledge and expertise that can be supported by the data gathered in evaluations. Career professionals will define the limits of their reports or testimony, especially when an examination of the individual has not been conducted.

E.13.b. Consent for Evaluation Individuals being evaluated are informed in writing that the relationship is for the purposes of an evaluation, not to provide career services. Entities or individuals who will receive the evaluation report are identified. Written consent to be evaluated is obtained from those being evaluated unless a court orders evaluations to be conducted without the written consent of individuals being evaluated. When children or vulnerable adults are being evaluated, informed written consent is obtained from a parent or guardian. *(See A.2. B.2.c., B.5.)*

E.13.c. Client Evaluation Prohibited Career professionals do not evaluate current or former clients for forensic purposes. Career professionals do not accept as clients, individuals they are evaluating or have previously evaluated for forensic purposes.

E.13.d. Avoid Potentially Harmful Relationships Career professionals who provide forensic evaluations avoid potentially harmful professional or personal relationships with family members, romantic partners, and close friends of individuals they are evaluating or have evaluated in the past. *(See A.5.)*

Section F: Use of the Internet in the Provision of Career Services

INTRODUCTION Career professionals have always been at the forefront in using new technologies to assist in serving clients. More and more, technology (and specifically the Internet) is being used to provide and/or support services offered by career professionals. However, the Internet should typically be only one component of the career services process and then its use must be evaluated based on the client's personal and cultural context. Above all, career professionals must practice ethically and continually promote the well-being of individual clients or groups of clients.

F.1. GENERAL

F.1.a. Benefits and Limitations Career professionals inform clients of the benefits and limitations of using information technology applications in their professional relationship and in business/billing procedures. Such technologies include but are not limited to computer hardware and software, telephones, the Internet, online assessment instruments, and other communication devices.

F.1.b. Capability to Utilize and Benefit from Technology-Assisted Services When providing technology-assisted distance career services, career professionals determine that clients are intellectually, emotionally, and physically capable of using, and are likely to benefit from, the application and that the application is appropriate for the needs of clients. Where possible, career professionals utilize multiple methods of contact (i.e., telephone, video conference, and email), in assessing the best means of providing career services to a particular client.

F.2. TECHNOLOGY APPLICATIONS

F.2.a. Types of Technology-Assisted Services Multiple means of online provision of career services currently exist, the most common of which are email, newsgroups, bulletin boards, instant messaging, chat rooms, blogs (web logs), web cams (video cameras) and websites offering a wide variety of services. Telephone or audiovisual linkages supported by the Internet continue to grow in popularity as the technology improves and the costs decline. Based on readily-available capabilities at the time of this writing, the Internet could be used in at least four ways to provide and/or support career services. These include:

1. Delivering information about occupations, the world of work, career planning, and job searching. This may include occupational/job descriptions, employment prospects, skills requirements, estimated salary, resume writing, job interviewing techniques, etc. Delivery may come through one or a combination of media including text, still images, graphics, and/or video. In providing these services, the standards for information development and presentation are the same as those for other print and audiovisual materials as stated in other NCDA documents.
2. Providing assessments and/or online searches of academic, occupational, or other databases to identify career, educational, or other alternatives. In providing these services, other standards developed by NCDA (i.e., *Section E of this Code*) and the Association of Computer-based Systems for Career Information (ACSCI) apply.

3. Delivering interactive career services. This use assumes that clients, either as individuals or as part of a group, have intentionally placed themselves in direct communication with a career professional. Standards for using the Internet for these purposes are addressed in this section.
4. Providing a database of job openings. Guidelines for this application are included in this section as well.

F.2.b. Alternative Services When technology-assisted distance career services are deemed inappropriate by the career professional or client, career professionals provide appropriate alternatives, including face-to-face service and/or a referral to career professionals who can provide in-person services. *(See A.10.)*

F.2.c. Access Career professionals ensure reasonable access to computer applications when providing technology-assisted distance career services. If they are unable to do so they provide an alternative method of service delivery, including referrals to career professionals who would be able to provide face-to-face services. *(See A.10.)*

F.2.d. Laws and Statutes Career professionals ensure that the use of technology services with clients is in accordance with all applicable federal, state, local, and/or institutional statutes, laws, regulations, and procedures, particularly when the services offered via technology cross state and/or national boundaries.

F.2.e. Outside Assistance Career professionals seek business, legal, and technical assistance (when necessary and appropriate) when using technology applications, particularly when the use of such applications crosses state or national boundaries.

F.2.f. Informed Consent & Confidentiality As part of the process of establishing informed consent and defining confidentiality and its limits, career professionals who provide technology-assisted distance career services:

1. Provide information to clients about their credentials.
2. Work with clients to establish goals and determine if a technology-assisted distance modality is appropriate.
3. Where applicable, define the fees for service and billing procedures.
4. Provide clients with information regarding where and how they can report any behavior on the part of the career professional that they consider unethical.
5. Where feasible, address issues related to maintaining the confidentiality of electronically transmitted communications (e.g., the use of encryption).
6. Inform clients of the inherent difficulty of maintaining absolute confidentiality when conducting electronically transmitted communication.
7. Urge clients to be aware of all authorized or unauthorized users (including family members and fellow employees) who may have access to any technology clients use in the professional relationship.
8. Inform clients of pertinent legal rights and limitations governing the practice of a profession over state lines or international boundaries, when necessary and appropriate.
9. Inform clients if and for how long archival storage of transaction records will be maintained.
10. Discuss the possibility of technology failure and alternate methods of service delivery.
11. Inform clients of emergency procedures, such as calling 911 or a local crisis hotline, when the career professional is not available, should circumstances warrant.
12. Discuss time zone differences, local customs, and cultural or language differences that might impact service delivery.
13. Establish a method for verifying identity.
14. Obtain the written consent of the legal guardian or other authorized legal representative prior to rendering services in the event the client is a minor child, an adult who is legally incompetent, or an adult incapable of giving informed consent.

F.3. QUALIFICATIONS OF DEVELOPER OR PROVIDER
Websites and other services designed to assist clients with career planning and job searching should be developed with content input from career professionals. The service should clearly state the qualifications and credentials of the developers.

F.4. ACCESS AND UNDERSTANDING OF ENVIRONMENT
Career professionals have an obligation to be aware of free and/or low cost public access points to the Internet within the community, so that a lack of financial resources does not create a significant barrier to clients accessing career services or information, assessments, or instructional resources over the Internet.

F.5. CONTENT OF CAREER SERVICES ON THE INTERNET

F.5.a. Appropriateness of Internet Content The content of a website or other online career information or planning services should be reviewed for the appropriateness of offering the material in this medium. Some types of content have been extensively tested for online delivery including searching databases by relevant variables; displaying occupational information; developing a resumé; assessing interests, abilities, personality, and other characteristics and linkage of these to occupational titles; relating school majors to occupational choices; and the completing of forms such as a financial needs assessment questionnaire or a job application.

When a website offers content or a service that has not been extensively tested for online delivery, is not grounded in theory, is not generally considered to be established professional practice in the fields of counseling and career development, and/or does not have an empirical or scientific foundation, career professionals must define the content or service as "unproven" or "developing" and explain the potential risks and ethical considerations of using such content or service and take steps to protect clients from possible harm.

F.5.b. Maintaining Internet Sites Career professionals maintaining sites on the Internet do the following:

1. Regularly check that electronic links are working and are professionally appropriate.
2. Provide electronic links to relevant state licensure and professional certification boards to protect consumer rights and facilitate addressing ethical concerns.
3. Provide a site that is accessible to persons with disabilities, when feasible.
4. Provide translation capabilities (when feasible) for clients who have a different primary language while also acknowledging the imperfect nature of such translations.
5. Assist clients in determining the validity and reliability of information found on the Internet and in other technology applications.
6. If a website includes links to other websites, the career professional who creates this linkage is responsible for ensuring that the services to which the site is linked meet all applicable ethical standards. If this is not possible, career professionals should post a disclaimer explaining that the linked site may not meet all applicable ethical standards and (if known) which standards are not met by the site.

F.6. ONGOING CLIENT SUPPORT When providing technology-assisted distance career services, career professionals periodically monitor clients' progress. Should career professionals determine that little or no progress is being made toward stated goals, career professionals will discuss the need for a referral to a face-to-face service provider. Career professionals will assist clients in identifying appropriate providers and will facilitate the transition. (See A.10., E.6.b., F.2.b.)

F.7. USE OF ASSESSMENT When using assessments on the Internet, career professionals are responsible for knowing and abiding by other standards developed by NCDA (i.e., *Section E of this Code*) and the Association of Computer-based Systems for Career Information (ACSCI). Where applicable and possible, career professionals should:

1. Determine if the assessments have been tested for online delivery and ensure that their psychometric properties are the same as in print form; or the client must be informed that the assessments have not yet been tested for this mode of delivery.
2. Abide by the same ethical guidelines as if administering and interpreting these assessments in person or in print form.
3. Make every effort to protect the confidentiality of client results.
4. Refer clients to qualified career professionals in his or her geographic area, if there is evidence that the client does not understand the assessment results.
5. Determine if the assessments have been validated for self-help use or that appropriate counseling intervention is provided before and after completion of the assessment resource if the resource has not been validated for self-help use.

F.8. INTERNET JOB POSTING AND SEARCHING All job postings must represent a valid opening for which those searching on the Internet have an opportunity to apply. It is encouraged that job postings be removed from the database within 48 hours of the time that the announced position is filled. Names, addresses, resumés, and other information that may be gained about individuals should not be used for any purposes other than provision of further information about job openings.

F.9. UNACCEPTABLE BEHAVIORS ON THE INTERNET Career professionals have a responsibility to act in an ethical manner at all times. Because a behavior is not expressly prohibited, this does not imply that it is ethical. The following behaviors are deemed unacceptable for career professionals:

1. Use of a false e-mail identity when interacting with clients and/or other professionals. When acting in a professional capacity on the Internet, career professionals have a duty to identify themselves honestly.
2. Accepting a client who will not identify him/herself and/or is unwilling to arrange for a telephone conversation as well as online interchange.
3. Anonymously monitoring chat rooms, web logs (blogs), bulletin board services, and/or other web-based communities and offering career planning and related services when no request has been made for such services. This includes sending out mass unsolicited emails to individuals with whom you do

not have an already established professional relationship. Career professionals may advertise their services but must do so observing proper online "netiquette" and standards of professional conduct.

Section G: Supervision, Training, and Teaching

INTRODUCTION Career professionals foster meaningful and respectful professional relationships and maintain appropriate boundaries with supervisees and students. Career professionals have theoretical and pedagogical foundations for their work and aim to be fair, accurate, and honest in their assessments of students.

G.1. SUPERVISION AND CLIENT WELFARE

G.1.a. Client Welfare A primary obligation of supervisors is to monitor the services provided by other career professionals or students for whom they have responsibility. Supervisors also monitor client welfare and supervisee performance and professional development. To fulfill these obligations, supervisors meet regularly with supervisees to review case notes, samples of work, or live observations. Supervisees have a responsibility to understand and follow the *NCDA Code of Ethics*.

G.1.b. Credentials Supervisors work to ensure that clients are aware of the qualifications of the supervisees who render services to clients. *(See A.2.b.)*

G.1.c. Informed Consent and Client Rights Supervisors make supervisees aware of client rights including the protection of client privacy and confidentiality in the professional relationship. Supervisees provide clients with professional disclosure information and inform them of how the supervision process influences the limits of confidentiality. Supervisees make clients aware of who will have access to records of the professional relationship and how these records will be used. *(See A.2.a., A.2.b., B.1.d. D.3.)*

G.2. SUPERVISOR COMPETENCE

G.2.a. Supervisor Preparation Prior to offering supervision services, career professionals are trained in supervision methods and techniques. Career professionals who offer supervision services regularly pursue continuing education activities including both career services and supervision topics and skills. *(See C.2.a., C.2.f.)*

G.2.b. Multicultural Issues/Diversity in Supervision Supervisors are aware of and address the role of multiculturalism/diversity in the supervisory relationship.

G.3. SUPERVISORY RELATIONSHIPS

G.3.a. Relationship Boundaries with Supervisees Supervisors clearly define and maintain ethical professional, personal, and social relationships with their supervisees, although they avoid and/or keep to a minimum nonprofessional relationships with current supervisees. If supervisors must assume other professional roles (e.g., clinical and administrative supervisor, instructor, etc.) with supervisees, they work to minimize potential conflicts and explain to supervisees the expectations and responsibilities associated with each role. They do not engage in any form of nonprofessional interaction that may compromise the supervisory relationship.

G.3.b. Sexual Relationships Sexual or romantic interactions or relationships with current supervisees are prohibited.

G.3.c. Harassment Supervisors do not condone or subject supervisees to harassment, sexual or otherwise. *(See C.6.a.)*

G.3.d. Close Relatives and Friends Supervisors avoid accepting close relatives, romantic partners, or friends as supervisees.

G.3.e. Potentially Beneficial Relationships Supervisors are aware of the power differential in their relationships with supervisees. If they believe nonprofessional relationships with a supervisee may be potentially beneficial to the supervisee, they take precautions similar to those taken by career professionals when working with clients. Examples of potentially beneficial interactions or relationships include attending a formal ceremony; hospital visits; providing support during a stressful event; or mutual membership in a professional association, organization, or community. Supervisors engage in open discussions with supervisees when they consider entering into relationships with them outside of their supervisory roles. Before engaging in nonprofessional relationships, supervisors discuss with supervisees and document the rationale for such interactions, potential benefits or drawbacks, and anticipated consequences for the supervisee. Supervisors clarify the specific nature and limitations of the additional role(s) they will have with the supervisee. *(See A.5.d.)*

G.4. SUPERVISOR RESPONSIBILITIES

G.4.a. Informed Consent for Supervision Supervisors are responsible for incorporating into their supervision the principles of informed consent and participation. Supervisors inform supervisees of the policies and procedures to which they are to adhere and the mechanisms for due process appeal of individual supervisory actions.

G.4.b. Emergencies and Absences Supervisors establish and communicate to supervisees procedures for contacting them or, in their absence, alternative on-call supervisors to assist in handling crises.

G.4.c. Standards for Supervisees Supervisors make their supervisees aware of professional and ethical standards and legal responsibilities. Supervisors of post-degree career professionals encourage these individuals to adhere to professional standards of practice. *(See C.1.)*

G.4.d. Termination of the Supervisory Relationship Supervisors or supervisees have the right to terminate the supervisory relationship with adequate notice. Reasons for withdrawal are provided to the other party. When cultural, professional, or other issues are crucial to the viability of the supervisory relationship, both parties make efforts to resolve differences. When termination is warranted, supervisors make appropriate referrals to possible alternative supervisors.

G.5. SUPERVISION EVALUATION, REMEDIATION, AND ENDORSEMENT

G.5.a. Evaluation Supervisors document and provide supervisees with ongoing performance appraisal and evaluation feedback and schedule periodic formal evaluative sessions throughout the supervisory relationship.

G.5.b. Limitations Through ongoing evaluation and appraisal, supervisors are aware of the limitations of supervisees that might impede performance. Supervisors assist supervisees in securing remedial assistance when needed. They recommend dismissal from training programs, applied practice settings, or state or voluntary professional credentialing processes when those supervisees are unable to provide competent professional services. Supervisors seek consultation and document their decisions to dismiss or refer supervisees for assistance. They ensure that supervisees are aware of options available to them to address such decisions. *(See C.2.g.)*

G.5.c. Multiple Roles/Relationships with Supervisees If supervisees request counseling, career services, or any other professional service which a supervisor may ordinarily offer, the supervisor will provide the supervisee with acceptable referrals. Career professionals do not typically engage in multiple roles/relationships with supervisees. If supervisors must provide a service to a supervisee in addition to providing supervision, they work to minimize potential conflicts and explain to supervisees the expectations and responsibilities associated with each role. In addition, the supervisor must address participation in multiple roles/relationships with the supervisee in terms of the impact of these issues on clients, the supervisory relationship, and professional functioning. *(See G.3.a.)*

G.5.d. Endorsement Supervisors endorse supervisees for certification, licensure, employment, or completion of an academic or training program only when they believe supervisees are qualified for the endorsement. In addition, supervisors do not withhold endorsement of qualified supervisees for certification, licensure, employment, or completion of an academic or training program for any reason unrelated to their fitness as a student or professional. Regardless of qualifications, supervisors do not endorse supervisees whom they believe to be impaired in any way that would interfere with the performance of the duties associated with the endorsement.

G.6. RESPONSIBILITIES OF EDUCATORS

G.6.a. Educators Educators who are responsible for developing, implementing, and supervising educational programs are skilled as teachers and practitioners. They are knowledgeable regarding the ethical, legal, and regulatory aspects of the profession, are skilled in applying that knowledge, and make students and supervisees aware of their responsibilities. Educators conduct education and training programs in an ethical manner and serve as role models for professional behavior. *(See C.1., C.2.a., C.2.c.)*

G.6.b. Integration of Study and Practice Educators establish education and training programs that integrate academic study and supervised practice.

G.6.c. Teaching Ethics Educators make students and supervisees aware of the ethical responsibilities and standards of the profession and the ethical responsibilities of students to the profession. Educators infuse ethical considerations throughout the curriculum. *(See C.1.)*

G.6.d. Peer Relationships Educators make every effort to ensure that the rights of peers are not compromised when students or supervisees lead career groups or provide supervision. Educators take steps to ensure that students and supervisees understand they have the same ethical obligations as educators, trainers, and supervisors.

G.6.e. Innovative Theories and Techniques When educators teach techniques/procedures that are innovative, without an empirical foundation, or without a well-grounded theoretical foundation, they define the techniques/procedures as "unproven" or "developing" and explain to students the potential risks and ethical considerations of using such techniques/procedures. *(See C.6.e.)*

G.6.f. Field Placements Educators develop clear policies within their training programs regarding field placement and other clinical experiences. Educators provide clearly stated roles and responsibilities for the student or supervisee, the site supervisor, and the program supervisor. They confirm that site supervisors are qualified to provide supervision and inform site supervisors of their professional and ethical responsibilities in this role. In addition, educators do not accept any form of professional services, fees, commissions, reimbursement, or remuneration from a site for student or supervisee placement.

G.6.g. Professional Disclosure Before initiating career services in a field placement, students disclose their status and explain how this status affects the limits of confidentiality. Educators ensure that the clients at field placements are aware of the services rendered and the qualifications of the students and supervisees rendering those services. Students and supervisees obtain client permission before they use any information concerning the professional relationship in the training process. *(See A.2.b.)*

G.7. STUDENT WELFARE

G.7.a. Orientation Educators recognize that orientation is a developmental process that continues throughout the education and training of students. Faculty provide prospective students with information about the educational program's expectations including but not necessarily limited to:

1. the type and level of skill and knowledge acquisition required for successful completion of the training;
2. training program goals, objectives, and mission, and subject matter to be covered;
3. bases for evaluation;
4. training components that encourage self-growth or self-disclosure as part of the training process;
5. the type of supervision settings and requirements of the sites for required clinical field experiences;
6. student and supervisee evaluation and dismissal policies and procedures; and
7. up-to-date employment prospects for graduates.

G.7.b. Self-Growth Experiences Education programs delineate requirements for self-disclosure or self-growth experiences in their admission and program materials. Educators use professional judgment when designing training experiences they conduct that require student and supervisee self-growth or self-disclosure.

Students and supervisees are made aware of the ramifications their self-disclosure may have when career professionals whose primary role as teacher, trainer, or supervisor requires acting on ethical obligations to the profession. Evaluative components of experiential training activities explicitly delineate predetermined academic standards that are separate from and do not depend on the student's level of self-disclosure. Educators may require trainees to seek professional help to address any personal concerns that may be affecting their competency.

G.8. STUDENT RESPONSIBILITIES

G.8.a. Standards for Students Students have a responsibility to understand and follow the *NCDA Code of Ethics* and adhere to all applicable federal, state, local, and/or institutional statutes, laws, regulations, and procedures governing professional staff behavior at the agency or placement setting. Students have the same obligation to clients as those required of career professionals. *(See C.1.)*

G.8.b. Impairment Students refrain from offering or providing career services when their physical, mental, or emotional problems are likely to harm a client or others. They are alert to the signs of impairment, seek assistance for problems, and notify their program supervisors when they are aware that they are unable to effectively provide services. In addition, they seek appropriate professional services for themselves to remediate the problems that are interfering with their ability to provide services to others. *(See A.1.a., C.2.d., C.2.g.)*

G.9. EVALUATION AND REMEDIATION OF STUDENTS

G.9.a. Evaluation Career professionals clearly state to students, prior to and throughout the training program, the levels of competency expected, appraisal methods, and timing of evaluations for all areas of competency. Educators provide students with ongoing performance appraisal and evaluation feedback throughout the training program.

G.9.b. Limitations Educators, through ongoing evaluation and appraisal, are aware of and address the inability of some students to achieve the level of competencies needed for successful continued performance. Educators

1. assist students in securing remedial assistance when needed,
2. seek professional consultation and document their decision to dismiss or refer students for assistance, and
3. ensure that students have recourse in a timely manner to address decisions to require them to seek assistance or to dismiss them and provide students with due process according to institutional policies and procedures.

G.9.c. Counseling for Students If students request counseling or if counseling services are required as part of a remediation process, educators provide acceptable referrals.

G.10. ROLES AND RELATIONSHIPS BETWEEN EDUCATORS AND STUDENTS

G.10.a. Sexual or Romantic Relationships Sexual or romantic interactions or relationships with current students are prohibited.

G.10.b. Harassment Educators do not condone or subject students to harassment, sexual or otherwise. *(See C.6.a.)*

G.10.c. Relationships with Former Students Educators are aware of the power differential in the relationship between faculty and students. Faculty members foster open discussions with former students when considering engaging in a social, sexual, or other intimate relationship. Faculty members discuss with the former student how their former relationship may affect the change in relationship.

G.10.d. Nonprofessional Relationships Educators avoid nonprofessional or ongoing professional relationships with students in which there is a risk of potential harm to the student or that may compromise the training experience or grades assigned.

G.10.e. Career Services Educators do not serve as career professionals to current students unless this is a brief role associated with a training experience or in their role as an academic advisor.

G.10.f. Potentially Beneficial Relationships Educators are aware of the power differential in the relationship between faculty and students. If they believe a nonprofessional relationship with a student may be potentially beneficial to the student, they take precautions similar to those taken by career professionals when working with clients. Examples of potentially beneficial interactions or relationships include, but are not limited to, attending a formal ceremony; hospital visits; providing support during a stressful event; or mutual membership in a professional association, organization, or community.

Educators engage in open discussions with students when they consider entering into relationships with students outside of their roles as teachers and supervisors. They discuss with students the rationale for such interactions, the potential benefits and drawbacks, and the anticipated consequences for the student. Educators clarify the specific nature and limitations of the additional role(s) they will have with the student prior to engaging in a nonprofessional relationship. Nonprofessional relationships with students should be time-limited and initiated with student consent. *(See G.3.e.)*

G.11. MULTICULTURAL/DIVERSITY COMPETENCE IN EDUCATION AND TRAINING PROGRAMS

G.11.a. Faculty Diversity Educators are committed to recruiting and retaining a diverse faculty. Additionally, educators do not condone or engage in discrimination based on age, culture, mental/physical disability, ethnicity, race, religion/spirituality, creed, gender, actual or perceived gender identity or expression, actual or perceived sexual orientation, marital/partnership status, language preference, socioeconomic status, any other characteristics not specifically relevant to job performance, or any basis prohibited by law.

G.11.b. Student Diversity Educators actively attempt to recruit and retain a diverse student body. Educators demonstrate commitment to multicultural/diversity competence by recognizing and valuing diverse cultures and types of abilities students bring to the training experience. Educators provide appropriate accommodations that enhance and support diverse student well-being and academic performance.

G.11.c. Multicultural/Diversity Competence Educators actively infuse multicultural/diversity competency in their training and supervision practices. They actively train students to gain awareness, knowledge, and skills in the competencies of multicultural practice. Educators include case examples, role-plays, discussion questions, and other classroom activities that promote and represent various cultural perspectives.

Section H: Research and Publication

INTRODUCTION Career professionals who conduct research are encouraged to contribute to the knowledge base of the profession and promote a clearer understanding of the conditions that lead to a healthy and more just society. Career professionals support efforts of researchers by participating fully and willingly whenever possible. Career professionals minimize bias and respect diversity in designing and implementing research programs.

H.1. RESEARCH RESPONSIBILITIES

H.1.a. Use of Human Research Participants Career professionals plan, design, conduct, and report research in a manner that is consistent with pertinent ethical principles, all applicable federal, state, and local statutes, laws, regulations, and/or procedures, host institutional regulations, and scientific standards governing research with human research participants. For one source of online training regarding information about the rights and welfare of human participants in research, see the attached web references section.

H.1.b. Need for Research and Review Career professionals have an obligation to contribute to periodic evaluations of the services they provide to their clients. The interventions, techniques, and methods of service delivery they use should be evaluated to establish evidence-based practice. Career professionals also have an obligation to periodically review the evaluation and research literature in their area of expertise so that the career services they provide to their clients reflect established best practice.

H.1.c. Deviation from Standard Practice Career professionals seek consultation and observe stringent safeguards to protect the rights of research participants when a research problem suggests a deviation from standard or acceptable practices.

H.1.d. Independent Researchers When independent researchers do not have access to an Institutional Review Board (IRB), they should consult with researchers who are familiar with IRB procedures to provide appropriate safeguards.

H.1.e. Precautions to Avoid Injury Career professionals who conduct research with human participants are responsible for the welfare of participants throughout the research process and should take reasonable precautions to avoid causing injurious psychological, emotional, physical, or social effects to participants.

H.1.f. Principal Researcher Responsibility The ultimate responsibility for ethical research practice lies with the principal researcher. All others involved in the research activities share ethical obligations and responsibility for their own actions.

H.1.g. Minimal Interference Career professionals take reasonable precautions to avoid causing disruptions in the lives of research participants that could be caused by their involvement in research.

H.1.h. Multicultural/Diversity Considerations in Research When appropriate to research goals, career professionals are sensitive to incorporating research procedures that take into account cultural considerations. They seek consultation when appropriate.

H.2. RIGHTS OF RESEARCH PARTICIPANTS (See A.2.)

H.2.a. Informed Consent in Research Individuals have the right to consent to become research participants. In seeking consent, career professionals use language that

1. Accurately explains the purpose and procedures to be followed.
2. Identifies any procedures that are experimental or relatively untried.
3. Describes any attendant discomforts and risks.
4. Describes any benefits or changes in individuals or organizations that might be reasonably expected.
5. Discloses appropriate alternative procedures that would be advantageous for participants.
6. Offers to answer any inquiries concerning the procedures.
7. Describes any limitations on confidentiality.
8. Describes the format and potential target audiences for the dissemination of research findings.
9. Instructs participants that they are free to withdraw their consent and to discontinue participation in the project at any time without penalty.

H.2.b. Deception Career professionals do not conduct research involving deception unless alternative procedures are not feasible and the prospective value of the research justifies the deception. If such deception has the potential to cause physical or emotional harm to research participants, the research is not conducted, regardless of prospective value. When the methodological requirements of a study necessitate concealment or deception, the investigator explains the reasons for this action as soon as possible during the debriefing.

H.2.c. Student/Supervisee Participation Researchers who involve students or supervisees in research make clear to them that the decision regarding whether or not to participate in research activities does not affect one's academic standing or supervisory relationship. Students or supervisees who choose not to participate in educational research are provided with an appropriate alternative to fulfill their academic or other requirements.

H.2.d. Client Participation Career professionals conducting research involving clients make clear in the informed consent process that clients are free to choose whether or not to participate in research activities. Career professionals take necessary precautions to protect clients from adverse consequences of declining or withdrawing from participation.

H.2.e. Confidentiality of Information Information obtained about research participants during the course of an investigation is confidential. When the possibility exists that others may obtain access to such information, ethical research practice requires that the possibility, together with the plans for protecting confidentiality, be explained to participants as a part of the procedure for obtaining informed consent.

H.2.f. Persons Not Capable of Giving Informed Consent When a person is not capable of giving informed consent, career professionals provide an appropriate explanation to, obtain agreement for participation from, and obtain the appropriate consent of a legally authorized person.

H.2.g. Commitments to Participants Career professionals take reasonable measures to honor all commitments to research participants.

H.2.h. Explanations After Data Collection After data are collected, career professionals provide participants with full clarification of the nature of the study to remove any misconceptions participants might have regarding the research.

Where scientific or human values justify delaying or withholding information, career professionals take reasonable measures to avoid causing harm.

H.2.i. Informing Sponsors Career professionals inform sponsors, institutions, and publication channels regarding research procedures and outcomes. Career professionals ensure that appropriate bodies and authorities are given pertinent information and acknowledgment.

H.2.j. Disposal of Research Documents and Records Within a reasonable period of time following the completion of a research project or study, career professionals take steps to destroy records or documents (audio, video, digital, and written) containing confidential data or information that identifies research participants in accordance with all applicable federal, state, local, and/or institutional statutes, laws, regulations, and procedures. When records are of an artistic nature, researchers obtain participant consent with regard to handling of such records or documents. Career professionals are encouraged to purge their files according to the time frame required by federal, state, local, and/or institutional statute, law, regulation, or procedure, particularly when there is no reasonable expectation that anyone will benefit from maintaining the records any longer. *(See B.6.a, B.6.g.)*

H.3. RELATIONSHIPS WITH RESEARCH PARTICIPANTS (WHEN RESEARCH INVOLVES INTENSIVE OR EXTENDED INTERACTIONS)

H.3.a. Nonprofessional Relationships Nonprofessional relationships with research participants should be avoided as these interactions may set up dual relationships and role confusion that may be harmful to the emotional health of participants.

H.3.b. Relationships with Research Participants Sexual or romantic interactions or relationships between career professionals/researchers and current research participants are prohibited.

H.3.c. Harassment and Research Participants Researchers do not condone or subject research participants to harassment, sexual or otherwise. *(See C.6.a.)*

H.3.d. Potentially Beneficial Interactions When a nonprofessional interaction between the researcher and the research participant may be potentially beneficial, the researcher must document, prior to the interaction (when feasible), the rationale for such an interaction, the potential benefit, and anticipated consequences for the research participant. Such interactions should be initiated with appropriate consent of the research participant. Where unintentional harm occurs to the research participant due to the nonprofessional interaction, the researcher must show evidence of an attempt to remedy such harm.

H.4. REPORTING RESULTS

H.4.a. Accurate Results Career professionals plan, conduct, and report research accurately. They provide thorough discussions of the limitations of their data and alternative hypotheses. Career professionals do not engage in misleading or fraudulent research, distort data, misrepresent data, or deliberately bias their results. They explicitly mention all variables and conditions known to the investigator that may have affected the outcome of a study or the interpretation of data. They describe the extent to which results are applicable for diverse populations.

H.4.b. Obligation to Report Unfavorable Results Career professionals report the results of any research of professional value. Results that reflect unfavorably on institutions, programs, services, prevailing opinions, or vested interests are not withheld.

H.4.c. Reporting Errors If career professionals discover significant errors in their published research, they take reasonable steps to correct such errors in a correction erratum, or through other appropriate publication means.

H.4.d. Identity of Participants Career professionals who supply data, aid in the research of another person, report research results, or make original data available take due care to disguise the identity of respective participants in the absence of specific authorization from the participants to do otherwise. In situations where participants self-identify their involvement in research studies, researchers take active steps to ensure that data is adapted/changed to protect the identity and welfare of all parties and that discussion of results does not cause harm to participants.

H.4.e. Replication Studies Career professionals are obligated to make available sufficient original research data to qualified professionals who may wish to replicate a study.

H.5. PUBLICATION

H.5.a. Recognizing Contributions When conducting and reporting research, career professionals are familiar with and give recognition to previous work on the topic, observe copyright laws, and give full credit to those to whom credit is due.

H.5.b. Plagiarism Career professionals do not plagiarize; that is, they do not present another person's work as their own.

H.5.c. Review/Republication of Data or Ideas Career professionals fully acknowledge and make editorial reviewers aware of prior publication of ideas or data where such ideas or data are submitted for review or publication.

H.5.d. Contributors Career professionals give credit through joint authorship, acknowledgment, footnote statements, or other appropriate means to those who have contributed significantly to research or concept development in accordance with such contributions. The principal contributor is listed first, and minor technical or professional contributions are acknowledged in notes or introductory statements.

H.5.e. Agreement of Contributors Career professionals who conduct joint research with colleagues or students/supervisees establish agreements in advance regarding allocation of tasks, publication credit, and types of acknowledgment that will be received.

H.5.f. Student Research For articles that are substantially based on students' course papers, projects, theses, or dissertations, and on which students have been the primary contributors, they are listed as principal authors.

H.5.g. Duplicate Submission Career professionals submit manuscripts for consideration to only one journal at a time. Manuscripts that are published in whole or in substantial part in another journal or published work are not submitted for publication without acknowledgment and permission from the previous publication.

H.5.h. Professional Review Career professionals who review material submitted for publication, research, or other scholarly purposes respect the confidentiality and proprietary rights of those who submitted it. Career professionals use care to make publication decisions based on valid and defensible standards. Career professionals review article submissions in a timely manner and based on their scope and competency in research methodologies. Career professionals who serve as reviewers at the request of editors or publishers make every effort to review only materials that are within their scope of competency and use care to avoid personal biases.

Section I: Resolving Ethical Issues

INTRODUCTION Career professionals behave in a legal, ethical, and moral manner in the conduct of their professional work. They are aware that client protection and trust in the profession depend on a high level of professional conduct. They hold other career professionals to the same standards and are willing to take appropriate action to ensure that these standards are upheld. Career professionals work to resolve ethical dilemmas with direct and open communication among all parties involved and seek consultation with colleagues and supervisors when necessary. Career professionals incorporate ethical practice into their daily work. They engage in ongoing learning and development regarding current topics in ethical and legal issues in the profession.

I.1. STANDARDS AND THE LAW

I.1.a. Knowledge Career professionals understand the *NCDA Code of Ethics* and other applicable ethics codes from professional organizations or from certification and licensure bodies of which they are members and/or which regulate practice in a state or territory. Career professionals ensure that they are knowledgeable of and follow all applicable federal, state, local, and/or institutional statutes, laws, regulations, and procedures. Lack of knowledge or misunderstanding of an ethical responsibility is not a defense against a charge of unethical conduct.

I.1.b. Conflicts Between Ethics and Laws If ethical responsibilities conflict with laws, regulations, or other governing legal authorities, career professionals make known their commitment to the *NCDA Code of Ethics* and take steps to resolve the conflict. If the conflict cannot be resolved by acknowledging and discussing the pertinent principles in the *NCDA Code of Ethics*, career professionals must adhere to the requirements of all applicable federal, state, local, and/or institutional statutes, laws, regulations, and procedures.

I.2. SUSPECTED VIOLATIONS

I.2.a. Ethical Behavior Expected Career professionals expect colleagues to adhere to the *NCDA Code of Ethics*. When career professionals possess knowledge that raises doubts as to whether another career professional is acting in an ethical manner, they take appropriate action, as noted in I.2.b–I.2.g.

I.2.b. Informal Resolution When career professionals have reason to believe that another career professional is violating or has violated an ethical standard, they attempt first to resolve the issue informally with the other career professional if feasible, provided such action does not violate confidentiality rights that may be involved.

I.2.c. Reporting Ethical Violations If an apparent violation has substantially harmed, or is likely to substantially harm, a person or organization and is not appropriate for informal resolution or is not resolved properly, career professionals take further action appropriate to the situation. Such action might include referral to state or national committees on professional ethics, voluntary national certification bodies, state licensing boards, law enforcement or other appropriate institutional authorities. This standard does not apply when an intervention would violate confidentiality rights or when career professionals have been retained to review the work of another career professional whose conduct is in question.

I.2.d. Consultation When uncertain as to whether a particular situation or course of action may be in violation of the *NCDA Code of Ethics*, career professionals consult with others who are knowledgeable about ethics and the *NCDA Code of Ethics*, with colleagues, and/or with appropriate authorities.

I.2.e. Organizational Conflicts If the demands of an organization with which career professionals are affiliated pose a conflict with the *NCDA Code of Ethics*, career professionals specify the nature of such conflicts and express to their supervisors or other responsible officials their commitment to the *NCDA Code of Ethics*. When possible, career professionals work toward change within the organization to allow full adherence to the *NCDA Code of Ethics*. In doing so, they are mindful of and address any confidentiality issues.

I.2.f. Unwarranted Complaints Career professionals do not initiate, participate in, or encourage the filing of ethics complaints that are made with reckless disregard or willful ignorance of facts that would disprove the allegation.

I.2.g. Unfair Discrimination Against Complainants and Respondents Career professionals do not deny persons employment, advancement, admission to academic or other programs, tenure, or promotion based solely upon their having made or their being the subject of an ethics complaint. This does not preclude taking action based upon the outcome of such proceedings or considering other appropriate information.

I.3. COOPERATION WITH ETHICS COMMITTEES Career professionals assist in the process of enforcing the *NCDA Code of Ethics*. Career professionals cooperate with investigations, proceedings, and requirements of the NCDA Ethics Committee or ethics committees of other duly constituted associations or licensing/certifications boards having jurisdiction over those charged with a violation. Career professionals are familiar with the *NCDA Policy and Procedures for Processing Complaints of Ethical Violations* and use it as a reference for assisting in the enforcement of the *NCDA Code of Ethics*.

Glossary of Terms

NOTE: NCDA has members in various career services positions (see Career Professionals), as well as in instructional (counselor educators, counseling psychology professors, etc.) and supervisory roles (Director, Associate Director, Career Supervisor, etc.). The term "career professional" will be used throughout this document both as a noun and as an adjective to refer to anyone holding NCDA membership and who is therefore expected to abide by these ethical guidelines.

Advocacy—promotion of the well-being of individuals and groups, and the career counseling profession within systems and organizations. Advocacy seeks to remove barriers and obstacles that inhibit access, growth, and development.

Assent—to demonstrate agreement, when a person is otherwise not capable or competent to give formal consent (e.g., informed consent) to a career counseling service or plan.

Career Counselor—a professional (or a student who is a career counselor-in-training) engaged in a career counseling practice or other career counseling-related services. Career counselors fulfill many roles and responsibilities such as career counselor educators, researchers, supervisors, practitioners, and consultants.

Career Professionals—this term includes career counselors, career coaches, career consultants, career development facilitators, and anyone else who is a member of NCDA and provides career counseling, career advice/advising, career coaching, career planning, job search assistance, and/or related services.

Career Services—all activities delivered by career professionals to individuals, groups and organizations. Services may include, but are not necessarily limited to, career counseling, career planning, assessment, job search assistance, skills practice, workshops and training, homework assignments, bibliographies, journaling, and overall career program development.

Career Services Plan—a document created by a career professional and a client that outlines goals, steps, time frames and outcome measures whereby a client can learn and apply an orderly process for reaching career goals.

Client(s)—individuals seeking or referred to the services of a career professional. Clients willfully enter into a defined professional relationship with a career professional or are included by means of informed consent by a parent or guardian.

Educator—a professional engaged in developing, implementing, and supervising the educational preparation of students and/or supervisees.

Supervisor—a professional who engages in a formal relationship with a practicing career professional or a student for the purpose of overseeing that individual's career services work and/or clinical skill development.

Culture—membership in a socially constructed way of living, which incorporates collective values, beliefs, norms, boundaries, and lifestyles that are co-created with others who share similar worldviews comprising biological, psychosocial, historical, psychological, and other factors.

Distance Career Services—The use of technology (including but are not limited to computer hardware and software, telephone, the Internet, online assessment instruments, and other communication devices) to provide career services to clients who are not located in the same room with the career professional.

Diversity—the similarities and differences that occur within and across cultures, and the intersection of cultural and social identities.

Documents—any written, digital, audio, visual, or artistic recording of the work within the career services relationship between career professional and client.

Dual Relationships—relationships and/or interactions with clients, students, supervisees, and/or research participants that involve the career professional in more than one professional role or a combination of professional and nonprofessional roles.

Examinee—a recipient of any professional career service that includes educational, psychological, and career appraisal utilizing qualitative or quantitative techniques.

Forensic Evaluation—any formal assessment conducted for court or other legal proceedings.

Multicultural/Diversity Competence—a capacity whereby career professionals possess cultural and diversity awareness and knowledge about self and others, and how this awareness and knowledge is applied effectively in practice with clients and client groups.

Netiquette—the etiquette of online/Internet communication.

Professional Relationship—a relationship in which the roles of client and career professional are defined, activities and services are selected, and fees are charged to a client, an employer, or a referring organization.

Student—an individual engaged in formal educational preparation as a career professional.

Supervisee—a career professional or student whose career services work and/or clinical skill development is being overseen in a formal supervisory relationship by a qualified trained professional.

Supervisor—Career professionals who are trained to oversee the work of other career professionals and students/supervisees.

Teaching—all activities engaged in as part of a formal educational program for career professionals.

Training—the instruction and practice of skills related to the work of career professionals. Training contributes to the ongoing proficiency of students and career professionals.

Working Relationship—a current agreement between a career professional and a client in which the roles, responsibilities and activities of both career professional and client are clearly defined.

Web References

ACA's Ethics Code: http://www.counseling.org/Resources

Introduction: An ethical decision-making model from the Ethics Resource Center http://www.ethics.org/resources/decision-making-model.asp

H.1.a. Use of Human Research Participants

http://cme.cancer.gov/clinicaltrials/learning/humanparticipant-protections.asp

APPENDIX D

American School Counselor Association Student Standards in the Career Development Domain

STANDARD A: Students will acquire the skills to investigate the world of work in relation to knowledge of self and to make informed career decisions.

Competency A:1 Develop Career Awareness
- A1.1 Develop skills to locate, evaluate, and interpret career information
- A1.2 Learn about the variety of traditional and nontraditional occupations
- A1.3 Develop an awareness of personal abilities, skills, interests, and motivations
- A1.4 Learn how to interact and work cooperatively in teams
- A1.5 Learn to make decisions
- A1.6 Learn how to set goals
- A1.7 Understand the importance of planning
- A1.8 Pursue and develop competency in areas of interest
- A1.9 Develop hobbies and vocational interests
- A1.10 Balance between work and leisure time

Competency A:2 Develop Employment Readiness
- A2.1 Acquire employability skills such as working on a team, problem-solving and organizational skills
- A2.2 Apply job readiness skills to seek employment opportunities
- A2.3 Demonstrate knowledge about the changing workplace
- A2.4 Learn about the rights and responsibilities of employers and employees
- A2.5 Learn to respect individual uniqueness in the workplace
- A2.6 Learn how to write a resume
- A2.7 Develop a positive attitude toward work and learning
- A2.8 Understand the importance of responsibility, dependability, punctuality, integrity, and effort in the workplace
- A2.9 Utilize time and task-management skills

STANDARD B: Students will employ strategies to achieve future career goals with success and satisfaction.

Competency B:1 Acquire Career Information
- B1.1 Apply decision-making skills to career planning, course selection, and career transition
- B1.2 Identify personal skills, interests, and abilities and relate them to current career choice
- B1.3 Demonstrate knowledge of the career planning process
- B1.4 Know the various ways in which occupations can be classified
- B1.5 Use research and information resources to obtain career information
- B1.6 Learn to use the Internet to access career planning information
- B1.7 Describe traditional and nontraditional occupations and how these relate to career choice
- B1.8 Understand how changing economic and societal needs influence employment trends and future training

Competency B:2 Identify Career Goals
- B2.1 Demonstrate awareness of the education and training needed to achieve career goals
- B2.2 Assess and modify their educational plan to support career

- B2.3 Use employability and job readiness skills in internship, mentoring, shadowing, and/or other work experience
- B2.4 Select course work that is related to career interests
- B2.5 Maintain a career planning portfolio

STANDARD C: Students will understand the relationship between personal qualities, education, training, and the world of work.

Competency C:1 Acquire Knowledge to Achieve Career Goals
- C1.1 Understand the relationship between educational achievement and career success
- C1.2 Explain how work can help to achieve personal success and satisfaction
- C1.3 Identify personal preferences and interests which influence career choice and success
- C1.4 Understand that the changing workplace requires lifelong learning and acquiring new skills
- C1.5 Describe the effect of work on lifestyle
- C1.6 Understand the importance of equity and access in career choice
- C1.7 Understand that work is an important and satisfying means of personal expression

Competency C:2 Apply Skills to Achieve Career Goals
- C2.1 Demonstrate how interests, abilities and achievement relate to achieving personal, social, educational, and career goals
- C2.2 Learn how to use conflict management skills with peers and adults
- C2.3 Learn to work cooperatively with others as a team member
- C2.4 Apply academic and employment readiness skills in work-based learning situations such as internships, shadowing, and/or mentoring experiences

APPENDIX E

National Career Development Guidelines Framework

UNDERSTANDING THE NCDG FRAMEWORK

Domains and Goals

Domains, goals and indicators organize the NCDG framework. The **three domains**: Personal Social Development (PS), Educational Achievement and Lifelong Learning (ED) and Career Management (CM) describe content. Under each domain are **goals** (eleven in total). The goals define broad areas of career development competency.

PERSONAL SOCIAL DEVELOPMENT DOMAIN

- GOAL PS1 Develop understanding of self to build and maintain a positive self-concept.
- GOAL PS2 Develop positive interpersonal skills including respect for diversity.
- GOAL PS3 Integrate growth and change into your career development.
- GOAL PS4 Balance personal, leisure, community, learner, family and work roles.

EDUCATIONAL ACHIEVEMENT AND LIFELONG LEARNING DOMAIN

- GOAL ED1 Attain educational achievement and performance levels needed to reach your personal and career goals.
- GOAL ED2 Participate in ongoing, lifelong learning experiences to enhance your ability to function effectively in a diverse and changing economy.

CAREER MANAGEMENT DOMAIN

- GOAL CM1 Create and manage a career plan that meets your career goals.
- GOAL CM2 Use a process of decision-making as one component of career development.
- GOAL CM3 Use accurate, current and unbiased career information during career planning and management.
- GOAL CM4 Master academic, occupational and general employability skills in order to obtain, create, maintain and/or advance your employment.
- GOAL CM5 Integrate changing employment trends, societal needs and economic conditions into your career plans.

Indicators and Learning Stages

Under each goal in the framework are indicators of mastery that highlight the knowledge and skills needed to achieve that goal. Each indicator is presented in **three learning stages** derived from *Bloom's Taxonomy*: knowledge acquisition, application and reflection. The stages describe learning competency. They are not tied to an individual's age or level of education.

Knowledge Acquisition (K). Youth and adults at the knowledge acquisition stage expand knowledge awareness and build comprehension. They can recall, recognize, describe, identify, clarify, discuss, explain, summarize, query, investigate and compile new information about the knowledge.

Application (A). Youth and adults at the application stage apply acquired knowledge to situations and to self. They seek out ways to use the knowledge. For example, they can demonstrate, employ, perform, illustrate and solve problems related to the knowledge.

Reflection (R). Youth and adults at the reflection stage analyze, synthesize, judge, assess and evaluate knowledge in accord with their own goals, values and beliefs. They decide whether or not to integrate the acquired knowledge into their ongoing response to situations and adjust their behavior accordingly.

Coding System

The NCDG framework has a simple **coding system** to identify domains, goals, indicators and learning stages. The coding system makes it easy for you to use the NCDG for program development and to track activities by goal, learning stage and indicator. However, you do **not** need to know or include the codes to use the NCDG framework.

DOMAINS

- PS—Personal Social Development
- ED—Educational Achievement and Lifelong Learning
- CM—Career Management

GOALS Coded by domain and then numerically.

For example, under the Personal Social Development domain:
- Goal PS1: Develop understanding of yourself to build and maintain a positive self-concept.
- Goal PS2: Develop positive interpersonal skills including respect for diversity.

INDICATORS AND LEARNING STAGES Coded by domain, goal, learning stage and then numerically.

Learning Stages:
- K—Knowledge Acquisition
- A—Application
- R—Reflection

For example, the second indicator under the first goal of the Personal Social Development domain:
- PS1.K2 Identify your abilities, strengths, skills, and talents.
- PS1.A2 Demonstrate use of your abilities, strengths, skills, and talents.
- PS1.R2 Assess the impact of your abilities, strengths, skills, and talents on your career development.

If you have questions about the NCDG framework, in general, or its technical development, please contact the National Training Support Center (703.416.1840).

THE FRAMEWORK

National Career Development Guidelines Revision 09/30/04	
Personal Social Development Domain	
Goal PS1	Develop Understanding of Yourself to Build and Maintain a Positive Self-Concept.
PS1.K1	Identify your interests, likes, and dislikes.
PS1.A1	Demonstrate behavior and decisions that reflect your interests, likes, and dislikes.
PS1.R1	Assess how your interests and preferences are reflected in your career goals.
PS1.K2	Identify your abilities, strengths, skills, and talents.
PS1.A2	Demonstrate use of your abilities, strengths, skills, and talents.
PS1.R2	Assess the impact of your abilities, strengths, skills, and talents on your career development.
PS1.K3	Identify your positive personal characteristics (e.g., honesty, dependability, responsibility, integrity, and loyalty).
PS1.A3	Give examples of when you demonstrated positive personal characteristics (e.g., honesty, dependability, responsibility, integrity, and loyalty).
PS1.R3	Assess the impact of your positive personal characteristics (e.g., honesty, dependability, responsibility, integrity, and loyalty) on your career development.
PS1.K4	Identify your work values/needs.
PS1.A4	Demonstrate behavior and decisions that reflect your work values/needs.
PS1.R4	Assess how your work values/needs are reflected in your career goals.

PS1.K5	Describe aspects of your self-concept.
PS1.A5	Demonstrate a positive self-concept through your behaviors and attitudes.
PS1.R5	Analyze the positive and negative aspects of your self-concept.
PS1.K6	Identify behaviors and experiences that help to build and maintain a positive self-concept.
PS1.A6	Show how you have adopted behaviors and sought experiences that build and maintain a positive self-concept.
PS1.R6	Evaluate the affect of your behaviors and experiences on building and maintaining a positive self-concept.
PS1.K7	Recognize that situations, attitudes, and the behaviors of others affect your self-concept.
PS1.A7	Give personal examples of specific situations, attitudes, and behaviors of others that affected your self-concept.
PS1.R7	Evaluate the affect of situations, attitudes, and the behaviors of others on your self-concept.
PS1.K8	Recognize that your behaviors and attitudes affect the self-concept of others.
PS1.A8	Show how you have adopted behaviors and attitudes to positively affect the self-concept of others.
PS1.R8	Analyze how your behaviors and attitudes might affect the self-concept of others.
PS1.K9	Recognize that your self-concept can affect educational achievement (i.e., performance) and/or success at work.
PS1.A9	Show how aspects of your self-concept could positively or negatively affect educational achievement (i.e., performance) and/or success at work.
PS1.R9	Assess how your self-concept affects your educational achievement (performance) and/or success at work.
PS1.K10	Recognize that educational achievement (performance) and/or success at work can affect your self-concept.
PS1.A10	Give personal examples of how educational achievement (performance) and/or success at work affected your self-concept.
PS1.R10	Assess how your educational achievement (performance) and/or success at work affect your self-concept.
GOAL PS2	**Develop Positive Interpersonal Skills Including Respect for Diversity.**
PS2.K1	Identify effective communication skills.
PS2.A1	Demonstrate effective communication skills.
PS2.R1	Evaluate your use of effective communication skills.
PS2.K2	Recognize the benefits of interacting with others in a way that is honest, fair, helpful, and respectful.
PS2.A2	Demonstrate that you interact with others in a way that is honest, fair, helpful, and respectful.
PS2.R2	Assess the degree to which you interact with others in a way that is honest, fair, helpful, and respectful.
PS2.K3	Identify positive social skills (e.g., good manners and showing gratitude).
PS2.A3	Demonstrate the ability to use positive social skills (e.g., good manners and showing gratitude).
PS2.R3	Evaluate how your positive social skills (e.g., good manners and showing gratitude) contribute to effective interactions with others.
PS2.K4	Identify ways to get along well with others and work effectively with them in groups.
PS2.A4	Demonstrate the ability to get along well with others and work effectively with them in groups.
PS2.R4	Evaluate your ability to work effectively with others in groups.
PS2.K5	Describe conflict resolution skills.
PS2.A5	Demonstrate the ability to resolve conflicts and to negotiate acceptable solutions.
PS2.R5	Analyze the success of your conflict resolution skills.
PS2.K6	Recognize the difference between appropriate and inappropriate behavior in specific school, social, and work situations.
PS2.A6	Give examples of times when your behavior was appropriate and times when your behavior was inappropriate in specific school, social, and work situations.
PS2.R6	Assess the consequences of appropriate or inappropriate behavior in specific school, social, and work situations.

(Continued)

	National Career Development Guidelines Revision 09/30/04 (*Continued*)
PS2.K7	Identify sources of outside pressure that affect you.
PS2.A7	Demonstrate the ability to handle outside pressure on you.
PS2.R7	Analyze the impact of outside pressure on your behavior.
PS2.K8	Recognize that you should accept responsibility for your behavior.
PS2.A8	Demonstrate that you accept responsibility for your behavior.
PS2.R8	Assess the degree to which you accept personal responsibility for your behavior.
PS2.K9	Recognize that you should have knowledge about, respect for, be open to, and appreciate all kinds of human diversity.
PS2.A9	Demonstrate knowledge about, respect for, openness to, and appreciation for all kinds of human diversity.
PS2.R9	Assess how you show respect for all kinds of human diversity.
PS2.K10	Recognize that the ability to interact positively with diverse groups of people may contribute to learning and academic achievement.
PS2.A10	Show how the ability to interact positively with diverse groups of people may contribute to learning and academic achievement.
PS2.R10	Analyze the impact of your ability to interact positively with diverse groups of people on your learning and academic achievement.
PS2.K11	Recognize that the ability to interact positively with diverse groups of people is often essential to maintain employment.
PS2.A11	Explain how the ability to interact positively with diverse groups of people is often essential to maintain employment.
PS2.R11	Analyze the impact of your ability to interact positively with diverse groups of people on your employment.
GOAL PS3	**Integrate Personal Growth and Change into Your Career Development.**
PS3.K1	Recognize that you will experience growth and changes in mind and body throughout life that will impact on your career development.
PS3.A1	Give examples of how you have grown and changed (e.g., physically, emotionally, socially, and intellectually).
PS3.R1	Analyze the results of your growth and changes throughout life to determine areas of growth for the future.
PS3.K2	Identify good health habits (e.g., good nutrition and constructive ways to manage stress).
PS3.A2	Demonstrate how you have adopted good health habits.
PS3.R2	Assess the impact of your health habits on your career development.
PS3.K3	Recognize that your motivations and aspirations are likely to change with time and circumstances.
PS3.A3	Give examples of how your personal motivations and aspirations have changed with time and circumstances.
PS3.R3	Assess how changes in your motivations and aspirations over time have affected your career development.
PS3.K4	Recognize that external events often cause life changes.
PS3.A4	Give examples of external events that have caused life changes for you.
PS3.R4	Assess your strategies for managing life changes caused by external events.
PS3.K5	Identify situations (e.g., problems at school or work) in which you might need assistance from people or other resources.
PS3.A5	Demonstrate the ability to seek assistance (e.g., with problems at school or work) from appropriate resources including other people.
PS3.R5	Assess the effectiveness of your strategies for getting assistance (e.g., with problems at school or work) from appropriate resources including other people.
PS3.K6	Recognize the importance of adaptability and flexibility when initiating or responding to change.
PS3.A6	Demonstrate adaptability and flexibility when initiating or responding to change.
PS3.R6	Analyze how effectively you respond to change and/or initiate change.

GOAL PS4	**Balance Personal, Leisure, Community, Learner, Family, and Work Roles.**
PS4.K1	Recognize that you have many life roles (e.g., personal, leisure, community, learner, family, and work roles).
PS4.A1	Give examples that demonstrate your life roles including personal, leisure, community, learner, family, and work roles.
PS4.R1	Assess the impact of your life roles on career goals.
PS4.K2	Recognize that you must balance life roles and that there are many ways to do it.
PS4.A2	Show how you are balancing your life roles.
PS4.R2	Analyze how specific life role changes would affect the attainment of your career goals.
PS4.K3	Describe the concept of lifestyle.
PS4.A3	Give examples of decisions, factors, and circumstances that affect your current lifestyle.
PS4.R3	Analyze how specific lifestyle changes would affect the attainment of your career goals.
PS4.K4	Recognize that your life roles and your lifestyle are connected.
PS4.A4	Show how your life roles and your lifestyle are connected.
PS4.R4	Assess how changes in your life roles would affect your lifestyle.

Educational Achievement and Lifelong Learning Domain

GOAL ED1	**Attain Educational Achievement and Performance Levels Needed to Reach Your Personal and Career Goals.**
ED1.K1	Recognize the importance of educational achievement and performance to the attainment of personal and career goals.
ED1.A1	Demonstrate educational achievement and performance levels needed to attain your personal and career goals.
ED1.R1	Evaluate how well you have attained educational achievement and performance levels needed to reach your personal and career goals.
ED1.K2	Identify strategies for improving educational achievement and performance.
ED1.A2	Demonstrate strategies you are using to improve educational achievement and performance.
ED1.R2	Analyze your educational achievement and performance strategies to create a plan for growth and improvement.
ED1.K3	Describe study skills and learning habits that promote educational achievement and performance.
ED1.A3	Demonstrate acquisition of study skills and learning habits that promote educational achievement and performance.
ED1.R3	Evaluate your study skills and learning habits to develop a plan for improving them.
ED1.K4	Identify your learning style.
ED1.A4	Show how you are using learning style information to improve educational achievement and performance.
ED1.R4	Analyze your learning style to develop behaviors to maximize educational achievement and performance.
ED1.K5	Describe the importance of having a plan to improve educational achievement and performance.
ED1.A5	Show that you have a plan to improve educational achievement and performance.
ED1.R5	Evaluate the results of your plan for improving educational achievement and performance.
ED1.K6	Describe how personal attitudes and behaviors can impact educational achievement and performance.
ED1.A6	Exhibit attitudes and behaviors that support educational achievement and performance.
ED1.R6	Assess how well your attitudes and behaviors promote educational achievement and performance.
ED1.K7	Recognize that your educational achievement and performance can lead to many workplace options.
ED1.A7	Show how your educational achievement and performance can expand your workplace options.
ED1.R7	Assess how well your educational achievement and performance will transfer to the workplace.
ED1.K8	Recognize that the ability to acquire and use information contributes to educational achievement and performance.
ED1.A8	Show how the ability to acquire and use information has affected your educational achievement and performance.
ED1.R8	Assess your ability to acquire and use information in order to improve educational achievement and performance.

(Continued)

	National Career Development Guidelines Revision 09/30/04 (*Continued*)
GOAL ED2	**Participate in Ongoing, Lifelong Learning Experiences to Enhance Your Ability to Function Effectively in a Diverse and Changing Economy.**
ED2.K1	Recognize that changes in the economy require you to acquire and update knowledge and skills throughout life.
ED2.A1	Show how lifelong learning is helping you function effectively in a diverse and changing economy.
ED2.R1	Judge whether or not you have the knowledge and skills necessary to function effectively in a diverse and changing economy.
ED2.K2	Recognize that viewing yourself as a learner affects your identity.
ED2.A2	Show how being a learner affects your identity.
ED2.R2	Analyze how specific learning experiences have affected your identity.
ED2.K3	Recognize the importance of being an independent learner and taking responsibility for your learning.
ED2.A3	Demonstrate that you are an independent learner.
ED2.R3	Assess how well you function as an independent learner.
ED2.K4	Describe the requirements for transition from one learning level to the next (e.g., middle school to high school, high school to postsecondary).
ED2.A4	Demonstrate the knowledge and skills necessary for transition from one learning level to the next (e.g., middle to high school, high school to postsecondary).
ED2.R4	Analyze how your knowledge and skills affect your transition from one learning level to the next (e.g., middle school to high school, high school to postsecondary).
ED2.K5	Identify types of ongoing learning experiences available to you (e.g., two- and four-year colleges, technical schools, apprenticeships, the military online courses, and on-the-job training).
ED2.A5	Show how you are preparing to participate in ongoing learning experiences (e.g., two- and four-year colleges, technical schools, apprenticeships, the military, on-line courses, and on-the-job training).
ED2.R5	Assess how participation in ongoing learning experiences (e.g., two- and four-year colleges, technical schools, apprenticeships, the military, on-line courses, and on-the-job training) affects your personal and career goals.
ED2.K6	Identify specific education/training programs (e.g., high school career paths and courses, college majors, and apprenticeship programs).
ED2.A6	Demonstrate participation in specific education/training programs (e.g., high school career paths and courses, college majors, and apprenticeship programs) that help you function effectively in a diverse and changing economy.
ED2.R6	Evaluate how participation in specific education/training programs (e.g., high school career paths and courses, college majors, and apprenticeship programs) affects your ability to function effectively in a diverse and changing economy.
ED2.K7	Describe informal learning experiences that contribute to lifelong learning.
ED2.A7	Demonstrate participation in informal learning experiences.
ED2.R7	Assess, throughout your life, how well you integrate both formal and informal learning experiences
Career Management Domain	
GOAL CM1	**Create and Manage a Career Plan that Meets Your Career Goals.**
CM1.K1	Recognize that career planning to attain your career goals is a life-long process.
CM1.A1	Give examples of how you use career-planning strategies to attain your career goals.
CM1.R1	Assess how well your career planning strategies facilitate reaching your career goals.
CM1.K2	Describe how to develop a career plan (e.g., steps and content).
CM1.A2	Develop a career plan to meet your career goals.
CM1.R2	Analyze your career plan and make adjustments to reflect ongoing career management needs.
CM1.K3	Identify your short-term and long-term career goals (e.g., education, employment, and lifestyle goals).
CM1.A3	Demonstrate actions taken to attain your short-term and long-term career goals (e.g., education, employment, and lifestyle goals).

CM1.R3	Re-examine your career goals and adjust as needed.
CM1.K4	Identify skills and personal traits needed to manage your career (e.g., resiliency, self-efficacy, ability to identify trends and changes, and flexibility).
CM1.A4	Demonstrate career management skills and personal traits (e.g., resiliency, self-efficacy, ability to identify trends and changes, and flexibility).
CM1.R4	Evaluate your career management skills and personal traits (e.g., resiliency, self-efficacy, ability to identify trends and changes, and flexibility).
CM1.K5	Recognize that changes in you and the world of work can affect your career plans.
CM1.A5	Give examples of how changes in you and the world of work have caused you to adjust your career plans.
CM1.R5	Evaluate how well you integrate changes in you and the world of work into your career plans.
GOAL CM2	**Use a Process of Decision-Making as One Component of Career Development.**
CM2.K1	Describe your decision-making style (e.g., risk taker, cautious).
CM2.A1	Give examples of past decisions that demonstrate your decision-making style.
CM2.R1	Evaluate the effectiveness of your decision-making style.
CM2.K2	Identify the steps in one model of decision-making.
CM2.A2	Demonstrate the use of a decision-making model.
CM2.R2	Assess what decision-making model(s) work best for you.
CM2.K3	Describe how information (e.g., about you, the economy, and education programs) can improve your decision-making.
CM2.A3	Demonstrate use of information (e.g., about you, the economy, and education programs) in making decisions.
CM2.R3	Assess how well you use information (e.g., about you, the economy, and education programs) to make decisions.
CM2.K4	Identify alternative options and potential consequences for a specific decision.
CM2.A4	Show how exploring options affected a decision you made.
CM2.R4	Assess how well you explore options when making decisions.
CM2.K5	Recognize that your personal priorities, culture, beliefs, and work values can affect your decision-making.
CM2.A5	Show how personal priorities, culture, beliefs, and work values are reflected in your decisions.
CM2.R5	Evaluate the affect of personal priorities, culture, beliefs, and work values in your decision-making.
CM2.K6	Describe how education, work, and family experiences might impact your decisions.
CM2.A6	Give specific examples of how your education, work, and family experiences have influenced your decisions.
CM2.R6	Assess the impact of your education, work, and family experiences on decisions.
CM2.K7	Describe how biases and stereotypes can limit decisions.
CM2.A7	Give specific examples of how biases and stereotypes affected your decisions.
CM2.R7	Analyze the ways you could manage biases and stereotypes when making decisions.
CM2.K8	Recognize that chance can play a role in decision-making.
CM2.A8	Give examples of times when chance played a role in your decision-making.
CM2.R8	Evaluate the impact of chance on past decisions.
CM2.K9	Recognize that decision-making often involves compromise.
CM2.A9	Give examples of compromises you might have to make in career decision-making.
CM2.R9	Analyze the effectiveness of your approach to making compromises.
GOAL CM3	**Use Accurate, Current, and Unbiased Career Information During Career Planning and Management.**
CM3.K1	Describe the importance of career information to your career planning.
CM3.A1	Show how career information has been important in your plans and how it can be used in future plans.
CM3.R1	Assess the impact of career information on your plans and refine plans so that they reflect accurate, current, and unbiased career information.

(Continued)

National Career Development Guidelines Revision 09/30/04 (*Continued*)

CM3.K2	Recognize that career information includes occupational, education and training, employment, and economic information and that there is a range of career information resources available.
CM3.A2	Demonstrate the ability to use different types of career information resources (i.e., occupational, educational, economic, and employment) to support career planning.
CM3.R2	Evaluate how well you integrate occupational, educational, economic, and employment information into the management of your career.
CM3.K3	Recognize that the quality of career information resource content varies (e.g., accuracy, bias, and how up-to-date and complete it is).
CM3.A3	Show how selected examples of career information are biased, out-of-date, incomplete, or inaccurate.
CM3.R3	Judge the quality of the career information resources you plan to use in terms of accuracy, bias, and how up-to-date and complete it is.
CM3.K4	Identify several ways to classify occupations.
CM3.A4	Give examples of how occupational classification systems can be used in career planning.
CM3.R4	Assess which occupational classification system is most helpful to your career planning.
CM3.K5	Identify occupations that you might consider without regard to your gender, race, culture, or ability.
CM3.A5	Demonstrate openness to considering occupations that you might view as nontraditional (i.e., relative to your gender, race, culture, or ability).
CM3.R5	Assess your openness to considering non-traditional occupations in your career management.
CM3.K6	Identify the advantages and disadvantages of being employed in a nontraditional occupation.
CM3.A6	Make decisions for yourself about being employed in a non-traditional occupation.
CM3.R6	Assess the impact of your decisions about being employed in a non-traditional occupation.
GOAL CM4	**Master Academic, Occupational, and General Employability Skills in Order to Obtain, Create, Maintain, and/or Advance Your Employment.**
CM4.K1	Describe academic, occupational, and general employability skills.
CM4.A1	Demonstrate the ability to use your academic, occupational, and general employability skills to obtain or create, maintain, and advance your employment.
CM4.R1	Assess your academic, occupational, and general employability skills and enhance them as needed for your employment.
CM4.K2	Identify job seeking skills such as the ability to: write a resume and cover letter, complete a job application, interview for a job, and find and pursue employment leads.
CM4.A2	Demonstrate the following job seeking skills: the ability to write a resume and cover letter, complete a job application, interview for a job, and find and pursue employment leads.
CM4.R2	Evaluate your ability to: write a resume and cover letter, complete a job application, interview for a job, and find and pursue employment leads.
CM4.K3	Recognize that a variety of general employability skills and personal qualities (e.g., critical thinking, problem solving, resource, information, and technology management, interpersonal skills, honesty, and dependability) are important to success in school and employment.
CM4.A3	Demonstrate attainment of general employability skills and personal qualities needed to be successful in school and employment (e.g., critical thinking, problem solving, resource, information, and technology management, interpersonal skills, honesty, and dependability).
CM4.R3	Evaluate your general employability skills and personal qualities (e.g., critical thinking, problem solving, resource, information, and technology management, interpersonal skills, honesty, and dependability).
CM4.K4	Recognize that many skills are transferable from one occupation to another.
CM4.A4	Show how your skills are transferable from one occupation to another.
CM4.R4	Analyze the impact of your transferable skills on your career options.
CM4.K5	Recognize that your geographic mobility impacts on your employability.
CM4.A5	Make decisions for yourself regarding geographic mobility.
CM4.R5	Analyze the impact of your decisions about geographic mobility on your career goals.

CM4.K6	Identify the advantages and challenges of self-employment.
CM4.A6	Make decisions for yourself about self-employment.
CM4.R6	Assess the impact of your decision regarding self-employment on your career goals.
CM4.K7	Identify ways to be proactive in marketing yourself for a job.
CM4.A7	Demonstrate skills that show how you can market yourself in the workplace.
CM4.R7	Evaluate how well you have marketed yourself in the workplace.
GOAL CM5	**Integrate Changing Employment Trends, Societal Needs, and Economic Conditions into Your Career Plans.**
CM5.K1	Identify societal needs that affect your career plans.
CM5.A1	Show how you are prepared to respond to changing societal needs in your career management.
CM5.R1	Evaluate the results of your career management relative to changing societal needs.
CM5.K2	Identify economic conditions that affect your career plans.
CM5.A2	Show how you are prepared to respond to changing economic conditions in your career management.
CM5.R2	Evaluate the results of your career management relative to changing economic conditions.
CM5.K3	Identify employment trends that affect your career plans.
CM5.A3	Show how you are prepared to respond to changing employment trends in your career management.
CM5.R3	Evaluate the results of your career management relative to changes in employment trends.

APPENDIX F

Secretary's Commission on Achieving Necessary Skills (SCANS)—Employability Skills

Foundational Skills	
Basic skills	Reading, writing, arithmetic and mathematical operations, speaking and listening
	A. *Reading*—locates, understands, and interprets written information in prose and in documents such as manuals, graphs, and schedules
	B. *Writing*—communicates thoughts, ideas, information, and messages in writing; and creates documents such as letters, directions, manuals, reports, graphs, and flow charts
	C. *Arithmetic/Mathematics*—performs basic computations and approaches practical problems by choosing appropriately from a variety of mathematical techniques
	D. *Listening*—receives, attends to, interprets, and responds to verbal messages and other cues
	E. *Speaking*—organizes ideas and communicates orally
Thinking skills	Thinking creatively, making decisions, solving problems, seeing things in the mind's eye, knowing how to learn, and reasoning
	A. *Creative Thinking*—generates new ideas
	B. *Decision Making*—specifies goals and constraints, generates alternatives, considers risks, and evaluates and chooses best alternative
	C. *Problem Solving*—recognizes problems and devises and implements plan of action
	D. *Seeing Things in the Mind's Eye*—organizes, and processes symbols, pictures, graphs, objects, and other information
	E. *Knowing How to Learn*—uses efficient learning techniques to acquire and apply new knowledge and skills
	F. *Reasoning*—discovers a rule or principle underlying the relationship between two or objects and applies it when solving a problem
Personal qualities	Individual responsibility, self-esteem, sociability, self-management, and integrity
	A. *Responsibility*—exerts a high level of effort and perseveres towards goal attainment
	B. *Self-Esteem*—believes in own self-worth and maintains a positive view of self
	C. *Sociability*—demonstrates understanding, friendliness, adaptability, empathy
	D. *Self-Management*—assesses self accurately, sets personal goals, monitors progress, and exhibits self-control
	E. *Integrity/Honesty*—chooses ethical courses of action

Workplace Competencies

Resources — Allocating time, money, materials, space, and staff
- A. *Time*—Selects goal-relevant activities, ranks them, allocates time, and prepares and follows schedules
- B. *Money*—Uses or prepares budgets, makes forecasts, keeps records, and makes adjustments to meet objectives
- C. *Material and Facilities*—Acquires, stores, allocates, and uses materials or space efficiently
- D. *Human Resources*—Assesses skills and distributes work accordingly, evaluates performance and provides feedback

Interpersonal — Working on teams, teaching others, serving customers, leading, negotiating, and working well with people from culturally diverse backgrounds
- A. *Participates as Member of a Team*—contributes to group effort
- B. *Teaches Others New Skills*
- C. *Serves Clients/Customers*—works to satisfy customers' expectations
- D. *Exercises Leadership*—communicates ideas to justify position, persuades and convinces others, responsibly challenges existing procedures and policies
- E. *Negotiates*—works toward agreements involving exchange of resources, resolves divergent interests
- F. *Works with Diversity*—works well with men and women from diverse backgrounds

Information — Acquiring and evaluating data, organizing and maintaining files, interpreting and communicating, and using computers to process information
- A. *Acquires and Evaluates Information*
- B. *Organizes and Maintains Information*
- C. *Interprets and Communicates Information*
- D. *Uses Computers to Process Information*

Systems — Understanding social, organizational, and technological systems, monitoring and correcting performance, and designing or improving systems
- A. *Understands Systems*—knows how social, organizational, and technological systems work and operates effectively with them
- B. *Monitors and Corrects Performance*—distinguishes trends, predicts impacts on systems operations, diagnoses deviations in systems' performance and corrects malfunctions
- C. *Improves or Designs Systems*—suggests modifications to existing systems and develops new or alternative systems to improve performance

Technology — Selecting equipment and tools, applying technology to specific tasks, and maintaining and troubleshooting technologies
- A. *Selects Technology*—chooses procedures, tools or equipment including computers and related technologies
- B. *Applies Technology to Task*—understands overall intent and proper procedures for setup and operation of equipment
- C. *Maintains and Troubleshoots Equipment*—prevents, identifies, or solves problems with equipment, including computers and other technologies

Source: Secretary's Commission on Achieving Necessary Skills. (1991a). *What work requires of schools: A SCANS report for America 2000.* Washington, DC: U.S. Department of Labor. (ED332054)

APPENDIX G

Sample Form for an Educational Development Plan

Name _____ Student # _____ Grade _____

EDUCATIONAL DEVELOPMENT PLAN

Date _____ Counselor _____

Career Pathway (based on assessment results)

1.
2.

Occupations/Careers of Interest in Selected Pathway

1.
2.
3.

Michigan Merit Curriculum
High School Graduation Requirements

4.0 English
- 1.0 9th Grade English ☐ ☐
- 1.0 10th Grade English ☐ ☐
- 1.0 11th Grade English ☐ ☐
- 1.0 12th Grade English ☐ ☐

4.0 Mathematics
- 1.0 Algebra I ☐ ☐
- 1.0 Algebra II ☐ ☐
- 1.0 Geometry ☐ ☐
- 1.0 12th Grade Math ☐ ☐

3.0 Science
- 1.0 Biology ☐ ☐
- 1.0 Physics or Chemistry ☐ ☐
- 1.0 Additional Science ☐ ☐

3.0 Social Studies
- 0.5 Civics ☐
- 0.5 Economics ☐
- 1.0 U.S. History and Geography ☐ ☐
- 1.0 World History and Geography ☐ ☐

1.0 Health and Physical Education ☐ ☐

1.0 Visual, Performing & Applied Arts ☐ ☐

2.0 Language Other than English ☐ ☐

Online Learning Experience ☐

*Athletes—Check NCAA Requirements!

Educational/Training Goals

___ High school diploma
___ Career/Technical Center certificate
___ On-the-job training
___ Apprenticeship
___ Trade and technical certification
___ Two-year associate's degree
___ Tech Prep (2 + 2, 2 + 4)
___ Four-year bachelor's degree
___ Master's degree
___ Doctoral degree
___ Military
___ Other: _____

GRADE 9		GRADE 10		GRADE 11		GRADE 12	
Semester 1	Semester 2	Semester 1	Semester 2	Semester 1	Semester 2	Semester 1	Semester 2

Student Signature _____ Counselor Signature _____ Guardian Signature _____

Source: Hobson, S. M., and Phillips, C. A. (2004). Educational planning: Helping students build lives by choice, not by chance. In B. T. Erford (Ed.), *Professional school counseling: A handbook of theories, programs & practices* (pp. 325–339). Austin, TX: Pro-Ed, Inc.

REFERENCES

Achieve Texas. (2007). *Ensuring success for every student: A resource guide for school counselors.* Austin, TX: Texas Education Agency. Retrieved July 12, 2013, from http://www.achievetexas.org/Resources.htm

ACT. (2000). *Workplace essential skills: Resources related to the SCANS competencies and foundational skills.* Iowa City, IA: U.S. Department of Labor.

ACT. (2009). *ACT interest inventory technical manual.* Iowa City, IA: Author.

ACT. (2010). *The condition of college & career readiness 2010.* Iowa City, IA: Author.

ACT, Inc. (2012). *ACT WorkKeys* [Measurement instrument]. Iowa City, IA: Author.

Adams, E. M., Cahill, B. J., & Ackerlind, S. J. (2005). A qualitative study of Latino lesbian and gay youths' experiences with discrimination and the career development process. *Journal of Vocational Behavior, 66,* 199–218.

Adams, S. (2012, November 20). 7 keys to rejoining the workforce after a long break. *Forbes.com.* Retrieved May 29, 2013, from http://www.forbes.com/sites/susanadams/2012/11/20/7-keys-to-rejoining-the-workforce-after-a-long-break/

Akos, P., Niles, S. G., Miller, E. M., & Erford, B. T. (2011). Promoting educational and career planning in schools. In B. T. Erford (Ed.), *Transforming the school counseling profession* (3rd. ed., pp. 202–221). Upper Saddle River, NJ: Pearson Education.

Alamprese, J. A. (2005). *Helping adult learners make the transition to postsecondary education. Adult education background papers.* Washington, DC: U.S. Department of Education.

Albertson, E. (2008). *How to open doors with a brilliant elevator speech* (2nd ed.). Portland, OR: SucceedingInBusiness, LLC.

Aley, C. (2013). *10 tips for cleaning up your online reputation.* Retrieved August 9, 2013, from http://comerecommended.com/2013/05/10-tips-for-cleaning-up-your-online-reputation/

Alliance for Board Diversity. (2013). *Missing pieces: Women and minorities on Fortune 500 boards.* Catalyst, The Prout Group, The Executive Leadership Council, the Hispanic Association on Corporate Responsibility, and Leadership Education for Asian Pacifics, Inc. Retrieved November 11, 2013, from theabd.org/Reports.html

Alzheimer's Association. (2013). *Planning for care costs.* Retrieved May 29, 2013, from http://www.alz.org/care/alzheimers-dementia-common-costs.asp

American Association for University Women. (2013). *The simple truth about the gender pay gap.* Washington, DC: Author. Retrieved November 11, 2013, from aauw.org/research/the-simple-truth-about-the-gender-pay-gap/

American Bar Association. (2006). *Guide to workplace law* (2nd ed.). New York, NY: Random House Reference.

American Counseling Association. (2005). *ACA Code of Ethics.* Alexandria, VA: Author.

American Counseling Association. (2010). *Licensure requirements for professional counselors—2010.* Alexandria, VA: Author.

American Mental Health Counselors Association. (2010). *AMHCA Code of Ethics.* Alexandria, VA: Author.

American Psychiatric Association. (2000). *DSM-IV-TR: Diagnostic and statistical manual of mental disorders* (4th ed.). [Text Revision]. Washington, DC: Author.

American Psychiatric Association. (2013). *Diagnostic and statistical manual of mental disorders* (*DSM-5*; 5th ed.). Washington, DC: Author.

American School Counselor Association. (2010). *Ethical standards for school counselors.* Alexandria, VA: Author.

American School Counselor Association. (2012). *The ASCA national model: A framework for school counseling programs* (3rd ed.). Alexandria, VA: Author.

Americans with Disabilities Act. (1990). Public Law 101–336, §2, 104 Stat. 328.

Americans with Disabilities Amendments Act. (2008). Public Law 110–325, 122 Stat. 3553.

Amundson, N. E., & Borgen, W. A. (1982). The dynamics of unemployment: Job loss and job search. *Personnel and Guidance Journal, 60,* 562–564.

Anderson, M. L., Goodman, J., & Schlossberg, N. K. (2012). *Counseling adults in transition: Linking Schlossberg's theory with practice in a diverse world.* New York, NY: Springer Publishing Company.

Annie E. Casey Foundation. (2014). *KIDS COUNT data book.* Baltimore, MD: Author. Retrieved from http://datacenter.kidscount.org/publications/databook/2013

Antonoff, S. R., & Friedemann, M. A. (2006). *College match: A blueprint for choosing the best school for you* (9th ed.). Alexandria, VA: Octameron Associates.

Ao, D. (2007). *Social capital and getting a job: A revisit and new direction.* (Doctoral dissertation). Retrieved from ProQuest. (UMI No. 3318850)

Arbona, C. (1996). Career theory and practice in a multicultural contexts. In M. L. Savickas (Ed.), *Handbook of career counseling theory and practice* (pp. 45–54). Palo Alto, CA: Davies-Black Publishing.

Archer, J., & Rhodes, V. (1995). A longitudinal study of job loss in relation to the grief process. *Journal of Community & Applied Social Psychology, 5*, 183–188.

Arnett, J. J. (2002). The psychology of globalization. *American Psychologist, 57*, 774–783.

Arrington, K. (2000). Middle grades career planning. *Journal of Career Development, 27*, 103–109.

Arthur, M. B., & Rousseau, D. M. (Eds.). (1996). *The boundaryless career: A new employment principle for a new organizational era.* Oxford, England: Oxford University Press.

Arthur, N., & Collins, S. (2011). Infusing culture in career counseling. *Journal of Employment Counseling, 48*, 147–149.

Arthur, N., & Popadiuk, N. (2010). A cultural formulation approach to career counseling with international students. *Journal of Career Development, 37*, 423–440.

Aspen Institute, The. (2014). *Robert B. Schwartz*. Retrieved August 1, 2014, from http://www.aspeninstitute.org/people/robert-schwartz

Asplund, J., Lopez, S. J., Hodges, T., & Harter, J. (2009). *The Clifton StrengthsFinder® 2.0 technical report: Development and validation.* Omaha, NE: Gallup Organization.

Astin, A. W., & Holland, J. L. (1961). The Environmental Assessment Technique: A way to measure college environments. *Journal of Educational Psychology, 52*, 308–316.

Astin, H. S. (1984). The meaning of work in women's lives: A sociopsychological model of career choice and work behavior. *The Counseling Psychologist, 12*, 117–126.

Athanasou, J. A., & Hoskiug, K. (1998). *Using a career interest card sort for vocational assessment and counselling.* Sydney, Australia. (ERIC Document Reproduction Services No. ED419960)

Atkinson, D. R., Morten, G., & Sue, D. W. (1979). *Counseling American minorities: A cross-cultural perspective.* Dubuque, IA: Wm. C. Brown.

Atkinson, M. J. (2003). Test review of the California Psychological Inventory (3rd ed.). In B. S. Plake, J. C. Impara, & R. A. Spies (Eds.), *The fifteenth mental measurements yearbook* [Electronic version]. Retrieved from the Buros Institute's Mental Measurement Yearbook Online database.

Azrin, N. H., & Besalel, V. A. (1980). *Job Club leader's manual: A behavioral approach to vocational counseling.* Baltimore, MD: University Park Press.

Bailey, T. (1990). Jobs of the future and the skills they require. *American Educator, 14*(1), 10–15, 40–44.

Baker, D. B. (2009). Choosing a vocation at 100: Time, change, and context. *Career Development Quarterly, 57*, 199–206.

Balderrama, A. (2009). *The full-time job of finding a job.* Retrieved August 7, 2013, from http://www.careerbuilder.com/Article/CB-1144-Job-Search-The-Full-Time-Job-of-Finding-a-Job/

Bandura, A. (1961). Transmission of aggression through imitation of aggressive models. *The Journal of Abnormal and Social Psychology, 63*, 575–582.

Bandura, A. (1977a). Self-efficacy: Toward a unifying theory of behavioral change. *Psychological Review, 84*, 191–215.

Bandura, A. (1977b). *Social learning theory.* Englewood Cliffs, NJ: Prentice Hall.

Bandura, A. (1978). Social learning theory of aggression. *Journal of Communication, 28*(3), 12–29.

Bandura, A. (1986). *Social foundations of thought and action: A social cognitive theory.* Englewood Cliffs, NJ: Prentice Hall.

Bandura, A. (1989). Human agency in social cognitive theory. *American Psychologist, 44*, 1175–1184.

Bardos, A. N. (2004). Test review of the Basic Achievement Skills Inventory. In K. F. Geisinger, R. A. Spies, J. F. Carlson, & B. S. Plake (Eds), *The seventeenth mental measurements yearbook* [Electronic version]. Retrieved from the Buros Institute's Mental Measurement Yearbook Online Database.

Barge, J. D. (2012). *Elementary career cluster activities guidance: Elementary career awareness.* Atlanta, GA: Georgia Department of Education. Retrieved July 12, 2013, from http://www.doe.k12.ga.us/Curriculum-Instruction-and-Assessment/CTAE/Documents/Elementary-Career-Guidance-document.pdf

Baruch, Y. (2006). Career development in organizations and beyond: Balancing traditional and contemporary viewpoints. *Human Resource Management Review, 16*, 125–138.

Bates, R. A., & Phelan, K. C. (2002). Characteristics of a globally competitive workforce. *Advances in Developing Human Resources, 4*(2), 121–132.

Baum, S., & Flores, S. M. (2011). Higher education and children in immigrant families. *The Future of Children, 21*(1), 171–193.

Beale, A. V., & Williams, J. C. (2000). The anatomy of an elementary school career day. *Journal of Career Development, 26*, 205–213.

Becker, R. L. (2000). *Reading-Free Vocational Interest Inventory: 2.* Columbus, OH: Elbern Publications.

Becker, R. L. (2005). Test review of the Becker Work Adjustment Profile: 2. In K. F. Geisinger, R. A. Spies, J. F. Carlson, & B. S. Plake (Eds), *The seventeenth mental measurements yearbook* [Electronic version]. Retrieved from the Buros Institute's Mental Measurement Yearbook Online Database.

Bennett, G. K., Seashore, H. G., & Wesman, A. G. (1992). *Differential aptitude tests* (5th ed.). San Antonio, TX: Pearson Assessments.

Berg-Kolin, H., Krueger, G., Thomas-Clark, C., & Finck, B. (2001). *The majors fair: Helping college students decide on majors.* Retrieved from ERIC database. (ED458486)

Berry, J. W. (1997). Immigration, acculturation, and adaptation. *Applied Psychology: An International Review, 46,* 5–68.

Bertrand, M., & Mullainathan, S. (2004). Are Emily and Greg more employable than Lakisha and Jamal? A field experiment on labor market discrimination. *The American Economic Review, 94,* 991–1013.

Betsworth, D. G., Bouchard, T. J., Jr., Cooper, C. R., Grotevant, H. D., Hansen, J.-I. C., Scarr, S., & Weinberg, R. A. (1994). Genetic and environmental influences on vocational interests assessed using adoptive and biological families and twins reared apart and together. *Journal of Vocational Behavior, 44,* 263–278.

Betsworth, D. G., & Fouad, N. A. (1997). Vocational interests: A look at the past 70 years and a glance at the future. *The Career Development Quarterly, 46,* 23–47.

Betz, N. E., & Borgen, F. H. (2010). The CAPA integrative online system for college major exploration. *Journal of Career Assessment, 18,* 317–327.

Betz, N. E., Klein, K. L., & Taylor, K. M. (1996). Evaluation of a short form of the career decision-making self-efficacy scale. *Journal of Career Assessment, 4,* 47–57.

Betz, N. E., Borgen, F. H., & Harmon, L. W. (2005). *Skills confidence inventory* (rev. ed.). Palo Alto, CA: Consulting Psychologists Press.

Betz, N. E., & Taylor, K. M. (1994). *Career decision-making self-efficacy scale.* Columbus, OH: The Ohio State University.

Bhat, C. S. (2010). Assisting unemployed adults find suitable work: A group intervention embedded in community and grounded in social action. *The Journal for Specialists in Group Work, 35,* 246–254.

Bianchi, S. M. (2011). Changing families, changing workplaces. *The Future of Children, 21*(2), 15–36.

Bikos, L. H., Krieshok, T. S., & O'Brien, K. M. (1998). Evaluating the psychometric properties of the Missouri Occupational Card Sort. *Journal of Vocational Behavior, 52,* 135–155.

Blustein, D. L. (2001). Extending the reach of vocational psychology: Toward an inclusive and integrated psychology of working. *Journal of Vocational Behavior, 59,* 171–182.

Blustein, D. L., Chavez, A. P., Diemer, M. A., Gallagher, L. A., Marshall, K. G., Sirin, S., & Bhati, K. S. (2002). Voices of the forgotten half: The role of social class in the school-to-work transition. *Journal of Counseling Psychology, 49,* 228–240.

Blustein, D. L., Coutinho, M. T. N., Murphy, K. A., Backus, F., & Catraio, C. (2011). Self and social class in career theory and practice. In P. J. Hartung and L. M Subich (Eds.), *Developing self in work and career: Concepts, cases, and contexts* (pp. 213–229). Washington, DC: American Psychological Association.

Blustein, D. L., Kenna, A. C., Gill, N., & DeVoy, J. E. (2008). The psychology of working: A new framework for counseling practice and public policy. *The Career Development Quarterly, 56,* 294–308.

Blustein, D. L., Medvide, M. B., & Wan, C. M. (2012). A critical perspective of contemporary unemployment policy and practices. *Journal of Career Development, 39,* 341–356.

Bolles, R. N. (1991). *Job-hunting tips for the so-called handicapped or people who have disabilities.* Berkeley, CA: Ten Speed Press.

Bordin, E. S. (1984). Psychodynamic model of career choice and satisfaction. In D. Brown, L. Brooks, & Associates (Eds.), *Career choice and development: Applying contemporary theories to practice* (pp. 94–136). San Francisco, CA: Jossey-Bass.

Bordin, E. S., Nachmann, B., & Segal, S. J. (1963). An articulated framework for vocational development. *Journal of Counseling Psychology, 10,* 107–116.

Borgen, W. A., & Amundson, N. E. (1987). The dynamics of unemployment: Job loss and job search. *Journal of Counseling and Development, 66,* 180–184.

Bouchard, T. J., Jr. (1998). Genetic and environmental influences on adult intelligence and special mental abilities. *Human Biology, 70*(2), 257–279.

Bowen, M. (1978). *Family therapy in clinical practice.* New York, NY: Jason Aranson.

Brady, R. P. (2002). *Work orientation and values survey.* Indianapolis, IN: JIST Publishing.

Brady, R. P. (2008). *Work motivation scale.* Indianapolis, IN: JIST Publishing.

Bragg, D. D. (2006). Transitioning to college: Academic pathways from high school to the community college. *Journal of Applied Research in the Community College, 13,* 117–132.

Brewington, J. O., Nassar-McMillan, S. C., Flowers, C. P., & Furr, S. R. (2004). A preliminary investigation of factors associated with job loss grief. *Career Development Quarterly, 53,* 78–83.

Bridgstock, R. (2009). The graduate attributes we've overlooked: Enhancing graduate employability through career management skills. *Higher Education Research & Development, 28,* 31–44.

Brigance, A. H. (1994). *BRIGANCE diagnostic life skills inventory.* North Billerica, MA: Curriculum Associates.

Brigance, A. H. (1995). *BRIGANCE diagnostic employability skills inventory.* North Billerica, MA: Curriculum Associates.

Brigance, A. H. (2010). *BRIGANCE transition skills inventory.* North Billerica, MA: Curriculum Associates.

Briggs Myers, I., McCaulley, M. H., Quenk, N. L., & Hammer, A. L. (1998). *MBTI® manual: A guide to the development and use of the Myers-Briggs Type Indicator® instrument* (3rd ed.). Palo Alto, CA: Consulting Psychologists Press.

Briscoe, J. P., & Hall, D. T. (2006). The interplay of boundaryless and protean careers: Combinations and implications. *Journal of Vocational Behavior, 69,* 4–18.

Brooks, K. (2010). *You majored in what? Mapping your path from chaos to career.* New York, NY: Penguin.

Brown, C. (2011). Vocational psychology and ex-offenders' reintegration: A call for action. *Journal of Career Assessment, 19,* 333–342.

Brown, D. (1990). Trait and factor theory. In D. Brown, L. Brooks, & Associates, *Career choice and development: Applying contemporary theories to practice* (2nd ed., pp. 13–36). San Francisco, CA: Jossey-Bass.

Brown, D. (2002a). Introduction to theories of career development and choice: Origins, evolution, and current efforts. In D. Brown & Associates, *Career choice and development: Applying contemporary theories to practice* (4th ed., pp. 3–23). San Francisco, CA: Jossey-Bass.

Brown, D. (2002b). The role of work and cultural values in occupational choice, satisfaction, and success: A theoretical statement. *Journal of Counseling & Development, 80,* 48–56.

Brown, D. (2007). *Career information, career counseling and career development* (9th ed.). Boston, MA: Pearson Education.

Brown, D. (2012). *Career information, career counseling, and career development* (10th ed.). Upper Saddle River, NJ: Pearson.

Brown, M. B. (2001). Review of the self-directed search (4th ed.). In B. Plake & J. C. Impara (Eds.), *The fourteenth mental measurements yearbook* [Electronic version]. Retrieved from the Buros Institute's Mental Measurement Yearbook Online database.

Brown, S. D., & Lent, R. W. (1996). A social cognitive framework for career choice counseling. *Career Development Quarterly, 44,* 354–366.

Bugaj, A. M. (2005). Test review of the Wide Range Interest and Occupation Test, second edition. In B. Plake, J. C. Impara, & R. Spies (Eds.), *The sixteenth mental measurements yearbook* [Electronic version]. Retrieved from the Buros Institute's Mental Measurement Yearbook Online database.

Bullock, E. E., Braud, J., Andrews, L., & Phillips, J. (2009). Career concerns of unemployed U.S. war veterans: Suggestions from a cognitive information processing approach. *Journal of Employment Counseling, 46,* 171–181.

Bullock-Yowell, E., Andrews, L., & Buzzetta, M. E. (2011). Explaining career decision-making self-efficacy: Personality, cognitions, and cultural mistrust. *Career Development Quarterly, 59,* 400–411.

Bullock-Yowell, E., Peterson, G. W., Reardon, R. C., Leierer, S. J., & Reed, C. A. (2011). Relationships among career and life stress, negative career thoughts, and career decision state: A cognitive information processing perspective. *Career Development Quarterly, 59,* 302–314.

Bunch, M. B. (2005). "Test review of the Woodcock-Johnson III." In B. Plake, J. C. Impara, & R. Spies (Eds.), *The sixteenth mental measurements yearbook* [Electronic version]. Retrieved from the Buros Institute's Mental Measurement Yearbook Online database.

Bushway, S. D., & Sweeten, G. (2007). Abolish lifetime bans for ex-felons. *Criminology & Public Policy, 6,* 697–706.

Business Roundtable. (2012). *Taking action for America: A CEO plan for jobs and economic growth.* Washington, DC: Author. Retrieved from ERIC database. (ED539813)

Byars-Winston, A. (2010). The vocational significance of Black identity: Cultural formulation approach to career assessment and career counseling. *Journal of Career Development, 37,* 441–464.

Calvert Investments, Inc. (2013, March). *Examining the cracks in the ceiling: A survey of corporate diversity practices of the S&P 100.* Bethesda, MD: Author. Retrieved November 10, 2013, from calvert.com/sr-examining-cracks.html

Campbell, D. (1992). *Campbell interest and skill survey (CISS).* San Antonio, TX: Pearson Assessments.

Campbell, D. P., & Borgen, F. H. (1999). Holland's theory and the development of interest inventories. *Journal of Vocational Behavior, 55,* 86–101.

Caniglia, J., & Leapard, B. (2009). Get real: Teaching financial literacy through Internet sites. *Meridian Middle School Computer Technologies Journal, 12*(2). Retrieved July 31, 2014, from http://www.ncsu.edu/meridian/summer2009/caniglia/print.html

Caplan, R. D., Vinokur, A. D., Price, R. H., & van Ryn, M. (1989). Job seeking, reemployment, and mental health: A randomized field experiment in coping with job loss. *Journal of Applied Psychology, 74,* 759–769.

Caplin, D., & Lewis, K. K. (2011). Coming home: Examining the homecoming experiences of young veterans. In D. C. Kelly, S. Howe-Barksdale, & D. Gitelson (Eds.), *Treating young veterans: Promoting resilience through practice and advocacy* (pp. 101–124). New York, NY: Springer Publishing Company.

Carne, G. L. (2011). *Coming back to college: Middle East veteran student involvement and culture shock.* (Doctoral dissertation). Retrieved from ProQuest. (UMI No. 3449946)

Carnevale, A. P. (2008). College for all? *Change: The Magazine of Higher Learning, 40*(1), 22–31.

Carnevale, A. P., Gainer, L. J., & Meltzer, A. S. (1990). *Workplace basics training manual. Best Practices Series: ASTD.* San Francisco, CA: Jossey-Bass.

Carson, E. A., & Sabol, W. J. (2012). *Prisoners in 2011.* Washington, DC: U.S. Department of Justice. (NCJ 239808)

Casner-Lotto, J., & Barrington, L. (2006). *Are they really ready to work? Employers' perspectives on the basic knowledge and applied skills of new entrants to the 21st century U.S. workforce.* Washington, DC: Partnership for 21st Century Skills. (ED519465)

Cass, V. C. (1979). Homosexual identity formation: A theoretical model. *Journal of Homosexuality, 4,* 219–235.

Cattell, R. B., Cattell, K., & Cattell, H. E. P. (2002). *16PF® (5th ed.).* Savoy, IL: Institute for Personality and Ability Testing.

Center for Credentialing and Education. (2010a). *Global career development facilitator—United States: Applicant information.* Retrieved August 28, 2010, from http://www.cce-global.org/credentials-offered/filter/gcdfus

Center for Credentialing and Education. (2010b). *GCDFs are specially trained.* Retrieved August 28, 2010, from http://www.cce-global.org/credentials-offered/filter/competencies

Center for Economic & Financial Education. (2014). *Mini-Society®.* Retrieved July 31, 2014, from http://www.cefe.illinois.edu/tools/ms.html

Center for Occupational Research and Development. (2009). *The ABCs of tech prep.* Waco, TX: Author. Retrieved from http://www.cord.org/uploadedfiles/ABCs%20of%20Tech%20Prep.pdf

Ceperley, A., & Schmidt, C. (2007). Adaptation of the career portfolio at the University of California, San Diego: A case study. *New Directions for Student Services, 119,* 65–72.

Chae, M. H. (2002). Counseling reentry women: An overview. *Journal of Employment Counseling, 39,* 146–152.

Chang, C. Y., & O'Hara, C. (2013). The initial interview with Asian American clients. *Journal of Contemporary Psychotherapy, 43,* 33–42.

Chartrand, J. M., Robbins, S. B., & Morrill, W. H. (1997). Test review of the Career Factors Inventory. In B. S. Plake, J. C. Impara, & R. A. Spies (Eds), *The fourteenth mental measurements yearbook* [Electronic version]. Retrieved from the Buros Institute's Mental Measurement Yearbook Online Database.

Chope, R. C. (2005). Qualitatively assessing family influence in career decision making. *Journal of Career Assessment, 13,* 395–414.

Chronister, K. M., Harley, E., Aranda, C. L., Barr, L., & Luginbuhl, P. (2011). Community-based career counseling for women survivors of intimate partner violence: A collaborative partnership. *Journal of Career Development, 39,* 515–539.

Cihon, P. J., & Castagnera, J. O. (2011). *Employment and labor law* (7th ed.). Mason, OH: South-Western Cengage Learning.

Clark, G. M., & Patton, J. R. (2006). *Transition planning inventory, updated version (TPI-UV).* Austin, TX: Pro-Ed.

Clemens, E. V., & Milsom, A. S. (2008). Enlisted service members' transition into the civilian world of work: A cognitive information processing approach. *The Career Development Quarterly, 56,* 246–256.

Cochran, D. J., Vinitsky, M. H., & Warren, P. M. (1974). Career counseling: Beyond "test and tell." *The Personnel and Guidance Journal, 52,* 659–664.

Cochran, L. (1994). What is a career problem? *Career Development Quarterly, 42,* 204–215.

Cochran, L. (1997). *Career counseling: A narrative approach.* Thousand Oaks, CA: Sage Publications.

Cohen, C. F., & Rabin, V. S. (2007). *Back on the career track: A guide for stay-at-home moms who want to return to work.* Boston, MA: Hachette Book Group USA.

Cohen, C. F., & Rabin, V. S. (2011). *iRelaunch comprehensive list of career reentry programs worldwide.* Retrieved May 29, 2013, from http://www.irelaunch.com/docs/complist.pdf

Cohen, C. F., & Rabin, V. S. (2013). *5 ways to relaunch your career after a career break.* Retrieved May 29, 2013, from http://www.womensconference.org/5-ways-to-relaunch-your-career/

College Board. (2009). Helping students research colleges. *College counseling sourcebook: Advice and strategies from experienced school counselors* (6th ed., Chapter 3). New York, NY: Author.

Colorado Department of Education. (2010). *Strategies for student engagement: A toolkit to implement quality service-learning in Colorado.* Retrieved July 31, 2014, from http://www.cde.state.co.us/search/node/service%20learning

Commission on Rehabilitation Counselor Certification. (2013). *Rehabilitation counseling.* Retrieved May 17, 2013, from http://www.crccertification.com/pages/rehabilitation_counseling/30.php

ConnectEd: The California Center for College and Career. (2010a). *A fact sheet on linked learning.* Berkeley, CA: Author. Retrieved August 1, 2014, from http://www.connectedcalifornia.org/downloads/LL_Fact_Sheet_web.pdf

ConnectEd: The California Center for College and Career. (2010b). *Certification criteria for linked learning pathways.* Berkeley, CA: Author. Retrieved from ERIC database. (ED509845)

Consortium for Entrepreneurship Education. (2014). *Sample entrepreneurship education programs in the United States.* Retrieved July 31, 2014, from http://www.entre-ed.org/_arc/states.htm

Constantine, M. G., Wallace, B. C., & Kindaichi, M. M. (2005). Examining contextual factors in the career decision status of African American adolescents. *Journal of Career Assessment, 13*, 307–319.

Corey, G., Corey, M. S., & Callahan, P. (2011). *Issues and ethics in the helping professions* (8th ed.). Belmont, CA: Thomson-Brooks/Cole.

Costa, P. T., Jr., & McCrae, R. R. (2010). *NEO Personality Inventory—3*. Port Huron, MI: Sigma Assessment Systems.

Costa, P. T., Jr., McCrae, R. R., & Kay, G. G. (1995). Persons, places, and personality: Career assessment using the revised NEO Personality Inventory. *Journal of Career Assessment, 3*, 123–139.

Cottone, R. R. (2001). A social constructivism model of ethical decision making in counseling. *Journal of Counseling & Development, 79*, 39–45.

Cottone, R. R., & Claus, R. E. (2000). Ethical decision-making models: A review of the literature. *Journal of Counseling & Development, 78*, 275–283.

Council for Accreditation of Counseling and Related Educational Programs (CACREP). (2009). *2009 Standards*. Alexandria, VA: Author.

Council for the Advancement of Standards in Higher Education. (2012). *CAS professional standards for higher education: Career services* (8th ed.). Washington, DC: Author.

Coutinho, M. T., Dam, U. C., & Blustein, D. L. (2008). The psychology of working and globalisation: A new perspective for a new era. *International Journal for Educational and Vocational Guidance, 8*, 5–18.

Crane, P. (2003, Summer). The best college—or the best fit? *The Journal of College Admission, 180*, 18–21.

Crites, J. O. (1981). *Career counseling: Models, methods, and materials*. New York, NY: McGraw-Hill.

Crites, J. O., & Savickas, M. L. (1996). Revision of the Career Maturity Inventory. *Journal of Career Assessment, 4*, 131–138.

Crites, J. O., & Savickas, M. L. (2012). *The career maturity inventory—The adaptability form (CMI Form C)*. Rootstown, OH: Vocopher.

Crompton, L. (1993). Gay and lesbian students, ROTC, and the new rules. *Academe, 9*(5), 8–12.

Crosby, O. (2002). Informational interviewing: Get the inside scoop on careers. *Occupational Outlook Quarterly, 46*(2), 32–37.

Crosby, O., & Dillon, T. (2010). Informational interviewing: Get the inside scoop on careers. *Occupational Outlook Quarterly, 54*(2), 22–29.

Cross, W. E., Jr. (1971). The negro-to-black conversion experience: Toward a psychology of Black liberation. *Black World, 20*, 13–27.

Croteau, J. M., & Hedstrom, S. M. (1993). Integrating commonality and difference: The key to career counseling with lesbian women and gay men. *The Career Development Quarterly, 41*, 201–209.

CTB/McGraw-Hill. (2004). Test review of the Test of Adult Basic Education, Forms 9 & 10. In Geisinger, K. F., Spies, R. A., Carlson, J. F., & Plake, B. S. (Eds), *The seventeenth mental measurements yearbook* [Electronic version]. Retrieved from the Buros Institute's Mental Measurement Yearbook Online Database.

Cueso, J. (2005). "Decided," "undecided," and "in transition": Implications for academic advisement, career counseling, and student retention. In R. S. Feldman (Ed.), *Improving the first year of college: Research and practice* (pp. 27–48). Mahwah, NJ: Erlbaum.

Cunningham, C. (2013). Using OES occupational profiles in a job search. *Occupational Outlook Quarterly, 57*(1), 36–44.

Curtis, R., & Simons, W. (2004). *The resume.com guide to writing unbeatable resumes*. New York, NY: McGraw-Hill.

Daire, A. P., LaMothe, S., & Fuller, D. P. (2007). Differences between black/African American students and white college students regarding influences on high school completion, college attendance, and career choice. *Career Development Quarterly, 55*, 275–279.

Dalton, J. C. (2001). Career and calling: Finding a place for the spirit in work and community. *New Directions for Student Services, 95*, 17–25.

Dannin, E. (2007). Why at-will employment is bad for employers and just cause is good for them. *Labor Law Journal, 58*(1), 5–16.

Dare, D. E. (2006). The role of career and technical education in facilitating student transitions to postsecondary education. *New Directions for Community Colleges, 135*, 73–80.

Datti, P. A. (2009). Applying social learning theory of career decision making to gay, lesbian, bisexual, transgender, and questioning young adults. *Career Development Quarterly, 58*, 54–64.

Davis, H. V. (1969). *Frank Parsons: Prophet, innovator, counselor*. Carbondale, IL: Southern Illinois University Press.

Davis, N. (2002). Writing cover letters with credibility. *Career Planning and Adult Development Journal, 17*(4), 20–28.

Dawis, R. V. (2002). Person-environment-correspondence theory. In D. Brown & Associates, *Career choice and development: Applying contemporary theories to practice* (4th ed., pp. 427–464). San Francisco, CA: Jossey-Bass.

Dawis, R. V. (2005). The Minnesota theory of work adjustment. In S. D. Brown & R. W. Lent (Eds.). *Career development and counseling: Putting theory and research to work* (pp. 3–23). Hoboken, NJ: John Wiley & Sons, Inc.

Dawis, R. V., & Lofquist, L. H. (1984). *A psychological theory of work adjustment.* Minneapolis, MN: University of Minnesota Press.

DD Form 2586. (2010). *Verification of military experience and training* (2010). Retrieved May 26, 2013, from http://www.dtic.mil/whs/directives/infomgt/forms/eforms/dd2586.pdf

DD Form 2648. (2011). *Preseparation counseling checklist for active component service members.* Retrieved May 21, 2013, from http://www.dtic.mil/whs/directives/infomgt/forms/eforms/dd2648t.pdf

DeLeire, T. (2000). The unintended consequences of the Americans with Disabilities Act. *Regulation, 23*(1), 21–24.

DeLuca, M. J., & DeLuca, N. (2010). *Best answers to the 201 most frequently asked interview questions* (2nd ed.). New York, NY: McGraw-Hill.

DeNavas-Walt, C., Proctor, B. D., & Smith, J. C. (2013). *Income, poverty, and health insurance coverage in the United States: 2012.* U.S. Census Bureau, Current population reports. Washington, DC: U.S. Government Printing Office.

DePaul, J., Walsh, M. E., & Dam, U. C. (2009). The role of school counselors in addressing sexual orientation in schools. *Professional School Counseling, 12*, 300–308.

DeSena, J. N., & Ansalone, G. (2009). Gentrification, schooling and social inequality. *Educational Research Quarterly, 33*(1), 61–76.

Detroit Service Learning Academy. (2011). College-bound initiative. Retreived May 13, 2011, from http://www.detroitsla.org/servicelearning/

DeVaney, S. B., & Hughey, A. W. (2000). Career development of ethnic minority students. In D. A. Luzzo (Ed.), *Career counseling of college students: An empirical guide to strategies that work* (pp. 233–252). Washington, DC: American Psychological Association.

Dewey, C. R. (1974). Exploring Interests: A non-sexist method. *Personnel and Guidance Journal, 52*, 311–315.

Diemer, M. A., & Hsieh, C. (2008). Sociopolitical development and vocational expectations among lower socioeconomic status adolescents of color. *Career Development Quarterly, 56*, 257–267.

Diemer, M. A., Wang, Q., Moore, T., Gregory, S. R., Hatcher, K. M., & Voight, A. M. (2010). Sociopolitical development, work salience, and vocational expectations among low socioeconomic status African American, Latin American, and Asian American youth. *Developmental Psychology, 46*, 619–635.

DiRamio, D., Ackerman, R., & Mitchell, R. L. (2008). From combat to campus: Voices of student-veterans. *NASPA Journal, 45*, 73–102.

Ditlevson, A. P. (1995). Real applause for an expanded "mock interview day." *Journal of Career Planning & Employment, 55*, 54–57.

Dixson, K. (2002). Every job searcher needs an e-résumé. *Career Planning and Adult Development Journal, 17*(4), 66–78.

Dolliver, R. H. (1967). An adaptation of the Tyler Vocational Card Sort. *Personnel and Guidance Journal, 45*, 916–920.

Donahue, M. P. (2009). *Investigating the grief process related to job loss* (Doctoral dissertation). Retrieved from ProQuest. (UMI No. 3387119)

Donohue, R., & Patton, W. (1998). The effectiveness of a career guidance program with long-term unemployed individuals. *Journal of Employment Counseling, 35*, 179–194.

Donnay, D. A. C., Morris, M. L., Schaubhut, N. A., Thompson, R. C., Grutter, J., & Hammer, A. L. (2005). *Strong interest inventory* [Newly revised]. Mountain View, CA: CPP, Inc.

Downing, N. E., & Rush, K. L. (1985). From passive acceptance to active commitment: A model of feminist identity development for women. *The Counseling Psychologist, 13*, 695–709.

Dugger, S. M., & Boshoven, J. B. (2010). Secondary and post-secondary educational planning. In B. T. Erford (Ed.), *Professional school counseling: A handbook of theories, programs & practices* (2nd ed., pp. 274–294). Austin, TX: Pro-Ed.

Dunn, M. G., Rochlen, A. B., & O'Brien, K. M. (2013). Employee, mother, and partner: An exploratory investigation of working women with stay-at-home fathers. *Journal of Career Development, 40*, 3–22.

Easton, B. (2010). Our world of work. *Library Journal, 135*(2), 32–34.

Eby, L. T., & Buch, K. (1995). Job loss as career growth: Responses to involuntary career transitions. *The Career Development Quarterly, 44*, 26–31, 34, 38–42.

Educational Testing Service. (2011). *GRE revised general test* [Measurement instrument]. Princeton, NJ: Author.

Emmel, A., & Cosca, T. (2010). The 2012 SOC: A classification system gets an update. *Occupational Outlook Quarterly, 54*, 13–19.

Entin, D. (2009). On realizing it's worse than I thought. *Journal of College Admission, 202*, 14–17.

Ericksen, K. S., Jurgens, J. C., Garrett, M. T., & Swedburg, R. B. (2008). Should I stay at home or should I go back to work? Workforce reentry influences on a mother's decision-making process. *Journal of Employment Counseling, 45*, 156–167.

Estrada-Hernandez, N., Wadsworth, J. S., Nietupski, J. A., Warth, J., & Winslow, A. (2008). Employment or economic success: The experience of individuals with disabilities in transition from school to work. *Journal of Employment Counseling, 45*, 14–24.

Evans, K. (2008). *Gaining cultural competence in career counseling.* Boston, MA: Houghton Mifflin.

Fabian, E. S. (2009). Occupational choice and the meaning of work. In I. Marini & M. A. Stebnicki (Eds.), *The professional counselor's desk reference* (pp. 421–430). New York, NY: Springer.

Fabian, E. S., & Liesener, J. J. (2005). Promoting the career potential of youth with disabilities. In S. D. Brown & R. W. Lent (Eds.), *Career development and counseling: Putting theory and research to work* (pp. 551–572). New York, NY: Wiley.

Farmer-Hinton, R. L., & Adams, T. L. (2006). Social capital and college preparation: Exploring the role of counselors in a college prep school for Black students. *The Negro Educational Review, 57*, 101–116.

Federal Bureau of Prisons. (2011). *Employment information handbook*. Washington, DC: Author. Retrieved June 6, 2013, from http://www.bop.gov/inmate_programs/emp_info_handbk.pdf

Federal Glass Ceiling Commission. (1995a). *A solid investment: Making full use of the nation's human capital*. Washington, DC: U.S. Government Printing Office.

Federal Glass Ceiling Commission. (1995b). *Good for business: Making full use of the nation's human capital*. Washington, DC: U.S. Government Printing Office.

Federal Trade Commission. (2011). *Choosing a career or vocational school*. Retrieved from http://www.ftc.gov/bcp/edu/pubs/consumer/products/pro13.shtm

Ferguson. (2011). *Encyclopedia of careers and vocational guidance* (15th ed.). New York, NY: Infobase Publishing.

Fischer, K. E., Kittleson, M., Ogletree, R., Welshimer, K., Woehlke, P., & Benshoff, J. (2000). The relationship of parent alcoholism and family dysfunction to stress among college students. *Journal of American College Health, 48*, 151–156.

Fitzpatrick, A. R. (1992). Test review of the Adult Basic Learning Examination, Second Edition. In J. J. Kramer & J. C. Conoley (Eds.), *The eleventh mental measurements yearbook* [Electronic version]. Retrieved from the Buros Institute's Mental Measurement Yearbook Online database.

Fitzpatrick, C., & Costantini, K. (2011). *Counseling 21st century students for optimal college and career readiness: A 9th–12th grade curricululm*. New York, NY: Routledge.

Flansburg, J. D. (2011). Vocational evaluation: A primer. *Journal of Employment Counseling, 48*, 114–143.

Fleenor, J. W. (2001). Test review of the Myers-Briggs Type Indicator, Form M. In B. Plake & J. C. Impara (Eds.), *The foureenth mental measurements yearbook* [Electronic version]. Retrieved from the Buros Institute's Mental Measurement Yearbook Online database.

Fleig-Palmer, M. M., Luthans, K. W., & Mandernach, B. J. (2009). Successful reemployment through resilience development. *Journal of Career Development, 35*, 228–247.

Fletcher, Jr., E. C., & Zirkle, C. (2009). The relationship of high school curriculum tracks to degree attainment and occupational earnings. *Career and Technical Education Research, 34*(2), 81–102.

Flores, L. Y., & Heppner, M. J. (2002). Multicultural career counseling: Ten essentials for training. *Journal of Career Development, 28*, 181–202.

Flores, L. Y., Navarro, R. L., & DeWitz, S. J. (2008). Mexican American high school students' postsecondary educational goals: Applying social cognitive career theory. *Journal of Career Assessment, 16*, 489–501.

Flores, L. Y., Ramos, K., & Kanagui, M. (2010). Applying the cultural formulation approach to career counseling with Latinas/os. *Journal of Career Development, 37*, 411–422.

Folds, R. E. (2013). *Your queer career: The ultimate career guide for lesbian, gay, bisexual, and transgender job seekers*. New York, NY: Riverdale Avenue Books.

Folsom, B., & Reardon, R. (2003). College career courses: Design and accountability. *Journal of Career Assessment, 11*, 421–450.

Foothill College Career Center. (2014). *Career workshops on wheels*. Retrieved August 4, 2014, from http://www.foothill.edu/career/documents/workshoponwheels.pdf

Forester-Miller, H., & Davis, T. (1996). *A practitioner's guide to ethical decision making*. Alexandria, VA: American Counseling Association. Retrieved August 24, 2010, from http://www.counseling.org/Counselors/PractitionersGuide.aspx

Fouad, N. A., & Bynner, J. (2008). Work transitions. *American Psychologist, 63*, 241–251.

Fouad, N., Cotter, E. W., & Kantamneni, N. (2009). The effectiveness of a career decision-making course. *Journal of Career Assessment, 17*, 338–347.

Fouad, N. A., Guillen, A., Harris-Hodge, E., Henry, C., Novakovic, A., Terry, S., & Kantamneni, N. (2006). Need, awareness, and use of career services for college students. *Journal of Career Assessment, 14*, 407–420.

Fox, R. S., Merz, E. L., Solórzano, M. T., & Roesch, S. C. (2013). Further examining Berry's model: The applicability of latent profile analysis to acculturation. *Measurement and Evaluation in Counseling and Development, 46*, 270–288.

Frame, M. W., & Williams, C. B. (2005). A model of ethical decision making from a multicultural perspective. *Counseling and Values, 49*, 165–179.

Frawley, T. A. (2009). Job shadowing introduces the realities of manufacturing. *Tech Directions, 68*(8), 15–17.

Freifeld, L. (2010). Warriors to workers. *Training, 47*(5), 14–18.

Friedman, T. L. (2005). *The world is flat: A brief history of the twenty-first century*. New York, NY: Farrar, Straus and Giroux.

Fry, R. (2013, September 18). Four takeaways from Tuesday's census income and poverty release. Pew Research Center. Retrieved September 21, 2013, from pewresearch.org/fact-tank/2013/09/18/four-takeaways-from-tuesdays-census-income-and-poverty-release/

Garcia, J. G., Cartwright, B., Winston, S. M., & Borzuchowska, B. (2003). A transcultural integrative model for ethical decision making in counseling. *Journal of Counseling & Development, 81*, 268–277.

Gardner, J. N., Van der Veer, G., & Associates. (1998). *The senior year experience: Facilitating integration, reflection, closure, and transition.* San Francisco, CA: Jossey-Bass.

Gati, I., Krausz, M., & Osipow, S. H. (1996). A taxonomy of difficulties in career decision-making. *Journal of Counseling Psychology, 43*, 510–526.

Geisinger, K. F. (2001). Test review of the Wonderlic Personnel Test and Scholastic Level Exam. In B. Plake & J. C. Impara (Eds.), *The fourteenth mental measurements yearbook* [Electronic version]. Retrieved from the Buros Institute's Mental Measurement Yearbook Online database.

Gelberg, S., & Chojnacki, J. T. (1996). *Career and life planning with gay, lesbian, & bisexual persons.* Alexandria, VA: American Counseling Association.

General Motors. (2012). *General Motors Company 2011 Annual Report: United States Securities and Exchange Commission form 10-K.* Retrieved December 2, 2013, from http://www.sec.gov/Archives/edgar/data/1467858/000146785812000014/gm201110k.htm#s96D4BEBC20E33527554E1031CB999789

Gibson, D. L., Weiss, D. J., Dawis, R. V., & Lofquist, L. H. (1970). *Minnesota satisfactoriness scales.* Minneapolis: University of Minnesota Press.

Gibson, R. L., & Mitchell, M. H. (2006). *Introduction to career counseling for the 21st century.* Upper Saddle River, NJ: Pearson.

Gilbride, D., & Hagner, D. (2005). People with disabilities in the workplace. In R. M. Parker, E. M. Szymanski, & J. B. Patterson, *Rehabilitation counseling: Basics and beyond* (4th ed., pp. 281–305). Austin, TX: ProEd.

Ginzberg, E. (1952). Toward a theory of occupational choice. *The Personnel and Guidance Journal, 30*, 491–494.

Ginzberg, E. (1972). Toward a theory of occupational choice: A restatement. *Vocational Guidance Quarterly, 20*, 169–176.

Ginzberg, E. (1984). Career development. In D. Brown & Associates (Eds.), *Career choice and development: Applying contemporary theories to practice* (pp. 169–191). San Francisco, CA: Jossey-Bass.

Ginzberg, E. (1988). Toward a theory of occupational choice. [Reprint of 1952 article]. *Career Development Quarterly, 36*, 358–363.

Ginzberg, E., Ginsburg, S. W., Axelrad, S., & Herma, J. L. (1951). *Occupational choice: An approach to a general theory.* New York, NY: Columbia University Press.

Glutting, J. J., & Wilkinson, G. (2003). *Wide range interest and occupation test* (2nd ed.) *(WRIOT-2).* San Antonio, TX: Pearson Assessments.

Goldman, B. A. (2007). Test review of the Career Direction Inventory. In K. F. Geisinger, R. A. Spies, J. F. Carlson, & B. S. Plake (Eds.), *The seventeenth mental measurements yearbook* [Electronic version]. Retrieved from the Buros Institute's Mental Measurement Yearbook Online database.

Goldman, L. (1983). The Vocational Card Sort technique: A different view. *Measurement & Evaluation in Guidance, 16*, 107–109.

Goldman Sachs. (2013). *Diversity and inclusion: Returnship® program.* Retrieved May 31, 2013, from http://www.goldmansachs.com/who-we-are/diversity-and-inclusion/recruiting/returnship/index.html

Goleman, D. (1995). *Emotional intelligence.* New York, NY: Bantam Books.

Goleman, D. (1998). *Working with emotional intelligence.* New York, NY: Bantam Books.

Goodrich, K. M., & Luke, M. (2009). LGBTQ responsive school counseling. *Journal of LGBT Issues in Counseling, 3*(2), 113–127.

Gordon, V. N. (2007). *The undecided college student: An academic and career advising challenge* (3rd ed.). Springfield, IL: Charles C Thomas.

Gordon, V. N., & Steele, G. E. (2003). Undecided first-year students: A 25-year longitudinal study. *Journal of the First-Year Experience, 15*(1), 19–38.

Gore, P. A., Jr., & Hitch, J. L. (2005). Occupational classification and sources of occupational information. In S. D. Brown & R. W. Lent (Eds.), *Career development and counseling: Putting theory and research to work* (pp. 382–413). Hoboken, NJ: John Wiley & Sons.

Gottfredson, G. D. (1996). The assessment of career status with the Career Attitudes and Strategies Inventory. *Journal of Career Assessment, 4*, 363–381.

Gottfredson, G. D., & Holland, J. L. (1991). *Position Classification Inventory professional manual.* Odessa, FL: Psychological Assessment Resources.

Gottfredson, G. D., & Holland, J. L. (1996). *Dictionary of Holland occupational codes* (3rd ed.). Odessa, FL: Psychological Assessment Resources.

Gottfredson, L. S. (1981). Circumscription and compromise: A developmental theory of occupational aspirations [Monograph]. *Journal of Counseling Psychology, 28*, 545–579.

Gottfredson, L. S. (1996). Gottfredson's theory of circumscription and compromise. In D. Brown, L. Brooks, & Associates (Eds.), *Career choice and development: Applying contemporary theories to practice* (3rd ed., pp. 179–232). San Francisco, CA: Jossey-Bass.

Gottfredson, L. S. (2000). Equal potential: A collective fraud. *Society, 37*(5), 19–28.

Gottfredson, L. S. (2002). Gottfredson's theory of circumscription, compromise, and self-creation. In D. Brown & Associates (Eds.), *Career choice and development: Applying contemporary theories to practice* (4th ed., pp. 85–148). San Francisco, CA: Jossey-Bass.

Gottfredson, L. S. (2005). Implications of cognitive differences for schooling within diverse societies. In C. L. Frisby & C. R. Reynolds (Eds.), *Comprehensive handbook of multicultural school psychology* (pp. 517–554). Hoboken, NJ: John Wiley & Sons.

Gottfredson, L. S. (2010). Lessons in academic freedom as lived experience. *Personality and Individual Differences, 49*, 272–280.

Gottfredson, L. S. (2011). Intelligence and social inequality: Why the biological link? In T. Chamorro-Permuzic, S. von Stumm, & A. Furnham (Eds.), *The Wiley-Blackwell handbook of individual differences* (pp. 538–575). Sussex, England: Wiley-Blackwell.

Gough, H. G. (1995). Career assessment and the California Psychological Inventory. *Journal of Career Assessment, 3*, 101–122.

Gough, H. G., & Bradley, P. (1996). *California psychological inventory* (3rd ed.) *(CPI 434)*. Palo Alto, CA: Consulting Psychologists Press.

Graduate Management Admission Council. (2012). *Graduate Management Admission Test*. [Measurement instrument]. Chicago, IL: Pearson VUE.

Grant-Vallone, E. J., & Ensher, E. A. (2011). Opting in between: Strategies used by professional women with children to balance work and family. *Journal of Career Development, 38*, 331–348.

Grier-Reed, T. L., & Skaar, N. R. (2010). An outcome study of career decision self-efficacy and indecision in an undergraduate constructivist career course. *The Career Development Quarterly, 59*, 42–53.

Grusec, J. E. (1992). Social learning theory and developmental psychology: The legacies of Robert Sears and Albert Bandura. *Developmental Psychology, 28*, 776–786.

Guindon, M. H., & Smith, B. (2002). Emotional barriers to successful reemployment: Implications for counselors. *Journal of Employment Counseling, 39*, 73–82.

Gushue, G. V., & Whitson, M. L. (2006). The relationship among support, ethnic identity, career decision self-efficacy, and outcome expectations in African American high school students: Applying social cognitive career theory. *Journal of Career Development, 33*, 112–124.

Hackett, G., & Betz, N. E. (1981). A self-efficacy approach to the career development of women. *Journal of Vocational Behavior, 18*, 326–336.

Hackney, H. L., & Cormier, S. (2013). *The professional counselor: A process guide to helping*. Upper Saddle River, NJ: Pearson.

Hall, D. T. (1976). *Careers in organizations*. Glenview, IL: Scott, Foresman.

Hammer, A. L. (1993). *Introduction to type® and careers*. Palo Alto, CA: Consulting Psychologists Press.

Hansen, R. N., & Johnston, J. A. (1989). *Missouri Occupational Card Sort* (College Form) (2nd ed.). Columbia, MO: Career Planning and Placement Center, University of Missouri–Columbia.

Hansen, J. T. (2004). Thoughts on knowing: Epistemic implications of counseling practice. *Journal of Counseling and Development, 82*, 131–138.

Hansen, J. C. (2005). Assessment of interests. In S. D. Brown & R. W. Lent (Eds.), *Career development and counseling: Putting theory and research to work* (pp. 281–304). Hoboken, NJ: John Wiley & Sons, Inc.

Hardy, K. V., & Laszloffy, T. A. (1995). The cultural genogram: Key to training culturally competent family therapists. *Journal of Marital and Family Therapy, 21*, 227–237.

Hardy, T. A., & Harley, D. A. (2009). A place at the blackboard: Including lesbian, gay, bisexual, transgender, intersex, and queer/questioning issues in the education process. *Multicultural education, 16*(4), 2–9.

Harlow, C. W. (2003). *Bureau of Justice Statistics special report: Education and correctional populations*. Washington, DC: U.S. Department of Justice. (NCJ 195670)

Harmon, L. W. (1996). A moving target: The widening gap between theory and practice. In M. L. Savickas & W. B. Walsh (Eds.), *Handbook of career counseling: Theory and practice* (pp. 37–43). Mountain View, CA: Davies-Black Publishing.

Harrington, J. C., Harrington, T. F., & Wall, J. E. (2012). *Ability explorer* (3rd ed.). Indianapolis, IN: JIST Publishing.

Harris, P. M., & Keller, K. S. (2005). Ex-offenders need not apply: The criminal background check in hiring decisions. *Journal of Contemporary Criminal Justice, 21*, 6–30.

Harrison, A., & Scorse, J. (2006). Improving the condition of workers? Minimum wage legislation and anti-sweatshop activism. *California Management Review, 48*, 144–160.

Harrison, B., & Schehr, R. C. (2004). Offenders and post-release jobs. *Journal of Offender Rehabilitation, 39*(3), 35–68.

Hartung, P. J., Fouad, N. A., Leong, F. T. L., & Hardin, E. E. (2010). Individualism-collectivism: Links to occupational plans and work values. *Journal of Career Assessment, 18*, 34–45.

Harvard Business School. (2013). *Career development: Charting your course*. Retrieved May 31, 2013, from http://www.alumni.hbs.edu/careers/cyc.html

Haycock, K. (2010). Introduction. In C. Theokas, *Shut out of the military: Today's high school education doesn't mean you're ready for today's army* (p. 3). Washington, DC: The Education Trust.

Haynie, M. J., & Shepherd, D. (2011). Toward a theory of discontinuous career transition: Investigating career transitions necessitated by traumatic life events. *Journal of Applied Psychology, 93*, 501–524.

Hees, C. K., Rottinghaus, P. J., Briddick, W. C., & Conrath, J. A. (2012). Work-to-school transitions in the age of the displaced worker: A psychology of working perspective. *Career Development Quarterly, 60*, 333–342.

Helford, M. C., Stewart, S. M. Gruys, M. L., & Frank, R. A. (2012). Perceptions of workforce re-entry, career progression, and lost income among stay-at-home moms and stay-at-home dads. *Journal of Leadership, Management & Organizational Studies, 2*(1), 1–14. Retrieved on May 28, 2013, from http://www.scientificjournals.org/journals2012/articles/1521.pdf

Helms, J. E. (1984). Toward a theoretical explanation of the effects of race on counseling: A Black and White model. *The Counseling Psychologist, 12*, 153–165.

Helms, J. E. (1992). *A race is a nice thing to have: A guide to being a white person or understanding the white persons in your life*. Topeka, KS: Content Communications.

Hemmings, A. (2007). Seeing the light: Cultural and social capital productions in an inner-city high school. *The High School Journal, 90*(3), 9–17.

Heppner, M. J., & Fu, C. (2010). Understanding the depth and richness of the cultural context in career counseling through the cultural formulation approach (CFA). *Journal of Career Development, 37*, 487–497.

Heppner, M. J., & Fu, C. (2011). The gendered context of vocational self-construction. In P. J. Hartung, & L. M. Subich (Eds.), *Developing self in work and career: Concepts, cases, and contexts* (pp. 177–192). Washington, DC: American Psychological Association.

Herlihy, B., & Remley, Jr., T. P. (1995). Unified ethical standards: A challenge for professionalism. *Journal of Counseling and Development, 74*, 130–133.

Herman, A. M., & Abraham, K. G. (1999, June). *Revising the standard occupational classification system. Report 929*. Washington, DC: U.S. Department of Labor. Retrieved July 1, 2013, from www.bls.gov/soc/socrpt929.pdf

Herman, D. O. (1985). Test review of the Career Decision Scale. In J. V. Mitchell (Es.), *The ninth mental measurements yearbook* [Electronic version]. Retrieved from the Buros Institute's Mental Measurement Yearbook Online database.

Herr, E. L. (2013). Trends in the history of vocational guidance. *Career Development Quarterly, 61*, 277–282.

Hetherington, C. (1991). Life planning and career counseling with gay and lesbian students. In N. J. Evans & V. A. Wall (Eds.), *Beyond tolerance: Gays, lesbians and bisexuals on campus* (pp. 131–145). Alexandria, VA: American College Personnel Association.

Hill, M., Glaser, K., & Harden, J. (1995). A feminist model for ethical decision making. In E. J. Rave & C. C. Larsen (Eds.), *Ethical decision making in therapy: Feminist perspectives* (pp. 18–37). New York, NY: Guilford Press.

Hirsch, A. E., Dietrich, S. M., Landau, R., Schneider, P. D., Ackelsberg, I., Bernstein-Bakerr, J., & Hohenstein, J. (2002). *Every door closed: Barriers facing parents with criminal records*. Philadelphia, PA: Community Legal Services, Inc. Retrieved June 2, 2013, from http://www.clasp.org/admin/site/publications_archive/files/0092.pdf

Hoachlander, G., Stearns, R. J., & Studier, C. (2008). *Expanding pathways: Transforming high school education in California*. Berkeley, CA: ConnectEd: The California Center for College and Career. Retrieved from ERIC database. (ED514485)

Hobson, S. M. (1996). Test anxiety: Rain or shine! *Elementary School Guidance and Counseling, 30*, 316–318.

Hobson, S. M., & Phillips, C. A. (2004). Educational planning: Helping students build lives by choice, not by chance. In B. T. Erford (Ed.), *Professional school counseling: A handbook of theories, programs & practices* (pp. 325–339). Austin, TX: Pro-Ed.

Hochschild, A. R. (2003). *The second shift*. New York, NY: Penguin Books.

Hodges, S., & Connelly, A. R. (2010). *A job search manual for counselors and counselor educators: How to navigate and promote your counseling career*. Alexandria, VA: American Counseling Association.

Hoff, K. S., Kroll, J., MacKinnon, F. J. D., & Rentz, A. L. (2004). Career services. In F. J. D. MacKinnon & Associates (Eds.), *Rentz's student affairs practice in higher education* (3rd ed., pp. 108–143). Springfield, IL: Charles C Thomas.

Holland, J. L. (1959). A theory of vocational choice. *Journal of Counseling Psychology, 6*, 35–45.

Holland, J. L. (1985). *Manual for the Vocational Preference Inventory*. Odessa, FL: Psychological Assessment Resources.

Holland, J. L. (1985). *Vocational preference inventory*. Odessa, FL: Psychological Assessment Resources.

Holland, J. L. (1994). *The Self-Directed Search technical manual* (4th ed.). Odessa, FL: Psychological Assessment Resources.

Holland, J. L. (1997). *Making vocational choices: A theory of vocational personalities and work environments* (3rd ed.). Lutz, FL: Psychological Assessment Resources.

Holland, J. L., & Associates. (1980). *Counselor's guide to the Vocational Exploration and Insight Kit (VEIK)*. Palo Alto, CA: Consulting Psychologists Press.

Holland, J. L., Daiger, D. C., & Power, P. G. (1980a). *My vocational situation*. Palo Alto, CA: Consulting Psychologists Press.

Holland, J. L., Daiger, D. C., & Power, P. G. (1980b). Some diagnostic scales for research in decision-making and personality: Identify, information and barriers. *Journal of Personality and Social Psychology, 39*, 1191–1200.

Holland, J. L., Fritzche, B. A., & Powell, A. B. (1994). *The Self-Directed Search technical manual*. Odessa, FL: Psychological Assessment Resources.

Holland, J. L., & Gottfredson, G. D. (1994). Test review of the Career Attitudes and Strategies Inventory. In J. C. Impara & B. S. Plake (Eds), *The thirteenth mental measurements yearbook* [Electronic version]. Retrieved from the Buros Institute's Mental Measurement Yearbook Online Database.

Holland, J. L., Johnston, J. A., & Asama, N. F. (1993). The Vocational Identity Scale: A diagnostic and treatment tool. *Journal of Career Assessment, 1*, 1–12.

Holland, J. L., & Powell, A. B. (1994). *Self-directed search career explorer*. Odessa, FL: Psychological Assessment Resources.

Holland, J. L., Powell, A. B., & Fritzche, B. A. (1997). *Self-directed search* (4th ed.). Odessa, FL: Psychological Assessment Resources.

Holland, K. (2013, March 30). Job-hunting toolkit for older workers. *CNBC News*. Retrieved August 20, 2013, from http://www.cnbc.com/id/100578929

Holzer, H. J., Raphael, S., & Stoll, M. A. (2003, May). *Employment barriers facing ex-offenders*. Paper presented at the Urban Institute Reentry Roundtable on Employment Dimensions of Reentry: Understanding the Nexus between Prisoner Reentry and Work, New York University Law School, New York.

Hopkins, G. (2010). *Hands-on career ed: Groundhog job shadow day*. Retrieved February 13, 2015, from http://www.educationworld.com/a_curr/curr050.shtml

Hopson, B., & Adams, J. D. (1977). Toward an understanding of transitions: Defining some boundaries of transition. In J. Adams, J. Hayes, & B. Hopson (Eds.), *Transition: Understanding and managing personal change* (pp. 1–19). Montclair, NJ: Allenheld & Osmun.

Hossler, D. (1984). *Enrollment management: An integrated approach*. New York, NY: College Board Publications.

Hossler, D., & Gallagher, L. (1987). Studying college choice: A three-phase model and the implications for policy makers. *College and University, 2*, 201–221.

Hossler, D., Schmit, J., & Vesper, N. (1999). *Going to college: How social, economic, and educational factors influence the decisions students make*. Baltimore, MD: Johns Hopkins University Press.

Howell, L. (2006). *Give your elevator speech a lift!* Bothell, WA: Book Publishers Network.

Hughes, E. (2006). Its time has come for you and your schools. *Techniques: Connecting Education and Careers, 81*(7), 35–39.

Human Rights Campaign. (2014). *Employment non-discrimination laws on sexual orientation and gender identity*. Retrieved July 14, 2014, from http://www.hrc.org/resources/entry/employment-non-discrimination-act.

Huyser, K. R., Sakamoto, A., & Takei, I. (2010). The persistence of racial disadvantage: The socioeconomic attainments of single-race and multi-race Native Americans. *Population Research and Policy Review, 29*, 541–568.

Imagine America Foundation. (2008). *Filling America's skilled worker shortage: The role of career colleges*. Boston, MA: Eduventures, Inc.

Industrial Psychology International Ltd. (1998). Test review of the Workplace Skills Inventory. In K. F. Geisinger, R. A. Spies, J. F. Carlson, & B. S. Plake (Eds), *The seventeenth mental measurements yearbook* [Electronic version]. Retrieved from the Buros Institute's Mental Measurement Yearbook Online Database.

Isaacson, L. E. (1985). *Basics of career counseling*. Boston, MA: Allyn & Bacon.

Ivey, A. E., Ivey, M. B., & Zalaquett, C. P. with Quirk, K. (2012). *Essentials of intentional interviewing: Counseling in a multicultural world* (2nd ed.). Belmont, CA: Brooks/Cole.

Jackson, D. N. (1994). *Jackson personality inventory—Revised (JPI-R)*. Port Huron, MI: Sigma Assessment Systems.

Jackson, D. N. (1999). *Jackson vocational interest survey (JVIS)*. Port Huron, MI: Sigma Assessment Systems.

Jackson, D. N. (2003). *Career Directions inventory*. Port Huron, MI: Sigma Assessment Systems.

Jackson, D. N., & Marshall, C. W. (1997). *Ashland interest assessment*. Port Huron, MI: Sigma Assessment Systems.

Jacobs, S. J., & Blustein, D. L. (2008). Mindfulness as a coping mechanism for employment uncertainty. *Career Development Quarterly, 57*, 174–180.

Jarvis, P. S. (2004). Educators use career "games" to teach lifelong career management skills. *Techniques, 79*(1), 34–36, 48.

Jenkins, J. A. (2005). Test review of the World of Work Inventory. In R. A. Spies & B. S. Plake (Eds.), *The sixteenth mental measurements yearbook* [Electronic version]. Retrieved from the Buros Institute's Mental Measurement Yearbook Online Database.

Job Accommodation Network. (2012). *Workplace accommodations: Low cost, high impact*. Morgantown, WV: Job Accommodation Network. Retrieved May 17, 2013, from http://askjan.org/media/downloads/LowCostHighImpact.pdf

Johansson, C. B. (1993). *Interest, determination, exploration, and assessment system (IDEAS)*. San Antonio, TX: Pearson Assessments.

Johansson, C. B. (2003a). *Career assessment inventory—The enhanced version (CAI)*. San Antonio, TX: Pearson Assessments.

Johansson, C. B. (2003b). *Career assessment inventory—The vocational version*. San Antonio, TX: Pearson Assessments.

Johnson, J., Rochkind, J., Ott, A., & DuPont, S. (2010). *Can I get a little advice here? How an overstretched high school guidance system is undermining students' college aspirations*. New York, NY: Public Agenda.

Jones, L. K. (1979). *The vocational counseling effects of the Occu-Sort on junior and senior high school students*. Raleigh, NC: North Carolina State University. (ERIC Document Reproductions Service No. ED189485)

Jones, L. K., & DeVault, R. M. (1979). Evaluation of a self-guided career exploration system: The Occu-Sort. *The School Counselor, 26*, 334–341.

Jung, C. G. (1923). *Psychological types; or, the psychology of individuation*. Princeton, NJ: Princeton University Press.

Juntunen, C. L., & Cline, K. (2010). Culture and self in career development: Working with American Indians. *Journal of Career Development, 37*, 391–410.

Kakiuchi, K. K. S., & Weeks, G. R. (2009). The occupational transmission genogram: Exploring family scripts affecting roles of work and career in couple and family dynamics. *Journal of Family Psychotherapy, 20*, 1–12.

Kanter, R. M. (1977). *Men and women of the corporation*. New York, NY: Basic Books.

Karlsen, B., & Gardner, E. F. (1986). *Adult basic learning examination* (ABLE, 2nd ed.). San Antonio, TX: Pearson Assessments.

Katz, J. (1985). The sociopolitical nature of counseling. *The Counseling Psychologist, 13*, 615–624.

Keim, M. C., & Strickland, J. M. (2004). Support services for two-year college student-athletes. *College Student Journal, 38*(1), 36–43.

Kelly, G. D. (1990). The cultural family of origin: A description of a training strategy. *Counselor Education and Supervision, 30*, 77–84.

Kerka, S. (2000). Middle school career education and development: Practice application brief no. 9, Eric Clearinghouse on Adult, Career, and Vocational Education. (ED 442 992)

Kern, C. W. (1995). Career decision-making course: Helping the undecided student. *College Student Affairs Journal, 14*(2), 75–82.

Kim, B. S. K. (2011). *Counseling & diversity: Counseling Asian Americans*. Belmont, CA: Brooks/Cole.

Kim, B. S. K., Li, L. C., & Liang, C. T. H. (2002). Effects of Asian American client adherence to Asian cultural values, session goal, and counselor emphasis of client expression on career counseling process. *Journal of Counseling Psychology, 49*, 342–354.

Kim, J., Ingersoll-Dayton, B., & Kwak, M. (2013). Balancing eldercare and employment: The role of work interruptions and supportive employers. *Journal of Applied Gerontology, 32*, 347–369.

King, N. J., & Madsen, E. (2007). Contextual influences on the career development of low-income African American youth. *Journal of Career Development, 33*, 395–411.

Kirby, K. M. (2002). Gay, lesbian, and bisexual employee issues in the workplace. In D. S. Sandhu (Ed.), *Counseling employees: A multifaceted approach* (pp. 169–184). Alexandria, VA: American Counseling Association.

Kitchener, K. S. (1984). Intuition, critical evaluation, and ethical principles: The foundation for ethical decisions in counseling psychology. *Counseling Psychologist, 12*, 43–55.

Klein-Collins, R. (2012). *New approaches for supporting the mature worker: The experiences of the U.S. Department of Labor's Aging Workforce Initiative grantees*. Chicago, IL: Council for Adult and Experiential Learning.

Knowdell, R. L. (2014). *Knowdell card sorts: Occupational Interests*. San Jose, CA: Career Research & Testing.

Kobylarz, L. (2004). *National career development guidelines: K–adult handbook*. Stillwater, OK: National Occupational Coordinating Committee Training and Support Center. Retrieved from http://associationdatabase.com/aws/NCDA/asset_manager/get_file/3384/ncdguidelines2007.pdf

Kochhar, R., Fry, R., & Taylor, P. (2011). *Twenty-to-one: Wealth gaps rise to record highs between Whites, Blacks and Hispanics*. Washington, DC: Pew Research Center.

Kolodinsky, P., Schroder, V., Montopoli, G., McLean, S., Mangan, P. A., & Pedersen, W. (2006). The career fair as a vehicle for enhancing occupational self-efficacy. *Professional School Counseling, 10*, 161–167.

Kolowich, S. (2009, February 13). Career centers see more students and fewer recruiters in tight job market. *The Chronicle of Higher Education*. Retrieved from http://www.chronicle.com

Kosine, N. R. (2007). Preparing students with learning disabilities for postsecondary education: What the research literature tells us about transition programs. *Journal of Special Education Leadership, 20*(2), 93–104.

Krannich, R., & Krannich, C. (2005). *The ex-offenders job hunting guide: 10 steps to a new life in the work world*. Manassas Park, VA: Impact Publishing.

Krieshok, T. S., Hastings, S., Ebberwein, C., Wettersten, K., & Owen, A. (1999). Telling a good story: Vocational rehabilitation with veterans. *The Career Development Quarterly, 47*, 204–214.

Krumboltz, J. D. (1979). A social learning theory of career decision making. In A. M. Mitchell, G. B. Jones, & J. D. Krumboltz (Eds.), *Social learning and career decision making* (pp. 19–49). Cranston, RI: Carroll Press.

Krumboltz, J. D. (1988). *Career beliefs inventory*. Palo Alto, CA: Consulting Psychologists Press.

Krumboltz, J. D. (1991). *Manual for the Career Beliefs Inventory*. Palo Alto, CA: Consulting Psychologists Press.

Krumboltz, J. D. (1994). The *Career Beliefs Inventory*. *Journal of Counseling and Development, 72*, 424–428.

Krumboltz, J. D. (1996). A learning theory of career counseling. In M. L. Savickas & W. B. Walsh (Eds.), *Handbook of career counseling theory and practice* (pp. 55–80). Palo Alto, CA: Consulting Psychologists Press.

Krumboltz, J. D. (1998). Serendipity is not serendipitous. *Journal of Counseling Psychology, 45*, 390–392.

Krumboltz, J. D. (2009a). *Career beliefs inventory (CBI)*. Palo Alto, CA: Consulting Psychologists Press.

Krumboltz, J. D. (2009b). The happenstance learning theory. *Journal of Career Assessment, 17*, 135–154.

Krumboltz, J. D., & Levin, A. S. (2004). *Luck is no accident: Making the most of happenstance in your life and career*. Atascadero, CA: Impact.

Krumboltz, J. D., Mitchell, A. M., & Jones, G. B. (1976). A social learning theory of career selection. *The Counseling Psychologist, 6*, 71–81.

Krumboltz, J. D., & Vidilakas, N. K. (2000). Expanding learning opportunities using career assessments. *Journal of Career Assessment, 8*, 315–327.

Kübler-Ross, E. (1969). *On death and dying*. New York, NY: Macmillan.

Kuder, Inc. (2012a). *Kuder career interests assessment (KCIA)*. Adel, IA: Author.

Kuder, Inc. (2012b). *Kuder skills confidence assessment (KSCA)*. Adel, IA: Author.

Kuder, Inc. (2012c). *Kuder skills confidence assessment–Adult (KSCA-A)*. Adel, IA: Author.

Kuder, Inc. (2012d). *Kuder work values assessment (KCIA)*. Adel, IA: Author.

Kuder, Inc. (2012e). *Kuder interest and skills confidence composite report*. Adel, IA: Author.

Kuder. (2013). *Kuder career planning system: Kuder journey*. Retrieved July 16, 2013, from http://www.kuder.com/product/kuder-career-planning-system/kuder-journey/

Kursmark, L. (2002). Writing effective résumés. *Career Planning and Adult Development Journal, 17*(4), 8–19.

Kursmark, L. (2013, April 25). *Resumes today: Best practices & current trends to create distinctive, competitive, effective documents for your clients*. Farmington Hills, MI: Michigan Career Development Association Professional Development Workshop.

Kurtz, A. (2013, January 4). Forget discouraged, 3 million workers hopelessly unemployed. *CNN Money*. Retrieved from http://money.cnn.com

Kyle, T. (2010, September 18). FDNY makes push for gay applicants amid discrimination claims. *DNAinfo.com New York*. Retrieved November 18, 2013, from dnainfo.com/new-york/20100918/manhattan/its-accused-of-discrimination-but-fdny-wants-gay-applicants

Laker, D., & Laker, R. (2007). The five-year resume: A career planning exercise. *Journal of Management Education, 31*, 128–141.

Lally, P. S., & Kerr, G. A. (2005). The career planning, athletic identity, and student role identity of intercollegiate student athletes. *Research Quarterly for Exercise and Sport, 76*, 275–285.

Lambie, G. W. (2006). Burnout prevention: A humanistic perspective and structured group supervision activity. *Journal of Humanistic Counseling, 45*, 32–44.

Latack, J. C., & Dozier, J. B. (1986). After the ax falls: Job loss as a career transition. *Academy of Management Review, 11*, 375–392.

Laux, J. M., Calmes, S., Moe, J. L., Dupuy, P. J., Cox, J. A., Ventura, L. A., Williamson, C., Benjamin, B. J., & Lambert, E. (2011). The career counseling needs of mothers in the criminal justice system. *Journal of Offender Rehabilitation, 50*, 159–173.

Law School Admission Council, Inc. (2012). *Law School Admission Test (LSAT)* [Measurement instrument]. Newtown, PA: Author.

Leach, M. M., Stoltenberg, C. D., Eichenfield, G. A., & McNeill, B. W. (1997). Self-efficacy and counselor development: Testing the integrated developmental model. *Counselor Education and Supervision, 37*, 115–124.

Leahy, M. J., Rak, E., & Zanskas, S. A. (2009). A brief history of counseling and specialty areas of practice. In I. Marini & M. A. Stebnecki (Eds.), *The professional counselor's desk reference* (pp. 3–13). New York, NY: Springer Publishing Company.

Lehker, T., & Furlong, J. S. (2006). Career services for graduate and professional students. *New Directions for Student Services, 115*, 73–83.

Lent, R. W. (2005). A social cognitive view of career development and counseling. In S. D. Brown & R. W. Lent (Eds.), *Career development and counseling: Putting theory and research to work* (pp. 101–127). Hoboken, NJ: John Wiley & Sons, Inc.

Lent, R. W., & Brown, S. D. (1996a). Applying social cognitive theory to career counseling: An introduction. *Career Development Quarterly, 44,* 307–309.

Lent, R. W., & Brown, S. D. (1996b). Social cognitive approach to career development: An overview. *Career Development Quarterly, 44,* 310–321.

Lent, R. W., & Brown, S. D. (2002). Social cognitive career theory and adult career development. In S. G. Niles (Ed.), *Adult career development: Concepts, issues, and practices* (3rd ed., pp. 77–97). Tulsa, OK: National Career Development Association.

Lent, R. W., Brown, S. D., & Hackett, G. (1994). Toward a unifying social cognitive theory of career and academic interest, choice, and performance [Monograph]. *Journal of Vocational Behavior, 45,* 79–122.

Lent, R. W., Brown, S. D., & Hackett, G. (1996). Career development from a social cognitive perspective. In D. Brown, L. Brooks, and Associates, *Career choice and development* (3rd ed., pp. 373–421). San Francisco, CA: Jossey-Bass.

Lent, R. W., Brown, S. D., & Hackett, G. (2000). Contextual supports and barriers to career choice: A social cognitive analysis. *Journal of Counseling Psychology, 47,* 36–49.

Lent, R. W., Brown, S. D., & Hackett, G. (2002). Social cognitive career theory. In D. Brown & Associates, *Career choice and development* (4th ed., pp. 255–311). San Francisco, CA: Jossey-Bass.

Lenz, J. G., & Shy, J. D. (2003). Career services and athletics: Collaborating to meet the needs of student-athletes. *NACE Journal, 63*(3), 36–40.

Leong, F. T. L. (2010). A cultural formulation approach to career assessment and career counseling: Guest editor's introduction. *Journal of Career Development, 37,* 375–390.

Leong, F. T. L. (2011). Cultural accommodation model of counseling. *Journal of Employment Counseling, 48,* 150–152.

Leong, F. T. L., Hardin, E. E., & Gupta, A. (2010). A cultural formulation approach to career assessment and career counseling with Asian American clients. *Journal of Career Development, 37,* 465–486.

Lester, J. (1999, January). *Guidelines for career development: Programs and services in the United States.* Paper presented at the Turning Points: Managing Career Change International Conference, Wellington, New Zealand. Retrieved from ERIC database. (ED445287)

Lester, J. N., Woods, J., & Carlson, B. L. (2013). The NOICC/SOICC network: Policy, programs, and partners, 1976–2000. *The Career Development Quarterly, 61,* 186–192.

Levitt, J. G., & Harwood, L. (2010). *Your career: How to make it happen.* Mason, OH: South-Western Cengage Learning.

Lewis, T., & Cheng, S.-Y. (2006). Tracking, expectations, and the transformation of vocational education. *American Journal of Education, 113,* 67–101.

Lichtenberger, E. (2012). Offender workforce development specialists and their impact on the post-release outcomes of ex-offenders. *Federal Probation, 76*(3), 31–36.

Lighthall, A. (2012). Ten things you should know about today's student veteran. *Thought & Action, 28,* 81–90.

Lindgren, A. (1995). *Cracking the hidden job market. Pocket Job Series No. 3.* St. Paul, MN: Prototype Career Press.

Linnemey, R. M., & Brown, C. (2010). Career maturity and foreclosure in student athletes, fine arts students, and general college students. *Journal of Career Development, 37,* 616–634.

Lipka, S. (2008, May 16). In tight employment market, career services gain clout. *The Chronicle of Higher Education.* Retrieved from http://www.chronicle.com

Liptak, J. J. (2009). *Job survival and success scale* (2nd ed.). Indianapolis, IN: JIST Publishing.

Liptak, J. J. (2011). *Barriers to success inventory.* Indianapolis, IN: JIST Publishing.

Liptak, J. (2012). *Transition-to-work inventory* (3rd ed.) (TWI-3) [Measurement instrument]. St. Paul, MN: JIST Publishing.

Livneh, H., & Cook, D. (2005). Psychosocial impact of disability. In R. M. Parker, E. M. Szymanski, & J. B. Patterson, *Rehabilitation counseling: Basics and beyond* (4th ed., pp. 187–224). Austin, TX: ProEd.

Lock, R. D. (2005). *Taking charge of your career direction: Career Planning Guide, Book 1* (5th ed.). Belmont, CA: Brooks/Cole.

Locke, W. S., & Gibbon, M. M. (2008). On her own again: The use of narrative therapy in career counseling with displaced new traditionalists. *The Family Journal: Counseling and Therapy for Couples and Families, 16,* 132–138.

Lofquist, L. H., & Dawis, R. V. (1991). *Essentials of person-environment-correspondence counseling.* Minneapolis, MN: University of Minnesota Press.

Lopez, S. J., & Tree, H. A. (2009). Test review of the Clifton StrengthsFinder. In E. A. Whitfield, R. W. Feller, & C. Wood (Eds.), *A counselor's guide to career assessment instruments* (pp. 390–394). Broken Arrow, OK: National Career Development Association.

Lorenz, K. (2009). *Warning: Social networking can be hazardous to your job search.* Career Builder.com. Retrieved February 14, 2015, from http://www.careerbuilder.com/Article/CB-533-Job-Search-Warning-Social-Networking-Can-Be-Hazardous-to-Your-Job-Search/

Lozada, M. (2001). Job shadowing: Career exploration at work. *Techniques: Connecting Education and Careers, 76*(8), 30–33.

Ludwikowski, W. M. A., Vogel, D., & Armstrong, P. A. (2009). Attitudes toward career counseling: The role of public and self-stigma. *Journal of Counseling Psychology, 56,* 408–416.

Lumsden, J. A. (2007). Development and implementation of an e-portfolio as a university-wide program. *New Directions for Student Services, 119,* 43–63.

Lunneborg, P. W. (1985). Test review of My Vocational Situation. From J. V. Mitchell (Ed.), *The ninth mental measurements yearbook* [Electronic version]. Retrieved from the Buros Institute's Mental Measurement Yearbook Online database.

Luthans, F., Luthans, K. W., & Luthans, B. C. (2004). Positive psychological capital: Beyond human and social capital. *Business Horizons, 47,* 45–50.

Luzzo, D. A. (2000). Career development of returning-adult and graduate students. In D. A. Luzzo (Ed.), *Career counseling of college students: An empirical guide to strategies that work* (pp. 191–200). Washington, DC: American Psychological Association.

Maddux, C. D. (2007). Test review of the Career Direction Inventory. In K. F. Geisinger, R. A. Spies, J. F. Carlson, & B. S. Plake (Eds.), *The seventeenth mental measurements yearbook* [Electronic version]. Retrieved from the Buros Institute's Mental Measurement Yearbook Online database.

Magnuson, C. S., & Starr, M. F. (2000). How early is too early to begin life career planning? The importance of the elementary school years. *Journal of Career Development, 27,* 89–101.

Magnuson, S., & Shaw, H. E. (2003). Adaptations of the multi-faceted genogram in counseling, training, and supervison. *The Family Journal: Counseling and Therapy for Couples and Families, 11,* 45–54.

Malott, K. M., & Magnuson, S. (2004). Using genograms to facilitate undergraduate students' career development: A group model. *Career Development Quarterly, 53,* 178–186.

Mandel, S. (2013). *The elevator pitch (EP): Engage people, move to action . . . in two minutes.* Retrieved August 6, 2013, from http://entrepreneurship.wfu.edu/old/newsletter/the-elevator-pitch.html

Marcus, E. (2005). *Is it a choice? Answers to the most frequently asked questions about gay & lesbian people* (3rd ed.). San Francisco, CA: Harper & Row.

Mariani, M. J. (1998). Job shadowing: Career sampling for students. *Occupational Outlook Quarterly, 42*(2), 42–49.

Martin, C. (2012). *Boost your interview IQ* (2nd ed.). New York, NY: McGraw-Hill.

Martin, C. (2013). *6 ways your online reputation could keep you from landing your dream job.* Retrieved August 9, 2013, from http://comerecommended.com/2013/01/6-ways-your-online-reputation-could-keep-you-from-landing-your-dream-job/

Martinez-Moncada, D. (2012). *How to brand yourself* [Infographic]. Retrieved August 10, 2013, from http://dailyinfographic.com/how-to-brand-yourself-infographic

Maslach, C., Jackson, S. E., Leiter, P. M., & Schaufeli, W. B. (1996). *Maslach burnout inventory* (3rd ed.). Palo Alto, CA: Consulting Psychologists Press.

Mastrangelo, P. M. (2001). Test review of the Myers-Briggs Type Indicator, Form M. In B. Plake & J. C. Impara (Eds.), *The foureenth mental measurements yearbook* [Electronic version]. Retrieved from the Buros Institute's Mental Measurement Yearbook Online database.

Mathison, D., & Finney, M. I. (2010). *Unlocking the hidden job market: 6 steps to a successful job search when times are tough.* Upper Saddle River, NJ: Pearson Education.

Mau, W. J. (2004). Cultural dimensions of career decision-making difficulties. *Career Development Quarterly, 53,* 67–77.

McAllister, S., & Ponterotto, J. G. (1992). A group career program for displaced homemakers. *Journal for Specialists in Group Work, 17,* 29–36.

McBain, L., Kim, Y. M., Cook, B. J., & Snead, K. M. (2012). *From soldier to student II: Assessing campus programs for veterans and service members.* Washington, DC: American Council on Education.

McCarn, S. R., & Fassinger, R. E. (1996). Revisioning sexual minority identity formation: A new model of lesbian identity and its implications for counseling and research. *The Counseling Psychologist, 24,* 508–534.

McCarney, S. B. (1989). *Transition Behavior Scale IEP and intervention manual.* Columbia, MO: Hawthorne Educational Services.

McCarney, S. B., & Arthaud, P. D. (2012). *The transition behavior scale* (3d ed.). Columbia, MO: Hawthorne Educational Services.

McCarthy, J., & Cluss, P. A. (2002). Motivational interviewing in the workplace. In D. S. Sandhu (Ed.), *Counseling employees: A multifaceted Approach* (pp. 65–81). Alexandria, VA: American Counseling Association.

McCormac, M. E. (1989). Information sources and resources. *Journal of Career Development, 16,* 129–138.

McCowan, R. J., & McCowan, S. C. (2001). Test review of the Ashland Interest Assessment. In B. Plake & J. C. Impara (Eds.), *The fourteenth mental measurements yearbook* [Electronic version]. Retrieved from the Buros Institute's Mental Measurement Yearbook Online database.

McCrae, R. R., & Costa, P. T., Jr., (1991). The NEO Personality Inventory: Using the five-factor model in counseling. *Journal of Counseling and Development, 69,* 367–372.

McEachern, A. G., & Kenny, M. C. (2007). Transition groups for high school students with disabilities. *The Journal for Specialists in Group Work, 32,* 165–77.

McIlveen, P., & Pensiero, D. (2008). Transition of graduates from backpack-to-briefcase: A case study. *Education & Training, 50,* 489–499.

McKee-Ryan, F. M., Song, Z., Wanberg, C. R., & Kinicki, A. J. (2005). Psychological and physical well-being during unemployment: A meta-analytic study. *Journal of Applied Psychology, 90*, 53–76.

Meeder, H. (2008). *The Perkins Act of 2006: Connecting career and technical education with the college and career readiness agenda. January 2008 Policy Brief*. Washington, DC: Achieve, Inc.

Michael, W. B. (2005). Test review of the Woodcock-Johnson III. In B. Plake, J. C. Impara, & R. Spies (Eds.), *The sixteenth mental measurements yearbook* [Electronic version]. Retrieved from the Buros Institute's Mental Measurement Yearbook Online database.

Miller, M. J., & Kerlow-Myers, A. E. (2009). A content analysis of acculturation research in the career development literature. *Journal of Career Development, 35*, 352–384.

Miller, R. J. (1992). Test review of the Woodcock-Johnson III. In J. J. Kramer & J. C. Conoley (Eds.), *The eleventh mental measurements yearbook* [Electronic version]. Retrieved from the Buros Institute's Mental Measurement Yearbook Online database.

Miller, W. R., C'de Baca, J., Matthews, D. B., & Wilbourne, P. L. (2001). *Personal values card sort*. Albuquerque, NM: University of New Mexico.

Milsom, A., & Hartley, M. T. (2005). Assisting students with learning disabilities transitioning to college: What school counselors should know. *Professional School Counseling, 8*, 436–441.

Minnesota Department of Employment and Economic Development. (2014). *Creative job search* (13th ed.). Saint Paul, MN: Author.

Mitchell, L. K., & Krumboltz, J. D. (1996). Krumboltz's learning theory of career choice and counseling. In D. Brown, L. Brooks, & Associates (Eds.), *Career choice and development* (3rd ed., pp. 233–280). San Francisco, CA: Jossey-Bass.

Mitchell, K. E., Levin, A. S., & Krumboltz, J. D. (1999). Planned happenstance: Constructing unexpected career opportunities. *Journal of Counseling and Development, 77*, 115–124.

Mitchell, L. K., & Krumboltz, J. D. (1996). Krumboltz's learning theory of career choice and counseling. In D. Brown, L. Brooks, & Associates (Eds.), *Career choice and development* (3rd ed., pp. 233–280). San Francisco, CA: Jossey-Bass.

Moon, S. M., Coleman, V. D., McCollum, E. E., Nelson, T. S., & Jenson-Scott, R. L. (1993). Using the genogram to facilitate career decisions: A case study. *Journal of Family Psychotherapy, 4*, 45–56.

Moore, E. J., Gysbers, N. C., & Carlson, P. (1980). *Missouri Occupational Preference Inventory*. Columbia, MO: Human Systems Consultants, Inc.

Moore, T. (2010). The entrepreneur fair: Fifth grade student businesses. *Social Studies and the Young Learner, 22*(3), 8–13.

Murphey, C. M., & Shillingford, M. A. (2012). Supporting unemployed, middle-aged men: A psychoeducational group approach. *Journal of Employment Counseling, 49*, 85–96.

Murphy, E., & Meisgeier, C. (2008). *MMTIC Manual: A guide to the development and use of the Murphy-Meisgeier Type Indicator for Children*. Gainesville, FL: Center for Applications of Psychological Type.

Myers, L. J., Speight, S. L., Highlen, P. S., Cox, C. I., Reynolds, A. R., Adams, E. M., & Hanley, C. P. (1991). Identity development and worldview: Toward an optimal conceptualization. *Journal of Counseling and Development, 70*, 54–63.

Nally, J. M., Lockwood, S. R., & Ho, T. (2011). Employment of ex-offenders during the recession. *The Journal of Correctional Education, 62*(2), 47–61.

National Association for College Admission Counseling. (2008). *Fundamentals of college admission counseling for graduate students and practicing counselors* (2nd ed.). Dubuque, IA: Kendall Hunt Publishing.

National Association of State Directors and Career Technical Education Consortium. (n.d.). *Authorized user's guide for the Career ClustersTM brand*. Retrieved July 1, 2013, from http://www.careertech.org/career-clusters/ccresources/users-guide.html

National Association of State Directors and Career Technical Education Consortium. (2013). *Career Clusters® & pathways*. Retrieved July 12, 2013, from http://www.careertech.org/career-clusters/glance/clusters-occupations.html

National Association of State Directors of Career and Technical Education Consortium & Association for Career and Technical Education. (2009). *CTE: Education for a strong economy*. Retrieved from https://www.acteonline.org/WorkArea/DownloadAsset.aspx?id=1908

National Association of Women Lawyers. (2013). *On-ramp programs*. Retrieved May 31, 2013, from http://www.nawl.org/content.asp?pl=311&sl=337&contentid=337

National Board for Certified Counselors. (2005). *NBCC code of ethics*. Greensboro, NC: Author.

National Career Development Association. (n.d.). *Guidelines for the preparation and evaluation of career and occupational information literature*. Broken Arrow, OK: Author. Retrieved on June 22, 2013, from http://ncda.org/aws/NCDA/pt/fli/4729/false

National Career Development Association. (1992). Guidelines for the preparation and evaluation of video career media. Retrieved from http://associationdatabasecom/aws/NCDA/asset_manager/get_file/3401/guidelinesforvideoevalation.pdf

National Career Development Association. (2000). Guidelines for the preparation and evaluation of career and occupational information literature. Retrieved from http://associationdatabasecom/aws/NCDA/asset_manager/get_file/3399/guidelines_for_the_preparation_and_evaluation_of_career_and_occupational_information_literature_.pdf

National Career Development Association. (2007) (p. 1) (p. 5); C.2.f. Continuing Education (p. 16); I.1.a. Knowledge (p. 45). *Code of ethics.* Broken Arrow, OK: Author Copyright © 2007 by National Career Development Association. Reprinted by permission.

National Career Development Association Code of Ethics (2007), Standard C.5., (p. 15). Copyright © 2008 by National Career Development Association. Reprinted by permission.

National Career Development Association (2007) (p. 4) (p. 7) (p. 10) (p. 16) (p. 18) (p. 32) (p. 33) (p. 46); C.5. Nondiscrimination (p. 18); C.2.a. Boundaries of Competence (p. 15). Copyright © 2007 by National Career Development Association. Reprinted by permission.

National Career Development Association. (2009). *Minumum competencies for multicultural career counseling and development.* Broken Arrow, OK: Author.

National Career Development Association. (2011). *Career development policy statement.* Broken Arrow, OK: Author. Retrieved February 1, 2015, from http://www.ncda.org/aws/NCDA/pt/fli/4728/false

National Career Development Association. (2014)(para 9). *Membership categories: Special designations.* Retrieved July 15, 2014, from http://associationdatabase.com/aws/NCDA/pt/sp/membership_categories_special. Copyright © 2008 by National Career Development Association. Reprinted by permission.

National Center for O*NET Development. (1999). *Stratifying occupational units by specific vocational preparation (SVP).* Raleigh, NC: Author. Retrieved July 13, 2013, from http://www.onetcenter.org/reports/SVP.html

National Center for O*NET Development. (2008). *Procedures for O*NET job zone assignment.* Raleigh, NC: Author. Retrieved July 13, 2013, from http://www.onetcenter.org/reports/JobZoneProcedure.html

National Center for Veterans Analysis and Statistics. (2010). *Unemployment rates of veterans: 2000–2009.* Washington, DC: United States Department of Veterans Affairs. Retrieved May 23, 2013, from http://www.va.gov/vetdata/docs/SpecialReports/Unemployment_Rates_FINAL.pdf

National Collegiate Athletic Association. (2013). *Estimated probability of competing in athletics the beyond high school interscholastic level.* Retrieved February 13, 2015, from http://www.ncaa.org/about/resources/research/probability-competing-beyond-high-school

National Institutes of Health. (2014). LifeWorks® career finder. Retrieved July 31, 2014, from http://www.science.education.nih.gov/Lifeworks.nsf/CareerFinder.htm

National Occupational Information Coordinating Committee. (1992). *The national career development guidelines project.* Washington, DC: Government Printing Office.

National Postsecondary Education Cooperative. (2007). *Deciding on Postsecondary Education: Final Report* (NPEC 2008–850), prepared by Keith MacAllum, Denise M. Glover, Barbara Queen, and Angela Riggs. Washington, DC: Author.

Nevill, D. D., & Super, D. E. (1986). *Manual for the Salience Inventory.* Palo Alto, CA: Consulting Psychologists Press.

Newseditor. (2011, February 2). Report calls for national effort to get millions of young Americans onto a realistic path to employability. *Harvard Graduate School of Education News & Impact.* Retrieved from http://www.gse.harvard.edu/news-impact

New York State Department of Labor. (2014). *Hours of work.* Retrieved July 14, 2014, from http://www.labor.ny.gov/workerprotection/laborstandards/workprot/hrswork.shtm

Nicholson, N. (1984). A theory of work role transitions. *Administrative Science Quarterly, 29,* 172–191.

Nielson, T. R. (2008). *Career trek.* Upper Saddle River, NJ: Pearson Education.

Nietupski, J., Warth, J., Winslow, A., Johnson, R., & Douglas, B. (2006). Iowa's high school super senior school-to-work transition program. *Journal for Vocational Special Needs Education, 29*(1), 17–29.

Niles, S. G., & Harris-Bowlsbey, J. (2009). *Career development interventions in the 21st century.* Upper Saddle River, NJ: Pearson Education, Inc.

North, A. B., & Worth, W. E. (2004). Trends in selected entry-level technology, interpersonal, and basic communication SCANS skills: 1992–2002. *Journal of Employment Counseling, 41,* 60–70.

Oakes, J., & Saunders, M. (Eds.). (2008). *Beyond tracking: Multiple pathways to college, career, and civic participation.* Cambridge, MA: Harvard Education Press.

O'Brien, K. M. (2001). The legacy of Parsons: Career counselors and vocational psychologists as agents of social change. *Career Development Quarterly, 50,* 66–76.

Occupational Safety and Health Administration. (2006). *All about OSHA.* Washington, DC: U.S. Department of Labor.

O'Connor, P. (2006). How community colleges can help your students. In *Fundamentals of college counseling* (pp. 154–161). Alexandria, VA: National Association for College Admission Counseling.

Okiishi, R. W. (1987). The genogram as a tool in career counseling. *Journal of Counseling and Development, 66,* 139–143.

O'Neil, H. F. (1997). *Workforce readiness: Competencies and readinesss.* Mahwah, NJ: Erlbaum.

Orthner, D. K., Akos, P., Rose, R., Jones-Sanpei, H., Merdado, M., & Wooley, M. E. (2010). CareerStart: A middle school student engagement and academic achievement program. *Children & Schools, 32,* 223–234.

Osborn, D. S. (2009). Workkeys. In J. T. Kapes, E. A. Whitfield, & R. Feller (Eds.), *A counselor's guide to career assessment instruments* (5th ed., pp. 214–222). Alexandria, VA: National Career Development Association.

Osborn, D. S., Dikel, M. R., Sampson, J. P., Jr., & Harris-Bowlsbey, J. (2011). *The Internet: A tool for career planning* (3rd ed.). Broken Arrow, OK: National Career Development Association.

Osborn, D. S., Howard, D. K., & Leierer, S. J. (2007). The effect of a career development course on the dysfunctional career thoughts of racially and ethnically diverse college freshman. *The Career Development Quarterly, 55,* 365–377.

Osborn, D. S., & Reardon, R. C. (2006). Using the Self-Directed Search: Career Explorer with high-risk middle school students. *The Career Development Quarterly, 54,* 269–273.

Osborn, D. S., & Zunker, V. G. (2006). *Using assessment results for career development* (7th ed.). Belmont, CA: Brooks/Cole, Cengage Learning.

O'Shea, T. F., & Feller, R. (2000). *Harrington O'Shea career decision making system–Revised* (CDM-R). San Antonio, TX: Pearson Assessments.

Osipow, S. H. (1998). *Occupational Stress Inventory—Revised.* Odessa, FL: Psychological Assessment Resources.

Osipow, S. H., Carney, C. G., Winer, J., Yanico, B., & Koschier, M. (1987). *Career decision scale.* Odessa, FL: Psychological Assessment Resources.

Osipow, S. H., & Fitzgerald, L. F. (1996). *Theories of career development* (4th ed.). Needham Heights, MA: Allyn & Bacon.

Osipow, S. H., & Winer, J. L. (1996). The use of the Career Decision Scale in career assessment. *Journal of Career Assessment, 4,* 117–130.

Ostovary, F., & Dapprich, J. (2011). Challenges and opportunities of Operation Enduring Freedom/Operation Iraqi Freedom veterans with disabilities transitioning into learning and workplace environments. *New Directions for Adult and Continuing Education, 132,* 63–73.

Overtoom, C. (2000). *Employability skills: An update.* (ERIC Digest No. 220). Retrieved from ERIC Database. (ED445236)

Padula, M. A. (1994). Reentry women: A literature review with recommendations for counseling and research. *Journal of Counseling and Development, 73,* 10–16.

Paivandy, S., Bullock, E. E., Reardon, R. C., & Kelly, F. D. (2008). The effects of decision-making style and cognitive thought patterns on negative career thoughts. *Journal of Career Assessment, 16,* 474–488.

Palmer, L. B., & Gaunt, D. (2007). Current profile of CTE and non-CTE students: Who are we serving? *Journal of Career and Technical Education, 23,* 35–43.

Palmer, P. J. (2000). *Let your life speak: Listening for the voice of vocation.* San Francisco, CA: Jossey-Bass.

Papa, A., & Maitoza, R. (2013). The role of loss in the experience of grief: The case of job loss. *Journal of Loss and Trauma, 18,* 152–169.

Paredes, D. M., Choi, K. M., Dipal, M., Edwards-Joseph, A. R. A. C., Ermakov, N., Gouveia, A. T., Jain, S., Koyama, C., Hinkle, J. S., & Benshoff, J. M. (2008). Globalization: A brief primer for counselors. *International Journal for the Advancement of Counselling, 30,* 155–166.

Parker, R. (2002). *Occupational attitude survey & interest schedule (OASIS-3).* Austin, TX: Pro-Ed.

Parker, R. M., & Bolton, B. (2005). Psychological assessment in rehabilitation. In R. M. Parker, E. M. Szymanski, & J. B. Patterson, *Rehabilitation counseling: Basics and beyond* (4th ed., pp. 307–328). Austin, TX: ProEd.

Parker, R. M., Szymanski, E. M., & Patterson, J. B. (2005). *Rehabilitation counseling: Basics and beyond.* Austin, TX: ProEd.

Parsons, F. (1909). *Choosing a vocation.* Boston, MA: Houghton Mifflin Company.

Paul, E. L., & Brier, S. (2001). Friendsickness in the transition to college: Precollege predictors and college adjustment correlates. *Journal of Counseling & Development, 79,* 77–89.

Paul, K. I., & Moser, K. (2009). Unemployment impairs mental health: Meta-analysis. *Journal of Vocational Behavior, 74,* 264–282.

Paycheck, J. (1977). Take this job and shove it. On *Take this job and shove it* [Album]. Nashville, TN: CBS Recording Studios.

Penick, N. (2000). The genogram technique: A therapeutic tool for the career counselor. In N. Peterson & R. C. Gonzalez (Eds.), *Career counseling models for diverse populations: Hands-on applications for practitioners* (pp. 137–149). Belmont, CA: Wadsworth.

Pérez, G. M. (2010). Hispanic values, military values: Gender, culture, and the militarization of Latino/a youth. In G. M. Pérez, F. A. Guridy, & A. Burgos, Jr. (Eds.), *Beyond el barrio* (pp. 168–186). New York, NY: New York University Press.

Pérez, P. A., & McDonough, P. M. (2008). Understanding Latina and Latino college choice: A social capital and chain migration analysis. *Journal of Hispanic Education, 7,* 249–265.

Peterson, G. W., Long, K. L., & Billups, A. (1999). The effect of three career interventions on educational choices of eighth grade students. *Professional School Counseling, 3,* 34–42.

Peterson, G. W., Sampson, J. P., Jr., Lenz, J. G., & Reardon, R. C. (2002). A cognitive information processing approach to career problem solving and decision making. In D. Brown, L. Brooks, & Associates, *Career choice and development* (4th ed., pp. 312–369). San Francisco, CA: Jossey-Bass.

Peterson, G. W., Sampson, J. P., Jr., & Reardon, R. C. (1991). *Career development and services: A cognitive approach.* Pacific Grove, CA: Brooks/Cole.

Peterson, G. W., Sampson, J. P., Jr., Reardon, R. C., & Lenz, J. G. (1996). A cognitive information processing approach to career problem solving and decision making. In D. Brown, L. Brooks, & Associates, *Career choice and development* (3rd ed., pp. 423–475). San Francisco, CA: Jossey-Bass.

Peterson, G. W., Sampson, J. P., Jr., Lenz, J. G., & Reardon, R. C. (2002). A cognitive information processing approach to career problem solving and decision making. In D. Brown, L. Brooks, and Associates, *Career choice and development* (4th ed., pp. 312–369). San Francisco, CA: Jossey-Bass.

Phillips, J., Braud, J., Andrews, L. & Bullock, E. E. (2007). Bridging the gap from job to career for U.S. veterans. *Career Convergence.* Retrieved May 21, 2013, from http://associationdatabase.com/aws/NCDA/pt/sd/news_article/5412/_self/layout_ccmsearch/false

Piaget, J. (1985). *Equilibration of cognitive structures.* Chicago, IL: University of Chicago Press.

Piehl, A. M. (2009). *Preparing prisoners for employment: The power of small rewards.* New York, NY: Manhattan Institute. Retrieved June 6, 2013, from http://www.manhattan-institute.org/html/cr_57.htm

Pierson, O. (2006). *The unwritten rules of the highly effective job search: The proven program used by the world's leading career services company.* New York, NY: McGraw-Hill.

Plano Independent School District. (2007, January 10). *College week 2007.* Retrieved from http://www.pisd.edu/news/archive/2006-07/college.week.shtml

Plomin, R., DeFries, J. C., McClearn, J. E., & McGuffin, P. (2001). *Behavioral genetics* (4th ed.). New York, NY: Worth.

Ponterotto, J. G., Rivera, L., & Sueyoshi, L. A. (2000). The career-in-culture interview: A semi-structured protocol for the cross-cultural intake interview. *Career Development Quarterly, 49,* 85–96.

Pope, M. (2011). The career counseling with underserved populations model. *Journal of Employment Counseling, 48,* 153–155.

Pope, M., Barret, B., Szymanski, D. M., Chung, Y. B., Singaravelu, H., Mclean, R., & Sanabria, S. (2004). Culturally appropriate career counseling with gay and lesbian clients. *Career Development Quarterly, 53,* 158–177.

Pope, M., Prince, J. P., & Mitchell, K. (2000). Responsible career counseling with lesbian and gay students. In D. A. Luzzo (Ed.), *Career counseling of college students: An empirical guide to strategies that work* (pp. 267–284). Washington, DC: American Psychological Association.

Pope, M., & Sveinsdottir, M. (2005). Frank, we hardly knew ye: The very personal side of Frank Parsons. *Journal of Counseling and Development, 83,* 105–115.

Power, S. J. (2009). Test review of the Wonderlic Basic Skills Test. In E. A. Whitfield, R. W. Feller, & C. Wood (Eds.), *A counselor's guide to career assessment instruments* (pp. 210–213). Broken Arrow, OK: National Career Development Association.

Prediger, D. J., & Swaney, K. B. (2004). Work task dimensions underlying the world of work: Research results for diverse occupational databases. *Journal of Career Assessment, 12,* 440–459.

Rayman, J., & Atanasoff, L. (1999). Holland's theory and career intervention: The power of the hexagon. *Journal of Vocational Behavior, 55,* 114–126.

Reardon, R. C., Vernick, S. H., & Reed, C. R. (2004). A Holland perspective on the U.S. workforce from 1960 to 1990. *Journal of Career Assessment, 12,* 99–112.

Redcross, C., Bloom, D., Jacobs, E., Manno, M., Muller-Ravett, S., Seefeldt, K., Yahner, J., Young, Jr., A. A., & Zweig, J. (2010). *Work after prison: One-year findings from the transitional jobs reentry demonstration (Executive Summary).* New York, NY: MDRC. Retrieved May 30, 2013, from http://www.mdrc.org/sites/default/files/Work%20After%20Prison%20ES.pdf

Reed, M. B., Bruch, M. A., & Haase, R. F. (2004). Five-factor model of personality and career exploration. *Journal of Career Assessment, 12,* 223–238.

Reese, R. J., & Miller, C. D. (2006). Effects of a university career development course on career decision-making self-efficacy. *Journal of Career Assessment, 14,* 252–266.

Reese, R. J., & Miller, C. D. (2010). Using outcome to improve a career development course: Closing the scientist-practitioner gap. *Journal of Career Assessment, 18,* 207–219.

Reese, S. (2005). Exploring the world of work through job shadowing. *Techniques: Connecting Education and Careers, 80*(2), 18–23.

Rehabilitation Services Administration. (2010). *Welcome to RSA.* Retrieved July 20, 2010, from http://rsa.ed.gov/

Remley, Jr., T. P., & Herlihy, B. (2010). *Ethical, legal, and professional issues in counseling* (3rd ed.). Upper Saddle River, NJ: Merrill.

Richmond, E. (2010). *Preparing students for college and career: Linked learning in California. Issue Brief.* Washington, DC: Alliance for Excellent Education. Retrieved from ERIC database. (ED510795)

Richmond, N., Peters, A. C., & Woods, S. (2013, July). *Get hired: Helping your clients rise to the top of Google rankings using social media.* Presentation at the annual conference of the National Career Development Association, Boston, MA.

Ripley, R. E., Neidert, G. P. M., & Ortman, N. L. (2004). *World of work inventory.* Tempe, AZ: World of Work.

Robertson, G. J. (1998). Test review of Career Anchors: Discovering your real values (rev. ed.). In J. C. Impara & B. Plake (Eds.), *The thirteenth mental measurements yearbook* [Electronic version]. Retrieved from the Buros Institute's Mental Measurement Yearbook Online database.

Robertson, H. C. (2013). Income and support during transition from a military to civilian career. *Journal of Employment Counseling, 50,* 26–33.

Robinson, C. H., & Betz, N. E. (2008). A psychometric evaluation of Super's Work Values Inventory—Revised. *Journal of Career Assessment, 16*(4), 456–473.

Robinson, E. T., & Keis, K. (2011). *Values preference indicator.* Sumas, WA: Consulting Research Group.

Robinson-Wood, T. L. (2009). *The convergence of race, ethnicity, and gender: Multiple identities in counseling* (3rd ed.). Upper Saddle River, NJ: Merrill/Prentice Hall.

Rockawin, D. (2012). Using innovative technology to overcome job interview anxiety. *Australian Journal of Career Development, 21*(2), 46–52.

Roe, A. (1957). Early determinants of vocational choice. *Journal of Counseling Psychology, 4,* 212–217.

Roe, A., & Lunneborg, P. W. (1984). Personality development and career choice. In D. Brown, L. Brooks, & Associates (Eds.), *Career choice and development: Applying contemporary theories to practice* (pp. 31–60). San Francisco, CA: Jossey-Bass.

Rogers, C. R. (1957). The necessary and sufficient conditions of therapeutic personality change. *Journal of Consulting Psychology, 21,* 95–103.

Rogers, W. (n.d.). 1-Famous-Quotes.com. Retrieved July 31, 2015, from http://www.1-famous-quotes.com/quote/1355312

Rojewski, J. W., & Kim, H. (2003). Career choice patterns and behavior of work-bound youth during early adolescence. *Journal of Career Development, 30,* 89–108.

Rosenbaum, J. E., & Person, A. E. (2003). Beyond college for all: Policies and practices to improve transitions into college and jobs. *Professional School Counseling, 6,* 252–60.

Rosenberg, H., & Brady, M. (2000). *Job observation and behavior scale.* Wood Dale, IL: Stoelting Co.

Rottinghaus, P. J., Buelow, K. L., Matyja, A., & Schneider, M. R. (2012). The Career Futures Inventory—Revised: Measuring dimensions of career adaptability. *Journal of Career Assessment, 20,* 123–139.

Rottinghaus, P. J., Day, S. X., & Borgen, F. H. (2005). The Career Futures Inventory: A measure of career-related adaptability and optimism. *Journal of Career Assessment, 13,* 3–24.

Rounds, J. B., Jr., Henly, G. A., Dawis, R. V., Lofquist, L. H., & Weiss, D. J. (1981). *Minnesota importance questionnaire.* Minneapolis: University of Minnesota Press.

Rutter, M. E., & Jones, J. V. (2007). The job club redux: A step forward in addressing the career development needs of counselor education students. *The Career Development Quarterly, 55,* 280–288.

Ruzek, N. A., Nguyen, D. Q., & Herzog, D. C. (2011). Acculturation, enculturation, psychological distress and help-seeking preferences among Asian American college students. *Asian American Journal of Psychology, 2,* 181–196.

Ryan, D. J. (2011). *Job search handbook for people with disabilities* (3rd ed.). Indianapolis, IN: JIST Works.

Ryan, S. W., Carlstrom, A. H., Hughey, K. F., & Harris, B. S. (2011). From boots to books: Applying Schlossberg's model to transitioning American veterans. *NACADA Journal, 31*(1), 55–63.

Ryan, R. (1996). Shaping alumni careers. *Journal of Career Planning & Employment, 56*(4), 44–48.

Sabbatino, E. D., & Macrine, S. L. (2007). Start on success: A model transition program for high school students with disabilities. *Preventing School Failure, 52*(1), 33–39.

Saks, A. M. (2005). Job search success: A review and integration of the predictors, behaviors, and outcomes. In S. Brown & R. Lent (Eds.), *Career development and counseling: Putting theory and research to work* (pp. 155–179). Hoboken, NJ: Wiley.

Salamone, P. R. (1996). Tracing Super's theory of vocational development: A 40-year retrospective. *Journal of Career Development, 22,* 167–184.

Sampson, J. P., Jr. (2008). *Designing and implementing career programs: A handbook for effective practice.* Broken Arrow, OK: National Career Development Association.

Sampson, J. P., Jr., Lenz, J. G., Reardon, R. C., & Peterson, G. W. (1999). A cognitive information processing approach to employment problem solving and decision making. *Career Development Quarterly, 48,* 3–18.

Sampson, J. P., Jr., Peterson, G. W., Lenz, J. G., & Reardon, R. C. (1992). A cognitive approach to career services: Translating concepts into practice. *The Career Development Quarterly, 41,* 67–74.

Sampson, J. P., Jr., Peterson, G. W., Lenz, J. G., Reardon, R. C., & Saunders, D. E. (1996a). *Career thoughts inventory.* Odessa, FL: Psychological Assessment Resources.

Sampson, J. P., Jr., Peterson, G. W., Lenz, J. G., Reardon, R. C., & Saunders, D. E. (1996b). *Improving your career thoughts: A workbook for the Career Thoughts Inventory.* Odessa, FL: Psychological Assessment Resources.

Sampson, J. P., Jr., Peterson, G. W., Lenz, J. G., Reardon, R. C., & Saunders, D. E. (1999). The use and development of the Career Thoughts Inventory. Retrieved from ERIC database. (ED447362)

Sampson, J. P., Jr., Peterson, G. W., Reardon, R. C., & Lenz, J. G. (2000). Using readiness assessment to improve career services: A cognitive information-processing approach. *Career Development Quarterly, 49,* 146–174.

Sampson, J. P., Jr., Reardon, R. C., Peterson, G. W., & Lenz, J. G. (2004). *Career counseling & services: A cognitive information processing approach.* Belmont, CA: Brooks/Cole.

Sanford, E. E. (2003). Test review of the Jackson Vocational Interest Survey. In B. S. Plake, J. C. Impara, & R. A. Spies (Eds.), *The fifteenth mental measurements yearbook* [Electronic version]. Retrieved from the Buros Institute's Mental Measurement Yearbook Online database.

Savickas, M. L. (1994). Donald Edwin Super: The career of a planful explorer. *Career Development Quarterly, 43,* 4–24.

Savickas, M. L. (1997). Career adaptability: An integrative construct for life-span, life-space theory. *Career Development Quarterly, 45,* 247–259.

Savickas, M. L. (2002). Career construction: A developmental theory of vocational behavior. In D. Brown, L. Brooks, & Associates, *Career choice and development* (4th ed., pp. 149–205). San Francisco, CA: Jossey-Bass.

Savickas, M. L. (2005). The theory and practice of career construction. In S. D. Brown & R. W. Lent (Eds.), *Career development and counseling: Putting theory and research to work* (pp. 42–70). New York, NY: Wiley.

Savickas, M. L. (2011a). *Career counseling.* Washington, DC: American Psychological Association.

Savickas, M. L. (2011b). Constructing careers: Actor, agent, and author. *Journal of Employment Counseling, 48,* 179–181.

Savickas, M. L. (2011c). The self in vocational psychology: Object, subject and project. In P. J. Hartung & L. M. Subich (Eds.), *Developing self in work and career: Concepts, cases, and contexts* (pp. 17–33). Washington, DC: American Psychological Association.

Savickas, M. L. (2012). Life design: A paradigm for career intervention in the 21st century. *Journal of Counseling and Development, 90,* 13–19.

Savickas, M. L. (2013). Career construction theory and practice. In S. D. Brown & R. W. Lent (Eds.), *Career development and counseling: Putting theory and research to work* (pp. 147–184). New York, NY: Wiley.

Savickas, M. L., Nota, L., Rossier, J., Dauwalder, J.-P., Duarte, M. E., Guichard, J., Soresi, S., Van Esbroek, R., & van Vianen, A. E. M. (2009). Life designing: A paradigm for career construction in the 21st century. *Journal of Vocational Behavior, 75,* 239–250.

Savickas, M. L., & Porfeli, E. J. (2011). Revision of the Career Maturity Inventory: The adaptability form. *Journal of Career Assessment, 19*(2), 355–374.

Savino, C. S., & Krannich, R. L. (2011). *The military to civilian transition guide: From army green to corporate gray, from navy blue to corporate gray, from air force blue to corporate gray.* Manassas Park, VA: Impact Publishing.

Schein, E. H. (2006a). *Career Anchors participant workbook* (3rd ed.). Hoboken, NJ: John Wiley Sons.

Schein, E. H. (2006b). *Career Anchors profile report.* Hoboken, NJ: John Wiley Sons.

Schein, E. H. (2006c). *Career Anchors self-assessment.* Hoboken, NJ: John Wiley Sons.

Schenck, P. (2009). Kuder career planning system. In E. A. Whitfield, R. W. Feller, & C. Woods (Eds.), *A counselor's guide to career assessment instruments* (5th ed., pp. 163–173). Broken Arrow, OK: National Career Development Association.

Schepp, B., & Schepp, D. (2010). *How to find a job on LinkedIn, Facebook, Twitter, MySpace and other social networks.* New York, NY: McGraw-Hill.

Schlossberg, N. K. (1981). A model for analyzing human adaptation to transition. *The Counseling Psychologist, 9*(2), 2–18.

Schlossberg, N. K. (2011). The challenge of change: The transition model and its applications. *Journal of Employment Counseling, 48,* 159–161.

Schmitt, J., & Warner, K. (2010, November). *Ex-offenders and the labor market.* Washington, DC: Center for Economic and Policy Research. Retrieved on June 1, 2013, from http://www.cepr.net/documents/publications/ex-offenders-2010-11.pdf

Schultheiss, D. E. P. (2009). To mother or matter: Can women do both? *Journal of Career Development, 36,* 25–48.

Schultz, M. (2010, June 30). Federal funding cuts will limit No Worker Left Behind. *Detroit News.* Retrieved July 22, 2013, from http://www.detroitnews.com/article/20100630/BIZ/6300356

Schutt, Jr., D. A., & Schwallie-Giddis, P. (2008). Career centers in educational settings. In D. A. Schutt, Jr. (Ed.), *How to plan & develop a career center* (pp. 91–104). New York, NY: Ferguson.

Scott, C. K. (2005). *Vocatio: Discovering your personal calling.* Sioux Falls, SD: Pine Hill Press.

Scott, C. K. (2010). Vocatio: The importance of exploring an ancient concept for community college students. *New Directions for Community Colleges, 151,* 101–110.

Scott, J. L., & Sarkees-Wircenski, M. (1996). *Overview of vocational and applied technology education.* Homewood, IL: American Technical Publishers.

Secretary's Commission on Achieving Necessary Skills. (1991a). *What work requires of schools: A SCANS report for America 2000.* Washington, DC: U.S. Department of Labor. (ED332054)

Secretary's Commission on Achieving Necessary Skills. (1991b). *SCANS blueprint for action: Building community coalitions.* Washington, DC: U.S. Department of Labor. (ED354299)

Secretary's Commission on Achieving Necessary Skills. (1991c). *Skills and tasks for jobs: A SCANS report for America 2000.* Washington, DC: U.S. Department of Labor. (ED350414)

Secretary's Commission on Achieving Necessary Skills. (1992). *Learning a living: A blueprint for high performance. A SCANS report for America 2000.* Washington, DC: U.S. Department of Labor. (ED346348)

Secretary's Commission on Achieving Necessary Skills. (1993). *Teaching the SCANS competencies.* Washington, DC: U.S. Department of Labor. (ED35440)

Sharf, R. S. (2010). *Applying career development theory to counseling* (5th ed.). Belmont, CA: Brooks/Cole, Cengage Learning.

Sharf, R. S. (2014). *Applying career development theory to counseling* (6th ed.). Belmont, CA: Brooks/Cole.

Shatkin, L. (2013). *300 best jobs without a four-year degree* (4th ed.). St. Paul, MN: JIST Works.

Shatkin, L., & Farr, M. (2010). *250 best-paying jobs* (2nd ed.). St. Paul, MN: JIST Works.

Shaw, S. F., Madaus, J. W., & Banerjee, M. (2009). Enhance access to postsecondary education for students with disabilities. *Intervention in School and Clinic, 44*, 185–190.

Shivy, V. A., Wu, J. J., Moon, A. E., Mann, S. C., Holland, J. G., & Eacho, C. (2007). Ex-offenders reentering the workforce. *Journal of Counseling Psychology, 54*, 466–473.

Shurts, W. M., & Shoffner, M. F. (2004). Providing career counseling for collegiate student-athletes: A learning theory approach. *Journal of Career Development, 31*, 95–109.

Simpson, C. G., & Spencer, V. G. (2009). *College success for students with learning disabilities.* Waco, TX: Prufrock Press.

Singleton, G. E., & Linton, C. (2006). *Courageous conversations about race: A field guide for achieving equity in schools.* Thousand Oaks, CA: Corwin Press.

Sjodin, T. L. (2012). *Small message, big impact: The elevator speech effect.* New York, NY: Penguin.

Skinner, B. F. (1938). *The behavior of organisms: An experimental analysis.* Englewood Cliffs, NJ: Prentice Hall.

Slaney, R. B. (1978). Expressed and inventoried vocational interests: A comparison of instruments. *Journal of Counseling Psychology, 25*, 520–529.

Slaney, R. B., & MacKinnon-Slaney, F. (2000). Using vocational card sorts in career counseling. In C. E. Watkins, Jr., & V. L. Campbell (Eds.), *Testing and assessment in counseling practice* (2nd ed., pp. 371–428). Mahwah, NJ: Erlbaum.

Sloan, T. (2005). Global work-related suffering as a priority for vocational psychology. *The Counseling Psychologist, 33*, 207–214.

Smith, S. S. (2005). "Don't put my name on it": Social capital activation and job-finding assistance among the black urban poor. *American Journal of Sociology, 111*, 1–57.

Social Security Administration. (2013). *Survivors benefits.* SSA Publication No. 05-10084. Washington, DC: Author.

Southern Regional Education Board. (2002). *High Schools That Work: An evidence-based design for improving the nation's schools and raising student achievement.* Atlanta, GA: Author. Retrieved from http://publications.sreb.org/2002/02V07_2002_HSTW_Brochure.pdf

Spielberger, C. D., & Vagg, P. R. (1999). *Job stress survey.* Odessa, FL: Psychological Assessment Resources.

Spokane, A. R., & Cruza-Guet, M. C. (2005). Holland's theory of vocational personalities in work environments. In S. D. Brown & R. W. Lent (Eds.). *Career development and counseling: Putting theory and research to work* (pp. 24–41). Hoboken, NJ: Wiley.

Spokane, A. R., Luchetta, E. J. & Richwine, M. H. (2002). Holland's theory of personalities in work environments. In D. Brown & Associates, *Career choice and development: Applying contemporary theories to practice* (4th ed., pp. 373–426). San Francisco, CA: Wiley.

State of New York Civil Rights Bureau. 2014. *The sexual orientation non-discrimination act.* Retrieved July 14, 2014, from http://www.ag.ny.gov/bureaus/civil_rights/sonda_brochure.html

State of Oklahoma. (2014). Career tech career activity files. Retrieved July 31, 2014, from http://www.okcareertech.org/educators/career-and-academic-connections/career-activity-files

Stebleton, M., & Henle, M. (2011). *Hired! The job hunting and career planning guide* (4th ed.). Boston, MA: Pearson Education.

Steinberg, W. J. (2003). Test review of the Jackson Vocational Interest Survey. In B. S. Plake, J. C. Impara, & R. A. Spies (Eds.), *The fifteenth mental measurements yearbook* [Electronic version]. Retrieved from the Buros Institute's Mental Measurement Yearbook Online database.

Stoltenberg, C. D., & Delworth, U. (1987). *Supervising counselors and therapists.* San Francisco: CA: Jossey-Bass.

Stone, III, J. R., & Aliaga, O. A. (2005). Career & technical education and school-to-work at the end of the 20th century: Participation and outcomes. *Career and Technical Education Research, 30*, 125–144.

Stone, J. R., & Lewis, M. V. (2012). *College and career ready in the 21st century.* New York, NY: Teachers College Press.

Stone, K. V. W. (2007). Revisiting the at-will employment doctrine: Imposed terms, implied terms, and the normative world of the workplace. *Industrial Law Journal, 36*(1), 84–101.

Stott, K. A., & Jackson, A. P. (2005). Using service learning to achieve middle school comprehensive guidance program goals. *Professional School Counseling, 9*, 156–159.

Strehlke, C. (2010). Social network sites: A starting point for career development practitioners. *Journal of Employment Counseling, 47*, 38–48.

Streufert, B., & Richmond, N. (2013, July). *Leveraging LinkedIn.* Presentation at the annual conference of the National Career Development Association, Boston, MA.

Sue, D. W., & Sue, D. (2008). *Counseling the culturally-different: Theory and practice* (5th ed.). New York, NY: Wiley.

Sueyoshi, L., Rivera, L., & Ponterotto, J. G. (2001). The family genogram as a tool in multicultural career counseling. In J. G. Ponterotto, J. M. Casas, L. A. Suzuki, & C. M. Alexander (Eds.), *Handbook of multicultural counseling* (2nd ed., pp. 655–671). Thousand Oaks, CA: Sage.

Super, D. E. (1950). Vocational adjustment: Implementing a self-concept. *Occupations, 30*(3), 88–92.

Super, D. E. (1953). A theory of vocational development. *American Psychologist, 8*, 185–190.

Super, D. E. (1957). *The psychology of careers.* New York, NY: Harper & Row.

Super, D. E. (1963). Self-concepts in vocational development. In D. E. Super, R. Starishevsky, N. Maitlin, & J. P. Jordaan, *Career development: Self-concept theory* (pp. 17–32). New York, NY: College Entrance Examination Board.

Super, D. E. (1980). A life-span, life-space approach to career development. *Journal of Vocational Behavior, 16*, 282–298.

Super, D. E. (1981). A developmental theory: Implementing a self-concept. In D. H. Montross & C. J. Shinkman (Eds.), *Career development in the 1980s: Theory and practice* (pp. 28–42). Springfield, IL: Charles C Thomas.

Super, D. E. (1983). Assessment in career guidance: Toward truly developmental counseling. *The Personnel and Guidance Journal, 61*, 555–562.

Super, D. E. (1984). Career and life development. In D. Brown, L. Brooks, & Associates (Eds.), *Career choice and development: Applying contemporary theories to practice* (pp. 192–234). San Francisco, CA: Jossey-Bass.

Super, D. E. (1988). Vocational adjustment: Implementing a self-concept. [Reprint of 1950 article]. *Career Development Quarterly, 36*, 351–358.

Super, D. E. (1990). A life-span, life-space approach to career development. In D. Brown, L. Brooks, & Associates (Eds.), *Career choice and development: Applying contemporary theories to practice* (2nd ed., pp. 197–261). San Francisco, CA: Jossey-Bass.

Super, D. E., Osborne, W. L., Walsh, D. J., Brown, S. D., & Niles, S. G. (1992). Developmental career assessment and counseling: The C-DAC model. *Journal of Counseling & Development, 71*, 74–80.

Super, D. E., Savickas, M. L., & Super, C. M. (1996). The life-span, life-space approach to careers. In D. Brown, L. Brooks, & Associates (Eds.), *Career choice and development: Applying contemporary theories to practice* (3rd ed., pp. 121–178). San Francisco, CA: Jossey-Bass.

Super, D. E., Thompson, A. S., & Lindeman, R. H. (1988a). *Adult career concerns inventory.* Palo Alto, CA: Consulting Psychologists Press.

Super, D. E., Thompson, A. S., & Lindeman, R. H. (1988b). *Adult Career Concerns Inventory: Manual for research and exploratory usage in counseling.* Palo Alto, CA: Consulting Psychologists Press.

Super, D. E., Thompson, A. S., Lindeman, R. H., Jordaan, J. P., & Myers, R. A. (1979). *Career Development Inventory: School form.* Palo Alto, CA: Consulting Psychologists Press.

Super, D. E., Thompson, A. S., Lindeman, R. H., Jordaan, J. P., & Myers, R. A. (1981). *Career Development Inventory: College form.* Palo Alto, CA: Consulting Psychologists Press.

Symonds, W. C., Schwartz, R. B., & Ferguson, R. (2011). *Pathways to prosperity: Meeting the challenge of preparing young Americans for the 21st century.* Report issued by the Pathways to Prosperity Project, Harvard Graduate School of Education. Retrieved from http://www.gse.harvard.edu/news_events/features/2011/Pathways_to_Prosperity_Feb2011.pdf

Takai, R., & Holland, J. L. (1979). Comparison of the Vocational Card Sort, the SDS, and the Vocational Exploration and Insight Kit. *The Vocational Guidance Quarterly, 27*, 312–318.

Talent Assessment. (2007). *Pictorial Inventory of Careers Pathfinder* [Measurement instrument]. Jacksonville, FL: Author.

Tarvydas, V. M. (1998). Ethical decision making processes. In R. R. Cottone & V. M. Tarvydas (Eds.), *Ethical and professional issues in counseling* (pp. 144–155). Upper Saddle River, NJ: Prentice-Hall.

Terkel, S. (1974). *Working.* New York, NY: Pantheon.

Texas Association of Business. (2014). *Nonsubscription.* Retrieved on July 14, 2014, from http://www.txbiz.org/advocacy/nonsubscription.aspx

Texas Department of Insurance Division of Workers' Compensation. (2014). *Non-covered employers.* Retrieved July 14, 2014, from http://www.tdi.state.tx.us/pubs/factsheets/noncoveremp.pdf

Theokas, C. (2010, Dec.). *Shut out of the military: Today's high school education doesn't mean you're ready for today's army.* Washington, DC: The Education Trust.

Theriot, M. T., & Segal, S. P. (2005). Involvement with the criminal justice system among new clients at outpatient mental health agencies. *Psychiatric Services, 56*, 179–185.

Thompson, A. S., Lindeman, R. H., Super, D. E., Jordaan, J. P., & Myers, R. A. (1988). *Career Development Inventory: Technical manual.* Palo Alto, CA: Consulting Psychologists Press.

Thompson, E., & Feldman, D. B. (2010). Let your life speak: Assessing the effectiveness of a program to explore meaning, purpose, and calling with college students. *Journal of Employment Counseling, 47*, 12–19.

Thompson, M. N., & Cummings, D. L. (2010). Enhancing the career development of individuals who have criminal records. *The Career Development Quarterly, 58*, 209–218.

Tomei, M. (2003). Discrimination and equality at work: A review of the concepts. *International Labour Review, 142*, 401–418.

Tomlinson, E. C., & Bockanic, W. N. (2009). Avoiding liability for wrongful termination: "Ready, aim, fire!" *Employee Responsibilities and Rights Journal, 21*(2), 77–87.

Top Recruiter TV. (2013). Episode 6. Retrieved August 9, 2013, from http://toprecruiter.tv/episode-6

Torpey, E. M. (2009). Gap year: Time off, with a plan. *Occupational Outlook Quarterly, 53*(3), 26–33.

Tovar-Murray, D., Jenifer, E. D., Andrusyk, J., D'Angelo, R., & King, T. (2012). Racism-related stress and ethnic identity as determinants of African American college students' career aspirations. *Career Development Quarterly, 60*, 254–262.

Troiden, R. R., (1989). The formation of homosexual identities. *Journal of Homosexuality, 17*, 43–73.

Trolley, B. C., Haas, H. S., & Patti, D. C. (2009). *The school counselor's guide to special education*. Thousand Oaks, CA: Corwin Press.

Trusty, J., Niles, S. G., & Carney, J. V. (2005). Education-career planning and middle school counselors. *Professional School Counseling, 9*, 136–143.

Tyler, L. E. (1961). Research explorations in the realm of choice. *Journal of Counseling Psychology, 8*, 195–201.

Unger, H. G. (2006). *But what if I don't want to go to college? A guide to success through alternative education* (3rd ed.). New York, NY: Ferguson.

United States Employment Service. (1986). *General aptitude test battery*. Washington, DC: U.S. Department of Labor.

University of Oregon. (2013). *What is intoCareers/CIS?* Retrieved August 14, 2013, from http://blogs.uoregon.edu/intocareers/about-intocareerscis/what-is-intocareerscis/

U.S. Bureau of Labor Statistics. (2008). *BLS Information: Glossary*. Retrieved May 3, 2013, from http://www.bls.gov/bls/glossary.htm

U.S. Bureau of Labor Statistics. (2009). *How the government measures unemployment*. Retrieved May 3, 2013, from http://www.bls.gov/cps/cps_htgm.pdf

U.S. Bureau of Labor Statistics. (2010). *2010 SOC User Guide*. Washington, DC: Author.

U.S. Bureau of Labor Statistics. (2011). *American time use survey: Eldercare in 2011*. Retrieved May 30, 2013, from http://data.bls.gov/cgi-bin/print.pl/tus/2011_eldercare_factsheet.htm

U.S. Bureau of Labor Statistics. (2012a). *Employment Situation of Veterans—2012*. Retrieved May 22, 2013, from http://www.bls.gov/news.release/pdf/vet.pdf

U.S. Bureau of Labor Statistics. (2012b). New school year, old story: Education pays. *Occupational Outlook Quarterly, 56*(3), 36.

U.S. Bureau of Labor Statistics. (2012c). *Persons with a disability: Labor force characteristics—2011*. Retrieved May 11, 2013, from http://www.bls.gov/news.release/pdf/disabl.pdf

U.S. Bureau of Labor Statistics. (2012d). Table 2. Employed full- and part-time workers by disability status and age, 2011 annual averages. Retrieved May 11, 2013, from http://www.bls.gov/news.release/disabl.t02.htm

U.S. Bureau of Labor Statistics. (2013a). *Employment characteristics of families—2012*. Retrieved May 30, 2013, from http://www.bls.gov/news.release/pdf/famee.pdf

U.S. Bureau of Labor Statistics. (2013b). *Employment situation summary*. Retrieved May 3, 2013, from http://www.bls.gov/news.release/empsit.nr0.htm

U.S. Bureau of Labor Statistics. (2013c). *Occupational outlook handbook: 2013-2014 edition*. St. Paul, MN: JIST Publishing.

U.S. Bureau of Labor Statistics. (2014). *K–12 career exploration*. Retrieved July 31, 2014, from http://www.bls.gov/k12/content/students/careers/career-exploration.htm

U.S. Census Bureau. (2011). *Net worth and asset ownership of households: 2011*. Retrieved September 22, 2013, from census.gov/people/wealth/

U.S. Department of Defense. (2013). *Active duty military personnel by rank/grade*. Retrieved May 23, 2013 from http://siadapp.dmdc.osd.mil/personnel/MILITARY/rg1302.pdf

U.S. Department of Education. (2011). *Funding your education: The guide to federal student aid*. Washington, DC: U.S. Government Printing Office.

U.S. Department of Education. (2014a). Gaining early awareness and readiness for undergraduate programs (GEAR UP). Retrieved July 31, 2014, from http://www2.ed.gov/programs/gearup/index.html

U.S. Department of Education. (2014b). *Tech-prep education*. Retrieved August 1, 2014, from http://www2.ed.gov/programs/techprep/index.html

U.S. Department of Health and Human Services. (2015). Births: Final data for 2013. *National Vital Statistics Reports, 64*(1). Retrieved January 31, 2015, from http://www.cdc.gov/nchs/products/nvsr.htm

U.S. Department of Labor. (1991a). *Dictionary of occupational titles* (4th ed., revised, 2 vols.). Washington, DC: U.S. Government Printing Office.

U.S. Department of Labor. (1991b). Employment and Training Administration. *Dictionary of occupational titles* (4th ed., revised, 2 vols.). Washington, DC: U.S. Government Printing Office.

U.S. Department of Labor. (2005a). Appendix B from *Employment information handbook for ex-offenders.* Washington, DC: Author. Retrieved June 6, 2013, from http://www.exoffender.org/up/docs/Exohandbook.pdf

U.S. Department of Labor. (2005b). *Employment information handbook for ex-offenders.* Washington, DC: Author. Retrieved June 6, 2013, from http://www.exoffender.org/up/docs/Exohandbook.pdf

U.S. Department of Labor. (2010). *Young person's occupational outlook handbook* (7th ed.). Indianapolis, IN: JIST Works, Inc.

U.S. Department of Labor. (2013a). *Prisoner reentry toolkit for faith-based and community organizations.* Washington, DC: Author. Retrieved June 1, 2013, from http://www.doleta.gov/PRI/PDF/Pritoolkit.pdf

U.S. Department of Labor. (2013b). *Secretary's Commission on Achieving Necessary Skills: Background.* Retrieved July 27, 2013, from http://wdr.doleta.gov/SCANS/

U.S. Department of Labor. (2013c). *Training: One-stop career centers.* Washington, DC: Author. Retrieved June 9, 2013, from http://www.dol.gov/dol/topic/training/onestop.htm

U.S. Department of Labor. (2013d). *VETS Fact Sheet 1: Transition Assistance Program.* Washington, DC: Author. Retrieved June 9, 2013, from http://www.dol.gov/vets/programs/tap/tap_fs.htm

U.S. Department of Labor. (2013e). *Youth services: 21st century youth.* Washington, DC: Author. Retrieved June 9, 2013, from http://www.doleta.gov/youth_services/

U.S. Department of Labor, Employment and Training Administration. (2000a). *Work Importance Locator: User's guide.* Washington, DC: Author.

U.S. Department of Labor, Employment and Training Administration. (2000b). *Work value card sorting sheet.* Washington, DC: Author.

U.S. Department of Labor, Employment and Training Administration. (2000c). *Work value worksheet.* Washington, DC: Author.

U.S. Department of Labor Wage and Hour Division. (2010). *Child labor provisions for nonagricultural occupations under the Fair Labor Standards Act.* Washington, DC: Author.

U.S. Department of Labor Employment and Training Administration. (2001a). *O*NET ability profiler.* Washington, DC: Author.

U.S. Department of Labor Employment and Training Administration. (2001b). *O*NET interest profiler.* Washington, DC: Author.

U.S. Department of Labor Employment and Training Administration. (2001c). *O*NET work importance locator.* Washington, DC: Author.

U.S. Department of Labor Employment and Training Administration. (2002). *O*NET Work Importance Profiler: User's guide.* Washington, DC: Author.

U.S. Department of Veterans Affairs. (n.d.). *Annual benefits summary: Fiscal year 2011.* Washington, DC: Author. Retrieved May 26, 2013, from http://www.vba.va.gov/REPORTS/abr/2011_abr.pdf

U.S. Department of Veterans Affairs. (2013). *Health benefits glossary.* Retrieved May 23, 2013, from http://www.va.gov/healthbenefits/resources/glossary.asp#v

U.S. Equal Employment Opportunity Commission. (2014). *Genetic information.* Retrieved July 10, 2010, from http://www.eeoc.gov/laws/types/genetic.cfm

U.S. Government Accountability Office. (2012). *Report to congressional committees: Inmate reentry programs.* Washington, DC: Author. GAO-13-93. Retrieved June 6, 2013, from http://www.gao.gov/assets/660/650900.pdf

U.S. Military Entrance Processing Command. (1997). *Armed services vocational aptitude battery.* North Chicago, IL: Author.

Valpar International. (2002). *Aviator 3.* Tucson, AZ: Author.

Valpar International. (2004). *Valpar Career Ability Test.* Tucson, AZ: Author.

Valverde, L. A. (2012). *Latino student's guide to college success* (2nd ed). Santa Barbara, CA: Greenwood.

Van Dam, K., & Menting, L. (2012). The role of approach and avoidance motives for unemployed job search behavior. *Journal of Vocational Behavior, 80,* 108–117.

Venable, M. A. (2010). Using technology to deliver career development services: Supporting today's students in higher education. *The Career Development Quarterly, 59,* 87–96.

Vernick, S. H., & Reardon, R. C. (2001). Career development programs in corrections. *Journal of Career Development, 27,* 265–277.

Veterans Benefits Administration. (2012). Post 9/11GI bill: *It's your future.* Retrieved May 26, 2013, from http://www.gibill.va.gov/documents/pamphlets/ch33_pamphlet.pdf

Vilorio, D. (2011). Focused jobseeking: A measured approach to looking for work. *Occupational Outlook Quarterly, 55,* 2–11.

Vinokur, A. D., Price, R. H., & Schul, Y. (1995). Impact of the JOBS intervention on unemployed works varying in risk for depression. *American Journal of Community Psychology, 23,* 39–74.

Virginia Department of Education. (2012). *Career clusters and academic and career plans of study: Virginia's best practices.* Retrieved July 12, 2013, from http://www.doe.virginia.gov/instruction/career_technical/career_clusters/

Visher, C., & Lattimore, P. (2007). Major study examines prisoners and their reentry needs. *National Institute of Justice*

Visher, C., & Lattimore, P. (2008). Study examines prisoners' reentry needs. *Corrections Today, 70*(2), 146–147.

Von Bergen, A. N., Von Bergen, C. W., & Ballaré, D.A. (2008). Family responsibilities discrimination: What employment counselors need to know. *Journal of Employment Counseling, 45*, 115–130.

Vondracek, F. W., Lerner, R. M., & Schulenberg, J. E. (1986). *Career development: A life-span developmental approach.* Hillsdale, NJ: Erlbaum.

Wachs, T. D. (1992). *The nature of nurture.* Newbury Park, CA: Sage.

Waldron, K., & Loomis, C. (2000). My vocational inheritance: A career genogram. In M. Pope, & C. W. Minor (Eds.), *Experiential activities for teaching career counseling classes and for facilitating career groups* (Vol. 1, pp. 69–70). Tulsa, OK: National Career Development Association.

Wall, B. (2008). *Working relationships: Using emotional intelligence to enhance your effectiveness with others* (rev. ed.). Mountain View, CA: Davies-Black Publishing.

Walls, J. (2002). *The senior experience: A transition to the world of work.* Retrieved from ERIC database. (ED465923)

Walsh, M. W. (2010, July 10). Maine giving social security another look. *New York Times.* Retrieved July 27, 2010, from http://www.nytimes.com/2010/07/21/business/economy/21states.html

Watkins, K. E. (1988). Supporting women's reentry to the workplace. *New Directions for Continuing Education, 39*, 49–64.

Wazny, L. (2010). The reality of re-entry for the ex-offenders in the United States. *Career Convergence Web Magazine.* Retrieved May 29, 2013, from http://ncda.org/aws/NCDA/pt/sd/news_article/32714/_PARENT/layout_details_cc/false

Weber, M. (1930). *The Protestant ethic and the spirit of capitalism.* New York, NY: Routledge Classics.

Weiss, D. J., Dawis, R. V., England, G. W., & Lofquist, L. H. (1977). *Minnesota satisfaction questionnaire—Revised long form.* Minneapolis, MN: University of Minnesota Press.

Welfel, E. R. (2002). *Ethics in counseling and psychotherapy: Standards, research, and emerging issues.* Pacific Grove, CA: Brooks/Cole.

Wendlandt, N. M., & Rochlen, A. B. (2008). Addressing the college-to-work transition: Implications for university career counselors. *Journal of Career Development, 35*, 151–165.

Whiston, S. C. (2009). *Principles and applications of assessment in counseling* (3rd ed.). Belmont, CA: Brooks/Cole, Cengage Learning.

Whiston, S. C., Sexton, T. L., & Lasoff, D. L. (1998). Career intervention outcome: A replication and extension of Oliver and Spokane (1988). *Journal of Counseling Psychology, 45*, 150–165.

Whitaker, A. (2013). *Calhoun poised to graduate first female lineman.* Retrieved February 13, 2015, from http://whnt.com/2013/09/27/calhoun-poised-to-graduate-first-female-lineman/

White House, The. (2011, August 31). *President's Council on Jobs and Competitiveness announces industry leaders' commitment to double engineering internships in 2012.* Retrieved from http://www.whitehouse.gov/the-press-office/2011/08/31/president-s-council-jobs-and-competitiveness-announces-industry-leaders

Whitfield, E. A., & Cato, S. (2009). A counselor's guide user's matrix: An alphabetical listing of career assessment instruments by category and type of use. In E. A. Whitfield, R. W. Feller, & C. Wood (Eds.), *A counselor's guide to career assessment instruments* (pp. 557–574). Broken Arrow, OK: National Career Development Association.

Whitfield, E. A., Feller, R., & Wood, C. (2009). *A counselor's guide to career assessment instruments* (5th ed.). Broken Arrow, OK: National Career Development Association.

Williams, A. P. (2013). *Reentry of substance abusing female ex-offenders from prison to an urban community.* (Unpublished doctoral dissertation). Retrieved from ProQuest. (UMI 3503066)

Williams, S. K. (1978). The Vocational Card Sort: A tool for vocational exploration. *The Vocational Guidance Quarterly, 26*, 237–243.

Williamson, E. G. (1939). *How to counsel students: A manual of techniques for clinical counselors.* New York, NY: McGraw-Hill.

Williamson, E. G. (1965). *Vocational counseling: Some historical, philosophical, and theoretical perspectives.* New York, NY: McGraw-Hill.

Williamson, E. G. (1972). Trait-factor theory and individual differences. In B. Steffire & W. H. Grant (Eds.), *Theories of Counseling* (pp. 136–176). New York, NY: McGraw-Hill.

Witt, M. A. (1992). *Job strategies for people with disabilities.* Princeton, NJ: Peterson's Guides.

Wnuk, S. M. (2003). Using the Intelligent Careers Card Sort® with university students. *The Career Development Quarterly, 51*, 274–284.

Wonderlic, Inc. (1999). *Wonderlic personnel test & scholastic level exam user's manual.* Libertyville, IL: Author.

Wonderlic, Inc. (2007a). *Wonderlic contemporary cognitive ability test.* Libertyville, IL: Author.

Wonderlic, Inc. (2007b). *Wonderlic personnel test—Revised: Administrator's guide.* Libertyville, IL: Author.

Wonderlic, Inc. (2011). *Wonderlic basic skills test (WBST), ability-to-benefit test: Administrator's examination.* Vernon Hills, IL: Author.

Wood, F. B. (2004). Preventing postparchment depression: A model of career counseling for college seniors. *Journal of Employment Counseling, 41*, 71–79.

Workers Rights Consortium. (2013, July). *Global wage trends for apparel workers, 2001–2011*. Retrieved from http://www.americanprogress.org/issues/labor/report/2013/07/11/69255/global-wage-trends-for-apparel-workers-2001-2011/

Working Mother. (2011). *2011 Working Mother 100 best companies: Turner Broadcasting System*. Retrieved August 9, 2013, from http://www.workingmother.com/best-companies/turner-broadcasting-system-3

Wrenn, C. G. (1962). The culturally-encapsulated counselor. *Harvard Educational Review, 32,* 444–449.

Wright, M. O., Crawford, E., & DelCastillo, D. (2009). Childhood emotional maltreatment and later psychological distress among college students: The mediating role of maladaptive schemas. *Child Abuse & Neglect: The International Journal, 33*(1), 59–68.

Yakushko, O., Backhaus, A., Watson, M., Ngaruiya, K., & Gonzales, J. (2008). Career development concerns of recent immigrants and refugees. *Journal of Career Development, 34,* 362–396.

Young, J. W., & Cline, F. (2009). *A concurrent validity study of the 2008 HSTW assessment scores*. Princeton, NJ: Educational Testing Service. Retrieved from ERIC database. (ED504171)

Young, R. A., Marshall, S. K., & Valach, L. (2007). Making career theories more culturally sensitive: Implications for counseling. *Career Development Quarterly, 56,* 4–18.

Zachar, P. (2009). Review of the Jackson Personality Inventory—Revised. In E. Whitfield, R. Feller, & C. Wood (Eds), *A counselor's guide to career assessment instruments* (5th ed.). (pp. 395–399). Columbus, OH: National Career Development Association.

Zalaquett, C. P., & Osborn, D. S. (2007). Fostering counseling students' career information literacy through a comprehensive career web site. *Counselor Education and Supervision, 46,* 162–171.

Ziering, N. (2013). *12 ways not to choose your college or university*. Retrieved February 13, 2015, from http://ezinearticles.com/?12-Ways-Not-to-Choose-Your-College-Or-University&id=4793534

Zikic, J., & Klehe, U. C. (2006). Job loss as a blessing in disguise: The role of career exploration and career planning in predicting reemployment quality. *Journal of Vocational Behavior, 69,* 391–406.

Zinn, H. (2010). *A people's history of the United States*. New York, NY: Harper Perennial Modern Classics.

Ziomek-Daigle, J., Black, L., & Kocet, M. M. (2007). "Let's dance": Race, faith, and sexual orientation. In S. M. Dugger & L. A. Carlson (Eds.). *Critical incidents in counseling children* (pp. 169–179). Alexandria, VA: American Counseling Association.

Zunker, V. G. (2006). *Career counseling: A holistic approach* (7th ed.). Belmont, CA: Brooks/Cole.

Zunker, V. G. (2012). *Career counseling: A holistic approach* (8th ed.). Belmont, CA: Brooks/Cole.

Zytowski, D. G. (2001). Frank Parsons and the progressive movement. *Career Development Quarterly, 50,* 57–65.

Zytowski, D. G. (2006). Career development on a three-legged stool. *Kuder User News, 5*(1), 1–2.

AUTHOR INDEX

A

Abraham, K. G., 296
Ackerlind, S. J., 132
Ackerman, R., 419
Adams, E. M., 132
Adams, J. D., 411
Adams, S., 435, 436
Adams, T. L., 359
Akos, P., 334
Alamprese, J. A., 322
Albertson, E., 398
Aley, C., 400
Aliaga, O. A., 357, 360
Amundson, N. E., 390–393
Anderson, M. L., 392, 410, 412, 414
Andrews, L., 111, 420–421
Andrusyk, J., 112
Ansalone, G., 357
Antonoff, S. R., 345, 347
Ao, D., 413
Aranda, C. L., 434
Arbona, C., 136
Archer, J., 392
Armstrong, P. A., 370
Arnett, J. J., 5
Arrington, K., 340, 342
Arthaud, P. D., 256
Arthur, M. B., 8
Arthur, N., 105, 107, 113, 125
Asama, N. F., 252
Asplund, J., 236, 237
Astin, A. W., 23
Astin, H. S., 66
Atanasoff, L., 18, 20
Athanasou, J. A., 268
Atkinson, D. R., 112
Atkinson, M. J., 236
Axelrad, S., 37, 469
Azrin, N. H., 394

B

Backhaus, A., 111
Backus, F., 106
Bailey, T., 323–324
Baker, D. B., 4, 18, 139
Balderrama, A., 405
Ballaré, D. A., 139
Bandura, A., 56, 57, 65, 66, 68
Banerjee, M., 350
Bardos, A. N., 243
Barge J. D., 299
Barr, L., 434
Barrington, L., 324
Baruch, Y., 3, 9
Bates, R. A., 323–324
Baum, S., 120, 136
Beale, A. V., 335
Becker, R. L., 234, 253
Bennett, G. K., 247
Berg-Kolin, H., 370, 376

Berry, J. W., 111
Bertrand, M., 123
Besalel, V. A., 394
Betsworth, D. G., 51
Betz, N. E., 65, 240, 248, 250, 378, 383
Bhat, C. S., 394
Bianchi, S. M., 433, 434
Bikos, L. H., 270
Billups, A., 337
Binet, A., 19
Black, L., 172
Blustein, D. L., 3, 8, 106, 108, 110, 120, 121,
    136, 390, 394
Bockanic, W. N., 144–146
Bolles, R. N., 416
Bolton, B., 415, 416
Bordin, E. S., 35, 36–37
Borgen, F. H., 19, 248, 254, 383
Borgen, W. A., 390–393
Borzuchowska, B., 168
Boshoven, J. B., 347, 348
Bouchard, T. J., Jr., 51
Bowen, M., 114
Bradley, P., 236
Brady, M., 254
Brady, R. P., 240
Bragg, D. D., 345
Braud, J., 420–421
Brewington, J. O., 391–392
Briddick, W. C., 3
Bridgstock, R., 381
Brier, S., 372
Brigance, A. H., 254
Briggs Myers, I., 237
Briscoe, J. P., 8
Brooks, K., 322, 370
Brooks, L., 40, 44, 45, 47, 79
Brown, C., 377, 423–427, 429, 430
Brown, D., 20, 35, 40, 44, 45, 47, 79, 104, 105,
    122, 162, 165, 318, 382, 469
Brown, M. B., 234
Brown, S. D., 29, 46, 65, 67–73, 82, 105,
    133, 179, 180, 190, 201, 250, 323,
    334, 437
Bruch, M. A., 238
Buch, K., 394
Buelow, K. L., 254
Bugaj, A. M., 235
Bullock, E. E., 81, 251, 420–421
Bullock-Yowell, E., 80, 111
Bunch, M. B., 248
Bushway, S. D., 427, 430
Butler, C., 472
Buzzetta, M. E., 111
Byars-Winston, A., 112, 113
Bynner, J., 411

C

Cahill, B. J., 132
Callahan, P., 104
Campbell, D., 231, 238, 247, 260

Campbell, D. P., 19
Caniglia, J., 338
Caplan, R. D., 394
Caplin, D., 420
Carlson, B. L., 315
Carlson, P., 270, 271
Carlstrom, A. H., 418
Carne, G. L., 419
Carnevale, A. P., 7, 323–324, 344
Carney, C. G., 250
Carney, J. V., 339
Carson, E. A., 424
Cartwright, B., 168
Casner-Lotto, J., 324
Cass, V. C., 112, 132–133, 172
Castagnera, J. O., 123, 133, 139–149, 151, 152,
    156, 416
Cato, S., 233, 248
Catraio, C., 106
Cattell, H. E. P., 238
Cattell, K., 238
Cattell, R. B., 238
C'de Baca, J., 291
Ceperley, A., 386
Chae, M. H., 432, 433, 436
Chang, C. Y., 129
Chartrand, J. M., 250
Cheng, S-Y., 357
Chojnacki, J. T., 376–377
Chope, R. C., 114, 115, 118–119
Chronister, K. M., 434
Cihon, P. J., 123, 133, 139–149, 151, 152,
    156, 416
Clark, G. M., 256
Claus, R. E., 168
Clemens, E. V., 417, 418, 420–422
Cline, F., 360
Cline, K., 113, 135
Cluss, P. A., 149
Cochran, D. J., 228
Cochran, L., 88–91, 94, 98–100, 179,
    180, 272
Cohen, C. F., 433, 435–438
Coleman, V. D., 114
Collins, S., 105, 125
Connelly, A. R., 452, 458, 460, 461
Conrath, J. A., 3
Cook, B. J., 418
Cook, D., 416
Corey, G., 104, 111
Corey, M. S., 104
Cormier, S., 174, 177
Cosca, T., 296
Costa, P. T., Jr., 237, 238
Costantini, K., 340–341
Cotter, E. W., 377, 378
Cottone, R. R., 168
Coutinho, M. T., 3–4, 8, 106
Crane, P., 347
Crawford, E., 372

Crites, J. O., 228, 251
Crompton, L., 144
Crosby, O., 320
Cross, W. E., Jr., 112
Croteau, J. M., 377
Cruza-Guet, M. C., 20
Cueso, J., 370
Cummings, D. L., 142, 429
Cunningham, C., 309
Curtis, R., 324, 396, 456

D

Daiger, D. C., 25, 251
Daire, A. P., 114
Dalton, J. C., 378
Dam, U. C., 3, 132
D'Angelo, R., 112
Dannin, E., 144
Dapprich, J., 421, 422
Dare, D. E., 354, 357, 360, 361
Datti, P. A., 132
Davis, G., 472
Davis, H. V., 4, 139
Davis, J. B., 18, 468
Davis, N., 379
Davis, T., 164, 168
Dawis, R. V., 18, 25–30, 122, 179, 240, 255, 271, 275, 291
Day, S. X., 254
DeFries, J. C., 51
DelCastillo, D., 372
DeLeire, T., 416
DeLuca, M. J., 400
DeLuca, N., 400
Delworth, U., 461
DeNavas-Walt, C., 108–109
DePaul, J., 132
DeSena, J. N., 357
DeVaney, S. B., 372
DeVault, R. M., 270
DeVoy, J. E., 390
Dewey, C. R., 270
DeWitz, S. J., 112
Diemer, M. A., 106–108, 110, 125, 126
Dikel, M. R., 295
Dillon, T., 320
DiRamio, D., 419, 421, 422–423
Ditlevson, A. P., 376
Dixson, K., 379
Dolliver, R. H., 269–272
Donahue, M. P., 391–392
Donnay, D. A. C., 234
Donohue, R., 393
Downing, N. E., 112
Dozier, J. B., 391–392, 410, 412
Dugger, S. M., 347, 348
Dunn, M. G., 432, 436
DuPont, S., 341

E

Easton, B., 317
Ebberwein, C., 421
Eby, L. T., 394
Eckert, T., 101
Eichenfield, G. A., 462
Emmel, A., 296
Engels, D., 472

England, G. W., 255
Ensher, E. A., 433
Entin, D., 372
Erford, B. T., 334, 348, 510
Ericksen, K. S., 435–438
Estrada-Hernandez, N., 349
Evans, K., 124–126

F

Fabian, E. S., 4, 416
Farmer-Hinton, R. L., 359
Farr, M., 315
Fassinger, R. E., 112
Feldman, D. B., 370, 377, 378
Feller, R., 232, 236, 258, 335
Ferguson, R., 7, 344, 345, 354
Finck, B., 370, 376
Finney, M. I., 324, 399, 404
Fischer, K. E., 372
Fitzgerald, L. F., 18, 19, 35, 37
Fitzpatrick, A. R., 243
Fitzpatrick, C., 340–341
Flansburg, J. D., 415
Fleenor, J. W., 237
Fleig-Palmer, M. M., 394, 412, 413
Fletcher, E. C., Jr., 357, 359
Flores, L. Y., 106, 112–114, 136, 137
Flores, S. M., 120, 136
Flowers, C. P., 391–392
Folds, R. E., 132
Folsom, B., 377
Forester-Miller, H., 164, 168
Fouad, N. A., 51, 106, 370, 372, 377, 378, 411
Fox, R. S., 111
Frame, M. W., 168
Frank, R. A., 432
Frawley, T. A., 342
Freifeld, L., 419
Friedemann, M. A., 345, 347
Friedman, T. L., 5, 6, 7
Fritzche, B. A., 25
Fritzsche, B. A., 234, 383
Fry, R., 108, 109
Fu, C., 113, 135
Fuller, D. P., 114
Furlong, J. S., 371
Furr, S. R., 391–392

G

Gainer, L. J., 323–324
Gallagher, L., 343, 359
Garcia, J. G., 168
Gardner, E. F., 242–243
Gardner, J. N., 379
Garrett, M. T., 435
Gates, B., 7
Gati, I., 370, 371, 378
Gaunt, D., 359
Geisinger, K. F., 245
Gelberg, S., 376–377
Gibbon, M. M., 130, 432, 434–437
Gibson, D. L., 255
Gibson, R. L., 6–9
Gilbride, D., 416
Gill, N., 390
Ginsburg, S. W., 37, 469
Ginzberg, E., 37–39, 469

Glaser, K., 168
Glutting, J. J., 235
Goldman, B. A., 231
Goldman, L., 269
Goleman, D., 255, 292
Gonzales, J., 111
Goodman, J., 392, 410
Goodrich, K. M., 132, 172
Gordon, V. N., 370, 371
Gore, P. A., Jr., 294, 296
Gottfredson, G. D., 23, 254, 298
Gottfredson, L. S., 48–52, 54, 120, 122, 133, 179, 180, 201, 254, 272, 334, 335, 340
Gough, H. G., 236
Grant-Vallone, E. J., 433
Grier-Reed, T. L., 378
Grusec, J. E., 57
Gruys, M. L., 432
Guerriero, J., 472
Guindon, M. H., 391–392
Gupta, A., 113
Gushue, G. V., 112
Gysbers, N. C., 270, 271

H

Haas, H. S., 347
Haase, R. F., 238
Hackett, G., 65, 67, 68, 82, 105, 133, 179, 180, 201, 250, 323, 334, 383, 437
Hackney, H. L., 174, 177
Hagner, D., 416
Haid, R. L., 293
Hall, D. T., 8
Hammer, A. L., 237
Hansen, J. C., 24
Hansen, J. T., 88
Hansen, R. N., 270, 271
Harden, J., 168
Hardin, E. E., 106, 113
Hardy, K. V., 114, 118–119
Hardy, T. A., 132
Harley, D. A., 132
Harley, E., 434
Harlow, C. W., 425–426, 429
Harmon, L. W., 6, 8, 9, 248
Harrington, J. C., 246
Harrington, T. F., 246
Harris, B. S., 418
Harris, P. M., 427, 428
Harris-Bowlsbey, J., 39, 165, 295
Harrison, A., 7
Harrison, B., 424–429
Harter, J., 236, 237
Hartley, M. T., 349
Hartung, P. J., 106, 107, 122
Harwood, L., 400
Hastings, S., 421
Haycock, K., 344
Hedstrom, S. M., 377
Hees, C. K., 3–4, 7, 8
Helford, M. C., 432, 435
Helms, J. E., 112, 127
Hemmings, A., 359
Henle, M., 406, 407
Henly, G. A., 240
Heppner, M. J., 106, 112, 113, 135

Herlihy, B., 163–165
Herma, J. L., 37, 469
Herman, A. M., 296
Herman, D. O., 250
Herr, E. L., 4, 8, 9
Herzog, D. C., 129
Hetherington, C., 377
Hill, M., 168, 169
Hirsch, A. E., 427, 430
Hitch, J. L., 294, 296
Ho, T., 424
Hoachlander, G., 363–364
Hobson, S. M., 73, 299, 339, 510
Hochschild, A. R., 436
Hodges, S., 452, 458, 460, 461
Hodges, T., 236, 237
Hoff, K. S., 370, 374, 376, 382, 386
Holland, J. L., 18, 20–26, 30–32, 38, 54, 92, 96, 98, 179, 180, 231–235, 238, 248, 251, 252, 254, 260, 268, 270, 271, 273, 289, 298–299, 335, 383, 469
Holland, K., 330
Holzer, H. J., 424–428, 431
Hopkins, G., 342
Hopson, B., 411
Hoskiug, K., 268
Hossler, D., 343, 344, 346, 359
Howard, D. K., 378
Howell, L., 324, 398
Hsieh, P., 108, 110, 125, 126
Hughes, E., 361
Hughey, A. W., 372
Hughey, K. F., 418
Huyser, K. R., 134

I

Ingersoll-Dayton, B., 434–435
Isaacson, L. E., 174
Ivey, A. E., 176
Ivey, M. B., 176

J

Jackson, A. P., 339
Jackson, D. N., 231, 232, 237
Jackson, S. E., 255
Jacobs, S. J., 8
James, L., 7
Jarvis, P. S., 339
Jenifer, E. D., 112
Jenkins, J. A., 238
Jenson-Scott, R. L., 114
Johansson, C. B., 231, 232
Johnson, J., 341, 346
Johnston, J. A., 252, 270, 271
Jones, G. B., 57–61
Jones, J. V., 459
Jones, L. K., 270
Jordaan, J. P., 48, 190, 250
Jung, C., 237
Juntunen, C. L., 113, 135
Jurgens, J. C., 435

K

Kakiuchi, K. K. S., 114, 118–119
Kanagui, M., 113
Kantamneni, N., 377, 378

Kanter, R. M., 123, 124
Karlsen, B., 242–243
Katz, J., 106
Katz, M., 383
Kay, G. G., 238
Keim, M. C., 377
Keis, K., 240
Keller, K. S., 427, 428
Kelly, F. D., 81, 251
Kelly, G. D., 114
Kenna, A. C., 390
Kenny, M. C., 349, 350
Kerka, S., 339
Kerlow-Myers, A. E., 111, 112
Kern, C. W., 377, 378
Kerr, G. A., 377
Kim, B. S. K., 128–129
Kim, H., 109
Kim, J., 434–436
Kim, Y. M., 418
King, N. J., 109, 125
King, T., 112
Kinicki, A. J., 392
Kirby, K. M., 377
Kitchener, K. S., 163, 164, 168–170
Klehe, U. C., 391, 393
Klein, K. L., 378
Klein-Collins, R., 330
Knowdell, R. L., 279, 289–291, 293
Kobylarz, L., 333
Kocet, M. M., 172
Kochhar, R., 109
Kolodinsky, P., 342
Kolowich, S., 370–371
Koschier, M., 250
Kosine, N. R., 348, 349
Krannich, C., 431–432
Krannich, R. L., 422, 431–432
Krausz, M., 370, 371, 378
Krieshok, T. S., 270, 421
Kroll, J., 370, 374, 376, 382, 386
Krueger, G., 370, 376
Krumboltz, J. D., 57–64, 69, 82, 84, 122, 139, 179, 180, 202, 249, 370
Kübler-Ross, E., 392
Kursmark, L., 379, 397, 399
Kurtz, A., 390
Kwak, M., 434–435
Kyle, T., 132

L

Laker, D., 463–465
Laker, R., 463–465
Lally, P. S., 377
Lambie, G. W., 172
LaMothe, S., 114
Lasoff, D. L., 382
Laszloffy, T. A., 114, 118–119
Latack, J. C., 391–392, 410, 412
Lattimore, P., 427, 430
Laux, J. M., 426
Leach, M. M., 462
Leahy, M. J., 165
Leapard, B., 338
Lehker, T., 371
Leierer, S. J., 80, 378
Leiter, P. M., 255

Lent, R. W., 18, 29, 65–74, 82, 105, 113, 120, 122, 126, 133, 179, 180, 201, 250, 323, 334, 437
Lenz, J. G., 75, 76, 78–81, 83, 91, 179, 180, 190, 192, 202, 251, 377, 378, 421, 472
Leong, F. T. L., 106, 107, 110, 111, 113, 114, 120, 122, 125, 128–129
Lerner, R. M., 66
Lester, J. N., 315, 333
Levin, A. S., 62, 139, 370
Levitt, J. G., 400
Lewis, K. K., 420
Lewis, M. V., 299
Lewis, T., 357
Li, L. C., 129
Liang, C. T. H., 129
Lichtenberger, E., 424
Liesener, J. J., 416
Lighthall, A., 418, 422–423
Lindeman, R. H., 48, 190, 250, 253
Lindgren, A., 404
Linnemey, R. M., 377
Linton, C., 194
Lipka, S., 370–371
Liptak, J., 253, 255, 256
Livneh, H., 416
Lock, R. D., 324, 404, 406
Locke, W. S., 130, 432, 434–437
Lockwood, S. R., 424
Lofquist, L. H., 18, 25–26, 28–30, 122, 240, 255, 271, 275, 291
Long, K. L., 337
Loomis, C., 119
Lopez, S. J., 236–237
Lorenz, K., 399
Lozada, M., 342
Luchetta, E. J., 23
Ludwikowski, W. M. A., 370
Luginbuhl, P., 434
Luke, M., 132, 172
Lumsden, J. A., 386
Lunneborg, P. W., 34, 35, 252
Luthans, B. C., 412
Luthans, F., 412, 413
Luthans, K. W., 412
Luzzo, D. A., 371, 373

M

MacKinnon, F. J. D., 370, 374, 376, 382, 386
MacKinnon-Slaney, F., 269, 270
Macrine, S. L., 348, 349
Madaus, J. W., 350
Maddox, T. E., 258
Maddux, C. D., 231
Madsen, E., 109, 125
Magnuson, C. S., 334, 337
Magnuson, S., 114, 118–119
Maitoza, R., 392
Makela, J., 472
Malott, K. M., 114, 118–119
Mandel, S., 399
Mandernach, B. J., 412
Marcus, E., 219
Mariani, M. J., 342
Marshall, C. W., 231
Marshall, S. K., 104

Martin, C., 400
Martinez-Moncada, D., 400
Maslach, C., 255
Maslow, A., 34
Mastrangelo, P. M., 237
Mathison, D., 324, 399, 404
Matthews, D. B., 291
Matyja, A., 254
Mau, W. J., 106, 107, 121, 129
McAllister, S., 437
McBain, L., 418, 422
McCarn, S. R., 112
McCarney, S. B., 256
McCarthy, J., 149
McCaulley, M. H., 237
McClearn, J. E., 51
McCollum, E. E., 114
McCormac, M. E., 294, 320
McCowan, R. J., 231
McCowan, S. C., 231
McCrae, R. R., 237, 238
McDonough, P. M., 359
McEachern, A. G., 349, 350
McGuffin, P., 51
McIlveen, P., 377, 380
McKee-Ryan, F. M., 392
McNeill, B. W., 462
Medvide, M. B., 394
Meeder, H., 357
Meisgeier, C., 237
Meltzer, A. S., 323–324
Menting, L., 394
Merrill, G., 468
Merz, E. L., 111
Michael, W. B., 233
Miller, C. D., 377, 378
Miller, E. M., 334
Miller, M. J., 111, 112
Miller, R. J., 232
Miller, W. R., 291
Milsom, A. S., 349, 417, 418, 420–422
Mitchell, A. M., 57–61
Mitchell, K. E., 62–64, 139, 370, 377
Mitchell, L. K., 60, 62, 249
Mitchell, M. H., 6–9
Mitchell, R. L., 419
Moon, S. M., 114, 118–119
Moore, E. J., 270, 271
Moore, T., 335
Morrill, W. H., 250
Morten, G., 112
Moser, K., 391–392
Mullainathan, S., 123
Murphey, C. M., 391–392, 394
Murphy, E., 237
Murphy, K. A., 106
Myers, L. J., 112
Myers, R. A., 48, 190, 250

N

Nachmann, B., 35
Nally, J. M., 424–427, 429, 431
Nassar-McMillan, S. C., 391–392
Navarro, R. L., 112
Neidert, G. P. M., 235, 238, 249
Nelson, T. S., 114
Nevill, D. D., 48
Ngaruiya, K., 111
Nguyen, D. Q., 129

Nicholson, N., 391–392
Nielson, T. R., 406, 407
Nietupski, J., 349
Niles, S. G., 39, 46, 165, 180, 190, 250, 334, 339
North, A. B., 323

O

Oakes, J., 362, 363, 368
O'Brien, K. M., 4, 139, 270, 432
O'Hara, C., 129
Okiishi, R. W., 114, 118–119
O'Neil, H. F., 323–324
Orthner, D. K., 337
Ortman, N. L., 235, 238, 249
Osborn, D. S., 250, 253, 258, 295, 337, 378
Osborne, W. L., 46, 180, 190, 250
O'Shea, T. F., 232
Osipow, S. H., 18, 19, 35, 37, 250, 256, 370, 371, 378
Ostovary, F., 421, 422
Ott, A., 341
Overtoom, C., 323
Owen, A., 421

P

Padula, M. A., 432, 433
Paivandy, S., 81, 251
Palmer, L. B., 359
Palmer, P. J., 378
Papa, A., 392
Paredes, D. M., 5
Parker, R., 233, 248
Parker, R. M., 415, 416
Parsons, F., 4, 18–20, 30, 75, 77, 78, 139, 229, 249, 294, 377, 384, 442, 468
Patterson, J. B., 415
Patti, D. C., 347
Patton, J. R., 256
Patton, W., 393
Paul, E. L., 372
Paul, K. I., 391–392
Paycheck, J., 170
Penick, N., 114, 116, 118–119
Pensiero, D., 377, 380
Pérez, G. M., 131
Pérez, P. A., 359
Perrone-McGovern, K. M., 472
Person, A. E., 344
Peters, A. C., 400
Peterson, G. W., 75–81, 83, 91, 179, 180, 190, 192, 202, 251, 337, 378, 421
Phelan, K. C., 323–324
Phillips, C. A., 299, 339, 510
Phillips, J., 420–421
Piaget, J., 77
Piehl, A. M., 424–430
Pierson, O., 398
Plomin, R., 51
Ponterotto, J. G., 114, 125, 437
Popadiuk, N., 107, 113
Pope, M., 4, 125, 138, 139, 377
Porfeli, E. J., 250, 251
Powell, A. B., 25, 234, 383
Power, P. G., 25, 251
Power, S. J., 245
Price, R. H., 394
Prince, J. P., 377
Proctor, B. D., 108–109

Q

Quenk, N. L., 237
Quirk, K., 176

R

Rabin, V. S., 433, 435–438
Rak, E., 165
Ramos, K., 113
Rao, J., 7
Raphael, S., 424
Rayman, J., 18, 20
Reardon, R. C., 23, 75, 76, 78–81, 83, 91, 179, 180, 190, 192, 202, 251, 298, 337, 377, 378, 421, 429
Redcross, C., 424–426, 428
Reed, A. Y., 468
Reed, C. A., 80
Reed, C. R., 23, 298
Reed, M. B., 238
Reese, R. J., 377, 378
Reese, S., 342
Reile, D. M., 472
Remley, T. P., Jr., 163–165
Rentz, A. L., 370, 374, 376, 382, 386
Rhodes, V., 392
Richards, S., 468
Richmond, E., 364
Richmond, N., 400
Richwine, M. H., 23
Ripley, R. E., 235, 238, 249
Rivera, L., 114, 125
Robbins, S. B., 250
Robertson, G. J., 239
Robertson, H. C., 419
Robinson, C. H., 240
Robinson, E. T., 240
Robinson-Wood, T. L., 183
Rochkind, J., 341
Rochlen, A. B., 380, 432
Rockawin, D., 324, 400
Roe, A., 34–36, 469
Roesch, S. C., 111
Rogers, C. R., 176
Rogers, W., 463
Rojewski, J. W., 109
Rosenbaum, J. E., 344
Rosenberg, H., 254
Rottinghaus, P. J., 3, 254
Rounds, J. B., Jr., 240
Rousseau, D. M., 8
Rush, K. L., 112
Rutter, M. E., 459
Ruzek, N. A., 129
Ryan, D. J., 415, 416
Ryan, R., 371, 387
Ryan, S. W., 418, 419, 421, 422

S

Sabbatino, E. D., 348, 349
Sabol, W. J., 424
Sakamoto, A., 134
Saks, A. M., 394, 406
Salamone, P. R., 39
Sampson, J. P., Jr., 75–83, 91, 179, 180, 190, 192, 202, 251, 295, 378, 421, 472
Sanford, E. E., 232
Sarkees-Wircenski, M., 355, 356–357, 360
Saunders, D. E., 81, 251, 378

Saunders, M., 362, 363, 368
Savickas, M. L., 39–43, 46, 88, 91–103, 176, 179, 180, 201, 250, 251, 253, 254, 272
Savino, C. S., 422
Schaufeli, W. B., 255
Schehr, R. C., 424–429
Schein, E. H., 239, 265
Schenck, P., 247
Schepp, B., 324, 399
Schepp, D., 324, 399
Schlossberg, N. K., 392, 410–412
Schmidt, C., 386
Schmit, J., 343
Schmitt, J., 424
Schneider, M. R., 254
Schul, Y., 394
Schulenberg, J. E., 66
Schultheiss, D. E. P., 130, 437
Schultz, M., 323
Schutt, D. A., Jr., 370, 472
Schwallie-Giddis, P., 370
Schwartz, R. B., 7, 344, 345, 354
Scorse, J., 7
Scott, C. K., 377, 378
Scott, J. L., 355, 356–357, 360
Seashore, H. G., 247
Segal, S. J., 35
Segal, S. P., 423
Sexton, T. L., 382
Sharf, R. S., 20, 35, 271, 272, 318
Shatkin, L., 315–316, 321, 322
Shaw, H. E., 114
Shaw, P. A., 468
Shaw, S. F., 350
Shillingford, M. A., 391–392, 394
Shivy, V. A., 424, 426–428, 430
Shoffner, M. F., 377
Shurts, W. M., 377
Shy, J. D., 377
Simons, W., 324, 396, 456
Simpson, C. G., 350
Singleton, G. E., 194
Sjodin, T. L., 324, 398
Skaar, N. R., 378
Skinner, B. F., 58
Slaney, R. B., 269, 270
Sloan, T., 148
Smith, B., 391–392
Smith, J. C., 108–109
Smith, S. S., 413
Smith-Keller, K., 472
Snead, K. M., 418
Solórzano, M. T., 111
Song, Z., 392
Spencer, V. G., 350
Spielberger, C. D., 254–255
Spokane, A. R., 20, 23
Starr, M. F., 334, 337
Stearns, R. J., 363–364
Stebleton, M., 406, 407
Steele, G. E., 370
Steinberg, W. J., 232
Stewart, S. M., 432
Stoll, M. A., 424
Stoltenberg, C. D., 461, 462
Stone, J. R., 299
Stone, J. R., III, 357, 360
Stone, K. V. W., 140

Stott, K. A., 339
Strehlke, C., 399, 400
Streufert, B., 400
Strickland, J. M., 377
Studier, C., 363–364
Sue, D., 106, 107
Sue, D. W., 106, 107, 112
Sueyoshi, L., 114
Sueyoshi, L. A., 125
Super, 93
Super, C. M., 40–43, 46, 179, 180, 250, 253
Super, D., 383, 469
Super, D. E., 39–48, 52, 53, 122, 135, 179, 180, 190, 204, 250, 253, 334, 437
Sveinsdottir, M., 4, 138, 139
Swedburg, R. B., 435
Sweeten, G., 427, 430
Symonds, W. C., 7, 344, 345, 354
Szymanski, E. M., 415

T

Takai, R., 270, 289
Takei, I., 134
Tarvydas, V. M., 168
Taylor, K. M., 250, 378
Taylor, P., 109
Terkel, S., 378
Theokas, C., 344
Theriot, M. T., 423
Thomas-Clark, C., 370, 376
Thompson, A. S., 48, 190, 250, 253
Thompson, E., 370, 377, 378
Thompson, M. N., 142, 429
Tomei, M., 122
Tomlinson, E. C., 144–146
Torpey, E. M., 340
Tovar-Murray, D., 112
Tree, H. A., 236–237
Troiden, R. R., 112, 132–133
Trolley, B. C., 347
Trusty, J., 339
Tyler, L. E., 268–270, 272, 274

U

Unger, H. G., 354, 365, 366, 385

V

Vagg, P. R., 254–255
Valach, L., 104
Valverde, L. A., 132
Van Dam, K., 394
Van der Veer, G., 379
van Ryn, M., 394
Venable, M. A., 382
Vernick, S. H., 23, 298, 429
Vesper, N., 343
Vidilakas, N. K., 62
Vilorio, D., 460
Vinitsky, M. H., 228
Vinokur, A. D., 394
Visher, C., 427, 430
Vogel, D., 370
Von Bergen, A. N., 139
Von Bergen, C. W., 139
Vondracek, F. W., 66

W

Wachs, T. D., 51
Wadsworth, J. S., 349
Waldron, K., 119, 120
Wall, B., 194, 196
Wall, J. E., 246
Walls, J., 377, 379–381
Walsh, D. J., 46, 180, 190, 250
Walsh, M. E., 132
Walsh, M. W., 152
Wan, C. M., 394
Wanberg, C. R., 392
Warner, K., 424
Warren, P. M., 228
Warth, J., 349
Watkins, K. E., 434, 435
Watson, M., 111
Wazny, L., 427, 431
Weaver, E., 468
Weber, M., 127
Weeks, G. R., 114, 118–119
Weiss, D. J., 240, 255
Welfel, E. R., 168
Wendlandt, N. M., 380
Wesman, A. G., 247
Wettersten, K., 421
Whiston, S. C., 229, 382, 383
Whitaker, A., 303
Whitfield, E. A., 233, 236, 248, 258
Whitson, M. L., 112
Wilbourne, P. L., 291
Wilkinson, G., 235
Williams, A. P., 424, 426
Williams, C. B., 168
Williams, J. C., 335
Williams, S. K., 270
Williamson, E. G., 19, 20, 25–26, 468
Winer, J. L., 250
Winslow, A., 349
Winston, S. M., 168
Witt, M. A., 415, 416
Wood, C., 236, 258
Wood, F. B., 377, 379, 381
Woods, J., 315
Woods, S., 400
Worth, W. E., 323
Wrenn, C. G., 105
Wright, M. O., 372

Y

Yakushko, O., 111
Yanico, B., 250
Young, J. W., 360
Young, R. A., 104, 107

Z

Zachar, P., 237
Zalaquett, C. P., 176, 295
Zanskas, S. A., 165
Ziering, N., 347
Zikic, J., 391, 393
Zinn, H., 135
Ziomek-Daigle, J., 172
Zirkle, C., 357, 359
Zuckerberg, M., 7
Zunker, V. G., 19, 250, 258, 318
Zytowski, D. G., 4, 139, 233

SUBJECT INDEX

A

Abilities. *See* Skills and abilities
Ability Explorer (AE) assessment, 246, 258
Academic ability, testing for, 241–245, 242t
Academic management, college students, 372–373
Acceptance letters for job offers, 408, 461
Acclimating to work. *See* Adjustment to career
Accommodations for people with disabilities, 143, 416
Accreditation of CTE programs, 367, 368t
Acculturation, 111–112, 111f, 127, 134–135
Achievement gaps, 343, 357, 359
ACT, Inc.
    tests, 235, 241–242, 343
    WorkKeys assessments, 253
    world-of-work map, 299
Activeness, adjustment behavior, 28
Actuarial approaches to counseling, 19–20
Adjustment to career, 252–257, 252t, 380–381, 461–463. *See also* Theory of work adjustment
Administrators, counselor consultations with, 387
Adolescents. *See* Children; K–12 educational settings
Adult Basic Learning Examination (ABLE), 242–243
Adult Career Concerns Inventory (ACCI), 48, 52–54, 253
Advancement, opportunities for, 302
Advertising and soliciting clients, 480–481
Affluence, 106
Age Discrimination in Employment Act (ADEA) of 1967, 143
Agency, 93, 106–107, 121
Age of clients. *See also* Retirement
    career development and, 133–134
    discrimination based on, 143
    midlife career change and, 42
    older workers, counseling (*See* Doris Bronner (fired))
Alcoholism, 143–144
American Bar Association, 142
American Counseling Association (ACA), 104, 165, 448, 472
American Diploma Project, 353–354
American dream, 106
American School Counselor Association (ASCA), 331–333t, 497–498
Americans with Disabilities Act (ADA) of 1990, 143, 349, 416
America's Career InfoNet, 309–312, 310f, 311t, 312–314f, 327
Anxiety, 73, 76
Applicant tracking systems (ATS), 396
Applications for jobs, 398, 451–453, 452t.
    See also Cover letters; Résumés
Archway of career determinants, 46, 47f, 53
Armed forces. *See* Military
Armed Forces Qualifying Test (AFQT), 344
Armed Services Vocational Aptitude Battery (ASVAB), 246–247, 344

Army Alpha and Army Beta tests of cognitive ability, 19
Arrests vs. convictions on background checks, 142, 428
The ASCA National Model (American School Counselor Association), 332
Ashland Interest Assessment (AIA), 231
Assessment instruments. *See also* Standardized tests
    for career-development assessment and counseling (C-DAC) model, 48
    for decision-making readiness, 81
    ethics and, 166–167, 483–485
    as helping strategies, 178–179
    for Krumboltz's learning theories, 62
    for people with disabilities, 415–416
    social cognitive career theory (SCCT) and, 71–73
    for Super's life-span, life-space approach, 46, 47t
    for theory of work adjustment (TWA), 27, 27t
    for veterans, 420–421
Assessment of readiness for CIP delivery sequence, 80–81, 80f, 86
Associative learning experiences (ALEs), 58, 59f, 62
At-will employment doctrine, 140, 144–146t, 155–156
Autonomy, 163–164, 171–172
Avocation, 2t

B

Background checks of applicants, 141–142, 428
Background information, gathering, 177, 185–187t. *See also* Intake assessments
Bandura's foundational learning theories, 56–57, 57f
Barriers and supports in SCCT, 68, 70, 72–74, 85–86
Barriers to employment. *See* Client issues
Barriers to Employment Success Inventory, 253
Basic Achievement Skills Inventory (BASI), 243
Becker Work Adjustment Profile: 2 (BWAP), 253–254
Behavior modification interventions, 430
Beliefs. *See also* Outcome expectations; Self-efficacy
    Career Beliefs Inventory (CBI) for, 62
    circumscription and, 48–50, 50f
    control over career choices and, 41
    modifying in counseling, 71
    self-observation generalizations (SOGs), 58, 60f, 62, 82–85
Beneficence, 164, 171, 173
Beneficiaries of pension plans, 152–153
Benefits, 380
Best Jobs book series (JIST Works, Inc.), 315
Bisexual individuals. *See* LGBT individuals
Bona fide occupational qualifications (BFOQs), 143

Bordin's psychodynamic model of career choice and satisfaction, 36–37
Boston Vocational Bureau, 18
Boundaryless career, 8–9
Brainstorming, 78, 85
Breadwinner's Institute, 18
Bridges/XAP computer-assisted career guidance system, 318
BRIGANCE Transition Skills Inventory (TSI), 254
Bureau of Labor Statistics, 305–309, 339, 390
Burnout, 172–173, 255, 393–394. *See also* Gillian Parker (burnout, seeking new direction)
Business cards, 397

C

Calculus between personality types, 25, 25f
California Psychological Inventory (CPI), 236
Campbell Interest and Skill Survey (CISS), 231, 247, 259–261
Campus Pride, 132
CandidCareer.com, 317
Capacities, tentative career choices and, 38, 42
Capital, types of, 359, 412–413
Card sorts, 268–293
    client examples and, 275–288
    constructivist theories and, 272
    history of, 268–271, 269t
    learning theories and, 271–272
    low-interest occupations, reconsidering, 72
    purchasing, 289, 289–293t
    steps for using, 272–275
    theory of circumscription and compromise and, 272
    trait factor theory and, 271
Career, defined, 2t
Career adaptability, 42, 48
Career adjustment, tests for, 252–257, 252t
Career Anchors Self-Assessment, 239, 265
Career and technical education (CTE), 353–369
    academic rigor of, 354–355
    accreditation of, 367, 368t
    as alternative to bachelor's degree, 344–345
    best practice programs for, 360–362
    career clusters for, 360
    counselor's role in, 364–367
    future of, 362–364
    history and legislation for, 355–359t
    sources of, 365, 366–367t
    as tracking system, 357, 359
Career Assessment Inventory (CAI), 231
Career Attitudes and Strategies Inventory (CASI), 254
Career Beliefs Inventory (CBI), 62, 84, 249–250, 259
Career clusters
    for career and technical education (CTE), 360
    national, 299, 300t
    standardized tests for career selection and, 231–235
    vocational aptitude tests and, 247–248

Career construction theory (Savickas), 91–100
  card sorts and, 272
  career interventions, 93–94
  client examples for, 101–103
  helping strategies for, 180
  life-design paradigm and, 94–99, 96t
  overview, 92–93, 93f, 95f
  standardized tests and, 254
Career counseling. *See also specific populations; specific theories and approaches*
  career planning vs., 160
  cognitive information-processing delivery sequence for, 80–82, 80f, 80t
  culture of client and, 112–120, 113t, 115–116t, 117–118f, 119t
  defined, 3, 160
  ethics and (*See* Ethics)
  history of, 3–6, 18–20, 468–469
  interviews for (*See* Career counseling interviews)
  issues addressed by, 2–3, 3t (*See also* Client issues)
  need for, 3, 9, 18
  process of, 174–200 (*See also* Stage model of counseling process)
  for transitions in life (*See* Transition counseling)
Career Counseling: A Narrative Approach (Cochran), 89
Career counseling interviews
  for CIP delivery sequence, 80
  cultural formulation, 114, 115t, 214–215, 215t
  culture of clients, understanding, 125
  for genograms, 115–116
  for intake assessment, 203
  motivational, 149
Career counselor education
  certification requirements, 161–163
  courses and instructors for, selecting, 445
  licensure requirements, 159
  pacing for, 445–446
  résumé content and, 454–455
  supervision, training, and teaching, 167, 488–491
Career counselors, 441–465, 442t
  career adjustment of, 461–463
  career preparation of, 442–449, 442t, 444t, 448–449t
  in community settings, 438–439
  competencies of, 442–443, 442t, 470–471, 480
  culture of client, responding to, 124–126, 124t
  education of (*See* Career counselor education)
  goals of, 463–465, 463t, 464f
  income information, 309
  job outlook for, 307–308, 308f
  job search process of, 449–461, 452t, 454t, 456t
  long-term career planning of, 463–465, 463t, 464f
  role of, 295, 364–367
  as social capital of students, 359
Career Cruising computer-assisted career guidance system, 318, 429
Career days, 319–320, 335
Career Decision Difficulties Questionnaire (CDDQ), 378
Career decision-making skills. *See* Cognitive information-processing (CIP) approach to counseling

Career Decision Making System–Revised (CDM-R), 232
Career Decision Scale (CDS), 250
Career Decision Self-Efficacy Scale (CDSE), 250, 378
Career development
  activities for, 3, 73–74 (*See also* Educational career planning activities)
  card sorts for, 292–293t (*See also* Card sorts)
  for career and technical education (*See* Career and technical education (CTE))
  of career counselors, 441–465 (*See also* Career counselors)
  in college settings (*See* College settings, career planning in)
  computer-assisted career guidance systems for, 382–383
  courses for, 377–381, 378t
  culture and, 120–121, 121f
  education for, 7, 136
  events for, 376
  for ex-offenders, 428–429
  groups for, 376–377
  history of, 3–6, 18–20, 468–469
  of K–12 students (*See* K–12 educational settings)
  sexual orientation and, 132
  socioeconomic status and, 131
  student competencies in, 332–333
  workshops for, 375–376
Career-development assessment and counseling (C-DAC) model, 46–48, 180
Career Development Inventory (CDI), 48, 52–53, 190, 250
Career Directions Inventory (CDI), 231–232
Career exploration for veterans, 420–421
Career Factors Inventory (CFI), 250
Career fairs, 342
Career Futures Inventory–Revised, 254
Career management for students, 373
Career maturity, 42, 48, 251
Career Maturity Inventory, 251
CareerOneStop Videos, 312, 315t
Career planning vs. career counseling, 160
Career preparation for ex-offenders, 429
Career problems. *See also specific problems*
  causes and analysis of, 81, 87
  Cochran's narrative approach and, 89
  defined, 77
  helping strategies for (*See* Helping strategies)
  identifying, 176–177
Careers in Focus series (Infobase/Ferguson), 317
Career stories
  assessment of, 97–98
  client examples of, 101–103
  interviews for, 94–97, 96t, 179
  life-design paradigm and, 94
Career Thoughts Inventory (CTI), 81, 86–87, 179, 251
Career transitions. *See* Transition counseling
Caretakers. *See* Homemakers and caretakers
Carl D. Perkins Career and Technical Education Improvement Act of 2006, 357
Carl D. Perkins Vocational and Applied Technology Education Act of 1990, 356–357
Carl D. Perkins Vocational Education Act of 1984, 356

CASVE (communication, analysis, synthesis, valuing, and execution)
  assessments and, 179
  client examples of, 87
  crystallization and, 91
  implementing, 190, 191–193t, 194
  overview, 77–80, 78f, 79t
Center for Credentialing and Education (CCE), 162–163, 163t
Centrality of work, 106
Certification, 161–163
Certified Clinical Mental Health Counselor (CCMHC), 161
Certified Professional Resume Writers (CPRWs), 396
Challenges. *See* Client issues
Chance events, 63, 84. *See also* Happenstance learning theory (HLT)
Change. *See* Transition counseling
Changes in world of work, 6–9
Child care, 438
Child labor, 148, 155
Children. *See also* Developmental theories; Students
  career construction theory and, 92–93, 95–96
  career counseling for (*See* K–12 educational settings)
  employment of, 148, 155
  Murphy Meisgeier Type Indicator for Children (MMTIC), 237
  survivor's benefits for, 154
Choice model of SCCT, 69–70, 70f
Choosing a Vocation (Parsons), 4, 18, 139, 229
Circumscription, 340. *See also* Theory of circumscription, compromise, and self-creation (Gottfredson)
Civil Rights Act of 1964, 123–124, 133, 142–143, 154–155
Classroom presentations, 319–320
Client-focused interventions, 125–126
Client issues
  career problems (*See also specific problems*)
    categories of, 2–3, 3t
    causes and analysis of, 81, 87
    Cochran's narrative approach and, 89
    defined, 77
    helping strategies for (*See* Helping strategies)
    culture, understanding, 112–120, 113t, 115–116t, 117–118f, 119t
    for ex-offenders, 425–428, 425t
  goals
    affluence as, 106
    career story assessment and, 97, 98
    cognitive information-processing and, 79, 81
    intake assessments and, 204, 218–219
    for job searches, 395
    social cognitive career theory and, 66, 71, 74, 85–86
  identifying, 176–177, 185, 186–187t (*See also* Intake assessments)
  motivators for counseling, 14
  for people with disabilities, 415
  personal issues and, 14–15
  theory, role of, 15
  for veterans, 419
Client scenarios, 9–14. *See also each client by first name*
  Doris Bronner (fired), 12–13

Client scenarios (*Continued*)
  Gillian Parker (burnout, seeking new direction), 13
  Juan Martinez (vocational rehabilitation after injury), 13–14
  Lakeesha Maddox (stay-at-home parent, widowed), 11
  Lily Huang Li Mei (undecided), 11
  Vincent Arroyo (gay student with military aspirations), 12
  Wayne Jensen (job security concerns), 10
Clifton StrengthsFinder (CSF), 236–237
Coat-buying metaphor for college selection, 347, 348t
Cochran's narrative approach. *See* Narrative approach to counseling (Cochran)
Coconstruction in life-design paradigm of CCT, 98–99
Code of Ethics (ACA), 104, 165
Code of Ethics (NCDA). *See* National Career Development Association (NCDA) Code of Ethics
Cognitive complexity, 23
A Cognitive Information Processing Approach to Career Problem Solving and Decision Making, 251
Cognitive information-processing (CIP) approach to counseling, 75–82
  client examples for, 86–87, 190, 191–193t
  decision-making course, 377–378
  decision-making model for, 77–80, 78f, 79t
  decision status taxonomy, 75–76, 75f
  helping strategies for, 179–180
  information-processing domains, pyramid of, 76–77, 76f
  seven-step delivery sequence for, 80–82, 80f, 80t, 83f
  for veterans, 421
Cognitive interventions, 62
Collective bargaining, 140, 145t
Collectivism, 106–107, 121–122, 129–130
College. *See* Postsecondary education
College and Career Transitions Initiative, 361–362
College Board tests, 243–244
College counselors. *See* Career counselors
College fairs, 345–346
College Match (Anonoff & Friedemann), 347
College settings, career planning in, 370–388
  career counseling programs, 375–382, 375t, 378t, 381t
  client example (*See* Lily Huang Li Mei (undecided))
  collaboration on campus, 387
  competencies and standards for, 374, 374t
  employer relationship and recruitment services, 386–387
  experiential learning, 385
  faculty and administrators, consultation services to, 387
  high school students, 371–373
  information resources for, 382–385
  job search services, 385–386
  returning students, 373–374
Commission on Rehabilitation Counselor Certification, 415
Commitment anxiety (CA), 81, 86–87, 251
Common law exceptions to wrongful discharge, 145, 146t
Communication, 166–167, 175

Community colleges, 345. *See also* Career and technical education (CTE)
Community setting counseling, 415, 438–439. *See also specific subpopulations*
Competencies
  of career counselors, 442–443, 442t, 470–471, 480
  in ethics, 158–159, 166
  of students, 497–498
  workplace, 509
Competition for jobs, 6, 459
Compromise, 38–39, 51, 54. *See also* Theory of circumscription, compromise, and self-creation (Gottfredson)
Compulsion, external pressures and, 37
Computer-assisted career guidance systems, 317–319, 338, 382, 383t
Concept congruence, 23–24
Confidence. *See* Self-efficacy
Confidentiality, 166, 171, 176, 477–479, 486
Consistency between personality types, 25
Consolidated Omnibus Budget Reconciliation Act (COBRA) of 1985, 149, 154
Constructing reality, 91
Construction in life-design paradigm of CCT, 94–97, 95f, 96f
Contextual factors, 135, 201. *See also* Distal contextual factors; Proximal contextual factors
Contextualized learning, 362–364
Contract exceptions to wrongful discharge, 144–145, 145t
Contracts, job offers and, 406
Convictions vs. arrests on background checks, 142
Coping resources for transitions, 412
Core curriculum, elementary, 334–335
Cost of living, 380
Council for Accreditation of Counseling and Related Educational Programs (CACREP), 158, 447
Council for the Advancement of Standards (CAS), 374–375, 375t, 384–387
Courageous conversations with coworkers, 196f, 197
Cover letters, 379, 397–398, 457
Credential file services, 386
Credentials, 161–163, 481. *See also* Licensure
Credit checks of applicants, 141–142
Crimes committed by clients. *See* Ex-offenders
Criminal background checks, 141–142, 428
Critical thinking, 125
Crystallization
  in CIP, 78
  in narrative approach, 91
  occupational choice stage of, 38
Cultural capital, 359
Cultural formulation approach (CFA) to counseling, 113–114, 113t
Cultural formulation interview, 114, 115t, 214–215, 215t
Culture, 104–137
  career counseling process and, 124–126, 124t
  career transitions and, 410–411
  of client, understanding, 112–120, 113t, 115–116t, 117–118f, 119t, 173
  client examples, 126–137
  defined, 104–105
  differences in, 107–110

diversity within, 110–112
impact of, 120–124
influence on career, 70
influence on self-view, 97
overview, 104–107, 105t
of work, 380
Curiosity, 41

D

Dawis's theory of work adjustment. *See* Theory of work adjustment
Decided clients, 75, 87
Decision making
  card sorts for (*See* Card sorts)
  courses for, 377–381, 378t
  culture and, 121–122
  for ethics, 168
  models for, 77–80, 78f, 79t, 86–87, 179
  social learning theory of career decision making, 57–60, 58t, 59–61f, 82
  standardized tests for, 249–252, 249t
Decision-making confusion (DMC), 81, 87, 251
Decline/disengagement stage of life-span model, 43, 53
Deconstruction in life-design paradigm of CCT, 97
Department of Education, 150, 322, 339–340
Department of Labor, 123, 233, 315, 323, 430
Depressed clients, 389
Developmental applications of SCCT, 73–74
Developmental considerations for K–12 students
  activities list, 351t
  elementary students, 333–334
  high school students, 340
  high school students transitioning to college, 371–373
  middle school students, 337
  returning students, 373–374
Developmental theories, 34–55
  Bordin's psychodynamic model of career choice and satisfaction, 36–37
  client examples of, 52–55
  defined, 34
  Ginzberg's theory of occupational choice, 37–39, 38t
  Gottfredson's theory of circumscription, compromise, and self-creation, 48–51, 50f, 54–55
  Roe's theory of personality development and career choice, 34–35, 35t, 36f
  Super's life-span, life-space approach, 39–48, 52–54 (*See also* Life-span, life-space approach to counseling (Super))
Developmental transition points, 177
Diagnostic and Statistical Manual of Mental Disorders (DSM-IV-TR), 113–114, 159, 214–215, 215t
Dictionary of Holland Occupational Codes (DHOC; Gottfredson & Holland), 23, 298–299
Dictionary of Occupational Titles (DOT; U.S. Department of Labor), 23, 233
Differential psychology, 19–20
Digital footprints, 397, 399–402t
Digital revolution, 4–5
Dignity USA, 172
Disabilities. *See* People with disabilities

Subject Index **547**

Disability insurance benefits, 150–152, 151t, 157
Disclosure statements, 176
Discouraged workers, 390, 391t, 393
Discovering Careers series (Infobase/Ferguson), 317
Discrimination
 age, 134
 background checks and, 142
 Code of Ethics (NCDA) on, 166, 172, 481
 cultural variables and, 122–124
 in employment-eligibility documentation requests, 141
 gender and, 133–134, 147, 154–155
 nondiscrimination laws, 142–144
 people with disabilities and, 143, 416
 race and ethnicity and, 136, 154–155
 sexual orientation and, 133, 155
 sociopolitical inequities and, 107–108
 work conditions and, 147, 148t
Disinterest, 71–72
Dismissals from employment. *See* Hiring and firing laws
Disparate treatment and impact, 143
Dissatisfied employees. *See* Theory of work adjustment
Distal contextual factors, 66–68, 70, 86, 113, 133
Diversity, 104–105, 110–112, 111f
Divorce, 149, 434
Dolliver, Robert H., 269–270
Dominant and nondominant culture groups, 105, 105t
"Don't ask, don't tell" policy of U.S. military, 144, 155
Doris Bronner (fired)
 card sorts for, 279, 284–288t, 285–288f, 288
 client overview, 12–13
 cognitive information-processing approach and, 87
 cultural dimensions and, 133–134, 133t
 employment law and, 155–156
 ethical considerations for, 170, 172–173
 information resources for, 329t
 intake assessment for, 220, 221f
 Krumboltz's learning theories and, 84
 life-span, life-space approach and, 53
 narrative theory and, 100–101
 person-environment fit theory, 31
 social cognitive career theory and, 85–86
 stage model of career counseling process and, 194, 194–196t, 197
 standardized tests for, 263–264, 264t
 theory of circumscription, compromise, and self-creation and, 54
 theory of work adjustment and, 32
Dropping out of college, 349, 354
Drug convictions, 424, 427
Drug dependence, 143–144, 424, 431
Drug-Free Workplace Act of 1988, 142
Drug testing, 142
Dual track education, 362–363

E

Earnings. *See* Income
Economic capital, 412
Economic disparities, culture and, 108–110
Education
 academic ability, testing for, 241–245, 242t
 barriers to, 70, 74

of career counselors (*See* Career counselor education)
for career development, 7, 136
on careers, 94
choosing college for, 347, 348t
of clients, intake assessments and, 201, 204, 205–208f, 208, 219–220
of clients in counseling session (*See* Psychoeducational interventions)
continuing education, 168, 462–463
ex-offenders and, 425–426, 429
financial aid for, 322–323, 422, 427, 429–430
homemakers and caretakers and, 436
importance of, 7, 321–322, 321f, 344–345, 354
information resources for, 321–323, 321f
multiple pathways approach to, 362–364
postsecondary (*See* Postsecondary education)
socioeconomic status and, 120
tracking systems, 357, 359, 359t, 362–364
transition to work from, 379, 381t
Educational Amendments Act of 1972, 133
Educational career planning activities
 elementary students, 335–337
 high school, 342t
 high school students, 342–350, 345t, 348t, 350t
 middle school students, 338–339
Educational development plans (EDPs), 339–340, 510
Educational level, job search by, 311–312
Educators, ethics and, 167
Effort, tolerable boundaries for, 49, 54–55
Ego, 37
Elaboration in CIP, 78
Electronic portfolios, 386
Elementary school students, 333–337. *See also* K–12 educational settings
 career planning activities for, 335–337
 developmental considerations, 333–334
 guidance lessons for, 334–335
 schoolwide programs for, 335, 336t
Elevator speeches, 398–399
Eligibility for work, documents for, 141
Emotional intelligence, 255
Emotional needs of clients
 decision making and, 86
 displaced homemakers and, 438
 job searching and, 391–394, 392f, 406
 veterans and, 421
Employability skills
 career development courses and, 380
 of ex-offenders, 426, 428, 430
 high school students and, 340
 information resources on, 323–324
 middle school students and, 338
 of SCANS, 508–509
 of veterans, 422
Employee Retirement Income Security Act (ERISA) of 1974, 153, 156
Employer relationship services, 386–387
Employers. *See also* Discrimination
 accessing, 385–386
 cognitive ability tests used by, 245
 contacting, 405
 ex-offenders, hiring, 142, 428, 431
 information resources for college students, 385
 people with disabilities, accommodations for, 143, 416

schools, relationship with, 357, 386–387
traits preferred by (*See* Employability skills; Skills and abilities)
unsatisfactory employees and, 27–28
Employment challenges. *See* Client issues
Employment counseling, defined, 3
Employment eligibility, 141
Employment gaps, 435–436
Employment history
 of career counselors, 455
 of clients, 208, 209f, 220, 221f, 426
Employment Information Handbook for Ex-Offenders (DOL), 430
Employment law, 138–157, 141t
 client examples for, 154–157
 discrimination and, 123–124
 evolution of, 140
 hiring and firing, 141–146 (*See also* Hiring and firing laws)
 list of, 146t
 in offshore holdings, 7, 148
 resources for, 153–154, 153t
 retirement and, 152–153
 unemployment and inability to work, 148–152
 work conditions and, 146–148
Encyclopedia of Careers and Vocational Guidance (Ferguson), 317
Ending stage of career counseling process, 181, 197–198
Engineering career and technical education, 360–361, 362t
Entire contract doctrine, 140
Entrance exams, 384, 384t. *See also specific exams*
Entrepreneurship, 335
Environmental assessment technique (EAT), 23
Environmental clues, 131–132
Environments. *See also* Work environments
 activeness and, 28
 calculus between, 25
 of counseling sessions, 176–177
 model (Holland), 23–24, 24t
 personality, influence on, 21
 as proximal contextual factors in SCCT, 67–68, 70
Equal Employment Opportunity Commission (EEOC), 142, 147
Equality of opportunities, 106–107, 123–124
Equal Pay Act of 1963, 147, 154
Establishment stage of life-span model, 42
Ethics, 158–173
 codes of, 104, 160, 164–168, 172, 472–496
 competence in, 158–159, 166
 continuing education for, 168
 credentials for, 159–163
 decision-making models for, 168
 general principles of, 163–165, 164t
Ethnicity. *See* Race and ethnicity
Evaluation of counseling experience, 181–182
Evaluations, ethics and, 166–167, 483–485
Executive-processing domain, 79–80
Ex-offenders
 challenges for, 425–428, 425t
 employment statistics for, 423–425, 425t
 helping strategies for, 428–432, 432t
Experiential learning, 385
Exploration stage of life-span model, 42, 52–53
Exploration stage of occupational choice, 38

Express contracts, 145t
External conflict (EC), 81, 87, 251
External cues, 77, 87
External influences on decision making, 81
External motivators for counseling, 14

F

Facebook, 399
Factors, defined, 18
Faculty, counselor consultations with, 387
FAFSA (Free Application for Federal Student Aid), 322
Fair Credit Reporting Act of 1970, 142
Fair Labor Standards Act (FLSA) of 1938, 147–148, 155
Families. *See also* Homemakers and caretakers
  background of clients, 208, 210–212f, 220, 222
  collectivism and, 106–107, 121–122, 129–130
  counseling of, 478
  genograms of, 114–120, 116t, 117–118f, 119t
  medical histories of, 142
  parent–child relationships, 92 (*See also* Theory of personality development and career choice (Roe))
Family and Medical Leave Act of 1993, 156
Fantasy career choices, 37–38
Fantasy period (Super's theory), 41–42
Fantasy techniques, 90
Federal Bonding Program, 431
Federal employees, 143
Federal Glass Ceiling Commission, 123
Feedback, for self-efficacy development, 74
Feedback loop in SCCT, 69–71
Fee structure, discussing, 176, 476
Felonies. *See* Ex-offenders
Ferguson career information resources, 316–317
Fidelity, 164–165, 171, 175
Fidelity bonding, 431
Field trips, 319–320, 335
Financial aid for education, 322–323, 422, 427, 429–430
Financial background checks, 141–142
Financial resources, influence on career, 70
First impressions, 398–399
Five-factor model (FFM) of personality, 237
Flexibility, adjustment behavior, 28
Following-up after interviews, 460
Foundational learning theories (Bandura), 56–57, 57f
Foundational skills, 508
Free Application for Federal Student Aid (FAFSA), 322
Freshman conferences (high school), 341
Friends, clients as, 173
Funding Your Education (Department of Education), 322
Future, preparing clients for, 181, 198–200t
Future narratives, 90–91, 179

G

Games, to simulate work, 338–339
Gay, Lesbian and Straight Education Network (GLSEN), 132
Gay people. *See* LGBT individuals
GEAR UP program, 339–340
Gender
  career choices and, 129–130, 135

discrimination and, 133–134, 147, 154–155
homemakers and, 432
Non-Sexist Vocational Card Sort, 270
occupational constraints, example of, 133–134
traditional roles of, 49, 137
wage gap and, 108–109, 123
General Aptitude Test Battery (GATB), 247
Generalization of CIP delivery sequence, 82
Generalizing, 124–125
Generational cohort, 133–134
Generic information-processing skills, 77
Genetic Information Nondiscrimination Act of 2008, 142
Genetics, abilities and, 51–52
Genograms, 114–120, 116t, 117–118f, 119t
Gillian Parker (burnout, seeking new direction)
  client overview, 13
  cognitive information-processing approach and, 87
  cultural dimensions and, 134–135, 134t
  employment law and, 156
  ethical considerations for, 170, 173
  intake assessment for, 219–220
  Krumboltz's learning theories and, 59, 59f, 84
  life-span, life-space approach and, 53
  narrative theory and, 101–103
  person-environment fit theory, 31
  social cognitive career theory and, 86
  stage model of career counseling process and, 197–198
  standardized tests for, 264–265, 265t
  theory of circumscription, compromise, and self-creation and, 54–55
  theory of work adjustment and, 32–33
Ginzberg's theory of occupational choice, 37–39, 38t
Glass ceiling, 123. *See also* Discrimination
Global Career Development Facilitators (GCDF), 162–163, 163t
Globalization, 5–6
Goals of clients
  affluence as, 106
  career story assessment and, 97, 98
  cognitive information-processing and, 79, 81
  identifying, 176–177, 185, 186–187t
  intake assessments and, 204, 218–219
  for job searches, 395
  social cognitive career theory and, 66, 71, 74, 85–86
Goodness of fit, 26, 99, 452, 460
Gottfredson's theory of circumscription, compromise, and self-creation, 48–51, 50f, 54–55, 179–180, 272
Government-issued documents for work eligibility, 141
Graduate school exams, 244, 384, 384t
Graduation requirements, 339, 344
Great Recession, 3
Greeting clients, 175
Grieving after job loss, 392
Grieving clients. *See* Lakeesha Maddox (stay-at-home parent, widowed)
Group counseling
  ethics and, 478
  for unemployed, 394, 406
Growth stage of life-span model, 41–42
Guidance lessons. *See* Lessons, guidance
Guided fantasy techniques, 90, 180

H

Happenstance learning theory (HLT), 62–64, 64t, 82–84, 179–180
Harassment, 147, 148t
Hazardous work, 147–148
Health insurance benefits, 149, 154
Health Insurance Portability and Accountability Act (HIPAA) of 1996, 142
Health status of clients
  client example, 225–226f, 225–227
  depression, 389
  ex-offenders, 426
  intake assessments and, 201, 215, 216–217f
Helping strategies
  for ex-offenders, 428–432, 432t
  for homemakers and caretakers, 436–438
  identifying, 177–180, 187–190t, 188f, 190
  implementing, 180–181, 190–197, 192f, 196f
  for people with disabilities, 415–417, 417t
  for veterans, 419–420, 421t, 423t
Hidden job market, 399, 404–405, 458–459
Hierarchy of needs (Maslow), 34
High Schools That Work (HSTW), 360, 361t
High school students, 340–350. *See also* K–12 educational settings; Theory of work adjustment
  career-development assessment and counseling (C-DAC) model for, 48
  career planning activities for, 342–350, 345t, 348t, 350t
  client example (*See* Vincent Arroyo (gay student with military aspirations))
  college, transitioning to, 371–373
  developmental considerations for, 340
  guidance lessons for, 340–341
  schoolwide programs for, 341–342, 342t
Hippocratic oath, 164
Hiring and firing laws
  background checks, 141–142
  immigration laws, 141, 157
  layoffs, advance notice of, 145–146
  wrongful discharge exceptions, 144–146t
History of career counseling, 3–6, 18–20, 468–469
Holland codes, 23, 54, 305
Holland's occupational classification systems, 298–299
Holland's theory. *See* Person-environment fit theory (Holland)
Homemakers and caretakers
  as career, 130, 154–155
  challenges for, 435–436
  definitions and statistics for, 432–435
  helping strategies for, 436–438
Housing situation of clients, 208, 212, 212f
How to Counsel Students (Williamson), 20
Human capital, 412
Human rights, 148
Humility, 124
Hypothetical clients. *See* Client scenarios

I

Id, 37
Identity, 25, 130, 137. *See also* Culture
Identity development, 112, 132–133, 172
Identity narratives, 94
Identity scores, 25
Identity statements, 99

Subject Index

Immigration, 111, 135, 137
Immigration Act of 1990, 141
Immigration and Reform Control Act (IRCA) of 1986, 141
Immigration law, 141, 157
Improving Your Career Thoughts (Sampson et al.), 82, 86–87
Inability to work, 149–152, 151t
Income
 education level and, 321–322, 321f
 information resources for, 307, 309–311, 315–316
 salaries, negotiating, 406–408
Income disparities
 culture and, 108–109, 108f, 123
 gender and, 147
Indecisiveness, 63, 76, 86, 250
Individual counseling for college career planning, 381–382
Individualism, 106–107
Individualized education plans (IEPs), 347–348
Individual learning plan (ILP), 81–82, 83f, 87
Individuals with Disabilities Education Act (IDEA) of 2004, 347
Industrial Revolution, 3–4, 18, 140
Inequality. *See* Equality of opportunities
Infobase/Ferguson career information resources, 316–317
Informational interviews, 320, 404–405
Information-processing domains of CIP, 76–77, 76f, 378
Information resources, 294–330
 on career counselors, 443
 on career development lessons, 337–338
 on careers, 382–384, 383f
 client examples for, 326–330
 on education and training, 321–323, 321f, 384–385, 384t
 ethics and, 167, 485–488
 on job searches (*See* Job search process)
 occupational and labor market information, 299–320 (*See also* Occupational and labor market information)
 occupational classification systems, 296–299
 role of counselor and, 295
 on skill-building information, 323–324, 325t
 types of, 295–296
Informed consent
 for assessments, 483
 in career counseling process, 165–167, 176
 professional relationships and, 474–475
 supervision, training, and teaching, 488
 technology assistance and, 486
Inhumane working conditions, 147–148
I-9 forms, 141, 157
Injuries at work, 150, 156–157. *See also* Juan Martinez (vocational rehabilitation after injury)
Instrumental learning experiences (ILEs), 58, 59f, 62, 84
Intake assessments, 201–227
 approaches to, 202–203, 203t
 challenges and obstacles, 213, 213f, 222–223, 223f
 client examples, 222–227
 concerns and goals, 204, 218–219
 cultural formulation interview, 214–215, 215f
 education and training, 204, 205–208f, 208, 219–220

 employment history, 208, 209f, 220, 221f
 family background, 208, 210–212f, 220, 222
 health status and medical information, 215, 216–217f, 225, 225–226f, 227
 living situation, 208, 212, 212f, 222
 overview, 201–202, 202t
 personal information, 203–204, 204f, 218, 218f
 strengths, 213–214, 214f, 223–224, 224f
Integrated career development for students, 333
Intelligence levels, genetics and, 51–52
Interest, Determination, Exploration, and Assessment System (IDEAS), 232
Interest level, assessing, 72
Interest model of SCCT, 69, 69f, 73
Interests
 career construction theory and, 95–97, 101–102
 ex-offenders career development and, 429
 future narratives and, 91
 standardized tests for, 229–230t, 229–235
 tentative career choices and, 38, 42
Internal cues, 77, 87
Internal motivators for counseling, 14
Internet
 career resources from, 167, 295, 485–488 (*See also* Information resources)
 globalization and, 5–6
 social media and, 397, 399–402t
Internships, 385
Interpersonal skills, 426–427
Interpretation of assessments, 166–167, 483–485
Interventions. *See also* Psychoeducational interventions
 for burnout, 394
 client-focused, 125–126
 cognitive, 62
 for ex-offenders, 430
 as helping strategies, 178–179t, 179–180
 for social cognitive career theory (SCCT), 71–73
Interviews. *See* Career counseling interviews; Job interviews
IQ tests, 52

J

Jackson Personality Inventory–Revised (JVI-R), 237
Jackson Vocational Interest Survey (JVIS), 232
Jargon, 176
JIST Works career information resources, 315–316, 316t
Job, defined, 2t
Job Accommodation Network (JAN), 416
Job applications, 398, 430
Job Club program, 394
Job clubs for graduates, 459
Job fairs, 386
Job interviews
 for career counseling positions, 460
 ex-offenders and, 430–431
 mock, 376, 379, 400
Job listings, 379, 402, 403–404t, 404, 458
Job loss. *See also* Unemployment
 as career transition, 413
 client example of (*See* Doris Bronner (fired))
 intake assessments, discussing in, 208

 laws for (*See* Hiring and firing laws)
 psychological reactions to, 391–394, 392f
Job Observation and Behavior Scale (JOBS), 254
Job offers
 acceptance letters for, 408, 461
 evaluating, 406
 negotiating, 380, 406–408, 407t
 responding to, 461
Job opportunities, 6–7, 402, 404–405
Job outlook, information resources for, 307–309, 307t, 308f
Job satisfaction, 26, 36–37, 255–256. *See also* Gillian Parker (burnout, seeking new direction); Theory of work adjustment
Job search process, 394–409
 for career counselors, 449–461, 452t, 454t, 456t
 closure of, 406–408, 407t
 college settings, career planning in, 385–386
 for ex-offenders, 430–433
 implementation of, 402–406, 405f
 overview of, 408, 408–409t
 for people with disabilities, 416–417, 417t
 preparation for, 395–401, 397t, 401–402t
 psychological reactions to, 392–393
 for veterans, 422
Job search skills, 324, 379–380
Job security, 8–9. *See also* Wayne Jensen (job security concerns)
Job shadowing, 320, 342, 342t
JOBS Intervention Project, 394
Job Stress Survey (JSS), 254–255
Job Survival and Success Scale, Second Edition (JSSS), 255, 264
Juan Martinez (vocational rehabilitation after injury)
 client overview, 13–14
 cognitive information-processing approach and, 87
 cultural dimensions and, 135–137, 136t
 employment law and, 156–157
 ethical considerations for, 170, 173
 information resources for, 327–328, 329f
 intake assessment for, 225, 226–227f, 227
 Krumboltz's learning theories and, 60, 61f, 84–85
 life-span, life-space approach and, 53
 narrative theory and, 101
 person-environment fit theory, 31
 social cognitive career theory and, 86
 stage model of career counseling process and, 187–190t, 188f, 190
 standardized tests for, 265–266, 266t
 theory of circumscription, compromise, and self-creation and, 55
 theory of work adjustment and, 33
Justice, 164, 172–173

K

K–12 educational settings, 331–352
 American School Counselor Association (ASCA) National Model, 331–333t
 American School Counselor Association (ASCA) Student Standards, 497–498
 career planning activities
  elementary, 335–337
  high school, 342–350, 345t, 348t, 350t
  middle school, 338–339

Subject Index

K–12 educational settings (*Continued*)
  client example (*See* Vincent Arroyo (gay student with military aspirations))
  college, transitioning to, 371–373
  developmental considerations
    elementary, 333–334
    high school, 340
    middle school, 337
  guidance lessons
    elementary, 334–335
    high school, 340–341
    middle school, 337–338
  integrated career development, 333
  occupational classification systems for, 299
  schoolwide programs
    elementary, 335, 336t
    high school, 341–342, 342t
    middle school, 338–339
  student competencies in career development, 332–333
  tracking systems for, 357, 359, 362–363
Knowdell Card Sort, 279
Knowledge-based professions, 6
Krumboltz's learning theories. *See* Learning theories of Krumboltz
Kuder Career Interests Assessment (KCIA), 232–233, 262–263
Kuder Career Planning System (KCPS), 318
Kuder Skills Confidence Assessment (KSCA), 247–248, 262–263
Kuder Work Values Assessment (KWVA), 239–240

L

Labor Department, 23
Labor market information, 299. *See also* Occupational and labor market information
Labor market participation. *See* Unemployment
Lakeesha Maddox (stay-at-home parent, widowed)
  client overview, 11
  cognitive information-processing approach and, 86–87
  cultural dimensions and, 129–130, 129t
  employment law and, 154–155
  ethical considerations for, 169, 171
  information resources for, 328–329
  intake assessment for, 222–224
  Krumboltz's learning theories and, 60, 60f, 84
  life-span, life-space approach and, 53
  narrative theory and, 100
  person-environment fit theory, 31
  social cognitive career theory and, 85
  stage model of career counseling process and, 185–187t
  standardized tests for, 259–262t
  theory of circumscription, compromise, and self-creation and, 54
  theory of work adjustment and, 32
Language, self-making and, 92
Language barriers, 101, 136, 173, 243
The Latino Student's Guide to College Success (Valverde), 132
Law. *See* Employment law; *specific laws*
Layoffs, 145–146, 154. *See also* Wayne Jensen (job security concerns)
Learning, role of in career counseling, 62, 63
Learning abilities, 51–52
Learning disabilities. *See* People with disabilities

Learning experiences
  happenstance learning theory and, 58, 59f, 62
  influences on, 67–68
  self-efficacy and, 65
Learning theories, 56–87
  Bandura's foundational learning theories, 56–57, 57f
  card sorts and, 271–272
  client examples for, 82–87
  cognitive information-processing approach, 75–82 (*See also* Cognitive information-processing (CIP) approach to counseling)
  defined, 56
  Krumboltz's learning theories, 57–64 (*See also* Learning theories of Krumboltz)
  social cognitive career theory, 64–75 (*See also* Social cognitive career theory (SCCT))
  social cognitive theory, 57
  social learning theory, 57
Learning theories of Krumboltz, 57–64
  on career counseling, 60, 62, 84, 179–180, 249–250
  client examples for, 82–85
  happenstance learning theory (HLT), 62–64, 64t, 82–84, 179–180
  helping strategies for, 179–180
  social learning theory of career decision making, 57–60, 58t, 59–61f
Learning theory of career counseling (LTCC), 60, 62, 84, 179–180, 249–250
Legal counsel for unemployment, 155–156
Leisure time activities, 97
Lesbians. *See* LGBT individuals
Lessons, guidance
  elementary students, 334–335
  high school students, 340–341
  middle school students, 337–338
LGBT-Friendly Campus Climate Index (Campus Pride), 132
LGBT individuals, 131–133, 144, 155, 172, 376–377. *See also* Vincent Arroyo (gay student with military aspirations)
Licensure
  documents showing, 458
  obtaining, 159–160, 161t, 446–449
  restrictions for, 427
Life balance, 3, 254, 329, 436, 438
Life-career rainbow, 45, 45f, 53
Life-design paradigm of CCT, 94–99, 96t
Life history, composing, 89–90, 179
Lifeline technique, 90
Lifelong learning, 8
Life portraits, 98
Life problems, 96
Life-span, life-space approach to counseling (Super), 39–48
  assessment instruments for, 46, 47t, 253
  career-development assessment and counseling (C-DAC) model, 46–48
  client examples for, 52–54
  helping strategies for, 179–180
  life-career rainbow, 45, 45f, 53
  life space, 43, 45, 45f, 53
  life span, 41–43, 41t, 44f
  propositions, 39, 40t, 41
  self-concept, 45–46, 46t, 47f
  theaters and roles in, 44t
Life structures, changing, 91
Lifestyle, defined, 2t

Lilly Ledbetter Fair Pay Act of 2009, 147, 154
Lily Huang Li Mei (undecided)
  card sort for, 279, 280–281f, 280–283t
  client overview, 11
  cognitive information-processing approach and, 86
  cultural dimensions and, 127–129, 128t
  employment law and, 154
  ethical considerations for, 169, 171
  information resources for, 326
  intake assessment for, 220, 222
  Krumboltz's learning theories and, 58, 60f, 83–84
  life-span, life-space approach and, 52–53
  narrative theory and, 100
  person-environment fit theory, 30–31
  social cognitive career theory and, 85
  stage model of career counseling process, 182–185t
  standardized tests for, 259
  theory of circumscription, compromise, and self-creation and, 54
  theory of work adjustment and, 32
LinkedIn profiles, 397, 400
Linked learning, 363–364, 363f
Living vs. minimum wage, 187
Lofquist's theory of work adjustment. *See* Theory of work adjustment
Log Cabin Republicans v. United States of America, 144
Long-term career management, 381, 463–465, 463t, 464f
Long-term unemployed people, 390
Loss of face, 129
Low-income students, 339–340
Low-interest occupations, reconsidering, 71–72
Low-skilled workers, 6–7, 135–136
Loyalty to employees, 8

M

Macronarratives, 97, 98–99
Maintenance stage of life-span model, 42–43, 52–53
Majors fairs, 376
Manufacturing jobs, scarcity of, 6
Marginally attached workers, 390, 391t
Maslach Burnout Inventory (MBI), 255
Maslow's hierarchy of needs, 34
Master Addictions Counselor (MAC), 161
Master Career Counselor (MCC), 161–162, 162t
Master Career Development Professional (MCDP), 161–162, 162t
Matching model (Parsons), 294
Matriculation, 349, 354
Mature workers. *See* Age of clients
Maxicycles of life-span model, 43, 44f
Means-ends strategies, 79
Medical history checks of employees, 141–142
Medical information of clients, 215, 216–217f, 225–226f, 225–227
Memories of childhood, 96–97, 102
Men and Women of the Corporation (Kanter), 123
Mental health counselors, 308f, 389
Mental health status of clients, 426
Metacognitions, 79–80, 92
Micronarratives, 97, 98

Subject Index

Microskills, 176
Middle-class lifestyle, requirements for, 344
Middle school students, 337–340. *See also* K–12 educational settings
  career-development assessment and counseling (C-DAC) model for, 48
  career planning activities for, 338–339
  developmental considerations for, 337
  guidance lessons for, 337–338
  schoolwide programs for, 338–339
Middle stage of career counseling process. *See* Helping strategies
Midlife, career change and, 42, 53
Military. *See also* Veterans
  as alternative to college, 344
  Armed Forces Qualifying Test (AFQT), 344
  Armed Services Vocational Aptitude Battery (ASVAB), 246–247, 344
  Army Alpha and Army Beta tests of cognitive ability, 19
  career searches for, 312–313
  client example (*See* Vincent Arroyo (gay student with military aspirations))
  "don't ask, don't tell" policy of, 144, 155
  postsecondary options in, 345
  skills translators for, 421, 421t
Minicycles of life-span model, 43, 44f, 53
Minimum wage, 147–148, 187
Minnesota Importance Questionnaire (MIQ), 240
Minnesota Mechanical Abilities Project, 19
Minnesota point of view, 19–20. *See also* Trait factor theories
Minnesota Satisfaction Questionnaire (MSQ), 255
Minnesota Satisfaction Scales (MSS), 255–256
Minnesota Stabilization Research Institute, 19
Minorities, 6. *See also* Gender; Race and ethnicity
Mission of college career services, 374, 374t
Mission statements, 90
Missouri Occupational Card Sort (MOCS), 270–271
Missouri Occupational Preference Inventory (MOPI), 270–271
Model environments (Holland), 23–24, 24t
Modeling, 73
Monitoring and control of decision-making process, 79–80
Motivational interviewing, 149
Motivators for counseling, 14
Mottos, 96, 98, 102
Murphy Meisgeier Type Indicator for Children (MMTIC), 237
Myers-Briggs Type Indicator (MBTI), 237
MyFuture.com, 312–313
My Vocational Situation (MVS), 25, 251–252

N

Names, discrimination and, 123, 136
Narrative approach to counseling (Cochran), 89–91
  card sorts and, 272
  career problem and, 89
  client examples for, 100–101
  crystallization, 91
  episodes within, 89, 89t
  future narrative for, 90–91
  helping strategies for, 179–180
  life history, composing, 89–90
  life structure, changing, 91
  reality, constructing, 91
  role, enacting, 91
  for veterans, 421
Narrative identity, 93
Narrative theories, 88–103
  career construction theory, 91–100 (*See also* Career construction theory (Savickas))
  client examples for, 91–100
  narrative approach of Cochran, 89–91 (*See also* Narrative approach to counseling (Cochran))
National Association for College Admission Counseling (NACAC), 346
National Board for Certified Counselors (NBCC), 161
National career clusters and pathways, 299, 300t
National Career Development Association (NCDA)
  counselor competencies, 470–471
  ethical career counseling and, 159–162, 164–168, 172
  occupational literature guidelines, 299, 301t
National Career Development Association (NCDA) Code of Ethics
  nondiscrimination and, 172
  overview, 160, 164–168
  reprinted, 472–496
    confidentiality, privileged communication, and privacy, 477–479
    evaluation, assessment, and interpretation, 483–485
    Internet use, 485–488
    professional relationships, 473–477
    professional relationships with other professionals, 482–483
    professional responsibility, 479–482
    research and publication, 491–494
    resolving ethical issues, 494–495
    supervision, training, and teaching, 488–491
National Career Development Guidelines (NCDG), 333, 374
National Career Development Guidelines (NCDG) Framework, 499–507
National Career Readiness Certificates (NCRC), 253
National Certified Career Counselors (NCCC), 161
National Certified Counselor (NCC), 161
National Certified School Counselor (NCSC), 161
National Counselor Examination (NCE), 17, 161
National Defense Education Act (NDEA) of 1958, 356
National Employment Counseling Association, 139
National Labor Relations Act of 1935, 140, 154
National Occupational Information Coordinating Committee (NOICC), 162, 313, 315, 332–333
Negligent hiring, 142, 428
Negotiating job offers, 380, 406–408, 407t
NEO Personality Inventory–3, 237–238
Network for Teaching Entrepreneurship (NFTE), 338
Networking
  for career counseling jobs, 458–459
  documents for, 395
  for ex-offenders, 426
  for hidden job market, 404–405, 405f
  of homemakers and caretakers, 435, 437
  social capital and, 359, 412–413, 426
  targeted opportunity profiles (TOPs) for, 399
Nondiscrimination laws, 142–144
Nonmaleficence, 164, 173
Non-Sexist Vocational Card Sort, 270
Nonverbal communication, 175

O

Objective self-assessment, 46
Observational learning, 57
Occupation, defined, 2t, 296
Occupational and labor market information, 299–320
  America's Career InfoNet, 309–312, 310f, 311t, 312–314f, 327
  CandidCareer.com, 317
  classroom presentations, career days, field trips, 319–320
  for college students, 384
  computer-assisted career guidance systems, 317–319, 338, 382, 383t
  Infobase/Ferguson resources, 316–317
  informational interviews, 320
  JIST Works resources, 315–316, 316t
  job shadowing, 320
  National Career Development Association (NCDA), 299, 301t
  Occupational Information Network (O*NET) for, 299–305, 302f, 303–305t, 306f
  Occupational Outlook Handbook (OOH; U.S. Bureau of Labor Statistics), 305–309, 307t, 308f, 310f
  other federal resources, 312–313
Occupational Attitude Survey & Interest Schedule (OASIS-3), 233, 248
Occupational classification systems, 296–299
Occupational Employment Statistics (OES), 309
Occupational information, 299
Occupational Information Network (O*NET)
  Ability Profiler, 247–248
  client examples for, 326
  counseling careers, as resource for, 443
  Interest Profiler, 233
  for job searches, 180
  for occupational and labor market information, 299–305, 302f, 303–305t, 306f
  OnLine, 302–305, 302f, 303–305t, 306f, 327–328
  work environments, assessing, 23
  Work Importance Locator, 271, 275, 279
  Work Importance Profiler, 240
Occupational knowledge, 77
Occupational level, 23
Occupational licensing, 142
Occupational Outlook Handbook (OOH; U.S. Bureau of Labor Statistics), 305–309, 307t, 308f, 310f
Occupational Safety and Health Act (OSHA) of 1970, 148
Occupational self-concept, 46, 46t
Occupational settings. *See* Work environments
Occupational Stress Inventory–Revised (OSI-R), 256
Occu-Sort (O-S), 270
Office for Special Education and Rehabilitative Services, 150

Subject Index

Open-mindedness, 63, 83–84
Opportunities. *See also* Happenstance learning theory (HLT)
  equality of, 106–107, 123–124
  for jobs, identifying, 6–7, 402, 404–405
Oppression, 107–108, 122
Optimal theory applied to identify development (OTAID) model, 112
Orienting clients to career counseling process, 175–176, 182–185t
Our Country's Needs (Parsons), 139
Outcome expectations, 65–66, 69, 71–74
Outsourcing jobs, 5–8
Overtime requirements, 147–148

P

Parent–child relationships, 92. *See also* Theory of personality development and career choice (Roe)
Parenting, 135, 329. *See also* Homemakers and caretakers; Lakeesha Maddox (stay-at-home parent, widowed)
Parsons, Frank, 4, 18–19, 138–139
Partners of companies, rights of, 156
Pathways to Prosperity study, 344, 354
Pension Benefit Guarantee Corporation, 153
Pensions, 152–153
People with disabilities. *See also* Vocational rehabilitation
  accommodations for, 143, 416
  Americans with Disabilities Act (ADA) of 1990, 143, 349, 416
  challenges for, 415
  client example of (*See* Juan Martinez (vocational rehabilitation after injury))
  discrimination and, 143, 416
  employment statistics for, 414–415, 414t
  helping strategies for, 415–417, 417t
  income of, 108–109
  insurance benefits for, 150–152, 151t, 157
  O*NET for, 302
  transition services for high school students, 347–350, 350t
  veterans, 418, 421–422
People with special needs, 231, 233, 253–254
Perceptions of skills. *See* Self-efficacy
Performance accomplishments, 71, 73
Performance model of SCCT, 70–71, 70f
Performance outcomes, 70–71
Perseverance, adjustment style, 29
Persistence, 70–71
Personal information of clients, 203–204, 204f, 218, 218f
Personal issues of clients, 14–15
Personality, career choice and, 36–37
Personality tests, 235–238, 236t
Personality traits, development of, 92
Personality types (Holland)
  assessment of, 22–23
  development of, 21, 21f
  Holland's six types, 22, 22t
  human complexity and Holland codes, 23
  matching types and environments, 23–24
  model environments and, 23, 24t
  similarity of, 24–25, 25f
  stability of, 24
Person-environment correspondence (PEC) theory, 29–30

Person-environment fit theory (Holland), 20–25
  card sorts and, 271
  client examples for, 30–31
  helping strategies for, 179–180
  key elements of, 21t
  model environments, 23, 24t
  personality development and, 21, 21f
  personality types, 22–23, 22t
  secondary concepts of, 24–25, 25f
  types and environments, matching, 23–24
Person input, 86
Person variables in SCCT, 65–66
Pictorial Inventory of Careers (PIC) Pathfinder, 233–234
Play activities, work preferences and, 37, 41–42
Pocket Guide series (JIST Works, Inc.), 316
Portable document files (pdfs), 398, 456
Portfolios, 386, 396–397
Position Classification Inventory (PCI), 23
Posted job positions, 402–404
Postmodernist theories, 88. *See also* Narrative theories
Postsecondary education. *See also* Career and technical education (CTE); College settings, career planning in
  graduate school exams for, 244, 384, 384t
  importance of, 7–8, 321–322, 321f
  planning stages for, 342–347, 348t
  professional degrees, 7, 244, 384, 384t
  for students with disabilities, 347–352, 350t
  transitioning to, 361–362
  for veterans, 422
Poverty, 109–110, 349, 426. *See also* Socioeconomic variables
Power roles, 49
Practical wisdom, 89
Predictive model of TWA, 26–27, 28t
Preliminary assessment for CIP delivery sequence, 80
Preseparation counseling, military, 420
Prestige levels, 49, 54
Privacy, 166, 477–479
Privileged communication, 166–167, 477–479
Problems. *See* Career problems
Problem solving
  barriers, addressing, 73
  brainstorming for, 78, 85
  CIP delivery sequence and, 82, 86–87
  as helping strategy, 180
Process model of TWA, 26–29, 29f
Professional degrees, 7, 244, 384, 384t
Professional relationships, 165, 170–173, 473–477, 482–483
Professional responsibility, 166, 479–482. *See also* Ethics
Progress, solidifying, 181, 197–198
Project Lead the Way (PLTW), 360–361, 362t
Propositions of Super, 39–41, 40t
Proprietary trade schools, 365
Protean career, 8–9
Proximal contextual factors, 67–68, 70–71, 85–86, 113, 122
Psychodynamic model of career choice and satisfaction (Bordin), 36–37
Psychoeducational interventions
  client example of, 190–194
  developmental applications of SCCT and, 73–74

for ex-offenders, 430
  as helping strategies, 179–180
Psychological capital, 413
Psychological conditions, 76, 201
Psychological reactions to unemployment, 391–394, 392f
Publication, ethics and, 167
Public responsibility, 481–482
Punctuality, 175

Q

Qualification for employment, counselors, 160
Questionnaires, 203
Quick response (QR) codes, 397
Quid pro quo systems, 147

R

Race and ethnicity. *See also* Culture
  achievement gap based on, 343, 357, 359
  cultural identity and, 129–130
  discrimination and, 136, 154–155
  learning ability based on, 51–52
Racial group differences, 51–52, 424
Racism, 107–108
Reactiveness, adjustment behavior, 28
Reading-Free Vocational Interest Inventory (R-FVII:2), 234
Realistic career choices, 38
Reality, constructing, 91
Reality testing, 73, 85–86
Recidivism rates, 425–426
Recommendation letters, 457–458
Reconstruction in life-design paradigm of CCT, 97–98
Reconstruction/reinterpretation of oneself, 77
Record keeping
  for counseling, 478–479
  for job searching, 406
Recruitment services, 386–387, 417
Reentry into workforce, 413, 424, 433, 437
References
  of career counselors, 457
  of clients, 141, 398, 435
Referring clients, 476–477
Rehabilitation Act of 1973, 143–144, 150
Rehabilitation counseling. *See* Vocational rehabilitation
Rehabilitation Services Administration (RSA), 150
Relationship management of college students, 372
Relocating for work, 310–311
Reputations vs. personality types, 92
Research and publication, 167, 479, 491–494
Reserve Officers' Training Corp (ROTC), 144
Résumés
  of career counselors, 453–457, 454t, 456t, 463–465, 463t, 464f
  information resources for, 395–397, 397t, 399
  job search skills and, 379
  for veterans, 422
Retirement
  card sorts for, 293t
  changes in, 9
  decline/disengagement stage of life-span model, 43
  forced, 143
  laws regarding, 152–153
Review of CIP delivery sequence, 82

Subject Index

RIASEC typologies
  Campbell's interest orientations vs., 261t
  Holland's occupational classification system and, 298–299
  job searches based on, 180
  personality types, 22, 22t, 96, 98
  standardized testing based on, 234, 248
  Vocational Card Sort (VCS) and, 270
  work environments, 23, 24t
Right-to-work legislation, 8
Roe's theory of personality development and career choice, 34–35, 35t, 36f
Role models, 92, 95, 97, 101, 132–133
Roles in life-span, life-space approach to counseling, 43, 44t

S

Safe-space stickers, 132, 132f
Salaries, negotiating, 406–408
Salience Inventory (SI), 48
Savickas's theory of career construction and counseling. *See* Career construction theory (Savickas)
Schema specialization and generalization, 77
School counselors, 308f, 309, 341, 364–367. *See also* K–12 educational settings
School-to-Work Opportunities Act of 1994, 357
Schoolwide programs
  elementary students, 335, 336t
  high school students, 341–342, 342t
  middle school students, 338–339
Scope of practice, 159–160, 160t
SDS Career Explorer (SDS CE), 234
Seasonal agricultural workers, 141
Second Chance Act of 2005, 429–430
Secretary's Commission on Achieving Necessary Skills (SCANS), 323–324, 325t, 380, 508–509
Self as actor, 92
Self as agent, 92–93
Self as author, 93
Self-assessment
  of career counselors, 444–445, 444t
  information and resources, 382–383
  subjective, 46
Self-awareness, 79, 124
Self-care of career counselors, 445
Self-concept
  Bordin's psychodynamic model of career choice and satisfaction, 36
  exploration stage of life-span model and, 42
  life-span, life-space approach, 45–46, 46t, 47f, 53
  theory of circumscription, compromise, and self-creation, 49–50
Self-creation, 51–52. *See also* Theory of circumscription, compromise, and self-creation (Gottfredson)
Self-Directed Search Career Explorer, 337
Self-Directed Search (SDS)
  client example of, 258
  Holland's occupational classification system and, 298
  overview of, 234
  person-environment fit theory and, 23, 25
  for self-assessment and career planning, 383
Self-disclosure, 170
Self-efficacy

Bandur's foundational learning theories and, 57
building, 323
Career Beliefs Inventory (CBI), 62, 84, 249–250, 259
career counseling, applying, 71
Career Decision Self-Efficacy Scale (CDSE), 250
  of counselors, 461–462
  helping strategies for, 179–180
  of homemakers and caretakers, 436–437
  narrative approach and, 89
  of nondominant racial and ethnic groups, 112, 120
  social cognitive career theory (SCCT) and, 65, 69, 71–74, 85–86
Self-knowledge, 77, 179, 337
Self-management
  of adults, 381
  of college students, 371–373
Self-observation generalizations (SOGs), 58, 60f, 62, 82–85
Self-reflection for counselors, 182
Self-talk, 79
Service learning projects for students, 339
Sex roles, 49, 54. *See also* Gender
Sexual harassment, 147
Sexual orientation. *See* LGBT individuals; Vincent Arroyo (gay student with military aspirations)
Sexual Orientation Non-Discrimination Act (SONDA) of 2003, 155
Shame of clients, 129
Shame of counselors, 126
$SIGI^3$ computer-assisted career guidance system, 318–319
Simulations, of job tasks, 320
Single parents, 329. *See also* Lakeesha Maddox (stay-at-home parent, widowed)
Situational assessments, 416
Sixteen Personality Factor (16PF), 238, 260–261
Skills and abilities. *See also* Employability skills
  accurate feedback for, 74
  activeness and, 28
  beliefs in (*See* Self-efficacy)
  for decision making, 77
  of ex-offenders, 425–426
  of homemakers and caretakers, 435–436
  performance model of SCCT and, 70–71
  reactiveness and, 28
  skill-building, 85–86, 323–324, 325t
  standardized tests for, 241–249, 242t, 246t, 256–257
  work satisfaction, predicting, 26
Skills Confidence Inventory, Revised Edition (SCI), 248
SkillsUSA, 324
Smith-Hughes Act of 1917, 355
Smith-Lever Act of 1914, 355
Social activism, 139, 148
Social capital, 359, 412–413, 426
Social cognitive career theory (SCCT), 65–75
  applications of, 71–73
  client examples of, 85–86
  contextual factors in, 66–68
  developmental applications of, 73–74
  helping strategies for, 179–180
  models of, 68–71

person variables in, 65–66
triadic reciprocality in, 68, 68f
Social cognitive theory, 57
Social constructivism, 92
Socialization, 51
Social learning theory, 57
Social learning theory of career decision making, 57–60, 58t, 59–61f, 82
A Social Learning Theory of Career Decision Making (SLTCDM; Krumboltz), 57–60
Social media, 397, 399–402t
Social Security Act of 1935, 151
Social security benefits, 152–154
Social Security Disability Insurance (SSDI), 150–152, 151t, 157
Social valuation of careers, 49
Society-focused interventions, 126
Socioeconomic variables
  achievement gap and, 343, 357, 359
  choice model of SCCT and, 70
  culture, differences in, 108–109
  as distal contextual factors of SCCT, 66–68
  example of, 131–133
Sociopolitical determinants, 106–108
Spanish resources, 243, 265, 301, 307
Special designations of NCDA, 161
Special populations, 231, 233, 253–254, 377. *See also specific populations*
Specification stage of occupational choice, 38
Spirituality, 106, 378
Stage model of counseling process, 174–200
  background information, gathering, 177, 185–186
  concerns and goals, identifying, 176–177, 185, 186–187t
  evaluating experience of counseling, 181–182
  future, preparing for, 181, 198–200t
  helping strategies, identifying, 177–180, 187–190t, 188f, 190
  helping strategies, implementing, 180–181, 190–197, 192f, 196f
  introduction, 174–175
  orienting clients, 175–176, 182–185t
  overview, 174, 175t
  progress, solidifying, 181, 197–198
Standardized tests, 228–267
  for academic abilities, 241–245, 242t
  for career adjustment, 252–257, 252t
  for career decision making, 249–252, 249t
  client examples for, 258–260t, 258–266, 263f, 264–266t
  in core curriculum, 337–338
  differentiation between scores, 25
  history of, 19–20
  for interests, 229–230t, 229–235
  leisure activity list vs., 97
  for personalities, 235–238, 236t
  publisher list, 257t
  resources for, 257–258
  for self-efficacy beliefs, 72
  types of, 228–229
  for vocational aptitude, 245–249, 246t
  for work values, 239–241, 239t
Standard Occupational Classification Revision Committee, 296
Standard Occupational Classification (SOC) system, 296–298f, 297t, 302–305
Stanford Binet Intelligence Scales, 19

Subject Index

Statistics for occupational employment, 309
Statuary exceptions to wrongful discharge, 144, 145t
Stay-at-home parents. *See* Homemakers and caretakers
STEM careers, 335, 336t
Stereotypes, 120, 128–129, 435–436
Stories of clients, 94–98, 96t
Strengths, identifying, 213–214, 214f, 223–224, 224f, 421
Stress
  career transitions and, 412
  of college students, 372
  job interviews and, 460–461
  tests for, 254–256
Strong Interest Inventory (SII), 23, 234–235, 270, 298
Students
  academic tests for, 241–245, 242t
  card sorts for, 270
  of career and technical education (*See* Career and technical education (CTE))
  career decision-making tests for, 249–252, 249t
  in college (*See* College settings, career planning in)
  convicted of crimes, 429–430
  developmental theories for, 34–55 (*See also* Developmental theories)
  interests tests for, 229–235, 230t
  K-12 (*See* K-12 educational settings)
  learning theories for, 75–82 (*See also* Cognitive information-processing (CIP) approach to counseling)
  occupational and labor market information, 299, 300t, 317–320
  personality tests for, 235–238, 236t
  returning to college, 373–374
  skill-building for, 323–324
  social cognitive career theory for, 73–74
  veterans as, 422
Style variables, work satisfaction and, 26
Subjective self-assessment, 46
Substance abuse, 143–144, 424, 426, 431
Success
  culture, effect of, 122–124
  predicting, 255 (*See also* Theory of work adjustment)
  satisfaction with job and, 26, 36–37, 255–256
  work ethic and, 106–107
Superego, 37
Super Senior School-to-Work Transition Program, 349
Super's life-span, life-space approach to counseling. *See* Life-span, life-space approach to counseling (Super)
Supervised reentry programs, 431–432
Supervisors, ethics and, 167, 488–491
Supplemental Security Insurance (SSI), 150–152, 151t
Survivor's benefits, 152–154

T

Targeted job search, 431
Targeted opportunity profiles (TOPs), 399
Task approach skills, 59–60, 60f, 62
Tax incentive programs for employers, 431
Teaching, ethics and, 167, 488–491
Technical education. *See* Career and technical education (CTE)
Techniques as helping strategies, 178–179t, 179–180
Technology, 436. *See also* Information resources
Tech prep programs, 360, 360t
Temporary help agencies, 431
Tentative career choices, 38
Terminating counseling relationship, 476–477
Tests of Adult Basic Education (TABE), 244–245
Theaters in life-span, life-space approach, 43, 44t
Theory of circumscription, compromise, and self-creation (Gottfredson), 48–51, 50f, 54–55, 179–180, 272
Theory of occupational choice (Ginzberg), 37–39, 38t
Theory of personality development and career choice (Roe), 34–35, 35t, 36f
Theory of work adjustment, 25–30
  adjustment styles, 28–29, 29t
  card sorts and, 271, 275
  client examples for, 32–33
  expansion of, 29–30
  helping strategies for, 180
  predictive model of, 27, 28f
  process model of, 27–29, 29f
  standardized testing and, 240
  traits and factors of, 26–27
  360-degree assessments, 62
Title protection, 159
Tolerable boundaries, 49, 54, 122
Tracking systems, 357, 359, 359t, 362–364
Trade schools. *See* Career and technical education (CTE)
Training. *See* Education
Training counselors, ethics and, 167, 488–491
Trait factor theories, 17–33
  card sorts and, 271
  comparison of, 30
  helping strategies for, 179
  historical roots of, 18–20
  person-environment fit theory, 20–25, 30–31 (*See also* Person-environment fit theory (Holland))
  theory of work adjustment (*See* Theory of work adjustment)
  theory of work adjustment (TWA), 25–30, 29t, 32–33
Traits, defined, 18
Transcripts, 458
Transgender individuals. *See* LGBT individuals
Transition Assistance Employment Workshops, 417
Transition assistance programs (TAPs), 420
Transition Behavior Scale, Third Edition (TBS-3), 256
Transition counseling, 410–440
  card sorts for, 289–291t
  career, adult, 410–413, 411t
  from college to work, 379–381, 381t
  in community setting, 438–439
  CTE programs to college, 361–362
  for ex-offenders, 423–432, 432t
  for homemakers and caretakers, 432–438
  for people with disabilities, 414–417, 414t, 417t
  for special needs high school students, 347–350, 350t
  for veterans, 417–423, 421t, 423t
Transition Planning Inventory, Updated Version (TPI-UV), 256
Transition stage of occupational choice, 38
Transition-to-Work Inventory, Third Edition (TWI-3), 256
Transportation barriers, 427
Treatment plans, 188, 188f
Triadic reciprocality, 57, 57f, 66, 67–68f, 68
Trust, 113–114, 164–165
Twitter, 399
Tyler, Leona E., 268–269
Tyler Vocational Card Sort (TVCS), 269

U

Undecided clients, 63, 75–76, 86–87. *See also* Decision-making; Lily Huang Li Mei (undecided)
Unemployment, 389–394. *See also* Job loss
  as career transition, 413
  client example of (*See* Doris Bronner (fired))
  definitions and statistics for, 390–391, 391t
  Great Recession and, 3
  group counseling for, 394
  helping strategies for, 393–394 (*See also* Job search process)
  laws regarding, 148–152
  of low-skilled workers, 7
  of people with disabilities, 349, 414–415
  psychological reactions to, 391–394
  veterans and, 418–419
Unemployment insurance, 149–150, 155–156, 390
UNICOR Bond Program, 431
Unions, 140
Unisex Edition of the ACT Interest Inventory (UNIACT), 235, 299
Universities. *See* College settings, career planning in; Postsecondary education
Unsafe working conditions, 147–148
Unsatisfactory employees. *See* Theory of work adjustment
Unskilled jobs, 6–7, 135–136

V

Valpar Career Ability Test (VCAT), 248–249, 265–266
Values
  acculturation level and, 111
  cognitive information-processing and, 78, 87
  work satisfaction, predicting, 26
  work values tests, 239–241, 239t
Values Preference Indicator (VPI), 240
Verification of eligibility to work, 141
Veterans
  challenges for, 419
  defined, 417
  employment statistics for, 417–419
  helping strategies for, 419–420, 421t, 423t
  occupational and labor information for, 302
Vicarious learning, 57
Videos, for career information, 310, 312, 315t, 317

Vincent Arroyo (gay student with military aspirations)
client overview, 12
cognitive information-processing approach, 87
cultural dimensions and, 131–133, 131t, 132f
employment law and, 155
ethical considerations for, 169, 172
intake assessment for, 218–219
Krumboltz's learning theories and, 59, 59f, 84
life-span, life-space approach and, 53
narrative theory and, 100
person-environment fit theory, 31
social cognitive career theory and, 85
stage model of career counseling process and, 190, 191–193t, 194
standardized tests for, 262–263, 263f
theory of circumscription, compromise, and self-creation and, 54
theory of work adjustment and, 32
Vocabulary, 1–2, 2t
Vocation, defined, 2t
Vocational aptitude tests, 245–249, 246t
Vocational Card Sort (VCS), 270
Vocational Counseling (Williamson), 20
Vocational education. *See* Career and technical education (CTE)
Vocational Education Act of 1963, 356
Vocational evaluation, 415–416
Vocational Exploration and Insight Kit (VEIK), 270
Vocational guidance, 3, 18–19, 93–94
Vocational identity, 46, 46t
Vocational interests, 26
Vocational Preference Inventory, 23, 25
Vocational rehabilitation, 25–30, 150, 157, 415, 431. *See also* Juan Martinez (vocational rehabilitation after injury)
Vocational Rehabilitation Act of 1973, 349
Vocational Technical Education Act of 1976, 434
Vocational trade schools, 345
Volition, 121

W

Wage gap, gender and, 108–109, 123, 147
Wayne Jensen (job security concerns)
card sort for, 275, 275–279t, 276–278f, 279
client overview, 10
cognitive information-processing approach, 86
cultural dimensions and, 126–127, 127t
employment law and, 154
ethical considerations for, 169, 170–171
information resources for, 327, 328t
intake assessment for, 218, 218f, 222
Krumboltz's learning theories and, 58, 59f, 82–83
life-span, life-space approach and, 52
narrative theory and, 100
person-environment fit theory and, 30
social cognitive career theory and, 85
stage model of career counseling process and, 198–200t
standardized tests for, 258–259, 259t
theory of circumscription, compromise, and self-creation and, 54
theory of work adjustment and, 32
Wealth, culture and, 109, 109f
Welcoming clients, 175–176, 182–185t
Wide Range Interest and Occupation Test (WRIOT-2), 235
Widows and widowers, 149, 434. *See also* Lakeesha Maddox (stay-at-home parent, widowed)
Williamson's trait factor approach to counseling, 20, 20t
Women, 6. *See also* Gender
Wonderlic tests, 245
Work, defined, 2t
Work environments
adjusting to, 252–257, 252t, 380–381, 461–463 (*See also* Theory of work adjustment)
assessment of, 23
helping strategies for, 180
of interest to client, 97, 101–102
Worker Adjustment and Retraining Act (WARN) of 1988, 146, 154
Worker's compensation, 150, 156–157
Work ethic, 106–107, 127
Work Importance Locator, 180
Work Motivation Scale (WMS), 240–241
Workplace competencies, 508
Workplace Skills Survey (WSS), 256–257
Work salience, 106
Work traumas, 93
Work values tests, 239–241, 239t
World of work, 5–9. *See also* Information resources
World of Work Inventory (WOWI), 235, 238, 249
World-of-work map, 299
Worldview, 107, 111–112
Wrongful discharge exceptions, 144–146t

Y

Young Person's Occupational Outlook Handbook (DOL), 315

Z

Zone of acceptable alternatives, 50, 50f, 54